COST ACCOUNTING
THEORY AND PRACTICE

COST ACCOUNTING
THEORY AND PRACTICE

R. PALANIAPPAN
Former - Head
Department of Commerce
Government Arts College, Salem

Visiting Faculty, Institute of Cost and Works Accountants of India

and

Institute of Company Secretaries of India
[Salem Chapter]

N. HARIHARAN
Professor & Head - Finance
Amplify Mindware Academy for Development of Education and Research (AMADER), Pune
Director i/c, CIMA Programme, Amplify Study Centre, Pune
[Chartered Institute of Management Accountants, London]

Former Vice-Principal
Shree Chandraprabhu Jain College, Chennai

Visiting Faculty, Institute of Company Secretaries of India
Southern India Regional Council, Chennai

I.K. International Publishing House Pvt. Ltd.

NEW DELHI • BANGALORE

Published by

I.K. International Publishing House Pvt. Ltd.
S-25, Green Park Extension
Uphaar Cinema Market
New Delhi–110 016 (India)
E-mail: info@ikinternational.com
Website: www.ikbooks.com

ISBN 978-93-80578-34-7

10 9 8 7 6 5 4 3 2 1

Published by Krishan Makhijani for I.K. International Publishing House Pvt. Ltd., S-25, Green Park Extension, Uphaar Cinema Market, New Delhi–110 016 and Printed by Rekha Printers Pvt. Ltd., Okhla Industrial Area, Phase II, New Delhi–110 020.

Preface

Indian business is operating in a globally competitive environment. Indian companies are under great pressure to control and reduce their operating costs. Hence, the study of cost accounting is gaining more importance. Recognising this fact, many Indian universities and professional bodies have included cost accounting in their curriculum and have also updated the contents of the subject.

Keeping the above in mind this FIRST EDITION is brought out as a comprehensive text book to cover the syllabi of all universities and professional bodies. Theory part of the book is written in a simple language. Solved numerical problems in large numbers are given in illustrations in each chapter to help the students for their easy understanding of the subject. Many exercises (both theory and numerical questions) are given at the end of each chapter. One special feature of the book is that numerous objective types' questions, short answer theory questions and short answer practical problems are given to suit the needs of the students of many universities. Especially the short answer problems given at the end of each chapter will help even a beginner to understand and solve comprehensive numerical problems in an easy way. We have also included recent development in the subject at appropriate places.

This book has been divided into 05 parts containing 22 chapters as mentioned below:

PART-1: COST CONCEPTS

- C-1: Introduction
- C-2: Cost Analysis, Classification and Cost Sheet

PART-2: ELEMENTS OF COST

- C-3: Materials Cost Control
- C-4: Materials Costing
- C-5: Labour Cost Control
- C-6: Methods of Wage Payment
- C-7: Overheads - Nature and Classification
- C-8: Accounting for Overheads and Control
- C-9: Administration, Selling and Distribution Overheads

PART-3: ACCOUNTING METHODS

- C-10: Cost Ledger
- C-11: Reconciliation of Cost and Financial Accounts
- C-12: Integral Accounting

PART-4: METHODS OF COSTING

C-13: Output/Unit/Single Costing

C-14: Job and Batch Costing

C-15: Contract/Terminal Costing

C-16: Process Costing

C-17: Joint Products, By-Products and Main Products Costing

C-18: Service/Operating Costing

PART-5: TECHNIQUES OF COSTING

C-19: Marginal Costing and Cost Volume Profit Analysis

C-20: Budgetary Control

C-21: Standard Costing and Variance Analysis

C-22: Miscellaneous Topics

The following are the main highlights of the book:

- Simple and Lucid style of presentation
- Self-Explanatory notes
- Logical organization of Topics
- Numerous Illustrations for Graduate, Postgraduate and Professional Courses
- Numerous exercises including Objective Type Questions, Short answer theory and practical problems along with comprehensive problems to practice and solve
- Step by step approach in solving practical problems
- Various University and Professional Courses Questions are adopted in Illustrations and Exercises
- Proforma, Tables and Charts at appropriate places

This book will be useful for the students pursuing the courses of B.Com, B.C.S, B.B.A, (Hons), M.Com, MCS, M.B.A., MCA, PGDBM, PGDFM, PGDM, CA (Inter), ICWA (Inter) and ACS (Inter).

R. PALANIAPPAN
N. HARIHARAN

Acknowledgements

We thank Mr. Krishan Makhijani, Managing Director of I. K. International Publishing House for publishing this book.

We thank Ms. Shruti Raj, Mr. Babu VR, Mr. Kalimuthu of I. K. International Publishing House and Mr. M. Srinivasan, typesetter for their excellent time integrity in bringing out this edition.

We thank our friend Mr. A. K. Sukumaran, General Manager, UBS Publishers' Distributors Pvt. Ltd, Coimbatore, for introducing us to the publisher.

Special thanks to our PGDFM students Ms. Garima Parmar, Ms. Parul Sharma, Ms. Priya Mehta, Ms. Aparna Gupta, Mr. Ankit Singh Lohiya, Mr. Sudhanshu Upadhyah, Mr. Anil Singh Rawat and Mr. Sahil Sharma for helping towards proof reading in this Edition.

We also thank all other students who have helped us to bring out this edition successfully.

We thank our family members for co-operating with us to make this attempt a success.

Finally we wish to thank all others who were helpful to us in some way or the other to complete this project successfully.

WE WELCOME YOUR COMMENTS AND SUGGESTIONS FOR FURTHER IMPROVEMENT OF THE BOOK

R. PALANIAPPAN
N. HARIHARAN

R. Palaniappan - Mobile: +91 9442140387
Mail: `rp.gurupala@gmail.com`

N. Hariharan - Mobile: +91 9960522279/+91 9444210843
Mail: `hariharan59@bsnl.in/hariharan.vp@gmail.com`

CONTENTS

1 INTRODUCTION

- Evolution of cost accounting
- Cost accounting
- Objectives of cost accounting
- Need and importance of cost accounting
- Advantages and disadvantages of cost accounting
- Methods of cost accounting
- Essentials of good cost accounting system
- Various terms
- Cost accounting vs. Financial accounting
- Cost accounting vs. Management accounting

1.1 EVOLUTION OF COST ACCOUNTING

Nathan Kranowski (1977) claims that the contemporary cost accounting began around 1885 though it had been in use for many years or centuries prior in a limited form. Previts and Merino (1998) support Kranowski's assertion that cost accounting came into use after 1800 and expanded during the American industrial revolution in the mid to late 1800's. The industrial revolution had a major impact on methods and costs of manufacturing. Because of this enormous development in manufacturing processing, both engineers and accountants began to look at the complete process. Both groups worked to detail the process for both the production and accounting flow process. As the industrial revolution evolved, trusts, such as the Standard Oil Trust and U.S. Steel, dominated the economy. The Olds Motor Works began in Detroit in 1899 using interchangeable parts that would lead the way to mass manufacturing and the need for more advanced cost accounting. In addition, Ford made the first Model T in 1908. Various literatures towards cost accounting tells that the main reason for dissemination of cost accounting systems in the late 1800's and early 1900's was that often firms considered their accounting systems to be secrets that were not to be made available to competing firms. Most companies did not even reveal their system to their own labourers.

It is said that during the seventeenth century in France, the Royal Wallpaper Manufactory had a Cost Accounting System. Some iron masters and potters in the eighteenth century in England too began to produce Cost Accounting information before the Industrial Revolution. Subsequently, with the advent of the industrial revolution, large sized process industries performing single activities (e.g. textiles, railways etc.,) came into being. During this period, there was a lack of market for intermediary products because of which cost information gained importance as a tool for measuring efficiency of different processes. The period, 1880 - 1925 saw the development of complex product designs and the emergence of multi-activity diversified corporations like Du Pont, General Motors etc. It was during this period that scientific management was developed which led accountants to convert physical standards into cost standards, the latter being used for variance analysis and control.

Widespread growth of industrialisation in the western world during the last half of the nineteenth century gave rise to the development of cost accounting. With the advent of the factory system, necessity for accurate cost information was felt to bring efficiency in production. In spite of that, there was slow development of cost accounting during the nineteenth century. To quote Eldon S. Hendriksen, "Not until the last 20 years of the nineteenth century was there much literature on the subject of cost accounting in England and even then very little was to be found in the United States". The most rapid development in cost accounting took place after 1914 with the growth of heavy industry and mass production methods when costs (i.e. overheads) other than materials and labour constituted a significant portion of the total cost of production. The scientific management movement led by Taylor gave impetus to the development of cost accounting because it contributed to the use of standard costs in planning manufacturing operations and in evaluating performances.

1.1.1 Cost Accounting in Indian Context

The need for the application of cost accounting methods in Indian industries was felt in the beginning of the twentieth century. The development of cost accounting in India started gaining importance after the independence of the country when the Indian Government started laying emphasis on the industrial development of the country. Further, provisions of cost audit under section 233B of the Companies Act gave impetus to the development of cost accounting in India. The Vivian Bose Enquiry Commission brought to light the various malpractices prevalent in the manufacturing establishments and it was thought that the audit of financial accounts at the end of the year was insufficient to judge the real efficiency of the working and manufacturing organisations as a result, the concept of cost audit emerged best utilise the resources of the country, and the government was given the power for ordering cost audit under section 233B of the Companies Act, 1956.

The following factors have accelerated the system of cost accounting in our country.

1. Increased awareness of cost consciousness by Indian industrialists with a view to ascertain costs more accurately for each product or job.
2. Growing competition among manufacturers led to fixation of prices at a lower level so as to attract more customers.
3. Economic policy of government which laid emphasis on planned economy with a view to achieve the targets led to cost reduction programmes by Indian industrialists.
4. Increased government control over pricing led the Indian manufacturers to give utmost importance to the installation of cost accounts.
5. The establishment of National Productivity Council in 1958 and the statutory recognition of Institute of Cost and Works Accountants of India in 1959 gave further encouragement to instal cost accounting system in Indian industries.

1.2 COST ACCOUNTING

"Cost accounting is the process of determining and accumulating the cost of product or activity. It is a process of accounting for the incurrence and the control of cost. It also covers classification, analysis, and interpretation of cost. In other words, it is a system of accounting, which provides the information about the ascertainment, and control of costs of products, or services. It measures the operating efficiency of the enterprise. It is an internal aspect of the organisation."

"Cost accounting is accounting for cost aimed at providing cost data, statement and reports for the purpose of managerial decision making."

The Institute of Cost and Management Accounting, London (CIMA) defines "Cost accounting is the process of accounting from the point at which expenditure is incurred or committed to the establishment of its ultimate relationship with cost centres and cost units. In the widest usage, it embraces the preparation of statistical data, application of cost control methods and the ascertainment of profitability of activities carried out or planned."

1.3 OBJECTIVES OF COST ACCOUNTING

The following are the main objectives of cost accounting:

1. To ascertain cost (cost of production) of every unit, job, process, service or department.
2. To control cost by using various techniques such as budgetary control, standard costing and inventory control.
3. To help management in taking decisions based on CVP relationship (cost volume profit).

4. To identify costing profit.

5. To identify stock of raw material, semi-finished and finished goods as and when required.

6. To study profit relationship based on capacity operations (say profit at 60% or 80% operating capacity).

7. To compare actual cost with budgeted cost to identify the variances.

8. To help the management in budgetary control.

9. To ascertain sales mix to maximise profit.

10. To facilitate preparation of financial and other statements.

1.4 NEED AND IMPORTANCE OF COST ACCOUNTING

Cost accounting provides valuable help to the management. It is not easy to quantify the need and importance since it cannot be concluded about where the work of a cost accountant comes to an end. The following points can be taken under the concept of "need". The same points are also the main advantages of cost accounting.

- ※ Helps to ascertain cost
- ※ Helps in price fixation
- ※ Helps to eliminate wastages
- ※ Helps to identify and eliminate unprofitable activities
- ※ Helps to check statement accuracy
- ※ Helps in inventory control
- ※ Helps for cost and revenue estimation
- ※ Helps to increase productivity and earning capacity
- ※ Helps investor's, moneylenders and other financial institutions to know about the business
- ※ Helps in formulating efficient policy for day-to-day business activities
- ※ Helps cost control

1.5 ADVANTAGES AND DISADVANTAGES OF COST ACCOUNTING

1.5.1 Advantages

※ Helps to identify idle capacity

※ Helps inter-firm comparison

※ Helps to ascertain cost

※ Helps in price fixation

※ Helps to eliminate wastages

※ Helps to identify and eliminate unprofitable activities

※ Helps to check statement accuracy

※ Helps in inventory control

※ Helps for cost and revenue estimation

※ Helps to increase productivity and earning capacity

※ Helps investor's, moneylenders and other financial institutions to know about the business

※ Helps in formulating efficient policy for day-to-day business activities

※ Helps cost control

※ Helps to increase production by comparing records of output

※ Helps to develop pricing strategy

※ Helps to generate information based on

a. Products
b. Periods
c. Departments/sections etc.

※ Helps to prepare production plan

※ Helps to identify and allocate overhead costs to respective departments/sections/products

※ Helps to reconcile cost and financial results

※ Helps in anticipating profits

※ Helps to provide proper performance records

1.5.2 Disadvantages

※ Involves heavy expenditure since the system has to maintain numerous records

※ Not applicable for all types of industry

※ No standard system for all industry

※ It is mechanical in nature

※ It is stereotyped

※ Common notion is that it cannot control costs and can contribute for operating efficiency. But can only give information on the same.

※ "Cost Concept Terminology" interpretation during decision making according to the convenience of cost accountants acts as a hurdle for standards

※ Considered "Empirical Science"

1.6 METHODS OF COST ACCOUNTING

Different industries follow different methods for ascertaining cost of their products. The method to be adopted by business organisations will depend on the nature of the production and the type of output. The following are the important methods of costing.

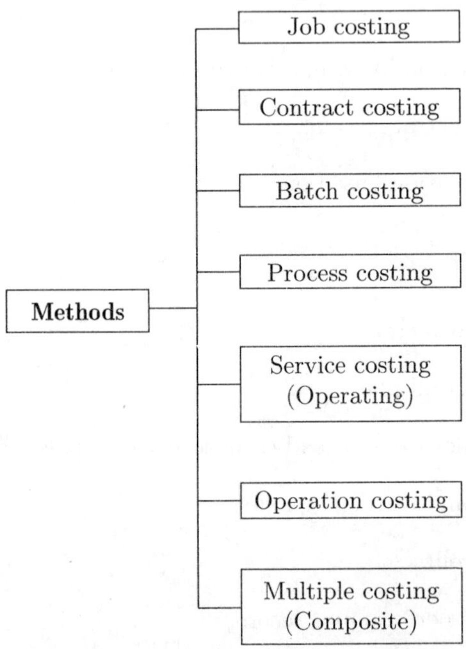

1. **Job Costing:** Job costing is concerned with finding the cost of a specific job or work order. This method is followed by those concerns where work is carried on the customer's request. Under this system a job cost sheet is prepared to find out profit or losses for each job or work order. Duration of the job will be short. Example: Printing job in a printing press, repair job in a garage etc.,

2. **Contract Costing:** Contract costing is applied for contract work like construction of dam, building civil engineering contract etc. Each contract or job is treated as separate cost unit for cost ascertainment and control. It is also called "Terminal Costing". Firms engaged in ship-building, civil engineering for roads, industrial estates and factory construction follow this type of costing.

3. **Batch Costing:** A batch is a group of identical products. Under batch costing a batch of similar products is treated as a separate unit for the purpose of ascertaining cost. The total costs of a batch are divided by the total number of units in a batch to arrive at the costs per unit. This type of costing is generally used in industries like bakery, toy manufacturing etc. Other examples include engineering equipment, drugs and footwear.

4. **Process Costing:** This method is used in industries where production is carried on through different stages or processes before becoming a finished product. Costs are determined separately for each process. The main feature of process costing is that output of one process becomes the raw materials of another process until the final product is obtained. This type of costing is generally used in industries like textile, chemicals, paper, oil refining etc.

5. **Service (Operating) Costing:** This method is used in those industries which render services instead of producing goods. Under this method cost of providing a service is also determined. It is also called service costing. Undertakings such as transport, electricity, gas, hospitals, educational institutions etc., are examples of this type.

6. **Operation Costing:** This is suitable for industries where production is continuous and units are exactly identical to each other. Examples: Mines or drilling, cement works, manufacture of bicycles, ceiling fans etc.

7. **Multiple Costing:** This refers to the combination of two or more of the above-mentioned methods of costing or mix of any methods mentioned above. Where a product comprises many assembled parts or components (as in case of motor car) costs have to be ascertained for each component as well as for the finished product for different components for which different methods of costing may be used. This composition comes under multiple costing method. It is also known as composite costing. This type of costing is applicable to soft drinks, automobiles and similar products.

1.7 ESSENTIALS OF GOOD COST ACCOUNTING SYSTEM

An ideal system of costing is that which achieves the objectives of a costing system and brings all the advantages of costing to the business. The following are the main characteristics which an ideal system of costing should possess or the points which should be taken into consideration before installing a costing system.

- ※ It should be tailor-made
- ※ It should be practical, simple and capable of meeting business requirements
- ※ Data used should be accurate enough for its intended purpose
- ※ Co-operation and participation of various department executives are a must for a good system
- ※ Cost of installing and operating should justify the results to have a good system
- ※ The system should not have or introduce unnecessary procedures. Overloading should be avoided
- ※ System should be complete in all aspects. Say the system should provide all users wealth of information that is necessary and required.
- ※ For system information to be valuable, it should be relevant to the objective and for the intended user
- ※ It should have clarity so that the user can understand and comprehend the information properly
- ※ Timely information is essential since it helps effective decision making
- ※ System should validate the information so that competence and integrity can be evolved to produce confidence among auditors
- ※ It should be cost-efficient. Say valuable information should not cost more to produce than it is worth
- ※ The system should have an appropriate communication channel which should adhere to standards

1.8 VARIOUS TERMS

1.8.1 Cost

It refers to the actual or notional expenditure incurred on or attributable to a given thing. In other words, cost is the amount of resources used for something which can be measured in terms of money.

1.8.2 Costing

It is defined as "the technique and process of ascertaining costs". In other words "costing is classifying, recording, allocation and appropriation of expenses for the determination of cost of products or services and for the presentation of suitably arranged data for the purpose of control and guidance of management."

1.8.3 Cost Accounting

It is defined as "the establishment of budgets, standard costs and actual costs of operations, processes, activities or products and the analysis of variances, profitability or the social use of funds". It mainly accounts for the cost of products, services or operations.

1.8.4 Cost Accountancy

It is defined as "the application of costing and cost accounting principles, methods and techniques to the science and art and practice of cost control and the ascertainment of profitability as well as presentation of information for the purpose of managerial decision making". In simple words it is the application of costing and cost accounting principles with specific purpose of cost control to facilitate decision making.

1.8.5 Cost Centre

It refers to location, person or item of equipment for which the cost may be ascertained and used for the purpose of cost control. Cost centre is a sub-unit for which cost allocation is attempted. Examples, each department in an organization can be considered cost centre. Say, production department, selling department etc.

A cost centre in which a specific process or continuous sequence of operations is carried out is known as "Process Cost Center".

1.8.6 Profit Centre

It is defined as "a segment of the business entity by which both revenues received and expenses incurred are controlled". It is a sub-unit of an organization to which both revenues and costs are assigned. This centre helps to evaluate actual and budgeted performance.

Note: "Cost centre" is one where only "costs" are assigned whereas "profit centre" is one where both "costs and revenues" are assigned.

1.8.7 Historical Costing

It is a system where costs are ascertained only after they are incurred. It is helpful for analysis (post-mortem) of costs incurred in the past. This system will help to identify the trend movement of costs over a period of time and will also be useful to estimate costs for future, based on the trends.

1.8.8 Absorption Costing

It is also known as "Full Cost Method". Absorption costing method is an inventory valuation and costing model which includes all costs irrespective of whether they are variable or fixed in nature. It is based on the principle that costs should be charged or absorbed to whatever is being, whether it is a cost unit or cost centre.

1.8.9 Marginal Costing

This is also called "Direct costing method" or "Variable costing method". In this only variable costs are considered for unit cost of a product and decisions are mostly based on variable costs. The principle followed in this case is that since fixed costs are largely period costs, they should not enter into the production units.

1.8.10 Uniform Costing

It is not a distinct method of costing. It is adoption of identical costing principles and procedures by several units of the same industry or by several undertakings by mutual agreement in order to facilitate easy comparison. The principles and methods of compilation, analysis, apportionment and absorption of overheads differ from one concern to the other in the same industry; but if a common or uniform pattern is adopted by all, it will mutually help in cost control and cost reduction.

1.9 COST ACCOUNTING vs. FINANCIAL ACCOUNTING

S. No.	Cost Accounting	Financial Accounting
1.	It is prepared mostly for internal management	It is prepared mostly for outsiders like investors, government, creditors, owners etc.
2.	The reports prepared are on the formats as required and designed by the management.	The reports prepared are specific in format prescribed by GAAP (Generally Accepted Accounting Principles) or IFRS (International Financial Reporting Standards)
3.	Focuses on the financial position of specific products, product lines etc.	Focuses on the entire financial position of the company
4.	No regulatory framework	Regulated mostly by GAAP and IFRS
5.	Cost reports can be prepared as and when required at frequent intervals. There is no specific time	Financial reports are prepared once in every twelve months
6.	Past data and future aspects are taken into consideration while preparing reports	Only past data are taken into consideration while preparing reports
7.	Cost of raw material, WIP and finished goods are compiled by cost accounting	It only incorporates the information compiled (in cost accounting) into the Balance Sheet
8.	Main purpose is to analyse, ascertain and control cost	Main purpose is to record financial transactions and find out profit or loss
9.	It is voluntary to meet the requirements of the management	It is compulsory to meet the requirements of Companies Act and Income Tax Act
10.	It is objective in nature towards recording transactions (costs)	It is subjective in nature towards recording transactions (nature of expenses)

11.	It aims at computing cost of production	It aims at finding out results in the form of profit or loss
12.	It is subject to cost audit to verify whether cost accounts disclose true and fair view of the cost of production	It is subject to statutory audit to verify whether financial accounts disclose true and fair view of the profit and loss as well as financial position
13.	Stocks are valued at cost price	Stocks are valued at cost or market price whichever is lesser
14.	Monetary and non-monetary data are considered	Only monetary data is considered

1.10 COST ACCOUNTING vs. MANAGEMENT ACCOUNTING

Usually the terms, cost accounting and management accounting, are used interchangeably and are used in one and the same sense. Therefore, cost accounting supports management accounting and in turn management accounting pushes cost accounting further according to the needs of the management. Because of this strong bondage between the cost accounting and management accounting are one and the same thing nowadays. However, the following points can be taken as differences.

S. No.	Cost Accounting	Management Accounting
1.	It precedes management accounting	It starts where cost accounting ends
2.	It deals with calculation of cost per unit using various cost techniques	It gathers information from cost accounting to take decisions
3.	It focus mainly on cost control keeping within budgeted and standard limits	It focus mainly on decision making from the given set of courses of action
4.	It does not use much financial accounting	It uses both financial and cost accounting
5.	Application of statistics and operation research towards control is very much limited in use	Application of statistics and operation research towards control is very much used in wider scope as compared to cost accounting
6.	Calculation of cost of production dominates cost accounting	Planning and control for decision making dominates management accounting

1.11 EXERCISE

Short Questions

1. What is cost accounting?
2. Explain the various objectives of cost accounting.
3. Write short notes on
   (a) Cost
   (b) Costing
   (c) Cost accounting
   (d) Cost accountancy
   (e) Cost centre
   (f) Profit centre
   (g) Historical costing
   (h) Absorption costing
   (i) Marginal costing
   (j) Uniform costing.
4. What are the advantages of cost accounting?
5. What are the limitations of cost accounting?

Essay Questions

1. Discuss the evolution of cost accounting.
2. Bring out the advantages and disadvantages of cost accounting.
3. Discuss the need and importance of cost accounting with suitable examples.
4. Explain the various methods of cost accounting with suitable example.
5. Discuss the prerequisite of ideal cost accounting system with suitable example.
6. Bring out the difference between cost accounting and financial accounting.
7. Bring out the difference between cost accounting and management accounting.

Cost Analysis: Cost Classification and Cost Sheet 2

- ☞ Cost Classification—Basis
- ☞ Miscellaneous Cost Terms
- ☞ Cost Sheet/Cost Statement
- ☞ Cost Sheet—Advantages

Cost analysis and cost classification involve grouping of costs into various logical groups on some suitable basis. Cost analysis and classification are essential for the purpose of cost control and managerial decision making.

There are various methods of classification of costs. The method selected is based on the purpose for which it is needed. The important bases of classification are:

1. By nature or element
2. By relation to cost centre or product
3. By function
4. By behaviour or variability
5. By time
6. By controllability
7. For decision making purpose
8. By payment
9. By normality.

2.1 CLASSIFICATION BY NATURE OR ELEMENT

On the basis of nature costs are classified into three categories:

(a) Materials cost
(b) Labour cost and
(c) Expenses.

(a) Materials Cost

Materials are the physical things, articles or commodities used in production. It includes raw materials, consumable stores, spare parts and components. It is further classified into direct materials cost and indirect materials cost.

(i) Direct materials cost: Direct materials include raw materials, components and spare parts entering the body of the finished product. They become part and parcel of the finished product. They are directly identified with a product, cost centre, process or a job. Direct materials cost is allocated to a cost object in whole.

Some materials may form part of finished product but their costs may be very small. As a matter of convenience and economy in accounting they are treated as indirect materials, e.g., small screws, washers, nails and sewing threads. But primary packing materials which are essential for convenient handling of the finished products are treated as direct materials.

(ii) Indirect materials cost: Cost of materials which do not enter the body of the finished product and which are incurred with reference to two or more products, cost centres, processes or jobs are called indirect materials cost. They cannot be charged to a specific cost object. They are to be apportioned over cost objects. These include consumable stores, secondary packing materials, lubricants, cotton waste, stationery, advertising materials etc. Usually costs of indirect materials are small compared to direct materials cost.

(b) Labour Cost

Labour cost includes all remuneration paid to employees. They include all rewards provided to employees in different forms such as salary, wages, allowances, bonus, commission, fees, contribution to PF, ESI and superannuation funds, cost of perquisites like free transport, medical facilities, reading rooms etc. Labour cost is classified into direct labour cost and indirect labour cost.

(i) Direct labour cost: Direct labour cost is identified or linked wholly with a particular product, cost centre, process or job. It includes all labour engaged in changing or altering of the composition of raw materials into finished products. It also includes wages of all employees engaged in a contract work. It is allocated in full to a cost centre or a cost object.

(ii) Indirect labour cost: It includes all labour cost incurred in relation to two or more products, processes, jobs or cost centres. Indirect labour assists or helps the direct labour in production process, e.g., works manager, supervisor, attenders, security staff, office people, staffs in stores department, time office and sales department. Indirect wages are apportioned to products, processes, jobs or cost centres.

(c) Expenses

It includes all costs other than materials and labour cost. It is the cost of various services consumed by an undertaking. It is further classified into direct expenses and indirect expenses.

(i) Direct expenses: It includes cost of all services specifically incurred for a product, process, job or cost centre. They are directly identified with a particular cost object. It is conveniently allocated to a particular cost object in whole. It is also called chargeable expenses. It includes excise duty, royalty, hire charges and repairs and maintenance of special equipment required for a job; cost of special drawings, designs, moulds and patterns.

(ii) Indirect expenses: Indirect expenses are expenses incurred in relation to two or more products, processes, jobs or cost centres. It is apportioned to various cost objects. It includes rent, rates, taxes, insurance, lighting, depreciation, power, fuel, advertisement and repairs and maintenance.

2.2 BY RELATION TO COST CENTRE

On the basis of relation to cost centre, costs are classified as direct costs and indirect costs.

(a) Direct Costs

Direct costs are incurred in relation to a specific product, process, job or cost centre. They consists of direct materials, direct labour and direct expenses. The total of all direct costs is called prime cost.

(b) Indirect Costs

Indirect costs are general expenses incurred for two or more products, processes, jobs or cost centres. They are apportioned to various cost objects on suitable basis. They include indirect materials, indirect labour and other indirect expenses. The total of all indirect costs is also called overheads, oncost or burden.

2.3 BY FUNCTION

All indirect costs are called overheads and can be classified on functional basis into:

(a) Factory overheads
(b) Office and administration overheads
(c) Selling overheads
(d) Distribution overheads.

(a) Factory Overheads

Factory overheads is also called production overheads, works overheads or manufacturing overheads. It includes all indirect expenses in relation to production activity. It includes all indirect materials used in production, indirect labour expended in production, works manager's salary and allowances, repairs, maintenance, depreciation and insurance of factory building, plant, equipment and machinery, supervision, cost of designing and drawing, cost of fuel, power, oil, water, gas and steam and consumable stores.

(b) Office and Administration Overheads

These include expenses incurred in connection with formulation of policies, overall administration and control of an organisation. This includes office salary, printing and stationery, repairs, maintenance, depreciation and insurance of office equipment, building and furniture, General Manager's or managing director's salary and allowances, postage, general travelling expenses, telephone and telegram, audit fees, bank charges, legal expenses and secretarial department expenses.

(c) Selling Expenses

These expenses are incurred for creating and stimulating demand for a product. Sometimes it is also called 'marketing cost'. These include advertisement, salesmanship, market research, showroom expenses, cost of free samples, commission and discount to distributors.

(d) Distribution Expenses

These are expenses incurred to take the goods from production centre to consumers place. They include warehouse expenses, packing, carriage outward and all expenses in connection with delivery van and trucks.

2.4 BY BEHAVIOUR OR VARIABILITY

Expenses respond in varying degrees to changes in production or activity level. Some expenses change in direct proportion to changes in production level, some expenses change in a lesser proportion to changes in production level and some expenses do not change at all. On the variability basis costs are classified into variable costs, fixed costs and semi-variable costs.

(a) Variable Costs

Variable costs change in direct proportion to changes in production. These include all direct materials, direct labour, direct expenses and a portion of indirect expenses. As these costs respond directly in relation to changes in production, variable cost is also called "product cost". They change in total amount only. Variable cost per unit remains constant at all levels of activity.

(b) Fixed Costs

Fixed costs remain constant in total or do not change even when production or activity level changes. They remain unaffected in total to changes in production level. But fixed cost per unit changes in inverse proportion to changes in production level. These expenses respond to passage of time. They are called *period cost* or *time cost.*

(c) Semi-Variable Costs

These expenses are partly variable and partly fixed. They change but not in direct proportion to changes in production level. They remain constant up to a certain production level and rise suddenly when production increases beyond a production level. So it is also called "Step Cost".

2.5 BY TIME

On time basis, costs are classified as follows:

(a) Historical Costs

These are the costs actually incurred during a certain period. These represent the cost of actual performance. It is also called "Postmortem" costs.

(b) Predetermined Costs

Predetermined costs are costs determined in advance of production. Predetermined cost is classified into

(i) Standard Costs and
(ii) Estimated Costs

(i) Standard costs: Standard costs are the desired costs or reasonable costs. These are the costs ought to be incurred for a given volume of production. They are fixed on scientific basis.

(ii) Estimated costs: The cost likely to be incurred in the future is determined on the basis of past experience. It is a simple assessment of what the cost will be.

2.6 BY CONTROLLABILITY

Costs are classified into controllable costs and uncontrollable costs.

(a) Controllable Costs

Controllable costs are those costs which can be influenced by the people within an organization. All direct expenses and variable overheads are normally controllable. They can be increased or reduced by the executive action of the management.

(b) Uncontrollable Costs

Uncontrollable costs are those costs which cannot be influenced by the managerial action.

The distinction between controllable and uncontrollable costs is not permanent. Some expenses which are uncontrollable in the short term may be controllable in the long term. Similarly uncontrollable expenses at the lower level in an organization may be influenced by people at higher level in an organization, e.g., wages and salaries of employees.

2.7 FOR DECISION MAKING PURPOSE

For enabling the management in decision making, costs are classified into the following groups:

(a) Marginal Cost

It is the total of all variable expenses. It includes all direct expenses and variable overheads. Marginal cost possesses all the characteristics of variable cost.

(b) Differential Cost

The change in the cost of two alternatives is called differential cost. The increase in the total cost due to increase in output is called 'incremental cost'. The decrease in the total cost due to decrease in output is called 'decremental cost'.

(c) Relevant Cost and Irrelevant Costs

Cost items taken into consideration while making a decision are called relevant costs. Costs which are not necessary for a particular decision making are called irrelevant costs. A cost relevant for a particular decision may be irrelevant for another decision. A cost irrelevant for a decision may be relevant for another decision. For example rent for own premises may be relevant for comparison of profitability with another firm paying rent. But it is irrelevant for computing tax liability of a firm using own building.

(d) Opportunity Cost

The benefit foregone due to an alternative decision taken is called opportunity cost. For example, a person decides to start a business of his own. For the purpose he resigns his present employment and withdraws his savings kept in a bank deposit. Due to this decision to start a business he foregoes his salary income and interest income. The loss of salary and interest income is opportunity cost for the business.

2.8 BY PAYMENT

On the basis of payment involved costs are classified as follows:

(a) Out of Pocket Costs or Explicit Costs

The costs result in actual outflow of cash, e.g., salary, wages, rent, advertisement, etc. paid.

(b) Imputed Costs or Notional Costs or Implicit Costs

These expenses are considered for decision making purpose only. They do not result in any cash outflow, e.g., rent for own premises, interest on own capital and depreciation on fully depreciated asset.

2.9 BY NORMALITY

Costs are classified into the following two groups:

(a) Normal Costs

Expenses incurred in a normal business condition is called normal costs. These costs are included in cost of production.

(b) Abnormal Costs

These costs are occasional and occur due to the happening of some unforeseen event, e.g., loss due to fire, theft, accident etc. These costs are not included in the cost of production. They are debited to costing profit and loss account.

2.10 MISCELLANEOUS COST TERMS

(a) Avoidable Cost and Unavoidable Cost

Avoidable costs: These are the costs which can be postponed or dispensed without impairing the operating efficiency of a firm. Usually controllable cost comes under this category.

Unavoidable costs: These expenses are necessary for maintaining the current operating efficiency. All uncontrollable costs come under this category.

(b) Sunk Costs

The cost incurred in the past but could not be recovered due to an alternative decision taken. The cost of an outmoded plant less its scrap value is a sunk cost. Sunk cost is irrelevant for decision making

(c) Replacement Cost

It is the cost of replacing an asset at current market price.

(d) Conversion Cost

It is the cost incurred for converting raw material into finished product. It includes direct labour, direct expenses and production overheads. It is equal to factory cost less materials consumed.

(e) Policy Cost or Discretionary Cost

These costs arise due to policy taken by the management. For example, bad debts will arise if the company takes a policy to sell goods on credit. These costs can be avoided by taking a reverse decision.

(f) Cost, Expense and Loss

Cost: The value of various resources and services expended or sacrificed to produce an article or to render a unit of service.

The term 'cost' is also used in different contexts to mean purchase cost or sale price.

Expenses: Costs incurred for which matching benefit has been received. There is neither reduction nor increase in owner's equity.

Loss: It refers to costs incurred without receipt of matching benefit. This results in reduction of owner's equity.

(g) Cost Centre

For purpose of cost ascertainment, an organisation is divided into various sub-units or divisions. These subunits or divisions are called 'cost centres'. A cost centre maybe a place, a person, a group of persons, a machine, a group of machines, a department or a process. Costs are accumulated in relation to a cost centre. The following is the important classification of cost centres:

(i) Personal and impersonal cost centre: Personal cost centre stands for a person or a group of persons. Impersonal cost centre refers to a place, a machine or a group of machines.

(ii) Production cost centre and service cost centre Production cost centre refers to a place where goods are produced. They actually stand for a production department.

Service cost centre stands for divisions which help the production departments by providing various services like maintenance department, time office, boiler house, canteen etc.

(iii) Operation and process cost centre Operation cost centre stands for the total activities carried out in a production department is divided into smaller functions or operation in relation to which costs are accumulated, e.g., cutting, welding, machining, boring etc.

Process cost centre stands for a department where production is carried on continuously. Costs are collected for a process as a single unit.

(h) Profit Centre

Profit centre is a place or division in an organisation which brings revenue.

(i) Value Added

Value added refers to increase in the market value of a product in excess of the cost incurred for altering or changing the composition of the product.

(j) Stock-Out Cost

Stock-out cost refers to the loss suffered by a company due to stoppage of production due to non-availability of raw materials.

(k) Shut-Down Cost

Shut-down cost refers to expenses continued to be incurred even after temporary closure of production facilities, e.g., insurance, security, management expenses like director's fees, managing director's salary, salary and wages to skilled employees, Audit fees, etc.

The following chart shows classification of costs:

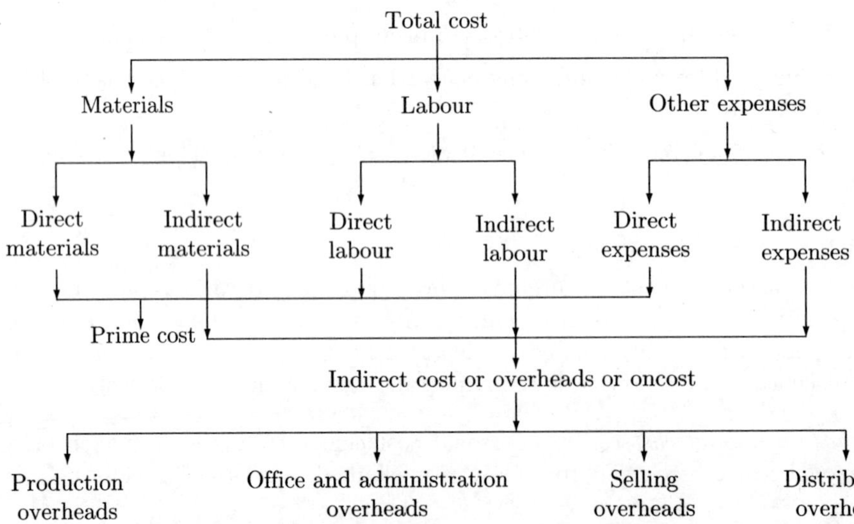

2.11 NON-COST ITEMS

The following expenses and revenues are not included in cost books:

1. **Finance expenses:** Expenses on issue of shares and debentures, discounts on issue of shares and debentures and interest paid on borrowings.
2. **Intangible assets written off:** Goodwill, preliminary expenses written off, etc.
3. **Provisions:** Provision for investments, provision for doubtful debts, etc.
4. **Appropriation of profits:** Transfer to reserves, proposed dividend, etc.
5. **Abnormal losses:** Loss by fire, theft etc.
6. **Capital losses:** Loss on sale of fixed assets and loss on sale of investments.
7. **All incomes:** Income from investments, profit on sale of assets, commissions and discounts earned.
8. **Income tax paid:** Provision for income tax.
9. **Others:** Fines, penalties, damages, gifts, presents, charity and donation.

2.12 COST SHEET OR COST STATEMENT

Cost sheet is a statement showing costs incurred during a period presented in a logical order arranged under proper headings. It is prepared to give maximum details like number of units produced and cost per unit of various cost groupings. Cost sheets may also be prepared for a job, a batch or a process. There is no fixed format for a cost sheet. It may be modified to suit the requirements. The following is the specimen of a cost sheet:

Proforma of a simple cost sheet or cost statement		
Particulars	**Total Cost (₹)**	**Cost per Unit (₹)**
Direct materials	xxx	xxx
Direct labour/wages/factory wages/manufacturing wages	xxx	xxx
Direct expenses/chargeable expenses	xxx	xxx
Prime cost	xxx	xxx
Add: Factory OHS/works OHS/production OHS/ manufacturing OHS	xxx	xxx
Works cost/factory cost	xxx	xxx
Add: Administration OHS	xxx	xxx
Cost of production	xxx	xxx
Add: Selling and distribution OHS	xxx	xxx
Cost of sales/total cost	xxx	xxx
Profit/loss	xxx	xxx
Sales	xxx	xxx

Proforma of a comprehensive cost sheet or cost statement			
Particulars		**Total Cost (₹)**	**Cost per Unit (₹)**
Materials consumed:			
Opening stock of raw materials/direct materials	xxx		
Add: Purchase of raw matcrials/direct materials	xxx		
Add: All purchase related expenses (carriage inward, import duty, insurance in transit and handling charge)	xxx		
Materials available for use	xxx		
Less: Closing stock of raw materials/direct materials	xxx	xxx	xxx
Direct labour		xxx	xxx
Direct expenses/chargeable expenses		xxx	xxx
Prime cost		xxx	xxx
Add: Factory overheads:			
Indirect materials, indirect wages, factory rent, rates and lighting, power, fuel, coal, gas, steam and water	xxx		
Depreciation, repairs and maintenance of factory building, plant, machinery and equipment	xxx		
Drawing office expenses, haulage	xxx		
Less: Sale of scrap	xxx	xxx	xxx
		xxx	xxx
Add: Opening stock of work-in-progress		xxx	xxx
Cost of total goods processed		xxx	xxx
Less: Closing stock of work-in-progress		xxx	xxx
Works cost/factory cost		xxx	xxx
Add: Administration overheads:			
Office rent, rates, lighting and insurance	xxx		
Depreciation, repairs and maintenance of office furniture and equipment	xxx		
Director's fees, office salary	xxx	xxx	xxx
Cost of production		xxx	xxx

Add: Opening stock of finished goods		xxx	xxx
Cost of goods available for sale		xxx	xxx
Less: Closing stock of finished goods		xxx	xxx
Cost of goods sold		xxx	xxx
Add: Selling and Distribution overheads:			
Advertisement, free samples, showroom expenses	xxx		
Sales office salary and allowances	xxx		
Salesmen's salary and commission	xxx		
Travelling expenses (for sales purpose)	xxx		
Warehouse rent and rates	xxx		
Carriage outward, delivery van expenses	xxx	xxx	xxx
Cost of sales/total cost		xxx	xxx
Profit/loss		xxx	xxx
Sales		xxx	xxx

Advantages of a cost sheet

1. It helps to ascertain total cost and cost per unit.
2. Costs are classified under proper headings and presented in a logical order.
3. It enables inter-firm and intra-firm comparison of costs.
4. It helps in price fixation.
5. It helps to ascertain profit or loss for a period.
6. It helps in preparing tenders and quotations.
7. It helps in preparing budgets.
8. It enables close watch over cost for cost control.

Production or manufacturing accounts

If information for a period relating to cost of production is presented in a ledger format, it is called production account or manufacturing account. All production expenses are debited to this account. Opening stock of work-in-progress is shown on the debit side. Closing stock of work-in-progress is shown on the credit side. The following is a proforma of a production account.

Proforma of production or manufacturing account

Particulars		Total Cost (₹)	Particulars	Total Cost (₹)
To opening work-in-progress		xxx	By closing stock of work-in-progress	xxx
To Materials consumed:				
Purchase of materials	xxx		By production cost c/d (Balancing figure)	xxx
Add: Opening stock of materials	xxx			
Add: Purchase related expenses	xxx			
	xxx			
Less: Closing stock of materials	xxx	xxx		
To Direct labour		xxx		
To Production overheads	xxx			
Less: Sale of scrap	xxx	xxx		
		xxx		xxx
To production cost b/d To administration overheads		xxx xxx	By cost of production (Balancing figure)	xxx
		xxx		xxx

Illustration-1

(Computation of materials consumed)

Calculate materials consumed from the following information:

	₹
Opening stock of raw materials	18,000
Purchase of raw materials	2,30,000
Carriage inward	27,000
Sale of raw material scrap	8,000
Closing stock of materials	20,000

Solution

Statement showing cost of raw materials consumed:

		₹
Opening stock of raw materials		18,000
Add: Purchase of raw materials		2,30,000
Add: Carriage inward		27,000
		2,75,000
Less: Sale of raw material scrap	8,000	
Less: Closing stock of materials	20,000	28,000
Materials consumed		2,47,000

Illustration-2

(Computation of materials consumed)

From the following information calculate the cost of materials consumed:

	₹
Stock on materials on 1.4.09	50,000
Purchase of materials	4,00,000
Import duty and clearing charges	1,00,000
Carriage on purchase	60,000
Transit insurance and handling charges	25,000
Return of defective materials to supplier	40,000
Sale of raw materials scrap	20,000
Stock of materials on 31.3.10	60,000

Solution

Statement showing cost of materials consumed

	₹
Stock on materials on 1.4.09	50,000

Add: Purchase of materials		4,00,000
Add: Import duty and clearing charges		1,00,000
Add: Carriage on purchase		60,000
Add: Transit insurance and handling charges		25,000
		6,35,000
Less: Return of defective materials to supplier	40,000	
Less: Sale of raw materials scrap	20,000	
Less: Stock of materials on 31.3.10	60,000	1,20,000
Cost of materials consumed		5,15,000

Illustration-3

(Computation of prime cost)

From the following calculate the prime cost:

	₹
Stock on materials on 1.4.09	28,000
Purchase of materials	1,60,000
Expenses in connection with purchases	20,000
Direct materials returned to supplier	20,000
Stock of direct materials on 31.3.10	35,000
Manufacturing wages	90,000
Royalty charges	75,000
Hire and maintenance charges of a special machinery	45,000

Solution

Statement showing computation of prime cost:

	₹	₹
Materials consumed:		
Stock on materials on 1.4.09	28,000	
Add: Purchase of materials	1,60,000	

Add: Expenses in connection with purchases		20,000	
		2,08,000	
Less: Direct materials returned	20,000		
Less: Stock of direct materials on 31.3.10	35,000	55,000	1,53,000
Manufacturing wages			90,000
Direct expenses: Royalty charges		75,000	
Hire and maintenance charges of a special machinery		45,000	1,20,000
Prime cost			3,63,000

Illustration-4

(Computation of prime cost)

From the following information calculate the prime cost:

	₹
Opening stock of raw materials	40,000
Purchase of raw materials	7,50,000
Carriage inward	25,000
Closing stock of raw materials	35,000
Carriage outward	30,000
Chargeable expenses	65,000
Indirect expenses	50,000
Factory wages	2,25,000
Factory rent	16,000

Solution

Statement showing prime cost:

	₹	**Total ₹**
Materials consumed:		
Opening stock of materials	40,000	
Add: Purchase of raw materials	7,50,000	

Add: Carriage inward	25,000	
	8,15,000	
Less: Closing stock of raw materials	35,000	7,80,000
Factory wages		2,25,000
Chargeable expenses		65,000
Prime cost		10,70,000

Illustration-5

(Cost sheet with grouping of expenses)

From the following information prepare a cost sheet showing (i) Prime cost, (ii) Works cost, (iii) Cost of production, (iv) Cost of sales and (v) Profit:

	₹
Purchase of materials	5,35,000
Stock of materials on 1.4.09	28,000
Stock of materials on 31.3.10	32,500
Manufacturing wages	2,85,000
Indirect materials	21,000
Indirect wages	42,700
Office salaries	57,600
Carriage inward	18,300
Chargeable expenses	53,000
Internal transport (factory)	27,500
Drawing office expenses	25,500
Advertisement	44,600
Printing and stationery	16,400
Works manager's salary	30,000
Carriage outward	18,500
Officer rent, rates and insurance	21,600
Director's fees	22,000

Foreman's salary	16,500
Income-tax paid	17,100
Depreciation, repairs and maintenance:	
Factory building	24,500
Plant and machinery	28,000
Office equipment and furniture	14,900
Transfer to reserves	20,000
Warehouse expenses	19,500
Motive power	24,000
Experimental expenses	13,000
Cotton waste	1,500
Oil, fuel and gas	8,600
Provision for bad and doubtful debts	9,300
Managing director's salary (40% to factory, 30% to office and 30% to selling)	45,000
Free samples distributed	3,700
Sale of scrap	2,500
Preliminary expenses written off	8,000
Packing and forwarding expenses	12,300
Lighting-factory	13,000
Lighting-office	9,000
Consumable stores	11,200
Sales	16,50,000

Solution

Cost sheet for the year ending 31.03.10		
	₹	**Total (₹)**
Materials consumed:		
Stock of materials on 1.4.09	28,000	
Add: Purchase of raw materials	5,35,000	
Add: Carriage inward	18,300	

	5,81,300	
Less: Stock of materials on 31.3.10	32,500	5,48,800
Manufacturing wages		2,85,000
Chargeable expenses		53,000
Prime cost		8,86,800
Factory overheads:		
Indirect materials	21,000	
Indirect wages	42,700	
Internal transport (factory)	27,500	
Drawing office expenses	25,500	
Works manager's salary	30,000	
Foreman's salary	16,500	
Depreciation, repairs and maintenance:		
Factory building	24,500	
Plant and machinery	28,000	
Motive power	24,000	
Experimental expenses	13,000	
Cotton waste	1,500	
Oil, fuel and gas	8,600	
Managing director's salary	18,000	
Lighting-factory (40%)	13,000	
Consumable stores	11,200	
	3,05,000	
Less: Sale of scrap	2,500	3,02,500
Factory cost/Works cost		11,89,300
Office and administration overheads:		
Office salaries	57,600	
Printing and stationery	16,400	
Office rent, rates and insurance	21,600	
Director's fees	22,000	
Depreciation, repairs and maintenance:		

Office equipment and furniture	14,900	
Managing director's Salary (30%)	13,500	
Lighting - office	9,000	1,55,000
Cost of production		13,44,300
Selling and distribution overheads:		
Advertisement	44,600	
Salesmen's salary, allowances and expenses	23,700	
Carriage outward	18,500	
Warehouse expenses	19,500	
Managing director's salary (30%)	13,500	
Free samples distributed	3,700	
Packing and forwarding expenses	12,300	1,35,800
Cost of sales/total cost		14,80,100
Profit (bf)		1,69,900
Sales		16,50,000

Illustration-6

(Simple cost sheet with stocks)

The following information is taken from the records of Arthi Ltd. for the month of April 2009.

	01.04.2009 ₹	**30.04.2009** ₹
Stock of raw materials	37,500	41,250
Stock of work-in-progress	28,700	23,200
Stock of finished goods	46,400	53,200
Transactions during the month are:		
Indirect materials	17,550	
Productive wages	97,500	
Indirect wages	20,900	
Purchase of materials	1,46,500	
Other factory expenses	24,800	

Administration expenses	41,600	
Sale of factory scrap	2,400	
Advertisement	26,500	
Carriage outward	5,000	
Sales	**4,35,000**	

Prepare a cost sheet showing (a) Prime cost, (b) Works cost, (c) Cost of production, (d) Cost of sales and (e) Profit.

Solution

Cost sheet for the month of April, 2009		
Particulars		**Total ₹**
Materials Consumed:		
Stock of materials on 1.4.09	37,500	
Add: Purchase of materials	1,46,500	
	1,84,000	
Less: Stock of materials on 30.4.09	41,250	1,42,750
Productive wages		97,500
Prime cost		2,40,250
Production overheads:		
Indirect materials	17,550	
Indirect wages	20,900	
Other factory expenses	24,800	
	63,250	
Less: Sale of factory scrap	2,400	60,850
		3,01,100
Add: Stock of work-in-progress on 1.4.09		28,700
		3,29,800
Less: Stock of work-in-progress on 30.4.09		23,200
Works cost		3,06,600
Administration overheads:		41,600
Cost of production		3,48,200

Add: Stock of finished goods on 1.4.09		46,400
		3,94,600
Less: Stock of finished goods on 30.4.09		53,200
Cost of goods sold		3,41,400
Selling and distribution overheads:		
Advertisement	26,500	
Carriage outward	5,000	31,500
Cost of sales		3,72,900
Profit (bf)		62,100
Sales		4,35,000

Illustration-7

(Apportionment of common expenses)

Arya Ltd. is producing two models of a product: model 'A' and model 'B'. The following cost information is taken from their records for 6 months period ending 31.3.09:

	1.10.2008 ₹	**31.3.2009** ₹
Stock of materials	29,800	21,970
Transactions during the month are:		
Purchase of materials	1,24,500	
Direct labour	81,900	
Office overheads	62,100	
Selling overheads	35,700	

The company wants to earn a profit of 20% on sales on both the products. The number of units produced were model 'A' 2,500 and model 'B' 3,000. Other information:

(a) Model 'B' consumes 20% more materials than model 'A'.
(b) Time spent for model 'B' is 25% more than model 'A'.
(c) Factory overheads are apportioned in the direct labour ratio over the two models.
(d) Administration overheads apportioned equally over the two models.
(e) Selling overheads apportioned in 2:3 ratio.

Prepare a cost sheet showing selling price of each model.

Solution

Cost sheet for 6 months ending 31.3.2009					
Particular		**Total (₹)**	**Ratio**	**Model 'A' (₹)**	**Model 'B' (₹)**
Materials Consumed:					
Stock of materials					
On 1.10.08	29,800				
Add: Purchase of materials	1,24,500				
	1,54,300				
Less: Stock of materials on 31.3.09	21,970	1,32,330	5:6	60,150	72,180
Direct labour		81,900	4:5	36,400	45,500
Prime cost				96,550	1,17,680
Factory overheads		62,100	4:5	27,600	34,500
Works cost				1,24,150	1,52,180
Office overheads		43,000	1:1	21,500	21,500
Cost of production				1,45,650	1,73,680
Selling overheads		35,700	2:3	14,280	21,420
Total cost				1,59,930	1,95,100
Profit: 20% on sales (or) 20/80 on cost				39,983	48,775
Sales				1,99,913	2,43,875
Number of units produced				2,500	3,000
Selling price per unit				79.97 (Approx.)	81.29 (Approx.)

Illustration-8

(Overhead expenses given as %)

The following expenses were taken from the account books of Nortan Ltd. for the year ending 31.3.2010:

	₹
Direct materials	6,00,000
Direct labour	4,25,000
Direct expenses	65,000

Charge factory overheads at 60% of direct labour, office overheads at 20% on factory cost and selling overheads at 15% of factory cost.

Prepare a cost sheet showing profit earned if the company earns a profit of 25% on sales.

Solution

Cost sheet for the year ended 31.3.2010	
	Total (₹)
Direct materials	6,00,000
Direct labour	4,25,000
Direct expenses	65,000
Prime cost	10,90,000
Factory overheads - 60% of direct labour	2,55,000
Works cost	13,45,000
Office overheads - 20% on works cost	2,69,000
Cost of production	16,14,000
Selling overheads - 15% on works cost	2,01,750
Total cost	18,15,750
Profit - 25% on sales or 25/75 on total cost	6,05,250
Sales	24,21,000

Illustration-9

(Finding the value of closing stock of finished goods)

The management of Jaihind Ltd. gives you the following information for the year ending 31.3.09. You are required to prepare a cost sheet.

	₹
Direct materials	3,75,000
Direct labour	2,40,000
Factory overheads	95,000

Administration overheads	60,000
Selling overheads	36,000
Sales	8,97,000

Additional information:

1. 3,500 units were produced during the year
2. Stock of finished goods 350 units valued at ₹70,000 as on 01.04.2008
3. Stock of finished goods as on 31.03.2009 are 400 units.

Solution

(i) Valuation of stock of finished goods on current cost basis:

Cost Sheet for the year ending 31.3.2009		
	Units	**Total ₹**
Direct materials	3,500	3,75,000
Direct labour	-	2,40,000
Prime cost	3,500	6,15,000
Factory overheads	-	95,000
Works cost	3,500	7,10,000
Administration overheads	-	60,000
Cost of production	3,500	7,70,000
Add: Opening stock of finished goods	350	70,000
	3,850	8,40,000
Less: Closing stock of finished goods	400	88,000
Cost of goods sold	3,450	7,52,000
Selling overheads	-	36,000
Cost of sales	3,450	7,88,000
Profit (bf)	-	1,09,000
Sales	3,450	8,97,000

(ii) Valuation of stock of finished goods on average cost basis:

Cost sheet for the year ending 31.3.2009		
	Units	**Total ₹**
Cost of production (Same as in (i))	3,500	7,70,000
Add: Opening stock of finished goods	350	70,000
	3,850	8,40,000
Less: Closing stock of finished goods	400	87,272
Cost of goods sold	3,450	7,52,728
Selling overheads	-	36,000
Cost of sales	3,450	7,88,728
Profit (bf)	-	1,08,272
Sales	3,450	8,97,000

Note:

Valuation of closing stock of finished goods:

(i) Current cost of production per unit $= \dfrac{\text{Cost of production during the year}}{\text{Number of units produced during the year}}$

$$= \frac{7{,}70{,}000}{3{,}500} = ₹220$$

Value of closing Stock $= 400 \times 220 =$ ₹88,000

(ii) Average cost of production per unit $= \dfrac{\text{Cost of production + Value of opening stock}}{\text{Units produced + Opening stock units}}$

$$= \frac{8{,}40{,}000}{3{,}850} = ₹218.18 \text{ (Approx.)}$$

Value of closing stock $= 400 \times 218.18 =$ ₹87,272

Illustration-10

(Finding the missing information)

The books of Adarsh Manufacturing Company presents the following data for the month of April, 2001.

Direct Labour Cost ₹17,500 being 175% of works overhead and cost of goods sold excluding administration expenses ₹56,000. Inventory accounts showed the following opening and closing balances:

	April 1 ₹	April 30 ₹
Raw materials	8,000	10,600
Work-in-progress	10,500	14,500
Finished goods	17,600	19,000
Other data:		
Selling expenses	3,500	
General and administration expenses	2,500	
Sales for the month	75,000	

You are required to:

(i) Compute the value of raw materials purchased
(ii) Prepare a cost statement showing the various elements of cost and also the profit.

(CA-Inter)

Solution

(i)

Computation of value of materials purchased		
	₹	₹
Cost of goods sold	-	56,000
Add: Closing stock of raw materials	-	10,600
Closing stock of work-in-progress	-	14,500
Closing stock of finished goods	-	19,000
		1,00,100
Less: Opening stock of raw materials	8,000	
Opening stock of work-in-progress	10,500	
Opening stock of finished goods	17,600	
Direct labour	17,500	
Works overhead (17,500×100/175)	10,000	63,600
Raw materials purchase	-	36,500

Note:

(1) All items added in the cost sheet till cost of goods sold is deducted.
(2) All items deducted in the cost sheet till cost of goods sold is added.
(3) Since administration cost is not included in cost of goods sold, it is not deducted.

(ii)

Cost statement for the month of April 2001		
		Total ₹
Materials consumed:		
Opening stock of raw materials	8,000	
Add: Purchase of materials	36,500	
	44,500	
Less: Closing stock of raw materials	10,600	33,900
Direct labour		17,500
Prime cost		51,400
Factory overheads (17,500×100/175)		10,000
		61,400
Add: Opening stock of work-in-progress		10,500
		71,900
Less: Closing stock of work-in-progress		14,500
Works cost		57,400
General and administration overheads		2,500
Cost of production		59,900
Add: Opening stock of finished goods		17,600
		77,500
Less: Closing stock of finished goods		19,000
Cost of goods sold		58,500
Selling expenses		3,500
Cost of sales		62,000
Profit (bf)		13,000
Sales		75,000

Illustration-11

(Finding missing information)

The following data relate to XYZ Ltd.

	Inventories	
	Beginning ₹	Ending ₹
Finished goods	1,10,000	95,000
Work-in-progress	70,000	80,000
Raw materials	90,000	95,000
Additional information:		
Cost of goods available for sale	6,84,000	
Total goods processed during the period	6,54,000	
Factory overheads	1,67,000	
Direct materials used	1,93,000	

Requirements:

(i) Determine raw materials purchased.
(ii) Determine the direct labour cost incurred.
(iii) Determine the cost of goods sold.

(B.Com. (Hons.), Delhi University)

Solution

(i)

Computation of raw materials purchased	
	₹
Direct materials used	1,93,000
Add: Closing stock of raw materials	95,000
	2,88,000
Less: Opening stock of raw materials	90,000
Raw materials purchase	1,98,000

(ii)

Determination of labour cost incurred	
	₹
Total goods processed during the period	6,54,000
Less: Opening stock of work-in-progress	70,000
	5,84,000
Less: Factory overheads	1,67,000
Prime cost	4,17,000
Less: Direct materials used	1,93,000
Direct labour cost	2,24,000

(iii)

Determining the cost of goods sold	
	₹
Cost of goods available for sale	6,84,000
Less: Closing stock of finished goods	95,000
Cost of goods sold	5,89,000

2.13 EXERCISES

I. Objective Type Questions

A. State whether the following statements are true or false

1. Cost centre is a place where direct materials are expended.
2. Direct materials enter the finished product.
3. The total of direct labour, direct expenses and production overheads is called conversion cost.
4. Hire charges paid for a special machinery is part of production overheads.
5. Royalty payable on production is production overheads.
6. Imputed cost results in outflow of cash.
7. Semi-variable cost is also called step cost.
8. The total of all direct expenses is called prime cost.
9. Valued added refers to cost incurred in the production of a product.
10. Variable cost per unit increases due to increase in production.
11. Fixed cost is also called period cost.

12. Standard cost is a predetermined cost.
13. Fixed costs are generally uncontrollable.
14. Sunk costs result in cash payment.
15. Office overheads are unavoidable costs.

(**Ans:** True - 2, 3, 7, 8, 11, 12, 13, 15; False - 1, 4, 5, 6, 9, 10, 14)

B. Fill in the blanks

1. Prime cost refers to total of all ___________ expenses.
2. Works cost is the total of prime cost and ___________.
3. Costs which result in actual payment of cash is called ___________.
4. Period cost or time cost is ___________ cost.
5. The benefit foregone due to an alternative decision is called ___________.
6. Labour cost incurred for conversion of raw materials into finished goods is called ___________.
7. Bad debts is an example of ___________ cost.
8. Costs remaining constant per unit is called ___________.
9. Place, a person, a machine or a group of these in relation to which cost is ascertained is called ___________.
10. The division which brings or earns revenue for a business is called ___________.
11. Costs which can be influenced by managerial action is called ___________.
12. Travelling expenses incurred specifically for a particular job is called ___________.
13. Expenses incurred for two or more jobs or cost centres is called ___________.
14. Increase in the market value of a product in excess of costs incurred for changing or altering its composition is known as ___________.
15. The difference in the total cost between two levels of production is called ___________.

(**Ans:** 1. Direct, 2. Factory overheads, 3. Out of pocket cost, 4. Fixed, 5. Opportunity cost, 6. Direct labour, 7. Policy, 8. Variable cost, 9. Cost centre, 10. Profit centre, 11. Controllable cost, 12. Direct expenses, 13. Indirect expenses, 14. Value added, 15. Differential cost)

II. Theory Questions

A. Short answer type questions

1. What is cost centre? Explain the various types of cost centre.
2. Explain direct materials.
3. What is direct labour?
4. What is direct expense? Give few examples.
5. What is prime cost?
6. Explain opportunity cost.
7. What is policy cost?
8. What is imputed cost?
9. What is cost classification?
10. Define out-of-pocket cost.

11. Define semi-variable cost.
12. All costs are controllable, comment.
13. What is value added? Explain.
14. What is conversion cost?
15. What is cost sheet?

B. Long answer type questions

1. Write short notes on: (a) Cost centre; (b) Opportunity cost; (c) Notional cost; (d) Out of pocket cost; and (e) Policy cost.
2. What do you understand by cost classification? Explain the various cost elements on the basis of variability.
3. Explain the functionwise classification of overheads.
4. Explain cost sheet. What are its uses?
5. All costs are controllable. Explain.
6. Explain what do you understand by chargeable expenses and state its treatment in cost accounts. **(CA-Inter)**
7. Explain various costs used in decision making and explain their characteristics. **(B.Com. (Hons), Delhi University)**
8. What is the purpose of classifying costs?

III. Practical Problems

A. Short answer type questions

1. Compute materials consumed from the following:

	₹
Opening stock of materials	20,000
Purchase of materials	1,25,000
Carriage on purchases	15,000
Sale of materials scrap	7,000
Closing stock of materials	18,000

(**Ans:** Materials consumed ₹1,35,000)

2. Compute materials consumed from the following:

	₹
Purchase of direct materials	3,50,000
Carriage inward	27,000
Carriage outward	18,000

Sale of factory scrap	10,000
Sale of direct materials scrap	15,000
Materials returned to supplier	30,000
Indirect materials	25,000
Opening stock of direct materials	50,000
Closing stock of direct materials	40,000

(**Ans:** Materials consumed ₹3,42,000)

3. Compute prime cost:

	₹
Opening Stock of materials	35,000
Purchase of materials	4,10,000
Import duty and Clearing charges	1,50,000
Other purchase expenses	25,000
Closing stock of materials	30,000
Factory wages	2,40,000
Factory overheads	1,60,000
Royalty paid on production	1,20,000
Hire charges for special machinery	40,000

(**Ans:** Prime cost ₹9,90,000)

4. Find the gross cost of goods processed during the period:

	₹
Prime cost	80,000
Factory overheads	45,000
Opening stock of work-in-progress	30,000
Closing stock of work-in-progress	25,000
Office overheads	70,000

(**Ans:** Gross cost of goods processed ₹1,55,000)

Note: Gross cost of goods processed = Prime Cost + Factory Overheads + Opening Stock of Work-in-Progress.

5. Find the net works cost:

	₹
Prime cost	1,50,000
Production overheads	60,000
Opening stock of work-in-progress	27,000
Closing stock of work-in-progress	30,000

(**Ans:** Net works cost ₹2,07,000)

6. Prepare a cost sheet from the following:

	₹
Raw materials consumed	80,000
Wages	20,000

Works expenses charged at 100% of wages, office overheads charged at 25% on works cost and selling overheads at 10% on works cost.

(**Ans:** Cost of sales ₹1,62,000)

7. Calculate profit and sales from the following:

	₹
Cost of sales	5,00,000
Profit 20% on sales	

(**Ans:** Profit ₹1,25,000; Sales - ₹6,25,000)

8. In a factory a standard product is manufactured. From the following particulars prepare a cost sheet showing total cost and profit made:

	₹
Raw materials consumed	30,000
Labour	60,000

Works overhead is charged at 40% of works cost and office overheads is taken at 20% of total cost. The standard product sold during the period is 180 units at ₹1200 each.

(B.Com., Bharathidasan University)

(**Ans:** Total cost ₹1,87,500; Total profit - ₹28,500; Cost per unit ₹1041.67; Profit per unit ₹158.33)

Note :

(a) Works cost = 40/60 on prime cost
(b) Office overheads = 20/80 on works cost.

9. The following information is taken from the records of X Ltd. for the year ending 31.3.2010:

Raw materials consumed	₹20,000
Direct wages	₹16,000
Production overheads	150% of direct wages
Office overheads	25% on works cost
Selling overheads	₹2 per unit sold
Opening stock of finished goods	500 units valued at ₹4,000
Units produced during the period	₹10,000
Units sold during the period	9,500 units at ₹10 per unit.

Prepare a cost sheet.

(**Ans:** Cost of production - ₹75,000; Closing stock - 1,000 units; Value - ₹7,500; Cost of sales-₹90,500; Profit - ₹4,500)

B. Comprehensive questions

1. **Simple cost sheet-with detailed cost elements**

From the following particulars taken from the books of United Engineering Ltd., prepare a cost sheet for the year ending 31.3.2010.

	₹
Stock of materials on 1.4.2009	65,700
Stock of materials on 31.3.2010	48,500
Purchase of materials	3,79,000
Productive wages	2,83,000
Hire charges and maintenance of a special equipment	46,000
Royalty paid	84,000
Carriage on purchases	21,500
Carriage outward	24,900
Indirect materials	34,000
Indirect wages	30,000
Foreman salary	20,000

Depreciation, repairs and maintenance	
Of Plant and machinery	42,000
Of office furniture and equipment	27,500
Drawing office salaries	18,000
Motive power, fuel and oil	39,000
Lubricants and cotton waste	13,400
Office salaries	52,000
Printing and stationery	11,300
Warehouse expenses	26,000
Advertisement	31,600
Travelling expenses	
General	12,700
Sales promotion	17,500
Samples and gifts	14,000
Bad debts written off	10,000
General manager's salary	60,000

General manager's salary to be apportioned in the ratio of 4 : 3 : 3 to factory, office and sales departments. Sale of finished goods amounted to ₹15,00,000.

(**Ans:** Prime cost - ₹8,30,700; Works cost - ₹10,51,100; Cost of production - ₹11,72,600; Cost of sales - ₹13,14,600; and Profit - ₹1,85,400)

2. **Simple cost sheet with opening and closing stocks**

From the following particulars, prepare a cost sheet for the year ending 31.03.2010:

	1.4.2009 ₹	**31.3.2010** ₹
Stock of materials	22,750	26,300
Stock of work-in-progress	18,200	15,700
Stock of finished goods	37,600	34,500

	₹
Purchase of raw materials	6,20,000
Carriage inward	21,400
Factory manager salary	25,000
Depreciation of plant and machinery	27,100
Office rent, rates and insurance	14,600

Salesman travelling expenses	21,900
Carriage outward	13,800
Debenture interest	16,500
Directors fee	24,000
General manager salary	25,000
Transfer to general reserve	20,000
Wages	3,70,000
Power expenses	1,15,000
Office salaries	28,000
General expenses	17,300
Dividend paid	35,000
Warehouse expenses	29,000
Income tax	41,000
Goodwill written off	10,000
Bank charges	6,000
Printing and stationery	12,500
Sales for the year	16,00,000

(**Ans:** Prime cost - ₹10,07,850; Works cost - ₹11,77,450; Cost of production - ₹13,04,850; Cost of goods sold - ₹13,07,950; Cost of sales - ₹13,72,650; Profit ₹2,27,350)

3. Dev Ltd. provides the following particulars for the month of August, 2009. Prepare a cost sheet:

	1.8.2009 ₹	**31.8.2009** ₹
Stock of raw materials	75,000	60,000
Stock of work-in-progress	27,000	36,500
Stock of finished goods	50,000	62,000

Transactions during the month of August 2009:

	₹
Purchase of raw materials	2,50,000
Factory expenses	82,000
Depreciation of plant and machinery	41,000
Selling and distribution overheads	27,500

Direct labour	1,70,000
Sale of factory scrap	16,000
Office overheads	34,500
Sales	6,00,000

(**Ans:** Prime cost - ₹4,35,000; Works cost - ₹5,32,500; Cost of production - ₹5,67,000; Cost of goods sold - ₹5,55,000; Cost of sales - ₹5,82,500; Profit - ₹17,500)

4. **Apportionment of Common Expenses**

TV Ltd. produces television sets in two models - Deluxe and Premium. The following information is taken from their records for the year ending 31.3.2010.

	1.4.2009 ₹		31.3.2010 ₹	
	Deluxe	**Premium**	**Deluxe**	**Premium**
Stock of work-in-progress	70,000	40,000	90,000	80,000
Stock of finished goods	1,65,000	1,10,000	2,10,000	1,70,000

Purchase of materials - ₹12,00,000; Direct labour - ₹7,50,000. Materials consumed were in proportion of 5 : 7 and wages incurred were in the ratio of 2 : 3 for the two models. Factory overheads is charged at 80% of direct labour, Administration overheads charged at 25% on works cost and selling and distribution overheads estimated at 15% on works cost.

The company wants to earn a profit of 25% on sales. Find the profit of each model for the year 2009.

(**Ans:** Profit - Deluxe: ₹4,61,000; Premium - ₹6,66,000)

5. **Valuation of Closing Stock**

Sri Ram Ltd. produces a standard product. It furnished the following cost information for 6 months ending 30.9.09:

	₹
Materials consumed	80,000
Direct labour	55,000
Factory overheads	33,000
Selling overheads at ₹2 per unit	
Number of units produced 4,200	
Number of units sold - 4,000 at ₹45 per unit	

You are required to prepare a cost sheet from the above showing (a) Cost of production for the period, (b) Cost per unit; (c) Profit for the period; (d) Profit per unit.

(**Ans:** Total cost of production - ₹1,68,000; Cost of production per unit - ₹40; Total profit - ₹12,000; Profit per unit - ₹3)

6. **Valuation of closing stock**

The following data relate to the manufacture of a Standard product during the four weeks ended 26th March, 1991:

Raw materials consumed	₹15,000
Direct wages	₹9,800
Machine hours worked	2,300 hours
Machine hour rate	₹0.50
Office on cost	10% of works cost
Selling on cost	₹0.10 per unit
Units produced - 19,030	
Units sold - 11,418 at ₹2 each.	

You are required to prepare a cost sheet in respect of the above showing the cost production and profit per unit. (**B.Com., Madras University**)

(**Ans:** Cost of production per unit - ₹1.50; Profit per unit - ₹0.40)

7. **Finding missing information**

The books and records of the Anand Manufacturing Company present the following data for the month of August, 2007:

Direct Labour Cost - ₹16,000 (160% of factory overhead)
Cost of goods sold - ₹56,000

	August 1 ₹	**August 31** ₹
Raw materials	8,000	8,600
Work-in-progress	8,000	12,000
Finished goods	14,000	18,000

Other Data:

	₹
General and administration expenses	2,600
Selling expenses	3,400
Sales for the month	75,000

You are required to prepare a statement showing cost of goods manufactured and sold and profit earned. **(CA-Inter)**

(**Ans:** Cost of goods sold - ₹56,000; Profit - ₹15,600)

Note: Purchase of raw materials - ₹36,000.

8. **Finding missing information**

On June 30, 2006 a flash flood damaged the warehouse and factory of ABC Corporation completely destroying the work-in-progress inventory. There was no damage to either raw materials or finished goods inventories. A physical verification taken after the flood revealed the following valuations:

	₹
Raw materials	62,000
Work-in-progress	?
Finished goods	1,19,000

The inventory on January 1, 2006 consisted of the following:

	₹
Raw materials	30,000
Work-in-progress	1,00,000
Finished goods	1,40,000

A review of the books and records disclosed that the gross profit margin historically approximated 25% of sales. The sales for the first six months of 2006 were ₹3,40,000. Raw material purchases were ₹1,15,000. Direct labour cost for this period were ₹80,000 and manufacturing overheads has historically been 50% of direct labour.

Compute the cost of work-in-progress inventory lost at June 30, 2006 by preparing a statement of cost and profit. **(B.Com. (Hons.), Delhi University)**

(**Ans:** Closing stock of work-in-progress - ₹69,000 and Profit - ₹85,000)

MATERIALS COST CONTROL

3

- Material Cost—Meaning
- Objectives of Materials Control
- Purchase Control
- Purchase Department—Functions
- Store Keeping
- Duties of Store Keeper
- Stores Records
- Inventory control—Types
- Stock Level—Settings
- EOQ—Economic Order Quantity
- ABC analysis
- JIT System
- VED System
- FNSD analysis

3.1 MEANING

Materials cost forms the major part of the total cost of production of almost all goods. Materials include direct materials, indirect materials, components and spare parts. Direct materials are the raw materials entering the body of finished product. Indirect materials are those items like office stores and supplies which do not enter the body of finished products. Materials of very minor value entering the body of the finished product like sewing threads, gums, glues, screws etc. are treated as indirect materials. Components are items purchased from outside suppliers and fitted into the final product, e.g. tyres, tubes and wind screens of a car. Spare parts are items either produced locally or purchased from outside and used in the maintenance of plant and machinery. The term inventory is a wider term. It includes all material items and stock of finished goods.

3.1.1 Objectives of Materials Control

Since materials is a major element of cost, it presents a great scope for controlling cost of production. The following are the important objectives of materials control:

1. Adequate quantity of materials must be made available to ensure continuous production. Production should not suffer for want of materials.
2. Materials of suitable quality must be purchased at lowest possible price by availing trade discount and quantity discount.
3. Materials control must also avoid overstocking of materials resulting in unnecessary locking up of large working capital in inventory.
4. Wastage of materials during handling and storage must be reduced to the minimum
5. Proper safety measures should be taken to prevent loss by fire, theft and pilferage.
6. Materials purchased earlier should be exhausted first to avoid materials becoming obsolete.
7. Proper records of materials movements must be maintained.
8. Proper control system should be established to ensure correct payment to suppliers.

3.1.2 Requirements of Materials Control

1. **Coordination:** There should be close co-operation and coordination of all related departments viz. purchasing, stores, inspection, accounting and payment.
2. **Purchase Scheduling:** Materials are to be purchased at proper intervals of time to ensure timely availability of materials for continuous production.
3. **Stock levels:** Proper stock levels must be maintained to avoid excessive investment in materials.
4. **Standard Norms:** Standard norms should be followed in purchasing, storage and issue of materials.
5. **Internal Check:** A suitable internal check system should be established to prevent misappropriation of materials.

6. **Standard Forms:** Proper materials forms must be used for recording various transactions.
7. **Proper Storage facilities:** Suitable storage facilities must be arranged so that loss of materials by theft, fire and pilferage is prevented.
8. **Materials issues:** Materials must be issued only against suitable requisitions.
9. **Pricing of Issue:** A suitable method of pricing the materials issued should be followed for correct valuation of materials consumed and stock of materials.
10. **Inspection:** Stocks are to be verified continuously to locate discrepancies in stocks.
11. **Production Process control:** Material wastages must be reduced to the minimum through proper production procedures.
12. **Accounting:** Suitable accounting procedure is established to record all materials transactions.
13. **Payment to supplier:** Payment procedure followed should ensure correct payment to suppliers.
14. **Reporting to Management:** Various reports relating to materials transactions must be prepared and sent to suitable authorities, enabling management to take corrective actions.

Materials control is broadly divided into four stages—purchase control, stores control, issue control and material loss control.

3.2 PURCHASE CONTROL

Materials control begins with purchase of materials.

3.2.1 Purchase Department

A separate department is established in medium and large concerns to procure materials on behalf of all user departments. A user department may be allowed to buy materials of small quantity which are required urgently. Centralised purchasing brings the following advantages:

1. Persons with suitable skills and knowledge is appointed to purchase materials.
2. Economy in purchase is ensured due to large scale purchase.
3. Specialisation in purchase is made possible.
4. Avoids excessive purchase.
5. Avoids duplication in purchase function.
6. It also ensures better control over purchasing.

The following are the disadvantages of centralised purchasing:

1. There will be delay in purchasing as user departments are not allowed to buy their materials requirements.
2. Centralised purchasing is not suitable when user departments are widely dispersed.

3. Chances of wrong purchase are many due to misunderstanding in the purchase department about the materials required by a user department.
4. Cost of operating a purchase department will be more.

Irrespective of the above disadvantages a centralised purchasing is more suitable except where user departments are located at distant places.

3.2.2 Functions of Purchase Department

1. Preparation of purchase budget

Purchase budget helps a purchase department to ascertain the type of materials to be purchased, their quantity and value. Finance required for purchase of materials is estimated in advance and arrangements for meeting financial requirements will be made.

2. Receiving purchase requisition

The following is a specimen of a standard purchase requisition:

<table>
<tr><td colspan="5">Purchase Requisition
Regular
Date: xxx   Occasional
No: xxx   Date by which material is required :xxx</td></tr>
<tr><th>Sl. No.</th><th>Code No.</th><th>Description of Materials</th><th>Quantity required</th><th>Remarks</th></tr>
<tr><td></td><td></td><td></td><td></td><td></td></tr>
<tr><td colspan="5">Requested by: xxx   Approved by : xxx
Purchase manager: xxx</td></tr>
</table>

Purchase requisition is a formal request made to purchase department to buy materials. Purchase requisition for regular materials is prepared by stores department when a material reaches reorder level. For special materials required occasionally, purchase requisition is prepared by the production department under authorisation from production manager.

A purchase requisition gives basic details like description of materials, quantity and time when materials are needed.

Purchase requisitions are prepared in triplicate. One copy is sent to the purchase department, the second copy is retained by the department which prepared the requisition and the third copy is sent to the authorising authority.

3. Choosing suppliers

The purchase department usually maintains up-to-date list of suppliers for each material. The purchase manager sends letters calling for tenders/quotations from suppliers. A comparative statement of all quotations is prepared. A supplier is selected whose price is lower and other terms like date of delivery, credit period etc. are favourable. The following factors are also considered while selecting a supplier:

1. Reliability based on past experience
2. Financial strength
3. Price and discount offered
4. Credit period
5. Time of delivery.

4. Placing purchase order

The following is a specimen of a purchase order:

XYZ Ltd

Purchase Order

No: xxx — Date: xxx

To: xxx — Ref. No:xxx

Sl. No.	Description	Quantity	Price per unit	Total value	Remarks

Delivery terms: xxx

Discount: xxx

Excise duty: xxx

Mode of transport: xxx

Mode of payment: xxx

Others: xxx

Please acknowledge the receipt of this order

For XYZ Ltd

Signature

It is a request in writing sent to supplier to supply certain specified materials at a certain price and conditions specified therein. When the supplier accepts the order it amounts to a legally binding contract between the buyer and supplier. The purchase order is prepared in five copies. These copies are sent to:

1. Supplier
2. Stores or requisitioning department
3. Receiving department
4. Accounting department
5. One copy is retained by the purchase department.

5. Receiving and inspection of materials

A separate receiving and inspection division is created in the purchase department in a large undertaking. Receiving department takes delivery of goods received from the supplier and checks the quantity and physical condition of materials received. The inspection team carries out quality checking. If quantity and qualities of materials are in order a Goods Received Note or Materials Inward Note or Receiving Report is prepared in five copies by the receiving and inspection department. The copies are sent as under:

1. One copy is retained by receiving and inspection department.
2. Four copies are sent to stores department with the materials. The storekeeper will check the materials received and verify the correctness of entries in goods received note. He will counter-sign the copies and will send one copy to purchase department, one copy to accounts department, one copy to requisitioning department and one copy is retained by the storekeeper. The following is the specimen of a Goods Received Note:

Goods Received Note

Supplier's name: xxx — No: xxx

Purchase order No: xxx — Date: xxx

Sl. No.	**Description**	**Code No.**	**Quantity**	**Rate (₹)**	**Amount (₹)**	**Remarks**

Received by: xxx — Inspected by: xxx

Stores ledger posted by: xxx — Store-keeper: xxx

Costed by: xxx

6. Checking and passing of the bills for payment

The invoice received from the supplier is sent to stores accounting section for verifying the authenticity and accuracy. The correctness of quantity of materials is checked with reference to goods received note. The correctness of price is checked by referring to purchase order. Then the accounting section passes the invoice for payment. The cashier makes the payment.

Computation of landed cost of materials

The invoice price of materials is not the effective cost of materials. To arrive at the effective cost of materials (landed cost/issue price of materials), all costs connected with purchase and receiving and stores overheads are added to net invoice price. The various costs forming the landed cost of materials are:

(i) Net invoice price (quotation price less trade discount)
(ii) Sales tax and excise duty
(iii) Carriage inward, loading and unloading charges.
(iv) Octroi, transit insurance etc.,
(v) Packing charges and cost of containers.
(vi) Stores overhead.

The following items are deducted from the total of the above:

(i) Sale of containers when no separate charge is made by supplier.
(ii) Credit given by supplier on return of containers.
(iii) CENVAT exercise credit available.
(iv) Normal wastage of materials deducted from the quantity of materials purchased only.

Abnormal loss of materials is valued at full cost and debited to costing profit and loss account.

Illustration-1: (Computation of issue price with normal loss)

ABC Chemicals Ltd, Delhi, purchased chemicals from a Varanasi supplier. Invoice particulars are given below:

	₹
Chemical A 3,000 kg at ₹4.20 per kg	12,600
Chemical B 5,000 kg at ₹3.80 per kg	19,000
Chemical C 2,000 kg at ₹4.75 per kg	9,500
Sales tax	2,055
Railway freight	1,000
Total	44,155

Other particulars are as under:

Chemicals	A	B	C
1. Transit loss (kg)	200	280	100
2. Carriage paid (₹)	270	650	325
3. Entry tax at Delhi	10 paise per kg	10 paise per kg	10 paise per kg

A provision for deterioration is to be made at 5% of chemicals. Calculate the rate of pricing of the chemicals **(CA-Inter)**

Solution

Computation of issue price					
Particulars	**Ratio**	**Chemicals**			**Total**
		A (₹)	**B (₹)**	**C (₹)**	
Purchase cost of materials	given	12,600	19,000	9,500	41,100
Add: Sales tax	Purchase cost	630	950	475	2,055
Railway freight	quantity purchased	300	500	200	1,000
carriage paid	given	270	650	325	1,245
Entry tax	quantity purchased	300	500	200	1,000
Total cost of materials		14,100	21,600	10,700	46,400
		Kg	Kg	Kg	Kg
Total quantity purchased		3,000	5,000	2,000	10,000
Less: Loss in transit		200	280	100	580
Total quantity received		2,800	4,720	1,900	9,420
Less: Deterioration in storage 5%		140	236	95	471
	Net quantity available for issue	2,660	4,484	1,805	8,949
Issue price per kg. $= \frac{\text{Total materials cost}}{\text{Net quantity available for issue}}$		₹5.30	₹4.82	₹5.93	-

Note: Loss in transit and deterioration in storage is treated as normal loss.

Illustration-2: (Computation of landed cost with normal and abnormal loss)

X Ltd purchased two materials 'A' and 'B' and the following information is available from the invoice:

	₹
Materials 'A'–2500 units at ₹5 per unit	12,500
Materials 'B'–4000 units at ₹8 per unit	32,000
Insurance	1,335
Freight and landing charge	3,250
Sales tax	1,780

Due to careless handling 50 units of material 'A' and 30 units of material 'B' were damaged in the premises of X Ltd.

You are required to

a) Calculate issue price of these materials.
b) Also calculate the issue price of these materials assuming a normal loss of 10%.

Solution

Statement of materials issue price

Particulars	Total (₹)	Material 'A'			Material 'B'		
		Units	Rate (₹)	Total (₹)	Units	Rate (₹)	Total (₹)
Purchase cost	44,500	2,500	5	12,500	4,000	8	32,000
Insurance (apportioned on value basis)	1,335	-	-	375	-	-	960
Freight and handling (apportioned on units basis)	3,250	-	-	1,250	-	-	2,000
Sales tax (apportioned on value basis)	1,780	-	-	500	-	-	1,280
Total	50,865	2,500	5.85	14,625	4,000	9.06	36,240
Less: Damage due to careless handling (abnormal loss)	564.3	50	5.85	292.50	30	9.06	271.80
	50,300.70	2,450	5.85	14,332.50	3,970	9.06	35,968.20
Less: Normal loss 10%	-	245	-	-	397	-	-
Total	50,300.70	2,205	6.50	14,332.50	3,573	10.07	35,968.20

a) Issue price when there is no normal loss: materials 'A' ₹5.85 and materials 'B' ₹9.06.
b) Issue price when there is normal loss of 10%: material 'A' ₹6.50 and materials 'B' ₹10.07.

Illustration-3: (Trade discount and cost of returnable containers)

The following are the details relating to a material purchased by a manufacturer.

(i) Purchase 2,000 kg at ₹40 per kg.
(ii) Trade discount 10%
(iii) Sales tax at 4%
(iv) Insurance 1% on total price.

(v) Loading and unloading ₹2,000

(vi) Cost of container at ₹50 per container for 100 kg of materials. Rebate is allowed at ₹35 per container if returned within 30 days. Containers are normally returned.

(vii) Normal loss of materials in stores 5%.

Compute landed cost and issue price of materials.

Solution

Calculation of issue price of materials		
	Units (kg)	**Total (₹)**
Purchase price (2,000 kg × ₹40)	2,000	80,000.00
Less: Trade discount 10%	-	8,000.00
	2,000	72,000.00
Add: Sales tax 4%		2,880.00
Total Price	2,000	74,880.00
Add: Insurance 1%	-	748.80
Add: Loading and unloading charges	-	2,000.00
	2,000	77,628.80
Add: Cost of container at ₹50 x 20	-	1,000.00
	2,000	78,628.80
Less: Credit for containers returned (₹35 × 20)	-	700.00
Landed cost	2,000	77,928.80
Less: Normal loss 5%	100	-
Total Cost	1,900	77,928.80

$$\text{Issue price per kg} = \frac{77{,}928.80}{1{,}900} = ₹41.02 \text{ approx}$$

Illustration-4: (Apportionment of purchase cost)

A lorry load of materials of mixed goods were purchased for ₹90,000. These were sorted into the following grades whose market rate is shown against each:

Grade A - 5,000 units selling rate at ₹12
Grade B - 3,000 units selling rate at ₹10
Grade C - 2,000 units selling rate at ₹5.

Find the purchase rate per unit of each grade of the materials assuming that all grades yield same rate of profit.

(B.Com., Madurai University)

Solution

Computation of profit%	
	₹
Sales value of materials purchased	
Grade A = 5,000 × 12	60,000
Grade B = 3,000 × 10	30,000
Grade C = 2,000 × 4	10,000
Total	1,00,000
Less: Cost of materials purchased	90,000
Profit	10,000

$$\% \text{ of profit on sales} = \frac{\text{Profit}}{\text{Sales}} \times 100$$

$$= \frac{10,000}{1,00,000} \times 100 = 10\%$$

Computation of purchase cost				
Grades	**Sales Value** ₹	**Profit** ₹	**Total Cost** ₹	**Cost p/u** ₹
Grade 'A'	60,000	6,000	54,000	10.80
Grade 'B'	30,000	3,000	27,000	9.00
Grade 'C'	10,000	1,000	9,000	4.50

3.3 RECEIVING AND INSPECTION

In small concerns the responsibility of receiving and inspecting of materials is entrusted to store keeper. In large organisations a separate Receipt and Inspection Department is created to receive and inspect the materials. The Receipt and Inspection Department usually performs the following functions.

1. Receives and inspects materials with purchase order and delivery challan received from the supplier. A copy of delivery challan is signed by an authorised person in Receipt and Inspection Department and sent to the supplier as a proof of receipt of materials.
2. Inspection department verifies the condition and quality of materials.
3. Inspection department will prepare an inspection report specifying the quality of materials received.

4. After completion of inspection, Goods Received Note is prepared in five copies. One copy is retained by the receiving department. The goods received are handed over to storekeeper with four copies of Goods Received Note. After receiving materials as per Goods Received Note, the storekeeper retains one copy of Goods Received Note and sends the other three copies to the following departments:

   (a) The Purchase Department
   (b) The Accounts Department
   (c) The Department which requisitioned the materials.

The following are the specimen of Materials Inspection Report and Goods Received Note:

Materials Inspection Report

Purchase order No: xxx — Goods Received Note No: xxx

Date: xxx — Date: xxx

Name of supplier: xxx

Sl. No.	**Description**	**Code No.**	**Quantity**			**Remarks**
			Received	**Accepted**	**Rejected**	

Date: xxx

Inspected by: xxx

Goods Received Note

Supplier name: xxx — Date: xxx

Purchase order No:

Sl. No.	**Description**	**Code No.**	**Quantity**	**Rate**	**Amount**	**Remarks**

Received by: xxx — Inspected by: xxx

Storekeeper: xxx — Costed by: xxx

Stores Ledger posted by: xxx

3.4 BILL OF MATERIALS

Bill of materials is a comprehensive list of materials required for a job or a product. It gives details of materials like description, quantity, quality and other specifications of materials. It is also known as "material specification list" or "materials list". This is prepared by Engineering and Planning Department. It is prepared in five copies and one copy is retained by Engineering and planning department and other copies are sent to each of the following departments:

(i) Stores department
(ii) Purchase department
(iii) Cost accounting department
(iv) Production control department

Advantages

1. It helps the stores department in preparing materials purchase requisitions.
2. It acts as authorisation to issue material to production department.
3. It helps the purchase department in placing materials purchase orders.
4. It helps to control the quantity of materials consumed in production.
5. It helps to control materials cost.
6. It helps in submission of tenders and quotations.

The following is the specimen of Bill of Materials:

Bill of Materials

Job/work order No: xxx — No: xxx

Description of Job: xxx — Date: xxx

Sl. No.	Description	Code No.	Details of issue			Remarks
			Date	Rate (₹)	Amount (₹)	

Prepared by : xxx — Stores department — Cost department

Checked by : xxx

3.4.1 Storekeeping

Stores department is responsible for receiving the materials purchased, storing them and issue for production whenever required. Stores department plays an important role in reducing materials cost. Suitable storage space and facilities for maintaining the quality of materials are to be provided. Proper safety measures are to be provided against loss of materials by theft, loss by fire etc.

3.4.1.1 Duties of storekeeper

The following are the brief list of functions or duties of a storekeeper:

1. Receive the materials purchased and store them in appropriate places.
2. Maintain proper stores records showing up-to-date details of materials received, issued, and quantities of materials in stores.
3. Proper facilities should be made for preventing materials losses like evaporation, shirnkage, deterioration in quality and loss by termites and pests.
4. Proper safety measures are also to be arranged for safekeeping of materials. Loss by abnormal causes like theft, accident, fire etc are to be prevented.
5. Unauthorised persons should not have accessibility to stores.
6. Proper arrangement for efficient and economical handling and movement of materials while receiving and issuing of materials.
7. Stores should be kept neat and tidy.
8. He should cooperate with purchase and production departments.
9. Frequent review of stock levels and prepare and send material purchase requisition notes to the purchase department.

3.4.1.2 Stores location

Location of stores is also important in reducing the materials cost. Stores should be located in a place which is easily accessible for receiving the materials purchased and also near to the production departments. So materials handling and transport cost is kept to the minimum.

3.4.1.3 Stores layout

Space and facilities available in stores should also be properly utilised for storing materials. Each material should be allotted a bin. A bin is a place for keeping materials. A bin may be a rack, a box, a fridge, a safe or an open space. Depending upon the nature, value and bulk of materials, proper storage space should be arranged. Bins should be serially numbered. Similar materials should be stored in a particular area. Stores should have adequate ventilation and light. There should be adequate space for free movement and easy handling of materials.

3.4.1.4 Classification and codification of materials

When the number of stores items handled are large, it is necessary to classify and codify them into different groups for proper stores control.

Materials may be classified as raw materials, consumable stores, spare parts, lubricating oil etc.

Codification and classification of materials may be done by using alphabetic, numeric or alpha-numerical methods. Each stores item should be given a distinct code number.

3.4.1.5 Types of stores

Stores are broadly classified into the following three categories:

1. Central or main stores
2. Sub-stores
3. Departmental stores.

1. Central or main stores

(a) Central or main store is centrally located and is easily accessible to all departments.
(b) It is suitable when the number of stores items are not large.
(c) It is also suitable to store items used by all or many departments.

2. Sub-stores

(a) It is a branch of the main stores when workplaces are distributed over a wide area.
(b) It is easily accessible for various works spots.
(c) Stores regularly used and needed urgently items are kept in sub-stores.

3. Departmental Stores

(a) Departmental stores are created to minimise the time required for drawing materials.
(b) Materials required for a particular department is kept in departmental stores.
(c) Materials of bulky nature and materials used regularly in large quantities in a department are suitable for departmental stores.
(d) It is also suitable when the central stores and production departments operate in different shifts.
(e) It is necessary when the control over the consumption of materials rests with a particular department.

3.4.2 Stores Records

The following are the three important stores records:

(a) Bin card
(b) Stock control card
(c) Stores ledger.

(a) Bin card

A bin card is a quantitative record of receipts, issues and closing balance of all items of stores. A bin is a place allotted for keeping a stores item. It may be a rack, shelf, tray, a container, open space etc. Separate bin cards are maintained for each stores item and kept nearer the bin where materials are stored. All material transactions like receipts and issues are recorded immediately in the chronological order and balance quantity of materials in stores is arrived after every transaction.

A specimen of the bin card is given below:

Bin Card

Description: xxx	Bin No : xxx
Normal quantity: xxx	Code No: xxx
Stores ledger: xxx	Maximum quantity : xxx
Order quantity: xxx	Minimum quantity : xxx
	Re-order level : xxx

Receipts			**Issues**			**Balance**	
Date	**GRN No.**	**Qty**	**Date**	**Reg. No**	**Qty**	**Qty**	**Remarks**

Merits of bin card

1. It helps the storekeeper in controlling the stock. Overstocking and understocking is avoided.
2. It helps the storekeeper to send materials purchase requisitions.
3. It helps the storekeeper in ascertaining actual stock position without actual physical counting.

Two-bin System

Under the two-bin system each bin is divided into two parts. In the first part materials equal to minimum stock or reorder level is kept. In the second part balance materials are stored. It is a supplement to ordinary bin system. It acts like a visual indicator. Materials are issued first from the second part. When materials in the second part is exhausted, it acts as an indicator to the storekeeper to send purchaser requisition to the purchase department.

(b) Stock control card

Stock control card is also a quantitative record of stores transactions like receipts, issues and balance of materials available in stock. In addition it contains particulars like materials on order. A separate card is maintained for each material. These cards are kept in a cabinet or a tray and not with materials in the bins.

(c) Stores ledger

Stores ledger is a stock record showing receipts, issues and balance of materials in hand showing both quantity and value. It is maintained in loose leaf form in the cost accounting department. A separate stores ledger leaf is maintained for each material. Each stores ledger is given a number for easy location and prevent risk of loss. Receipt column is written with the details in Goods Received Note and Issue column is written with details in materials requisition slip. The following is the specimen of a stores ledger.

Stores Ledger

Code No: xxx	Maximum level: xxx	Supplier's name: xxx
Description: xxx	Minimum level: xxx	1. xxx
Location: xxx	Danger level: xxx	2. xxx
	Ordering level: xxx	3. xxx
	Ordering quantity : xxx	

Date	Receipts				Issues				Balance			Remarks
	G.R. No.	Qty	Rate (₹)	Value (₹)	M.R. No.	Qty	Rate (₹)	Value (₹)	Qty	Rate (₹)	Value (₹)	

3.5 INVENTORY CONTROL

Inventory control is the systematic control and regulation of purchase, storage and usage of materials in such a way to ensure continuous availability of raw materials and components for smooth flow of production at economical cost. Materials constitute a significant part of total cost of production of a product. Hence it presents a great scope for control of production cost. Efficient material purchases and storage reduces purchase cost, storage cost and loss of materials. Lack of control over inventory leads to excessive investment in inventories and wastage.

Objectives of inventory control

The following are the objectives of a good inventory control system:

(a) To provide continuous flow of materials, components and parts for smooth and uninterrupted flow of production.

(b) To minimise the cost of purchase.

(c) To minimise the storage cost.
(d) To avoid loss and wastage of materials.
(e) To prevent overstocking and obsolete items.

Techniques of inventory control

The following are the common techniques of inventory control:

(a) Setting various stock levels.
(b) Determination of economic order quantity.
(c) Use of perpetual inventory system, periodical and continuous stock verifications.
(d) Use of materials management techniques
(i) ABC analysis (ii) JIT (iii) VED (iv) FNSD

3.5.1 Setting Various Stock Levels

Various stock levels are fixed for each item of regular materials. The various stock levels fixed are:

1. Re-order level
2. Minimum level or safety stock level
3. Maximum level
4. Danger level
5. Average stock level.

These stock levels are flexible and are subject to change when factors like price, availability, lead time etc change.

Objects of fixing stock levels

1. To minimise materials purchase cost and stocking of materials.
2. To avoid overstocking or understocking of materials.
3. To enable the storekeeper to initiate materials purchase requisitions.

Factors influencing setting of stock levels

a) Lead time

Lead time is the time required to receive materials from the time when steps are initiated to buy materials. It is the time lag between indenting and receipt of materials. There are two types of time lag.

(i) *Internal time lag:* Delay within the firm. It is equal to the time required for placing advertisement, receiving quotations, and preparation of purchase orders.
(ii) *External time lag:* Delay outside the firm. Time taken by the a supplier to execute the order and transit time for materials to reach buyers place from supplier's place.

(b) Rate of consumption or usage of materials

It is the quantity of materials used in production during a specific period (say, a day, week, or month). Consumption of main or regular materials will be more. It is expressed in three terms as maximum usage, minimum usage and average or normal usage.

(c) Ordering cost

It is the cost incurred for placing and receiving materials for one order. It includes staff salary, stationery, postage, telephone, cost of materials handling and inspection of materials received.

(d) Carrying or storage cost

It is the cost of storing and preserving the materials. It includes staff salary, rent, insurance, upkeep and maintenance.

(e) Investment

Money locked up in the form of materials.

3.5.1.1 Re-order level

It is the stock level at which steps are to be taken to place a fresh purchase order. When the actual stock level reaches this level, the storekeeper will send materials purchase requisition to the purchase department. It indicates when orders for purchase of materials is to be placed.

Formula:

$$\text{Re-order level} = \text{Maximum consumption} \times \text{maximum lead time}$$

(or)

$$\text{Minimum level} + \text{normal consumption during normal lead time}$$

Re-order level is also called "order level" or "ordering level" or "re-order point". Factors considered for fixing this level are:

(a) Maximum/normal lead time.
(b) Maximum/normal consumption or usage.

3.5.1.2 Maximum level

It is also called 'summit level'. It indicates the maximum quantity of a material to be maintained at any time. Actual stock should not be allowed to go above this level. It helps to avoid overstocking.

The disadvantages of overstocking are:

(a) Large capital is locked up in the form of materials.
(b) More storage space is required.
(c) Loss due to obsolescence due to change in production plan or product mix.
(d) More storage insurance, upkeep and maintenance.
(e) Loss of materials due to shrinkage, evaporation, pilferage, etc.
(f) Heavy loss due to fire, theft, accident, etc.

Formula:

$$\text{Maximum level} = \text{Re-ordering level} + \text{Re-order quantity} - (\text{Minimum consumption} \times \text{Minimum lead time})$$

The following factors are considered for fixing maximum level

(a) Minimum rate of consumption
(b) Minimum lead time
(c) Re-order level
(d) Re-order quantity
(e) Amount of capital available
(f) Storage space available.

3.5.1.3 Minimum level or safety level

This refers to minimum quantity of materials to be maintained at all times. This stock level helps to avoid stock out position. This level is also called safety level or buffer level.

Formula:

$$\text{Minimum level} = \text{Re-order level} - (\text{Normal consumption} \times \text{Normal lead time})$$

3.5.1.4 Danger Level

This level indicates that the stock level has reached a level that materials will last for a very short period only. Purchase department has to take emergency steps to procure materials to avoid stock out position. The available materials should be used for important jobs only under special instructions.

Formula:

$$\text{Danger level} = \text{Minimum usage} \times \text{Minimum lead time}$$

(or)

$$= \text{Average usage} \times \text{Minimum lead time}$$

(or)

$$= \text{Minimum usage} \times \text{Average lead time}$$

(or)

$$= \text{Average consumption} \times \text{Maximum lead time for emergency purchase}$$

Of the above formulas, the last one is most commonly followed.

3.5.2 Average Level

Average level is not an actual stock level. It is only an arithmetic level.

Formula:

$$\text{Average level} = \frac{\text{Minimum level} + \text{Maximum level}}{2}$$

$$\text{(or)} = \text{minimum level} + \frac{1}{2} \text{ of re-order quantity}$$

The following shows various stock levels:

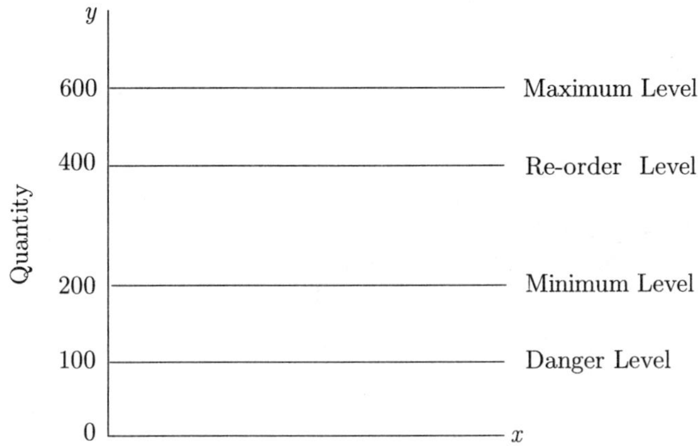

Illustration-5

From the following data compute (i) Re-order level, (ii) Minimum level, (iii) Maximum level and (iv) Average stock level.

Normal usage - 50 units per week each
Minimum usage - 25 units per week each
Maximum usage - 75 units per week each
Re-order Quantity - 300 units
Re-order period - 4 to 6 weeks

(B.Com. - Madras University)

Solution

(i) Re-order level

$$\text{Re-order level} = \text{Maximum consumption} \times \text{Maximum lead time}$$
$$= 75 \times 6 = 450 \text{ units.}$$

(ii) Minimum level

$$\text{Minimum level} = \text{Re-order level} - (\text{Normal consumption} \times \text{Normal lead time})$$
$$= 450 - (50 \times 5) = 200 \text{ units.}$$

(iii) Maximum level

$$\text{Maximum level} = \text{Re-order level} + \text{Re-order quantity} - (\text{Minimum consumption} \times \text{Minimum lead time})$$
$$= 450 + 300 - (25 \times 4) = 650 \text{ units.}$$

(iv) Average stock level

$$\text{Average stock level} = \frac{\text{Minimum level} + \text{Maximum level}}{2}$$
$$= \frac{200 + 650}{2} = 425 \text{ units}$$
$$\text{(or)} = \text{Minimum level} + \frac{1}{2}\text{of Re-order quantity}$$
$$= 200 + \left(\frac{1}{2} \text{ x } 300\right) = 350 \text{ units.}$$

Illustration-6

Calculate the maximum level and buffer level from the following information:

Maximum consumption - 75 units per day
Minimum consumption - 25 units per day
Average consumption - 50 units per day
Ideal order size - 125 units
Re-order levels - 375 units
Lead time - 1 to 3 days

Solution

$$\text{Maximum level} = \text{Re-order level} + \text{Re-order quantity (ideal order size)} - (\text{Minimum consumption} \times \text{Minimum lead time})$$
$$= 375 + 125 - (25 \times 1) = 475 \text{ units.}$$

$$\text{Buffer level (Minimum level)} = \text{Re-order level} - (\text{Average consumption} \times \text{Average lead time})$$
$$= 375 - (50 \times 2) = 275 \text{ units.}$$

Illustration-7: (Computation of lead time and usage rates, reverse working)

X Ltd provides you the following information:

(a) Re-order level - 64,000 units, Re-order quantity - 40,000 units, minimum stock - 34,000 units and maximum stock - 94,000 units.
(b) Average lead time - 2.5 days.
(c) The difference between maximum and minimum lead times is 3 days.

Determine minimum and maximum lead time and usages.

Solution

(a) **Computation of minimum and maximum lead times**

$$\text{Average lead time} = \frac{\text{Minimum} + \text{Maximum lead time}}{2} = 2.5$$

$\therefore$ Total of minimum and maximum lead times = Average lead time $\times$ 2

$$= 2.5 \times 2 = 5 \text{ days}$$

Difference between minimum lead time and maximum lead time = 3 days.

Maximum lead time = 4 days.

Minimum lead time = 1 day.

$$\text{Maximum lead time} = \text{Average lead time} + \frac{1}{2} \text{ of difference between maximum and minimum lead times}$$

$$= 2.5 + \left(\frac{1}{2} \times 3\right) = 4 \text{ days}$$

$$\text{Minimum lead time} = \text{Average lead time} - \frac{1}{2} \text{ of difference between maximum and minimum lead times}$$

$$= 2.5 - \left(\frac{1}{2} \times 3\right) = 1 \text{ day}$$

Alternatively:

(b) **Computation of minimum and maximum usages and average usages**

$$\text{Re-order level} = \text{Maximum usage} \times \text{Maximum lead time}$$

$$64{,}000 = ? \times 4$$

$$\therefore \quad \text{Maximum usage} = \frac{64,000}{4} = 16,000 \text{ units}$$

$$\text{Maximum level} = \text{ROL} + \text{ROQ} - (\text{Minimum usage} \times \text{Minimum lead time})$$

$$94,000 = 64,000 + 40,000 - (\ ? \ \times 1)$$

$$\therefore \quad \text{Minimum usage} = 10,000 \text{ units}$$

$$\text{Minimum level} = \text{Re-order level} - (\text{Average usage} \times \text{Average lead time})$$

$$34,000 = 64,000 - (? \text{ x } 2.5)$$

$$\therefore \quad \text{Average usage} = \frac{30,000}{2.5}$$

$$= 12,000 \text{ units}$$

3.5.3 Determination of Economic Order Quantity

Another area for effective control of materials cost is purchase of materials. Materials may be purchased in large quantities or in small quantities. There are merits and demerits in both cases.

The following are the merits and demerits of large orders:

Merits

(a) Large trade discounts can be obtained.
(b) Order cost will be less due to less number of orders.
(c) Economy in transport and materials handling charges.

Demerits

(a) Large capital is locked up in inventory resulting in loss of interest.
(b) More storage space is required resulting in more rent.
(c) As materials are stored for longer period loss due to obsolescence, deterioration in quality, loss by shrinkage, evaporation, pilferage, etc., will be more.
(d) Storage expenses like maintenance, insurance, etc., will be more.

The following are the merits and demerits of small orders:

Merits

(a) Less capital investment resulting in lower interest loss.
(b) Less storage space required resulting in less rent.
(c) Loss by shrinkage, evaporation, pilferages will be less.
(d) Storage expenses like maintenance, insurance will be less.

Demerits

(a) More ordering cost due to large number of orders.
(b) Transport and material handling charges increase.
(c) More entries in stores records.

The above costs can be classified into two basic groups as:

(a) Ordering Costs

Staff salaries and wages in the purchase department, cost of stationery, postage and telephone, transportation and receiving and inspection costs.

(b) Carrying Costs

Rent of stores department, salaries and wages of stores department, loss of interest, maintenance and insurance, loss by obsolescence, weight loss and loss due to fire accidents, etc.

3.6 ECONOMIC ORDER QUANTITY (EOQ)

It refers to the quantity of materials to be purchased through a single order which minimises the ordering cost and carrying cost. It is also known as optimum order size or ideal order quantity. It avoids the demerits of both small orders and large orders. It helps the purchase department in deciding the number of units to be ordered while placing purchases order for a material.

There are three ways of calculating Economic Order Quantity. They are:

(a) Mathematical Model
(b) Graphical Model
(c) Trial and Error Model.

3.6.1 Mathematical Model

The EOQ can be calculated by using the following formula derived by the mathematician Mr. Wilson:

$$\text{EOQ} = \sqrt{\frac{2\text{AO}}{\text{C}}}$$

where,

EOQ = Economic Order Quantity
A = Annual Usage or Consumption (units)
O = Cost of placing one order (Buying cost per order)
C = Cost of carrying one unit of materials per annum (i.e. loss of interest, insurance, storage expenses etc.)

The above formula is followed in the following circumstances:

(a) Consumption of materials is uniform and regular and the quantity consumed is known.
(b) Cost of placing an order is known and fixed.
(c) Cost of carrying is known and is proportionate to the quantity stored.

3.6.2 Graphical Model

EOQ can be arrived by plotting ordering cost and carrying cost of different order sizes in a graph. The ideal order size will be where the total of ordering cost and carrying cost is minimum i.e. the point at which ordering cost line and carrying cost line intersects each other. This is graphically shown as under:

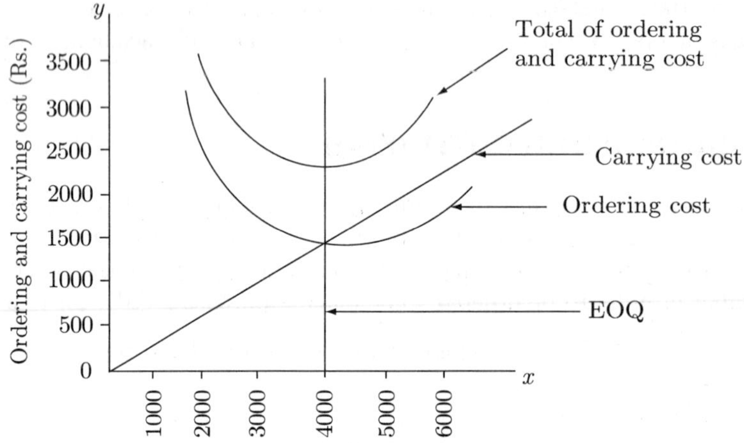

3.6.3 Trial and Error Model

This procedure is followed when the materials price and trade discount vary according to the order size. Invoice price (net of trade discount), number of orders, cost of ordering, average carrying cost for different order sizes are computed. The total materials cost for an year is arrived. The order size where total annual materials cost is lower is the optimum order size.

EOQ vs Re-Order Quantity

Normally re-order quantity (i.e. actual quantity ordered) will be equal to EOQ. When orders are placed equal to EOQ the inventory cost will be lower. But in the following circumstances the re-order quantity may be different from EOQ:

(i) When higher trade discounts are offered for large purchases.

(ii) When availability of materials are uncertain, large quantities may be purchased to avoid stock out position.

(iii) When materials price has decreased considerably. Large quantity may be purchased to take advantage of cheaper price.

(iv) The minimum quantity for which the supplier will accept order is higher than EOQ.

EOQ vs Re-Order Level

EOQ	ROL
1. It stands for the number of units to be purchased in an order.	1. It helps to initiate fresh purchase.
2. It stands for how much to be ordered	2. It indicates when a purchase order is to be initiated.
3. $EOQ = \sqrt{\frac{2AO}{C}}$	3. ROL = Maximum consumption × Maximum lead time

Illustration-8

From the following information calculate the Economic Order Quantity and the number of orders to be placed in one year:

(i) Quarterly consumption of materials - 2,000 kg.
(ii) Cost of placing one order - ₹50
(iii) Cost per unit - ₹40
(iv) Storage and carrying cost - 8% on average inventory value.

(B.Com. (Hons.), Delhi University)

Solution

$$EOQ = \sqrt{\frac{2AO}{C}} = \sqrt{\frac{2 \times 8{,}000 \times 50}{3.20}} = 500 \text{ kg.}$$

$$\text{Number of orders per quarter} = \frac{\text{Quarterly consumption}}{\text{EOQ}} = \frac{2{,}000}{500} = 4 \text{ orders}$$

$$\text{Number of orders in a year} = 4 \times 4 = 16 \text{ orders.}$$

Note:

(i) Annual consumption = 2,000 × 4 = 8,000 kg.

(ii) Carrying cost per unit per annum $= 40 \times \frac{8}{100} =$ ₹3.20

Illustration-9

A company purchases 1,000 units of a material at ₹70 per unit in a year. The cost of placing one order is ₹35. Cost of investment is 6%. The cost of insurance, rent and other storage expenses ₹2.80 per unit per annum.

Calculate:

(i) Economic Order Quantity
(ii) Number of orders to be placed in a year
(iii) Frequency of orders.

Solution

(i) $\text{EOQ} = \sqrt{\dfrac{2\text{AO}}{\text{C}}}$

$= \sqrt{\dfrac{2 \times 1{,}000 \times 35}{7}}$

$= 100$ units

Note:

() Carrying cost i.e. (c):

Interest $= 70 \times 6/100 =$ ₹4.20

Insurance, rent, etc. = ₹2.80

Total = ₹7.00

(ii) Number of orders in a year $= \dfrac{\text{Annual consumption}}{\text{EOQ}}$

$= \dfrac{1{,}000}{100} = 10$ orders

(iii) Frequency of orders $= \dfrac{\text{No. of days in a year}}{\text{No. of orders in a year}}$

$= \dfrac{360 \text{ days}}{10} = 36$ days or 1.2 months

Note: 360 days a year is assumed.

Illustration-10

A factory requires 50,000 units of a material annually at a cost of ₹12 per unit. The cost of placing and receiving an order is ₹45. Inventory carrying cost is 1.5% of the inventory value per annum. Calculate the EOQ with proof.

Solution

(i) $\text{EOQ} = \sqrt{\dfrac{2\text{AO}}{\text{C}}}$

$= \sqrt{\dfrac{2 \times 50{,}000 \times 45}{0.18}}$

$= 5{,}000$ units

Note:

Carrying cost (C) $= 12 \times \dfrac{1.5}{100} =$ ₹0.18.

Proof:

Sl. No.	Order Size	No. of orders	Ordering cost (₹)	Average inventory (units)	Inventory Carrying cost (₹)	Total of Ordering cost and carrying cost
1.	12,500	4	45 × 4 = 180	12,500/2 = 6,250	6,250 × 0.18 = 1,125	1,305
2.	10,000	5	45 × 5 = 225	10,000/2 = 5,000	5,000 × 0.18 = 900	1,125
3.	5,000	10	45 × 10 = 450	5,000/2 = 2,500	2,500 × 0.18 = 450	900
4.	4,000	12.5	45 × 12.5 = 562.50	4,000/2 = 2,000	2,000 × 0.18 = 360	922.5
5.	2,000	25	45 × 25 = 1,125	2,000/2 = 1,000	1,000 × 0.18 = 180	1,305

EOQ is 5,000 units since the total of ordering and carrying cost is lower.

3.6.4 Use of Perpetual Inventory System and Continuous Stock Verifications

(a) Perpetual Inventory System

Perpetual inventory system is a method of recording stores balances after every receipt and issue, to facilitate regular checking and to obviate closing down for stock taking. The perpetual inventory system records changes in materials on a daily basis. Hence managerial control and preparation of interim financial statements is easier. It involves keeping stores records such as bin card and stores ledger.

The following are the advantages of perpetual inventory:

(i) The stock of various materials can be easily ascertained. It helps in the preparation of interim financial statements like profit and loss account and balance sheet without delay.
(ii) It eliminates stoppage of production for stock taking.
(iii) Stores records are reliable due to internal check.
(iv) Discrepancies in stores records are promptly discovered and remedial steps are taken immediately.
(v) It helps the management to exercise control over materials cost.
(vi) It reveals the existence of surplus, dormant and slow moving items.

(b) Periodical Stocktaking

Periodical stocktaking refers to physical verification of all inventories at the end of a specific period. Since it is usually taken at the end of a year, it is called 'Annual Stocktaking'. It is difficult to detect discrepancies and fraud. It is carried out by a team temporarily formed by people drawn from different departments. As the time of stocktaking is known, there is no element of surprise. This may encourage the staff in the stores department to indulge in malpractice. It also involves stoppage of production till stocktaking is completed which may take a few days.

(c) Continuous Stock Verification

A permanent team is formed with people qualified in stock verification. This team carries out physical verification of materials on a daily basis, hence it is called continuous stocktaking. The stock verifying team estimates the workload and divides the work among themselves. The stock verification is done throughout the year continuously. There is an element of surprise. The staff in the stores department will know the item of material to be verified only at the time of actual verification. Continuous stocktaking is possible only under perpetual inventory system.

Continuous Stocktaking vs Periodic Stocktaking

	Continuous Stocktaking		Periodic Stocktaking
1.	A separate team is formed on permanent basis	1.	Stock verifying team is formed on temporary basis.
2.	Members of the team are well qualified.	2.	Members are drafted from various departments, hence not qualified in stock verification.
3.	Stock verification is carried through-out the year.	3.	Stock verification is done at the end of the specified period only.
4.	It is a continuous process.	4.	It is a one time function.
5.	Normal production is not affected.	5.	Production has to be stopped for a few days till all stocks are verified.
6.	There is an element of surprise.	6.	There is no element of surprise.
7.	Discrepancies are detected immediately.	7.	Discrepancies are detected only at the end of the specified period.
8.	Small firms cannot afford it.	8.	It is suitable for small firms.

Discrepancies in the physical stock

Avoidable causes

1. Wrong recording or omission of transactions.
2. Pilferage and theft.
3. Careless handling of materials.
4. Wrong measurement and counting.

Unavoidable causes

1. Shortage due to shrinkage, evaporation, spillage and bulk breaking.
2. Surplus due to absorption of moisture.

Treatment of discrepancies

Stock shortage or surplus slip is prepared. On the basis of this stock adjustment accounts are opened. Stock adjustment account is debited for shortage and credited for surplus. Opposite entry is made in stores control account.

3.6.5 Use of Material Management Techniques

3.6.5.1 ABC analysis

It is a system of materials management where stores items are grouped into three categories, namely, A, B and C. This classification is based on the importance of a material to the organisation. Some items of materials may constitute only small part in physical quantity, say 10%, but in their value they may constitute 70% in the total value of all materials. Such materials are placed under category 'A'. Some items of materials may constitute only a moderate portion say 20% in their physical quantity and amount to 20% in their value also. These materials are placed under category 'B'. Some items of materials may constitute 70% in their physical quantity and their value may constitute only 10% in the total value of materials.

This can also be explained with the help of the following graph:

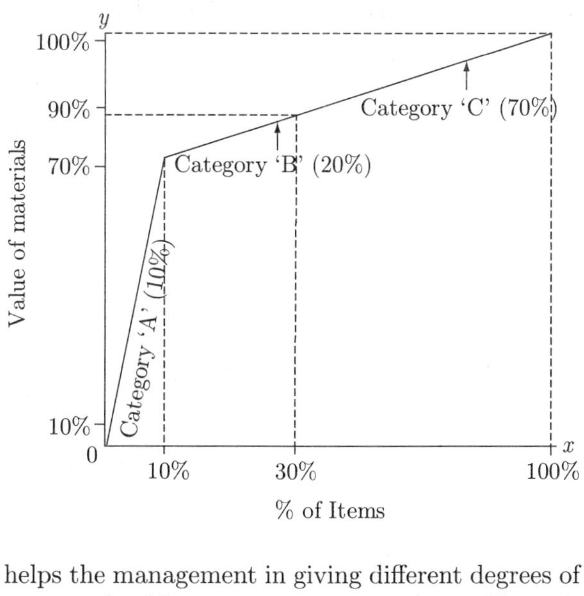

The above classification helps the management in giving different degrees of importance in materials management. The management should concentrate more on controlling materials in category 'A'. A small quantity saved will result in more savings in materials cost. A still less importance is given in controlling materials in category 'B'. Least importance is given in controlling materials in category 'C'.

This method is called Always Better Control or selective value approach or pareto analysis or 70-20-10 analysis. The above classification of materials may be presented in a table as under:

Category	% of items (units)	% of costs
A	10%	70%
B	20%	20%
C	70%	10%

Advantages of ABC analysis are:

1. It helps the management to concentrate more on controlling more important items.
2. Considerable savings in management time is made.
3. It improves inventory planning and control.
4. It helps in reducing the inventory costs.

Illustration-11: (ABC Analysis)

Classify the following inventory items into A, B and C categories.

Item	1	2	3	4	5	6	7	8	9	10	11	12	13	14
Quantity (units)	500	300	1,400	1,500	400	250	150	250	900	350	650	1,150	100	600
Price p/u (₹)	45	350	12	8	120	500	900	100	13	25	35	20	3,000	157.50

Solution

ABC Analysis

Category 'A' - items 2,6,7 and 13 - 850 units (10%), Value ₹6,65,000 (70%)
Category 'B' - items 1,5,8 and 14 - 1700 units (20%), Value ₹1,90,000 (20%)
Category 'C' - items 3,4,9,10,11 and 12 - 5,950 units (70%), Value ₹95,000 (10%)

Material Item	Quantity (unit)	% in Qty	Rate p/u (₹)	Value (₹)	% of value	Category
1	500	5·882	45	22,500	2.368	B
2	300	3·529	350	1,05,000	11.053	A
3	1,400	16·471	12	16,800	1.768	C
4	1,500	17·647	8	12,000	1.263	C
5	400	4·706	120	48,000	5.053	B
6	250	2·941	500	1,25,000	13.158	A
7	150	1·765	900	1,35,000	14.211	A

8	250	2·941	100	25,000	2.631	B
9	900	10·588	13	11,700	1.232	C
10	350	4·118	25	8,750	0.921	C
11	650	7·647	35	22,750	2.395	C
12	1,150	13·530	20	23,000	2.421	C
13	100	1·176	3000	3,00,000	31.579	A
14	600	7·059	157.50	94,500	9.947	B
Total	8,500	100·000	-	9,50,000	100.000	

3.6.5.2 Just-in-time purchase (JIT)

JIT purchase means materials and components required for production are purchased just when they are required for production. This involves evolving a closer relationship between the manufacturer and the suppliers. The manufacturer has to select a few reliable suppliers and assure them of continuous purchase order. On the other hand the suppliers have to assure timely supply and quality of materials. This system was practised by Japanese manufacturers first.

Advantages of JIT

1. Investment in stock of materials reduced considerably. So the interest on investment on materials is reduced.
2. This results in savings of rent for storage space, insurance, etc.
3. This also prevents loss of materials by evaporation, shrinkage, pilferage, etc.
4. Risk of obsolescence is avoided.
5. Close relationship between the manufacturer and the supplier is established.
6. It reduces wastage of time in inspection of materials.

3.6.5.3 VED inventory analysis

In VED inventory analysis, materials and components are classified into three groups, namely vital, essential and desirable. Some materials and components are very important for continued production. The absence of these materials will lead to immediate stoppage of production. Such materials and components are classified as vital materials. The availability of these materials and components must be ensured always. Certain materials and components are needed for production. The absence of these materials may not affect the production for a few hours or days. Such materials are called essential materials. There are certain materials and components, their absence will not affect production for longer period, say, a few weeks. Production can be continued with alternative materials and components. Such items are classified is desirable materials.

This system of inventory management ensures timely availability of all important materials. This avoids stock out position.

3.6.5.4 FNSD analysis

In FNSD analysis, materials and stores are divided into four categories, namely, fast moving, normal moving, slow moving and dead stocks.

(i) **F** — Fast moving items are used in production in large quantities on a regular basis. Stock position of these materials are to be watched continuously. Adequate quantities of materials are to be purchased to ensure continuous production.

(ii) **N** — Normal moving items are used in production in moderate quantities. Stock position of these materials are to be reviewed at periodical intervals.

(iii) **S** — Slow moving items are used only occasionally or in small quantities. Care should be taken to avoid overstocking of these materials.

(iv) **D** — Dead stock items - These materials are no longer required in production. This position might have arisen due to change in production patterns. Alternative uses are to be found for these materials or disposed of immediately to avoid loss of value.

FNSD analysis also helps in reviewing stock position periodically. It helps to avoid stockout position. It also prevents over stocking. Obsolescence loss is minimised.

3.7 COMPREHENSIVE ILLUSTRATIONS

Illustration-12: (Computation of issue price - normal loss and treatment of cost of containers)

X Ltd received the following quotation for the supply of material 'A':

Invoice price - 1,000 kg - ₹28 per kg
- 2,500 kg - ₹25 per kg
- 5,000 kg - ₹21 per kg

Trade discount is 10% of invoice price. One container is required for every 100 kg of materials. Separate charge is made at ₹50 per container and ₹40 credit will be given if returned within 50 days. Sales tax is 4%. Other expenses are:

Transport charge - ₹2,000
Insurance - ₹1,000
Loading and unloading charges - ₹500.

It is expected that normally 5% weight is lost. Compute the total cost of materials and cost per kg. The company needs 2,500 kg of materials.

Solution

Statement showing materials cost			
		Qty (kg)	Total (₹)
Invoice price 2,500 × 25		2,500	62,500
Less: Trade discount 10%		-	6,250
Net invoice price		2,500	56,250
Sales tax 4%		-	2,250
Cost of container	25 × 50 = 1,250	-	
Less: Credit for return	25 × 40 = 1,000	-	250
Transport charges		-	2,000
Insurance		-	1,000
Loading and unloading charges		-	500
		2,500	62,250
Less: Loss of weight 5%		125	-
Total Cost		**2,375**	**62,250**

$$\text{Cost per kg} - \frac{62,250}{2,375} = ₹\ 26.21$$

Illustration-13: (Materials Issue Price - Normal and abnormal loss)

The following are the particulars relating to purchase of 2,000 kg of material 'x'

(i) Invoice price ₹40 per unit
(ii) Trade discount 10%
(iii) Sales tax is 3% on net invoice price
(iv) Insurance 2% of net invoice value
(v) 60 units were damaged in transit due to an accident. Insurance company admitted a claim of ₹1,800 only.
(vi) Other expenses were: Freight ₹2,500, loading and unloading ₹600, octroi ₹1,000.
(vii) Stores overheads applied at 5% on total cost of materials.
(viii) 10% of weight is lost in stores due to shrinkage and evaporation.

Calculate the total cost of materials and cost per kg.

Solution

Statement showing materials cost			
		Qty (kg)	Total (₹)
Invoice price 2000 × 40		2,000	80,000
Less: Trade discount 10%		-	8,000
Net invoice price		2,000	72,000
Insurance 2% of net invoice price		-	1,440
Sales tax 3% of net invoice price		-	2,160
Freight		-	2,500
Loading and unloading		-	600
Octroi		-	1,000
	Total	2,000	79,700
Less: Loss in transit due to accident	$\frac{79{,}700 \times 60}{2{,}000}$	60	2,391
		1,940	77,309
Add: Stores overheads	$\frac{77{,}309 \times 5}{100}$	-	3,865
		1,940	81,174
Less: Loss in weight 10%		194	-
	Total materials Cost	**1,746**	**81,174**

Materials cost per kg $= \frac{81{,}174}{1{,}746} =$ ₹46.49

Loss due to accident	
	₹
Value of materials lost in accident	2,391
Less: Insurance claims received	1,800
Net loss - debited to costing profit and loss account	591

Illustration-14: (Joint cost of purchase)

Materials of different grades were purchased at a total cost of ₹3,00,000. The materials were sorted into following grades showing their market price.

Grade	Units (Nos)	Selling price per unit (Rs)
Grade 'A'	15,000	₹10
Grade 'B'	7,000	₹6
Grade 'C'	20,000	₹8
Grade 'D'	9,600	₹5

Assuming that all materials yield same rate of grass profit, find out the purchase cost per unit of each grade materials.

Solution

Sales value of materials purchased	
	₹
Grade A = 15,000 × 10	1,50,000
Grade B = 7,000 × 6	42,000
Grade C = 20,000 × 8	1,60,000
Grade D = 9,600 × 5	48,000
Total	**4,00,000**
Less: Total purchase cost	3,00,000
Gross profit	**1,00,000**

$$\% \text{ of gross profit on sales} = \frac{\text{Gross profit}}{\text{Sales}} \times 100$$

$$= \frac{1,00,000}{4,00,000} \times 100 = 25\%$$

Table showing purchase cost per unit			
Grade	**Selling price p/u (₹)**	**Cross profit p/u**	**Cost price p/u (₹)**
A	10	$10 \times \frac{25}{100} = 2.50$	7.50
B	6	$6 \times \frac{25}{100} = 1.50$	4.50
C	8	$8 \times \frac{25}{100} = 2.00$	6.00
D	5	$5 \times \frac{25}{100} = 1.25$	3.75

Illustration-15: (Bin Card)

From the following transactions relating to material x, prepare the bin card.

1.3.2008	opening stock	200 tonnes
6.3.2008	Issued	140 tonnes
7.3.2008	Purchased	350 tonnes
8.3.2008	Condemned due to deterioration in quality and transferred to scrap	30 tonnes
9.3.2008	Issued	80 tonnes
14.3.2008	Issued	120 tonnes
17.3.2008	Purchased	200 tonnes
20.3.2008	Issued	280 tonnes
25.3.2008	Purchased	280 tonnes
28.3.2008	Issued	280 tonnes

Stock was verified on 21.03.2008. Actual stock amounted to 143 tonnes.

Solution

Bin Card No. xxx

Material - x
Reorder quantity: xxx
Reorder level: xxx

Maximum level: xxx
Minimum level: xxx

Date	Receipts		Issues		Balance (Tonnes)
	G.R. No.	Tonnes	Req. No.	Tonnes	
1.3.08	-	-	-	-	200
6.3.08	-	-	-	140	60
7.3.08	-	350	-	-	410
8.3.08	-	-	Scrapped	30	380
9.3.08	-	-	-	80	300
14.3.08	-	-	-	120	180
17.3.08	-	200	-	-	380
20.03.08	-	-	-	280	100
21.3.08	Surplus	43	-	-	143
25.3.08	-	280	-	-	423
28.3.08	-	-	-	280	143

Illustration-16: (Stock levels)

From the following information calculate the four important level of stores:

(a) Average delivery time - 20 days
(b) Maximum delivery time - 30 days
(c) Minimum delivery time - 15 days
(d) Maximum delivery time for emergency purchases - 5 days
(e) Average rate of consumption per day - 25 units.
(f) Maximum rate of consumption per day - 35 units
(g) Minimum rate of consumption per day - 14 units
(h) Standard ordering quantity - 600 units

(B.Com., - Bangalore University - Oct 2002)

Solution

(a) Reorder level = Maximum consumption × Maximum reorder period.

$= 35 \times 30 = 1{,}050$ units.

(b) Minimum level = Reorder level – (Normal consumption × Normal reorder period)

$= 1{,}050 - (25 \times 20) = 550$ units.

(c) Maximum level = Reorder level + Reorder quantity – (Minimum consumption × Minimum reorder period)

$= 1{,}050 + 600 - (14 \times 15) = 1{,}440$ units.

(d) Danger level = Maximum delivery period for emergency purchase × Average consumption

$= 5 \times 25 = 125$ units.

(e) $$\text{Average level} = \frac{\text{Minimum level} + \text{Maximum level}}{2}$$

$$= \frac{500 + 1{,}440}{2}$$

$= 970$ units.

(or)

$$\text{Average level} = \text{Minimum level} + \frac{1}{2}\text{of reorder quantity}$$

$$= 550 + \left(\frac{1}{2} \times 600\right)$$

$= 850$ units.

Illustration-17: (Stock levels)

In respect of material M-4, the following data are available:

Budgeted consumption:

Maximum - 300 units per month
Minimum - 50 units per month
Average - 150 units per month
Annual - 1,800 units
Lead time - 2 to 4 months

Storage cost is 25% p.a. of average stock value.

Ordering cost ₹2 per order.

Price per unit of material ₹0.32

Calculate :

(a) Reorder level
(b) Minimum level
(c) Maximum level.

(B.Com., - Bangalore University - Oct 2003)

Solution

Calculation of EOQ

$$\text{EOQ} = \sqrt{\frac{2\text{AO}}{\text{C}}}$$

$$= \sqrt{\frac{2 \times 1{,}800 \times 2}{0.08}}$$

$$\text{EOQ} = 300 \text{ units}$$

Note: C = 0.32 × 25% = ₹0.08

(a) Reorder level = Maximum consumption × Plan delivery time.
= 300 × 4 = 1,200 units.

(b) Minimum level = Reorder level – (Normal consumption × Normal delivery time)
= 1200 – (150 × 3)= 750 units.

(c) Maximum level = Reorder level+Reorder quantity
– (Minimum consumption × Minimum delivery time)
= 1200 + 300 – (50 × 2) = 1,400 units.

Illustration-18: (Computation of maximum level)

The following data relate to material x:

Supply period 4 to 8 months

Consumption Rate:

Maximum - 600 units per month.
Minimum - 100 units per month
Normal - 300 units per month
Yearly - 3,600 units.
Storage cost 50% of stock value.
Ordering cost - ₹400 per order.
Price per unit of material - ₹64.

Compute the maximum stock level. **(B.Com. (Hons.), - Delhi University)**

Solution

$$\text{EOQ} = \sqrt{\frac{2\text{AO}}{\text{C}}}$$

$$= \sqrt{\frac{2 \times 3,600 \times 400}{64 \times \frac{50}{100}}}$$

$$\text{EOQ} = 300 \text{ units}$$

Reorder level = Maximum consumption × Maximum delivery time.
= 600 × 8 = 4,800 units.

Maximum level = Reorder level+Reorder quantity
– (Minimum consumption × Minimum delivery time)
= 4800 + 300 – (100 × 4) = 4,700 units.

Illustration-19: (EOQ - with discount offer)

Annual requirements of a particular item of inventory is 10,000 units. Inventory carrying cost per unit per year is 20% and ordering cost is ₹40 per order. The price quoted by the supplier is ₹4 per unit. However the supplier is ready to give a discount of 5% for orders of 1,500 units or more. Is it worthwhile to avail the discount offer? **(B.Com. (Hons.), - Delhi University-2006)**

Solution

$$\text{EOQ} = \sqrt{\frac{2\text{AO}}{\text{C}}}$$

$$= \sqrt{\frac{2 \times 10,000 \times 40}{4 \times 20\%}}$$

$$= 1,000 \text{ units}$$

Statement showing materials cost

Order size (Units)	No. of orders	Ordering cost (₹)	Average Carrying Cost (₹)	Purchase Cost (Rs)	Total Cost (₹)
1,000	10	$10 \times 40 = 400$	$1{,}000 \times \frac{1}{2} \times 4 \times \frac{20}{100} = 400$	$10{,}000 \times 4 = 40{,}000$	40,800
1,500	$6\frac{2}{3}$	$6\frac{2}{3} \times 40 = 267$	$1{,}500 \times \frac{1}{2} \times 3.80 \times \frac{20}{100} = 570$	$10{,}000 \times 3.80 = 38{,}000$	38,837

Ans: Since total materials cost is cheaper under the discount offer, it is better to accept discount offer and buy in lots of 1,500 units.

Illustration-20: (EOQ with discount offer)

The quarterly production of a company's product which has a steady market is 20,000 units. Each unit of a product requires 0.5 kg of raw material. The cost of placing one order for raw materials is ₹100 and the inventory carrying cost is ₹2 per annum. The lead time for procurement of materials is 36 days and a safety stock of 1000 kg raw materials is maintained by the company. The company has been able to negotiate the following discount structure with the raw materials supplier:

Order quantity Kg	Discount ₹
upto 6,000	Nil
6,000 - 8,000	400
8,000 - 16,000	2,000
16,000 - 3,2000	3,200
30,000 - 45,000	4,000

You are required to

(i) Calculate the reorder point taking 30 days a month.

(ii) Prepare a statement showing the total cost of procurement and storage of raw materials after considering the discount if the company elects to place one, two, four or six orders in the year.

(iii) State the number of orders which the company should place to minimise the costs after taking EOQ also into consideration. **(CA-PE II - May 2002)**

Solution

(i) Reorder point = Safety stock + Lead time consumption

= 1,000 + 36 × 111.11

= 1,000 + 3,999.96

= 4,999.96 (or) 5,000 units

Note:

(a) Annual production = 20,000 × 4 = 80,000 units.
(b) Normal production per day = 80,000/360 days = 222.22 units.
(c) Materials consumption per day = 222.22 × 0.5 = 111.11 kg.
(d) Annual materials consumption = 8,000 units × 0.5 kg = 40,000 kg.

Statement showing cost of procurement and storage					
No. of Orders	**Order size (units)**	**Ordering cost (₹)**	**Storage cost (₹)**	**Discount (₹)**	**Total of ordering cost and storage cost (₹)**
1.	40,000	1 × 100 = 100	$40{,}000 \times \frac{1}{2} \times 2 = 40{,}000$	4000	$100 + 40,000 - 4,000 =$ 36,100
2.	20,000	2 × 100 = 200	$20{,}000 \times \frac{1}{2} \times 2 = 20{,}000$	3,200	$200 + 20,000 - 3200 =$ 17,000
4.	10,000	4 × 100 =400	$10{,}000 \times \frac{1}{2} \times 2 = 10{,}000$	2,000	$400 + 10{,}000 - 2{,}000 =$ 8,400
6.	6666.67	6 × 100 = 600	$6666.67 \times \frac{1}{2} \times 2 = 6667$	400	$600 + 6667 - 400 =$ 6,867
(EOQ 20 orders)	2,000	20 × 100 = 2,000	$2{,}000 \times \frac{1}{2} \times 2 = 2{,}000$	-	$2,000 + 2,000 = 4,000$

Ans: Total cost of procurement and storage is lower when the order is placed for 2,000 units (i.e. EOQ). Total 20 orders are to be placed in a year.

Note:

$$\text{EOQ} = \sqrt{\frac{2\text{AO}}{\text{C}}} = \sqrt{\frac{2 \times 40,000 \times 100}{2}} = 2,000 \text{ kg}$$

3.8 EXERCISE

I. Objective Type Questions

A. State whether the following statements are true or false.

(i) Materials control refers to controlling the cost price of materials.

(ii) Materials control reduces the materials cost of a product.
(iii) Perpetual inventory system refers to continuous stocktaking
(iv) Under perpetual inventory receipts, issues and balance of materials are recorded on a regular basis.
(v) Maintaining bin cards and stores ledger is part of perpetual inventory system.
(vi) Bin refers to a place where material is stored.
(vii) Bin card shows the value of materials received, issued and in stock.
(viii) Bin card is maintained in the stores department.
(ix) Stores ledger is maintained by purchase department.
(x) Stores ledger shows the quantity and value of materials received, issued and in stock.
(xi) Issue price of material consists of invoice price only.
(xii) Issue price of materials consists of invoice price, purchase cost and storage cost.
(xiii) Unavoidable stores loss is added to the materials cost or included in stores overheads.
(xiv) EOQ refers to optimum purchase quantity.
(xv) Reorder level and Reorder quantity are same.
(xvi) Reorder quantity indicates when a purchase order is to be placed.
(xvii) Reorder quantity indicates how many units are to be ordered in a single order.
(xviii) Safety stock stands for danger stock level.
(xix) Stores ledger is a perpetual inventory record.
(xx) Under ABC analysis, materials are graded into three categories on the basis of their importance.

[**Ans:** *True:* (ii), (iv), (v) (vi), (viii), (x), (xii), (xii) (xiii), (xiv), (xvii), (xix), (xx)
False: (i), (iii), (vii), (ix), (xi), (xv), (xvi), (xviii).]

B. Fill in the blanks

(i) Materials are issued to user departments against the document called ________.
(ii) A statement showing a comprehensive list of materials required for a job or production is called ________.
(iii) A record showing quantity of materials receipt, issues and in balance is called ________.
(iv) Bin card is a record showing receipt, issues and balance of materials in ________. terms.
(v) Stores ledger shows ________ and ________ of materials received, issued and in balance.
(vi) Bind card is maintained by ________.
(vii) Stores ledger is maintained in ________.
(viii) The quantity of materials purchased in an order which minimises the purchase cost and storage cost is called ________.
(ix) The stock level which helps avoid overstocking is ________.
(x) The stock level which indicates when steps are to be initiated to buy materials ________.
(xi) The place where materials are stored is called a ________.
(xii) The stock level which prevents stock out position is called ________.
(xiii) In ________ purchase system, materials and components are procured just before

production commences.

(xiv) In ______________ analysis materials are grouped into three categories on the basis of their importance.

(xv) The system of record keeping where materials movements are recorded on a continuous basis is called ______________ inventory.

(xvi) Stock adjustment account is debited with ______________ and credited with ______________.

[**Ans:** (i) Materials Requisition, (ii) Bill of materials, (iii) Bin card, (iv) Quantitative, (v) Quantity and value, (vi) Stores department, (vii) Cost accounting department, (viii) EOQ, (ix) Maximum level, (x) Reorder level, (xi) Bin, (xii) Minimum level, (xiii) JIT, (xiv) ABC, (xv) perpetual, (xvi) Shortage, surplus.]

II. Theory Questions

A. Short answer type questions

1. What is bill of material?
2. What is Goods Received Note?
3. Who prepares bill of materials?
4. Who prepares materials purchase requisition for regular production?
5. What is EOQ?
6. Name the carrying costs?
7. Name the ordering cost?
8. When carrying cost and ordering cost will be equal?
9. What is a bin?
10. What is bin card?
11. What is stores ledger?
12. Name the stock level?
13. What is reorder level?
14. What is ABC analysis?
15. What is JIT purchase?
16. Explain VED analysis?
17. Explain double bin system?
18. When reorder quantity will be different from EOQ?

B. Long answer type questions

1. What is materials control? Explain the objectives of materials control.
2. Explain the various stock levels
3. Differentiate between:
   (a) Reorder level and Reorder quantity.
   (b) Bind card and stores ledger.

(c) Reorder quantity and economic order quantity.

4. Explain the periodic stock verification and continuous stocktaking. Which of the two is more useful and advantageous to the business and why? **(ICWA-Inter)**
5. (a) What are the factors that should be considered while fixing maximum ad minimum stock level?

   (b) What is meant by reordering level? **(ICWA-Inter)**
6. What is perpetual inventory? Explain the advantages.
7. What is bin card? Give a specimen form of the bin card and discuss its utility. **(B.Com., - Bangalore)**
8. Explain ABC analysis and its advantages.
9. Explain the various techniques used for inventory control. **(CS-Inter)**
10. Distinguish between:

    (a) Perpetual inventory system and continuous stocktaking.

    (b) Bin card and stores ledger.

    (c) Perpetual and periodic inventory systems. **(B.Com. (Hons.), - Delhi)**
11. What is JIT inventory system? Explain how it eliminates wastage of resources.
12. To be able to calculate a basic EOQ certain assumptions are necessary. List down these assumptions. **(CA-Inter)**
13. What is Just-In-Time inventory system? How JIT differs from EOQ?
14. What are obsolete, slow moving and dormant materials? How do you deal with them?
15. What is EOQ? Explain the various procedures for computing EOQ.
16. What are the duties and responsibilities of a storekeeper?
17. Discuss the functions of a storekeeper. **(B.Com., - Madras University)**
18. Discuss the pros and cons of centralised and decentralised stores.
19. How do you classify the materials into categories A, B and C?

III. Practical Problems

A. Short answer type questions

1. From the following figures, calculate economic order quantity and number of orders to be placed in a year.

   Annual consumption of materials - 4,000 units.
   Cost of buying per order - ₹5
   Cost per unit - ₹2 per unit.
   Storage and carrying cost - 8% of inventory value **(B.Com., - Madras)**
   (**Ans:** EOQ = 500 units, 8 orders in a year)

2. Find out the reorder level from the following:
   Maximum consumption of materials - 250 units per week, minimum delivery time 4 weeks and maximum reorder period 6 weeks:

   (**Ans:** Reorder level 1500 units)

3. Compute the minimum stock level:

   Normal usage of materials - 250 units per week
   Normal Reorder period - 4 weeks
   Maximum reorder period - 6 weeks
   Minimum reorder period - 2 weeks
   Reorder level - 2,000 units.

   (**Ans:** Minimum level - 1,000 units)

4. Calculate inventory carrying cost per unit from the following:

   Cost of raw materials per unit ₹60.
   Average rate of return on investment - 10%
   Buying cost per order ₹75

   (**Ans:** Carrying cost ₹6 per unit)

5. Calculate the maximum stock level:

   Reorder level 2,500 units, reorder quantity 1,500 units, minimum reorder period 3 weeks, minimum usage per week 200 units.

   (**Ans:** Maximum stock level - 3,400 units)

6. Find out the carrying cost of inventory:

   Cost materials per unit - ₹80
   Average rate of return on investment 10%
   Rent, taxes insurance etc. - ₹2 per unit p.a.

   (**Ans:** Carrying cost ₹10 per unit p.a.)

7. Total of ordering cost and carrying cost at EOQ is ₹5,000. What is ordering cost and carrying cost?

   (**Ans:** Ordering cost ₹2,500, carrying cost ₹2,500)

8. Find the EOQ from the following:

   Purchase price of a materials ₹50 per units. Annual cost of carrying one unit - 10% of purchase price. Total cost of carrying and ordering per annum ₹5,000. The company is following EOQ policy.

   (**Ans:** EOQ = 500 units.)

9. Find the economic order quantity and frequency of orders from the following information.

   Monthly consumption - 3,000 units.
   Cost per unit - ₹54
   Ordering cost - ₹150 per order
   Inventory carrying cost 20% of average inventory.

   (**Ans:** EOQ = 1,000 units, frequency of orders one in 10 days)

10. From the following information compute EOQ

    Cost per unit of material ₹1 per unit
    Consumption of materials per annum - ₹1,600
    Buying cost per order - ₹20.
    Storage and carrying cost per annum 10% of inventory value.

    (**Ans:** EOQ ₹800)

B. Comprehensive questions

1. *(Computation of landed cost of materials)*
   In a truck load, the following materials were received:

Code No.	Materials	Quantity (kg)	Rate per kg (₹)
M 2010	Carbon black	3,050	4.00
P 5025	S.H. Phosphate	2,060	3.00

   Sales tax was charged at 5%
   Transport charges - ₹100
   Railway freight - ₹1,050
   Loading and unloading - ₹50

   The Goods Received Note received from the storekeeper showed the following quantity:
   M 2010 - 3,000 kg P 5025 - 2,000 kg

   From the above figures you are required to calculate the purchase rate per kg of carbon black and S.H. Phosphate. **(M.Com., - Madras University)**

   (**Ans:** Cost per kg - Carbon black - ₹4.51, S.H. phosphate - ₹3.48)

2. *(Choosing a supplier)*
   The following quotations were received from two different suppliers:
   Supplier M - ₹15 per unit
   Supplier N - ₹14.75 per unit plus ₹5,000 fixed charges irrespective of units ordered. Calculate:

   (i) Purchase quantity at which materials cost will be same from both suppliers
   (ii) When purchase quantity is 18,000 units, to whom the order should be placed.
   (iii) When order quantity is 25,000 units, whom will you select.

   (**Ans:**(i) 20,000 units, (ii) Supplier 'M' should be selected. (iii) Supplier 'N' should be selected).

3. *(Joint purchase cost)*
   Materials of different grades were purchased at a total cost of ₹4,00,000. These materials were sorted into three grades, the details of which are given below:

Grades	Quantity (units)	Selling price p/u (₹)
Grade 'A'	40,000	7.00
Grade 'B'	25,000	5.00
Grade 'C'	10,000	9.50

   Calculate purchase cost per unit of each grade materials

(**Ans:** Cost price - Grade 'A' - ₹5.60, Grade 'B' - ₹4.00, Grade 'C' - ₹7.60)

4. *(Stock levels)*
The following information is obtained relating to material 'A':
Maximum consumption - 600 units per week
Minimum consumption - 400 units per week
Average consumption - 450 units per week
Lead time 2 to 6 weeks.
Reorder quantity - 1,500 units.

Maximum lead time for emergency purchase 1 week calculate.

a) Reorder level b) Maximum level c) Minimum level d) Average level e) Danger level.

(**Ans:** Reorder level 3,600 units, maximum level 4,300 units, minimum level 1,800 units, Average level 3,050 units or 2,550 units, danger level 450 units)

5. *(Stock level - Two materials)*
Two materials 'A' and 'B' are used as follows:
Reorder quantity - A 1,200 units, B - 1,000 units.
Reorder period - A - 2 to 4 months, B - 3 to 6 months.
Normal usage - 300 units per month each
Minimum usage - 150 units per month each.
Maximum usage - 450 units per month each.

You are required to calculate the following for each of the materials:
(a) Reorder level, (b) Maximum level, (c) Minimum level (d) Average stock level.

(**Ans:** Reorder level A - 1,800 units, B - 2,700 units, maximum level - A -2,700 units, B - 3,250 units, minimum level A - 900 units, B - 1,350 units, average level A - 1,800 units. B - 2,300 units.)

6. *(Stock Levels)*
Two components x and y are used as follows:
Minimum usage - 50 units per week each
Maximum usage - 150 units per week each
Normal usage - 100 units per week each
Ordering quantities - x - 600 units
y - 1,000 units
Delivery period x - 4 to 6 weeks
y - 2 to 4 weeks

Maximum reorder period for emergency purchases x - 2weeks, y - 2weeks. Calculate for each component:
a) Reorder level, b) Maximum level, (c) Minimum level d) Danger level **(CA - Inter)**

(**Ans:** Reorder level x - 900 units, y - 600 units;
Maximum level - x 1,300 units, y - 1,500 units;
Minimum level - x 400 units, y - 300 units;
Danger level x 200 units, y - 200 units)

7. *(EOQ - with discount offer)*
RST Limited has received an offer of quantity discount on its orders of materials as under:

Price per tonne	Tonnes number
₹9,600	Less than 50
₹9,360	50 and less then 100
₹9,120	100 and less than 200
₹8,880	200 and less than 300
₹8,640	300 and above

The annual requirement for the material is 500 tonnes. The ordering cost per order is ₹12,500 and the stock holding cost is estimated at 25% of the materials cost per annum.

Required:

(i) Compute the most economical purchase level
(ii) Compute EOQ if there are no quantity discounts and the price per tonne is ₹10,500.

(CA-PEII, - Nov 2004)

(**Ans:** (i) Most economical purchase quantity 300 tonnes (iii) EOQ 69.01 tonnes)

8. *(Stock level and EOQ)*
A company manufactures 5,000 units of a product per month. The cost of placing an order is ₹100. The purchase price of raw materials is ₹10 per kg. The reorder period is 4 to 8 weeks. The consumption of raw materials varies from 100 kg to 450 kg per week, the average consumption being 275 kg. The carrying cost of inventory is 20% per annum.

You are required to calculate:
(i) Reorder quantity, (ii) Reorder level, (iii) Maximum level, (iv) Minimum level, (v) Average stock level. **(CA-PE II)**

(**Ans:** (i) Reorder quantity 2449.49 kg. (ii) Reorder level 3,600 kg, (iii) Maximum level 5,649.49 kg, (iv) Minimum level 1,950 kg, (v) Average level = 3,800 kg (or) 3,175 kg

9. *(Stock levels)*
For the manufacture of a certain product two components A and B used. The following particulars about these components are available:

	A	B
Normal usage (per week)	60nos.	60 nos.
Maximum usage (per week)	80 nos.	80 nos.
Minimum usage (per week)	30 nos.	30 nos.
Reorder quantity	400 nos.	600 nos.
Reorder period	4 to 6 weeks	2 to 4 weeks

You are required to calculate for each component:
(i) Reordering level, (ii) Minimum level, (iii) Maximum level, (iv) Average stock level.

(ICWA - Inter - June 2004)

(**Ans:** (i) Reorder level - A 480 nos., B 320 nos, (ii) Minimum level A 180 nos, B 140 nos, (iii)

Maximum level A 760 nos, B 860 nos. (iv) Average level A - 470 nos, B - 500 nos)

10. *(Stock levels)*
Two components A and B are used as follows :
Normal usage - 50 units per week each.
Minimum usage - 25 units per week each.
Maximum usage - 75 units per week each.
Reorder quantity A - 300 units, B - 500 units.
Reorder period - A 4 to 6 weeks, B -2 to 4 weeks.

Calculate for each component:
(i) Reordering level, (ii)Minimum level, (iii) Maximum level, (iv) Average stock level.
(B.Com., - Madras University)

(**Ans:**(i) Reorder level - A - 450 nos., B - 300 nos, (ii) Minimum level A 200 nos, B 150 nos, (iii) Maximum level A 650 nos, B 750 nos. (iv) Average level A - 425 nos, B - 450 nos)

11. *(Stock levels)*
From the following information calculate, reorder minimum and maximum stock levels:

Minimum consumption - 100 units per day
Maximum consumption - 150 units per day
Normal consumption - 120 units per day
Reorder period - 10 to 15 days
Normal reorder period - 12 days
Reorder quantity - 1500 units. **(B.Com., - Madras University)**

(**Ans:** Reorder level 2,250 units, Minimum level 750 units, and max level 2,750 units)

12. *(Stock levels)*
From the following information calculate
1) Maximum level, 2) Minimum level, 3) Reorder level, 4) Average stock level.

Normal consumption - 800 units per week
Minimum consumption - 400 units per week
Maximum consumption - 1,200 units per week
Reorder quantity - 4,800 units.

Time required for delivery :
Minimum - 4 weeks and
Maximum - 6 weeks. **(B.Com., - Bangalore University, April 2003)**

(**Ans:** 1) Max. Level 10,400 units, 2) Minimum level - 3,200 units, 3) Re-order level 7,200 units, 4) Average level 6,800 units)

13. *(Bin card)*
Following are the transactions relating to material x, code No. 456 m, prepare bin card. Bin card No. x 456:

2009 June 1 - Opening balance 300 units
2 - Purchased 500 units.
5 - Issued - 500 units.

9 - Purchased 900 units.
12 - Issued 800 units.
15 - Purchased 600 units.
19 - Issued 400 units
22 - Issued 300 units
26 - Purchased 500 units
29 - Issued 600 units
30 - Purchased - 400 units.

(**Ans:** Balance 600 units)

14. *(EOQ and discount offer)*
A manufacturer requires 9,600 units of a certain component annually. This is currently purchased from a regular supplier at ₹ 50 per unit. The cost of placing an order is ₹ 60 per order and annual carrying cost is ₹5 per piece. What is economic order quantity for placing an order?
Recently the supplier has expressed his willingness to reduce the price to ₹48, if the total requirements are obtained from him in two equal orders and to ₹47, if the entire quantity required is purchased in one lot. Analyse the costs of the three options and recommend the best course.
What other factors should also be considered before the decision is taken?
(ICWA-Inter, Dec. 2003)

(**Ans:** EOQ - 480 units, 2 orders per annum should be placed)

15. *(ABC analysis)*
Categorise the following items of materials on the basis of ABC analysis:

Material No.	Quantity (nos)	Price p/u (₹)
1	300	100
2	200	400
3	2,000	13
4	150	150
5	300	800
6	250	50
7	400	500
8	1,400	15
9	400	75
10	2,100	10
11	600	140
12	300	600
13	1,400	10
14	1,500	12
15	700	30

Ans:

	A	B	C	Total
Items	2,5,7,12	1,4,6,9,11,15	3,8,10,13,14	15
Quantity	1,200 units	2,400 units	8,400 units	12,000 units
Value (₹)	7,00,000	2,00,000	1,00,000	10,00,000
% of quantity	10%	20%	70%	100%
% of value	70%	20%	10%	100%

4 MATERIALS COSTING

- Material Costing—Pricing
- Pricing Methods—Types
- FIFO
- LIFO
- HIFO
- Base Stock Method
- Simple Average Price Method
- Weighted Average Price Method
- Standard Price Method
- Inflated Price Method
- Specific Price Method
- Materials Transactions—Miscellaneous
- Material and Production Losses
- Scrap - Accounting Treatment
- Material Control Ratios

4.1 NEED FOR PRICING

Value of materials used in a job, a process or a product is to be valued correctly to find the correct cost of the jobs, processes or products. There will be no problem in valuing the materials when a particular material in the stores is purchased at a single price only. But in practice this will not be the case. If a particular material in the stores has been purchased at different rates on different occasions, the question arises as to fixing price for a particular lot of materials issued for production. Then a suitable price is to be applied for valuation of materials issued for jobs or work orders. Various methods are available for pricing material issues. They are:

1. Actual price methods
   (a) First In First Out (FIFO)
   (b) Last In Last Out (LIFO)
   (c) Highest In First Out (HIFO)
   (d) Base stock
2. Average price methods
   (a) Simple average
   (b) Weighted average
   (c) Periodic simple average
   (d) Periodic weighted average
   (e) Moving simple average
   (f) Moving weighted average
3. Market price or replacement price method
4. Standard price method
5. Inflated price method
6. Specific price method.

Choosing a price method

The following points should be kept in mind while choosing a method:

1. A method selected should ensure full recovery of materials cost.
2. The method should be suitable to frequency and range of changes in market price of a material.
3. There should be no over-recovery or under-recovery of materials cost. So materials cost variance is avoided.

4.2 ACTUAL PRICE METHODS

4.2.1 First In First Out (FIFO) Method

When a material purchased on different occasions at different prices is in stores, it is assumed that materials purchased first is issued first. The price of the first lot is applied for the materials issued. When the first lot is exhausted the next lot is taken up for issue. Materials are issued in the order of the time of purchase of materials. So materials purchased first go out first.

Advantages

1. Materials are issued at actual price. So there will be no over-pricing or under-pricing of material issues.
2. This is the most logical and simple method.
3. This method is suitable when number of purchases are a few.
4. It is also suitable when prices are falling.
5. Closing stock of material issued will closely resemble the market price.

Disadvantages

1. The chances of clerical error in computing issue prices are more when the number of purchases are many.
2. It is not suitable when prices are increasing. The materials purchased earlier at lower price will be exhausted first and costlier material will be in hand.
3. Materials charged to production will be lower and the book profit will be higher. It leads to higher tax liability.
4. Cost of materials charged to different jobs will differ. It will be difficult to compare the cost and profit of different jobs.
5. Sometimes materials issued for a job are charged at different prices.

Illustration-1: (Stores ledger-FIFO method)

A Ltd. provides the following transactions relating to material 'X' during the month of October 2008:

October 1	Opening balance 40 units at ₹45 per unit
2	Issued 15 units Req. No. 101
3	Purchased 75 units at ₹46 per unit, GRN No. 51
5	Issued 20 units Req. No. 103
8	Purchased from X Co. 90 units at ₹48, GRN No. 56
10	Returned defective materials to X Co. - 15 units
14	Received from Y Co. 60 units at ₹47 per unit, GRN No.59
18	Received replacements from X Co. MRR - No. 30
21	Purchased 125 units at ₹48, GRN No. 70
23	Issued - 95 units, Req. No. 118
24	Issued - 90 units, Req. No. 120
26	Transferred 15 units from Department A to Department B, MTN No. 27
28	Stock verification revealed a shortage of 7 units, Audit Note No. 15
29	Received from B Co. 35 units at ₹50 per unit, GRN No. 81
31	Issued 60 units, Req. No. 141

Prepare stores ledger account using FIFO method of pricing issues.

Solution

Stores ledger-FIFO method

Date	Particulars	Receipts			Issues			Balance		
		Qty. (units)	Rate ₹	Value ₹	Qty. (units)	Rate ₹	Value ₹	Qty. (units)	Rate ₹	Value ₹
Oct 1	Opening Balance	-	-	-	-	-	-	40	45	1,800
2	Issue Req. No. 101	-	-	-	15	45	675	25	45	1,125
3	Purchase GRN No. 51	75	46	3,450	-	-	-	25	45	1,125
								75	46	3,450
5	Issue Req. No. 103	-	-	-	20	25	500	5	45	225
								75	46	3,450
8	Purchase GRN 56	90	48	4,320	-	-	-	5	45	225
								75	46	3,450
								90	48	4,320
10	Return to X & Co.	-	-	-	15	48	720	5	45	225
								75	46	3,450
								75	48	3,600
14	Received GRN 59	60	47	2,820	-	-	-	5	45	225
								75	46	3,450
								75	48	3,600
								60	47	2,820
18	Receipt from X & MRR No. 30	15	48	720	-	-	-	5	45	225
								75	46	3,450
								90	48	4,320
								60	47	2,820
21	Purchase GRN 70	125	48	6,000	-	-	-	5	45	225
								75	46	3,450
								90	48	4,320
								60	47	2,820
								125	48	6,000

23	Issue Req. 115	-	-	-	5	45	225	75	48	3,600
					75	46	3,450	60	47	2,820
					15	48	720	125	48	6,000
24	Issue Req. 120	-	-	-	75	48	3,600	45	47	2,115
					15	47	705	125	48	6,000
28	Shortage - Audit Note No.15	-	-	-	7	47	329	38	47	1,786
								125	48	6,000
29	Receipt GRN No. 81	35	50	1,750	-	-	-	38	47	1,786
								125	48	6,000
								35	50	1,750
31	Issue Req. 141	-	-	-	38	47	1,786	103	48	4,944
					22	48	1,056	35	50	1,750

Note:

1. Materials returned to X & Co. on 10th October is priced at actual purchase price and deducted from the respective batch.
2. Replacement received from X & Co. is priced at actual cost and added to quantity received from X & Co. and not treated as fresh purchase.
3. Shortage is treated like an issue and priced as per FIFO rules.
4. Transfer of materials from department 'A' to 'B' on 26th October, should not be entered in stores ledger.

4.2.2 Last In First Out (LIFO) Method

Under this method materials purchased last are issued first. In this method material issues are priced at the last purchase price. After exhausting the materials in the last lot, the materials from the next previous lot is applied for issue. It is reverse of FIFO method.

Advantages

1. This method is also simple and easy to operate.
2. The value of materials issued relates to the latest market price.
3. As actual price is used for valuing issue of materials, there will be no over-pricing or under-pricing of material issues.
4. This method is suitable when prices are increasing.
5. The risk of loss is less as the costly materials are exhausted first and materials purchased earlier at cheaper price are in hand.
6. As the costly materials are charged to jobs, the profit will be less and tax liability is also reduced.

Disadvantages

1. The chances of clerical errors will be more if the number of purchases and issues are more, as in FIFO.
2. Sometimes materials for a job may be charged at different rates.
3. The cost of materials charged to different jobs will vary, making the comparison of cost and profitability of similar jobs difficult.
4. This method is not accepted for income tax purpose and not recognised in Accounting Standards.

Illustration-2: (Stores ledger-LIFO method)

The following transactions took place during the month of March 2009 relating to material 'X-70'.

March 1	Materials in hand 50 units valued at ₹625
2	Purchased 75 units at ₹13, GRN No. 205
4	Issued 40 units, Req. No. 711
7	Purchased 100 units at ₹13.50, GRN No. 210
9	Issued 125 units, Req. No. 740
10	Materials returned: 10 units from departments out of materials issued on 4th March
11	Purchased 50 units at ₹13.25, GRN No. 225
13	Transfer of 25 units from Job 101 to Job 102
15	Stock verification revealed a loss of 5 units
18	Issued 60 units, Req. No. 755
21	Issued 25 units, Req. No. 760
22	Purchased 35 units at ₹14, GRN No. 230
25	Issued 45 units, Req. No. 755
28	Purchased 60 units at ₹13.75, GRN No. 240
30	Issued 40 units, Req. No. 245
31	Issued 25 units, Req. No. 248

Prepare stores ledger account using LIFO method of pricing the material issues.

Solution

Stores ledger-LIFO method										
Date	Particulars	Receipts			Issues			Balance		
		Qty. (units)	Rate ₹	Value ₹	Qty. (units)	Rate ₹	Value ₹	Qty. (units)	Rate ₹	Value ₹
Mar 1	Opening balance	-	-	-	-	-	-	50	12.50	625.00
2	Purchase GRN No. 205	75	13.00	975.00	-	-	-	50	12.50	625.00
								75	13.00	975.00
4	Issue Req. No. 711	-	-	-	40	13.00	520.00	50	12.50	625.00
								35	13.00	455.00
7	Purchase GRN No. 210	100	13.50	1,350	-	-	-	50	12.50	625.00
								35	13.00	455.00
								100	13.50	1,350.00
9	Issue Req. No. 740	-	-	-	100	13.50	1,350.00	50	12.50	625.00
					25	13.00	325.00	10	13.50	135.00
10	Return from job	10	13.00	130.00	-	-	-	10	13.00	130.00
								50	12.50	625.00
								10	13.50	135.00
11	Purchase GRN 225	50	13.25	662.50	-	-	-	10	13	130
								50	12.50	625
								10	13.50	135
								50	13.25	662.50
15	Shortage	-	-	-	5	13.25	66.25	10	13.00	130.00
								50	12.50	625.00
								10	13.50	135.00
								45	13.25	596.25
18	Issue Req. No. 755	-	-	-	45	13.25	596.25	10	13.00	130.00
					10	13.50	135.00	45	12.50	562.50
					5	12.50	62.50			
21	Issue Req. No. 760	-	-	-	25	12.50	312.50	10	13.00	130.00
								20	12.50	250.00

22	Purchase GRN	35	14.00	490.00	-	-	-	10	13.00	130.00
								20	12.50	250.00
								35	14.00	490.00
25	Issue Req. No.755	-	-	-	35	14.00	490.00	10	13.00	130.00
					10	12.50	125.00	10	12.50	125.00
28	Purchase GRN No. 240	60	13.75	825.00	-	-	-	10	13.00	130.00
								10	12.50	125.00
								60	13.75	825.00
30	Issue Req. No. 245	-	-	-	40	13.75	550.00	10	13.00	130.00
								10	12.50	125.00
								20	13.75	275.00
31	Issue Req. No. 248	-	-	-	20	13.75	275.00	10	13.00	130.00
					5	12.50	62.50	5	12.50	62.50

Note:

1. Return from job on March 10, treated as first lot and priced at original issue price.
2. Transfer from job 101 to job 102 on 13th March, is not entered in stores ledger.
3. Shortage on stock verification is treated like an issue, and priced as per LIFO rules.

4.2.3 Highest In First Out (HIFO) Method

Materials purchased at highest price are issued first. Cost of materials consumed will always be higher. The value of materials in stores will be low. The result obtained in this method will be similar to result obtained under LIFO method during inflationary period.

4.2.4 Base Stock Method

Under this method a certain quantity of material purchased earlier is kept as minimum stock (reserve stock) and this is not available for issue. The stock reserved and not available for issuing is called 'base stock'.

Base stock method is not a separate method. This method operates with either FIFO or LIFO method.

Illustration-3: (Base stock-FIFO and LIFO method)

The stock of materials on 1.4.2009 was 750 units at ₹ 30 per unit. The following receipts and issues were recorded. You are required to prepare the stores ledger account under FIFO and LIFO methods. The base stock is 500 units.

2.4.2009	Purchased 250 units at ₹ 33
4.4.2009	Issued 200 units
7.4.2009	Issued 150 units
10.4.2009	Purchased 500 units at ₹ 32
14.4.2009	100 units returned to supplier out of materials purchased on 10th April
15.4.2009	Issued 200 units
17.4.2009	Received back 50 units from departments, out of materials issued on 4.4.2009
20.4.2009	Purchased 300 units at ₹ 34
22.4.2009	Issued 450 units
25.4.2009	Stock verification revealed a loss of 10 units
30.4.2009	Issued 50 units

Solution

Stores ledger account-Base stock-FIFO method

Date	Particulars	Receipts			Issues			Balance		
		Qty. (units)	Rate ₹	Value ₹	Qty. (units)	Rate ₹	Value ₹	Qty. (units)	Rate ₹	Value ₹
Apr 1	Opening Balance	-	-	-	-	-	-	750	30	22,500
2	Purchase	250	33	8,250	-	-	-	750	30	22,500
								250	33	8,250
4	Issued	-	-	-	200	30	6,000	550	30	16,500
								250	33	8,250
7	Issued	-	-	-	50	30	1,500	500	30	15,000
					100	33	3,300	150	33	4,950
10	Purchased	500	32	16,000	-	-	-	500	30	15,000
								150	33	4,950
								500	32	16,000
14	Return to supplier	-	-	-	100	32	3,200	500	30	15,000
								150	33	4,950
								400	32	12,800

15	Issued	-	-	-	150	33	4,950	500	30	15,000
					50	32	1,600	350	32	11,200
17	Return from department	50	30	1,500	-	-	-	550	30	15,000
								350	32	11,200
20	Purchase	300	34	10,200	-	-	-	550	30	15,000
								350	32	11,200
								300	34	10,200
22	Issue	-	-	-	50	30	1,500	500	30	15,000
					350	32	11,200	250	34	8,500
					50	34	1,700			
25	Shortage	-	-	-	10	34	340	500	30	15,000
								240	34	8,160
30	Issue	-	-	-	50	34	1,700	500	30	15,000
								190	34	6,460

Stores ledger account-Base stock-LIFO method

Date	Particulars	Receipts			Issues			Balance		
		Qty. (units)	Rate ₹	Value ₹	Qty. (units)	Rate ₹	Value ₹	Qty. (units)	Rate ₹	Value ₹
Apr 1	Opening Balance	-	-	-	-	-	-	750	30	22,500
2	Purchase	250	33	8,250	-	-	-	750	30	22,500
								250	33	8,250
4	Issued	-	-	-	200	33	6,600	750	30	22,500
								50	33	1,650
7	Issued	-	-	-	50	33	1,650	650	30	19,500
					100	30	3,000			
10	Purchase	500	32	16,000	-	-	-	650	30	19,500
								500	32	16,000
14	Return to supplier	-	-	-	100	32	3,200	600	30	19,500
								400	32	12,800
15	Issued	-	-	-	200	32	6,400	650	30	19,500
								200	32	6,400

17	Return from department	50	33	1,650	-	-	-	650 200 50	30 32 33	19,500 6,400 1,650
20	Purchase	300	34	10,200	-	-	-	650 200 50 300	30 32 33 34	19,500 6,400 1,650 10,200
22	Issue	-	-	-	300 50 100	34 33 32	10,200 1,650 3,200	650 100	30 32	19,500 3,200
25	Shortage	-	-	-	10	32	320	650 90	30 32	19,500 2,880
30	Issue	-	-	-	50	32	1,600	650 40	30 32	19,500 1,280

4.3 AVERAGE PRICE METHODS

Under average price method actual purchase price is not applied for pricing issues. Cost of all materials is averaged and issues are priced on average price arrived. There are various methods for calculating average price. The following are the various average pricing methods:

4.3.1 Simple Average Price Method

Prices of all materials in stores are divided by the number of prices of materials in stores to arrive at simple average price. New average price is to be calculated by omitting the price of a material lot that has been exhausted. For this purpose it is assumed that materials purchased first are exhausted first. After every new purchase and issue a new average price is calculated.

Advantages

1. This method is simple and easy to operate.
2. It is suitable when the price of materials fluctuates in a narrow range.
3. The cost of materials charged to jobs will not vary widely as the materials cost are averaged.

Disadvantages

1. Quantity of materials purchased is ignored. If the quantity of materials purchased are not uniform, the average price arrived will not give a correct price.

2. This method is not suitable when prices are fluctuating widely.
3. This method leads to over- or under-absorption of materials cost.
4. The value of closing stock may not correspond to current market value of materials.

4.3.2 Weighted Average Price Method

Quantity of materials purchased is given importance. The total value of materials in stores is divided by the number of units of material in store, to calculate weighted average price. This method gives a correct average price. But in simple average price method, a small quantity of materials needed urgently might have been purchased at a higher price. This will inflate the issue price of materials. But in weighted average price method as the value is spread over all the units, the average price arrived is more accurate. A new average price is calculated after every new purchase.

Advantages

1. The weighted average price is more reliable.
2. The wide fluctuation in price of materials purchased at different points of time is averaged over all units in stock. So issue price will not change widely.
3. New average price is calculated only after every new purchase.
4. The question of over- recovery or under-recovery does not arise.
5. In times of frequent price fluctuations, this method is more suitable.

Disadvantages

1. The issue price will not correspond to market price of materials prevailing at the time of issue.
2. Calculation of average price may be cumbersome if the number of purchases are many.

4.3.3 Periodic Simple Average Price Method

Under simple average price method the issue price will change when a particular lot of material is exhausted or a new purchase is made. But under periodic simple average price method a single average price is calculated for a specific period at its end. The purchase price of materials during a period are added and divided by the number of prices. This price is known as periodic simple average price. This price is applied for all issues made during the period.

4.3.4 Periodic Weighted Average Price Method

Under weighted average price method a new average price is calculated after every new purchase. But under the periodic weighted average price method. Single average price is calculated for a specific period at its end. This price is calculated by dividing the value of all the materials purchased by the total quantity of materials purchased during the period. All issues are made at the same average price during the period.

4.3.5 Moving Periodic Simple Average Price Method

First, periodic simple average prices are calculated for a number of periods. To the calculate moving periodic simple average price, the periodic simple average prices are added and the total is divided by the number of periodic simple average prices.

4.3.6 Moving Periodic Weighted Average Price Method

In this method also first periodic weighted average prices for a number of periods are calculated. Then the total of periodic weighted average prices are divided by the number of periodic weighted average prices to calculate the moving periodic weighted average price.

Illustration-4: (Simple average price method)

From the following particulars prepare stores ledger account using simple average price method of material issues.

2009, May 1	Balance of materials in stores 250 units at ₹40 per unit
2	Issued 100 units
5	Purchased 350 units at ₹42
8	Issued 200 units
9	Returned to supplier 50 units which was purchased on 5th May
12	Issued 100 units
16	Purchased 200 units at ₹43
20	Issued 300 units
25	Stock verification revealed a loss of 10 units
28	Purchased 300 units at ₹45
29	Issued 250 units
30	Purchase 100 units at ₹44

Solution

Stores ledger account-Simple average price method

Date	Particulars	Receipts			Issues			Balance		
		Qty. (units)	Rate ₹	Value ₹	Qty. (units)	Rate ₹	Value ₹	Qty. (units)	Rate ₹	Value ₹
May 1	Opening balance	-	-	-	-	-	-	250	40	10,000
2	Issued	-	-	-	100	40	4,000	150	40	6,000

5	Purchase	350	42	14,700	-	-	-	500	-	20,700
8	Issued	-	-	-	200	41	8,200	300	-	12,500
9	Return to supplier	-	-	-	50	42	2,100	250	-	10,400
12	Issue	-	-	-	100	42	4,200	150	-	6,200
16	Purchase	200	43	8,600	-	-	-	350	-	14,800
20	Issue	-	-	-	300	42.50	12,750	50	-	2,050
25	Shortage	-	-	-	10	42.50	425	40	-	1,625
28	Purchase	300	45	13,500	-	-	-	340	-	15,125
29	Issue	-	-	-	250	44	11,000	90	-	4,125
30	Purchase	100	44	4,400	-	-	-	190	-	8,525

Note:

1. Issue prices
   (a) 8th May $= (40 + 42) \div 2 = 41$
   (b) 12th May $= 42$
   (c) 20th May $= (42 + 43) \div 2 = 41.50$
   (d) 29th May $= (43 + 45) \div 2 = 44$
2. It is assumed that materials purchased first are exhausted first.
3. Return to supplier is made at actual purchase price.

Illustration-5: (Weighted average price method)

From the following receipts and issues relating to material '$M-123$', during the month of September 2009, prepare stores ledger account valuing materials issue under weighted average method.

September 1	Opening balance 1,500 units at ₹8 per unit
2	Issued 500 units
3	Purchased 800 units at ₹8.50
5	Issued 600 units
9	Issued 400 units
12	Received back 100 units out of issue made on 9th September
13	Purchased 1,500 units at ₹9.00 per unit.
15	Issued 900 units
19	Issued 700 units
22	Returned to supplier 50 units out of purchase made on 13th September

25	Purchased 500 units at ₹8.75 per unit
27	Physical verification revealed a loss of 20 units
30	Issued 600 units

Solution

Stores ledger account-weighted average price method										
Date	Particulars	Receipts			Issues			Balance		
		Qty. (units)	Rate ₹	Value ₹	Qty. (units)	Rate ₹	Value ₹	Qty. (units)	Rate ₹	Value ₹
1	Opening Balance	-	-	-	-	-	-	1,500	8	12,000
2	Issue	-	-	-	500	8	4,000	1,000	8	8,000
3	Purchase	800	8.50	6,800	-	-	-	1,800	8.222	14,800
5	Issue	-	-	-	600	8.222	4,933	1,200	8.222	9,867
9	Issue	-	-	-	400	8.222	3,289	800	8.222	6,578
12	Return from jobs	100	8.222	822	-	-	-	900	8.222	7,400
13	Purchase	1,500	9	13,500	-	-	-	2,400	8.708	20,900
15	Issue	-	-	-	900	8.708	7,837	1,500	8.708	13,063
19	Issue	-	-	-	700	8.708	6,096	800	8.708	6,967
22	Return to supplier	-	-	-	50	9	450	750	8.689	6,517
25	Purchase	500	8.75	4,375	-	-	-	1,250	8.714	10,892
27	Shortage	-	-	-	20	8.714	174	1,230	8.714	10,718
30	Issue	-	-	-	600	8.714	5,228	630	8.714	5,490

Illustration-6: (Periodic simple average price method)

The following are the purchase and issue of materials 'Z' during the month of December 2009:

December 1	Balance in hand 400 units at ₹50 per unit
2	Issued 250 units
3	Purchased 500 units at ₹55
6	Issued 450 units
9	Purchased 700 units at ₹57 per unit
11	Purchased 300 units at ₹58 per unit

14	Issued 800 units
17	Purchased 600 units at ₹56 per unit
20	Issued 500 units
24	Purchased 300 units at ₹56.50
29	Issued 450 units

Prepare a store ledger account under periodic simple average price method.

Solution

Stores Ledger Account - Periodic Simple Average Price Method										
Date	Particulars	Receipts			Issues			Balance		
		Qty. (units)	Rate ₹	Value ₹	Qty. (units)	Rate ₹	Value ₹	Qty. (units)	Rate ₹	Value ₹
Dec 1	Opening Balance	-	-	-	-	-	-	400	50	20,000
2	Issue	-	-	-	250	56.50	14,125	150	-	5,875
3	Purchase	500	55	27,500	-	-	-	650	-	33,375
6	Issue	-	-	-	450	56.50	25,425	200	-	7,950
9	Purchase	700	57	39,900	-	-	-	900	-	47,850
11	Purchase	300	58	17,400	-	-	-	1,200	-	65,250
14	Issue	-	-	-	800	56.50	45,200	400	-	20,050
17	Purchase	600	56	33,600	-	-	-	1,000	-	53,650
20	Issue	-	-	-	500	56.50	28,250	500	-	25,400
24	Purchase	300	56.50	16,950	-	-	-	800	-	42,350
29	Issue	-	-	-	450	56.50	25,425	350	-	16,925

Note:

1. Periodic Simple Average Price $= \frac{55 + 57 + 58 + 56 + 56.50}{5} =$ ₹56.50
2. Price of opening balance materials is not considered for calculating periodic simple average price.

Illustration-7: (Periodic weighted average price method)

The following transactions took place relating to material 'x' during the month of January 2009. You are required to prepare a stores ledger account under periodic weighted average price method.

January 1	Opening balance 500 units at ₹25 per unit.
3	Issued 200 units.
4	Purchased 400 units at ₹26 per unit.
5	Issued - 300 units
8	Purchased 300 units of ₹25.50
10	Returned 25 units to supplier out of purchase made on 8th January.
12	Issued 400 units.
13	Purchased 250 units at ₹26.50 per unit.
15	Issued 300 units
19	Issued 150 units.
23	Purchased 500 units at ₹27.00 per unit.
27	Purchased 300 units at ₹27.50 per unit.
30	Issued - 600 units.

Solution

Stores Ledger Account - Periodic Weighted Average Price Method

Date	Particulars	Receipts			Issues			Balance		
		Qty. (units)	Rate ₹	Value ₹	Qty. (units)	Rate ₹	Value ₹	Qty. (units)	Rate ₹	Value ₹
Jan 1	Opening Balance	-	-	-	-	-	-	500	25	12,500
3	Issue	-	-	-	200	26.529	5,306	300	-	7,194
4	Purchase	400	26	10,400	-	-	-	700	-	17,594
5	Issue	-	-	-	300	26.529	7,959	400	-	9,635
8	Purchase	300	25.50	7,650	-	-	-	700	-	17,285
10	Returned to supplier	-	-	-	25	25.50	638	675	-	16,647
12	Issue	-	-	-	400	26.529	10,612	275	-	6,035
13	Purchase	250	26.50	6,625	-	-	-	525	-	12,660
15	Issue	-	-	-	300	26.529	7,959	225	-	4,701

19	Issue	-	-	-	150	26.529	3,979	75	-	722
23	Purchase	500	27	13,500	-	-	-	575	-	14,222
27	Purchase	300	27.50	8,250	-	-	-	875	-	22,472
30	Issue	-	-	-	600	26.529	15,917	275	-	6,555

Note:

1. Periodic Simple Average Price $= \frac{\text{Value of materials purchased}}{\text{No. of units purchased}} = \frac{46,425}{1,750} =$ ₹26.529.
2. Value of opening materials is ignored for calculation of weighted average price.

3. Market price or Replacement price method

In this method materials are issued at the current market price. This method can be followed only in case of materials for which market price is readily available.

Advantages:

1. Issue prices correspond to current market price. So this method is suitable for preparing tenders and quotations.
2. It helps in fixing the correct selling price of finished products.
3. This helps to evaluate the efficiency of purchase departments.

Disadvantages:

1. This method can be followed only when market price of a material is available regularly.
2. It results in either overvaluation or undervaluation of materials issued.
3. The value of closing stock will not reveal the correct value.

Illustration-8: (Market price method)

The following is an extract of the record of receipts and issues of a material during November 2009:

November 1	Opening balance 800 units at ₹15 per unit
3	Purchase 400 units at ₹14.50 per unit
4	Issued 600 units (Market price ₹14.60)
6	Purchased 340 units at ₹15.75 per unit
9	Issued 450 units (Market price ₹15.40)
11	Purchased 300 units at ₹16 per unit

14	Issued 400 units (Market price ₹15.60)
17	Purchased 400 units at ₹15.90 per unit
20	Purchased 250 units at ₹16.20 per unit
23	Issued 200 units (Market price ₹16.50 per unit)
27	Issued 500 units (Market price ₹16.50 per unit)
30	Purchased 400 units at ₹16.10 per unit.

Prepare stores ledger account under market price method.

Solution

Stores Ledger Account - Market Price Method

Date	Particulars	Receipts			Issues			Balance		
		Qty. (units)	Rate ₹	Value ₹	Qty. (units)	Rate ₹	Value ₹	Qty. (units)	Rate ₹	Value ₹
Nov 1	Opening Balance	-	-	-	-	-	-	800	15	12,000
3	Purchase	400	14.50	5,800	-	-	-	1,200	-	17,800
4	Issue	-	-	-	600	14.60	8,760	600	-	9,040
6	Purchase	340	15.75	5,355	-	-	-	940	-	14,395
9	Issue	-	-	-	450	15.40	6,930	490	-	7,465
11	Purchase	300	16	4,800	-	-	-	790	-	12,265
14	Issue	-	-	-	400	15.60	6,240	390	-	6,025
17	Purchase	400	15.90	6,360	-	-	-	790	-	12,385
20	Purchase	250	16.20	4,050	-	-	-	1,040	-	16,435
23	Issue	-	-	-	200	16.50	3,300	840	-	13,135
27	Issue	-	-	-	500	16.50	8,250	340	-	4,885
30	Purchase	400	16.10	6,440	-	-	-	740	-	11,325

4.3.7 Standard Price Method

Under this method management fixes a price for valuing all material issued during a particular period. This predetermined price is called Standard Price. Current market price, expected future trend in prices, discounts in price and purchase related expenses are considered while fixing the standard price. This method is suitable when price of a material is stable with only minor changes in either way. If price fluctuations are large, the standard price is to be fixed for a short period only. Standard price is fixed for each material.

Advantages

1. This method is simple and easy to operate.
2. A material issued to different jobs are priced at the same price. Comparison of cost of various jobs is possible.
3. The efficiency of purchase department can be measured.
4. It reduces clerical work in connection with computation of issue price for each material issues.

Disadvantages

1. The issue price does not correspond to actual price. This results in either over-pricing or under-pricing of material issues.
2. This method is not suitable when price fluctuations are frequent and wide.

Illustration-9: (Standard price method)

The following particulars have been extracted in respect of the material 'X'. Prepare a stores ledger account for the month of October 2009. Use the Standard Price of ₹8 for pricing the issues:

Receipts

1.10.2009	Opening Stock 500 units at ₹7.50 per unit
4.10.2009	Purchase - 400 units at ₹7.75 per unit
8.10.2009	Purchase - 600 units at ₹8.00 per unit
11.10.2009	Purchase - 350 units at ₹8.25 per unit
16.10.2009	Purchase - 400 units at ₹8.10 per unit
27.10.2009	Purchase - 500 units at ₹8.20 per unit

Issues

5.10.2009	Issued - 550 units
10.10.2009	Issued - 700 units
14.10.2009	Issued - 400 units
18.10.2009	Issued - 500 units
29.10.2009	Issued - 400 units

Solution

Stores Ledger Account - Standard Price Method										
Date	Particulars	Receipts			Issues			Balance		
		Qty. (units)	Rate ₹	Value ₹	Qty. (units)	Rate ₹	Value ₹	Qty. (units)	Rate ₹	Value ₹
Oct 1	Opening Balance	-	-	-	-	-	-	500	7.50	3,750
4	Purchase	400	7.75	3,100	-	-	-	900	-	6,850
5	Issue	-	-	-	550	8.00	4,400	350	-	2,450
8	Purchase	600	8.00	4,800	-	-	-	950	-	7,250
10	Issue	-	-	-	700	8.00	5,600	250	-	1,650
11	Purchase	350	8.25	2,887.50	-	-	-	600	-	4537.50
14	Issue	-	-	-	400	8.00	3,200	200	-	1,337.50
16	Purchase	400	8.10	3,240	-	-	-	600	-	4,577.50
18	Issue	-	-	-	500	8.00	4,000	100	-	577.50
27	Purchase	500	8.20	4,100	-	-	-	600	-	4,677.50
29	Issue	-	-	-	400	8.00	3,200	200	-	1,477.50

4.3.8 Inflated Price Method

Under this method the issue price of materials is adjusted to cover the normal loss of materials and stores overhead.

Illustration-9: (Inflated price method)

From the following particulars, work out the issue rate for 1,000 of first class and second class bricks:

(a) Paid for supply at the kiln site for 30 lakh first class bricks at ₹300 per 1,000 bricks.
(b) Paid for supply at the kiln site for 60 lakh second class bricks at ₹250 per 1,000 bricks.
(c) Paid carriage charges for carrying all bricks from the kiln to store yard at ₹15 per 1,000 bricks.
(d) Paid unloading charges ₹900 (lump sum)
(e) Paid for stacking in the store yard ₹1,800 (lump sum).
(f) Breakage in handling 1% for first class bricks and 2% for second class bricks.

(ICWA-Inter)

Solution

Statement showing computation of Issue Price for 1,000 Bricks		
Particulars	**First Class** ₹	**Second Class** ₹
Supply Cost:		
First class - 30 lakh bricks at ₹300 per 1,000 bricks	9,00,000	
Second class - 60 lakh bricks at ₹250 per 1,000 bricks	-	15,00,000
Carriage charges at ₹15 per 1,000 bricks	45,000	90,000
Unloading charges - ₹ 900		
Stocking charges - ₹1,800		
Total - ₹2,700	900	1,800
Apportioned in the ratio of number of units i.e.1:2		
Total Cost	**9,45,900**	**15,91,800**

Computation of Good Units		
Particulars	**First Class units**	**Second Class units**
Number of units produced	30,00,000	60,00,000
Less: Breakage in handling:		
First class - 1%	30,000	-
Second class - 2%	-	1,20,000
Good Units	**29,70,000**	**58,80,000**

$$\text{Issue rate per } 1,000 \text{ bricks} = \frac{\text{Total cost}}{\text{Good unit (in'000s)}}$$

$$\text{First class} = \frac{9,45,900}{2,970} = ₹\ 318.50 \text{ (approx)}$$

$$\text{Second class} = \frac{15,91,800}{5,880} = ₹\ 270.70 \text{ (approx)}$$

Note : Breakage in handling is treated as normal loss.

4.3.9 Specific Price Method

This method is applied when materials are purchased for a particular job or work order. The actual purchase cost is applied for materials used in the job or work order.

Selection of a Pricing Method

There is no hard and fast rule for selecting a method for pricing issues. The method selected should be suitable and give results desired by the management. The following factors influence the selection of a suitable pricing method:

(a) The method of costing used and the policy of management.
(b) The frequency of purchases and issues
(c) The value of materials
(d) The extent of price fluctuations
(e) The amount of clerical work involved in computation of issue prices
(f) The result expected - whether the materials consumed should reflect current cost, historical cost or average cost
(g) The method of cost in use
(h) The method of pricing followed by other firms in the industry

Miscellaneous Materials Transactions

1. Returns to Supplier

Materials received from the supplier may be of poor quality or in damaged condition. Such goods are returned to the supplier at the original price at which it was purchased. When supplier sends replacement materials it is also taken into stock at original purchase price.

2. Return from departments or jobs

After completion of a work, a part of materials received for the job may be found surplus. Such materials are returned to stores. These materials are entered in receipt column of stores ledger at the original issue price. Later, when these materials are issued for some other job, it is priced at the original price.

3. Transfer of materials from one job or to another job

Surplus materials of a job is to be returned to stores. To have a control over movement of materials, transfer of materials from one job to another is not allowed. Sometimes as a case of expediency, to avoid delay or save cost in movement of materials, transfer may be allowed with advice to stores, costing and receiving departments. It is not entered in stores ledger.

4. Deficiency or Shortage of Materials

Physical verification of materials in stores may reveal shortage. Shortage is entered in issue column of stores ledger and valued according to the pricing method followed. Later on it is transferred and debited to costing profit and loss account.

5. Surplus

Surplus may araise when materials absorb moisture from atmosphere or due to use of under measurement in issue of materials. Surplus material found in stores is entered in the receipt column of stores ledger and valued by applying the latest purchase price. This is later on transferred to the credit of costing profit and loss account.

Material and Production Losses

1. Waste

Waste refers to loss of materials in the production process that does not possess any realisable value. It is of two types. Some wasted material may be physically available in the form of residue materials. Sometimes wasted materials may not be available physically, e.g, loss by evaporation, spillage, shrinkage, etc. Waste may further be classified into normal and abnormal wastes.

Accounting Treatment

(a) *Normal Waste*

Normal waste of materials is that part of material wasted always in the production process and it cannot be avoided due to the inherent nature of materials. Cost of normal wastage is spread over good units produced.

(b) *Abnormal Waste*

Wastage over and above the normal level is called abnormal wastage. It is not a regular feature. It arises only occasionally due to reasons like careless handling, poor quality, wrong instruction by foremen or bad machine working condition. Abnormal waste is valued at full cost and debited to costing profit and loss account. It is not allowed to influence the cost of production.

2. Scrap

Part of materials wasted in production process and having some realisable value is called scrap. Based on the past experience a standard is fixed for scrap. Examples of scraps are - paper cuttings in printing presses, saw dust and wood pieces, metal pieces and splits due to cutting, boring, turning etc. in engineering industries.

Scraps are classified into three types such as:

(a) *Legitimate Scrap*

This arises due to nature of processing operations performed.

(b) *Administrative Scrap*

This arises due to changes made in the method of production by the management.

(c) *Defective Scrap*

This arises due to poor quality of materials, carelessness on the part of machine operator, wrong instruction by foreman or poor working condition of machines.

Accounting Treatment

A. Normal Scrap

(i) *Other Income*

When the value of scrap is insignificant it is credited to profit and loss account as other income. This procedure is followed as a matter of accounting convenience.

(ii) *Credited to Materials Cost or Production Overheads*

When the value of scrap is considerable it may either be deducted from production overheads or from materials cost.

(iii) *Credited to Specific Process or Job*

When the scrap is identifiable to a particular job or process, the scrap value is credited to that specific job or process.

B. Abnormal Scrap

If scrap is in excess of normal level it is called abnormal scrap. It is valued at full cost less scrap value. Its net value is debited to costing profit and loss account.

3. Defectives

Defectives stand for units produced which do not conform to dimensional or quality standards specified for the product. These products come out with some deficiency. The deficiency in the product can be cured by spending additional amount of labour, materials and other services.

Accounting Treatment

a) *Normal Defectives:*

When the defectives are within the normal level, the additional cost expended for curing the defect is treated as production cost. It is absorbed by all units produced.

b) *Abnormal Defectives:*

Defectives may be in excess of normal level due to causes like poor workmanship, faulty instruction by foreman, or poor machine working conditions. The additional cost incurred for curing the abnormal defective units is debited to costing profit and loss account.

4. Spoilable

Spoilage refers to products produced which do not conform to dimensional or quality standards specified for the product. The defects in the product cannot be rectified or cost of rectification may be large and not economical.

Spoilages may possess some value and it is sold as seconds or saleable rejections. Sometimes it may not possess any realisable value and is thrown away.

Sometimes spoilage is also used to refer to materials badly damaged after it has gone through some production process. These damaged materials may be reused as materials for the same product or others. In some cases it cannot be reused and is sold.

Spoilage should not be confused with scrap. Scrap arises in the initial stage of production itself.

Accounting Treatment

a) *Normal Spoilage:*

The cost of normal spoilage is debited to the concerned process, job or production overheads. Any amount realised from the sale of normally spoilt units is credited to process, job or production overheads account.

b) *Abnormal Spoilage:*

Abnormal spolage is valued at full cost less realisible value. It is debited to costing profit and loss account.

Materials Control Ratios

Various ratios are computed to exercise a control over materials cost. The various material control ratios are:

1. **Inventory Turnover Ratio or Material Turnover Ratio**

   Inventory turnover ratio refers to the rate of consumption of materials compared to the average stock of materials held. The stock turnover ratio is computed by using the following formula:

   $$= \frac{\text{Cost of materials consumed}}{\text{Cost of average stock held}}$$

   Material turnover ratio in quantitative terms may also be calculated as follows:

   $$= \frac{\text{Quantity of materials consumed}}{\text{Quantity of average stock held}}$$

   Number of days average stock held is also calculated as follows:

   $$= \frac{365}{\text{Inventory turnover ratio}}$$

   Inventory turnover ratio is used to exercise control over cost of materials. High inventory ratio indicates that the materials are used regularly. But a very high turnover indicates the lower level of stock. This may lead to "Stock Out" position. Low inventory turnover ratio refers to overstocking. It also helps to identify slow moving, dormant and obsolete stocks.

   "Slow Moving Stocks" are materials used in small quantities or used irregularly.

   "Dormant Stocks" are materials used only when need arises e.g., spare parts and tools.

   "Obsolete Stocks" are materials not in current use. A material may have become out of date due to change in the product, change in the method of production or change in the product design.

   Control over slow moving, dormant and obsolete items:

   (a) Find alternative use or substitute use for these items.
   (b) Sell them as early as possible if they cannot be put to alternative use.

2. **Input - Output Ratio**

   Material consumed is compared with output obtained. This helps to find out the efficiency in consumption of materials. By comparing with standard ratios the excessive wastage of materials can be identified. Input-output ratio is calculated as follows:

$$= \frac{\text{Materials consumed}}{\text{Output}}$$

3. **Yield Ratio**

   Yield ratio is the reverse of Input-output ratio. The output is compared with the material consumed. It helps to find out production efficiency. By comparing with standard yield ratio, the production inefficiency can be identified. This ratio is calculated as follows:

$$= \frac{\text{Output}}{\text{Materials consumed}}$$

Illustration-11: (Material turnover ratio)

From the following information for the year 2009-10 compute materials turnover ratio and number of days average stock is held and comment on it:

	Materials 'A' ₹	Materials 'B' ₹
Materials in hand on 1.4.2009	60,000	90,000
Materials in hand on 31.3.2010	24,000	75,000
Materials purchased during 2009-10	5,10,000	2,32,500

Solution

Computation of Materials Consumed		
Particulars	**Materials 'A'** ₹	**Materials 'B'** ₹
Purchase of materials	5,10,000	2,32,500
Add: Stock of materials on 1.4.09	60,000	90,000
	5,70,000	3,22,500
Less: Stock of materials on 31.3.10	24,000	75,000
Materials consumed	5,46,000	2,47,500
Average stock $= \frac{\text{Opening stock} + \text{Closing stock}}{2}$	$\frac{60,000 + 24,000}{2}$ = 42,000	$\frac{90,000 + 75,000}{2}$ = 82,500

$$\text{Materials turnover ratio} = \frac{\text{Materials consumed}}{\text{Average stock}}$$

$$\text{Materials 'A'} = \frac{5,46,000}{42,000} = 13 \text{ times}$$

$$\text{Materials 'B'} = \frac{2,47,500}{82,500} = 3 \text{ times}$$

$$\text{Number of days of average stock held} = \frac{365}{\text{Materials turnover ratio}}$$

$$\text{Materials 'A'} = \frac{365}{13} = 28 \text{ days (Approx.)}$$

$$\text{Materials 'B'} = \frac{365}{3} = 122 \text{ days (Approx.)}$$

Comment:

Materials 'A' is fast moving item. Stocks are held equal to 28 days materials requirements.

Materials 'B' is a slow moving item or it indicates overstocking. Materials are held equal to 122 days consumption. Stock level of material 'B' is to be reduced after considering normal delivery time required.

Illustration-12: (Materials turnover ratio)

The following are the transactions relating to Material 'A' during the month of April 2009:

1.4.2009	Opening balance	500 units
8.4.2009	Purchased	600 units
11.4.2009	Issued	700 units
15.4.2009	Purchased	900 units
18.4.2009	Issued	400 units
22.4.2009	Purchased	300 units
28.4.2009	Issued	800 units

Number of units produced during the month of April 2009 is 1,750 units. Compute materials turnover ratio in quantitative terms. Also compute yield ratio and input output ratio.

Solution

$$\begin{aligned}\text{Closing stock} &= \text{Opening stock} + \text{Purchases} - \text{Issues}\\ &= 500 + 1800 - 1900\\ &= 400 \text{ units.}\end{aligned}$$

$$\begin{aligned}\text{Average stock} &= \frac{\text{Opening stock} + \text{Closing stock}}{2}\\ &= \frac{500 + 400}{2}\\ &= 450 \text{ units}\end{aligned}$$

$$\begin{aligned}\text{Materials consumed} &= \text{Materials issued}\\ &= 1900 \text{ units}\end{aligned}$$

$$\begin{aligned}\text{Materials turnover ratio} &= \frac{\text{Materials consumed}}{\text{Average stock}}\\ &= \frac{1900}{450}\\ &= 4.22 \text{ times}\end{aligned}$$

$$\begin{aligned}\text{Yield ratio} &= \frac{\text{Output}}{\text{Materials consumed}} \times 100\\ &= \frac{1750}{1900} \times 100\\ &= 92.11\%\end{aligned}$$

$$\begin{aligned}\text{Input output ratio} &= \frac{\text{Materials consumed}}{\text{Output}}\\ &= \frac{1900}{1750} \times 100\\ &= 108.57\%\end{aligned}$$

COMPREHENSIVE ILLUSTRATIONS

Illustration-13: (FIFO, LIFO and weighted average methods)

You are presented with the following information by OM Engineering related to the first week of December, 1995. The transactions in connection with a material are as follows:

Days	Receipts		Issues (Unit)
	Units	Rate per Unit (₹)	
1st	40	15.00	-
2nd	20	16.50	-
3rd	-	-	30
4th	50	17.10	-
5th	-	-	20
6th	-	-	40

Calculate the cost of materials issued under (i) FIFO method; (ii) LIFO method and (iii) Weighted average method of issue of materials and value of closing stock under the methods aforesaid. **(CS-Inter)**

Solution

Stores Ledger - FIFO Method										
Date	Particulars	Receipts			Issues			Balance		
		Qty. (units)	Rate ₹	Value ₹	Qty. (units)	Rate ₹	Value ₹	Qty. (units)	Rate ₹	Value ₹
Dec 1	Purchase	40	15.00	600	-	-	-	40	15.00	600
2	Purchase	20	16.50	330	-	-	-	40	15	600
								20	16.50	330
3	Issue	-	-	-	30	15	450	10	15	150
								20	16.50	330
4	Purchase	50	17.10	855	-	-	-	10	15	150
								20	16.50	330
								50	17.10	855
5	Issue	-	-	-	10	15	150	10	16.50	165
					10	16.50	165	50	17.10	855
6	Issue	-	-	-	10	16.50	165	20	17.10	342
					30	17.10	513			
	Total	110	-	1,785	90	-	1,443	20	-	342

Stores Ledger - LIFO Method										
Date	Particulars	Receipts			Issues			Balance		
		Qty. (units)	Rate ₹	Value ₹	Qty. (units)	Rate ₹	Value ₹	Qty. (units)	Rate ₹	Value ₹
Dec 1	Purchase	40	15.00	600	-	-	-	40	15.00	600
2	Purchase	20	16.50	330	-	-	-	40 20	15 16.50	600 330
3	Issue	-	-	-	20 10	16.50 15.00	330 150	30	15.00	450
4	Purchase	50	17.10	855	-	-	-	30 50	15.00 17.10	450 855
5	Issue	-	-	-	20	17.10	342	30 30	15.00 17.10	450 513
6	Issue	-	-	-	30 10	17.10 15.00	513 150	20	15.00	300
	Total	110	-	1,785	90	-	1,485	20	-	300

Stores Ledger - Weighted Average Method										
Date	Particulars	Receipts			Issues			Balance		
		Qty. (units)	Rate ₹	Value ₹	Qty. (units)	Rate ₹	Value ₹	Qty. (units)	Rate ₹	Value ₹
Dec 1	Purchase	40	15.00	600	-	-	-	40	15.00	600
2	Purchase	20	16.50	330	-	-	-	60	15.50	930
3	Issue	-	-	-	30	15.50	465	30	15.50	465
4	Purchase	50	17.10	855	-	-	-	80	16.50	1,320
5	Issue	-	-	-	20	16.50	330	60	16.50	990
6	Issue	-	-	-	40	16.50	660	20	16.50	330
	Total	110	-	1,785	90	-	1,455	20	-	330

Illustration-14: (LIFO method)

Prepare a stores ledger account from the following details using LIFO.

April 1	Opening balance 10,850 kg at ₹130 per unit
2	Purchased 20,000 kg ₹134 per kg.
3	Issued 6,750 kg to production
5	Issued 8,500 kg to production
6	Received back 550 kg from production being surplus
7	Purchased 17,550 kg at ₹128 per kg
8	Issued 11,250 kg to production
9	Physical verification revealed a loss of 250 kg
10	Issued 8,950 kg to production
12	Issued 6,300 kg to production
15	Purchased 10,000 kg at ₹132 per kg
16	Issued 7,750 kg to production

(ICWA-Inter)

Solution

Stores Ledger Account - LIFO Method

Date	Particulars	Receipts			Issues			Balance		
		Qty. (units)	Rate ₹	Value ₹	Qty. (units)	Rate ₹	Value ₹	Qty. (units)	Rate ₹	Value ₹
Apr 1	Opening Balance	-	-	-	-	-	-	10,850	130	14,10,500
2	Purchase	20,000	134	26,80,000	-	-	-	10,850 20,000	130 134	14,10,500 26,80,000
3	Issued	-	-	-	6,750	134	9,04,500	10,850 13,250	130 134	14,10,500 17,75,500
5	Issued	-	-	-	8,500	134	11,39,000	10,850 4,750	130 134	14,10,500 6,36,500
6	Return from production	550	134	73,700	-	-	-	10,850 5,300	130 134	14,10,500 7,10,200
7	Purchase	17,550	128	22,46,400	-	-	-	10,850 5,300	130 134	14,10,500 7,10,200

								17,550	128	22,46,400
8	Issue	-	-	-	11,250	128	14,40,000	10,850	130	14,10,500
								5,300	134	7,10,200
								6,300	128	8,06,400
9	Shortage	-	-	-	250	128	32,000	10,850	130	14,10,500
								5,300	134	7,10,200
								6,050	128	7,74,400
10	Issue	-	-	-	6,050	128	7,74,400	10,850	130	14,10,500
					2,900	134	3,88,600	2,400	134	3,21,600
12	Issue	-	-	-	2,400	134	3,21,600	6,950	130	9,03500
					3,900	130	5,07,000			
15	Purchase	10,000	132	13,20,000	-	-	-	6,950	130	9,03500
								10,000	132	13,20,000
16	Issue	-	-	-	7,750	132	10,23,000	6,950	130	9,03500
								2,250	132	2,97,000

Illustration-15: (Valuation of closing stock under FIFO, LIFO and weighted average methods)

The following transactions in respect of material 'Y' occurred during the six months ended 30th June 1988:

Days	Purchase		Issued (Unit)
	Units	Rate per Unit (₹)	
January	200	25	-
February	300	24	250
March	425	26	300
April	475	26	550
May	500	25	800
June	600	20	400

Required:

The chief accountant urges that the value of closing stock remains the same, no matter which method of pricing of materials issues is used. Do you agree? Why or Why not? Detailed Stores ledger account is not required. **(CA-Inter)**

Solution

Month	Opening Balance (Units)	Purchase (Units)	Issues (Units)	Closing Balance (Units)
January, 1988	-	200	-	200
February	200	300	250	250
March	250	425	300	375
April	375	475	300	550
May	300	500	800	-
June	-	600	400	200

There is no opening stock in the month of June. So closing stock of 200 units of June is out of purchases made in June.

Hence closing stock of June will be valued at ₹20 under FIFO, LIFO weighted average and simple average price methods.

So the argument of chief accountant is correct.

Illustration-16: (Selecting a suitable method of pricing issues)

The following are the transactions in respect of purchase and issue of components forming part of an assembly of a product manufactured by a firm which requires to update its cost of production, very often for bidding tenders and finalising cost plus contracts:

Date	Quantity (Nos.)	Particulars
1986, January 5	1,000	Purchased at ₹1.20 each
11	2,000	Issued
February 1	1,500	Purchased at ₹1.30 each
18	2,400	Issued
26	1,000	Issued
March 8	1,000	Purchased at ₹1.40 each
17	1,500	Purchased at ₹1.30 each
28	2,000	Issued

The stock on January 1, 1986 was 5000 nos. valued at ₹1.10 each. State the method you would adopt in pricing the issue of components giving reasons. What value would you place on stocks as on March 31, which happens to be the financial year end and how would you treat the difference in value, if any, on the stock account?

Solution

The purchase prices are fluctuating up and down. So it is advisable to adopt weighted average method of pricing issues.

Stores Ledger Account - Weighted Average Method										
Date	Particulars	Receipts			Issues			Balance		
		Qty. (units)	Rate ₹	Value ₹	Qty. (units)	Rate ₹	Value ₹	Qty. (units)	Rate ₹	Value ₹
Jan 1	Opening Stock	-	-	-	-	-	-	5,000	1.10	5,500
5	Purchase	1,000	1.20	1,200	-	-	-	6,000	1.1167	6,700
11	Issued	-	-	-	2,000	1.1167	2,233	4,000	1.1167	4,467
Feb 1	Purchased	1,500	1.30	1,950	-	-	-	5,500	1.1667	6,417
18	Issued	-	-	-	2,400	1.1667	2,800	3,100	1.1667	3,617
26	Issued	-	-	-	1,000	1.1667	1,167	2,100	1.1667	2,450
Mar 8	Purchased	1,000	1.40	1,400	-	-	-	3,100	1.2419	3,850
17	Purchase	1,500	1.30	1,950	-	-	-	4,600	1.2609	5,800
28	Issued	-	-	-	2,000	1.2609	2,522	2,600	1.2609	3,278

Weighted average cost of closing stock is ₹3,278. Its market value is (2,600 × 1.30) ₹3,380. For balance sheet purpose it is valued at cost or market price whichever is lower i.e. ₹3,278.

Illustration-17: (FIFO, LIFO and cumulative weighted average method)

Movewell Ltd, is a distributor of bicycles. At 30th June stock-in-hand was 200 units which had a value of ₹8,400.

The transactions for the six months to 31st December were as follows:

Date	Purchase Quantity (units)	Cost per unit (₹)
July	200	46.00
August	500	49.40
September	1,000	52.50

The purchase manager obtained a bulk purchase discount of ₹7.50 per unit on the September purchase.

Date	Sales Quantity (units)	Cost per unit (₹)
October	500	66.00
November	700	70.00
December	500	75.00

There were no sales during the first three months of the period. Using the FIFO, LIFO and cumulative weight average methods of stock valuation, you are required to:

(a) Show the stores ledger records, including the closing stock valuation.
(b) Prepare trading account for the six months period, using each of the three valuation methods.
(c) Indicate which valuation method is the best measure of profit and why? **(CS-Inter)**

Solution

Stores Ledger FIFO Method

Date	Particulars	Receipts			Issues			Balance		
		Qty. (units)	Rate ₹	Value ₹	Qty. (units)	Rate ₹	Value ₹	Qty. (units)	Rate ₹	Value ₹
July	Opening Balance	-	-	-	-	-	-	200	42	8,400
July	Purchase	200	46	9,200	-	-	-	200	42	8,400
								200	46	9,200
August	Purchase	500	49.40	24,700	-	-	-	200	42	8,400
								200	46	9,200
								500	49.40	24,700
September	Purchase	1000	52.50	52,500	-	-	-	200	42	8,400
								200	46	9,200
								500	49.40	24,700
								1000	52.50	52,500
October	Issue	-	-	-	200	42	8,400	400	49.40	19,760
					200	46	9,200	1,000	52.50	52,500
					100	49.40	4,940			

November	Issue	-	-	-	400 300	49.40 52.50	19,760 15,750	700	52.50	36,750
December	Issue	-	-	-	500	52.50	26,250	200	52.50	10,500

Stores Ledger LIFO Method

Date	Particulars	Receipts			Issues			Balance		
		Qty. (units)	Rate ₹	Value ₹	Qty. (units)	Rate ₹	Value ₹	Qty. (units)	Rate ₹	Value ₹
July	Opening Balance	-	-	-	-	-	-	200	42	8,400
July	Purchase	200	46	9,200	-	-	-	200 200	42 46	8,400 9,200
August	Purchase	500	49.40	24,700	-	-	-	200 200 500	42 46 49.40	8,400 9,200 24,700
September	Purchase	1,000	52.50	52,500	-	-	-	200 200 500 1000	42 46 49.40 52.50	8,400 9,200 24,700 52,500
October	Issue	-	-	-	500	52.50	26,250	200 200 500 500	42 46 49.40 52.50	8,400 9,200 24,700 26,250
November	Issue	-	-	-	500 200	52.50 49.50	26,250 9,900	200 200 300	42 46 49.40	8,400 9,200 14,820
December	Issue	-	-	-	300 200	49.40 46	14,820 9,200	200	42	8,400

Stores Ledger - Cumulative Weighted Average Method										
Date	Particulars	Receipts			Issues			Balance		
		Qty. (units)	Rate ₹	Value ₹	Qty. (units)	Rate ₹	Value ₹	Qty. (units)	Rate ₹	Value ₹
July	Opening Balance	-	-	-	-	-	-	200	42	8,400
July	Purchase	200	46	9,200	-	-	-	400		17,600
August	Purchase	500	49.40	24,700	-	-	-	900		42,300
September	Purchase	1,000	52.50	52,500	-	-	-	1,900	49.8947	94,800
October	Issue	-	-	-	500	49.8947	24,947	1400		69,853
November	Issue	-	-	-	700	49.8947	34,926	700		34,927
December	Issue	-	-	-	500	49.8947	24,947	200		9,980

Note:

$$\text{Cumulative weighted average price} = \frac{\text{Value of opening stock + Value of all purchases}}{\text{Total number of units}}$$

$$= \frac{94,800}{1,900} = ₹49.8947$$

Trading account for 6 months ending 31st December							
Particulars	FIFO ₹	LIFO ₹	C.W. Average ₹	Particulars	FIFO ₹	LIFO ₹	C.W. Average ₹
To Opening stock	8,400	8,400	8,400	By Sales	1,19,500	1,19,500	1,19,500
To Purchases	86,400	86,400	86,400	By Closing stock	10,500	8,400	9,980
To Gross profit	35,200	33,100	34,680				
	1,30,000	1,27,900	1,29,480		1,30,000	1,27,900	1,29,480

Note:

(1) Purchase - July = 200 units × ₹46 = ₹9,200

August = 200 units × ₹6 = ₹24,700

September = 1,000 units × ₹52.50 = ₹52,500

Total = ₹86,400

(2) Sales-October	= 500 units × ₹66	= ₹33,000
November	= 700 units × ₹70	= ₹49,000
December	= 500 units × ₹75	= ₹37,500
	Total	= ₹1,19,500

Comment: Of the three methods LIFO method gives good results due to the following reasons:

(a) Purchase prices are increasing. Issue price correspond to market price.
(b) As cost of materials consumed is more and profit will be less and tax liability is also reduced.
(c) Value of materials in hand is at lower price, reducing the risk.

Illustration-18: (Treatment of shortage and surplus)

After the annual stock taking you come to know of some significant discrepancies between book stock and physical stock, you gather the following information:

Items	Stock card (units)	Stores ledger (units)	Physical check (units)	Cost per unit (₹)
A	600	600	560	60
B	380	380	385	40
C	750	780	720	10

1. What action should be taken to record the information above?
2. Recommend a possible course of action by the management to prevent future losses.

(CA-Inter)

Solution

1. **Actions to be taken are:**
   (a) Stock card and stores ledger is to be compared periodically to check the accuracy of entries made in them.
   (b) Physical verification of stocks to be carried out and compared with stock card to find stock discrepancies.
   (c) Investigate the discrepancies to find the possible causes for the same.
   (d) The following accounting treatment is suggested:

      i. *Shortage of materials:*

      Production OHS control a/c - Dr. (if normal loss)
      Costing P & L a/c - Dr. (if abnormal loss)
      Work-in-progress a/c - Dr. (Omission or short recording of issues)
      To Raw materials control a/c

ii. *Surplus materials:*

Raw materials control Account - Dr.
To production OHS control a/c (if normal)
To costing P&L a/c (if abnormal)
To WIP control a/c (For excess recording of issues)

The following entries are to be made for the above case.

Materials 'A':

There is shortage in physical verification only. The shortage is below 10%, may be treated as normal loss:

Accounting entry:

Production OHS control a/c Dr 2400
To Raw materials control a/c 2400

Material 'B':

There is discrepancy in physical verification only. Surplus is below 5% and treated as normal gain accounting entry:

Raw materials control a/c Dr 200
To Production OHS control a/c 200

Material 'C':

There is discrepancy in stock card and stores ledger entry and also in physical verification.

If we take entry in stock card is correct, then there should be under recording/omission to record issue of 30 units (780-750). It is corrected by giving the following entry:

WIP Control a/c Dr 300
To Raw materials control a/c 300.

There is shortage of 30 units found in physical verification (750-720) and treated as normal loss. The following entry is made:

Production OHS control a/c Dr 300
To Raw materials control a/c 300

2. Measures suggested to prevent discrepancies in future:

   (a) Proper recording of materials movement and verification of the records at reasonable intervals.
   (b) Materials should be issued against requisitions authorised by a specified authority.
   (c) Unauthorised persons should not have access to stores records.
   (d) Materials received earlier should be exhausted first to prevent deterioration in quality, shrinkage, and materials becoming obsolete.
   (e) Suitable internal control system should be established.

Illustration-19: (Different pricing methods and impact on profit)

Oil India is a bulk distributor of high octane petrol. A periodic inventory of petrol in hand is taken when the books are closed at the end of each month. The following summary of information is available for the month:

	₹
Sales	9,45,000
General administration cost	25,000
Opening stock 1,00,000 litres at ₹3 per litre	3,00,000

Purchases (including freight inward)

June 1 . 2,00,000 litres at ₹2.85 per litre.
June 30. 1,00,00 litres at ₹3.03 per litre.
June 30. Closing stock 1,30,000 litres

Compute the following data by the FIFO, weighted average and LIFO methods of inventory costing:

(a) Value of inventory on June 30
(b) Amount of cost of goods sold for June
(c) Profit or loss for June **(CA-Inter)**

Solution

(a) Value of stock on June 30 and cost of goods sold.

Stores Ledger - FIFO Method									
Date	Receipts			Issues (Cost of goods sold)			Balance		
	Litre (units)	Rate ₹	Value ₹	Litre (units)	Rate ₹	Value ₹	Litre (units)	Rate ₹	Value ₹
June 1	-	-	-	-	-	-	1,00,000	3	3,00,000
June 1	2,00,000	2.85	5,70,000	-	-	-	1,00,000 2,00,000	3 2.85	3,00,000 5,70,000
June 30	-	-	-	1,00,000 1,70,000	3 2.85	3,00,000 4,84,500	30,000	2.85	85,500
June 30	1,00,000	3.03	3,03,000	-	-	-	30,000 1,00,000	2.85 3.03	85,500 3,03,000
Total	3,00,000	-	-	2,70,000	-	7,84,500	1,30,000	-	3,88,500

Stores Ledger - Weighted Average Method									
Date	Receipts			Issues (Cost of goods sold)			Balance		
	Litre (units)	Rate ₹	Value ₹	Litre (units)	Rate ₹	Value ₹	Litre (units)	Rate ₹	Value ₹
June 1	-	-	-	-	-	-	1,00,000	3	3,00,000
June 1	2,00,000	2.85	5,70,000	-	-	-	3,00,000	2.90	8,70,000
June 30	-	-	-	2,70,000	2.90	7,83,000	30,000	2.90	87,000
June 30	1,00,000	3.03	3,03,000	-	-	-	1,30,000	3.00	3,90,000
Total	3,00,000	-	8,73,000	2,70,000	-	7,83,000	1,30,000	3.00	3,90,000

Stores Ledger - LIFO Method									
Date	Receipts			Issues (Cost of goods sold)			Balance		
	Litre (units)	Rate ₹	Value ₹	Litre (units)	Rate ₹	Value ₹	Litre (units)	Rate ₹	Value ₹
June 1	-	-	-	-	-	-	1,00,000	3	3,00,000
June 1	2,00,000	2.85	5,70,000	-	-	-	1,00,000	3	3,00,000
							2,00,000	2.85	5,70,000
June 30	-	-	-	2,00,000	2.85	5,70,000	30,000	3.00	90,000
				70,000	3.00	2,10,000			
June 30	1,00,000	3.03	3,03,000	-	-	-	30,000	3.00	90,000
							1,00,000	3.03	3,03,000
Total	3,00,000	-	8,73,000	2,70,000	-	7,80,000	1,30,000	-	3,93,000

(a) Inventory on June 30

(i) FIFO - ₹3,88,500
(ii) Weighted average ₹3,90,000
(iii) LIFO - ₹3,93,000

(b) Cost of goods sold

(i) FIFO - ₹7,84,500
(ii) Weighted average ₹7,83,000
(iii) LIFO - ₹7,80,000

Statement showing profit for June			
	(i) FIFO ₹	(ii) Weighted Average ₹	(iii) LIFO ₹
Sales	9,45,000	9,45,000	9,45,000
Less: Cost of goods sold	7,84,500	7,83,000	7,80,000
Gross profit	1,60,500	1,62,000	1,65,000
Less: General and administration cost	25,000	25,000	25,000
Net profit	1,35,500	1,37,000	1,40,000

Illustration-20: (Choosing a suitable pricing method)

The following transactions relating to material 'A' took place during the month of September 2009.

September 1.	Opening balance	1000 units at ₹10 per unit.
2	Issued	500 units
5	Purchased	700 units at ₹11 per unit
8	Issued	600 units
12	Purchased	500 units at ₹12 per unit.
15	Issued	600 units
20	Purchased	700 units at ₹13 per unit
26	Issued	400 units
30	Issued	200 units

Prepare stores ledger account by choosing an appropriate method of pricing issues.

Solution

Stores Ledger - LIFO Method										
Date	Particulars	Receipts			Issues			Balance		
		Qty. (units)	Rate ₹	Value ₹	Qty. (units)	Rate ₹	Value ₹	Qty. (units)	Rate ₹	Value ₹
Sep 1	Opening Balance	-	-	-	-	-	-	1,000	10	10,000

2	Issue	-	-	-	500	10	5,000	500	10	5,000
5	Purchase	700	11	7700	-	-	-	500 700	10 11	5,000 7,700
8	Issue	-	-	-	600	11	6,600	500 100	10 11	5,000 1,100
12	Purchase	500	12	6000	-	-	-	500 100 500	10 11 12	5,000 1,100 6,000
15	Issue	-	-	-	500 100	12 11	6,000 1,100	500	10	5,000
20	Purchased	700	13	9,100	-	-	-	500 700	10 13	5,000 9,100
26	Issue	-	-	-	400	13	5,200	500 300	10 13	5,000 3,900
30	Issue	-	-	-	200	13	2,600	500 100	10 13	5,000 1,300

Note: Material prices are increasing. LIFO method is more suitable in inflationary condition.

Illustration-21

The following are the purchases and issues made relating to a material in the month of July 2009.

July 1	Opening balance	2000 units at ₹7.50 per unit.
3	Issued	800 units
6	Purchased	3000 units at ₹8 per unit
8	Issued	1,500 units
10	Issued	1,200 units
14	Purchased	1,800 units at ₹7.75 per unit.
16	Issued	2,000 units
21	Purchased	1,500 units at ₹8.25 per unit
25	Issued	1,900 units
29	Issued	500 units

Prepare stores ledger accounts in the following circumstances (a) Stock of materials in hand should be closely related to current market price. (b) The value of materials issued should relate to current market price.

Solution

(a) FIFO method should be followed when closing stock of materials should relate to current market price.

Stores Ledger - FIFO Method

Date	Particulars	Receipts			Issues			Balance		
		Qty. (units)	Rate ₹	Value ₹	Qty. (units)	Rate ₹	Value ₹	Qty. (units)	Rate ₹	Value ₹
July 1	Opening Balance	-	-	-	-	-	-	2,000	7.50	15,000
3	Issue	-	-	-	800	7.50	6,000	1,200	7.50	9,000
6	Purchase	3,000	8	24,000	-	-	-	1,200	7.50	9,000
								3,000	8.00	24,000
8	Issue	-	-	-	1,200	7.50	9,000	2,700	8.00	21,600
					300	8.00	2,400			
10	Issue	-	-	-	1,200	8	9,600	1500	8.00	12,000
14	Purchase	1,800	7.75	13,950	-	-	-	1,500	8.00	12,000
								1,800	7.75	13,950
16	Issue	-	-	-	1,500	8	12,000	1,500	7.75	11,625
					300	7.75	2,325			
21	Purchase	1,500	8.25	12,375	-	-	-	1,500	7.75	11,625
								1,500	8.25	12,375
25	Issue	-	-	-	1,500	7.75	11,625	1,100	8.25	9,075
					400	8.25	3,300			
29	Issue	-	-	-	500	8.25	4,125	600	8.25	4,950

(b) LIFO method is followed if the value of materials issued should closely relate to market price.

Stores Ledger - LIFO Method

Date	Particulars	Receipts			Issues			Balance		
		Qty. (units)	Rate ₹	Value ₹	Qty. (units)	Rate ₹	Value ₹	Qty. (units)	Rate ₹	Value ₹
July 1	Opening Balance	-	-	-	-	-	-	2,000	7.50	15,000
3	Issue	-	-	-	800	7.5	6,000	1,200	7.50	9,000
6	Purchase	3,000	8	24,000	-	-	-	1,200	7.50	9,000
								3,000	8.00	24,000
8	Issue	-	-	-	1,500	8	12,000	1,200	7.50	9,000
								1,500	8.00	12,000
10	Issue	-	-	-	1,200	8	9,600	1,200	7.50	9,000
								300	8.00	2,400
14	Purchase	1,800	7.75	13,950	-	-	-	1,200	7.50	9,000
								300	8.00	2,400
								1,800	7.75	13,950
16	Issue	-	-	-	1,800	7.75	13,950	1,200	7.50	9,000
								300	8.00	2,400
21	Purchase	1,500	8.25	12,375	-	-	-	1,200	7.50	9,000
								300	8.00	2,400
								1,500	8.25	12,375
25	Issue	-	-	-	1,500	8.25	12,375	1,100	7.50	8,250
					300	8.00	2,400			
					100	7.50	750			
29	Issue	-	-	-	500	7.50	3,750	600	7.50	4,500

Illustration-22: (Inventory turnover ratio)

From the following information calculate the inventory turnover ratio and also the number of days the average stock of each material is held:

	Materials 'M' ₹	Materials 'N' ₹
Opening stock	60,000	75,000
Purchases	5,50,000	3,40,000
Closing stock	40,000	65,000

Solution

(1) Computation of materials consumed

	Materials 'M' ₹	Materials 'N' ₹
Opening Stock	60,000	75,000
Add: Purchases	5,50,000	3,40,000
	6,10,000	4,15,000
Less: Closing stock	40,000	65,000
Materials consumed	5,70,000	3,50,000

(2)

$$\text{Computation of average stock} = \frac{\text{opening stock} + \text{closing stock}}{2}$$

$$M = \frac{60{,}000 + 40{,}000}{2} = ₹50{,}000$$

$$N = \frac{75{,}000 + 65{,}000}{2} = ₹70{,}000$$

(3)

$$\text{Inventory turnover ratio} = \frac{\text{materials consumed}}{\text{average stock}}$$

$$M = \frac{5{,}70{,}000}{50{,}000} = 11.4 \text{ times}$$

$$N = \frac{3{,}50{,}000}{70{,}000} = 5 \text{ times}$$

4.4 EXERCISES

I. Objective Type Questions

A. State whether the following questions are true or false

1. There is only one method for pricing material issues.
2. Materials requisition is sent by purchase department.
3. Materials requisition is sent to stores department
4. Under LIFO method, the value of materials issued closely relate to current market price.
5. When market price of materials prices are fluctuating the LIFO method is suitable for pricing materials issue.
6. FIFO method is followed for pricing materials issues in times of rising prices.

7. Under LIFO method, the value of closing stock will correspond to current market price.
8. Under FIFO method, the value of closing stock will correspond to current market prices
9. Weighted average price method is suitable for valuing materials issues in times of price fluctuations.
10. Normal loss of materials is avoidable.
11. Simple average price method of pricing issue of materials may result in either overpricing or underpricing.
12. The materials wasted in the initial stage of production is called spoilage.
13. The products, produced with some defects that cannot be made good, is called defectives.
14. Abnormal wastage and scrap of materials are controllable.
15. Scrap has no sale value.
16. Normal loss is part of cost of production.
17. Base stock method is a distinct method of valuing materials issues.
18. Transfer of materials from one job to another job is not recorded in stores ledger.
19. For preparing tenders and quotation, replacement price method is suitable.
20. Profit will be more under FIFO method of pricing issue of materials.

(**Ans: True:** 3,4,8,9,11,14,16,18,19,20. **False:** 1,2,5,6,7,10,12,13,15,17)

B. Fill in the blanks

1. ________ method of pricing is suitable when loss of materials in storage and stores overheads are large.
2. ________method of pricing is followed in times of inflation.
3. The method of pricing followed when prices of materials are fluctuating is called ________
4. Under ________ method, cost of materials issued is closely related to current market price.
5. Under FIFO method, the ________ of materials will correspond to current market price.
6. The ________ scrap of materials is uncontrollable.
7. The abnormal loss is charged to ________
8. Completely damaged raw materials after it has undergone some production operations is called ________.
9. The numerical relationship between materials put in and output obtained is called ________.
10. The cost of rectifying normal defectives is part of ________.
11. The number of times the average stock of a material consumed is called ________.

(**Ans:** 1. Inflated price, 2. LIFO, 3. Weighted average price method, 4. LIFO, 5.Closing stock, 6. Normal, 7. Costing profit and loss a/c, 8. Spoilage, 9. Input-output ratio, 10. Cost of production, 11. Materials/Inventory turnover ratio)

II. Theory Questions

A. Short answer type questions

1. What is LIFO Method?
2. What is FIFO Method?
3. Name the average price methods.
4. What is Materials turnover ratio?
5. What method of pricing is suitable in times of inflation?
6. How materials returned to supplier are treated in stores ledger?
7. What price is applied for return of surplus materials from departments?
8. What is materials requisition slip?
9. Write a brief note on materials transfer note.
10. What is spoilage?
11. What is wastage?
12. What is defectives?
13. What is Input - Output Ratio?
14. What is normal loss of materials?
15. What is abnormal loss of materials?

B. Long answer type questions

1. Explain various methods of pricing issues.
2. What is FIFO method of pricing issues? Explain its advantages and disadvantages.
3. What is weighted average price method? Explain its advantages and disadvantages.
4. Compare the effect on profit, value of closing stock and cost of materials issued under FIFO and LIFO methods of pricing issues.
5. Write short notes on:
   (a) Waste (b) Scrap (c) Spoilage and (d) Defectives.
6. What is materials turnover ratio? What are its uses.
7. Explain the steps for controlling abnormal spoilage and defectives.
8. How will you treat the following items in cost accounts (a) Scrap, (b) Spoilage (c) Defectives and (d) Wastage.
9. How will you treat the cost of rectifying defectives in cost accounts?
10. What factors are considered while choosing a pricing method for issue of materials?
11. Explain the following:

    (a) Replacement Price Method
    (b) Standard Price Method.

III. Practical Problems

A. Short answer type questions

1. Ascertain the value of closing stock under FIFO method.

Opening Stock	1,000 units at ₹15 per unit.
Purchases	2,000 units at ₹16 per unit.
Issues	2,600 units.

(**Ans:** Closing stock 400 units valued at ₹16 per unit i.e ₹6400)

2. Find the value of closing stock under LIFO method.

Opening Stock	500 units at ₹12 per unit.
Purchases	1,800 units at ₹13 per unit.
Issues	1,600 units.

(**Ans:** Closing stock 700 units valued at ₹8,600 (500 units at ₹12 + 200 units at ₹13)

3. Find the value of materials issued under FIFO method.

1.7.2009	Opening Stock	800 units at ₹20 per unit.
10.7.2009	Purchases	1,500 units at ₹21 per unit.
12.7.2009	Issues	1,500 units.

(**Ans:** Value of materials ₹30,700 (800 units at ₹20 + 700 units at ₹21)

4. Find the value of materials issued under LIFO method:

1.10.09	Opening stock of materials	500 units at ₹8 per unit.
7.10.09	Purchases	800 units at ₹9 per unit.
10.10.09	Issues	1,000 units.

(**Ans:** Value of materials issued: ₹8,800 (800 units at ₹9 + 200 units at ₹8 per unit).

5. Calculate the closing stock under simple average price method:

1.5.09	Opening stock	750 units at ₹16 per unit.
10.5.09	Purchases	1,000 units at ₹18 per unit.
15.5.09	Issues	1,250 units

(**Ans:** Closing stock 500 units valued at ₹17 per unit i.e. ₹8,500)

6. Calculate materials turnover ratio and the number of days the average stock is held:

	₹
Opening stock	25,000
Purchases	2,72,000
Closing stock	21,000

(**Ans:** Materials turnover ratio: 12 times, number of days average stock held 30 days)

Note: Assumed 360 days a year.

7. Calculate materials turnover ratio and the number of days average stock is held:

Opening stock	13,000 units
Purchases	1,44,000 units
Closing stock	7,000 units

(**Ans:** Materials turnover ratio : 15 times, number of days average stock held 24 days)

Note: Assumed 360 days a year.

8. Calculate yield ratio and input-output ratio

Opening stock	12,000 kg
Purchases	60,000 kg
Closing stock of materials	10,000 kg
Output obtained	55,000 kg

(Yield ratio = 88.7%, Input-output ratio = 112.72%)

B. Comprehensive questions

1. *(FIFO and LIFO Methods)*

From the following information, prepare stores ledger accounts under each of the methods - FIFO and LIFO.

January 1	Opening balance 300 units at ₹5 per unit.
5	Purchased 500 units at ₹6 per unit.
17	Issued 300 units.
24	Purchased 400 units at ₹5.50 per unit.
27	Issued 500 units.
31	Purchased 600 units at ₹6.50 per unit.

(**Ans:** Value of closing stock a) FIFO ₹6,100, b) LIFO ₹6,000)

2. *(FIFO and LIFO Methods)*

The following transactions occur in the purchase and issue of a materials.

October 1	Purchased 4,000 units at ₹4.00 per unit.
15	Purchased 500 units at ₹5.00 per unit.
23	Issued 2,000 units.
November 5	Purchased 6,000 units at ₹6.00 per unit.
11	Issued 4,000 units.
21	Issued 1,000
29	Issued 2,000
December 15	Purchased 4,500 units at ₹5.50 per unit.
25	Issued 3,000 units.

Prepare stores ledger under FIFO and LIFO methods.

(**Ans:** Closing stock - FIFO methods; 3000 units, valued at ₹16,500 and LIFO method: 3000 units valued at ₹14,250)

3. *(Selecting a suitable method of pricing issues)*

The following transactions took place during the month of November 2009 relating to materials 'EXE':

2009 January 1	Opening balance 2,000 units at ₹20 per unit.
2	Issued 1,100 units.
5	Purchased 1,600 units at ₹21 per unit.
8	Issued 1,300 units
10	Purchased 1,000 units at ₹21.50 per unit.
12	Issued 1,500 units.
14	Received back 200 units from production, originally issued on 8th January
17	Purchased 500 units at ₹22 per unit
20	Stock verification revealed a loss of 50 units.
24	Issued 900 units.
27	Purchased 500 units at ₹23 per unit.
31	Issued 400 units.

Prepare stores ledger selecting a suitable method of pricing issues.

(**Ans:** Closing stock - 550 units valued at ₹11,300)

Note:

(a) Since materials prices are increasing, LIFO method has been selected.
(b) Materials received back from production is treated as a new purchase.

4. *(Weighted average price method)*

From the following receipts and issues of materials 'EXE' in a manufacturing unit, prepare stores ledger using weighted average method of valuing the issues:

November 1	Opening balance 2,000 units at ₹5.00 each.
3	Issued 1,500 units to production.
4	Received 4,500 units at ₹6.00 each
8	Issued 1,600 units to production.
9	Returned to stores 100 units by production department (from the issue of Nov.3)
16	Received 2,400 units at ₹6.50 each
19	Returned to supplier 200 units out of the quantity received on November 4
20	Received 1,000 units at ₹7.00 each
24	Issued to production 2,100 units.
27	Received 1,200 units at ₹7.50 each.
29	Issued to production 2,800 units.

(Use rates upto two decimal places) **(ICWA-Inter)**

(**Ans:** Closing stock 3,000 units, value ₹19,558)

5. *(Simple average price method and LIFO method)*

1987 January 5	Purchased 4,000 units at ₹4 per unit.
20	Purchased 500 units at ₹5 per unit.
February 5	Issued 2,000 unit
10	Purchased 6,000 units at ₹6 per unit.
15	Issued 4,000 units
18	Issued 1,000 units
March 4	Issued 2,000 units
12	Purchased 4,500 units at ₹5.50 per unit.
24	Issued 3,000 units

From the above particulars prepare stores ledger account under (i) LIFO Method, (ii) Simple average method. **(B.Com., - Madras University)**

(**Ans:** Closing stock (i) LIFO method 3000 units value ₹14,250. (ii) Simple average method 3,000 units value ₹15,000)

February 5	(4 + 5)/2 = ₹4.50
15	(4 + 5)/3 = ₹3.00
18	= ₹6.00
March 4	= ₹6.00
24	(6 + 6.50)/2 = ₹6.25

6. *(Standard price method)*

The following transactions relating to material 'M' took place during the month of August 2009.

August 2	Purchased 500 units at ₹9.00
5	Issued 300 units
7	Purchased 700 units at ₹9.25 per unit
10	Issued 500 units
12	Purchased 700 units at ₹8.80 per unit
15	Issued 400 units
19	Purchased 300 units at ₹9.50 per unit
23	Issued 500 units
28	Purchased 600 units at ₹9.10 per unit

The management decided to follow standard price method for pricing material issues. The standard price fixed for the month of August is 9.00. Determine the value of closing stock by preparing stores ledger. Also determine the purchasing efficiency of materials department.

(**Ans:** Value of closing stocks ₹10,145, Materials price variance ₹225 adverse)

Note:

$$\begin{aligned}\text{Material price variance} &= \text{Actual quantity} \times \text{std price} - \text{Actual cost of purchase}\\ &= 2{,}800 \times 9 - 25{,}445\\ &= (-)225\end{aligned}$$

Since actual cost of materials purchased is more, it is adverse variance. Adverse variance denotes inefficiency in purchase.

7. *(Replacement price method)*

The following is a summary of the receipts and issue of materials in a factory during the month of April:

April 1	Opening balance 700 units at ₹25 per unit
3	Issued 400 units (Market price ₹26)
6	Purchased 1,200 units at ₹27 per unit
9	Issued 800 units (Market price ₹25)
12	Purchased 1,000 units at ₹26 per unit.
14	Issued 500 units (Market price ₹28)
20	Purchased 700 units at ₹27 per unit.
24	Issued 1,000 units (Market price ₹28.50)
27	Purchased 500 units at ₹29 per unit.
29	Issued 900 units (Market price ₹30)

Prepare stores ledger account using market prices.

(**Ans:** Closing stock 500 units value ₹9,400)

8. *(FIFO method)*

The following is a summary of receipts and issues of materials in a factory during a month.

1st	Opening balance 500 units at ₹25 per unit
3rd	Issue 70 units
4th	Issue 100 units
8th	Issue 80 units
13th	Received from supplier 200 units at ₹24.50 per unit.
14th	Returned to stores 15 units at ₹24 per unit.
16th	Issue 180 units.
20th	Received from supplier 240 units at ₹24.75 per unit.
24th	Issue 304 units
25th	Received from supplier 320 units at ₹24 per unit.
26th	Issue 112 units.
27th	Returned to stores 12 units at ₹24.50 per unit.
28th	Received from supplier 100 units at ₹25.00 per unit.

Prepare stores ledger on the basis of 'First-In-First-Out'. Stock verification revealed that on 15th there was a shortage of 5 units and another on 27th of 8 units. **(CA-Inter)**

(**Ans:** Closing Stock - 528 units value ₹12,850)

9. *(Base stock method)*

The stock of materials on hand on 1.4.2008 was 400 units at ₹50 per unit. The following receipts and issues were recorded. You are required to prepare the stores ledger account, showing how the value of issues would be calculated under base stock method, both through FIFO and LIFO, base being 100 units.

3.4.2008	Purchased 100 units at ₹55 per unit
8.4.2008	Issued 400 units
11.4.2008	Purchased 600 units at ₹60 per unit
13.4.2008	Issued 500 units
19.4.2008	Purchased 500 units at ₹65 per unit
26.4.2008	Issued 600 units
8.5.2008	Purchased 800 units at ₹70 per unit
12.5.2008	Issued 500 units
14.5.2008	Issued 200 units
20.5.2008	Purchased 500 units at ₹75 per unit
25.5.2008	Issued 400 units
28.5.2008	Purchased 300 units at ₹80 per unit

(**Ans:** Closing stock - Base stock (FIFO) - 600 units value 44,000, Base stock (LIFO) - 600 units value 43,500)

10. *(Inventory turnover ratio)*

From the following particulars compute inventory turnover ratio and number of days average stock is held:

	Materials 'M' ₹	**Materials 'N'** ₹
Opening stock of materials	2,50,000	3,00,000
Purchase of materials	34,10,000	13,60,000
Closing stock of materials	2,10,000	2,60,000

(**Ans:** Stock turnover ratio - Material 'M' - 15 times and Material 'N' - 5 times. Number of days average stock held - Material 'M' 24 days and Material 'N' - 72 days)

Note: 360 days a year assumed.

11. *(Inventory turnover ratio)*

From the following particulars calculate materials turnover ratio and number of days average stock is held:

Opening stock	15,500 units
Purchases	1,28,500 units.
Closing stock	13,500 units

(**Ans:** Inventory turnover ratio 9 times, number of days average stock held - 41 days (approx).

LABOUR COST CONTROL 5

- Labour Cost Control—Meaning
- Types of Labour
- Labour Turnover—Casus/Effects/Cost/Remedial Steps
- Rate or Time Study
- Job Evaluation—Meaning/Importance/Merits and Demerits
- Timekeeping—Meaning/Methods/Essentials
- Time Booking—Meaning/Records used
- Idle Time—Types/Treatments
- Over Time—Meaning/Causes/Control/Treatment
- Pay Roll or Wage Sheet—Meaning/Precautions
- Wages and Treatments of Wages
- Labour Cost Rate—Calculations
- Labour Productivity—Calculations

5.1 INTRODUCTION

Labour cost constitutes a significant element of cost next only to materials cost. Hence there is great scope for controlling cost. But it is very difficult to control the labour cost because it concerns with human beings. All other factors of production are inanimates and are subject to strict control.

Also the utilisation of all inanimate factors of production depend on labour. Similarly materials, machines and money not used now can be used in the future. But labour is a wasting asset. Labour time unused goes waste and cannot be recovered and increases the cost of production. Labour as a factor of production is capable of expansion. Through proper training and motivation productivity can be increased to reduce the cost per unit of output.

5.1.1 Labour Cost Components

All costs incurred to procure and retain the services of employees is included in labour cost. Remuneration may be paid in the form of wages, salary, allowances, fees, commission, bonus, contribution to provident fund, ESI, pension fund, etc.

Labour cost also includes cost of perquisites provided like free transport facilities from home to office and back, medical facilities, rent-free house, free use of car, rest rooms, indoor games, creches, etc.

5.2 TYPES OF LABOUR

Labour cost is classified into (a) Direct labour and (b) Indirect labour.

(a) Direct Labour

Remuneration paid to employees who are directly engaged in conversion of raw materials into finished products is direct labour cost. Direct labour cost is identifiable and allocated to a particular product or division or department in a company.

(b) Indirect Labour

Remuneration paid to all employees who are not directly connected with production is indirect labour cost. It includes remuneration paid to people engaged in providing various supporting services like security service, timekeeping, canteen, stores, warehousing, office, etc. Indirect labour cost is not directly related to production function and cannot be identified with a product, process or division in a company.

5.3 LABOUR COST CONTROL

Labour cost is the second most important cost in many industries. In knowledge based industries like software development and other services industries labour cost is the single largest cost. Labour cost control is essential for achieving the following objectives:

1. To reduce labour cost by exercising control over idle time, labour turnover, overtime, etc.
2. To increase the labour productivity through proper training and motivation.
3. Ascertaining correct direct labour cost helps in absorption of overheads.
4. Determining labour cost of various jobs, processes, and products.

Labour cost control is a multi-disciplinary function. It needs the co-ordinated efforts of the following departments:

1. The personnel department
2. The engineering department
3. The rate or time and motion study department
4. The timekeeping department
5. The pay-roll department
6. The cost accounting department.

5.4 PERSONNEL DEPARTMENT

ABC Ltd.

Employee Placement Requisition

Department: ________ Date: ________

Please arrange for workers of the under mentioned categories with effect from ________.

S. No.	Number of employees required	Categories	Job Specification	Job Description

Requisitioned by ________ Authorised by ________

Personnel department is responsible for recruitment, placement, training and promotion of employees. Only workers with suitable qualification and experience are to be selected and placed in required numbers. Personnel department initiates steps to recruit workers after receiving requisitions of workers from various departments. A standard proforma of employee placement requisition is given at above table.

The number of workers to be recruited depends on the number of employees leaving the organisation and increased workload due to growth and expansion of a company.

The following precautions are to be taken before recruitment of workers:

(a) Recruitments are made according to the employee placement requests received from various departments.
(b) Recruitment is also to be based on labour budget.
(c) Proper channels and procedures are to be followed for recruiting different categories of workers.
(d) Additional workers over labour budget and casual workers are to be recruited with proper approval from appropriate authorities.

5.4.1 Labour Turnover

Labour turnover is the change in labour force of an organisation during a period. Change in labour force takes place due to the following reasons—resignation by present employees, dismissal of employees by the management, recruitment of employees in place of resignation and dismissal and to meet the needs of expansion if any. Following methods are used for computation of labour turnover ratio:

(a) Separation Method

In this method number of employees who left the organisation in the normal course due to retirement, those resigned and those discharged by the organisation is expressed as a percentage of average number of employees.

$$\text{Labour turnover ratio} = \frac{\text{Number of employees separated}}{\text{Average number of employees}} \times 100$$

$$= \frac{(\text{Nos. retired} + \text{resigned} + \text{discharged})}{\text{Average number of employees}} \times 100$$

(b) Replacement Method

In this method number of employees recruited in the place of employees who left the organisation is expressed as a percentage of average number of employees. This method is also called "Net Labour Turnover Method".

$$\text{Labour turnover ratio} = \frac{\text{Number of employees replaced}}{\text{Average number of employees}} \times 100$$

In the above method number of workers newly appointed on account of expansion of business is not considered. But this new appointment also causes a change in composition of labour force. Some authorities take into account the newly appointed workers for computation of labour turnover. The total number of workers replaced and newly appointed is called accession. The labour turnover will be calculated as follows:

$$\text{Labour turnover ratio} = \frac{\text{Number of accessions}}{\text{Average number of workers}} \times 100$$

(c) Flux Method

In this method total number of workers separated and accessions are expressed as a percentage of average number of workers.

$$\text{Labour turnover ratio} = \frac{\text{Number of separations} + \text{Number of accessions}}{\text{Average number of workers}} \times 100$$

Illustration-1

From the following information calculate the labour turnover rate under (a) Separation method, (b) Replacement method and (c) Flux method.

Number of workers at the beginning of the year - 1750
Number of workers at the end of the year - 1850

During the year 50 workers left, 40 workers were discharged and 270 workers recruited. Of the workers recruited 180 workers were recruited in the place of those left and discharged, while the rest were appointed for an expansion scheme.

Solution

(a) Separation Method:

$$\text{Labour turnover ratio} = \frac{\text{Number of employees separated}}{\text{Average number of employees}} \times 100$$

$$= \frac{50 + 40}{1{,}800} \times 100 = 5\%$$

(b) Replacement Method:

$$\text{Labour turnover ratio} = \frac{\text{Number of employees replaced}}{\text{Average number of employees}} \times 100$$

$$= \frac{180}{1{,}800} \times 100 = 10\%$$

(or) Alternatively

$$\text{Labour turnover ratio} = \frac{\text{Number of accessions}}{\text{Average number of workers}} \times 100$$

$$= \frac{270}{1{,}800} \times 100 = 15\%$$

(c) Flux Method:

$$\text{Labour turnover ratio} = \frac{\text{Number of separations} + \text{Number of accessions}}{\text{Average number of workers}} \times 100$$

$$= \frac{90 + 270}{1{,}800} \times 100 = 20\%$$

Workings:

$$\text{Average No. of workers} = \frac{\begin{pmatrix}\text{(No. of workers in the beginning of the year} \\ + \\ \text{No. of workers at the end of the year)}\end{pmatrix}}{2}$$

$$= \frac{1{,}750 + 1{,}850}{2} = 1{,}800$$

Illustration-2

The cost accountant of Y Ltd. calculated labour turnover rates for the quarter ended 31st March 2007 as 10%, 5% and 3% respectively under 'Flux Method', 'Replacement Method' and 'Separation Method' respectively. If the number of workers replaced during that quarter is 30, find out the number of:
(1) Workers recruited and joined and (2) workers left and discharged.

Solution

Computation of average No. of workers:

Under Replacement Method

$$\text{Labour turnover ratio} = \frac{\text{Number of employees replaced}}{\text{Average number of employees}} \times 100 = \frac{5}{100} = 5\%$$

$$\text{No. of replacements} = 5\% = 30$$

$$\text{Average no. of workers } 100\% = \frac{30}{5} \times 100 = 600$$

(1) No. of workers recruited and joined

Under Flux Method

$$\text{Labour turnover ratio} = \frac{\text{Number of separations} + \text{Number of replacements}}{\text{Average number of workers}} \times 100$$

$$\frac{10}{100} = 10\% = 600$$

$$\text{No. of workers separated and joined } 10\% = 600 \times \frac{10}{100} = 60$$

(2) No. of workers left and discharged

Under Separation Method

$$\text{Labour turnover ratio} = \frac{\text{Number of employees separated}}{\text{Average number of employees}} \times 100 = \frac{3}{100} = 3\%$$

$$\text{Average no. of workers } 100\% = 600$$

$$\text{No. of workers separated } 3\% = 600 \times \frac{3}{100} = 18$$

5.4.2 Causes of Labour Turnover

The main causes for the labour turnover is broadly classified under the following three heads.

(a) Personal causes
(b) Unavoidable causes
(c) Avoidable causes.

(a) Personal causes

Some employees leave the organisation voluntarily due to the following causes:

(i) When workers get better job elsewhere.
(ii) Superannuation.
(iii) Disability due to illness or accident.
(iv) Domestic problems and family responsibilities.
(v) Women employees may quit the job after marriage and childbirth.
(vi) Dislike for the job due to poor working environment.

(b) Unavoidable causes

Sometimes the management sends out some employees under the following circumstances:

(i) Disability and unfit for the job.
(ii) Insubordination and continuous violation of organisational rules.
(iii) Seasonal nature of business.
(iv) Economic recession and down trend in business.

(c) Avoidable causes

Avoidable causes make the workers dislike the job and force them to quit the job. The management should give importance for removing these conditions. They are:

(i) Poor wages and allowance.
(ii) Lack of job security.
(iii) Lack of promotional avenues.
(iv) Poor working environments.
(v) Lack of facilities like transport, recreation, medical facilities, workmen compensation, etc.
(vi) Strained relationship with the management.
(vii) Long hours of work.
(viii) Hazardous nature of work and non-provisioning of safety devices.

5.4.3 Effects of Labour Turnover

Labour turnover due to superannuation, ill health and family problems cannot be avoided. Labour turnover should be kept to the minimum. High labour turnover is an indication of dissatisfied workers. This will bring down the morale of the workers and productivity of the organisation. The following are the ill effects of high labour turnover:

1. Low labour productivity.
2. Disrupts regular production due to delay in recruitment.
3. Experienced workers go out and new workers are recruited. Productivity of new workers will be less.
4. Wastage of materials and frequent breakdown of machines due to faulty handling of materials and machines by inexperienced workers.
5. Selection and training cost increases.

5.4.4 Cost of Labour Turnover

Two types of costs are associated with labour turnover. They are:

(i) Preventive costs.
(ii) Replacement costs.

(i) Preventive costs

These costs are incurred to retain the employees in the organisation and reduce the labour turnover to the minimum. They are:

1. Cost of providing free transport, medical facilities, educational facilities to children, recreational facilities, canteen, reading rooms, etc.
2. Improving the working conditions.
3. Providing safety devices to prevent industrial accidents and injury to workers.
4. Proper medical treatment and giving compensation in case of grievous injuries.
5. Providing retirement benefits like pension, gratuity and provident fund.

(ii) Replacement Costs

Replacement cost is incurred for recruitment and training of new workers. They include:

1. Cost incurred for selection and recruitment of new workers
2. Cost of training new workers
3. Material wastage increases due to improper handling by new workers
4. Repairs and machine breakdown also increase due to faulty operation by new workers.
5. Production, sales and profit decrease due to delay in recruitment of new workers

Illustrations-3

The management of First Flight Ltd is worried about the increasing labour turnover in their factory and they want to find the impact of labour turnover on profit as a result of labour turnover.

Sales in the last year amounted to ₹70,00,000 and P/V ratio was 20%. The total number of actual hours worked by direct labour force was 3,60,000 hours. The actual number of direct labour hours included 20,000 hours attributable to training new recruits, out of which half of the hours were unproductive. As a result of delays in filling the vacancies due to labour turnover 75,000 potentially productive hours were lost.

The cost incurred consequent on labour turnover revealed on analysis the following:

	₹
Settlement cost due to leaving	35,000
Recruitment costs	21,000
Selection costs	18,000
Training costs	26,000

Assuming that the potential production lost as a consequence of labour turnover could have been sold at prevailing prices, find the profit foregone last year on account of labour turnover.

Solution

Calculation of actual productive hours	
Total actual hours worked by direct labour	3,60,000
Less: unproductive training hours	10,000
Actual productive hours	**3,50,000**

$$\text{Sales per productive hour} = \frac{70{,}000{,}000}{3{,}50{,}000} = ₹\ 20$$

$$\text{Sales lost due to loss of potential productive hours of } 75{,}000 = 20 \times 75{,}000$$
$$= ₹\ 15{,}00{,}000$$

$$\text{Contribution foregone} = 15{,}00{,}000 \times \frac{20}{100} = ₹3{,}00{,}000$$

Statement showing loss of profit on account of labour turnover

	₹
Contribution foregone	3,00,000
Settlement cost due to leaving	35,000
Recruitment costs	21,000
Selection costs	18,000
Training costs	26,000
Total profit foregone	**4,00,000**

5.4.5 Remedial Steps to Reduce Labour Turnover

Labour turnover should be kept at a reasonable level to increase the labour productivity and reduce the cost of production. The following steps may be initiated to keep the labour turnover at reasonable level:

(i) **Proper recruitment policy:** A proper recruitment policy helps in selecting only suitable workers. It helps in avoiding recruitment of unsuitable workers.

(ii) **Proper training:** New workers are to be properly trained before being placed. When workers are promoted they are also to be trained.

(iii) **Promotion:** When suitable workers are at lower level they should be considered for promotion to higher posts when vacancy araises.

(iv) **Providing good working conditions:** Provision of good ventilation, lighting, proper tools and safety devices to improve the workers efficiency and their morale.

(v) **Good labour relationship:** Frequent consultation with labour union, providing grievances solving mechanism, calling for suggestions from workers for improving productivity and incentives for hard work will make the workers satisfied.

(vi) **Fair remuneration:** Suitable remuneration should be given for the work done.

5.5 ENGINEERING DEPARTMENT

Engineering department is concerned with product designing and preparing production plans. This department usually performs the following functions:

(i) Preparing production budgets and schedules for jobs.
(ii) Supervises and controls production activities.
(iii) Inspection of quality of products produced.
(iv) Ensuring suitable safety conditions and minimising industrial accidents.
(v) Ensuring proper working conditions.
(vi) Conducting research and experiments to improve the methods of production.

5.6 THE RATE OR TIME AND MOTION STUDY DEPARTMENT

This department is concerned with improving the efficiency of workers. It works in close co-operation with personnel, production and cost accounting departments. The following functions are carried out by this department:

(a) Work Study

Work study is conducted to find the best way of doing a job. It is a detailed analysis of nature of jobs, methods of production and equipment and tools used. Work study includes methods study and time and motion study.

(i) Methods study:

It aims at improving the method of production, remove unnecessary operations and standardising the work procedure. It helps in better utilisation of materials, men and machines. It helps in maximising the production.

(ii) Time and motion study:

Time study: Its aim is to find the effective time required to do a job. Total work is divided into small operations. The time taken by a worker of average efficiency to do the various operations are calculated and totalled to find the time needed to complete the job. Time taken by an efficient or slow worker is not taken. Some additional time should also be allowed for fatigue and for attending to personal needs. Total time so arrived is called standard time for the job. Fixing standard time helps in introducing incentive wage payment schemes.

Motion study: It is a study of the workers while they are at their job. The bodily movement of workers are recorded with the help of a camera and their movements are analysed. It helps to identify the necessary and best bodily movements and helps avoiding unnecessary and wasteful movements.

(b) Job Analysis

It is a process of finding the nature of the job, tasks involved and qualification, skill and experience required for doing the job. The responsibility involved in the job is also determined. Job analysis helps the personnel department to recruit suitable workers for the job. It also helps in fixing the position of a job and its relationship with other positions. It includes job description and job specification.

(c) Job Evaluation

Job evaluation is the process of finding the true worth and money value of jobs. It is a method of determining wage structure of different jobs. Qualifications, skill and experience required and responsibility attached to the job are considered in the evaluation of a job. The following are the objectives of job evaluation.

1. It aims at fixing wage structure for all jobs rationally.
2. It helps to establish parity with similar and equal jobs in the industries and in the surrounding area.
3. It helps in fixing fair remuneration to all employees depending on the skill and responsibility required for the jobs.
4. It also promotes better employer and employee relationship.
5. It helps in recruiting suitable persons for various jobs.

(d) Merit Rating

Merit rating is concerned with evaluating the effectiveness of workers at work. It analyses the job related strength and weakness of workers. Individual abilities of workers are evaluated. The following qualities are considered in merit rating:

1. Education, skill and experience.
2. Attendance and regularity.
3. Quality and quantity of work done.
4. Creative skills.
5. Integrity and character.
6. Cooperation and discipline.

5.6.1 Importance of Merit Rating

1. It helps to find out the strength and weakness of individual workers. Workers are ranked on the basis of their strength and suitable jobs may be assigned to workers.
2. It is possible to improve the worker productivity through proper training to overcome their weaknesses.
3. It helps in framing suitable promotion policy.
4. It helps in introducing productivity based incentive schemes.
5. Efficient and hard workers are highly rewarded. This acts as a self-motivation to the employees.

5.6.2 Limitations of Job Evaluation

1. The rating may be subjective and may lead to dissatisfaction among the workers.
2. Evaluator may evaluate on the basis of a single trait, ignoring other qualities of an worker.
3. Ratings may be based on the views of rater. He may ignore the improvement made by an worker.

5.6.3 Difference between Job Evaluation and Merit Rating

1. Job evaluation is finding the worth of a job and ranking them. Merit rating is finding competence and worth of individual workers.
2. Job evaluation helps in fixing rational wage structure. Merit rating helps to fix the wages of individual workers according to their efficiency.
3. Job evaluation helps in fixing uniform wage rates for similar jobs. Merit rating helps in fixing uniform wages for workers having similar efficiency.

5.7 TIMEKEEPING DEPARTMENT

Timekeeping is recording the attendance time of workers. Time of arrival, time of departure, days absent and total time spent by a worker in a concern during a period are recorded. Timekeeping is necessary for purpose of calculating overtime, absence and wages payable. Even when wages are paid on piece rate basis timekeeping is necessary for maintaining discipline. The following are the objectives of timekeeping:

(i) Preparation of pay rolls.
(ii) Calculation of overtime and overtime wages.
(iii) Meeting statutory requirements.

(iv) Maintaining discipline.
(v) Helps overheads distribution based on direct labour hour basis.

Methods of Timekeeping

Timekeeping is classified into the following two categories:

(a) Manual methods.
(b) Mechanical methods.

5.7.1 Manual Methods

The following are the manual methods of timekeeping:

(a) Attendance Register method

This is the oldest method of timekeeping. The attendance register is kept at the entry of the factory gate or nearer the departments. The details like name, worker number, the department, designation and rate of pay are shown in the register. The workers have to sign in 'IN' column while arriving and in 'OUT' column while leaving the factory. A single register will be kept when the number of workers are small. Separate attendance register for each department is maintained when number of workers are many.

This method is very simple and inexpensive. This method is not suitable when the number of workers are large because workers have to wait longer to sign the register. This may also lead to dishonest practice when there is collision between a worker and timekeeper.

(b) Metal Disc Method

Under this method, a metal disk bearing worker's number is given to all workers. In the morning while arriving, workers have to put the disc in a box kept at the factory gate. After the official arrival time is over another box will be kept in the place of the first box. Latecomers have to put the disc in this box.

This method is also simple and inexpensive. But there are chances that a worker may insert the disc of another worker in the box while entering the factory gate. There is possibility of including dummy workers in the mustor roll by the foreman.

5.7.2 Mechanical Method

The following are the mechanical methods for timekeeping of workers:

(a) Time Recording Clock

A specimen of time and pay roll card is given below:

Combined Time and Pay Roll Card

Name of the worker: xxxxx | Week ending: xxxxx

No. of the worker: xxxxx

Department: xxxxx

Day		**Regular**		**Overtime**		**Total Time**	
		In	**Out**	**In**	**Out**	**Normal Time**	**Overtime**
Monday	AM						
	PM						
Tuesday	AM						
	PM						
Wednesday	AM						
	PM						
Thursday	AM						
	PM						
Friday	AM						
	PM						
Saturday	AM						
	PM						
Sunday	AM						
	PM						
Calculation of wages			**Hours worked**	**Rate**	**Amount**	**Deductions**	**Net Amount**
		Normal time					
		Over-time					
Total							

Timekeeper ____________ | Pay roll clerk ____________

Foreman ____________ | Worker ____________

Time recording machine is a mechanical device. Every worker is given a time card. Time cards serially arranged are kept at the factory gate. At the time of entering the factory gate the worker has to pick up his card and insert it in the time recording clock. The clock will automatically record the time of arrival. This procedure is to be repeated at the time of departure also. Late arrivals, early departure and overtime are recorded in red ink to attract the attention of the management. The time card may be prepared with two divisions. The upper part is record of workers attendance time. In the lower part workers wage rate, allowances and deduction from gross wages are given. This part helps in calculation of workers pay roll. This card is called combined time and pay roll card.

This method is useful when the number of workers is large. Time recorded is accurate and reliable. In this method also there is chance for misuse. A worker may punch the time card of his friend also.

(b) Dial Time Recorder

This machine has a dial around the clock. The dial has about 150 holes and each hole bears a number corresponding to the identification number of the worker concerned. The dial has a radial arm at the centre. The worker has to place the radial arm at the hole of this number and his time is automatically recorded on a roll of paper against the worker's number. The time of worker is transferred by the machine to the wage sheet. The machine also calculates the wages of workers. It provides great accuracy and saves time. This machine is costly and can be used for a small number of workers only.

5.7.3 Essentials of a Good Timekeeping System

1. A good timekeeping system should be simple, reliable and inexpensive.
2. It should be suitable to record the time of arrival and departure without delay.
3. It should not give room for the entry of proxy or dummy workers.
4. A good timekeeping system should record the attendance of even piece workers and causal workers to ensure smooth and continuous production and to maintain discipline.
5. Mechanical methods should be introduced to avoid disputes.
6. It should record the late arrival and early departure of workers.
7. There should be a continuous check by a responsible officer.

5.7.4 Time Booking

Time booking is recording the total time spent by workers in the factory for on various jobs or works. The following are the objectives of time booking.

1. Ascertaining the time spent by workers on different jobs or work orders.
2. Ascertaining the labour cost of different jobs or work orders.
3. Allocation of overheads over various jobs on labour hour basis.
4. Finding idle time by comparing attendance time and time booked.
5. Helps to allocate labour cost as direct labour and indirect labour cost.
6. Measuring the efficiency of a worker by comparing time taken with budgeted time.
7. To calculate overtime wages, bonus payable and total wages.

The following records are used for time booking:

(i) Daily time sheets.
(ii) Weekly time sheets.
(iii) Job tickets or job cards.

(i) Daily Time Sheets

Each worker is given a daily time sheet in which time spent on different jobs in a day are recorded by the workers and signed by the foremen after verifying it. The following is the specimen of a daily time sheet:

<table>
<tr><td colspan="7">Daily Time Sheet
Name of the worker: xxxxx — Date: xxxxx
No. of the worker : xxxxx — Time sheet no: xxxxx
Department: xxxxx</td></tr>
<tr><th rowspan="2">Jobs</th><th rowspan="2">Description of the work</th><th colspan="2">Time</th><th rowspan="2">Hour</th><th rowspan="2">Rate</th><th rowspan="2">Amount</th></tr>
<tr><th>On</th><th>Off</th></tr>
<tr><td></td><td></td><td></td><td></td><td></td><td></td><td></td></tr>
<tr><td colspan="7">Worker: xxx — Foreman: xxx — Cost dept: xxx</td></tr>
</table>

(ii) Weekly Time Sheet

To reduce the volume or number of time sheets, a single time sheet is given for a week. Weekly time sheets are kept in the department concerned and entries in the time sheets are made by the department clerk to avoid incorrect entries. The following is the specimen of a weekly time sheet:

<table>
<tr><td colspan="7">Weekly Time Sheet
Name of the worker: xxxxx — Date: xxxxx
No. of the worker : xxxxx — Time sheet no: xxxxx
Department: xxxxx</td></tr>
<tr><th rowspan="2">Jobs</th><th rowspan="2">Description of the work</th><th colspan="2">Time</th><th rowspan="2">Hour</th><th rowspan="2">Rate</th><th rowspan="2">Amount</th></tr>
<tr><th>On</th><th>Off</th></tr>
<tr><td>Monday
Tuesday
Wednesday
Thursday
Friday
Saturday
Sunday</td><td></td><td></td><td></td><td></td><td></td><td></td></tr>
<tr><td>Total</td><td></td><td></td><td></td><td></td><td></td><td></td></tr>
<tr><td colspan="7">Worker: xxx — Foreman: xxx — Cost dept: xxx</td></tr>
</table>

(iii) Job Ticket or Job Cards

Job tickets or job cards are maintained to ascertain time spent by various workers on a job. It helps to ascertain the labour cost of each job separately. Job cards are maintained on various models. They are:

(a) Job card for each job

Each job is allotted a separate card wherein the time spent by various workers is recorded. This helps to find the labour cost of a job easily. The following is the specimen of a job card:

Job card for each job

Job no: xxxxx | Started on: xxxxx

Job description: xxxxx

Date	Dept.	Operation	Worker No.	Time		Total	Cost Office	
				On	Off		Rate	Amount

Checked and verified: xxx | Foreman: xxx | Cost dept: xxx

(b) Job card for each worker

Job card is issued for each worker to ascertain the time spent by a worker on various jobs. The following is the specimen of a job card.

Job card for each worker

Worker name: xxxxx | Date: xxxxx

Worker no : xxxxx | Jobcard no: xxxxx

Department : xxxxx

Day	Job No.	Description	Time		Hours	For Cost Office	
			On	Off		Rate	Amount

Checked and verified: xxx | Foremen: xxx | Cost dept: xxx

(c) Combined time and job card

In small companies one combined time card and job card is used for both timekeeping and time booking. This card may be issued for a day or for a week. The following is the specimen of a combined time and job card:

Combined Time and Job card

Worker name: xxxxx — Date: xxxxx

Worker no: xxxxx — Card no: xxxxx

Department : xxxxx

Day	Job No.	Time		Time		For Cost Office	
		In	Out	Normal	Overtime	Rate	Amount
Monday							
Tuesday							
Wednesday							
Thursday							
Friday							
Saturday							
Sunday							

Checked and verified: xxx — Foreman: xxx — Cost dept: xxx

(d) Piece work card

Piece work card is maintained by firms where workers are paid on piece rate basis. In this card quantity of production is recorded. Workers, attendance time is also recorded ensure smooth production and to maintain discipline. The following is the specimen of piece work card.

Piece work card

Worker name: xxxxx — Date: xxxxx

Worker no : xxxxx — Card no: xxxxx

Department : xxxxx

Day	Job No.	Description of job	Time		No. of Units			For Cost Office	
			In	Out	Made	Rejected	Accepted	Rate	Amount
Monday									
Tuesday									
Wednesday									
Thursday									
Friday									

Saturday									
Sunday									
Checked and verified: xxx				Foreman: xxx				Cost dept: xxx	

Reconciliation of Timekeeping and Time booking

The total time spent by a worker should tally with the time booked on different jobs but rarely it does. The difference in time is called idle time. Idle time is the time spent in the factory and paid for but not spent in production. Idle time should be reduced to the minimum. For the purpose of analysing and controlling idle time card is prepared. The following is the specimen of idle time card:

Idle Time Card

Worker name: xxxxx　　Date: xxxxx

Worker no: xxxxx　　Job Card no: xxxxx

Department : xxxxx

Reason for idle time	**Time**		**Time cost**	**For Office**		**Remarks**
	On	**Off**		**Rate**	**Amount**	
1. Waiting for (a) Materials (b) Tools (c) Instructions 2. Machine breakdown 3. Power failure 4. Inspection 5. Other reasons						
Checked and verified: xxx			Foremen: xxx		Cost dept: xxx	

5.7.5 Idle Time

Time booked by an worker on different jobs will be less than the time spent by him in the factory. This time not spent on production is called idle time. It is also called unproductive time or wasted time. Workers are paid for the idle time also. Idle time arises due to many reasons. Idle time should be kept to the minimum. Idle time is classified into two types as follows:

(a) Normal Idle Time

Time wasted due to unavoidable reasons is called normal idle time. Normal idel time is regular and expected. Normal idle time cannot be avoided. Normal idle time arises due to:

1. Time taken to move from factory gate to workspot.
2. Time taken to receive instructions from foremen.
3. Time taken to collect materials and tools necessary for the job.

4. Time taken to attend to personal needs and tea-breaks.
5. Time taken to move from one job to another.
6. Time taken to set up and adjust the machine.

Treatment of normal idle time cost in cost accounts

Normal idle time cost cannot be avoided. It is treated as production cost. There are two ways to add normal idle time cost to production cost. They are:

(i) Normal idle time wages is treated as direct labour cost by loading the normal idle time wages over productive hours. For example, time booked by a worker is 7 hours in a day of 8 hours and day rate is: ₹15 per hour. The effective labour rate will by $(8 \times 15)/7 =$ ₹ 17.14.

(ii) Normal idle time wages is ascertained separately and included in the production overheads. It is recovered by various jobs on some suitable basis.

(b) Abnormal Idle Time

Idle time in excess of normal idle time is called abnormal idle time. Its occurance is irregular and not expected. Abnormal idle time arises only occasionally. It arises due to avoidable reasons. The causes for abnormal idle time are:

1. Loss of time due to power failure.
2. Loss of time due to machine breakdown.
3. Loss of time due to non-availability of materials.
4. Loss of time due to accidents.
5. Loss of time due to strikes and lockout.

Treatment of abnormal idle time cost in cost accounts

Abnormal idle time wages is not related to production function. It should be charged to costing profit and loss account.

Illustration-4

The capacity usage ratio and the capacity utilisation ratio in respect of a machine for a particular month is 80% and 90% respectively. The available working hours in a month are 240 hours:

The break-up of idle time is as follows:

Waiting for job	6 hours
Breakdown	5 hours
Waiting for tools	5 hours.

Calculate idle time cost and present the same in a tabular form when the hourly fixed cost of running the machine is ₹ 10. **(ICWA - Inter-adapted)**

Solution

Total hours available	240 hours
Capacity usage ratio	80%
Standard working hours expected 80% of 240 hours	192 hours
Normal idle time (unavoidable idle time, 240 hours−192 hours)	48 hours
Capacity utilisation ratio 90%	
Actual hours worked (192 × 90/100)	173 hours (approx)
Abnormal idle time (avoidable time, 192-173 kms)	19 hours
Analysis of avoidable idle time:	
Idle time due to waiting for job	6
Idle time due to breakdown	5
Idle time due to waiting for tools	5
	16
Idle facility (BF)	3
Total avoidable idle time	**19**

Idle time Report		
	Idle hours	**Idle Time cost at ₹ 10 per hour**
Normal idle time (a)	48	480
Abnormal idle time:		
Waiting for job	6	60
Breakdown	5	50
Waiting for tools	5	50
Idle facilities	3	30
(b)	19	190
Total = (a+b)	**67**	**670**

5.7.6 Overtime

Usually 8 hours working time per day is considered as normal working time. Any time worked over and above the normal time is called overtime. Overtime wage rate is always higher than the normal time rate. According to Factory Act and Shop Establishment Act workers are to be paid at normal rate for 9 hours work a day or 48 hours work a week whichever is beneficial to workers. Workers are paid at double the normal rate over 9 hours work a day. Wages paid over and above the normal rate is called overtime premium. Overtime premium will increase the cost of production. Generally overtime work should not be encouraged.

Causes for overtime work

Overtime is allowed in the following circumstances:

1. On the request of a customer to complete a rush order.
2. To meet the rising demand for the company's product in the market.
3. Due to faulty planning by the production department.
4. Due to unavoidable reasons like power failure, etc.
5. Due to seasonal nature of demand for the company's product.

Control of overtime

1. Production should be streamlined through proper production planning thus avoiding overtime work.
2. As a rule overtime should be allowed only by a higher level official.

Limitations of overtime work

1. Overtime work increases overhead expenses like lighting, supervision etc.
2. Workers may work slowly during normal time to earn overtime work.
3. There may be partiality in granting overtime workers leading to frustration among workers.
4. During overtime workers are tired and their productivity will be less but paid more.

Treatment of overtime premium in cost accounts

(a) When overtime is allowed to complete a job within a specified time at the request of a customer, the overtime premium should be charged to that job.

(b) When overtime is allowed more or less regularly to meet the increased demand for the company's product, the overtime premium should be treated as production overheads.

(c) Overtime premium maybe treated as direct wages if it is allowed due to seasonal demand for the product.

(d) If overtime is necessitated due to faulty production planning, the overtime premium should be charged to costing profit and loss account.

(e) When overtime is allowed because of natural causes like flood, earthquake, etc., overtime premium should be charged to costing profit and loss account.

(f) When overtime is allowed due to shortage of labour, overtime premium is treated as direct labour cost by applying inflated wage rate. Inflated wage rate is calculated by adding overtime premium to normal wage rate.

Illustration-5

Three workers P, Q and R have put in the following hours during a week:

	Worker 'P' (Paid at ₹ 8 per day of 8 hours)	**Worker 'Q' (Paid at ₹ 6 per day of 8 hours)**	**Worker 'C' (Paid at ₹ 12 per day of 8 hours)**
Monday	10 hours	11 hours	9 hours
Tuesday	$10\frac{1}{2}$ hours	$9\frac{1}{2}$ hours	8 hours
Wednesday	8 hours	8 hours	$10\frac{1}{2}$ hours
Thursday	9 hours	10 hours	11 hours
Friday	11 hours	8 hours	10 hours
Saturday	8 hours	6 hours	9 hours
Total	$56\frac{1}{2}$ hours	$52\frac{1}{2}$ hours	$57\frac{1}{2}$ hours

Dearness allowance at a fixed rate of ₹50 per week is payable to all workers irrespective of their individual wage rate. Full-day wages are paid for 8 hours during weekdays and 4 hours on Saturdays. Full-day wages are paid for 4 hours work on Saturday. Workers are paid overtime according to the Factories Act for hours worked in excess of normal working hours on each day.

Compute the weekly earnings of workers.

Solution

Computation of normal hours and overtime hours									
Days	**Normal Hours**			**Overtime Single Rate**			**Overtime Double Rate**		
	P	**Q**	**R**	**P**	**Q**	**R**	**P**	**Q**	**R**
Monday	8	8	8	1	1	1	1	2	-
Tuesday	8	8	8	1	1	-	$1\frac{1}{2}$	$\frac{1}{2}$	-
Wednesday	8	8	8	-	-	1	-	-	$1\frac{1}{2}$
Thursday	8	8	8	1	1	1	-	1	2
Friday	8	8	8	1	-	1	2	-	1
Saturday	4	4	4	4	2	5	-	-	-
Total	44	44	44	8	5	9	$4\frac{1}{2}$	$3\frac{1}{2}$	$4\frac{1}{2}$

(ii)

Computation of weekly earnings			
	Worker 'P'	Worker 'Q'	Worker 'R'
Normal wage rate per hour	₹ 1.00	₹ 0.75	₹ 1.50
Normal working hours	44	44	44
Overtime hours - Single rate	8	5	9
Overtime hours - Double rate	$4\frac{1}{2}$	$3\frac{1}{2}$	$4\frac{1}{2}$
Normal time wages	44.00	33.00	66.00
Overtime wages at single rate	8.00	3.75	13.50
Overtime wages at double rate	9.00	5.25	13.50
Dearness allowance	50.00	50.00	50.00
Weekly earnings	111.00	92.00	143.00

Note: According to Factories Act double wages are paid for hours worked over 9 hours in a day. So for 9th hour worked is paid at single rate.

Illustration-6

A company's basic wage rate is ₹ 0.45 per hour and its overtime rates are:

Evenings - Time and one third.
Weekends - Double time.

During the previous year the following hours are worked:

Normal time - 4,40,000 Clock hours
Time plus one-third - 40,000 Clock hours
Double time - 20,000 Clock hours

The following times have been worked on the stated jobs:

	Job X	Job Y	Job Z
Normal time	6,000	10,000	8,000
Evening overtime	600	1,200	2,100
Weekend overtime	200	100	600

You are required to calculate the labour cost chargeable to each job in each of the following circumstances:

(a) Where overtime is worked regularly throughout the year as company policy due to labour shortage.

(b) Where overtime is worked irregularly to meet spasmodic production requirements.
(c) Where overtime is worked specifically at the customer's request to expedite delivery.

(ICWA - Inter)

Solution

Computation of average wage rate			
	Hours	**Wage rate**	**Wages ₹**
Normal time	4,40,000	₹ 0.45 per hour	1,98,000
Evening time	40,000	₹ 0.60 per hour (Normal rate + 1/3 rd)	24,000
Weekend time	20,000	₹ 0.90 per hour (Normal rate × 2)	18,000
Total	5,00,000		2,40,000

$$\text{Average wage rate per hour} = \frac{\text{Total wages paid}}{\text{Total hours worked}}$$

$$= \frac{2,40,000}{5,00,000} = ₹\ 0.48$$

(a) Overtime is allowed regularly due to labour shortage

Wages are charged to all jobs at average wage rate. Thus overtime premium is spread over all jobs done during the period. Wages chargeable to jobs are follows:

	Job X	**Job Y**	**Job Z**
Normal time	6,000	10,000	8,000
Evening overtime	600	1,200	2,100
Weekend overtime	200	100	600
Total time (hours)	6,800	11,300	10,700
Average wage rate per hour	₹0.48	₹0.48	₹0.48
Total wages of jobs	₹3,264	₹5,424	₹5,136

(b) Overtime is allowed to meet spasmodic production requirements

Jobs are charged at normal wage rate. Overtime premium is treated as production overheads. Wages chargeable to jobs are as follows:

	Job X	**Job Y**	**Job Z**
Total hours worked	6,800	11,300	10,700
Normal wage rate per hour	₹0.45	₹0.45	₹0.45
Total wages of jobs	₹3060	₹5,085	₹4,815

(c) Overtime is allowed at the customer's specific request to expedite delivery

Overtime premium is also included in wages cost of respective jobs and is also included in wages cost of respective jobs.

Wages chargeable to jobs are as follows:

	Job X	Job Y	Job Z
Normal time	(6,000 hrs × ₹ 0.45) = ₹ 2,700	(10,000 hrs × ₹ 0.45) = ₹ 4,500	(8,000 hrs × ₹ 0.45) = ₹ 3,600
Evening time	(600 × ₹ 0.45 × 1 1/3) = ₹ 360	(1,200 hrs × ₹ 0.45 × 1 1/3) = ₹ 720	(2,100 hrs × ₹ 0.45 × 1 1/3) = ₹ 1,260
Weekend time	(200 × ₹ 0.45 × 2) = ₹ 180	(100 hrs × ₹ 0.45 × 2) = ₹ 90	(600 hrs × ₹ 0.45 × 2) = ₹ 540
Total wages	₹ 3,240	₹ 5,310	₹ 5,400

Illustration-7

From the following data calculate the normal and overtime wages payable to a workman:

	Hours worked
Monday	9 hours
Tuesday	11 hours
Wednesday	8 hours
Thursday	10 hours
Friday	10 hours
Saturday	8 hours
Total	56 hours

Normal working hours per day are 8 hours. Wages are paid at single rate up to 9 hours each day and at double rate over 9 hours each day or at single rate upto 48 hours a week and at double rate for hours worked over 48 hours a week whichever is more beneficial to workman is paid. Worker's normal wage rate is ₹ 20 per day of 8 hours.

Solution

Normal wage rate per hour = ₹20/8 hours = ₹2.50

Computation of normal and overtime worked				
Days	**Total hours**	**Normal time hours**	**Overtime hours**	
			Single rate	**Double rate**
Monday	9	8	1	-
Tuesday	11	8	1	2
Wednesday	8	8	-	-
Thursday	10	8	1	1
Friday	10	8	1	1
Saturday	8	8	-	-
Total	56	48	4	4

Computation of wage payable to workman:

Normal time wages 48 hrs × ₹ 2.50 = ₹ 120
Overtime wages at Single rate 4 hrs × ₹2.50 = ₹ 10
Overtime wages at double rate 4 hrs × ₹2.50 × 2 = ₹ 20

Total wages = **₹ 150**

(or)

Wages for 48 hours per week at single rate 48 hrs × ₹ 2.50 = ₹ 120
Wages for 8 hours overtime at double rate 8 hrs × ₹ 2.50 × 2 = ₹ 40

Total wages = **₹ 160**

Wages payable to workman is ₹ 160 (more beneficial to workman).

5.8 PAY ROLL DEPARTMENT

The pay roll department carries out the following functions:

1. Keeping record of all workers showing their job description, wage rate and department.
2. Ascertaining the time worked by the workers from time card.
3. Classifying the total time worked into normal time and overtime.
4. Calculating the gross wages of workers.
5. Preparing the pay roll of various departments.
6. Computing net wages payable after various deductions.
7. Making payments for wages.

Preparing pay roll or wages sheet:

Wages sheet or pay roll is prepared on the basis of time card or piece work card. Pay roll is prepared department-wise showing the gross wages payable, deductions to be made and net wages payable.

Specimen of a pay roll is given below:

Pay Roll														
Department: xxx														Period ending: xxx
									Deductions					
Name	**Worker Number**	**Wage rate**	**Total Hours**	**Overtime Hours**	**Wage**	**D.A.**	**Other allowances**	**Gross wages**	**ESI**	**PF**	**IT**	**Others**	**Total Deductions**	**Net Wages**
Total														
Prepared by : xxx														Checked by : xxx

Precautions to be taken in wage payment to avoid frauds

Chances of committing fraud in payment of wage payment is more than in any other area. Proper procedure should be established to prevent frauds and irregularities in wage payment. The following are the type of frauds and irregularities committed in connection with wage payment:

(i) Inclusion of dummy or ghost workers in the pay roll and claiming wages
(ii) Making double payment to a worker
(iii) Failure to make proper deductions.
(iv) Claiming overtime wages when there is no overtime.
(v) Omitting to record the absence of workers.
(vi) Making wrong entries in recording workers' attendance.

The following steps may be taken to prevent frauds in wage payment:

(i) There should be proper control and supervision in marking the workers attendance time.
(ii) Proper mechanical device must be installed to prevent improper marking in workers attendance time.
(iii) Time cards and job cards are to be compared.
(iv) Permission from proper authority is to be obtained for giving overtime work.
(v) When piece rate system of wage payment is followed, actual quantity produced should be compared with that shown in piece work cards.

(vi) Timekeeping and preparation of pay roll should not be entrusted to the same person.
(vii) Proper internal check system should be introduced.
(viii) Sample or test checks are to be made by a higher level official.
(ix) Wage payment should be made in the presence of a higher level official.
(x) The cashier should withdraw exact amount from the bank for payment of wages.
(xi) Unclaimed wages should be accounted and handed over to a higher level officer. Subsequent payment of unclaimed wages should be made by the higher level officer only.
(xii) Workers are to be identified before making payment.

6. The Cost Accounting Department

Cost accounting department collects and classifies the labour cost of various departments, processes, jobs and work orders. Time cards, job tickets, piece work cards and pay roll form the basis for ascertaining labour cost.

Wages analysis or wages abstract

Labour cost incurred during a period is to be analysed for achieving the following objectives:

(i) Classification of labour cost into direct labour cost and indirect labour cost.
(ii) Allocation and apportionment of labour cost to various departments, processes, products, work orders etc.
(iii) Determining proper method for recovery of indirect labour cost.

The following is the specimen of a wages abstract:

Wages abstract or Wages Analysis Sheet															
No : xxx												Period ending : xxx			
Job No. 1			Job No. 2			Job No. 3			Job No. 4			Overheads			Cost Ledger Folio
Clock No	Hrs	Amt ₹	Clock No	Hrs	Amt ₹	Clock No	Hrs	Amt ₹	Clock No	Hrs	Amt ₹	Clock No	Hrs	Amt ₹	
Total			Total			Total			Total			Total			
Prepared by : xxx					Cost ledger posted by : xxx							Checked by : xxx			

Accounting Entries for Wages

Wages incurred is debited to wages control account and credited to cost ledger control account. Direct wages of various jobs are debited to work-in-progress account, indirect wages are debited to respective overhead control accounts. The wages of abnormal idle time is debited to costing profit and loss account. Entries in cost ledger are as follows:

(i)	For wages incurred - paid and outstanding: Wages control account To Cost ledger control account	 Dr.
(ii)	Allocation of direct and indirect wages: Work-in-progress control account (Direct wages of various jobs)	 Dr.
	Overheads control account (For indirect wages)	Dr.
	Costing profit and loss account (For abnormal idle time wages) To Wages control account	Dr.

When Integral Accounting System is followed the entries for wages will be as follows:

(i)	For wages incurred - paid and outstanding: Wages control account To Cash account (Paid) To O/s Wages account (Not paid)	 Dr.
(ii)	For allocation of direct and indirect wages: Work-in-progress control account (For direct wages of various jobs)	 Dr.
	Overheads control account (For indirect wages)	Dr.
	Profit and loss account (For abnormal idle time wages) To Wages control account	Dr.

Illustration-8

Enter the following transactions in cost ledger:

	₹
Gross wages	18,000
Employer and employee's contribution P.F. (each)	900
Employer's contribution to ESI	270
Employee's contribution to ESI	180

Income tax liability of employee	1,000
Wages abstract reveals the following:	
Direct wages	10,000
Indirect factory wages	4,000
Administrative staff salary	2,000
Selling and distribution staff salary	1,000

Solution

		₹
Gross Wages		18,000
Less: Deductions		
Employee's contribution to provident fund	900	
Employee's contribution to ESI	180	
Income tax payable	1,000	2,080
Net wages payable		15,920

Total Wages Cost	
	₹
Gross wages	18,000
Add: Employer's contribution to provident fund	900
Employee's contribution to ESI	270
	19,170

Journal Entries				
(i)	Wages control account	Dr.	19,170	
	To Cash			15,920
	To Provident fund payable			1,800
	To ESI payable			450
	To Income tax payable			1,000
	(Being wages incurred)			
(ii)	Work-in-progress control account	Dr.	18,000	
	Factory overheads control account	Dr.	4,000	
	Office and administration overheads control account	Dr.	2,000	

	Selling and distribution overheads control account	Dr.	1,000	
	To Wages control account			25,000
	(Being direct wages and indirect wages transferred)			

Treatment of other relevant items in Cost Accounts

Holiday Wages

Workers are allowed certain holidays like weekly holidays, holidays on important occasions like Independence day, Republic day etc. Wages are paid for these holidays. Even though holiday wages are unproductive, they are included in the cost of production. There are two methods of treating holiday wages:

1. Treated as direct labour cost by using inflated wages rate.
2. Treated as indirect wages and included in factory overheads.

Leave Wages

Workers are entitled to certain leaves with pay. They are personal leave and medical leave. Earned leave is allowed to be accumulated and cash is paid for the unavailed leave. These leave wages are also unproductive but included in cost of production. These wages may be treated either as direct wages or indirect wages.

Night Shift Allowance

Some extra allowance is given for work in night shift. It is not allowed for a particular job. So night shift allowance may be treated as production overheads and charged to all jobs.

Learner's Wages

Learners take more time for doing a job. So a part of wages paid to learners should be treated as direct wages and included in the prime cost of respective jobs. The remaining wages is treated as production overheads.

Fringe Benefits

Workers are provided some benefits or services either free of cost or at concessional rates. These facilities are transport facility from home to office and back, medical treatment to self and family members, company car and free residential accommodation or at concenssional rent. The cost of providing those facilities and services are treated as indirect wages and included in production overheads.

Casual Workers

Sometimes workers are appointed on temporary basis to do some extra work arising occasionally. These workers are called casual workers. Separate attendance records are to be maintained. A proper check must be maintained over employment of casual workers. When casual workers are appointed for production jobs, their wages should be treated as direct wages. When workers are appointed to do some miscellaneous jobs, their wages should be treated as overheads.

Outworkers

Outworkers may be classified into two types as below:

1. On-site workers
2. Workers who work from their homes

(i) On-site workers

Workers of some organisations engaged in construction activities work at contract site. Proper check should be exercised on recording the attendance and payment of wages. A responsible person should visit the site to check the number of workers working on-site with the number of people sent to site. There is chance for inclusion of dummy workers. All workers should be given identity cards.

(ii) Workers who work from their homes

Some people take materials from office and complete the work in their homes using their own tools and equipment. These people are not workers of the organization. They are paid for the volume of work done. So maintenance of attendance register is not necessary. The organization does not provide any work space. There is savings in lighting, tools and equipment maintenance cost etc. But proper control should be exercised in the following matters:

(i) The delivery of work must be made within the stipulated time.
(ii) Proper control should be exercised over issue of materials and volume of output turned out.
(iii) Quality of work should be checked. Defective and substandard work should be rejected.

5.9 COMPUTATION OF LABOUR COST RATE FOR ABSORPTION OF LABOUR COST

Labour cost includes monetary benefits like basic pay, allowances, etc. and non-monetary benefits like subsidised canteen services, medical facilities, accommodation at concessional rate, free commutation etc. Monetary and non-monetary benefits provided to indirect workers are included in overheads. But monetary and non-monetary benefits provided to direct workers is treated as direct labour cost. For this purpose an inflated labour hour rate is computed as below:

$$\text{Labour cost rate per hour} = \frac{\text{Monetary benefits + Cost of non-monetary benefits}}{\text{Budged productive labour hours}}$$

(Total labour hours – Normal idle time)

Illustration-9

(a) Calculate the labour hour rate of a worker from the following data:

Basic pay - ₹200 p.m.
D.A. - ₹150 p.m.
Fringe benefits - ₹100 p.m.

Number of working days in a year is 300. 30 days leave with full pay and 20 days half-pay leave in a year is availed and allowed. (Assume 8 hours day.)

(b) What would be the effect on hourly rate if only 30 days full pay leave is availed? **(CS-Inter)**

Solution

(a)

Computation of Effective Working Hours		
Total working days in a year		300 days
Less: Leave with full pay	30 days	
Leave with half pay	20 days	50 days
Effective working days		250 days
Effective working hours	250 × 8	2,000 hours

Computation of total wages paid in a year	
	₹
Basic wages: 200 × 12	2,400
DA - 150 × 12	1,800
Fringe benefits - 100 × 12	1,200
Gross wages	5,400
Less: 20 days half pay (or) 10 days full pay (5,400 × 10/300)	180
Net wages paid	5,220
Labour hour rate = 5,220/2,000	₹2.61

(b) Hourly rate when 30 days leave with full pay is only availed

(i)

Computation of effective working hours	
Total working days	300
Less: Leave availed	30
Effective working days	270
Effective working hours (270 × 8)	2,160 hours.

(ii)

Computation of total wages paid in a year	
	₹
Basic wages (200 × 12)	2,400
DA (150 × 12)	1,800
Fringe benefits	1,200
Total wages	5,400
Labour hour rate (5,400/2,160)	₹2.50

Effect on labour rate per hour

Labour rate per hour decreases by ₹0.11 (i.e. 2.61 – 2.50) when only 30 days leave with fully pay only availed.

5.9.1 Labour Productivity

Labour productivity is measured by comparing volume of output obtained from a given input. It helps to measure the efficiency of workers. Workers are paid on the basis of their efficiency. Measuring labour productivity helps in fixing suitable wages to workers with different efficiency ratings. Increase in labour productivity helps to increase the output and thus reduces cost of production per unit.

Labour productivity is computed as follows:

$$= \frac{\text{Standard time for actual production}}{\text{Actual time}} \times 100$$

(or)

$$= \frac{\text{Actual Output}}{\text{Standard Output}} \times 100$$

Steps for improving labour productivity

1. Selection and employment of workers with suitable skill.
2. Providing proper training to new workers as well as retraining to existing workers.
3. Avoid employment of excessive workers or labour shortage by conducting work measurement study.
4. Take steps to simplify and standardisation of work.

Labour Cost Control Reports

Management has to take many steps to control cost. For this purpose it needs many information. Information required by the management is submitted through various reports. These reports may be submitted weekly, monthly or quarterly. The following are important reports:

Title of Report	Frequency	Submitted to	Contents of the report	Purpose of the reports
1. Training and recruitment cost report	Monthly	Top management	Cost incurred for recruitment and training.	To find ways to reduce the cost
2. Idle time report	Weekly	Production manager	Time wasted with causes for idle time	To reduce idle time
3. Labour efficiency and productivity report	Monthly	Production manager	Actual efficiency of workers	To improve labour efficiency
4. Labour utilisation report	Monthly	Top management	Details excessive labour or labour shortage	To avoid surplus workers (or) labour shortage

5. Absenteeism report	Weekly	Production manager	Details of workers absent	To take control steps to reduce absenteeism
6. Unclaimed wages report	Weekly	Top management	Details of wages not claimed	Prevention of bogus or dummy workers
7. Labour turnover report	Monthly	Top management	Details of workers resigned, discharged and recruited	To reduce labour turnover
8. Overtime report	Weekly	Top management	Details of overtime allowed	To avoid overtime work
9. Report on accidents	Monthly	Production manager	Details of accidents, causes and frequency	To take steps to prevent accidents.
10. Labour Cost ratios	Quarterly	Top management	Ratios of output to input, labour cost to output, total wages to sales etc.	To find the excessive labour cost if any and controlling it.

5.10 COMPREHENSIVE ILLUSTRATIONS

Illustration-10: (Computation of standard time and time allowed)

The time taken for a particular operation for operator 'X' in the process division of a manufacturing concern on three different counts was 24, 22 and 27 minutes. While that of operator 'Y' was 20, 23 and 26 minutes. It has been ascertained that the rating of 'X' is 70/60 and that of 'Y' is 55/60. Allowances for fatigue, personal needs are assumed at 15%. Calculate, using the above information as a base, for that particular operation:-

(i) the standard time and

(ii) the time allowed under an incentive allowance of 30% of standard time.

(ICWA-Inter, June 1992)

Operator	Time taken (in minutes)	Rating	Normal time (in minutes)	Average time (in minutes)
X	24	70/60	28.00	
	22	70/60	25.67	
	27	70/60	31.50	
			85.17/3	28.39

Y	20	50/60	18.33	
	23	50/60	21.08	
	26	50/60	23.84	
			63.25/3	21.08
			Total	49.47
		Average time	49.47/2 = 24.735	

(i) Computation of standard time

Average time	24.735 minutes
Add: 15% allowance for fatigue	3.656 minutes
	28.391 minutes

Standard time = 28.39 minutes

(ii) Computation of time allowed under incentive scheme

Standard time	28.39 minutes
Add: 30% incentive allowance	8.52 minutes
Time allowed	36.91 minutes

Illustration-11: (Labour turnover - No expansion)

From the following data given by the labour department calculate the labour turnover rate by applying:

(a) Separation method (b) Replacement method (c) Flux method

Number of workers at the beginning of the year - 1,500
Number of workers at the end of the year - 1,700

During the year 40 workers resigned, 80 workers were discharged and 100 were recruited in the place of those leaving.

Solution

$$\text{(a) Separation method} = \frac{\text{Nos. resigned} + \text{Nos. discharged}}{\text{Average number of workers}} \times 100$$

$$= \frac{120}{1,600} \times 100 = 7.5\%$$

$$\text{(b) Replacement method} = \frac{\text{Number of employees replaced}}{\text{Average number of employees}} \times 100$$

$$= \frac{100}{1{,}600} \times 100 = 6.25\%$$

$$\text{(c) Flux method} = \frac{\text{Nos. separated + Nos. replaced}}{\text{Average no. of workers}} \times 100$$

$$= \frac{220}{1{,}600} \times 100 = 13.75\%$$

Note :

$$\text{Average No. of workers} = \frac{\text{No. of workers in the beginning of the year + No. of workers at the end of the year}}{2}$$

$$= \frac{1{,}500 + 1{,}700}{2} = 1{,}600$$

Illustration-12: (Labour turnover - with expansion)

Number of workers as on 1st January are 4,750 and number of workers on 31st December are 5,250. During the year, 60 workers left while 190 workers were discharged. 650 workers were recruited including 150 workers recruited in the place of vacancies arising due to resignation and discharge. The rest were recruited for expansion of production facility.

From the above information calculate labour turnover rate under various methods.

Solution

Labour Turnover rate:

$$\text{(i) Separation method} = \frac{\text{Nos. separated}}{\text{Average number of workers}} \times 100$$

$$= \frac{250}{5{,}000} \times 100 = 5\%$$

Note :

$$\text{Average No. of workers} = \frac{\text{No. of workers in the beginning of the year+ No. of workers at the end of the year}}{2}$$

$$= \frac{4{,}750 + 5{,}250}{2} = 5{,}000$$

$$\text{(b) Replacement method} = \frac{\text{Number of employees replaced}}{\text{Average number of employees}} \times 100$$

$$= \frac{150}{5{,}000} \times 100 = 3\%$$

(c) Accession method $= \dfrac{\text{No. of Accession (Nos. separated + Nos. recruited for expansion)}}{\text{Average no. of workers}} \times 100$

$= \dfrac{650}{5{,}000} \times 100 = 13\%$

(d) Flux method $= \dfrac{\text{Nos. separated + Nos. accession}}{\text{Average no. of workers}} \times 100$

$= \dfrac{250 + 650}{5{,}000} \times 100 = 18\%$

Illustration-13: (Loss of profit due to labour turnover)

The management of Come-in and Go-out are worried about their increasing labour turnover in the factory and before analysing the causes and taking remedial steps, they want to have an idea of the profit foregone as a result of labour turnover in the last year.

Last year's sales amounted to ₹83,03,300 and P/V ratio was 20%. The total number of actual hours worked by the direct labour force was 4.45 lakhs. As a result of the delays by the personnel department in filling vacancies due to labour turnover, 1,00,000 potentially productive hours were lost. The actual direct labours included 30,000 hours attributable to training new recruits, out of which half of the hours were unproductive.

The costs incurred consequent on labour turnover revealed, on analysis, the following:

	₹
Settlement costs due to leaving	43,820
Recruitment costs	26,740
Selection costs	12,750
Training costs	30,490

Assuming that the potential production lost as a consequence of labour turnover could have been sold at prevailing prices, find the profit foregone last year on account of labour turnover.

Solution

(i)

Determination of Productive Hours	
Actual hours worked	4,45,000
Less: Unproductive training hours (30,000 × 1/2)	15,000
Actual productive hours	4,30,000

(ii)

Loss of Contribution	
Total sales	₹83,03,300
PV ratio	20%
Total contribution	83,03,300 × 20/100 = ₹16,60,660
Loss of contribution due to loss of productive hours	$\frac{16,60,660}{4,30,000} \times 1,00,000$ = ₹3,86,200

(iii)

Statement showing loss of profit due to labour turnover	
	₹
Loss of contribution as per (ii) above	3,86,200
Settlement costs due to leaving	43,820
Recruitment costs	26,740
Selection costs	12,750
Training costs	30,490
Total profit lost	5,00,000

Illustration-14: (Computation of labour cost rate)

From the particulars given below, prepare the labour cost per man day of 8 hours and per hour.

(a) Basic salary: ₹2.00 per day
(b) Dearness allowance: 25 paise per every point over 100 cost of living index for working class - current cost of living index - 700 points
(c) Leave salary: 10% of (a) and (b)
(d) Employer's contribution to provident fund: 8% of (a), (b) and (c)
(e) Employer's contribution to state insurance: 2.5% of (a), (b) and (c)
(f) Expenditure on amenities to labour: ₹20 per head per month
(g) Number of working days in a month: 25 days of 8 hours each.

(B.Com., Madras University)

Solution

Statement showing labour cost		
Particulars	**Total (p.m.) ₹**	**Per day (₹)**
(a) Basic salary (25 × 2)	50.00	2.00
(b) Dearness allowance (600 × 0.25)	150.00	6.00
(c) Leave salary (200 × 10%)	20.00	0.80
(d) Employer's contribution to PF (220 × 8%)	17.60	0.70
(e) Employer's contribution to state insurance (220 × 2.5%)	5.50	0.22
Labour cost	243.10	9.72

Labour cost per day = ₹9.72

Labour cost per hour = 9.72/8 = ₹1.215

Illustration-15

A worker is paid ₹300 per month in addition to dearness allowance of ₹ 75 per month. He is entitled to bonus @ 10% of basic pay. Employer's contribution is 8 1/3% of basic pay towards contributory provident fund to which worker also contributes an equal amount. The contribution for ESI is 1% for employer and 0.5% for worker. The employer maintains a canteen where subsidised tea and lunch are provided to workers and a monthly subsidy of ₹3,000 is provided by the employer to the canteen. The total number of employees taking advantage of the canteen is 400. Normal working days in a year should be taken to be 300 days of 8 hours each. Normal idle time amounts to 20%. The worker is entitled to 15 days' earned leave during the year.

Find the labour cost per hour.

Solution

(i)

Computation of effective labour hours during a month	
Working days in a year	300 days
Working hours per day	8 hours
Total working hours in a year (300 × 8)	2,400 hours
Less: Earned leave (15 days of 8 hours)	120 hours
	2,280 hours
Less: 20% idle time (2280 × 20/100)	456 hours
Effective working hours in a year	1,824 hours
Effective working hours in a month (1,824/12)	152 hours

(ii)

Computation of labour cost per month	
	₹
Wages	300.00
Bonus 10% basic pay (300 × 10%)	75.00
Dearness allowance	30.00
Employers contribution to PF 8 1/3% (300 × 25/300)	25.00
Employer's contribution to ESI - 1% of Basic pay (300 × 1/100)	3.00
Canteen subsidy per worker (3000/400)	7.50
Total	440.50

(iii) Labour cost per hour = 440.50/152 = ₹2.90

Illustration-16: (Allocation of labour cost to jobs)

Calculate the earnings of workers 'A' and 'B' from the following particulars for a month and allocate the earnings to each job X, Y and Z.

Particulars	A	B
(a) Basic wages	₹100	₹100
(b) Dearness allowance	50%	55%
(c) Provident fund (on basic wages)	8%	8%
(d) Employee's state insurance (on basic wages)	2%	2%
(e) Overtime	10 hrs.	-
(f) Idle time and leave	-	16 hrs.

The normal working hours for a month are 200 hours. Overtime is paid at double the normal wages plus dearness allowance. Employee's contributions to state insurance and provident fund are at equal rate with the employer's contributions. The month contains 25 working days and one paid holiday. The two workers were employed on jobs X, Y and Z in the following proportions:

Jobs	X	Y	Z
Worker 'A'	80	60	60
Worker 'B'	100	40	60

Overtime was done on Job 'Y'. **(ICWA-Inter)**

Solution

(i)

Computation of workers' earnings		
	Worker 'A' ₹	**Worker 'B'** ₹
Basic wages	100	100
Dearness allowance	50	55
Overtime (*See* WN-2)	15	-
	165	155

(ii)

Computation of labour cost (excluding overtime)		
	₹	**Worker 'B'** ₹
Earnings (excluding overtime	150	155
Employer's contribution to:		
(a) PF - 8% of basic wages	8	8
(b) ESI - 2% of basic wages	2	2
	160	165
Normal working hours per month (WN−1)	200 hrs	200 hrs.
Labour cost per hour	160/200 = ₹0.80	165/200 = ₹0.825

(iii)

Allocation of labour cost to jobs				
	Total ₹	Job X ₹	Job Y ₹	Job Z ₹
Worker 'A':				
Ordinary labour cost	160.00	64.00	48.00	48.00
Overtime wages	15.00	-	15.00	-
Worker 'B':				
Ordinary labour cost	165.00	82.50	33.00	49.50
Total	340.00	146.50	96.00	97.50

Working note:

(1) Computation of normal working hours

$$= 25 \text{ days} \times 8 \text{ hours} = 200 \text{ hrs}$$

(2) Computation of overtime wages

	₹
Basic wages per month	100
Dearness allowance	50
Total	150

Normal working hours per month = 200 hours.

Normal rate per hour = 150/200 = ₹0.75

Overtime rate (double the normal rate) = 0.75 × 2 = ₹1.50

Overtime wages for 10 hours = 1.50 × 10 = ₹15.00

Illustration-17: (Work measurement and labour budgeting)

An article passes through five hand operations as follows:

Operation No.	Time per article	Grade of worker	Wage rate per hour
1	15 minutes	A	₹6.50
2	25 minutes	B	₹5.00
3	10 minutes	C	₹4.00
4	30 minutes	D	₹3.50
5	20 minutes	E	₹3.00

The factory works 40 hours a week and the production target is 600 dozen per week. Prepare a statement showing for each operation and in total, the number of operators required, the labour cost per dozen and the total labour cost per week to produce the targeted output.

Solution

Operation No.	**Time required for production of 600 dozens (i.e. 7,200 units)**	**Labour cost per week ₹**	**No. of operators required (Grade)**	**Labour cost per dozen ₹**
1	7,200 ×15/60 = 1,800 Hrs.	1,800 × 6.50 = ₹11,700	1,800/40= 45 (A)	11,700/600 = ₹19.50
2	7,200 ×25/60 = 3,000 Hrs.	3,000 × 5.00 = ₹15,000	3,000/40=75 (B)	15,000/600 = ₹25.00
3	7,200 ×10/60 = 1,200 Hrs.	1,200 × 4.00 = ₹4,800	1,200/40=30 (C)	4,800/600 = ₹8.00

4	7,200 ×30/60 = 3,600 Hrs.	3,600 × 3.50 = ₹12,600	3,600/40=90 (D)	12,600/600 = ₹21.00
5	7200 ×20/60 = 2,400 Hrs.	2,400 × 3.00 = ₹7,200	2,400/40=60 (E)	7,200/600 = ₹12.00
	Total	51,300	-	85.50

5.11 EXERCISES

I. Objective Type Questions

A. State whether the following statements are true or false

(i) Employee placement requisition is prepared by personnel department.

(ii) Labour cost is classified into direct labour cost and indirect labour cost.

(iii) High labour turnover is beneficial to a firm.

(iv) Fringe benefits are incurred in cash.

(v) Time study is conducted to find out the time required to do a job.

(vi) Motion study is conducted to find the movement of machine parts in a factory.

(vii) Recording of total time spent by workers in the factory is called timekeeping.

(viii) Time booking and timekeeping is same.

(ix) Wages are not paid to workers for idle time.

(x) Treatment of idle time cost depends on the causes of idle time.

(xi) Extra payment made for overtime work is overtime premium.

(xii) Job cards are maintained to find the time spent by various workers on a job.

(xiii) Labour is a wasting asset.

(xiv) Job evaluation and job description are same.

(xv) Merit rating is used to find the worth of a job.

(xvi) Overtime premium is always treated as indirect labour cost.

(xvii) Wages abstract is prepared by cost accounting treatment.

(xviii) Abnormal idle time wages is debited to costing profit and loss account.

Ans: True - (i), (ii), (v), (vii), (x), (xi), (xii), (xiii), (xvii), (xviii)
False - (iii), (iv), (vi), (viii), (ix), (xiv), (xv), (xvi).

B. Fill in the blanks

(i) Workers engaged in production function are called ________

(ii) Wages of ________ workers are always treated as overheads.

(iii) Rate of change in labour force is called ________

(iv) Method used to calculate labour turnover rate of outgoing workers is called ________

(v) Production capacity of workers is ________

(vi) Time for which workers are paid but no work is done is called ________

(vii) Recording the time spent by workers in the factory is called ________

(viii) Uncontrollable idle time is called ________

(ix) Idle time arising only occasionally is called ________

(x) According to Factories Act workers are paid at single rate upto ________ hours work per day.

(xi) Idle time due to power failure is ________

(xii) Study conducted to find the reasonable time to do a job is called ________

(xiii) Recording the time spent by a worker in the factory is called ________

(xiv) Card used to record the time spent by workers on a job is called ________

(xv) Reconciliation of time recorded in time card and job card is to find out ________

(xvi) Abnormal idle time cost is charged to ________

(xvii) Finding the worth of a job is called ________

(xviii) Measuring the efficiency and productivity of individual workers is called ________

(xix) Workers working at customer's place or at work site are called ________

(xx) Workers employed temporarily are called ________

(**Answer:** (i) Direct workers, (ii) indirect workers, (iii) labour turnover rate, (iv) separation method, (v) elastic, (vi) idle time, (vii) timekeeping, (viii) normal idle time, (ix) abnormal idle time, (x) 9, (xi) abnormal idle time, (xii) time study, (xiii) timekeeping, (xiv) job card, (xv) idle time, (xvi) costing profit and loss account, (xvii) job evaluation, (xviii) merit rating, (xix) out workers, (xx) casual workers)

II. Theory Questions

A. Short answer type questions

1. What is timekeeping?
2. What is time booking?
3. What is job card?
4. What is time card?
5. What is idle time?
6. What is abnormal idle time?
7. What is overtime?
8. Explain wages abstract.
9. Give a list of various types of job cards.
10. What are fringe benefits?
11. Give a few example of non-monetary benefits to workers?
12. What is normal idle time?
13. What is abnormal idle time?
14. What is time and motion study?
15. What is merit rating?
16. What is job evaluation?

B. Long answer type questions

1. What is timekeeping and time booking? Explain the importance of timekeeping and time booking.
2. Explain the various methods of timekeeping? Explain the difference between timekeeping and time booking.
3. Write short notes on : (a) Time and motion study, (b) Job evaluation, (c) Merit rating.
4. Distinguish job evaluation from merit rating.
5. What do you understand by labour turnover? Discuss the causes of labour turnover and its effect on the cost of production.
6. What is overtime? Explain the treatment of overtime premium in cost accounts.
7. What is idle time? Explain the causes of idle time and explain its treatment in cost accounts.

8. What do you understand by time and motion study? Explain how standard time is set under time study. State how time and motion study is useful to the management.
9. Distinguish between: (a) Direct labour andindirect labour; (b) Casual workers and out workers; (c) Timekeeping and time booking; (d) Time card and job card; and (e) Normal and abnormal idle time.
10. What do you understand by labour turnover? How is it measured? What steps should be taken to check the increasing rate of labour turnover?
11. Explain the steps to prevent fraud in wage payment.
12. Explain the treatment of holiday and leave pay in cost accounts.
13. Write short notes on: (a) Pay roll; (b) Fringe benefits; (c) Wages abstract; (d) Labour productivity.
14. (a) Define job evaluation and explain its advantages to the employer and the employees.
    (b) What is standard time? Explain how standard time is determined.
15. What are the steps that should be taken for preventing fraud and irregularities in pay roll?
16. What do you understand by fringe benefits? What are the various items of fringe benefits. Explain the treatment of cost of fringe benefits in cost accounts.

III. Practical Problems

A. Short answer type questions

1. The extract from the pay roll of a company gives the following information:

Number of employees at the beginning of 2004	240
Number of employees at the end of 2004	310
Number of employees discharged during the year	5
Number of employees resigned during the year	26
Number of employees replaced due to quits and discharges	25

Calculate the net annual labour turnover rate. **(B.Com., Madras University)**

[**Ans:** Net labour turnover rate (Replacement method) = 9.1%]

2. Calculate labour turnover rate under separation method.

Number of employees at the beginning of 2008	600
Number of employees at the end of 2008	800
Number of employees resigned	15
Number of employees discharged	55

[**Ans:** Labour turnover rate 10%]

3. Calculate standard time from the following: A worker with an efficiency rating of 80% produced 20 units in a day of 8 hours. Allow 10% idle time allowance.

   [**Ans:** Standard time 21 minutes per unit]

   Note :

   Actual time taken = 8 × 60/20 = 24 minutes
   Efficiency rating = 80%

Normalised time for 100% efficiency rating = 24 × 80/100	= 19.20 minutes
Add: 10% allowance for idle time	= 1.92 minutes
Standard time	= 21.12 minutes

4. Calculate net wages payable from the following:

Basic wages	₹2000 p.m.
Dearness allowance	30% of basic pay
House rent allowance	10% of basic pay
Employee's and Employer's contribution	10% each to P.F.
Employer's contribution to ESI	2% of basic pay
Employee's contribution to ESI	1% of basic pay

   [**Ans:** Net wages payable ₹2,580]

   Note: Gross wages = Basic wages + DA + HRA + = ₹2,800
   Net wages = Gross wages - Employee's contribution to PF and ESI.

B. Comprehensive Practical Problems

1. Calculate labour turnover rate under various methods from the following information for the month of October, 1998:

Number of employees at the beginning of the month	950
Number of employees at the end of the month	1,050
Number of employees resigned during the year	10
Number of employees replaced in the vacancies	20
Number of employees discharged during the year	30
Number of employees replaced due to expansion scheme	120

(B.Com., Madras University)

[**Ans:** Labour turnover rate: (a) Separation method - 4%; (b) Replacement method - 2%; (c) Accession method - 14%; (d) Flux method - 18%]

2. From the following data provided to you, find out the labour turnover rate by applying: (a) Flux method, (b) Replacement method, (c) Separation method.

Number of workers on the pay roll:	
At the beginning of the month	500
At the end of the month	600

During the month 5 workers left, 20 persons were discharged and 75 workers were recruited. Of these 10 workers were recruited in the vacancies of those leaving, while the rest were engaged for an expansion scheme. **(ICWA-Inter)**

[**Ans:** (a) Flux method - 18.18%; (b) Replacement method - 1.82%; (c) Separation method - 4.55%]

3. From the following particulars prepare a statement showing cost per man day of 8 hours and cost per hour:

   (a) Basic salary and dearness allowance - ₹5,000
   (b) Leave salary 6% of basic salary and DA.
   (c) Employer's contribution to PF 8% of basic salary and DA.
   (d) Employee's contribution to PF 8% of basic salary and DA.
   (e) Employer's contribution to state insurance 2% of basic salary and DA.
   (f) Employee's contribution to state insurance 1% of basic salary and DA.
   (g) Pro-rata expenditure on amenities to labour ₹100 per head per month.
   (h) Number of working hours in a month 200.

[**Ans:** Cost per man day ₹236, Cost per hour ₹29.50]

Note: Employee's contribution to PF and ESI ignored for ascertaining labour cost.

4. A worker is paid a basic salary of ₹6,000 and a dearness allowance of ₹900 per month. He is entitled to a bonus of 15% on basic salary and D.A. Employer's contribution to recognised provident fund is $8\frac{1}{3}$% of basic salary and DA, to which employee contributes an equal amount. Employer also contributes 2% of basic salary and DA towards state insurance and employee's contribution is 1% of basic salary and DA. The company also provides canteen facility at subsidised rates at monthly subsidy of ₹9,000. The number of employees using the canteen are 300.

The total number of working days in a year is 300 days of 8 hours each. Workers are entitled to 20 days leave with full pay. Workers are also given 20 days additional leave with half pay. Normal idle time amounted to 20%. Compute labour cost per man hour when,

   (a) Additional leave with half pay availed
   (b) Additional leave with half pay not availed

[**Ans:** (a) ₹60.85; (b) ₹58.11]

Note: Assumed number of days in a month is 30.

5. Calculate the standard labour hour rate for workman of grade 'A' from the following data:

Basic pay	₹4,000 p.m.
D.A.	₹1,000 p.m.
Fringe benefits	₹100 p.m.
Number of working days per year	300

Leave rules:

30 days personal leave with full pay
20 days sick leave with half pay

What would be the labour cost per hour if:

(a) Sick leave is fully availed.
(b) Sick leave is not availed.

[**Ans:** Labour cost per hour (a) Sick leave fully availed - ₹29.75; (b) Sick leave not availed - ₹28.33]

6. X Ltd. Provides the following emoluments and benefits to worker "Pee".

(a) Basic salary ₹4,500 per month
(b) Dearness allowance:
On first ₹2,000 of salary - ₹1,500
On second ₹2,000 of salary - ₹750
On balance of salary - 40%
(c) Employer's contribution to:
Provident Fund - 8% of salary and D.A.
E.S.I. - 2% of salary and D.A.
(d) Bonus - 20% of salary and D.A.
(e) Other allowances - ₹7,500 per annum.

'Pee' works for 2,250 hours per annum, out of which 300 hours are non-productive but treated as normal idle time. 'Pee' worked for 18 effective hours in Job No. 77, where the cost of direct materials is ₹3,000, overhead is charged at 200% of direct labour. The job is priced to earn a profit of 10% on sales value.

You are requested to find out:

(a) Effective hourly labour cost
(b) Sales value of Job. 77

[**Ans:** (a) Effective hourly labour cost per hour - ₹59.45; (b) Sales value of Job. 77 - ₹6,900.33]

7. Normal working hours in a factory are 44 hours per week. Worker 'X' is paid at ₹10 per hour and overtime is paid at double the above rate. In addition, a production bonus of ₹5.00 per 100 units produced in excess of 2,000 units per week. The time and job cards show the following details:

Days	Morning Time		Evening Time		Output (Units)
	In	Out	In	Out	
Monday	8.00 am	12.30 noon	2.00 pm	5.30 pm	600
Tuesday	8.30 am	1.00 pm	2.00 pm	6.00 pm	650
Wednesday	8.00 am	12.00 noon	1.00 pm	5.30 pm	650
Thursday	8.00 am	12.00 noon	1.00 pm	6.30 pm	550
Friday	8.00 am	12.00 noon	1.00 pm	5.00 pm	450
Saturday	8.00 am	12.00 noon	1.00 pm	6.00 pm	600

Calculate earnings of worker 'X' for the week.

[**Ans:** Weekly earnings - ₹665]

Note: 1) Normal time wages (44 × 10) = ₹440

2) Overtime wages (7 1/2 × 10 × 2) = ₹150

3) Production Bonus(1500 × 5/100) = ₹ 75

Total = ₹665

8. The following details are available for the year 2008:

	₹
Sales	50,00,000
Direct materials	17,00,000
Direct labour	11,00,000
Variable overheads	7,00,000
Fixed overheads	5,00,000

Actual hours worked during the year amounted to 1,60,000 hours.

As a result of labour turnover 10,000 hours were lost due to delay in recruitment. Actual hours worked includes 20,000 hours relating to training of new workers which is reckoned as equal to 10,000 productive hours.

The following expenses were incurred relating to labour turnover:

	₹
Settlement cost	25,000
Recruitment cost	10,000
Training cost	15,000

Find the effect of labour turnover on profit, assuming that all products produced can be sold at prevailing prices.

[**Ans:** Loss of profit – ₹2,50,000]

Note:

(a) Productive hours = 1,60,000 – 10,000 (unproductive training time) = 15,00,000 hours.
(b) Loss of productive hours

(i) Due to delay in recruitment	- 10,000 hours.
(ii) Unproductive training time	- 10,000 hours
Total	- 20,000 hours

(c) Total Contribution (Sales – Variable Cost) = ₹15,00,000
(d) Loss of contribution due to unproductive hours = $\frac{15,00,000}{1,50,000} \times 20,000$ = ₹2,00,000.
(e) Loss of profit = Loss of contribution + Expenses due to labour turnover

9. From the following data calculate the total monthly remuneration of 3 workers X, Y and Z.

   (a) Standard production per month per worker is 1,000 units.
   (b) Actual production during a month: X - 800 units; Y - 700 units; and Z - 900 units.
   (c) Piece work rate per unit of production - 15 paise.
   (d) D.A. - ₹40 per month (fixed)
   (e) House rent allowance ₹20 per month (fixed).
   (f) Additional production bonus at the rate of ₹5 for each percentage of actual production exceeding 75% over standard production.

(ICWA-Inter)

[**Ans:** Monthly earnings of workers : X - ₹205, Y - ₹165, and Z - ₹270]

10. Job card of worker 'X' reveals the following for a week of 44 hours:

    (a) Time booked - 44 hours (including 4 hours overtime)
    (b) Loss of time - 4 hours due to machine breakdown.

    The worker is paid at ₹15 per hour. Overtime is paid at double the normal rate.

    You are required to allocate total wages paid to the worker between direct and indirect labour. Also show the amount charged to costing profit and loss account.

    [**Ans:** Total wages - ₹780, wages for 44 hours at normal rate (44 × 15) - ₹660 treated as direct labour, overtime premium for 4 hours (4 × 15) - ₹60 treated as indirect labour. Idle time due to machine breakdown is abnormal, hence idle time cost (4 × 15) ₹60 is debited to costing profit and loss account].

11. Workers X and Y are engaged on job 'A'. The following hours were worked by workers on Job 'A' during a week.

Days	Worker 'X'	Worker 'Y'
Monday	8 hrs.	10 hrs.
Tuesday	10 hrs.	9 hrs.
Wednesday	9 hrs.	11 hrs.
Thursday	11 hrs.	8 hrs.
Friday	9 hrs.	9 hrs.
Saturday	9 hrs.	6 hrs.

(a) Normal working hours on week days 8 hours and on Saturday 4 hours.

(b) Normal daily wages - X - ₹100, Y - ₹120

(c) 4 hours work on Saturday is paid at full day wages. Work on Saturday in excess of 4 hours is treated as overtime and is paid at 1 1/2 times the normal wages and at double the rate over 8 hours.

(d) Dearness allowance paid at 50% on wages including overtime wages.

Calculate the weekly earnings of workers X and Y. Also calculate the labour cost of Job 'A'.

[**Ans:** Weekly earnings - Worker 'X' - ₹1312.50, Worker Y - ₹1462.50, Labour cost of Job 'A' - ₹2,775]

METHODS OF WAGE PAYMENT 6

- Wage Payment Methods/System—Characteristics
- Methods of Wage Payment System
- Time Rate System
- Piece Rate System
- Incentive and Bonus Plans
- Other Incentive Schemes:
  - Profit Sharing Plan
  - Co-partnership
  - Non-monetary Incentive

6.1 INTRODUCTION

There are many methods for paying wages to workers. A company should follow a wage payment system which best suits its labour policy. The wage payment system must satisfy both the workers and the management. It should ensure fair remuneration to workers after considering individual worker's efficiency. It should also ensure higher labour productivity and lower labour cost per unit.

Characteristics of a good wage payment system

The main characteristics of a good wage payment system are:

1. It should be simple and easy to understand by workers.
2. It should be flexible and capable of being modified when the situation changes.
3. It should be economical.

4. It should ensure fair remuneration for their efforts.
5. It should help to keep the labour turnover to the minimum.
6. It should provide incentive for high efficiency and hard work.
7. It should fulfill the legal requirements like payment of minimum wages, payment of bonus etc.
8. It should be acceptable to trade unions also.
9. It should also be based on the company's capacity to pay.
10. It should ensure a good labour relation in the company.

Factors to be considered while introducing a good wage payment system

1. **Industry standards**

   The wage structure prevailing in the industry and wages prevailing in local area should be considered in introducing a wage payment system.

2. **Productivity**

   Workers' efficiency and productivity should be the main criteria in a wage system.

3. **Cost of living**

   Inflation reduces the value of money. So workers, wages should be linked with the rate of inflation. Thus workers are to be compensated for increased cost of living.

4. **Ability to pay**

   There will be no difficulty in paying increased wages during business prosperity. During periods of recession and industrial downtrend, there may be difficulty in meeting higher wage bills. So company's financial strength should be considered while fixing wage structure.

5. **Attitude of trade unions**

   Attitude of labour and trade unions towards the wage payment system is also important. Labour and trade union acceptance is essential for maintaining good labour relationship and industrial peace.

6.2 METHODS OF WAGE PAYMENT

Wage payment systems are mainly grouped under the following three heads:

(A) Time rate system
(B) Piece rate system
(C) Incentive and premium bonus plans.

6.2.1 Time Rate System

It is the simplest and most common method of wage payment being followed in many organisations for long. In this method time spent by a worker in the organisation is the main factor for paying wages. The effort and output of individual worker is not considered for payment of wages. For each category of workers separate rates of wages are fixed for a unit of time. The unit of time may be an hour, a day, a week or a month. The earning of a worker is computed by using the following step:

$$\text{Earnings} = \text{Time taken} \times \text{Time rate}$$

There are four variations of time rate system. They are:

(i) Simple time rate or flat time rate system.
(ii) High wage plan
(iii) Differential time rate system.
(iv) Measured day rate system.

(i) Simple Time Rate (or) Flat Time Rate System

A single time rate is fixed for all workers belonging to a particular grade. All workers are paid at the same time rate irrespective of the effort put in or individual efficiency. It is one of the oldest methods. **This has the following merits and demerits**

1. It is very simple and easy to understand.
2. It is inexpensive.
3. It is acceptable to trade unions, as it does not create divisions among workers.
4. Quality of output is maintained.
5. Repairs and maintenance of machines and wastage of material is minimum since the workers do not rush through the work.

Demerits

1. There is no incentive for hard work and efficiency.
2. Productivity will be less resulting in higher labour cost per unit.
3. Workers will go slow during normal working time with an intention to earn overtime.
4. Close supervision is necessary to extract work from workers.
5. This method does not promote honesty and efficiency among workers.

Suitability of Time Rate System

Irrespective of many demerits this method suffers, it is being followed in many organisations. The reasons for its following are:

1. Where the output of individual workers cannot be measured, e.g., general helpers, supervisory staff, etc.
2. Where workers are engaged in rendering skilled services, e.g., Tool making, inspection and testing etc.
3. Where quality of output is more important than the quantity produced.
4. Where materials used are very costly.

(ii) High wage plan

High time rates are fixed to attract highly efficient workers. High rate will be substantially higher than the industrial average rates. Productivity increases due to employment of efficient workers. A standard output is fixed which can be easily achieved by efficient workers. There is incentive for higher production. All merits and demerits of the flat time rate system is applicable to this method also except that there is incentive for higher productivity.

(iii) Differential Time Rate System

Workers of a grade are paid at different time rates depending on their efficiency. Efficient workers are paid at high time rate and less efficient workers are paid at lower time rate. This method rewards efficient workers. Other merits and demerits of the flat time rate system are applicable to this system also.

(iv) Measured Day Rate System

Time rates are fixed for achieving a particular level of output. Workers are paid for the level of performance achieved by a worker. This method also recognises the efficiency level of individual workers. Other merits and demerits of the flat time rate system are applicable to this system also.

6.2.2 Piece Rate System

Piece rate system is also known as payment by result. Wage rate payable per unit of production is fixed which is called 'piece rate'. Workers are paid on the basis of volume of output produced. The time taken to produce the output is not considered. Earnings of a worker are calculated by the following step:

$$\text{Earning} = \text{Output} \times \text{Piece rate}$$

The following are variants of piece rate system:

(i) Simple piece rate system.
(ii) Taylor's differential piece rate system.
(iii) Merrick's multiple piece rate system.
(iv) Gantt's task and bonus plan.

(i) Simple Piece Rate System

Simple piece rate system is also known as straight piece rate system. A single wage rate per unit of an article produced is fixed. All workers are paid at this rate irrespective of number of units produced by them. The following are the merits and demerits of simple piece rate system:

Merits

1. Every worker is paid according to his efforts. So there is incentive for hard work and efficiency.
2. Close supervision is not necessary as every worker will try to maximise his output.
3. As productivity increases, cost per unit decreases.

4. Amount of wages earned by workers increases.
5. Idle time comes down.
6. All production facilities like machines, tools are fully utilised.

Demerits

1. This method can be applied only when the output of individual workers are to be measured.
2. When the jobs are dissimilar there will be difficulty in fixing piece rates.
3. There is no guaranteed minimum wages.
4. There will be division among workers as more efficient and less efficient. This is not liked by trade unions.
5. Workers will rush through the work. As a result materials wastage will be more.
6. Due to high speed of operations, machine breakdown and their repairs and maintenance will be more.
7. Workers may not give importance for quality of output turned out. So close quality inspection is required.
8. Workers' earnings will be affected due to no fault of theirs like power failure, machine breakdown, non-availability of materials etc.

(ii) Taylor's differential piece rate system

This system was introduced by F.W. Taylor, the father of scientific management. By using time and motion study a standard output is fixed. Two piece rates, one high piece rate and another low piece rate are fixed. Wages are paid at high piece rate to workers whose output is equal to or more than the standard. Wages are paid at low piece rate to workers whose output is less than the standard. Taylor wants to discourage the less efficient workers because production facilities are under utilised resulting in higher cost per unit. Efficient workers are highly rewarded and at the same time the management also benefits through reduced cost per unit. Punishment by way of lower wages is severe even for a slight fall in production. So workers resent this system. Earnings are calculated by using the following step:

$$\text{Earnings} = \text{Actual output} \times \text{High piece rate or Low piece rate}$$

Illustration-1

Calculate the earnings of workers under (a) straight piece rate system and (b) taylor's differential piece rate system from the following information:

Hourly rate per hour	₹24
Standard time per unit	10 minutes

Differentials to be applied are:

90% of piece rate below standard and
110% of piece rate at or above standard.

In a day of 8 hours the output of the workers are as below:

Worker 'x' - 40 units, worker 'y' - 48 units and worker 'z' - 55 units.

Solution

Standard output per 10 minutes	1 unit
Standard output per hour	$60 \div 10 = 6$ units.
Standard output per day of 8 hours	48 units.

$$\text{Normal piece rate} = \frac{\text{Wages per hour}}{\text{Standard output per hour}}$$

$$= \frac{24}{6} = ₹4.00$$

$$\text{Low price rate} = \text{Normal piece rate} \times \frac{90}{100}$$

$$= 4 \times \frac{90}{100} = ₹3.60$$

$$\text{High price rate} = \text{Normal piece rate} \times \frac{110}{100}$$

$$= 4 \times \frac{110}{100} = ₹4.40$$

Earning of workers

Worker 'x'

Worker 'x' will be paid at low piece rate since his output is below standard.

$$\text{Earnings} = \text{Output} \times \text{Low piece rate}$$

$$= 40 \times 3.60 = ₹144$$

Worker 'y'

Worker 'y' will be paid at high piece rate since his output is equal to standard.

$$\text{Earnings} = \text{Output} \times \text{High piece rate}$$

$$= 48 \times 4.40 = ₹211.20$$

Worker 'z'

Worker 'z' will be paid at high piece rate since his output is above standard.

$$\text{Earnings} = \text{Output} \times \text{High piece rate}$$

$$= 55 \times 4.40 = ₹242$$

(iii) Merrick's Multiple Piece Rate System

This system moderates the severity of punishment for small fall in efficiency. Under this method workers are paid at three piece rates according to their efficiency. They are:

	Efficiency%	Piece rates
1.	For efficiency upto 83% of standard output	Workers are paid at normal piece rate.
2.	For efficiency above 83% and upto 100% of standard output.	Workers are paid at 110% of normal piece rate.
3.	For efficiency above 100% of standard output	Workers are paid at 120% of normal piece rate system.

This method encourages efficient workers. But slow workers are not punished as in Taylor's system. Slow workers are paid at normal piece rates. This method has all the merits and demerits of a piece rate system.

Illustration-2

Compute the earnings of three workers A, B and C under Merrick's multiple piece rate system from the following information:

Standard production per hour - 10 units.
Normal wage rate per hour ₹10.

Output of workers on a day of 8 hours are as below:

Worker A - 60 units
Worker B - 70 units
Worker C - 85 units.

Solution

$$\text{Normal piece rate} = \frac{\text{Normal wages per hour}}{\text{Std. production per hour}} = \frac{10}{10} = ₹1.00$$

Standard output per day $= 10 \times 8 = 80$ units.

$$\%\text{ of efficiency of workers} = \frac{\text{Actual output}}{\text{Standard output}} \times 100$$

$$\text{Worker A} = \frac{60}{80} \times 100 = 75\%$$

$$\text{Worker B} = \frac{70}{80} \times 100 = 87.5\%$$

$$\text{Worker C} = \frac{85}{80} \times 100 = 106.25\%$$

Computation of earnings of workers

Worker 'A'

His percentage of efficiency is below 83% of standard. He will be paid at Normal piece rate.

$$\text{Earnings} = \text{Output} \times \text{normal piece rate}$$
$$= 60 \times 1.00 = ₹60$$

Worker 'B'

His percentage of efficiency is between 83% to 100% of standard. He will be paid at 110% of normal piece rate.

$$\text{Earnings} = \text{Output} \times \text{Normal piece rate} \times \frac{110}{100}$$
$$= 70 \times 1 \times \frac{110}{100} = ₹77$$

Worker 'C'

His percentage of efficiency is above 100% of standard. He will be paid at 120% of normal piece rate.

$$\text{Earnings} = \text{Output} \times \text{Normal piece rate} \times \frac{120}{100}$$
$$= 85 \times 1 \times \frac{120}{100} = ₹102$$

(iv) Gantt's Task and Bonus Plan

This method is a combination of time rate system and piece rate system. Wages are paid to workers as below based on workers efficiency:

Sl.No.	Efficiency %	Wage rates
1.	For output below the standard output (i.e. efficiency below 100%)	Workers are paid at normal time rate for actual time taken.
2.	For output equal to the standard output (i.e efficiency equal to 100%)	Workers are paid at 120% of normal time rate for actual time taken.
3.	For output above 100% of standard output (i.e efficiency above to 100%)	Workers are paid at high piece rate system.

Illustration-3

The following are the particulars applicable to a work process:

Time rate per hour ₹5.
High task 40 units per week.
Piece rate above the high task ₹6.50 per unit.

In a 40-hour week, the production of workers are as follows:

Worker 'A' - 35 units, Worker 'B' - 40 units, Worker 'C' - 41 units and Worker 'D' 52 units.

Calculate the wages of workers under Gantt's task and bonus plan.

Solution

$$\% \text{ of efficiency of workers} = \frac{\text{Actual output}}{\text{Standard production}} \times 100$$

$$\text{Worker A} = \frac{35}{40} \times 100 = 87.5\%$$

$$\text{Worker B} = \frac{40}{40} \times 100 = 100\%$$

$$\text{Worker C} = \frac{41}{40} \times 100 = 102.5\%$$

$$\text{Worker D} = \frac{52}{40} \times 100 = 130\%$$

Earnings of workers

Worker 'A'

His efficiency percentage is below 100%. He will be paid time wages only.

$$\text{Earnings} = \text{Time taken} \times \text{Time rate}$$
$$= 40 \times 5 = ₹200$$

Worker 'B'

His efficiency percentage is equal 100%. He will be paid time wages and a bonus of 20% on time wages.

$$\text{Earnings} = \text{Time taken} \times \text{Time Rate} + 20\% \text{ bonus}$$
$$= 40 \times 5 + (40 \times 5)\frac{20}{100}$$
$$= 200 + 40 = ₹240$$

Worker 'C'

His efficiency percentage is above 100%. He will be paid at high piece rate.

$$\text{Earnings} = \text{Output} \times \text{High piece rate}$$
$$= 41 \times 6.50 = ₹266.50$$

Worker 'D'

His efficiency is above 100%. He will be paid at high piece rate.

$$\text{Earnings} = \text{Output} \times \text{High piece rate}$$
$$= 52 \times 6.50 = ₹338$$

6.2.3 Incentive and Bonus Plans

Under time rate systems all workers are paid alike irrespective their individual effort. There is no incentive for higher efficiency and hard work. Under piece rate systems workers are paid for their effort. But there is no guaranteed minimum wages. Incentive and bonus plans are a combination of time rate system and piece rate system. Under this system standard time to complete a task or job is fixed. The standard time is the time a worker of ordinary skill will take to complete a job, which is fixed under time and motion study. All workers are paid for the actual time taken to complete the job. An incentive is given to workers who complete the job within the standard time. Under this method all workers are guaranteed time wages and bonus is given to efficient workers.

A good incentive wage payment system should have the following characteristics:

1. The system should be simple and easy to understand.
2. The system should ensure reasonable wages to workers and beneficial to the employer also by means of reduced labour cost per unit.
3. It should provide incentive for higher efficiency and hard work.
4. It should guarantee minimum wages to lead a decent living.
5. Standard time and standard outputs fixed should be reasonable and achievable by workers of average skill.
6. The system should be fully explained to workers and their co-operation is to be obtained.
7. It should also ensure quality of production.
8. The incentive scheme should be introduced for indirect workers also.

Some important incentive and bonus systems are explained below:

1. Halsey Premium Bonus Plan

F.A. Halsey introduced this plan. Under this plan standard time for doing a job is fixed. All workers are paid for actual time worked. Additionally a bonus is paid to those workers who complete the job with in the standard time. Bonus is paid at 50% of wages for time saved.

Advantages

(i) It is simple to understand and easy to operate.
(ii) Time wages are guaranteed for all workers for actual time taken.
(iii) Efficient workers are paid incentive bonus.
(iv) The wages for time saved equally shared by workers and the management.
(v) Cost per unit is reduced by increased productivity.

Disadvantages

(i) There is difficulty in fixing standard time for different types of jobs.
(ii) Quality of output suffers as workers will rush through the job.
(iii) Workers are not given full benefit for time saved.

Illustration-4

From the following data calculate the earnings of workers A, B and C under Halsey plan:

Standard time per unit: 10 minutes
Wage rate per hour ₹15
Time worked 8 hours
Output of workers A, B and C are 45 units, 60 units and 75 units respectively.

Also calculate the effective earnings per hour.

Solution

	Worker A	Worker B	Worker C
Standard time for actual output	$\left(\frac{45 \times 10}{60}\right)$ = 7.5 hours	$\left(\frac{60 \times 10}{60}\right)$ = 10 hours	$\left(\frac{75 \times 10}{60}\right)$ = 12.5 hours
Time taken	8 hours	8 hours	8 hours
Time Saved	-	2 hours	4.5 hours

Computation of earnings of workers			
	Worker A ₹	Worker B ₹	Worker C ₹
Time wages = Time taken × Time rate (8 × 15)	120	120	120
Bonus = Time saved × Time rate × $\frac{50}{100}$	-	$\left(2 \times 15 \times \frac{50}{100}\right) = 15$	$\left(4.5 \times 15 \times \frac{50}{100}\right) = 33.75$
Total earnings	120	135	153.75
Effective earnings per hour	$\frac{120}{8}$ = ₹15	$\frac{135}{8}$ = ₹16.88	$\frac{153.75}{8}$ = ₹19.22

2. Halsey-Weir premium Bonus Plan

This plan is similar to Halsey plan. The only difference is in payment of bonus. Bonus under this plan is only 30% of wages for time saved instead of 50% in Halsey plan.

3. Rowan system

David Rowan introduced this scheme. Under this method standard time is fixed for doing a job. All workers are paid for time taken. Bonus is paid on time wage in proportion that time saved bears to standard time. The following formula is applied for calculating bonus:

$$\text{Bonus} = \frac{\text{Time saved}}{\text{Standard time}} \times \text{Time taken} \times \text{Time rate}$$

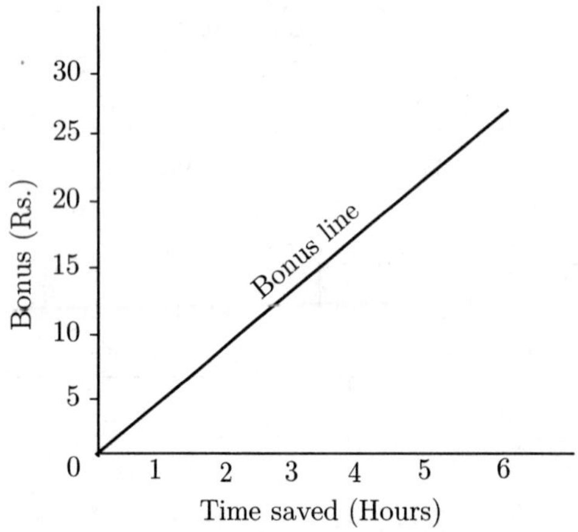

Bonus under Halsey plan

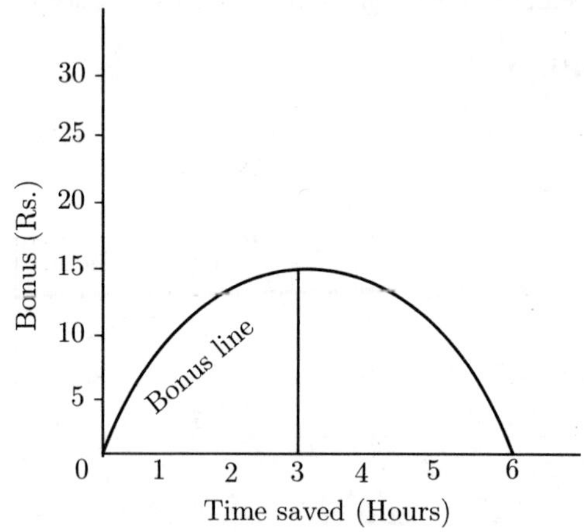

Bonus under Rowan plan

One special feature of this scheme is that bonus will increase till the time saved is upto 50% of standard time of a job. If the time saved exceeds 50% of standard time, the bonus amount starts declining. Under this plan workers are encouraged to save time upto 50% of standard time only and discourages reckless speed in doing the job. This is presented in a chart as given above. (Standard time assumed 6 hours)

Advantages

1. It is simple and easy to operate.
2. Time wages are guaranteed to all workers.
3. Bonus is paid to efficient workers.
4. Cost per unit will be less.
5. Over-speeding is controlled.

Disadvantages

1. Computation of bonus is complex.
2. The ability to earn more bonus is limited to 50% of standard time.
3. It does not encourage highly efficient workers.

Comparison of Rowan plan with Halsey

Sl.No.	Points	Halsey Plan	Rowan Plan
1	Rate of bonus	Paid at 50% of time saved	Rate of bonus progressively increases as time saved increases
2	Maximum bonus	No limit to maximum bonus.	Maximum bonus is paid when time saved is equal to 50% of standard time.
3.	Decrease in bonus	Bonus goes on increasing as time saved increases	Bonus starts declining when time saved exceeds 50% of standard time.
4.	Rate of earnings	Rate of earnings is faster	Rate of earnings is slow

4. Bedeaux point premium plan

Standard time is fixed for a job. The time is expressed in terms of 'B'. Each 'B' represent one minute. All workers are paid time wages. 75% bonus is paid for time saved. Under this scheme 25% bonus is paid for time saved to foreman. This method recognises the role of foremen in helping the workers to save time.

5. Barth Scheme This scheme ensures incentives to beginners and trainees whose efficiency may be below standard. Earnings of workers are calculated by applying the following formula:

$$\text{Earnings} = \text{Time rate} \times \sqrt{\text{Standard time} \times \text{Time taken}}$$

6. Emerson's Efficiency plan

Under this method standard time is fixed to complete a job. Worker's efficiency is measured and expressed in percentage of standard. All workers are paid time wages. No bonus is paid for efficiency upto 66 2/3%, bonus percent gradually increases as efficiency % increases. The rate of bonus payable for different levels of efficiency is given in Emerson's Efficiency Table. Its main feature is given below:

Schedule of Bonus

S.No.	Efficiency %	Bonus %
1.	For efficiency upto $66\frac{2}{3}$%	No bonus
2.	For efficiency above $66\frac{2}{3}$% up to 99%	Bonus varies from 0.01 to 18.81% of time wages.
3.	For efficiency equal to 100%	Bonus is 20% of time wages
4.	For efficiency above 100%	Bonus% increases by 1% for every 1% increase in efficiency over 100%

Merits

(i) All workers are given guaranteed time wages.

(ii) Bonus is given to efficient workers.

(iii) Bonus is given to even average workers, as bonus is given even for 67% efficiency.

Illustration-5

X Ltd employs Emerson's Efficiency Scheme in its factory. Standard output per day of 8 hours is fixed at 50 units. Normal time wages is ₹5 per hour.

Four workers M, N, O and P produced goods as follows on a specific day:

M - 30 units, N - 45 units, O - 50 units and P - 58 units.

Ascertain the earnings of workers under Emerson's efficiency plan. You may assume 0.6% as bonus for every additional 1% efficiency between $66\frac{2}{3}\%$ and 100%. **(B.Com., - Karnataka University)**

Solution

$$\text{Worker's efficiency } \% = \frac{\text{Actual output}}{\text{Standard output}} \times 100$$

$$\text{Worker M} = \frac{30}{50} \times 100 = 60\%$$

$$\text{Worker N} = \frac{45}{50} \times 100 = 90\%$$

$$\text{Worker O} = \frac{50}{50} \times 100 = 100\%$$

$$\text{Worker P} = \frac{58}{50} \times 100 = 116\%$$

(ii) Worker's Bonus %

M = Nil

N = Efficiency over 66 ⅔ %

$= 90 - 66\,{}^{2}\!/_{3} \times 0.6 = 14\%$

O = 20%

P = 20 + 16 = 36%

(iii) Worker's earnings

M = 8 × 5 = ₹40

$$N = 8 \times 5 + (8 \times 5)\,\frac{14}{100} = 40 + 5.60 = ₹45.60$$

$$O = 8 \times 5 + (8 \times 5)\,\frac{20}{100} = 40 + 8 = ₹48$$

$$P = 8 \times 5 + (8 \times 5)\,\frac{36}{100} = 40 + 14.4 = ₹54.40$$

Group Bonus Scheme

Sometimes a job is to be completed by a team of workers of different grades and working for different times. It is difficult to measure the effort of individual workers. Here group bonus scheme is used.

The following are the main group bonus schemes:

1. Budgeted expenses bonus
2. Cost efficiency bonus (or) Scanlon plan
3. Priestman bonus system
4. Towne's gain sharing plan
5. Waste reduction plan.

(i) Budgeted expenses bonus

Under this method expenses budgeted for a period are determined. Actual expenses are compared with budgeted expenses to find the savings in cost. Bonus is paid to workers in the group as a percentage of savings in cost in addition to time wages. This method may be applied for indirect workers also.

(ii) Cost efficiency bonus or Scanlon Plan

Under this plan percentage of wages on sales is fixed on the basis of past experience. During each period this percentage wages are applied on sales during the period. Actual wages paid is deducted from the above amount. The excess of this amount over actual wages is called value-added. Workers are paid a bonus as a percentage on value added.

Illustration-6

Good Eagle Co Ltd has introduced Scanlon plan of incentive bonus plan for its employees from 1987. The relevant information for the three previous years are as follows:

Year	Sales Revenue ₹	Total Salaries and Wages
1984	2,40,000	72,000
1985	2,50,000	70,000
1986	2,70,000	86,400

For 1987, the sales revenue has been ₹3,25,000 and the total salaries and wages paid ₹90,000. What is the amount due to the employees under the Scanlon plan if 50% is set aside in a bonus equalisation reserve fund, how much money is to be paid out for 1987 as Scanlon plan?

Solution

% of average salaries and wage for the past 3 years

$$= \frac{72,000 \ + 70,000 + 86,400}{2,40,000 + 2,50,000 + 2,70,000} \times 100$$

$$= \frac{2,28,400}{7,60,000} \times 100 \ = \ 30.05\%$$

Salaries and wages at 30.05% on 1987 sales $= 3,25,000 \times \frac{30.05}{100}$

	=	97,662.50
Less: Actual salaries and wages paid in 1987	=	90,000.00
Value added	=	7,662.50
Less: 50% transferred to bonus equalisation fund	=	3,831.25
Bonus payable to employees	=	3,831.25

(iii) Priestman Bonus System

Under this method standard production of the group is fixed. Actual output is compared with the standard to find excess production over standard. This excess production is expressed in percentage terms. A part of this percentage is paid as bonus to workers in addition to time wages. If actual production is below standard workers are paid time wages only.

Illustration-7

Twenty men work as a group. Standard production for the team is 100 units per hour. When the actual production exceeds standard, a bonus is paid to all workers in the team in addition to their time wages.

The bonus is computed thus: The percentage of actual production in excess of standard is computed and bonus is paid at half this percentage. Time wages are paid applying worker individual day wage rates. The standard wage rate for the group is ₹5.00 per hour. Bonus% is applied on standard wage rate. The following is the production of the team in a particular week:

Days	Hours worked	Output (Units)
Monday	175 hours	19,500 units
Tuesday	200 hours	24,000 units
Wednesday	190 hours	23,600 units
Thursday	220 hours	26,500 units
Friday	210 hours	25,900 units
Saturday	185 hours	23,280 units

(a) Compute the total bonus for the week and bonus per hour.

(b) Compute the earnings of workers Balaji and Prasad who worked in the team as follows:

Balaji worked 42 hours and his day rate wage is ₹ 8 per hour and Prasad worked for 44 hours and his rate wage is ₹ 10 per hour.

Actual production	1,42,780 units
Standard production $(1,180 \times 100)$	1,18,000 units
Excess production	**24,780 units**

Solution

$$\% \text{ of excess production} = \frac{24,780}{1,18,000} \times 100 = 21\%$$

$$\% \text{ of Bonus} = 21 \times \frac{1}{2} = 10.5\%$$

$$\text{Bonus rate per hour} = \text{Std. wage rate} \times \text{bonus}\%$$
$$= 5 \times 10.5\% = ₹0.525$$

Earnings of workers

Worker	Time wages	Bonus	Total earnings
Balaji	$42 \times 8 =$ ₹336	$42 \times 0.525 =$ ₹22.05	₹358.05
Prasad	$44 \times 10 =$ ₹440	$44 \times 0.525 =$ ₹23.10	₹463.10

(iv) Towne's Gain sharing Plan

This plan was introduced in USA in the year 1886 by H.R. Towne. Foremen and workers are encouraged to save cost. Workers are paid bonus at 50% of savings in labour cost which is distributed to workers in the ratio of their basic wages. Foremen were also paid a bonus.

Illustration-8

A team of 5 workers undertook a work on piece rate basis for ₹ 2,500. All workers in the team work for 50 hours each. Their day wage rates are ₹ 9, ₹ 8, ₹ 7, ₹6 and ₹5 respectively. Workers are paid bonus equal to half the savings in labour cost which is distributed to the workers in the ratio of their time wages. Show the earnings of workers.

Solution

(i) Time wages = Time taken × Time rate

Worker-1 = $50 \times 9 =$ ₹ 450

Worker-2 = $50 \times 8 =$ ₹ 400

Worker-3 = $50 \times 7 =$ ₹ 350

Worker-4 = $50 \times 6 =$ ₹ 300

Worker-5 = $50 \times 5 =$ ₹ 250

Total = **₹ 1,750**

Ratio of time wages 9 : 8 : 7 : 6 : 5

(ii) Group bonus

Group piece rate - ₹ 2,500

Group Time wages - ₹ 1,750

Group Bonus - ₹ 750

(iii) Bonus to workers

Worker-1 $= 750 \times \frac{9}{35} =$ ₹ 192.85

Worker-2 $= 750 \times \frac{8}{35} =$ ₹ 171.43

Worker-3 $= 750 \times \frac{7}{35} =$ ₹ 150.00

Worker-4 $= 750 \times \frac{6}{35} =$ ₹ 128.57

Worker-5 $= 750 \times \frac{5}{35} =$ ₹ 107.14

(iv) Earnings of workers = Time wages + Bonus

Worker-1 = 450 + 192.86 = ₹ 642.86

Worker-2 = 400 +171.43 = ₹ 571.43

Worker-3 = 350 +150.00 = ₹ 500.00

Worker-4 = 300 + 128.57 = ₹ 428.57

Worker-5 = 250 +107.14 = ₹ 357.14

(v) Waste Reduction Plan

This method encourages workers to reduce materials wastages. Standard materials wastage is fixed. Actual waste is measured and compared with standard to find the savings in materials cost. A percentage of savings in materials cost is paid to workers as bonus.

6.3 OTHER INCENTIVE SCHEMES

(A) Profit Sharing Plan

A part of the profit is paid as bonus as per the agreement between labour union and the management. In India profit sharing bonus is governed by Payment of Bonus Act 1965. According to this act minimum bonus payable is 8.33% of wages and maximum bonus is 20% of wages. There is no restriction in payment of bonus in excess of 20% if the management is willing.

Merits

1. It promotes employer and employee co-operation.
2. A sense of attachment with the company is established in the minds of workers.
3. It induces workers to improve their efficiency.

Demerits

1. Bonus payable is ascertained only at the end of the year. During the year the workers are in the dark about the amount of bonus they will get. This delayed payment of bonus does not motivate the workers sufficiently.
2. Often there is dispute between management and workers in fixing the rate of bonus payable.
3. Workers may not get any bonus in the year of loss. The loss may be due to various market conditions, but workers are denied bonus.
4. All workers get same rate of bonus irrespective of their individual efficiency.

(B) Co-partnership

Under this scheme workers become co-partners of the business by contribution to the capital of the company. Thus employees become co-owners of the business and get a share in the profit. Employees stock option plan is an example of co-partnership.

Merits

1. It reduces the labour - management misunderstanding.
2. It instils a sense of oneness with the business.
3. Labour turnover is reduced considerably.
4. Employees themselves are interested in increasing the profit of the business.

(C) Non-monetary Incentives

Workers can also be motivated by providing good facilities. The following are few examples of non-monetary incentives:

(i) Good working conditions, (ii) Free medical care, (iii) Free transport facilities, (iv) Subsidised canteen facilities, (v) Promotion, (vi) Free or subsidised housing facilities, (vii) Welfare schemes.

Merits

1. It does not increase the wage payment.
2. It creates satisfaction in workers mind and improves the morale of employees.
3. It helps to reduce the labour turnover.
4. Helps in attracting the skilled and efficient workers.
5. It reduces workers absenteeism.

Comprehensive illustrations

Illustration-9

(Time, piece rate, Halsey and Rowan plan)

Calculate the earnings of workers from the following information:

Standard time for a job - 40 hours
Time taken to complete the job - 30 hours

Hourly rate of wages is ₹10 per hour. Dearness allowance at the rate of ₹2 per hour actually worked is given. Compute the earnings of the worker under the following methods (i) Time rate method, (ii) Piece rate method, (iii) Halsey plan, (iv) Rowan plan.

Solution

(i) Time Rate Method

	₹
Time wages = TT×TR= 30 × 10	300
Dearness allowance 30 × 2	60
Total earnings	**360**

(ii) Piece Rate Method

	₹
Piece rate wages = Standard time×Time rate = 40 × 10	400
Dearness allowance= 30 × 2	60
Total earnings	**460**

(iii) Halsey Plan

	₹
Time wages = TT×TR= 30 × 10	300
Bonus = TS×TR×$\frac{1}{2}$ =10 × 10 × $\frac{1}{2}$	50
Dearness allowance 30 × 2	60
Total earnings	**410**

Note : Time saved (TS) = Standard time – Time taken
= 40 – 30 = 10 hours.

(iv) Rowan Plan

	₹
Time wages = TT×TR = 30 × 10	300
Bonus = TS/ST×TT×TR=10/40 × 30 × 10	75
Dearness allowance 30 × 2	60
Total earnings	**435**

Illustration-10

(Halsey, Halsey-Weir, Rowan plan and barth scheme)

From the following information, compute the earnings of a worker under

(i) Halsey plan (ii) Halsey-Weir plan (30% to worker) (iii) Rowan plan and (iv) Barth scheme.

Normal wage rate per hour ₹12
Standard time to produce 1 article is 16.5 minutes
In a week of 44 hours a worker produced 220 articles.

Also compute effective earnings per hour.

Solution

Standard time for actual production $\left(\frac{200 \times 16.5}{60}\right)$	55 hours
Time taken	44 hours
Time saved	**11 hours**

Computation of earnings

(i) Halsey plan

	₹
Time wages = TT×TR= 44 × 12	528
Bonus = TS×TR×$\frac{1}{2}$=11 × 12 × $\frac{1}{2}$	66
Total earnings	**594**

Effective earnings per hour = 594 ÷ 44 = ₹ 13.50

(ii) Halsey - Weir Plan

	₹
Time wages = TT×TR= 44 × 12	528.00
Bonus = TS×TR×30/100 =11 × 12 × 30/100	39.60
Total earnings	**567.60**

Effective earnings per hour = 567.60 ÷ 44 = ₹ 12.90

(iii) Rowan Plan

	₹
Time wages = TT×TR= 44 × 12	528.00
Bonus = TS/ST×TT×TR = 11/55 × 44 × 12	105.60
Total earnings	**633.60**

Effective earnings per hour = 633.60 ÷ 44 = ₹ 14.40

(iv) Barth Scheme

$$\text{Total earnings} = \text{Time Rate} \times \sqrt{\text{Standard time} \times \text{time taken}}$$
$$= 12 \times \sqrt{55 \times 44} = \text{Rs. } 590.32$$

Effective earnings per hour = 590.32 ÷ 44 = ₹ 13.41.

Illustration-11

(Time rate, Piece rate, Rowan plan and halsey plan)

In a week of 48 hours, a worker produced 160 articles. The estimated time to produce one article is 20 minutes and under incentive schemes time allowed is increased by 10%. Normal day rate wages is ₹ 20 per hour. Calculate his gross wages and earnings per hour Under: (i) Time rate, (ii) Piece work with guaranteed weekly wage (iii) Rowan plan and (iv) Halsey-plan.

Solution

(i) Time Rate Plan

Time wages = TT × TR = 48 × 20 = ₹ 960

Earnings per hour ₹ 20.

(ii) Piecework with guaranteed weekly wages

$$\text{Normal Piece rates} = \frac{\text{Normal wage rate per hour}}{\text{Standard output per hour}}$$

$$= \frac{20}{3} = ₹6.67$$

Note: Standard output per 20 minutes = 1 unit.

Standard out per hour = 3 units.

Piecerate wages = Output × Piece rate
= 160 × 6.67 = ₹1067.20

Guaranteed weekly wages = TT × TR
= 48 × 20 = ₹ 960.

Worker will be paid higher of the above.

Earning payable to worker = ₹ 1,067.20
Earnings per hour = 1067.20 ÷ 48 = ₹ 22.23.

(iii) Rowan plan

Estimated time per unit	20 minutes
Add: 10% time for incentive scheme	2 minutes
Standard time	**22 minutes**
Standard time for actual output = $\frac{22 \times 160}{60}$	58.67 hours
Time taken	48.00 hours
Time saved	**10.67 hours**
Time wages = TT×TR= 48 × 20	₹960.00
Bonus = TS/ST×TT×TR=10.67/58.67×48 × 20	₹174.59
Total earnings	**₹1,134.59**

Earnings per hour = 1,134.59 ÷ 48 = ₹ 23.64.

(iv) Halsey Plan

Time wages = TT×TR= 48 × 20	₹960.00
Bonus = TS×TR×$\frac{1}{2}$ = 10.67 × 20 × $\frac{1}{2}$	₹106.70
Total earnings	**₹1,066.70**

Earnings per hour = 1,066.70 ÷ 48 = ₹ 22.22.

Illustration-12

(Halsey and Rowan schemes - Comparative cost statement)

A worker takes 10 hours to complete a job under a scheme of payment by result. Same worker takes 15 hours to complete the job under time rate system. His wage rate is ₹ 20 per hour. Materials cost for the job is ₹ 200 and overhead are recovered at 50% of direct wages. Calculate the factory cost of the job under (a) Rowan and (b) Halsey plans.

Solution

Standard time	-	15 hours
Time taken	-	10 hours
Time saved	-	5 hours

Earnings of workers				
Particulars	**(a) Rowan Plan**		**(b) Halsey Plan**	
Time wages	TT×TR= 10 × 20	₹200.00		₹200
Bonus	TS/ST×TT×TR 5/15 × 10 × 20	₹66.67	$TS \times TR \times \frac{1}{2}$ $5 \times 20 \times \frac{1}{2}$	₹50
Total earnings		**₹266.70**		**₹250**

Comparative cost statement of the Job		
Particulars	**(a) Rowan Plan**	**(b) Halsey Plan**
Direct materials	₹ 200.00	₹ 200
Direct wages	₹ 266.67	₹ 250
Prime cost	₹ 466.67	₹ 450
Overheads: 50% of Direct wages	₹ 133.33	₹ 125
Factory cost	600.00	575

Illustration-13

(Accelerated premium bonus scheme)

A worker takes 110 hours to do a job for which standard time allowed is 200 hours. His day wage rate is ₹ 18 per hour. He is paid bonus for time saved on a sliding scale as under:

(a) Within first 10% savings in standard time, the bonus is 30% of the time saved.

(b) Within second 10% savings in standard time, the bonus is 40% of the time saved.
(c) Within third 10% of savings in standard time, the bonus is 50% of the time saved.
(d) Within the fourth 10% of savings in standard time, the bonus is 60% of the time saved.
(e) For savings over 40% of standard time, the bonus is 75% of the time saved.

Solution

Standard time	-	200 hours
Time taken	-	110 hours
Time saved	-	90 hours

Computation of workers earnings

Time wages = TT×TR= 110 × 18	=	₹1,980
Bonus		
(a) For first 10% savings in standard time (i.e. for 20 hours)= $20 \times 18 \times \frac{30}{100}$	=	₹108
(b) For second 10% savings in standard time (i.e. next 20 hours)= $20 \times 18 \times \frac{40}{100}$	=	₹144
(c) For third 10% savings in standard time (i.e. next 20 hours)= $20 \times 18 \times \frac{50}{100}$	=	₹180
(d) For fourth 10% savings in standard time (i.e. next 20 hours)= $20 \times 18 \times \frac{60}{100}$	=	₹216
(e) For savings in excess of 40% in standard time (i.e. next 10 hours) = $10 \times 18 \times \frac{75}{100}$	=	₹135
Total earnings	=	**₹ 2763**

Illustration-14

(Rowan and Halsey plan - Computation of time taken)

The standard time for a job is 50 hours. The hourly rate of guaranteed wages is ₹9. Because of savings in time, a worker x gets an hourly wages of ₹10.80 under Rowan premium bonus system. For the same savings in time calculate the hourly rate of wages a worker 'Y' will get under Halsey premium bonus system assuming 50 percent bonus to worker. **(CA-PEII, June 2009)**

Solution

Let time taken be = x

$$\text{Time saved} = \text{Standard time} - \text{Time taken}$$
$$= (50 - x) \text{ hours.}$$

$$\text{Bonus under Rowan premium Plan} = \frac{\text{Time saved}}{\text{Standard time}} \times \text{Time taken} \times \text{Time rate}$$

$$= \frac{(50 - x)}{50} \times x \times 9$$

$$\text{Time wages} = \text{TT} \times \text{TR}$$

$$= (x \times 9)$$

$$\text{Total earnings} = x \times 9 + \left(\frac{50 - x}{50}\right) x \times 9$$

$$\text{Effective hourly wages} = ₹\ 10.80$$

$$\text{Total earnings} = 10.80 \times x$$

$$\therefore \quad 10.80 \times x = x \times 9 + \frac{50 - x}{50} \times x \times 9$$

Dividing both sides by x we get

$$10.80 = 9 + \frac{50 - x}{50} \times 9$$

$$10.80 = \frac{450 + 450 - 9x}{50}$$

$$540 = 900 - 9x$$

$$9x = 900 - 540 = 360$$

$$x = \frac{360}{9} = 40$$

Hence time taken = 40 hours.

Earnings of 'Y' under Halsey Plan	
	₹
Time wages = TT×TR= 40 × 9	360
Bonus = TS×TR×$\frac{1}{2}$=10 × 9 × $\frac{1}{2}$	45
Total earnings	405

Effective Hourly Rate = 405 ÷ 40 = ₹10.125

Alternatively the time taken may be computed as below

Under Rowan Plan	
	₹
Effective hourly wages per hour	10.80
Hourly wages	9.00
Bonus per hour	**1.80**

$$\text{Rate of bonus} = \frac{\text{Bonus}}{\text{Hourly wages}} \times 100$$
$$= \frac{1.80}{9} \times 100 = 20\%$$

Under Rowan plan rate of bonus is equal to rate of savings in standard time. Hence time saved is 20% of standard time.

Standard time	50 hours
Less: Time saved	10 hours
∴**Time taken**	**40 hours**

Illustration-15

(Halsey and Rowan plans - computing hourly wage rate and materials cost)

Two workmen, Sachin and Saurav, produce the same product using the same material. Their normal wage rate is also the same. Sachin is paid bonus according to the Rowan system, while Sourav is paid bonus according to the Halsey system. The time allowed to make the product is 100 hours. Sachin takes 60 hours while Saurav takes 80 hours to complete the product. The factory OH rate is ₹ 10 per man-hour actually worked. The factory cost for the product of Sachin is ₹ 7,280 and for Saurav it is ₹ 7,600. You are required to (a) find the normal rate of wages and (b) compute the cost of materials. **(CA-PEII, May 98)**

Solution

(i) Let the materials cost be - x

(ii) Let the hourly wage rate be - y

(iii) Time wages = TT × TR
Sachin = 60 × y = 60y
Saurav = 80 × y = 80y

(iv) Bonus:

$$\text{Sachin (Rowan plan)} = \frac{\text{TS}}{\text{ST}} \times \text{TT} \times \text{RT}$$
$$= \frac{40}{100} \times 60 \times y = 24y$$

$$\text{Saurav (Halsey plan)} = \text{TS} \times \text{TR} \times \frac{1}{2}$$
$$= 20 \times y \times \frac{1}{2} = 10y$$

(v) Total earnings = Time wages + Bonus
Saurav = $60y + 24y = 84y$
Sachin = $80y + 10y = 90y$

(vi) Factory overheads = Time taken × OH rate
Saurav = 60 × 10 = ₹ 600
Sachin = 80 × 10 = ₹ 800.

(vii) Statement showing factory cost

Particulars	Sachin	Saurav
Materials	x	x
Wages	84y	90y
Prime cost	$x + 84y$	$x + 90y$
Factory OHS	600	800
Factory cost	$x + 84y + 600$	$x + 90y + 800$
Factory cost (given)	7,280	7,600

We form two equations from the above

$$\begin{array}{rrcl} \text{(i)} & x + 84y + 600 & = & 7{,}280 \\ \text{(ii)} & x + 90y + 800 & = & 7{,}600 \\ \hline \text{Subtracting (ii)} - \text{(i)} & (-)6y(-)200 & = & (-)320 \end{array}$$

$$y = \frac{120}{6} = 20$$

Time rate = ₹ 20 per hour.

Cost of materials - taking equation (i) substitute value of y - we get value of materials.

$$x + 84y + 600 = 7{,}280$$
$$x + 84 \times 20 + 600 = 7{,}280$$
$$x + 1{,}680 + 600 = 7{,}280$$
$$x = 7{,}280 - 1{,}680 - 600$$
$$x = 5{,}000$$

Value of materials is ₹ 5,000

Wages

$$\text{Saurav} = 84y = 84 \times 20 = 1{,}680$$
$$\text{Sachin} = 90y = 90 \times 20 = 1{,}800$$

Comparative Cost Sheet		
Particulars	**Sachin** ₹	**Saurav** ₹
Materials	5,000	5,000
Wages	1,680	1,800
Prime cost	6,680	6,800
Factory OHS	600	800
Factory cost	7,280	7,600

Illustration-16

(Comparative cost under Halsey and Rowan plan)

The finishing shop of a company employs 60 direct workers. Each worker is paid ₹400 as wages per week of 40 hours. When necessary overtime is worked upto a maximum of 15 hours per week per worker at time rate plus one-half as premium.

The current output on an average is 6 units per man-hour which may be regarded as standard output. If bonus scheme is introduced it is expected that the output will increase to 8 units per man hour. The workers will, if necessary, continue to work overtime upto the specified limit although no premium or incentives will be paid.

The company is considering introduction of either Halsey or Rowan scheme of wages incentive system. The budgeted weekly output is 19,200 units.

The selling price is ₹ 11 per unit and the direct materials cost is ₹ 8 per unit. The variable overheads amount to ₹ 0.50 per direct labour hour and the fixed overhead is ₹ 9,000 per week.

Prepare a statement to show the effect on the company's weekly profit of the proposal to introduce (a) Halsey scheme and (b) Rowan scheme. **(CA-Inter, May 2002)**

Solution

Computation of wages

(i)

Present system	
Budgeted output	19,200 units
Output per hour	6 units
∴ Total production hours = 19,200 ÷ 6	3,200 hours
Normal weekly manhours (60×40)	2,400 hours
Overtime hours	800 hours

Normal time wages = 2,400×60	₹24,000
Add: Overtime wages = $\frac{400}{40} \times 800 \times 1\frac{1}{2}$	₹12,000
Total wages	**₹36,000**

(ii)

Halsey Schemes	
Budgeted output	19,200 units
Budgeted time $\left(\frac{19{,}200}{6}\right)$	3,200 hours
Actual time taken $\frac{19{,}200}{8}$	2,400 hours
Time saved	800 hours

Earnings	
	₹
Time wages = TT×TR= 2,400 × 10	24,000
Bonus = TS×TR×$\frac{1}{2}$=800 × 10 × $\frac{1}{2}$	4,000
Total earnings	**28,000**

(iii)

Rowan Scheme	
	₹
Earnings	₹
Time wages = TT×TR = 2,400 × 10	24,000
Bonus = $\frac{TS}{ST}$×TT×TR =$\frac{800}{3{,}200}$ × 2,400 × 10	6,000
Total earnings	**30,000**

Comparative Statement showings profit under various Schemes			
Particulars	**Present**	**Halsey scheme** ₹	**Rowan Scheme** ₹
D. Materials (19,200 × 8)	1,53,600	1,53,600	1,53,600
D. Wages	36,000	28,000	30,000
Prime Cost	1,89,600	1,81,600	1,83,600
Variable overhead	1,600	1,200	1,200
Fixed overhead	9,000	9,000	9,000
Total Cost	2,00,200	1,91,800	1,93,800
Profit (BF)	11,000	19,400	17,400
Sales (19,200 × 11)	2,11,200	2,11,200	2,11,200

Illustration-17

(Straight piece rate, Time rate and Taylor's differential piece rate systems)

Standard Production - 6 units per hour
Normal time rate - ₹ 18 per hour.

In a 9 hour day 'A' produces 50 units, 'B' produces 54 units and 'C' produces 60 units. From the above information compute the earnings of workers under (i) Straight Piece Rate System, (ii) Time Rate System and (iii) Taylor's Differential Piece Rate System.

Differentials to be applied

1. 80% of piece rate below standard.
2. 120% of piece rate at or above standard.

Solution

(i) Straight Piece Rate System

$$\text{Normal piece rate} = \frac{\text{Normal wages per hour}}{\text{Standard output per hour}}$$

$$= \frac{18}{6} = ₹3$$

Earnings = Output × Normal piece rate

Worker 'A' = 50 × 3 = ₹150

Worker 'B' = 54 × 3 = ₹162

Worker 'C' = 60 × 3 = ₹180

(ii) Time Rate System

Earnings = TT × TR

Worker 'A' = 9 × 18 = ₹162

Worker 'B' = 9 × 18 = ₹162

Worker 'C' = 9 × 18 = ₹162

(iii) Taylor's Differential Piece Rate System

Standard production per day = 9 × 6 = 54 units.

Earnings:

Worker 'A' - his output is below standard and will be paid at 80% of normal piece rate.

Earnings = Output × Low price rate
= 50 × 2.40 = ₹120

Worker 'B' - His output is equal to standard and will be paid at high piece rate.

Earnings = 54 × 3.60 = ₹194.40

Worker 'C' - His output is above standard and will be paid at high piece rate.

Earnings = Output × High piece rate
= 60 × 3.60 = ₹216

Note:

1. Low piece rate = Normal piece rate × $\frac{80}{100}$

$= 3 \times \frac{80}{100} =$ ₹2.40

2. High piece rate = Normal piece rate × $\frac{120}{100}$

$= 3 \times \frac{120}{100} =$ ₹3.60

Illustration-18

(Piece rate, Differential rate, Halsey and Rowan plans)

From the following particulars you are required to work out the earnings of a worker for a week under (a) Straight piece rate, (b) Differential piece rate, (c) Halsey premium scheme (50% sharing) and (d) Rowan premium scheme.

Weekly working hours	-	48
Hourly wage rate	-	₹7.50

Piece rate per unit	-	₹3.00
Normal time taken per piece	-	20 minutes
Normal output per week	-	120 pieces
Actual output for the week	-	150 pieces

Differential piece rate - 80% of piece rate when output is below normal and 120% piece rate when output is above normal. **(ICWA-Inter)**

Solution

(a) Straight piece rate:

$$\text{Earnings} = \text{Output} \times \text{Normal piece}$$
$$= 150 \times 3 = ₹450$$

(b) Differential piece rate

$$\text{Low piece rate} = \text{Normal piece rate} \times \frac{80}{100}$$
$$= 3 \times \frac{80}{100} = ₹2.40$$
$$\text{High piece rate} = \text{Normal piece rate} \times \frac{120}{100}$$
$$= 3 \times \frac{120}{100} = ₹3.60$$

Since the worker output is above standard he will be paid at high piece rate.

$$\text{Earnings} = \text{Output} \times \text{High piece rate}$$
$$= 150 \times 3.60 = ₹540$$

(c) Halsey Premium Scheme

Standard time for actual output $= \frac{150 \times 20}{60}$	50 hours
Time taken	48 hours
Time saved	**2 hours**

Earnings	
	₹
Time wages = TT×TR= 48 × 7.50	360.00
Bonus $= \text{TS} \times \text{TR} \times \frac{1}{2} = 2 \times 7.50 \times \frac{1}{2}$	7.50
Total earnings	**367.50**

d) Rowan Premium Scheme

	₹
Earnings–Time wages = TT×TR= 48 × 7.50	360.00
Bonus = $\frac{TS}{ST}$ ×TT×TR=$\frac{2}{50}$ × 48 × 7.50	14.40
Total earnings	**374.00**

Illustration-19

(Emerson's efficiency scheme)

A Ltd is paying its workers under Emerson's efficiency plan. The standard output fixed for a week of 48 hours is 500 units. Hourly wage rate is ₹12. The output of workers during the week are: worker A - 300 units, worker 'B' - 450 units, Worker 'C' - 500 units and worker 'D' 550 units. The daily wage rate is paid without bonus to workers who show upto $66\frac{2}{3}$ percent of the standard. Beyond this there is a bonus payable in a graded scale in a fixed ratio to the increased output as follows:

Efficiency	Bonus
90%	10%
100%	20%

Further increase of bonus by 1% for every 1% further rise in efficiency. Find out the weekly earnings of workers A, B, C and D.

Solution

$$\text{Workers efficiency } \% = \frac{\text{Actual output}}{\text{Standard output}} \times 100$$

$$\text{Worker 'A'} = \frac{300}{500} \times 100 = 60\%$$

$$\text{Worker 'B'} = \frac{450}{500} \times 100 = 90\%$$

$$\text{Worker 'C'} = \frac{500}{500} \times 100 = 100\%$$

$$\text{Worker 'D'} = \frac{550}{500} \times 100 = 110\%$$

Statement showing earnings of workers				
	A ₹	B ₹	C ₹	D ₹
Time wages (TT × TR) = (48 × 12)	576	576	576	576
Bonus (Time wages × Bonus %)	Nil	$\left(576 \times \frac{10}{100}\right)$ = 57.60	$\left(576 \times \frac{20}{100}\right)$ =115.20	$\left(576 \times \frac{30}{100}\right)$ = 172.80
Total earnings	576	633.60	691.20	748.80

Illustration-20

(Computation of earnings)

An employee working under a bonus scheme saves 10 hours in a job for which standard time is 60 hours. Calculate the rate per hour worked and wages payable to him if incentive bonus of 10% on the hourly rate is payable when standard (namely 100% efficiency) is achieved, and a further incentive of 1% on hourly rate for each 1% in excess of that 100% efficiency is payable. Assume that normal rate of payment is ₹ 5 per hour. **(B.Com., Madras University)**

Solution

$$\text{Efficiency \%} = \frac{\text{Standard time}}{\text{Time Taken}} \times 100$$
$$= \frac{60}{50} \times 100 = 120\%$$

Worker will get a bonus of = 30% on hourly rate.

	₹
Earnings	₹
Time wages = TT×TR = 50 × 5	250
Bonus =250 × $\frac{30}{100}$	75
Total earnings	**325**

Earnings per hour = 325 ÷ 50 = ₹6.50.

Illustration-21

(Bonus at slab rates)

The standard production in a factory is 10 units per day of 8 hours. The wage is ₹6 per day. Bonus rated on efficiency is paid according to a scale as follows:

Level of efficiency	Bonus %
upto 60% of standard	Nil
above 60% and upto 75%	5%
above 75% and upto 90%	10%
above 90% and upto 100%	15%

For an increase of every 1% efficiency beyond 100% the bonus also rises by 1%. Output of 3 workers on a day was as follows:

A - 40 units
B - 75 units
C - 100 units

Calculate the earnings of the workers. **(B.Com., Madras University)**

Solution

Standard production per hour = 10 units.

Standard production per day of 8 hours = 10 × 8 = 80 units

$$\text{Workers efficiency } \% = \frac{\text{Actual output}}{\text{Standard output}} \times 100$$

$$\text{Worker 'A'} = \frac{40}{80} \times 100 = 50\%$$

$$\text{Worker 'B'} = \frac{75}{80} \times 100 = 93.75\%$$

$$\text{Worker 'C'} = \frac{100}{80} \times 100 = 125\%$$

Workers earnings

Worker 'A'	
	₹
Time wages per day	6.00
Bonus (efficiency below 60%)	Nil
Total earnings	**6.00**

Worker 'B'	
	₹
Time wages per day	6.00
Bonus-15% of time wages	0.90
Total earnings	**6.90**

Worker 'C'	
	₹
Time wages per day	6.00
Bonus-(15 + 25) = 40% of time wages	2.40
Total earnings	**8.40**

Illustration-22

(Merrick's multiple piece rate system)

Calculate the earnings of three workers A, B and C under Merrick's multiple piece rate system given the following:

Standard production - 120 units
Production of 'A' - 90 units
Production of 'B' - 100 units
Production of 'C' - 130 units
Ordinary piece rate - ₹0.10

(B.Com., Madras University)

Solution

$$\text{Worker's efficiency \%} = \frac{\text{Actual output}}{\text{Standard output}} \times 100$$

$$\text{Worker 'A'} = \frac{90}{120} \times 100 = 75\%$$

$$\text{Worker 'B'} = \frac{100}{120} \times 100 = 83.33\%$$

$$\text{Worker 'C'} = \frac{130}{120} \times 100 = 108.33\%$$

Earnings of workers

Worker 'A'

Efficiency below 83% paid at normal piece rate.

$$\text{Earnings} = \text{Output} \times \text{Normal piece rate}$$
$$= 90 \times 0.10 = ₹9.00$$

Worker 'B'

His efficiency is above 83% but below 100%. He is paid at 110% of normal piece rate.

$$\text{Earnings} = \text{Output} \times \text{Normal piece rate} \times 110\%$$
$$= 100 \times 0.10 \times \frac{110}{100} = ₹11.00$$

Worker 'C'

His efficiency is above 100%. He is paid at 120% of normal piece rate.

$$\text{Earnings} = \text{Output} \times \text{Normal piece rate} \times 120\%$$
$$= 130 \times 0.10 \times \frac{120}{100} = ₹15.60$$

Illustration-23

(Group Bonus Scheme)

In a manufacturing concern, 20 men work in a group. The concern follows a group bonus system whereby each workman belonging to the group is paid a bonus on the excess output over the hourly production standard of 250 pieces, in addition to is normal wages at hourly rate. The excess of production over standard is expressed as a percentage and two-thirds of this percentage is considered to be the share of workman and is applied on the notional hourly rate of ₹ 6 considered only for the purpose of computation of bonus. The output for a week are stated below:

Days	Man hours worked	Output (in pieces)
Monday	160	48,000
Tuesday	172	53,000
Wednesday	164	40,000
Thursday	168	52,000
Friday	160	46,000
Saturday	160	42,000
Total	984	2,81,000

You are required to:

1. Work out the amount of bonus for the week and the average rate at which each workman is paid the same.
2. Compute the total wages including bonus payable to Ram Jadav who worked for 48 hours at an hourly rate of ₹ 2.50 and to Francis Williams who worked for 52 hours at an hourly rate of ₹ 3. **(ICWA-Inter)**

Solution

$$\text{Standard output } (984 \times 250) = 2{,}46{,}000 \text{ units}$$
$$\text{Actual output} = 2{,}81{,}000 \text{ units}$$
$$\text{Excess production} = 35{,}000 \text{ units}$$

$$\%\text{ of excess production} = \frac{35{,}000}{2{,}46{,}000} \times 100 = 14.22\%$$

$$\text{Bonus } \% = 14.22 \times \frac{2}{3}$$
$$= 9.49\%$$

$$\text{Bonus per hour} = 6 \times 9.49\%$$
$$= ₹0.57$$

$$\text{Bonus for the week} = 984 \times 0.57$$
$$= ₹560.88$$

Earnings of workers:

Ram Jadav-

Time wages = 48 hrs × ₹2.50 = ₹120.00
Bonus = 48 hrs × ₹0.57 = ₹27.36
Total = ₹147.36

Francis Williams-

Time wages = 52 hrs × ₹3.00 = ₹156.00
Bonus = 52 hrs × ₹0.57 = ₹29.67
Total = ₹185.67

Illustration-24

(Allocation of labour cost to jobs)

Calculate the earnings of 'A' and 'B' from the following particulars for a month and allocate the labour cost to each job x, y and z.

		Worker A ₹	Worker B ₹
(i)	Basic wages	200	300
(ii)	Dearness allowance	50%	50%
(iii)	Contribution P.F. (on basic wages)	8%	8%
(iv)	Contribution to employee's state insurance (On basic wages)	2%	2%
(v)	Overtime (hours)	10	-

The normal working hours for the month are 200. Overtime is paid at double the total of normal wages and dearness allowance. Employer's contribution to state insurance and provident fund are at equal rate with employee's contribution. The two workers were employed on jobs x, y and z in the following proportions:

	Jobs		
	x	y	z
Worker 'A'	40%	30%	30%
Worker 'B'	50%	20%	30%

Overtime was done on job y.

Solution

Statement showing earnings of workers		
	A ₹	B ₹
Basic wages	200	300
Dearness allowance	100	150
Overtime wages $\left[\frac{(\text{Basic wages} + \text{DA}) \times 2 \times 10}{200}\right]$	30	-
Gross wages	330	450

Statement showing labour cost		
	A ₹	B ₹
Gross wages (excluding overtime)	300	450
Employer's contribution to PF	16	24
Employer's contribution to ESI	4	6
Total	320	480
Labour cost per hour	320/200 = ₹1.60	480/200 = ₹2.40

Statement showing allocation of labour cost to jobs				
	Jobs			Total
	x	y	z	
Worker 'A' (4 : 3 : 3)	120	90	90	300
Overtime wages	-	30	-	30
Worker 'B' (5 : 2 : 3)	225	90	135	450
Total	345	210	225	780

Illustration-25

(Computation of Bonus to managers and workers)

Components for an assembly are produced under the control of the production manager. These are assembled and sold under the supervision of the sales manager. The production manager is entitled for a bonus payment for himself at 1/8th and the workers 7/8th of the difference between the notional value and cost of production of the delivered components. The notional value is assessed at ₹ 5,18,500 for the components issued to assembly. The sales manager is entitled to a bonus of $2\frac{1}{2}$% of the profits for himself and $12\frac{1}{2}$% is distributed among his sales staff. The sales during the period amount to ₹ 6,50,000.

From the above-mentioned particulars, show the calculations involved in arriving at the bonus for both managers and the staff. Also find the impact of such bonus as a percentage of sales.

	₹
Raw materials at the beginning of the period	22,800
Raw materials at the end of the period	16,400
Purchases during the period	2,48,600
Wages - Production	46,200
Wages - Assembly	18,100
Overheads - Production	2,12,500
Overheads - Sales	45,200
Credit for scrap realisation pertaining to components	8,700
Work-in-progress of production at the beginning	12,500
Work-in-progress of production at the end	18,200
Completed assemblies at the beginning	36,000
Completed assemblies at the end	24,030
Net realisation on assemblies sold	6,50,000

(ICWA - Inter)

Solution

Computation of cost of production and bonus to production manager and workers:

Cost of Materials Consumed		₹
Purchase of raw materials	2,48,600	
Add: Opening stock of raw materials	22,800	
	2,71,400	
Less: Closing stock of raw materials	16,400	2,55,000

Wages-Production		46,200
Prime Cost		3,01,200
Production overheads		2,12,500
Add: Work-in-progress at the beginning		12,500
		5,26,200
Less: Work-in-progress at the end	18,200	
Scrap realised pertaining to components	8,700	26,900
Cost of production (before bonus)		4,99,300
Notional value of cost of production (given)		5,18,500
Bonus to production manager and workers		19,200
Bonus to production manger 19,200 × 1/8		2,400
Bonus to workers 19200 × 7/8		16,800
Total production bonus		19,200

Statement showing profit and bonus to Sales Manager and Sales staff	
	₹
Cost of production of components	5,18,500
Wages - Assembly	18,100
Over heads - Sales	45,200
Completed assemblies at the beginning	36,000
	6,17,800
Less: Completed assemblies at the end	24,030
Cost of sales	5,93,770
Profit (before bonus)	56,230
Sales	6,50,000
Bonus to sales manager $56{,}230 \times \frac{2.5}{100}$	1,406
Bonus to sales staff $56{,}230 \times \frac{12.5}{100}$	7,029
Total sales bonus	8,435

Total Bonus

	₹
Production bonus	19,200
Sales bonus	8,435
Total bonus	27,635

$$\% \text{ of Bonus on Sales} = \frac{27,635}{6,50,000} \times 100 = 4.25\%$$

Illustration-26

(Suggestion of suitable incentive scheme)

Zed Limited is working by employing 50 skilled workers. It is considering the introduction of incentive scheme - either Halsey scheme (with 50% bonus) or Rowan scheme of wage payment for increasing the labour productivity to cope up the increasing demand for the product by 40%. It is believed that proposed incentive scheme could bring about an average 20% increase over the present earnings of the workers; it could act as sufficient incentive for them to produce more.

Because of assurance, the increase in productivity has been observed as revealed by the figures for the month of April, 2004.

Hourly rate of wages (guaranteed)	30
Average time for producing one unit by one worker at the previous performance (This maybe taken as time allowed)	1.975 hours
Number of working days in the month	24
Number of working hours per day for each worker	8
Actual production during the month	6,120 units

Required:

(i) Calculate the effective rate of earnings under the Halsey scheme and Rowan scheme.
(ii) Calculate the savings to the Zed ltd in terms of direct labour cost per piece.
(iii) Advise Zed Ltd about the selection of the scheme to fulfil its assurance.

(CA-Interm May 2004)

Solution

Halsey Scheme - Total wages payable	
Standard time for actual production = 6,120 units × 1.975 hours	12,087 hours

Actual time worked (24 days×8 hours×50 workers)	9,600 hours
Time saved	2,487 hours
Bonus payable under Halsey plan $= \text{Time saved} \times \text{Time rate} \times \frac{50}{100}$ $= 2487 \times 30 \times \frac{50}{100}$	₹37,305
Time wages = Time taken×Time rate = 9600×30	₹2,88,000
Total wages	**₹3,25,305**

$$\% \text{ increase in wages} = \frac{37,305}{2,88,000} \times 100 = 12.95\%$$

Rowan scheme - Total wages payable	
	₹
$\text{Bonus} = \frac{TS}{ST} \times TT \times TR = \frac{2,487}{12,087} \times 9,600 \times 30$	59,258.38
Time wages	2,88,000.00
Total wages	**3,47,258.38**

$$\% \text{ increase in wages} = \frac{59,258.38}{2,88,000} \times 100 = 20.58\ \%$$

(i)

Effective hourly rate of wages	
	₹
Halsey plan = 3,25,305 ÷ 9,600	33.89
Rowan plan = 3,47,258.38÷ 9,600	36.17

(ii)

Savings in Labour cost	
	₹
Labour cost per unit	
Under time rate system (per unit) = 30×1.975	59.25
Under Halsey plan = 3,25,305÷ 6,120	53.15
Savings in labour cost per unit:	
Under Halsey plan = 59.25 – 53.15	6.10
Under Rowan plan = 59.25 – 56.74	2.51

(iii) Recommendation

Savings under Halsey plan is more but it gives an increase in wages at 12.95% only. But workers are to be given an increase of 20% or more. Under Rowan scheme increase in wages is 20.58%. Hence Rowan scheme is recommended for implementation.]

6.4 EXERCISES

I. Objective Type Questions

A. State whether the following statements are true or false

(i) There are two principal wages payment systems.

(ii) There is incentive for hard work under the time rate system.

(iii) Piece rate system is also called payment by results.

(iv) Time rate system is suitable if efforts of individual workers cannot be measured.

(v) Piece rate system motivates the workers to produce more.

(vi) High wages means higher cost of production per unit.

(vii) Piece rate system guarantees minimum wages.

(viii) A flat rate of bonus is given for time saved under Rowan scheme.

(ix) Bonus is equal under Halsey plan and Rowan plan when time saved is equal to 50% of time saved.

(x) Under Rowan plan bonus declines when time saved exceeds 50% of standard time.

(xi) Amount of bonus increases faster under Rowan plan than under Halsey plan.

(xii) Priestman bonus system is applied when workers work as a team.

(xiii) Bonus for time saved is given to foreman also under Rowan plan.

(xiv) Efficiency of individual workers is recognised under group bonus system.

(xv) Payment of bonus on the basis of profit is voluntary in India.

(xvi) Premium bonus schemes benefit only employees.

(xvii) There are two piece rates under Merricks multiple piece rate system.

(xviii) Gantt task and bonus scheme is a combination of time rate and piece rate systems.

(xix) Under Emerson's efficiency plan no bonus is given for efficiency below 100% of the standard.

(xx) Bonus at a fixed rate is paid for time saved under Halsey plan.

[**Ans:** True - (i), (iii), (iv), (v), (ix), (x), (xi), (xii); (xviii), (xx)
False - (ii), (vi), (vii), (viii), (xiii), (xiv), (xv), (xvi), (xvii), (xix)]

B. Fill in the blanks

(i) The two principal wages payment systems are (a) Time Rate System and (b) ________.

(ii) The wages payment system is suitable when work is of clerical nature and involves mental work is ________.

(iii) The bonus system used when output of individual workers cannot be measured is called ________.

(iv) Gantt task and bonus system is a combination of ________ and ________.

(v) Number of piece rates applied is ________ in Taylor's differential piece rate system.

(vi) There is no incentive for higher efficiency and hard work under ________ system.

(vii) Under Emerson's efficiency scheme no bonus is given upto ________ % of efficiency.

(viii) For efficiency upto ________ %, basic piece rate is applied under Merrick's multiple piece rate system.

(ix) Individual efficiency of workers is not considered under ________ bonus system.

(x) Towne plan is a ________ bonus system.

[**Ans:** (i) Piece Rate System, (ii) Time rate System, (iii) Group bonus scheme), (iv) Time rate system, Piece rate system, (v) Two, (vi) Time rate, (vii) 66 2/3, (viii) 83, (ix) group, (x) group.]

II. Theory Questions

A. Short answer type questions

1. Explain the traditional wage payment systems.
2. What is time rate system?
3. What is straight piece rate system?
4. What is differential piece rate system?
5. What is Taylor's Differential piece rate system?
6. What is group bonus system?

7. When can workers be remunerated under piece rate system?

8. When the workers cannot be remunerated under piece rate system?

9. Where time rate system is suitable?

10. Explain Halsey plan.

11. What is 'profit sharing scheme'?

12. Explain 'co-partnership' system.

B. Long answer type questions

1. Explain the merits and demerits of time rate system and piece rate system.

2. What are the features of a good wage payment system.

3. Explain Halsey plan and Rowan plan. What are their merits and demerits and also compare the two plans.

4. What are the characteristics of a good incentive scheme?

5. What is Taylor's differential piece rate system and Merick's multiple piece rate system. Explain their merits and demerits and compare them.

6. Discuss the relative merits of paying bonus to an individual worker according to his efficiency and a similar payment to a 'gang' or 'group' of workers. **(CA-Inter)**

7. What precautionary steps are to be taken when an incentive wage payment scheme is to be introduced for the first time in a manufacturing organisation? **(B.Com., Andhra)**

8. "Increased productivity as a result of premium bonus plans benefits both employer and employees". Discuss **(ICWA-Inter)**

9. Under the Rowan premium system, a less efficient worker can obtain the same bonus as a high efficient worker - Discuss **(ICWA-Inter)**

10. Out of Halsey and Rowan plans of wage payment which method will be more beneficial to a worker who saves less than 50% of the standard time? Illustrate your answer? **(CS-Inter)**

11. Write short note on: (a) Profit sharing schemes, (b) Co-partnership schemes, and (c) Group bonus schemes.

12. Write short notes on: (i) Halsey plan, (ii) Rowan plan, (iii) Taylor's differential piece rate system, (vi) Merrick's multiple piece rate system.

III. Practical Problems

(A) Short answer type questions

1. From the following information compute the earnings of a worker under

   (i) Time rate system and
   (ii) Halsey Plan

Standard time	20 hours
Time taken	15 hours
Hourly wage rate	₹20

   [**Answer:** (i) ₹300, (ii) ₹350]

2. Compute bonus under Rowan Scheme

Standard time	16 hours
Time taken	10 hours
Time rate	₹18 per hour

   [**Answer:** ₹67.50]

3. Calculate time saved.

Actual production	75 units
Standard time per unit	10 minutes
Time taken	8 hours

   [**Ans:** 4.5 hours]

4. From the following compute standard time:

Actual production	120 units.
Time given under straight piece the system	15 minutes

   Time given is increased by 20% under incentive schemes

   [**Ans:** 36 hours]

5. Compute the earnings of a worker under Barth scheme:

Standard time	25 hours
Time taken	18 hours
Time rate	₹12 per hour

   [**Ans:** ₹254.56]

6. From the following information calculate the share of group bonus to each worker in the group:

   Group bonus ₹ 2,000, Time wages of workers in the group are - Worker 'A' ₹ 1500, Worker 'B' ₹ 2,000, Worker 'C' ₹ 1800, Worker 'D' ₹ 2,200 and Worker 'E' ₹ 2,500.

   [**Ans:** Bonus to A - ₹300, B - ₹400, C - ₹360, D - ₹440, E - ₹500]

7. Five men work as a team. Group piece rate is ₹13,500. Time worked and their individual time rates of the workers are as follows

   Worker 'A' - 80 hours at ₹30 per hour

   Worker 'B' - 75 hours at ₹25 per hour

   Worker 'C' - 60 hours at ₹40 per hour

   Worker 'D' - 50 hours at ₹45 per hour

   Worker 'E' - 45 hours at ₹40 per hour

   Compute group bonus.

   [**Ans:** Group bonus ₹2,775]

8. From the following compute the total bonus and the bonus payable of worker and foreman under Bedeaux point premium plan:

Time allowed	900 'B's
Time taken	540 'B's
Time rate	₹15 per hour.

   [**Ans:** Total bonus ₹ 90, bonus to worker (75%) ₹ 67.50, bonus to foremen (25%) ₹ 22.50]

B. Comprehensive Practical Problems

1. *(Time Rate, Piece rate, Halsey and Rowan plan)*

   Calculate the earnings of a worker from the following information under (a) time rate method (b) piece rate method (c) Halsey plan and (d) Rowan plan.

Standard time	40 hours
Time taken	30 hours
Hourly wage rate	₹10 per hour

   [**Ans:** (a) ₹300, (b) ₹400, (c) ₹350 (d) ₹375]

2. *(Rowan, Halsey and Hasley-Weir plans)*

   Calculate the earnings of a worker under (a) Rowan premium bonus system (b) Halsey premium bonus system (c) Halsey-Weir plan (30% to workman), from the following particulars:

Hourly rate of wages ₹7.50
Standard time to produce 1 dozen articles is 5 hours.
Actual time taken to produce 10 dozen articles is 40 hours.

[**Ans:** a) ₹360, (b) ₹337.50, (c) ₹322.50]

3. *(Time Rate, Piece rate with guaranteed weekly wages, Rowan and Halsey plans)*

   During one week the workman 'x' produced 200 articles. He received wages for guaranteed 44 hour week at the rate of ₹ 21 per hour. The estimated time to produce one unit is 15 minutes and under incentive scheme the time allowed is increased by 20%. Calculate his gross wages under each of the following methods of remuneration: (a) Time Rate, (b) Piece work rate with a guaranteed weekly wages (c) Rowan premium bonus (d) Halsey premium bonus.

   [**Ans:** (a) ₹924, (b) ₹1,050, (c) ₹1,170.40, (d) ₹1,092]

4. *(Straight piece rate and Taylor's differential piece rate)*

   Calculate the earnings of a worker under (i) Straight piece rate system and (ii) Taylors differential piece rate system, from the following particulars:

Normal hourly rate	₹24
Standard time per unit	- 30 seconds

   Differentials to be applied:

   90% of piece rate for below standard and
   110% of piece rate at or above standard.

   Worker 'A' produces 900 units per day and worker 'B' produces 1100 units per day.

   [**Ans:** (i) A - ₹180, B - ₹220, (ii) A - ₹162, B - ₹242]

5. *(Accelerated premium scheme)* What will be the earnings of a worker at ₹5.50 per hour when he takes 140 hours to do a volume of work for which the standard time allowed is 200 hours. The plan of payment of bonus on a sliding scale is as under:

   (a) Within the first 10% saving in standard time, the bonus is 40% of the time saved.
   (b) Within the second 10% saving in standard time, the bonus is 50% of the time saved.
   (c) Within the third 10% saving in standard time, the bonus is 60% of the time saved.
   (d) Within the fourth 10% saving in standard time, the bonus is 70% of the time saved.
   (e) For the rest the bonus is 75% of the time saved.

   [**Ans:** ₹935]

6. *(Merrick's multiple piece rate system)*

   On the basis of the following information, calculate the earnings of A, B, C and D under Merrick's multiple piece rate system.

Standard production per hour	12 units.
Normal rate per hour	₹7.50

In a 8 hour day:

A produced 75 units, B produced 96 units.
C produced 90 units, D produced 100 units.

[**Ans:** A - ₹ 46.88, B - ₹ 66, C - ₹ 61.88, D - ₹ 75]

7. *(Merrick's multiple piece rate system)*

Calculate the earnings of workers A, B and C under straight piece rate system and Merrick's multiply piece rate system from the following particulars:

Normal rate per hour ₹5.40
Standard time per unit 1 minute **Output per day is as follows:**

Worker 'A'	390 units
Worker 'B'	450 units
Worker 'C'	600 units

Working hours per day are 8 hours.

(**Ans:** (i) Straight piece rate system A - ₹35.10, B - ₹40.50, C - ₹54 (ii) Merrick's multiple piece rate system A - ₹35.10, B - ₹44.55, C - ₹64.80)

8. *(Gantt's task and bonus plan)*

From the information given below, calculate the earnings of three workers x, y and z under Gantt's task and bonus plan:

(a) Time rate ₹15 per hour.
(b) High task per day of 8 hours - 80 units.
(c) High piece rate ₹2 per unit.
(d) Day's output: x - 70 units, y - 80 units, z - 90 units

(B.Com., Karnataka)

[**Ans:** x - ₹120, y - ₹144, z - ₹180]

9. *(Emerson's efficiency plan)*

In a manufacturing concern the daily wages guaranteed for workers is ₹ 40. The standard output for the month is 1,000 articles representing 100% efficiency. The rate of wages is paid without bonus to those workers who show upto $66\frac{2}{3}\%$ efficiency. Beyond this, bonus is payable in a graded scale.

Efficiency	Bonus
90%	10%
100%	20%

Further rise of 1% of bonus for every 1% further rise in efficiency. Calculate the total earnings of A, B, C and D who have worked 26 days in a month and produced as follows: A - 500 units, B - 900 units, C - 1,000 units, D - 1,200 units.

(B.Com., Mysore)

[**Ans:** A - ₹1,040; B - ₹1,144; C - ₹1,248; D - ₹1,456]

10. *(Bedeaux's point premium plan)*

Standard time for a job is 1,200 'B's
Time taken is 900 'B's
Time rate is ₹20 per hour

Calculate the earnings of the worker under Bedeaux's premium plan.

[**Ans:** ₹375]

11. *(Barth, Halsey and Rowan plan)*

Calculate the earnings of a worker under (a) Barth Scheme, (b) Halsey plan and (c) Rowan plan from the following information:

Standard time per unit	30 minutes
Actual output	40 units
Time taken	15 hours
Time rate	₹12 per hour

[**Ans:** (a) ₹207.85; (b) ₹210; (c) ₹225].

12. *(Accelerated premium system)*

The standard hours of job X is 100 hours. The job has been completed by Amar in 60 hours. Akbar in 70 hours and Anthony in 95 hours. The bonus system applicable to the job is as follows:

Percentage of time saved to time allowed	**Bonus**
Savings upto 10%	10% of time saved
Savings from 11% to 20%	15% of time saved
Savings from 21% to 40%	20% of time saved
Savings from 41% to 100%	25% of time saved

The rate of pay is ₹1 per hour. Calculate the total earnings of each workers and also the rate of earnings per hour. **(B.Com., Madras University)**

Ans:

	Amar	**Akbar**	**Anthony**
Total earnings	68	76	95.50
Earnings per hour	1.1333	1.0857	1.0052

13. *(Emerson's efficiency plan)*

    In a manufacturing company a daily wage rate guaranteed for a worker is ₹ 50 and the standard output fixed for the month is 1,000 articles representing 100% efficiency. The daily wage rate is paid without bonus to those workers who show upto 66 2/3% of the efficiency standard. Beyond this there is a bonus payable in a graded scale in a fixed ratio to the increased output as follows:

Efficiency	**Bonus Payable**
90%	10%
100%	20%

    Further increase of 1% for every 1% further increase in efficiency. Find out the earnings of A, B, C and D who have worked for 26 days in a month. Worker's output is : A - 500 articles, B - 900 articles, C - 1,000 articles and D - 1,100 articles.

    [**Ans:** Worker A - ₹1,300; Worker B - ₹1,430; Worker C -₹1,560; Worker D - ₹ 1,690]

14. *(Emerson's scheme modified)*

    An employee working under a bonus scheme saved 20 hours in a job for which the standard time is 80 hours. Calculate the rate per hour worked and wages payable to a worker, if incentive bonus of 15% on the hourly rate is payable when the standard time (namely 100% efficiency) is achieved and a further incentive bonus of 1% on hourly rate for each 1% in excess of 100% efficiency is payable. The actual hours worked are 60. Assume that the normal rate of payment is ₹ 15 per hour.

    [**Ans:** ₹1,335; Bonus% - 48.33%]

15. *(Computation of earnings and factory cost)*

    In an engineering works the standard time for a job is 16 hours and the basic wage is ₹ 1 per hour. A bonus scheme is instituted so that the worker is to receive normal rate for hours actually worked and for half of hours saved. Materials for the job cost ₹ 20 and factory overhead is charged on the basis of ₹ 2 per hour.

    Calculate the wages and effective earnings per hour if job is completed (a) in 12 hours and (b) in 14 hours.

    Also ascertain factory cost of the job on the same basis.

    (M.Com., Kanpur, Agra)

Ans:

	A	B
	₹	₹
(a) Total earnings	14	15
(b) Earnings per hour	1.17	1.07
(c) Factory cost	58	63

16. *(Merrick's multiple piece rate)*

The multiple piece rate plan is operated as follows:

(a) Basic price rate below 85% efficiency level.
(b) 110% of basic piece rate from 85% to below 100% efficiency level.
(c) 120% of basic piece rate at 100% efficiency level or more.

Minimum guaranteed day wages are equal to 70% efficiency level. Assuming that 100% of efficiency is 100 pieces per day and the piece rate is ₹ 1 per piece. Calculate the labour cost per piece at 20% intervals from 60% to 120% (including 100%) efficiency levels.

[**Ans:** Wages per piece at 60% efficiency level - ₹1.17, at 80% efficiency level ₹1.00; at 100% efficiency level ₹1.10, at 120% efficiency level ₹1.20]

17. *(Group bonus scheme)*

Ten men work as a group. When the weekly production of the group exceeds the standard - 200 piece per hour - each man in the group is paid a bonus for the excess production in addition to his wages at hourly rates.

The bonus is computed thus: the percentage of production in excess of the standard amount is found and one half this percentage is regarded as the men's share. Each man in the group is paid at the wage rate of ₹0.35 per hour. There is no relationship between the individual workman's hourly rate and the bonus rate.

The following is one week's record:

Day	**Hours worked**	**Production (units)**
Monday	90	22,100
Tuesday	88	20,600
Wednesday	90	24,200
Thursday	84	20,100
Friday	88	20,400
Saturday	40	10,200
Total	480	1,17,600

(a) Compute the rate and amount of bonus for the week;

(b) Ascertain the total pay of Jones, who worked $41\frac{1}{2}$ hours and was paid at ₹ 0.25 per hour and that of Smith, who worked $44\frac{1}{2}$ hours and was paid ₹ 0.30 per hour.

[**Ans:** (a) Rate of bonus per hour ₹ 0.0394; Amount of bonus ₹ 18.91; (b) Jones - ₹ 12.02; Smith - ₹ 15.10]

18. *(Allocation of labour cost to jobs)*

A worker is paid 50 paise per hour and the 5 days working week contains 42 hours. The daily allowance for approved absence from his place of work, maintenance of machine etc., is 12 minutes and his job card shows that his time chargeable during the week to various jobs is as follows:

Job No. 305	- 20 hours
Job No. 310	- 10 hours
Job No. 320	- 8 hours

The unascertained time is caused by a power failure. Show how his wages for the week would be dealt with in cost accounts. **(B.Com. (Hons.), Delhi University, 2003)**

Ans:

	₹
Wages chargeable to Job No. 305	10.00
Wages chargeable to Job No. 310	5.00
Wages chargeable to Job No. 320	4.00
Normal idle time (treated as OHS)	0.50
Abnormal idle time due to power failure transferred to costing P & L a/c	1.50
Total wages	21.00

19. *(Productivity Bonus)*

XYZ Co. employs its workers for a single shift of 8 hours per day for 25 days in a month. The company has recently fixed the standard output of 40 units per day per worker for a mass production item and introduced an incentive scheme to boost output. Details of wages payable to the workers are as follows:

(i) Basic wages: ₹3 per unit subject to a guaranteed minimum wages of ₹80 per day worked.
(ii) Dearness allowance : ₹40 per day worked.
(iii) Incentive bonus upto 80% efficiency : Nil
(iv) For efficiency above 80% : ₹50 for every 1% increase above 80%.

The details of performance of 2 workers for a particular month are as follows:

Workers	No. of days worked	Output (Units)
A	25	820
B	18	500

Calculate the total earnings of both the workers for the month.

(B.Com. Hons., Delhi University, 2004)

[**Ans:** A - ₹3,560; B - ₹2,220]

20. *(Computation of rate of wages and materials cost)*

In a factory Ram and Sham produce the same product using the same input of same material and at the same normal wage rate:

Bonus is paid to both of the them in the form of normal time wage adjusted by the proportion which time saved bears to the standard time for the completion of the product. The time allotted to the product is 50 hours. Ram takes 30 hours and Sham takes 40 hours to produce the product. The factory cost of the product for Ram is ₹ 3,100 and for Sham ₹ 3,280. The factory overhead rate is ₹ 12 per man hour.

Calculated (i) Normal wage rate, (ii) Cost of materials used for the product and, (iii) the input of material if the unit material cost is ₹ 16.

(B.Com. (Hons.), Delhi University, 1997)

[**Ans:** (i) ₹10 per hour, (ii) ₹2,320, (iii) 145 units.]

21. *(Computation of time taken and total earnings)*

A skilled worker in XYZ Ltd is paid a guaranteed wage rate of ₹ 30 per hour. The standard time per unit for a particular product is 4 hours. P, a machine man has been paid wages under the Rowan plan and he had earned an effective hourly rate of ₹ 37.50 on the manufacture of that product.

What could have been his total earnings and effective hourly rate, had he been put on Halsey Incentive scheme (50%)?

[**Ans:** Total earnings under Halsey Plan ₹105, effective hourly rate ₹35]

22. *(Bonus on the basis of cost reduction)*

Calculate the earnings of workers x and y from the following information:

Output by each worker	300 units
Standard conversion cost per unit	₹50

Overhead charged at 200% of wage rate hour. Time rate for A ₹ 25 per hour and for 'B' ₹ 30 per hour. Time taken to complete the jobs: Worker 'A' 150 hours and 'B' 140 hours.

There is an incentive system based on the reduction of conversion cost in the following scale:

Savings in conversion cost	**Bonus%**
Upto 10%	5% of wages
Upto 20%	10% of wages
Upto 40%	20% of wages

[**Ans:** x - ₹ 4,500, y - ₹ 4,620]

Hint:

	x	y
Time wages	3,750	4,200
Overheads	7,500	8,400
Actual conversion cost	11,250	12,600
Standard conversion cost	15,000	15,000
Reduction in conversion	3,750	2,400
% of reduction in conversion cost	25%	16%
Bonus % on wages	20%	10%
Bonus amount	750	420
Total earnings (Time wages + Bonus)	4,500	4,620

OVERHEADS: NATURE AND CLASSIFICATION

7

- Meaning
- Importance
- Classifications
  - Element-wise
  - Functional-wise
  - Controllability-wise
  - Behaviour-wise
- Segregation of Semi-Variable Expenses
- Collection and Codification
- Methods of codification

7.1 INTRODUCTION

7.1.1 Meaning

Total expenses incurred in a firm may be classified broadly into direct costs and indirect costs. Direct costs are those costs which are conveniently related to or traced to a product, a job order or services provided. Direct costs consists of direct materials, direct labour and direct expenses. Total of all direct expenses is called prime cost. All expenses other than direct expenses are grouped as indirect costs viz., indirect materials, indirect labour and indirect expenses. Total of all indirect expenses are called Overheads. Overheads can not be conveniently identified with or traced to or related to a product or a cost unit or a specific job order. Overheads are also known in other terms such as oncost, burden and supplementary cost. Overheads are in the nature of general expenses incurred commonly for two or more products, job orders or cost centres.

CIMA defines overhead costs as "Expenditure on labour, materials or services which cannot be economically identified with a specific saleable cost per unit".

7.1.2 Importance

In the past the term cost is used to mean only prime cost. Due to scientific inventions production is being carried on large scale. This necessitated the increased use of machines, mobilisation of large financial resources, employing professional managers for framing corporate policies and planning, transportation of materials and products, personnel management, marketing, adherence to various business laws, tax laws, labour laws etc. This resulted in incurring of large indirect costs like plant maintenance, technical consultancy, legal advices, secretarial services, and marketing research. It forms a large part of total cost incurred in a firm. To ascertain the correct cost of production, it is necessary to establish a detailed system for collection and accounting for overheads.

7.2 CLASSIFICATION OF OVERHEADS

Overheads cost can be classified under various basis. The basis of classification of overheads costs depends upon the type and nature of business, nature of product or services rendered. Overheads classification is shown in the following table:

A) Element-wise classification	B) Functional-wise classification	C) Controllability-wise classification	D) Behavior-wise classification
(i) Indirect materials	(i) Factory overheads	(i) Controllable overheads	(i) Fixed overheads
(ii) Indirect labour	(ii) Office and administration overheads	(ii) Uncontrollable overheads	(ii) Variable overheads
(iii) Indirect expenses	(iii) Selling overheads		(iii) Semi-variable overheads
	(iv) Distribution overheads		

A. Element-wise classification

(i) Indirect materials: Indirect materials are not exclusively incurred for a particular product, job or cost centre. Indirect materials do not form part of the body of finished products. It cannot be identified with a product, job or cost centre. Indirect materials cannot be allocated but can only be apportioned over products or cost centres. They are : stores consumed in repairs and maintenance, lubricants, cotton waste, stationery, packing materials, normal loss of materials, tools for general use etc. Some materials of small value may be directly identified with a product but for convenience and economy in accounting they are treated as indirect materials e.g., sewing threads in garments, rivets, glues, washers, bolts, nuts etc.

(ii) **Indirect labour:** Wages paid to workers who are not engaged in conversion of raw materials into finished products is indirect labour cost. They cannot be allocated to a product but can be apportioned over products or cost centres. They are: works manager's salary, foremen's salary, salary to people working in general office, sales department, stores department, labour department, security department etc.; leave pay, and employer's contribution to P.F, ESI, and labour welfare expenditures.

(iii) **Indirect expenses:** All indirect expenses other than indirect materials and indirect labour are classified as indirect expenses. They are rent, rates, insurance, taxes, advertisement, depreciation, lighting etc.

B. Functional-wise classification

(i) **Factory overheads:** All indirect materials, indirect labour and indirect expenses incurred in the production process are called factory overheads. They are: indirect materials, indirect labour, works manager salary, supervisor salary, oil, fuel, lubricants, depreciation and repairs and maintenance of factory building, plant and machinery, factory supplies, drawing office expenses, welfare expenses, haulage etc. Factory overheads is also called manufacturing overheads, production overheads and work overheads.

(ii) **Office and administration overheads:** All expenses incurred in connection with overall governance and control of a company is administration and office overheads. They are- directors fees & remuneration, general manager or managing director salary & remuneration, office salaries including salary to accountant, legal advisor, secretary and finance controller; audit fees, stationery, bank charges, telephone, depreciation and insurance of furniture and office machinery and equipment.

(iii) **Selling overheads:** Selling expenses are incurred to create demand for the products and induce the customers to buy the products. They are advertising, travelling, salesman's salary, commission, free samples, window display, after-sales service expenses, etc.

(iv) **Distribution overheads:** It includes all expenses incurred to take the goods from production centre to consumer's place. They are: rent, rates, insurance of warehouse; depreciation, running cost and repairs & maintenance of delivery van; carriage outward, packing expenses, storage expenses, discount allowed, bad debts etc.

C. Controllability-wise classification

(i) **Controllable overheads:** These overheads come under the influence of the management. The management can at its discretion either increase or reduce these expenditures. All direct expenses and some overheads are controllable.

(ii) **Uncontrollable overheads:** These overheads do not come under the influence of management. These are mostly determined by external factors. They are rent, insurance, tax, etc.

Controllability-wise classification is not rigid or permanent. They may change depending upon variation in corporate policies, level of activity and length of time. Expenditure may be uncontrollable in short periods but may be controllable in the long run.

D. Behaviour-wise classification

(i) Fixed overheads
(ii) Variable overheads
(iii) Semi-variable overheads.

(i) Fixed overheads: Expenses which remain constant in total irrespective of changes in volume of activity are called fixed overheads. They do not change when volume of production changes within the present capacity. Even if there is no production these expenses are incurred. They are: rent, insurance, office salary, security staff salary, etc. These expenses are incurred in relation to time factor. So they are called time cost or period cost. These expenses are mostly uncontrollable. Fixed overheads in total will change if rate of these expenses are revised like,

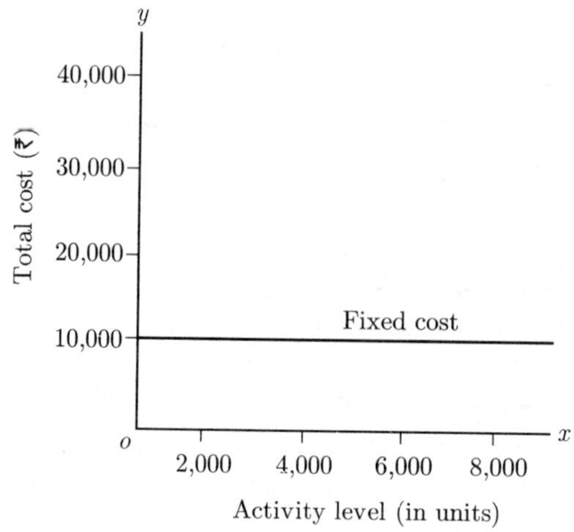

Total fixed cost chart

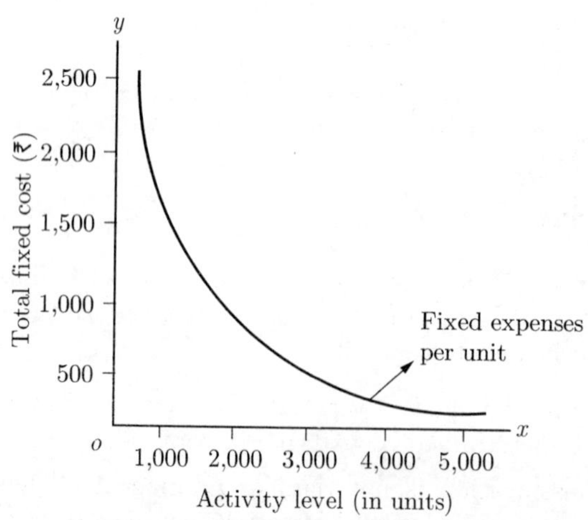

Fixed overheads per unit chart

salary scale, rate of premium, rent charges etc. Fixed overheads per unit will change in inverse proportion to changes in production volume. When production increases fixed overheads are borne by larger number of units and fixed overheads per unit will decrease as the amount of expenses is borne by larger number of units and vice versa.

(ii) **Variable overheads:** Variable overheads change in total in direct proportion to changes in volume of production. If production increases variable overheads also increase proportionately. If production decreases variable overheads will also decrease in the same proportion. Variable overheads per unit will be same at all levels of production. But practically variable overheads per unit at lower level of production will be more. Variable overheads per unit will be lower at higher levels of production due to economy in large scale production. As variable overheads are related to production, they are also called product cost or production cost.

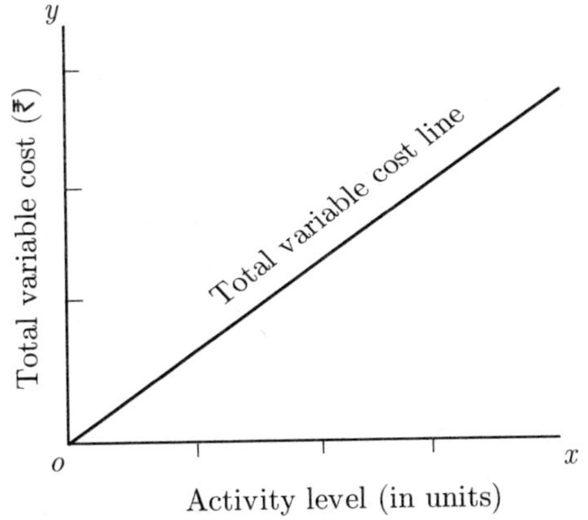

Total variable cost chart

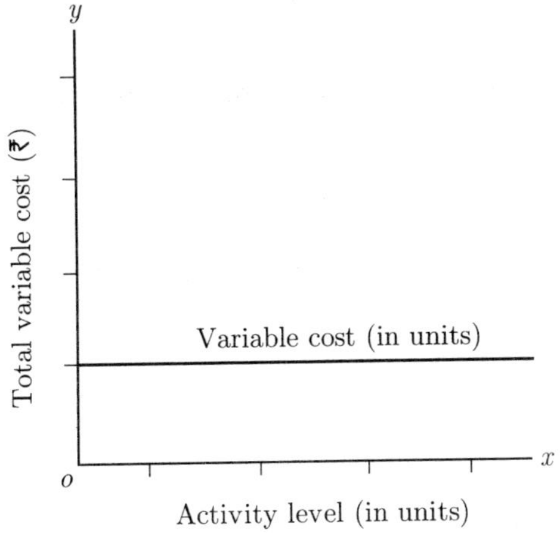

Variable cost per unit chart

(iii) Semi-variable overheads: There are certain expenses which are partly variable and partly fixed. They have the characteristics of both fixed and variable costs. They are supervisor salary, telephone charges and electricity. Semi-variable expenses are further classified into two groups. They are:

(a) Some semi-variable expenses change in relation to change in production level but they change less than proportionately to changes in production e.g.: repairs & maintenance, store handling etc.

(b) Some semi-variable expenses remain stable within a certain range of production, then increases to next level when production range increases to next level. So semi-variable expenses are also called stage costs or step costs.

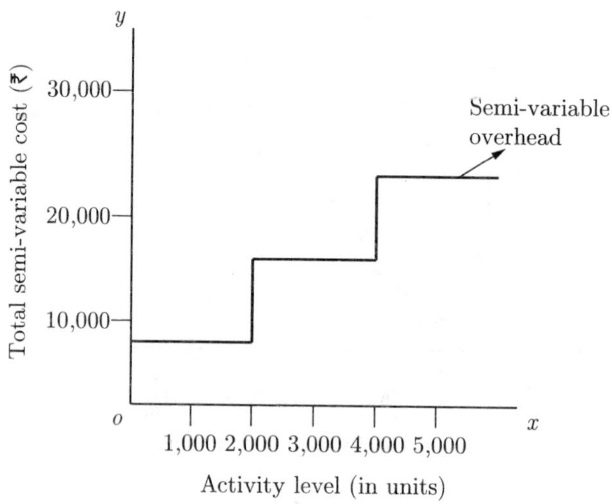

Total semi-variable overheads chart

Segregation of semi-variable expenses into fixed and variable costs

Methods

For effective control of costs semi-variable overheads need to be further divided into fixed and variable costs. Several methods are used to segregate semi-variable expenses into variable and fixed costs. They are:

1. High and low points methods
2. Method of averages
3. Equation method
4. Graphic presentation method
5. Least square method
6. Survey method.

(1) High and low points method

For a given period the output and costs at lower level and at higher level of production are taken. The difference in the units of output and costs between the two levels is arrived. This difference in cost is divided by difference in units. This gives the variable cost per unit. Fixed cost is arrived by subtracting variable cost from total semi-variable cost. The following is the formula for calculating variable cost and fixed costs:

$$\text{Variable cost} = \frac{\text{Difference in semi-variable cost}}{\text{Difference in units of production}}$$

$$\text{Fixed cost} = \text{Total semi-variable cost} - \text{variable cost}$$

Illustration-1

The following figures have been extracted from books of Sri Ram Industries Ltd for the half year ended 30th Sept, 2008.

Month 2008	**Volume (units)**	**Repairs & maintenance cost (Semi-variable) ₹**
April	1,000	2,500
May	800	2,300
June	1,200	2,700
July	1,400	2,900
August	1,500	3,000
September	1,600	3,100

Solution

	Units	**Cost (₹)**
High point (Sept 08)	1,600	3,100
Low point (May 08)	800	2,300
Difference	**800**	**800**

$$\text{Variable cost p/u} = \frac{\text{Difference in semi-variable cost}}{\text{Difference in units}} = \frac{800}{800} = ₹1$$

$$\text{Fixed cost} = \text{Total semi-variable cost for 1600 units} - \text{Variable cost} = 3{,}100 - 1{,}600 = ₹1{,}500$$

(2) Method of Averages

Under this method the semi-variable cost for a given period is divided into different sub-periods. Average cost is arrived for each sub-period. Then the average cost of these sub-periods are plotted on a graph. For example figures given in illustration-1 are divided into three sub-periods of two months each. Average units and costs will be as follows.

Sub-periods	Average Units	Average Cost ₹
April & May	900 (1000 + 800÷2)	2,400 (2500 + 2300÷2)
June & July	1,300 (1200 + 1400÷2)	2,800 (2700 + 2900÷2)
Aug & Sep	1,550 (1500 + 1600÷2)	3,050 (3000÷3100÷2)

The above average units and costs are plotted on a graph. We get fixed cost line cutting the vertical axis at ₹1,500.

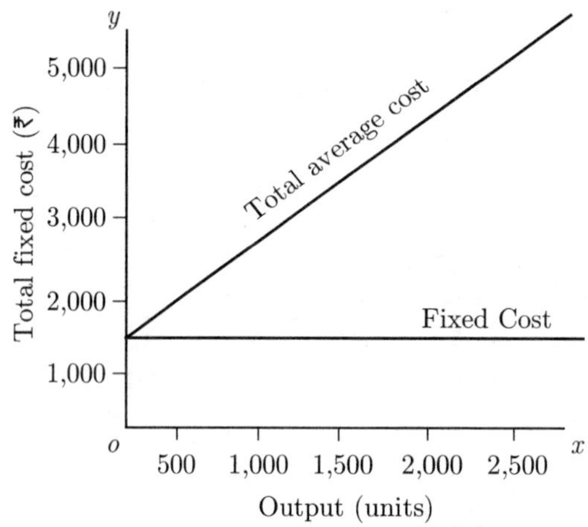

(3) Equation Method: (Simultaneous Equation Method)

The equation for a straight line is:

$$Y = mX + c$$

Y = Total semi-variable overheads
X = Volume of output
c = Fixed cost and
m = Slope of variable cost line (variable cost per unit)

From illustration 1 above, substituting two set of values we get two equations as below:

$$3{,}100 = m(1,600) + c - \text{equation (i)} - \text{(September value taken)}$$
$$3{,}000 = m(1,500) + c - \text{equation (ii)} - \text{(August value taken)}$$

By subtracting value in (ii) from (i) we get

$$100 = m(100)$$
$$m = \text{Re. } 1$$

Variable cost per unit = ₹1

Fixed cost = Total semi-variable cost (for September) – Variable cost for 1600 units
= 3,100 – 1,600 = 1,500

So the fixed cost is ₹1,500 per month.

(4) Graphic presentation method

The semi-variable costs for various levels of activity are plotted on a graph. X axis represents volume of output and 'Y' axis the semi-variable cost. A straight line is drawn covering as many points as possible. This line is called line of best fit. The point at which straight line cuts Y axis represents fixed cost. The slope of straight line represents variable cost.

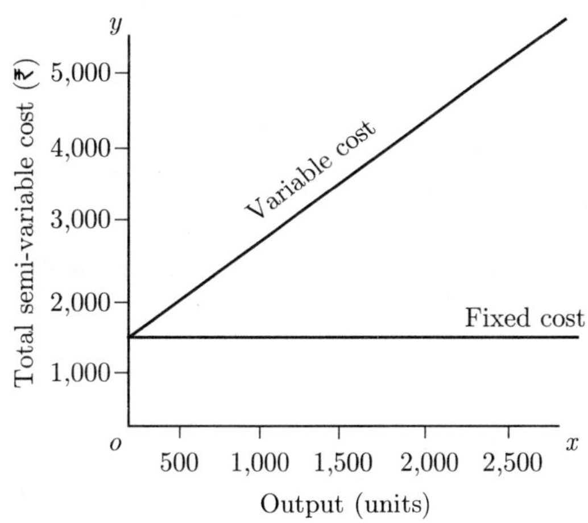

(5) Least square method

Under graphic presentation method line of best fit (line of regression) is drawn by vision arbitrarily. In least square method line of best fit is drawn by using linear equation (i.e. straight line equation). The equation is

$$y = mx + c$$

where
y = Total semi-variable overheads
x = Volume of output
c = Fixed cost and
m = Slope of variable cost line (variable cost per unit).

Values of different periods/activity levels are substituted in the above equation. The mean (simple average) of output and semi-variable expenses is calculated and deviations of output (x) and semi-variable cost from the mean is calculated. Then the deviation of mean output (x) of each period/activity level is squared (x^2) and total of x^2 is calculated. Next the deviation output (x) and semi-variable expenses (y) is multiplied and products of xy for each period are totalled. Variable cost per unit is obtained by dividing the total of xy by total of x^2. By substituting the variable cost per unit (m) in the above equation the amount of fixed cost (c) can be calculated. This is a statistical method. It gives more accurate and reliable result then other methods.

Illustration-2

The following expenses were incurred in a factory during the 6 month period ending June, 2008.

Month	Output	Indirect Material Cost
Jan'08	600	2,200
Feb	700	2,400
Mar	750	2,500
Apl	900	2,800
May	960	2,920
June	1,010	3,020

Analyse the indirect materials cost into variable costs and fixed costs using least square method.

Solution

Month	Output	Indirect Material Cost	Deviation of Output from the mean	Deviation of cost from the mean	x^2	xy
1	2	3	4	5	6 (4 × 4)	7 (4 × 5)
Jan	600	2,200	(−)220	(−)440	48,400	96,800
Feb	700	2,400	(−)120	(−)240	14,400	28,800
Mar	750	2,500	(−)70	(−)140	4,900	9,800
Apl	900	2,800	80	160	6,400	1,28,000
May	960	2,920	140	280	19,600	39,200
June	1,010	3,020	190	380	36,100	72,200
Total	4,920	15,840			$\Sigma x^2 = 1,29,800$	$\Sigma xy = 2,59,600$
Mean (Average)	820 (4,920 ÷ 6)	2,640 (15,840 ÷ 6)				

$$\text{Variable charges per unit } \frac{\Sigma xy}{\Sigma x^2} = \frac{2,59,600}{1,29,800} = ₹2 \text{ p/u.}$$

$$\text{Fixed cost} = \text{Mean expenses (Mean output} \times \text{Variable cost p/u)}$$
$$= 2{,}640 - (820 \times 2) = 1{,}000$$

Thus, the line on the graph will be represented by

$$y = Mx + c$$
$$2{,}640 = 2 \times 820 + 1{,}000$$

(6) Analytical Method

The variability of each group of expenses is judged. The judgement is based on past experience, the present conditions and expected changes in future. This method involves an element of arbitrariness. The correctness of the judgement also depends on the perception of the person making the judgement. So this method is not reliable.

Advantages of segregating overheads into fixed and variable overheads

1. **Cost control**

   Splitting semi-variable overheads into fixed costs and variable costs helps the management in understanding the behavior of expenses. Fixed expenses are incurred on time basis and are uncontrollable. Variable expenses are related to volume of production and are controllable.

2. **Decision making**

   The management has to take decisions relating to volume of production, profit planning, fixing prices etc. Differentiating overheads into fixed costs and variable cost helps the management in taking correct decisions.

3. **Application of marginal costing**

   Marginal costing is an important tool in the hands of the management for future planning. Marginal costing is based on classification of costs into fixed costs and variable costs.

4. **Flexible budget**

   Like marginal costing, budgeting is also a useful costing technique. Segregation of overheads into fixed and variable costs helps in preparing flexible budgets.

5. **Quotation and Tenders**

   Very often firms are asked to quote price for supplying their products. Differentiating overheads into fixed and variable helps in easy estimation of costs for preparing tenders and quotations. This is very essential where goods are produced according to customer's orders.

6. **Overheads absorption rates**

   Establishing single overhead for all overheads is not desirable. Segregation of overheads into fixed and variable overheads help in establishing overhead absorption rates separately for fixed overheads and variable overheads.

7.3 COLLECTION AND CODIFICATION OF OVERHEADS

Overheads in a period are to be gathered from different sources. It is called collection of overheads. Records where actual expenses are recorded or estimated are sources of overheads. Overheads gathered are grouped under various heads and subheads.

Codification: To ensure accurate, timely, economical collection and grouping of overheads using codes for various expenses is necessary. Using codes reduce is clerical work.

Standing number: For every expenditure a separate identification number or letter or combination of letter and number is allotted. This number or letter allotted is called standing number or standing order. Standing number signifies the general authorisation given for incurring an expense.

7.3.1 Methods of Codification

1. **Mnemonic method:** Few letters are assigned for an overhead which suggests the name of the expenditure e.g., DEP for depreciation. This helps in easy recollection.
2. **Numerical codes:** A block of numbers is assigned for each group of overheads say 1 to 25 for stores expenses etc.
3. **Decimal codes:** Each group of expenses is given a whole number and decimal is given for a sub-group expenditure. For example:

(1) Stores expenses

1.1 Lubricants

1.2 Cotton wastes

1.3 Pasting materials

1.4 Factory stationery.

(2) Indirect labour

2.1 PF contribution

2.2 ESI contribution

2.3 Medical expenses

2.4 Indoor games

2.5 Free commutation.

4) Alpha numerical codes: Both letter and numbers are allotted for easy identification and grouping. For example

(i) Factory Overheads

F.1 Indirect materials

F.1.1 Tools
F.1.2 Oil
F.1.3 Lubricants.

F.2 Indirect labour

F.2.1 Contribution to PF
F.2.2 Contribution to ESI
F.2.3 Leave salary
F.2.4 Indoor games.

(ii) Administration Overheads

A.1 Office repairs & maintenance

A.1.1 Computer maintenance
A.1.2 Building maintenance
A.1.3 Air-conditioner maintenance.

A.2 Office stationery

A.2.1 Typewriter ribbon
A.2.2 White sheet
A.2.3 Forms.

COMPREHENSIVE ILLUSTRATIONS

Illustration-3

(High and low points methods)

The standard departmental overhead rate is ₹ 15 per hour. Based on the following details provided to you, work out the capacity level at which the overhead rate has been fixed:

Activity Level	Overhead Allowance ₹
6,000 hrs	1,20,000
8,000 hrs	1,44,000
10,000 hrs	1,68,000

	Activity Level	Overhead Allowance
		₹
	10,000 hrs	1,68,000
	6,000 hrs	1,20,000
Difference	**4,000 hrs**	**48,000**

Solution

$$\text{Variable overheads per unit} = \frac{\text{Difference in overheads}}{\text{Difference in activity level (hrs)}}$$

$$= \frac{48{,}000}{4{,}000}$$

$$= ₹.\ 12 \text{ per hour}$$

Fixed expenses

	₹
Total overheads (at 6,000 hrs activity level)	1,20,000
Less: Variable expenses = 6,000 × ₹12	72,000
Fixed expenses	48,000

Activity level at which departmental overhead rate of ₹ 15 is computed:

$$\text{Total overheads per unit} = \text{Variable overhead per unit} + \text{Fixed overhead per unit}$$

$$₹\ 15 = ₹12 + \text{Fixed overhead per unit}$$

$$\text{Fixed overhead per unit} = ₹\ 15 - 12 = ₹3$$

$$\text{Number of units} = \frac{\text{Total fixed overheads}}{\text{Fixed overhead rate per unit}}$$

$$= \frac{48{,}000}{3} = 16{,}000 \text{ units}$$

Illustration-4

(High and low point method)

Meera Industries Limited is a single product company having a manufacturing capacity of 6,000 units per week of 48 hours.The output data vis-à-vis different elements of cost for three consecutive weeks are given below:

Units produced	Direct materials ₹	Direct labour ₹	Total factory overheads ₹
2,400	4,800	6,000	37,200
2,800	5,600	7,000	38,400
3,600	7,200	9,000	40,800

As a cost accountant, you are asked by the company to work out the selling price assuming an activity level of 4,000 units per week and a profit of 20% on selling price.

Solution

Total overheads given is to be segregated into variable and fixed overheads

$$\text{Variable overheads per unit} = \frac{\text{Difference in factory overheads}}{\text{Difference in production level}}$$

$$= \frac{40,800 - 37,200}{3,600 - 2,400} = \frac{3,600}{1,200} = ₹3 \text{ per unit}$$

$$\text{Fixed factory overhead} = \text{Total overheads for 3600 units} - \text{Variable overheads}$$
$$= 40{,}800 - 3{,}600 \times 3$$
$$= 40,800 - 10,800 = 30,000$$

Computation of selling price per unit at production level of 4,000 units

	₹
Direct materials (₹2×4,000)	8,000
Direct labour (₹2.50×4,000)	10,000
Variable overheads (₹3×4,000)	12,000
Fixed factory overheads	30,000
Total cost	60,000
Profit at 20% on S.P or at 25% on cost $\frac{60{,}000 \times 25}{100}$	15,000
Sales	75,000

Selling price per unit $\frac{75{,}000}{4{,}000} = ₹18.75$

Note:

1. Direct materials p/u $= \dfrac{4{,}800}{2{,}400} =$ ₹2.00 (details in the first level is taken)

2. Direct labour p/u $= \dfrac{6{,}000}{2{,}400} =$ ₹2.50

Illustration-5

In a factory Type A and Type B machines have been designed to produce the same product but Type A is less automatic than Type B and requires somewhat more labour to operate. Pertinent cost are as follows:

	Type A ₹	Type B ₹
Set up cost	400	600
Variable cost per unit	4.90	4.40

Which type of machine should be used for processing various orders?

(ICWA-Inter, 1984)

Solution

Difference inset up cost (fixed) = ₹600 − ₹400 = ₹200

Difference in variable cost per unit = ₹4.90 − 4.40 = ₹0.50

$$\text{Indifference point} = \frac{\text{Difference in set-up cost}}{\text{Difference in variable cost per unit}}$$

$$= \frac{200}{0.50} = 400 \text{ units}$$

Proof:

	Type A ₹	Type B ₹
Set-up cost	400	600
Variable cost (400 units×rate per unit)	1,960	1,760
Total	**2,360**	**2,360**

Machine A should be used if production is less than 400 units since its set-up cost is less. Machine B should be used if production is more than 400 units, since its variable cost per unit is lower.

Verification:

	Production levels (Machine)			
	A	B	A	B
	399 units	399 units	401 units	401 units
	₹	₹	₹	₹
Set up cost	400	600	400	600
Variable cost (400 units×rate per unit)	1,955.10 (399×4.90)	1,755.60 (399× 4.40)	1,964.90 (401×4.90)	1,764.40 (4014×4.40)
Total Cost	**2,355.10**	**2,355.60**	**2,364.90**	**2,364.40**

At production level of 399 units the total cost of Machine A is less, hence machine 'A' should be preferred if order is for less than 400 units. When production order is for more than 400 units product should be produced with machine 'B' since the cost is less.

7.4 EXERCISES

I. Objectives Type questions

A. State whether the following statements are true or false

(a) All indirect expenses are called prime cost.

(b) Factory overheads include all expenses like raw materials, manufacturing wages and other expenses incurred in factory.

(c) Variable cost per unit does not change.

(d) Fixed overhead is also called time cost.

(e) Fixed expenses per unit remain same at all levels of activity.

(f) Fixed expenses in total do not change even if the activity level changes.

(g) Variable expenses in total changes in direct proportion to changes in volume of output.

(h) Semi-variable expenses are also called step cost.

(i) Variable overheads vary with time.

(j) Fixed cost changes in relation to volume of activity.

(k) Fixed costs are policy costs.

(l) Fixed overheads are controllable.

(m) Administration costs are mostly fixed.

(n) Direct costs can be identified with and charged to a particular cost unit.

(o) Period costs are not assigned to products.

(p) Abnormal cost is controllable.

(q) Cost of floppy disk used for office computer is administration overhead.

Answers: True: c, d, f, g, h, k, m, n, q
False: a, b, e, i, j, l, o, p

B. Fill in the blanks

(a) ________ cost in total does not change even if the volume of activity changes.

(b) Expenses incurred exclusively for a job is called ________.

(c) Expenses incurred commonly for two or more jobs, products are called ________.

(d) Expenses incurred in relations to time or period is known as ________.

(e) Variable cost per unit remains ________ at all levels of activity

(f) ________ costs per unit changes in inverse proportion to change in level of activity.

(g) Semi-variable cost has the characteristic of both ________.

(h) The aggregate of indirect materials, indirect wages and indirect expenses is ________.

(i) ________ costs are partly fixed and partly variable.

(j) Unit fixed cost takes ________ shape in graphical presentation.

(k) ________ diagram is used for segregation of fixed and variable costs.

(l) Period costs are ________.

Answers: (a) Fixed, (b) Direct cost, (c) Indirect cost or overheads, (d) Fixed cost, (e) Constant, (f) Fixed cost (g) Fixed and variable costs (h) Overheads, (i) Semi-variable, (j) Downward curve (k) Scatter, (l) Fixed costs.

II. Theory Questions

A. Short answer type questions

(a) What is overhead?

(b) Explain variable overheads.

(c) Give the characteristics of fixed overheads with examples.

(d) Explain semi-variable overheads.

(e) Name the functional-wise classification of overheads.

(f) Name the various methods of segregation of semi-variable overheads into fixed costs and variable costs.

(g) Distinguish between fixed and variable overheads.

(h) What is chargeable expenses?

(i) Write short notes on administration overheads.

B. Long answer type questions

(a) Explain the various methods of classification of overheads.

(b) What do you understand by factory overheads?

(c) What is the necessity for classification of overheads into fixed costs and variable costs?

(d) "Classification of overheads into fixed costs and variable costs is highly helpful to the management for efficient functioning of factory." Discuss.

III. Practical Problems

1. B & Co., has recorded the following data in the most recent periods:

Total cost of production ₹	**Volume of production** (units)
14,600	800
19,400	1,200

What is the best estimate of firms variable costs per unit and fixed cost?

[**Ans:** Variable overheads per unit ₹ 12 and fixed overheads = ₹5,000]

2. Firm X manufactures surgical goods, its normal production is 2,600 units per month at a total cost of ₹ 32,000. At full capacity it can manufacture 3,400 units per month at a total cost of ₹ 38,000. Calculate:

   (i) Average cost per instrument under normal operating conditions
   (ii) Average variable cost per instrument
   (iii) Total fixed cost and

(iv) Average fixed cost per unit under normal operating conditions.

(CS-Inter, June 1985)

[**Ans:** (i) ₹ 12.31 (ii) ₹ 7.50 per unit (iii) ₹ 12,500 (iv) ₹ 4.81 per unit]

3. The following information is extracted from the books of XY Ltd for 6 months ending Dec 31, 2007 :

Month	Volume (Units)	Semi-Variable (₹)
July	150	2,700
Aug	300	3,900
Sep	450	5,100
Oct	750	7,500
Nov	1,050	9,900
Dec	1,350	12,300

Find the fixed and variable cost under a) High and low points method and b) Least square method .

[**Ans:** Variable cost P/U ₹ 8, Fixed overheads ₹ 1,500.]

4. The following are the maintenance costs incurred in a machine shop per six months with corresponding machine hours.

Month	Machine Hour	Maintenance Costs (₹)
January	2,000	300
February	2,200	320
March	1,700	270
April	2,400	340
May	1,800	280
June	1,900	290
	12,000	1,800

Analyse the maintenance cost which is semi-variable into fixed and variable elements.

[**Ans:** b] Variable cost 10 paise per hour; Fixed costs ₹ 100) **(CA-Inter)**

5. XY Ltd supplies the following information for two succeeding periods :
Segregate the semi-variable overheads into fixed and variable overheads. Also determine the total overheads of producing 50,000 units.

	Period-I	Period-II
No. of Units Produced	40,000	15,000
Semi Variable Overheads (₹)	5,20,000	3,20,000

[**Ans:** Variable Cost P/u: ₹ 8, Fixed cost: ₹ 2,00,000. Total overheads for production of 50,000 units: ₹ 6,00,000]

6. From the data given below segregate the semi-variable overheads into fixed cost and variable costs by using (i) High and low point method and (ii) Simultaneous equation method.

	Capacity (%)	Machine Hours	Semi-variable overheads (₹)
January	75%	750	19,500
February	90%	1,000	22,000

[**Ans:** Variable cost per hour ₹ 10; Fixed cost ₹ 12,000]

7. AB Ltd supplies you the following information for three successive months:

Unit Produced	Direct Material (₹)	Direct Labour (₹)	Total factory Overheads (₹)
3,600	7,200	9,000	55,800
4,200	8,400	10,500	57,600
5,400	10,800	13,500	61,200

You are requested to determine the sales volume for an activity level of 4,000 units and assuming a profit of 25% on selling price, also determine the selling price P/U.

[**Ans:** Total cost for 4000 units ₹ 75,000; Sales ₹ 1,00,000, Selling price p/u ₹ 25].

Note:

(a) Direct materials and direct labour are variable costs, since their cost per unit remains same at all levels of production.

(b) Factory overheads is semi-variable because it changes in different proportion to changes in volume of production. Variable factory overheads is ₹ 3.00 per unit. Fixed factory overheads is ₹ 45,000.

ACCOUNTING FOR OVERHEADS AND CONTROL 8

- Meaning
- Allocation and Apportionment
- Process of charging
- Apportionment of Service department overheads to Production Departments
- Absorption
- Methods of absorption
- Machine hour rate - Computation
- Under-absorbed / Over-absorbed - Overheads Treatment
- Concept of Capacity and Overheads Recovery Rates

8.1 INTRODUCTION

8.1.1 Meaning

Factory overheads is an important item of cost next to direct materials and direct labour. Factory overheads should be collected and analysed into different groupings. Proper codification should be made for proper recording in account books. Then factory overheads should be charged to various departments, cost centres and products. It involves allocation, apportionment and absorption of overheads.

8.1.2 Allocation and Apportionment

Direct expenses are incurred exclusively for a particular product, particular cost centre or a particular job order. So the whole of direct costs is charged to that product or job order. Charging the whole of direct expenses to a particular product or cost centre or job order is called allocation of overheads. Indirect costs are common to two or more products or cost centres or job orders. To ascertain the correct amount of production overheads, they are distributed to products or Cost centres or job orders proportionately on some suitable basis. This process of charging a portion of indirect costs to cost centres is called overheads apportionment.

Differences between allocation and apportionment

Allocation	Apportionment
1) Allocation is charging of entire direct expenses to a particular product or a cost centre or a job order.	1) Apportionment means distribution of indirect costs over many products or cost centres or job orders.
2) It is concerned with charging direct expenses.	2) It is concerned with charging indirect expenses.
3) Allocation is accurate.	3) It is only approximate.
4) No necessity for choosing a base.	4) Overheads is apportioned on some suitable basis.

8.1.3 Sources of Factory Overheads

Cost data of Indirect materials are collected from stores requisition. An analysis of stores requisition helps in departmentalisation of materials consumed.

Cost data of Indirect labour is obtained from the job cards or job tickets.

Cost data of Indirect expenses are gathered from cash book. Expenses like depreciation are collected from fixed assets registers.

8.2 PROCESS OF CHARGING OVERHEADS TO COST UNITS

Overheads in a firm should be included in the total cost of a cost unit. This involves three stages. They are:

1. Departmentalisation of overheads
2. Apportionment of service department overheads to production departments
3. Allotting the production department overheads to cost unit.

8.2.1 Departmentalisation of Overheads

Expenses are to be collected department-wise to judge the efficiency of various departments. Some overheads like indirect materials, machinery repairs, etc are incurred wholly for a specific department.

They are allotted to that department; some expenses are common to two or more departments. These common expenses are to be apportioned to various departments on some suitable basis. This step is also known as primary distribution of overheads or departmental distribution of overheads. Examples of some common expenses incurred and their basis of apportionment are:

Expenses	Basis of apportionment
1) Indirect materials	Direct materials
2) Indirect labour	Direct labour
3) All labour welfare expenses (or) amenities to labour	No. of employees
4) Supervision	No. of employees
5) PF and ESI contribution Group insurance, workmen compensation	Direct labour
6) Repairs & maintenance and depreciation of capital assets.	Value of capital assets
7) Insurance of assets	Asset value
8) Insurance of stock of materials and stores	Value of stock of material and stores
9) Rent	Area
10) Lighting	Light & fan point/area
11) Power	KWH/HP of machines X machine hours/HP of machines
12) Materials handling and storekeeping	No. of stores requisition/weight of materials handled
13) Miscellaneous expenses	Direct labour
14) Canteen expenses	Number of employees

8.2.2 Principles of Apportionment of Overheads

The criteria on which the allocation and apportionment of overheads are based is as follows:

1. **Volume of services received**

   Under this method the services or benefits received by each department is the basis for apportionment of overheads. The department receiving more benefits bears more overheads and department receiving lesser service is assigned less overheads. This principle is considered to be more appropriate and equitable.

2. **Analysis or survey method**

   Sometimes it may not be possible to quantify services received by various departments from an expenditure. Such expenses are to be apportioned only arbitrarily. Analysis is made periodically to determine the basis of apportionment.

3. **Ability to pay method**

   Under this principle the department earning more revenue is allotted more expenses. This method is considered unfair in the sense that more efficient department is penalised and less efficient department is rewarded. Various departments in a company might have been started at different points of time. Some departments might have been started earlier and are well established, may be earning more income. Some departments may be new and earns less revenue. In this situation it is advisable to use the ability to pay method.

4. **Efficiency method**

   Standard production is fixed as a tool of control. Actual output is compared with the standard to measure the efficiency of the departments. Unit cost of more efficient department will be less as the overheads are distributed among more units and cost will be more in the less efficient departments as overheads are distributed among lesser number of units. This method is considered to be more equitable.

   The following is the list of some service departments and basis used to apportion their overheads.

Service Department	Basis of Apportionment
1) Stores department	1) No of material requisitions or value of materials
2) Purchase department	2) No of purchase order/value of materials
3) Timekeeping	3) No of employees
4) Labour department	4) Number of employees
5) Canteen, labour welfare	5) Number of employees
6) Asset maintenance	6) Asset value/machine hours
7) Internal transport	7) Weight of materials handled
8) Building service	8) Area

8.3 APPORTIONMENT OF SERVICE DEPARTMENT OVERHEADS TO PRODUCTION DEPARTMENTS

Service departments provide services to other departments. They do not produce any products. To ensure that service department expenses are also fully recovered, their expenses are to be distributed to production departments. This step is also called secondary distribution of overheads or reapportionment of overheads. Various methods are used to distribute services department costs to production departments. They are:

1. Non-reciprocal methods

(a) Direct distribution method
(b) Step method or step ladder method

2. Reciprocal methods
   (a) Simultaneous equation method or mathematical equation method or algebraic method
   (b) Repeated distribution method or continuous distribution method
   (c) Trial and error method

1. Non-reciprocal Methods

(a) Direct distribution method

Under this method overheads cost of service departments are distributed to production departments only. One service department may provide service to an another service department. For example labour department will be managing employees in stores department also. But this factor of service rendered by one service department to another service department is ignored. This method will not give correct result.

Illustration-1

(Direct distribution method)

ABC Ltd has three production departments and four service departments. The expenses of the department as per primary distribution summary are as follows:

Production Departments

P - 50,000
Q - 45,000
R - 60,000

Service Departments

1. Stores department ₹24,000.
2. Timekeeping and pay roll ₹24,000.
3. Power ₹24,000.
4. Labour welfare ₹9,000.

The following further information is available

Particulars	Service Departments				Production Departments		
	1	2	3	4	P	Q	R
Value of materials requisitioned (₹)	-	-	15,000	-	40,000	40,000	20,000
No of employees	30	30	60	30	180	120	60
Horsepower of machines	-	-	-	-	500	700	400

Prepare a statement showing distribution of service department overheads to production departments under direct distribution method.

Solution

(A)

Secondary overheads distribution summary					
Particulars	**Basis of apportionment**	**Total ₹**	**Production Departments**		
			P (₹)	**Q (₹)**	**R (₹)**
Departmental Overheads	Given	1,55,000	50,000	45,000	60,000
Stores department overheads	Value of materials requisitioned:2 : 2 : 1	24,000	9,600	9,600	4,800
Timekeeping & pay roll dept	No. of employees: 3 : 2 : 1	24,000	12,000	8,000	4,000
Power	Horse power of machines5 : 7 : 4	24,000	7,500	10,500	6,000
Labour welfare	No. of employees 3 : 2 : 1	9,000	4,500	3,000	1,500
	Total Overheads	2,36,000	83,600	76,100	76,300

(B) Step method or step ladder method

Under direct distribution method the service rendered by one service department to another service department is completely ignored, even though the service department may help another service department. For example, stores department, timekeeping and labour welfare departments help other service departments. Under the step method the service departments are arranged in their order of decreasing importance.

In the overheads distribution summary all departments are arranged vertically beginning with service departments arranged in their order of importance and next production departments are taken in the given order. Then the overheads of first service department is distributed to other subsequent departments. Next the overheads of second service department (including the share received from the first service department) are distributed to other subsequent departments. It should be noted the second service department's overheads are not distributed to first service department. Similarly the overheads of other service departments are distributed to subsequent departments only. Finally, we get the total overheads of production departments. In this method services rendered by one service department to another service department is considered only partially. The overheads distribution summary looks like the steps of a ladder, so this method is called step method or step ladder method. Let us do the sum given in illustration 1 under this method:

Solution

Overheads Distribution Summary

Service Departments	Departmental overheads					Total overheads
Timekeeping	24,000	(–)24,000				
Labour welfare	9,000	1,500	(–)10,500			
Stores	24,000	1,500	700	(–)26,200		
Power	24,000	3,000	1,400	3,418	(–)31,818	
Production Departments						
P	50,000	9,000	4,200	9,112	9,943	82,255
Q	45,000	6,000	2,800	9,112	13,920	76,832
R	60,000	3,000	1,400	4,558	7,955	76,913

Alternatively the above overheads distribution summary can be prepared in the following format, where departments are arranged horizontally:

Overhead Distribution Summary

Particulars	Ratio	Service Department				Production Department		
		Time-keeping	Labour welfare	Stores	Power	P	Q	R
Departmental overheads	-	24,000	9,000	24,000	24,000	50,000	45,000	60,000
Timekeeping	1:1:2:6:4:2	(–)24,000	1,500	1,500	3,000	9,000	6,000	3,000
Labour welfare	1:2:6:4:2		(–)10,500	700	1,400	4,200	2,800	1,400
Stores	3:8:8:4			(–)26,200	3,418	9,112	9,112	4,558
Power	5:7:4				(–)31,818	9,943	13,920	7,955
Total	-	-	-	-	-	82,255	76,832	76,913

Workings:

(1) No. of departments helped by a service department

Stores department	-	4
Timekeeping & payroll	-	6
Power	-	3
Labour welfare	-	6

(2) Service departments in the order of their importance

Department	Rank
Timekeeping	1
Labour welfare	2
Stores department	3
Power	4

Note:

(i) Service departments are ranked on the basis of number of departments they help.
(ii) A department helping more number of other department is taken as more important.
(iii) Labour welfare and timekeeping pay roll department helped equal number of departments. Total expenses of time keeping department is more, so it is ranked first.

(3) Basis of apportionment

	Departments						
	Time-keeping	**Labour welfare**	**Stores**	**Power**	**P**	**Q**	**R**
Timekeeping: No. of employees (1:1:2:6:4:2)	-	30	30	60	180	120	60
Labour welfare: No. of employees (1:2:6:4:2)	-	-	30	60	180	120	60
Stores department (value of materials requisitioned) (3:8:8:4)	-	-	-	15,000	40,000	40,000	20,000
Power (horsepower of machine)(5:7:4)	-	-	-	-	500	700	400

2. Reciprocal Methods

Under the reciprocal methods the services rendered by one service department to another service department is fully considered while apportioning the service department overheads. There are three methods which are used to apportionment the service department overheads to production departments. They are:

(a) Simultaneous equation method or mathematical equation method or algebraic method
(b) Repeated distribution method or continuous distribution method.
(c) Trial-and-error method

(a) Simultaneous equation method

Under this method two stages are involved. Under the first step the total overheads of service departments are found by completing the distribution among the service departments by using simultaneous equation. In the second stage the total overheads of service departments are distributed among production departments as per the percentages given.

Illustration-2

There are three production departments and two service departments. The expenses incurred by them during the 3 months from 1.1.2008 to 31.3.2008 are:

Production Departments:

A - ₹80,000.
B - ₹70,000.
C - ₹50,000.

Service Departments:

X - ₹23,400.
Y - ₹30,000.

The expenses of service departments are apportioned to other departments on the following basis:

	A	B	C	X	Y
Service dept-X	20%	40%	30%	-	10%
Service dept-Y	40%	20%	20%	20%	-

Show clearly as to how service department expenses are apportioned to production departments.

Solution

Let the total overheads of service department X be - x

(after receiving its share of expenses from service department Y)

Let the total overheads of service department Y be - y

(after receiving its share of expenses from service department X)

$$\therefore\ x = 23{,}400 + \frac{20}{100}y(\text{or})23{,}400 + 0.2y \tag{8.1}$$

$$\therefore\ y = 30{,}000 + \frac{10}{100}x(\text{or})30{,}000 + 0.1x \tag{8.2}$$

Take equation (i) for solving

$$x = 23{,}400 + 0.2y$$

Substitute the value of y in equation (8.1)

$$x = 23{,}400 + 0.2(30{,}000 + 0.1x)$$
$$x = 23{,}400 + 6{,}000 + 0.02x$$
$$x - 0.02x = 29{,}600$$
$$x = \frac{29{,}600}{0.98} = 30{,}000$$

Total overheads of service department x = ₹30,000

Substitute the value of x in equation (8.2)

$$y = 30,000 + 0.1(30{,}000) = 33{,}000$$

Overhead distribution summary				
Particular	**Total**	**Production department**		
		A	B	C
	₹	₹	₹	₹
Department overheads	2,00,000	80,000	70,000	50,000
Service department X	30,000	6,000	12,000	9,000
Service department Y	33,000	13,200	6,600	6,600
Total Overheads	-	99,200	88,600	65,600

(b) Repeated distribution method/continuous distribution method

Under this method the total overheads determined as per primary distribution are arranged horizontally. Then service department expenses are distributed to other departments at given percentages. A share in the overheads of first service department is distributed to second service department. While distributing the overheads of second service department a share is given to the first service department. This process of distributing one service department overhead to another service department will continue endlessly. To stop this cycle, when the share of one service department becomes very small, the amount is distributed to production departments only.

Illustration-3

X Ltd has three production departments and two service departments. Their overheads for a period after primary distribution are:

Production departments

A - ₹90,000.

B - ₹1,20,000.
C - ₹1,50,000.

Service departments

X - ₹50,000.
Y - ₹30,000.

The expenses of service department are distributed to other departments on a percentage basis as follows:

	Production Dept			Service Dept	
	A	B	C	X	Y
Service dept X	30%	30%	25%	-	15%
Service dept Y	40%	20%	30%	10%	-

Prepare an overheads distribution summary showing the apportionment of two service departments under "Repeated Distribution Method".

Solution

	Production Dept			Service Dept	
	A	B	C	X	Y
Departmental overheads	90,000.00	1,20,000.00	1,50,000.00	50,000.00	30,000.00
Service Dept X	15,000.00	15,000.00	12,500.00	(−)50,000.00	7,500.00
Service Dept Y	15,000.00	7,500.00	11,250.00	3,750.00	(−)37,500.00
Service Dept X	1,125.00	1,125.00	937.50	(−)3,750.00	562.50
Service Dept Y	225.00	112.50	168.75	56.25	(−)562.50
Service Dept X	16.88	16.88	14.06	(−)56.25	8.43
Service Dept Y	3.75	1.87	2.81	-	(−)8.43
Total OHS	1,21,370.63	1,43,756.25	1,74,873.12	-	-

C) Trial-and-Error method

Under this method also there are two stages in apportionment of service department overheads to production departments. First total overheads of service departments are found by distributing one service department cost to another service department by applying the percentages given. Next total overheads of service department are distributed to production departments.

Illustration-4

You are supplied with the departmental overheads of various departments in a factory. Apportion the service department overheads to production departments under trial-and-error method:

Production departments

P - 78,000
Q - 1,25,000
R - 45,000

Service departments

S - 40,000
R - 26,000

The expenses of service departments are apportioned as under:

	P	Q	R	S	T
Service department 'S'	30%	40%	20%	-	10%
Service department 'T'	10%	20%	50%	20%	-

Estimated working hours of production departments are as under:

Departments

P - 1,000 hrs
Q - 2,500 hrs
R - 1,400 hrs

Also compute overhead recovery rate per working hour.

Solution

Statement showing distribution of overheads among service departments

	Service Departments	
	S	**T**
Departmental overheads	40,000.00	26,000.00
Service departmental		
Overheads apportionment:		
From S to T 10%	-	4,000.00
From T to S 20%	6,000.00	30,000.00
From S to T 10%	-	600.00

From T to S 20%	120.00	-
From S to T 10%	-	12.00
From T to S 20%	2.40	-
From S to T 10%	-	0.24
From T to S 20%	0.05	-
Total	46,122.45	30,612.24

Overheads distribution summary

Particulars	Total Overheads	Basis	Production Department		
			P (₹)	Q (₹)	R (₹)
Departmental overheads	2,48,000.00	Given	78,000.00	1,25,000.00	45,000
Service department 'S'	46,122.45	30%, 40%, 20%	13,836.74	18,448.98	9,224.49
Service department 'T'	30,612.24	10%, 20%, 50%	3,061.22	6,122.45	15,306.12
Total overheads	-	-	**94,897.96**	**1,49,571.43**	**69,530.61**

$$\text{Overheads recovery rate per working hour} = \frac{\text{Total overheads}}{\text{Working hours}}$$

$$\text{Department P} = \frac{94{,}897.96}{1{,}000} = ₹94.90$$

$$\text{Department Q} = \frac{1{,}49{,}571.43}{2{,}500} = ₹59.83$$

$$\text{Department R} = \frac{69{,}530.61}{1{,}400} = ₹49.66$$

8.4 ABSORPTION OF OVERHEADS

After apportionment of service department overheads to production departments, the total overheads of production departments are known. The next stage in overheads accounting is to distribute the overheads of production departments to the units of products or jobs passing through it. Charging production department overheads to cost units is called absorption of overheads. Absorption of overheads is also known as recovery, levy, and charge. Absorption involves calculation of overhead rates on some basis.

8.4.1 Overheads absorption rate

Overheads absorption rates are calculated by relating the overheads of a production department to the budgeted activity level of that department. The activity level may be expressed in number of units, labour hours, machine hours etc. Overheads absorption rates are calculated so that production department expenses are charged to products or jobs accurately. It also helps in easing out the seasonal fluctuations in rates of expenses during a period. Economy, accuracy and suitability should be the criteria in selecting an overhead absorption rate. The following are the various overhead rates applied:

(1) Actual overhead rate

Under this method actual overheads incurred during a period is totalled and this total is divided by volume of activity selected. The following is the formula for calculating actual overhead rate:

$$\text{Actual overhead rate} = \frac{\text{Actual overhead expenses incurred in a given period}}{\text{Volume of activity during the period (units, machine hours, etc.)}}$$

Actual overhead rate does not help in preparation of plans, budgets, tender or quotations.

Limitations

Actual overhead rates can be calculated only after the period is over. It does not help the management in controlling the cost or in price fixation. It acts as a record of past activity only.

In case of seasonal industries expenses vary during different seasons. Using the actual rates will result in different prices for the products in different seasons. Some expenses are not incurred evenly throughout the year like: bonus, workmen compensation, sick leave salary, leave wages etc. Applying actual overheads absorption rate leads to many difficulties.

(2) Predetermined overhead rates

Overhead expenses likely to be incurred during a future period are determined in advance, which is called budgeted overheads. Budgeted production is also determined. The following formula is used for calculating predetermined overhead rates:

$$\text{Predetermined overhead rate} = \frac{\text{Budgeted overhead expenses}}{\text{Budgeted activity level (units, machine hour, etc.)}}$$

Predetermined overhead rate helps in preparing cost estimates, tenders or quotations. It is useful in cost control as the actual cost may be compared with budgeted cost.

(3) Blanket or single overhead rate

All production expenses are totalled and it is divided by the activity level. Calculating a single overhead rate for all production expenses is called blanket overhead rate or single overhead rate. It is calculated as under:

$$\text{Blanket overhead rate} = \frac{\text{Total overheads of a production department}}{\text{Budgeted activity level. (units, machine hours, etc.)}}$$

This is easy to calculate and less costly. Using a blanket overhead rate is advisable only where all products pass through all manufacturing processes and production is carried on small scale.

(4) Multiple overhead rates

Production expenses incurred are classified under different groups based on the similarity or nature of expenses or similarity of purpose for which they are incurred. For example, expenses may be classified as follows: indirect materials, stores and materials handling expenses, all expenses related to machines like repairs & maintenance, depreciation, insurance etc. All indirect labour expenses like foremen salary, works manager salary, group insurance, workmen compensation, PF and ESI contribution, labour welfare expenses, fixed overheads, variable overheads.

Expenses may also be classified under cost centres, production departments or service departments.

Separate overhead rate is calculated for each group of expenses, cost centre or production department. It is calculated as under:

$$\text{Multiple overhead rate} = \frac{\begin{array}{c}\text{Total expenses of a/}\\ \text{cost centre/production department/service department}\end{array}}{\text{Relevant base (units, hours, etc.)}}$$

A product or a job may pass through all cost centres or production departments. Overheads are charged to the products or jobs using all overhead rates. Some products or jobs may pass through only a few cost centres, then overhead rates of those cost centres through which the product or job pass are applied for calculating overhead charges of the product.

Application of multiple overhead rates for charging overheads to products or jobs is more scientific and gives accurate result.

Illustration-5

PB Ltd is a manufacturing company and the product passes through three departments melting, machining and finishing. The manufacturing expenses are as follows.

	Melting	Machining	Finishing	Total
Direct wages	20,000	80,000	90,000	1,90,000
Factory overheads	20,000	1,60,000	1,05,000	2,85,000

The factory cost of product produced has been calculated by a new cost clerk. It is as under:

	₹	₹
Materials		500.00
Direct wages		

Melting	75	
Machining	100	
Finishing	50	225.00
Prime cost		725.00
Factory overheads: 150% of direct wages = $\left(\frac{2,85,000}{1,90,000} \times 100\right)$		337.50
Factory cost		**1,062.50**

You, being a newly appointed cost accountant of the company, are required to verify the correctness of the works cost of the product calculated.

Solution

The cost clerk has used a blanket overhead rate for charging overhead. Here the product passes through three departments. It is advisable to apply separate overhead rates for each department they are:

Overhead rates as a % on wages:

$$\text{Melting} = \frac{20,000}{20,000} \times 100 = 100\%$$

$$\text{Machining} = \frac{1,60,000}{80,000} \times 100 = 200\%$$

$$\text{Finishing} = \frac{1,05,000}{90,000} \times 100 = 116.67\%$$

Revised cost sheet showing correct factory cost

	₹	₹
Materials		500.00
Wages		
Melting	75	
Machining	100	
Finishing	50	225.00
Prime cost		725.00
Factory overheads		
Melting= 75 × 100%		75.00
Machining= 100 × 200%		200.00

Finishing= 50 × 116.67%		58.33
		333.33
Factory cost		**1,058.33**

Illustration-6

The following information relates to the activities of a production department for a certain period in a factory:

Materials used - ₹1,25,000
Direct wages - ₹80,000
Machine hours - 25,000 hrs
Labour hours - 20,000 hrs

Production overheads apportioned to the department ₹1,00,000. The information relating to an order carried out in this period is as under:

Materials used - ₹10,000
Labour hours - 2,000 hrs
Direct wages - ₹8,000
Machine hours - 3,000 hrs

Prepare a comparative statement of cost of this order by applying the following methods of absorption of overheads:

(a) Direct materials cost method
(b) Direct labour cost method
(c) Prime cost method
(d) Direct labour hour method
(e) Machine hour rate method.

Solution

Overhead absorption rates:

(a) Direct materials cost method:

$$\text{Overhead rate} = \frac{\text{Overheads}}{\text{Direct materials cost}} \times 100$$

$$= \frac{1{,}00{,}000}{1,25,000} \times 100 = 80\%$$

(b) Direct labour cost method:

$$\text{Overhead rate} = \frac{\text{Overheads}}{\text{Direct labour cost}} \times 100$$
$$= \frac{1{,}00{,}000}{80{,}000} \times 100 = 125\%$$

(c) Prime cost method:

$$\text{Overhead rate} = \frac{\text{Overheads}}{\text{Prime cost}} \times 100$$
$$= \frac{1{,}00{,}000}{2{,}05{,}000} \times 100 = 48.78\%$$

(d) Direct labour hour rate method:

$$\text{Overhead rate} = \frac{\text{Overheads}}{\text{Direct labour hours}} \times 100$$
$$= \frac{1{,}00{,}000}{20{,}000} \times 100 = ₹5$$

(e) Machine hour rate method:

$$\text{Overhead rate} = \frac{\text{Overheads}}{\text{Machine hours}} \times 100$$
$$= \frac{1{,}00{,}000}{25{,}000} \times 100 = ₹4$$

Statement showing cost of the order

Methods	(a) ₹	(b) ₹	(c) ₹	(d) ₹	(e) ₹
Direct materials	10,000	10,000	10,000	10,000	10,000
Direct wages	8,000	8,000	8,000	8,000	8,000
Prime cost	18,000	18,000	18,000	18,000	18,000
Production OHS	8,000 (10,000 × 80%)	10,000 (8,000 × 125%)	8,780 18,000 × 48.78%)	10,000 (2,000 hrs × 5)	12,000 (3,000 hrs × 4)
Works cost	26,000	28,000	26,780	28,000	30,000

(5) Supplementary overhead rate

Some times actual expenses incurred may have increased or decreased considerably or actual production may be much less or more than the budgeted overheads. This results in substantial under-

or over-absorption of overheads. To ensure full recovery of overheads to products, and overhead rate may be calculated for the under-absorbed or over-absorbed overheads. This overhead rate is called supplementary overhead rate. Supplementary overhead rate is calculated by using the following formula

$$\text{Supplementary overhead rate} = \frac{\begin{array}{c}\text{Under- or over-absorbed overheads}\\ \text{(Actual ohs} - \text{Absorbed ohs)}\end{array}}{\text{Activity level (units, machine hours, etc.)}}$$

(6) Normal overhead rate

This overhead rate is calculated for expenses expected to be incurred at normal activity level. This is calculated as follows:

$$\text{Normal overhead rate} = \frac{\text{Normal overheads}}{\text{Normal activity level (machine hours, units, etc.)}}$$

8.5 METHODS OF OVERHEAD ABSORPTION

(1) Units Cost Method

Under this method total factory overheads (actual or predetermined) are divided by the number of units produced or budgeted units. For example:

Total factory overheads	-	₹1,00,000
No. of units produced	-	20,000 units

$$\text{Overhead rate per unit} = \frac{\text{Total factory overheads}}{\text{No of units produced}}$$

$$= \frac{1,00,000}{20,000} = ₹5 \text{ per unit}$$

This method is simple and easy to apply. This method is suitable if a single product with uniform specifications are produced and all units pass through all production operations.

This method is not suitable when goods of heterogeneous nature are produced, where some units may pass through all production processes and some other products may pass through only a few production processes.

(2) Percentage of Direct Materials Cost Method

Under this method total factory overheads is related to direct materials cost of units produced and expressed as a percentage. It is calculated as follows:

$$\begin{array}{l}\text{Overhead rate as a percentage of}\\ \text{direct materials cost}\end{array} = \frac{\text{Total factory overheads}}{\text{Total direct materials}} \times 100$$

Example:

Factory overheads - ₹50,000
Direct materials - ₹2,00,000

$$\text{Overhead absorption rate} = \frac{50{,}000}{2,00,000} \times 100 = 25\%$$

If a product requiring direct materials ₹200 is produced, the overhead charged to that product will be 25% of ₹200 or ₹50.

Merits

1. It is simple and easy to calculate.
2. Suitable to industries where raw materials cost forms the major part of the product cost.
3. It is suitable when price of raw materials are stable and materials mix ratio remains same in units produced.

Demerits

1. Materials prices do not remain stable. They change very frequently; this will distort the absorption of overheads.
2. There is no direct relationship between production expenses and materials. Product requiring costly materials may need only simple production process but results in over-absorption of overheads.
3. Some factory overheads like rent, rates and insurance are time based. Under this method time factor is completely ignored.
4. This method is also not suitable when materials mix ratio changes.

(3) Percentage on Direct Wages Method

Under this method total factory overhead is divided by total direct wages and multiplied by hundred. It is calculated as follows:

$$\%\text{ of direct wages} = \frac{\text{Factory overheads}}{\text{Direct wages}} \times 100$$

Example:

Factory overheads - ₹80,000
Direct wages - ₹1,00,000

$$\%\text{ of overhead absorption rate} = \frac{80,000}{1,00,000} \times 100 = 80\%$$

When a job requiring direct wage of ₹1000 is completed, the share of its overhead charges will be 80% of ₹1000 or ₹800.

Merits:

1. There is a direct relationship between production and direct wages. When production is more, more wages are payable. When production is more, production expenses will also be more.
2. Wage is paid on time basis. So time factor is included in computing overhead absorption rate.
3. It is also simple and easy to understand and operate.
4. Information required for calculation of overhead absorption rate is readily available.
5. This method is suitable when workers with different grades or skills are employed. When compared with direct materials cost, wages rates fluctuate less frequently.

Demerits:

1. Many factory expenses like indirect materials, rent, rates, insurance, and depreciation are not related to direct wages.
2. If labour mix ratio changes, this method will distort the overhead absorption.
3. Labour productivity is also ignored.

(4) Percentage on Prime Cost Method

Total factory overheads are compared with prime cost and it is expressed as a percentage on prime cost. It is calculated as follows:

$$\text{Overhead absorption rate} = \frac{\text{Factory overheads}}{\text{Prime cost}} \times 100$$

Example:

Factory overheads	-	₹90,000
Direct materials	-	₹2,00,000
Direct wages	-	₹1,60,000

$$\text{Overhead absorption rate} = \frac{\text{Factory overheads}}{\text{Prime cost}} \times 100$$

$$= \frac{90{,}000}{3,60{,}000} \times 100 = 25\%$$

Product X is produced in a factory. Its direct materials and direct wages are ₹500 and ₹600 respectively. The overhead charged to product X will be 25% on prime cost of the product.

$$\text{Prime cost} = \text{Direct materials} + \text{Direct wages}$$

$$= 500 + 600 = ₹1{,}100$$

$$\text{Overheads absorbed} = 1{,}100 \times \frac{25}{100} = ₹275$$

This method gives equal importance to direct materials and direct wages. This method may be applied when direct materials cost and direct wages are incurred equally in producing a product. This method is simple and easy to operate and understand. But this method suffers from the draw-backs of both direct materials cost method and direct wages cost method.

(5) Direct Labour Hour Rate Method

Labour hour rate is computed by dividing the total factory overheads by number of effective direct labour hours. Normal idle time hours are to be deducted from total labour hours for calculating effective labour hours. This method is suitable where workers with uniform skill and experience are employed. Time factor is fully considered for calculation of overheads absorption rate.

The advantages and disadvantages applicable to percentage of direct wages cost method is also applicable to this method.

(6) Machine Hour Rate Method

It is calculated as under:

$$= \frac{\text{Total factory overheads}}{\text{No. of machine hours}}$$

For calculating machine hour rate, the factory overheads are widely classified into two groups as:

(i) Fixed expenses or standing charges.
(ii) Operating expenses or machine expenses.

Fixed expenses or standing charges

These are incurred even when the machine is idle. They are supervisor/foremen salary, helper wages, rent, rates and insurance, interest on borrowed capital, lighting etc.

Operating expenses or machine expenses

These expenses are incurred only when the machines are operated. They are depreciation, repairs and maintenance, power, oil, fuel, lubricants, cotton waste, special chemicals and consumable stores.

8.6 COMPUTATION OF MACHINE HOUR RATES

Machine expenses are classified into standing charges and operating expenses.

1. Standing charges like rent, supervision, lighting, interest on borrowed capital, shop cleaning and building service are expenses incurred for the entire work shop. A part of this expense is to be apportioned to a machine or a group of machines. Total standing charges is divided by number of machine hours. We get a machine hour rate for the standing charges for the period

2. Operating expenses are direct to the machine and a rate per machine hour is computed for each expenses.

   The total of machine hour rate for standing charges and operating expenses gives the machine hour rate.

8.6.1 Computation of Number of Machine Hours

From the total machine hours available normal idle time and setup time should be deducted to arrive at effective machine hours.

8.6.2 Types of Machine Hour Rates

1. **Ordinary machine hour rate:** Only direct expenses of a machine like depreciation, repairs & maintenance, power, fuel are taken for calculating ordinary machine hour rate.

2. **Composite machine hour rate:** When standing charges per machine hour is added to ordinary machine hour rate, the resulting machine hour rate is called composite machine hour rate.

3. **Comprehensive machine hour rate:** When machine operator wages are added to composite machine hour rate, it is called comprehensive machine hour rate.

   Many authorities do not favour the inclusion of operator wages in machine hour rate computation. The reason is operator wages is considered direct wages and forms part of prime cost. It should not be included in factory overheads again in calculation of machine hour rate. When operator wage is not included in the direct labour cost of a product or a job, it may be included in computation of machine hour rate.

4. **Group machine hour rate:** Usually a machine is taken as a cost centre and machine hour rate is computed for each machine separately. Sometimes machines of similar type are grouped into one cost centre and a single machine hour rate is calculated for this group of machines. Using this method results in less accounting and clerical work. It is more economical.

Merits

1. Goods are produced mainly with the help of machines. So using machine hour rate is more suitable.
2. Most of factory expenses are related to machine operations. Machine hour rate is more appropriate.
3. Time factor is fully considered.
4. Absorption will indicate the extent to which machines were under- utilised.
5. This method is more scientific and logical.

Demerits

1. This method is not suitable when goods are produced with labour.

2. More work is involved in determining the number of machine hours operated.
3. There is a difficulty in ascertaining machine cost.
4. When products pass through different machine operations i.e., some products may pass through all machine operations, some products may pass through only a few machine operations, there will be inaccuracy in overhead absorption.
5. This method increases costing work. So it is time consuming and costly also.

Illustration-7

Cost of machine	₹1,75,000
Cost of installation	₹10,000
Scrap value after 15 years of useful life	₹5,000
Working hours per month	200 hrs
Lighting for the shop	₹800 pm
Rent for the shop	₹2,000 pm
Insurance premium for the machine	₹7,200 pa
Repair charges	50% of depreciation
Other standing charges allocated to the machine	₹1,000 pm

Power is used by the machine at 5 units per hour at ₹3.50 per unit

The machine occupies one-fourth of the floor space of the shop supervisor is expected to devote one-fifth of his time to oversee this machine.

Solution

	Total (pm) ₹	Per hour ₹
Standing charges		
Lighting - $800 \times 1/4$	200	
Rent - $2,000 \times 1/4$	500	
Insurance premium - $7,200/12$	600	
Other standing charges	1,000	
Total standing charges	2,300	
Standing charges per hour = 2,300/200		11.50
Operating charges		
Depreciation=cost of the machine−scrap value/life $= \dfrac{1,85,000 - 5,000}{15 \times 12}$	1,000	5.00
Repair charges -50% of depreciation		2.50

Power - 5 × 3.50		17.50
Machine hour rate		**36.50**

Illustration-8

Calculate machine hour rate from the following:

a) Cost of machine	₹19,200
b) Estimated scrap value	₹1,200
c) Average repair and maintenance charges per month	₹150
d) Standing charges allocated to this machine per month	₹50
e) Effective working life of machine	10,000 hrs
f) Running time per month	166 hrs
g) Power used by the machine	5 units per hour at 19 paise per unit

(B.Com., Madras University)

Solution

	Total (pm) ₹	**Per hour** ₹
Standing charges	50	0.30
Running expenses:		
Depreciation		
(Cost of machine −scrap)/life		
$=\frac{19{,}200-1{,}200}{10{,}000\text{ hrs}}$		1.80
Repairs and maintenance	150	0.90
Power - 5 units×19 paise		0.95
Machine hour rate		**3.95**

Illustration-9

Compute the machine hour rate from the following data:

	₹
Cost of the machine	1,00,000
Installation charges	10,000
Estimated scrap value after the expiry of life of 15 years)	5,000
Rent and rates of the shop per month	200
General lighting for the shop per month	300
Insurance premium for the machine per annum	960
Repairs and maintenance per annum	1,000
Power consumption - 10 units per hr Rate of power per 100 units	20
Estimated working hours per annum This includes setting up time of 200 hrs	2,200 hrs
Shop supervisor salary per month	600

The machine occupies one-fourth of the total area. The supervisor is expected to devote one fifth of his time for supervising the machine. **(B.Com., Madras University)**

Solution

Computation of machine hour rate		
	Total (pa) ₹	**Per hour** ₹
Standing charges		
Rent and rates - 200 × 12/4	600	
General lighting - 300 × 12/4	900	
Insurance premium	960	
Shop supervisor salary - 600 × 12/5	1,440	
Total	3,900	
Standing charges per hour - 3,900/2,000	-	1.95
Operating expenses:		
Depreciation = (Cost of the machine−scrap value)/life		
$=\dfrac{1,10,000-5,000}{15}$	7,000	3.50
Repairs and maintenance	1,000	0.50
Power−10 units*20 /100		2.00
Machine hour rate		**₹7.95**

Note: Effective machine hours

Estimated working hours per annum	=	2,200
(−) Setting up time	=	200
Effective machine hours	=	**2,000**

(7) Sale Price Method

Under this method factory overhead are recovered as a % on sales value. It is calculated as under.

$$\text{Overhead absorption rate} = \frac{\text{Factory overheads}}{\text{Sales}} \times 100$$

Factory overheads have no direct relationship with sales value of a product. So it is not suitable and not applied widely.

Selecting a suitable overhead absorption rate

Selecting an appropriate overhead absorption rate depends upon the following factors:

1. Nature of manufacturing operations involved, e.g., labour operated production or machine operated production.
2. Type of labour employed, skilled workers or unskilled workers.
3. Nature of expenses involved.
4. The production process through which a product passes.
5. The length of time involved in production process (i.e., production cycle).
6. Policy of management.
7. The method must be flexible to incorporate the change when change takes place.

Under-absorption or over-absorption of overheads

Overheads are absorbed by using predetermined overhead rates. The following formula is used for calculation of absorbed overheads.

$$\text{Absorbed overheads} = \text{Actual activity level (unit or hours)} \times \text{predetermined overhead rate}$$

If actual overhead rate is applied, there will be no under- or over-absorption of overheads.

When predetermined overhead rates are used for absorption of overheads, normally there will be difference between actual overheads incurred and absorbed overheads. If absorbed overheads is less than actual overheads it is called under-absorption of overheads. If absorbed overheads are more than actual overheads it is called over-absorption of overheads.

Causes for under-absorption or over-absorption of overheads

Under- or over- absorption of overheads arise due to the following reasons:

(a) **Error in estimating the level of activity:** There may be vast difference between budgeted level of activity and actual level of activity. This results in either under- or over-absorption of overheads.

(b) **Error in estimating the overhead expenses:** Due to change in rate of various overheads or due to new overheads being incurred under- or over-absorbed take place.

(c) **Seasonal nature of work:** Volume of work done may change in different seasons. So overheads may change from season to season.

(d) **Change in method of production:** When proportion of work done is changed by increasing or reducing the machine or labour work. This leads to over- or under-absorption of overheads.

(e) **Use of unsuitable method of absorption:** When production is done with machines but percentage of direct materials method is applied and material prices fluctuate widely, then there will be under- or over-absorption of overheads.

(f) **Change in activity level:** When activity increases than budgeted level, there will be over-absorption of overheads. If activity level is less than the budgeted level, it will cause under-absorption of overheads.

Treatment of under- or over-absorbed overheads

Disposal of under- or over-absorbed overheads depends upon the causes for over- or under-absorption. Three methods are available for treatment of under- or over-absorption. They are:

(1) Use of supplementary overhead rates

When the amount of under- or over-absorbed overhead is large, a supplementary overhead rate may be used to dispose the under- or over-absorbed overheads. The following step is followed for calculation of supplementary overhead rate:

$$\text{Supplementary overhead rate} = \frac{\text{Under or over-absorbed overheads}}{\text{Actual activity level (hours or units)}}.$$

In case of over-absorption, the supplementary overhead rate will be negative. It is used to reduce the absorbed overheads. In case of under-absorption the supplementary overhead rate calculated will be positive. It is used to increase the absorbed overheads.

When there is change in the rates of various expenses, change in method of production, or change in level of activity, supplementary overhead rate should be applied to correct the under- or over-absorption of overheads.

But if under- or over-absorption arises due to faulty estimation of overhead expenses or level of activity, supplementary overhead rate should not be used to dispose under- or over-absorption of overheads. The under- or over-absorbed overheads should be transferred to costing profit and loss account.

(2) Carry forward to subsequent year

This method is followed when the amount of under- or over-absorbed overheads is very small in a particular gear. The overheads carried forward in one year may get balanced in the next year due to an opposite effect in actual expenses in subsequent year. This method is not favoured if the amount is large since the overhead of one period is carried to another period.

(3) Transfer to costing profit and loss account

This method is followed when under- or over-absorption occurs due to some abnormal factors or faulty estimation of overhead expenses or activity level. This method causes wrong valuation of work in progress and finished goods stock.

Illustration-10

In a factory overheads of a particular department are recovered on the basis of ₹5 per machine hour. The total expenses incurred and the actual machine hours for the department for the month of August were ₹80,000 and 10,000 hours respectively. Of the amount of ₹80,000, ₹15,000 became payable due to an award of the labour court and ₹5,000 was in respect of expenses of the previous year booked in the current month (August). Actual production was 40,000 units, of which 30,000 units were sold. On analysing the reasons, it was found that 60% of the under-absorbed overhead was due to defective planning and the rest was attributed to normal cost increase. How would you treat the under- absorbed overhead in cost accounts. **(CA-Inter)**

Solution

Under-absorbed overheads during the month of August			
		₹	₹
(a)	**Total Expenditure**		80,000
	Non-recurring expenses		
	Amount paid due to court award	15,000	
	Expenses of previous year	5,000	20,000
	Actual expenditure for the month		60,000
	Overhead recovered		
	Actual machine hours×hourly rate i.e., 10,000×5		50,000
	Under-absorbed overhead		10,000
(b)	**Causes of under-absorption**		
	Due to defective planning 60% of ₹10,000		6,000
	Normal cost-increase (balancing)		4,000
			10,000

c) Treatment of under-absorbed overhead in cost accounts

1. Under-absorption due to defective planning is treated as abnormal cost. Abnormal cost is written off to costing profit & loss account. ₹6,000 of under-absorption is due to defective planning.

2. Under-absorption due to normal cost increase is to be adjusted in cost of production: Normal cost increases ₹4000 is to be apportioned between cost of sales and financial goods in the ratio of units sold and finished stock i.e., 3 : 1.

$$\text{Cost of sale: ₹}4000 \times \frac{3}{4} = \text{₹}3{,}000$$

$$\text{Finished goods: ₹}4000 \times \frac{1}{4} = \text{₹}1,000$$

Note: Usually supplementary rates should be used. It will be (₹4000/50,000) × 100, i.e. 8% of absorbed overheads. Alternatively supplementary rate per unit is calculated i.e. ₹4000/40,000 or 0.10 per unit.

Illustration-11

The factory overhead costs of four production departments of a company engaged in job orders for an accounting year are as follows:

Dept A - ₹19,300, Dept B - ₹4,200, Dept C - ₹4,000, Dept D - ₹2,000,

Overheads have been applied as under:

Dept A ₹1.50 per machine hour for 14,000 hours.
Dept B ₹1.30 per direct labour for 3,000 hours.
Dept C 80% of direct labour cost of ₹6,000.
Dept D ₹2 per piece for 950 pieces.

Find out the amount of department-wise under- or over-absorbed factory overheads.

(ICWA-Inter adapted)

Solution

Statement showing under- or over-absorbed factory overheads

Department	**Factory Overheads incurred (₹)**	**Factory Overheads Absorbed (₹)**	**Under(−)/Over(+) absorption of factory overheads (₹)**
A	19,300	21,000 i.e. 14,000 × 1.50	(+) 1700
B	4,200	3,900 i.e. 3,000 × 1.30	(−) 300
C	4,000	4,800 i.e. 6,000 × 80%	(+) 800
D	2,000	1,900 i.e. 950 × 2	(−) 100
Total	29,500	31,600 -	(+) 2,100

8.7 CONCEPT OF CAPACITY AND OVERHEAD RECOVERY RATES

Calculation of overhead recovery rates is a prerequisite for absorption of overheads to cost units. For calculation of overhead recovery rates two factors are necessary. One is the total amount of overheads and the other is production capacity level assumed. Overhead recovery rate depends on the capacity level assumed. Capacity can be expressed in terms of units produced, labour hours or machine hours worked. There are different capacity levels.

(a) Maximum capacity or theoretical capacity

This is the capacity at which a plant can operate when there is no constraint to production. The plant is supposed to run all the days in a year. No allowance is given for holidays, leave, machine setup time etc. This is an ideal capacity which cannot be attained practically. This capacity is also called rated capacity or installed capacity.

(b) Practical capacity

This is the capacity that can be attained after giving allowances for plant maintenance, plant set-up, leaves and holidays. It is also called operating capacity or net capacity or available capacity. Normally practical capacity ranges from 80% to 90% of maximum capacity.

(c) Normal capacity

It is the capacity actually utilised during a long period of time, usually covering a business cycle, say 3 to 5 years. This capacity is usually based on sales expectancy. Overhead recovery rates are calculated by using normal capacity.

(d) Capacity based on sales expectancy

Plant capacity will be used to meet the actual demands for the products. This capacity is calculated on immediate sales potential. But normal capacity considers long term sales demand for the products, usually covering a business cycle.

(e) Actual capacity

Actual capacity utilised need not be equal to capacity based on sales expectancy. Sometimes there may be constraints in production like power cut, non-availability of raw materials, shortage of skilled man power etc. This capacity sometimes may be normal capacity based on sales expectancy.

(f) Idle capacity

Practical capacity remaining unutilised for want of demand, power cut, labour shortage and non-availability of raw materials is called idle capacity. It is the difference between practical capacity and actual capacity.

Idle capacity cost: It is calculated as follows,

$$\text{Idle capacity cost} = \frac{\text{All fixed overheads related to plant}}{\text{Normal plant capacity}} \times \text{Idle capacity}$$

Treatment of idle capacity cost: Treatment of idle capacity cost depends upon the reasons for idle capacity

1. Idle capacity cost due to power failure, major machine breakdown, faulty planning, accidents etc., are abnormal. It is charged to costing P&L a/c.

2. Idle capacity cost due seasonal nature of business is charged to production overheads.
3. Idle capacity cost due to normal factors like leave, holiday, plant set-up, repairs & maintenance are charged to production overheads.

Idle time and idle capacity: Idle time refers to the time for which workers are paid but spent unproductively. This may be normal idle time arising due to time taken for machine set-up, moving from one job to another, lunch and tea breaks etc., or abnormal idle time due to loss of time due to accident, non-availability of materials, power failure etc.

Idle capacity refers to plant capacity available for production but remaining unutilised. This may also be due to normal causes like repairs and maintenance, leave, holidays etc or may be abnormal due to faulty planning, power failure, non-availability of materials, power lack of demand for the product, etc.

Illustration-12

ABC Ltd is producing an article at the rate of 5 units per hour. It was producing and selling 10,000 units on an average in the past 5 years. Due to slackness in demand for the product during the year 2007 it produced and sold only 9,000 units. The company works single shift of 8 hours per day and 6 days a week. The number of holidays declared in the year 2007 is 15 days. Production has been stopped for 60 hours per quarter for carrying out periodic repairs and maintenance work. The fixed overheads during the year 2007 amounted to ₹4,50,000. You are required to.

1. Calculate the maximum, practical, normal and actual capacities in 2007 in terms of hours.
2. Compute the idle capacity and hourly rate for recovery of overhead rates for each of the capacity computed at (a) above and
3. Prepare a statement showing the idle capacity cost assuming that the overhead rates of recovery are based on the various capacity levels arrived at (a) above.

Solution

(a) Calculation of various capacity levels in terms of hours

(i) Maximum Capacity

$$\begin{aligned}\text{Maximum capacity} &= \text{No. of days in 2007} \times \text{No. of hours per day}\\ &= 365 \times 8\\ &= 2{,}920 \text{ hours}\end{aligned}$$

(ii) Practical capacity

Maximum capacity		2,920 hours
Normal idle capacity days:		
Sundays = 52 × 8	= 416 hours	

Holidays = 15 × 8	= 120 hours	
Repairs & maintenance = 60 × 4	= 240 hours	
		= 776 hours
Practical capacity (2,920 – 776)		= 2,144 hours

(iii) **Normal capacity** $= \dfrac{\text{Normal production and sales}}{\text{Rate of production per hour}}$

$$= \frac{10{,}000}{5}$$

$$= 2{,}000 \text{ hours}$$

(iv) **Actual capacity** $= \dfrac{\text{Production and sales in 2007}}{\text{Rate of production per hour}}$

$$= \frac{9{,}000}{5}$$

$$= 1{,}800 \text{ hours}$$

(b)

Statement showing idle capacity and overhead recovery rates

Base Capacity	**Base Capacity (hours)** (1)	**Capacity utilised (hours)** (2)	**Idle Capacity (hours) (1) - (2)**	**Overhead Recovery Rate[Fixed overheads/ Base Capacity(hours)]** ₹
Maximum	2,920	1,800	1,120	$\frac{4{,}50{,}000}{2{,}920} = 154.11$
Practical	2,144	1,800	344	$\frac{4{,}50{,}000}{2{,}144} = 209.89$
Normal	2,000	1,800	200	$\frac{4{,}50{,}000}{2{,}000} = 225.00$
Actual	1,800	1,800	-	$\frac{4{,}50{,}000}{1{,}800} = 250.00$

(c)

Statement showing idle capacity cost

Base Capacity	**Overhead recovery rate ₹(1)**	**Idle Capacity (hours) (2)**	**Idle capacity Cost ₹(1 × 2)**
Maximum	154.11	1120	1,72,603.20
Practical	209.89	344	72,202.16
Normal	225	200	45,000.00
Actual	250	-	

COMPREHENSIVE ILLUSTRATIONS

Illustration-13

The Modern Manufacturing Company has three production departments A,B and C and two service departments D and E.

The following are the abstracts from the records of the company for the month of March 1998:

	₹
Rent and rates	20,000
Indirect wages	6,000
Depreciation on machinery	40,000
Power	6,000
General lighting	2,400
Sundries	40,000

The following further details are also available:

Particulars	Total	A	B	C	D	E
Floor space(sq.ft)	20,000	4,000	5,000	6,000	4,000	1,000
Horse power of machines	300	120	60	100	20	20
Light points	120	20	30	40	20	10
Direct wages (₹)	20,000	6,000	4,000	6,000	3,000	1,000
Value of machinery (₹)	5,00,000	1,20,000	1,60,000	2,00,000	10,000	10,000

Apportion the expenses to the departments on suitable basis. **(B.Com - Madras University)**

Solution

Primary distribution of overheads							
Particulars	Basis of apportionment	Total	Production departments			Service departments	
			A	B	C	D	E
		₹	₹	₹	₹	₹	₹
D. Wages	Actual	4,000	-	-	-	3,000	1,000
Rent and rates	floor space 4:5:6:4:1	20,000	4,000	5,000	6,000	4,000	1,000
Indirect wages	D .Wages 6:4:6:3:1	6,000	1,800	1,200	1,800	900	300

Dep. of machinery -	Value of machinery 12:16:20:1;1	40,000	9,600	12,800	16,000	800	800
Power	HP of machines 12:6:10:2:2	6,400	2,400	1,200	2,000	400	400
General lighting	light points 2:3:4:2:1	2,400	400	600	800	400	200
Sundries	D Wages 6:4:6:3:1	40,000	12,000	8,000	12,000	6,000	2,000
Departmental overheads		1,18,800	30,200	8,800	38,600	15,500	5,700

Note: Direct wages of production departments are not included in overhead distribution summary.

Illustration-14

In an engineering factory, the following particulars have been extracted for the year ended 31.12.97. Compute the departmental overhead rate for each of the production departments assuming that overheads are recovered as a percentage of direct wages:

Particulars	Production departments			Service departments	
	A	B	C	X	Y
Direct wages (₹)	30,000	45,000	60,000	15,000	30,000
Direct materials (₹)	15,000	30,000	30,000	22,500	22,500
Staff number	1,500	2,250	2,250	750	750
Electricity (kwh)	6,000	4,500	3,000	1,500	1,500
Assets value (₹)	60,000	40,000	30,000	10,000	10,000
Light points	10	16	4	6	4
Area (sq.metres)	150	250	50	50	50

The expenses for the period were:

	₹		₹
Power	11,000	Depreciation	30,000
Lighting	2,000	Repairs	6,000
Stores overhead	8,000	General overheads	12,000
Staff welfare	30,000	Rent and rates	5,500

Apportion the expenses of service department Y according to direct wages and those of service department X in the ratio of 5:3:2 to the production departments.

Solution

Overhead distribution summary							
Particulars	Basis of apportionment	Total	Production departments			Service departments	
			A	B	C	X	Y
		₹	₹	₹	₹	₹	₹
Direct wages	Actual	45,000	-	-	-	15,000	30,000
Direct materials	Actual	45,000	-	-	-	22,500	22,500
Power	kWH 12:9:6:3:3	11,000	4,000	3,000	2,000	1,000	1,000
Lighting	Light points 5:8:2:3:2	2,000	500	800	200	300	200
Stores overheads	Direct materials 2:4:4:3:3	8,000	1,000	2,000	2,000	1,500	1,500
Staff welfare	Staff number 2:3:3:1:1	30,000	6,000	9,000	9,000	3,000	3,000
Depreciation	Asset value 6:4:3:1:1	30,000	12,000	8,000	6,000	2,000	2,000
Repairs	Asset value	6,000	2,400	1,600	1,200	400	400
General Overhead	Direct wages 2:3:4:1:2	12,000	2,000	3,000	4,000	1,000	2,000
Rent and taxes	Area 3:5:1:1:1	5,500	1,500	2,500	500	500	500
Department overheads		1,94,500	29,400	29,900	24,900	47,200	63,100
Service Department x	5:3:2	-	23,600	14,160	9,440	(–) 47,200	-
Service Department y	2:3:4	-	14,022	21,033	28,045	-	(–) 63,100
Total overheads		1,94,500	67,022	65,093	62,385	-	-

Illustration-15

Electronics Limited furnishes you the following information. It has three production departments A,B and C and two service departments D and E. The following figures are extracted from the records of the company:

	₹		₹
Rent and rates	40,000	Power	24,000
General lighting	12,000	Depreciation on machinery	30,000
Indirect wages	18,000	Sundries	25,000

The following further details are available:

Particulars	Total	A	B	C	D	E
Floor area (sq. metres)	10,000	2,000	2,500	3,000	2,000	500
Light points	60	10	15	20	10	5
Direct wages (₹)	40,000	12,000	8,000	12,000	6,000	2,000
HP of machines	160	60	30	50	10	10
Value of machinery (₹)	2,50,000	60,000	80,000	1,00,000	5,000	5,000
Working hours	-	6,000	4,000	4,000	-	-

The service department expenses are allocated as follows:

	A	B	C	D	E
Service department D	20%	30%	40%	-	10%
Service department E	40%	20%	30%	10%	-

What is the total cost of an article if its raw materials cost is ₹500, labour cost ₹300 and it passes through departments A, B and C 4, 5 and 3 hours respectively.

Solution

Overhead distribution summary							
Particulars	Basis of apportionment	Total	Production departments			Service departments	
			A	B	C	D	E
		₹	₹	₹	₹	₹	₹
Direct wages	actual	-		-	-	6,000	2,000

Rent and rates	floor area 4:5:6:4:1	40,000	8,000	10,000	12,000	8,000	2,000
General lighting	light points 2:3:4:2:1	12,000	2,000	3,000	4,000	2,000	1,000
ID.wages	D .wages 6:4:6:3:1	18,000	5,400	3,600	5,400	2,700	900
Power	HP of machines 6:3:5:1:1	24,000	9,000	4,500	7,500	1,500	1,500
Dep. on machinery	value of machinery 12:16:20:1:1	30,000	7,200	9,600	12,000	600	600
Sundries	D.wages 6:4:6:1:1	25,000	7,500	5,000	7,500	3,750	1,250
Departmental overheads		1,57,000	39,100	35,700	48,400	24,550	9,250
Service department D		-	4,910	7,365	9,820	(−)24,550	2,455
Service department E		-	4,682	2,341	3,512	1,170	(−)11,705
Service department D		-	234	351	468	(−)1,170	117
Service department E		-	47	23	35	12	(−)117
Service department D		-	3	4	5	(−)12	-
Total overheads		1,57,000	48,976	45,784	62,240	-	-

Working hours	6,000	4,000	4,000
Overhead rate per hour	₹8.16	₹11.45	₹15.56

Cost sheet of job

	₹
Raw materials	500
Labour	300
Prime cost	800
Overheads:	
Dept A - $8.16 \times 4 = 32.64$	
Dept B - $11.45 \times 5 = 57.25$	
Dept C - $15.56 \times 3 = 46.68$	
	136.57
Total cost	936.57

Illustration-16

In a factory there are two service departments P and Q and three production departments A,B and C. The department overheads as per primary distribution are:

Production departments

A - ₹6,50,000
B - ₹6,00,000
C - ₹5,00,000

Service departments

P - ₹1,20,000
Q - ₹1,00,000

The expenses are distributed to production departments on a percentage basis as follows:

	A	B	C	P	Q
Service department P	30%	40%	15%	-	15%
Service department Q	40%	30%	20%	10%	-

Prepare a statement showing the distribution of service department overheads to production departments on the basis of a) Repeated distribution, b)Simultaneous equation, and c) Trial-and-error methods.

Solution

(a) Repeated distribution method

Overhead distribution summary					
Particulars	**Production departments**			**Service departments**	
	A ₹	**B** ₹	**C** ₹	**P** ₹	**Q** ₹
Departmental overheads	6,50,000	6,00,000	5,00,000	1,20,000	1,00,000
Service department P	36,000	48,000	18,000	(−)1,20,000	18,000
Service department Q	47,200	35,400	23,600	11,800	(−)1,18,000
Service department P	3,540	4,720	1,770	(−)11,800	1,770
Service department Q	708	531	354	177	(−)1,770
Service department P	53	71	27	(−)177	26

Service department R	11	9	6	-	(−)26
Total overheads	7,37,512	6,88,731	5,43,757	-	-

(b) Simultaneous equation method

Let the total overheads of service department P be - x
Let the total overheads of service department Q be - y

$$x = 1,20,000 + 0.1y \quad (8.3)$$
$$y = 1,00,000 + 0.15x \quad (8.4)$$

Substituting the value of y in equation (8.1) we get

$$\begin{aligned} x &= 1,20,000 + 0.1(1,00,000 + 0.15x) \\ &= 1,20,000 + 10,000 + 0.15x \\ x - 0.15x &= 1,30,000 \end{aligned}$$

$$x = \frac{1,30,000}{0.985}$$
$$x = 1,31,980$$

Substituting the value of x in equation (8.2) we get y = 1,19,797

Overhead distribution summary					
Particulars	**Total overheads**	**Basis**	**Production departments**		
			A	**B**	**C**
Departmental overheads	17,50,000	given	6,50,000	6,00,000	5,00,000
Service department 'P'	1,31,980	30%, 40%, 15%	39,594	52,792	19,797
Service department 'Q'	1,19,797	40%, 30%, 20%	47,919	35,939	23,959
Total overheads	-	-	7,37,513	6,88,731	5,43,756

(c)

Trial-and-error method		
	Service departments	
	P	**Q**
Departmental overheads	1,20,000	1,00,000
Apportionment - P to Q -15%		18,000
		1,18,000
Q to P - 10%	11,800	-

P to Q - 15%	-	1,770
Q to P - 10%	177	-
P to Q - 15%	-	27
Q to P - 10%	3	-
Total	1,31,980	1,19,797

Overhead distribution summary					
Particulars	**Total overheads**	**Basis**	**Production departments**		
			A	B	C
Departmental overheads	17,50,000	given	6,50,000	6,00,000	5,00,000
Service department 'P'	1,31,980	30%, 40%, 15%	39,594	52,792	19,797
Service department 'Q'	1,19,797	40%, 30%, 20%	47,919	35,939	23,959
Total overheads	-	-	7,37,513	6,88,731	5,43,756

Illustration-17

Deccan Manufacturing Ltd. has three departments which are regarded as production departments. Service departments costs are distributed to these production departments using step ladder method of distribution. Estimates of factory overhead costs to be incurred by each department in the forthcoming year are as follows. Data for distribution is also shown against each department:

Departments	Factory overheads (₹)	Direct labour hours	Number of employees	Area (sq.metres)
Production- X	1,93,000	4,000	100	3,000
Y	64,000	3,000	125	1,500
Z	83,000	4,000	85	1,500
Service- P	45,000	1,000	10	500
Q	75,000	5,000	50	1,500
R	1,05,000	6,000	40	1,000
S	30,000	3,000	50	1,000

The overhead costs of the four service departments are distributed viz., P, Q, R and S respectively on the following basis:

Departments	Basis
P	Number of employees
Q	Direct labour hours
R	Area in square metres
S	Direct labour hours

You are required to:

(a) Prepare a schedule showing the distribution of overhead costs of the four service departments to the three production departments

(b) Calculate the overhead recovery rate per hour for each of the three production departments.

(CA-Inter)

Solution

(a)

Service Departments	Overheads ₹					Total overheads ₹
P	45,000	(–)45,000				
Q	75,000	5,000	(–)80,000			
R	1,05,000	4,000	24,000	(–)1,33,000		
S	30,000	5,000	12,000	19,000	(–)66,000	
Production departments						
X	1,93,000	10,000	16,000	57,000	24,000	3,00,000
Y	64,000	12,500	12,000	28,500	18,000	1,35,000
Z	83,000	8,500	16,000	28,500	24,000	1,60,000

(b) Direct labour hour rate overheads/direct labour hours

Production departments

X - 3,00,000/4,000 = ₹75
Y - 1,35,000/3,000 = ₹45
Z - 1,60,000/4,000 = ₹40

Illustration-18

In a factory the following expenses were incurred in respect of machine Z:

(a) Power consumption ₹9,000 p.a. and oil, waste etc. ₹1,800.
(b) Repairs for the entire life of the machine ₹16,000.

Other expenses for the entire factory for the year:

(i) Rent and rates - ₹27,000
(ii) Lighting - ₹1,200
(iii) Supervision - ₹3,750
(iv) Sundry expenses - ₹10,000

Other information:

Area of the factory - 10,000 sq.ft. Area occupied by this machine is 2,000 sq.ft. cost of the machine is ₹60,000. Estimated life of the machine is 10 years. There are 16 workers in the factory out of them 4 attend to this machine. The degree of supervision is 2/5th to this machine. The factory will work for 2,000 hours per annum. Calculate machine hour rate. **(B.Com, Madras university)**

Solution

Computation of machine hour rate		
Standing charges	**Total p.a** ₹	**Per hour** ₹
Rent and rates = 27,000 × 2,000/10,000	5,400	
Lighting = 1,200 × 2/10	240	
Supervision = 3,750 × 2/5	1,500	
Sundry expenses = 10,000 × 4/16	2,500	
Total standing charges	9,640	
Standing charges per hour = 9,640/2,000		4.82
Running expenses:		
Depreciation = 60,000/10	6,000	3.00
Repairs = 16,000/10	1,600	0.80
Power	9,000	4.50
Oil, waste etc.	1,800	0.90
Machine hour rate		14.02

Note: Sundry expenses apportioned on the basis of number of workers.

Illustration-19

The following information relating to Nalanda Fabricators for the 2001 at standard capacity has been collected:

	Departments		
	Machining	**Assembling**	**Factory Office**
Direct labour Cost	₹1,00,000	50,000	-
Floor space occupied	60%	30%	10%
Factory overheads traceable to departments	₹92,000	53,000	42,000

Factory overheads not traceable to departments:

Rent, rates, taxes and insurance: ₹10,000

It has been decided that the cost of factory office, which is a service a department, can be equitably apportioned to other departments on direct labour cost basis.

The machining department operates on a 40 hour week. There are five machines in the department and every machine has remained idle for 280 hours in the year 2001 for vacations, holidays, repairs, etc. Calculate overhead absorption rate based on machine hours for machining departments and overhead rate based on direct labour cost for assembling department. **(B.Com (Hons.), Delhi)**

Solution

Overhead distribution statement			
	Production departments		**Service department**
	Machining ₹	**Assembling** ₹	**Factory Office** ₹
Departmental overheads	92,000	53,000	41,000
Factory rent, rates, taxes and insurance (6 : 3 : 1) (Floor space)	6,000	3,000	1,000
Total overheads	98,000	56,000	42,000
Factory office OHs apportioned in 2:1 ratio (Direct labour cost rate)	28,000	14,000	(−)42,000
Total overheads	1,26,000	70,000	-

Machine hours - (40×5×52)	10,400 hours
Less: holidays - (280×5)	1,400 hours
Effective machine hours	**9,000 hours**

Overhead absorption rates	
Machine Dept: Machine hour rate.(1,26,000/9,000)	₹14
Assembly Dept: Direct labour cost rate: 70,000/50,000×100	140%

Illustration-20

The following particulars related to the production department of a factory for the month of June, 1985.

Materials used	₹80,000
Direct wages	₹72,000
Labour hours	₹20,000
Hours of machine operation	₹25,000
Factory charges allocated to the machine	₹90,000

Cost data of a particular work order carried out in the department during June 1985 are given below:

Material used	₹8,000
Direct wages	₹6,250
Labour hours booked	₹3,300
Machine hours booked	₹2,400

What would be the factory cost of the work order under the following methods of charging overheads: (i) Direct labour cost rate, (ii) Machine hour rate and, (iii) Direct labour hour rate

(ICWA-Interm Dec, 1985)

Solution

Overhead absorption rates:

(i) Direct labour cost rate $= \dfrac{\text{Factory overheads}}{\text{direct wages}} \times 100$

$$= \frac{90{,}000}{72{,}000} \times 100 = 125\%$$

(ii) Machine hour rate $= \dfrac{\text{Factory overheads}}{\text{number of machine hours}}$

$$= \frac{90{,}000}{25{,}000}$$

$= ₹3.60$

(iii) Direct labour hour rate $= \dfrac{\text{Factory overheads}}{\text{Number of labour hours}}$

$$= \frac{90{,}000}{20{,}000} = ₹4.50$$

Factory cost of work order P:	(i)	(ii)	(iii)
Direct materials	8,000	8,000	8,000
Direct wages	6,250	6,250	6,250
Prime cost	14,250	14,250	14,250
Factory overheads			
(i) 6,250 × 125%	7,812.50		
(ii) 2,400 × 3.60		8,640	
(iii) 3,300 × 4.50			14,850
Factory cost	22,062.50	22,890	29,100

Illustration-21

In a factory department there are three machines to which the following expenses have been allocated: A - ₹639; B - ₹607; C - ₹951

In addition, there is an overhead crane to bring materials to the machines as necessary. The expenses allocated to this crane are ₹570.

During the period of this expenditure the machines were used as follows:

	A Hours	B Hours	C Hours
With the use of crane	160	130	480
Without the use of crane	428	577	-
	588	707	480

Calculate a machine hour rate for each machine, distinguishing between the hours in which the crane is used and those in it is not. **(CA-Inter)**

Solution

	A ₹	B ₹	C ₹
Total expenses allocated	639	607	951
Total machine hours	588	707	480

Machine hour rate (excluding crane expenses) (A)	1.087 $\left(\frac{639}{588}\right)$	0.859 $\left(\frac{607}{707}\right)$	1.981 $\left(\frac{570}{480}\right)$
Crane expenses per hour (570/770) (B)	0.740	0.740	0.740
Machine hour rate with use of crane (A) + (B)	₹1.827	1.599	2.721

Note: Total machine hours used with crane are - 160 + 130 + 480 = 770 hours

Illustration-22

A machine shop cost centre contains six machines of equivalent capacities. Three operators are employed on each machine, one at ₹10 an hour and two at ₹5 per hour each. The factory works for forty hours week which includes four hours for set-up time. The work is done jointly by the operators are paid fully for hours. In addition they are paid a bonus of 10% on productive time. Costs are reported for this company on the basis of thirteen weekly period.

The company for the purpose of computing machine hour rate includes the direct wages of the operators and also recoups the factory overheads allocated to the machines. The following details of factory overheads applicable to the cost centre are available:

1. Set-up time as described above.
2. Depreciation 10% per annum on original cost of machine. Original cost of machine is ₹13,000.
3. Maintenance and repairs per week per machine is ₹25.
4. Consumables stores per week per machine ₹36.
5. Power 20 units per hour per machine at 40 paise.
6. Apportionment to the cost centre:

	₹
Rent per annum	3,000
Heat and light per annum	5,400
Foreman's salary per annum	7,200

You are required to:

(a) Calculate the cost of running one machine for a four week period and,

(b) The machine hour rate.

Solution

(a)

Cost of running one machine for a four-week period		
	₹(p.a)	₹
Standing charges:		
Rent	3,000	
Heat and light	5,400	
Foreman's salary	7,200	
Total expenses for six machines	15,600	
Charges per machine per four-week period $= \dfrac{15,600}{6} \times \dfrac{4}{52}$		200
Wages (See Note -1)		3,200
Bonus (See Note - 4)		288
Total standing charges per machine per four-week period		3,688
Operating expenses:		
Depreciation $13{,}000 \times \dfrac{10}{100} \times \dfrac{4}{52}$		100
Repairs and maintenance (₹25 × 4)		100
Consumable stores (₹36 × 4)		144
Power (144 hrs × 20 units × 40 paise)		1,152
Total machine expenses per four-week period		5,184

$$\text{Machine hour rate} = \frac{5{,}814}{144} = ₹36$$

Note:

1. Operator wages: No. of hrs × wage rate

(i) 160 × 10	= 1,600
(ii) 160 × 5 × 2	= 1,600
Total	= 3,200

2. No. of hours per four week period = 40 × 4 = 160 hrs

3. Productive time per week

Total time per week	-	40 hrs
Loss set time per week	-	4 hrs
Productive time	-	36 hrs

% of productive time $\frac{36}{40} \times 100 = 90\%$

Productive time for 4 week period $= 36 \times 4 = 144$ hrs

4. Bonus $= 3{,}200 \times 10\% \times 90\% =$ ₹288.

   (Operator wages × Bonus% × % of productive time)

5. It is assumed that machine consumes powers during productive times only.

Illustration-23

For a factory, which has three production departments (two machine shops and one assembly shop) and three service departments, one of which engineering service department, serving the machine shops only. You are required to:

(a) Prepare an overhead analysis sheet, showing the bases of apportionment of overheads to production departments.
(b) Calculate suitable overhead absorption rates for the production departments, ignoring the apportionment of service department overheads among service departments.
(c) Calculate the overheads to be absorbed by two products - x and y, whose cost sheet shows the following times spent in different departments.

	x	y
Machine shop - A	5 machine hours	3 machine hours
Machine shop - B	2 machine hours	7 machine hours
Assembly shop	7 direct labour hours	9 direct labour hours

The annual budgeted overhead cost for the year are:

	Indirect wages (₹)	**Consumable stores (₹)**
Machine shop- A	23,260	6,300
Machine shop-B	20,670	9,100
Assembly shop	8,110	2,100
Stores	4,100	1,400
Engg. services	2,670	2,100
General services	3,760	1,600

Depreciation of machinery	22,000
Insurance of machinery	4,000

Insurance of building	1,800 (see note - 1)
Power	3,600
Light and heat	3,000
Rent	7,050 (see note 2)

Note:

1. Because of special fire risk, machine shop A is responsible for a special loading of insurance on the building insurance cost for machine A as one-third of the annual premium.
2. The general services department is located in a building owned by the company. It is valued at ₹6,000 and is charged into costs at a notional value of 8% per annum. This cost is additional to the rent and rates shown above.
3. The value of issues of materials to the production departments are in the same proportion as shown above for consumables stores.

The following data are also are available:

Department	Book value of machinery (₹)	Area (Sq.ft)	Effective H.P hours (%)	Production direct labour hrs	Capacity machine hrs
Machine shop A	60,000	5,000	50	2,00,000	40,000
Machine shop B	45,000	6,000	$33\frac{1}{3}$	1,50,000	50,000
Assembly shop	15,000	8,000	$4\frac{1}{6}$	3,00,000	-
Stores	6,000	2,000	-	-	-
Engg. service	18,000	2,500	$12\frac{1}{2}$	-	-
General service	6,000	1,500	-	-	-

(ICWA-Inter)

Solution

(a)

Overhead distribution summary								
Particulars	Basis of apportionment	Total ₹	Production departments			Service departments		
			Mach. shop A ₹	Mach. shop B ₹	Assem. shop ₹	Stores ₹	Engg. service ₹	General service ₹
Indirect wages	given	62,570	23,260	20,670	8,110	4,100	2,670	3,760
Consumables stores	given	22,600	6,300	9,100	2,100	1,400	2,100	1,600

Dep. of machines	Value of machines (60:45:15:6:18:6)	22,000	8,800	6,600	2,200	880	2,640	880
Insurance of machineries	Value of machines (60:45:15:6:18:6)	4,000	1,600	1,200	400	160	480	160
Insurance of building	1/3 to machine shop A and balance on area basis	1,800	600	360	480	120	150	90
Power	H.P. hrs	3,600	1,800	1,200	150	-	450	-
Light and heat	Area (10:12:16:4:5:3)	3,000	600	720	960	240	300	180
Rent and rates	Area (10:12:16:4:5:3)	7,050	1,500	1,800	2,400	600	750	-
Rent of general service dept.	8% on building value (notional)	480	-	-	-	-	-	480
Departmental overheads		1,27,100	44,460	41,650	16,800	7,500	9,540	7,150
Stores department	Value of con. stores (63:91:21)	-	2,700	3,900	900	(-) 7,500	-	-
Engineering service	Machine hrs of shop A & B only (4:5)	-	4,240	5,300	-	-	(-) 9,540	-
General service	Labour hours (4:3:6)	-	2,200	1,650	3,300	-	-	(-)7,150
Total OHS of production depts.		1,27,100	53,600	52,500	21,000	-	-	

(b) Overhead absorption rates

Machine hour rate = Total overheads/no. of machine hrs

Machine shop A = 53,600/40,000 = ₹1.34

Machine shop B = 52,500/50,000 = ₹1.05

Labour hour rate = Total OHS/No. of labour hours

Assembly shop = 21,000/3,00,000 = Re. 0.07

(c)

Statement showing overheads absorbed by products x and y		
	Product x ₹	**Product y ₹**
Machine shops = Machine hours × MHR overheads		
A = 5 × 1.34	6.70	
= 3 × 1.34		4.02
B = 2 × 1.05	2.10	
= 7 × 1.05		7.35
Assembly shop = Labour hours × LHR		
= 7 × 0.07	0.49	
= 9 × 0.07		0.63
Total overheads charged to products	9.29	12.00

Illustration-24

In a manufacturing concern, the predetermined rate of overhead recovery is ₹40 per machine hour. During the year total factory overhead amounted to ₹88,96,000 and machine hours actually worked were 1,86,000 only.

Actual production and sales during the year were 1,20,000 units and 1,05,000 units respectively. The production shop had 36,000 unfinished units based on technical estimates these were considered as 50% complete.

Analysis of the data revealed that 37.5% of the unabsorbed overheads were attributable to initial inaccuracies in the planning and the balance was due to rising price levels.

Show the treatment of unabsorbed overheads in cost accounts. **(ICWA-Inter)**

Solution

	₹
Actual overheads incurred	88,96,000
Overheads absorbed (1,86,000 × 40)	74,60,000
Unabsorbed overheads	14,36,000

Disposal of unabsorbed overheads

(i) Unabsorbed overheads 37.5% due to inaccuracies in planning charged to profit and loss account ₹14,36,000 × 37.5% = ₹5,38,500.

(ii) Unabsorbed overheads due to rise in price levels = ₹14,36,000 × 62.5% = 8,97,500, to be spread over cost of goods sold, stock of finished goods and stock of unfinished goods in the ratio of units:

	Equivalent units	Unabsorbed overheads (₹)
Cost of goods sold	1,05,000	6,82,881
Stock of finished goods	15,000	97,554
Stock of unfinished goods (36,000 × 50%)	18,000	1,17,065
Total	1,38,000	8,97,500

Illustration-25

The budgeted activity and cost data for half year was as follows:

Direct labour hours	68,000
Direct wages	₹42,500
Overheads:	
Fixed	₹37,400
Variable	₹64,600

During the six months from January to June the following actual results were achieved:

Direct labour hours	65,000
Direct wages	₹45,500
Overheads:	
Fixed	₹38,700
Variable	₹65,800

The existing method of absorbing overhead is direct wages % rate. A proposal has been made to change the overhead absorption to a direct labour hour rate analysed into fixed and variable overhead.

You are required for the period January to June to calculate under new proposal (i.e. using direct labour hour rate of absorption):

(i) The budgeted direct labour hour rate of overhead absorption of fixed and variable overheads.
(ii) The absorbed overhead and
(iii) The over- or under-absorbed overhead.

(B.Com. (Hons.), Delhi, April 2002)

Solution

(i) Budgeted labour hour rate $= \dfrac{\text{Budgeted overheads}}{\text{Budgeted labour hours}}$

$$\text{Fixed} = \frac{37,400}{68,000} = ₹0.55$$

$$\text{Variable} = \frac{64,600}{68,000} = ₹0.95$$

(ii) Absorbed overhead = Budgeted labour hour rate × Actual labour hours

Fixed = ₹0.55 × 65,000	₹35,750
Variable = ₹0.95 × 65,000	₹61,750
Total absorbed overheads	₹97,500

(iii)

	Fixed	Variable
Actual overheads	₹38,700	65,800
Absorbed overheads	₹35,750	61,750
Under-absorbed overheads	₹2,950	4,050

Total under-absorbed overheads = (i.e. 2,950 + 4,050) = ₹7,000

Illustration-26

In a manufacturing unit overhead was recovered at a predetermined rate of ₹25 per man day. The total factory overhead incurred and the man days actually worked were ₹41,50,000 and 1,50,000 respectively.

Out of the 40,000 units produced during the period 30,000 units were sold. There were also 30,000 incomplete units which may be reckoned as $66\frac{2}{3}\%$ complete. On analysing the reasons, it was found that 40% of the unabsorbed overheads were due to defective planning and the rest were attributable to increase in overhead cost.

How would unabsorbed overheads be treated in cost accounts?

Solution

Actual overheads incurred	41,50,000
Absorbed overheads (1,50,000 mondays × ₹25)	37,50,000
Under-absorbed overheads	4,00,000

Treatment in cost accounts

(i) 40% of unabsorbed overheads due to defective planning is charged to costing profit and loss account - (4,00,000 × 40%) = ₹1,60,000.

(ii) 60% of unabsorbed overheads (4,00,000 × 60%) =₹2,40,000, due to increase in overhead cost is spread over cost of goods sold, finished goods stock and stock of incomplete units, through supplementary overhead rate as follows:

Equivalent completed units

	Units
Completed units sold	30,000
Stock of completed units (40,000 – 30,000)	10,000
Stock of incomplete units (30,000 × $66\frac{2}{3}$%)	20,000
	60,000

Supplementary overhead rate = 2,40.000/60,000 = ₹4.

Treatment of unabsorbed overheads in cost accounts.

		₹
Unabsorbed overheads charged to cost of goods sold	30,000 × 4 =	1,20,000
Unabsorbed overheads charged to stock of completed units	10,000 × 4 =	40,000
Stock of incomplete units	20,000 × 4 =	80,000
	Total	2,40,000

Accounting entries in cost books for the above				
1.	Costing Profit and Loss account	Dr.	1,60,000	
	To Overheads control account			1,60,000
(Being 40% of unabsorbed overheads due to defecting planning debited to Costing P&L a/c)				
2.	WIP control a/c	Dr	80,000	
	Finished goods stock a/c	Dr	40,000	
	Cost of goods sold a/c	Dr	1,20,000	
	To Overheads control a/c			2,40,000
(Being 60% of unabsorbed overheads due to increase in cost debited to stock of uncompleted units, stock of completed goods and cost of goods sold).				

Illustration-27

PQR Manufacturers, a small scale enterprise, produces a single product and has adopted a policy to recover the production overheads of the factory by adopting a single blanket rate based on machine hours. The budgeted production overheads of the factory are ₹10,08,000 and budgeted machine hours are 96,000.

For a period of first six months of the financial year 2007-08, following information was extracted from the books:

Actual production overheads ₹6,79,000

Amount included in the production overheads

Paid as per court's order	₹45,000
Expenses of previous year booked in current year	₹10,000
Paid to workers for strike period under an award	₹42,000
Obsolete stores written off	₹18,000

Production and sales data of the concern for the first six months are as under

Production:	
Finished goods	22,000 units
Works-in-progress	16,000 units
(50% completed in every respect)	
Sale:	
Finished Goods	18,000 units

The actual machine hours worked during the period were 48,000 hrs. It is revealed from the analysis that $\frac{1}{4}$ of the under-absorption was due to defective production policies and the balance was attributable to increase in costs.

You are required:

(i) to determine the amount of under-absorption of production overheads for the period.
(ii) to show the accounting treatment of under-absorption of the production overheads, and
(iii) to apportion the unabsorbed overheads to the items. **(CA-Inter, May 2008)**

Solution

(i)

Budgeted production overheads of the factory		10,08,000
Budgeted machine hours		96,000
Budgeted production overheads absorption rate per machine hour: ₹10,08,000/96,000 = ₹10.50		

Production overheads absorbed/recovered during the first 6 months of 2007-08:		
Actual machine hours worked		48,000
Production overheads rate per hour		₹10.50
Production overheads recovered		48,000 × 10.50 = ₹5,04,000
Production overheads incurred:		₹6,79,000
Less: Items not to be included		
Paid as per court's order	₹45,000	
Previous year expenses	₹10,000	
Award wages for strike period	₹42,000	
Obsolete stores write off	₹18.000	₹1,15,000
Normal production overheads for the period	-	₹5,64,000
Under-absorption of overheads: (5,64,000 – 5,04,000)		₹60,000

(ii) Accounting treatment of under-absorption of overheads:

The under-absorption of overheads consists of two elements as under:

(a) One-fourth is due to defective production polices and as such the amount involved should be written off to costing profit/loss account to costing P/L Account (60,000 × 0.25) = ₹15,000

(b) The balance of under-absorption is attributable to increase in costs and hence should be charged to work-in-process, finished goods stock and cost of sales - ₹45,000.

(iii)

Apportionment of under-absorbed overheads	
	Units
Production	22,000
Sales	18,000
Finished goods stock (22,000 – 18,000)	4,000
Production	22,000
Work-in-progress 16,000 × 52% complete	8,000
Total equivalent units	30,000
Under-absorbed overheads	₹45,000
Supplementary OH rate per unit (45,000/30,000)	₹1.50

Items	Equivalent units (a)	Overhead apportionment (b) = (a) × 1.50 ₹
Work-in-progress	8,000	12,000
Finished goods stocks	4,000	6,000
Cost of goods sold	18,000	27,000
Total	30,000	45,000

8.8 EXERCISES

I. Objective Type Questions

A. State whether the following statements are true or false

(a) Cost unit and cost centre are the same.

(b) A term synonymous with factory overhead is 'other expenses'.

(c) Pre-determined overhead rate is used for collection of overhead costs.

(d) Direct expenses are apportioned to various departments.

(e) Apportionment is related to distribution of overheads to various departments.

(f) Primary distribution is apportionment of prime cost to various departments.

(g) The use of actual overhead absorption rate results in delay in determining cost of production.

(h) The use of predetermined overhead rate results in under- or over-absorption of overheads.

(i) Pre-determined overhead absorption rate helps in preparation of cost estimates and quotations.

(j) Allocation of direct cost is only approximate.

(k) Apportionment of overheads is only approximate.

(l) Allocation of direct cost is accurate.

(m) Direct materials of very small value used in production is treated as indirect materials cost.

(n) A blanket overhead rate is a single overhead rate computed for the entire factory overheads.

(o) Blanket overhead rate is suitable when many products are produced on large scale.

(p) Under-absorption or over-absorption of overhead arise when actual overhead absorption rate is used.

(q) If actual overheads is less, it is called under-absorption of overheads.

(r) Primary packing cost is selling overheads.

(s) If an expense is identified with a specific cost unit, it is treated as direct expense

(t) Fixed cost vary with volume rather than time.

(u) Variable cost vary with time.

(v) The use of actual overhead absorption rate may be suitably applied in small firms which are manufacturing a single product.

[**Ans:** a)False b)False c)False d)False e)True f)False g)True h)True i)True j)False k)True 1)True m)True n)True o)False p)False q)False r)False s)True t)False u)False v)True.]

B. Fill in the blanks

(a) Distribution of indirect expenses to various departments is called ____________

(b) Allocation of whole items of cost to cost centres or cost units is called ____________.

(c) Basis of apportionment of labour welfare expenses is ____________

(d) Comprehensive machine hour rate includes ____________

(e) Under step method of secondary distribution of overheads the last service department overheads is apportioned to ____________ department only.

(f) Basis of apportionment of group insurance is ____________

(g) A negative supplementary overhead rate is computed when there is ____________

(h) Machine hour rate is used for absorption of overheads when production is carried on with the help of ____________

(i) Generally an item of expense, when identified with a specific cost unit is treated as ____________

[**Ans:** a) Apportionment of overheads b) Allocation c) No of employees d) Operator wages e) Production f) Direct wages g) Over-absorption h) Machines. i) Direct expenses.]

C. Multiple choice questions

(i) The allotment of whole items of cost to cost centres or cost units is called

(a) Cost allocation
(b) Cost apportionment
(c) Overhead absorption
(d) Cost classification.

(ii) Packing cost is a

(a) Production cost
(b) Selling cost
(c) Distribution cost
(d) None of these.

(iii) Administration overheads are recovered as a percentage of

(a) Direct materials (b) Direct wages
(c) Works cost (d) Prime cost

(iv) Which of the following is not a selling overhead?

(a) Insurance to cover sold goods while in transit (b) Royalty on sales
(c) Legal costs for debt realisation (d) Distribution of samples

(v) When under- or over-absorption is significant it should be disposed of by

(a) Transferring to costing profit and loss account
(b) The use of supplementary overhead rate
(c) Carried over to next accounting year
(d) None of the above

(vi) Idle capacity of a plant refers to the difference between.

(a) Maximum capacity and practical capacity
(b) Practical capacity and normal capacity
(c) Practical capacity and capacity based on sales expectancy
(d) Practical capacity and actual capacity.

(vii) Maximum possible production capacity without making allowance for leave, holidays, normal repairs etc is.

(a) Practical capacity (b) Rated capacity
(c) Actual capacity (d) Normal capacity.

(viii) Packing expenses is an example of

(a) Production overheads (b) Administration overheads
(c) Selling overheads (d) Distribution overheads

(ix) The capacity based on immediate sales expectancy is

(a) Practical capacity (b) Maximum expectancy
(c) Normal capacity (d) Actual capacity

(x) Overhead absorption rate calculated on the basis of estimated cost is

(a) Blanket overhead rate (b) Predetermined overhead rate
(c) Single overhead rate (d) Supplementary overhead rate

(xi) Over-absorption of overheads takes place when

(a) Absorbed overheads is more (b) Actual overheads is more
(c) Pre-determined overhead rate is more
(d) Pre-determined overhead rate is less.

(xii) Primary distribution of overheads is

(a) Apportionment of indirect expenses to various departments
(b) Apportionment of service department overheads to production departments
(c) Apportionment of indirect expenses to cost units (d) None of the above

(xiii) Staff welfare expenses are apportioned in the ratio of

(a) Number of employees (b) Direct materials
(c) Machine hours (d) Prime cost

(xiv) General expenses are apportioned in the ratio of

(a) Direct wages (b) Direct materials (c) Prime cost
(d) Works cost.

[**Ans:** i) a, ii) c, iii) c, iv) b, v) b, vi) d, vii) b, viii) d, ix) d, x) b, xi) a, xii) a, xiii) a, xiv) a]

II. Theory Question

A. Short answer type question

1. What is cost allocation?
2. What is cost apportionment?
3. What is primary distribution of overheads?
4. What is secondary distribution of overheads?
5. What is the suitable basis for apportionment of canteen expenses?
6. What are the various methods of distribution of service department overheads to production department?
7. What is reapportionment of overheads?
8. What do you mean by recovery or absorption of production department overheads?
9. What is over-absorption of overheads?
10. What is under-absorption of overheads?
11. What is machine hour rate?
12. What is composite machine hour rate?
13. What is labour hour rate?
14. What is blanket overhead rate?
15. What is supplementary overhead rate?

16. Explain multiple overhead rate?
17. Discuss predetermined overhead rate?
18. What is actual overhead rate?
19. Explain the term capacity.
20. What is rated capacity?
21. What is practical capacity?
22. What is idle capacity?
23. Explain normal capacity?
24. Explain composite machine hour rate.
25. Explain non-reciprocal methods of distribution of service department overheads?
26. Explain group machine hour rate.

B. Short answer type question

1. What are factory overheads?. Explain.
2. What do you mean by cost allocation?
3. What is apportionment of overheads?
4. Explain the difference between allocation and apportionment.
5. Explain the various bases used for departmental distribution of indirect expenses.
6. What do you understand by "primary distribution of overheads"?
7. What is secondary distribution of overheads?
8. Mention the various methods used for apportionment of service department overheads to production departments.
9. Explain the reciprocal method of re-apportionment of service department overheads to production departments.
10. Explain the features of step method of reapportionment of overheads?
11. What do you mean by absorption of overheads? Explain the various methods of overheads absorption.
12. Explain the objectives of overheads absorption.
13. Write short notes on
    a) pre-determined overhead rate b) Machine hour rate and c) Labour hour rate.

14. Explain the suitability of various methods of overheads absorption.
15. What is supplementary overhead rate? When supplementary overhead rate is used?
16. Explain the causes for under- or over-absorption of overheads.
17. Explain the various methods used for disposal of under- or over-absorption of overheads in cost accounts.
18. What are the merits of using pre-determined overhead rates?
19. What are the merits of actual overhead rate?
20. Explain the various capacity levels.
21. Explain the procedure for calculation of different capacity levels.
22. What is idle capacity?
23. Differentiate idle capacity and idle time.
24. What do you understand by classification, allocation and apportionment in relation to overheads?
25. What do you understand by production department and service department?
26. Write short notes on

    (a) Blanket overhead rate
    (b) Idle capacity
    (c) Supplementary overhead rate and
    (d) Rated capacity.

III. Practical Problems

A. Short answer type questions

1. There are four production departments. The machines installed in each departments are 30HP, 40HP, 20HP and 35HP respectively. During a period the machines operated for 100 hrs, 75 hrs, 90 hrs and 80 hrs respectively.

   The power charges amounted to ₹26,500. Apportion the power charges to various departments on suitable basis.

   [**Ans:** ₹7,500, ₹7,500, ₹4,500 and ₹7,000]

   Note: Ratio of apportionment 3,000, 3,000, 1,800, 2,800. (i.e - HP x machine hours).

2. There are four departments in a company. Number of employees working in each department are 200, 250, 400 and 350 respectively. All the employees used the company canteen. Canteen expenses amounted to ₹84,000 during a period. Direct wages paid to them in each department amounted to ₹1,50,000, ₹1,00,000, ₹1,75,000 and ₹2,25,000.

   Apportion the canteen expenses to various departments.

   [**Ans:** ₹14,000, ₹17,500, ₹28,000, ₹24,500]

3. There are three production departments A, B and C and two service departments P and Q. Floor space occupied by each department is

   A - 500 sq.ft
   B - 750 sq.ft
   C - 600 sq.ft
   P - 400 sq.ft
   Q - 450 sq.ft

   Rent paid during a particular period amounted to ₹21,600. Apportion the rent to each of the departments.

   [**Ans:** A - ₹4,000, B - ₹6,000, C - ₹4,800, P - ₹3,200, Q - ₹3,600]

4. There are three production departments A, B and C. The power charges of the three departments amounted to ₹22,000.

   Other details are

Departments	A	B	C
HP of machines	20	30	25
Working hours	40	40	40
Power consumed (kWH)	500	700	800

   Apportion the power charges to production departments.

   [**Ans:** A - ₹5,500, B - ₹7,700, C - ₹8,800]

5. Direct materials consumed in three production departments are:

   Department x - ₹1,00,000
   Department y - ₹2,00,000
   Department z - ₹2,50,000

   Total production overheads amounted to ₹60,500. Company follows the policy of recovering production overheads as a percentage on direct materials cost. Compute the percentage of production overheads on direct materials. Also apportion the production overheads to all the production departments.

   [**Ans:** % of production overhead on direct materials]

$$\left(\frac{60,500}{5,50,000}x100\right) = 11\%$$

   Production overheads: x - ₹11,000, y - ₹22,000, z - ₹27,500]

6. X Ltd has 90 workers on its roll. The company works for 6 days in a week. Normal working hours per day is 8 hours on an average. Normal idle time amounted to 30 minutes per day. Calculate labour hours for a four weekly period.

   [**Ans:** Labour hours - 16,200]

7. You are required to find out direct labour hour rate from the following information:

   (a) Total number of operators working in the department 200.
   (b) Department works for 300 days in a year and the number of hours worked in a day is 8.
   (c) Total departmental overheads are ₹22,800
   (d) From the total number of hours 5% are to be deducted for idle time.

   [**Ans:** Direct labour hour rate Re. 0.05]
   Note: Direct labour hours - 4,56,000

8. Indirect labour cost for the current year in a company amounted to ₹95,000. This includes arrear wages relating to last year ₹12,000 and compensation paid to an worker as per court decree ₹7,000. Total direct labour hours for the current year is 3,80,000 hours. Compute labour hour rate.

   [**Ans:**Labour hour rate = ₹0.20 per hour]

   Note: Non-recurring items - Arrear wages and compensation excluded.

9. Ordinarily a machine is expected to run for 2,400 hours per annum. It is estimated that 200 hours will be lost for normal repairs and maintenance and further 600 hours will be lost due to set-up and staggering. Compute effective machine hours.

   [**Ans:** Effective machine hours - 1,600]

10. A machine runs 2,200 hours in a year. Normal idle time of the machine is 5%. During the year 50 hours were lost due to power failure. Total machine expenses amounted to ₹26,125. Compute machine hour rate.

    [**Ans:** Machine hour rate ₹12.50]

    Note: Loss of time due to power failure is abnormal idle time. It is not considered for computing machine hour rate. Effective machine hours 2090.

11. A tractor is operated for 200 hours with a sowing machine. The tractor is operated without the sowing machine 800 hrs. Other details are:

    Total tractor expenses - ₹30,000
    Sowing machine expenses - ₹10,000

    Compute machine hour rate without the use of sowing machine and with the use of sowing machine.

    [**Ans:** Machine hour rate - without use of sowing machine (30,000 ÷ 1000) = ₹30, with the use of sowing machine ₹80]

    Note: Sowing machine expenses per hour $= \dfrac{10,000}{200} =$ ₹50

12. A Ltd employs 150 workers. Company works 40 hours per week and 50 weeks a year. Budgeted Overhead rate is ₹1.60 per hour. Actual overheads for a year amounted to ₹5,00,000. Compute under- or over recovery of overheads.

    [**Ans:** Under recovery of overheads ₹20,000]

13. Factory overheads of three production departments for a year are:

    Department - P - ₹57,500
    Department - Q - ₹54,750
    Department - R - ₹67,400

    The basis of absorption of overheads are given below:

    Department - P - ₹6 per machine hour for 10,000 hour
    Department - Q - 80% of direct labour cost of ₹70,000
    Department - R - ₹5 per unit for 12,600 units.
    Calculate under- or over-absorption of overheads.

    [**Ans:** Over-absorption, Dept P - ₹2,500 and Q - ₹1,250 over absorption Dept R - ₹4,400]

14. Compute under- or over-absorption of overheads from the following:

    Machine hour rate ₹6
    Actual machine hours worked - 2,300 hours
    Machine hours lost due to non-availability of materials - 100 hours
    Actual factory overheads amounted to ₹16,000.
    (Ans: Under-absorption of overheads ₹1,600)

    Note: Machine hours lost due to non-availability of materials is abnormal idle time. Total machine hours (i.e. 2300 +100) 2400 is taken.

B. Comprehensive Practical Problems

1. *(Primary overhead distribution)*

   Sri Ram Ltd., an engineering company has three production departments A,B and C, two service departments D and E. The following expenses were incurred during six months ended 30th September 2008:

	₹
Rent and rates	15,000
Supervision	8,000
Lighting	13,500
Power	36,000
Depreciation	27,000
Labour welfare expenses	24,000
Repairs and maintenance	22,500
Fire insurance of stock	19,500
General expenses	18,000
Indirect wages	17,100

   Following additional information were available:

Particulars	Production departments			Service departments	
	A	B	C	D	E
Area occupied (sq.ft)	2,000	3,000	4,000	2,000	1,000
Number of employees	300	250	200	150	100
Number of light and fan points	12	10	15	4	4
Value of assets (₹in lakhs)	5	4	6	2	1
Direct wages (₹)	20,000	30,000	25,000	8,000	7,000
Value of stock (₹)	20,000	30,000	50,000	15,000	10,000
H.P. of machines	30	35	25	5	5

Prepare primary overhead distribution summary, showing clearly the basis of apportionment of various expenses.

[**Ans:** Dept. A - ₹51,170, B - ₹54,730, C - ₹58,950, D - ₹29,260 and E - ₹21,490]

2. *(Primary overhead distribution)*

The following details were extracted from the books of Nanda Ltd, a manufacturing company for the year ended 31st, March 2008:

Particulars	Production departments			Service departments	
	P	Q	R	X	Y
Direct materials (₹)	20,000	25,000	30,000	15,000	15,000
Direct labour (₹)	17,000	19,000	20,000	6,000	5,000
No of employees	400	500	300	200	150
No of light points	15	15	10	8	7
Power (KWH)	10,000	6,000	8,000	3,000	2,000
Plant value (₹)	2,00,000	1,50,000	1,00,000	50,000	50,000
Floor space (sq.ft)	1,250	500	500	250	250

The following are the expenses for the year:

Indirect materials ₹10,500, indirect labour ₹13,400, supervision ₹6,200, lighting expenses ₹1,650, labour welfare expenses ₹9,300, power ₹29,000, depreciation of plant and machinery ₹22,000, rent and rates ₹11,000,other expenses - ₹10,050 and repairs and maintenance ₹16,500. You are required to prepare primary overhead distribution summary.

[**Ans:** Dept.P - ₹41,400, Q - ₹33,100, R - ₹30,300, X - ₹34,340 and Y - ₹31,460]

3. *(Secondary distribution - various methods)*

RST Ltd has two production departments: Machining and finishing. There are three service departments: human resource (HR), maintenance and design. The budgeted costs in these service departments are as follows :

	HR ₹	**Maintenance** ₹	**Design** ₹
Variable	1,00,000	1,60,000	1,00,000
Fixed	4,00,000	3,00,000	6,00,000
	5,00,000	4,60,000	7,00,000

The usage of these department's output during the year completed is as follows:

User of service	**HR**	**Maintenance**	**Design**
HR	-	-	-
Maintenance	500	-	-
Design	500	500	-
Machining	4,000	3,500	4,500
Finishing	5,000	4,000	1,500
	10,000	8,000	6,000

Requested:

(i) Use the direct method to re-apportion RST Ltd's service department cost to its production departments,

(ii) Determine the proper sequence to use in re-apportioning the firm's service department cost by step-down method.

(iii) Use the step-down method to re-apportion the firm's service department cost.

(CA-Inter, Nov 2006)

Ans:

(i) Direct distribution method: Machining department- ₹9,61,889; Finishing - ₹6,98,111

(ii) Sequencing of departments - HR, Maintenance and Design.

(iii) Step method - Machining - ₹9,78,672; Finishing - ₹6,81,328.

4. *(Secondary distribution)*

A company has three production departments and two service departments. Department overheads as per primary distribution are as follows:

Production Departments

A = ₹13,600
B = ₹14,700
C = ₹12,800

Service Departments

X = ₹9,000
Y = ₹3,000

The expenses of service departments are charged on a percentage basis which is as follows:

	A	B	C	X	Y
X Department	40%	30%	20%	-	10%
Y Department	30%	30%	20%	20%	-

Apportion the cost of service departments using

(a) Repeated distribution method
(b) Simultaneous equation method and
(c) Trial-and-error method

(ICWA-Inter, 1998)

[**Ans:** (A) 18,712, (B) 18,833, (C) 15,555]

5. *(Primary distribution, secondary distribution and absorption of overheads)*

Primier Ltd. has three production departments A, B and C and two service departments D and E. The following figures are extracted from the records of the company:

	₹
Rent and rates	5,000
General lighting	600
Indirect wages	1,500
Power	1,500
Depreciation	10,000
Sundries	10,000

Following additional informations is available:

	Total	A	B	C	D	E
Floor area (Sq.ft)	10,000	2,000	2,500	3,000	2,000	500
Light points (nos.)	60	10	15	20	10	5
Direct wages (₹)	10,000	3,000	2,000	3,000	1,500	500
Horse power of machine	150	60	30	50	10	-
Value of machinery (₹)	2,50,000	60,000	80,000	1,00,000	5,000	5,000
Working hours	-	6,225	4.027	4,066	-	-

The expenses of service departments D and E are allocated using repeated distribution method as follows:

	A	B	C	D	E
D	20%	30%	40%	-	10%
E	40%	20%	30%	10%	-

What is the cost of an article if its raw material cost is ₹50, labour cost ₹30 and it passes through departments A, B and C for 4, 5 and 3 hours respectively? **(CA Inter May 2002)**

[**Ans:** Total cost of article ₹104.54]

6. *(Secondary distribution Step down method)*

Excellent Manufacturing Works have two production departments: Mixing and curing and three service departments: Time office, store and maintenance. The following details are available from the departmental distribution summary for the month of July 2001:

		₹	₹
Production departments	Mixing	1,44,000	
	Curing	96,000	**2,40,000**
Service departments	Time office	48,000	
	Stores	60,000	
	Maintenance	36,000	**1,44,000**

The following relevant data are also available:

	Production Departments		**Service Departments**		
	mixing	**curing**	**Time Office**	**Stores**	**Maintenance**
No. of employees	20	15	10	8	5
No. of stores Requisition Processed	120	100			30
Machine hours	3,600	2,400			

The company consistently follows the method of secondary distribution on non-reciprocal basis. Show the apportionment of the cost of service departments to production departments stating the basis of computation in the form of a note at the end of the exercise.

(ICWA,Inter,2001-Dec)

[**Ans:** Total cost - Mixing ₹2,26,136 & curing ₹1,57,864]

Note: Ratio of apportionment

Time office - 8:5:20:15

Stores - 3:12:10
Maintenance - 3:2

7. *(Secondary distribution - Simultaneous equation method)*

A factory has three production departments A, B and C and also two service departments 'x' and 'y'. The primary distribution of the estimated overheads in the factory has just been completed. These details and the quantum of service rendered by the service departments, to the other departments are given below:

	Departments				
	A	**B**	**C**	x	**y**
Primary distribution (₹)	2,40,000	2,10,000	2,50,000	1,40,000	96,000
Service rendered by					
Dept 'x'	30%	20%	35%	-	15%
Dept 'y'	25%	40%	25%	10%	-

Prepare a statement showing the distribution of service department overheads to the production departments, by the simultaneous equation method. **(ICWA-Inter, Dec 2004)**

[**Ans:** Total cost A ₹3,15,259, B ₹2,87,889, C ₹3,32,853.]

8. A company has three production departments P, Q, R and two service departments M and C. The following details in respect of indirect expenses incurred are furnished for a typical month.

Item of Expenses	**Amount (₹)**
Indirect labour	9,000
Lighting	1,200
Rent & rates	12,000
Power	6,000
Depreciation	24,000
Sundry expenses	7,800

Following further data are available for the distribution of overheads.

Particulars	**Departments**				
	P	Q	R	M	C
Value of machinery ('000 of ₹)	60	50	40	10	-
H.P. of Machines	40	45	60	15	-
Light points (Nos.)	20	30	40	20	10
Floor space (sq. meters)	150	200	250	100	50
Direct wages ('000 of ₹)	30	20	40	4	6

Machine hrs worked	2,940	2,060	2,150	-	-

The service department costs are apportioned as follow:

Departments	P	Q	R	M	C
M	20%	30%	40%	-	10%
C	40%	20%	30%	10%	-

You are required to calculate:

(a) Overhead recovery rates showing the basis of apportionment.
(b) Total cost of job no. 234, the job card of which has revealed the following data:

	Departments		
	P	**Q**	**R**
Machine consumed (₹)	228	136	100
Direct wages (₹)	162	144	256
Machine hrs worked	10	8	12

(ICWA-Inter, Dec 2006)

Ans:

(a) Dept P = ₹8.01 or 8
Dept Q = ₹10.02 or 10
Dept R = ₹11.99 or 12

(b) ₹1,330.26 or ₹1,330

9. *(Secondary distribution - Simultaneous equation method)*

ABC Ltd budgets the following amounts for its two service departments (legal and personnel) in supporting each other and the two production divisions, the Micro Computer Divisions (MCD) and the Peripheral Equipment Division (PED).

	Budgeted Capacity				
To be supplied by	**MCD**	**PED**	**Legal**	**Personal**	**Total**
Legal (hours)	3,000	1,500	-	500	5,000
Legal (%)	60%	30%	-	10%	100%
Personnel (hours)	45,000	50,000	5,000	-	1,00,000
Personnel (%)	45%	50%	5%	-	100%

Details on actual usage are as follow:

	Budgeted Capacity				
To be supplied by	MCD	PED	Legal	Personal	Total
Legal (hours)	800	2,400	-	800	4,000
Legal (%)	20%	60%	-	20%	100%
Personnel (hours)	53,200	22,800	4,000	-	80,000
Personnel (%)	66.5%	28.5%	5%	-	100%

The actual expenses were:

	Fixed	Variable
Legal	₹7,20,000	₹4,00,000
Personnel	₹9,50,000	₹12,00,000

Fixed expenses are allocated on the basis of budgeted capacity. Variable expenses are allocated on the basis of actual usage.

Required:
Prepare a statement showing apportionment of expenses of service department (legal and personnel) to production divisions MCD and PED by using simultaneous equation method.

(CA-Inter, May 2003)

[**Ans:** MCD - ₹18,77,752 and PED ₹13,92,248]

10. *(Primary distribution, secondary distribution and absorption)*

ABC Ltd has three production departments P1, P2, and P3 and two service departments S1 and S2. The following data are extracted from the records of the company for the month of October 2007:

	₹
Rent and rates	62,500
General lighting	7,500
Indirect wages	18,750
Power	25,000
Depreciation on machinery	50,000
Insurance of machinery	20,000

Other information:

	P1	P2	P3	S1	S2
Direct wages (₹)	37,500	25,000	37,500	18,750	6,250
Horse power of machines used	60	30	50	10	-

Costs of machinery (₹)	3,00,000	4,00,000	5,00,000	25,000	25,000
Floor space (sq.ft)	2,000	2,500	3,000	2,000	500
Number of light points	10	15	20	10	5
Production hours worked	6,225	4,050	4,100	-	-

Expenses of the service departments S1 and S2 are reapportioned as below:

	P1	**P2**	**P3**	**S1**	**S2**
S1	20%	30%	40%	-	10%
S2	40%	20%	30%	10%	-

Required:

(i) Compute overheads absorption rate per production hour of each production department.
(ii) Determine the total cost of product X which was processed for manufacture in department P1, P2 and P3 for 5 hours, 3 hours and 4 hours respectively, given that its direct materials cost is ₹625 and direct labour cost is ₹375.

(CA-Inter, Nov 2007)

Ans:
(i) Overhead rate per hour - P1 - ₹9.75, P2 - ₹15.77 and P3 - ₹20.52.
(ii) Total cost of product x ₹1,178.17.

11. *(Primary distribution and secondary distribution - various methods)*

The following cost information for a period is available for a small engineering unit.

(a) Allocated expenditure:

	Total ₹	**Production Department**		**Service Department**	
		Machine shop ₹	**Assembling** ₹	**General Plant Service** ₹	**Stores & Maintenance** ₹
Indirect wages	29,300	8,000	6,000	4,000	11,300
Store Consumed	6,700	2,200	1.700	1,100	1,700
Supervisory salaries	14,000	-	-	14,000	-

(b) Other expenses to be apportioned

Power and fuel	15,000
Rent	15,000

Insurance	3,000
Depreciation	1,00,000

(c) Additional information available

	Floor Area Sq.ft	H.P. hours	No. of Employees	Investment in Asst (₹)
Machine shop	2,000	3,500	30	6,40,000
Assembling	1,000	500	15	2,00,000
General plant	500	-	5	10,000
Stores & maintenance	1,500	1,000	10	1,50,000

(d) Basis of apportionment of service department costs

	Machine shop	Assembling	General Plant service	Store & Maintenance
Store & Maintenance	50%	20%	30%	-

General plant service - in proportion to the number of employees.

You are required to prepare an overhead distribution statement in detail. Service department costs are to be distributed by a) Continued distribution method and b) Simultaneous equation method. Calculations are to be shown to the nearest rupee.

[**Ans:** Total overheads - machine shop ₹1,41,249, Assembling ₹41,751]

12. *(Secondary distribution and absorption)*

RST Ltd produces machine parts on a job order basis'. Most of the business is obtained through bidding. Most of the firms competing with RST Ltd. bid full cost plus a 20% mark-up. Recently, with the expectation of gaining more sales, RST Ltd, reduce its mark-up from 25% to 20%. The company operates two service departments and two producing departments. The budgeted costs and the normal service levels of activity for each department are given below:

	Machine shops		Production Departments	
	A	B	C	D
Overheads costs (₹)	5,00,000	10,00,000	5,00,000	7,50,000
Number of employees	40	35	150	150
Maintenance hours	10,000	1,000	32,000	8,000
Machine hours	-	-	50,000	5,000
Labour hours	-	-	5,000	5,000

The direct costs of Department A are allocated on the basis of employees. Those of department B are allocated on the basis of maintenance hours. Department overhead rates are used to assign costs to products. Department C uses machine hours, and department D uses labour hours. The firm is preparing to bid on a job (job Z) that requires three machine hours per unit produced in department C and no time in department D. The expected prime costs per unit are ₹85. Required:

(i) Allocate the service costs to the production departments using the direct method.
(ii) What will be the bid for job Z, if the direct method of allocation is used?
(iii) Allocate the service costs to the producing departments using the sequential method.
(iv) What will the bid be for job Z, if the sequential method is used?
(v) Allocate the service department costs to the production departments using the reciprocal method.
(vi) What will be the bid for job Z, if the reciprocal method is used?

(CA-Inter, Nov. 2002)

[**Ans:** (i) ₹15,50,000, ₹12,00,000 (ii) ₹211.20 (iii) ₹15,65,672, ₹11,84,328 (iv) ₹214.72 (v) ₹15,07,966, ₹12,42,108, (vi) ₹210.58]

13. PQR Ltd. has its own power plant, which has two users, cutting department and welding department. When the plans were prepared for the power plant, the top management decided that its practical capacity should be 1,50,000 machine hours. Budgeted practical fixed costs are ₹9,00,000 and budgeted variable costs are ₹4 per machine-hour. The following data are available:

	Cutting Department	**Welding Department**	**Total**
Overheads costs (₹)	5,00,000	10,00,000	15,00,000
Actual usage In 2002-03 (machine hours)	60,000	40,000	1,00,000
Practical capacity for each department (machine hours)	90,000	60,000	1,50,000

Required:

(i) Allocate the power plant's cost to the cutting and welding department using a single rate method in which the budgeted rate is calculated using practical capacity and costs are allocated based on actual usage.
(ii) Allocate the power plant's cost to the cutting and welding departments, using the dual-rate method in which fixed cost are allocated based on practical capacity and variable costs are allocated based on actual usage.
(iii) Allocate the power plant's cost to the cutting and welding departments, using the dual-rate method in which fixed cost rate is calculated using practical capacity, but fixed costs are allocated to cutting and welding department based on actual usage. Variable costs are allocated based on actual usage,
(iv) Comment on your results in requirements (i), (ii) and (iii).

[**Ans:** (i) ₹11,00,000, ₹14,00,000 (ii) ₹12,80,000, ₹15,20,000 (iii) ₹12,20,000, 14,80,000 (iv) option (ii) is selected. option (i) and (ii) results in under absorption of overheads]

(CA-Inter, May 2005)

14. *(Labour hour rate)*

Prabhu Limited, a manufacturer of furniture, mainly on job order basis, manufactures furniture with the help of labourers. The company works all the 52 weeks in a year at 6 days a week. There are 7 paid holidays in a year. Official leave permitted is 12 days per annum. Normal idle time is 40 minutes per day. On the basis of past experience it is found that absenteeism per worker is 5 days. The company employs 50 workers. The company follows the policy of recovery of overheads on predetermined labour hour rate basis. The annual budgeted overheads of the company is estimated at ₹7,92,000. You are required to work out labour hour rate.

[**Ans:** Labour hour rate - ₹7.50]

15. *(Overhead rate - Different methods)*

The following information relates to the activities of a production department of a factory for a certain period:

Direct material used	₹4,000
Direct wages	₹6,000
Direct labour hours worked	24,000 Hrs
	(including 2,000 hrs of machine operation)
Overheads chargeable to the department	₹5,000

For order no. 156 carried out in the department the relevant figures are:

Direct material used	₹200
Direct wages	₹165
Direct labour hour	820 hrs
	(including 80 machine hours)

You are requested to calculate the overheads chargeable to order no. 156 and works cost by four different cost rates.

[**Ans:** Overhead rates
1) % on direct materials cost -125%
2)% on direct labour cost 83.33%
3) Direct labour hour rate Re. 0.208 and
4) Machine hour rate ₹2.50.
Works cost ₹615, ₹502.50, ₹535.56 and ₹565 respectively.]

16. *(Dual Machine hour rate)*

X Ltd having fifteen different machines, furnish the information as under for 2006-07.

(i) Overheads expenses: Factory rent ₹96,000 (floor area 80,000 Sq.ft.), heat and gas ₹45,000 and supervision ₹1,20,000

(ii) Wages of the operator are ₹48 per day of 8 hours. He attends to one machine when it is under set-up and two machines while they are under operation.

In respect of machine 'B' (one of the above machines) the following particulars are furnished:

(i) Cost of machine ₹45,000, life of machine 10 years and scrap value at the end of its life ₹5,000

(ii) Annual expenses on special equipment attached to the machine are estimated at ₹3,000

(iii) Estimated operation time of the machine is 3,600 hours and setup time is 400 hours per annum..

(iv) The machine occupies 5,000 sq.ft of floor area.

(v) Power costs ₹2 per hour while machine is in operation. Find out the comprehensive machine hour rate of machine 'B'. Also find out the machine costs to be absorbed in respect of use of machine 'B' on the following two work orders:

	Work orders No. 31	**Work order No. 32**
Machine set-up time (hrs)	10	20
Machine operation time (hrs)	90	180

[**Ans:** Total cost - Work order No: 31 ₹1,110, work order No:32 ₹2,220, Comprehensive machine hour rate - setup-time ₹12, operation time ₹11]

17. *(Machine hour rate)*

A machine was purchased on 1st September, 2007, for ₹5 lakhs. The total cost of all machineries inclusive of the new machinery was ₹75 lakh. The following further particulars are available:

Expected life of the machine 10 years
Scrap value at the end of ten years ₹5,000.
Repairs and maintenance of the machine for the year ₹2,000.
Expected number of working hours of the machine per year 4,000 hours.
Insurance premium annually for all the machines ₹4,500.
Electricity consumption for the machine per hour (@ 75 paise per unit) 25 units.
Area occupied by the machine 100 sq. ft.
Area occupied by other machines 1,500 sq. ft.
Rent per month of the department ₹600.
Lighting charges for 20 points for the whole department (out of which three points are for the machine) ₹120 per month.
Compute the machine hour rate for the new machine on the basis of the data given above.

(B.Com. (Hons.), Delhi)

[**Ans:** ₹31.87]

18. *(Machine hour rate)*

Compute machine hour rate from the following data:

	₹
Cost of the machine	1,00,000
Installation charges	10,000
Scrap value after 15 years of life	5,000
Rent and rates for shop per month	200
General lighting for shop per month	300
Insurance for the machine per annum	960
Repairs and maintenance per annum	1,000
Power consumption 10 units per hour	-
Rate of power per 100 units	20
Estimated working hours per annum 2,000 hours	
Supervisors salary per month	600

The machine occupies 1/4 of the total area of the shop. The supervisor is expected to devote 1/5 of his time on this machine. **(B.Com., Madras, 1992)**

(**Ans:** ₹7.95)

19. *(Comprehensive machine hour rate)*

From the details provided below you are requested to compute a comprehensive machine hour rate:

(i) Original purchase price of the machine (subject to depreciation of 10% per annum on original cost) ₹21,600
(ii) Normal working hours for the month (the machine works to only 75% of capacity) 200 hours
(iii) Wages of machine man ₹4 (per day of 8 hours)
(iv) Wages of a helper (machine attendant) ₹2(per day of 8 hours)
(v) Power consumption estimated at ₹150 per mensem for the time worked,
(vi) Supervision charges apportioned for the machine centre ₹300 p.m
(vii) Electricity and lighting ₹75 p.m
(viii) Repairs and maintenance (machine) including consumable stores per mensem ₹150
(ix) Other general expenses (overhead) per annum ₹1,000
(x) Insurance of plant and building Rs. 2,160 per anuum
(xi) Production bonus payable to workers $33\frac{1}{3}\%$ in terms of an award of basic wages and dearness allowance
(xii) Workers are also paid a fixed dearness allowance of ₹75 per month
(xiii) Add 10% of the wages and dearness allowance against leave wages and holidays with pay to arrive at a comprehensive labour cost for debit to production.

(B. Com., Madras University, April 1998)

(**Ans:** ₹10.32)

20. *(Composite machine hour rate)*

From the following details,compute a composite machine hour rate:

(i) Cost of the machine ₹1,00,000, estimated life 15 years,residual value ₹10,000.
(ii) Machine running hours: 2040 hours per machine per annum including idle time of 40 hours due to routine repairs and maintenance and 20 hours due to break down of machine,
(iii) Power consumption of the machine per hour: 20 units. Rate of power per 100 units ₹80.
(iv) There are two operators in the shop and wages, workmen's compensation, insurance etc of an operator who is in charge of two machines is ₹12,000 p.a.
(vi) Rent, rates and taxes of the shop ₹4,800 p.a.
(vii) Insurance premium for the machine - ₹400 per quarter,
(viii) General lighting of the shop per month ₹600.
(ix) Repairs and maintenance expenses for the machine per month ₹400 for the shop.
(x) Shop supervisor salary per month ₹1,500.
(xi) Other factory overheads allocated for the shop ₹6,000. p.a.

There are four identical machines in the machine shop.The supervisor devotes 1/5 of his time for supervising the machine. **(B.Com. (Hons), Calcutta)**

[**Ans:** ₹27.57]

Note:

(a) Effective machine hours 1,980. Machine breakdown considered normal

(b) If machine breakdown is taken as abnormal, effective machine hours 2,000 hrs, machine hour rate ₹27.45

21. *(Dual machine hour rate)*

A manufacturing unit has purchased and installed a new machine of ₹12,70,000 to its fleet of 7 existing machines. The new machine has an estimated life of 12 years and is expected to realise ₹70,000 as scrap at the end of its working life. Other relevant data are as follows:

(i) Budgeted working hours are 2,592 based on 8 hours per day for 324 days. This includes 300 hours for plant maintenance and 92 hours for setting up of plant,
(ii) Estimated cost of maintenance of the machine is ₹25,000(p.a).
(iii) The machine requires a special chemical solution, which is replaced at the end of each week (6 days in a week) at a cost of ₹400 each time.
(iv) Four operators control the operations of 8 machines and the average wages per person amounts to ₹420 per week plus 15% fringe benefits.
(v) Electricity used by the machine during the production is 16 units per hour at a costs of ₹3 per unit. No current is taken during maintenance and setting up.
(vi) Department and general works overheads allocated to the operation during last year was ₹50,000. During the current year it is estimated to increase 10% of this amount.

Calculate machine hour rate, if (a) setting up time is unproductive; (b) setting up time is productive. **(CA-Inter, May 2005)**

[**Ans:** Machine hour rate (a) Setting uptime is unproductive ₹123.69 and (b) Setting-up time is productive ₹118.72]

22. *(Dual machine hour rate)*

In a factory a machine is considered to work for 208 hours in a month. It includes maintenance time of 8 hours and set-up time of 20 hours. The expenses data relating to the machine are as under:

(i) Cost of the machine is ₹5,00,000, life 10 years. Estimated scrap value at the end of life is ₹20,000
(ii) Repairs and maintenance per annum ₹60,480
(iii) Consumable stores per annum ₹47,520
(iv) Rent of building per annum (the machine under reference occupies 1/6 of the area) ₹72,000
(v) Supervisor's salary per month (common to three machines) ₹6,000
(vi) Wages of operator per month per machine ₹2,500
(vii) General lighting charges per month allocated to the machine ₹1,000
(viii) Power 25 units per hour at ₹2 per unit

Power is required for productive purpose only. Set-up time, though productive, does not require power. The supervisor and operator are permanent. Repairs and maintenance and consumable stores vary with the running of the machine. **(CA-Inter, May 2002)**

(**Ans:** Set-up time machine hour rate ₹52.50 and Running time machine hour rate ₹152.50)

23. *(Comprehensive machine hour rate)*

Calculate the comprehensive machine hour rate of a machine from the following:

(i) Cost of the machine ₹25 lakh, having a scrap value of ₹1 lakh after 10 years
(ii) The machine will be operated for three shifts of 7 hrs. each for 300 working days in a year of which 300 hrs. will be utilised for minor repairs and maintenance
(iii) **Wage payable:** ₹8,000 p.m for an operator and ₹3,000 p.m. for a helper for every shift

₹16,000 p.m. to one supervisor per shift for the department accommodating four machines including the above machine

(iv) **Other details:**

Power consumption	25 units (kWH) @ ₹4.80 per unit
Repairs & Maintenance	₹30,000 per annum for the machine.
General lighting and heating	₹4,000 p.m. for the whole department having the four machines.
Insurance	₹18,000 per machine per annum.
Rent, rates and taxes	₹3,000 p.m. for the department.
Factory overheads	₹36,000 per annum for the department.

(ICWA-Inter, June 2007)

[**Ans:** Comprehensive machine hour rate - ₹263]

24. *(Under-absorption of overheads)*

In a factory overheads of a particular department are recovered on the basis of ₹5 per machine hour. The total expenses incurred and actual machine hours for the department for the month of August were ₹80,000 and 10,000 hours respectively. Of the amount of ₹80,000, ₹15,000 became payable due to an award of the labour court and ₹5,000 was in respect of the expenses of the previous year booked in the current month (August). Actual production was 40,000 units of which 30,000 units were sold. On analysing the reasons, it was found that 60% of unabsorbed overheads was due to defective planning and the rest was attributed to normal cost increase. How would you treat the unabsorbed overheads in cost accounts? **(CA-Inter)**

[**Ans:** 60% of unabsorbed overheads i.e, ₹6,000 - due to defective planning is debited to costing P & L a/c and the balance 40%(i,e. ₹4,000) debited to cost of goods sold a/c and stock of finished goods a/c through a supplementary overhead rate of ₹0.10 per unit.]

25. *(Under-absorption of overheads)*

Based on the data given below compute (i) overheads absorption rate and (ii) the amount of under- or over-absorbed overheads

Budgeted labour hours	8,500
Budgeted overheads	1,48,750
Actual labour hours	7,928
Actual overheads	1,46,200

[**Ans:**(i) Labour hour rate ₹17.50 (ii) Under-absorbed overheads ₹7,460]

26. *(Under-absorption of overheads)*

ABC Ltd manufacturing a single product and absorbed the production overheads at a pre-determined overhead rate of ₹10 per machine hour.

At the end of the financial years 2007-08,it has been found that actual production overheads incurred were ₹6,00,000. It includes ₹45,000 on account of written off obsolete stores and ₹30,000 being the wage paid for the strike period under an award.

The production and sales data for the year 2007-08 is as under:

Production:

Finished goods - 20,000 units
Work-in-progress (50% Completed) - 8,000 units

Sales:

Finished goods - 18,000 units

The actual machine hours worked during the period were 48,000, it has been found that one third of the under-absorption of production overheads was due to lack of production planning and the rest was attributed to normal increase in costs. You are required to:

(i) Calculate the amount of under-absorption of production overheads during the year 2007-08 and
(ii) Show the accounting treatment of under-absorption of production overheads

Ans:

(i) Under-absorption of production overheads - ₹45,000.
(ii) Accounting entry:

WIP control a/c	Dr 5,000
Fin. goods control a/c	Dr 2,500
Cost of sales a/c	Dr 22,500
Profit and loss a/c	Dr 15,000
To production overheads control a/c	45,000

Administration, Selling And Distribution Overheads

9

- ☞ Meaning
- ☞ Collection and apportionment
- ☞ Administration overheads - accounting methods/control
- ☞ Selling and distribution overheads - apportionment basis/control
- ☞ Depreciation - objectives/other Terms
- ☞ Methods of depreciation
- ☞ Treatment of miscellaneous items

9.1 OFFICE AND ADMINISTRATION OVERHEADS

9.1.1 Meaning

CIMA-London defines administration overheads as, "the cost of formulating policy, directing the organization and controlling the operations of an undertaking, which is not related directly to a production, selling, distribution, research, or development activity or function".

Office and administration overheads are incurred for formulation of organisational policy, framing plans and overall control of operations of an organization. It is the expenditure incurred for overall guidance and control of an undertaking. In recent times the amount of office and administration overheads has increased considerably and acquired importance in its accounting and control. The reasons for increase in office and administration overheads are due to the following reasons:

1. Increase in size of industrial concerns.
2. Increased complexity in business law, labour laws, tax laws etc.

3. Increase in complexions in managing large labour force.
4. Increase in necessity for utilizing specialised services like technical consultants, management consultants, legal advisors etc.

Most of office and administration expenses are in the nature of period cost and are fixed.

9.1.2 Collection and Apportionment

Each expenditure is allotted a standing number and expenses are collected by standing number-wise. For easy control and achieving specialisation office is divided into various divisions or departments such as:

(a) General office
(b) Accounting and finance
(c) Filing and records keeping
(d) Secretarial and legal etc.

Administration overheads are apportioned to various divisions in the office, as is done in the case of factory overheads. The following are some important office and administration expenses and bases used for their apportionment.

Expenses	Basis
Office rent, rates and taxes	Floor area
Salaries and allowance	No. of employees
Depreciation and repairs of office building	Floor area
Depreciation and repairs of office machinery and equipment	Value of Machines
Invoicing	No. of invoices
Legal expenses	No. of cases handled
Typing	No. of letters typed

9.1.3 Absorption of Administration Overheads

Administration overheads may be absorbed by following any one of the methods given below. They are:

(a) Number of units
(b) Prime cost
(c) Conversion cost
(d) Cost of production
(e) Works cost
(f) Sales value

Since administration overheads are fixed and depends on policies of the management, they have no direct bearing on production or sales volume. The methods suggested for absorption of administration overheads are only arbitrary. Of the above methods, conversion cost method may be used more gainfully.

9.1.4 Accounting for Administration Overheads

Usually three methods are used for accounting of administration overheads. They are,

1. **Apportionment to production and selling overheads**

   Under this method only production and selling functions are recognised as primary functions. Administration service is regarded as a supplementary service. It is apportioned to production departments and sales departments. The idea behind this method is the services of administration are received by production and sales departments and the amount of administration overheads is small. This method suffers from the following limitations,

   (a) For effective functioning of any organization, administration function is the base. But administration function is not considered a primary function under this method. Administration function is not given its due importance.

   (b) When administration overheads are distributed over production overheads and sales overheads, the administration overheads distributed to production department form part of cost of production and are included in the valuation of stock of finished goods. The administration overheads distributed to selling overheads is treated as part of cost of sales, hence it does not enter the value of stock of finished goods. Administration overheads are treated differently in different places.

2. **Transfer to profit and loss account**

   Administration overheads are period costs and have no direct relationship with production and sales. So they are charged to profit and loss account of the period in which administration expenses are incurred. This is a simple and convenient method. But it suffers from the following disadvantages:

   (a) Administration function is a primary function for effective functioning of an undertaking. But this factor is ignored.

   (b) Cost of production and stock of finished goods are understated resulting in under-absorption of overheads.

   (c) Control of administration overheads is not possible.

9.1.5 Control of Administration Overheads

Since administration overheads are generally fixed and incurred as a result of the management policy decisions, it is more difficult to exercise effective control over them. However some degree of control can be ensured by following any of the steps given below:

1. **Comparison with past results**

   Current administration costs are collected and classified under standing numbers and are compared with previous year costs. This reveals the increase or decrease in expenses. The difference is analysed for causes. If causes are internal to the organization corrective actions are initiated to control the expenses.

2. **Use of budgetary controls**

   Administration overheads are fixed in advance using budgetary control device. Actual expenses are compared with budgets. Causes for deviation in expenses are analysed and the responsibility is fixed. Deviations from budgeted expenses are noted and corrective actions are taken when causes are internal to the organization. If deviations are due to external factors then budgets are revised.

3. **Use of standard costs**

   The reasonable expenses, to be incurred in the given situation is determined, and is called standard cost. Standard cost is fixed scientifically. Actual costs are collected and compared with standard cost to find deviations, if any and causes for deviations. Control measures are initiated to correct the deviations. Standard cost technique helps in measuring efficiency and effectiveness of administrative overheads.

9.2 SELLING AND DISTRIBUTION OVERHEADS

Selling overheads are incurred for increasing the demand for the products and sale of products. Distribution expenses are expenses incurred for taking the goods to customer's place. Selling expenses and distribution expenses represent two different functions. For costing purpose these two expenses are grouped as one under the head "Selling and distribution overheads". This is also called marketing overheads. These expenses were used to be small in the past. But in recent times it forms a major part in the total cost incurred in an undertaking. The reasons for increase in selling and distribution overheads are:

1. Goods are produced on large scale for sale in distant markets.
2. Increased competition forces a company to incur heavy expenses on advertising and sales promotion.

9.2.1 Collection and Apportionment of Selling and Distribution Overheads

Various selling expenses are also given distinct standing numbers as in the case of production overheads. Expenses are collected standing number wise. Sales department is also classified into different divisions like:

1. Direct selling
2. Packing and forwarding

3. Transportation
4. Advertising
5. Accounting and collection etc.

Overheads collected are apportioned to various departments using suitable basis. Further expenses may be analysed on product basis and territory basis. The following are some expenses and the basis of apportionment

Expenses	Basis
Transportation expenses	No. of units
Discount allowed	Sales value
Bad debts	Debtor/sales value
Billing cost	No. of orders
Dispatch cost	No. of dispatches
Advertisement	Sales value

9.2.2 Absorption of Selling and Distribution Overheads

The following are the methods for absorption of selling and distribution overheads:

1. Number of unit basis
2. Percentage of sales basis
3. Percentage of works cost basis.

9.2.3 Control of Selling and Distribution Overheads

Selling and distribution overheads are classified into variable, fixed and semi-variable. Control of selling and administration overheads is also difficult because of the following reasons:

1. Amount of selling and distribution overheads is influenced by the extent of competition from others. This is an external factor.
2. Estimation of sales potential is also difficult.
3. Sales depends on customer's preferences and tastes. The organization has no influence over consumer's behaviour.
4. The amount of expenses like advertising, discount allowed to customers, credit period etc all depend on the management policy decisions. So many expenses are related to policies.
5. It is difficult to determine market trend.

The following steps may be followed for control of selling and distribution overheads:

1. **Comparison with past results**

   The selling and distribution overheads of current period are collected and compared with previous year figures. This shows the variation in expenses. If variation is due to some internal factors, corrective action is taken to control them.

2. **Use of budgetary control**

   Sales budget (quantitative and monetary) is taken as the base for preparing selling and distribution overheads budget. Actual expenses are compared with budgeted expenses and corrective action is taken to control deviation in expenses.

3. **Use of standard cost**

   Standard cost is fixed in advance and actual expenses are compared with the standard cost. If there are any adverse deviations, the reasons are analysed and the responsibilities are fixed. It is very difficult to fix standard cost for selling and distribution overheads.

Illustration-1

A company manufactures three products PRIMA, DONNA and MEGA. Its market has three zones-North, South and East. The estimated sales for 1985 are as below:

	North ₹	South ₹	East ₹
PRIMA	20,000	8,000	-
DONNA	12,000	-	32,000
MEGA	-	28,000	16,000

Budgeted advertising outlay is as given below:

	North ₹	South ₹	East ₹	Total ₹
Local cost	1,280	1,800	1,680	4,760
General	-	-	-	2,320

Work out a statement to present the advertising cost per cent on sales for each product and for each territory. **(B.Com., Madurai University, 1986)**

Solution

Statement showing apportionment of advertising cost–Territory basis					
		Sales territories			
	Basis of apportionment	North ₹	South ₹	East ₹	Total ₹
Local cost	given	1,280	1,800	1,680	4,760
General	2% on sales (see note)	640	720	960	2,320
Total advertising cost		1,920	2,520	2,640	7,080
Estimated sales		32,000	36,000	48,000	1,16,000
% of advertising cost on estimated sales		6%	7%	5.5%	6.1%

Statement showing advertising cost—Product basis					
		PRIMA ₹	DONNA ₹	MEGA ₹	Total ₹
North	6% on sales	1,200	720	-	1,920
South	7% on sales	560	-	1,960	2,520
East	5.5% on sales	-	1,760	880	2,640
Total advertising cost		1,760	2,480	2,840	7,080
Estimated sales		28,000	44,000	44,000	1,16,000
% of advertising cost on estimated sales		6.29%	5.64%	6.45%	6.1%

Note: Percentage of general advertisement cost on total estimated sales

$$= \frac{\text{General advertisement cost}}{\text{Total estimated sales}} \times 100 = \frac{2{,}320}{1{,}16{,}000} \times 100$$

$$= 2\%$$

Illustration-2

Progressive Company Ltd manufactures three products A, B and C and sells them through own sales force in three zones X, Y and Z. The overall control of distribution and sales is taken care of at head-quarters, also responsible for sales promotion.

You are presented with the following data for the year ended 31st March, 1992.

		Sales ₹	Direct Selling and Distribution ₹
Zone-X	Product -A	1,50,000	10,200
	-B	1,00,000	10,500
	-C	50,000	5,300
		3,00,000	26,000
Zone-Y	Product -A	2,00,000	14,200
	-B	2,00,000	18,800
	-C	1,00,000	10,500
		5,00,000	43,500
Zone-Z	Product -A	50,000	4,200
	-B	40,000	3,400
	-C	1,10,000	14,400
		2,00,000	22,000

Selling and distribution expenses at the headquarters are as follows:

	₹
Selling expenses	18,000
Advertisement expenses	20,000
Other expenses	24,000

While advertisement expenses are allocated to zones and products on the basis of sales, the other two types of expenses are allocated equally to zones and products.

Cost of sales should be taken as the following percentages of sales:

Product A	80%
B	75%
C	70%

You are required to tabulate the information to present comparative profit and loss statements for each zone and each product. **(ICWA-Inter, June 1992)**

Solution

Statement showing profit/loss for each zone for the year ended 31st March 1992				
Particulars	**Zone X** ₹	**Zone Y** ₹	**Zone Z** ₹	**Total** ₹
Sales	3,00,000	5,00,000	2,00.000	10,00,000
Cost of sales				
Product A (80% of sales)	1,20,000	1,60,000	40,000	3,20,000
Product B (75% of sales)	75,000	1,50,000	30,000	2,55,000
Product C (70% of sales)	35,000	70,000	77,000	1,82,000
Total	2,30,000	3,80,000	1,47,000	7,57,000
Gross margin (Sales-cost of sales)	70,000	1,20,000	53,000	2,43,000
Less: Selling and distribution expenses				
Direct	26,000	43,500	22,000	91,500
Advertisement (3:5:2)	6,000	10,000	4,000	20,000
Selling (equal)	6,000	6,000	6,000	18,000
Others (equal)	8,000	8,000	8,000	24,000
Net profit	24,000	52,500	13,000	89,500

Statement showing profit/loss for each product for the year ended 31st March 1992				
Particulars	**Product A** ₹	**Product B** ₹	**Product C** ₹	**Total** ₹
Sales-Zone X	1,50,000	1,00,000	50,000	3,00,000
Zone Y	2,00,000	2,00,000	1,00,000	5,00,000
Zone Z	50,000	40,000	1,10,000	2,00,000
Total sales	4,00,000	3,40,000	2,60,000	10,00,000
Less: Cost of sales	3,20,000	2,55,000	1,82,000	7,57,000
Gross margin	80,000	85,000	78,000	2,43,000
Less: Selling and distribution expenses				
Direct	28,600	32,700	30,200	91,500
Advertisement (sales)	8,000	6,800	5,200	20,000
Selling (equal)	6,000	6,000	6,000	18,000
Others (equal)	8,000	8,000	8,000	24,000
Net profit	29,400	31,500	28,600	89,500

Note: Cost of sale

$$\text{Product 'A'} = 4{,}00{,}000 \times \frac{80}{100} = 3{,}20{,}000$$

$$\text{Product 'B'} = 3{,}40{,}000 \times \frac{75}{100} = 2{,}55{,}000$$

$$\text{Product 'C'} = 2{,}60{,}000 \times \frac{70}{100} = 1{,}82{,}000$$

9.3 DEPRECIATION

Depreciation is the fall in value of a fixed asset due to wear and tear in use or passage of time or any other cause. The fall in the value of fixed asset is permanent, gradual and of continuing nature. The amount of depreciation or rate of depreciation to be charged in a year depends on the following factors:

1. **Cost of asset**

   The cost of asset includes purchase price, freight, loading and unloading, installation cost and repairs cost till the asset is ready for use.

2. **Salvage value or residual value or scrap value**

   The salvage value means the estimated amount for which the fixed asset can be sold or exchanged for new assets at the end of its useful life.

3. **Estimated life**

   The length of time during which an asset is expected to be used in business is called its life. The life of an asset depends on its intensity of use (e.g. an asset used in one shift will have longer life than an asset used in double shift), the level of maintenance and the policy of management with regard to replacement of assets.

9.3.1 Objectives of Providing Depreciation

1. **Calculation of true income**

   Depreciation is a necessary cost of using fixed asset. Depreciation is charged to product costs to calculate the true profit of a given accounting period.

2. **Ascertaining true cost of production**

   Depreciation is an important expenses and forms part of cost of production. So a manufacturing firm should charge depreciation in order to calculate correct cost of production.

3. **To meet legal requirements**

   Indian Companies Act makes it compulsory to provide depreciation at prescribed rate before declaring dividend.

4. To determine the tax liability

Depreciation is an allowable expenditure for calculation of taxable business income.

5. To provide funds for replacement of assets

A fixed asset sooner or later will become useless. Therefore it must be replaced with a new asset. Provision of depreciation does not result in outflow of cash and cash equivalent to depreciation remains in business and is available to buy new assets when the existing asset becomes useless.

6. To show true and fair value in balance sheet

An auditor has to certify that the assets in balance sheet are shown at its true and fair value. Provision of depreciation becomes necessary to show assets at their true and fair value.

9.3.2 Other Terms Relevant to Depreciation

Depletion: Depletion is reduction in the value of an asset due to decrease in its physical quantity. The natural assets like mines, quarries, oil wells etc. will decrease in value according to the quantity of resources extracted or exhausted. Reduction in value due to depletion of natural assets is also taken as depreciation.

Amortisation: The word amortisation is used in relation to decrease in the value of intangible assets such as goodwill, patents, trade-marks, copyright etc. Intangible assets have limited useful life. The process of writing off the value of intangible assets over its useful life is called amortisation.

Obsolescence: The term obsolescence refers to decrease in value of an asset due to factors such as invention of machines with new technique or machines with large capacity with reduced operating cost; change in fashion and taste of consumers; change in law resulting in an asset becoming unusable etc. The decrease in value due to obsolescence is sudden, irregular and not expected. It is called external depreciation. Separate procedure should be followed for charging obsolescence loss. They are:

1. In some industries such as information technology, the technology has not matured. Continuous improvements are made resulting in old model asset becoming obsolete, redundant and costly to continue to operate etc. In such a case, the regular rate of depreciation may be suitably hiked to cover obsolescence loss.
2. If obsolescence is only occasional, a fixed amount may be charged to profit and loss account every year and credited to obsolescence reserve account. The actual obsolescence will be charged against this reserve.
3. The actual obsolescence loss may be charged to profit and loss account of the year in which it arises. This procedure may be followed if the loss is very small.
4. When obsolescence loss is big, it may be treated as deferred revenue charge and spread over a number of years.

9.4 METHODS OF DEPRECIATION

Depreciation is not an actual expenditure. It is based on estimates. The estimates as to life and scrap value are subjective. It may vary from person to person. There are various types of assets with different cost, life, and scrap value. To calculate depreciation on various types of assets, the following methods are used.

9.4.1 Straight Line Method (Fixed or Equal Instalment Method)

This method assumes that business receives equal benefit from using the assets every year. A fixed rate of depreciation is applied on original cost of assets to calculate depreciation. The amount of depreciation will be same in all years over its useful life. When rate of depreciation is not given, the following formula may be used for calculating depreciation.

$$\text{Depreciation} = \frac{\text{Original cost} - \text{Estimated scrap value}}{\text{Estimated useful life}}$$

The following are the main advantages of this method:

(i) This method is easy and simple to use.
(ii) As depreciation is uniform, the comparison of cost of production over years becomes realistic.
(iii) This method is recognised by the Institute of Chartered Accountants of India and also by Indian Companies Act.
(iv) The value of assets shown in balance sheet is considered to be reasonable.

The following are the disadvantages of this method:

(i) It is assumed benefit received from an asset is equal over the life of the assets. But during the initial years of the life of an asset benefits received will be more and in the latter part of the assets life the benefit will be less. But charge to profit and loss account including repairs and maintenance will be less in initial years and more in later years. This method is illogical.
(ii) This method is not recognised under the Income Tax Act.
(iii) When additions are made to assets often, the depreciation calculation becomes complicated.

Suitability

(i) When repairs and maintenance charges are uniform over the life of the assets.
(ii) The chances of obsolescence is less.
(iii) Life of the asset can be determined accurately.
(iv) Asset is used uniformly from year to year and the benefit received is equal in all the years.

For example, if a machine is purchased for ₹80,000 on April 1 and installation charges are ₹30,000 with an estimated scrap value of ₹10,000. The estimated life of the machine is 5 years. The annual depreciation charge over the life of the asset will be as follows:

$$\text{Depreciation} = \frac{80{,}000+30{,}000-10{,}000}{5}$$
$$= \frac{1,00,000}{5}$$
$$= ₹20{,}000$$

9.4.2 Diminishing Balance Method (Written Down Value or Reducing Balance Method)

Under this method, depreciation is calculated at a fixed percentage on the original cost in the first year and on the book value from second year onwards. The amount of depreciation goes on decreasing each year.

Advantages

(i) Higher depreciation is charged in the initial years of machine's life when the machine is more efficient. Depreciation is less in the latter part of machine's life when the machine is less efficient.

(ii) Repairs and maintenance charge is less in the earlier years and more in the later years. The charge to profit and loss account (deprecation plus repairs and maintenance) will be uniform throughout the life of the asset. This is more equitable.

(iii) When new machines are purchased the cost of new machine is added to the book value of existing machines for calculation of depreciation. Calculation of depreciation is simple and easy.

(iv) This method is recognised under AS-6 and Indian Companies Act, 1956 and is used for income tax purpose.

(v) As the machine is never fully written off the asset account appears in the books till it is disposed of.

Demerits

(i) It does not take into account loss of interest on the amount invested in the asset.

(ii) If the life of the asset is short the depreciation charge in the earlier years will be heavy.

(iii) Depreciation is not uniform through the life of the asset.

Suitability

(i) When repairs and maintenance are less in the beginning years and heavy in the later years of the machine life.

(ii) When the possibility of obsolescence is more.

9.4.3 Annuity Method

This method takes into account the loss of interest on the amount invested in the asset. Interest calculated at a fixed rate on the book value of the asset in the beginning of the year and debited to the assets account every year. Depreciation is charged at a fixed amount, so that the book value of the asset is reduced to the salvage value of the asset at the end of its life.

9.4.4 Sinking Fund Method (Depreciation Fund Method)

This method provides necessary cash for replacement of an asset at the end of its useful life. The amount of depreciation, which is same every year, is calculated with reference to sinking fund table. Cash equal to annual depreciation is set aside and invested in outside securities. The interest earned on the investment every year is also reinvested. The accumulated amount will be equal to the cost of original assets at the end of its useful life. At the end of the last years investment made in outside securities will be realised and used to buy a new asset.

9.4.5 Insurance Policy Method

Under this method an insurance policy is taken for an amount needed to replace an existing asset. Premium is paid to insurance company. Policy is taken for a period equal to the useful life of the existing asset. When the useful life of existing asset expires the insurance policy also matures. The policy amount is used to purchase a new asset in the place of the old asset.

9.4.6 Machine Hour Rate Method

This method is used when the useful life of an asset can be measured in terms of hours of operation and not in years. When the intensity of use of machine varies from year to year this method is more suitable. Depreciation per machine hour is calculated by dividing the total value of the asset by life in terms of machine hours. Depreciation charge for an year will be computed as follows:

$$\begin{aligned}\text{Depreciation} = {} & \text{No. of machine hours operated during the year} \\ & \times \text{Depreciation rate per machine hour}\end{aligned}$$

In some cases life of an asset may be expressed in terms of miles for a vehicle and flying hours for an aircraft.

9.4.7 Depletion Method

This method is used to calculate depreciation of natural assets like mines, quarries, oil wells etc. Depreciation per unit (tonnes, gallons or numbers) is calculated first by dividing the total cost of the asset by the capacity of the asset. Annual depreciation charge is calculated as follows:

$$\text{Depreciation} = \text{Quantity of resources extracted during the year} \times \text{Depreciation rate p/u}$$

The amount of depreciation will vary from year to year depending on the volume of resources extracted.

9.4.8 Revaluation Method

This method is applied to calculate depreciation on the assets of small value like loose tools, bottles, corks, packages etc. It is not possible to calculate the useful life of loose tools accurately. Some tools may last for long and some may be broken in a short period. Procedure for calculating depreciation is different in this method. Cost of additions to the asset during the year is added to the opening value and the value of assets at the end of the year is calculated. The decrease in the closing value is the depreciation expenses.

9.4.9 Sum of the Years Digits Method

Under this method it is assumed that the efficiency of the machine will be more in the initial years and less in the later years of machine life. Depreciation is charged in the ratio of benefits received. When the life of machine is say, 4 years, weight 4 is assigned for the first year, weight 3 is assigned for the second year and so on. The ratio of weights will be 4 : 3 : 2 : 1. The total of weights is $4 + 3 + 2 + 1 = 10$.

For example: value of asset is ₹1,50,000, life of the asset is 4 years and scrap value is nil. This depreciation charge would be as follows:

I year: $1{,}50{,}000 \times 4/10 = 60{,}000$

II year: $1{,}50{,}000 \times 3/10 = 45{,}000$

III year: $1{,}50{,}000 \times 2/10 = 30{,}000$

IV year: $1{,}50{,}000 \times 1/10 = 15{,}000$

9.5 TREATMENT OF MISCELLANEOUS ITEMS IN COST ACCOUNTS

9.5.1 Depreciation on Fully Depreciated Asset

Due to better maintenance and the asset may be in usable condition even after its estimated useful life. Sometimes an asset may continue to be used due to non-availability of a replacement. In such a case depreciation is not charged in financial account books. But in cost accounts, depreciation is charged for having received benefits from the use of asset, whether it is fully depreciated or not. It also makes comparison of cost data comparable and suitable over years.

9.5.2 Depreciation on Replacement Value of Assets

Depreciation is calculated on the original cost of assets. But some accountants favour charging depreciation on replacement value of the assets. For example: a machine costing ₹50,000 is depreciated on original cost basis and the life of machine is 5 years. In the beginning of the sixth year the cost of the asset may be more, say ₹1,00,000 or more. The depreciation charged on the original cost will not provide adequate funds for purchase of new assets.

Arguments in favour of charging depreciation on replacement value:

1. The object of providing depreciation is to save cash for replacement of assets. This method provides adequate amount for replacement of assets.
2. True profit is not arrived when depreciation is calculated on the original cost.
3. Two firms might have purchased identical assets in different years. Due to inflation, cost of machines will vary. Depreciation differs even though assets used are identical and benefits received are the same.
4. In times of inflation profit is overstated as depreciation on the original cost remains static.
5. All revenues and costs are incurred on current price basis. But depreciation is charged on historical cost basis. This distorts the true profit.

Arguments against charging depreciation on the replacement value:

1. It is very difficult to estimate the replacement value at the first year itself.
2. Replacement value will also change from year to year depending on the rate of inflation or deflation.
3. Provision of depreciation on replacement value is not accepted under Income Tax Act .
4. Depreciation on replacement value is not near to actual. It is only imaginary.

Depreciation on replacement value is not permitted under Indian laws. If it is desired to provide adequate funds for replacement of assets, then an additional provision may be made every year and credited to replacement reserve account

9.5.3 Accelerated Rate of Depreciation

This is a higher rate of depreciation which consists of normal depreciation rate augmented for additional depreciation suffered due to increased use of asset. Normal rate of depreciation is adequate for normal use of assets. For increased use of assets, depreciation rate should be suitably increased. When an asset usually operated in a single shift is used in double shifts or triple shifts, depreciation rate should be increased for additional shifts. The Income Tax Act also provides for the accelerated rate of depreciation in case of double shifts and triple shifts.

9.5.4 Interest on Capital

There is wide difference of opinion as to inclusion of interest on capital in computation of cost of production (borrowed as well as own fund). The following are the points in favour and against the inclusion of interest:

9.5.5 Arguments In Favour

1. Capital is an essential factor of production like labour and land. Interest is a reward for the use of capital as wages is for the use of labour. So interest should be included in cost.
2. In some industries materials and finished products are to be stored for long for improving their quality or suitability (seasoning). Capital is locked up for long time resulting in loss of interest.
3. In some industries production process may be lengthy taking more time. It locks up large sum of money in work-in-progress. Interest is an important element of cost.
4. Sometimes goods are stored for long before sale as in the case of seasonal industries. Interest is to be considered for calculating correct profit.
5. Comparison of cost on equitable basis cannot be made without including interest on the capital in the cost of production.
6. While comparing jobs requiring different amount of capital, it is essential to consider interest while computing profits.

9.5.6 Arguments Against

1. Wages and salaries are the reward for labour. The profit is the reward for own capital. Interest should not be considered in cost.
2. Interest is matter of pure finance, it should not be considered.
3. It is difficult to estimate the capital employed in various processes or departments or for different products.
4. Rate of interest is not same. It varies from long-term loan to short-term loan or overdrafts. Rate of interest also varies from season to season.
5. There is different concept of capital like working capital, gross capital employed, net capital employed, own capital and borrowed capital to be considered for charging interest.
6. Inclusion of interest leads to unnecessary complications in the calculation of cost of production.

9.5.7 Research and Development Cost

1. **Research cost:**

   CIMA defines "Research cost is the cost for new and improved products, new application of materials, or new or improved methods". It is incurred for searching new or improved products or new methods of production or new plants. Research may of two types. They are:

   (a) **Basic research or pure research:** It is carried to improve the quality, technique of production, etc not directed towards any particular aim.

(b) **Applied research:** It is carried out to achieve a particular aim. Usually it is related to the area in which the firm is operating.

Treatment of research cost in cost accounting

i. When research and development is carried on a regular basis, it is charged to production overheads.

ii. Cost of applied research for a particular product may be charged to that product cost.

iii. If research and development is done on behalf of a customer, it is charged to that particular job cost.

iv. If heavy expenditure is incurred and the results are uncertain, it may be charged to costing profit and loss.

v. When research and development is done to develop a new product. The cost may be accumulated till the commercial production commences. The cost is treated as deferred revenue expenses and spread over a specified number of years.

2. **Development costs**

It is the cost of the process which begins with the implementation of the decision to produce a new or improved product or to employ a new or improved method of production and ends with the commencement of formal production of that product.

It begins where research ends. It begins with the implementation of the decision to produce a new or improved product.

Treatment of development cost

It is charged to the particular product or process for which it is incurred.

9.5.8 Packing Expenses

1. **Primary packing:** Primary packing is essential to protect the quality of the product and for convenient handling. Cost of primary packing is included in the direct materials cost of the product.

2. **Secondary packing:** It is an additional packing. It is made to improve the image of the product or easy transportation of the product. It is included in the selling and distribution overheads.

3. **Special packing:** If a customer needs a particular type of packing, it is included in the cost of that particular order or job.

9.5.9 Carriage and Freight Charges

1. When carriage and freight charges are incurred for bringing the raw materials purchased. It is included in the direct materials cost.

2. When carriage and freight are incurred for bringing a machine purchased. The expenditure is capitalised and added to the cost of machine purchased.

3. When carriage and freight charges are paid to take the finished products to markets, it is treated as distribution overheads.

4. When carriage and freight are paid for large number of stores and materials purchased, it is treated as indirect materials cost and included in the production overheads.

9.5.10 Cost of Rectification of Defective Products

Some units produced may not conform to the standards specified. Some additional cost is to be incurred to cure the defect. If defectives are within the normal level, cost of rectification is included in production overheads. If defectives are beyond the normal level, cost of rectifying the abnormal defective is charged to costing profit and loss account.

9.5.11 Bad Debts

There are two views as to the treatment of bad debts. They are,

1. Bad debts arise due to credit sales. So it is a matter of pure finance and should not be considered in cost accounts.

2. Nowadays almost all transactions between the manufacturer and the wholesaler is on credit basis. It should be considered selling and distribution overheads. But heavy bad debts should be charged to costing profit and loss account.

9.5.12 After-Sales Services Cost

Firms producing and marketing consumer durables and machineries provide after-sales services. It is undertaken to satisfy the customers and improve the sales. For this purpose separate divisions are maintained. It results in staff salaries, replacement of spares, visit to customers place etc. These expenses are included in selling and distribution overheads.

9.5.13 Advertisement Cost

The treatment of advertisement costs are as follows:

1. When advertisement is incurred for a particular product, it is allocated to that product.

2. When advertisement is of a general nature incurred for all products, it is apportioned to products on some equitable basis such as sales value, number of units sold etc.

3. When heavy expenditure is incurred for launching a new product, it is treated as deferred revenue expenditure and spread over a number of years.

4. When expenditure of capital nature like installation of neon lights are incurred, it is capitalised and debited to fixed asset account. This amount is written off over the useful life of the asset as depreciation.

9.5.14 Market Research Cost

Market research is undertaken usually before launching a new product or entering a new market. It is undertaken to collect the information like competition, customer taste and preference, market trend, trading practices etc. It helps a company to device its own market strategy. The amount of expenditure depends on the management policy. If the expenditure is small it is included in selling and distribution cost of the year in which it is incurred. If the amount is heavy it is treated as deferred revenue expenditure and spread over two or three years.

9.5.15 Rent

Rent paid for leased premises is an actual expenditure and it is included in appropriate overheads. If premises is owned, there is difference of opinion in charging rent for own premises. To ensure uniformity in inter-firm comparison of cost and profit, it is advisable to include notional rent for own premises in cost accounting.

9.5.16 Training Expenses

Trainings are of various types such as training to new employees and retraining the old employees when new machineries or new methods of production are introduced. Training is also given to employees promoted to new positions. These training costs are routine and normal in all organisations. Training cost should be included in appropriate overheads and loaded to job or product costs.

9.5.17 Canteen Expenses

When food, beverages and refreshments are provided to employees at subsidised rate, the subsidy borne by the management is part of labour cost. It is treated as indirect labour cost and apportioned to various departments according number of employees using the canteen from each department.

9.5.18 Fringe Benefits

This is the cost of additional payment or benefits provided to workers. It is provided in the form of rent-free house, medical facilities, recreations, free education to employees children etc. This is part of indirect labour cost. It is apportioned to various departments in the ratio of number of employees in the respective departments.

9.6 EXERCISES

I. Objective Type Questions

A. State whether the following statements are true or false

(a) Expenses incurred for sales promotion are distribution expenses.

(b) Packing expenses are distribution expenses.

(c) Primary packing is selling overheads.

(d) Warehousing cost is distribution expenses.

(e) Obsolescence arises due to actual use of plant and machinery.

(f) Pure research is connected with the business activity of a company.

(g) Development cost is incurred to develop a new method of production.

(h) Secondary packing is selling overheads.

(i) Salary of the general manager is treated as factory overheads.

(j) Development activity begins where research ends.

[**Ans:** *True:* b, d, h, j *False:* a, c, e, f, g, i]

B. Fill in the blanks

(a) Decrease in the value of machinery due to development of a new machinery with improved operating capacity is called ____________.

(b) Research of general nature is also called ____________ research.

(c) Heavy advertisement cost incurred at the time of launching a new product may be treated as ____________.

(d) Interest on capital is ____________ from cost accounts.

(e) Heavy bad debts of exceptional nature is charged to ____________.

(f) Obsolescence is also called ____________ depreciation.

[**Ans:** (a) obsolescence (b) pure (c) deferred revenue expenditure (d) excluded (e) costing profit and loss account (f) external]

II. Theory Questions

A. Short answer type questions

1. Administration costs are mostly of fixed nature. Do you agree? explain.

2. What is selling overheads?

3. What is distribution overheads?

4. Is packing expenses selling overheads or distribution overheads? Explain.

5. Is warehousing expenses selling overheads or distribution overheads? Explain.
6. What is amortisation? Explain.
7. What is obsolescence?
8. What is depletion? Explain.
9. How research cost is treated in cost accounts?
10. What is development cost? Explain its treatment in cost accounts.
11. How fringe benefits are treated in cost accounts?
12. How depreciation on fully depreciated asset is treated in cost accounts?
13. What is accelerated rate of depreciation? Explain.

B. Long answer type of questions

1. What is administration overheads? Explain the accounting treatment of administration overheads.
2. Explain the various methods of control of administration overheads.
3. Define selling and distribution overheads. Discuss the accounting for selling and distribution expenses. **(CA-Inter)**
4. What is the distinction between selling cost and distribution cost? Explain with examples.
5. Explain the accounting treatment of selling and distribution expenses.
6. What are the arguments for and against the inclusion of interest on capital in the cost accounts? **(CA-Inter)**
7. Wheat is research and development cost? Explain its treatment in cost accounts.
8. Explain the accounting treatment of the following items in cost accounts:
   (a) Packing expenses (b) Bad debts
   (c) Patent and trade mark acquisition cost
   (d) Expenses on removal and re-erection of machinery **(CA-Inter)**
9. Distinguish between research cost and development cost.
10. What is amortisation? Explain.
11. Explain the different types of researches and their accounting treatment in cost accounts.
12. Explain the various circumstances under which you would favour the inclusion of interest on capital in cost accounting. **(CA-Inter)**
13. Explain the causes for obsolescence and its accounting treatment in cost accounts.
14. What are the steps to be followed in controlling administration overheads?

III. Practical Problems

1. A company is making a study of the relative profitability of the two products A and B. In addition to direct costs, indirect selling and distribution costs to be allocated between the two products are as under:

	₹
Insurance charges for inventory (finished)	78,000
Storage costs	1,40,000
Packing and forwarding charges	7,20,000
Salesmen salaries	8,50,000
Invoicing costs	4,50,000

Other details are:

	Product A	Product B
Selling price per unit (₹)	500	1,000
Cost per unit (excluding selling and distribution cost) (₹)	300	600
Annual sales (in units)	10,000	8,000
Average inventory (in units)	1,000	800
Number of invoices	2,500	2,000

One unit of product A requires a storage space twice as much as product B. The cost to pack and forward one unit is same for both the products. Salesmen are paid salary plus commission at 5% on sales and equal amount of efforts are put forth on the sales of each of the products.

Required:

(a) Set up a schedule showing the apportionment of the indirect selling and distribution costs between the two products.

(b) Prepare a statement showing the relative profitability of the two products. **(CA-Inter)**

[**Ans** (a) Product A-₹14,55,000; B-₹14,33,000 (b) Product A-₹5,45,000; B-₹17,67,000]

2. XYZ Ltd., a manufacturing company, having an extensive marketing network throughout the country sells its products through four zonal sales offices viz. A, B, C and D. The budgeted expenditure for the year is given below:

	₹
Sales manager's salary	1,20,000
Expenses relating to sales manager's office	80,000
Travelling salesmen's salaries	3,20,000
Travelling expenses	36,000

Advertisement			30,000
Godown rent—zone-A		15,000	
	B	25,200	
	C	9,800	
	D	18,000	68,000
Insurance on inventories			20,000
Commission on sales at 5% on sales			6,00,000

The following particulars are also available:

Zone	**Sales in ₹ lakhs**	**No. of salesmen**	**Total mileage covered**	**Allocation of advertisement**	**Average stock ₹ lakhs**
A	36	5	6,000	30%	6
B	48	6	14,000	30%	8
C	16	2	4,500	20%	4
D	20	3	5,500	20%	2

Based on the above details, compute zone-wise selling overheads as percentage to sales.

(ICWA-Inter)

[**Ans:** Selling overheads: Zone A-₹3,77,200; B-₹4,99,000; C-₹1,71,867 and D-₹2,25,933
Selling overheads as percentage on sales A-10.48%; B-10.40%; C-10.74% and D-11.30%]

10 Cost Ledger

- Meaning
- Main and subsidiary ledgers
- Various control accounts
- Journal entries in cost ledger—comparison of financial and cost books
- Cost ledger—advantages

10.1 INTRODUCTION

When a company decides to introduce cost accounts, two methods of keeping cost accounts are available. In the first method cost accounting books are maintained independently of financial accounts. Then there will be two sets of account books, one for cost accounts and the other for financial accounts. This method of keeping cost accounting books is called Cost Ledger Accounting or Non-integrated Accounting. In the second method of accounting cost accounts and financial accounts are maintained in a single ledger. The second method of accounting is called Integral or Integrated Accounting or Inter-locking Accounts. In this chapter we are concerned with Cost Ledger Accounting method.

In financial accounting real accounts, personal accounts and nominal accounts are maintained. Cost accountant is concerned with only costs. So in cost accounts only impersonal accounts are maintained.

10.1.1 Cost Accounting Ledgers

1. Cost ledger control account or general ledger adjustment account

This is the main ledger in cost accounting books. In this ledger various control accounts are maintained for various subsidiary ledgers opened in cost books. Cost information like purchase of materials, wages & salaries paid, various expenses paid are taken from financial account books and these expenses are debited in cost books. Credit entry will be missing. To give the missing credits and to make the cost ledger self-balancing a control account is opened which is called general ledger adjustment account or cost ledger control account or financial ledger control account.

2. Subsidiary ledgers

To reduce the number of accounts in the main ledger a number of subsidiary ledgers are opened for each important element of cost. They are:

(a) Stores ledger
(b) WIP ledger
(c) Finished goods ledger
(d) Overheads ledger etc.

(a) Stores ledger

Individual accounts are opened for each item of materials and stores. All transactions like purchases, purchase returns, issue of materials and stores are recorded and balances are extracted at the end of the period.

(b) Work-in-progress ledger

Separate accounts are opened for each job undertaken. Various expenses incurred for the jobs like direct materials, direct wages, manufacturing expenses are debited in respective job accounts. The jobs completed are debited to finished goods control account and credited to work-in-progress control account. The balance in this account represents cost of jobs commenced and remaining incomplete.

(c) Finished goods ledger

Similar to WIP ledger, separate accounts are opened for each item of finished goods. Goods finished during the year are debited to respective finished goods account. Goods sold are credited to respective finished goods account. At the end of the period, balances are extracted. This balance represents cost of finished goods remaining unsold.

(d) Overheads ledger

Overheads ledger is classified into various subdivisions for each overhead like production overheads, office and administration overheads and selling and distribution overheads. The expenses incurred during the period are debited to respective overheads account. Factory overheads recovered are credited in factory overheads account and debited to work-in-progress account, office and administration overheads recovered are credited to office and administration overheads account and debited to finished goods account. Selling and distribution expenses recovered are credited to selling and distribution overheads and debited to cost of sales control account.

10.1.2 Control Accounts

Various control accounts are opened in cost ledger for various subsidiary ledgers. In control accounts totals of all transactions in subsidiary ledgers are posted in control accounts. Hence, control accounts are only summary of various accounts maintained in each subsidiary ledger. The following are the various control accounts opened in cost ledger.

1. Stores ledger control account

Opening balance of materials and stores items appear on the debit side of this account. All purchases are debited to this account. All direct materials issued for various jobs are credited to stores ledger control account and debited to WIP ledger control account. Total of indirect materials issued are credited in this account and debited to various overheads accounts. For example packing materials issued is debited to selling and distribution overheads control account and office stationery's issued is debited to office and administration overheads control account. Similarly indirect materials issued for production is debited to production overheads ledger control account. At the end closing balance is extracted, it represents the cost of all materials and stores in hand.

2. Wages control account

All wages and salaries, allowances etc paid to employees are debited in this account. Direct wages allocated for production is credited to this account and debited to WIP ledger control account. All indirect wages are credited in this account and debited to concerned overheads control accounts. For example, office salaries and allowances recovered are debited to finished goods ledger control account. All indirect manufacturing wages recovered is debited to production overheads ledger control account.

3. Production overheads/Factory overheads/works overhead/Manufacturing overheads ledger control account

All indirect materials issued for production, indirect wages and all factory expenses incurred are debited to this account and production overheads recovered are credited in this account and debited to work-in-progress ledger control account. The difference in this account will represent either under absorption or over absorption of production overheads.

4. WIP ledger control account

All direct materials issued, materials purchased directly for jobs, direct wages allocated and production overheads recovered are debited to this account. The cost of jobs completed during the period are credited to this account and debited to finished goods ledger control account. The closing balance in this account represents the cost of various jobs remaining incomplete.

5. Finished goods ledger control account

The opening balance of all finished goods unsold appears on the debit side. All jobs completed during the period is debited to this account. The cost of all finished stock sold are credited to this account. The closing balance in this account represents cost of all finished stocks remaining unsold.

6. Office and administration overheads ledger control account

All office salaries, stationeries and all office expenses are debited to this account. Office and administration overheads recovered is credited to this account and debited to finished stock ledger control account. The difference in this account represents over- or under-absorption of administration overheads.

7. Selling and distribution overheads ledger control account

All sales office salaries and allowances, cost of packing materials and other selling expenses are debited to this account. Selling and distribution overheads recovered are credited to this account. and debited to cost of sales control account. Alternatively the selling and distribution overheads recovered may be debited to costing and profit and loss account instead of debiting to cost of sales control account. The difference in this account also represents either over- or under-absorption of selling and distribution overheads.

8. Cost of sales control account

The cost of finished stocks sold and selling and distribution overheads are debited to this account. The total sales value of the finished stock sold are credited to this account and debited to general ledger adjustment account. The difference in this account represents the profit earned from the sale of finished stock and it is transferred to costing and profit and loss account.

9. Costing profit and loss account

Profit from cost of sales control account is credited to this account. All abnormal losses like loss of materials by fire, theft etc and all abnormal wages are debited to this accounting. All under-recovery of various overheads are debited to costing profit and loss account. All over-absorption of various overheads are credited to costing profit and loss account. Sometimes over- or under-absorption of overheads may be carried forward to next period instead of transferring to costing profit and loss account. The difference in costing profit and loss account represents either profit or loss for the period. If there is profit it is credited to general ledger adjustment account. If there is loss it is debited to general ledger adjustment account.

10. General ledger adjustment account/Cost ledger control account/financial ledger control account

This is a control account opened in the main ledger. All expenses incurred are debited to various expenses control account and credited to general ledger adjustment account. Sales are debited in general ledger adjustment account. The balance in this ledger represents the total of all personal accounts in the financial ledger.

10.2 JOURNAL ENTRIES IN COST LEDGER

To facilitate easy understanding of accounting entries made in cost ledger let us see the journal entries made in the financial ledger and the cost ledgers comparatively. The entries in financial and cost books are tabulated below:

Transactions	Financial books	Cost book
A. Entries relating to materials		
1. Purchase of materials	Purchases a/c Dr To cash or creditors a/c	Stores ledger control a/c Dr To General ledger adj. a/c
2. Materials purchased for special job	-do-	WIP ledger control a/c Dr To General ledger adj. a/c

3. Materials returned to suppliers	Creditors a/c Dr To purchase returns a/c	General ledger adj. a/c Dr To Stories ledger control a/c
4. Direct materials issued to production	No entry	WIP ledger control a/c Dr To Stores ledger control a/c
5. Materials returned from production to stores	No entry	Stores ledger control a/c Dr To WIP ledger control a/c
6. Materials transfer from one job to another job	No entry	Receiving job a/c Dr To Giving job a/c
7. Indirect materials issued to production	No entry	Production overheads ledgers control a/c Dr To Stores ledger control a/c
8. Abnormal loss of materials	Profit and loss a/c Dr Insurance claims Dr To purchase a/c	Costing profit and loss a/c Dr To Stores ledger control a/c
B. Entries relating to wages		
1.Wages,salaries,allowances, etc. incurred	Wages a/c Dr Salaries a/c Dr Allowances a/c Dr To cash or outstanding expenses a/c	Wages ledger control a/c Dr To General ledger adj. a/c
2. Direct wages allotted to production	No entry	WIP progress ledger control a/c Dr To Wages ledger control a/c
3. Indirect wages charged to various overheads	No entry	Factory overheads control a/c Dr Administration overheads control a/c Dr Selling overheads control a/c Dr To Wages ledger control a/c
4. Abnormal wages	No entry	Costing p & l a/c Dr To Wages control a/c
C. Entries relating to overheads		
1. Indirect expenses incurred	Expenses a/c Dr To cash or outstanding expenses a/c	Production overheads control a/c Dr Admn. overheads control a/c Dr Selling overheads control a/c Dr To General ledger adj. a/c
2. Production overheads recovered	No entry	WIP progress led control a/c Dr To Production overheads control a/c
3. Admn. overheads recovered	No entry	Finished stock ledger control a/c Dr To Admn. overheads control a/c
4. Selling overheads recovered Dr	No entry	Cost of sales control a/c or Costing profit and loss a/c Dr To Selling overheads control a/c
5. Over-recovery of overheads	No entry	Concerned overheads control a/c Dr To Costing p & l a/c

6. Under-recovery of overheads	No entry	Costing P & L a/c Dr To Concerned overheads control a/c
D. Transfer of finished jobs	No entry	Finished stock ledger control a/c Dr To WIP ledger control a/c
E. Cost of finished goods sold	No entry	Cost of sales control a/c Dr To Finished stock ledger control a/c
F. Finished goods sold	Cash a/c or Debtors a/c Dr To sales a/c	General ledger adj. a/c Dr To Cost of sales control a/c
G. Transfer of difference in cost of sales control a/c	No entry	Cost of sales control a/c Dr To Costing P & L a/c
H. Transfer of difference in costing profit and loss a/c	No entry	Costing P & L a/c (profit) Dr To General ledger adj. a/c

Advantages of maintaining cost ledger

The following are the advantages of maintaining cost ledger:

1. It provides necessary cost data for ascertainment of cost of jobs, process, products, cost centre and departments.
2. It helps in establishing standards and establishing control over materials, labour and overheads is made possible.
3. Establishing proper cost control helps in elimination of wasteful expenditures.
4. It helps the management in taking policy decisions relating to production planning, profit planning and cost control measures.
5. It provides ready information about the value of closing stock of materials, work-in-progress and finished goods. It helps in prompt preparation of profit and loss account and balance sheet at regular intervals.
6. It acts as a check over financial accounts.
7. Costing data are available from books of original entry and hence no delay is caused in obtaining cost information.

Illustration-1

The following transaction took place during the month of March 2009 in M/S. Nadan Ltd. Enter the transactions in the cost and financial books.

		₹
1.	**Materials purchased:**	
	a) Credit purchases	15,000
	b) Cash purchases	10,000
	c) Credit purchases for job no: 20	5,000
	d) Cash purchase for repair works:	2,000
2.	Return to suppliers	3,000
3.	Carriage inward paid on direct	
	Materials purchases	500
4.	Direct materials issued to jobs	20,000
5.	Indirect materials issued to jobs	3,000
6.	Materials returned from jobs to stores	1.000
7.	Materials transferred from job no: 15 to 25	1,000

Solution

S.No.	Financial books	Cost books
1.	(a) Purchases a/c Dr 15,000 To Creditors a/c 15,000 (Being credit purchases)	Stores ledger control a/c Dr 15,000 To General ledger adj. a/c 15,000
	(b) Purchases account Dr 10,000 To Cash a/c 10,000 (Being cash purchases)	Stores ledger control a/c Dr 10,000 To General ledger adj. a/c 10,000
	(c) Purchases a/c Dr 5,000 To Creditors a/c 5,000 (Being materials purchased on credit)	WIP ledger control account Dr 5,000 To General ledger adj. a/c 5,000
	(d) Repairs a/c Dr 2,000 To cash a/c 2,000 (Being materials purchased for repair works)	Production overheads a/c Dr 2,000 To General ledger adj. a/c 2,000
2.	Creditors a/c Dr 3,000 To purchase returns a/c 3,000 (Being materials returned to suppliers)	General led adj. a/c Dr 3,000 To Stores ledger control a/c 3,000
3.	Carriage inward account Dr 500 To Cash a/c 500 (Being carriage inward paid)	Stores ledger control account Dr 500 To General ledger adj. a/c 500
4.	No entry	Work in progress led. Cont. a/c Dr 20,000 To Stores led cont a/c 20,000 (Being direct materials issued for job)

5.	No entry	Production overheads led. cont. Dr 3,000 To general ledger adj. a/c 3,000 (Being indirect materials issued for jobs)
6.	No entry	Stores ledger control a/c Dr 1,000 To work in progress led. cont a/c 1,000 (Being materials returned from jobs)
7.	No entry	Job No: 25 account Dr 1,000 To Job No. 15 a/c 1,000 (Being materials transferred from Job No: 15 to 25)

Illustration-2

The following transactions are taken from the books of M/S. Shankar Ltd for the month of March 2009:

	₹	₹
Gross wages		30,000
Less-Deduction:		
Employee's contribution to P.F	3000	
Employee's contribution to ESI	450	
Income tax deducted at source	600	4,050
Net wages payable in cash		25,950
Employer's contribution to P.F	3,000	
Employer's contribution to ESI	300	3,300

Following details were obtained from the wages analysis book:

	₹
1. Direct labour	22,000
2. Indirect factory labour	6,000
3. Salaries to administration staff	3,500
4. Salaries to selling and distribution staff	1,800
	33,300

Show journal entries in the cost books

Solution

Journal entries in cost books		
1.	Wages control account Dr 33,300 To General ledger adjustment a/c (Being total wages recorded)	 33,300
2.	Work-in-progress ledger control a/c Dr 22,000 To Wages ledger control a/c (Being direct wages debited to WIP ledger control account)	 22,000
3.	Production overheads ledger control a/c Dr 6,000 Administration overheads ledger control a/c Dr 3,500 Selling and distribution overheads ledger control a/c Dr 1,800 To Wages ledger control account (Being indirect wages transferred to various overheads control accounts)	 11,300

Illustration-3

Pass journal entries in cost books from the following information regarding overheads. Prepare a statement of recovery of overheads and pass suitable entries for under/over-recovery:

(i)

	₹
(a) Outstanding expenses	5,000
(b) Cash expenses	20,000

(ii)

Analysis of the above			
	Outstanding expenses ₹	Cash expenses ₹	Total ₹
Factory overheads	2,000	12,000	14,000
Administration overheads	1,500	5,000	6,500
Selling and distribution overheads	1,500	3,000	4,500
	5,000	20,000	25,000

(iii)

Recovery of overheads as under	
	₹
Factory overheads	14,400
Administration overheads	6,200
Selling and distribution overheads	4,300
	24,900

Solution

Journal entries in cost books

(i)	Factory overheads ledger control account Admn. overheads ledger control account Selling and distribution overheads led. cont. a/c To general ledger adjustment account (Being actual overheads incurred)	Dr 14,000 Dr 6,500 Dr 4,500	25,000
(ii)	Work-in-progress ledger control account To Factory overheads control account (Being factory overheads recovered)	Dr 14,400	14,400
(iii)	Finished goods ledger control account To Administration overheads control account (Being administration overheads recovered)	Dr 6,200	6,200
(iv)	Cost of sales control account To Selling and distribution overheads led.cont a/c (Being selling and distribution overheads recovered)	Dr 4,300	4,300

Statement showing recovery of overheads				
	Overheads incurred (₹)	**Overheads recovered (₹)**	**Under recovery (₹)**	**Over recovery (₹)**
Factory overheads	14,000	14,400	-	(+)400
Administration overheads	6,500	6,200	(−)300	-
Selling and distribution	4,500	4,300	(−)200	-
	25,000	24,900	(−)500	(+)400

Journal entry for under-recovery and over-recovery of overheads			
(i)	Costing profit and loss account	Dr 500	
	To administration overheads ledger control account		500
	To selling and distribution overheads ledger control account		300
	(Being under-recovered overheads transferred to costing P & L account)		
(ii)	Factory overheads ledger Control account	Dr 400	
	To Costing profit and loss account		400
	(Being over-recovered overheads transferred to costing P & L account)		

Illustration-4

The following balances are shown in the cost ledger of K. Ltd. on 31st March, 2009:

	Dr ₹	Cr ₹
Finished goods ledger control a/c	20,000	
WIP progress ledger control a/c	40,000	
Stores ledger control a/c	1,00,000	
General ledger adjustment a/c		1,60,000
	1,60,000	1,60,000

Transactions for the year ending 31st March 2009 were:

Purchase of materials		5,90,000
Purchase of materials for special jobs		36,000
Returns to suppliers from stores		4,000
Wages and salaries paid		
Direct	4,10,000	
Factory indirect	90,000	
Administration staff	78,000	
Selling and distribution	48,000	
Abnormal idle time	6,000	6,32,000
Expenses (direct)		44,000
Production expenses		1,02,000
Administration expenses		82,000
Selling and distribution expenses		52,000
Materials issued to production		6,10,000
Materials lost by fire from stores		8,000
Stores issued to maintenance		26,000

Production overhead applied to production at 20% on prime cost		
Administration overheads recovered from finished goods		1,56,000
Selling and distribution overheads recovered		1,04,000
Finished goods produced		13,20,000
Finished goods sold at cost		14,00,000
Sales		16,00,000

Write up necessary accounts in the cost ledger to record the above transactions and prepare a Trial balance as at 31st March 2009.

Solution

Cost ledger

General ledger adjustment account					
		₹			₹
April 1, 08	To Stores ledger control a/c	4,000	April 1	By Balance b/d	1,60,000
	To Costing profit and loss a/c	16,00,000		By Stores ledger control a/c	5,90,000
March 31, 09	To Balance c/d	1,78,000		By WIP ledger control a/c	36,000
				By Wages control a/c	6,32,000
				By WIP ledger control a/c	44,000
				By Production overheads control a/c	1,02,000
				By Admn. overheads control a/c	82,000
				By Sell & dist overheads control a/c	52,000
				By Costing Profit and loss a/c	84,000
		17,82,000			17,82,000

Stores ledger control account					
		₹			₹
April 1	To Balance b/d	1,00,000	March 31	By General ledger adj a/c	4,000
March 31	To General ledger adj a/c	5,90,000		By WIP Progress ledger cont a/c	6,10,000

				By Costing profit and loss a/c	8,000
				By Production overheads control a/c	26,000
				By Balance c/d	42,000
		6,90,000			6,90,000

WIP Progress ledger control account					
		₹			₹
April 1	To Balance b/d	40,000	March 31	By Finished goods led cont a/c	13,20,000
March 31	To General ledger adj /c	36,000		By Balance c/d	40,000
	To Wages control a/c	4,10,000			
	To General led. adj a/c	44,000			
	To Stores led cont. a/c	6,10,000			
	To Production overheads cont a/c	2,20,000			
		13,60,000			13,60,000

Finished goods ledger control account					
		₹			₹
April 1	To Balance b/d	20,000	March 31	By Cost of sales cont a/c	14,00,000
	To Admn overheads control a/c	1,56,000		By Balance c/d	96,000
	To WIP led control a/c	13,20,000			
		14,96,000			14,96,000

Wages control account					
		₹			₹
March 31	To General led adj a/c	6,32,000	March 31	By WIP led cont a/c	4,10,000
				By Production overheads cont a/c	90,000
				By Admn. Ohs .cont. a/c	78,000
				By Sell & dist. Ohs cont. a/c	48,000
				By Costing P & L a/c	6,000
		6,32,000			6,32,000

Production overheads control account					
		₹			₹
March 31	To Wages control a/c	90,000	March 31	By WIP ledger control a/c	2,20,000
	To General led adj a/c	1,02,000			
	To Stores led control a/c	26,000			
	To Costing P & L a/c	2,000			
		2,20,000			2,20,000

Administration overheads control account					
		₹			₹
March 31	To Wages control a/c	78,000	March 31	By Finished goods led cont a/c	1,56,000
	To General led adj a/c	82,000		By Costing profit and loss a/c	4,000
		1,60,000			1,60,000

Selling and distribution overheads control account					
		₹			₹
March 31	To Wages control a/c	48,000	March 31	By Cost of sales control a/c	1,04,000
	To General led. Adj. a/c	52,000			
	To Costing profit and loss a/c	4,000			
		1,04,000			1,04,000

Cost of sales control account				
		₹		₹
March 31	To Sell & dist overheads cont a/c	1,04,000	By General led adj a/c	16,00,000
	To Finished goods led cont a/c	14,00,000		
	To Costing profit and loss a/c	96,000		
		16,00,000		16,00,000

Costing profit and loss account			
	₹		₹
		By Cost of sales control a/c	96,000
		By Production overheads cont. a/c	2,000
To Administration overheads cont a/c	4,000	By Sell & dist overheads cont a/c	4,000
To Stores ledger cont a/c	8,000		
To Wages led control a/c	6,000		
To General led adj a/c (net profit)	84,000		
	1,02,000		1,02,000

Trial balance as on 31st March 2009		
	Dr ₹	Cr ₹
Stores ledger control account	42,000	
Work-in-progress ledger control account	40,000	
Finished goods ledger control account	96,000	
General ledger control account		1,78,000
	1,78,000	1,78,000

Working

1.

	₹
Prime Cost	
Materials issued to production	6,10,000
Materials purchased for special jobs	36,000
Direct wages	4,10,000
Direct expenses	44,000
	11,00,000

2. Production overheads applied = Prime cost × 20%

= 11,00,000 × 20% = ₹2,20,000

Illustration-5

The following balances appeared in the books of X.Ltd, as at the beginning of the financial year ending April 1, 2008:

	₹	₹
General ledger adjustment account		76,185
Stores ledger control account	43,755	
WIP progress control account	21,435	
Finished goods ledger control account	10,995	
	76,185	76,185

At the end of the year the following information is supplied:

Purchase for stores	2,88,200	
Purchase for special job		8,750
Direct wages	1,93,135	
Indirect factory wages	47,715	
Administrative salaries	33,655	
Selling and distribution salaries	21,260	2,95,765
Production expenses		62,160
Administrative expenses		42,730
Selling and distribution expenses		27,185
Stores issued to production		2,73,505
Stores issued to maintenance account		12,380
Return to supplier		1,035
Production overheads absorbed by production		1,22,500
Administrative overheads absorbed by finished goods		76,250
Selling overheads recovered on sales		48,000
Products finished during the year		5,88,585
Finished goods sold at cost		6,61,460
Sales		7,50,000

You are required to prepare necessary ledger accounts in the cost ledger and prepare a trial balance.

Solution

In cost ledger-General ledger adjustment account					
		₹			₹
March 31	To Stores led cont a/c	1,035	April 1	By Balance b/d	76,185
	To profit and loss a/c-sales	7,50,000	March 31	By Stores led cont. a/c	2,88,200
	To Balance c/d	90,145		By WIP led cont a/c	8,750

				By Wages control a/c	2,95 765
				By Production overheads cont. a/c	62,160
				By Admn overheads cont. a/c	42,730
				By Selling overheads cont. a/c	27,185
				By Costing P & La/c-profit	40,205
		8,41,180			8,41,180

Stores ledger control account					
		₹			₹
April 1	To Balance b/d	43,755	March 31	By WIP Led. Cont. a/c	2,73,505
March 31	To General led adj a/c	2,88,200		By Production overheads led cont a/c	12,380
				By General led adj a/c	1,035
				By Balance c/d	45,035
		3,31,955			3,31,955

Wages control account					
		₹			₹
March 31	To General led adj a/c	2,95,765	April 31	By WIP Progress led cont a/c	1,93 135
				By Production overheads led cont a/c	47,715
				By Admn. overheads led cont a/c	33,655
				By Selling overheads led cont a/c	21,260
		2,95,765			2,95,765

Production overheads ledger control account					
		₹			₹
March 31	To General led adj a/c	62,160	March 31	By WIP Progress led cont a/c	1,22,500
	To Stores ledger cont. a/c	12,380			
	To Wages control a/c	47,715			
	To Costing profit and loss a/c	245			
		1,22,500			1,22,500

Administration overheads ledger control account					
		₹			₹
March 31	To General led. Adj. a/c	42,730	March 31	By Finished goods led cont. a/c	76,250
	To Wages led cont a/c	33,655		To Costing profit and loss a/c	135
		76,385			76,385

Selling and distribution overheads ledger control account					
		₹			₹
March 31	To General led adj. a/c	27,185	March 31	By Cost of sales control a/c	48,000
	To Wages led cont a/c	21,260		By Costing profit and loss a/c	445
		48,445			48,445

Work-in-progress ledger control account					
		₹			₹
April 1	To Balance b/d	21,435	March 31	By Finished goods led cont a/c	5,88,585
March 31	To General led adj a/c	8,750		By Balance c/d	30,740
	To Stores led cont a/c	2,73,505			
	To Wages led cont. a/c	1,93,135			
	To Production overheads led cont a/c	1,22,500			
		6,19,325			6,19,325

Finished goods ledger control account					
		₹			₹
April 1	To Balance b/d	10,995	March 31	By Cost of sales control a/c	6,61,460
March 31	To Administration overheads cont. a/c	76,250		By Balance c/d	14,370
	To WIP led cont. a/c	5,88,585			
		6,75,830			6,75,830

Cost of sales control account					
		₹			₹
March 31	To Selling overheads cont. a/c	48,000	March 31	By General led adj. a/c	7,50,000
	To Finished goods led cont a/c	6,61,460			
	To Costing profit and loss a/c	40,540			
		7,50,000			7,50,000

Costing profit and loss account					
		₹			₹
March 31	To Admn. overheads cont. a/c	135	March 31	By Cost of sale cont a/c	40,540
	To Selling overheads led cont a/c	445		By Production overheads cont a/c	245
	To General led adj. a/c	40,205			
		40,785			40,785

Trial balance as on 31st March 2009		
	Dr ₹	Cr ₹
Stores ledger control account	45,035	
Work-in-progress ledger control account	30,740	
Finished goods ledger control account	14,370	
General ledger control account		90,145
	90,145	90,145

Illustration-6

The following balances are taken from the books of X Ltd., as on 1st April, 2008:

	Dr (₹)	Cr (₹)
Work-in-progress ledger control account	7,055	
Factory overheads suspense account	360	
Finished goods ledger control account	5,275	
Stores ledger control account	9,450	
Administration overheads suspense account	180	
General ledger adjustment account		22,320

The transactions for the year ended 31st March, 2009 are as follows:

Stores issued to production	45,370
Stores purchased	52,400
Materials purchased for special jobs	1,135
Wages paid (including indirect wages ₹2,520)	57,600
Finished goods sold	1,18,800
Administration expenses	5,400
Selling expenses	6,000
Factory overheads	15,600
Stores issued for capital work-in-progress	1,500
Finished goods transferred to warehouse	1,08,000
Stores issued for factory repairs	2,000
Factory overheads applied to production	16,830
Administration overheads charged to production	4,580
Factory overheads applicable to unfinished work	3,080
Selling overheads allocated to sales	5,500
Stores lost due to fire in stores (not insured)	150
Administration expenses on unfinished work	850
Finished goods stock on 31-3-2009	14,274

You are required to record the entries in the cost ledger for the year ending 31-3-2009 and prepare a trial balance as on 31-3-2009.

Solution

In cost ledger-General ledger adjustment account					
		₹			₹
March 31	To Cost of sales control a/c	1,18,800	April 1	By Balance b/d	22,320
	To Balance c/d	54,585	March 31	By Stores led cont a/c	52,400
				By Wages led control a/c	57,600
				By Factory overheads control a/c	15,600
				By WIP led cont. a/c	1,135
				By Admn. overheads led control a/c	5,400
				By Selling overheads led control a/c	6,000
				By Costing profit and loss a/c	12,930
		1,73,385			1,73 385

Stores ledger control account					
		₹			₹
April 1	To Balance b/d	9,450	March 31	By WIP Progress led cont a/c	45,370
March 31	To General led adj a/c	52,400		By Capital WIP a/c	1,500
				By Factory overheads led cont. a/c	2,000
				By Costing profit and loss a/c	150
				By Balance c/d	12,830
		61,850			61,850

Wages ledger control account					
		₹			₹
April 31	To General led adj. a/c	57,600	March 31	By WIP Led cont a/c	55,080
				By Factory overheads led cont. a/c	2,520
		57,600			57,600

Factory overheads control account					
		₹			₹
April 1	To Factory overheads suspense a/c	360	March 31	By WIP led cont a/c	16,830
	To General led adj a/c	15,600		By Factory overheads suspense a/c	3,080
	To Stores ledger control a/c	2,000		By Costing profit and loss a/c	570
	To Wages led cont a/c	2,520			
		20,480			20,480

Work-in-progress ledger control account					
		₹			₹
April 1	To Balance b/d	7,055	March 31	By Finished goods led cont a/c	1,08,000
March 31	To General led adj a/c	1,135		By Balance c/d (b.f)	22,050
	To Stores led cont. a/c	45,370			
	To Wages led cont. a/c	55,080			
	To Factory overheads led cont a/c	16,830			
	To Admn. overheads cont. a/c	4,580			
		1,30,050			1,30,050

Administration overheads ledger control account					
		₹			₹
April 1	To Admn. overheads suspense a/c	180	March 31	By WIP led cont a/c	4,580
March 31	To General led adj. a/c	5,400		By Admn. overheads suspense a/c	850
				By Costing profit and loss a/c (b.f)	150
		5,580			5,580

Finished goods ledger control account					
		₹			₹
April 1	To Balance b/d	5,275	March 31	By Cost of sales control a/c (b.f)	99,000
March 31	To WIP led cont a/c	1,08,000		By Balance c/d	14,275
		1,13,275			1,13,275

Selling overheads ledger control account					
		₹			₹
March 31	To General led adj a/c	6,000	March 31	By Cost of sales control a/c	5,500
				By Costing P & L a/c (b.f)	500
		6,000			6,000

Cost of sales control account					
		₹			₹
March 31	To Finished goods led cont. a/c	99,000	March 31	By General led adj a/c-sales	1,18,800
	To Selling overheads led cont. a/c	5,500			
	To Costing profit and loss a/c (b.f)	14,300			
		1,18,800			1,18,800

Costing profit and loss account					
		₹			₹
March 1	To Stores led cont a/c	150	March 31	By Cost of sales control a/c	14,300
	To Factory overheads led cont a/c	570			
	To Admn overheads led cont. a/c	150			
	To Selling overheads led cont a/c	500			
	To General led adj a/c	12,930			
		14,300			14,300

Factory overheads suspense account					
		₹			₹
April 1	To Balance b/d	360	March 31	By Factory overheads led cont. a/c	360
March 31	Factory overheads cont. a/c	3,080		By Balance c/d	3,080

Administration overheads suspense account					
		₹			₹
April 1	To Balance b/d	180	March 31	By Admn. Ohs cont a/c	180
March 31	To Admn. overheads cont. a/c	850		By Balance c/d	850

Capital Work-in-Progress account					
		₹			₹
March 31	To Admn. overheads led cont. a/c	1,500	March 31	By Balance c/d	1,500

Trial balance as on 31st March 2009		
	Dr (₹)	**Cr (₹)**
Stores ledger control account	12,830	
Work-in-progress ledger control account	22,050	
Finished goods ledger control account	14,275	
Factory overheads suspense account	3,080	
Administration overheads suspense account	850	
Capital work in progress account	1,500	
General ledger adjustment account		54,585
	54,585	54,585

Illustration-7

The balances in cost ledger of a manufacturing company on January 1, 2009 were:

	₹
Stores ledger control account	7,000
Work-in-progress account	12,600
Finished stock account	2,200
Cost ledger control account	21,800

You are given the following information for the year 1989:

Purchase for materials	40,000
Direct factory wages	60,000
Manufacturing expenses	34,600
Selling and distribution expenses	5,400
Materials issued to production	37,200
Manufacturing expenses recovered	34,440
Selling and distribution expenses recovered	5,320
Sales	1,50,000
Stock of materials at December 31,2009	9,800
Stock of finished goods at December 31,2009	4,700
Work-in-progress at December 31,2009	14,700

You are required to show the (i) work-in-progress ledger control account (ii) Finished stock ledger control account and (iii) Cost of goods sold account in the cost ledger for the year 2009.

Solution

Work-in-Progress Ledger Control Account			
	₹		₹
To balance b/d	12,600		
To Stores ledger control account	37,200	By finished goods ledger	
		led a/c (b.f)	1,29,540
To Wages ledger control account	60,000	By balance c/d	14,700
To Manufacturing overheads control account	34,440		
	1,44,240		1,44,240

Finished stock ledger control account			
	₹		₹
To Balance b/d	2,200	By cost of goods sold account (b.f)	1,27,040
To WIP ledger control account	1,29,540	By balance c/d	4,700
	1,31,740		1,31,740

Cost of goods sold account			
	₹		₹
To Finished stock ledger Control account	1,27,040	By general ledger adjustment account	1,50,000
To Selling and distribution overheads ledger control account	5,320		
To Costing profit and loss account (b.f)	17,640		
	1,50,000		1,50,000

10.3 EXERCISES

I. Objective Type Questions

A. State whether the following statements are true or false

(i) Cost ledger accounting is also known as non-integrated account.

(ii) General ledger adjustment account is opened in integrated accounting system.

(iii) Reconciliation of accounts books are necessary under non-integral accounting system.

(iv) Materials purchased for a special job is directly debited to work-in-progress account.

(v) Direct materials issued, Direct wages and factory overheads recovered are debited to finished goods control account.

(vi) Closing balance in WIP ledger control account represents prime cost of incomplete jobs.

(vii) Stores ledger account is a subsidiary book in cost ledger.

(viii) Main source of costing information is financial books.

(ix) Double entry system of book keeping is not followed in cost ledger accounting.

[**Ans:** True: (i), (iii), (iv), (vi), (viii) False: (ii), (v), (vii), (ix)]

B. Fill in the blanks

(i) ______________ account is prepared with goods received note and materials requisition slips.

(ii) Reconciliation of financial books and cost books are not required under ______________ accounting system.

(iii) ______________ account is debited with cost of jobs completed.

(iv) ______________ ledger contains accounts of all jobs/work undertaken.

(v) Materials issued for repairs work is debited to production overheads ledger control account and credited to ______________ account.

(vi) ______________ account makes the cost ledger self-balancing.

(vii) Cost of finished goods sold is ______________ to cost of sales control account and ______________ to finished goods ledger control account.

[**Ans:** (i) stores ledger control account (ii) integrated (iii) finished goods ledger (iv) work in progress control (v) stores ledger control (vi) general ledger adjustment (vii) debited, credited]

C. Long Answer Theory Questions

1. What is cost ledger accounts? Explain its advantages.
2. What are control accounts? What purpose do they serve?
3. Explain the various subsidiary ledgers maintained in cost books.
4. What are cost control accounts? Describe their advantages.

Practical Problems

1. During the month of January, 2009, the following transactions took place in Union Ltd. Enter the following transactions in the financial and cost books:

	₹
(i) Materials purchased:	
Credit purchases	50,000
Cash purchases	40,000
Cash purchases for repair work	10,000
Credit purchase for job no: 123	8,000
(ii) Materials returned to suppliers	5,000
(iii) Direct materials issued to jobs	60,000

(iv)	Indirect materials issued to jobs	12,000
(v)	Materials returned from jobs to stores	2,500
(vi)	Materials destroyed by fire	7,500
(vii)	Materials transferred from job no: 20 to job no: 25	2,000
(viii)	Carriage inward	1,500

2. Enter the following transactions in financial and cost books:

		₹
Gross wages		25,000
Employee's contribution to P.F	3,000	
Employee's contribution to ESI	1,500	
Income tax deducted at source	1,000	5,500
Employer's contribution to P.F	3,000	
Employer's contribution to ESI	750	3,750
Total		34,250

Wages analysis sheet gives the following details:

	₹
(i) Direct labour	15,000
(ii) Indirect factory labour	2,300
(iii) Office salaries	3,500
(iv) Salaries to sales department staff	3,000
(v) Abnormal idle time	1,000
Total	24,800

3. Pass journal entries in financial and cost books from the following information regarding overheads. Prepare a statement of recovery of overheads and pass suitable entries for under/over recovery of overheads.

(i)

	₹
(i) Outstanding expenses	2,000
Cash expenses	10,000

(ii) Analysis of the above

	Cash expenses (₹)	Outstanding expenses (₹)	Total ₹
Factory overheads	5,500	1,000	6,500
Administration overheads	2,200	700	2,900
Selling and distribution overheads	2,300	300	2,600
	10,000	2,000	12,000

(iii) Absorption of overheads is as under:

	₹
(a) Factory overheads	6,800
(b) Administration overheads	2,750
(c) Selling and distribution overheads	2,800
	12,350

4. From the following figures ascertained from the costing and financial books of a company. You are required to pass necessary entries in the cost journal under non-integral accounting system:

	₹
Purchases	5,00,000
Carriage inward	20,000
Stores issued for production	3,90,000
Productive wages	6,00,000
Unproductive labour	1,50,000
Work overheads incurred	4,00,000
Materials issued for repair works	15,000
Cost of completed jobs	11,00,000
Work overheads recovered	3,95,000

5. The balances in the cost ledger of a manufacturing company on January 1,2008 were:

	₹
Stores ledger control account	7,000
Work-in-Progress ledger control account	12,800

Finished goods ledger control account	2,000
Cost ledger control account	21,800

You are given the following information for the year 2008:

Purchase of materials	40,000
Direct factory wages	60,000
Manufacturing expenses	34,600
Selling and distribution expenses	5,400
Sales	1,50,000
Materials issued to production	37,200
Manufacturing expenses recovered	34,440
Selling and distribution expenses recovered	5,320
Stock of materials on 31,12.2008	9,800
Stock of finished goods on 31,12.2008	4,700
Work-in-Progress on 31.12.2008	14,700

You are required to show the accounts in the cost ledger for the year 2008.

[**Ans:** Cost of goods finished ₹1,29,740, Cost of finished goods sold ₹1,27,040, Under recovery of factory overheads ₹160, Under-recovery of selling and distribution overheads ₹80 Profit ₹17,400, Trial balance total ₹29,200.]

6. From the following details show the necessary accounts in the cost ledger:

	Opening balance ₹	**Closing balance** ₹
Work-in-progress	5,000	9,000
Materials	8,000	11,000
Finished goods	10,000	12,000

Transactions during the period:

	₹
Materials purchased	25,000
Wages paid (including indirect wages ₹2,000)	10,000
Overheads incurred	8,000
Overheads recovered	9,000
Sales	50,000

[**Ans:** Materials issued ₹22,000, Cost of goods finished ₹35,000, Cost of goods sold ₹33,000, Under recovery of overheads ₹1,000, Profit ₹16,000, Trial balance total ₹32,000.]

7. From the following information gathered from the cost record of an industrial unit prepare necessary ledger accounts in the cost ledger of the company:

Opening balances:		₹
Work-in-progress	3,800	
Materials	22,000	
Finished stock	17,000	42,800
Materials purchased		58,000
Direct labour		21,000
Electricity charges		20,000
Factory overhead expenses incurred		27,000
Factory overhead expenses applied to production		26,000
Selling, distribution and administration expenses		28,000
Selling, distribution and admn. expenses charged to finished stock		29,000
Sales		1,86,000
Closing balances:		
Work-in-progress	2,500	
Materials	15,000	
Finished stock	32,000	49,500

[**Ans:** Profit ₹38,700, finished goods completed ₹1,33,300 finished goods sold ₹1,18,300]

8. Acme Manufacturing Co Ltd. opens the costing records, with the balances as on 1st April, as follows:

	Dr ₹	**Cr** ₹
Materials control account	1,24,000	
Work-in-progress account	62,500	
Finished goods account	1,24,000	
Production overheads account	8,400	
Administration overheads account		12,000
Selling and distribution overheads account	6,250	
General ledger adjustment account		3,13,150
	3,25,150	3,25,150

The following are transactions for the year ending 31st March:

	₹
Materials purchased	4,80,100
Materials issued to jobs	4,77,400
Materials issued to work maintenance	41,200
Materials issued to administration office	3,400
Materials issued to selling departments	7,200
Wages direct	1,49,300
Wages indirect	65,000
Transportation for incoming materials	8,400
Production overheads	2,42,250
Absorbed production overheads	3,59,100
Administration overheads	74,000
Administration overheads allocation to production	52,900
Administration overheads allocation to sales	14,800
Sales overheads	64,200
Sales overhead absorbed	82,000
Finished goods produced	9,58,400
Finished goods sold	9,77,300
Sales	14,43,000

[**Ans:** General leger adjustment a/c balance ₹3,37,100 (Cr), Stores ledger control a/c ₹83,300 (Dr), Production overheads ledger control a/c ₹₹2,250 (Cr), Work-in-progress ledger control a/c ₹89,900 (Dr), Administration overheads ledger control a/c ₹2,300 (Cr), Selling overheads ledger control a/c ₹10,450, Finished goods ledger control a/c ₹1,58,000 (Dr)]

RECONCILIATION OF COST AND FINANCIAL ACCOUNTS

11

- Meaning
- Need
- Reasons for Disagreement in Two sets of account books
- Reconciliation - Procedure and Model Statement
- Memorandum Reconciliation - Procedure and Model Statement

11.1 RECONCILIATION

In a non-integral accounting system, cost accounts and financial accounts are maintained separately. Though both accounts are maintained under double entry principles, the profits disclosed in cost accounts is not the same as disclosed by financial accounts. The principles followed for recording incomes and expenses between both the sets of accounts vary. In financial accounts all incomes and all expenses are recorded on actual basis, but in cost accounts only those expenses relating to production, administration and selling and distribution activities are recorded and all incomes are omitted. Therefore it becomes necessary that these two sets of accounts should be reconciled.

11.1.1 Need for Reconciliation

1. To find out the reasons for variance in profits in the two sets of accounts.
2. To check the accuracy of the information in cost accounting books. It ensures the reliability of cost informations recorded in cost accounting books.

When cost and financial accounts are kept under integral accounting system, there will be only one set of accounts. So there is no need for reconciling the two sets of accounting books.

11.1.2 The Reasons for Disagreement in Profits in Two Sets of Account Books

The following are the various reason which result in disagreement in profits between the two sets of accounts:

1. **Some expenses are recorded in financial books only and not in cost accounts**

   They are:

   (a) **Expenses of pure financial nature**

   They include interest paid on bank loans, mortgages, debentures, overdrafts, share and debenture issue expenses written off, discount on issue of shares and debenture discounts written off etc.

   (b) **Intangible assets written off**

   They are: Preliminary expenses, goodwill, deferred revenue expenditures written off.

   (c) **Abnormal Loss**

   They are: Loss by fire, accident, theft, natural calamities etc.,

   (d) **Capital Loss**

   They are: Loss on sale of fixed assets and investments.

   (e) **Appropriations**

   They include: Provisions for income tax, income tax paid, transfer to reserves, dividends paid, proposed dividend etc.

   (f) **Provisions**

   They are: Provision for bad and doubtful debts, provision for discounts, etc.

   (g) **Others**

   Fines and penalties paid for infraction of law, presents, gifts, charity, donations, obsolescence loss, etc.

   Effect on profit

   Cost profit more and financial profit less.

2. **Expenses appearing in cost accounts only and not in financial accounts**

   They are called notional expenses or imputed costs. They are:

   (a) Rent charged for own building

   (b) Interest charged on own capital.

   (c) Depreciation charged on fully depreciated assets.

   (d) Salary for proprietor charged in cost accounts but not actually drawn.

   Effect on profit

   Cost profit less and financial profit more.

3. Some expenses appear in both account books but the amounts differ

(a) **Over-recovery or over-absorption of overheads**

In financial accounts expenses are shown on actual basis, but in cost accounts expenses are shown on some estimated basis which is called recovery or absorption of overheads. This may result in showing more or less expenses than the actual in cost account books. If expenses recovered in cost accounts are more, it is called over-recovery or over-absorption.

Effect on Profit

Cost profit less and financial profit more.

(b) **Under-recovery or under-absorption of overheads** If expenses charged in cost accounts are less, it is called under-recovery or under-absorption of overheads.

Effect on Profit

Cost profit more and financial profit less.

4. Difference in valuation of stock

There are different methods for valuation of stock such as FIFO, LIFO, average cost methods etc, cost accountant may follow any of the above methods for valuation of stock. But financial accountant will follow the policy of valuing the stock at cost price or market price whichever is lower. As a result the profits in two sets of account books differ.

(a) Under-valuation of opening stock in cost accounts

Effect on profit

Cost profit more and financial profit less.

(b) Over valuation of opening stock in cost accounts

Effect on profit

Cost profit less and financial profit more.

(c) Under-valuation of closing stock in cost accounts

Effect on profit

Cost profit less and financial profit more.

(d) Over-valuation of closing stock in cost accounts

Effect on profit

Cost profit more and financial profit less.

5. Over- or under-recovery of depreciation

There are different methods for calculation and charging of depreciation. Cost accountant may follow one method and financial accountant may follow another method. This results in charging different amounts of depreciation in the two sets of account books.

(a) **Over recovery of depreciation**

The depreciation charged in cost accounts will be more

Effect on profit

Cost profit less and financial profit more.

(b) **Under-recovery of depreciation**

The depreciation charged in cost accounts will be less

Effect on profit

Cost profit more and financial profit less.

6. **All incomes (except sales and scrap value of materials) are shown in financial accounts only and not in cost accounts**

   They are: Interest, dividends, rent etc, received, discount received, commission earned, profit on sale of fixed assets and investments, transfer fees, difference in exchange (cr) etc.

   Effect on Profit

   Cost Profit less and financial profit more.

11.1.3 Procedure for Reconciliation

Reconciliation statement commences with profit as per one set of account books. The transactions which result in difference in profits are either added or deducted from the given profit to find the profit as per the other set of account books.

The profit we take as starting point in reconciliation statement is usually called base profit or starting profit. The profit to be found is called opposite profit. Transactions causing difference in profits which have the effect of reducing base profit are to be added and those transactions causing difference in profits which have the effect of increasing the base profit is to be deducted. Transactions which have the effect of reducing the opposite profit are to be deducted and those transactions which have the effect of increasing the opposite profit are to be added.

In case loss as per one set of account books is given reverse procedure is to be followed.

The following is the proforma of a "Reconciliation Statement"

Reconciliation Statement		
	₹	₹
Profit as per cost accounts	-	xxxx
Add: i) Over-recovery of overheads in cost accounts	-	xxxx
ii) Incomes credited in financial accounts only	-	xxxx
iii) Over-valuation of opening stock in cost accounts	-	xxxx
iv) Under-valuation of closing stock in cost accounts	-	xxxx

v) Notional expenses charged in cost accounts only	-	xxxx
		xxxxx
Less: i) Under-recovery of overheads in cost accounts	xxxx	-
ii) Expenses charged in financial accounts only	xxxx	-
iii) Under-valuation of opening stock in cost accounts	xxxx	-
iv) Over-valuation of closing stock in cost accounts	xxxx	xxxx
Profit as per financial accounts	-	xxxx

Note:

(i) When profit as per financial accounts is given, all items added above are to be deducted and all items deducted are to be added to find the profit as per cost accounts.

(ii) When the reconciliation statement is started with profit in one set of account books and the final answer is in minus amount, it is called loss as per other set of account books.

11.1.4 Memorandum Reconciliation Account or Statement

If reconciliation statement is prepared in a ledger format, it is called Memorandum Reconciliation Account (or) Statement. Starting profit or base profit is taken on the credit side of the memorandum reconciliation account. All items to be added are shown on the credit side of the Memorandum Reconciliation account. All items to be deducted are shown on the debit side. Since it is only a memorandum account the prefixes "To" on the debit side and "By" on the credit side need not be used.

The following is the proforma of a Memorandum Reconciliation Account

Memorandum Reconciliation Account (or) Statement			
	₹		₹
Loss as per cost accounts	xxxx	Profit as per cost accounts	xxxx
Under-recovery of overheads in cost accounts	xxxx	Over-recovery of overheads in cost accounts	xxxx
Expenses charged in financial accounts only	xxxx	Incomes credited in financial accounts only	xxxx
Under-valuation of opening stock in cost account	xxxx	Over-valuation of opening stock in cost accounts	xxxx
Over-valuation of closing stock in cost accounts	xxxx	Under-valuation of closing stock in cost accounts	xxxx
Profit as per financial accounts (Balancing amount)	xxxx	Notional expenses charged in cost accounts only	xxxx

		Loss as per financial accounts (Balancing amount)	xxxx
	xxxxx		xxxx

Illustration-1

Ascertain the profit as per financial books from the following information:

	₹
Profit as per cost accounts	25,000
Closing stock over-valued in cost books	12,500
Preliminary expenses written off	3,000
Profit on sale of building	30,000
Administrative expenses over-recovered in cost books	50,375
Works overhead under-recovered in cost books	30,375
Bank interest and transfer fees in financial books	5,000
Interest on investments recorded in financial books	10,000
Depreciation shown excess in cost books	4,000
Provision made for income tax	40,000

(B.Com., Madras University, April-2002)

Solution

Reconciliation Statement

	₹	₹
Profit as per cost accounts	-	25,000
Add: Profit on sale of building	30,000	
Administrative expenses over-recovered in cost books	50,375	
Bank interest and transfer fees credited in financial books	5,000	
Interest on investments recorded in financial books	10,000	
Depreciation shown excess in cost books	4,000	99,375
		1,24,375
Less: Closing stock over-valued in cost books	12,500	
Preliminary expenses written off	3,000	
Works overhead under-recovered in cost book	30,375	

Provision made for income tax	40,000	85,875
Profit as per financial accounts	-	38,500

Illustration-2

The following figures are available in respect of ABC Ltd for the year ended 31.12.1986.

	Financial records	Cost records
	₹	₹
Opening stock:		
Raw materials	6,000	5,000
Work-in-progress	7,000	6,500
Finished goods	5,000	4,500
Closing Stock:		
Raw materials	4,000	4,300
Work-in-progress	3,000	3,700
Finished goods	5,900	6,200
Purchases	40,000	-
Direct wages	20,000	-
Indirect wages	3,000	-
Factory overheads	17,000	21,000
Sales	1,10,000	-
Administrative expenses	3,000	2,800
Selling expenses	4000	4,500
Financial expenses	1,000	-
Interest received	1,600	-
Transfer to reserve	4,000	-
Dividend paid	9,000	-

Compute profits in financial accounts as well as in cost accounts and prepare a reconciliation statement. **(B.Com. - Madras University, May 1987 and March 1991)**

Profit and Loss Account			
	₹		₹
To Opening Stock:-		By Sales	1,10,000

Raw materials	6,000	By Closing Stock :-	
Work-in-progress	7,000	Raw materials	4,000
Finished goods	5,000	Work-in-progress	3,000
To Purchases	40,000	Finished goods	5,900
To Direct wages	20,000	By Interest received	1,600
To Indirect wages	3,000		
To Factory overheads	17,000		
To Administrative expenses	3,000		
To Selling expenses	4,000		
To Financial expenses	1,000		
To Transfer to reserves	4,000		
To Dividend paid	9,000		
To Profit	5,500		
	1,24,500		1,24,500

Cost Sheet

		₹
Material Consumed:		
Opening stock of raw materials	5,000	
Add: Purchases	40,000	
	45,000	
Less: Closing stock of raw materials	4,300	
	40,700	40,700
Direct wages	—	20,000
Prime cost	—	60,700
Factory overhead	—	21,000
	—	81,700
Add: Opening stock of work-in-progress	—	6,500
	—	88,200
Less: Closing stock of work-in-progress	—	3,700
Works cost	—	84,500
Administrative expenses	—	2,800
Cost of production	—	87,300

Add: Opening stock of finished goods	—	4,500
	—	91,800
Less: Closing stock of finished goods	—	6,200
Cost of goods sold	—	85,600
Selling expenses	—	4,500
Cost of sales	—	90,100
Profit (bf)	—	19,900
Sales	—	1,10,000

Reconciliation Statement

	₹	₹
Profit as per cost accounts	—	19,900
Add: Factory overheads over-recovered	1,000	
Selling expenses over-recovered	500	
Interest received	1,600	3,100
		23,000
Less:		
Under valuation of opening stock in cost accounts		
Raw materials	1,000	
Work-in-progress	500	
Finished goods	500	
Over-valuation of closing stock in cost accounts:		
Raw materials	300	
Work-in-progress	700	
Finished goods	300	
Administrative expenses under-recovered	200	
Financial expenses	1,000	
Transfer to reserves	4,000	
Dividend paid	9,000	17,500
Profit as per financial records		5,500

Note: Indirect wages is also factory overheads.

Illustration-3

From the following figures prepare a reconciliation statement:

	₹
Net Profit as per financial book	1,28,755
Net Profit as per cost book	1,72,400
Works overhead under recovered in cost book	3,120
Administration overheads recovered in excess	1,700
Depreciation charged in financial books	11,200
Depreciation charged in cost books	12,500
Interest received not included in cost books	8,000
Obsolescence loss charged in financial books	5,700
Income tax provided in financial books	40,300
Bank interest credited in financial books	750
Stores adjustments (credited in financial books)	475
Depreciation of stock charged in financial book	6,750

(B.Com., Madras, April 2002)

Solution

Reconciliation Statement

	₹	₹
Profit as per cost records	—	1,72,400
Add: Administrative overheads recovered in excess	1,700	
Depreciation recovered in excess in cost books	1,300	
Interest received not included in cost books	8,000	
Bank interest credited in financial books	750	
Stores adjustment (credit in financial books)	475	12,225
Less: Works overhead under-recovered in cost books	3,120	1,84,625
Obsolescence loss charged in financial books	5,700	
Income tax provided in financial books	40,300	
Depreciation of stock charged in financial books	6,750	55,870
Profit as per financial books		1,28,755

Illustration-4

The following is the summarized version of trading and profit and loss accounts of Continental Enterprise Ltd, for the year ending March 31, 2008:

	₹			₹
To Materials	48,000	By Sales		96,000
To Wages	36,000	By Closing stock of finished goods		20,400
To Works expenses	24,000	By Closing stock of Work-in-progress:		
To Gross profit	14,400			
		Materials	3,000	
		Wages	1,800	
		Works expenses	1,200	6,000
	1,22,400			1,22,400
To Selling expenses	3,000	By Gross profit b/d		14,400
To Administrative expense	6,000			
To Net profit	5 ,400			
	14,400			14,400

During the year 6,000 units were manufactured and 4,800 were sold.

The costing records show that works overheads have been estimated at ₹3 per unit produced and administrative overheads at ₹1.50 per unit produced. The selling expenses were estimated at ₹0.50 per unit sold. The costing books show a profit of ₹8,640.

Prepare cost sheet showing profit as per cost books and a reconciliation statement reconciling the profits as shown in cost books and financial books.

(B.Com. (Hons), Delhi University, adapted)

Solution

Cost Sheet		
	₹	₹
Materials	48,000	
Less: Materials included in closing stock of work-in-progress	3,000	45,000
Wages	36,000	
Less: Wages included in closing stock of work-in-progress	1,800	34,200
Prime cost		79,200
Works overhead - 6,000 × 3		18,000

Works cost		97,200
Administrative overheads - 6,000 × 1.50		9,000
Cost of production		1,06,200
Less: Closing stock of finished goods $\frac{1,06,200 \times 1,200}{6,000}$		21,240
Cost of goods sold		84,960
Selling expenses - 4,800 × 0.50		2,400
Cost of sales		87,360
Profit		8,640
Sales		96,000
Reconciliation Statement		
Profit as per cost books		8,640
Add: Administration overheads over-recovered	3,000	3,000
		11,640
Less: Works overhead under-recovered - (6,000 – 1,200)	4,800	
Closing stock of finished goods over-valued in cost book	840	
Under-recovery of selling expenses	600	6,240
Profit as per financial books		5,400

Illustration-5

The financial records of Modern Manufacturers Ltd., reveal the following for the year ended 30.06.2006:

		(₹in thousands)
Sales (20,000 unit)		4,000
Materials		1,600
Wages		800
Factory overheads		720
Office and administrative overheads		416
Selling and distribution overheads		288
Closing stock of finished goods (1,230 units)		240
Closing stock of work-in-progress:		
Material	48	
Labour	32	
Factory overheads	32	112
Goodwill written off		320
Interest paid on capital		32

In Costing records factory overheads is charged at 100% of wages, office and administrative overheads at 10% of factory cost and selling and distribution overheads at the rate of ₹16 per unit sold.

Find out the profit as per costing and financial records and prepare a statement reconciling the same. **(CA-Inter, adapted)**

Solution

Profit and Loss account (₹in thousands)

	₹			₹
To Materials	1,600	By Sales		4,000
To Wages	800	By Stock of finished goods		240
To Factory overheads	720	By Stock of work-in-progress		
To Office and administration overheads	416	Materials	48	
To Selling and distribution overheads	288	Wages	32	
To Goodwill written off	320	Factory overheads	32	112
To Interest on capital	32			
To Profit	176			
	4,352			4,352

Cost Sheet

		₹
Materials	1,600	
(-) Material included in closing stock of work-in-progress	48	1,552
Wages	800	
(-) Wages included in closing stock of WIP	32	768
Prime cost		2,320
Factory overheads 100% of wages		768
Factory cost		3,088
Office and administration overheads: 10% of work cost		308.8
Cost of production		3396.8
Less: Closing Stock of finished goods $\frac{3,396.8 \times 1,230}{21,230}$		196.8
Cost of goods sold		3200.0
Selling and distribution overheads 20,000 × 16		320.0
Cost of Sales		3,520.0
Profit		480.0
Sales		4,000.0

Reconciliation Statement		
	₹	₹
Profit as per cost accounts		480.0
Add: Factory overheads recovered in excess (720-32-768)	80.0	
Selling and distribution overheads recovered in excess	32.0	
Under-valuation of closing stock of		
finished goods in cost account	43.2	155.2
Less: Under-recovery of office and administration overheads	107.2	635.2
Goodwill written off	320.0	
Interest on capital	32.0	459.2
Profit as per financial accounts		176.0

Illustration-6

The following figures have been extracted from the cost records of a manufacturing Company:

	₹
Stores:	
Opening Balance	63,000
Purchases	3,36,000
Transfer from work-in-progress	1,68,000
Issues to work-in-progress	3,36,000
Issues to repairs and maintenance	42,000
Deficiencies found in stock taking	12,600
Work-in-Progress:	
Opening balance	1,26,000
Direct wages applied	1,26,000
Overheads applied	5,04,000
Closing balance	84,000

Finished Products

Entire output is sold at a profit of 10% on actual cost.

Others

Wages incurred ₹1,47,000, Overheads incurred ₹5,25,000, Income from investments ₹21,000, Loss on sale of fixed assets ₹42,000.

Draw the Stores Control Account, Work-in-Progress Control Account, Costing Profit and loss Account, Profit and Loss Account and Reconciliation Statement. **(CA-Inter - May 2008)**

Solution

Stores Control Account

	₹		₹
To Opening balance	63,000	By Work in progress a/c	3,36,000
To General ledger adjustment a/c		By Overheads control a/c	42,000
Purchase	3,36,000	By Overheads control (deficiency) a/c	12,600
To w-in-p control a/c - returns	1,68,000	By Closing balance (bf)	1,76,400
	5,67,000		5,67,000

Work-in-Progress Control Account

	₹		₹
To Opening balance	1,26,000	By Stores control a/c	1,68,000
To Stores control a/c	3,36,000	By Costing profit and loss a/c (bf)	8,40,000
To Wages control a/c	1,26,000	By Closing balance	84,000
To Overheads control a/c	5,04,000		
	10,92,000		10,92,000

Overheads Control Account

	₹		₹
To Stores control a/c	42,000	By Work-in-progress control a/c	5,04,000
To Stores control a/c	12,600	By Costing profit and loss a/c	
To Wages control a/c (WN 1)	21,000	(under-recovery) (bf)	96,600
To General ledger adjustment a/c			
overheads	5,25,000		
	6,00,600		6,00,600

Costing Profit and Loss Account			
	₹		₹
To Work-in-progress control a/c	8,40,000	By General ledger adjustment a/c - Sales (WN 2)	9,24,000
To Overheads control a/c	96,600	By General ledger adjustment a/c- Loss (bf)	12,600
	9,36,600		9,36,600

Note: 1	Total Wages Paid	1,47,000
	(-) Direct wages charged to work-in-progress	1,26,000
	Balance wages being indirect - charged to overheads	21,000
Note: 2	Total cost of goods sold	8,40,000
	Add: Profit 10% on cost	84,000
	Sales	9,24,000

Note: 3 Deficiency is treated as normal loss. It may also be treated as abnormal loss, in that case deficiency should be transferred to costing profit and loss account.

Financial Profit and Loss Account			
	₹		₹
To Opening balance:		By Sales	9,24,000
Stores	63,000	By Investment income	21,000
Work-in-progress	1,26,000	By Closing balance:	
To Purchases	3,36,000	Stores	1,76,400
To Wages	1,47,000	Work-in-progress	84,000
To Overheads	5,25,000	By Loss	33,600
To Loss on sales of fixed assets	42,000		
	12,39,000		12,39,000

Reconciliation Statement	
	₹
Loss as per cost accounts	12,600
Add: Loss on sales of fixed assets	42,000
	54,600
Less: Investment income	21,000
Loss as per financial accounts	33,600

Illustration-7

The following is the profit and loss account of Sri Ram Industries Ltd., for the year ending 31.03.2009:

Profit and Loss Account

	₹		₹
To Office salaries	26,500	By Gross profit b/d	1,35,585
To General expenses	18,200	By Dividend received	5,000
To Salesman salaries	15,300	By Interest on bank deposit	3,450
To Sales	23,750		
To Distribution expenses	11,550		
To Loss on sale of machinery	5,475		
To Fines	1,360		
To Discount on debentures	3,000		
To Net profit	38,900		
	1,44,035		1,44,035

The cost records revealed a different profit, ascertain the cost profit by preparing a Memorandum Reconciliation Statement.

Solution

Memorandum Reconciliation Statement

	₹		₹
Dividend received	5,000	Profit as per financial records	38,900
Interest on bank deposits	3,450	Loss on sale of machinery	5,475
Profit as per cost records	40,285	Fines	1,360
		Discount on debentures	3,000
	48,735		48,735

Illustration-8

X Ltd., furnishes the summary of Trading and Profit and Loss Account for the year ending 31.03.2009.

Trading and Profit and Loss Account

	₹		₹
To Raw materials	1,52,000	By Sales (15,000 unit)	4,75,000
To Direct wages	1,20,000	By Closing stock (1000 unit)	27,500

	₹			₹
To Factory overheads	63,500	By Work-in-progress:		
To Administration overheads	47,250	Materials	14,500	
To Selling and distribution overheads	54,000	Wages	8,250	
To Preliminary expenses written off	14,000	Overheads	2,500	25,250
To Goodwill written off	13,000	By Income from investments		34,000
To Dividend	28,000	By Rent received		43,000
To Income tax	15,000			
To Transfer to reserve	25,000			
To profit	73,000			
	6,04,750			6,04,750

The scrutiny of cost records for the period revealed the following:

(i) Factory overheads have been recovered at 50% of direct wages.

(ii) Administration overheads have been charged at ₹3 per unit produced.

(iii) Selling and distribution expenses have been charged at ₹3.75 per unit sold.

You are requested to prepare a statement of cost to work out profit as per cost accounts and to reconcile the same with that shown in the financial accounts.

Solution

Statement of Cost

		₹
Raw Materials	1,52,000	
(−) Cost of materials included in closing stock of W.I.P	14,500	1,37,500
Direct wages	1,20,000	
(−) Wages included in closing stock of W.I.P	8,250	1,11,750
Prime cost		2,49,250
Factory overheads - 50% of direct wages.		55,875
Works cost		3,05,125
Administrative overheads (16,000 × 3)		48,000
Cost of production		3,53,125
Less: Closing stock of finished goods $\frac{3,53,125}{16,000} \times 1,000$		22,070
Cost of goods sold		3,31,055

Selling expenses (15,000 × 3.75)		56,250
Cost of sales		3,87,305
Profit		87,695
Sales		4,75,000

Reconciliation Statement		
	₹	₹
Profit as per Statement of Cost		87,695
Add: Over-recovery of administration overheads		750
Over-recovery of selling and distribution overheads		2,250
Under-valuation of closing stock in cost accounts		5,430
Income from investments		34,000
Rent received		43,000
		1,73,125
Less: Under recovery of factory overheads		
(63,500 – 2,500 – 55,875)	5,125	
Preliminary expenses written off	14,000	
Goodwill written off	13,000	
Dividend	28,000	
Income tax	15,000	
Transfer to reserve	25,000	1,00,125
Profit as per financial accounts		73,000

Illustration-9

From the following information (a) prepare a statement of cost to determine profit as per cost accounts and (b) prepare a statement reconciling it with profit shown by financial accounts assuming that indirect expenses are absorbed on the basis of normal production capacity in cost accounts.

Profit and Loss account for the year ended 31.03.2009			
	₹		₹
To Material consumed	1,50,000	By Sales (75,000 units)	3,10,000
To Direct wages	80,000	By Interest received	25,000
To Works expenses	48,000	By Rent received	7,000
To Office expenses	24,000		
To Selling and distribution expenses	15,000		

To Debenture interest	9,000		
To Provision for doubtful debts	6,000		
To Profit	10,000		
	3,42,000		3,42,000

The normal output of the factory is 1,00,000 unit. Works expenses are fixed to the extent of ₹32,000. Office expenses are for all practical purposes constant. Selling and distribution expenses are constant to the extent of ₹10,000 and the balance varies directly with sales.

Solution

Statement of Cost

		₹
Materials consumed		1,50,000
Direct wages		80,000
Prime cost		2,30,000
Works expenses:		
Fixed $32,000 \times \frac{75,000}{1,00,000}$	24,000	
Variable (48,000 – 32,000)	16,000	40,000
Works cost		2,70,000
Office expenses $\frac{24,000 \times 75,000}{1,00,000}$		18,000
Cost or production		2,88,000
Selling and distribution expenses :		
Fixed $\frac{10,000 \times 75,000}{1,00,000}$	7,500	
Variable	5,000	12,500
Cost of sales		3,00,500
Profit		9,500
Sales		3,10,000

Reconciliation Statement

	₹	₹
Profit as per cost statement		9,500
Add: Interest received		25,000
Rent received		7,000
		41,500
Less: Under-recovery of		

Works expenses	8,000	
Office expenses	6,000	
Selling and distribution expenses	2,500	
Debenture interest	9,000	
Provision for doubtful debts	6,000	31,500
Profit as per financial accounts		10,000

Illustration-10

From the following information (a) prepare a statement showing profit as per cost accounts and (b) a statement reconciling the costing profit with that shown by financial accounts.

Trading and Profit and Loss accounts for the year ending 31.03.2009

	₹		₹
To Direct materials consumed	5,00,000	By Sales (500000 Units)	14,40,000
To Direct wages	4,50,000	By commission earned	6,800
To Factory expenses	2,80,000	By Profit on sale of investments	13,700
To Office expenses	75,000		
To Selling and distribution expenses	75,000		
To Donations	10,000		
To Fines and penalty	7,500		
To Transfer to reserves	15,000		
To Profit	48,000		
	14,60,500		14,60,500

Normal output of the factory is 4,00,000 units. Factory expenses are fixed upto ₹2,00,000. All office expenses are fixed. Selling and distribution expenses are constant to the extent of ₹50,000 and the balance are variable. Prepare a statement reconciling the profits as per cost and financial accounts assuming that indirect expenses are absorbed on the basis of normal production capacity in cost accounts.

Solution

Cost Sheet

		₹
Direct materials consumed		5,00,000
Direct wages		4,50,000

Prime cost		9,50,000
Factory expenses:		
Fixed $2,00,000 \times \frac{5,00,000}{4,00,000}$	2,50,000	
Variable	80,000	3,30,000
Works cost		12,80,000
Office expenses $75,000 \times \frac{5,00,000}{4,00,000}$		93,750
Cost of production		13,73,750
Selling and distribution expenses :		
Fixed $50,000 \times \frac{5,00,000}{4,00,000}$	62,500	
Variable	25,000	87,500
Cost of sales		14,61,250
Loss (bf)		(−) 21,250
Sales		14,40,000

Reconciliation Statement

	₹	₹
Loss as per cost accounts		(−) 21,250
Add: Over-recovery of :		
Factory expenses		50,000
Office expenses		18,750
Selling and distribution expenses		12,500
Commission earned		6,800
Profit on sale of investments		13,700
		80,500
Less: Donations	10,000	
Fines and penalty	7,500	
Transfer to reserves	15,000	32,500
Profit as per financial accounts		48,000

Illustration-11

In a factory two types of radios are manufactured, Viz. "Popular" and "Deluxe" models. From the following particulars, prepare a statement showing cost per radio and profit per radio sold. There is no opening or closing stocks.

	Popular	Deluxe
	₹	₹
Labour	46,800	62,920
Materials	81,900	1,08,680

Works overhead is charged at 80% on labour and office overheads taken at 15% on works cost.

"Popular" radios sold during the period are 234 at ₹1,000 each and "Deluxe" radios sold are 286 at ₹1,100 each. Ascertain the total profit as per cost books from the above particulars. If the works expenses are ₹87,000 and office expenses ₹58,000 find out the actual profit made and prepare a reconciliation statement to reconcile the cost profit with the profits disclosed by the financial books.

(B.Com., Madras University)

Solution

Statement of Cost

	Popular	Deluxe	Total
	₹	₹	₹
Materials	81,900	1,08,680	1,90,580
Labour	46,800	62,920	1,09,720
Prime cost	1,28,700	1,71,600	3,00,300
Works expenses : 80% of wages	37,440	50,336	87,776
Work cost	1,66,140	2,21,936	3,88,076
Office overheads : 15% on Work cost	24,921	33,290	58,211
Cost of production	1,91,061	2,55,226	4,46,287
Profit	42,939	59,374	1,02,313
Sales	2,34,000	3,14,600	5,48,600
	$\frac{1,91,061}{234}$	$\frac{2,55,226}{286}$	
Cost of production per unit	₹816.50	₹892.40	
	$\frac{42,939}{234}$	$\frac{59,374}{286}$	
Profit per unit	₹183.50	₹207.60	

Note: Calculations were made to the nearest rupee.

Profit and Loss Account

	₹		₹
To Materials :		By Sales :	
Popular	81,900	Popular	2,34,000
Deluxe	1,08,680	Deluxe	3,14,600
To Labour :			
Popular	46,800		
Deluxe	62,920		
To Works overhead	87,000		
To Office overheads	58,000		
To Net profit	1,03,300		
	5,48,600		5,48,600

Profit Reconciliation Statement

	₹
Profit as per cost accounts	1,02,313
Add: Works overhead over-recovered	776
Office overheads over-recovered	211
Profit as per financial accounts	1,03,300

11.2 EXERCISES

I. Theory Questions

1. Explain the need for reconciliation of cost and financial profit.
2. What is meant by reconciliation of cost and financial profit?
3. What are the expenses appearing in cost books only?
4. What are the expenses and incomes appearing in financial books only?
5. What is "Memorandum Reconciliation statement"?
6. How over-valuation and under-valuation of closing stock is cost accounts is treated in profit reconciliation statement?

7. How under-valuation and over-valuation of opening stock in cost accounts is treated in profit reconciliation statement?

8. How under-absorption of overheads is treated in profit reconciliation statement?

9. How over-absorption of overheads is treated in profit reconciliation statement?

II. Practical Problems

1. The profits as per cost accounts was ₹1,50,000. Calculate the profit as per financial accounts on the basis of the following information.

   (a) Works overheads under-recovered in cost accounts by ₹6,200.

   (b) Administration expenses under-recorded in financial accounts by ₹2,750.

   (c) Depreciation charges over-recovered in cost accounts ₹1,900.

   (d) Interest received on investments ₹1,000. **(B.Com., Madras University)**

   [**Ans:** Profit as per financial accounts ₹1,49,450]

2. The profit shown by cost ledger for the year ending 31st March 2009 is ₹18,400 but profit as per financial accounts is ₹16,600.

   Closing stock is over-valued in financial books by ₹2,100. Works overhead under-absorbed amounts to ₹3,000. Bank charges and interest on loan paid during the year was ₹250 and ₹1,200 respectively. Interest and dividends received on investment amounted to ₹550.

   Prepare a statement reconciling cost and financial profits.

   [**Ans:** Reconciliation: $₹18,400 + 2,100 + 550 - 3,000 - 250 - 1,200 =$ ₹16,600]

3. In a factory, works overheads are absorbed at 60% of labour cost and office overheads at 20% of works cost. Prepare (i) cost sheet, (ii) profit and loss account, (iii) Reconciliation statement if total expenditure consists of materials ₹2,00,000, wages ₹1,50,000, factory expenses ₹1,00,000 and office expenses ₹85,000.

   10% of the output is in stock at the end. Sales are ₹5,20,000.

   (B.Com. Hons, Delhi Universty)

   [**Ans:** Cost profit ₹44,800, financial profit ₹38,500]

4. The following is the profit and loss account of 'X' Ltd. for the year ended 31st March 2010.

Profit and Loss Account			
	₹		₹
To Opening stock	2,50,000	By Sales	10,00,000
To Purchases	4,00,000	By Closing stock	1,00,000
To Direct wages	2,50,000		
To Factory expenses	1,25,000		
To Cross profit	75,000		
	11,00,000		11,00,000
To Office expenses	22,000	By Gross profit	75,000
To Selling expenses	14,000	By Dividend received	11,000
To Interest on Loan	15,000		
To Profit	35,000		
	86,000		86,000

Cost records show the following:

(i) Closing stock in cost books ₹1,10,000
(ii) Direct labour ₹2,40,000
(iii) Factory expenses ₹1,40,000
(iv) Administration expenses and selling expenses each are calculated at 2% of sales.

Find the cost profit by preparing a profit reconciliation statement.

[**Ans:** Cost profit ₹40,000]

5. **Profit** as per financial accounts is ₹65,000. Find the profit as per cost accounts from the following information:

		Cost accounts	Financial Accounts
		₹	₹
(i)	Opening stock of raw materials	15,000	17,000
(ii)	Closing stock of raw materials	21,000	19,500
(iii)	Opening stock of finished goods	31,500	26,000
(iv)	Closing stock of finished goods	28,000	24,500

[**Ans:** Profit as per cost accounts: ₹66,500]

6. Profit as per cost books is ₹45,600. Calculate the profit as per financial books from the following information:

		₹
(i)	Dividend received	4,200
(ii)	Loss on sale of machinery	1,600
(iii)	Loss by obsolescence of assets	7,100
(iv)	Under-absorption of selling overheads	2,300

[**Ans:** Profit as per financial books: ₹38,800]

7. The profit disclosed by financial books is ₹26,740 and by cost books is ₹25,470.

On examination of account books, the following differences were found:

	Cost accounts	Financial accounts
	₹	₹
Factory overheads	14,350	16,140
Opening stock	6,790	8,130
Closing stock	5,880	6,270
Income from investment	-	2,750
Loss on sale of machinery	-	1,100
Depreciation on fully depreciated machinery	2,360	

Prepare a reconciliation statement.

[**Ans:** Reconciliation statement: ₹26,740 + 1,340 + 1,100 + 1,790 − 390 − 2, 750 − 2, 360 = ₹25,470]

8. From the following information prepare a reconciliation statement:

	₹
Profit as per financial accounts	1,23,500
Works overhead under-recovered	7,800
Office overheads over-recovered	4,500
Interest earned	3,250
Rent received	2,400
Bad debts written off	3,000
Preliminary expenses written off	7,500

[**Ans:** Profit as per cost accounts ₹1,31,650]

9. The following information is made available to you from the financial books of S.V. Ltd for the year ended March 31, 2007:

	₹		₹
To Direct materials used	3,00,000	By Sales (2,00,000 units)	7,50,000
To Direct wages	2,00,000		
To Factory expenses	1,20,000		
To Office expenses	40,000		
To Selling and distribution exp.	80,000		
To Net profit	10,000		
	7,50,000		7,50,000

Normal output of the factory is 2,50,000 units. Factory overheads are fixed upto ₹60,000 and office expenses are fixed for all practical purposes.

Selling and distribution expenses are fixed to the extent of ₹50,000 and the rest are variable.

Prepare a statement reconciling the profits as per cost and financial accounts assuming that indirect expenses are absorbed on the basis of normal production capacity in cost accounts.

(B.Com., Delhi University)

[**Ans:** Profit as per cost accounts ₹40,000]

12

INTEGRAL ACCOUNTING

- Meaning
- Advantages
- Scheme of making entries
- Comparison table of journal entries—non-integral vs. integral system

12.1 INTRODUCTION

The system of recording transactions may be devised in such a way that information recorded are suitable for financial accounting purposes and for cost accounting purposes also. Such a system of maintaining single accounting book is called Integral Accounting or Integrated Accounting. When financial accounts are kept separately, the expenses are recorded as in vouchers without making any classification and analysis of costs. In the Integrated Accounts cost information are recorded after classifying them under proper heads, so that cost information in the Integrated Accounts are readily usable for cost accounting purposes.

In financial accounts to reduce the burden of the main ledger usually only two subsidiary ledgers under self-balancing system are opened. They are sales ledger (debtors ledger) and purchases ledger (creditors ledger). In integrated accounting more subsidiary ledgers are opened to reduce the burden of the main ledger. They are stores ledger, stock ledger, jobs ledger and expenses ledger. For each subsidiary ledger a control account (or total account) is opened in the main ledger.

12.2 SCHEME OF MAKING ENTRIES

1. All transactions affecting personal accounts need no modification. They are recorded in the usual way as in financial accounts.

2. All incomes not required for costing purpose are also recorded in the usual way as in financial accounts.

3. All non-cost expenses not required for costing purposes are also recorded in the usual way as in financial accounts.

4. All appropriations and writing off of intangible assets are also recorded in the usual way as in financial accounts.

5. All cost transactions are recorded through respective subsidiary ledgers and totals of all transactions are posted to control accounts maintained in the main ledger. They are:

   (a) Stores ledger

   Separate accounts are opened for each material and store. All transactions relating to materials and stores are recorded in these accounts. In the main ledger a total account called stores ledger control account is opened. Total of all purchases are debited to this account. Total purchase returns and issue of materials and stores are credited to this account. The closing balance represents the value of materials and stores in hand at the end of the period.

   (b) Stock ledger

   Separate accounts are opened for each type of finished goods. All transactions relating to finished goods are recorded in these accounts. In the main ledger a control account called finished stock ledger control account is opened. The total of all goods finished are debited to this account. All goods sold are credited in this account .The closing balance in this account represents the value of finished goods in hand.

   (c) Job ledger (or) work-in-progress ledger

   Separate accounts are opened for each job undertaken. Expenses incurred for these jobs are debited in respective job accounts. Completed jobs will be credited in work-in-progress ledger and transferred to the debit of finished stock accounts kept in stock ledger.

   (d) Expenses ledger or overheads ledger

   This ledger is subdivided into various parts for each class of overheads like, production overheads, office and administration overheads and selling and distribution overheads. All expenses incurred are classified under proper heads and debited in respective overheads accounts. Overheads recovered are credited in these accounts. In the main ledger separate control accounts like, production overheads control account, office and administration overheads control account and selling and distribution overheads control account are opened. Total of all expenses incurred are debited in the respective control accounts. Overheads recovered are credited in the respective control accounts. The closing balance in these control accounts represents over- or under-recovery of overheads which will be transferred to profit and loss account.

   Cost classification and analysis sheets, notional costs considered for costing purpose only will not form part of accounting records.

Advantages of integrated accounts

1. There is considerable savings in cost, time and effort in accounting work.
2. There is no duplication in accounting work.
3. As there is only one profit and loss account, there is no need for preparation of reconciliation statement.
4. Cost information is taken from books of original entry. Accuracy in cost accounting information is ensured.
5. Close relationship is established between financial accounting department and cost accounting department.
6. It facilitates introduction of mechanised accounting.
7. Accounting procedures are simplified to suit the needs of financial accountant and cost accountant.

12.3 JOURNAL ENTRIES

Journal entries made in financial accounts, cost ledger accounting system and integral accounting system are given in the following table for easy understanding:

Transaction	Non Integral system		Integral system
	Financial Books	Cost books	
1. Credit purchase of materials	Purchase a/c. ...Dr To Sundry creditors a/c	Stores ledger control a/c. ...Dr To Cost Ledger control a/c. (or) General ledger adjustment a/c.	Stores ledger control a/c...Dr To Creditors a/c.
2. Cash purchase of materials	Purchase a/c...Dr To Cash a/c	-do-	Stores ledger control a/c...Dr To Cash a/c
3. Purchase of materials for a special job	Purchase a/c...Dr To Sundry creditors or Cash a/c	Work in progress ledger control a/c...Dr To Cost ledger control or General ledger adjustment a/c	Work in progress ledger control a/c...Dr. To Creditors or cash a/c
4. Materials purchased for repairs	-do-	Works overhead control a/c...Dr To Cost ledger control a/c	Work overhead control a/c...Dr To Creditors or cash

5. Materials returned to suppliers	Sundry creditors a/c. . . Dr To Purchase returns a/c	Cost ledger or Gen. ledger adjustment a/c. . . Dr To Stores ledger control a/c	Sundry creditors a/c. . . Dr To stores Ledger Control a/c
6. Payment to creditors	Sundry creditors a/c. . . Dr To Cash a/c	No entry	Creditors a/c. . . Dr To cash a/c
7. Issue of direct materials for production	No entry	Work in progress ledger control a/c. . . Dr To Stores ledger control a/c	Work in progress ledger control a/c. . . Dr To Stores ledger control a/c
8. Issue of indirect materials	No entry	Work overhead control a/c. . . Dr To Stores ledger control a/c.	Work-in-progress ledger control a/c. . . Dr To Stores ledger control a/c.
9. Return of direct material to stores	No entry	Stores ledger control a/c. . . Dr To work-in-progress ledger control a/c	Stores ledger control a/c. . . Dr Work-in-progress ledger control a/c.
10. Return of indirect material to stores	No entry	Stores ledger control a/c. . . Dr To works overhead control a/c.	Stores ledger control a/c. . . Dr To works overhead control a/c.
11. Abnormal loss of materials	Profit and loss a/c. . . Dr To Purchase a/c	Costing Profit and Loss a/c. . . Dr To Stores ledger control a/c.	Profit and Loss a/c. . . Dr To Stores ledger control a/c.
12. Payment of wages	Wages a/c . . . Dr To Cash To Provident fund a/c To Wages payable a/c To TDS a/c	Wages control a/c. . . Dr To Cost ledger control or Gen. ledger adjustment a/c	Wages control a/c. . . Dr To Insurance a/c To Provident fund a/c To wages payable a/c (for unpaid wages) To Tax a/c To Cash a/c

13. Allocation and distribution of wages	No entry	Work-in-progress Ledger control (for direct labour) a/c. . . Dr Works overhead control (for indirect labour) a/c. . . Dr Administration overhead control (for office salary) a/c. . . Dr Selling & distribution overhead control (for sales staff salaries) a/c. . . Dr To Wages control a/c.	Work-in-progress ledger control a/c. . . Dr Works overhead control a/c. . . Dr Administration overheads Control a/c. . . Dr Selling & distribution overhead control a/c. . . Dr To wages control a/c.
14. Payment of expenses like rent, fuel, repairs etc.	Expenses a/c. . . Dr To Sundry creditors To Cash	Works overhead control a/c. . . Dr Administration overhead control a/c. . . Dr Selling and distribution overhead control a/c. . . Dr To Cost ledger control a/c. or Gen ledger adj. a/c	Overhead control (factory) Administration or selling and distribution) a/c. . . Dr To Creditors To Cash
15. Abnormal Idle time	No entry	Costing profit and loss a/c. . . Dr To Wages control a/c	Profit and Loss a/c. . . Dr To wages control a/c.
16. Depreciation charged	Depreciation a/c. . . Dr To capital assets a/c	Works overhead control a/c. . . Dr Administration overhead control a/c. . . Dr Selling and distribution overhead control a/c. . . Dr To Cost ledger control a/c. or Gen. ledger adj. . . a/c	Works overhead control a/c. . . Dr Administration over head control a/c or selling and distribution overhead control a/c. . . Dr To Capital assets a/c
17. Recovery of works overheads by predetermined overheads rate	No entry	Work-in-progress control a/c. . . Dr To works overhead control a/c.	Work-in-progress ledger control a/c. . . Dr To factory overhead control a/c
18. Finished goods transferred from work in progress a/c	No entry	Finished goods ledger control a/c. . . Dr To work-in-progress ledger control a/c	Finished goods control a/c. . . Dr To work-in-progress ledger control a/c.

19. Cost of goods sold	No entry	Cost of sales a/c... Dr To Finished goods (at cost) led. control a/c	Cost of sales a/c... Dr To finished goods led. control (at cost) a/c.
20. Transfer of balance in cost of sales control a/c.	No entry	Profit and Loss a/c... Dr To Cost of sales a/c	Profit and Loss a/c... Dr To Cost of sales a/c
21. Sales	Debtor or cash a/c... Dr To Sales a/c	Cost ledger control or Gen. ledger adj. a/c... Dr To Cost of sales a/c (at sales price) (or) To Costing profit and loss a/c.	Debtors or cash (at Selling price) a/c... Dr To Sales a/c (at sales price)
22. Allocation of administration overheads	No entry	Finished goods control a/c... Dr To Administration overhead control a/c.	Finished goods control a/c... Dr To Administration overhead control a/c.
23. Allocation of selling and distribution overheads	No entry	Cost of sales a/c... Dr To selling and distribution overhead control a/c.	Cost of sales a/c... Dr To selling and distribution overhead control a/c.

Illustration-1

Following transactions are taken from the books of Ram Ltd relating to materials during the month of March, 2010. Ram Ltd maintains integrated accounting system. Give journal entries.

		₹
March 1	Materials purchased on credit	1,00,000
March 2	Materials purchased on cash	2,50,000
March 4	Direct materials issued for production	2,40,000
March 5	Indirect materials issued for production	50,000
March 6	Secondary packing materials issued to sales department	10,000
March 9	Stationery issued to office	5,000
March 11	Materials returned to supplier	25,000
March 13	Direct materials received back from production	7,000
March 14	Materials purchased for Job No. 29	4,000
March 17	Materials transferred from Job No. 15 to Job No. 21	7,500
March 20	Cash paid to creditors	60,000

Solution

Journal entries

Date	Particulars		Debit ₹	Credit ₹
March 1, 2010	Stores Ledger control a/c To creditor a/c (Being materials purchased on credit)	Dr	1,00,000	1,00,000
March 2	Stores ledger control a/c To bank (Being materials purchased for cash)	Dr	2,50,000	2,50,000
March 4	Work-in-progress control a/c To Stores ledger control a/c (Being direct materials issued to production)	Dr	2,40,000	2,40,000
March 5	Factory overheads control a/c To Stores ledger control a/c (Being indirect materials issued for production)	Dr	50,000	50,000
March 6	Selling overheads control a/c To Stores Ledger control a/c (Being packing materials issued to sales department)	Dr	10,000	10,000
March 9	Administration overheads control To Stores ledger control a/c (Being stationery issued to office)	Dr	5,000	5,000
March 11	Creditor a/c To Stores ledger control a/c (Being materials returned to supplier)	Dr	25,000	25,000
March 13.	Stores ledger control a/c To work-in-progress control a/c (Being direct materials received back from production)	Dr	7,000	7,000
March 14	Work-in-progress control a/c To Bank a/c (Being materials purchased for a specific job)	Dr	4,000	4,000
March 17	Work-in-progress control a/c (Job No. 21) To work-in-progress control a/c (Job No. 15) (Being materials transferred form Job No. 15 to Job No. 21)	Dr	7,500	7,500
March 20	Creditors a/c To Bank (Being cash paid to creditors)	Dr	60,000	60,000

Illustration-2

The following are the transactions relating to wages and salaries of X Ltd,

(a) Wages incurred ₹2,50,000, out of which ₹2,40,000 was paid of the above, direct wages amounted to ₹2,25,000 and indirect wages ₹25,000.

(b) Salaries paid to:

Office staff - ₹75,000
Selling staff - ₹40,000

(c) Indirect wages paid - ₹25,000

Journalise the above transactions. The account books are maintained under integrated accounting system.

Solution

Journal Entries

			₹	₹
a) (i)	Wages control account	Dr	2,50,000	
	To Bank a/c			2,40,000
	To Outstanding wages a/c (Being wages incurred)			10,000
(ii)	Work -in-progress control a/c	Dr	2,25,000	
	Factory overheads control a/c	Dr	25,000	
	To Wages control a/c (Being wages allocated to WIP and factory overheads)			2,50,000
b) (i)	Wages control a/c	Dr	1,15,000	
	To Bank a/c (Being salaries paid)			1,15,000
(ii)	Administration overheads control a/c	Dr	75,000	
	Selling overheads control a/c	Dr	40,000	
	To Wages control a/c (Being salaries charged to overheads)			1,15,000
c) (i)	Wages control a/c	Dr	25,000	
	To Bank a/c (Being indirect wages paid)			25,000

(ii)	Factory overheads control a/c To wages control a/c (Being indirect wages charged to factory overheads)	Dr	25,000	25,000

Illustration-3

Jorunalise the following transactions under integrated accounting system:

(i) Production expenses incurred ₹80,000
(ii) Office expenses paid ₹17,000 and office expenses not yet paid ₹5,000
(iii) Selling and distribution expenses paid ₹15,000
(iv) Production expenses recovered ₹84,000
(v) Office expenses recovered ₹20,000
(vi) Selling and distribution expenses recovered ₹15,000

Solution

Journal Entries

			₹	₹
(i)	Production overheads control a/c To Cash a/c (Being production expenses incurred)	Dr	80,000	80,000
(ii)	Administration overheads control a/c To Cash a/c To outstanding office expenses a/c (Being office expenses incurred)	Dr	22,000	17,000 5,000
(iii)	Selling and distribution overheads control a/c To Cash a/c (Being selling and distribution expenses paid)	Dr	15,000	15,000
(iv)	a) Work-in-progress control a/c To Production overheads control a/c (Being production expenses recovered)	Dr	84,000	84,000
	b) Production overheads control a/c To Profit and loss a/c (Being over-recovery of production overheads)	Dr	4,000	4,000
(v)	a) Finished goods control a/c To Administration overheads control a/c	Dr	20,000	20,000

	(Being office overheads recovered)		
	b) Profit and loss a/c Dr	2,000	
	To Administration overheads control a/c		2,000
	(Being under-recovery of administration overheads)		

Note: Entry in (v) b) is passed assuming finished goods are valued on cost of production basis. If finished goods are valued on works cost basis, the following entry is made, instead of the above:

		₹	₹
	Profit and loss a/c Dr	22,000	
	To Administration overheads control a/c		22,000
	(Being administration expenses charged to P & L a/c)		
(vi)	(a) Cost of sales control a/c Dr	15,000	
	To selling and distribution overheads control a/c		15,000
	(Being Selling and distribution overheads charged to cost of sales a/c)		

Alternatively: The following entry may be made:

		₹	₹
	(b) Profit and loss a/c Dr	15,000	
	To selling and distribution overheads control a/c		15,000
	(Being selling and distribution expenses charge to P&L a/c)		

Illustration-4

Give journal entries under integrated accounting system for the following transactions:

	Particulars	₹
	Cost of goods finished during the period	4,50,000
	Cost of goods sold during the period	4,20,000
	Goods sold at selling price:	
	a. Cash sales	2,00,000
	b. Credit sales	4,00,000
	Sales return	30,000
	Cash received from debtors	2,75,000

Solution

Journal Entries

	Particulars		₹	₹
1.	Finished goods control a/c To Work-in-progress control a/c (Being cost of goods finished)	Dr	4,50,000	4,50,000
2.	Cost of sales control a/c To Finished goods control a/c (Being cost of goods sold)	Dr	4,20,000	4,20,000
3.	Cash a/c Debtors a/c To Cost of sales control a/c (Being sales made)	Dr. Dr	2,00,000 4,00,000	6,00,000
4.	Cost of sales control a/c To Debtors a/c (Being sales return received)	Dr	30,000	30,000
5.	Cash a/c To Debtors a/c (Being cash received from debtors)	Dr	2,75,000	2,75,000

Illustration-5

The following balances appeared in the books of modern Ltd. as on 1.4.09:

Particulars	Debit ₹	Credit ₹
Stores ledger control a/c	5,000	-
Finished goods control a/c	35,000	-
Work-in-progress control a/c	16,000	-
Creditors	-	35,000
Debtors	70,000	-
Fixed assets	3,00,000	-
Cash	20,000	-
Reserves	-	61,000

Capital	-	3,50,000
	4,46,000	4,46,000

Transactions for the year ending on 31.3.10 were:

Particulars	₹
Purchase of materials:	
For cash	75,000
For credit	1,00,000
Purchase return	4,000
Wages paid:	
Dircct	1,50,000
Indirect	42,000
Salaries paid:	
Office	27,000
Selling	39,000
Direct materials issued to production	1,40,000
Indirect materials issued to production	10,000
Factory expenses incurred and paid	35,000
Administration expenses incurred and paid	27,000
Selling and distribution expenses paid and incurred	20,000
Factory expenses recovered	80,000
Administration expenses recovered to finished goods	53,000
Selling and distribution expenses recovered	60,500
Goods finished during the year at cost	3,66,000
Cost of goods sold	3,61,000
Sale of goods at selling price:	
On cash	80,000
On credit	4,00,000
Cash paid to creditors	80,000
Cash received from debtors	4,15,000
Depreciation on fixed assets (factory)	30,000
Provision for income tax	18,000

Prepare necessary ledger accounts under integrated accounting system.

Solution

Modern Ltd.
Integrated Ledger Accounts

		₹			₹
Stores Ledger Control a/c					
1.4.09	To Balance b/d	5,000	31.3.10	By Creditors	4,000
31.3.10	To Cash	75,000	31.3.10	By WIP Control a/c	1,40,000
31.3.10	To Creditors	1,00,000	31.3.10	By Factory overheads Control a/c	10,000
			31.3.10	By Balance c/d	26,000
		1,80,000			1,80,000
1.4.10	To Balance b/d	26,000			

Wages Control account					
		₹			₹
31.3.10	To Cash	2,58,000	31.3.10	By WIP control a/c	1,50,000
			31.3.10	By Factory overheads Control a/c	42,000
			31.3.10	By Administration OHS Control a/c	27,000
			31.3.10	By Selling overheads Control a/c	39,000
		2,58,000			2,58,000

Factory Overheads Control account					
		₹			₹
31.3.10	To Wages control a/c	42,000	31.3.10	By WIP control a/c	80,000
31.3.10	To Stores ledger control a/c	10,000	31.3.10	By Profit and loss a/c (Under recovery)	37,000
31.3.10	To Cash a/c	35,000			
31.3.10	To fixed assets a/c	30,000			
		1,17,000			1,17,000

Administration Overheads Control account					
		₹			₹
31.3.10	To Wages control a/c	27,000	31.3.10	By Finished goods control a/c	53,000
31.3.10	To Cash a/c	27,000	31.3.10	By Profit and loss a/c (under recovery)	1,000
		54,000			54,000

Selling Overheads Control account					
		₹			₹
31.3.10	To Wages control a/c	39,000	31.3.10	By Cost of sales a/c	60,500
31.3.10	To Cash a/c	20,000			
31.3.10	To Profit and loss a/c (over recovery)	1,500			
		60,500			60,500

Work-in-Progress Control account					
		₹			₹
1.4.09	To Balance b/d	16,000	31.3.10	By Finished goods control a/c	3,66,000
31.3.10	To Wages control a/c	1,50,000			
31.3.10	To Stores ledger control a/c	1,40,000	31.3.10	By Balance c/d	20,000
31.3.10	To Factory overheads control a/c	80,000			
		3,86,000			3,86,000
1.4.10	To Balance b/d	20,000			

Finished Goods Control account					
		₹			₹
1.4.09	To Balance b/d	35,000	31.3.10	By Cost of sales a/c	3,61,000
31.3.10	To Administration overheads control a/c	53,000			
31.3.10	To WIP control a/c	3,66,000	31.3.10	By Balance c/d	93,000
		4,54,000			4,54,000
1.4.10	To Balance b/d	93,000			

Cost of Sales account

		₹			₹
31.3.10	To Selling overheads control a/c	60,500	31.3.10	By Cash	80,000
31.3.10	To Finished goods control a/c	3,61,000	31.3.10	By Debtors a/c	4,00,000
31.3.10	To Profit & loss a/c	58,500			
		4,80,000			4,80,000

Profit and Loss account

		₹			₹
31.3.10	To Factory overheads control a/c	37,000	31.3.10	By Cost of sales a/c	58,500
31.3.10	To Administration overheads control a/c	1,000	31.3.10	By Selling overheads control a/c	1,500
31.3.10	To Provision for income tax	18,000			
31.3.10	To Profit - transferred to reserves	4,000			
		60,000			60,000

Debtors account

		₹			₹
1.4.09	To Balance b/d	70,000	31.3.10	By Cash	4,15,000
31.3.10	To Cost of sales	4,00,000	31.3.10	By Balance c/d	55,000
		4,70,000			4,70,000
1.4.10	To Balance b/d	55,000			

Creditors account

		₹			₹
31.3.10	To Stores ledger control a/c	4,000	1.4.09	By Balance b/d	35,000
31.3.10	To Cash a/c	80,000	31.3.10	Stores ledger control a/c	1,00,000
31.3.10	To Balance c/d	51,000			
		1,35,000			1,35,000
			1.4.10	By Balance b/d	51,000

Fixed Assets account					
		₹			₹
1.4.09	To Balance b/d	3,00,000	31.3.10	By Factor overheads control a/c	30,000
			31.3.10	By Balance c/d	2,70,000
		3,00,000			3,00,000
1.4.10	To Balance b/d	2,70,000			

Reserves account					
		₹			₹
			1.4.09	By Balance b/d	61,000
31.3.10	To balance c/d	65,000	31.3.10	By Profit & Loss a/c	4,000
		65,000			65,000
			1.4.10	By Balance b/d	65,000

Cash account					
		₹			₹
1.4.09	To Balance b/d	20,000	31.3.10	By Stores ledger control a/c	75,000
31.3.10	To Cost of sales a/c	80,000	31.3.10	By Wage control a/c	2,58,000
31.3.10	To Debtors a/c	4,15,000	31.3.10	By Factory overheads control a/c	35,000
			31.3.10	By Administration overheads control a/c	27,000
			31.3.10	By Selling overheads control a/c	20,000
			31.3.10	By Creditors a/c	80,000
			31.3.10	By Balance c/d	20,000
		5,15,000			5,15,000
1.4.10	To Balance b/d	20,000			

Capital account					
		₹			₹
			1.4.09	By Balance b/d	3,50,000
31.3.10	To balance c/d	3,50,000			
		3,50,000			3,50,000
			1.4.10	By Balance b/d	3,50,000

Provision for Income Tax account					
		₹			₹
31.3.10	To balance c/d	18,000	31.3.10	By Profit & loss a/c	18,000
		18,000			18,000
			1.4.10	By Balance b/d	18,000

Trial Balance as on 31.3.2010		
Particulars	**Debit** ₹	**Credit** ₹
Stores ledger control a/c	26,000	-
Work-in-progress control a/c	20,000	-
Finished goods control a/c	93,000	-
Debtors	55,000	-
Creditors	-	51,000
Fixed assets	2,70,000	-
Cash	20,000	-
Reserves	-	65,000
Capital	-	3,50,000
Provision for income tax	-	18,000
	4,84,000	4,84,000

12.4 EXERCISE

I. Objective Type Questions

A. State whether the following statements are true or false.

(i) Cost ledger adjustment account is opened in integrated accounting system

(ii) Only one profit and loss account is prepared in integrated accounts.

(iii) Reconciliation statement is not necessary under integrated accounting system.

(iv) Control accounts are opened for each class of important expenses.

(v) Notional cost is recorded in integrated accounts book.

(vi) Expenses of pure financial nature are not recorded in integrated accounts.

(vii) Only impersonal accounts are opened in integrated accounting system.

(viii) Reconciliation of cost and financial accounts does not arise under integrated accounting.

(ix) Under integrated accounting system only nominal accounts will be maintained.

(x) Personal accounts are not maintained under integral accounting system.

(xi) Over-absorption or under-absorption will not arise under integral accounting system.

(xii) Purchase of materials is debited to stores ledger control a/c.

(xiii) Debit balance of factory overheads a/c represents under-absorption of factory overheads.

(xiv) There is no need for general ledger adjustment a/c, under integrated accounting system.

[**Ans: True:** (ii), (iii), (iv), (viii), (xii), (xiii), (xiv) **False:** (i), (v), (vi), (vii), (ix), (x), (xi)]

B. Fill in the blanks

(i) The accounting system where cost and financial accounts are kept in one ledger is called ______________.

(ii) Preparation of ______________ statement is not required under integral accounting system.

(iii) For every subsidiary ledger a ______________ account is opened in the main ledger.

(iv) ______________ accounting system results in avoiding duplication of accounting work.

(v) Stores control account is ______________ for purchase of materials.

(vi) Direct materials issued for production is debited in ______________ account.

(vii) Cost of jobs completed is credited to ______________ .

(viii) Credit sales in debited to ______________ account.

(ix) Question of reconciling cost and financial accounts does not arise under ______________ accounting system.

(x) Stores ledger control account always shows ______________ balance.

(xi) Credit balance in administration overheads control a/c represent ______________ recovery.

[**Ans:** (i) Integrated accounts (ii) Reconciliation (iii) Control (iv) Integrated (v) Debited (vi) Work-in-progress (vii) Work-in-progress control account (viii) Debtors, (ix) integrated; (x) debit; (xi) over]

II. Theory Questions

A. Short Answer type Questions

1. What do you understand by integrated accounts?
2. Explain the advantages of integrated accounting system.
3. State the differences between integrated accounts and non-integrated accounts.
4. Explain the basic requirements of integrated accounting system
5. Write a short note on integrated accounting system.
6. Define integrated accounting system and advantages of the same.

III. Practical Problems

A. Short answer type questions

1. Give journal entry for purchase of raw materials on credit under integrated accounting system:
   [**Ans:** Stores control account debit and Creditors a/c credit]
2. Give journal entry for wages incurred under integrated accounting system.
   [**Ans:** wages control account debit and wages payable account credit]
3. Give Journal entry for factory expenses incurred under integral accounting system.
   [**Ans:** Factory overheads control a/c Debit and cash account or creditors account credit]
4. Give journal entry for works overhead recovered under integral accounting system.
   [**Ans:** work-in-progress control account debit and works overhead control account credit]
5. Give journal entry for goods finished during the period, under integrated accounts.
   [**Ans:** Finished goods control account debit and work-in-progress control account credit]
6. Give journal entry for the following:

   (i) Cost of goods finished during the year - ₹3,00,000
   (ii) Cost of goods sold during the year - ₹4,50,000

   Ans:

   (i) Finished good control a/c Dr 3,00,000
   To work-in-progress control a/c 3,00,000

   (ii) Cost of sales a.c Dr 4,50,000
   To finished goods control a/c 4,50,000
7. Journalise the following transactions:
   Purchase of goods on credit - ₹1,50,000
   Purchase of goods on cash - ₹70,000

Ans:

Stores ledger control a/c Dr
To creditors a/c - 1,50,000
To cash - 70,000

8. Give journal entry for the following:

   (i) Issue of materials to production - ₹60,000
   (ii) Factory overheads absorbed - ₹45,000

   Ans:

   (i) Work-in-progress a.c Dr - 60,000
   To stores ledger control a/c - 60,000
   (ii) Work-in-progress control a/c Dr - 45,000
   To factory overheads control a/c 45,000

9. Journalise the following:
   Sale of goods for cash - ₹2,00,000
   Sale of goods for credit - ₹3,00,000

Ans:

Cash a/c Dr 2,00,000
Debtors a/c Dr 3,00,000
To cost of sales a/c 5,00,000

B. Long answer type questions

1. Give journal entries for entering the following transactions in an integrated accounting system.

	₹
Purchase of direct materials on credit	50,000
Raw materials issued to production	40,000
Maintenance materials issued	5,000
Depreciation of plant and machinery	20,000
Production overheads recovered	30,000

2. Journalise the following transactions assuming cost and financial accounts are integrated:

	₹
Wages paid (40% Indirect)	75,000
Raw materials purchased on credit	1,00,000
Direct materials issued to production	70,000

Wages charged to production	45,000
Administrative expenses incurred	50,000
Administrative expenses recovered	47,000
Manufacturing overheads paid	60,000
Manufacturing expenses outstanding	20,000
Manufacturing expenses recovered	85,000

3. From the following information you are required to pass journal entries and prepare necessary accounts under the system of integrated accounts:

	₹
Materials purchased on credit	2,50,000
Wages paid	1,25,000
Wages productive	90,000
Wages unproductive	35,000
Finished goods at cost	4,50,000
Materials issued to production	2,20,000
Factory expenses incurred	1,55,000
Factory expenses absorbed	1,60,000
Office and administration expenses paid	1,40,000
Office and administration expenses recovered	1,36,000
Selling and distribution overheads paid	80,000
Selling and distribution expenses recovered	80,000
Sales (all credit)	6,00,000

[**Ans:** Stores control account: ₹30,000, Factory overheads control account ₹30,000. Office overheads control a/c ₹4,000, WIP control account ₹20,000]

4. BPR Ltd. keeps books on integrated accounting system: The following balances appeared in the books as on April 1, 2009:

	Dr ₹	Cr ₹
Stores control account	40,950	-
WIP control account	38,675	-
Finished goods control account	52,325	-

Bank account	-	22,750
Creditors account	-	18,200
Fixed assets account	1,47,875	-
Debtors account	27,300	-
Share capital account	-	1,82,000
Provision for depreciation account	-	11,375
Provision for doubtful debts account	-	3,725
Factory overheads outstanding account	-	6,250
Prepaid administration overheads account	9,975	-
Profit and loss account	-	72,800
	3,17,100	3,17,100

The transaction for the year ended March 31, 2009 were as given below:

	₹	₹
Direct wages	1,97,925	
Indirect wages	11,375	2,09,300
Purchase of materials (on credit)		2,27,500
Materials issued to production		2,50,250
Materials issued for repairs		4,550
Goods finished during the year (at cost)		4,89,125
Credit sales		6,82,500
Cost of goods sold		5,00,500
Production overheads absorbed		1,09,200
Production overheads paid during the year		91,000
Production overheads outstanding at the end of the year		7,775
Administration overheads paid during the year		27,300
Selling overheads incurred		31,850
Payment to creditors		2,29,775
Depreciation of machinery		14,789
Administration overheads outstanding at the end of the year		2,225
Provision for doubtful debts at the end of the year		4,590
Receipt from debtors		6,59,750

Required: Write up accounts in the integrated ledger of BPR Ltd and prepare a trial balance.
(CA inter)

[**Ans:** Balance-stores control account ₹13,650, WIP control account ₹1,06,925, Finished goods account ₹80,450, Bank account ₹47,775, Creditors account ₹15,925, Fixed assets account

1,47,875, Debtors account 50,050, Share capital account 1,82,000, Provision for depreciation a/c ₹26,164, Trial balance total ₹4,46,725].

5. A company maintains costing system fully integrated with financial accounts. The following information is taken from its books for the year ending 31.3.2009:

Balance at the beginning of the year:	₹
Stores ledger control account	25,000
Work-in-progress control account	20,000
Finished goods control account	35,000
Prepaid production overheads brought forward from the previous month	3,000

Transaction during the year are:

		₹
Materials purchased		75,000
Materials issued:		
to production	30,000	
to factory maintenance	4,000	34,000
Materials transferred between batches		5,000
Total wages paid:		
to direct workers	25,000	
to indirect workers	5,000	30,000
Direct wages charged to batches		20,000
Recorded non-productive time of direct workers		5,000
Selling and distribution overheads incurred		6,000
Other production overheads incurred		12,000
Sales		1,00,000
Cost of finished goods sold		80,000
Cost of goods completed		65,000
Value of WIP at the end of the year		40,000

The production overhead absorption reate is 150% of direct wages charged to work-in-progress.

Required:
(a) Store control account (b) WIP control account (c) Finished goods control account (d)Production overheads control account (e) Profit and loss account.

[**Ans:** (a) ₹66,000, (b) ₹40,000, (c) ₹20,000, (d) over absorption ₹1,000, (e) profit ₹20,000]

OUTPUT COSTING / UNIT COSTING / SINGLE COSTING 13

- ☞ Meaning
- ☞ Sources of cost information
- ☞ Treatment of stocks
- ☞ Cost sheet specimen
- ☞ Treatment of defective materials, scarp, by products and defective products
- ☞ Cost sheet - tender/quotation/estimation

13.1 MEANING

There are certain industries where a single product is produced on large scale mostly in continuous process. Units produced are identical in quality, design and size. Materials consumed, labour rates and overheads charges absorbed will be same on all units produced. The method of costing applied to ascertain the cost of such goods produced is simple. It is called unit costing or output costing or single costing.

In this method, expenses incurred during a particular period are accumulated and the number of units produced are also ascertained. To arrive at the cost per unit the total cost for the period is divided by the total number of units produced during the period.

The following are a few examples of industries where the output costing is followed: Brick making, collieries, mineral oil extraction, paper industry, cement, steel manufacture, breweries etc.

The units of measurement used in some of the industries are as follows:

Brick making industry - 1,000 bricks

Paper Collieries, Steel	} Tons
Breweries	- Barrels
Mineral oil extraction	- Gallon.

13.2 SOURCES OF COST INFORMATION

(i) Materials: Materials purchased, opening stock of materials, closing stock of materials , expenses relating to materials purchased are available in financial records. Abnormal loss of materials is deducted from materials cost.

(ii) Labour: Labour charges incurred are available in cash book.

(iii) Overheads: Overheads are also available in cash book and nominal accounts in financial books. These expenses are analysed and classified as production overheads, office and administration overheads and selling and distribution overheads.

13.3 TREATMENT OF STOCKS

The stocks of raw materials, stock of work-in-progress and stocks of finished goods are treated as follows for cost determination:

(i) **Stock of raw materials:** For calculation of cost of materials used in production during the period (i.e. Materials consumed), opening stock of the materials is added to the purchases and closing stock of materials is deducted from the purchase of materials.

(ii) **Stock of work-in-progress:** Opening value of work-in-progress is added to the total amount got after adding factory overheads to prime cost. Closing stock of work-in-progress is deducted from the above total amount.

    Work-in-progress refers to partly finished goods or incomplete units. Its cost includes materials used, proportion of wages and factory overheads incurred till this stage. Alternatively work-in-progress stock may be valued on prime cost basis. The total cost we get after adjusting the stock of work-in-progress is called works cost or factory cost.

(iii) **Stock of finished goods:** The cost of opening stock of finished goods is added to cost of production and cost of closing stock of finished goods is deducted from cost of production. The closing stock is always valued on current cost basis. Sometimes it is valued on average cost basis also.

13.4 COST SHEET

This is a statement of cost incurred during a period. The expenses incurred during the period are arranged in a logical order. The cost sheet broadly consists of two parts. In the first part all direct expenses like direct materials, direct labour and direct expenses are added. The total of all direct expenses is called Prime Cost. In the second part all indirect expenses, usually classified on functional basis are added one after another in the order of their importance. factory overheads is added to prime cost and the total is called factory cost or works cost. Office and administration overhead is added to works cost and the total is called cost of production. Lastly selling and distribution overhead is added. The total is called cost of sales or total cost. Then sales is compared with total cost to find the profit or loss for the period.

The cost sheet may be provided with additional column to show the cost per unit for each element of cost. Another additional column may also be added in the cost sheet to show the corresponding previous period cost. This helps the management to find the causes for increase in various expenses and helps in taking cost control measures.

Cost sheets may be prepared for any period according to the requirements of the management. The period for which cost sheets prepared may be for a week, month, a quarter, a half year or a year.

Specimen cost sheet

		No.of units	Total cost (₹)	Cost per unit (₹)
Materials consumed:				
Purchase of materials	xxx			
Add: opening stock of materials	xxx			
Add: Carriage inward	xxx			
Add: Other expenses in connection with purchase	xxx			
	xxx			
Less: Closing stock of materials	xxx			
Less: Abnormal loss of materials	xxx			
		xxx	xxx	xxx
Direct wages		-	xxx	xxx
Direct expenses/chargeable expenses		-	xxx	xxx
Prime Cost		xxx	xxx	xxx
Factory overheads		-	xxx	xxx
		xxx	xxx	xxx
Add: Opening stock of work-in-progress		-	xxx	xxx
		xxx	xxx	xxx
Less: Closing stock of work-in-progress		-	xxx	xxx
Works cost		xxx	xxx	xxx
Office and administration overheads		-	xxx	xxx
Cost of production	-	xxx	xxx	xxx
Add: Opening stock of finished goods		xxx	xxx	xxx
		xxx	xxx	xxx
Less: Closing stock of finished goods		xxx	xxx	xxx
Cost of goods sold		xxx	xxx	xxx
Selling and distribution overheads		-	xxx	xxx
Cost of sales		xxx	xxx	xxx
Profit/loss		-	xxx	xxx
Sales		xxx	xxx	xxx

Valuation of closing stock of finished goods

Closing stock of finished goods is the goods produced during the period but remaining unsold. It is valued on current cost basis. The step for valuation of closing stock of finished goods is:

$$\text{Value of closing stock} = \frac{\text{Cost of production}}{\text{Total production (units)}} \times \text{Closing stock (units)}$$

Sometimes closing stock is valued on average cost basis. Then the step for valuation of closing stock is:

$$\text{Value of closing stock} = \frac{\text{Cost of production + Value of opening stock of fin. goods}}{\text{Units produced during the period + Opening stock units}} \times \text{Closing stock (units)}$$

Treatment of scrap

When materials undergo some production process and such are wasted or lost, it may possess some value. It is deducted from the factory overheads. Sometimes raw materials in the beginning of the production stage itself may be wasted or lost. It may posses some value. It may be deducted from factory overheads or it may be deducted from materials cost while calculation of materials consumed.

Production (or) Manufacturing Account

When cost information is presented in a ledger format it is called production or manufacturing account. When sales is credited to this account, this account may also be called profit and loss account.

Specimen production or manufacturing account

		No.of units	**Total cost ₹**	**Cost per unit ₹**		**No. of units**	**Total cost ₹**	**Cost per unit ₹**
To Purchase of materials	xxx							
Add: Opening stock of materials	xxx				By Cost of production c/d	xxx	xxx	xxx
Add: Carriage inward	xxx							
Add: Expenses on purchase	xxx							
	xxx							
Less: Closing stock of materials	xxx							
Materials consumed To direct wages	xxx	xxx	xxx	xxx				
Price cost		xxx	xxx	xxx				
To Factory overheads		-	xxx	xxx				

Add: Opening stock of WIP		-	xxx	xxx				
Less: Closing stock of WIP								
Works cost		xxx	xxx	xxx				
To Office and administration over heads		-	xxx	xxx				
		xxx	xxx	xxx		xxx	xxx	xxx
To Opening stock of finished goods		xxx	xxx	xxx	By Sales	xxx	xxx	xxx
To Cost of production b/d		xxx	xxx	xxx	By Closing stock of finished goods	xxx	xxx	xxx
To Selling and distribution expenses		-	xxx	xxx		xxx	xxx	xxx
To Profit		-	xxx	xxx				
		xxx	xxx	xxx		xxx	xxx	xxx

Illustration-1

The following information was taken from the cost records of A Ltd for the year ending 31st March 2009. You are required to prepare a cost sheet showing cost per unit for each element of cost:

	₹
Raw materials purchased	2,15,000
Stock of raw materials on 1.4.2008	25,000
Stock of raw materials on 31.3.2009	50,000
Carriage on purchase	10,000
Factory wages	1,20,000
Fuel	55,000
Electric power	32,000
Plant repairs and depreciation	17,000
Haulage	21,000
Indirect materials	18,000
Unproductive wages	30,000
Salaries and office expenses	43,000
Sale of scrap realised	15,000

Director's fee and managing director's salary	60,000
Rent, rates, taxes and insurance:	
Factory	17,000
Office	6,000
Provision for income tax	25,000
Bad debts written off	10,000
Packing and forwarding expenses	46,000
Warehouse expenses	22,000
Advertisement	30,000
Discount allowed	4,000
Salesmen salary and commission	70,000
Travelling expenses	18,000
Sales	8,70,000

Number of units produced during the year were 20,000 units.

Also compute,

(a) Percentage of factory overheads on wages,

(b) Percentage of office and administration overheads on works cost,

(c) Percentage of selling and distribution of overheads on works cost, and

(d) Percentage of profit on sales.

Solution

Cost sheet of A Ltd for the year ending 31.3.09			
		Total Cost ₹	Cost per Unit ₹
Materials consumed:			
Raw materials purchase	2,15,000		
Add: Stock of raw materials - opening	25,000		
Carriage on purchases	10,000		
	2,50,000		
Less: Stock of raw materials–closing	50,000	2,00,000	10.00
Factory wages		1,20,000	6.00
Prime cost		3,20,000	16.00
Factory overheads			

Fuel	55,000		
Electric power	32,000		
Plant repairs and depreciation	17,000		
Haulage	21,000		
Indirect materials	18,000		
Rent, rates, tax and insurance factory	17,000		
Unproductive wages	30,000		
	1,90,000		
Less: Sale of scrap	15,000	1,75,000	8.75
Works cost		4,95,000	24.75
Office and administration overheads:			
Salaries and office expenses	43,000		
Director's fees and M.D.'s Salary	60,000		
Rent, rates, tax and insurance-office	6,000	1,09,000	5.45
Cost of production		6,04,000	30.20
Selling and distribution overheads:			
Packing and forwarding charges	46,000		
Warehouse expenses	22,000		
Advertisement	30,000		
Salesmen salary and commission	70,000		
Travelling expenses	18,000	1,86,000	9.30
Cost of sales/total cost		7,90,000	39.50
Profit		80,000	4.00
Sales		8,70,000	43.50

(a) Percentage of factory overheads to wages $= \dfrac{\text{Factory overheads}}{\text{Wages}} \times 100$

$$= \frac{1,75,000}{1,20,000} \times 100 = 145.83\%$$

(b) Percentage of office and administration overheads to works cost $= \dfrac{\text{Office and administration overheads}}{\text{Works cost}} \times 100$

$$= \frac{1,09,000}{4,95,000} \times 100 = 22.02\%$$

(c) Percentage of selling and distribution overheads to works cost $= \dfrac{\text{Selling and distribution overheads}}{\text{Works cost}} \times 100$

$$= \frac{1,86,000}{4,95,000} \times 100 = 37.58\%$$

(d) Percentage of profit on sales $= \dfrac{\text{Profit}}{\text{Sales}} \times 100$

$$= \frac{80,000}{8,70,000} \times 100 = 9.195\%$$

Note: Provision for income tax, bad debts written off and discount allowed are expenses of pure financial nature and not included in cost computation.

Illustration-2

Prepare a cost sheet showing cost per machine and profit per machine from the following particulars:

	Ordinary Machine	Automatic Machine
Number of machines produced and sold	640	810
Materials used (₹)	90,000	1,40,000
Manufacturing wages (₹)	75,000	1,25,000
Selling price per machine (₹)	600	750

Production overheads is charged at 125% of wages. Administration overheads at 20% of works cost and selling overheads at 10% of cost of production.

Solution

Cost Sheet				
	Ordinary Machine (output - 640 units)		Automatic Machine (output - 810 units)	
	Total Cost ₹	Cost Per Machine ₹	Total Cost ₹	Cost per Machine ₹
Materials	90,000	140.63	1,40,000	172.84
Manufacturing wages	75,000	117.19	1,25,000	154.32
Prime cost	1,65,000	257.82	2,65,000	327.16
Production overheads:				

125% on wages	93,750	146.48	1,56,250	192.90
Works cost	2,58,750	404.30	4,21,250	520.06
Administration overheads:				
20% on works cost	51,750	80.86	84,250	104.01
Cost of production	3,10,500	485.16	5,05,500	624.07
Selling overheads:				
10% on cost of production	31,050	48.52	50,550	62.41
Cost of sales	3,41,550	533.68	5,56,050	686.48
Profit	42,450	66.32	51,450	63.52
Sales	3,84,000	600.00	6,07,500	750.00

Illustration-3

Hindustan Gears Ltd produces two types of gear boxes namely 'Super' and 'Deluxe'. The total cost incurred during a period are as follows:

	₹
Materials consumed	1,59,900
Direct wages	1,40,000
Indirect materials	24,600
Indirect wages	35,000
Depreciation of plant and machinery	20,000
Power	28,000
Administration expenses	45,000

Additional Information:

	Super	**Deluxe**
No. of units produced	4,000	5,000
Materials consumption ratio per unit	4	5
Direct wages	3	4
Machine hours used per unit	2hrs	3 hrs

Prepare a cost sheet showing cost per unit of each type of gear box.

Solution

Workings

1. Materials allocation Ratio = Materials consumption Ratio per unit × number of units

   Super = 4,000×4 = 16,000

   Deluxe = 5,000×5 = 25,000

   Ratio = 16 : 25
2. Direct wages (given) = 3 : 4
3. Depreciation and power = Machine hours per unit × No. of units

   Super = 4,000×3 = 12,000

   Deluxe = 5,000×4 = 20,000

   Ratio = 3 : 5
4. Administration expenses = No. of units basis

   Ratio = 4,000 : 5,000

   = 4 : 5
5. Indirect wages = Direct wages ratio
6. Stores overhead = Materials ratio

Cost Sheet

	Total Cost ₹	Ratio	Super Ouput: 4,000 units		Deluxe Output: 5,000 units	
			Total Cost ₹	Per Unit ₹	Total Cost ₹	Per Unit ₹
Materials consumed	1,59,900	16:25	62,400	15.60	97,500	19.50
Direct wages	1,40,000	3:4	60,000	15.00	80,000	16.00
Indirect materials	24,600	16:25	9,600	2.40	15,000	3.00
Indirect wages	35,000	3:4	15,000	3.75	20,000	4.00
Depreciation of plant and machinery	20,000	3:5	7,500	1.88	12,500	2.50
Power	28,000	3:5	10,500	2.62	17,500	3.50
Administration expenses	45,000	4:5	20,000	5.00	25,000	5.00
Total cost	4,52,500	-	1,85,000	46.25	2,67,500	53.50

Illustration-4

The following is the data relating to the manufacture of a standard product during three months ended 31.03.09.

Direct materials used	=	₹3,20,000
Direct wages	=	₹1,48,000
Machine hours worked	=	4,750 hours
Machine hour rate	=	₹14 per hour

Administration overheads at 20% of factory cost

Selling overheads	=	₹2.20 per unit
Units produced	=	16,000 units
Units sold	=	14,500 at ₹46 per unit

Prepare a cost sheet showing cost and profit per unit and profit for the period.

Solution

Cost Sheet (For 3 months ended 31.03.2009)		
	Total Cost (₹)	Cost Per Units (₹)
Direct materials used	3,20,000	20.00
Direct wages	1,48,000	9.25
Prime cost	4,68,000	29.25
Factory overheads:		
Machine hours × machine hours rate $(4,750 \times 14)$	66,500	4.16
Works cost	5,34,500	33.41
Administration overheads:		
20% of works cost	1,06,900	6.68
Cost of production	6,41,400	40.09
Less: Closing stock of finished goods: $\frac{(6{,}41{,}400 \times 1,500)}{16{,}000}$	60,131	40.09
Cost of goods sold	5,81,269	40.09
Selling overheads (14,500 × 2.20)	31,900	2.20
Cost of sales	6,13,169	42.29
Profit	53,831	3.71
Sales	6,67,000	46.00

13.5 TREATMENT OF DEFECTIVE MATERIALS, SCRAP, BY PRODUCTS AND DEFECTIVE PRODUCTS

Defective Materials

Materials received from the supplier may be in damaged condition and is returned to the supplier. The cost of materials returned to the supplier is deducted from materials cost. Material received from the supplier may be in good condition, but while in stores, due to its inherent nature a portion of the materials may perish or become defective due to deterioration in quality and become unsuitable for use in factory. Such materials may possess sales value, the sale value should be deducted from materials cost. If defective materials is over and above the normal level due to poor storage, careless handling etc it should be debited to costing profit and loss account.

Scrap

If raw materials is scrapped in the introduction stage itself, it is called materials scrap. Its sale value is deducted from raw materials consumed. Sometimes materials may become defective after under-going some production process. The sale value of this material (usually called factory scrap) is deducted from production overheads. If defectives are due to abnormal causes, the cost of such defective materials is debited to costing profit and loss account.

Byproducts

Some raw materials while being processed in production process may give rise to some additional products of insignificant value. The sale of such products is deducted from production overheads.

Defective Products

Products coming out of factory may have defects. The defects in the finished products may be cured by spending additional materials and/or labour. The cost of such additional work should be added to factory overheads if defectives is within normal level. If defectives are due to abnormal reasons, the cost of rectifying abnormal defectives is charged to costing profit and loss account. Sometimes defects in the finished product cannot be cured or cost of rectification will be more than the additional revenue received. In this case the defectives will be sold as seconds or as scrap. The amount realised from the sale of defectives is deducted from total manufacturing cost.

Illustration-5

The following particulars were taken from the cost books of an Iron foundry for the year ending 31.03.2009.

Works overhead at 60% of direct labour.

Stores overhead at 15% of direct materials.

10% of castings were rejected being not upto the specification and a sum of ₹2,500 realized from sale of scrap.

	₹
Raw materials purchased	50,000
Stock of raw materials:	
On 01.04.2008	15,000
On 31.03.2009	10,000
Direct labour	75,000

10% of finished castings were found to be defective in manufacture and rectified by expenditure on additional works overheads to the extent of 20% on the proportionate direct wages.

The good output during the period was 1,000 tonnes.

Find out the cost of good castings per tonne.

Solution

Cost sheet for the year ending 31.03.2009 (Output: 1,000 tons)			
		Total Cost ₹	**Cost per Unit** ₹
Materials consumed: Raw materials purchased	50,000		
Add: Opening stock of raw materials	15,000		
	65,000		
Less: Closing stock of raw materials	10,000	55,000	55.00
Direct labour		75,000	75.00
Prime cost		1,30,000	130.00
Works overheads: at 60% of direct labour		45,000	45.00
Stores overheads: at 15% of direct materials		8,250	8.25
		1,83,250	183.25
Less: Sale of rejected casting		2,500	2.50
		1,80,750	180.75

Additional works overheads: $75{,}000 \times \frac{10}{100} \times \frac{20}{100}$		1,500	1.50
Manufacturing cost or works cost		1,82,250	182.25

13.6 TENDER OR QUOTATION OR ESTIMATED COST SHEET

A manufacturer has to estimate the price at which he is willing to supply the articles he is producing in response to a tender or quotation floated by various parties. The manufacturer has to take great care while submitting tender or quotation for supply of articles. The articles are to be manufactured in the future if his tender is accepted. The cost of materials, labour and overheads is to be estimated by taking present cost and probable changes in the prices of materials, rates of labour and overheads.

Estimated cost sheet is different from a tender or quotation. Tender or quotation is prepared by a producer for submission to outsiders in order to procure orders from them. Estimated cost sheet is prepared by the management for its own use. Total cost for a future period is estimated for the volume of production budgeted. The likely changes in rates of materials, labour and overheads are also taken into consideration. Estimated cost sheets are prepared mainly for the purpose of controlling costs.

Direct wages is also to be estimated by considering the likely changes in wage rates anticipated.

Overheads are charged by using any of the suitable method of absorption of overheads like machine hour rate, labour hour rate, percentage on direct wages etc. Due attention is to be given to the behaviour of overheads in the estimation of overheads costs like fixed, variable and semi-variable overheads. Sometimes cost sheet for future period is prepared as a part of production and profit planning.

Illustration-6

The following is the cost incurred by a manufacturer during the year ending 31.03.2009.

	₹		₹
Direct materials	6,00,000	Factory overheads	2,25,000
Direct labour	4,50,000	Administration overheads	2,55,000

The manufacturer has received an order for the supply of a machine. The materials cost and wages cost is estimated at ₹60,000 and ₹45,000 respectively. Factory overheads is recovered as a percentage on direct labour and administration overheads recovered as a percentage on works cost. What price the manufacturer has to quote if he wants to make a profit of 15% on selling price?

Solution

Cost sheet for the year ending 31.03.2009	
	₹
Direct materials	6,00,000
Direct labour	4,50,000
Prime cost	10,50,000
Factory overheads	2,25,000
Works cost	12,75,000
Administration overheads	2,55,000
Cost of production	15,30,000

Overhead recovery percentages

1. Percentage of factory overheads to direct labour

$$= \frac{\text{Factory overheads}}{\text{Direct labour}} \times 100$$

$$= \frac{2{,}25{,}000}{4{,}50{,}000} \times 100$$

$$= 50\%$$

2. Percentage of administration overheads on works cost

$$= \frac{\text{Administration overheads}}{\text{Works cost}} \times 100$$

$$= \frac{2{,}55{,}000}{12{,}75{,}000} \times 100$$

$$= 20\%$$

Tender or quotation for a machine	
	₹
Direct materials	60,000
Direct wages	45,000
Prime cost	1,05,000
Factory overheads	
50% on direct wages	22,500
Works cost	1,27,500
Administration overheads	
20% on works cost	25,500
Cost of production	1,53,000
Profit: 15% on selling price i.e.	
15/85 on cost of production	27,000
Selling price	1,80,000

Illustration-7

Following are the particulars for the production of 2,000 sewing machines during the year ended 31.03.2008.

	₹
Materials	1,60,000
Wages	2,40,000
Manufacturing expenses	1,00,000
Salaries	1,20,000
Rent, rates etc.	20,000
Selling expenses	60,000
General expenses	40,000
Sales	8,00,000

The company plans to manufacture 3,000 machines during the year ended 31.03.2009. You are required to submit a statement showing price at which the machines should be sold so as to show a profit of 10% on selling price.

The following additional information is supplied to you:

(a) Price of materials is expected to increase by 20%
(b) Wage rates are expected to show an increase of 5%
(c) Manufacturing expenses will rise in proportion to combined cost of materials and wages.
(d) Selling expenses per unit will remain the same.
(e) All other expenses will remain unaffected by the rise in output.

(B.Com. Madras University)

Solution

Estimated cost sheet for the year ending 31.03.2009 Production: 3,000 machines		
	Total Cost ₹	Cost per Unit ₹
Materials $= 1{,}60{,}000 \times \frac{3{,}000}{2{,}000} \times \frac{120}{100}$	2,88,000	96.00
Wages $= 2{,}40{,}000 \times \frac{3{,}000}{2{,}000} \times \frac{105}{100}$	3,78,000	126.00
Prime Cost	6,66,000	222.00
Manufacturing Expenses: $\frac{\text{Manufacturing cost for previous year}}{\text{Prime cost of previous year}} \times$ prime cost of current year	1,66,500	55.50

$= \frac{1,00,000}{4,00,000} \times 6,66,000$		
Works cost	8,32,500	277.50
Administration overheads:		
Salaries = 1,20,000		
Rent, Rates etc., = 20,000		
General expenses = 40,000	1,80,000	60.00
Cost production	10,12,500	337.50
Selling overheads:		
$\frac{60,000}{2000} =$ ₹30 P/u ×3000	90,000	30.00
Cost of sales	11,02,500	367.50
Profit: 10% on selling price (i.e. 10/90 on cost of sales	1,22,500	40.83
Sales	12,25,000	408.33

Illustration-8

The following information has been supplied by *A* Ltd from its costing records for the year ending 31.03.2009.

	₹
Rates of factory	1,400
Lighting of factory	2,600
Depreciation of plant	3,500
Clerical salaries	12,000
Management expenses	6,000
Power	4,500
Factory indirect wages	12,250
Plant repairs and maintenance	10,000
Rectification of defective work	2,800
Consumable stores	7,500
Selling expenses	4,600
General expenses	4,600
Receipts from sale of scrap	1,200
Profits from canteen	500

Production has been 1,00,000 units, the prime cost of which has been materials 90 paise and wages 60 paise per unit and selling price was ₹2.35 per unit, all units being sold.

In the year ending 31.03.2010 selling price is reduced to ₹2.25 per unit and production increased by 50 percent without extra shift.

Prepare a statement showing:

1. Various elements of cost in the year ending on 31.03.2009.
2. The estimated cost and profit for the year ending 31.03.2010, assuming that 1,50,000 units will be produced and sold.

Solution

Cost sheet for the year ending 31.03.2009 Output: 1,00,000 units		
	₹	**Total Cost** ₹
Materials (0.90 × 1,00,000)		90,000
Wages (0.60 × 1,00,000)		60,000
Prime cost		1,50,000
Production overheads: Rates of factory	1,400	
Lighting of factory	2,600	
Depreciation of plant	3,500	
Power	4,500	
Factory indirect wages	12,250	
Plant repairs and maintenance	10,000	
Rectification of defective work	2,800	
Consumable stores	7,500	
	44,550	
Less: Sale of scrap – 1200	1,200	43,350
Works cost		1,93,350
Office and administration overheads: Clerical salaries	12,000	
Management expenses	6,000	
General expenses	4,600	22,600
Cost of production		2,15,950
Selling and distribution overheads: Selling expenses		4,600
Cost of sales		2,20,550
Profit:		14,450
Sales (1,00,000 × 2.35)		2,35,000

Estimated cost sheet for the year ending 31.03.2010	
	₹
Materials (0.90 × 1,50,000)	1,35,000
Wages (0.60 × 1,50,000)	90,000
Prime cost	2,25,000
Factory overheads: $43{,}350 \times \frac{1{,}50{,}000}{1{,}00{,}000}$	65,025
Works cost	2,90,025
Office and administration overheads:	22,600
Cost of production	3,12,625
Selling & distribution overheads: $4{,}600 \times \frac{1{,}50{,}000}{1{,}00{,}000}$	6,900
Cost of sales	3,19,525
Estimated profit (bf)	17,975
Sales (1,50,000 × 2.25)	3,37,500

Note: It is assumed that all factory expenses and selling overheads are directly variable. All office overheads are fixed.

Illustration-9

A factory is engaged in production of two standard products which pass through three departments. The cost figures for the factory for the month of November are furnished below:

	Total ₹	Dept A ₹	Dept B ₹	Dept C ₹
Direct materials	18,600	7,500	6,400	4,700
Labour cost	15,000	6,000	5,000	4,000
Overheads	7,500	3,000	2,500	2,000
Total cost	41,100	16,500	13,900	10,700

Prepare a simple cost sheet for products X and Y on the basis of the data furnished below:

		Dept. 'A' (₹)	Dept. 'B' (₹)	Dept. 'C' (₹)
Product - 'X':	Materials	100	200	300
	Labour	50	60	70

Product - 'Y':	Materials	50	90	140
	Labour	70	60	80

Solution

Cost sheet		
	Product X (₹)	Product Y (₹)
Materials	600	280
Labour	180	210
Prime cost	780	490
Overheads - 50% of labour cost	90	105
Total Cost	870	595

Illustration-10

A factory produces a standard machine. The following information is given to you from which you are required to prepare a cost sheet for the quarter ended 31.03.09:

	₹
Raw materials purchase	1,80,000
Stock of raw materials - opening	45,000
Stock of raw materials - closing	25,000
Direct wages	1,60,000
Other direct expenses	40,000
Manufacturing expenses	100% of direct wages
Office overheads	10% on works cost
Selling and distribution overheads	₹4 per unit

Opening stock of finished goods - 1,500 units valued at ₹45,000
Production during the period - 20,000 units
Closing stock of finished goods - 2,200 units

Also find out the selling price per unit on the basis that profit margin is uniformly made to give a return of 20% on the selling price. There is no stock of work-in-progress either at the beginning or at the end of the period.

Solution

Cost sheet for 3 months ending 31.03.09				
		No.of units	Total Cost ₹	Cost P/U ₹
Raw materials consumed:				
Purchase of raw materials	1,80,000			
Add: Opening stock of raw materials	45,000			
	2,25,000			
Less: Closing stock of raw materials	25,000	20,000	2,00,000	10.00
Direct wages	-	-	1,60,000	8.00
Other direct expenses		-	40,000	2.00
Prime cost		20,000	4,00,000	20.00
Manufacturing overheads:				
100% on direct wages		-	1,60,000	8.00
Works cost		20,000	5,60,000	28.00
Office overheads:				
10% on works cost		-	56,000	2.80
Cost of production		20,000	6,16,000	30.80
Add: Opening stock of finished goods		1,500	45,000	30.00
		21,500	6,61,000	60.80
Less: Closing stock of finished goods		2,200	67,760	30.80
Cost of goods sold		19,300	5,93,240	30.74
Selling overheads		-	77,200	4.00
Cost of sales		19,300	6,70,440	34.74
Profit: 20% on selling price i.e. 20/80 on cost price		-	1,67,610	8.68
Sales		19,300	8,38,050	43.42

Illustration-11

A foundry has received orders for three different types of castings namely A, B and C weighing 36, 45 and 54 tons respectively. 10% of raw materials used are wasted in manufacturing and are sold as scrap for 50% of cost price of raw materials. The cost of raw materials is ₹4,500 per ton, the wages for three types of castings are ₹64,000, ₹81,000 and ₹1,08,000 respectively.

Factory overheads are charged at 50% of wages and office and administration overheads at 15% of works cost. The cost of moulds for the three types of castings are ₹9,000, ₹12,000, ₹15,500. If the factory wants to earn a profit of 25% on selling price, find the selling price per ton of each type of castings.

Solution

Estimated cost sheet						
	Castings 'A'		Castings 'B'		Castings 'C'	
	Tons	Total Cost ₹	Tons	Total Cost ₹	Tons	Total Cost ₹
Raw materials	40	1,80,000	50	2,25,000	60	2,70,000
Less: Raw materials scrap	4	9,000	5	11,250	6	13,500
Net materials cost	360	1,71,000	45	2,13,750	54	2,56,500
Wages	-	64,000	-	81,000	-	1,08,000
Cost of moulds	-	9,000	-	12,000	-	15,500
Prime cost	36	2,44,000	45	3,06,750	54	3,80,000
Factory overheads:						
50% of wages	-	32,000	-	40,500	-	54,000
Works cost	36	2,76,000	45	3,47,250	54	4,34,000
Office and administration overheads - 15% on works cost	-	41,400	-	52,088	-	65,100
Cost of production	36	3,17,400	45	3,99,338	54	4,99,100
Add: Profit 25% on selling price i.e., 25/75 on cost	-	1,05,800	-	1,33,112	-	1,66,367
Sales	36	4,23,200	45	5,32,450	54	6,65,467
Selling price per ton		11,755.56	-	11,832.22	-	12,323.46

Illustration-12

A factory can produce 60,000 units per annum at its optimum capacity (100%). The estimated cost of production is as follows:

Direct materials ₹3 per unit
Direct labour - ₹2 per unit (subject to a minimum of ₹6,000 pm)

Overheads:

Fixed - ₹1,00,000 p.a
Variable - ₹2 per unit

Semi-variable - ₹40,000 upto 50% capacity and an additional cost of ₹10,000 per every 20% increase in capacity or part thereof. Each unit of raw materials yields scrap, which is sold at the rate of 20 paise per unit.

In 2009 the factory worked at 50% capacity for the first 3 months but it was expected that it would work at 80% capacity for the remaining 9 months. During the first three months the selling price per unit was ₹12. What should be the price for the remaining 9 months to produce a total profit of ₹1,00,000? **(ICWA - Inter)**

Solution

Estimated statement of cost and selling price for the year 2009		
		Total Cost ₹
Direct materials (WN. 2)	1,30,500	
Less: Materials scrap (WN. 6)	8,700	1,21,800
Direct Labour (WN. 3)		90,000
Prime Cost		2,11,800
Overheads:		
Fixed	1,00,000	
Variable (WN. 4)	87,000	
Semi-variable (WN. 5)	55,000	2,42,000
Total cost		4,53,800
Profit		1,00,000
Sales for the year		5,53,800
Less: Sales in first 3 months (WN. 7)		90, 000
Sales in remaining 9 months		4,63,800
Selling price per unit in the remaining 9 Months		= 4,63,800/36,000 = ₹12.88

Workings

1. **Production in Units**

   Fixed 3 months - $60{,}000 \times \frac{3}{12} \times \frac{50}{100}$ = 7,500 units

   Remaining 9 months - $60{,}000 \times \frac{9}{12} \times \frac{80}{100}$ = 36,000 units

   Total production = 43,500 units

2. **Material cost**— $43{,}500 \times 3$ = ₹1,30,500

3. Direct labour

	On production	Minimum	Payable
3 months	7,500 × 2 = 15,000	6,000 × 3 = 18,000	18,000
9 months	36,000 × 2 = 72,000	6,000 × 9 = 54,000	72,000
		Total	₹ 90,000

4. Variable overheads— 43,500 × 2 = ₹87,000

5. Semi-variable overheads

3 months - for 50% capacity = 40,000 × 3/12 = ₹10,000

9 months - for 50% capacity = 40,000 × 9/12 = ₹30,000

- for 20% capacity = 10,000 × 9/12 = ₹ 7,500

- for 10% capacity = 10,000 × 9/12 = ₹ 7,500

Total = ₹55,000

6. Materials scrap— 43,500 × 0.20 = ₹8,700

7. Sales in first 3 months— 7,500 × 12 = ₹90,000

Illustration-13

The cost structure of an article the selling price of which is ₹45,000 is as follows:

Direct materials	50%
Direct labour	20%
Overheads	30%

An increase of 15% in the cost of materials and of 25% in the cost of labour is anticipated. These increased cost in relation to the present selling price would cause 25% decrease in the amount of present profit per article. You are required to:

1. Prepare a statement of profit per article at present, and
2. The revised selling price to produce the same percentages of profit to sales as before.

(ICWA - Inter)

Solution

Statement of profit-present	
	₹
Materials	15,000
Labour	6,000
Prime cost	21,000
Overheads	9,000

Total cost	30,000
Profit	15,000
Sales	45,000

Statement showing revised selling price		
		₹
Materials cost at present	15,000	
Add: Increase 15%	2,250	17,250
Labour at present	6,000	
Add: Increase 25%	1,500	7,500
Prime cost		24,750
Overheads		9,000
Total cost		33,750
Add: Profit - 50% on cost		16,875
Revised selling price		50,625

Workings

1. Let the present total cost be x.

2. Cost Structure:

	Present	Change	Future
Direct materials	$0.5x$	$0.075x$	$0.575x$
Direct labour	$0.2x$	$0.050x$	$0.250x$
Overheads	$0.3x$	-	$0.300x$
Total	$1.0x$	$0.125x$	$1.125x$

3. Profit at present = Sales − Cost

$$= 45{,}000 - x$$

4. Decrease in profit due to increase in cost $= (45{,}000 - x)\dfrac{25}{100}$

$$= 11{,}250 - 0.25x$$

$$\begin{aligned} \text{Increase in cost} &= \text{Decrease in profit} \\ 0.125x &= 11{,}250 - 0.25x \\ 0.125x + 0.25x &= 11{,}250 \end{aligned}$$

$$0.375x = 11{,}250$$

$$x = \frac{11,250}{0.375}$$

$$\text{Present total cost} = ₹30{,}000$$

5. Present profit = 45,000 – 30,000

= ₹15,000

6. % of profit on cost at present= $\frac{15,000}{30,000} \times 100 = 50\%$

Illustration-14

X Ltd manufactures four brands of toys A, B, C and D. If the company limits the manufacture to just one brand, the monthly production will be:

A - 50,000 units B - 1,00,000 units C - 1,50,000 units D - 3,00,000 units

You are given the following set of information from which you are requested to find out the profit or loss made on each brand showing clearly the following elements:

a. Direct cost b. Works cost c. Total cost

	Brands			
	A	B	C	D
Actual production (units)	6,750	18,000	40,500	94,500
Direct wages (₹)	15,000	27,500	37,500	1,05,000
Direct materials cost (₹)	50,000	92,500	1,27,500	3,80,000
Selling price per unit (₹)	20	15	10	8

Factory overheads for the month was ₹1,62,000. Selling and distribution cost should be assumed at 20% of works cost. Factory overheads should be allocated to each brand on the basis of units which could have been produced in a month when single brand production was in operation.

(ICWA - Inter)

Solution

Working notes

1. When production is limited to one product, the production of D - 3,00,000 units, but the production of 'A' is only 50,000 units. It means each unit of product 'A' is equal to 6 units of 'D' (i.e. 3,00,000/50,000 = 6). Similarly 1 unit of product 'B' is equal to 3 units of 'D' (i.e. 3,00,000/1,50,000 = 2). So the weight assigned for each product is A – 6, B– 3, C – 2 and D–1.

2. Let us convert actual production of each product in terms of 'D'.

Product	Weight	Actual production (Units)	Equivalent production in terms of 'D' (units)
A	6	6,750	40,500
B	3	18,000	54,000
C	2	40,500	81,000
D	1	94,500	94,500
		Total	2,70,000

Total factory overhead is ₹1,62,000.

3. Factory overheads for each unit of product 'D'$=\dfrac{1,62,000}{2,70,000}=0.60$

4. Factory overheads apportioned for each product for actual production - in terms of equivalent production:

Product	Equivalent Production (units)	Overhead rate per unit ₹	Factory Overheads ₹
A	40,500	0.60	24,300
B	54,000	0.60	32,400
C	81,000	0.60	48,600
D	94,500	0.60	56,700
		Total	1,62,000

Statement of profit or loss				
	Products			
	A ₹ (6,750 units)	B ₹ (18,000 units)	C ₹ (40,500 units)	D ₹ (94,500 units)
Direct materials	50,000	92,500	1,27,500	3,80,000
Direct wages	15,000	27,500	37,500	1,05,000
(a) Direct cost/prime cost	65,000	1,20,000	1,65,000	4,85,000
Factory overheads	24,300	32,400	48,600	56,700
(b) Works cost	89,300	1,52,400	2,13,600	5,41,700
Selling and distribution overheads	17,860	30,480	42,720	1,08,340
(c) Total cost	1,07,160	1,82,880	2,56,320	6,50,040
Profit	27,840	87,120	1,48,680	1,05,960
Sales	1,35,000	2,70,000	4,05,000	7,56,000

Illustration-15

The cost of manufacturing 5,000 units of a commodity comprises:

	₹
Materials	20,000
Wages	25,000
Chargeable expenses	400
Fixed overheads	16,000
Variable overheads	4,000

For manufacturing every 1,000 extra units of the commodity the cost of production increases as follows:

Materials	:	Proportionately
Wages	:	10% less than proportionally
Chargeable expenses	:	No extra cost
Fixed overheads	:	₹200 extra
Variable overheads	:	25% less than proportionately

Calculate the estimated cost of producing 8,000 units of the commodity and show by how much it would differ if a flat rate of factory overheads based on wages were charged.

(B.Com., Madras University)

Solution

Statement of Cost

	Present cost (5,000 units) ₹	Additional cost (3,000 units) ₹	Total cost (8,000 units) ₹
Materials	20,000	$\frac{20,000}{5,000} \times 3,000 = 12,000$	32,000
Wages	25,000	$\frac{25,000}{5,000} \times 3,000 \times \frac{90}{100} = 13,500$	38,500
Chargeable expenses	400		400
Prime cost	45,400	25,500	70,900
Fixed overheads	16,000	$200 \times 3 = 600$	16,600
Variable overheads	4,000	$\frac{4,000}{5,000} \times 3,000 \times \frac{75}{100} = 1,800$	5,800
Total cost	65,400	27,900	93,300

Illustration-16

The following details have been obtained from the cost records of Comet Paints Ltd.:

	₹
Stock of raw materials on 1.4.2008	75,000
Stock of raw materials on 31.3.2009	91,500
Direct wages	52,500
Indirect wages	2,750
Sales	2,11,000
Work-in-progress on 1.4.2008	28,000
Work-in-progress on 31.3.2009	35,000
Purchase of raw materials	66,000
Factory rent, rates and power	15,000
Depreciation of plant and machinery	3,500
Expenses on purchase	1,500
Carriage outward	2,500
Advertising	3,500
Office rent and taxes	2,500
Travellers' wages and commission	16,500
Stock of finished goods on 1.4.2008	54,000
Stock of finished goods on 31.3.2009	31,000

Prepare a production account giving the maximum break up of costs and profit.

(B.Com.(Hons)., Delhi University)

Solution

Comet Paints Ltd

Production account for the year ended 31.03.2009

		₹		₹
To Materials consumed:				
Purchase of raw materials	66,000		By prime cost c/d	1,03,500
Add: Opening stock of RM	75,000			
Add: Carriage on purchase	1,500			
	1,42,500			
Less: Closing stock of RM	91,500	51,000		

Particulars			Particulars	
To Direct wages		52,500		
		1,03,500		1,03,500
To prime cost b/d		1,03,500		
To Factory overheads:				
Indirect wages	2,750		By work cost c/d	1,17,750
Factory rent, rates and power	15,000			
Depreciation on plant and machinery	3,500	21,250		
		1,24,750		
Add: Opening stock of WIP		28,000		
		1,52,750		
Less: Closing stock of WIP		35,000		
		1,17,750		1,17,750
To Works cost b/d		1,17,750	By cost of production c/d	1,20,250
Office rent and taxes		2,500		
		1,20,250		1,20,250
To Cost production b/d		1,20,250	By cost of goods sold c/d	1,43,250
Add: Opening stocked of finished goods		54,000		
		1,74,250		
Less: Closing stock of finished goods		31,000		
		1,43,250		1,43,250
To Cost goods sold b/d		1,43,250	By sales	2,11,000
To Selling and distribution overheads:				
Carriage outward	2,500			
Advertising	3,500			
Travellers wages and commission	6,500	12,500		
Cost of sales		1,55,750		
To profit transferred to costing profit and loss account		55,250		
		2,11,000		2,11,000

13.7 EXERCISE

I. Objective Type Questions

A. Fill in the blanks

(i) Unit costing or output costing is applied in industries where goods produced are ______________.

(ii) Carriage inward and expenses on purchase are added to ______________ cost.

(iii) Closing stock of finished goods is valued on ______________ cost basis.

(iv) Total of all direct expenses in called ______________ cost.

(v) Factory cost is the total of prime cost plus ______________.

[**Ans:** (i) Identical (ii) Direct materials (iii) Current (iv) Prime (v) Factory overheads]

B. State whether the following statements are true or false

(i) Raw materials scrap is added to direct materials cost.

(ii) Unit costing is followed in industries where goods produced are similar to one another in all aspects.

(iii) The method of costing followed in brick making industry is unit costing.

(iv) Opening stock of finished goods is valued on current cost basis.

(v) Factory scrap is deducted from production overheads.

(vi) Cost sheet is prepared for a specified period.

[**Ans: True:** (ii), (iii), (v), (vi) **False:** (i), (iv)]

II. Theory Questions

A. Short answer type questions

1. What is cost sheet?
2. What is prime cost?
3. What is works cost or factory cost?
4. What is conversion cost?
5. What is materials scrap? How is it treated in cost accounts?
6. What is factory scrap? How is it treated in cost accounts?
7. What are defectives?
8. What is tender or quotation?

9. What is estimated cost sheet? How is it different from quotation or tender?

B. Long answer type questions

1. Explain the features of unit costing. What are the various industries in which unit costing method is followed?
2. What is cost sheet? Explain its uses.
3. What is production account? Distinguish it from cost sheet.
4. What is materials scrap and factory scrap. How are they treated in cost accounts?
5. What is tender or quotation? What are the points to be kept is mind while preparing tender or quotation? Explain.

III. Practical Problems

A. Short answer type questions

1. Find the works cost from the following:

   Materials consumed - ₹75,000
   Direct wages - ₹1,00,000
   Factory overheads - 75% of direct wages.

   [**Ans:** works cost ₹2,50,000]

2. Find the cost of production from the following details:

   Direct materials - ₹1,50,000
   Direct labour - ₹1,00,000
   Factory overheads - 30% on prime cost
   Administration overheads - 20% of works cost.

   [**Ans:** ₹3,90,000]

3. From the following details ascertain manufacturing cost:

   Direct materials - ₹2,00,000
   Manufacturing wages - ₹80,000
   Works overhead - 50% on manufacturing wages
   Opening work-in progress - ₹20,000
   Closing work-in-progress - ₹25,000

   [**Ans:** Manufacturing cost ₹3,15,000)]
   Note: Manufacturing cost is also called work cost.

4. Factory overheads for the year 2009 is ₹50,000.

   Direct wages for the year 2009 amounted to ₹2,00,000.

   Factory overheads is recovered on direct wages basis.

Find out the rate of factory overheads on direct wages.
Also find out the factory overheads recovered in the year 2010, if direct wages for the year 2010 amounted to ₹3,60,000.

[**Ans:** Rate of factory OHS on direct wages 25%. Factory overheads recovered in 2010 ₹90,000]

5. The following details are extracted from the books of *X* Ltd for the year 2010.

Cost of production for 8,000 units - ₹2,00,000
Opening stock 1,500 units valued at ₹24 per unit
Closing stock in 1,200 units

Find out the closing stock value and cost of goods sold.

[**Ans:** Value of closing stock ₹30,000. Cost of goods sold ₹2,06,000]

B. Long answer type questions

1. The following informations have been taken from the books of Apollo Industries Ltd for the year ending 31.03.2009:

	₹
Stock of raw materials on 1.4.2008	62,000
Stock of raw materials on 31.3.2009	47,000
Purchase of raw of materials	3,20,000
Carriage inward	26,000
Direct labour	2,25,000
Indirect labour	54,000
Indirect materials	43,000
Other direct charges	51,000
Rent, rates and insurance - Factory	60,000
Rent, rates and insurance - Office	45,000
Depreciation - Plant and machinery	72,500
Depreciation - Office equipment	41,400
Salary - Office	52,500
Salary - Salesmen	60,000
Loss on sale of fixed assets	13,000
Other factory expenses	28,000
Other office expenses	19,000
Cash discount allowed to debtors	15,000
Manager salary and allowances	66,000
Travelling expenses of salesmen	8,000

Warehouse rent, rates and insurance	25,000
Advertising expenses	35,000
Carriage and freight outward	7,500
Sales	14,00,000

Manager's salary and allowances are apportioned between factory and office as 70% and 30% respectively. From the above particulars prepare a cost sheet showing (a) prime cost (b) works cost (c) cost of production (d) cost of sales and (e) profit.

[**Ans:**

(a) Prime cost ₹6,37,000
(b) Works cost ₹9,40,700
(c) Cost of production ₹11,18,400
(d) Cost of sales ₹12,53,900
(e) Profit ₹1,46,100]

2. The following informations have been taken from the records of XYZ Ltd for the year ended 31.03.2009:

	01.04.2008 ₹	31.03.2009 ₹
Stock of raw materials	65,000	72,000
Work-in-progress	43,000	41,500
Stock of finished goods	76,300	81,400

	₹		₹
Indirect wages	13,700	Sale of scrap	6,450
Factory rent and rates	16,800	Purchase of materials	1,47,000
Office salaries	24,600	Direct labour	1,14,000
General expenses	17,100	Plant repairs	16,570
Office rent	5,900	Depreciation of plant	19,380
Rent of showroom	4,200	Factory lighting	13,510
Salesmen salary	21,250	Advertisement	28,460
Sales	5,38,500	Carriage inward	16,340
Carriage outward	19,320		

Prepare a cost sheet showing (a) prime cost (b) factory cost (c) cost of production (d) cost of goods sold (e) cost of sales (f) profit.

[**Ans:**

(a) Prime cost ₹2,70,340
(b) Factory cost ₹3,45,350
(c) Cost of production ₹3,92,950
(d) Cost of goods sold ₹3,87,850
(e) Cost of sales ₹4,61,080
(f) Profit ₹77,420]

3. M/s. Indu Industries Ltd is the manufacturers of Moonlight torches. The following data relate to manufacture of torches during the month of March, 2009.

Raw materials consumed	₹20,000
Direct wages	₹12,000
Machine hours worked	9,500 hours
Machine hour rate	₹2
Office overheads	20% on works cost
Selling overheads	50 paise per unit
Units produced	20,000 units
Units sold	18,000 units at ₹5 per unit

Your are required to prepare cost sheet showing the cost and profit per unit and the total profit earned. **(B.Com., Madras University)**

[**Ans:** Cost per unit ₹3.06, Profit per unit ₹1.44 and Total profit ₹25,920]

4. The accounts of Nanda Ltd., a machine manufacturer shows the following cost data for the year ending on 31.03.2009:

Direct materials used	₹7,50,000
Direct labour	₹6,20,000
Works overheads	₹4,65,000
Office and administration overheads	₹3,21,125

Prepare a cost sheet showing works cost, and cost of production and percentage of office and administration overheads to works cost and factory overheads to direct labour.

In April 2009, the company received an enquiry for the supply of a machine. The machine will require direct materials costing ₹16,500 and direct labour accounting to ₹9,750. What price the company should quote for the supply of the machine when overheads are charged on above percentages. The company wants to earn a profit of 20% on selling price.

[**Ans:**

Works cost - ₹18,35,000
Cost of production - ₹21,56,125
% of factory overheads on direct labour - 75%
Percentage of office and administration overheads on works cost - 17.5%
Tender price of the machine - ₹49,294.91]

5. The following cost data are taken from M/s. Raj Industries for the year ending on 31.03.2009:

	₹
Purchase of Raw Materials	14,50,000
Stock of Raw Materials on 1.4.2008	1,35,000

Stock of Raw Materials on 31.3.2009	1,42,000
Manufacturing wages	11,70,000
Factory overheads	9,36,000
Office and general expenses	3,54,900
Stock of finished goods on 1.4.2008	94,000
Stock of finished goods on 31.3.2009	86,000
Sale of finished goods	43,03,090

The company is about to send a tender for a large plant. The costing department estimates that the materials required would cost ₹75,000 and wages to workmen for making the plant would cost ₹40,000. The tender is to be made to include the same percentage of profit the company earned in the year ended 31.03.2008. The company follows the policy of recovering factory overheads as a percentage on manufacturing wages and office overheads as a percentage on works cost. Calculate the selling price the company would quote for the plant.

[**Ans:**

Percentage of works overheads on direct wages	-	80%
Percentage of office overheads on works cost	-	10%
Percentage of profit on cost	-	10%
Tender price	-	₹1,77,870]

6. Following are the informations relating to the manufacture of 1,000 units of UPS produced by by Premier Industries Ltd., during the year ending on 31.03.2009:

Cost of materials	₹80,000	Direct wages	₹60,000
Works overheads	₹40,000	Office salaries	₹12,000
Rent and taxes	₹8,000	General expense	₹16,000
Selling expenses	₹10,000	Sales	₹2,50,000

Following estimates were made by the costing department of the company for the year ending on 31.03.2010.

(i) The output and sales would be 1,200 UPS.
(ii) The price of materials will rise by 20% on the previous year's level.
(iii) Wages will rise by 15%
(iv) Manufacturing expenses will rise in proportion to combined cost of materials and wages.
(v) Selling expenses per unit will remain unchanged.
(vi) Other expenses will remain unaffected by the rise in output.

From the above information prepare a cost statement for the year ending 31.03.2009 and estimated cost sheet for the year ending 31.03.2010, showing selling price per unit so as to show a profit of 10% on selling price.

[**Ans:** Total cost ₹2,26,000 and Profit ₹24,000 in the year ending on 31.03.2009 selling price p/u in the year ending 31.03.2010 ₹280.16]

7. Victory Ltd., produces emergency lamps. The production capacity is 5,000 units per month. The following are the production and cost data for the first 3 months of the year 2009.

Month	**Production** (units)	**Direct Materials** ₹	**Direct Wages** ₹	**Production overheads (semi-variable)** ₹
January	2,500	25,000	15,000	17,000
February	3,200	32,000	19,200	20,500
March	3,500	35,000	21,000	22,000

You are asked to find out the selling price per unit when the monthly output averages at 4,000 units. The profit desired is $12\frac{1}{2}\%$ on selling price.

[**Ans:** Selling price p/u ₹25.29]

Hint: *Variable factory overheads ₹5 p/u, fixed factory overheads ₹4,500*

8. An umbrella manufacturer produces two types 'Super' and 'Special'. The manufacturing cost for the year ended on 31.03.2009 are as follows:

Raw materials	₹5,40,000
Direct wages	₹3,00,000
Factory overheads	₹2,70,000

There is no work-in-progress at the beginning or at the end of the year. It is ascertained that (i) Direct materials of type 'Super' is twice as much as direct materials of type 'Special' (ii) Direct wages for type 'Special' are 60% of those for type 'Super' (iii) Production overheads was ₹15 per unit for both types. (iv) Administration expenses are 30% of works overheads for both types. (v) selling expense is ₹3 per unit for both types. (vi) Production during the year is: Super 10,000 units and Special 8,000 (vii) Units sold are : 'Super' 8,000 units and 7,200 units of 'Special' (viii) Selling price of Super is ₹100 per unit and special is ₹75 per unit.

Prepare a statement showing cost per unit and profit per unit of both types of umbrellas.

Ans:

	Super ₹	Special ₹
Cost per unit	93.68	70.03
Profit per unit	6.32	4.97

9. The production cost of 10,000 units of a product are: Materials ₹50,000, wages ₹40,000, chargeable expenses ₹2,500, fixed overheads ₹34,000 ,Variable overheads ₹20,000.

For manufacturing every 1,000 extra units of the commodity the cost of production increases as follows:

Materials	Proportionately
Wages	6% less than proportionately
Chargeable expenses	₹250

Fixed overheads	₹400
Variable overheads	10% less than proportionately

Calculate the estimated cost of production of 15,000 units and show how much it would differ if a flat rate of factory overheads based on wages are charged.

[**Ans:** Estimated production cost ₹2,02,550, difference (Increase) ₹14,380]

10. The following information has been taken from the cost records of Micro Technologies Ltd for the year ending 31.03.2009:

	₹		
Direct materials	3,50,000	Factory overheads	1,95,000
Direct labour	2,60,000	Administration overheads	1,44,900
Selling expense	96,600		
Distribution expenses	68,425		
Profit	2,35,000		

An work order has been executed in 2009-10 and the expenses incurred are - materials ₹45,000 and direct wages ₹36,000

Assuming that in 2009-10 the rate of factory overheads went up by 15%, distribution charges went down by 10%, administration and selling expenses increased by 16%. Find the selling price if the company wants to earn a profit of 20% on selling price. Factory overheads are based on direct wages and administration, selling and distribution expenses are based on works cost.

[**Ans:** Selling price: ₹1,99,519]

11. A manufacturing company has an installed capacity of 1,20,000 units per annum. The cost structure of the product manufactured is as under:

(i) Variable costs per unit:-

Materials	-	₹8
Labour (Subject to a minimum of ₹56,000 per month)	-	₹8
Overheads	-	₹3

(ii) Fixed overheads ₹1,04,000 p.a

(iii) Semi-variable overheads ₹48,000 per annum at 60% capacity, which increases by ₹6,000 per annum for increase of every 10% of the capacity utilization or any part thereof. The capacity utilization for the next year is estimated at 60% for 2 months, 75% for 6 months and 80% for the balance part of the year. If the company is planning to have a profit of 25% on the selling price, calculate the estimated selling price for each unit of production. Assume there is no opening and closing stock.

[**Ans:** Selling price ₹28.00]

12. A Television manufacturer makes 2 models, 21-inch and 29-inch models. From the following particulars, prepare a statement showing cost and profit per unit (per model) sold. There are no opening or closing stocks.

	21-inch ₹	29-inch ₹
Materials	27,300	1,08,680
Labour	15,600	62,920

Works overhead is charged at 80% on labour and office overheads is taken at 15% on works cost. The selling price of both the models is ₹1,000. 78 units of 21-inch and 286 units of 29-inch models were sold.

(B.Com., Madras University)

[**Ans:**

	21 inch ₹	29 inch ₹
Cost per unit	816.50	892.40
Profit per unit	183.50	107.60

]

13. Prepare a cost sheet for the year 2008 from the following showing the total cost and cost per unit. Number of units produced 2,000.

	₹
Opening stock of raw materials	10,000
Purchases	1,80,000
Direct wages	56,000
Indirect wages	48,000
Closing stock of raw materials	12,000
Work-in-progress on 1.1.2008	5,000
Work-in-progress on 31.12.2008	6,000
Factory overheads	26,000
Office overheads	45,000
Selling overheads	16,000
Opening stock of finished goods (100 units)	20,000
Closing stock of finished goods	120 units
Profit 10% on sales	

During the year 2009, it is decided to increase the production to 2,400 units. It is anticipated that:

(a) Materials prices will increase by 10%

(b) Wages will reduce by 20%

(c) Other expenses will remain constant per unit.

(d) Expected profit 20% on sales.

Ascertain the selling price to be fixed per unit. **(B.Com., Madras University)**

[**Ans:** Sales in 2008 - ₹3,57,511, Total cost in 2009 - ₹3,93,120, Profit - ₹98,280 and sales - ₹4,91,400, Selling price per unit - ₹204.75]

14. A manufacturer of scooter finds that in 2008, it costs him ₹72,00,600 to manufacture 350 scooters, which he sold for ₹27,000 each. The cost was made up of:

	₹
Materials	28,20,000
Direct wages	32,40,000
Factory overheads	4,86,000
Office overheads	6,54,600

For the next year he estimates that:

(a) Each scooter will require materials of ₹8,000 and labour ₹9,000.

(b) The factory overheads will bear the same relation to wages as in previous period

(c) The office overheads percentage on factory cost will be the same as in the past.

Prepare a statement showing the profit he would make per unit if he reduces the price of the scooter by ₹1,000. **(B.Com., Mysore University)**

[**Ans:** Profit per scooter ₹5,815]

15. A company's record shows the following particulars for the year 2008.

Production and sales	100 fans
	₹
Direct materials	25,000
Direct labour	10,000
Direct charges	1,000
Works overheads	9,000
Office overheads	5,000
Selling overheads	5,000
Profit	11,000

You ascertain that 80% of the works overheads fluctuates directly with production and 70% of selling overheads fluctuate with sales.

It is anticipated that the company would produce 500 fans per annum for the year 2009 and direct labour charges per unit will be reduced by 10% while fixed works overhead charges will increase by ₹2,400. Office overheads and fixed selling overhead charges are expected to show an increase of 10% and 20% respectively but otherwise no changes are anticipated.

Prepare a statement of cost and profit for the year 2009, assuming same percentage of profit as in 2008.

[**Ans:** 2009 - sales - ₹2,88,000, Profit ₹48,000]

Note: % of profit 20% on cost.

16. The following budgeted cost informations are available from the records of a manufacturing concern:

	(₹in lakhs)	
Direct materials	61.20	
Direct wages:		
Rolling shop (1,20,000 hrs)	6.00	
Milling shop (2,40,000 hrs)	14.40	20.40
Works overhead (allocation on labour hours)		
Rolling shop	9.60	
Milling shop	28.80	38.40
Administrative overheads		24.00
Selling overheads		28.80
Distribution overhead		14.40

The concern follows the absorption method of costing. On the basis of the above data, prepare a schedule of overhead rates. The sales division of the concern requires a cost estimate for a product for which the following information are available:

Direct materials: Materials X - 120 kg at ₹30 per kg.
Materials Y - 72 kg at ₹55 per kg.
Direct labour: Rolling shop - 40 hours at ₹6 per hour.
Milling shop - 70 hours at ₹5 per hour.

You are required to work out the cost estimate showing cost per unit using the above information and the overhead rates so computed. **(ICWA-Inter)**

[**Ans:** Cost of sales ₹14,523.60]

17. Cool Wind Ltd., manufacture fans which are sold at ₹400 per piece. The cost of sale is composed of 40% of direct materials, 30% wages and 30% overheads.

An increase in material price by 25% and in wage rate by 10% is expected in the forthcoming year. As a result of which the profit at current selling price may dwindle by 39% of present gross profit.

With the above information, you are required to (a) prepare a statement showing current and future cost and profit at present selling price and (b) determine the future selling price, if the present rate of gross profit is to be maintained. **(CA-Inter)**

[**Ans:** Present cost: 300, Profit ₹100 and gross profit % on cost 33.33%, Future selling price ₹452]

18. Mr. Rohit has a small furniture factory. He specialises in the manufacture of small dining tables of standard size of which he can make 15,000 a year. The cost per table worked out as under for the year 2007-08, when he made and sold 10,000 tables.

Materials	₹30
Labour	₹10
Overhead (fixed) recovered at 50% of materials cost	₹15
Total	₹55

Prices is fixed by adding a standard margin of 10% to total cost arrived at as above.

In 2008-09 due to fall in cost of materials, total cost worked out as under:

Materials	₹20
Labour	₹10
Overhead (fixed) recovered at 50% of materials cost	₹10
Total	₹40

Rohit maintained his standard margin of 10% on the cost of sales. Sales were at the same level as in 2007-08. You are asked to:

(a) Determine profit or loss for the year 2007-08 and 2008-09

(b) Compute the price which should have been charged in 2008-09 to yield the same profit or loss as in 2007-08 **(CA-Inter, May 2003) (ICWA-Inter)**

[**Ans:** Profit 2007-08 ₹55,000, 2008-09 ₹45,000 (loss). Revised selling price 2008-09 ₹50.50 per unit]

19. A manufacturing company has an installed capacity of 1,50,000 units per annum. Its structure is given below:

(i) Variable cost per unit:-

Materials	-	₹10
Labour (subject to a minimum of ₹1,00,000 per month)	-	₹10
Overheads	-	₹4

(ii) Fixed overheads ₹1,92,300 p.a

(iii) Semi-variable overheads per annum at 75% capacity (it will increase by ₹4,000 per annum for an increase of every 5% of the capacity utilization or part there of) - ₹60,000

The capacity utilisation for the next year is budgeted at 75% for first three months, 80% for the next six months and 90% for the remaining three months.

Required: If the company is planning to have a profit of 20% on the selling price, calculate the selling price for the next year. **(CA-Inter, Nov 2006)**

[**Ans:** Sales ₹40,01,312.50, Selling price per unit ₹32.83]

20. A re-roller produced 400 metric tons of M.S. bars spending ₹36,00,000 towards materials and ₹6,20,000 towards rolling charges. Ten per cent of output was found to be defective, which had to be sold at 10% less than the price for good production. If the sales realisation should give the firm an over all profit of 12.5% on cost, find the selling price per metric ton of both the categories of bars. The scrap raised during the rolling process fetched a realisation of ₹60,000.

(CA (PE. II), Nov 2005)

[**Ans:** Selling price per metric ton - good production ₹11,818.18, defective production ₹10,636.36]

Note: Convert the defective output into equivalent good units i.e. $40 \times \frac{90}{100} = 36$ metric tons. Total output: $360 + 36 = 396$ tons.

21. The following details have been extracted from the records of M/s Vijay Industries Ltd:

	₹
Stock of raw materials on 01.04.2008	90,000
Stock of raw materials on 31.03.2009	93,500
Direct materials purchased	2,46,000
Direct wages	1,75,000
Indirect wages	26,500
Indirect materials	38,700
Factory rent and rates	27,500
Power	22,000
Depreciation on plant and machinery	17,500
Expenses on purchase	15,000
Carriage outward	7,600
Salary - office	14,000
Salary - selling	12,500
Sales	7,25,000
Office rent and rates	16,000
Advertising	19,000
Travelling salesmen's salary and commission	23,800
Stock of finished goods on 01.04.2008	67,500
Stock of finished goods on 31.03.2009	61,000

Prepare a cost sheet showing prime cost, works cost, cost of production, cost of goods sold, cost of sales and profit.

[**Ans:** Prime cost ₹4,32,500, Works cost ₹5,64,700, Cost of production ₹5,94,700, Cost of goods sold ₹6,01,200, Cost of sales ₹6,64,100, Profit ₹60,900]

Job Costing and Batch Costing 14

- ☞ Job Costing - Meaning
- ☞ Features
- ☞ Objectives/Advantages & Limitations
- ☞ Cost Accumulation
- ☞ Job Cost Sheet-model/Summary
- ☞ Routines
- ☞ Batch Costing-meaning
- ☞ EBQ or EBS

There are certain industries where goods are produced against orders received from customers. An order received from a customer for a product/products is called a job. Each order received will be different from others in respect of materials to be used, production process involved, machines and tools to be employed, the departments through which it is to pass etc. So costs are accumulated for each job separately. For identification purpose each job is assigned a distinct number. The method of costing used to ascertain the cost of each job (or) work order is called job costing, or specific order costing (or) lot costing (or) job lot costing.

The following are the industries where job costing method is followed:

Shipbuilding, printing press, vehicle repair jobs, furniture producers, interior decoration, special machine tool manufacturers, foundries etc.

Features of Job Costing

1. Each job or work order is unique, different from each other requiring different production facilities.
2. Production commences after receiving orders from customers. Production is not for stock and future sale. So production process is not continuous.
3. Various elements of costs are estimated in advance to find the total cost of each job. Later profit desired is added to determine the price of jobs. Price of job is fixed in advance before production is taken up.
4. Usually prices of the jobs are fixed in advance before production is taken up.
5. All jobs may not go through all production processes.
6. The type of machines and tools to be used and level of skill required will be different for each job.
7. Each job or work order is a separate cost unit. Costs are collected separately for each job to find the cost and profit of each job.
8. Each job is given a district number for identification through various stages of production and cost accumulation.

Objectives of Job Costing

1. Ascertaining the cost and determine the profit or loss of each job separately.
2. Determining the value of work-in-progress.
3. Helps in collection, apportionment and absorption of overheads more accurately.
4. Detailed production control is established.
5. Helps in identification of weakness and wastage in production, thereby it helps to control costs.

Advantages of Job Costing

1. It helps to find the cost and profit of each job separately.
2. It helps to find the reasons for increase or decrease in costs. It helps in taking cost control measures.
3. Helps in comparing actual costs with estimated costs to find variances and taking measures to correct the deviations in future.
4. It helps in fixing the responsibility.
5. It helps in accurate estimating of cost of future jobs.
6. Detailed production planning is made and steps are taken to remove inefficiencies.
7. Helps in preparing tenders, quotation and estimates for cost plus contracts.

Limitations of Job Costing

1. As separate cost records are to be maintained it involves more accounting work.
2. Price for job is fixed in advance. As work is done in future, the actual cost may vary substantially if rates of various elements of costs have changed.
3. Determining overheads of each job is difficult because each job requires different production facilities.
4. Application of cost control technique is difficult as jobs differ from one another.

14.1 COST ACCUMULATION

Each job is charged with its cost. Each job is given a separate number. Cost accounting department prepares a separate cost sheet for each job. Materials cost are collected from materials requisition slips and materials analysis sheets. Labour cost is collected from job tickets or job cards. Overtime wages paid at customers request is to be charged as direct labour cost of that particular job. Overheads are to be charged for jobs by using a suitable method of recovery of overheads. A model of Job cost sheet is given below:

Job Cost Sheet

Job/Production order No: ________________ Quantity: ________________

Name of customer: ________________ Details of product: ________________

Commencement date: ________________ Date completed: ________________

Materials				Labour				Overheads				Remarks
Date	Department	Material requisition number	Amount ₹	Date	Department	Job Ticket No.	Amount ₹	Date	Department	Rate ₹	Amount ₹	
Total			xxxx				xxxx				xxxx	

Summary			
Particulars	**Estimated Cost**	**Actual Cost**	**Variance**
Materials Labour Overheads			
Total			

14.2 ROUTINES OF JOB COSTING

14.2.1 Receiving customer's enquiry

Usually customers visit the producer's place and enquire about the price, quality, time of delivery and other terms and conditions before placing an order. Some large organisations call for tender or quotation for the supply of products through newspapers by way of advertisement.

14.2.2 Preparing cost estimates, tender or quotation

In response to enquiries received from customers the cost accountant has to estimate the likely cost of production. Cost estimates are to be made with due care. Error in estimation may lead to under-pricing resulting in lower profit or even loss. Over-pricing will lead to loss of order. While estimating the cost rate, the future likely changes are to be considered.

14.2.3 Receiving customer's order

If price quoted and other terms and conditions are satisfactory to the customer, he will place order.

14.2.4 Production order

Production Order

Product: ________________ Quantity: ________________

Job no: ________________ Date of order: ________________

Materials requisition No: ____________ Date of commencement: ____________

Machine no: ____________ Date of completion: ____________

Clock Time	Operation No.	Department No.	Operation		Quantity	
			No.	Details	Made	Rejected

After the receipt of orders from customers, production order will be issued. Production order is an authorisation to production department to commence the production process. Production order will consist of details about the job, materials to be used, number of units to be produced, time by which work is to be completed etc. A standard production order format is shown in the table above.

14.2.5 Completion of job

After the work is completed, the production department will send a completion report to the costing department.

14.2.6 Computation of profit/loss

The cost accounting department compares the actual cost with the price of job. The difference is either profit or loss.

Illustration-1

X Ltd is to quote for job No: 123. The following are the direct costs estimated for the job.

Direct materials : 15 kg at ₹5 per kg
Direct labour : Department '*A*' - 8 hours at ₹6 per hour
Department '*B*' - 12 hours at ₹7.50 per hour

The following additional information is taken from the company's budget:

	₹
Department '*A*' variable overhead	48,000
Hours budgeted	16,000
Department '*B*' variable overhead	57,000
Hours budgeted	38,000
Fixed overheads budgeted	1,35,000

You are required to prepare a quotation for the job.

Solution

Job cost sheet. Job No. 123		
		₹
Direct Materials (15 Kg × ₹5)		75.00
Direct Wages - Dept. '*A*' (8 hrs × ₹6)	48	
- Dept. '*B*' (12 hrs × ₹7.50)	90	138.00
Prime Cost		213.00
Overheads :		

Variable - Dept. '*A*' (8 hrs × ₹3)	24	
- Dept. '*B*' (12 hrs × ₹1.50)	18	42.00
Fixed (20 hrs × ₹2.50)		50.00
Total Cost		305.00
Profit - 20% on selling price i.e. 20/80 on cost		76.25
Selling Price		**381.25**

Working Note

1. Variable Overhead rate per hour

$$\text{Dept. 'A'} - \frac{48{,}000}{16{,}000} = ₹3.00$$

$$\text{Dept. 'B'} - \frac{57{,}000}{38{,}000} = ₹1.50$$

2. Fixed Overhead Rate per hour $= \dfrac{1{,}35{,}000}{54{,}000} = ₹2.50$

Illustration-2

A foundry has received two jobs, work on which commenced on 1st July 2009. The following details of cost incurred are available:

	Job 56 (₹)	Job 89 (₹)
Materials issued from stores	5,000	7,500
Materials purchased direct	1,000	1,500
Direct wages	3,000	3,900
Materials returned to stores	250	250
Transfer of materials from Job No. 56 to Job No. 89	400	400

Overheads recovered at 50% on direct wages. Job No. 56 has been completed. Prepare accounts showing total cost and profit or loss on completed job. The price quoted for the job 56 is ₹11,000.

Solution

Job 56 account

	₹		₹
To Materials issued	5,000	By Materials returned	250
To Materials purchased	1,000	By Materials transferred to Job: 89	400

To Direct wages	3,000	By Sales	11,000
To Overheads -50% on direct wages	1,500		
To Profit transferred to P & L a/c	1,150		
	11,650		11,650

Job 89 account			
	₹		₹
To Materials issued	7,500	By Materials returned	250
To Materials purchased	1,500		
To Materials transfer from Job.56	400	By Balance c/d	15,000
To Direct wages	3,900		
To Overheads 50% on direct wages	1,950		
	15,250		15,250
To balance b/d	15,000		

Illustration-3

The following are the cost information relating to Job No: 345.

Direct materials - ₹2,000
Direct wages - Dept. X - 15 hrs at ₹10 per hour
Dept. Y - 12 hrs at ₹15 per hour
Dept. Z - 20 hrs at ₹20 per hour.

The estimated variable expenses for these departments are as follows:

Dept. X ₹15,000 for 5,000 labour hours.
Dept. Y ₹30,000 for 7,500 labour hours.
Dept. Z ₹20,000 for 10,000 labour hours.

The estimated fixed overheads are ₹1,68,750 for 22,500 hours. Add 20% on cost for profit. Draw up a cost sheet.

Solution

Job cost sheet - Job No: 345	
	₹
Direct materials	2,000.00
Direct wages: Dept X - 15 hrs × ₹10	150.00

Dept Y - 12 hrs × ₹15	180.00
Dept Z - 20 hrs × ₹20	400.00
Prime cost	2,730.00
Variable overheads:	
Dept × $\frac{15,000}{5,000} \times 15 = 45$	
Dept × $\frac{30,000}{7,500} \times 12 = 48$	
Dept × $\frac{20,000}{10,000} \times 20 = 40$	133.00
Fixed overheads $\frac{1,68,750}{22,500} \times 47$	352.50
Total cost	3,215.50
Profit 20% on cost	643.10
Selling price	3,858.60

Illustration-4

The following data are taken from the records of M/s Vijay Engineering Ltd which is using job costing for the year ending 31.03.2009.

	₹
Direct materials	7,50,000
Direct wages	6,00,000
Direct expenses	1,25,000
Factory overheads	4,80,000
Administration overheads	3,91,000
Selling and Distribution overheads	4,88,750
Profit	5,66,950

(a) Prepare a job cost sheet for the year ending on 31.3.2009.

(b) In April 2009, the company received an order for a job no. 222 requiring materials estimated at ₹1,50,000, direct labour will be ₹1,20,000 and directs expenses ₹30,000 selling and distribution expenses is expected to increase by 10%. The company recovers factory overheads as a percentage on direct wages and administration and selling and distribution overheads as a percentage on works cost. What price the company should quote for the job if it wants to earn the same rate of profit as in the year ending on 31.03.09.

Solution

Job cost sheet for the year ending 31.03.2009	
	₹
Direct materials	7,50,000
Direct wages	6,00,000
Direct expenses	1,25,000
Prime cost	14,75,000
Factory overheads	4,80,000
Works cost	19,55,000
Administration overheads	3,91,000
Cost of production	23,46,000
Selling and distribution overheads	4,88,750
Cost of sales	28,34,750
Profit	5,66,950
Sales	34,01,700

% of factory overheads on direct wages= $\frac{4,80,000}{6,00,000} \times 100 = 80\%$

% of administration overheads on works cost= $\frac{3,91,000}{19,55,000} \times 100 = 20\%$

% of selling and distribution overheads on works cost= $\frac{4,88,750}{19,55,000} \times 100 = 25\%$

% of profit on cost= $\frac{5,66,950}{28,34,750} \times 100 = 20\%$

Job cost sheet - Job N0. 222

	₹
Materials	1,50,000
Direct labour	1,20,000
Direct expenses	30,000
Prime Cost	3,00,000
Factory overheads - 80% Direct wages	96,000
Works Cost	3,96,000
Administration overheads- 20% on works cost	79,200
Cost of Production	4,75,200

Selling and distribution overheads - 25% on works cost	99,000
	5,74,200
Profit 20% on cost	1,14,840
Job Quotation Price	6,89,040

Illustration-5

The following information for the year ended 31st March 2009 is obtained from the books and records of a factory:

	Completed Jobs ₹	**Work-in-Progress** ₹
Direct materials issued	2,50,000	75,000
Direct wages	2,00,000	60,000
Direct expenses	50,000	10,000
Materials transferred to work-in-progress	4,000	4,000
Materials returned to stores	2,000	-

Factory overheads are 75% on wages and office overheads at 25% on factory cost. The value of jobs executed during 2008-09 was ₹9,50,000.

You are required to prepare:

(a) Consolidated completed job account

(b) Consolidated work-in-progress account

Solution

Consolidated Completed Job Account				
To Direct materials issued	2,50,000		By Customer's a/c (value of completed jobs)	9,50,000
(−) Materials transferred to work-in-progress	4,000			
	2,46,000			
(−) Materials returned to stores	2,000	2,44,000		
Direct wages		2,00,000		
Direct expenses		50,000		
Factory overheads (75% on wages)		1,50,000		

Factory Cost		6,44,000		
Office Overheads (25% on factory cost)		1,61,000		
Profit		1,45,000		
		9,50,000		9,50,000

Consolidated Work-in-Progress Account			
To Direct materials issued	75,000	By Balance c/d	2,42,500
Materials transferred from completed job	4,000		
Direct wages	60,000		
Direct expenses	10,000		
Factory overheads (75% on wages)	45,000		
Factory Cost	1,94,000		
Office overheads (25% on wages)	48,500		
	2,42,500		2,42,500

Illustration-6

The following information relates to a factory consisting of two departments - assembly and galvanising. All products pass through the two departments:

	Assembly	Galvanising
Materials	₹7,000	₹600
Direct wages	₹3,500	₹1,800
Works overheads	₹1,750	₹1,200
Direct labour hours	14,000	7,200
Machine hours	28,000	14,400

One of the job completed in the factory was No. 1177 and the following data relate to this job:

	Assembly	Galvanising
Materials	₹100	₹20
Direct wages	₹50	₹25
Direct labour hours	300	100
Machine hours	250	300

There are five methods by which works overhead could be recovered as a % of material, as a % of direct wages, as a % of prime cost, by direct labour hour rate and by machine hour rate. Using these methods, calculate the production cost of Job No. 1177.

(BBA, Bharathidasan, April 1992)

Solution

Calculation of Overhead Recovery Rates		
Basis of Apportionment	**Assembly**	**Galvanising**
(a) % on Materials cost	$\left(\frac{1,750}{7,000}\right) \times 100 = 25\%$	$\left(\frac{1,200}{600}\right) \times 100 = 200\%$
(b) % on labour cost	$\left(\frac{1,750}{3,500}\right) \times 100 = 50\%$	$\left(\frac{1,200}{1,800}\right) \times 100 = 66.67\%$
(c) % on prime cost	$\left(\frac{1,750}{10,500}\right) \times 100 = 16.67\%$	$\left(\frac{1,200}{2,400}\right) \times 100 = 50\%$
(d) Direct labour hour rate	$\left(\frac{1,750}{14,000}\right) =$ ₹0.125	$\left(\frac{1,200}{7,200}\right) =$ ₹0.167
(e) Machine hour rate	$\left(\frac{1,750}{28,000}\right) =$ ₹0.062	$\left(\frac{1,200}{14,400}\right) =$ ₹0.083

Job Cost Sheet - Job No. 1177 - under different methods of overheads recovery			
	Assembly	Galvanising	Total
(a) Material Cost Rate Method:			
Materials	100	20	120
Direct wages	50	25	75
Prime cost	150	45	195
Works overhead	25	40	65
Production cost	175	85	260
(b) Labour Cost Rate Method:			
Prime cost (see (a))	150	45.00	195.00
Works overhead	25	16.67	41.67
Production cost	175	61.67	236.67
(c) % of Prime Cost Method:			
Prime cost	150	45.00	195.00
Works overhead	25	22.50	47.50
	175	67.50	242.50

(d) **Labour Hour Rate Method:**			
Prime cost	150.00	45.00	195.00
Works overhead	37.50	16.70	54.20
Production cost	187.50	61.70	249.20
(e) **Machine Hour Rate Method:**			
Prime cost	150.00	45	195.00
Works overhead	15.50	25	40.50
Production cost	165.50	70	235.50

Note: Works overheads under various methods

	Assembly	**Galvanising**
(a) % of Materials cost	$100 \times \frac{25}{100} = ₹25$	$20 \times \frac{200}{100} = ₹40$
(b) % on Labour of cost	$50 \times \frac{50}{100} = ₹25$	$25 \times \frac{66.67}{100} = ₹16.67$
(c) % on prime cost	$150 \times \frac{16.67}{100} = ₹25$	$45 \times \frac{50}{100} = ₹22.50$
(d) Direct labour hour rate	$300 \times 0.125 = ₹37.50$	$100 \times 0.167 = ₹16.70$
(e) Machine hour rate	$250 \times 0.062 = ₹15.50$	$300 \times 0.083 = ₹25$

Illustration-7

Following data refer to the month of December 2008:

1.

	Job 410	**Job 411**	**Total**
Opening Balance of jobs on 1.12.08			
Direct materials	80	420	500
Direct wages	150	450	600
Factory overheads	200	400	600
	430	1,270	1,700

2. Direct materials requisition during the month of December 2008:

Job No.	₹
410	120
411	280
412	225
413	300
	925

3. Direct labour distribution:

Job No.	Hours	₹
410	400	600
411	200	450
412	300	675
413	100	225
	1,000	1,950

4. Factory overheads are applied to jobs on production according to direct labour hour rate which is ₹2

5. Factory overheads incurred in December 2008 ₹2100

6. Job Nos. 411 and 412 were completed during the month. They were billed to customers at a price which included 15% of the price of the job for selling and distribution expenses and another 10% price for the profit.

Prepare:

(a) Job cost sheets for Job Nos. 411 and 412.

(b) Determine the price of the job.

(c) Calculate the value of work-in-progress and

(d) Prepare an income statement showing gross profit for the month of December, 2008.

Solution

Job Cost Sheet		
	Job 411	Job 412
Opening balance on 1.12.08	1,270	-
Direct materials in the month	280	225
Direct labour	450	675
Factory overheads at ₹2 per hour	400	600

Factory cost	2,400	1,500
Selling and distribution expenses (i.e. 15/75 of factory cost)	480	300
Cost of sales	2,880	1,800
Profit (10/90 on cost of sales)	320	200
Billing price of jobs	3,200	2,000

Work-in-Progress

	₹	₹
Opening balance on 1.12.08		1,700
Expenses in December:		
Materials		925
Labour		1,950
Overhead (1,000 × ₹2)		2,000
		6,575
Less: Factory cost of jobs completed:		
Job No. 411	2,400	
Job No. 412	1,500	3,900
Closing balance on 31.12.08		2,675

Income Statement

	₹	₹
Selling price - Job No. 411	3,200	
- Job No. 412	2,000	5,200
Less : Factory cost - Job No. 411	2,400	
- Job No. 412	1,500	3,900
Gross profit		1,300

Working Note

1.

		₹
Let Selling price be		100
Less : Selling exp.	15	
Profit	10	25
Factory cost		75

2. Selling and distribution expenses: $\frac{15}{75}$ of factory cost:

$$\text{Job 411} = 2400 \times \frac{15}{75} = ₹480$$

$$\text{Job 412} = 1500 \times \frac{15}{75} = ₹300$$

3. Profit $= \frac{10}{75}$ of factory cost (or) $\frac{10}{90}$ of cost of sales.

$$\text{Job 411} = 2880 \times \frac{10}{90} = ₹320$$

$$\text{Job 412} = 1800 \times \frac{10}{90} = ₹200$$

14.3 BATCH COSTING

Batch costing is an extension of job order costing. Batch costing is followed in industries where spare parts, small tools etc. are produced in specific lot sizes. There are many producers specialising in production of various auto spare parts and components. These spare parts and components are produced for supply to producers of vehicles as original equipment, in addition these are also produced for sale in replacement market. Sometimes goods are produced against orders received from customers. Critical components are produced internally for own consumption in assembly shop. A lot or batch is production of a specific number of similar units of a product. Production of various components are taken up for production one after another in certain specific quantity. The following are the industries where batch costing is followed:

Automobile spare parts and components production (ancillary units), garments production, shoe manufacturing, watches, toys production, pharmaceutical industries etc.

Cost Accumulation

Each batch is a unit of cost. Costs are calculated for each batch separately. Total cost of a batch is divided by the number of units produced in that batch to find the cost per unit. As in job costing, each batch is also given a number for identification and cost accumulation. Cost accumulation in batch costing is similar to procedure followed in job costing.

14.3.1 Economic Batch Quantity (EBQ) (or) Economic Batch Size

Spare parts and components are produced one after another with the help of same production facilities. But machines and tools are to be reset and adjusted each time when production is changed from one component to another. In this process machine operator and his assistant has to spend time and incur some expenditures for resetting the machines and tools. So machines will be reset only when a minimum number of units are to be produced and also maximum number of units to be produced in a batch will also be fixed. Production of large quantities in a batch will be uneconomical since goods produced are to be stored for long before sale and more capital is locked up. Setting up production for small quantities will also be uneconomical since set-up costs are to be borne by few units. So a quantity is to be fixed which is neither big nor small, that quantity will bring economy in production cost. That quantity to be produced in a batch is called Economic Batch Quantity (EBQ) or Economic Lot Size. Economic Batch Quantity can be calculated in three ways. One is trial-and-error method. Other way is using an equation which is similar to EOQ. The equation is as follows:

$$\text{Economic Batch Quantity} = \sqrt{\frac{2AS}{C}}$$

$A =$ Annual usage or annual demand
$S =$ Setting up cost per batch
$C =$ Carrying and storage cost per unit per annum

Third method of calculation of Economic Batch Quantity is presenting the relevant information in a graph. The relevant informations are inventory holding cost, setting up cost and annual demand for the component.

Illustration-8

Annual demand for a component is 30,000 units. Cost of set-up per batch is ₹600. Inventory carrying cost per unit per annum is ₹1.

(a) Calculate the total cost assuming batch size of 4,000 units, 5,000 units, 6,000 units, 7,000 units, 8,000 units, 9,000 units and 10,000 units. Also find the economic batch quantity.

(b) Using mathematical formula calculate economic batch quantity.

Solution

(a)

Batch Size (units)	No. of set-ups	Set-up costs ₹	Average carrying cost per annum	Total cost ₹
4,000	7.50	4,500	$\frac{4{,}000}{2} \times 1 = 2{,}000$	6,500
5,000	6.00	3,600	$\frac{5{,}000}{2} \times 1 = 2{,}500$	6,100
6,000	5.00	3,000	$\frac{6{,}000}{2} \times 1 = 3{,}000$	6,000
7,000	4.30	2,580	$\frac{7{,}000}{2} \times 1 = 3{,}500$	6,080
8,000	3.75	2,250	$\frac{8{,}000}{2} \times 1 = 4{,}000$	6,250

9,000	3.33	2,000	$\frac{9{,}000}{2} \times 1 = 4{,}500$	6,500
10,000	3.00	1,800	$\frac{10{,}000}{2} \times 1 = 5{,}000$	6,800

[**Ans:** Total cost is lower when batch size is 6,000 units. Hence economic batch size is 6,000 units.]

(b) Using EBQ formula,

$$\text{Economic batch quantity} = \sqrt{\frac{2AS}{C}} = \sqrt{\frac{2 \times 30{,}000 \times 600}{1}}$$
$$= 6{,}000 \text{ units}$$

Illustration-9

Calculate economic batch quantity from the following data:

Annual demand	20,000 units
Set-up cost per batch	₹10
Cost per unit	₹100
Cost of carrying inventory	10% of cost

Also calculate the number of batches to be set in a year.

Solution

$$\text{Economic batch quantity} = \sqrt{\frac{2AS}{C}}$$
$$= \sqrt{\frac{2 \times 20{,}000 \times 10}{10}}$$
$$= 200 \text{ units}$$

$$\text{No. of batches to be set in a year} = \frac{\text{Annual demand}}{\text{EBQ}}$$
$$= \frac{20{,}000}{200}$$
$$= 100 \text{ batches}$$

Note: Carrying cost $= 100 \times \frac{10}{100} =$ ₹10.

Illustration-10

A Ltd. is committed to supply 24,000 bearings per annum to B Ltd. on a steady basis. It is estimated that it costs 10 paise as inventory holding cost per bearing per month and that the set-up cost per run of bearing manufacture is ₹324.

(i) What should be the optimum run size for bearing manufacture.

(ii) What would be the interval between two consecutive optimum runs?

(iii) Find out the minimum inventory holding cost per annum.

(CA-Inter, Nov. 2000)

Solution

(i) Economic batch quantity $= \sqrt{\frac{2AS}{C}} = \sqrt{\frac{2 \times 24{,}000 \times 324}{1.20}}$

$= 3{,}600$ units

Note: Inventory holding cost $= 0.10 \times 12 =$ ₹1.20 per unit per annum.

(ii) Interval between two consecutive optimum runs $= \frac{\text{No. of days in a year}}{\text{No. of batches in a year}}$

$= \frac{365}{6.67} = 55$ days

Note: Number of batches in a year $= \frac{24{,}000}{3{,}600} = 6.67$ batches.

(iii) Minimum inventory holding cost per annum $= \frac{3{,}600}{2} \times 1.20 =$ ₹2,160

Illustration-11

Following information relates to manufacture of a component 101 in a cost centre:

Cost of materials	6 paise per unit
Operator wages	72 paise an hour
Machine hour rate	₹1.50
Setting up time of the machine	2 hours 20 minutes
Manufacturing time	10 minutes per component

Prepare a cost sheet showing both production and setting up cost, total cost and cost per unit when batch consists of (i) 10 components, (ii) 100 components and (iii) 1,000 components.

Solution

Batch Cost Sheet						
	10 Units		100 Units		1,000 Units	
	Total ₹	Per unit ₹	Total ₹	Per unit ₹	Total ₹	Per unit ₹
Setting up costs:						
(i) Operator wages for 2 hours 20 minutes (see WN)	1.68		1.68		1.68	
(ii) Machine expenses for 2 hours 20 minutes	3.50		3.50		3.50	
	5.18	0.52	5.18	0.05	5.18	0.005
Production costs:						
(i) Materials at 6 paise per unit	0.60	0.06	6.00	0.06	60	0.060
(ii) Wages at 72 paise per hour	1.20	0.12	12.00	0.12	120	0.120
(iii) Machine expenses at ₹1.50 per hour	2.50	0.25	25.00	0.25	250	0.250
	4.30	0.43	43.00	0.43	430	0.43
Total cost	9.48	0.948	48.18	0.4818	435.18	0.43518

Note: Operator wages for 2 hrs 2 minutes $= \frac{72}{60} \times 140 = 168$ paise or ₹1.68.

Illustration-12

Leo Ltd. undertakes to supply 1,000 units of a component per month for the month of January, February and March. Every month a batch order is opened against which materials and labour cost are booked at actual. Overheads are levied on the basis of labour hours. The selling price is contracted at ₹15 per unit.

From the following data, present the cost and profit per unit of each batch order and overall position of the order for 3,000 units. Ignore set-up costs.

Month	Batch Output (Numbers)	Materials Cost (₹)	Labour Cost (₹)
January	1,250	6,250	5,000
February	1,500	9,000	6,000
March	1,000	5,000	4,000

Labour is paid at the rate of ₹4 per hour. The other details are:

Month	Overhead (₹)	Total labour hours
January	12,000	4,000
February	9,000	4,500
March	15,000	5,000

(CA-Inter)

Solution

Statement showing cost and profit on each month				
	January (1,250 units) ₹	February (1,500 units) ₹	March (1,000 units) ₹	Total (3,750 units) ₹
Materials	6,250	9,000	5,000	20,250
Wages	5,000	6,000	4,000	15,000
Overheads	3,750	3,000	3,000	9,750
Total cost	15,000	18,000	12,000	45,000
Sales at ₹15 per unit	18,750	22,500	15,000	56,250
Profit	3,750	4,500	3,000	11,250
Profit per unit	3.00	3.00	3.00	3.00
Cost per unit	12.00	12.00	12.00	12.00

Overall position for 3 months for supply of 3,000 units

Sales 3,000 units × ₹15 = 45,000
(−) Cost 3,000 units × ₹12 = 36,000
Profit = 9,000

Illustration-13

You are required to prepare a job cost sheet showing the actual cost, estimated cost and variances of a batch of 1,000 units from the following information relating to M/s. Siva Engineering Co. Ltd.

Preparation work is undertaken in three departments, X, Y and Z.

Materials used for the batch:

Department X - 400 units at ₹20 per unit
Department Y - 100 units at ₹10 per unit

Direct labour charges:

Department X - 200 hours at ₹5 per unit
Department Y - 100 hours at ₹12.50 per unit
Department Z - 100 hours at ₹10 per unit

Factory overheads:

Department X - 125% of direct labour
Department Y - at 200% of direct labour
Department Z - at ₹20 per labour per hour.

Surplus materials 50 units found in Department X is returned to stores.

A comparison of the actual costs with the estimated cost of direct materials and factory overheads has shown that the actual costs exceeded the respective estimated costs by 25 percent, whereas the actual labour cost has gone down by 10% over the estimated costs.

Solution

Batch Cost Sheet - 1,000 units			
	Actual (₹)	**Estimated** (₹)	**Variances Adverse (A)/ Favourable (F)**
Materials:			
Department X - $(400 \times 20) = 8{,}000$			
Less: Return to stores $(50 \times 20) = 1{,}000$	7,000	5,600	1,400 (A)
Department Y - (100×10)	1,000	800	200 (A)
Direct Labour:			
Dept. X - (200×5)	1,000	1,111	111 (F)
Dept. Y - (100×12.50)	1,250	1,389	139 (F)
Dept. Z - (100×10)	1,000	1,111	111 (F)
Factory Overheads:			
Dept. X - $(1000 \times \frac{125}{100})$	1,250	1,000	250 (A)
Dept. Y - $(1250 \times \frac{200}{100})$	2,500	2,000	500 (A)
Dept. Z - (100×20)	2,000	1,600	400 (A)
Total	17,000	14,611	2,389 (A)

14.4 EXERCISE

I. Objective Type Questions

A. State whether the following statements are true or false

(i) Job costing is followed in industries where production is continuous and repetitive.
(ii) Each job is different from other jobs.
(iii) Job costing is a specific order costing.
(iv) Total cost incurred during period is divided by the number of jobs completed during the period to find the cost of each job.
(v) Job costing is suitable for vehicle repair shops.
(vi) Prices of jobs are fixed in advance before production is taken up.
(vii) Batch costing is followed in industries producing spare parts, small tools and components.
(viii) All units produced in a batch are similar to each other.
(ix) Set-up cost and holding are same at economic batch quantity.

[**Ans:** *False:* (i), (iv) *True:* (ii), (iii), (v), (vi), (vii), (viii), (ix)]

B. Fill in the blanks

(i) Unit costing or output costing is applied in industries where goods produced are ____________.

(ii) Method of costing followed in industries where goods are produced according to customers specifications ____________.

(iii) The cost statement opened to ascertain the cost of each job is called ____________.

(iv) The batch size where production cost is minimum is called ____________.

[**Ans:** (i) Similar/homogenous, (ii) Job costing, (iii) Job cost sheet, (iv) EBQ]

II. Theory Questions

A. Short answer type questions

1. Name the industries suitable for job costing .
2. Name the industries suitable for batch costing.
3. Explain the special features of job costing.
4. What is economic batch quantity?

B. Long answer type questions

1. What is job costing?
2. Explain the special features of job costing.
3. Specify the industries where job costing is more suitable.
4. What are the objectives of job costing?
5. Explain the prerequisites of a job costing.
6. Explain the importance of 'estimating' in job costing.
7. What is batch costing?
8. List out the industries where batch costing is applied.
9. What is economic batch quantity? How it is computed?
10. What are the important features of job costing?
11. Explain the advantages and limitations of job costing.
12. Explain the various methods of calculating economic batch quantity.
13. Distinguish between job costing and process costing.

III. Practical Problems

A. Short answer type questions

1. Find the cost of job no. 505, from the following details:

Materials issued for the job	₹20,000
Surplus materials returned to stores	₹750
Materials transferred to other jobs	₹1,250
Wages	₹12,000

   Factory overheads charged at 75% on wages
   Administration overheads recovered at 10% of work cost

   [**Ans:** Total cost of job no. 505 - ₹42,900]

2. The following informations are available for the job no. 222.

Direct materials	₹40,000
Direct labour	₹25,000

   Factory overheads 40% of direct labour. Profit desired is 20% on selling price. Find the selling price of job no. 222.

   [**Ans:** selling price ₹93,750]

3. From the following details calculate profit from job no. 99.

Materials issued from stores	₹13,000
Materials received from other jobs	₹2,000
Direct wages	₹9,000
Factory overheads	50% on direct wages

Administration overheads 20% on works cost, Profit 20% on selling price.

[**Ans:** Profit ₹8,550]

B. Long answer type questions

1. The following information for the year ended 31st March 2009 is obtained from the books of a factory:

	Completed Jobs ₹
Raw materials supplied from stores	90,000
Wages	1,00,000
Chargeable expenses	10,000
Materials transferred to work-in-progress	2,000
Materials returned to stores	1,000

Factory overheads is 80% of the wages and office overheads 25% of factory cost. The value of the executed contracts during 2008-09 was ₹4,10,000.

Prepare consolidated completed jobs account showing the profit made or loss incurred on the contracts. **(B.Com., Madras University)**

[**Ans:** Factory cost - ₹2,77,000, Total cost - ₹3,46,250, Profit - ₹63,750]

2. The following particulars are given in respect of job number 505 of an engineering company:
Materials - ₹4,010

Wages:

Dept. A - 60 hours at ₹3 per hour
Dept. B - 40 hours at ₹4 per hour
Dept. C - 20 hours at ₹5 per hour

Variable overhead expenses for three departments were estimated as follows:

Dept. A - ₹5,000 for 5000 labour hours
Dept. B - ₹3,000 for 1500 labour hours
Dept. C - ₹2,000 for 500 labour hours

Fixed overheads:

Estimated at ₹20,000 for 10,000 normal working hours.

You are required to calculate the cost of Job No. 505 and calculate the price to give profit of 20% on selling price. **(B.Com., Madras University, Sep. 1988)**

[**Ans:** Total cost - ₹4,910, Profit - ₹1,227.50, Selling price - ₹6,137.50)]

3. From the records of a manufacturing company, the following budgeted details are available for the year 2010:

		₹
Direct materials		1,90,000
Direct wages:		
Machine shop (12000 Hours)	63,000	
Assembly shop (10000 Hours)	48,000	1,11,000
Works overhead:		
Machine shop	88,200	
Assembly shop	51,800	1,40,000
Administration overheads		90,000
Selling overheads		81,000
Distribution overheads		62,100

Assuming that the company follows the absorption method of costing, you are required to:

(a) Prepare a schedule of overhead rates from the figures available stating the basis of overhead recovery rates used under given circumstances:

(b) Work out a cost estimate for the following job no. 444 based on overhead rates so computed:

Direct materials X - 25 kg at ₹16.18 per kg
Y - 15 kg at ₹20.00 per kg
Direct labour - Machine shop 30 hours
- Assembly shop 42 hours

[**Ans:** (a) Overhead rates: Works overhead per direct labour hour - Machine shop ₹7.35, Assembly Shop - ₹5.18, Percentage of administration overheads on works cost 20.41%; Percentage of selling and distribution overheads on works cost - 32.45%.

(b) Total cost of Job : ₹2,295.44]

4. An engineering firm has three departments. The budgeted expenses for the ensuing year are:

		Dept. A	Dept. B	Dept. C
Materials	(₹)	10,000	10,000	7,970
Direct wages	(₹)	13,664	8,784	7,930
Direct expenses	(₹)	176	228	90
Works expenses	(₹)	9,760	6,484	6,110
Administration	(₹)	2,688	2,560	1,989
Labour hours		1,220	1,621	611

Works expenses are charged to output at a man hour rate and administrative expenses are charged as a percentage on works cost. What price should be charged to Job No. 61 to include a profit of 10% on cost, on which direct costs are as follows:

	Dept. A	Dept. B	Dept. C
Materials	420	300	240
Direct wages	450	350	335
Direct expenses	10	-	-
Direct labour hours	240	216	200

(B.Com., Madras University, May 1994)

[**Ans:** Price - ₹8,246.43; Profit - ₹749.68; Total cost - ₹7,496.75]

5. The following details are taken from Falcon Engineering Ltd. for the year 2008:

	₹
Materials used	1,50,000
Direct wages	90,000
Total overheads	75,000
Labour hours worked	25,000
Machine hours worked	30,000

The following are the details relating to Job No. 25:

Materials used (₹)	15,000
Labour hours	3,500
Direct labour (₹)	10,000
Machine hours	4,000

Calculate the total cost of the job using the following methods of recovery of overheads:

(a) Direct labour hour basis

(b) Direct wages basis

(c) Machine hour basis

[**Ans:** Total cost - D. Labour hour method - ₹35,500; Direct wages basis - ₹33,333, Machine hour basis - ₹35,000]

6. The following information was taken from Patel Engineering Ltd. for the year ended on 31st March 2009:

	Completed Jobs (₹)	Incomplete Jobs (₹)
Materials issued from stores	1,45,000	12,000

Direct wages	1,30,000	20,000
Direct expenses	17,500	6,000
Materials returned to stores	5,000	-

Factory overheads are 80% of wages, office overheads are 35% of factory cost and selling and distribution overheads are 10% of cost of production. The completed jobs realised ₹6,50,000.

Required:

(i) Prepare work-in-progress ledger control a/c

(ii) Prepare completed jobs ledger control a/c and

(iii) Cost of sales control a/c

[**Ans:** WIP ledger balance - ₹54,000; Completed jobs ledger -₹5,28,525; Cost of sales control ₹5,81,377.50]

7. A Ltd. received a job order for 500 units, the production of which has to pass through three production departments X, Y and Z. Machine hour rate is used to charge factory overheads to jobs. The machine hour rates for the departments are: Department X - ₹10, Department Y - ₹12, Department Z - ₹20.

   The production department spent the following machine hours on this job: Department X - 75 hours, Department Y - 60 hours, Department Z - 50 hours.

   The direct expenses for the job are direct materials ₹12,000 and direct wages ₹10,000.

   Administration Overheads are used to be charged at 30% on works cost. Due to rise in cost administration cost is expected to increase by 50%. From past experience it is found that 10% of gross production will be scrapped and sale of which will fetch 25% of its cost. Find the selling price of the job after adding 20% profit on cost. Also find the price per unit.

   [**Ans:** Price of the job: ₹41,513.35; Selling price per unit: ₹83.03]

8. Modern Industries Ltd. gives the following information relating to Job No. 25.

   Direct materials - ₹12,500

   Direct wages:

   Dept. A - 1,000 hours at ₹12 per hour
   Dept. B - 600 hours at ₹15 per hour

   Variable overheads:

   Dept. A - ₹40,000 for 10,000 labour hours
   Dept. B - ₹60,000 for 12,000 labour hours

   Fixed overheads:

   Estimated at ₹20,000 for 10,000 normal working hours.
   Calculate the cost of Job No. 25 and find the profit and profit percentage on sales. The selling price of the job is ₹52,000.

   [**Ans:** Total Cost - ₹43,700, Profit - ₹8,300, Percentage of profit sales 15.96%]

9. Easun Engineering undertook two jobs during the month of July 2009. The following are the cost data relating to the jobs.

	Job No. 44 (₹)	Job No. 45 (₹)
Materials issued	15,000	18,000
Direct wages	7,500	9,000
Factory overheads	4,500	5,000
Materials returned to stores	1,000	1,200
Material transfer from Jobs 44 to 45	2,500	2,500

Calculate the cost of jobs.

[**Ans:** Total cost: Job 44 - ₹23,500; Job 45 - ₹33,300]

10. Anand Ltd. supplies the following information relating to various jobs completed in the year ended 31st March 2009:

	₹
Materials used	3,00,000
Direct wages	2,50,000
Factory overheads	2,00,000
Administration overheads	75,000
Selling and distribution overheads	90,000
Profit	1,09,800

(a) Prepare a job cost sheet for the year ending on 31.03.2009. Also calculate factory overheads, percentage on direct wages, administration and selling and distribution overheads percentages on works cost.

(b) The company received many job orders for the year 2009-10. Estimated direct expenses for the job are - Direct materials ₹4,00,000 and Direct wages ₹3,60,000. Overheads are recovered on above percentages. During the year 2009-10, it is anticipated that factory overheads will go up by 15%, administration expenses will remain constant, and selling and distribution expenses are likely to come down by 10%. If the company wants to earn same percentage of profit on cost as in 2008-09, what should be the sale price of the jobs in 2009-10.

Ans: (a) 2008-09 - Total cost ₹9,15,000; Percentage of factory overheads on wages 80%; Percentage of administration overheads on works cost 10%; Percentage of selling and distribution overheads on works cost 12%, Percentage of profit on cost 12%.

(b) 2009-2010 - Sale Price ₹14,76,349.95; Profit ₹1,58,180.35

11. In a factory following the job costing method, an abstract from the work-in-progress account as on 30th September was prepared as under:

Job No.	Materials	Direct Labour		Factory Overheads
		Hours	₹	applied (₹)
115	1,325	400	800	640
118	810	250	500	400
120	765	300	475	380
	2,900		1,775	1,420

Materials used in October were as follows:

Materials requisition no.	Job No.	Cost (₹)
54	118	300
55	118	425
56	118	515
57	120	665
58	121	910
59	124	720
		3,535

A summary of labour hours deployed during October is as under:

Job No.	Number of Hours	
	Shop *A*	Shop *B*
115	25	25
118	90	30
120	75	10
121	65	-
124	20	10
	275	75
Indirect Labour:		
Waiting for materials	20	10
Machine breakdown	10	5
Idle time	5	6
Overtime premium	6	5
	316	101

A shop credit slip was issued in October, that materials issued in October under requisition No. 54, was returned back to stores as being not suitable. A material transfer note issued in October indicated that material issued under requisition no. 55 for Job 118 was directed to Job 124.

The hourly rate in Shop A per labour is ₹3 per hour while at Shop B, it is ₹2 per hour. The factory overhead is applied at the same rate as in September. Jobs 115, 118 and 120 were completed in October.

You are required to compute the factory cost of the completed jobs. It is the practice of the management to put 10% on the factory cost to cover administration and selling overheads and invoice the job to the customer on a total cost plus 20% basis. What would be the invoice price of these three jobs?

[**Ans:** Invoice prices: Job 115 ₹3,946.80, Job 118 ₹3,721.08, Job No. 120 - ₹3,598.32]

Batch Costing

12. Compute the economic batch quantity for a company using batch costing with the following information:

Monthly demand for the component	2,000 units
Set-up cost per batch	₹120
Annual rate of interest	6%
Cost of manufacture per unit	₹6

(B.Com., Madras University, Sep. 1992)

[**Ans:** Economic batch quantity - 4,000 units)]

13. From the following particulars find out the economic batch size:

Annual demand	12,000 units
Set-up cost per batch	₹120
Inventory carrying cost per unit per annum	₹6

[**Ans:** 693 units]

14. Leo Limited undertakes to supply 1,000 units of a component per month for the month of January, February and March. Every month a batch order is opened against which materials and labour cost are booked at actual. Overheads are levied at a rate per labour hour. The selling price is contracted at ₹15 per unit. From the following data, present the cost and profit per unit of each batch order and the overall position of the order for the 3,000 units.

Month	Batch Output (Numbers)	Material Cost (₹)	Labour Cost (₹)
January	1,250	6,250	2,500
February	1,500	9,000	3,000
March	1,000	5,000	2,000

Labour is paid at the rate of ₹2 per hour. The other details are

Month	Overheads Total (₹)	Labour Hours
January	12,000	4,000
February	9,000	4,500
March	15,000	5,000

(CA-Inter, May 87)

[**Ans:** Cost p/u - ₹10, Profit p/u ₹- 5, Total cost - ₹30,000, Total profit ₹15,000]

15. A company following batch costing supplies the following information relating to the production of component - X.15:

Materials cost per unit	₹9.50
Labour cost of machine operator per hour	₹7.20
Rate of production	5 units per hour
Machine hour rate	₹15
Machine set-up time	5 hours

Prepare a comparative batch cost sheet for the production of (i) 100 units, (ii) 500 units and (iii) 1000 units per batch.

Also calculate the cost per unit in each batch showing setup cost and production cost separately.

Ans:

	Batch (i) 100 units (₹)	Batch (ii) 500 units (₹)	Batch (iii) 1,000 units (₹)
Setup Cost	111	111	111
Production Cost	1,394	6,970	13,940
Total Cost	1,505	7,081	14,051
Cost per unit	15.05	14.162	14.051

16. The demand for an item is uniform at the rate of 25 units per month. The fixed cost is ₹30 each time production is made. The production cost is ₹3 per unit and the inventory carrying cost is 50 paise per unit per month. If storage cost is ₹3 per item per month, determine how often to make a production run and of what size (EBQ). **(ICWA-Inter)**

[**Ans:** EBQ - 55 units, Production run - One in every 66 days (or) 3.5 production runs in a year]

CONTRACT COSTING OR TERMINAL COSTING

15

- ☞ Meaning
- ☞ Features
- ☞ Contract costing and job costing - difference
- ☞ Important cost items - treatment
- ☞ Incomes of contract
- ☞ Cost of maintenance and rectification of defective work
- ☞ Incomplete contract - profit calculation methods
- ☞ Terms involved in contract

15.1 CONTRACT COSTING

Contract costing is a special type of job costing. It is followed in construction and erection industries, where works like construction of buildings, dams, canals, bridges, shopping complexes, ships, road laying, sewerage plants etc. are taken up. Contract costing is also called terminal costing. Each contract is a unit of costing.

15.1.1 Features of Contract Costing

1. It is mainly connected with construction work.
2. Scale and size of contracts are large.
3. Each contract is a unit of cost.

4. Materials and labour costs form the major part of contract cost.
5. Major part of contract costs are direct costs.
6. Overhead cost forms only a small part of contract cost.
7. Works are done outside the contractor's office.

A contract may be defined as an agreement where one party agrees to do some work for another for an agreed sum. The person agreeing to do the work is called the contractor. The person for whom the work is done is called contractee. The price agreed for the work is called contract price.

A contractor will open a contract ledger wherein a separate account will be opened for each contract. Each contract is given a separate number.

15.1.2 Difference between Job Costing and Contract Costing

S.No	Points of Difference	Job Costing	Contract Costing
1	Size	Value of jobs is comparatively small.	Value of work is large.
2	Period	Each job takes a shorter period for completion.	As the contract is for a large work, it takes longer period for completion.
3	Place of work	Work is done in the contractor's place of business.	Work is done outside the contractor's place - work is done at the place allotted by contractee.
4	Elements of cost	Overhead cost is considerable.	Materials and labour costs are major elements of cost. Overheads form only a small part.
5	Nature of expenses	Indirect cost forms a sizeable part.	Major costs are direct to the contract. Indirect costs form only a small part.
6	Cost ascertainment	Detailed and lengthy work is involved in the evaluation of overhead recovery rates.	Since all expenses are direct. Cost ascertainment is simple.
7	Profit ascertainment	The profit or loss of a job is computed after the work is completed.	Almost all contracts take more than a year for completion, there is a need for calculating profit on incomplete contracts.
8	Payment of price	Usually the price agreed is received in advance before commencement of work.	Payments are made in instalments as work progresses.

15.1.3 Nature of Contract Account

Separate contract accounts are opened for each contract in the contract ledger. All expenses relating to contracts are debited in the respective contract accounts and incomes are credited in the contract account. The difference between the debit and credit side is either profit or loss.

15.2 TREATMENT OF IMPORTANT COST ITEMS

15.2.1 Materials Cost

Materials cost is the major cost of a contract. Materials may be issued from stores or purchased directly which is debited to contract. Some materials may turnout to be unsuitable for the contract or surplus. These are returned to stores and credited to contract account. Sometimes surplus or unsuitable materials may be sold at contract spot itself, the cost price of materials sold is credited to contract account. The profit or loss on sale of materials is transferred to profit and loss account.

15.2.2 Abnormal Loss of Materials

Materials may be damaged or lost due to accident, fire, theft etc. The cost of these materials are treated as Abnormal loss and debited to profit and loss account and credited to contract account. When damaged materials realise some amount, it is credited to profit and loss account. Abnormal loss is not allowed to influence the contract profit.

15.2.3 Normal Loss of Materials

Some materials may be lost which is normal to the contract work. The cost of these materials is part of contract cost. If residue materials like wood chipping, metal rod pieces, empty cement bags etc., are sold, the sale price is credited to contract account.

15.2.4 Transfer of Materials from One Contract to Another

Surplus materials from a contract should normally be returned to stores as a measure of cost control. In times of emergency and as a matter of expediency surplus materials of a contract may be allowed to be transferred to another contract under advice to stores and costing department.

All materials are specific to a contract and forms the direct materials cost of the contract. Materials at site at the end is credited to contract accounts.

15.2.5 Labour Cost

All workers usually spend their whole time on a particular contract. All wages will be direct labour cost of the contract. Some people like engineers, supervisors may spend their time on two or more contracts. Their wages and salaries are to be apportioned to the respective contracts on the basis of time devoted to each contract.

15.2.6 Special Plant and Equipment

When a plant and equipment is purchased for exclusive use in a particular contract, then its cost price is debited to the contract and its book value at the end is credited to the contract account. A machinery may be used for two or more contracts, then its depreciation is apportioned on some suitable basis over the contracts and debited to the contract account. Value of plants returned, transferred to other contracts and damaged plants are credited to the contract account. Value of machines at the site is credited to the contract account at its book value on the last date of the period.

15.2.7 Subcontract Cost

A main contractor may do some work through subcontracting like foundation laying, electrical work, plumbing work etc. subcontract price paid by the main contractor is a direct charge and debited to the contract account.

15.2.8 Overheads

General office expenses, management staff salaries and fees, interest on loans borrowed are common expenses. It is apportioned to various contracts on some suitable overhead recovery methods.

15.3 INCOMES OF CONTRACTS

(a) When a contract is completed, the contract price is the income and is credited to the contract account.

(b) When contract is incomplete.

When work completed reaches certain agreed stages, the surveyor or architect of contractee will inspect the work and will issue a certificate stating the value of work completed. It is called work certified. It is debited to work-in-progress account and credited to contract account. Some work done after certification but yet to be certified is called work uncertified. It is also debited to work-in-progress account and credited to contract account. Work uncertified is valued at cost. The various expenses incurred since certification to the last day of the year is the cost of work uncertified.

15.3.1 Cost of Maintenance and Rectification of Defective Work

Sometimes a contractor may be under contractual obligation to maintain the assets for a certain agreed period. Similarly a contractor has to rectify the defective work by spending some additional amount. These costs are debited to the contract account.

15.3.2 Profit from Contract

(a) **Contract Completed:** When a contract is completed during the financial year and credit side of contract is more, the excess of the credit side over debit side is profit and it is transferred to the credit of profit and loss account. If the debit side of the contract account is more than the credit side, it is loss and transferred to the debit of profit and loss account.

(b) Contract is Incomplete: It is the usual practice to take credit for profit on incomplete contract in every financial year. If profit is recognised after the contract is completed it gives rise to many difficulties. Profit will be more in the year of completion and lower profits in other years where contract completed are less. More income tax is to be paid. To overcome the above difficulties profit are recognised every year for the value of work completed. Many methods are there for calculation of profit on incomplete contract.

15.3.3 Methods of calculating profit on incomplete contract

(a) No profit is recognised if the value of work completed and certified is less than 25% of total contract price.

(b) When work completed and certified is 25% or more but less than 50% of the contract price, ⅓ of notional profit is taken to the credit of profit and loss account. This ⅓ amount is also further reduced in proportion to cash received bears to work certified. This profit is called realised profit or profit on cash basis. The following step is used to calculate the profit on contract:

$$= \text{Notional profit} \times \frac{1}{3} \times \frac{\text{Cash received}}{\text{Work certified}}$$

(c) When work completed and certified is 50% or more, ⅔ of the notional profit as reduced in proportion to cash received is recognised. The following step is followed for calculating profit:

$$= \text{Notional profit} \times \frac{2}{3} \times \frac{\text{Cash received}}{\text{Work certified}}$$

(d) Profit on estimated basis may also be calculated. The following step is followed for calculation of profit:

$$= \text{Estimated profit} \times \frac{\text{Cost incurred till date}}{\text{Total estimated contract cost}}$$

(or)

$$= \text{Estimated profit} \times \frac{\text{Cost incurred till date}}{\text{Total estimated contract cost}} \times \frac{\text{Cash received}}{\text{Work certified}}$$

(e) Profit on contract which is almost complete and only a small part of work is pending.

It is possible to estimate the cost to complete the contract with reasonable accuracy. Total cost for completion of contract is calculated by adding future estimated cost for completion with actual cost incurred so far. The total cost is compared with contract price to arrive the total estimated profit. Profit is calculated by using the following step:

$$\text{Profit} = \text{Estimated profit} \times \frac{\text{Work certified}}{\text{Contract price}}$$

(or)

$$\text{Profit} = \text{Estimated profit} \times \frac{\text{Work certified}}{\text{Contract price}} \times \frac{\text{Cash received}}{\text{Work certified}}$$

(or)

$$\text{Profit} = \text{Estimated profit} \times \frac{\text{Cash received}}{\text{Contract price}}$$

The last step is commonly used for calculating profit on contract which is almost complete.

Loss on incomplete contract

Loss on incomplete contract is fully transferred to profit and loss account.

15.4 OTHER TERMS RELATED TO CONTRACT

15.4.1 Retention Money

Contractee makes payment to contractor in instalments as the work progresses based on the certificate issued by the contractee's architect or surveyor as to the work completed. Contractee does not make full payment for the work completed and certified. He may make payment equal to, say, 80% or 90% of work certified. The balance amount is retained to ensure that the contractor continues the work even if the contract cost increases. This amount retained is like a caution deposit. It will be released after the satisfactory completion of the work. This amount retained by the contractee is called retention money.

Notional profit

The excess of credit side over the debit side of an incomplete contract is called notional profit.

Reserve profit

A part of notional profit is kept as reserve to meet future contingency. The profit kept as reserve is called reserve profit.

Work-in-progress

1. When value of the work completed is less than 25% of contract price (or) no work has been certified. Value of work-in-progress is equal to the net expenditure incurred. So work-in-progress = Direct expenses + Indirect expenses incurred − Value of materials and plant in hand at the end of the financial year.

2. When value of work-in-progress is 25% or more of the contract price, Work-in-progress = Net Expenditure + Profit/(−) Loss transferred to P&L a/c

(or)
Work-in-progress = Work certified + Work uncertified – Profit/(+) Loss transferred to P&L a/c

15.4.2 Work certified

When work done reaches certain agreed stages in construction, the architect of the contractee will assess the work done and issue a certificate specifying the value of the work completed. The value of work completed and certified by the architect is called work certified.

15.4.3 Work uncertified

Some work might have been done till the end of the financial year after certification. But the work may not have reached next stage in construction for certification. So the work remains uncertified. This work is called work uncertified.

Illustration-1

The following information was extracted from the contract ledger of Surya Engineering Ltd. for the year ending 31.03.2009.

	₹
Materials issued from stores	5,75,000
Materials purchased direct for the contract	2,10,000
Direct Labour	60,000
Supervision	50,000
Administration expenses apportioned	90,000
Plant purchased on 1.10.2008	2,50,000
Materials returned to stores	15,000
Materials at site on 31.03.09	20,000

The contract price is ₹10,00,000. The contract work commenced on 01.07.08. The work was completed on 31.03.09. Charge depreciation at 20% per annum on plant. Plant was returned to stores on 31.03.09. Prepare the contract account.

Solution

Contract account			
	₹		₹
To Materials issued	5,75,000	By Contractee a/c (contract price)	10,00,000
To Materials purchased	2,10,000	By Materials returned	15,000

To Direct labour	60,000	By Materials at site		20,000
To Supervision	50,000	By Plant returned at cost	2,50,000	
To Administration expenses	90,000	(−) Depreciation	25,000	2,25,000
To Plant purchased	2,50,000			
To Profit-transferred to Profit and loss a/c	25,000			
	12,60,000			**12,60,000**

Illustration-2

IVCL Engineering Ltd., civil contractors, undertook a contract for ₹12,00,000. Work commenced on the contract on 01.04.2008. Other information relating to the contract for the year ending on 31.03.2009 are as below:

	₹
Materials issued	3,40,000
Direct wages paid	2,20,000
Direct expenses	25,000
Office overheads charged	40,000
Plant purchased on 01.07.08	1,00,000
Materials returned to stores	10,000
Cost of plant returned to stores on 31.12.08	40,000
Materials at site on 31.03.09	5,000
Cash received being 90% of work certified	7,20,000
Work uncertified	50,000
Depreciate plant at 10% p.a.	
Direct wages due on 31.03.09	15,000
Direct expenses due on 31.03.09	5,000

Prepare contract account for the year 2008-09 showing profit to be taken to profit and loss account of the year.

Solution

Contract account for the year ending 31.03.2009					
		₹			₹
To Materials issued		3,40,000	By Work-in-progress		
To Direct wages paid	2,20,000		Work certified - $7,20,000 \times \frac{100}{90}$		8,00,000
Add: Due	15,000	2,35,000	Work uncertified		50,000
To Direct expenses paid	25,000		By Materials returned		10,000
Add: Due	5,000	30,000	By Materials at site		5,000
To Office overheads		40,000	By Plant returned at cost	40,000	
To Plant purchased		1,00,000	(−) Dep. $\left(40,000 \times \frac{10}{100} \times \frac{6}{12}\right)$	2,000	38,000
To Notional profit		2,13,500	By Plant at site cost	60,000	
			(−) Dep. $\left(60,000 \times \frac{10}{100} \times \frac{9}{12}\right)$	4,500	55,500
		9,58,500			**9,58,500**
To Profit- transferred to Profit and loss a/c		1,28,100	By Notional profit b/d		2,13,500
To Reserve - (bf)		85,400			
		2,13,500			**2,13,500**

Note:

1) Profit $= \text{Notional Profit} \times \frac{2}{3} \times \%$ of cash received

$$= 2{,}13{,}500 \times \frac{2}{3} \times \frac{90}{100}$$

$$= ₹1,28,100$$

2) Since value of work certified is more than 50% of contract price $\frac{2}{3}$rd of notional profit is taken as profit.

Illustration-3

Vasudev, a civil contractor undertook a contract for the construction of a shopping complex for ₹20,00,000. The work commenced on 01.04.2008. The following data was extracted from his books for the year ending on 31.03.2009.

	₹
Materials issued from stores	2,40,000
Wages paid	1,10,000
Direct expenses paid	65,000
Wages unpaid on 31.3.09	15,000
Direct expenses due on 31.3.09	10,000
Machineries purchased on 1.4.08	75,000
Machinery transferred to other contract on 31.12.08	25,000
Machinery returned to stores on 30.9.08	10,000
Materials received from other contract	20,000
Materials at site on 31.3.09	9,000
Work certified	6,00,000
Cash received from contractee	5,25,000
Work uncertified	18,000
Machinery is to be depreciated at 10%	
Supervisor Salary	60,000 p.a.

Supervisor had spent approximately 7 months on this contract.

Prepare contract account for the year 2008-09 showing the profit transferred to costing profit and loss account. Also show the relevant items in the balance sheet.

Solution

Contract Account for the year ending 31.03.09

		₹			₹
To Materials issued		2,40,000	By Work in progress:		
To Wages paid	1,10,000		Work certified	6,00,000	
Add unpaid	15,000	1,25,000	Work uncertified	18,000	6,18,000
To Materials received from other contract		20,000	By machinery transferred:		
			at cost	₹25,000	22,500
			Less: Depreciation	₹2,500	
To Direct expenses paid	₹65,000		By Machinery Returned		
			at cost	₹10,000	9,000
Add Due	₹10,000	75,000	Less: Depreciation	₹1,000	
To Supervisor salary		35,000	By machinery at site		
			at cost	₹40,000	36,000
To Machinery at cost		75,000	Less: Depreciation	₹4,000	

To Notional profit		1,24,500	By Materials at site		9,000
		6,94,500			6,94,500
To profit - transferred to costing profit and loss a/c		36,313	By Notional profit b/d		1,24,500
To Reserve c/d (b/f)		88,187			
		1,24,500			1,24,500

Note:

1) Full depreciation has been charged on machinery transferred, machinery returned and machinery at site, since depreciation percentage is not expressed as per annum.

2) 1/3rd of notional profit is taken as profit as the value of work certified is above 25% but below 50% of contract price.

3) Profit $= \text{Notional Profit} \times \frac{1}{3} \times \frac{\text{Cash received}}{\text{Work certified}}$

$$= 1{,}24{,}500 \times \frac{1}{3} \times \frac{5{,}25{,}000}{6{,}00{,}000}$$

$= ₹36{,}313$

Balance Sheet (Extract) as on 31.03.09				
Liabilities	**₹**	**Assets**		**₹**
Profit and loss a/c	36,313	Work in Progress:		
Reserve	88,187	Work certified	₹6,00,000	
		Work uncertified	₹18,000	
			₹6,18,000	
Wages unpaid	15,000	Less: Cash received	5,25,000	93,000
Direct expenses due	10,000	Material at site		9,000
		Plant at site		36,000

Illustration-4

The following information were taken from the books of Canara Civil Engineers for the year ending 31.03.09.

	₹
Contract price	15,00,000
Cash received being 80% of work certified	6,00,000
Work uncertified	25,000

Materials purchased	3,45,000
Direct wages	2,80,000
Subcontract cost	40,000
Site expenses	70,000
Machineries purchased 01.07.08	90,000
Machinery returned to stores on 31.12.08	20,000
Materials returned to stores	20,000
Materials at site on 31.03.09	22,500

Materials costing ₹8,000 and machinery costing ₹10,000 were damaged in an accident. The damaged materials and machinery is sold for ₹1,250 and ₹2,000 respectively. Charge depreciation at 25% per annum on machinery.

Prepare contract account and show how the relevant items will appear in balance sheet.

Solution

Contract Account for the year ending 31.03.09

	₹			₹
To Materials purchased	3,45,000	By Work in progress:		
To Direct wages	2,80,000	Work certified $\left(6,00,000 \times \frac{100}{80}\right)$		7,50,000
To Subcontract cost	40,000	Work uncertified		25,000
To Site expenses	70,000	By Materials returned		20,000
To Machineries purchased	90,000	By Machinery Returned at cost	₹20,000	
		Less: Depreciation $20,000 \times \frac{25}{100} \times \frac{6}{12}$	₹2,500	17,500
To Notional profit	76,750	By Abnormal Loss:		
		By Materials damaged		8,000
		By Machinery damaged		10,000
		By Materials at site		22,500
		By Machinery at site at cost	60,000	
		$60,000 \times \frac{25}{100} \times \frac{9}{12}$		
		(−) Depreciation	11,250	48,750
	9,01,750			9,01,750

	₹			₹
To profit - transferred to costing profit and loss a/c $76{,}750 \times \frac{1}{2} \times \frac{80}{100}$	30,700	By Notional profit b/d		76,750
To Reserve c/d (b/f)	46,050			
	76,750			76,750

Balance sheet as on 31.03.09				
Liabilities	**₹**	**Assets**		**₹**
Profit and Loss a/c	15,950	Work in Progress:		
Reserve	46,050	Work certified	₹7,50,000	
		Work uncertified	₹25,000	
			₹7,75,000	
		Less: Cash received	6,00,000	
			1,75,000	
		(−) Reserve	46,050	1,28,950
		Material at site		22,500
		Machinery at site		48,750
	-			-

Working

1)

Abnormal loss account			
	₹		₹
To Contract a/c:		**By Cash:**	
Materials	8,000	Sale of materials	1,250
Machinery	10,000	Sale of machinery	2,000
		By abnormal loss transferred to costing P&L a/c	14,750
	18,000		18,000

2) Contract profit $= \text{Notional profit} \times \frac{1}{2} \times \text{Cash received \%}$

$$= 76{,}750 \times \frac{1}{2} \times \frac{80}{100}$$

$= ₹30{,}700$

3)

Profit transferred to Balance Sheet:	₹
Contract profit	30,700
(−) abnormal loss	14,750
Profit	15,950

Illustration-5

The following is the trial balance of ABC construction company engaged on one contract only, for the year ended 31.03.09.

	Dr ₹	Cr ₹
Contractee's account (amount received)		4,00,000
Buildings	2,00,000	-
Creditors	-	60,000
Bank balance	40,000	-
Materials	2,50,000	-
wages	2,20,000	-
Overheads	50,000	-
Plant and machinery	2,00,000	-
Capital account	-	5,00,000
	9,60,000	9,60,000

The work on the contract commenced on 1.4.08 materials costing ₹2,25,000 were sent to contract. Materials costing ₹5,000 destroyed in an accident. Wages of ₹2,20,000 were paid during the year. Plant costing ₹75,000 was used from 1.4.08 to 31.12.08 and was then returned to stores. Materials costing ₹5,000 were on site on 31.3.09.

The contract was for ₹7,50,000. 80% of contract work was certified. Work uncertified was estimated at ₹20,000.

Overheads charged to the contract was 20% of wages. Plant and machinery is depreciated at 20% for the whole year.

Prepare contract account and balance sheet.

Solution

Contract Account for the year ended 31.03.09			
	₹		₹
To Materials	2,25,000	By Work in progress:	
To Wages	2,20,000	Work certified	6,00,000
To Plant & machinery	2,00,000	Work uncertified	20,000
To Overhead 20% of wages	44,000	By Abnormal loss: Materials destroyed in accident	5,000
To Notional profit	1,04,750	By Plant returned to stores a Cost ₹75,000	
		(−) Depreciation ₹11,250	63,750

		By Plant at site at cost ₹1,25,000	
		(−) Depreciation ₹25,000	1,00,000
		By Materials at site	5,000
	7,93,750		7,93,750
To Profit transferred to costing profit and loss a/c	46,556	By Notional profit	1,04,750
To Reserve c/d (b/f)	58,194		
	1,04,750		1,04,750

Costing profit and loss Account			
	₹		₹
To Abnormal loss material damaged in accident	5,000	By contract profit	46,556
To Depreciation on plant returned to stores	3,750		
To overheads (50,000 – 44,000)	6,000		
To Net profit	31,806		
	46,556		46,556

Note:

1) Contract profit $= \text{Notional profit} \times \frac{2}{3} \times \frac{\text{Cash received}}{\text{Work certified}}$

$$= 1,04,750 \times \frac{2}{3} \times \frac{4,00,000}{6,00,000}$$

$= ₹46,556$

2) Depreciation on plant returned to stores - 9 months depreciation charged to contract account and 3 months depreciation charged to costing profit and loss account.

Balance Sheet as on 31.03.2009				
Liabilities	₹	**Assets**		₹
Capital	5,00,000	Building		2,00,000
Creditors	60,000	Work-in-progress:		
Profit and loss account	31,806	Work certified	₹6,00,000	
		Work uncertified	₹20,000	
			₹6,20,000	
		Less: Cash received	4,00,000	
			2,20,000	
		(−) Reserve	58,194	1,61,806
		Plant in stores at cost	75,000	

		(−) Depreciation	15,000	60,000
		Plant at site	1,25,000	
		(−) Depreciation	25,000	1,00,000
		Bank Balance		40,000
		Materials in stores		25,000
		Materials at site		5,000
	5,91,806			5,91,806

Illustration-6

ABC Ltd. began to trade on 1st January 2006. During 2006 the company was engaged on only one contract of which the contract price was ₹5,00,000. Of the plant and materials charged to the contract, plant which cost ₹5,000and materials which cost ₹4,000 were lost in an accident. On 31st December 2006 plant which cost ₹5,000 was returned to stores, the cost of work done but uncertified was ₹2,000 and materials costing ₹4,000 were in hand on site. Charge 10% depreciation on plant. Prepare contract account and balance sheet from the following:

Trial balance as on 31st December 2006:

	₹	₹
Share capital		1,20,000
Creditors		10,000
Cash received (80% of work certified)		2,00,000
Land and buildings	43,000	
Bank balance	25,000	
Charged to contract		
Materials	90,000	
Plant	25,000	
Wages	1,40,000	
Expenses	7,000	
	3,30,000	3,30,000

(B.Com., Madras University 1996)

Solution

Contract account for the year ending 31.12.2006				
	₹			₹
To Materials	90,000	By Work in progress:		
To Wages	1,40,000	By Work certified		2,50,000
To Plant	25,000	By Work uncertified		2,000

To Expenses	7,000	By Abnormal loss:		
To Notional profit c/d	21,000	Plant cost		5,000
		Materials cost		4,000
		By Plant returned - cost	5,000	
		(−) Depreciation	500	
				4,500
		By Materials in hand		4,000
		By plant at site - cost	15,000	
		(−) Depreciation	1,500	
				13,500
	2,83,000			2,83,000
To Profit - transferred to costing P&L a/c $21{,}000 \times \frac{2}{3} \times \frac{80}{100}$	11,200	By Notional profit b/d		21,000
To Reserve c/d	9,800			
	21,000			21,000

Balance Sheet as on 31.12.2006

Liabilities		₹	Assets		₹
Share capital		1,20,000	Land and building		43,000
Profit	11,200		Work-in-progress		
(-)Abnormal loss	9,000	2,200	Work certified	2,50,000	
			Work uncertified	2,000	
Creditors		10,000		2,52,000	
			Less: Cash received	2,00,000	
				52,000	
			Less: Reserve	9,800	42,200
			Bank		25,000
			Plant at store		4,500
			Materials in hand		4,000
			Plant at site		13,500
		1,32,200			1,32,200

Illustration-7

A contractor who prepares his accounts on 31st December each year, commenced a contract on 1st April 2005. The costing records concerning the said contract reveal the following information on 31st December 2005.

	₹
Materials charged to site	2,58,100
Labour engaged	5,60,500
Foreman's salary	79,300

Plant costing ₹2,60,000 has been on site for 146 days. Their working life is estimated at 7 years and their final scrap valued at ₹15,000. A supervisor, who is paid ₹4,000 p.m. has devoted approximately 3/4th of his time to this contract. The administrative and other expenses amounted to ₹1,40,000. Material in hand at site on 31st December 2005 cost ₹25,400. Some of the material costing ₹4,500 was found unsuitable and was sold for ₹4,000 and part of the plant costing ₹5,500 (on 31.12.2005) unsuited to the contract was sold at a profit of ₹1,000.

The contract price was ₹20,00,000. On 31st December 2005, two-thirds of the contract was completed. Architects certificate has been issued covering 50% of the contract price and ₹7,50,000 has so far been paid on account. Prepare contract account and contractee's account. Show how these accounts will appear in the Balance Sheet as on 31st December 2005. Depreciation charged on time basis.

Solution

Contract Account for the year ending 31.12.2005

	₹		₹
To Materials	2,58,100	By Materials site	25,400
To Labour	5,60,500	By Materials sold - cost	4,500
To Foreman's salary	79,300	By Cost of contract (bf)	10,49,000
To Supervisor's salary (see WN-1)	27,000		
To Depreciation on plant (see WN -2)	14,000		
To Administration and other expenses	1,40,000		
	10,78,900		10,78,900
		By Work-in-progress:	
To Cost of contract b/d	10,49,000	Work Certified	10,00,000
To Notional profit c/d	2,13,250	Work uncertified (see WN 3)	2,62,250
	12,62,250		12,62,250
To Profit transferred to costing profit and loss	1,06,625	By Notional profit b/d	2,13,250
To Reserve c/d	1,06,625		
	2,13,250		2,13,250

Balance Sheet as on 31.12.2005					
Liabilities		₹	**Assets**		₹
Profit	1,06,625		Work-in-progress		
Add: Profit on sale of plant	1,000		Work certified	10,00,000	
			Work uncertified	2,62,250	
	1,07,625			12,62,250	
Less: Loss on sale of materials	500		Less: Cash received	7,50,000	
		1,07,125		5,12,250	
			Less: Reserve	1,06,625	4,05,625
			Materials at site		25,400
			Plant at cost	2,60,000	
			(–) Plant sold	5,500	
				2,54,500	
			(–) Depreciation	14,000	2,40,500
		–			–

Working Note

1. Supervisor's salary $= 4{,}000 \times 12 \times \frac{9}{12} \times \frac{3}{4} = ₹27{,}000$

2. Depreciation on plant $= \frac{2{,}60{,}000 - 15{,}000}{7} \times \frac{146}{365} = ₹14{,}000$

3. Work uncertified:

   Cost of 2/3 contract = ₹10,49,000

   Cost of full contract $= 10{,}49{,}000 \times \frac{3}{2} = ₹15{,}73{,}500$

   Cost of 50% on contract certified $= \frac{15{,}73{,}500}{2} = ₹7{,}86{,}750$

   Cost of uncertified work = 10,49,000 – 7,86,750 = ₹2,62,250

4. Profit $= \text{Notional profit} \times \frac{2}{3} \times \frac{\text{Cash received}}{\text{Work certified}}$

   $= 2,13,250 \times \frac{2}{3} \times \frac{7,50,000}{10,00,000}$

   $= ₹1{,}06{,}625$

Contractee Account			
	₹		₹
To Balance c/d	7,50,000	By Bank	7,50,000
	7,50,000		7,50,000

Illustration-8

Premier Constructions Ltd undertook a contract. The work commenced on the contract on 1st April 2008. The following information was taken from the contract ledger as on 31st March 2009.

(i) The contract price was ₹3,00,000.

(ii) The architect had issued a certificate stating that 3/4th of contract had been completed on 20th March.

(iii) Depreciation of plant was ₹8,000.

(iv) Cash received on contract ₹2,00,000

(v) The expenses incurred on the contract up to 31st March 2009 were:

	₹
Materials purchased	90,000
Direct wages	75,000
Materials issued from stores	30,000
Plant purchased	50,000
Administration overheads	30,000
Materials returned to stores	10,000
Materials at site on 31st March	11,000

(vi) The above summary of expenses includes the following expenses incurred after 20th March 2009:

	₹
Materials	20,000
Direct wages	15,000
Administration	12,000

(vii) A fine of ₹2,500 in likely to be imposed for delay in completion.

(viii) Ignore depreciation on plant for the valuation of uncertified work.

You are required to prepare the contract account for the year ending on 31.03.2009.

Solution

Contract Account for the year ending 31.03.2009			
	₹		₹
To Materials purchased	90,000	Work in progress:	
To Materials issued	30,000	Work certified	2,25,000
To Direct wages	75,000	Work uncertified	47,000
To Administration overheads	30,000	Materials returned	10,000
To Plant depreciation	8,000	Materials at site	11,000
To notional profit c/d	60,000		
	2,93,000		2,93,000
To Profit transferred to costing profit and loss a/c	35,556	By Notional profit b/d	60,000
To Reserve c/d	24,444		
	60,000		60,000

Note:

1) Work uncertified (Cost incurred after 20th March)

Materials	₹20,000
D. wages	₹15,000
Administration overheads	₹12,000
	₹47,000

2) $$\text{Profit} = \text{Notional profit} \times \frac{2}{3} \times \frac{\text{Cash received}}{\text{Work certified}}$$

$$= 60,000 \times \frac{2}{3} \times \frac{2,00,000}{2,25,000}$$

$$= ₹35,556$$

Illustration-9

Engineers Ltd. undertook several contracts during the year 2002. The following information relate to contract no. 107.

Direct materials		₹20,250
Direct wages		₹15,500
Stores issued		₹10,500
Loose tools		₹2,400
Tractor expenses:		
Running expenses	2,300	
Wages of driver	3,000	₹5,300
Other direct charges		₹2,650

The contract took 13 weeks for its completion. The values of loose tools and stores returned at the end of the period were ₹200 and ₹3,000 respectively. The plant was also returned at a value of ₹16,000 after charging depreciation at 20%. The value of tractor was ₹20,000 and the depreciation was to be charged to the tractor at 15% per annum. The administration and office expenses are to be provided at 10% on works cost. Profit is to be charged at 20% of the total cost.

Calculate the contract price and prepare the contract account assuming the contract price was duly received from the contractee. **(B.Com. (Hons.), Delhi University, modified)**

Solution

Computation of contract price		
Direct materials		₹20,250
Direct wages		₹15,500
Stores issued	₹10,500	
(−) Returned	₹3,000	₹7,500
Loose tolls	₹2,400	
(−) Returned	₹200	₹2,200
Depreciation - plant		₹4,000
Depreciation - Tractor $20{,}000 \times \frac{15}{100} \times \frac{13}{52} =$		₹750
Tractor expenses		₹5,300
Other direct charges		₹2,650
Work cost		₹58,150
Administration and office expenses - 10% of works cost		₹5,815
Total cost		₹63,965
Profit 20% of total cost		₹12,793
Contract price		₹76,758

Contract Account No. 107			
	₹		₹
To Direct materials	20,250	By Contractee account (Contract price)	76,758
To Direct wages	15,500	By Loose tools returned	200
To Stores	10,500	By Stores returned	3,000
To Loose tools	2,400		

To Tractor expenses	5,300		
To Depreciation - Tractor	750		
- Plant $\left(16{,}000 \times \frac{20}{80}\right)$	4,000		
To Other direct charges	2,650		
To Administration expenses	5,815		
Profit - transferred to costing P&L a/c	12,793		
	79,958		79,958

Illustration-10

An expenditure of ₹1,94,000 has been incurred on a contract to the end of March 2003. The value of work certified is ₹2,20,000. The cost of work done but not yet certified is ₹6,000. It is estimated that the contract will be completed by 30th June, 2003 and an additional expenditure of ₹40,000 will have to be incurred to complete the contract. The total estimated expenditure on the contract is to include a provision of $2\frac{1}{2}\%$ for contingencies. The contract price is ₹2,80,000 and ₹2,00,000 has been realised in cash up to 31st March 2003.

Calculate the proportion of profit to be taken to the profit and loss account as on 31st 2003 under different methods. **(B.Com. (Hons.), Delhi University)**

Solution

Contract Account			
To Contract cost	1,94,000	By Work-in-progress:	
To Notional profit	32,000	Work certified	₹2,20,000
		Work uncertified	₹6,000
	2,26,000		₹2,26,000

Methods of calculating profit:

1. Profit $= \text{Notional profit} \times \frac{2}{3}$

$= 32,000 \times \frac{2}{3}$

$=$ ₹21,333

2. Profit $= \text{Notional profit} \times \frac{2}{3} \times \frac{\text{Cash received}}{\text{Work certified}}$

$= 32,000 \times \frac{2}{3} \times \frac{2,00,000}{2,20,000}$

$=$ ₹19,394

3. Profit $= \text{Estimated profit} \times \dfrac{\text{Work certified}}{\text{Contract price}}$

$= 40,000 \times \dfrac{2,20,000}{2,80,000}$

$=$ ₹31,429

4. Profit $= \text{Estimated profit} \times \dfrac{\text{Work certified}}{\text{Contract price}} \times \dfrac{\text{Cash received}}{\text{Work certified}}$

$= 40,000 \times \dfrac{2,20,000}{2,80,000} \times \dfrac{2,00,000}{2,20,000}$

$=$ ₹28,571

5. Profit $= \text{Estimated profit} \times \dfrac{\text{Contract cost incurred}}{\text{Total estimated cost}}$

$= 40,000 \times \dfrac{1,94,000}{2,34,000}$

$=$ ₹33,162

6. Profit $= \text{Estimated profit} \times \dfrac{\text{Contract cost incurred}}{\text{Total estimated cost}} \times \dfrac{\text{Cash received}}{\text{Work certified}}$

$= 40,000 \times \dfrac{1,94,000}{2,34,000} \times \dfrac{2,00,000}{2,20,000}$

$=$ ₹30,148

Note: Computation of estimated profit

	₹
Cost incurred upto 31st March 2003	1,94,000
Add: Estimated cost	40,000
	2,34,000
Add: Provision for contingencies 2,34,000 × $\frac{2.5}{97.5}$	6,000
Total cost	2,40,000
Estimated profit (bf)	40,000
Contract price	2,80,000

Illustration-11

Compute a conservative estimate of profit on a contract (which is 80% complete) from the following particulars. Illustrate at least four methods of computing profit:

		₹
(i)	Total expenditure to date	1,02,000
(ii)	Estimated further expenditure to complete the contract (including contingencies)	20,400

(iii)	Contract price	1,83,600
(iv)	Work certified	1,20,000
(v)	Work uncertified	10,200
(vi)	Cash received	97,920

Solution

Contract Account

	₹		₹
To Contract cost	1,02,000	Work-in-progress:	
To Notional profit	28,200	Work certified	1,20,000
		Work uncertified	10,200
	1,30,200		1,30,200

Methods of calculating profit

1. Profit $= \text{Notional profit} \times \frac{2}{3}$

$= 28,200 \times \frac{2}{3}$

$=$ ₹18,800

2. Profit $= \text{Notional profit} \times \frac{2}{3} \times \frac{\text{Cash received}}{\text{Work certified}}$

$= 28,200 \times \frac{2}{3} \times \frac{97,920}{1,20,000}$

$=$ ₹15,340

3. Profit $= \text{Estimated profit} \times \frac{\text{Work certified}}{\text{Contract price}}$

$= 61,200 \times \frac{1,20,000}{1,83,600}$

$=$ ₹40,000

4. Profit $= \text{Estimated profit} \times \frac{\text{Work certified}}{\text{Contract price}} \times \frac{\text{Cash received}}{\text{Work certified}}$

$= 61,200 \times \frac{1,20,000}{1,83,600} \times \frac{97,920}{1,20,000}$

$=$ ₹32,640

Note: Calculation of estimated profit

	₹
Cost incurred till date	1,02,000
Estimated further expenditure	20,400
Total cost	1,22,400

Estimated profit (b/f)	61,200
Contract price	1,83,600

Illustration-12

The following particulars relate to contract A are obtained at the year end:

	₹
Date of commencement April - 1	
Contract price	6,00,000
Materials delivered direct to site	1,20,000
Materials issued from stores	40,000
Materials returned to stores	4,000
Materials on site on December 31	22,000
Direct labour	1,40,000
Direct expenses	60,000
Architect's fees	2,000
Establishment charges	25,000
Plant installed at cost	80,000
Value of plant December 31	65,000
Accrued wages December 31	10,000
Accrued direct expenses December 31	6,000
Cost of contract not yet certified	23,000
Value of contract certified by architect	4,20,000
Cash received from contractee	3,78,000

During the period, materials amounting to ₹9,000 have been transferred from Contract A to Contract B.

You are required to show (i) Contract account, (ii) Contractee's account and (iii) Extract from the Balance Sheet as at December 31, clearly showing the calculation of work-in-progress.

Solution

Contract 'A' Account

		₹		₹
To Materials delivered		1,20,000	Work-in-progress:	
To Materials issued		40,000	Work certified	4,20,000
To Direct labour paid	1,40,000		Work uncertified	23,000
Accrued wage	10,000	1,50,000	By Materials returned	4,000
			By Materials onsite	22,000

To Direct expenses paid	60,000		By Materials transferred to contract 'B'	9,000
Add: Accrued expenses	6,000	66,000		
To Establishment charges		25,000		
To Architect fees		2,000		
To Plant depreciation		15,000		
To Notional profit c/d		60,000		
		4,78,000		4,78,000
To Profit transferred to costing profit and loss $\left(60,000 \times \frac{2}{3} \times \frac{3,78,000}{4,20,000}\right)$		36,000	By Notional profit b/d	60,000
To Reserve c/d		24,000		
		60,000		60,000

Contractee Account			
	₹		₹
To Balance c/d	3,78,000	By Bank	3,78,000
	3,78,000		3,78,000
		By balance b/d	3,78,000

Balance Sheet as on December 31			
Liability	₹	**Assets**	₹
Profit and loss A/c	36,000	Work-in-progress:	
Accrued wages	10,000	Work certified	4,20,000
Accrued direct expenses	6,000	(+) Work uncertified	23,000
			4,43,000
		(−) Cash received	3,78,000
			65,000
		(−) Reserve	24,000
			41,000
		Plant at site	65,000
		Materials at site	22,000

Illustration-13

Shiva construction company was engaged on three contracts A, B and C. The following information was taken from the company's contract ledger:

Date of Commencement	Contract A January 1	Contract B July 1	Contract C October 1
	₹	₹	₹
Contract price	7,50,000	4,50,000	5,50,000
Materials issued	1,30,000	1,15,000	40,000
Wages	1,90,000	2,10,000	25,000
Office expenses	6,000	7,000	2,500
Plant installed	50,000	60,000	20,000
Materials on hand	5,500	6,250	3,000
Wages accrued	1,500	2,000	750
General expenses accrued	1,000	1,700	300
Work certified	4,00,000	3,20,000	90,000
Cash received	3,40,000	2,20,000	65,000
Work not yet certified	15,000	10,000	4,000

The accounts are closed on December 31 each year. The plants were installed on the dates of commencement of contract. Charge depreciation at 10% per annum. Prepare contract account in the columnar form.

Solution

Contract Account

	A	B	C		A	B	C
To Materials	1,30,000	1,15,000	40,000	By Work-in-progress: Work not certified	15,000	3,20,000	90,000
Wages paid and accrued	1,91,500	2,12,000	25,750	Work certified	4,00,000	10,000	4,000
Office expenses	6,000	7,000	2,500	Materials on-hand	5,500	6,250	3,000
Plant installed	50,000	60,000	20,000	Plant at site - Cost less Dep.	45,000	57,000	19,500
General expenses accrued	1,000	1,700	300	Loss transferred to costing P&L a/c	-	2,450	-
Notional profit c/d	87,000	-	27,950				
	4,65,500	3,95,700	1,16,500		4,65,500	3,95,700	1,16,500

To Profit transferred to costing P&L a/c	49,300	-	27,950	By Notional Profit b/d	87,000	-	27,950
Reserve c/d	37,700	-	-				
	87,000	-	27,950		87,000	-	27,950

Note:

1. Depreciation on plant

Contract A - Cost of plant	50,000
(-) Depreciation at 10%	5,000
Closing balance	45,000

Contract B - Cost of plant	60,000
(-) 6 month depreciation at 10%	3,000
Closing balance	57,000

Contract C - Cost of plant	20,000
(-) 3 month depreciation at 10%	500
Closing balance	19,500

2. Profit from Contract 'B' $= \text{Notional profit} \times \frac{2}{3} \times \frac{\text{Cash received}}{\text{Work certified}}$

$$= 87,000 \times \frac{2}{3} \times \frac{3,40,000}{4,00,000}$$

$= ₹49,300$

3. No profit is taken for Contract 'C', since value of the work certified is below 25% of contract price.

4. In case of loss, the whole loss should be transferred to profit and loss account. So all loss of contract 'B' is transferred to profit and loss account.

Illustration-14

The following particulars relate to two houses which a firm of builders had in course of construction under contract:

	House A	**House B**
	₹	₹
Work-in-progress on 1st Jan 1998 (Excluding ₹800 estimated profit which was taken to profit and loss account in 1997)	14,000	-

Materials purchased	23,000	16,600
Wages	20,000	14,000
Electrical services and fittings	1,400	300
Road making charges	8,000	-
Contract price (including road making)	60,000	40,000
Cash received upto 31.12.98	60,000	24,000
Percentage of cash received	100	$66\frac{2}{3}$
Value of materials on hand on 31.12.98	400	540
Completed work not certified	-	2,500
Value of plant used in site	12,000	6,000
Period of plant remained on site during the year	10 months	12 months

The total establishment expenses incurred during the year 1998 amounted to ₹12,240. These are to be charged to the two contracts in proportion to wages. Depreciation of plant is to be taken at the rate of 10% per annum. Prepare the two contract accounts in columnar form showing profit or loss on each house for the year 1998.

Solution

Contract Account

	A ₹	B ₹		A ₹	B ₹
To Work-in-progress on 01.01.98 - (14,000 + Profit 800)	14,800	-	By Contractee a/c	60,000	-
Materials purchased	23,000	16,600	By Work-in-progress:		
Wages	20,000	14,000	Work certified	-	36,000
Electrical services & fittings	1,400	300	Work uncertified	-	2,500
Road making charges	8,000	-			
Establishment expenses	7,200	5,040	Materials on hand	400	540
Depreciation on plant	1,000	600	Loss transferred to costing P&L a/c	15,000	-
Notional profit c/d	-	2,500			
	75,400	39,040		75400	39,040
To Profit transferred to costing P&L a/c	-	1,111	By Notional profit b/d	-	2,500
Reserve (bf)	-	1,389			
		2,500		-	2,500

Illustration-15

MVP Construction Ltd. commenced a contract on April 1, 1999. The total contract was for ₹17,50,000. It was decided to estimate the total profit and to take to the credit of P&L a/c the proportion of estimated profit on cash basis, which work completed bore to the total contract. Actual expenditure in 1999-2000 and estimated expenditure in 2000-2001 are given below:

	1999-2000 (Actual)	**2000-2001 (Estimated)**
	₹	₹
Materials issued	3,00,000	5,50,000
Labour paid	2,00,000	2,50,000
Labour outstanding	20,000	30,000
Plant purchased	1,50,000	-
Expenses paid	75,000	1,50,000
Expenses prepaid at end	15,000	-
Plant returned to store (historical cost)	50,000	1,00,000 (On 31st Dec 2009)
Materials at site	20,000	50,000
Work certified	8,00,000	Full
Work uncertified	25,000	-
Cash received	6,00,000	Full

The plant is subject to annual depreciation at 25% of WDV cost. The contract is likely to be completed on December 31, 2000. Prepare the contract account.

Determine the profit on the contract for the year 1999-2000 on prudent basis, which has to be credited to P&L a/c. **(ICWA-Inter, Sep. 2000)**

Solution

MNP Construction Ltd.

Contract Account for the year ending 31.3.2000				
		₹		₹
To Materials issued		3,00,000	By Plant returned to store (WN :2)	37,500
To Labour paid	2,00,000			
Add: Outstanding	20,000	2,20,000	By Materials at site	20,000
To Expenses paid	75,000			
Less: Prepaid	15,000	60,000	By Plant at site (WN:3)	75,000

To Plant purchased		1,50,000	By Cost of contract c/d	5,97,500
		7,30,000		7,30,000
To Cost of contract b/d		5,97,500	By Work-in-progress:	
			Work certified	8,00,000
To Notional profit c/d		2,27,500	Work uncertified	25,000
		8,25,000		8,25,000
To Profit transferred to costing profit and loss a/c		66,321	By Notional profit b/d	2,27,500
To Reserve c/d		1,61,179		
		2,27,500		2,27,500

Working Note

1. Estimated Profit:

	₹	₹
Actual cost upto 31.3.2000		5,97,500
Add: Estimated expenditure on 31.12.2000		
Materials issued	5,50,000	
Add: Materials at site on 31.3.2000	20,000	
	5,70,000	
Less: Materials at site on 31.12.2001	50,000	5,20,000
Labour paid	2,50,000	
Add: Outstanding on 31.12.2001	30,000	
	2,80,000	
Less: Outstanding on 31.3.2000	20,000	2,60,000
Expenses paid	1,50,000	
Add: Prepaid on 31.3.2000	15,000	1,65,000
Plant depreciation $75,000 \times 25\% \times 9/12$		14,063
Total estimated cost	-	15,56,563
Estimated profit (bf)	-	1,93,437
Contract price	-	17,50,000

2. Plant returned to stores at cost - 50,000
   Less: 25% Depreciation - 12,500
   37,500

3. Plant at site cost - 1,00,000
   Less: 25% Depreciation - 25,000
   75,000

4. Profit $= \text{Estimated profit} \times \frac{\text{Work certified}}{\text{Contract price}} \times \frac{\text{Cash received}}{\text{Work certified}}$

$= 1,93,437 \times \frac{8,00,000}{17,50,000} \times \frac{6,00,000}{8,00,000}$

$=$ ₹66,321

Illustration-16

Three contracts commenced on the following months : I - 1st January, II - 1st July and III - 1st October. They were undertaken by a contractor and their accounts on 31st December 2006 showed the following position:

	Contract I	**Contract II**	**Contract III**
	₹	₹	₹
Contract price	4,00,000	2,70,000	3,00,000
Expenditure:			
Materials	72,000	58,000	20,000
Wages paid	1,10,000	1,12,400	14,000
General charges	4,000	2,800	1,000
Plant	20,000	16,000	12,000
Materials on hand	4,000	4,000	2,000
Wages accrued	4,000	4,000	1,800
Work certified	2,00,000	1,60,000	36,000
Cash received in respect thereof	1,50,000	1,20,000	27,000
Work finished but not certified	6,000	8,000	2,100

The plant was installed on the date of commencement of each contract. Depreciation is to be taken at 10%. You are required to prepare the contract account in columnar form.

(B.Com., Madras University)

Solution

Contract Account for the year ending 31.12.2006							
	I	II	III		I	II	III
To Materials	72,000	58,000	20,000	By Work-in-progress:			
To Wages paid and accrued	1,14,000	1,16,400	15,800	Work certified	2,00,000	1,60,000	36,000
To General charges	4,000	2,800	1,000	Work uncertified	6,000	8,000	2,100
To Plant depreciation	2,000	1,600	1,200	By Materials on hand	4,000	4,000	2,000

To Notional profit c/d	18,000	-	2,100	By loss transferred to costing profit a/c		6,800	
	2,10,000	1,78,800	40,100		2,10,000	1,78,800	40,100
To Profit	9,000	-	-	By Notional profit b/d	18,000	-	2,100
To Reserve c/d	9,000	-	2,100				
	18,000	-	2,100		18,000	-	2,100

Note:

1) Full depreciation has been charged on plant as time factor is not specified for depreciation.

2) Profit - Contract I = $\text{Notional profit} \times \frac{2}{3} \times \frac{\text{Cash received}}{\text{Work certified}}$

$$= 18,000 \times \frac{2}{3} \times \frac{1,20,000}{1,60,000} = ₹9,000$$

Illustration-17

The following information relates to a building contract for ₹10,00,000 and for which 80% of the value of work-in-progress as certified by the architect is being paid by the contractee:

	2001	2002	2003
	₹	₹	₹
Materials issued	1,20,000	1,45,000	84,000
Direct wages	1,10,000	1,55,000	1,10,000
Direct expenses	5,000	17,000	6,000
Indirect expenses	2,000	2,600	500
Work certified - December 31	2,35,000	7,50,000	1,00,000
Work done but not certified	2,800	8,000	-
Materials at site	2,000	5,000	8,000
Value of plant issued	14,000	-	-

The value of plant at the end of 2001, 2002 and 2003 was ₹11,200, ₹7,000 and ₹3,000 respectively. Prepare contract account for the three years taking into account such profit as you think proper on incomplete contract. Also prepare contractee account.

(B.Com., Madras University, adopted)

Solution

Contract Account for the year ending 31.12.2001			
	₹		₹
To Materials issued	1,20,000	By Work-in-progress:	
To Direct wages	1,10,000	Work certified	2,35,000
To Direct expenses	5,000	Work uncertified	2,800
To Indirect expenses	2,000	By Materials at site	2,000
To Plant issued	14,000	By Plant at site	11,200
To Notional profit	-		
	2,51,000		2,51,000

Contract Account for the year ending 31.12.2002			
	₹		₹
To Opening Balance			
Work-in-progress:		By Work-in-Progress:	
Work certified	2,35,000	Work certified	7,50,000
Work uncertified	2,800	Work uncertified	8,000
Materials at site	2,000	By Materials at site	5,000
Plant at site	11,200	By Plant at site	7,000
To Materials issued	1,45,000		
To Direct wages	1,55,000		
To Direct expenses	17,000		
To Indirect expenses	2,600		
To Notional profit	1,99,400		
	7,70,000		7,70,000
To Profit transferred to costing profit and loss	1,06,347	By Notional profit b/d	1,99,400
To Reserve c/d	93,053		
	1,99,400		1,99,400

Contract Account for the year ending 31.12.2003			
	₹		₹
To Opening Balance			
Work-in-progress:		By Work-in-progress:	
Work certified	7,50,000	Work certified	93,053
Work uncertified	8,000	By contractee a/c	10,00,000
Materials at site	5,000	By Materials at site	8,000
Plant at site	7,000	By Plant at site	3,000

To Materials issued	84,000		
To Direct wages	1,10,000		
To Direct expenses	6,000		
To Indirect expenses	500		
To Profit transferred to costing profit and loss a/c	1,33,553		
	11,04,053		11,04,053

Contractee Account

2001	₹	**2001**	₹
To Balance c/d	1,88,000	By Bank	1,88,000
	1,88,000		1,88,000
2002		**2002**	
		By Balance b/d	1,88,000
To Balance c/d	6,00,000	By Bank	4,12,000
	6,00,000		6,00,000
2003		**2003**	
		By Balance b/d	6,00,000
To contract a/c	10,00,000	By Bank	4,00,000
	10,00,000		10,00,000

Illustration-18

Mr. Bhawandas undertook a contract for ₹15,00,000 on an arrangement that 80% of the value of work done as certified by the architect of the contractee, should be paid immediately and that the remaining 20% be retained until the contract was completed.

In 1998, the amount expended were - Materials ₹1,80,000, wages ₹1,70,000, carriage ₹6,000, Cartage ₹1,000, Sundry Expenses ₹3,000. The work was certified for ₹3,75,000 and 80% of this was paid as agreed.

In 1999, the amount expended were - Materials ₹2,20,000, wages ₹2,30,000, carriage ₹23,000, Cartage ₹2,000, Sundry Expenses ₹4,000. Three-fourths of the contract was certified as done by 31st December and 80% of this was received accordingly. The value of work uncertified was ascertained at ₹20,000.

In 2000, the amount expended were - Materials ₹1,26,000, Wages ₹1,70,000, carriage ₹6,000, Sundry Expenses ₹3,000 and on 30th June the whole contract was completed.

Prepare contract a/c for all the three years, Balance sheet as on 31.12.98 and as on 31.12.99 and also prepare contractee account. **(B.Com., Madras University, Modified)**

Solution

Contract Account for the year ending 31.12.1998			
	₹		₹
To Materials issued	1,80,000	By Work-in-progress:	
To Wages	1,70,000	Work certified	3,75,000
To Carriage	6,000		
To Cartage	1,000		
To Sundry expenses	3,000		
To Notional profit	15,000		
	3,75,000		3,75,000
To Reserve c/d	15,000	By Notional profit b/d	15,000
	15,000		15,000

Contract Account for the year ending 31.12.1999			
	₹		₹
To Opening balance		By Opening balance :	
Work-in-progress:		Reserve b/d	15,000
Work certified	3,75,000	By Work-in-progress:	
To Materials issued	2,20,000	Work certified	11,25,000
To Wages	2,30,000	Work uncertified	20,000
To Carriage	23,000		
To Cartage	2,000		
To Sundry expenses	4,000		
To Notional profit	3,06,000		
	11,60,000		11,60,000
To Profit $\left(3,06,000 \times \frac{2}{3} \times \frac{80}{100}\right)$	1,63,200	By Notional profit b/d	3,06,000
To Reserve c/d	1,42,800		
	3,06,000		3,06,000

Contract Account for the year ending 31.12.2000			
	₹		₹
To Opening balance		By Opening balance :	
Work-in-progress:		Reserve b/d	1,42,800

	₹		₹
Work certified	11,25,000	By Contractee a/c	
Work uncertified	20,000	(Contract price)	15,00,000
To Materials issued	1,26,000		
To Wages	1,70,000		
To Carriage	6,000		
To Sundry expenses	3,000		
To Profit transferred to costing profit and loss account	1,92,800		
	16,42,800		16,42,800

Balance Sheet (Extract) as on 31.03.1999

Liabilities	₹	Assets		₹
Profit and Loss a/c	1,63,200	Work-in-progress:		
		Work certified	₹11,25,000	
		Work uncertified	₹20,000	
			₹11,45,000	
		Less: Cash received	₹9,00,000	
			₹2,45,000	
		Less : Reserve	₹1,42,800	
				1,02,200

Balance Sheet (Extract) as on 31.03.1998

Liabilities	₹	Assets		₹
		Work-in-progress:		
		Work certified	₹3,75,000	
		Less: Cash received	₹3,00,000	
			₹75,000	
		Less : Reserve	₹15,000	
				60,000

Contractee Account

31.12.1998	₹	31.12.1998	₹
To Balance c/d	3,00,000	By Bank	3,00,000
	3,00,000		3,00,000

31.12.1999		1999	
		By Balance b/d	3,00,000
To Balance c/d	9,00,000	By Bank	6,00,000
	9,00,000		9,00,000
30.06.2000		**2000**	
		By Balance b/d	9,00,000
To Contract a/c	15,00,000	By Cash(BF)	6,00,000
	15,00,000		15,00,000

Illustration-19

Brock Construction Ltd. commenced a contract on November 1, 2003. The total contract was for ₹39,37,500. It was decided to estimate the total profit on the contract and to take to the credit of P&L a/c that proportion of estimated profit on cash basis, which work completed bore to the total contract. Actual expenditure for the period November 1, 2003 to October 31, 2004 and estimated expenditure on November 1, 2004 to March 31, 2005 are given below:

	Nov 01, '03 to Oct 31, '04 (Actual)	Nov 01, '04 to Mar 31, '05 (Estimated)
	₹	₹
Materials issued	6,75,000	12,37,500
Labour paid	4,50,000	5,62,500
Labour prepaid	25,000	-
Labour outstanding	-	2,500
Plant purchased	3,75,000	-
Expenses paid	2,00,000	3,50,000
Expenses outstanding	50,000	25,000
Plant returned to store (historical cost)	75,000	3,00,000
	(On 31.03.04)	(On 31.03.05)
Work certified	20,00,000	Full
Work uncertified	75,000	-
Materials at site	75,000	37,500
Cash received	17,50,000	-

The plant is subject to annual depreciation at 33.33% on WDV method. The contract is likely to be completed on March 31, 2005.

Required

Prepare the contract account. Determine the profit on the contract for the year November, 2003 to October 2004 on prudent basis, which has to be credited to P&L a/c.

Solution

Contract Account for the year ended October 30, 2004					
		₹			₹
To Materials issued		6,75,000	By Plant returned to store at cost	75,000	
To Labour paid	4,50,000		(-) Dep. (WN:1)	10,417	64,583
Less: Prepaid	25,000	4,25000	By Materials at site		75,000
To Expenses paid	2,00,000		By Plant at site at cost	3,00,000	
Add: Outstanding	50,000	2,50,000	(-) Depreciation	1,00,000	2,00,000
To Plant purchased		3,75,000	By Cost of contract c/d		13,85,417
		17,25,000			17,25,000
To Cost of contract b/d		13,85,417	By Work-in-progress:		
			Work certified		20,00,000
To Notional profit c/d		6,89,583	Work uncertified		75,000
		20,75,000			20,75,000
To Profit transferred to costing profit and loss (WN:2)		3,43,025	By Notional profit b/d		6,89,583
To Reserve c/d		3,46,558			
		6,89,583			6,89,583

Working Note

1. Depreciation on plant returned on March 31, 2004

$$= 75{,}000 \times \frac{33.33}{100} \times \frac{5}{12}$$

Estimated profit = ₹10,417

2. Profit = Estimated profit $\times \dfrac{\text{Cash received}}{\text{Contract price}}$

$$= 7{,}71{,}805 \times \frac{17{,}50{,}000}{39{,}37{,}500}$$

$$= ₹3{,}43{,}025$$

3. Estimated Profit:

	₹	₹
Actual cost up to 31.10.2004		13,85,417
Add: Estimated cost for Completion		
Materials issued	12,37,500	
Add: Materials at site on 31.10.2004	75,000	
	13,12,500	
Less: Materials at site on 31.03.2005	37,500	12,75,000
Labour paid	4,50,000	
Add: Prepaid on 31.10.2004	25000	
	4,75,000	
Add: Outstanding on 31.03.2005	2,500	4,77,500
	2,80,000	
Plant depreciation $2,00,000 \times \frac{33.33}{100} \times \frac{5}{12}$		27,778
Total estimated cost	-	31,65,695
Estimated profit	-	7,71,805
Contract price	-	39,37,500

Escalation Clause

Contract price is fixed in advance. In case of large contracts construction period may be long. It is very difficult to estimate the price of materials and rates of labour for long periods in future. Due to some unexpected factors the prices of materials and rates of labour and other expenses may increase abnormally. In such cases the contractor stands to suffer. So a provision may be included in the contract to increase the contract price when prices of materials and rate of labour increases beyond a certain agreed level.

Provision included in the contract to increase the contract price if materials prices and rates of labour and other expenses increase over and above certain agreed level, is called Escalation Clause. Escalation clause protects the interest of the contractor. It also helps to avoid dispute between contractor and contractee.

Illustration-20

A Limited undertook a contract for ₹50,00,000 on 1st April 2006. On 31st March 2007, when accounts were closed the following details were available:

	₹
Materials purchased	10,00,000
Wages paid	4,50,000

General expenses	1,00,000
Plant purchased	5,00,000
Material on hand at closing	2,50,000
Wages outstanding at closing	50,000
Work certified	20,00,000
Cash received	15,00,000
Work uncertified	1,50,000
Depreciation of plant	50,000

The Escalation clause in the contract was as follows:

In the event of prices of materials and wages increase by more than 5%, the contract price would be increased by 25% of the rise in cost of materials and wages beyond 5% in each case.

It was found that since the date of signing the agreement the price of materials and wage rates increased by 25%. The value of work certified does not take into account the effect of the above clause.

Prepare Contract account (show the working). **(ICWA-Inter, June 2008)**

Solution

Contract Account

		₹		₹
To Materials purchased		10,00,000	By Work-in-progress:	
To Wages paid	4,50,000		Work certified	20,00,000
Add: Outstanding	50,000	5,00,000	Work uncertified	1,50,000
To General expenses		1,00,000	By materials on hand	2,50,000
To Depreciation of plant		50,000	By Escalation in	
To Notional profit c/d		8,00,000	Contract price (See WN-1)	50,000
		24,50,000		24,50,000
To Profit carried to costing profit and loss a/c (See WN-2)		2,00,000	By Notional profit b/d	8,00,000
To Reserve c/d		6,00,000		
		8,00,000		8,00,000

Working Note

1. Increase in contract price allowed due to escalation clause:

   Increase in materials price and wage rates - 25%

   Current material price and rates of wages - 125%

		₹
Materials purchased		10,00,000
Less: Materials on hand		2,50,000
Materials used		7,50,000
Increase in materials cost	$7,50,000 \times \frac{25}{125}$	1,50,000
Less: 5% increase	$1,50,000 \times \frac{5}{25}$	30,000
Increase in materials cost over 5%		1,20,000
Increase in wages	$5,00,000 \times \frac{25}{125}$	1,00,000
Less: 5% increase	$1,00,000 \times \frac{5}{25}$	20,000
Increase in wages over 5%		80,000

Escalation in Contract Price:

Increase in materials price over 5% = ₹1,20,000

Increase in wages over 5% = ₹80,000

Total = ₹2,00,000

Increase in contract price $= 2,00,000 \times \frac{25}{100} =$ ₹50,000

2. Profit $=$ Estimated profit $\times \frac{1}{3} \times \frac{\text{Cash received}}{\text{Work certified}}$

$= 8,00,000 \times \frac{1}{3} \times \frac{15,00,000}{20,00,000}$

= ₹2,00,000

Cost Plus Contract

Cost plus contract is an arrangement whereby actual cost incurred is reimbursed to the contractor and contractor is assured of a reasonable profit which may be a fixed amount or a fixed percentage on cost of contract. Cost plus contracts are given in times of emergency like war or the nature of work is such, it is extremely difficult to estimate the cost in advance. The contractee has the right to inspect the cost records. The agreement will also specify the type and quantity of materials to be used, type of labour and time and rates of labour and other expenses. This type of contract is beneficial both to contractor and contractee. The contractor is assured of a reasonable profit. The contractee is also assured of the timely completion of the contract at reasonable price.

Merits

1. There is no risk to the contractor due to increase in costs.
2. The contractor is assured of a reasonable profit.
3. The contractee stands to benefit if there is decrease in costs.
4. The chances of dispute between contractor and contractee are reduced.
5. There is no bargaining problem.
6. Completion of the contract is assured irrespective of increase in materials prices and labour rates.

Demerits

1. It involves maintaining detailed cost records.
2. Dispute may arise as to the type of expenses to be incurred.
3. Chances of falsification of records are more. So it needs periodic inspection of records by contractee.
4. Contractee stands to lose by rise in costs.
5. There is no incentive to reduce or control the cost.

Illustration-21

From the following details prepare the contract account

	₹
Materials used	75,000
Wages incurred	60,000

Provide 50% on wages for works overhead and 15% on works cost for office expenses. Contractor is assured of 20% profit on total cost.

Solution

Contract Account

	₹		₹
To Materials used	75,000	By Contractee a/c	2,27,700
To wages incurred	60,000		
To Works overhead - 50% on wages	30,000		
Works cost	1,65,000		
To Office expenses - 15% on works cost	24,750		
Total cost	1,89,750		
To Profit and loss a/c - 20% on total cost	37,950		
	2,27,700		2,27,700

15.5 EXERCISE

I. Objective Type Questions

A. State whether the following statements are true or false

(i) Contract costing is an extension of job costing.

(ii) Contractee agrees to do the contract work for a fixed price.

(iii) Subcontract cost is debited to contract account.

(iv) Cost of extra work is debited to contract account.

(v) Contractor benefits if prices of materials and labour rates decrease in cost plus contract.

(vi) A part of the profit of incomplete contract is kept as reserve to meet future contingencies.

(vii) Contract price is fixed in advance in cost plus contract.

(viii) Provision is made to increase the contract price if prices of materials and labour rates increase abnormally in cost plus contracts.

(ix) Contractor will incur loss if material prices and labour rates increase in fixed price contracts.

(x) Most of costs are direct costs in contract costing.

(xi) There is no difference between notional profit and estimated profit.

(xii) Escalation clause in a contract provides that contract price is fixed.

[**Ans: True:** (i), (iii), (vi), (ix), (x) **False:** (ii), (iv), (v), (vii), (viii), (xi), (xii)]

B. Fill in the blanks

(i) A part of work certified retained by contractee while making payment is called ____________.

(ii) Contract price is not fixed in advance in ____________ contract.

(iii) The provision to increase the contract price in case of increase in material prices and labour rates over an agreed level is called ____________.

(iv) Most of the expenses in contract are ____________.

(v) Contract costing is an extension of ____________ costing.

(vi) Every contract is a unit of ____________.

(vii) No profit is taken credit to profit and loss account when work certified is less than ____________ of the contract price.

(viii) Abnormal loss is ____________ in the contract.

(ix) ____________ Contract provides for payment of actual cost plus a stipulated profit.

(x) Work-in-progress appears on the ____________ side of contract account.

(xi) In contract costing, each ____________ is a cost unit.

[**Ans:** (i) Retention money, (ii) cost-plus, (iii) Escalation clause, (iv) direct, (v) Job, (vi) cost, (vii) 25%, (viii) credited, (ix) cost plus contract, (x) credit side, (xi) contract]

II. Theory Questions

A. Short answer type questions

1. Explain the distinct features of contract costing.
2. Name the industries where contract costing is followed.
3. Contract costing is a special type of job costing. Do you agree? Explain.
4. How abnormal loss of materials is treated in contract accounts?
5. What is notional profit?
6. What is work certified?
7. How value of uncertified work is computed?
8. What is cost plus contract?
9. What is escalation clause in a contract?
10. Explain the treatment of normal loss in a contract.
11. What is retention money? What is its purpose?
12. Explain the terms: contractor, contractee and architect certificate.
13. What is progress payment in contracts?

B. Long answer type questions

1. What is contract costing? Explain its special features.
2. Distinguish between job costing and contract costing.
3. What is cost-plus contract? Explain its advantages and disadvantages.
4. What is escalation clause in contract? explain.
5. Explain the various methods of calculating profit on incomplete contract.
6. Write short notes on: (a) Subcontract cost, (b) Retention money, (c) Cost of extra work, (d) Work certified, (e) Cost plus contract, (f) Escalation clause.
7. Explain the treatment of cost of machinery, plant and tools used exclusively in a contract.
8. Discuss the principles to be followed while taking credit for profit on incomplete contracts.

III. Practical Problems

A. Short answer type questions

1. Calculate the profit that can be reasonably taken to profit and loss account from the following details:

	₹
Notional profit	50,000
Work certified	4,00,000
Work uncertified	25,000
Contract price	6,00,000
Cash received	3,20,000

[**Ans:** Profit credited to profit and loss a/c - ₹26,667]

2. Calculate notional profit and profit transferred to profit and loss a/c, from the following details:

	₹
Contract price	10,00,000
Cash received from contractors being 90% of work certified	7,20,000
Uncertified work	50,000
Contract cost	7,00,000

[**Ans:** Notional Profit - ₹1,50,000; Profit transferred to Profit and loss a/c ₹90,000]

3. Calculate notional profit from the following particulars:

	₹
Contract price	15,00,000
Cost incurred till date	7,50,000
Cash received	6,40,000
80% of work certified is received in cash	
Work uncertified	30,000

[**Ans:** Notional Profit - ₹80,000]

4. From the following details calculate estimated profit and profit credited to profit and loss a/c for the year ended 31st March, 2009. Also calculate the amount of profit retained as reserve.

	₹
Contract price	15,00,000
Work certified upto 31st March 2009	14,00,000
Expenses incurred on contract till 31st March 2009	12,00,000
Further expenses to be incurred after 31st March 2009 for completion of the contract is estimated at	75,000
Cash received	12,00,000

[**Ans:** Estimated profit - ₹2,25,000; Profit credited to profit and loss a/c - ₹1,92,857, Amount retained as reserve - ₹7,143, Notional profit - ₹2,00,000]

Note: Profit $= \text{Estimated profit} \times \dfrac{\text{Cash received}}{\text{Work certified}}$

5. From the following information calculate the value of uncertified work:

   Contract price - ₹20,00,000
   Value of work certified on 28.2.2009 - ₹12,00,000

   Expenses incurred since work certified to 31.3.2009 are,
   Materials - ₹60,000
   Labour - ₹50,000

   Overheads usually charged at 10% of materials and labour.

   [**Ans:** Work uncertified ₹1,21,000]

6. A contractor supplies you the following information relating to a contract for the year ended 31st March 2010:

	₹
Contract price	20,00,000
Cost incurred for completion of 2/3rd of the contract	11,50,000
Architects certificate has been issued for 50% of contract and cash paid by contractor amounted to	8,00,000

   Compute the value of work uncertified.

   [**Ans:** Value of work uncertified - ₹1,91,667]

   Note:

   (a) Uncertified work = Total work completed − Work certified

$$= \frac{2}{3} - \frac{1}{2} = \frac{4}{6} - \frac{3}{6}$$

$$= \frac{1}{6}$$

   (b) Value of work uncertified (on cost basis)

$$= 11{,}50{,}000 \times \frac{1}{6}$$

$$= ₹1{,}91{,}667$$

B. Long answer type questions

1. When a contract is large enough to extend over a number of years, what proportion of profit should be taken to the profit and loss account at the end of each year under each of the following cases?

(a) When the work has just started and the cost of work done is only about 10% of the contract price.

(b) When the work was reasonably advanced and about 60% of work has been completed.

(c) When the work is nearing completion and 95% has been completed.

(ICWA-Inter, June 2008)

[**Ans:** (a) profit nil; (b) two-thirds of notional profit as reduced to percentage of cash received; (c) estimated profit in proportion to cash received bears to total contract price]

2. From the following information calculate the amount of profit to be transferred to profit and loss account:

(a)

	₹
Notional profit	1,20,000
Work certified	5,00,000
Contract price	9,00,000
Cash received	4,50,000

[**Ans:** Notional profit $\times \frac{2}{3} \times \frac{\text{Cash received}}{\text{Work certified}}$; ₹72,000]

(b)

	₹
Notional profit	50,000
Estimated profit	60,000
Work certified	9,00,000
Contract price	10,00,000
Cash received	8,10,000

[**Ans:** Estimated profit $\times \frac{\text{Cash received}}{\text{Contract price}}$; ₹48,600]

Note: Since work certified is 90% and contract is nearing completion, estimated profit has been taken.

(c)

	₹
Notional profit	45,000
Cash received	2,00,000
Work certified	2,25,000
Contract price	8,00,000

[**Ans:** Profit $=$ Notional profit $\times \frac{1}{3} \times \frac{\text{Cash received}}{\text{Work certified}} =$ ₹13,333.33]

(d)

	₹
Notional profit	25,000
Work certified	2,00,000
Cash received	1,80,000
Contract price	10,00,000

[**Ans:** Profit - nil; Since work certified is 20% of contract price no credit is taken for profit]

(e)

	₹
Contract price	20,00,000
Work certified	19,00,000
Cash received	16,00,000
Estimated profit	4,00,000
Notional profit	3,00,000

[**Ans:** Profit $= \text{Estimated profit} \times \frac{\text{Cash received}}{\text{Contract price}}$; ₹3,20,000]

Note: Work certified is 95% of contract price and nearing completion. Hence estimated profit is taken for calculation profit.

3. Construction Ltd. undertook a contract for the construction of a house on April 2008. The construction was completed on 31st March 2009. The following information was available from their cost records.

	₹
Materials sent to site	5,00,000
Labour charges paid	4,20,000
Direct expenses paid	50,000
Establishment expenses	60,000
Plant installed on 01.04.08	1,50,000
Materials returned to stores	12,000
Plant returned to stores on 31.12.08	50,000
Materials at site on 31.03.09	15,000
Wages accrued on 31.03.09	25,000
Direct expenses accrued on 31.03.09	7,500

The contract price was agreed at ₹14,00,000. Charge depreciation on plant at 20% per annum. Prepare contract account.

[**Ans:** Profit - ₹3,37,000]

4. A construction company undertook a contract at an estimated profit of ₹1,08,00,000, which includes a budgeted profit of ₹18,00,000. The relevant data for the year ended 31.03.2005 are as under:

	(₹ in '000)
Materials issued on site	5,000
Direct wages paid	3,800
Plant issued	700
Site office expenses	270
Materials returned from site	100
Direct expenses	500
Work certified	10,000
Progress payments received	7,200

A special plant was purchased specifically for this contract at ₹8,00,000 and after use on this contract till the end of 31.3.2005, it was valued at ₹5,00,000. The cost of materials at site at the end of the year was estimated at ₹18,00,000. Direct wages accrued as on 31.3.2005 was ₹1,10,000.

Required:

Prepare the contract account for the year ended 31st March 2005 and compute the profit to be taken to the Profit and Loss account.

(B.Com., (Hons.), Delhi University, 2005)

[**Ans:** Notional profit - ₹12,20,000, Profit - ₹8,13,333]

Note: $$\text{Profit} = \text{Notional profit} \times \frac{\text{Work certified}}{\text{Contract price}} \times \frac{\text{Cash received}}{\text{Work certified}}$$
$$= 12{,}20{,}000 \times \frac{1{,}00{,}00{,}000}{1{,}08{,}00{,}000} \times \frac{72{,}00{,}000}{1{,}00{,}00{,}000}$$
$$= ₹8{,}13{,}333$$

5. A contractor obtained a contract for ₹6,00,000 on 1st January 2008. The expenses incurred during the year ending on December 31, 2008 were as under:

	₹
Materials	1,80,000
Wages paid	1,60,000
Wages accrued	10,000
Other expenses	25,000

The plant specially installed for the contract worth ₹45,000 was returned to the stores subject to a depreciation of 20%. Materials on 31st December 2008 were valued at ₹24,000.

Up to 31st December 2008, the contractor had received ₹3,60,000 in cash representing 80% of the work certified. Work uncertified was estimated at ₹4,000.

Prepare contract account, showing the profit for the year. Also show how the value of work-in-progress would appear in the Balance Sheet as on 31st December 2008.

(B.Com., Madras University)

[**Ans:** Notional profit - ₹94,000, Profit - ₹50,133, Reserve - ₹43,867, WIP (after deduction of cash and reserve) ₹50,133]

6. Following particulars relate to Contract No. 703

	₹
Contractor price	6,00,000
Materials	1,20,000
Wages	1,64,000
Machinery	20,000
General expenses	8,600

Cash received ₹2,40,000, which is equal to 80% of work certified. Materials not used amounted to ₹10,000. Write off depreciation on machinery at 10%. Prepare contract account.

[**Ans:** Notional profit - ₹15,400; Profit - ₹8,213; Reserve - ₹7,187]

7. A undertook several large contracts and his ledger contained, therefore, a separate account for each contract. On 31.12.2008, the account of contract no. 22 showed the following amounts as expended thereon:

	₹
Materials directly purchased	1,80,000
Materials issued from stores	50,000
Wages	2,44,000
Direct expenses	24,000
Plant purchased	1,60,000
Subcontract cost	14,000
Establishment charges apportioned	40,000

The contract was for ₹15,00,000 and up to 31.12.2008 ₹6,00,000 have been received in cash which represented 80% of work certified.

The materials at site unconsumed were valued at ₹15,000. The contract plant was to be depreciated by ₹16,000.

Prepare contract account showing what profits thereon have been earned to date.

(B.Com., Madras University)

[**Ans:** Notional profit - ₹1,97,000; Profit - ₹1,05,067, Reserve - ₹91,933]

8. The following balances were extracted from the book of a building contractor on 31st March 2009:

	₹
Materials issued to site	67,720
Wages paid	73,455
Wages outstanding on 31.3.2009	720
Plant issued to site	6,000
Direct charges	2,725
Establishment charges	5,650
Stock of materials at site on 31.3.09	1,200
Value of work certified at 31.3.09	1,65,000
Cost of work not yet certified	8,500
Cash received from contractee	1,41,075

The work commenced on 1st April, 2008 and the contract price agreed was ₹2,45,000.

Prepare contract account for the year, providing for depreciation of plant at 25%. Set out the contractors balance sheet so far as it relates to the contract.

[**Ans:** Notional profit ₹22,930, Profit ₹13,070, Reserve ₹9,860, WIP (after deducting cash received and reserve) ₹22,565]

9. The following expenditures were incurred on the contract No. 77 to 31st March 2009:

	₹
Direct materials	25,000
Direct wages	30,000
Indirect materials	9,500
Materials returned	900
Plant issued	20,000
Office and administration overheads apportioned	15,000

The following further information were obtained:

(a) The contract price is ₹1,50,000 and the work commenced on 1st April 2008.

(b) Depreciation on plant charged at 20%.

(c) The architect issued a completion certificate for four-fifths of the contract price on 20th March 2009.

(d) The contract expenses given above included expenses incurred after 20th March 2009 are given below:

Wages - ₹1,200

Materials - ₹2,000
Establishment charges at 50% of wages.

(e) Ignore depreciation on plant for valuation of work uncertified.

(f) Materials at site on 31st March 2009 amounted to ₹6,500.

(g) A fine of ₹2,000 is likely to be imposed for delay on completion.

(h) Cash received is 90% of work certified.

Required:

(i) Prepare contract account

(ii) Show profit taken to the credit of profit and loss account.

(iii) Value of uncertified work.

[**Ans:** Notional profit - ₹47,700; Profit ₹28,620; Reserve - ₹19,080; Value of uncertified work - ₹3,800]

Note:

(a) Fine is not actual amount for the year, hence not considered.

(b) Value of uncertified work (cost incurred from 21st March 2009 to the end of the year)

	₹
Materials	2,000
Wages	1,200
Establishment charges (50% of wages)	600
Cost of uncertified work	3,800

10. The following is the summarised information relating to Contract No.100:

	₹
Contract price	6,00,000
Wages	1,64,000
General expenses	8,600
Materials	1,20,000
Cash received (80% of work certified)	2,40,000
Materials at site	6,000
Plant	20,000
Materials transferred to other contract	4,000

Included in the above information are wages ₹3,500, Materials ₹4,000 and other expenses ₹2,500 which were incurred since certification. Depreciate plant at 10%.

Prepare contract account. **(B.Com. (Hons.), Delhi University, 2004)**

[**Ans:** Notional profit - ₹25,400; Profit - ₹13,547; Reserve - ₹11,853; Value of work uncertified - ₹10,000]

11. Surya Construction Ltd. with a paid up share capital of ₹50 lakh undertook a contract to construct MIG apartments. The work commenced on the contract on 1st April 2002. The contract price was ₹60 lakh. Cash received on the contract upto 31st March, 2003 was ₹18 lakh (being 90% of work certified). Work completed but not certified was estimated at ₹1,00,000. As on 31st March 2009 materials at site was estimated at ₹30,000, machinery costing ₹2,00,000 was returned to stores and wages outstanding was ₹5,000. Plant and machinery is to be depreciated at 5%.

    The following were the ledger balances (Dr.) as per trail balance as on 31st March 2003:

	₹
Land and building	23,00,000
Plant and machinery at site (60% at site)	25,00,000
Furniture	60,000
Materials	12,00,000
Materials received from other contract	2,00,000
Fuel and power	1,25,000
Site expenses	5,000
Office expenses	12,000
Rates and taxes	15,000
Cash at bank	1,33,000
Wages	2,50,000

    Prepare contract account and balance sheet.

(B.Com. (Hons.), Delhi University, 2001)

[**Ans:** Notional profit - ₹2,43,000; Profit - ₹72,900; Reserve - ₹1,70,100; Balance sheet total - ₹50,27,900]

12. From the following information prepare the contract account for the year ended on 30.09.2002:

	₹
Contract price	50,00,000
Work certified	20,00,000
Cash received 90% of work certified	
Materials at site on 30.9.2002	30,000
Wages paid	2,55,000
Materials sent to site	14,00,000
Site expenses	5,000
Power and fuel	1,25,000
Office expenses	12,000
Rates and taxes	15,000

(ICWA - Inter, adopted)

[**Ans:** Notional profit - ₹2,18,000; Profit - ₹65,400]

13. A firm of building contractors undertook a contract on 01.04.2008. The contract price is ₹10,00,000. The following information was taken from their records:

	₹
Materials issued to site	2,25,000
Materials purchased direct	60,000
Wages paid	1,70,000
Direct expenses paid	25,000
Plant installed at cost	2,50,000
Wages accrued on 31.3.2009	15,000
Direct expenses accrued on 31.3.2009	7,000
Cash received 90% of work certified	5,40,000
Work uncertified	10,000

Of the plant and materials charged to the contract, materials worth ₹7,500 and plant costing ₹10,000 were destroyed in a fire accident. Some materials costing ₹6,000 were sold at a profit of ₹1,000. Plant returned to stores on 30.9.2008 was ₹40,000. Depreciate plant at 20% per annum. Materials at site on 31.3.2009 ₹20,000.

You are required to prepare contract account and contractee account.

[**Ans:** Notional profit - ₹97,500; Profit - ₹58,500; Reserve - ₹39,000; Contractee a/c balance (Cr.) ₹5,40,000]

14. The following is the trial balance of Premier Construction Company engaged on the execution of Contract No. 1047 for the year ended 31st December 2005:

	₹	₹
Contractee's account (amount received)	-	3,00,000
Buildings	1,60,000	-
Creditors	-	72,000
Bank balance	35,000	-
Capital account	-	5,00,000
Materials	2,00,000	-
Wages	1,80,000	-
Expenses	47,000	-
Plant	2,50,000	-
	8,72,000	8,72,000

The work on the contract 1047 commenced on 1st January 2005. Materials costing ₹1,70,000 were sent to the site of the contract but those of ₹6,000 were destroyed in an accident. Wages of ₹1,80,000 were paid during the year. Plant costing ₹50,000 was used on the contract all through the year. Plant with a cost of ₹2,00,000 was used from 1st January to 30th September and was then returned to stores. Materials of the cost of ₹4,000 were at site on 31st December 2005.

The contract was for ₹6,00,000 and the contractee pays 75% of the work certified. Work certified was 80% of the total contract at the end of 2005. Uncertified work was estimated at ₹15,000 on 31st December 2005. Expenses are charged to the contract at 25% of wages. Plant is to be depreciated at 10% p.a.

Prepare contract account No. 1047 account for the year 2005 and make out the balance sheet as on 31st December 2005.

[**Ans:** Notional profit - ₹90,000; Profit ₹45,000; Balance sheet total ₹6,04,000]

15. Sanjay builders obtained a contract on 01.04.2008, who close their accounts on 31st March every year. The following are the information relating to the contract on 31st March 2009.

	₹
Materials issued from stores	1,50,000
Labour	90,000
Supervision	24,000
Establishment charges	66,000

A machine costing ₹40,000 has been used in the contract for 146 days. Its working life is estimated at 7 years and its final scrap value is ₹5,000.

A supervisor who is paid at ₹4,000 per month had spent approximately half of his time on this contract.

Materials on hand on 31st March 2009 amounted to ₹5,000.

The contract price is ₹6,50,000. By 31st March 2009 two-thirds of the contract was completed but architect issued certificate covering 50% of the contract. Cash received on the contract amounted to ₹3,00,000.

Prepare contract account and show the profit to be taken to profit and loss account.

[**Ans:** Notional profit - ₹79,750, Profit - ₹49,077, Reserve - ₹30,673, Cost of uncertified work - ₹81,750]

Note:

(a) Depreciation on plant

$$= \frac{\text{Cost} - \text{Scrap}}{\text{Life}} \times \frac{146}{365}$$

$$= \frac{40{,}000 - 5{,}000}{7} \times \frac{146}{365}$$

$$= ₹2{,}000$$

16. Balaji Builders undertook a contract for ₹7,40,000. The work was commenced on 1st July 2007. The company closes its accounts on 31st March every year. The cost details were extracted from their books on 31st March, 2008:

	₹
Materials issued to contract	2,00,000
Materials purchased direct	50,000
Wages paid	1,75,000
Direct expenses paid	75,000
Plant purchased on 01.07.2007	1,60,000
Materials returned to stores	15,000
Plant returned to stores on 31.12.2007	60,000
Wages outstanding on 31.03.2008	13,000
Direct expenses accrued on 31.03.2008	5,000
Materials at site on 31.03.08	20,000
Cash received	4,00,000

Charge depreciation at 20% p.a. on plant. Three-fourths of contract work has been completed but the architect issued certificate covering 60% of contract price.

Prepare contract account showing the profit taken to profit and loss account. Also show contractee account.

[**Ans:** Notional profit ₹40,800; Profit - ₹24,505; Reserve - ₹16,295]

Note:

(a) Depreciation on plant returned $= 60{,}000 \times \frac{20}{100} \times \frac{6}{12} =$ ₹6,000

(b) Depreciation on plant at site $= 1{,}00{,}000 \times \frac{20}{100} \times \frac{9}{12} =$ ₹15,000

(c) Value of work uncertified:

Cost incurred for 3/4th of contract = ₹5,04,000

Cost of whole contract $= 5{,}04{,}000 \times \frac{4}{3} =$ ₹6,72,000

Cost of 60% of contract certified $= 6{,}72{,}000 \times \frac{60}{100} =$ ₹4,03,200

Cost of uncertified work = Cost incurred − Cost of 60% work certified

= 5,04,000 − 4,03,200

= ₹1,00,800.

17. The following information relates to a building contract for ₹10,00,000.

	2004	2005
	₹	₹
Materials	3,00,000	84,000
Wages	2,30,000	1,05,000
Direct expenses	22,000	10,000
Indirect expenses	6,000	1,000
Work certified	7,50,000	10,00,000
Work uncertified	8,000	-
Materials at site	5,000	7,000
Plant issued	14,000	2,000
Cash received	6,00,000	10,00,000

Value of plant at the end of 2004 and 2005 were ₹7,000 and ₹5,000 respectively.

Prepare (a) Contract account and (b) Contractee's account for two years taking into consideration such profit for transfer to the profit and loss account as you think proper.

(B.Com., Madras University, Oct. 1986)

[**Ans:** Notional profit 2004 - ₹1,98,000; Profit 2004 - ₹1,05,600; Profit 2005 - ₹1,32,400]

18. The following information relates to a contract for ₹75,00,000. (The contractee pays 90% of the value of work done as certified by the architect).

	1999	2000	2001
	₹	₹	₹
Materials	9,00,000	11,00,000	6,30,000
Wages	8,50,000	11,50,000	8,50,000
Direct expenses	35,000	1,25,000	45,000
Indirect expenses	15,000	20,000	-
Work certified	17,50,000	56,50,000	75,00,000
Work in progress uncertified	-	10,000	-
Plant issued	1,00,000	-	-

The value of plant at the end of 1999, 2000 and 2001 was respectively ₹80,000; ₹50,000 and ₹20,000. Prepare the contract accounts for all three years and show the relevant figures in the Balance Sheet.

(B.Com., Madras University, Oct. 1992)

[**Ans:** Notional profit 1999 - ₹70,000; Profit 2000 - ₹8,91,000; 2001 - ₹8,79,000; WIP 1999 - ₹1,75,000; 2000 - ₹5,65,000]

19. P Ltd undertook a contract for the construction of a building at a contract price of ₹15,00,000. During the first year, the following amounts were spent against which a sum of ₹5,62,500 (representing 90% of the work certified) was received by the contractor:

	₹
Materials used	2,62,500
Wages paid to the workers	1,50,000
Overhead expenses	37,500

During the second year the contractor spent the following amounts:

	₹
Materials used	3,75,000
Wages paid to the workers	3,00,000
Overhead expenses	75,000

In the second year the contract was completed and a sum of ₹8,75,000 was received by the contractor.

You are required to prepare the contract account and determine the profits.

(M.Com., Periyar University, April 2008)

[**Ans:** I year - Notional profit ₹1,75,000; Profit ₹52,500, Reserve - ₹1,22,500; II year - Profit ₹2,47,500]

Note :

Since cash received on contract in the two years total ₹14,37,500. Profit on realisation basis may be taken at ₹2,37,187.50. $\left(2,47,500 \times \frac{14,37,500}{15,00,000}\right)$

20. Constructors Ltd. is engaged in two contracts A and B during the year. The following particulars are obtained at the year end 31st December:

Date of commencement	**Contract A April 1**	**Contract B September 1**
	₹	₹
Contract price	6,00,000	5,00,000
Materials issued	1,60,000	60,000
Materials returned	4,000	2,000
Materials on site (Dec. 31)	22,000	8,000
Direct labour	1,50,000	42,000
Direct expenses	66,000	35,000
Office expenses	25,000	7,000

Plant installed	80,000	70,000
Value of plant (Dec. 31)	65,000	64,000
Cost of contract not certified	23,000	10,000
Work certified	4,20,000	1,35,000
Cash received	3,78,000	1,25,000
Architect fees	2,000	1,000

During this period materials costing ₹9,000 have been transferred from contract 'A' to contract 'B'.

You are required to prepare contract accounts and contractee's accounts.

(B.Com., Madras University, September 1988)

[**Ans:** Contract A - Loss ₹5,000; Contract B - Notional Profit ₹60,000; profit - ₹36,000]

21. Compute a conservative estimate of profit on a contract (which is 80% complete) from the following particulars. Illustrate at least four methods of computing the profit:

	₹
Total expenditure to date	1,02,000
Estimated further expenditure to complete the contract (including contingencies)	20,400
Contract price	1,83,600
Work certified	1,20,000
Work uncertified	10,200
Cash received	97,920

(B.Com., (Hons.) Delhi University, 1997)

Ans:

$$\begin{aligned} \text{Notional profit} &= \text{Work certified} + \text{Work uncertified} - \text{Total expenditure to date} \\ &= 1{,}20{,}000 + 10{,}200 - 1{,}02{,}000 \\ &= ₹28{,}200 \end{aligned}$$

$$\begin{aligned} \text{Estimated profit} &= \text{Contract price} - \text{Total estimated cost} \\ &= 1{,}83{,}600 - 1{,}22{,}400 \\ &= ₹61{,}200 \\ \text{Total estimated cost} &= \text{Total expenditure to date} + \text{Estimated further expenditure} \\ &= 1{,}02{,}000 + 20{,}400 \\ &= ₹1{,}22{,}400 \end{aligned}$$

Profit:

$$\text{Method I} = \text{Notional profit} \times \frac{2}{3}$$
$$= 28{,}200 \times \frac{2}{3}$$
$$= ₹18{,}800$$

$$\text{Method II} = \text{Notional profit} \times \frac{2}{3} \times \frac{\text{Cash certified}}{\text{Work certified}}$$
$$= 28{,}200 \times \frac{2}{3} \times \frac{97,920}{1,20,000}$$
$$= ₹15{,}341$$

$$\text{Method III} = \text{Estimated profit} \times \frac{\text{Work certified}}{\text{Contract price}}$$
$$= 61{,}200 \times \frac{1,20,000}{1,83,600}$$
$$= ₹40{,}000$$

$$\text{Method IV} = \text{Estimated profit} \times \frac{\text{Work certified}}{\text{Contract price}} \times \frac{\text{Cash received}}{\text{Work certified}}$$
$$= 61{,}200 \times \frac{1,20,000}{1,83,600} \times \frac{97,920}{1,20,000}$$
$$= ₹32{,}640$$

22. An expenditure of ₹2,34,000 has been incurred on a contract to the end of 31st March 2003. The value of work certified is ₹2,60,000. The cost of work done but not yet certified is ₹6,000. It is estimated that the contract will be completed by 30th June 2003 and an additional expenditure of ₹60,000 will have to be incurred to complete the contract. The total estimated expenditure on the contract is to include a provision of $2\frac{1}{2}$% for contingencies. The contract price is ₹3,20,000 and ₹2,20,000 has been realised in cash up to 31st March 2003.

    Calculate the proportion of profit to be taken to the profit and loss account as on 31st March 2003 under different methods.

    [**Ans:** Notional profit = 32,000; Estimated profit = 18,650]

    Profit:

$$\text{Method I} = \text{Notional profit} \times \frac{2}{3} \times \frac{\text{Cash certified}}{\text{Work certified}}$$
$$= 32{,}000 \times \frac{2}{3} \times \frac{2,20,000}{2,60,000}$$
$$= ₹18{,}051$$

$$\text{Method II} = \text{Notional profit} \times \frac{2}{3}$$
$$= 32{,}000 \times \frac{2}{3}$$
$$= ₹21{,}333$$

$$\text{Method III} = \text{Estimated profit} \times \frac{\text{Work certified}}{\text{Contract price}}$$
$$= 18{,}650 \times \frac{2,60,000}{3,20,000}$$
$$= ₹15{,}153$$

$$\text{Method IV} = \text{Estimated profit} \times \frac{\text{Cash received}}{\text{Contract price}}$$
$$= 18{,}650 \times \frac{2,20,000}{3,20,000}$$
$$= ₹12{,}822$$

23. The contract ledger of M/s. XYZ showed the following expenditure on account of contract on 31st December 2006:

	₹
Materials	2,10,000
Wages	2,93,000
Plant	70,000
Sundry expenses	15,000
Establishment charges	10,000

The contract was started on 1st January 2006 and the contract price was ₹10,00,000. Cash received on account to date was ₹4,80,000 representing 80% of work certified, remaining 20% being retained until completion. Value of plant on 31st December 2006 was ₹20,000 and the value of materials in hand was ₹6,000. The cost of work finished but not certified on said date was ₹50,000.

Some of the materials costing ₹20,000 were found unsuitable and were sold for ₹16,000 and a part of plant costing ₹5,000 unsuited for the contract was sold at a profit of ₹1,000.

The contractor estimated a further expenditure that would be incurred in completing the contract and took to the credit of P & L a/c for the year 2006 that portion of estimated net profit on contract which the value of work certified bears to the contract price. This is to be further reduced by proportion of cash received that bears to work certified. The estimates of further expenditure were as follows:

(a) that the contract would by completed by 30th June 2007.
(b) that a further sum of ₹30,000 would have to be spent on plant and its residual value on completion of the contract would be ₹12,000.

(c) that materials in addition to those in hand on 31st December 2006 would cost ₹1,00,000 and that further sundry expenses of ₹7,000 would be incurred.

(d) that the wages for the completion of the contract would amount to ₹1,69,900.

(e) that the establishment expenses would cost the same amount per year as in the previous year.

(f) that ₹18,000 would be sufficient to provide for contingencies.

Prepare contract account for the year ended 31st December 2006 and show the amount to be credited to P & L a/c for the year. Also show how the relevant figures would appear in the balance sheet as on that date.

(B.Com. (Hons.) Delhi University, 2007)

[**Ans:** Notional profit - ₹1,03,000; Estimated profit - ₹1,09,100; Profit - ₹52,368; Reserve - ₹50,632; WIP - ₹1,19,368]

24. Modern Construction Ltd. obtained a contract no. B.37 for ₹40 lakhs. The following balances and information relate to the contract for the year ended 31st March 2008:

	01.04.2007 ₹	**31.03.2008** ₹
Work-in-progress		
Work certified	9,40,000	30,00,000
Work uncertified	11,200	32,000
Materials at site	8,000	20,000
Accrued wages	5,000	3,000

Additional information relating to the year 2007-2008 are:

	₹
Materials issued from stores	4,00,000
Materials directly purchased	1,50,000
Wages paid	6,00,000
Architect fees	51,000
Plant hire charges	50,000
Indirect expenses	10,000
Share of general overheads for B.37	18,000
Materials returned to stores	25,000
Materials returned to supplier	15,000
Fines and penalties paid	12,000

The contractee pays 80% of work certified in cash. You are required to prepare:

(a) Contract account showing clearly the amount of profits transferred to profit and loss account.

(b) Contractee's account

(c) Balance sheet

(CA-PE II, May 2008)

[**Ans:** Notional profit - ₹8,43,800; Profit - ₹4,50,027; WIP-₹2,38,227]

25. One of the building contracts currently engaged in by a construction company commenced 15 months ago and remain unfinished. The following information relating to the work on the contract has been prepared for the year just ended:

	(₹in '000)
Contract price	2,500
Value of work certified at the end of the year	2,200
Cost of work not yet certified at the end of the year	40
Cost incurred: Opening Balances	
Cost of work completed	300
Materials at site	10
During the year:	
Materials delivered to site	610
Wages	580
Hire of plant	110
Other expenses	90
Closing Balance:	
Materials on site	20

As soon as materials are delivered to the site, they are charged to the contract account. A record is also kept of materials as they are actually used on the contract. Periodically a stock check is made and any discrepancy between book stock and physical stock is transferred to a general contract material discrepancy account. This is absorbed back to each contract, currently at the rate of 0.5% of materials booked. The stock check at the year end revealed a stock shortage of ₹5,000.

In addition to the direct charges listed above, general overheads are charged to contracts at 5% of the value of certified work. General overheads ₹15,000 had been absorbed into the cost of work completed at the beginning of the year.

It has been estimated that further costs to complete the contract will be ₹2,20,000. This estimate includes the cost of materials on site at the end of the year just finished and also a provision for rectification.

Required:

(a) Explain briefly the distinguishing features of contract costing.

(b) Determine the profitability of the above contract and recommend how much profit (to the nearest ₹'000) should be taken for the year just ended. (Provide a detailed schedule of cost).

(c) State how your recommendation in (b) would be affected if the contract price was ₹40,00,000 (rather than ₹25,00,000) and if no estimate has been made of costs to completion. (If required, suitable assumption may be made).

(ICWA-Inter, Nov. 1995)

[**Ans:** (b) Profit - ₹4,51,034. $\left(\text{Estimated profit} \times \dfrac{\text{Cost of work to date}}{\text{Estimated total cost}}\right)$ (c) Profit - ₹2,49,067]

Working Notes

(a)

Cost of materials booked:	
Materials delivered to site	₹6,10,000
Add: Opening materials at site	₹10,000
	₹6,20,000
Less: Closing materials at site	₹20,000
	₹6,00,000
Less: Shortage	₹5,000
Materials booked	₹5,95,000

(b) Stock discrepancy charged to the contract is $595 \times \dfrac{0.5}{100} = ₹3{,}000$

(c) Cost of contract to date = ₹1,773

(d) Total estimated cost = ₹1,993

(e) Notional profit = Value of work certified + Work not certified − Cost of contract to date

$$= ₹22{,}00{,}000 + 40{,}000 - 17{,}73{,}000$$
$$= ₹4{,}67{,}000$$

(f) Profit for question (c) = $\text{Notional profit} \times \dfrac{2}{3} \times \dfrac{\text{Cash received}}{\text{Work certified}}$

$$= 4{,}67{,}000 \times \frac{2}{3} \times \frac{80}{100}$$
$$= ₹2{,}49{,}067$$

26. RST Construction Ltd. commenced a contract on April 1, 2005. The total contract was for ₹49,21,875. It was decided to estimate the total profit on the contract and to take to the credit of P & L a/c that proportion of estimated profit on cash basis, which work completed bore to the total contract. Actual expenditure for the period April 1, 2005 to March 31, 2006 and estimated expenditure on April 1, 2006 to September 30, 2006 are given below:

	Apr 1, 2005 to Mar 31, 2006 (Actual)	Apr 1, 2006 to Sep 30, 2006 (Estimated)
	₹	₹
Materials issued	7,76,250	12,99,375
Labour paid	5,17,500	6,18,750
Labour prepaid	37,500	-
Labour outstanding	12,500	5,750
Plant purchased	4,00,000	-
Expenses paid	2,25,000	3,75,000
Expenses outstanding	25,000	10,000
Expenses prepaid	15,000	-
Plant returned to store (historical cost)	1,00,000 (On 30.9.05)	3,00,000 (On 30.9.06)
Work certified	22,50,000	Full
Work uncertified	25,000	-
Cash received	18,75,000	-
Materials at site	82,500	42,500

The plant is subject to annual depreciation at 25% on written down value method. The contract is likely to be completed on September 30, 2006.

Required:

Prepare the contract account. Determine the profit on the contract for the year 2005-06 on prudent basis, which has to be credited to P & L a/c. **(CA-PE II, May 2006)**

[**Ans:** Notional profit - ₹7,66,250; Profit - ₹3,89,000; Reserve - ₹3,77,250]

Note:

(a) Estimated profit = ₹10,21,125

(b) $\text{Profit} = \text{Estimated profit} \times \dfrac{\text{Cash received}}{\text{Contract price}}$

$$= 10{,}21{,}125 \times \frac{18{,}75{,}000}{49{,}21{,}875}$$

$$= ₹3{,}89{,}000$$

27. The following information relates to contract no. 333. You are required to prepare the contract account. The contractor is assured of a profit of 20% on total cost. The following are the expenses relating to the contract:

	₹
Materials purchased	75,000
Materials issued from stores	1,00,000
Indirect materials	25,000
Wages paid	1,10,000
Loose tools issued	6,000
Other direct charges	30,000

The contract took 3 months for completion. The value of tools and materials returned to stores were ₹500 and ₹6,000 respectively. It is the practice to charge administration and office expenses at 20% on works cost.

[**Ans:** Profit - ₹81,480; Contract price - ₹4,88,880]

Note:

(a) Works cost = ₹3,39,500

(b) Administration overheads = ₹67,900

(c) Total cost = ₹4,07,400

28. *X* Ltd. obtained contract for ₹75,00,000. The work on the contract commenced on 1st April 2008. The following information was taken from the cost ledger of the company for the year ending 31.3.2009.

	₹
Materials purchased	16,00,000
Direct wages paid	8,00,000
Administration expenses	2,75,000
Plant purchased	7,00,000
Materials at site on 31.3.2009	40,000
Wages outstanding on 31.3.2009	40,000
Work certified	32,00,000
Cash received	25,00,000
Work uncertified	50,000
Depreciation on plant	1,40,000

There is an escalation clause in the contract deed. It contained the following provision:

In the event of materials prices increasing over 5% of the prevailing price and wage rates increasing beyond 4% of the prevailing rate, the contract price would be increased by 50% of the material price increase over 5% and by 40% of increases in wages over 4%.

Materials prices have gone by 30% since signing the contract. Wage rates have gone up by 20% since signing the contract. The value of work certified does not take into account the increase in materials price and wage rates.

Prepare contract account.

[**Ans:** Notional profit - ₹6,29,800; Profit - ₹1,64,010; Reserve - ₹4,65,790]

Note:

(a) 30% increase in material price $= 15{,}60{,}000 \times \frac{30}{130} =$ ₹3,60,000

(b) Increase in materials price over 5% $= 3{,}60{,}000 \times \frac{25}{30} =$ ₹3,00,000

(c) Escalation in contract price for increase in materials price over 5% $= 3{,}00{,}000 \times \frac{50}{100} =$ ₹1,50,000

(d) Increase in wages (20%) $= 8{,}40{,}000 \times \frac{20}{120} =$ ₹1,40,000

(e) Increase in wages over 4% $= 1{,}40{,}000 \times \frac{16}{20} =$ ₹1,12,000

(f) Escalation allowed in contract price for wages increase = ₹1,12,000 $\times \frac{40}{100} =$ ₹44,800

(g) Total escalation allowed in contract price = 1,50,000 + 44,800 = ₹1,94,800.

29. A construction company undertaking a number of contracts, furnish the following data relating to its uncompleted contracts as on 31st March 2009:

	Contract Numbers (₹ in lakhs)			
	723	**726**	**729**	**731**
Total contract price	23.20	14.40	10.08	28.80
Estimated cost on completion of contract	20.50	11.52	12.60	21.60
Expenses for the year ended 31.03.09:				
Direct materials	5.22	1.80	1.98	0.80
Direct wages	2.32	4.32	3.90	2.16
Overheads (excluding depreciation)	1.06	2.60	2.62	1.05
Profit reserve on 01.04.2008	1.50	-	-	-
Plant installed at cost	5.00	3.50	2.75	3.00
Materials at site 01.04.2008	0.75	-	-	-
Materials at site 31.03.2009	0.45	0.20	0.08	0.05
Work certified 31.03.2008	4.65	-	-	-
Work certified during the year 2008-2009	12.76	13.26	7.56	4.32
Work uncertified 31.03.2009	0.84	0.24	0.14	0.18
Progress payments received during the year	9.57	9.00	5.75	3.60

Depreciation at 20% per annum is to be charged on plant issued. While the Contract No. 723 was carried over from last year, the remaining contracts were started in the first week of April, 2008.

Required:

(a) Determine the profit/loss in respect of each contract for the year ended 31.3.2009.

(b) State the profit/loss to be carried to profit and loss account for the year ended 31st March 2009. **(CA-Inter)**

Ans:

	723	**726**	**729**	**731**
(i) Notional profit/(loss) (₹in lacs)	5.20	4.28	(1.27)	(0.06)
(ii) Profit to P/L a/c (₹in lacs)	2.60	1.80	(1.27)	(0.06)

30. Paramount Engineers are engaged in construction of a bridge under a long-term contract. The cost incurred up to 31.03.2009 was as under:

Fabrication:	(₹in lakhs)
Direct materials	280
Direct labour	100
Overheads	60
	440
Erection cost to date	110
	550

The contract price is ₹11 crores and the cash received on account till 31.03.2009 was ₹6 crore. A technical estimate of the contract indicates the following degree of completion of work:

Fabrication: Materials - 70%, Direct labour and overheads - 60%, Erection - 40%.

You are required to estimate the profit that could be taken to profit and loss account against this partly completed contract as at 31.03.2009. **(CA-Inter)**

[**Ans:** (i) Estimated profit - ₹158.33 lakh; (ii) Profit - ₹86.36 lakh]

31. A firm of building contractors began to trade on 1st January 2008. The following was the expenditure on a contract for ₹6,00,000.

	₹
Materials issued from stores	1,00,000
Materials purchased for the contract	90,000
Plant installed at cost	70,000
Wages paid	2,00,000
Wages accrued on 31.12.2008	80,000
Direct expenses paid	20,000
Direct expenses due on 31.12.2008	5,000
Establishment	13,000

Of the plant and materials charged to the contract, plant which cost ₹4,000 and materials costing ₹3,000 were lost. Certain of the materials costing ₹4,000 were sold for ₹5000. On 31.12.2008 plant which cost ₹10,000 was returned to the stores and a part of the plant which cost ₹4,000 was damaged and could not be used.

The work certified was for ₹4,80,000 and 80% of the same was received in cash. The cost of work done but uncertified was ₹2,000. Depreciation on plant was charged at 10% p.a.

Prepare the contract account for the year ending 31.12.2008 by transferring to the profit and loss account the portion of profit which you think is reasonable.

Show these details of the contract which would appear in the Balance Sheet of the firm as on 31.12.2008. **(B.Com., Madras University, March 1988)**

[**Ans:** Loss - ₹25,200; WIP - ₹98,000]

32. The Manufacturers Ltd., began to trade on 1st January 2008. During 2008 the company was engaged in only one contract of which the contract price was ₹10,00,000.

Of the plant and materials charged to the contract, plant which cost ₹10,000 and materials which cost ₹8,000 were lost in an accident.

On 31st December 2008 plant costing ₹10,000 was returned to stores, the cost of work uncertified but finished was ₹4,000 and materials costing ₹8,000 were in hand on site.

Charge 10% depreciation on plant and compile contract account and balance sheet from the following:

	₹	₹
Share capital		2,40,000
Creditors		20,000
Cash received (80% of work certified)		4,00,000
Land and buildings	86,000	
Bank balance	50,000	
Charged to contract:		
Materials	1,80,000	
Plant	50,000	
Wages	2,80,000	
Expenses	14,000	
	6,60,000	6,60,000

[**Ans:** Notional profit - ₹42,000; Profit - ₹22,400; Reserve - ₹19,600; WIP - ₹84,400; Balance sheet total - ₹2,64,400]

Process Costing

16

- Meaning
- Process costing-Suitability
- Characteristics/Prerequisites/Advantages/Disadvantages
- Process costing and Job costing-Distinction
- Accounting Procedure for Process Costing
- Calculation of Abnormal Gain or Loss-Steps
- Inter-Process Profit-Meaning/Justifications
- Arguments against transfer at Market Price
- Preparation of Process Accounts-Procedures
- Valuation of WIP and Equivalent Production Concept
- Valuation of WIP-Steps involved
- Valuation of WIP-Methods

16.1 MEANING

Process costing is followed in process industries. In process industries products of identical units are produced after they pass through different distinct and well defined stages in production. Each distinct stage of production is called a process. The raw materials introduced in a process come out in semifinished condition. The output obtained in a process which is in partly finished condition is passed on to the next process till they are completed. The output of a previous process becomes the raw material for the subsequent process. So in process industries identical units of a product is produced on large scale. The various batches of materials introduced in a process can not be identified to a particular batch of output. On each unit same amount of materials, labour and overheads are expended. The total cost incurred in a process is spread over the units produced in that process during that period. So the cost gets averaged. Process costing is concerned with ascertaining the cost of production of each process separately.

In certain industries, e.g. textiles, the semi-finished goods in an intermediary process may be passed on to the next process in full or a part and the balance may be sold in the market. Similarly, for an intermediary process additional materials may be introduced through purchase in the market.

Industries Suitable for Process Costing

1. Production industries - textiles, vegetable oil, paper, cement, iron and steel, rubber etc.
2. Mining industries like gold, sulphur, mineral oil etc.
3. Chemicals like soap, medicines etc.
4. Public utility undertakings such as water supply, electricity generation and supply of gas etc.

Characteristics of Process Costing

1. Continuous production of identical units of a product on large scale for sale is made.
2. The output which is in semi-finished condition become raw materials for the subsequent process.
3. The amount of materials, labour and overheads incurred on all units are same.
4. Each process is a unit of costing. The expenses incurred during a particular period in each process are accumulated separately.
5. The units produced in a process during a period is ascertained. Total cost of production during the period in a process is divided by the number of units produced in that period to arrive the cost per unit. The total cost is averaged over the units produced.
6. The output of one process becomes the raw materials for the next process till it is finished.

Prerequisites for the Use of Process Costing

1. The products must pass through two or more specific clearly identifiable production stages. Each stage of production is called a process.
2. The output of each process in semifinished condition should become the raw materials for the subsequent process.
3. The products produced must be identical and standardized.
4. The production of goods must be continuous and on large scale.

Advantages of Process Costing

1. It facilitates easy calculation of product cost for a particular period.
2. This also helps to collect the cost of each process separately.
3. It helps to find the cost effectiveness of a particular process.
4. Cost control measures can be implemented with ease as actual and standard costs are available process-wise.
5. Computation of cost of production in each process is easy as the products produced are homogeneous.
6. It helps to identify the more efficient process.
7. Standard costing technique can be conveniently introduced for cost control purposes.

Disadvantages

1. Only average cost of production in a period is found. This does not help the management in cost control.
2. Only historical costs are available. It is not of much use in control and planning for future.
3. There will always be stock of work-in-progress in the beginning and at the end of every period. It complicates the calculation of cost of finished product and valuation of partly finished goods.
4. All units of work-in-progress may not be in the same completion stage. So an element of arbitrariness is introduced in valuing them.
5. When finished product of a process is passed on to next process at cost price, it become difficult to judge the efficiency and profitability of each process.

16.1.1 Distinction between Job Costing and Process Costing

	Process costing	Job costing
1.	Goods are produced continuously on a large scale.	Production is not continuous.
2.	Goods are produced for sale.	Gods are produced against customers orders.
3.	Units of products produced are homogeneous.	Each job is different from other.
4.	Same amount of materials, labour and overheads are incurred on each unit.	The amount of materials, labour and overheads incurred differ from job to job.
5.	Costs are collected process-wise.	The cost are accumulated for each job separately.
6.	Total cost of each process is accumulated for a period.	The cost are accumulated for each job separately.

7.	The output of one process becomes the raw materials for the subsequent process.	There is no transfer of partly finished goods from one job to another.
8.	As the production is continuous, normally there will be stock of partly finished goods at the beginning and at the end of a period.	Stock of partly completed jobs may be there occasionally and on a small scale.
9.	Total cost incurred during a period is divided by number of units produced during the period. So average cost of units produced are calculated.	Specific costs of each job are ascertained separately.
10.	As only average cost for a period is calculated, the accounting work is simple.	As cost of each job is ascertained separately, the accounting work is complicated and lengthy

16.2 ACCOUNTING PROCEDURE

A separate account is opened for each process. The expenses direct to various process are debited to respective process accounts. The common expenses of the firm is apportioned to the processes on some suitable methods of overheads apportionment. Value of units produced is credited in process account. Each process account may have an additional column to show the quantities of raw materials introduced and quantities of output obtained and process losses. It is only an analytical column to facilitate the management to exercise control over process production and loss. The various elements of expenses are as follows:

16.2.1 Materials

Materials cost is the major component. Materials issued in the first process passes through all processes till completion stage. Occasionally additional materials may be issued in a subsequent process. The details of materials issued to various departments are ascertained from materials issue analysis sheet. Indirect materials issued for various processes are also treated as direct cost of respective processes and debited to them.

16.2.2 Wages

Remuneration of employees working exclusively in a process is direct cost of that process. Only few people attend to work in two or more processes. Their wages are distributed to various processes on some equitable basis.

16.2.3 Overheads

Many of the production expenses are incurred separately for each process and forms direct expenses of that process. Only few expenses like office and administration costs are common to all departments. They are apportioned to the processes on some suitable basis.

16.2.4 Determination of Process Cost when there is no Process Loss

All costs of a process like materials, labour and overheads are debited to the process. The total of these costs becomes the cost of production of that process and becomes the raw materials cost of the next processes.

Illustration-1

(Without process loss)

Product A passes through three processes for completion. The following informations relating to the process for the month of March is given:

	Total	Process 'X'	Process 'Y'	Process 'Z'
	₹	₹	₹	₹
Direct materials	50,000	30,000	12,000	8000
Direct labour	30,000	18,000	7,000	5,000
Direct expenses	10,000	5,500	3,000	1,500
Manufacturing overheads	24,000	-	-	-

Manufacturing overheads are apportioned to processes on direct wages basis.

Neither there is opening nor closing stocks of raw material or work-in-progress. During the month 1,000 units were completed.

Prepare process accounts showing cost per unit in each process.

Solution

Process 'X' account					
Particulars	**Cost per unit**	**Total**	**Particulars**	**Cost per unit**	**Total**
	₹	₹		₹	₹
To Direct materials	30.00	30,000	By Transfer to process 'Y' a/c (bf)	67.90	67,900
To Direct labour	18.00	18,000			
To Direct expenses	5.50	5,500			
To Manufacturing overheads	14.40	14,400			
	67.90	67,900		67.90	67,900

Process 'Y' a/c					
Particulars	**Cost per unit** ₹	**Total** ₹	**Particulars**	**Cost per unit** ₹	**Total** ₹
To Process 'X' a/c	67.90	67,900	By Transfer to process 'Z' a/c (bf)	95.50	95,500
To Direct materials	12.00	12,000			
To Direct labour	7.00	7,000			
To Direct expenses	3.00	3,000			
To Manufacturing overheads	5.60	5,600			
	95.50	95,500		95.50	95,500

Process 'Z' a/c					
Particulars	**Cost per unit** ₹	**Total** ₹	**Particulars**	**Cost per unit** ₹	**Total** ₹
To Process 'Y' a/c	95.50	95,500	Transfer to finished stock a/c (bf)	114.00	1,14,000
To Direct materials	8.00	8,000			
To Direct labour	5.00	5,000			
To Direct expenses	1.50	1,500			
To Manufacturing overheads	4.00	4,000			
	114.00	1,14,000		114.00	1,14,000

Working Note

$$\begin{aligned}\text{\% of manufacturing overheads on direct labour} &= \frac{\text{Total manufacturing overheads}}{\text{Total direct labour}} \times 100\\ &= \frac{24{,}000}{30{,}000} \times 100\\ &= 80\%\end{aligned}$$

Process losses

A small part of materials introduced into a process may be lost due to evaporation, dusting or shrinkage. If the lost material is not available for sale it is called wastage. Some part of the materials may be scrapped or discarded in production process. The scrapped materials may possess some sale value or may not.

Normal loss

The loss of materials is estimated on the basis of past experience. The loss of materials which are expected and which cannot be avoided is called normal loss. If normal loss possess some sale value, it is credited to the concerned process account.

Accounting treatment

Amount realised from sale of normal loss is credited to the concerned process account. The net cost of production of a process is dividedly by good units produced. The cost of normally lost materials is spread over good units produced in the process.

Abnormal loss

When the loss of materials is in excess of normal loss, it is called abnormal loss. Abnormal loss occurs only occasionally due to causes like poor quality of raw materials, poor machine working condition, carelessness on the part of operator and foreman, accident etc. As it is not regular, it should not be allowed to influence the process cost. The abnormal loss units should be valued on par with good units produced. The amount of abnormal loss should be credited to the concerned process account and debited to abnormal loss account. The sale value of abnormally wasted units is credited to abnormal loss account. Abnormal loss account is balanced and the net abnormal loss is transferred to the debit of costing profit and loss account.

Abnormal gain

Some times the actual loss in a process may be less than the normal loss (i.e. actual output is more than the normal output). The savings in normal loss i.e. extra units produced over normal output is called abnormal gain or abnormal effectiveness.

Accounting treatment

Abnormal gain units are also valued like good units of production. It is debited to concerned process account and credited to abnormal gain account. The scrap value of abnormal gain units is credited to normal loss account and debited to abnormal gain account. The abnormal gain account is balanced and net abnormal gain is transferred to the credit of costing profit and loss account.

16.2.5 Steps for Calculation of Abnormal Loss or Abnormal Gain

Step-1: Computation of abnormal loss or Gain units

Input/units introduced	- xxx units
Less: Normal loss	- xxx units
Normal production	- xxx units

Actual production given - xxx units

Abnormal loss/(−) gain - xxx units

Step-2: Computation of abnormal loss (or) gain value in rupees:

$$\text{Abnormal loss/gain (₹)} = \frac{\text{Total cost} - \text{Normal scrap value}}{\text{Normal production (units)}} \times \text{Abnormal loss/gain (units)}$$

Illustration-2

(With normal loss but no scrap value)

In a chemical industry one product passes through two processes 'A' and 'B'. The finished product of process 'A' becomes raw materials for the process 'B'. The finished product of process 'B' is sent to finished stock for sale. Find out the cost of production of each process from the following data:

	Process 'A'	Process 'B'
Raw materials	1,000 kg at ₹5 per kg	200 kg at ₹6 per kg
Direct wages	₹4,000	₹2,150
Direct expenses	₹2,300	₹1,500
Factory overheads at	100% of direct labour	50% of direct labour
Normal process loss	10% of input	5% of input
Scrap value of normal loss	Nil	Nil

Solution

Process 'A' Account

Particulars	Units (kg)	Total (₹)	Particulars	Units (kg)	Total (₹)
To Raw materials at ₹5 per kg	1,000	5,000		-	-
To Direct wages	-	4,000	By Normal loss	100	-
To Direct expenses	-	2,300	By Transfer to process B a/c	900	15,300
To Factory overheads	-	4,000	(bf)		
(Cost per kg = 15,300/900= ₹17)					
	1,000	15,300		1,000	15,300

Process 'B' Account					
Particulars	**Units (kg)**	**Total (₹)**	**Particulars**	**Units (kg)**	**Total (₹)**
To Process 'A' a/c	900	15,300	By Normal loss ($1,100 \times 5\%$)	55	-
To Raw materials (at ₹6 per kg)	200	1,200	By Transfer to finished stock a/c	1,045	21,225
To Direct wages	-	2,150	(Cost per kg (bf) = 20,900/1045 = ₹20)		
To Direct expenses		1,500			
To Factory overheads (50% of Direct wages)		1,075			
	1,100	21,225		1,100	21,225

Illustration-3

(With normal loss and with scrap value)

A product passes though three processes I, II and III. The details of expenses incurred and other details of the three processes for the year ending 31st March 2009:

	Process I	Process II	Process III
Raw materials introduced	5,000 Units	-	-
Cost per unit	₹10	-	-
Indirect materials (₹)	22,000	17,000	13,000
Wages (₹)	30,000	21,000	16,000
Manufacturing expenses (₹)	27,500	19,375	10,474
Normal loss: Loss in weight	5%	4%	10%
Scrap	10%	10%	10%
Scrap value per unit (₹)	4	5	8

Prepare process accounts and compute cost per unit.

Solution

Process I Account					
Particulars	**Units**	**Total (₹)**	**Particulars**	**Units**	**Total (₹)**
To Raw materials (at ₹10 p/u)	5,000	50,000	By Normal loss: Loss in weight 5%	250	-

To Indirect materials	-	22,000	Scrap 10% (at ₹4 p/u)	500	2,000
To Wages	-	30,000	By transfer to process II a/c (bf) [cost per unit = 1,27,500/4,250 = ₹30]	4,250	1,27,500
To Manufacturing expenditure	-	27,500			
	5,000	**1,29,500**		**5,000**	**1,29,500**

Process II Account					
Particulars	**Units**	**Total (₹)**	**Particulars**	**Units**	**Total (₹)**
To Process I a/c	4,250	1,27,500	By Normal loss: Loss in weight 4%	170	-
To Indirect materials	-	17,000	Scrap 10% (at ₹5 p/u)	425	2,125
To Wages	-	21,000	By transfer to process III a/c (bf) [cost per unit = 1,82,750/3,655 = ₹50]	3,655	1,82,750
To Manufacturing expenditure	-	19,375			
	4,250	**1,84,875**		**4,250**	**1,84,875**

Process III Account					
Particulars	**Units**	**Total (₹)**	**Particulars**	**Units**	**Total (₹)**
To Process II a/c	3,655	1,82,750	By Normal loss: Loss in weight 10%	365.50	-
To Indirect materials	-	13,000	Scrap 10% (at ₹8 p/u)	365.50	2,924
To Wages	-	16,000	By transfer to process II a/c (bf) [cost per unit = 2,19,300/2,924 = ₹75]	2,924	2,19,300
To Manufacturing expenditure	-	10,474			
	3,655	**2,22,224**		**3,655**	**2,22,224**

Illustration-4

(Part of output transferred to stock account)

A company manufactures a product which involves three process P, Q and R. The following are the details of the three processes for three months Jan-March 2009.

	Process 'P'	Process 'Q'	Process 'R'
Raw materials introduced	15,000 Units	2,550 Units	660 Units
Cost per unit	₹8	₹10	₹15
Indirect materials (₹)	25,000	19,000	20,000
Direct wages (₹)	60,000	45,000	32,000
Production overheads (₹)	17,750	22,475	10,010
Output transferred to stock for sale	30%	40%	100%
Output transferred to next process	70%	60%	-
Normal loss on input	10%	5%	6%

Prepare process accounts and finished stock account.

Solution

Process 'P' account					
Particulars	Units	Total (₹)	Particulars	Units	Total (₹)
To Raw materials (at ₹8 p/u)	15,000	1,20,000	By Normal loss 10%	1,500	-
To Indirect materials		25,000	Production: Transfer to finished stock - 30% (WN-1)	4,050	66,825
To Direct wages		60,000	Transfer to process(WN-1)	9,450	1,55,925
To Production overheads	-	17,750	'Q' - 70% (₹16.50 per Unit)		
	15,000	2,22,750		15,000	2,22,750

Process 'Q' account					
Particulars	Units	Total (₹)	Particulars	Units	Total (₹)
To Process 'P'	9,450	1,55,925	By Normal Loss 5%	600	-
To Raw materials (at ₹10 P/u)	2,550	25,500	By Production: Transfer to finished stock 40% (WN-2)	4,560	1,07,160
To Indirect materials	-	19,000			
To Direct wages	-	45,000	Transfer to process 'R' 60% (₹23.50 per unit) (WN-2)	6,840	1,60,740
To Production over leads	-	22,475			
	12,000	2,67,900		12,000	2,67,900

Process 'R' account					
Particulars	**Units**	**Total (₹)**	**Particulars**	**Units**	**Total (₹)**
To Process 'Q'	6,840	1,60,740	By Normal loss 6%	450	-
To Raw materials (at ₹15 p/u)	660	9,900	By Production transferred to finished stock a/c (cost per unit ₹33)	7,050	2,32,650
To Indirect materials	-	20,000			
Direct wages		32,000			
To Production overheads		10,010			
	7,500	2,32,650		7,500	2,32,650

Finished stock account					
Particulars	**Units**	**Total (₹)**	**Particulars**	**Units**	**Total (₹)**
To Process 'P' a/c	4,050	66,825			
To Process 'Q' a/c	4,560	1,07,160			
To process 'R' a/c	7,050	2,32,650			

Working Note

1. **Process 'P'**

Total cost of production = ₹2,2,750

Total units produced (15,000 – 1,500) = 13,500 Unit

Cost per unit = 2,22,750/13,500 = ₹16.50

Cost of units transferred to process 'Q' = 9,450 × 16.50 = ₹1,55,925

Cost of units transferred to stock = 4,050 × 16.50 = ₹66,825

2. **Process 'Q'**

Total cost of production = ₹2,67,900

Total units produced (9,450 + 2,550 – 600) = 11,400 Unit

Cost per unit = 2,67,900/11,400 = ₹23.50

Cost of units transferred to stock = 4,560 × 23.50 = ₹1,07,160

Cost of unit transferred to process 'R' = 6,840 × 23.50 = ₹1,60,740

Illustration-5

(With abnormal loss)

500 units of raw material at ₹20 per unit was introduced in process 'A'. The normal loss of process 'A' was 10% of input and the scraps were realised at the market rate of ₹5 per unit. Direct wages and production overheads amounted to ₹8,500 and ₹4,250 respectively. The actual output was 435 units. [Prepare process 'A' account and abnormal loss account.

Solution

Process 'A' account

	Units	Total (₹)		Units	Total (₹)
To Raw materials (at ₹20 per unit)	500	10,000	By Normal loss 10%	50	250
To Direct wages	-	8,500	By abnormal loss (see wn)	15	750
To production overheads	-	4,250	By production (at ₹50 p/u)	435	21,750
	500	22,750		500	22,750

Abnormal loss account

	Units	Total (₹)		Units	Total (₹)
To Process 'A' a/c	15	750	By cash (sale of scrap at ₹5 p/u)	15	75
			By net abnormal loss transferred to costing profit and loss a/c (bf)	-	675
	15	750		15	750

Working Note

1. Abnormal loss (units):

Input	= 500 units
(−) Normal loss 10%	= 50 units
Normal production	= 450 units
Actual production	= 435 units
Abnormal loss	= 15 units

2. Normal cost of production p/u $= \dfrac{\text{Total cost} - \text{Normal scrap value}}{\text{Normal production (units)}}$

$= \dfrac{22{,}750 - 250}{450}$

$=$ ₹50

3. Value of abnormal loss = 15 units × ₹50 = ₹750

4. Value of production = 435 units × ₹50 = ₹21,750

Illustration-6

(Abnormal loss and abnormal gain)

A Ltd produces and sells its products produced through two consecutive processes 'A' and 'B'. The following are the expenses and other relevant data for the month of July 2008:

	Process 'A'	Process 'B'
Raw materials introduced	1,800 tons	320 tons
Cost per unit	₹15	₹20
Indirect materials	₹4,500	₹2,000
Direct wages	16,000	9,000
General expenses	1,820	2,616
Normal loss on input	10%	5%
Normal scrap value per ton	₹4	₹5.50
Actual output	1,600 tons	1,850 tons

Prepare process accounts. Also prepare normal loss, abnormal loss and abnormal gain account.

Solution

Process 'A' account					
Particulars	Units (Tons)	Total (₹)	Particulars	Units (Tons)	Total (₹)
To Raw materials (at ₹15 per ton))	1,800	27,000	By Normal loss -10%	180	720
To Indirect materials	-	4,500	By Abnormal loss (WN-1)	20	600
To Direct wage	-	16,000	By Transfer to process 'B' a/c (cost per unit ₹30) (WN-1)	1,600	48,000
To general expenses	-	1,820			
	1,800	49,320		180	49,320

Process 'B' a/c					
Particulars	**Units** (Tons)	**Total** (₹)	**Particulars**	**Units** (Tons)	**Total** (₹)
To process 'A' a/c	1,600	48,000	By normal loss 5% (at ₹5.50 per ton)	96	528
To Raw materials (at ₹20 per ton)	320	6,400	By Transfer to finished stock a/c (cost per unit ₹37)	1,850	68,450
To Indirect materials	-	2,000			
To Direct wages	-	9,000			
To General expenses		2,616			
To Abnormal gain	26	962			
	1946	68,978		1,946	68,978

Abnormal loss account					
Particulars	**Units** (Tons)	**Total** (₹)	**Particulars**	**Units** (Tons)	**Total** (₹)
To Process 'A' a/c	20	600	By cash (sale of scrap at ₹4 per ton)	20	80
			By Net abnormal loss transferred to costing profit and loss a/c	-	520
	20	600		20	600

Abnormal gain account					
Particulars	**Units** (Tons)	**Total** (₹)	**Particulars**	**Units** (Tons)	**Total** (₹)
To Normal loss a/c (scrap value) at ₹5.50 per ton)	26	143	By process 'B' a/c	26	962
To Net abnormal gain transferred to costing profit and loss a/c	-	819			
	26	962		26	962

Normal loss a/c					
Particulars	**Units** (Tons)	**Total** (₹)	**Particulars**	**Units** (Tons)	**Total** (₹)
To Process 'A'	180	720	By Abnormal gain	26	143

To Process 'B'	96	528	By Cash (Process 'A' scrap)	180	720
			By Cash (Process 'B' scrap)	70	385
	276	1,248		276	1,248

Working Note

1. Abnormal loss units - Process A:

$$\begin{aligned}
&\text{Input} &&= \text{1,800 tons}\\
&(-)\ \text{Normal loss 10\%} &&= \text{180 units}\\
&\text{Normal production} &&= \text{1,620 units}\\
&\text{Actual production} &&= \text{1,600 units}\\
&\text{Abnormal loss} &&= \text{20 units}
\end{aligned}$$

$$\text{Cost of production p/u} = \frac{\text{Total cost} - \text{Normal scrap value}}{\text{Normal production (units)}}$$

$$= \frac{49{,}320 - 720}{1620} = ₹30$$

Abnormal loss value$(20 \times 30) = ₹600$

Value of units transferred to process B$(1,600 \times 30) = ₹48{,}000$

2. Abnormal loss units - Process B:

$$\begin{aligned}
&\text{Input} &&= \text{1,920 tons}\\
&(-)\ \text{Normal loss 5\%} &&= \text{96 units}\\
&\text{Normal production} &&= \text{1,824 units}\\
&\text{Actual production} &&= \text{1,850 units}\\
&\text{Abnormal gain} &&= (-)\ \text{26 units}
\end{aligned}$$

$$\text{Cost of production p/u} = \frac{\text{Total cost} - \text{Normal scrap value}}{\text{Normal production (units)}}$$

$$= \frac{68{,}016 - 528}{1,824} = ₹37$$

Abnormal gain value$(26 \times 37) = ₹962$

Cost of production transferred to finished stock$(1,850 \times 37) = ₹68{,}450$

Illustration-7

(Abnormal gain)

A product passes through three processes before completion 5,000 units were introduced into the first process 'X' at a cost of ₹5 per unit. Direct wages and other expenses incurred in the process are ₹7,500 and ₹5,100 respectively. The normal process loss is 8% of input which is sold at ₹2 per unit in the market. Actual output amounted to 4,750 units.

Prepare process 'X' account and abnormal gain account.

Solution

Process 'X' account

Particulars	Units (Tons)	Total (₹)	Particulars	Units (Tons)	Total (₹)
To Raw materials	5,000	25,000	By Normal loss 8% (at ₹2 per unit)	400	800
To Direct wages	-	7,500	By Transfer to process 'Y'	4,750	38,000
To Other expenses	-	5,100			
To Abnormal gain (See WN)	150	1,200			
	5,150	38,800		5,150	38,800

Abnormal gain account

Particulars	Units (Tons)	Total (₹)	Particulars	Units (Tons)	Total (₹)
To Normal loss a/c (scrap value)	150	300	By Process 'X' a/c	150	1,200
To Net abnormal gain transferred to costing profit and loss a/c	-	900			
	150	1,200		150	1,200

Working Note

1. Abnormal loss (units):

Input	= 5,000 units
(−) Normal loss 8%	= 400 units
Normal production	= 4,600 units
Actual production	= 4,750 units

Abnormal gain = 150 units

2. $\text{Cost of production p/u} = \dfrac{\text{Total cost} - \text{Normal scrap value}}{\text{Normal production (units)}}$

$$= \frac{37{,}600 - 800}{4{,}600} = ₹8$$

3. Value of abnormal gain = 150 units × ₹8 = ₹1,200

4. Value of production = 4750 units × ₹8 = ₹38,000

Illustration-8

(With stock of raw materials)

The product of a company pass through three processes P, Q and R. It is ascertained from the past experience that process loss computed on input including opening stock of the respective process will be process P–5%, Process Q–10% and Process R–15%. The process loss fetch a scrap value of ₹2, ₹3 and ₹5 respectively from processes P, Q and R. 5,000 units of Raw material at ₹15 per unit is introduced in Process P. The other details of production and expenses are as follows:

	Process P (₹)	Process Q (₹)	Process R (₹)
Indirect materials	13,000	11,000	12,500
Wages	15,000	13,500	9,000
Direct expenses	6,750	7,000	6,225
	Units	**Units**	**Units**
Opening stock of raw materials	-	250	350
Closing stock of raw materials	-	350	200

Solution

Process 'P' account

Particulars	Units	Total (₹)	Particulars	Units	Total (₹)
To Raw materials (at ₹15 per unit)	5,000	75,000	By Normal loss 5% (at ₹2 per unit)	250	500
To Indirect materials	-	13,000	By Transfer to process Q a/c (Cost per unit ₹23) (bf)	4,750	1,09,250
To Wages	-	15,000			
To Direct expenses	-	6,750			
	5,000	1,09,750		5,000	1,09,750

Process 'Q' account					
Particulars	**Units**	**Total (₹)**	**Particulars**	**Units**	**Total (₹)**
To Opening stock (at ₹23 per unit)	250	5,750	By Normal loss 10% (at ₹3 per unit)	500	1,500
To Process P a/c	4,750	1,09,250			
To Indirect materials	-	11,000	By Transfer to process R a/c (Cost per unit ₹33) (bf)	4,150	1,36,950
To Wages	-	13,500	By Closing stock	350	8,050
To Direct expenses	-	7,000	(Cost per unit ₹23)		
	5,000	1,46,500		5,000	1,46,500

Process 'R' account					
Particulars	**Units**	**Total (₹)**	**Particulars**	**Units**	**Total (₹)**
To Process P a/c	4,150	1,36,950	By Normal loss 15% (at ₹5 per unit)	675	10,125
To Opening stock (at ₹33 per unit)	350	11,550			
To Indirect materials	-	12,500	By Transfer to process R a/c (Cost per unit ₹44) (bf)	3,625	1,59,500
To Wages	-	9,000	By Closing stock	200	6,600
To Direct expenses	-	6,225	(Cost per unit ₹33)		
	4,500	1,76,225		4,500	1,76,225

Illustration-9

(Valuation of closing stock of finished goods)

Product 'X' is produced in a chemical manufacturing company after the raw materials passes through three process R, S and T. 6,000 units of raw materials at ₹12 per unit were introduced and other production details for the month of April 2009 are given below:

	Process R (₹)	Process S (₹)	Process T (₹)
Direct materials consumed	32,000	27,500	23,600
Direct wages	43,000	39,500	31,400
Indirect expenses	6,000	10,350	3,675

Normal process loss on total input (including opening stock)	10%	5%	8%
Scrap value of process loss	₹3	₹4	₹4.50
	Units	**Units**	**Units**
Stock of finished production: 1st April 2009	350	200	300
30th April 2009	250	175	200
Value of stock on 1st April 2009	₹27	₹42	₹57

Prepare process account.

Solution

Process 'R' account					
Particulars	**Units**	**Total (₹)**	**Particulars**	**Units**	**Total (₹)**
To Raw materials (at ₹12 per unit)	6,000	72,000	By Closing stock (at ₹28 per unit)	250	7,000
To Indirect materials	-	32,000	By Transfer to process S a/c (bf)	5,500	1,53,650
To Direct wages	-	43,000			
To Indirect expenses	-	6,000			
Total	6,000	1,53,000			
Less: Normal loss 10%	600	1,800			
Cost of production (₹28 per unit)	5400	1,51,200			
Add: Opening stock	350	9,450			
	5,750	1,60,650		5,750	1,60,650

Process 'S' account					
Particulars	**Units**	**Total (₹)**	**Particulars**	**Units**	**Total (₹)**
To Process R a/c	5,500	1,53,650	By Closing stock (at 44 per unit)	175	7,700
To Indirect materials	-	27,500	By Transfer to process T a/c (bf)	5,250	2,30,600
To Direct wages	-	39,500			
To Indirect expenses	-	10,350			

	5,500	2,31,000			
Less: Normal loss 5%	275	1,100			
Cost of production (₹44 per unit)	5,225	2,29,900			
Add: Opening stock	200	8,400			
	5,425	2,38,300		5,425	2,38,300

Process 'T' account

Particulars	Units	Total (₹)	Particulars	Units	Total (₹)
To Process S a/c	5,250	2,30,600	By Closing stock (at ₹9.50 per unit)	200	11,900
To Indirect materials	-	23,600	By Transfer to finished stock a/c (bf)	4,930	2,92,585
To Direct wages	-	31,400			
To Indirect expenses	-	3,675			
	5,250	2,89,275			
Less: Normal loss 8%	420	1,890			
Cost of production (₹59.50 per unit)	4,830	2,87,385			
Add: Opening stock	300	17,100			
	5,130	3,04,485		5,130	3,04,485

Inter-Process Profit

In process costing each process is treated as cost centre and profit centre. To find the profit of each process, output of one process is transferred to next process at an inflated price over the cost. The inflated price may be fixed at market price or cost plus a fixed percentage of profit desired. The following are the justifications for transfer of finished product of a process to next process at inflated price:

1. To find the profit of each process
2. To find the operating efficiency of each process.
3. To decide whether a particular process is to be discontinued or not.
4. The last process is not loaded with the whole of the profit.
5. It creates a competitive environment between various processes.
6. The inefficiency of one process is not passed on to other processes.
7. Raw materials are charged at current market price to each process.

Arguments against Transfer at Market Price

1. Accounting work involved is time consuming and complicated.
2. There is difficulty in valuing stocks of each process.
3. The unearned profit included in stocks are to be eliminated for accounting purposes.

Procedure for preparing process accounts are:

1. All expenses including materials received from previous process in debited to process account.
2. All expenses are totalled and normal loss in deducted to find cost of production.
3. Closing stock is deducted from the cost of production, opening stock is added to find the cost of goods transferred to the next process.
4. Profit at agreed rate is added to cost of goods transferred to find the transfer price.
5. Process account is prepared with three columns total, cost and profit.
6. The cost and profit columns are only memorandum columns which helps to find the unrealised profit included in the stock of each process. It helps to calculate the realised profit and valuation of stocks at cost price.

Illustration-10

The product 'M' is produced in a company after the raw materials undergoing operations in three consecutive processes. It is the policy of the company to transfer goods from one process to another at a price calculated to give profit. The output of process I is transferred at a profit of 20% on transfer price and at 20% on cost price from process II to process III and from process III to finished stock. The following data was obtained for the month of August 2008:

	Process I (₹)	Process II (₹)	Process III (₹)
Direct materials	50,000	40,000	30,000
Direct wages	30,000	20,000	15,000
Stock on 31st August	12,000	10,000	9,000

Finished goods are sold for ₹2,50,000. Closing stock of finished goods is ₹20,000. Stocks are valued on prime cost basis.

Required:

(a) Prepare process accounts
(b) Stock at cost price for balance sheet purpose and
(c) Calculate realised profit.

Solution

Process 'I' account							
Particulars	Total (₹)	Cost (₹)	Profit (₹)	Particulars	Total (₹)	Cost (₹)	Profit (₹)
To Direct materials	50,000	50,000	-	By Transfer to process II a/c	85,000	68,000	17,000
To Direct wages	30,000	30,000	-				
Prime cost	80,000	80,000	-				
Less: Closing stock	12,000	12,000	-				
	68,000	68,000	-				
Profit 20% on transfer price	17,000	-	17,000				
	85,000	68,000	17,000		85,000	68,000	17,000

Process 'II' account							
Particulars	Total (₹)	Cost (₹)	Profit (₹)	Particulars	Total (₹)	Cost (₹)	Profit (₹)
To Process I a/c	85,000	68,000	17,000				
To Direct materials	40,000	40,000	-	By Transfer to process II a/c	1,62,000	1,19,172	42,828
To Direct wages	20,000	20,000	-				
Prime cost	1,45,000	1,28,000	17,000				
Less: Closing stock	10,000	8,828	1,172				
	1,35,000	1,19,172	15,828				
Profit 20% on cost price	27,000	-	27,000				
	1,62,000	1,19,172	42,828		1,62,000	1,19,172	42,828

Process 'III' account							
Particulars	Total (₹)	Cost (₹)	Profit (₹)	Particulars	Total (₹)	Cost (₹)	Profit (₹)
To Process II a/c	1,62,000	1,19,172	42,828				
To Direct materials	30,000	30,000	-	By Transfer to process II a/c	2,37,600	1,57,034	80,566
To Direct wages	15,000	15,000	-				
Prime cost	2,07,000	1,64,172	42,828				

Less: Closing stock	9,000	7,138	1,862				
	1,98,000	1,57,034	40,966				
Profit 20% on cost price	39,600	-	39,600				
	2,37,600	1,57,034	80,566		2,37,600	1,57,034	80,566

(a)

Finished stock account

Particulars	Total (₹)	Cost (₹)	Profit (₹)	Particulars	Total (₹)	Cost (₹)	Profit (₹)
To Process III a/c	2,37,600	1,57,034	80,566	By Sales	2,50,000	1,43,816	1,06,184
To Profit	32,400	-	32,400	By Closing stock	20,000	13,218	6,782
	2,70,000	1,57,034	1,12,966		2,70,000	1,57,034	1,12,966

(b)

Valuation of stock at cost price

Process	Closing Stock (1)	Unrealised Profit (2)	Cost Price (3) = (1−2)
	(₹)	(₹)	(₹)
I	12,000	-	12,000
II	10,000	$\frac{17,000}{1,45,000} \times 10,000 = 1,172$	8,828
III	9,000	$\frac{42,828}{2,07,000} \times 9,000 = 1,862$	7,138
Finished stock	20,000	$\frac{80,566}{2,37,600} \times 20,000 = 6,782$	13,218
		Total	41,184

(c)

Realised profit

Process	Total Profit (1)	Unrealised Profit (2)	Realised profit (3) = (1−2)
	(₹)	(₹)	(₹)
I	17,000	-	17,000

II	27,000	1,172	25,828
III	39,600	1,862	37,738
Finished stock	32,400	6,782	25,618
		Total	1,06,184

Illustration-11

Product 'Zed' is produced in three processes before it is transferred to finished stock. The following information is obtained for the month of April 2009:

	Process I (₹)	Process II (₹)	Process III (₹)	Finished stock (₹)
Opening stock	30,000	36,000	24,000	90,000
Direct materials	60,000	63,000	90,000	-
Direct wages	45,000	45,000	48,000	-
Production overheads	42,000	18,000	1,20,000	-
Closing stock	15,000	18,000	12,000	30,000
% of profit on Cost	33 1/3%	25%	25%	-
Inter-process profit for opening stock	-	6,000	6,000	33,000

Stock in processes are valued at prime cost and finished stock has been valued at price at which it is received from process III. Sales during the period was ₹10,50,000.

Required:

(a) Prepare process account

(b) Compute cost of closing stock for balance sheet purpose and

(c) Find the realised profit.

Solution

Process 'I' a/c							
Particulars	Total (₹)	Cost (₹)	Profit (₹)	Particulars	Total (₹)	Cost (₹)	Profit (₹)
To Opening stock	30,000	30,000	-				
To Direct materials	60,000	60,000	-	By Transfer to process II a/c	2,16,000	1,62,000	54,000
To Direct wages	45,000	45,000	-				
Prime cost	1,35,000	1,35,000	-				
Less: Closing stock	15,000	15,000	-				

	1,20,000	1,20,000	-				
To Production overheads	42,000	42,000	-				
	1,62,000	1,62,000	-				
To Profit (33 1/3% on cost price)	54,000	-	54,000				
	2,16,000	1,62,000	54,000		2,16,000	1,62,000	54,000

Process 'II' a/c

Particulars	Total (₹)	Cost (₹)	Profit (₹)	Particulars	Total (₹)	Cost (₹)	Profit (₹)
To Opening stock	36,000	30,000	6,000				
To Process I a/c	2,16,000	1,62,000	54,000	By Transfer to process II a/c	4,50,000	3,03,000	1,47,000
To Direct materials	63,000	63,000	-				
To Direct wages	45,000	45,000	-				
Prime Cost	3,60,000	3,00,000	60,000				
Less: Closing stock	18,000	15,000	3,000				
	3,42,000	2,85,000	57,000				
To Production overheads	18,000	18,000	-				
	3,60,000	3,03,000	57,000				
To Profit (25% on cost)	90,000	-	90,000				
	4,50,000	3,03,000	1,47,000		4,50,000	3,03,000	1,47,000

Process 'III' a/c

Particulars	Total (₹)	Cost (₹)	Profit (₹)	Particulars	Total (₹)	Cost (₹)	Profit (₹)
To Opening stock	24,000	18,000	6,000				
To Process II a/c	4,50,000	3,03,000	1,47,000	By Transfer to process II a/c	9,00,000	5,70,000	3,30,000
To Direct materials	90,000	90,000	-				
To Direct wages	48,000	48,000	-				
Prime cost	6,12,000	4,59,000	1,53,000				

Less: Closing stock	12,000	9,000	3,000				
	6,00,000	4,50,000	1,50,000				
To Production overheads	1,20,000	1,20,000	-				
	7,20,000	5,70,000	1,50,000				
To Profit (25% on cost)	1,80,000	-	1,80,000				
	9,00,000	5,70,000	3,30,000		9,00,000	5,70,000	3,30,000

(a)

Finished stock account

Particulars	Total (₹)	Cost (₹)	Profit (₹)	Particulars	Total (₹)	Cost (₹)	Profit (₹)
To Opening stock	90,000	57,000	33,000	By Sales	10,50,000	6,08,000	3,97,000
To Process III a/c	9,00,000	5,70,000	3,30,000				
Total	9,90,000	6,27,000	3,63,000				
To Profit	45,000	-	45,000	By Closing stock	30,000	19,000	11,000
	10,35,000	6,27,000	4,08,000		10,35,000	6,27,000	4,08,000

(b)

Computation of cost of closing stock

Process	Closing Stock (1)	Unrealised Profit (2)	Cost Price (3) = (1–2)
	(₹)	(₹)	(₹)
I	15,000	-	15,000
II	18,000	$\frac{60,000}{3,60,000} \times 18,000 = 3,000$	15,000
III	12,000	$\frac{1,53,000}{6,12,000} \times 12,000 = 3,000$	9,000
Finished stock	30,000	$\frac{3,63,000}{9,90,000} \times 30,000 = 11,000$	19,000
		Total	58,000

(c)

Realised profit				
Process	Total Profit	Unrealised Profit		Realised Profit
		Opening Stock	Closing Stock	
	(₹)	(₹)	(₹)	(₹)
	(1)	(2)	(3)	(4) = (1+2−3)
I	54,000		-	54,000
II	90,000	6,000	3,000	93,000
III	1,80,000	6,000	3,000	1,83,000
Finished stock	45,000	33,000	11,000	67,000
			Total	3,97,000

16.3 VALUATION OF WORK-IN-PROGRESS AND CONCEPT OF EQUIVALENT PRODUCTION

In process industries production is continuous. There will be stock of incomplete units at the opening and closing day of a period. These incomplete units will be in various stages of production. On some units major part of work might have been completed and only a small part of work may be pending. On some other units work might have just started and major part of work is yet to be completed. The valuation of these incomplete units poses a difficult problem. One way of finding the value of incomplete units is to measure the actual value of materials, labour and overheads incurred. This is practically not possible as materials, labour and overheads incurred in a process industries cannot be traced direct to individual units. So the concept of equivalent production is applied. According to concept of equivalent production the incomplete units are expressed in terms of complete units. Say, if 100 units on which work completed is 40%, these 100 incomplete units may be taken as 40 completed units (i.e. 100 units × 40% = 40 units).

16.3.1 Steps Involved in Valuation of Work-in-Progress

Step 1: Calculation of equivalent units

(a) Note the number of opening work-in-progress, number of fresh units introduced into the process during the period, the number of units completed, abnormal loss/gain units and the number of units of closing work-in-progress.

(b) Opening Stock (FIFO Method): Note the degree of completion given for opening work-in-progress is (say 20%). Only the balance work (i.e. 80%) has to be completed during the period. So take the balance degree of work done during the period for finding the equivalent units for opening work-in-progress. If 200 units are in stock in the beginning of the period with 70% work complete. The equivalent units for opening work-in-progress for the current period will be 200 units × 30% = 60 units.

(c) Abnormal loss: Abnormal loss may have arisen before the work has been completed. Then the actual degree of completion is taken for calculation of equivalent units.

(d) Abnormal Gain: This is savings in normal loss converted into good units completed. The degree of completion is always 100%.

(e) Total equivalent units: The equivalent units of opening work-in-progress, closing work-in-progress, abnormal loss and completed units are added to find the equivalent units. The equivalent units of abnormal gain is deducted from the total equivalent units.

(f) One important point to be noted is sometimes materials will be issued in stages as the work progresses. In this case degree of completion for material, labour and overheads will be same. Sometimes entire raw material is issued in the beginning of production stage itself and labour work will be done in stages. In this case degree of completion for materials, labour and overheads will vary.

Step 2: Determining cost per equivalent unit for each elements of expenses:

(a) From the total cost of materials the sale of normal scrap is deducted. The net cost of materials is divided by total number of equivalent units of materials.

(b) Total labour cost is divided by total number of equivalent units of labour.

(c) Total overheads is divided by total equivalent units of overheads.

Step 3: Preparing statement of evaluation:

In this step value of units completed from opening work-in-progress, value of fresh units completed, value of closing work-in-progress and value of abnormal loss/gain is found by multiplying respective equivalent unit by respect cost per equivalent units.

Accounting treatment

(i) Value of opening stock of work-in-progress is debited to process account.

(ii) Value of closing stock of work-in-progress is credited to process account.

(iii) Treatment of process costs, normal loss, abnormal loss and abnormal gain is as per procedure already discussed.

16.4 METHODS OF VALUATION OF WORK-IN-PROGRESS

Three methods are used to value work-in-progress. They are,

1. **First In First Out Method (FIFO)**

   In this method, it is assumed that the work is done on the fresh units introduced during the period only after completing the opening stock of work-in-progress. So the closing work-in-progress is always from fresh units introduced during the period. This method is most logical and preferred one.

2. Average Cost Method

This method is useful when prices of materials, rates of labour and expenses fluctuates widely. The value of each element of cost included in opening work-in-progress is added to the respective elements of cost incurred during the period. Total cost of each element of cost is divided by equivalent elements of respective costs. This helps in averaging the cost. No separate equivalent unit is calculated for opening work-in-progress. Opening work-in-progress is included in total units completed and 100% degree of completion is used for calculation of equivalent units for completed units including opening work-in-progress.

3. Weighted Average Cost Method

This method is used when two or more dissimilar products are produced in a process. Each product is given a weightage for calculation of equivalent units. Total process cost is apportioned among the products using equivalent units.

4. Last-In-First Out Method (LIFO)

In this method it is assumed work is commenced on fresh units first. After the completion of all fresh units opening work-in-progress is taken up for completion. When the closing work-in-progress is equal to or less than the opening work-in-progress units, entire closing work-in-progress units are valued on the basis of the value of opening work-in-progress. If closing work-in-progress units are more than opening work-in-progress units, the excess units of closing work-in-progress over opening work-in-progress units are valued on current cost basis. If produced units is equal to or less than units introduced into the process, the entire output is from fresh units. If produced units are more than the fresh units introduced, the excess units are completed from opening work-in-progress. The value of completed units and work-in-progress will differ accordingly. This method is not logical and least preferred.

Problems under equivalent production are classified under the following groupings

1. There is closing work-in-progress only and no process loss.
2. There is closing work-in-progress and process loss.
3. There is opening and closing work-in-progress and process losses:
   (a) FIFO Method
   (b) Average Method
   (c) Weighted Average Method
   (d) LIFO Method

Illustration-12 (Closing work-in-progress and no process loss)

During April 2009, 5,000 units were introduced into process 'A'. 4,000 units were completed and transferred to process 'B' and 1,000 units remained incomplete. The materials were introduced in the beginning itself. The degree of labour and overheads work completed were 75%.

The expenses incurred during the month was as follows:

Direct materials - ₹27,500
Direct labour - ₹19,000
Overhead - ₹14,250

Required:

(a) Find the equivalent production units.

(b) Ascertain the cost per unit.

(c) Statement of evaluation.

(d) Process 'A' a/c.

Solution

(a)

Statement showing equivalent production						
Input (Units)	Output		Equivalent Production			
		Units	Materials		Labour and Overheads	
			%	Units	%	Units
5,000	Units completed	4,000	100%	4,000	100%	4,000
	Closing stock of WIP	1,000	100%	1,000	75%	750
5,000		5,000	-	5,000	-	4,750

(b)

Statement of cost			
Particulars	Total Cost (₹)	Equivalent Production (Units)	Cost per unit (₹)
Direct materials	27,500	5,000	5.50
Direct labour	19,000	4,750	4.00
Overheads	14,250	4,750	3.00
Total	60,750		12.50

(c)

Statement of evaluation					
Particulars	Elements of Cost	Equivalent Production (Units)	Cost per unit (₹)	Cost (₹)	Total (₹)
(i) Units completed	All costs	4,000	12.50	50,000	50,000

(ii) Closing WIP	D. Materials	1,000	5.50	5,500	
	D. Labour	750	4.00	3,000	
	Overheads	750	3.00	2,250	10,750

Process 'A' account

Particulars	Units	Total (₹)	Particulars	Units	Total (₹)
To Direct materials	5,000	27,500	Units completed	4,000	50,000
To Direct wages	-	19,000	Closing WIP	1,000	10,750
To Direct expenses	-	14,250			
	5,000	60,750		5,000	60,750

Illustration-13 (With closing stock and process loss)

SBL Ltd. furnishes you the following information relating to process B for the month of April, 2006:

(i) Opening work-in-progress: Nil

(ii) Units introduced - 10,000 units at ₹5 per unit.

(iii) Expenses debited to the process 'B': Process Materials - ₹24,600; Direct labour - ₹10,400; Overheads - ₹5,000.

(iv) 8,000 units of finished output were transferred to the next process during the month.

(v) Normal loss in process - 10% of input.

(vi) Closing work-in-progress - 800 units. Degree of completion: Materials 100% Labour and overheads - 50%.

(vii) Degree of completion of abnormal loss: Materials - 100%, labour and overheads - 80%.

(viii) Scrap realisation: Normal loss - at ₹2 per unit; abnormal loss at ₹4 per unit.

You are required to prepare:

(a) Statement of equivalent production

(b) Statement of cost of each element

(c) Statement of evaluation

(d) Process 'B' account

(e) Abnormal loss account **(ICWA-Inter, June, 2006)**

Solution

(a)

Statement showing equivalent production						
Input (Units)	Output		Equivalent Production			
		Units	Materials		Labour and Overheads	
			%	Units	%	Units
10,000	Units completed	8,000	100%	8,000	100%	8,000
	Closing stock of WIP	800	100%	800	50%	400
	Normal loss	1,000	-	-	-	-
	Abnormal loss (See WN-1)	200	100%	200	80%	160
10,000		10,000	-	9,000	-	8,560

(b)

Statement of cost			
Particulars	Total Cost (₹)	Equivalent Production (Units)	Cost per unit (₹)
Materials I value of units introduced (10,000 × 5) 50,000			
Less: Normal loss - Scrap value 2,000	48,000		
Materials - II - Process	24,600		
Materials	72,600	9,000	8.067
Direct labour	10,400	8,560	1.215
Overheads	5,000	8,560	0.584
Total	88,000	-	9.866

(c)

Statement of evaluation					
Particulars	Elements of Cost	Equivalent Production (Units)	Cost per unit (₹)	Cost (₹)	Total (₹)
(i) Units completed	All costs	8,000	9.866	78,926	78,926

(ii) Closing WIP	Materials	800	8.067	6,454	
	Labour	400	1.215	486	
	Overheads	400	0.584	234	7,174
(iii) Abnormal loss	Materials	200	8.067	1,612	
	Labour	160	1.215	194	
	Overheads	160	0.584	94	1,900

Process 'B' account

Particulars	Units	Total (₹)	Particulars	Units	Total (₹)
To Raw materials at ₹5 per unit	10,000	50,000	By Normal loss at ₹2 per unit	1,000	2,000
To Process materials	-	24,600	By Abnormal loss	200	1,900
To Direct labour	-	10,400	By Output transferred to next process	8,000	78,926
To Overheads	-	5,000	By Closing work-in-progress	800	7,174
	10,000	90,000		10,000	90,000

Abnormal loss account

Particulars	Units	Total (₹)	Particulars	Units	Total (₹)
To Process 'B' a/c	200	1,900	By Cash - Sale of scrap at ₹4 per unit	200	800
			By Net abnormal loss transferred to costing P&L a/c	-	1,100
	200	1,900		200	1,900

Working Note

1. Abnormal loss (units):

	Input	= 10,000 units
Less:	Normal loss: 1,000	
	Closing WIP: 800	= 1,800 units
	Normal production	= 8,200 units

Actual production	=	8,000 units
Abnormal loss	=	200 units

2. Calculations were made to the nearest rupee.

Illustration-14 (With closing stock, normal loss and abnormal gain)

In a manufacturing concern, 6,000 kg. of oil seeds were introduced at ₹5 per kg. in process I. There was no opening work-in-progress. The following information are available for the operation of a period:

(i) Expenses debited to process - I:

Direct materials - ₹10,800

Direct labour - ₹13,200

Overheads - ₹7,920

(ii) Normal loss 5% of input

(iii) Closing work-in-progress - 700 kg

Degree of completion:

Materials - 100%

Labour and overheads - 40%

(iv) Finished output transferred to process - II - 5,200 kg

(v) Units scrapped as normal loss was sold at ₹3 per kg.

Prepare,

(a) Statement of equivalent production
(b) Statement of cost
(c) Statement of evaluation
(d) Process account
(e) Abnormal loss or gain account. **(ICWA-Inter adapted)**

Solution

(a)

Statement showing equivalent production						
Input (Units)	**Output**		**Equivalent Production**			
		Units	**Materials**		**Labour and Overheads**	
			%	**Units**	**%**	**Units**
6,000	Units completed	5,200	100%	5,200	100%	5,200
	Closing WIP	700	100%	700	40%	280
	Normal loss	300	-	-	-	-
	Total	6,200	-	5,900	-	5,480
	(−) Abnormal gain (See WN-1)	200	100%	200	100%	200
6,000		6,000	-	5,700	-	5,280

(b)

Statement of cost				
Particulars		**Total Cost (₹)**	**Equivalent Production (Units)**	**Cost per unit (₹)**
Materials I (6,000×5) Less: Normal loss - Scrap value (300 × 3)	30,000 900			
 Materials II	29,100 10,800	39,900	5,700	7.00
Direct materials				
Direct labour		13,200	5,280	2.50
Overheads		7,920	5,280	1.50
Total		61,020	-	11.00

(c)

Statement of Evaluation					
Particulars	**Elements of Cost**	**Equivalent Production (Units)**	**Cost per unit (₹)**	**Cost (₹)**	**Total (₹)**
(i) Units completed	All costs	5,200	11.00	57,200	57,200
(ii) Closing WIP	Materials	700	7.00	4,900	

	Direct labour	280	2.50	700	
	Overheads	280	1.50	420	6,020
(iii) Abnormal Gain	All Cost	200	11.00	2,200	2,200

Process 'I' account

Particulars	Units	Total (₹)	Particulars	Units	Total (₹)
To Raw materials at ₹5 per unit	6,000	30,000	By Normal loss at ₹3 per kg	300	900
To Direct materials	-	10,800	By Production transferred to process II a/c	5,200	57,200
To Direct labour	-	13,200			
To Overheads	-	7,920	By Closing work-in-progress	700	6,020
To Abnormal gain	200	2,200			
	6,200	64,120		6,200	64,120

Abnormal gain account

Particulars	Units	Total (₹)	Particulars	Units	Total (₹)
To Normal loss - Scrap value	200	600	By Process I a/c	200	2,200
To Net abnormal gain transferred to costing profit and loss account	-	1,600			
	200	2,200		200	2,200

Working Note

1. Abnormal gain (units):

	Input	= 6,000 units
Less:	Normal loss: 300	
	Closing WIP: 700	= 1,000 units
	Normal production	= 5,000 units
	Actual production	= 5,200 units
	Abnormal loss	= (–) 200 units

Illustration-15 (With opening and closing work-in-progress but no process loss)

From the following information relating to process I of a factory for the month of January, 2009, prepare statement of equivalent production, statement of cost, statement of evaluation and process I account using average cost method:

(i) Opening work-in-progress - 1,000 units: valued at ₹60,000 consisting of:

Materials - ₹30,000

Labour - ₹20,000

Overheads - ₹10,000

(ii) Units introduced into the process 10,000 units

(iii) There is no process loss

(iv) Closing work-in-progress - 2,000 units
Degree of competition: Materials - 90%, Labour and overheads - 60%

(v) Expenses incurred in the process during the month:

Direct materials - ₹45,600

Direct labour - ₹46,300

Overheads - ₹33,350

Solution

(a)

Statement showing equivalent production					
Output		**Equivalent Production**			
	Units	**Materials**		**Labour and Overheads**	
		%	**Units**	**%**	**Units**
Units completed (See WN-1)	9,000	100%	9,000	100%	9,000
Closing WIP	2,000	90%	1,800	60%	1,200
	11,000	-	10,800	-	10,200

(b)

Statement of Cost			
Particulars	**Materials (₹)**	**Labour (₹)**	**Overheads (₹)**
(i) Cost included in opening WIP	30,000	20,000	10,000

Expenses incurred	45,600	46,300	33,350
Total	75,600	66,300	43,350
(ii) Equivalent production units	10,800	10,200	10,200
(iii) Cost per unit = (i) ÷ (ii)	7	6.50	4.25

(c)

Statement of Evaluation

Particulars	**Elements of Cost**	**Equivalent Production (Units)**	**Cost per unit (₹)**	**Cost (₹)**	**Total (₹)**
Units completed	All costs	9,000	17.75	1,59,760	1,59,750
Closing WIP	Materials	1,800	7.00	12,600	
	Direct labour	1,200	6.50	7,800	
	Overheads	1,200	4.25	5,100	25,500

Process 'I' account

Particulars	**Units**	**Total (₹)**	**Particulars**	**Units**	**Total (₹)**
To Opening WIP	1,000	60,000	By Production transferred to process II a/c	9,000	1,59,750
To Materials	10,000	45,600	By Closing WIP	2,000	25,500
To Labour	-	46,300			
To Overheads	-	33,350			
	11,000	1,85,250		11,000	1,85,250

Working Note

1. Abnormal gain units:

Opening WIP	- 1,000 units
Units Introduced	- 10,000 units
	- 11,000 units
Closing WIP	- 2,000 units
Units completed	- 9,000 units

Illustration-16 (With opening and closing work-in-progress and no process loss)

A company manufactures its sole product by passing it through three processes X, Y and Z. The following details relating to process 'Y' is obtained for the month of May 2009:

(i) Opening work-in-progress - 500 units - ₹25,500 consisting of:
Degree of completion - Materials - 100%, Labour and overheads - 75%

(ii) Received from process 'X' 5,000 units at ₹8 per unit.

(iii) There is no process loss.

(iv) Expenses incurred during the month:

Direct materials - ₹25,000

Direct labour - ₹34,300

Overheads - ₹24,500

(v) Closing work-in-progress 750 units.
Degree of completion - Materials - 100%, Labour and overheads - 70%

(vi) Units completed and transferred to process 'I' - 4,750 units. Using FIFO Method Prepare:

(a) Statement of equivalent production

(b) Statement of cost

(c) Statement of evaluation

(d) Process 'Y' account

Solution

(a)

Statement showing equivalent production					
Output		Equivalent Production			
	Units	Materials		Labour and Overheads	
		%	Units	%	Units
(i) Units completed from:					
(a) Opening WIP	500	-	-	25%	125
(b) Units introduced	4,250	100%	4,250	100%	4,250
(ii) Closing WIP	750	100%	750	70%	525
	5,500	-	5,000	-	4,900

(b)

Statement of Cost			
Particulars	Total Cost (₹)	Equivalent Production (Units)	Cost per unit (₹)
Materials I (5,000×8)	40,000		

Materials II - Incurred	25,000		
	65,000	5,000	13.00
Direct labour	34,300	4,900	7.00
Overheads	24,500	4,900	5.00
Total	1,88,800	-	25.00

(c)

Statement of Evaluation

Particulars	Elements of Cost	Equivalent Production (Units)	Cost per unit (₹)	Cost (₹)	Total (₹)
(i) Units completed					
(a) Opening stock	Opening value	-	-	-	25,500
	Labour	125	7	875	
	Overheads	125	5	625	1500
(b) Units introduced	All cost	4,250	25	1,06,250	1,06,250
Total					1,33,250
(ii) Closing WIP	Materials	750	13	9,750	
	Labour	525	7	3,675	
	Overheads	525	5	2,625	16,050

Process 'Y' account

Particulars	Units	Total (₹)	Particulars	Units	Total (₹)
To Opening WIP	500	25,500	By Production transferred to process Z a/c	4,750	1,33,250
To Process X	5,000	40,000	By Closing WIP	750	16,050
To Direct materials	-	25,000			
To Direct labour	-	34,300			
To Overheads	-	24,500			
	5,500	1,49,300		5,500	1,49,300

Illustration-17 (With opening and closing work-in-progress and with process loss)

From the following information relating to process I of a factory for the month of April 2003, prepare the statement of equivalent production, statement of cost, statement of evaluation, process accounts using average cost method:

(i) Opening work-in-progress : 500 units -

Materials	- ₹27,000
Labour	- ₹8,000
Overheads	- ₹12,500
	- ₹47,500

(ii) Cost incurred during April 2003:

Input of materials: 14,000 units	- ₹5,74,750
Labour	- ₹1,19,300
Overheads	- ₹1,78,450

(iii) Process loss: Normal loss - 10% of input including opening stock of work-in-progress

Value of scrapped units - ₹10 each.

Actual loss during April 2003; 1,500 units

Degree of completion: Materials 100%, Labour and overheads 60%.

(iv) Closing work-in-progress 1,000 units.
Degree of completion - Materials - 100%, Labour and overheads - 70%

(v) Processed units transferred to process II : 12,000 units during April 2003.

(ICWA-Inter, June 2003)

Solution

(a)

Statement showing equivalent production							
Input		**Output**		**Equivalent Production**			
				Materials		**Labour and Overheads**	
	Units		**Units**	**%**	**Units**	**%**	**Units**
Opening WIP	500	Units completed	12,000	100%	12,000	100%	12,000
Fresh units	14,000	Closing WIP	1,000	100%	1,000	70%	700
		Normal Loss	1,450	-	-	-	-

		Abnormal Loss	50	100%	50	60%	30
	14,500		14,500	-	13,050	-	12,730

(b)

Statement of Cost			
Particulars	**Materials (₹)**	**Labour (₹)**	**Overheads (₹)**
Cost icluded in opening WIP	27,000	8,000	12,500
Cost incurred during April	5,74,750	1,19,300	1,78,450
	6,01,750		
Less: Sale of normal scrap (1,450×10)	14,500		
(i) Total cost	5,87,250	1,27,300	1,90,950
(ii) Equivalent production units	13,050	12,730	12,730
(iii) Cost per unit	45	10	15

(c)

Statement of Evaluation					
Particulars	**Elements of Cost**	**Equivalent Production (Units)**	**Cost per unit (₹)**	**Cost (₹)**	**Total (₹)**
Units completed	All cost	12,000	70	8,40,000	8,40,000
Closing WIP	Materials	1,000	45	45,000	62,500
	Labour	700	10	7,000	
	Overheads	700	15	10,500	
Abnormal loss	Materials	50	45	2,250	3,000
	Labour	30	10	300	
	Overheads	30	15	450	

(d)

Process 'I' a/c							
	Units	**Rate (₹)**	**Total (₹)**		**Units**	**Rate (₹)**	**Total (₹)**
To Opening WIP	500	-	47,500	By Normal loss	1,450	10	14,500

To Input materials	14,000	-	5,74,750	By Output transfer to process II	12,000	70	8,40,000
To Labour	-	-	1,19,300	By Abnormal loss	50	-	3,000
To Overheads	-	-	1,78,450	By Closing WIP	1,000	-	62,500
	14,500	-	9,20,000		14,500	-	9,20,000

Illustration-18 (With opening and closing stock and with no process loss)

Following information is available regarding process 'A' for the month of February 1999:

Production Record:	
Units in process as on 1.2.1999	4,000
(All material used, 25% ccmplete for labour and overhead)	
New units introduced	16,000
Units completed	14,000
Units in process as on 28.2.1999	6,000
(All materials used $33\frac{1}{3}$% complete for labour and overhead)	
Cost Records:	
Work-in-process as on 01.02.1999	
Materials	₹6,000
Labour	₹1,000
Overhead	₹1,000
Cost during the month:	
Materials	₹25,600
Labour	₹15,000
Overhead	₹15,000
	₹55,600

Presuming that average method of inventory is used, prepare:

(a) Statement of equivalent production
(b) Statement of cost
(c) Statement of apportionment of cost
(d) Process cost accounts for process 'A'

Solution

(a)

Statement of equivalent production							
Input		Output		Equivalent Production			
	Units		Units	Materials		Labour and Overheads	
				%	Units	%	Units
Opening WIP	4,000	Unit completed	14,000	100%	14,000	100%	14,000
New units	16,000	Closing WIP	6,000	100%	6,000	33 1/3%	2,000
	20,000		20,000		20,000		16,000

(b)

Statement of Cost			
Particulars	Materials (₹)	Labour (₹)	Overheads (₹)
Cost of opening WIP	6,000	1,000	1,000
Cost incurred during the month	25,600	15,000	15,000
Total cost (A)	31,600	16,000	16,000
Equivalent unit (B)	20,000	16,000	16,000
Cost per equivalent unit (A÷B)	1.58	1	1

(c)

Statement of apportionment of cost					
Particulars	Elements of Cost	Equivalent Production (Units)	Cost per unit (₹)	Cost (₹)	Total (₹)
Units completed	All cost	14,000	3.58	50,120	50,120
Closing WIP	Materials	6,000	1.58	9,480	13,480
	Labour	2,000	1	2,000	
	Overheads	2,000	1	2,000	

Process 'A' a/c					
Particulars	Units	Total (₹)	Particulars	Units	Total (₹)
To Opening WIP	4,000	8,000	By Production - transferred to next	14,000	50,120
To Materials	16,000	25,600	By Closing w/p	6,000	13,480

To Labour	-	15,000			
To Overheads	-	15,000			
	20,000	63,600		20,000	63,600

Illustration-19 (Opening and closing WIP and process loss)

From the following information for May 2009, prepare (a) Statement of equivalent production (b) Statement of cost (c) valuation of production (d) process II Account (apply FIFO method).

Opening stock - 600 units	₹1,050
Degree of completion:	
Materials	80%
Labour	60%
Overhead	60%
Transfer from process I	11,000 unit at ₹5,500
Transfer to process III	8,800 units
Direct material added in process II	₹2,410
Direct labour amounted to	₹7,155
Production overhead incurred	₹9,540
Units scrapped	1,200
Degree of completion:	
Materials	100%
Labour	70%
Overhead	70%
Closing stock	1,600 units
Degree of completion:	
Materials	70%
Labour	60%
Overhead	60%

There was a normal cots in the process of 10% of production units scrapped realised at 50 paise per unit. **(B.Com, Madras University, October 1992)**

Solution

(a)

Statement of equivalent production									
Input		Output		Equivalent Production					
	Units		Units	Materials I		Materials II		Labour and Overheads	
				%	Units	%	Units	%	Units
Opening WIP	600	1) Unit completed							
Process I	11,000	from:							
		a) Opening WIP	600	-	-	20%	120	40%	240
		b) Process I	8,200	100%	8,200	100%	8,200	100%	8,200
			8,800						
		2) Closing WIP	1,600	100%	1,600	70%	1,120	60%	960
		3) Normal loss	1000	-	-	-	-	-	-
		4) Abnormal loss (see WN)	200	100%	200	100%	200	70	140
	11,600		11,600	-	10,000	-	9,640	-	9,540

(b)

Statement of Cost			
Particulars	Total Cost (₹)	Equivalent Production (Units)	Cost per unit (₹)
Materials I - Process I materials received 5,500			
Less Normal scrap value (1000 × 0.50) = 500	5,000	10,000	0.50
Materials II - Direct materials added in the process	2,410	9,640	0.25
Labour	7,155	9,540	0.75
Overheads	9,540	9,540	1.00
Total	24,105	-	2.50

Working Note

	Opening work-in-process	600 Units
Add:	Units received from process I	11,000 Units
	Total input	11,600 Units
Less:	Closing work-in-process	1,600 Units
	Gross production	10,000 Units
Less:	Normal less 10%	1,000 Units
	Normal production	9,000 Units
	Actual production	8,800 Units
	Abnormal loss	200 Units

(c)

Statement of valuation of production

Particulars	Elements of Cost	Equivalent Production (Units)	Cost per unit (₹)	Cost (₹)	Total (₹)
A) Units completed					
(i) Opening WIP	Opening value	-	-	-	1,050
	Materials II	120	0.25	30	
	Labour	240	0.75	180	
	Overhead	240	1.00	240	450
(ii) Process unit	All cost	8,200	2.50	20,500	20,500
Total					22,000
B) Closing WIP	Materials I	1,600	0.50	800	
	Materials II	1,120	0.25	280	
	Labour	960	0.75	720	
	Overhead	960	1.00	960	2,760
C) Abnormal loss	Materials I	200	0.50	100	
	Materials II	200	0.25	50	
	Labour	140	0.75	105	
	Overhead	140	1.00	140	395

Process II account					
Particulars	Units	Total (₹)	Particulars	Units	Total (₹)
To opening WIP	600	1,050	By normal loss at		
To process I a/c	11,000	5,500	₹0.5 per unit	1,000	500
To materials	-	2,410	By abnormal loss	200	395
To direct labour	-	7,155	By production transferred to process III	8,800	22,000
To overhead	-	9,540	By closing WIP	1,600	2,760
	11,600	25,655		11,600	25,655

Illustration-20

From the following information for the month ending October, 2005, prepare process cost accounts for process III. Use first-in-first-out (FIFO) method to value equivalent production.

Opening work-in-progress	2,000 units at ₹25,750
Transfer from process II	53,000 units at ₹4,11,500
Transfer to process IV	48,000 units
Closing stock of work-in-progress	5,000 units
Unit scrapped	2,000 units
Direct materials added in process III	₹1,97,600
Direct wages	₹97,600
Production overheads	₹48,800

Degree of completion:

	Opening Stock	Closing Stock	Scrap
Materials	80%	70%	100%
Labour	60%	50%	70%
Overheads	60%	50%	70%

The normal loss in the process was 5% of production and scrap was sold at ₹3 per unit.

(CA-PE II, November 2005)

Solution

(a)

Statement of equivalent production									
Input		Output		Equivalent Production					
	Units		Units	Materials I		Materials II		Labour and Overheads	
				%	Units	%	Units	%	Units
Opening WIP	2,000	1) Unit completed							
Transfer from Process I	53,000	from: a) Opening WIP	2,000	-	-	20%	400	40%	800
		b) Process II	46,000	100%	46,000	100%	46,000	100%	46,000
			48,000						
		2) Normal loss	2,500	-	-	-	-	-	-
		3) Closing WIP	5,000	100%	5,000	70%	3,500	50%	2,500
			55,500	-	51,000	-	49,900	-	49,300
		4) (-) Abnormal gain	500	100%	500	100%	500	100%	500
	55,000		55,000	-	50,500	-	49,400	-	48,800

(b)

Statement of cost			
Particulars	Total Cost (₹)	Equivalent Production (Units)	Cost per unit (₹)
Material I : Cost of units received from process II 4,11,500 Less : value of normal scrap: 7,500 (2500×3)	4,04,000	50,500	8
Material II: Direct material added in process III	1,97,600	49,400	4
Direct wages	97,600	48,800	2
Production overheads	48,800	48,800	1
Total	-	-	15

(c)

Statement of evaluation					
Particulars	**Elements of Cost**	**Equivalent Production (Units)**	**Cost per unit (₹)**	**Cost (₹)**	**Total (₹)**
A) Units completed					
From: (a) Opening WIP	Opening value	-	-	-	25,750
	Materials II	400	4	1,600	
	Labour	800	2	1,600	
	Overhead	800	1	800	4,000
(b) Process II Unit	All cost	46,000	15	6,90,000	6,90,000
					7,19,750
2) Closing WIP	Materials I	5,000	8	40,000	
	Materials II	3,500	4	14,000	
	Labour	2,500	2	5,000	
	Overhead	2,500	1	2,500	61,500
3) Abnormal gain	All cost	500	15	7,500	7,500

Process III account					
Particulars	**Units**	**Total (₹)**	**Particulars**	**Units**	**Total (₹)**
To opening WIP	2,000	25,750	By normal loss at		
To process II	53,000	4,11,500	₹3 per unit	2,500	7,500
To direct materials	-	1,97,600	By production		
To direct wages	-	97,600	transferred to process III	48,000	7,19,750
To production overheads		48,800	By closing WIP	5,000	61,500
To Abnormal gain	500	7,500			
	55,500	7,88,750		55,500	7,88,750

Working Note

1.		Opening work-in-process	2,000 Units
	Add:	Units received from process II	53,000 Units

	Total Input	55,000 Units
Less:	Closing work-in-process	5,000 Units
	Gross production	50,000 Units
Less:	Normal less 5%	2,500 Units
	Normal production	47,500 Units
	Actual Production	48,000 Units
	Abnormal gain	(−)500 Units

2. Material I represents cost of materials received from process II, opening WIP is already in the process so material I cost is not apportioned to opening WIP.

3. Material II represents cost of direct materials added in the process

Illustration-21

From the following information relating to process 'X' for the month of July 2009, prepare

(i) Statement of equivalent production

(ii) Statement of cost

(iii) Statement of evaluation and process 'x' account.

Opening work-in-progress (60% complete) 10,000 units

Materials	₹24,000
Labour	₹17,000
Overheads	₹11,000
	₹52,000

Units introduced into the process: 25,000 units. Cost incurred in process 'X' during the month:

Direct materials	₹48,400
Direct labour	₹32,480
Overheads	₹11,600

Normal loss - 1000 units, scrap realised ₹2 per unit
Closing work-in-progress 12,000 units - 60% complete.
Units completed and transferred to process 'y' - 22,000 units.

Use average cost method.

Solution

(a)

Statement of equivalent production					
Input		Output		Equivalent Production	
	Units		Units	%	Units
Opening WIP	10,000	Units completed	22,000	100%	22,000
Units introduced	25,000	Closing WIP			
		From (a) Opening WIP	10,000	-	-
		(b) Units introduced	2,000	60%	1,2000
		Normal loss	1,000		
	35,000		35,000	-	23,200

(b)

Statement of cost			
Particulars	Total Cost (₹)	Equivalent Production (Units)	Cost per unit (₹)
Direct materials - 48,400			
Less: Normal loss (1000 × 2) −2,000	46,400	23,200	2.00
Direct labour	32,480	23,200	1.40
Overheads	11,600	23,200	0.50
Total	90,480	-	3.90

(c)

Statement of evaluation					
Particulars	Elements of Cost	Equivalent Production (Units)	Cost per unit (₹)	Cost (₹)	Total (₹)
(1) Units completed	All costs	22,000	3.90	85,800	85,800
(2) Closing WIP From:					

(a) Opening WIP	Opening value	-	-	-	52,000
(b) Units introduced	Materials	1,200	2.00	2,400	
	Labour	1,200	1.40	1,680	
	Overheads	1,200	0.50	600	4,680
					56,680

Process III a/c

Particulars	Units	Total (₹)	Particulars	Units	Total (₹)
To opening WIP	10,000	52,000	By normal loss at ₹2 per unit	1,000	2,000
To direct materials	25,000	48,400			
To direct labour	-	32,480	By production transferred to process 'y' account	22,000	85,800
To overheads	-	11,600			
			By closing WIP	12,000	56,680
Total	35,000	1,44,480		35,000	1,44,480

Illustration-22 (Weighted average cost method)

Bharat Limited produces three products M, N and O which pass through three processes I, II and III. The following information shows the relative importance of each product in each process.

	Process I points	Process II points	Process III points
Product 'M'	4	2	3
Product 'N'	2	5	4
Product 'O'	7	5	3

Cost details for the month of July 2009, are as follows:

	Process I	Process II	Process III	Total
	₹	₹	₹	₹
Materials	31,500	46,700	54,800	1,33,000
Labour	20,600	31,500	36,400	88,500
Overheads	22,300	19,300	18,800	60,400
Total	74,400	97,500	1,10,000	2,81,900

Production during the month was

Product 'M'	500 units
Product 'N'	700 units
Product 'O'	400 units

Prepare (a) statement of weighted average production (b) statement showing cost of each type of product.

Solution

Statement showing weighted average production					
Product	Production (units)	Weighted Production (Points)			
		Process I	Process II	Process III	Total
M	500	2,000	1,000	1,500	4,500
N	700	1,400	3,500	2,800	7,700
O	400	2,800	2,000	1,200	6,000
Total	1,600	6,200	6,500	5,500	18,200

Statement of the cost of each type of product							
Sl. No	Particulars	Process I	Process II	Process III	Total ₹	Production (units)	Total cost ₹
1.	Total cost in each process	₹74,400	₹97,500	₹1,10,000			
2.	Total points in each process	6,200	6,500	5,500			
3.	Cost per unit (1 ÷ 2)	₹12	₹15	₹20			
4.	Weightage for one unit of product 'M'	4	2	3			
5.	Unit cost of Product 'M'	₹48	₹30	₹60	138	500	69,000
6.	Weightage for unit of product 'N'	2	5	4			
7.	Unit cost of product 'N'	₹24	₹75	₹80	179	700	1,25,300

8.	Weightage for one unit of product 'O'	7	5	3			
9.	Unit cost of product 'O'	₹84	₹75	₹60	219	400	87,600
	Total						2,81,900

Illustration-23

In a manufacturing unit, raw materials passes through four processes. The output of each process is the input of the subsequent processes. The loss in the four processes I, II, III and IV are respectively 25%, 20%, 20% and 16 2/3% of the input. If the end product at the end of process IV is 40,000 kg, what is the quantity of raw material required to be fed at the beginning of process I and the cost of same at ₹5 per kg. Also find out the effect of increase or decrease in the material cost of the end product for variation of every rupee in the end product for variation of every rupee in the cost of raw material. **(CA-Inter)**

Solution

Taking an input of 100 kg in process I, the output and input in the four processes will be as follows:

	Process I (kg)	**Process II (kg)**	**Process III (kg)**	**Process IV (kg)**
Input	100	75	60	48
Less : Process loss	25	15	12	8
Output	75	60	48	40

For an input of 100 kg in process I the output obtained in process IV is 40 kg. Therefore for an output of 40,000 kg in process IV the input required in process $I = 40{,}000 \times \frac{100}{40} = 1{,}00{,}000$ kg. For every 1 kg of output in process IV input required in process $I = \frac{1{,}00{,}000}{40{,}000} = 2.5$ kg. For every Rupee increase in cost of raw material the cost of final product will increase by ₹2.50.

Illustration-24

The product of a factory has to pass through three processes A, B and C. The normal wastage of each process is 2% in 'A', 5% in B and 10% in C. The percentage of waste is computed on the number of units entering each process.

The scrap value of wastage of process A, B and C are ₹10, ₹40 and ₹20 per 100 units respectively.

The output of each process is transferred to next process. The output from process C into stock. The following further information is obtained.

	Process 'A' (₹)	Process 'B' (₹)	Process 'C' (₹)
Materials consumed	12,000	4,000	4,000
Direct labour	8,000	6,000	6,000
Manufacturing expenses	2,000	4,000	2,000

20,000 units were put into process 'A' at a cost of ₹16,000. The output of each process has been as below:

A - 19,600 units

B - 18,400 units

C - 16,700 units

There is no stock of work-in-progress in any process.

(B.Com., Madras University, September 1992)

Solution

Process 'A' account					
Particulars	**Units**	**Total (₹)**	**Particulars**	**Units**	**Total (₹)**
To Consumed materials	20,000	16,000	By Normal loss 2% at ₹10 per 100 units	400	40
To Materials consumed	-	12,000			
To Direct labour	-	8,000	By Output-transferred to process 'B' account (bf)	19,600	37,960
To Manufacturing expenses	-	2,000			
	20,000	38,000		20,000	38,000

Process 'B' account					
Particulars	**Units**	**Total (₹)**	**Particulars**	**Units**	**Total (₹)**
To Process 'A' a/c	19,600	37,960	By Normal loss 5% at ₹40 per 100 units	980	392
To Materials consumed	-	4,000			
To Direct labour	-	6,000	By Abnormal loss	220	609

To Manufacturing expenses	-	4,000	By Production transferred to process 'C'	18,400	50,959
	19,600	51,960		19,600	51,960

Process 'C' account					
Particulars	**Units**	**Total (₹)**	**Particulars**	**Units**	**Total (₹)**
To Process 'B' a/c	18,400	50,959	By Normal loss 10% at ₹20 per 100 units	1840	368
To Materials consumed	-	4,000			
To Direct labour	-	6,000	By Production transferred to finished stock a/c	16,700	63,120
To Manufacturing expenses		2,000			
To Abnormal gain	140	529			
	18,540	63,488		18,540	63,488

Working Note

1. Process 'B'

(a) Abnormal loss (units)

	Input	19,600 Units
Less:	Normal loss 5%	980 Units
	Normal production	18,620 Units
	Actual production	18,400 Units
	Abnormal loss	220 Units

(b) Cost per unit $= \dfrac{\text{Total cost} - \text{Normal scrap value}}{\text{Normal production}}$

$$= \frac{51,960 - 392}{18,620}$$

$= ₹2.769$

(c) Value of abnormal loss $= 220 \times 2.769 =$ ₹609 (Approx)

(d) Value of production $= 18{,}400 \times 2.769 =$ ₹50,959 (Approx)

2. Process 'C'

(a)			
		Input	18,400 Units
	Less:	Normal loss 10%	1,840 Units
		Normal production	16,560 Units
		Actual production	16,700 Units
		Abnormal loss	(–) 140 Units

(b) $\text{Cost per unit} = \dfrac{\text{Total cost} - \text{Normal scrap value}}{\text{Normal production}}$

$= \dfrac{62,959 - 368}{16,560}$

$=$ ₹3.7796

(c) Value of Abnormal gain = 140 × 3.7796 = ₹529

(d) Value of production = 16,700 × 3.7796 = ₹63,120

Illustration-25

The Vega manufacturing co. uses FIFO method of inventory valuation in process costing. The following data relate to process I for the month of April, 2004.

(i) Beginning work-in-progress:

Quantity	1,500 units
Value	₹4,500

Degree of completion: Materials - 100%, Conversion cost - 80%

(ii) Units introduced during the month : 5,000 units

(iii) Transferred to process II : 5,500 units

(iv) Ending work-in-progress : 1,000 units

(v) Degree of completion: Materials - 100%, Conversion cost - 60%

(vi) Costs added during the month:

Materials	₹10,000
Labour	₹9,800
Overheads	₹4,900

You are required to

(a) Prepare the statement of equivalent production

(b) Prepare process I account **(B.com. (Hons.), Delhi University, 2004)**

Solution

(a)

Statement of equivalent production								
Input		**Output**		**Equivalent Production**				
				Materials		**Conversion cost**		
	Units		**Units**	**%**	**Units**	**%**	**Units**	
Opening WIP	1,500	1) Units completed						
	5,000	from:						
Units introduced		a) Opening WIP	1,500	-	-	20%	300	
		b) New units	4,000	100%	4,000	100%	4,000	
			5,500					
		2) Closing WIP	1,000	100%	1,000	60%	600	
	6,500		6,500	-	5,000	-	4,900	

Process 'I' account					
Particulars	**Units**	**Total (₹)**	**Particulars**	**Units**	**Total (₹)**
To Opening WIP	1,500	4,500	By Production transfer to process II	5,500	25,400
To Raw materials	5,000	10,000			
To Labour	-	9,800	By Closing WIP	1,000	3,800
To Overheads	-	4,900			
	6,500	29,200		6,500	29,200

Working Note

Statement of cost				
Particulars		**Total Cost (₹)**	**Equivalent Production (Units)**	**Cost per unit (₹)**
Materials		10,000	5,000	2
Conversion cost				
Labour	9,800			
Overheads	4,900	14,700	4,900	3
Total		24,700	-	5

Statement of Evaluation					
Particulars	**Elements of Cost**	**Equivalent Production (Units)**	**Cost per unit (₹)**	**Cost (₹)**	**Total (₹)**
Closing WIP	Materials	1,000	2	2,000	
	Conversion cost	600	3	1,800	3,800
Units completed:		-	-	-	
	Opening value	-	-	4,500	
(i) From opening WIP	Conversion cost	300	3	900	
(ii) units introduced	all cost	4,000	5	20,000	25,400

16.5 EXERCISE

I. Objective Type Questions

A. State whether the following statements are true or false

(i) Process costing is an extension of operation costing

(ii) Method of costing followed in industries where raw materials pass through various distinct stages in production before completion is called process costing.

(iii) Abnormal loss is debited to process account.

(iv) Abnormal loss affects cost of production of a process.

(v) Normal loss is credited to process account.

(vi) Normal loss does not affect the process production cost.

(vii) Producing equal number of units in each process is called concept of equivalent production.

(viii) Inter-process profit is an example of "transfer pricing".

(ix) Concept of equivalent production is applied when there is no stock of work-in-process either in the opening or closing.

(x) Each process is a cost centre.

(xi) All units produced in a process are always transferred to the next process.

(xii) The increase in the sale value of scrapped units is called abnormal gain.

(xiii) Value of abnormal gain is credited to process account.

(xiv) Abnormal loss is valued like good units produced in a process.

[**Ans: True:** (i), (ii), (v), (viii), (x), (xiv) **False:** (iii), (iv), (vi), (vii), (ix), (xi), (xii), (xiii)]

B. Fill in the blanks

(i) Method of costing followed in vegetable oil production firm is ______________

(ii) The loss of raw material over the normal level is called ______________

(iii) The ______________ of each process becomes the raw material for the next process.

(iv) Abnormal gain is also called abnormal ______________.

(v) To find profit of each process, the output of one process is transferred to next process at ______________.

(vi) The principle applied for valuation of incomplete units is called ______________.

(vii) The method where it is assumed that opening work-in-process is completed first is called ______________.

(viii) The value of abnormal effectiveness is ______________ to process account.

(ix) The sale value of normal scrap is ______________ to the process account.

(x) The value of abnormal loss is ______________ to process account.

[**Ans:** (i) Process costing, (ii) Abnormal loss, (iii) Output, (iv) Effectiveness, (v) Invoice price/sale price, (vi) concept of equivalent production, (vii) FIFO, (viii) debited, (ix) Credited, (x) credited.]

II. Theory Questions

A. Short answer type questions

1. Name the industries where process costing is followed.
2. What is a process industry?
3. Where abnormal loss is shown in process accounts?
4. Explain the treatment of abnormal gain in process accounts.
5. How normal loss is treated in process account?
6. What is the purpose of calculating inter process profit?
7. What is equivalent production?

B. Long answer type questions

1. What is process costing?. Explain its characteristics.
2. Explain the industries in which process costing is followed.

3. Explain the difference between process costing and job costing.

4. What are the advantages and disadvantages of process costing.

5. What is inter-process profit? Explain.

6. What is concept of equivalent production? Explain.

7. Explain the various methods of valuing incomplete units

8. What is abnormal loss? Explain its treatment in process costing.

9. What is abnormal gain? How it is treated in cost accounts? Explain.

10. Write short notes on:
    (a) Normal loss (b) abnormal loss (c) abnormal gain(d) inter process profit (e) equivalent production.

11. Distinguish between job costing and process costing.

12. What are the advantages and limitations of process costing.

III. Practical Problems

A. Short answer type questions

1. In a certain process 5,000 units were introduced at a cost of ₹75,000. Additional process cost incurred is ₹30,000. Actual units produced is 4,500 units. Normal process loss is 10% of input. Normal loss realised ₹3 per unit. Compute cost per unit. Show process account

   [**Ans:** Cost per unit ₹23]

2. 2,500 units were introduced into process 'A' at a cost of ₹8 per unit. Direct labour and departmental expenses amounted to ₹8,000. Normal process loss is 10% of input. Normal loss realised ₹4 per unit. Actual output during the period is 2,200 units. Compute abnormal loss and its value

   [**Ans:** Abnormal loss 50 units and abnormal loss amount ₹600]

3. 1,000 kgs of semi-finished goods is transfered from process 'A' to process 'B' at a cost of ₹25 per unit. The normal wastage in process 'B' is an under:

   Weight loss : 5% of input
   Scrap : 10% of input

   Scrapped units realised ₹2.50 per kg. Labour and other expenses in process 'B' amounted to ₹7,500. Actual output amounted to 900 kg. Compute cost per unit of finished units and abnormal gain.

   [**Ans:** cost per unit ₹37.94 abnormal gain 50 units valued at ₹1,897)

4. In process 'A' 4,000 units were introduced in the beginning of the year 2009. At the end of the year 2009, 3,000 units were completed and transfered to process 'B'. 1,000 units were in process, degree of completion being - materials 75% labour 60% and overheads 50%. Compute equivalent units of production for each element of cost for the year 2009.

   [**Ans:** Equivalent units - Materials - 3,750 units, labour - 3,600 units and overheads - 3,500 units]

5. Sri Ram Ltd. furnished you the following information relating to process 'X'

   (a) Opening work-in-progress - 3,000 units.

   Degree of completion:

   Materials - 80%
   Labour - 70%
   Overheads - 60%

   (b) Units introduced - 8,000 units.
   (c) Closing work-in-progress - 2,000 units.

   Degree of completion:

   Materials - 75%
   Labour - 60%
   Overheads - 50%

   (d) Number units produced and transferred to next process is 8,500 units, balance being normal loss.

   Compute equivalent units of production under FIFO method.

   [**Ans:** Equivalent units - materials - 7,600 units, Labour - 7,600 units, overheads - 7,700 units]

6. Find out the equivalent production from the following data under the FIFO method:

   (a) Opening work-in-progress - 2,000 units.

   Degree of completion:

   Materials - 80%
   Labour - 60%
   Overheads - 60%

   (b) Units introduced - 8,000 units.
   (c) Closing work-in-progress - 3,000 units.

   Degree of completion:

   Materials - 80%
   Labour - 60%
   Overheads - 60%

   Assume there are no process losses.

   (B.Com., (Hons.), Delhi University)

   [**Ans:** Equivalent production - materials - 7,800 units, Labour and overheads 7,600 units]

7. From the following information relating to process 'X' compute equivalent units of production using average cost method:

   (a) Opening work-in-progress - 1,000 units.

   Degree of completion:

   Materials - 100%
   Labour - 75%
   Overheads - 75%

   (b) Materials introduced into the process 'X' - 19,000 units
   (c) Units scrapped - 1,500 units.

   Degree of completion:

   Materials - 100%
   Labour - 80%
   Overheads - 80%

   (d) Closing work-in-progress - 1,000 units.

   Degree of completion:

   Materials - 100%
   Labour - 80%
   Overheads - 80%

   (e) Units finished and transferred to process 'Y' - 17,500 units.
   (f) Normal loss : 5% of total input including opening work-in-progress.

   [**Ans:** Equivalents units of production - materials - 19,000 units, labour and overheads - 18,700 units]

8. Find out abnormal gain/loss units.

   Input - 3,000 units
   output - 2,650 units
   Normal loss - 10% of input

   [**Ans:** Abnormal loss - 50 units]

9. Find out abnormal gain/loss units

   Input - 5,000 units
   Actual output - 4,600 units
   Normal loss - 10% of input

   [**Ans:** Abnormal gain - 100 unit]

10. Calculate the actual output

    Input - 7,000 units
    Opening stock - 3,000 units
    Normal Loss - 10% of total input including opening stock.
    Abnormal loss - 500 units

[**Ans:** Actual output - 8,500 units]

11. Find the input in the process.

    Opening stock - 1,000 units.
    Normal loss - 10% of total input
    Abnormal loss - 100 units
    Actual output - 8,900 units

[**Ans:** Input - 9,000 units]

B. Comprehensive Practical Problems

No Process Loss

1. A product passes through three processes A, B and C. 5,000 units of raw material are introduced in process 'A' at ₹8 per units. All units were completed. The following are the expenses incurred in the process:

	Process 'A'	Process 'B'	Process 'C'
Indirect materials	13,000	11,000	8,000
Direct wage	27,000	21,000	19,000

Total manufacturing expenses incurred during the period is ₹33,500. Manufacturing expenses are apportioned on direct wages basis to various processes. Prepare process accounts.

[**Ans:** Total cost process 'A' ₹93,500, process 'B' ₹1,36,000 process 'C' ₹1,72,500. Cost per unit process 'A' ₹18,70, process 'B' ₹27.20 process 'C' ₹34.50 normal loss-no scrap value.

2. Product 'zed' is produced in a company. The product passes through three process R, S and T before it is completed. The following are the expenses incurred during the month of September, 2009:

	Process R	Process S	Process T
Raw materials introduced	7,500 kgs	1,375 kgs	350 kgs
Cost per kg	16	20	23
Normal process loss on input	5%	10%	10%
Other materials added in the process (₹)	15,000	13,000	9,000
Direct labour (₹)	27,500	25,000	21,000
Production overheads (₹)	15,625	24,125	18,200

Prepare process accounts showing cost per unit of each process.

[**Ans:** Total cost process R ₹1,78,125, process 'S' ₹2,67,750 process T ₹3,24,000, cost per unit, process 'R' ₹25 process 'S' ₹35, process 'T' ₹45 output-process, R - 7,125 kg, S - 7,650 kg, T - 7,200 kg).

Normal loss with scrap value

3. Product 'A' passes through two processes 'A' and 'B'. The output of process 'B' is passed on to finished stock. 10,000 units of raw materials at ₹3 per unit was introduced in process 'A'. The other expenses incurred in the processes were:

	Process 'A'	Process 'B'
Direct wages	15,000	12,500
Factory overheads	13,500	10,300
Normal loss	5%	10%

Prepare process accounts. Scraps realised ₹3 per unit.

[**Ans:** Total cost - Process 'A' ₹57,000 and Process 'B' - ₹76,950, Cost per unit - Process 'A' - ₹6, Process 'B' - 9]

With normal losses and sale of product

4. At the end of process 'A', carried on in a factory during the week ending July 31st, 2002, the number of units produced was 850 units excluding 50 units damaged at the very end of the process. The damaged units realised ₹3 per unit as scrap. A normal wastage of 10 per cent occurs during the process, the wastage realised ₹2 per unit.

A unit of raw material costs ₹4. The other expenses for the week were:

Wages - ₹500
Power - ₹200
Production overheads - ₹450

40% of output is sold so as to show a profit of $16\frac{2}{3}$ per cent on the selling price, the rest of the output is transferred to process 'B'. Prepare the process 'A' account.

[**Ans:** cost of 850 units - ₹4800, sale of 340 units ₹2,304, profit ₹384, cost of 510 units transferred to process 'B' ₹2,880.]

Note: 1. Materials introduced = (850 + 50) × 100/90 = 1,000 units. 2. Units damaged is treated as normal loss.

With abnormal loss and normal loss

5. 500 units were introduced into process 'B' at ₹10 per unit labour ₹4,500 and other production expenses ₹950. Normal loss is estimated at 10% of input, scraps realised ₹2 per cent - 400 unit were produced and passed on to process 'C'. Prepare process 'B' account and abnormal loss account.

[**Ans:** Total cost of production ₹9,200. Cost per unit ₹23, abnormal loss 50 units ₹1,150]

6. 1,500 units were introduced into process I at a rate of ₹12 per unit. The direct labour amounted to ₹12,500. Production overhead was ₹7,600. The normal loss in the process is 10% of input but actual production amounted to 1,250 units. The scrap realised ₹2 per unit. Prepare process I account and abnormal loss account.

   [**Ans:** Total cost of production ₹35,000, cost per unit ₹28, abnormal loss 100 unit at ₹2,800]

With abnormal gain and normal loss

7. 800 units of a material was introduced into process 'M' at the rate of ₹2 per unit. The direct labour amounted to ₹4,500. The manufacturing expenses amounted to ₹1,980. The normal loss is 5% of input. The net production was 780 units. Prepare process 'M' account and abnormal loss/gain account assuming the process scrap realised ₹2.50 per unit.

   [**Ans:** Total cost of production ₹8,190, cost per unit ₹10.50, abnormal gain 20 units ₹210]

8. 1,000 units of raw materials at the rate of ₹7.50 were introduced in process 'N' during the month of January. The expenses incurred in the process are : Direct labour ₹6,200 and production overheads ₹2,500. The output of the process is 925 units. The normal loss is 10% of input.

   Prepare process account and abnormal loss or gain account.

   [**Ans:** Total cost of production ₹16,650, cost per unit ₹18, abnormal gain 25 units at ₹450]

With abnormal loss, abnormal gain and normal loss

9. The product CD is obtained after it passes three distinct processes. The following information is obtained from the accounts for the month ending December 31, 2008:

Items	Total	Process I	Process II	Process III
	₹	₹	₹	₹
Direct materials	7,542	2,600	1,980	2,962
Direct wages	9,000	2,000	3,000	4,000
Production overheads	9,000			

   1,000 units at ₹3 each were introduced to process I. There was no stock of materials or work-in-progress at the beginning or end of the period. The output of each process passes direct to the next process and finally to finished stores. Production overhead is recovered at 100% of direct wages. The following additional data are obtained:

Process	Output during the month	% of normal loss to input	Value of scrap per unit
I	950	5%	2
II	840	10%	4
III	750	15%	5

   Prepare process cost accounts and abnormal gain or loss accounts.

(B.Com., Madras University, March 1994)

Ans:

Items	Process I (₹)	Process II (₹)	Process III (₹)
Cost of production	9,500	16,800	28,500
Cost per unit	10	20	38
Abnormal loss	-	300	-
Abnormal gain	-	-	1,368

With abnormal gain and abnormal loss, sale of finished product

10. The following are the particulars relating to two processes X and Y for the month of January, 2005:

	Process X	Process Y
Total Input (units)	50,000 (at ₹1.50 per unit)	1,000
Normal loss (% of input)	10%	5%
Additional cost incurred:		
Materials	-	4,080
Direct labour	35,000	45,000
Overheads	27,500	39,500
Realizable value of scrap per unit	₹0.50	₹2
Output (units)	43,000	43,000

The entire output of process x was transferred to process y. The entire output of process y was sold at ₹6 per unit. Assume there was no opening or closing stock of any type in process 'x' and 'y'.

You are required to prepare the necessary accounts for the period.

(B.Com. (Hons.), Delhi University, 2005)

[**Ans:** Process 'x' cost per unit ₹3, abnormal loss (2,000 units) ₹6,000, process 'y' cost per unit ₹5.10 (approx), abnormal gain (1,200 units) ₹6,120, profit ₹38,700]

11. A product is produced in three consecutive processes. The details are given below:

Items	Process I	Process II	Process III
Raw materials used (1000 tons) ₹	2,00,000	-	-
Wages (₹)	87,500	39,500	10,710
Weight lost (% of input)	5%	10%	20%
Scrap (Sale price ₹50 per ton)	50 tons	30 tons	51 tons

Sale price per ton (₹)	350	500	850

Management expenses were ₹17,500 and selling expenses ₹10,000. Two-thirds of the output of process I and one half of the output of process II are passed on to the next process and the balances are sold. The entire output of process III is sold.

Prepare the three process accounts and a statement of profit.

(B.Com., Madras University, March 1993)

[**Ans:** Cost per unit process I - ₹316.67 (approx), process II ₹447.06 (Approx), Process III - ₹798.43 (Approx) - Profit ₹3,890]

With raw materials stock

12. From the following figures, calculate the cost of the three processes in which output of one process is passed on to the next process immediately on completion:

	Process 'A' ₹	Process 'B' ₹	Process 'C' ₹
Wages and materials	30,400	12,000	29,250
Works overhead	5,600	5,250	6,000
Production-in units	36,000	37,500	48,000
Stocks (units from proceeding process) 1st July 2008	Nil	4,000	16,500
Stocks (units from proceeding process) 31st July 2008	Nil	1,000	5,500

[**Ans:** Cost per unit: Process A - ₹1, Process B ₹1.50, Process C - ₹2.25. Normal loss: Process B - 1500 units, Process C - 500 units].

With no process loss

13. Product 'Z' requires three distinct processes and after the third process the product is transferred to finished stock. You are required to prepare various process accounts from the following information:

Items	Total ₹	Process I ₹	Process II ₹	Process III ₹
Materials	12,000	9,600	1,440	960
Labour	9,600	3,600	3,840	2,160
Direct expenses	1,920	1,200	720	-
Production overheads	14,400	-	-	-

Production overhead is to be allocated to different processes on the basis of labour.

Production during the period was 480 units but there is no opening or closing stock. Prepare process accounts for all the three processes.

(B.Com., Madras University, October 1988)

Ans:

	Process I ₹	**Process II** ₹	**Process III** ₹
Total cost of production	19,800	31,560	37,920
Cost per unit	41.25	65.75	79

14. A product is obtained after passing it through three processes. The following information is collected for January 2009:

	Process I ₹	**Process II** ₹	**Process III** ₹
Direct materials (₹)	5,200	3,960	5,924
Direct wages	4,000	6,000	8,000
Output in units during the month	950	840	750
Normal loss	5%	10%	15%
Value of scrap per unit (₹)	4	8	10

Additional information: 1000 units at ₹6 each were introduced in process I. Therefore no stock of materials or work-in-progress at the beginning or at the end of the month. The production overhead was ₹18,000 for that month. They are to be allocated on the basis of direct wages.

Prepare the process accounts indicating normal loss, abnormal loss and abnormal gain.

(B.Com., Madras University, October 1995)

Ans:

	Process I ₹	**Process II** ₹	**Process III** ₹
	Process I ₹	Process II ₹	Process III ₹
Total cost of production	19,000	33,600	57,000
Cost per unit	20	40	76
Normal loss	200	760	1,260
Abnormal loss	-	600 (15 units)	-
Abnormal gain	-	-	2,736 (36 units)

15. Prepare the necessary accounts from the following details

	Process 'A' ₹	Process 'B' ₹
Materials	30,000	3,000
Labour	10,000	12,000
Overheads	7,000	8,600
Input (units)	20,000	17,500
Normal loss	10%	4%

Sale value of wastage per unit ₹1. There was no opening of closing stock of work-in-progress. Final output from process 'B' was 17,000 units. Entire output of process 'A' was transferred to process 'B'.

(B.Com., Madras University, April 1987)

Ans:

	Process 'A' ₹	Process 'B' ₹
Cost of production	43,750	67,440
Cost per unit	2.50	3.967
Abnormal loss	1,250 (500 units)	
Abnormal gain	-	790 (200 units)

With normal loss only

16. A product passes through three processes A, B and C. 10,000 units at a cost of ₹1 per unit were issued to process A. The other direct expense were:

	Process 'A' ₹	Process 'B' ₹	Process 'C' ₹
Sundry materials	1,000	1,500	1,480
Direct labour	5,000	8,000	6,500
Direct expenses	1,050	1,188	1,605

The wastage of process A was 5%, process B 4%, and process 'C' 5%. The wastage of process A has sold at ₹0.25 per unit and that of B at ₹0.50 per unit and that of C at ₹1.00 per unit. Prepare process accounts. **(B.Com., Madras University, March 1989)**

Ans:

	Process 'A'	Process 'B'	Process 'C'
Total cost of production (₹)	16,925	27,423	36,552
Production (units)	9,500	9,120	8,664
Cost per unit (₹)	1.78	3.01	4.22
Normal loss (₹)	125	190	456

Normal loss and abnormal loss

17. A product passes through two processes. The output of process I becomes the input of process II and the output of process II is transferred to warehouse. The quantity of raw materials introduced into process I is 20,000 kg at ₹10 per kg. The cost and output data for the month under review are as under:

	Process I	Process II
Direct materials (₹)	60,000	40,000
Direct labour (₹)	40,000	30,000
Production overheads	39,000	40,250
Normal loss on input	8%	5%
Output (units)	18,000	17,400
Realisation of scrap per unit	2.00	3.00

The company's policy is to fix the selling price of the end product in such way as to yield a profit of 20% on selling price.

Required:

(i) Prepare the process accounts
(ii) Determine the selling price per unit of the end product.

(ICWA-Inter, November 2002)

Ans:

	Process I		Process II	
	Kg.	**₹**	**Kg.**	**₹**
Transfer to next process	18,000	3,28,500	17,400	4,43,700
Abnormal loss	400	7,300	-	-
Abnormal gain	-	-	300	7,650
Cost per kg	-	18.25	-	25.50

Selling price of end product $= 25.50 \times 100/80 =$ ₹31.875

Inter process profit

18. The manufacturing operations of Lovely Products Limited, involve three distinct processes for its product. The output of process P is charged to process 'Q' at a profit of 25% on cost and that of process 'Q' to process R on similar basis.

The completed production is transferred to stock at a price which gives process R a profit of 25% on cost.

From the following particulars, prepare process accounts and finished stock account. The stock in each process is valued at prime cost.

	Process P ₹	Process Q ₹	Process R ₹
Materials	14,000	21,000	7,000
Labour	21,000	14,000	27,000
Closing stock	7,000	14,000	21,000

Show also the actual realised profit to be taken to the credit of the profit and loss account.

(B.Com, Madras University, October, 1987)

Ans:

	Process P ₹	Process Q ₹	Process R ₹
Transferred to next process	35,000	70,000	1,03,750
Process profit	7,000	14,000	20,750
Realised profit	7,000	12,600	16,792

19. Product 'A' passes through three processes, before it is transferred to the finished stock. The following information is obtained for the month of july:

Items	Process I ₹	Process II ₹	Process III ₹	Finished stock ₹
Opening stock	5,000	8,000	10,000	20,000
Direct materials	40,000	12,000	15,000	-
Direct wages	35,000	40,000	35,000	-
Manufacturing overheads	20,000	24,000	20,000	-
Closing stock	10,000	4,000	15,000	30,000
Profit percentage on transfer price to next process	25%	20%	10%	-
Inter process profit for opening stock	-	1,395	2,690	6,534

Stock in process is valued at prime cost and finished stock has been valued at the price at which it is received from process III. Sales during the period were ₹4,00,000.

Required:

(i) Process accounts
(ii) Actual realised profit
(iii) Valuation of stock for balance sheet purpose.

(ICWA - Inter adapted)

Ans:

Items	Process I ₹	Process II ₹	Process III ₹	Finished stock ₹
Transfer to next process	1,20,000	2,50,000	3,50,000	-
Total profit	30,000	50,000	35,000	60,000
Realized profit	30,000	50,697	33,655	56,732
Closing stock at cost	10,000	3,302	10,965	20,198

Work-in-progress - computation of equivalent units only

20. During the month of April 2009, 15,000 units were introduced into process 'A' 13,500 units were completed and passed on to process 'B'. The remaining units were completed in all respects to the extent of 80%. Compute the equivalent units for the purpose of cost ascertainment.

[**Ans:** Equivalent units - 14,700 units]

With closing work-in-progress

21. Two processes are involved in the production of product 'max'. In A Limited 20,000 units are introduced in process X at ₹5 per unit. The other expenses incurred are direct labour ₹57,000 and production overheads amount to ₹47,500. 16,000 units were completed and passed on to process y. The balance units were 100% complete regarding materials and 75% regarding labour and overheads.

Required:

(i) Statement of equivalent production
(ii) Statement of cost
(iii) Statement of evaluation and
(iv) Process 'x' account

Ans:

(i) Equivalent units: Materials - 20,000 units & labour and overheads - 19,000 units
(ii) Cost per equivalent units - Materials ₹5, labour ₹3 and overheads ₹2.50.
(iii) Value of completed units - ₹1,68,000, work-in-progress ₹36,500.

With closing stock, normal loss and abnormal loss

22. During the month of April 2003, 4,000 units were introduced into process 'A' at a cost of ₹23,200. At the end of the month 3,000 units were completed and transferred to process 'B' account. 720 units were still in process and 280 units were scraped. A normal wastage of 5% was expected. It was estimated that the incomplete units have reached a stage in production as follows.

    Materials - 75%
    Labour and overheads - 50%

    The additional costs incurred were:

	₹
Materials	6,160
Wages	13,760
Overheads	6,880

    Units scrapped realized at ₹2 per unit.

    Prepare:

    (i) A statement showing equivalent production and
    (ii) Statement shaving cost per unit.

    Ans:

    (i) Equivalent production - materials 3,620 units and labour and overheads, 3,440 units.
    (ii) Cost per unit - materials ₹8, labour ₹4 and overheads ₹2

Equivalent units only - FIFO

23. The following data are available in respect of process Z for January, 2007.

    (i) Opening stock of work-in-progress 800 units at a cost of ₹4,000.
    (ii) The degree of completion of opening work-in-progress : materials 100%, labour 60% and overheads 60%.
    (iii) Input of materials 9,200 units.
    (iv) Units scraped 1,200 units. The stage of completion is materials 100%, labour 80% and overheads 80%.
    (v) Closing work-in-progress : 900 units. The stage of completion of these units was : materials 100%, labour 70% and overheads 70%.
    (vi) 7,900 units were completed and transferred to next process.
    (vii) Normal loss is 8% of the total input.

    Your are required to compute equivalent production under FIFO method.

    (B.Com., (Hons.), - Delhi University 2007)

    [**Ans:** Equivalent units - materials, 8400 units, labour and overheads - 8,370]

Equivalent unit only

24. The following particulars are extracted from the books of Y Limited for the month of August 1998:

(a) Opening stocks of WIP - 200 units.

Degree of completion:

Materials - 100%
Labour - 40%
Overheads - 40%

(b) Units introduced in August 1998 - 1,050
(c) Completed units in August 1998 - 1,100
(d) Closing WIP (units) - 150

Degree of completion:

Materials - 100%
Labour - 70%
Overheads - 70%

Prepare a statement of equivalent production.

[**Ans:** Equivalent units - materials - 1,050, labour and overheads - 1,125]

Note: FIFO method is used.

FIFO method - Abnormal Gain

25. From the following information for the month of October, 2003, prepare process III cost account.

Opening WIP in process III - 1,800 units at ₹27,000
Transfer from process II - 47,700 units at ₹5,36,625
Transferred to warehouse - 43,200 units
Closing WIP of process III - 4,500 units
Units scrapped - 1,800 units
Direct materials added in process III - ₹1,77,840
Direct wages - ₹87,840
Production overheads - ₹43,920
Degree of completion:

	Opening Stock	**Closing Stock**	**Scraped Units**
Materials	80%	70%	100%
Labour	60%	50%	70%
Overheads	60%	50%	70%

The normal loss in process was 5% of the production and scrap was sold at ₹6.75 per unit.

(CA-PEII, November 2003)

Ans:

	Material I	Material II	Labour	Overheads
Equivalent units	45,450	44,460	43,920	43,920
Cost per unit (₹)	11.473	4.00	2.00	1.00

Value of completed units ₹7,95,371, value of closing WIP ₹70,979, value of abnormal gain (450 units) ₹8,313.

Average Cost Method - Equivalent units only:

26. Following information is available regarding process 'A' for the month of June 2009.

    (i) Opening work-in-progress - 2,000 units

    Degree of completion:

    Materials - 100%
    Labour and overheads - 70%

    (ii) Unit introduced into the process - 16,000 units

    (iii) Units scrapped - 2,000 units. Degree of completion:

    Materials - 100%
    Labour and overheads - 60%

    (iv) Units transferred to next process - 16,000 units

    (v) Normal loss 10% of total input including opening stock of WIP.

    Prepare equivalent production using average method.

    [**Ans:** Equivalent production units : Materials - 16200, labour and overheads - 16,120]

27. The following information is given in respect of process III for the month of January 2001:

    (a) Opening stock - 2,000 units, made up of:

    Direct materials - I - ₹12,350
    Direct materials - II - ₹13,200
    Direct labour - ₹17,500
    Overheads - ₹11,000

    (b) Transfer from process No. 2: 20,000 units at ₹6.00 per unit.

    (c) Transfer to process no. 4: 17,000 units.

    Direct materials - ₹30,000
    Direct labour - ₹60,000
    Overheads - ₹60,000

    (d) Scrap - 1000 units

    Direct materials - 100%
    Direct labour - ₹60%
    Overheads - ₹60%

(e) Normal loss - 10% of production
(f) Scrapped units realised ₹4 per unit.
(g) Closing stock - 4,000 units.

Degree of completion:

Direct materials	- 80%
Direct labour	- ₹60%
Overheads	- ₹40%

Prepare process no. 3 Account using average price method, along with necessary supporting statement. **(CA - Inter May - 2001)**

Ans:

	Material I	Material II	Labour	Overheads
Equivalent units	20,300	19,500	18,700	17,900
Cost per unit (₹)	6.1847	2.2154	4.1444	3.9665

Value of output transferred to process no.4, ₹2,80,688, value of Abnormal gain (700 units) ₹11,548.

Note:

Output transfer to process 4	- 17,000 Units
Normal loss (10% of 17,000)	- 1,700 Units
Actual process loss	- 1,000 Units
Abnormal gain	- 700 Units

28. Process 2 receives units from process I and after carrying out works on the units, transfers them to process 3. For the accounting period the relevant data are as follows:

    Opening WIP 200 units (25% complete) valued at ₹5,000
    800 units received from process I value at ₹8,600
    840 units were transferred to process 3
    Closing WIP 160 units (50% complete)
    The cost of the period were ₹33,160 and no units were scrapped.

    Required:

    Prepare the process 2 account using average cost method of valuation.

    (ICWA - Inter - November 1995)

    [**Ans:** Equivalent units - materials 920, labour 920, overheads 920, total cost per unit ₹50.826].

FIFO Method

29. From the following details, prepare a statement of production, statement of cost and statement of evaluation.

Opening WIP 500 units at ₹6 per unit.
Transfer from processes no. 1 : 15,000 units at ₹32,175
Direct materials added in process No. 2 : ₹10,350
Direct wages: ₹27,260 and production overheads ₹21,845.
Units scrapped 800
Normal loss 5% of production.
Transfer to process no.3 : 13,200 units.
Closing stock - 1,500 units

Degree of completion

	Opening Stock	Closing Stock	Scraped Units
Materials	80%	100%	60%
Labour	50%	80%	40%
Overheads	50%	80%	40%

Units scrapped realised ₹2 per unit.

(M.Com, Periyar University, April, 2008)

Ans:

	Material I	Material II	Labour and Overheads
Equivalent units	14,300	14,360	14,190
Cost per unit (₹)	2.1521	0.7208	3.4605

Value of units transferred to next process ₹84,372, value of closing stock ₹8,462, abnormal loss (100 units) ₹396.

Joint Products, By-products and Main Products Costing 17

- Meaning - Joint Product, Main Product, By Product
- Joint Product Cost - Apportionment Methods
- By-Products accounting
- Cost Apportionment of Joint costs under By-Product accounting
- Production Planning

17.1 MEANING

In certain industries the raw materials introduced in a production process will give rise to two or more products. Raw materials after undergoing manufacturing operations upto a certain stage splits into two or more products of more or less of equal value and/or importance. The point at which the raw material splits into two or more products is called split-off point or separation stage. These products are called either as main products, joint products or by-products. Same raw materials and same manufacturing operations are involved upto split-off point. The expenses incurred upto split-off point is called joint cost. Joint cost is the cost incurred for all the products produced in the process.

Industries where joint product and by-product costing involved are:

Petroleum refining, vegetable oil production, milk products, food processing, chemical industries, coke production, sugar industry etc.

Let us discuss first the various important terms involved.

17.1.1 Joint Products

Two or more products produced in a process which are almost of equal value and importance are called joint products. Joint products usually require further processing before sale. Production of any one of the joint product cannot be avoided or cannot be increased without corresponding increase in the production of other products. These products are the result of the same raw materials and manufacturing process.

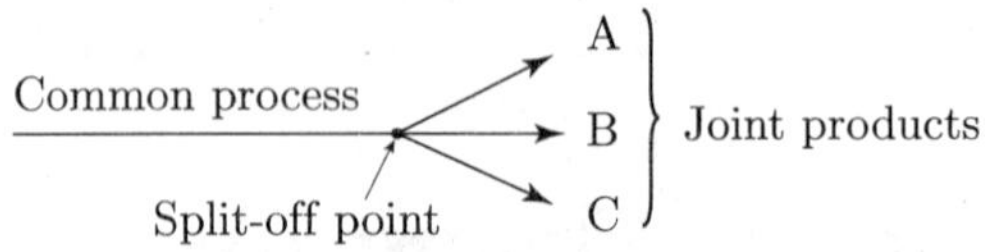

Joint products

17.1.2 Main Product

If any one of the products produced is of higher value than other products, it is called the main product. It may also be called major product or prime product. Production process is set-up to produce the main product.

17.1.3 By-product

When a product produced in a process is of smaller value or is insignificant value it is called a by-product. The production of by-products are incidental to the production of main product. So the emergence of by-product cannot be avoided. For example, oil cake obtained in vegetable oil production, molasses and bagasse in sugar industry and gas obtained in Coke making process are by-products. By-products are usually sold without further processing.

17.1.4 Joint Costs

Expenses incurred in the common process are called joint costs. Expenses like raw materials, labour and other manufacturing expenses incurred upto separation or split-off point is called joint costs. The joint costs are the expenses incurred for the production of all products (main product, joint product and by-products) in a process. Apportionment of joint costs accurately over the various products is important in determining the cost and profit of each product.

17.1.5 Split-off Point

Raw materials introduced in a process pass as a single product upto a certain stage. Thereafter it splits into two or more products. The point at which raw materials splits into two or more products is called split-off point or separation point. All the products may emerge at a single split-off point. Sometimes there may be more than one split off point. For example in Sugar industry bagasse emerge in crushing process and molasses emerge in refining process. Split-off point is important in determining joint cost and its apportionment over various products.

		Joint Products	By-Products
1.	Commercial value	Joint products are of equal commercial value	By-products are of lesser commercial value
2.	Production	Production facilities are created for producing all joint products	Production of by-product is only incidental to the production of main product.
3.	Further processing	Joint products need further processing before sale	Usually by-products are sold without further processing
4.	Quantity produced	All joint products are produced in large quantities	By-products are incidental to main product and produced in small quantities.

Objectives of joint products and by-products costing are:

1. Ascertaining the joint cost and its apportionment over the different products accurately.
2. Determining the cost of various products.
3. Determining profitability of the products.
4. Helps in cost control steps.
5. In deciding which products are to be processed further before sale and which products are to sold at split-off point.
6. Fixing the correct selling price of the products.

17.2 JOINT PRODUCTS COSTING

Main objective of joint product costing is determining the cost of production of joint products. This involves apportionment of joint costs more accurately over the joint products. The following are the various methods used for apportionment of joint costs:

Methods of apportionment of joint cost

1. Physical units method
2. Average unit cost method
3. Survey method
4. Contribution margin method.
5. Standard cost method.
6. Market value method:
   (a) At the point of separation
   (b) After further processing
   (c) Net realisable value (or) relative sales value
   (d) Net value or reverse cost method

17.2.1 Physical Units Method

This method is used when all the products absorb the same amount of raw materials and processing costs. Total joint expenses is divided by total number of units to ascertain cost per unit. To calculate total cost of each joint product, cost per unit is multiplied by number of units produced in each joint product.

Merits

This method is easy to understand and to apply.

Limitations

1. The joint products may vary in quality but cost per unit is the same.
2. It does not help in fixing correct selling price for the different joint products.
3. The products may be in different physical forms. So it is difficult to apportion the cost using same measurement unit.
4. It does not help the management in cost control and in decision making.

Illustration-1

Products M, N, O and P are produced from a common raw material. 4,500 kg of raw materials were used at a cost ₹34,200. Manufacturing overheads amounted ₹13,680. The quantity of products produced are M - 1,575 kg, N - 1,350 kg, O - 900 kg, P - 450 kg and 225 kg were lost in processing.

Calculated materials, manufacturing and total cost of each product.

Solution

Statement showing apportionment of joint cost

Products	Output (kg)	% of total output	Apportionment of joint cost		Total cost
			Raw materials	Manufacturing overheads	
			₹	₹	₹
M	1,575	35%	12,600	5,040	17,640
N	1,350	30%	10,800	4,320	15,120
O	900	20%	7,200	2,880	10,080
P	450	10%	3,600	1,440	5,040
Normal Loss	225	5%	-	-	-
	4,500	-	34,200	13,680	47,880

17.2.2 Average Unit Cost Method

Under this method total joint cost is divided by total number of units of all joint products. It gives average cost per unit of all joint products. The result obtained under this method is similar to the result obtained under physical units method. The merits and demerits of this method are similar to that of physical units method.

Illustration-2

Raw material 'X' is introduced into a process. It yields five products which are almost equal in their value. During a period 6,000 kg of raw material 'X' was introduced in a process at a cost of ₹59,400. 10% of materials put in is lost in the process. The output of various products are A - 1,300 kg, B - 1,280 kg, C - 1,100 kg, D - 1,050 kg and E - 670 kg. Labour cost and manufacturing cost in the process are ₹27,500 and ₹18,400 respectively. Calculate the cost per unit and total cost of each joint product.

Solution

	Input of material 'X'	- 6,000 kg
Less:	Normal loss	- 600 kg
	Total output	- 5,400 kg

Joint Cost

	₹
Cost of material 'X'	59,400
Labour cost	27,500
Manufacturing cost	18,400
Total	1,05,300

Average cost per unit - $\frac{1,05,300}{5,400}$ = ₹19.50.

Cost of Joint products

Joint product - 'A' = $1,300 \times 19.50$ = ₹25,350

'B' = $1,280 \times 19.50$ = ₹24,960

'C' = $1,100 \times 19.50$ = ₹21,450

'D' = $1,050 \times 19.50$ = ₹20,475

'F' = 670×19.50 = ₹13,065

Total = ₹1,05,300

17.2.3 Survey Method

Under this method a detailed survey is conducted to find the value of materials consumed, labour time expended and other production expenses incurred for each joint product and weights are assigned to each product. By considering number of units produced and weights assigned for each joint product, weighted average cost of each product is found. The weight assigned for each product is to be reviewed periodically since various factors of production may change.

Merits

1. This method helps in accurate apportionment of joint costs over various joint products.
2. It also helps in correct price fixation.
3. It enables the management in decision making.

Demerits

1. More time and effort is required for assigning weights for each product.
2. When various factors of production expended per product cannot be ascertained, weights are given arbitrarily.
3. Using arbitrariness results in inaccurate allocation of joint cost.
4. This also distorts the correctness of the decision taken by the management.

Illustration-3

A company produces four products in its manufacturing process: P, Q, R and S. The various expenses in common process during a period are:

	₹
Raw materials	35,000
Labour cost	19,500
Factory overheads	9,900

Number of units produced during the period are: P - 2,200, Q - 1,600, R - 1,000 and S - 800.

The following weights are assigned after a detailed survey: P - 5 points, Q - 3 points, R - 1 point and S - 2 points.

Required: Apportion the joint costs using weights assigned.

Solution

Joint Costs	₹
Raw materials	35,000
Labour cost	19,500
Factory overheads	9,900
Total	64,400

Statement showing apportionment of Joint Cost

Joint products	Number of units	Weighted points	Weighted production (Units)(2) × (3)	Cost per weighted unit $\left(\frac{64,400}{18,400}\right)$	Joint cost (4) × (5)	Cost per unit (6) ÷ (2)
(1)	(2)	(3)	(4)	(5)	(6)	(7)
				₹	₹	₹
P	2,200	5	11,000	3.50	38,500	17.50
Q	1,600	3	4,800	3.50	16,800	10.50
R	1,000	1	1,000	3.50	3,500	3.50
S	800	2	1,600	3.50	5,600	7.00
Total	5,600	-	18,400	-	64,400	-

17.2.4 Contribution Margin (or) Gross Margin Method

Total joint cost is grouped as variable cost and fixed cost. Variable costs are allocated on the basis of physical units. Fixed costs are apportioned in the ratio of contribution margin. Contribution margin is the excess of sales over variable cost. Therefore

$$\text{Contribution} = \text{Sales} - \text{Variable cost}$$

Merits

1. Apportionment of joint cost on behaviour basis is more appropriate.
2. Since marginal cost approach is followed, it helps the management in taking correct decisions.
3. It also helps correct measurement of profitability of each product.

Demerits

1. There is difficulty in dividing the joint costs into variable and fixed costs.
2. Incorrect apportionment of joint cost will distort the entire decision making process.

17.2.5 Standard Cost Method

Standard cost is a predetermined cost. The reasonable expenses to be incurred for each product is fixed in advance. This method helps in controlling cost and in fixing responsibility for excess expenses incurred.

Merits

1. It helps in controlling cost and avoiding wastages.
2. It helps in fixing responsibility.

Demerits

1. Fixing the standard cost is very difficult.
2. The standard cost becomes useless when rates of various expenses change widely.

Illustration-4

A company produces 3 grades of a product in a common process. The costs incurred are: variable cost ₹67,900 and fixed cost ₹33,300.

The number of units produced and their selling prices are,

Products	Units	Selling Price p/u ₹
A	4,000	15
B	3,200	12
C	2,500	10

Apportion the joint cost using a suitable method and ascertain the profit of each product.

Solution

Statement showing apportionment of joint cost				
	A ₹	B ₹	C ₹	Total ₹
Sales	60,000	38,400	25,000	1,23,400
Less: Variable cost (in units ratio)	28,000	22,400	17,500	67,900
Contribution	32,000	16,000	7,500	55,500
Less: Fixed cost (32:16:7.5)	19,200	9,600	4,500	33,300
Profit	12,800	6,400	3,000	22,200

17.2.6 Market Value Method

Under this method ability to pay is the criterion used to apportion the joint cost. The product bringing more sales revenue is allotted more cost. This method is considered to be more appropriate over other methods. There are three variants of this method. They are:

17.2.6.1 Market value at the point of separation

Sometimes products produced in a common process may have market immediately after separation. Sales value at the point of separation is used as the basis for apportionment of joint cost. When quantities of products produced are more or less equal, selling price per unit is used as the basis for apportioning joint cost.

Illustration-5

Three products X, Y and Z are produced at a joint cost of ₹50,560. These products does not require further processing. The following are the other details extracted from the books of the company:

Products	Quantity (Units)	Selling price per unit at the point of separation ₹
X	1,500	6
Y	2,000	5
Z	1,800	7

Apportion the joint cost on the basis of

(a) at sales value at the point of separation.

(b) at selling price per unit at the point of separation.

Solution

(a)

Apportionment of joint cost on sales value at the point of separation					
Products	Number of Units	Selling price p/u ₹	Sales value ₹	Ratio	Apportioned joint cost ₹
X	1,500	6	9,000	9/31.6	14,400
Y	2,000	5	10,000	10/31.6	16,000
Z	1,800	7	12,600	12.6/31.6	20,160
Total	5,300	-	31,600	-	50,560

(b)

Apportionment of joint cost on selling price basis			
Products	**Selling price p/u** ₹	**Ratio**	**Apportioned joint cost** ₹
X	6	6/18	16,853 (Approx)
Y	5	5/18	14,045 (Approx)
Z	7	7/18	19,662 (Approx)
Total	-	-	50,560

17.2.6.2 Market value after further processing

Sometimes joint products at split-off point may not have market. So it is difficult to ascertain the market value of joint products at split-off point. In such cases, the other alternative available to apportion the joint cost is using the market value of products after further processing. But this method is not logical because the expenses incurred in further processing may be in different proportions for different products.

Illustration-6

A Ltd produces three products in a joint process. The expenses incurred upto separation point are:

	₹
Raw materials	25,000
Labour charges	17,500
Manufacturing overheads	11,500
Total	54,000

During a period the company produced and sold the products after further processing as follows:

Products	**Units**	**Selling Price p/u**
X	7,500	6
Y	6,000	5
Z	5,000	3

Solution

Products	**Sales value** ₹	**Ratio**	**Apportioned joint cost** ₹
X	45,000	3/6	27,000

Y	30,000	2/6	18,000
Z	15,000	1/6	9,000
	-	-	54,000

17.2.6.3 Net realisable value (or) relative sales value method

In this method further processing cost is deducted from the sales value after further processing. It is a better method over market value after further processing. Net realisable value is the market value after further processing less further processing cost.

Illustration-7

PQR Ltd produces three joint products A, B and C and sells them at ₹14, ₹12 and ₹9 respectively. Number of units produced are 1,500, 1,200 and 1,000 respectively. The total joint cost incurred during a period is ₹4,980. Processing cost incurred after split-off point are ₹8,000, ₹6,500 and ₹5,000 respectively. Apportion the joint cost using relative sales value.

Solution

Products (1)	Sales value (2) ₹	Further processing cost (3) ₹	Relative sales value (4) = (2) – (3) ₹	Ratio	Apportioned joint cost ₹
A	21,000	8,000	13,000	130/249	2,600
B	14,400	6,500	7,900	79/249	1,580
C	9,000	5,000	4,000	40/249	800
Total	44,400	19,500	24,900	-	4,980

17.2.6.4 Net value or reverse cost method

In this method estimated cost of production at the split-off point is calculated by deducting the estimated profit, selling and distribution expenses and expenses incurred after separation from the final sales value of the joint products. Joint cost is apportioned on the estimated cost (net value) basis over the joint products.

Illustration-8

A factory produces three products which originate from a joint process. Costs incurred and other relevant details are:

Particulars	Joint costs	Subsequent processing costs		
		Product 'A'	Product 'B'	Product 'C'
	₹	₹	₹	₹
Materials	15,000	3,500	3,000	2,500
Labour	7,000	1,500	1,200	900
Production overheads	6,900	1,000	800	700
Total cost	28,900	6,000	5,000	4,100
Total sales value		28,000	22,000	15,000
Estimated profit on sales value		25%	20%	30%

Prepare a statement showing apportionment of joint cost.

Solution

Statement showing apportionment of joint cost				
Particulars	Product 'A' ₹	Product 'B' ₹	Product 'C' ₹	Total ₹
Sales value	28,000	22,000	15,000	65,000
Less: estimated profit	7,000	4,400	4,500	15,900
Estimated total cost	21,000	17,600	10,500	49,100
Less: Subsequent processing cost	6,000	5,000	4,100	15,100
Estimated cost at split-off point	15,000	12,600	6,400	34,000
Ratio of estimated cost at split-off point	15/34	12.6/34	6.4/34	—
Apportioned joint cost	12,750	10,710	5,440	28,900

17.3 BY-PRODUCTS ACCOUNTING

Products emerging from common processes which are of smaller value are called by-products. Joint costs are to be apportioned over main products and by-products. The following methods are used for apportionment of joint costs:

1. Non-cost methods (or) sales value method

   This method is further sub-divided into following methods:

   (a) Miscellaneous income or other income method.
   (b) Total sales less total cost method.
   (c) Total cost less sales value of by-product method.

(d) Sales value of by-product less selling expenses credited to process account are deducted from total cost.

(e) Sales value of by-product less selling expenses and further processing cost credited to process account.

(f) Reverse cost method.

2. Cost method

This method is further subdivided into the following methods:

(a) Replacement or opportunity cost method.

(b) Standard cost method.

(c) Apportionment on suitable basis.

17.3.1 Non-Cost Method or Sales Value Method

17.3.1.1 Miscellaneous income or other income method

Income from the sale of a by-product is credited to profit and loss account as other income or miscellaneous income. This method is followed when the quantity and sales value is very small. Stock of by-product is valued at nil cost and it will not appear in the balance sheet. So stock reporting is not accurate. By-product produced in one period may be sold in the next period. This distorts income reporting also.

17.3.1.2 Total sales less total cost method

Sales value of by-product is added to the sales value of the main product. Total cost of the process is deducted from the total sales to arrive at the profit. Stock of by-product is valued at nil cost and will not appear in the balance sheet.

17.3.1.3 Total cost less sales value of by-product method

Under this method sales value of the by-product is deducted from total cost of production or cost of sales. By-product stock is valued at nil cost. The stock of the main product is valued on the total cost basis.

Illustration-9

During a certain period 1,000 units of main a product are produced and out of this 750 units were sold at ₹40 per unit. The by-product emerging from the process is sold at ₹2,500. The total cost production of 1,000 units is ₹25,000. Calculate the amount of profit after crediting the sales value of the by-product:

(a) To cost of production and

(b) To cost of sales.

Solution

(a)

Sales value of by-product credited to cost of production		
		₹
Sales value of main product (750 × 40)		30,000
Less: Total cost of production	25,000	
Less: Sales value of by-product	2,500	
Net cost of production	22,500	
Less: Closing stock of main product $\frac{22{,}500}{1{,}000} \times 250$	5,625	16,875
Gross Profit		13,125

(b)

Sales value of by-products credited to cost of sales		
		₹
Sales value of main product (750 × 40)		30,000
Less: Cost of production	25,000	
Less: Stock of main product $\frac{25{,}000}{1{,}000} \times 250$	6,250	
Cost of Sales	18,750	
Less: Sales value of by-product	2,500	16,250
Gross Profit		13,750

The difference in gross profit is due to difference in valuation of closing-stock.

17.3.1.4 Sales value of by-product less selling expenses credited to process account or deducted from total cost

Under this method sales value of by-product less selling expenses is either credited to process account or deducted from total process cost. Closing stock of the by-product is valued at selling price less a reasonable expenses to be incurred for selling the stock.

17.3.1.5 Sales value of by-product less selling expenses and further processing cost credited to process Account

Under this method selling expenses and further processing cost of by-product is deducted from the sales value of by-product. Net sales value of by-product is credited to process account.

Illustration-10

In the course of manufacturing a main product, 500 units of the by-product were produced. Sales value of by-product was ₹30 per unit. Further processing cost incurred for the by-product was ₹4,000 and selling expenses incurred for sale of the by-product was ₹2,500. Find the amount to be credited to the process account in respect of the by-product:

Solution

			₹
Sales value of by-product (500 × 30)			15,000
Less:	Further processing cost	4,000	
	Selling expenses	2,500	6,500
Amount to be credited to process account			8,500

17.3.1.6 Reverse cost method

Under this method, estimated profit, selling expenses and further processing cost of the by-product is deducted from the sales value of the by-products to get the joint cost of the by-product.

Illustration-11

In manufacturing the main product 'A', a company processes the incidental waste into two by-products X and Y. From the following data relating to the products you are required to prepare a comparative profit and loss statement showing the individual costs and other details. The cost upto separation point was ₹1,55,200.

	Main Product	By-products	
	A	X	Y
	₹	₹	₹
Sales	4,00,000	32,000	48,000
Cost after separation	40,000	6,400	7,200
Estimated net profit percentage to sales value	-	20%	20%
Estimated selling expenses as percentage of sale value	20%	10%	15%

Reverse cost method to be applied for separation of joint cost. **(ICWA-Inter, June 2004)**

Solution

Statement showing joint costs of by-products				
	By-product X		By-product Y	
		₹		₹
Sales		32,000		48,000
Less: Estimated net profit	6,400		9,600	

Selling expenses	3,200		7,200	
Cost after separation	6,400	16,000	7,200	24,000
Share of joint cost	-	16,000	-	24,000

Statement showing joint cost of main product 'A'		
		₹
Total joint cost		1,55,200
Less: Joint cost of product 'X'	16,000	
Product 'Y'	24,000	40,000
Joint cost of main product 'A'		1,15,200

Comparative profit and loss statement			
	Main Product	**By-products**	
	A	X	Y
	₹	₹	₹
Sales (a)	4,00,000	32,000	48,000
Cost of sales : Joint cost	1,15,200	16,000	24,000
Costs after separation	40,000	6,400	7,200
Cost of production	1,55,200	22,400	31,200
Estimated selling expenses	80,000	3,200	7,200
Total cost (b)	2,35,200	25,600	38,400
c) Profit (a – b)	1,64,800	6,400	9,600

Illustration-12

A factory manufacturing article 'A' also obtains two by-products 'B' and 'C'. The costs incurred are:

	Joint cost	**Subsequent costs**		
		A	B	C
	₹	₹	₹	₹
Materials	10,000	1,500	1,300	1,000
Labour	1,600	200	150	100
Overheads	8,000	800	550	400
Total	19,600	2,500	2,000	1,500
Sales		30,000	24,000	20,000
Estimated profit % on sales		30%	25%	20%

Show how you would apportion the joint cost of manufacture.

Solution

Statement showing apportionment of joint cost				
Particulars	Main Product 'A' ₹	By-product 'B' ₹	By-product 'C' ₹	Total ₹
Sales	30,000	24,000	20,000	74,000
Less: Estimated profit	9,000	6,000	4,000	19,000
Cost of Sales	21,000	18,000	16,000	55,000
Less: Subsequent cost	2,500	2,000	1,500	6,000
Estimated cost at the point of separation	18,500	16,000	14,500	49,000
Ratio of estimated cost at the point of separation	185/490	160/490	145/490	-
Apportioned joint cost	7,400	6,400	5,800	19,600

17.3.2 Cost Methods

17.3.2.1 Replacement or opportunity cost method

This method is followed when the by-product obtained from the process can be reused as raw materials in some other process of the company. The market value of materials which are similar to the by-product is the replacement price. The replacement price of the by-product is credited to the process account.

Illustration-13

In the production of a main product, a by-product Y is obtained. In a certain period 500 units of the by-product are produced which are transferred to another process where the by-product is consumed. If the by-products were purchased from the market, the price would have been ₹8 per unit. Calculate the amount to be credited to the main product in respect of the by-product under the replacement cost method.

Solution

Amount to be credited in respect of by-product is 500 units × ₹8 = ₹4,000

17.3.2.2 Standard cost method

This method is followed when the by-product is consumed within the same company and the market price of similar products are changing frequently. A standard cost is fixed for the by-product. The standard cost of by-product is credited to the process account. This method helps to exercise control over the cost of the main product.

17.3.2.3 Apportionment on suitable basis

This method is applied when value of by-products are of considerable value. By-product is treated like a joint product. Joint cost is apportioned between the by-product and main product on some suitable basis after carefully evaluating the various factors of production consumed by each product.

17.4 PRODUCTION PLANNING

17.4.1 Sales after further processing (or) Sales at split-off point

A company has to decide whether a product is to be sold at split-off point or sold after further processing. The criteria is maximisation of profit. The additional cost in further processing and incremental sales revenue is to be compared. If incremental revenue is more than the additional cost the product is to be sold after further processing and vice-versa.

Illustration-14

In a chemical manufacturing company, three products A, B and C emerge at a single split-off stage in department P. Product A is further processed in department Q, product B in department R and 'C' in department S. There is no loss in further processing of any of the three products. The cost data for a month are as under:

		₹
Cost of raw materials introduced in department	'P'	12,68,800
Direct wages - Department	'P'	3,84,000
	'Q'	96,000
	'R'	64,000
	'S'	36,000

Factory overheads of ₹4,64,000 are to be apportioned to the departments on direct wages basis.

During the month under reference, the company sold all three products after processing them further as under:

Products	A	B	C
Output sold (kg)	44,000	40,000	20,000
Selling price per kg·₹	32	24	16

There are no opening or closing stocks. If these were sold at the split-off stage, that is, without further processing, the selling prices would have been ₹20, ₹22 and ₹10 each per kg respectively for A,B and C.

Required:

(i) Prepare a statement showing the apportionment of joint costs to joint products.

(ii) Present a statement showing product-wise and total profit for the month under reference as per the company's current processing policy.

(iii) What processing decision should have been taken to improve the profitability of the company.

(iv) Calculate the product-wise and total profit arising from your recommendation in (iii) above.

Solution

(i)

Statement showing apportionment of joint costs				
	Products			
	A	**B**	**C**	**Total**
Output sold (Kg): (i)	44,000	40,000	20,000	-
Selling price per kg at split-off stage (₹): (ii)	20	22	10	-
Sales value at split-off stage (₹): (i)×(ii)	8,80,000	8,80,000	2,00,000	19,60,000
Joint Cost, (Cost incurred in department P) Apportioned at sales value at split-off stage (₹) (22 : 22 : 5)	8,80,000	8,80,000	2,00,000	19,60,000

(ii)

Statement showing product-wise and total profit after further processing				
	Products			
	A	**B**	**C**	**Total**
Output sold (Kg): (a)	44,000	40,000	20,000	-
Selling Price per kg after further processing (₹): (b)	32	24	16	-
Sales value after further processing (₹) (c)= (a) × (b)	14,08,000	9,60,000	3,20,000	26,88,000
Joint costs (₹): (d)	8,80,000	8,80,000	2,00,000	19,60,000
Further processing costs (₹): (e) (See $WN-1$)	1,72,800	1,15,200	64,800	3,52,800
Total cost (₹) (f) = (d) + (e)	10,52,800	9,95,200	2,64,800	23,12,800
Profit/(Loss) (₹): (c) – (f)	3,55,200	(35,200)	55,200	3,75,200

Alternatively

	A	B	C	Total
	₹	₹	₹	₹
Incremental sales revenue	5,28,000 (44,000×12)	80,000 (40,000×2)	1,20,000 (20,000×6)	7,28,000
Less: Incremental cost (further processing cost)	1,72,800	1,15,200	64,800	3,52,800
Incremental profit	3,55,200	(35,200)	55,200	3,75,200

(iii) Processing decision to improve the profitability of the company

Products A and C should be sold after further processing since they generate additional profit. Product B should be sold at split-off stage itself since further processing results in loss.

(iv) Product-wise and total profit as per recommendation in (iii) above

	Products			Total
	A	B	C	
Profit (₹)	3,55,200	Nil	55,200	4,10,400

Working Notes

1. Statement showing joint costs and further processing costs:

	Joint costs	Further processing cost		
	Dept. 'P'	Dept. 'Q'	Dept. 'R'	Dept. 'S'
	₹	₹	₹	₹
Raw materials	12,68,800	-	-	-
Wages	3,84,000	96,000	64,000	36,000
Overheads	3,07,200	76,800	51,200	28,800
Total cost	19,60,000	1,72,800	1,15,200	64,800

Note: Overheads apportioned in wages ratio i.e., 96 : 24 : 16 : 9

Illustration-15

A company purchases raw materials worth ₹11.04 lakh and processes them into four products P, Q, R and S which have a unit sales value of ₹3, ₹9, ₹16 and ₹60 respectively at split-off point, as they could be sold as such to other processors. However, during a year, the company decided to further process and sell products P, Q and S while R was not to be processed further but sold at split-off point to other processors. The processing of raw materials into four products cost ₹28 lakh to the company. The other data for the year were as under:

Products	Output	Sales	Additional Process Cost (All variable)
	(Units)	(₹ in lakh)	(₹ in lakh)
P	10,00,000	46.00	12.00
Q	20,000	4.00	2.40
R	10,000	1.60	-
S	18,000	12.00	0.40

You are required to work out the following information for managerial decision making:

(i) If joint costs are allocated amongst four products on the basis of 'net realisable value' at split-off point, what would be the company's annual income?

(ii) If company had sold off all other three products at split-off stage, identify the increase/decrease in the company's annual income as compared to (i) above.

(iii) What sales strategy could the company have planned to maximise its profit in the year?

(iv) Identify the net increase in income if the strategy at (iii) above is adopted, as compared to (i) above.

Solution

(i)

Statement showing annual income - Products sold after further processing (₹ in lakh)					
Product	Sales	Share of joint cost	Additional processing cost	Total cost	Net income
	₹	₹	₹	₹	₹
P	46.00	27.20	12.00	39.20	6.80
Q	4.00	1.28	2.40	3.68	0.32
R	1.60	1.28	-	1.28	0.32
S	12.00	9.28	0.40	9.68	2.32
Total	63.60	39.04	14.80	53.84	9.76

(ii)

Statement showing annual income - Products sold at split-off point					
Particulars	Product P	Product Q	Product R	Product S	Total
1. Output (units)	10,00,000	20,000	10,000	18,000	-
2. Selling price per unit (₹)	3	9	16	60	-
3. Total sales value (₹)	30.00	1.80	1.60	10.80	44.20

4. Joint cost (₹)	27.20	1.28	1.28	9.28	39.04
5. Net profit (₹) (3–4)	2.80	0.52	0.32	1.52	5.16

Decrease in profit(9.76 – 5.16) = ₹4.60 lakhs

(iii) Sales strategy for maximising the profit

1. Product P and S should be sold after further processing since their profits are higher if sold after further processing.
2. Product Q should be sold at split-off point since its profit decreases if sold after further processing.
3. Product R should be sold at split-off point as its profit is same under both the alternatives.

(iv)

Statement showing annual income as per suggestion in (iii)

	Product P	Product Q	Product R	Product S	Total
Profits (₹ in lakh)	6.80	0.52	0.32	2.32	9.96

Annual income as in (i) above	=	₹9.76 lakhs
Annual income as per suggestion	=	₹9.96 lakhs
Increase in annual income	=	₹0.20 lakhs

Working Notes

1.

Statement showing 'Net realisable value' and apportionment of joint cost

	Products				Total
	P ₹	Q ₹	R ₹	S ₹	₹
Sales value (sold after further processing)	46.00	4.00	1.60	12.00	63.60
Less: Additional processing cost	12.00	2.40	-	0.40	14.80
Net realisable value	34.00	1.60	1.60	11.60	48.80
Joint cost (apportioned on net realisable value basis)	27.20	1.28	1.28	9.28	39.04

2.

Joint Cost

	(₹in lakh)
Cost of Raw materials purchased	11.04

Processing cost of four products	28.00
Total	39.04

17.5 COMPREHENSIVE ILLUSTRATIONS

Illustration-16

X Ltd manufactures a product 'A' which yields two by-products 'B' and 'C'. In a period the amount spent upto the point of separation was ₹20,600. Subsequent expenses are:

	A ₹	B ₹	C ₹
Materials	300	200	150
Direct wages	400	300	200
Overheads	300	270	280
	1000	770	630

Gross sales value of products A, B and C was ₹15,000, ₹10,000 and ₹5,000 respectively. It was estimated that the net profit as a percentage of sales in case of B and C would be 25% and 20% respectively. Ascertain the profit earned on 'A'. **(B.Com., Madras University, March 1988)**

Solution

Statement showing joint cost of by-products		
	By-products	
	B ₹	C ₹
Gross sales value	10,000	5,000
Less: Profit	2,500	1,000
Total cost	7,500	4,000
Less: Subsequent expenses	770	630
Joint cost	6,730	3,370

Statement showing joint cost of product 'A'		
		₹
Total joint cost		20,600
Less: Joint cost:		
By-product B	6,370	
By-product C	3,370	9,740
Joint cost of 'A'		10,860

Statement showing profit of 'A'	
	₹
Joint cost	10,860
Subsequent expenses	1,000
Total cost	11,860
Profit (b/f)	3,140
Gross sales value	15,000

Illustration-17

A factory is engaged in the production of a chemical X and in the course of its manufacture a by-product Y is produced, which after a separate process has a commercial value. Following are the information for the month of March:

	Joint Expenses	**Separate expenses**	
		X	**Y**
	₹	₹	₹
Materials	10,000	2,000	2,800
Labour	4,000	2,500	2,500
Expenses	2,500	1,400	1,000

The output for the month was 150 quintals of X and 50 quintals of Y. The selling price of product Y is ₹200 per quintal. The profit on Y is 33 1/3% on cost price.

Prepare necessary accounts to show the cost per quintal of X.

(B.Com., Madras University, May 1988)

Solution

Joint expenses account			
	₹		₹
To Materials	10,000	By Product X	1,200
To Labour	4,000	By Product Y (bf)	15,300
To Expenses	2,500		
	16,500		16,500

Product X account			
	₹		₹
To Materials	2,000	By Cost of production (bf)	21,200
To Labour	2,500	Cost per unit = ₹141.33	
To Expenses	1,400		
To Joint expenses	15,300		
	21,200		21,200

Product Y account			
	₹		₹
To Materials	2,800	By Cost of production	7,500
To Labour	2,500		
To Expenses	1,000		
To Joint expenses	1,200		
	7,500		7,500

Working Notes

Sales value of by Product Y (50 × 200)	₹10,000
Less: Profit $33\frac{1}{3}\%$ on cost $\left(\text{i.e. } \frac{33\frac{1}{3}}{133\frac{1}{3}} \text{ on sales}\right)$	2,500
Total cost of production	7,500
Less: Separate cost	6,300
Joint cost of by Product Y	1,200

Illustration-18

Calculate the estimated cost of by-products X and Y at the point of separation from the main product:

	By-products	
	X	Y
	₹	₹
Selling price per unit	12	24
Cost per unit after separation	3	5
Units produced	500	200

Selling expenses amount to 25% of total works cost i.e. including both separation and post-separation works cost. Selling prices are arrived after adding 20% of total cost i.e. the sum of works cost and selling expenses. Calculate estimated cost of products at the point of separation.

(B.Com., Bangalore University, Oct. 2002)

Solution

Statement showing apportionment of pre-separation Cost				
Particulars	**By-products X**		**By-product Y**	
	Per unit ₹	**Total (500 units)** ₹	**Per unit** ₹	**Total (200 units)** ₹
Sales	12.00	6,000	24.00	4,800
Less: Profit 20/120 on sales	2.00	1,000	4.00	800
Total cost	10.00	5,000	20.00	4,000
Less: Selling expenses 25/125 on Total cost	2.00	1,000	4.00	800
Total works cost	8.00	4,000	16.00	3,200
Less: After separation cost	3.00	1,500	5.00	1,000
Estimated cost at the point of separation	5.00	2,500	11.00	2,200

Illustration-19

A by-product Kappa is derived in the course of manufacturing a product 'Gamma'. The by-product is further processed for sale. From the following data available from cost records, prepare an account showing cost per kg of the product 'Gamma'.

	Joint Expenses	**Separate Expenses**	
	₹	**Gamma ₹**	**Kappa ₹**
Materials	20,000	12,000	1,000
Labour	14,000	10,000	4,000
Overheads	5,000	3,000	1,200

The quantities produced during the period under consideration were: Gamma - 400 kg and Kappa - 100 kg. The selling price of Kappa was ₹240 per kg on which the profit earned was estimated at 30% of the selling price.

Solution

Joint expenses account			
	₹		₹
To Materials	20,000	By-product Gamma (bf)	28,400
To Labour	14,000	By-product Kappa account	10,600
To Overheads	5,000		
	39,000		39,000

Product Gamma account			
	₹		₹
To Separate expenses:			
To Materials	12,000	By Cost of production (bf)	53,400
To Labour	10,000	Cost per kg $= \frac{53,400}{400} =$ ₹133.50	
To Overheads	3,000		
To joint expenses	28,400		
	53,400		53,400

Product Kappa account			
	₹		₹
To Separate expenses:			
To Materials	1,000	By cost of production (bf)	16,800
To Labour	4,000	Cost per quintal $= \frac{16,800}{100} =$ ₹168.00	
To Overheads	1,200		
To joint expenses	10,600		
	16,800		16,800

Working Note

	₹
Sales value of Kappa (100 kg × ₹240)	24,000
Less: Profit 30% on selling price	7,200
Total cost	16,800
Less: Separate expenses	6,200
Joint expenses of Kappa	10,600

Illustration-20

The following details are extracted from the costing books of Shiva Oil Products Ltd. for the year ended 31.03.2000. Purchase of Copra 5,400 tonnes for ₹4,40,000.

	Crushing process ₹	Refining process ₹	Finishing process ₹
Cost of labour	5,500	2,200	3,300
Electric power	1,320	792	528
Sundry material	220	4,400	308
Repairs to plant and machinery	616	726	-
Steam	1,320	990	990
Factory expenses	2,904	1,452	484
Cost of casks	-	-	16,500

3,200 tonnes of crude oil was produced in the crushing process, 2,600 tonnes of oil was produced by the refining process, 2,550 of refined oil was finished for delivery.

Copra sacks sold for ₹880.

1,925 tonnes of Copra residue sold for ₹24,200.

Loss in weight in crushing 275 tonnes.

500 tonnes of by-products obtained from the refining process valued at ₹14,850.

Your are required to show the accounts of each of the following processes concerned for the purpose of arriving at the cost of each process and a total cost per tonne of the finished oil:

1) Crushing process
2) Refining process and
3) Finishing process including casking. **(B.Com., Bangalore University, April, 2001)**

Solution

Crushing process account					
Particulars	**Units (Tonne)**	**Total ₹**	**Particulars**	**Units (Tonne)**	**Total ₹**
To Copra purchased	5,400	4,40,000	By Sale of Copra residue	1,925	24,200
To Wages		5,500	By Sale of sacks		880

To Electric power		1,320	By Loss in weight	275	-
To Sundry materials		220			
To Repairs to plant and machinery		616	By Refining process account (cost per tonne 4,26,800/3200 = ₹133.375)	3,200	4,26,800
To Steam		1,320			
To Factory Expenses		2,904			
	5,400	4,51,880		5,400	4,51,880

Refining process account

Particulars	Units (Tonne)	Total ₹	Particulars	Units (Tonne)	Total ₹
To Crushing process account	3,200	4,26,800	By Loss in weight (bf)	100	-
To Wages		2,200	By by-product account	500	14,850
To Electric power		792	By Finishing process a/c	2,600	4,22,510
To Sundry materials		4,400			
To Repairs to plant and machinery		726	Cost per tonne = 4,22,510/2,600 = ₹162.50		
To Steam		990			
To Factory expenses		1,452			
	3,200	4,37,360		3,200	4,37,360

Finishing process account

Particulars	Units (Tonne)	Total ₹	Particulars	Units (Tonne)	Total ₹
To Refining process account	2,600	4,22,510	By Loss in weight (bf)	50	-
To Wages		3,300	By finished stock a/c	2,550	4,44,620
To Electric power		528	Cost per tonne = 4,44,620/2550 = ₹174.36		
To Repairs to plant and machinery		308			
To Steam		990			

To Factory expenses		484			
To Cost of casks		16,500			
	2,600	4,44,620		2,600	4,44,620

Illustration-21

In the course of manufacturing the main product 'P', by-products 'A' and 'B' also emerge. The joint expenses of manufacture amount to ₹1,19,550. All the three products are processed further after separation and sold as per details given below:

	Main Product	By-products	
	P	A	B
	₹	₹	₹
Sales	90,000	60,000	40,000
Costs incurred after separation	6,000	5,000	4,000
Profit as percentage on sales	25%	20%	15%

The total fixed selling expenses are 10% of the total cost of sales are apportioned to the three products in the ratio of 20 : 40 : 40.

(i) Prepare a statement showing the apportionment of joint the costs to the main product and the two by-products.

(ii) If the by-product A is not subjected to further processing and sold at the point of separation for which there is a market at ₹58,500 without incurring any selling expenses, would you advise its disposal at this stage?

Show the workings. **(CA-Inter)**

Solution

(i)

Statement showing apportionment of joint cost

	Main Product	By-products		Total
	P	A	B	
	₹	₹	₹	₹
Sales	90,000	60,000	40,000	1,90,000
Less: Profit	22,500	12,000	6,000	40,500
Cost of Sales	67,500	48,000	34,000	1,49,500
Less: Selling expenses 10% of total cost of sales	2,990	5,980	5,980	14,950

Cost of production	64,510	42,020	28,020	1,34,550
Less: Cost incurred after separation	6,000	5,000	4,000	15,000
Share of joint cost	58,510	37,020	24,020	1,19,550

(ii)

Statement showing profit/loss due to further processing of by-product 'A'	
	₹
Incremental revenue from further processing of by-product 'A' (58,500 – 60,000)	1,500
Further processing cost	5,000
Loss due to further processing	3,500

By-product 'A' should be sold at the split-off point, because additional revenue from further processing is less than further processing cost.

Illustration-22

Three joint products are produced by passing chemicals through two consecutive processes. Output from process I is transferred to process II from which three products are produced and immediately sold. The data regarding the processes for April 2007 is given below:

	Process I ₹	**Process II** ₹
Direct materials 2,500 kg	10,000	-
Direct labour	6,250	6,900
Overheads	4,500	6,900
Normal loss	10% of input	Nil
Scarp value	₹2 per kg	-
		Joint products
Output	2,300 kg	A - 900 kg B - 800 kg C - 600 kg

There were no opening or closing stocks in either process and the selling prices of the output from process II were:

Joint product 'A'	₹24 per kg
Joint product 'B'	₹18 per kg
Joint product 'C'	₹12 per kg

Required

(a) Prepare an account for process I together with any loss or gain account you consider necessary.

(b) Calculate the profit attributable to each of the joint products by appropriating the total costs from process II:

(i) According to weight of output

(ii) By the market value of production.

Solution

(a)

Process I account					
Particulars	Units	Total ₹	Particulars	Units	Total ₹
To Direct materials	2,500	10,000	By Normal loss - 10% of input at ₹2 per kg	250	500
To Direct labour		6,250			
To overheads	-	4,500	Output - transferred to process II a/c	2,300	20,700
To Abnormal gain	50	450			
	2,550	21,200		2,550	21,200

(b) (i)

Apportioning total cost on the basis of weight of output			
	Process II - Joint products		
	A	B	C
Weight of output (apportionment of total cost in 9 : 8 : 6 ratio)	900 kg	800 kg	600 kg

Statement of Profit			
	Joint products		
	A	B	C
1. Output (Kg)	900	800	600
2. Selling price per kg (₹)	24	18	12

3. Sales value (₹)	21,600	14,400	7,200
4. Apportioned cost (₹)	13,500	12,000	9,000
Profit/(Loss) (3-4)	8,100	2,400	(1,800)

(b) (ii) Apportionment of joint cost on the basis of market value of production

Statement of Profit			
	Joint products		
	A	B	C
	₹	₹	₹
Sales	21,600	14,400	7,200
Less: Apportioned cost (WN-5)	17,250	11,500	5,750
Profit	4,350	2,900	1,450

Working Note

1. Abnormal gain/loss units: (process I)

	Input	- 2,500 units
Less:	Normal loss 10%	- 250 units
	Normal production	- 2,250 units
	Actual production	- 2,300 units
	Abnormal gain	- (−) 50 units

2. Cost per unit of normal production $= \dfrac{\text{Total cost} - \text{Normal scrap value}}{\text{Normal production}}$

$$= \frac{20{,}750 - 500}{2{,}250}$$

$$= ₹9 \text{ per unit}$$

3. Abnormal gain = 50 units × ₹9 = ₹450

4. Total cost of process II:

	₹
Input received from process I	20,700
(2300 units)	
Direct labour	6,900
Overheads	6,900
Total cost	34,500

5. Appointment of total cost to joint products:

	Joint products		
	A ₹	B ₹	C ₹
(i) Apportionment on weight basis (9 : 8 : 6 ratio)	13,500	12,000	9,000
(ii) Apportionment on market value of production (216 : 144 : 72 ratio)	17,250	11,500	5,750

Illustration-23

A chemical process yields the following products out of materials introduced in the process:

	Percentage or Material
Main product 'A'	60%
By-product 'B'	15%
By-product 'C'	20%
Wastage	5%

1. Following additional information has been given to you: The total costs incurred are:

   Input - 1,000 units - ₹4,600
   Direct labour - ₹4,100
   Overheads - ₹6,000

2. One unit of product 'C' requires half the raw materials required for one unit of product 'B', one unit of product 'A' requires one and half times the raw material required for product 'B'.

3. Product 'A' required double the time needed for the production of one unit of 'B' and one unit 'C'.

4. Product 'C' requires half the time required for the production of one unit of product 'B'.

5. Overheads are to be absorbed in the ratio of 6 : 1 : 1. You are required to calculate the total and per unit cost of each of the products. **(CS-Inter, Dec. 2005)**

Solution

Statement of Cost

Particulars	Ratio	Total Cost	Main Product A Output - 600 units		Main Product B Output - 150 units		Main Product C Output - 200 units	
			Total	Per unit	Total	Per unit	Total	Per unit
		₹	₹	₹	₹	₹	₹	₹
Raw materials	18 : 3 : 2 (WN - ii)	4,600	3,600	6.00	600	4.00	400	2.00

Labour	36 : 3 : 2 (WN - iii)	4,100	3,600	6.00	300	2.00	200	1.00
Overheads	6 : 1 : 1	6,000	4,500	7.50	750	5.00	750	3.75
Total cost	-	14,700	11,700	19.50	1,650	11.00	1,350	6.75

Working Note

(i) Number of units produced:

$$\text{Main product 'A'} \quad - 1{,}000 \times \frac{60}{100} = 600 \text{ units}$$

$$\text{By-product 'B'} \quad - 1{,}000 \times \frac{15}{100} = 150 \text{ units}$$

$$\text{By-product 'C'} \quad - 1{,}000 \times \frac{20}{100} = 200 \text{ units}$$

$$\text{Wastage} \quad - 1{,}000 \times \frac{5}{100} = \underline{50 \text{ units}}$$

$$\text{Total} \quad = \underline{1{,}000 \text{ units}}$$

(ii) Basis of apportionment of raw materials cost:

Product	Units	Weights	Weighted units
A	600	3	1,800
B	150	2	300
C	200	1	200

Ratio of apportionment = 18 : 3 : 2

(iii) Basis of apportionment of labour

Product	Units	Weights	Weighted units
A	600	6	3,600
B	150	2	300
C	200	1	200

Ratio of apportionment = 36 : 3 : 2

Illustration-24

A certain raw material on undergoing a chemical process yields three products A, B and C and a by-product X. The relevant particulars of the process for a month are given below:

Joint processing cost	
Raw materials input	20,000 kg at ₹15
Other materials	₹30,600
Direct labour	4,000 hours at ₹20
Production overheads	₹1,00,000

Output, selling price and other particulars				
Products	**Output**	**Selling price/kg if sold without further processing**	**Further processing cost**	**Selling Price/kg after further processing**
	(kg)	₹	₹	₹
A	8,000	28	56,000	38
B	6,000	30	60,000	42
C	5,000	32	60,000	43
X	500	6	1,500	8

(a) If the company apportions the joint cost after taking credit for the sale value of the by-product, in proportion to the sale value of the three main products at the point of separation, what is the cost per kg of each product at that stage?

(b) Which of the products should be processed further? Show workings.

(c) What is the profit earned if all the main products are sold without further processing? Give product-wise details.

(d) If further processing is done as suggested in (b), what is the total profit earned? Give product-wise details.

(IWCA-Inter, June-2004)

Solution

Joint costs

	₹
Raw materials (20,000 kg × ₹15 per kg)	3,00,000
Other materials	30,600

Direct labour (4,000 hrs × ₹20 per hour)	80,000
Production overheads	1,00,000
	5,10,600
Less: Sales value of by-product - X (500 kg × ₹6 per kg)	3,000
Net joint cost	5,07,600

(a)

Statement showing apportionment of joint cost

Products	Sales value of production			Apportionment of net joint cost	Cost per kg
	Output	Selling price per kg	Total sales value		
	(kg)	(₹)	(₹)	(₹)	(₹)
A	8,000	28	2,24,000	2,01,600	25.20
B	6,000	30	1,80,000	1,62,000	27.00
C	5,000	32	1,60,000	1,44,000	28.80
Total	19,000	-	5,64,000	5,07,600	-

(b)

Statement showing net gain/loss from further processing

Products	Incremental sales revenue			Further processing cost	Net gain (loss) from further processing
	Output	Incremental selling price per kg	Total		
	(kg)	(₹)	(₹)	(₹)	(₹)
A	8,000	10	80,000	56,000	24,000
B	6,000	12	72,000	60,000	12,000
C	5,000	11	55,000	60,000	(5,000)
X	500	2	1,000	1,500	(500)

Products A and B should be sold after further processing. Product C should be sold at the split-off point itself.

(c)

Statement showing profit if sold at split-off point

Products	Sales value at split-off point			Share of joint cost	Profit (loss)
	Units	Selling price per unit	Total		
	(kg)	(₹)	(₹)	(₹)	(₹)
A	8,000	28	2,24,000	2,01,600	22,400

B	6,000	30	1,80,000	1,62,000	18,000
C	5,000	32	1,60,000	1,44,000	16,000
Total	19,000	-	5,64,000	5,07,600	56,400

(d)

Statement showing profit as per suggestion in (b) above							
Products	**Units**	**Share of joint cost**	**Further processing cost**	**Total cost**	**Sales value per kg**	**Total sales**	**Profit/ loss**
	(kg)	(₹)	(₹)	(₹)	(₹)	(₹)	
A	8,000	2,01,600	56,000	2,57,600	38	3,04,000	46,400
B	6,000	1,62,000	60,000	2,22,000	42	2,52,000	30,000
C	5,000	1,44,000	-	1,44,000	32	1,60,000	16,000
Total	19,000	5,07,600	1,16,000	6,23,600	-	7,16,000	92,400

17.6 EXERCISE

I. Objective Type Questions

A. State whether the following statements are true or false

(i) Value of joint products are more or less of equal value.

(ii) Joint costs and common costs are same.

(iii) Main products are incidental to the production of by-products.

(iv) The point of production stage at which raw materials are separated into various products is called split-off point.

(v) By-products usually do not require further processing

(vi) The production process upto the stage of separation point is called common process.

(vii) Management has control over the quantities of by-products produced in a process.

(viii) In the common process many products are produced simultaneously.

[**Ans: True:** (i), (iv), (v), (vi) **False:** (ii), (iii), (vii), (viii)]

B. Fill in the blanks

(i) The quantity of ______________ product will be more than that of ______________.

(ii) The expenses incurred upto the point of separation is called ______________.

(iii) Two or more products produced in a common process which are more or less of equal value are called ______________.

(iv) The product produced in a process having more value is called ______________ product.

(v) The product produced in a process which is incidental to the production of main product is ______________.

(vi) The value of ______________ product is higher than ______________ product.

(vii) The expenses incurred after the separation point is called ______________ expenses.

(viii) The products which are usually sold after further processing are called ______________.

(ix) The production stage at which many products emerge from a common raw material is called ______________.

[**Ans:** (i) main, by-product, (ii) joint cost, (iii) joint products, (iv) main (v) By-product, (vi) main, by-product, (vii) separate, (viii) joint products or main products (ix) split-off point/separation point]

II. Theory Questions

A. Short answer type questions

1. What are joint products?
2. What is by-product?
3. What is a joint cost?
4. Explain split-off point or separation stage.
5. What is main product?
6. What is 'reverse cost method'?
7. What is relative sales value?
8. What is common process?

B. Long answer type questions

1. Explain joint products and by-products with examples.
2. What is joint cost? Explain the various methods of apportionment of joint costs over joint products.
3. Explain the importance of apportionment of joint cost.
4. Explain the various methods of by-products costing.
5. Distinguish between joint products and by-products. How are by-products costed? Write short notes on 'By-product Accounting'. **(CA-Inter)**
6. Explain the problems involved in joint product costing and by-product costing.

III. Practical Problems

A. Short answer type questions

1. A Ltd Co. produces four joint products. The cost of raw materials consumed is ₹12,500. Expenses incurred upto separation stage are ₹7,500. The number of units produced were: A - 650 units, B - 430 units, C - 520 units and D - 400 units. Apportion the joint cost.

   [**Ans:** Joint cost - 'A': ₹6,500, 'B': ₹4,300, 'C': ₹5,200 and 'D' ₹4,000]

2. | | | |
   |---|---|---|
   | Cost of process 'P' | : | ₹42,000 |
   | Joint products produced | : | 'Q' - 600 units and 'R' - 500 units |
   | Selling price per unit | : | 'Q' - ₹12 and 'R' - ₹17.10. |

   Apportion the joint cost on sales value basis.

   [**Ans:** Joint cost - 'Q': ₹19,200, 'R': ₹22,800]

3. In a chemical industry a by-product 'Y' is obtained while producing the main product 'X'. The total cost incurred upto the separation point is: ₹25,000. Further processing cost incurred for the main product is ₹5,000. The market value of the main product 'X' and by-product 'Y' is ₹38,000 and ₹1,500 respectively. Find the profit from the main product 'X' if the sales value of the by-product 'Y' is treated as other income.

   [**Ans:** Profit - ₹8,000]

   Note: Profit = Sales value of 'X' − Total cost.

4. In a dairy while producing the product 'M', by-product 'B' is obtained. The cost incurred in the common process upto split-off point is ₹35,000. Further processing cost incurred for the main product is ₹9,000. The market value of the products 'M' and 'B' are ₹50,000and ₹5,000 respectively. If sales revenue of by-product 'B' is added to the market value of main product 'M', find the profit.

   [**Ans:** Profit - ₹11,000]

   Note: Profit = Total sales value − Total cost.

5. 'X' Ltd produces four joint products A, B, C and D. Product C does not require further processing, hence sold at split-off point for ₹65,000. Products A, B and D were sold after further processing at cost of ₹18,000, ₹20,000 and ₹15,000 respectively. The sales values of the products A, B and D after further processing are ₹1,23,000, ₹92,000 and ₹85,000 respectively. Find the "relative sales value" of the joint products.

   [**Ans:** 'A': ₹1,05,000, 'B': ₹72,000, 'C': ₹65,000 and 'D': ₹70,000]

   Note: Relative sales value = Sales value after further processing − further processing cost.

6. 750 units of a joint product 'X' were produced in a process. The product could be sold at split-off point at ₹22 per unit. If further processing cost of ₹9,000 is incurred, the joint product can be sold at ₹30 per unit.

   State whether the product is to be sold at split-off point or after further processing.

   [**Ans:** Joint product 'X' should be sold at split-off point]

Note:

Increment revenue from further processing (750 × 8)	=	₹6,000
Additional processing cost	=	₹9,000
Loss from further processing	=	(–)₹3,000

B. Comprehensive problems

1. (Physical units basis) The following data have been extracted from the books of M/s. Eastern Coke Co. Ltd.

Joint products	Yield in lbs. of recovered products per tonne of coal
Coke	1,420
Coal tar	120
Benzol	22
Sulphate of ammonia	26
Gas	412

The price of coal is ₹80 per tonne. The direct labour and overhead costs to the point of split-off are ₹40 and ₹60 respectively per tonne of coal.

Calculate material, labour, overhead and total costs of each product on the basis of weight.

(B.Com., Madras University)

Ans:

	Coke	Coal tar	Benzol	Sulphate of ammonia	Gas	Total
	₹	₹	₹	₹	₹	₹
Materials	56.80	4.80	0.88	1.04	16.48	80
Labour	28.40	2.40	0.44	0.52	8.24	40
Overheads	42.60	3.60	0.66	0.78	12.36	60
Total	127.80	10.80	1.98	2.34	37.08	180

Note: Ratio of weight - 1420 : 120 : 22 : 26 : 412

2. (Sales value and selling price basis). The joint cost of making 50 units of product A, 100 units of product B and 150 units of product C are ₹900. The selling price per unit of the products are ₹2, ₹3 and ₹4 respectively. The products did not require any further processing costs after the split-off point.

You are required to apportion the joint cost (a) on selling price basis and (b) on sales value basis.

[**Ans:** (a) Selling price basis - 'A': ₹200, 'B': ₹300 and 'C': ₹400

(b) Sales value basis - 'A': ₹90, 'B': ₹270 and 'C': ₹540]

3. (Physical units and market value basis) Three joint products are produced by passing chemicals through two successive processes.

Output from process I is transferred to process II from which the three joint products are produced and immediately sold. The data regarding the processes for April 1990 is given below:

	Process I ₹	Process II ₹
Direct materials (2,500 kg at ₹4 per kg)	10,000	-
Direct labour	13,000	15,000
Overheads	9,000	15,800
Normal loss	10% of input	Nil
Scarpe value	₹2 per kg	-
Output	2,200 kg	**Joint products** X - 600 kg Y - 1,000 kg Z - 600 kg

There were no opening or closing stocks in either process and the selling price of the output from process II to were:

Joint product - 'X': ₹25, 'Y': ₹20 and 'Z': ₹15.

Required:

(a) Prepare an account for process I together with any abnormal loss or gain accounts

(b) Calculate the profit attributable to each of the joint products by apportioning the total costs form process II:

i. According to the weight of output and

ii. By the market value of the production.

[**Ans:** (a) Cost of production process I 2,200 kg at ₹30,800, abnormal loss 50 kg at ₹700.

(b) (i) Cost 'X': ₹16,800, 'Y': ₹28,000 and 'Z': ₹16,800. Loss X ₹1,800, Y ₹8,000, Z ₹7,800

(ii) Cost 'X': ₹21,000, 'Y': ₹28,000 and 'Z': ₹12,600. Loss X ₹6,000, Y ₹8,000, Z ₹3,600]

4. (Reverse cost method) A factory is engaged in the production of a product 'X' and in the course of its manufacture, a by-product 'Y' is produced which after a separate process has commercial value.

The following is the information for the month of December 2008:

	Joint Expenses	Separate Expenses	
		X	Y
	₹	₹	₹
Materials	10,000	2,000	2,500
Wages	4,000	2,500	2,500
Overheads	2,500	1,400	1,000

The output for the month was:

X - 150 tonnes, Y - 50 tonnes

The selling price of the product 'Y' is ₹200 per tonne. The profit on 'Y' is $33\frac{1}{3}\%$ on cost.

Prepare the necessary accounts to show the cost of X per tonne.

(B.Com., Bangalore University)

[**Ans:** Cost per tonne of 'X': ₹139.33]

5. A company produced the main chemical product M and in the process a by-product B is produced. The cost upto the point of separation ₹1,20,000.

   The separate additional costs incurred after separation point are ₹33,000 and ₹3,000 respectively.

   The quantities emerging at separation point 1,50,000 kg and 30,000 kg respectively. All the production was sold at the following prices:

   M at ₹1.96 per kg

   B at ₹0.20 per kg.

   Selling and distribution overheads applicable to the above quantities are ₹1,900 and ₹365 respectively.

   Prepare the statements of profit or loss for both M and B on each of the following basis:

   (a) Value of B nil at separation point

   (b) Apportion costs upto separation on quantity basis and

   (c) Apportion costs upto separation on the basis of sales.

(B.Com., Madras University)

Ans: Profit/(Loss):

	M	B
	₹	₹
(a)	1,39,100	2,635
(b)	1,59,100	(17,365)
(c)	1,41,500	235

6. (Reverse cost method) Two products A and B are obtained in crude form and require further processing at a cost of ₹5 for A and ₹4 for B per unit before sale.

   Assuming a net margin of 25% on cost, their sale prices are fixed at ₹13.75 and ₹8.75 per unit respectively. During the period the joint cost was ₹88,000 and the output were: A - 8,000 units and B - 6,000 units.

   Ascertain the joint cost per unit. **(B.Com. (Hons) Delhi University, 2002)**

   [**Ans:** Joint cost per unit A: ₹8, B: ₹4]

   Note: Ratio of value at the point of separation 8 : 3.

7. Strong Limited produces four joint products A, B, C and D all of which emerge from the processing of one raw material. The following are the relevant data:

   Production for the period:

Joint Products	**Number of units**	**Selling price per unit** ₹
A	500	18
B	900	8
C	400	4
D	200	11

   The company budgets for a profit of 10% of sales value. The other estimated costs are: (

	₹
Carriage inwards	1,000
Direct wages	3,000
Manufacturing overheads	2,000

   Administration overhead 10% of sales value.

   Calculate the maximum price that may by paid for the raw material.

   (B.Com. (Hons) Delhi University)

   [**Ans:** Raw materials cost ₹12,000]

   Note: Raw materials cost = Total sales value − Profit − All expenses given.

8. (Reverse cost method) A factory is engaged in the production of chemical X and in the course of its manufacture a by-product Y is produced, which after a separate process has commercial value. For the month of March 2007, the following are summarised cost data:

	Joint Expenses	Separate Expenses	
		X	Y
	₹	₹	₹
Materials	19,200	7,360	780
Labour	11,700	7,680	2,642
Overheads	3,450	1,500	544

The output of the month was 142 tonnes of X and 49 tonnes of Y. The selling price of Y averaged ₹280 per tonne.

Assuming the profit on Y is estimated at 50% of selling price, calculate the cost of X per tonne.

(B.Com. (Hons) Delhi University, 2007)

[**Ans:** Cost of X per tonne - ₹338]

9. Calculate the estimated cost of production of by-products X and Y at the point of separation from the following information:

	By-products	
	X	Y
Selling price per unit (₹)	28	20
Additional processing cost per unit	4	3
Number of units produced	600	400

Selling expenses amount to 20% on the cost of sales. Selling prices are fixed by adding a profit of 25% on sales.

[**Ans:** Value at the point of separation - X: ₹7,680, Y: ₹3,600]

10. (Reverse cost method) The chemical manufacturing company manufactures a main product and two by-products. Data for a month are shown below:

	Main Product	By-products	
		P	Q
	₹	₹	₹
Sales	3,00,000	40,000	30,000
Production cost:	-	-	-
After separation (₹)	40,000	5,000	3,000
Administration cost (₹)	20,000	2,000	1,000
Ratio of distribution and selling expenses	75%	15%	10%
Net profit on sales	20%	15%	10%

Expenses in the common process upto separation point is ₹1,95,500.

Apportion the joint cost among the main product and joint products.

[**Ans:** Joint cost—Main product ₹1,54,125, Joint product P: ₹21,825 and Q: ₹19,550]

Note:

(a) Value at the point of separation = Sales − Profit − Separate cost

(b) Distribution and selling cost = Value at the point of separation − Joint expenses

$$= 2,30,000 - 1,95,500 = 34,500.]$$

C. Decision involving further processing

11. Inorganic Chemicals purchases salt and processes it into more refined products such as caustic soda, chlorine and PVC (Polyvinyl Chloride). During the month of April, 2000, Inorganic Chemical purchases salt for ₹10,00,000. Conversion cost of ₹15,00,000 was incurred upto the split-off point, at which time two saleable products were produced: caustic soda and Chlorine. Chlorine can be further processed into PVC. The April production and sales information are as follows:

	Production	**Sales**	**Sale price per tonne**
Caustic soda	1,200 tonnes	1,200 tonnes	₹1,250
Chlorine	800 tonnes	-	-
PVC	500 tonnes	500 tonnes	₹5,000

All 800 tonnes of chlorine was further processed at an incremental cost of ₹5,00,000 to yield 500 tonnes of PVC. There were no by-products or scrap from this further processing of chlorine. There were no beginning or ending inventories of caustic soda, chlorine or PVC in April.

There is an active market for chlorine. Inorganic Chemicals could have sold all its April production of chlorine at ₹1,875 a tonne.

Required:

(a) Calculate, how the joint cost of ₹25,00,000 would be allocated between caustic soda and chlorine under each of the following methods:

i. Sales value at split-off

ii. Physical measure (tonnes) and

iii. Estimated net realisable value.

(b) What is the gross margin percentage of caustic soda and PVC under the three methods cited in requirement?

(c) Lifetime Swimming Pool Products offer to purchase 800 tonnes of chlorine in May 2000 at ₹1,875 a tonne. This sale would mean that no PVC would be produced in May. How would the offer affect May operating income?

(CA-Inter, May 2000)

[**Ans:** (a) Apportionment of joint cost:

	Caustic Soda	Chlorine
i. Sales Value method Ratio 1:1	12,50,000	12,50,000
ii. Physical measure (tons) Ratio 6 : 4	15,00,000	10,00,000
iii. Net realisable value method ratio 3 : 4	10,71,429	14,28,571

(b) Gross Margin and Gross Margin %

	Caustic Soda		Chlorine	
	₹	%	₹	%
i. Sales value method	2,50,000	16.67	7,50,000	30
ii. Physical measure	0	0	10,00,000	40
iii. Net realisable value	4,78,571	31.90	5,71,429	22.86

(c) Incremental profit from further processing of chlorine into PVC ₹5,00,000.

The operating income of Inorganic chemical will be reduced by R ₹5,00,000 if it accepts the offer of Lifetime Swimming Products.]

12. In a chemical plant four different products viz. AB, BC, CD and DD emerge from the input of crude oil. Product AB can be sold immediately, but the remaining three products require further processing before they can be marketed.

In a month, 40,000 litres of crude oil was produced at a cost of ₹30 per litre and processed at a cost or ₹3 lakh. The details of output obtained, further processing cost, selling price per unit etc are give below:

Product	Output	Further processing cost	Selling price at the point of sale
		₹	₹
AB	8,000 kg	-	45/kg
BC	10,000 kg	80,000	60/kg
CD	12,000 kg	1,20,000	70/kg
DD	5,000 litres	60,000	80/litre

Prepare:

(a) Statement showing apportionment of joint cost on suitable basis and product-wise profitability statement.

(b) If the company finds a market for CD at ₹63/kg without further processing, will it be advisable to accept it?

[**Ans:**

(a)

Product	Joint Cost ₹	Profit ₹
AB	2,78,000	82,000
BC	4,02,000	1,18,000
CD	5,57,000	1,63,000
DD	2,63,000	77,000

(b) Product CD should be sold at split-off point, since further processing cost is more by ₹36,000 over the incremental revenue from further processing]

13. A company produces two joint products X and Y, from the same basic raw materials. The processing is completed in three departments:

Materials are mixed in department I. At the end of this process X and Y get separated. After separation X is completed in the department II and Y is finished in department III. During a period 2,00,000 kg of raw materials were processed in department I at a total cost of ₹8,75,000 and the resultant 60% becomes X and 30% become Y and 10% normally lost in processing.

In department II 1/6 of the quantity received from department I is lost in processing. X is further processed in department II at a cost of ₹1,80,000.

In department III further materials of 60,000 kg were added. There was no processing loss. Further processing cost in department III amounted to ₹1,50,000

The details of sales during the year:

	Product 'X'	Product 'Y'
Quantity Sold (kg)	90,000	1,15,000
Sale price per kg (₹)	10	4

There were no opening stocks. If these products are sold at split-off point, the selling price of X and Y would be ₹8 and ₹4 per kg respectively.

Required:

(a) Prepare a statement showing the apportionment of joint cost to X and Y in proportion of sales value at split-off point.

(b) Prepare a statement showing the cost per kg of each product indicating joint cost, processing cost and total cost separately.

(c) Prepare a statement showing the product-wise profit for the year.

(d) On the basis of profits before and after further processing of products X and Y give your comment whether the products should be further processed or not.

(CA-PE II, May 2005)

[**Ans:**

(a) Apportioned joint cost (Sales value ratio 4 : 1) - Product X: ₹7,00,000
- Product Y: ₹1,75,000

(b)

Product	Product X	Product Y
Joint cost	7,00,000	1,75,000
Further processing cost	1,80,000	1,50,000
Total cost	8,80,000	3,25,000
Cost per unit	8.80	2.708

(c) Profit - Sold at split of point 2,60,000 6,500
Sold after further processing 1,08,000 1,48,540

(d) Product X should be sold at split-off point because profit decreases from ₹2,60,000 to ₹1,08,000. Product Y should be sold after further processing because its profit increases from ₹65,000 to ₹1,48,540.]

14. Tee Pee Ltd in the course of refining crude oil obtains four joint products A, B,C and D. The total cost till the split-off point was ₹97,600. The output and sale in the year 1990 were as follows:

Product	**Output (Gallons)**	**Sales ₹**	**Separate cost ₹**
A	5,00,000	1,15,000	30,000
B	10,000	10,000	6,000
C	5,000	4,000	-
D	9,000	30,000	1,000

Your are required to:

(a) Calculate the net income for each of the products if the joint costs are apportioned on the basis of sales value of the different products.

(b) What would be the net income of the company from each product if it decides to sell the products at the split-off point itself at A: 15 paise, B: 50 paise, C: 80 paise and D: ₹3 per gallon?

(c) In case the company expects to operate at the same level of production and sales in the year 1991, could the company increase the net income by altering its processing decisions? If so, what would be the expected overall income? Which products should be processed further and which would be sold at split-off? Assume that all costs incurred after the split-off point are variable.

(CS-Inter, December 1991)

[**Ans:**

(a) Net income - A: ₹14,408, B: ₹(2,138), C: ₹1,545 and D: ₹10,585.

(b) Net income if sold at split-off point - A: ₹4,408, B: ₹(1,138) C: ₹1,545 and D: ₹8,585.

(c) Products A and D should be sold after further processing. But products B and C should be sold at split-off point itself. Overall income ₹25,400]

Service Costing or Operating Costing 18

- Meaning
- Objectives
- Computation of Composite Measurement Unit
- Cost Accumulation
- Cost item-Treatments
- Operating Cost Sheet-Specimen

18.1 MEANING

Service costing or operating costing is concerned with ascertaining cost of providing service. Service costing is an extension of unit or output costing. Unit or output costing is followed in industries producing homogeneous goods. Service costing is followed in industries providing services either for internal use or to outside customers. In both unit costing and service costing, cost of producing goods or of rendering services are accumulated for a period. The total cost of a particular period is divided by number of units of goods produced or number of units of services rendered. One special problem connected with service costing is measuring quantum of services rendered.

Industries following service costing are: Transport, cinema, hotel, generation and supply of electricity, educational institution, gas and water supply,

18.1.1 Cost Unit

Nature of services provided vary from industry to industry. A suitable cost measurement unit is to be selected for each industry. Services are intangible. Ordinary measurement units cannot be used to measure the services. Usually a composite measurement unit is used which is a combination of two factors. The following are some examples of cost units used in various institutions:

	Organisation	Cost unit
1.	Passenger transport	Passenger kilometer
2.	Goods transport	Tonne kilometer/quintal kilometer
3.	Hotel - lodging	Room days
4.	Hotel - boarding, canteen	Man meals/per item
5.	Electricity	per KWH
6.	Water supply	per gallon/per litre
7.	Gas	per cubic metre/per kilogram
8.	Hospital	Patient day/bed day
9.	Cinema house	Man show

Objectives of service costing

1. Ascertaining accurate cost of providing services.
2. Provide basis for apportionment of service department expenses to production departments.
3. Providing cost information for correct price fixation.
4. Helps the management in decision making where alternatives are available (e.g. hiring vehicles or maintaining own vehicles)
5. Helps controlling cost and avoiding wastages.
6. Measuring efficiency of service departments.

18.2 TRANSPORT COSTING

Transport industry helps in taking people from one place to another and moving goods to various places. Transport industry includes road, railways, water and air transport. Some organisations maintain vehicles for their own use (for bringing raw materials, taking finished goods to markets, transport facility to employees). Some organisations provide services to the public. In both cases correct measurement of cost is important for decision making purpose or price fixation or giving quotations. When services are rendered to public, composite measurement units like passenger KM or tonne KM is used. In some cases vehicles are let on hire for a trip or for a few days. In such cases distance covered (in km/mile) or days are taken as measurement units.

Computation of Composite Measurement Unit

Passenger Transport

Cost unit used in passenger transport is passenger KM. It is calculated as follows:

$$\text{Passenger KM} = \text{Total distance covered during a period} \times \text{Actual seating capacity utilised}$$

$$\text{Distance covered} = \text{Number of vehicles} \times \text{Number of trips per day} \times \text{Distance per trip} \times \text{Number of days operated during the period}$$

$$\text{Actual seating capacity utilized} = \text{Total seating capacity} \times \text{\% of capacity full}$$

Illustration-1

A transport company operates 4 buses between two cities which are 60 km apart. Each bus makes 3 round trips per day. The seating capacity of the buses are 50 passengers. The buses operate on all days during the month of June 2009. On an average all buses run with 80% of seats full.

Calculate total kilometres run and passenger kilometres.

Solution

$$\begin{aligned}\text{Total kilometres} &= \text{Number of buses} \times \text{Number of trips} \times \text{Distance per trip} \times \text{Number of days}\\ &= 4 \times 3 \times 120 \times 30\\ &= 43{,}200 \text{ km}\\ \text{Passenger kilometres} &= \text{Total distance covered} \times \text{Total capacity} \times \text{\% of capacity full}\\ &= 43{,}200 \times 50 \times \frac{80}{100}\\ &= 17{,}28{,}000 \text{ passenger km}\end{aligned}$$

Goods Transport

Cost unit used in goods transport is tonne kilometre/quintal kilometre. There are two ways for calculating tonne kilometre. They are,

(i) **Absolute tonne kilometre (Synthetic method)**

= Actual distance covered × Actual load carried.

(ii) **Commercial tonne kilometre (Simple average method)**

= Total distance covered × Average load carried.

Illustration-2

A truck starts with a load of 12 tonnes from point 'X'. It unloads 3 tonnes of load at point 'Y' and the balance goods are unloaded at point 'Z'. It returns to point X with a load of 9 tonnes. The distance from X to Y is 50 km, from Y to Z is 70 km and from Z to X is 100 km.

Calculate (i) Absolute tonne km and (ii) Commercial tonne km.

Solution

(i) Absolute tonne km = Actual distance covered × Actual Load carried

From X to Y	= 50 × 12	= 600 tonne km
From Y to Z	= 70 × 9	= 630 tonne km
From Z to X	= 100 × 9	= 900 tonne km
Total absolute tonne km		= 2,130 tonne km

(ii) Commercial tonne km = Total distance covered × Average load carried

$$= 220 \times 10 = 2{,}200$$

$$\text{Average load carried} = \frac{12 + 9 + 9}{3} = \frac{30}{3} = 10 \text{ tonnes}$$

Load Factor

Some goods may be more bulky but less in weight. Such goods (e.g. synthetic water storage tank may occupy more space of the truck and its weight will be less. The transport operator will charge for the full loading capacity of the truck rather than for the actual weight of the load. For example, foam beds weighing 5 tonnes are loaded in a truck whose capacity is 10 tonnes. The transporter will charge for full capacity (i.e. 10 tonnes) even though actual weight of the goods is 5 tonnes. The actual weight of 5 tonnes is to be taken as equal to 10 tonnes while computing cost units. (i.e. tonne km). This is called standard load or equivalent load. For fixing freight charges and for comparing operating efficiency standard load factor is to be considered.

Illustration-3

Certain goods are sent by a businessman to a city which is 200 km away. Goods of 4 tonnes fills the entire loading space of the vehicle whereas its capacity is of 12 tonnes. The transport company charges a freight of ₹6 per standard tonne km.

Compute the standard load, tonne km and freight charges.

Solution

Actual weight of goods = 4 tonnes

Standard load (full capacity of the vehicle) = 12 tonnes

Tonne km = Distance covered × Standard load

= 200 × 12 = 2,400

Freight charges = 2,400 × 6

= ₹14,400

Illustration-4

A city municipality arranges for the removal of its garbage by means of motor vehicle transport. The following vehicles are maintained:

No. of vehicles	Specifications
20	5 tonne lorries
30	4 tonne lorries
50	3 tonne lorries
40	2 tonne lorries

On an average each lorry makes six trips a day and in each trip covers an average distance of five km. Each lorry carries garbage of 60% of its capacity. On an annual average, 20% of the lorries are laid up for repairs. The conservancy work is carried out daily. Calculate tonne km utilised for removal of garbage per month. **(B.Com. (Hons.) Delhi University, 2007)**

Solution

(i) Total capacity

$$
\begin{aligned}
20 \text{ vehicles} \times 5 \text{ tonnes} &= 100 \text{ tonnes} \\
30 \text{ vehicles} \times 4 \text{ tonnes} &= 120 \text{ tonnes} \\
50 \text{ vehicles} \times 3 \text{ tonnes} &= 150 \text{ tonnes} \\
40 \text{ vehicles} \times 2 \text{ tonnes} &= 80 \text{ tonnes} \\
\text{Total} &= 450 \text{ tonnes}
\end{aligned}
$$

$$
\begin{aligned}
\text{Tonne km} &= \text{Total capacity} \times \text{No. of trips} \times \text{Trip distance} \times \text{\% of capacity carried} \\
&\quad \times \text{\% of vehicle on the road} \times \text{No. of days per month} \\
&= 450 \times 6 \times 5 \times \frac{60}{100} \times \frac{80}{100} \times 30 \\
&= 1{,}94{,}400 \text{ tonne km}
\end{aligned}
$$

18.2.1 Cost Accumulation

Costs are collected for a period. Most of the costs are collected from the following registers maintained in a transport organization. They are:

(i) **Vehicle register:** This register shows the details like cost of vehicle, date of purchase, life of vehicle, depreciation, insurance etc.

(ii) **Workshop register:** Repairs and maintenance work done is recorded in this register.

(iii) Daily log sheets: It is maintained by the driver of the vehicle. Daily running details like trips made, distance run, fuel consumption, oil consumption etc. are recorded.

The costs collected are usually classified into three divisions as standing/fixed charges, Repairs and maintenance costs and running/variable expenses. There is no hard and fast rule for classification of costs. Sometimes costs are classified into two divisions only as fixed expenses and running/variable expenses. Again there is no definite rule for classification of certain expenses.

Fixed/standing charges are incurred on time basis. They will remain constant irrespective of the actual running of the vehicles. They include taxes, insurance, rent, office expenses, salary and wages of drivers, conductors, mechanic, clerk and manager, interest on borrowed capital, supervision, etc.

Maintenance and repair charges are in the nature of semi-variable expenses. They include repairs, spare parts, tyres, tubes, painting etc.

Running/variable expenses:

These expenses vary in proportion to operation of the vehicles. They include depreciation, fuel, oil, lubricants etc.

18.2.2 Treatment of Certain Items

Depreciation

If depreciation is calculated on operation basis (e.g. based on mileage run), it is variable cost. If it is calculated on time basis it is fixed cost. But most of the authors treat depreciation calculated on time basis as variable. So there is no clear rules for treatment of depreciation.

Salary and wages of driver and conductor

It is treated as fixed expenses when paid on monthly basis. Sometimes they may be paid on daily basis for actual days or hours worked. Then salary and wages paid is treated as variable. Commission is also allowed to drivers and conductors calculated as a percentage on collection. It is treated as variable cost.

Sale of old tyres, tubes and spare parts

The sale value is to be deducted from repairs and maintenance cost.

18.3 OPERATING COST SHEET

The costs collected for a period are presented in a statement where cost are grouped under proper divisions. It is called operating cost sheet. The following is the proforma of an operating cost sheet:

Particulars	Total ₹	Per passenger km/Tonne km ₹
(A) Fixed costs:		
Tax, insurance	xxx	
Garage rent	xxx	
Salary and wages	xxx	
Interest on capital	xxx	
Office expenses, supervision	xxx	
	xxx	xxx
(B) Repairs and maintenance:		
Tyres, tubes & spare parts	xxx	
Repairs, overhauling, paintings etc	xxx	
	xxx	
Less: Sale of old tyres, tubes and spare parts	xxx	
	xxx	xxx
(C) Running/operating expenses:		
Depreciation	xxx	xxx
Petrol, diesel, oil	xxx	xxx
Lubricants	xxx	xxx
Total	xxx	xxx
Kilometres run	xxx	
Load carried (tonnes/passengers)	xxx	
Number of days operated	xxx	
% of capacity utilisation	xxx	
Tonne km/passenger km	xxx	

Illustration-5

From the following data calculate the cost per kilometre of a vehicle:

Value of vehicle	₹15,000
Road licence fees per year	₹500
Insurance charges per year	₹100
Garage rent per year	₹600

Driver wages per month	₹200
Cost of petrol per litre	₹8
Kilometre per litre	8
Proportionate charges for tyres and maintenance per kilometre	₹0.20
Estimated life	1,50,000 km
Estimated annual kilometres	6,000

(B.Com., Madras University)

Solution

Operating Cost Sheet		
Particulars	**Total per annum** ₹	**Per kilometre** ₹
Standing Charges:		
Road licence fees	500	
Insurance charges	100	
Garage rent	600	
Driver wages (200 × 12)	2,400	
Cost per km - 3,600 ÷ 6,000	3,600	0.60
Repairs and Maintenance:		
Tyre and maintenance cost		0.20
Operating expenses:		
Depreciation $= \frac{\text{cost} - \text{scrap}}{\text{life}} = \frac{15,000}{1,50,000}$	-	0.10
Petrol 8 ÷ 8	-	1.00
Cost per km	-	1.90

Illustration-6

A transport company is running 4 buses between two towns which are 50 km away from each other. Seating capacity of each bus is 40 passengers. The following particulars are given from their books for April 2008:

	₹
Wages of drivers and conductors	2,400
Salaries	1,000
Diesel, oil	4,000
Repairs and expenses	800
Insurance and tax	1,600
Depreciation	2,600
Interest	2,000

Actual passengers carried were 75% of the seating capacity. All the buses ran on all the days of the month. Each bus made one round trip per day. Find out the cost per passenger km.

Solution

(i) Computation of passenger km

Total distance run = No. of buses × No. of trips × Trip distance × No. of days

$= 4 \times 1 \times 100 \times 30$

$= 12{,}000$ km

Passenger km = Total distance run × Seating capacity × % of capacity carried

$$= 12{,}000 \times 40 \times \frac{75}{100}$$

$= 3{,}60{,}000$

(ii)

Operating cost sheet for the month of April 2008		
Particulars	₹	**Total per month** ₹
1. Fixed costs:		
Wages of drivers and conducts	2,400	
Salaries	1,000	
Insurance and tax	1,600	
Interest	2,000	
	7,000	7,000
2. **Repairs and maintenance:**	800	
Repairs and expenses	800	800
3. Operating expenses:		
Depreciation	2,600	
Diesel, oil	4,000	

	6,600	6,600
Total cost		14,400

$$\text{Cost per passenger km} = \frac{\text{Total cost}}{\text{Passenger km}}$$
$$= \frac{14{,}400}{3{,}60{,}000}$$
$$= ₹0.04 \text{ (or) } 4 \text{ paise}$$

Illustration-7

From the following data calculate the cost per passenger mile in an appropriate cost sheet for the year 2008-09 for a fleet of passenger buses booked by a transport company:

5 passenger buses costing ₹50,000, ₹1,20,000, ₹45,000, ₹55,000 and ₹80,000 respectively. Yearly depreciation of vehicles 20% of the cost. Annual repair, maintenance and spare parts 80% of depreciation, diesel and oil ₹9,000 per month.

- Wages of 10 drivers at ₹100 each per month.
- Wages 20 cleaners at ₹50 each per month.
- Yearly rate of interest 4% on capital.
- Rent of 6 garages at ₹50 each per month.
- Director's fees at ₹400 per month.
- Office establishment at ₹1,000 per month.
- Licence and taxes at ₹1,000 every six months.
- Realisation by sale of old tyres and tubes at ₹3,200 every 6 months.
- 900 passengers were carried over 1,600 km during the year.

Solution

Operating cost sheet			
Particulars		₹	**Total per annum** ₹
Standing charges:			
Driver wages	10 × 100 × 12	12,000	
Cleaner wages	20 × 50 × 12	12,000	

Interest	$3,50,000 \times \frac{4}{100}$	14,000	
Rent of garages	$6 \times 50 \times 12$	3,600	
Director's fees	400×12	4,800	
Office establishment	$1,000 \times 12$	12,000	
Licence and taxes	$1,000 \times 2$	2,000	
		60,400	60,400
Repairs and maintenance:			
80% of depreciation	$70,000 \times \frac{80}{100}$	56,000	56,000
Operating expenses:			
Depreciation	$3,50,000 \times \frac{20}{100}$	70,000	
Diesel and oil	$9,000 \times 12$	1,08,000	
		1,78,000	1,78,000
	Total Cost	-	2,94,400

$$\text{Passenger km} = \text{Total km run} \times \text{No. of passengers carried}$$
$$= 1{,}600 \times 900 = 14{,}40{,}000$$

$$\text{Cost per passenger km} = \frac{2{,}94{,}400}{14{,}40{,}000} = ₹0.20 \text{ (Approx)}$$

Illustration-8

National Transport Company supplies the following details in respect of a truck of 5 tonne capacity:

Cost of truck	₹90,000
Estimated life	10 years
Diesel, oil, grease	₹15 per trip each way
Repairs and maintenance	₹500 per month
Driver wages	₹500 per month
Cleaner wages	₹250 per month
Insurance	₹4,800 per year
Tax	₹2,400 per year
General supervision charges	₹4,800 per year

The truck carries goods to and from city covering a distance of 50 miles each way. While going to the city freight is available to the extent of full capacity and on return 20% of capacity. Assuming that the truck runs on an average 25 days a month, work out:

(a) Operating cost per tonne mile

(b) Rate per tonne per trip that the company should charge if profit of 50% on freightage is to be earned.

Solution

Statement of operating cost			
Particulars		**Total per month** ₹	**Per tonne mile** ₹
Standing charges:			
Driver wages		500	
Cleaner wages		250	
Insurance	(4,800 ÷ 12)	400	
Tax	(2,400 ÷ 12)	200	
General supervision charges	(4,800 ÷ 12)	400	
		1,750	
Standing charges per tonne mile	(1,750 ÷ 7,500)	-	0.233
Running charges:			
Repairs and maintenance		500	
Diesel, oil, grease	(15 × 2 × 25)	750	
Depreciation $= 90,000 \times \frac{10}{100} \times \frac{1}{12}$		750	
		2,000	
Running expenses per tonne mile 2000 ÷ 7500			0.267
Total expenses per tonne mile		-	0.500
Add: Profit 50% on freightage			0.500
Freight charges per tonne miles			1.000
Freight charges per trip per tonne (both ways)	100 × 1	100	

Tonne miles

Going to city $= 5 \times 50 \times 25 = 6{,}250$

Return trip $= 5 \times 50 \times 25 \times \frac{20}{100} = 1{,}250$

Total tonne miles $= 7{,}500$

Illustration-9

Global Transport Ltd charges ₹90 per tonne for its 6 tonnes lorry load from city 'A' to 'B'. The charges for the return journey are ₹84 per tonne. No concession or reduction in these rates is made for any delivery of goods at the intermediate station 'C'. In January 2005, the truck made 12 outward journeys for city 'B' with full load out of which 2 tonnes were unloaded twice on the way at city 'C'. The truck carried a load of 8 tonnes in its return journey for 5 times but once caught by the police and ₹1,200 were paid as fine. For the remaining trips the truck carried full load out of which all the goods were unloaded at 'A' except once at city 'C'. The distance from city 'A' to city 'C' and city 'B' are 140 km and 300 km respectively. Annual fixed costs and maintenance charges are ₹60,000 and ₹12,000 respectively. Running charges spent during January 2005 are ₹2,944. You are required to find out the cost per absolute tonne km and the profit for January 2005.

(B.Com. (Hons.), Delhi University, 2006)

Solution

(i) Calculation of tonne km

Onward -	City A to B = $(300 \times 6 \times 10)$	= 18,000 tonne km
	City A to C = $(140 \times 6 \times 2)$	= 1,680 tonne km
	City C to B = $(160 \times 4 \times 2)$	= 1,280 tonne km
Return -	City B to A = $(300 \times 8 \times 5)$	= 12,000 tonne km
	City B to A = $(300 \times 6 \times 6)$	= 10,800 tonne km
	City B to C = $(160 \times 6 \times 1)$	= 960 tonne km
	Total tonne km	= 44,720 tonne km

(ii) Calculation of revenue

	₹
A to B = $12 \times 6 \times 90$	6,480
B to A = $6 \times 6 \times 84$	3,024
B to A = $5 \times 8 \times 84$	3,360
B to C = $1 \times 6 \times 84$	504
	13,368
Fine paid	1,200
Net revenue	12,168

Note: Carrying goods over the capacity and paying fine is a regular feature in transport industry. So fine paid is treated as a normal expenditure. It may be shown as deduction from total revenue or added to the operating cost. Profit arrived will be same in both cases.

(iii)

Operating cost sheet for the month of January 2005	
	₹
Fixed cost (60,000 ÷ 12)	5,000
Maintenance charges (12,000 ÷ 12)	1,000
Running charges	2,944
Total Cost	8,944

Cost per tonne km = ₹8,944 ÷ ₹44,720
= ₹0.20

(iv)

Calculation of profit	
	₹
Net revenue	12,168
Less: Operating cost	8,944
Profit	3,224

Illustration-10

The following expenses were incurred by a company in respect of two lorries for 25 days:

	Lorry A ₹	Lorry B ₹
Driver wages	120	125
Cleaner wages	130	130
Petrol	150	230
Oil	18	25
Depreciation	320	210
Repairs	140	140
Supervision	80	80
Garage overhead	140	120
Road tax	45	45
Other overhead expenses	35	40

Lorry A carried 100 tonnes of raw material and covered a distance of 3,000 kilometres in 25 days. Lorry B carried 120 tonnes of raw material and covered a distance of 4,500 kilometres in 25 days.

Find out the cost per kilometre. Prepare on operating cost sheet in summary form for the two vehicles. **(B.Com., Bangalore University, Nov. 2000)**

Solution

Operation cost sheet				
Particulars	Lorry A		Lorry B	
	Total	Per tonne km	Total	Per tonne km
	₹	₹	₹	₹
Standing charges:				
Depreciation	320		210	
Supervision	80		80	
Road tax	45		45	
Overhead expenses	35		40	
Garage overheads	140		120	
Total	620	0.0020	495	0.0009
Running and maintenance expenses:				
Repairs	140		140	
Driver wages	120		125	
Cleaner wages	130		130	
Petrol	150		230	
Oil	18		25	
Total	558	0.0019	650	0.0012
Cost per tonne km	-	0.0039	-	0.0021

Computation of tonne km

Lorry A = 100 × 3,000 km = 3,00,000 tonne km

Lorry B = 120 × 4,500 km = 5,40,000 tonne km

Illustration-11

Mr. Eswar owns a bus, which runs between Mysore and Bangalore and back for 10 days in a month. The distance from Mysore to Bangalore is 150 km. The bus completes the trip from Mysore to Bangalore and back the same day. The bus goes another 10 days in a month towards Hassan. The distance from Mysore to Hassan is 120 km. The trip is completed on the same day. For the next 4 days of its operation in a month it runs in the local city. Daily distance covered in the local city is 40 km. Calculate the rate Mr. Eswar should charge from passengers when he wants to earn profits of $33\frac{1}{3}\%$ of his takings. The other information is:

	₹
Cost of the bus	3,00,000
Depreciation 20% p.a.	
Salary of driver	1,750 p.m.
Salary of conductor	1,750 p.m.
Salary of clerk	9,600 p.a.
Diesel consumption 8 km per litre costing	₹10 per litre
Token tax	3,000 p.m.
Lubricating oil ₹50 per 100 km	
Repairs and maintenance	3,000 p.a.
Permit fees	1,420 p.m.
Insurance	8,400 p.a.

Normal capacity 50 passengers. The bus is generally occupied 90% of the capacity when it goes to Bangalore, 80% when it goes to Hassan and 100% in the local trip.

(B.Com., Bangalore University, April 2001)

Solution

Operating cost sheet			
Particulars		₹	**Total per month** ₹
Fixed charges:			
Permit fees		1,420	
Token tax		3,000	
Insurance (8,400 ÷ 12)		700	
Salary of driver		1,750	
Salary of conductor		1,750	
Salary of clerk		800	
		9,420	9,420
Repairs and maintenance (3,000 ÷ 12)		-	250
Running expenses:			
Depreciation	$3{,}00{,}000 \times \frac{20}{100} \times \frac{1}{12}$	5,000	
Diesel	$\frac{10}{8} \times 5{,}560$	6,950	

Lubricating oil	$\frac{50}{100} \times 5{,}560$	2,780	
		14,730	14,730
Total cost		-	24,400
Add: Profit $33\frac{1}{3}\%$ on taking or 50% on cost		-	12,200
Takings			36,600
Fare per passenger km		$\frac{36{,}600}{2{,}39{,}000}$	₹0.153

Total km

Mysore to Bangalore	= 150 × 2 × 10	= 3,000 km
Mysore to Hassan	= 120 × 2 × 10	= 2,400 km
Local city	= 4 × 40	= 160 km
	Total	= 5,560 km

Passenger km

Mysore to Bangalore	= 3,000 × 50 × 90/100	= 1,35,000
Mysore to Hassan	= 2,400 × 50 × 80/100	= 96,000
Local trip	= 160 × 50	= 8,000
	Total passenger km	= 2,39,000

Fares charged from passengers		
		₹
From Mysore to Bangalore	150 × 0.153	22.95
From Mysore to Hassan	120 × 0.153	18.36
Local city - round trip	40 × 0.153	6.12

18.4 HOTEL (LODGING) COSTING

Lodging houses provide room service to guests. The expenses incurred by a lodging house are office expenses, salary to manager, office and maintenance staff, attendants etc., lighting, power, repairs and maintenance, laundry, depreciation etc. The expenses may be classified as fixed, semi-variable and variable cost or may be classified on the basis of nature of expenses. A lodging house may provide additional services like swimming, beauty parlour, saloon, laundry etc. Additional charges may be levied for utilizing these services. Sometimes these services may be provided to all customers without additional charges. In such a case the cost of providing these services will be added to the total operating cost.

Cost Unit

The cost unit is room days. Various types of rooms may be available. They are single bedroom, double bedroom, family room, ordinary room, deluxe room and luxury room. These rooms may be provided with air-conditioners or without air-conditioners. Due weightage is to be given for various types rooms and room days are to be expressed in terms of equivalent room days or standard room days.

Illustration-12

Hotel Intercontinental Ltd has the following types of rooms:

Single rooms	120 Nos
Double rooms	90 Nos
Family rooms	40 Nos

From the following particulars calculate the rent to be charged for each type of room:

(a) Rooms occupied during different seasons are:

	Summer	**Winter**
Single rooms	100%	60%
Double rooms	80%	50%
Family rooms	70%	30%

(b) The annual expenses are as follows:

	₹
Staff salaries	4,00,000
Repairs and maintenance	75,000
Interior decoration	60,000
Laundry	50,000
General expenses	1,15,395

(c) Depreciation on fixed assets:

- At 5% on building costing ₹50,00,000
- At 10% on furniture and fittings costing ₹5,00,000
- At 25% on air-conditioners costing ₹2,00,000.

(d) Other expenses:

(i) Lighting:

- ₹75 per single room per month if occupied.
- ₹100 per double room per month if occupied.
- ₹120 per family room per month if occupied.

(ii) Power: Single room ₹50, double room ₹75 and family room ₹100 per month if occupied.

(iii) Room attendant's salary:

	Summer ₹	Winter ₹
Single rooms	20 per day	30 per day
Double rooms	25 per day	35 per day
Family rooms	30 per day	40 per day

Additional information:

(i) Summer may be assumed for 7 months and winter 5 months. Number of days in a month is taken as 30 days.

(ii) Percentage of profit on cost is 25%.

(iii) The rent of double room is $1\frac{1}{2}$ times the rent of single room and for family room the rent is double the rent of single room.

Solution

(1)

Calculation of room days			
	Single Room	**Double Room**	**Family Room**
Summer	$120 \times 7 \times 30 = 25{,}200$	$90 \times 7 \times 30 \times \frac{80}{100} =$ 15,120	$40 \times 7 \times 30 \times \frac{70}{100} =$ 5,880
Winter	$120 \times 5 \times 30 \times \frac{60}{100} =$ 10,800	$90 \times 5 \times 30 \times \frac{50}{100} =$ 6,750	$40 \times 5 \times 30 \times \frac{30}{100} =$ 1,800
Total room days	36,000	21,870	7,680
Rent charged - weightage	1	1.5	2
Room days in terms of single room	36,000	32,805	15,360

Total room days in terms of single room:

Single rooms	36,000
Double rooms	32,805
Family rooms	15,360
Total	84,165

(2)

Power expenses	
	₹
Single rooms	60,000
Double rooms	54,675
Family rooms	25,600
Total	1,40,275

(3)

Lighting expenses	
Single rooms	90,000
Double rooms	72,900
Family rooms	30,720
Total	1,93,620

(4)

Room attendants' salary			
	Summer	**Winter**	**Total** ₹
Single room	25,200 × 20 = 5,04,000	10,800 × 30 = 3,24,000	8,28,000
Double room	15,120 × 25 = 3,78,000	6,750 × 35 = 2,36,250	6,14,250
Family room	5,880 × 30 = 1,76,400	1800 × 40 = 72,000	2,48,400
		Total	16,90,650

(5)

Depreciation	
On Building	2,50,000
On Furniture and fittings	5,000
On Air-conditioners	50,000
Total	3,05,000

Operating Cost Sheet

	₹
Staff salaries	4,00,000
Repairs and maintenance	75,000
Interior decoration	60,000
Laundry	50,000
General expenses	1,15,395
Power expenses	1,40,275
Lighting expenses	1,93,620
Room attendants salary	16,90,650
Depreciation	3,05,000
Total operating cost	30,29,940
Add: Profit at 25% on cost	7,57,485
Total revenue from rent	37,87,425

Total number of single room days $= 84{,}165$

Room rent per single room per day $= \frac{37{,}87{,}425}{84{,}165}$

$=$ ₹45

Room rent per double room per day $= 45 \times 1.5$

$=$ ₹67.50

Room rent per family room per day $= 45 \times 2$

$=$ ₹90

Illustration-13

Hotel Paramount Ltd., Bangalore, gives you the following information:

1. Number of rooms - 100 ordinary rooms, 75 deluxe rooms and 60 luxury rooms. On an average 90% of rooms are full in summer and 75% rooms are full during winter. Summer and winter are taken as 6 months each. Normal days in a month are 30 days.

2. Staff salaries - ₹10,00,000.

3. Room attendants' salary at ₹50 per day when occupied. There are 1 attendant for every 5 rooms.

4. Lighting ₹200 per month per ordinary room if occupied.

5. Power ₹50 per month per ordinary room if occupied.
6. Linen, laundry etc., ₹5,000 per month.
7. Repairs and maintenance ₹1,25,000 per annum.
8. Miscellaneous expenses - ₹7,59,150 per annum.
9. Interior decoration ₹50,000 per annum.
10. Cost of fixed assets ₹2 crore, rate of depreciation 10%.
11. Interest on borrowed capital ₹50,000 per annum.

Calculate the rent the hotel should charge for each type of room if the company wants to earn a profit of 20% on cost. The rent charged for deluxe room is double the charge of ordinary room and rent charged for luxury room is thrice that of ordinary room.

Solution

1.

Room Days			
	Ordinary Room	Deluxe Room	Luxury Room
Summer	$100 \times 6 \times 30 \frac{90}{100} =$ 16,200	$75 \times 6 \times 30 \times \frac{90}{100} =$ 12,150	$60 \times 6 \times 30 \times \frac{90}{100} =$ 9,720
Winter	$100 \times 6 \times 30 \times \frac{75}{100} =$ 13,500	$75 \times 6 \times 30 \times \frac{75}{100} =$ 10,125	$60 \times 6 \times 30 \times \frac{75}{100} =$ 8,100
Total room days	29,700	22,275	17,820
Rent charged - weightage	1	2	3
Room days in terms of single room	29,700	44,550	53,460

Total room days	
Ordinary rooms	29,700
Deluxe rooms	44,550
Luxury rooms	53,460
Total ordinary rooms	1,27,710

2. Room attendants, salary $= 1{,}27{,}710 \times 50 \times \frac{1}{5} =$ ₹12,77,100

3. Lighting expenses $= 1{,}27{,}710 \times \frac{200}{30} =$ ₹8,51,400

4. Power expenses $= 1{,}27{,}710 \times \frac{50}{30} =$ ₹2,12,850

5. Linen, laundry, etc. $= 5{,}000 \times 12 =$ ₹60,000

6. Depreciation $= 2{,}00{,}00{,}000 \times \frac{10}{100} =$ ₹20,00,000

Operating cost sheet	
	₹
Staff salaries	10,00,000
Room attendants' salary	12,77,100
Lighting expenses	8,51,400
Power expenses	2,12,850
Linen, laundry, etc.	60,000
Repairs and maintenance	1,25,000
Miscellaneous expenses	7,59,150
Interior decoration	50,000
Depreciation	20,00,000
Interest on borrowed capital	50,000
Total operating cost	63,85,500
Add: Profit at 20% on cost	12,77,100
Total rent charges	76,62,600

Total ordinary room days $=$ 1,27,710

Rent per ordinary room per day $= \frac{76,62,600}{1,27,710}$

$=$ ₹60

Rent per deluxe room per day $= 60 \times 2$

$=$ ₹120

Rent per luxury room per day $= 60 \times 3$

$=$ ₹180

18.5 HOTEL - BOARDING/CANTEEN COSTING

Hotels and canteens provide food items. The expenses incurred are — wheat, rice, vegetable, oil, fuel, staff salaries, lighting and power, repairs and maintenance, egg, meat, depreciation etc. These expenses may also be classified on behaviour basis or on their nature. Simple measurement units are followed like per meal, per each item, per coffee etc. Canteens are maintained in business establishments for the benefit of employees. Food is served either at cost price or at below cost i.e. at subsidised rate. The subsidy is borne by the management. The following is a specimen operating cost sheet of a canteen:

Operating cost sheet of canteen	
	₹
Wages and salaries:	
Manager, supervisor, cooks	xxx
Waiters, security, cleaners, helpers	xxx
Provisions:	
Wheat, rice, fruits, vegetables, eggs, meat	xxx
oil, gas, tea, coffee, milk	xxx
Consumables stores	xxx
Repairs, lighting etc	xxx
Miscellaneous expenses	xxx
Total cost	xxx

Illustration-14

Sri Ram Industries runs a canteen for its employees. The following information relating to canteen were extracted from its books for the month of July 2008:

1. **Wages and salaries**
   - 5 cooks at ₹1,500 per month each
   - 1 manger at ₹4,000 per month
   - 1 clerk cum cashier at ₹2,000 per month
   - 4 assistants at ₹1,000 per month each
2. **Provisions**

Rice 200 kg at	₹20 per kg
Vegetables	₹750
Milk	₹1,000
Tea and coffee	₹600

Sugar	₹400
Bread and cakes	₹300
Meat and eggs	₹1,000
Oil	₹500

3. Service

Gas	₹1,200
Electricity	₹700
Steam	₹300

4. Consumable stores - ₹2,000

5. Overheads apportioned - ₹800

6. Miscellaneous expenses - ₹4,950

The canteen provided 3,000 meals at ₹10 per meal during the month. Find the subsidy to be borne by the management. Also find the subsidy per meal.

Solution

Operating cost sheet for the month of July 2008		
Particulars	₹	**Total per month** ₹
1. Wages and Salaries:		
Cooks 5 × 1,500	7,500	
Manager	4,000	
Clerk-cum-cashier	2,000	
Assistants 4 × 1,000	4,000	17,500
2. Provisions:		
Rice 200 kg × ₹20	4,000	
Vegetables	750	
Milk	1,000	
Tea and coffee	600	
Sugar	400	
Bread and cakes	300	
Meat and eggs	1,000	
Oil	500	8,550

3. Services:		
Gas	1,200	
Electricity	700	
Steam	300	2,200
4. Consumable stores	-	2,000
5. Overheads apportioned	-	800
6. Miscellaneous expenses	-	4,950
Total cost	-	36,000
Less: Amount collected from employees	-	30,000
Subsidy to be borne by the management	-	6,000

Subsidy per meal = 6,000 ÷ 3,000 = ₹2.00

18.6 HOSPITAL COSTING

Hospitals provide medical services to patients. An hospital has the following departments/divisions:

(i) Out-patient department (OPD)

(ii) Wards (in patient)

(iii) Supporting services like X-Ray, laboratory, scanning, pathology etc.

(iv) General services like power, catering, transport, laundry etc.

The expenses of hospitals include salaries and wages of doctors, nurses, technicians and office staff, cost of medicines, lighting, power, cost of oxygen, X-rays, insurance, laundry charges, depreciation and repairs and maintenance. The expenses are usually classified as fixed and variable costs.

Cost unit is a composite unit called patient day or bed day.

Illustration-15

A public health centre runs an intensive medical care unit. For this purpose, it has hired a building at a rent of ₹5,250 per month, with the understanding that it would bear the repairs and maintenance charges also.

The unit consists of 25 beds but 5 more beds can be comfortably accommodated when the occasion demands. The permanent staff attached to the unit is as follows:

- 2 supervisors, each at a salary of ₹2,500 per month
- 4 nurses, each at a salary of ₹1,500 per month
- 2 ward boys, each at a salary of ₹750 per month.

Though the unit remains open for the patients all the 365 days in a year, it has full capacity of 25 patients per day only for 120 days. For 245 days it has on average 20 beds occupied per day. But there are occasions when the beds are full and extra beds are hired from out side at a charge of ₹10 per bed per day. However this does not come to more than 5 extra beds above the normal capacity on any one day. The total hire charges for the extra beds hired for the year amount to ₹5,000.

The unit has engaged expert doctors from outside to attend on the patients. The fees are paid on the basis of the number of patients attended and time spent by them. On an average it works out to ₹22,500 per month.

The other expenses for the year are as under:

	₹
Repairs and maintenance	7,200
Food supplied to patients	88,000
Janitor and other services for them	25,000
Laundry charges for their bed linen	28,000
Medicines supplied	64,000
Cost of oxygen, X-rays etc, other than those directly born by patients	1,08,000
General administration charges allocated	99,000
Total	4,19,200

Required:

(i) If the unit recovered an overall amount of ₹150 per patient per day, what is the profit made by the unit (in nearest rupee)?

(ii) The unit wants to work on a budget for the next year, but the number of patients requiring intensive medical care is a very uncertain factor.

Assuming that the same revenue and expenses will prevail in the next year also, work out the number of patients required by the unit to break even. **(ICWA-Inter)**

Solution

Computation of number of patient days

For 120 days	= 120 × 25	= 3,000
For 245 days	= 245 × 20	= 4,900
Extra beds	= 5,000 ÷ 10	= 500
Total patient days		= 8,400

(i)

Operating cost sheet			
		₹	₹
Fixed costs:			
Rent	(5250 × 12)	63,000	
Salaries:			
Supervisor	(2 × 2500 × 12)	60,000	
Nurses	(4 × 1500 × 12)	72,000	
Ward boys	(2 × 750 × 12)	18,000	
Repairs and maintenance		7,200	
General administration charges		99,000	
	Total	3,19,200	3,19,200
Variable costs:			
Fees paid to expert doctors		2,70,000	
Hire charges for extra beds		5,000	
Food supplied to patients		88,000	
Janitor and other services		25,000	
Laundry charges		28,000	
Medicines supplied		64,000	
Cost of X-rays etc.		1,08,000	
	Total	5,88,000	5,88,000
	Total costs		9,07,200

$$\text{Average charges collected from patients} = 8{,}400 \times 150 = ₹12{,}60{,}000$$

$$\text{Profit for the year} = 12{,}60{,}000 - 9{,}07{,}200 = ₹3{,}52{,}800$$

(ii)

Computation of number of patients required to breakeven	
	₹
Charges per patient/day	150
Less: Variable cost per patient/day $\left(\frac{5,88,000}{8,400}\right)$	70
Contribution per patient/day	80

$$\text{Break even point} = \frac{\text{Fixed cost}}{\text{Contibution per patient/day}}$$

$$= \frac{3{,}19{,}200}{80} = 3{,}990 \text{ patient days}$$

18.7 POWERHOUSE COSTING

Powerhouse expenses are classified into generation cost, distribution cost, salaries and wages and administration. It may also be classified on the basis of variability as fixed costs and variable costs. The cost unit used is kilowatt-hour (KWH). The following is the specimen operating cost sheet of a powerhouse:

Operating cost sheet	
	₹
Fixed charges:	
Depreciation	xxx
Administration overheads	xxx
Interest on borrowed capital	xxx
Plant supervision	xxx
Salary and wages	xxx
Total (A)	xxx
Variable charges:	xxx
Coal, fuel and gas	xxx
Repairs and maintenance	xxx
Consumable stores	xxx
Operating wages	xxx
Total (B)	xxx
Total cost (A+B)	xxx

Illustration-16

The Iron and Steel Works which generates its own electricity for the purpose of using the same for running the factory, gives the following information:

(i) Fuel-coal consumed during the month 1,000 quintals at ₹12 per quintal.

(ii) Oil 15 quintals at ₹1,000 per quintal.

(iii) Water 2,00,000 litres at ₹1 per 1,000 litres.

(iv) Cost of steam boiler ₹50,000 which has the residual value of ₹2,000. The life of steam boiler is 10 years.

(v) Salaries and wages for the boiler house:

- 20 men at ₹150 per month
- 40 women at ₹60 per month.

(vi) Share of administration charges ₹1,050 per month.

(vii) Sale of ash ₹300.

(viii) Generating plant cost ₹1,50,000 and depreciation at 10%.

(ix) Repairs and maintenance of steam boiler and generating plant ₹1,000.

(x) Salaries and wages for generating plant:

- 10 skilled workers at ₹300 per month
- 15 unskilled workers at ₹100 per month.

(xi) Number of units generated 2,00,000.

(xii) 1/10th of units generated were used by generating department itself.

Calculate the cost of electricity generated per unit.

(M.Com., Madurai University, Nov. 2001)

Solution

Units Generated: 2,00,000 units

Operating cost sheet for the month			
		₹	₹
Operating cost:			
Cost of coal consumed - 1,000 × 12	= 12,000		
Less: Sale of ash	= 300	11,700	
Oil	(15 × 1,000)	15,000	
Water	$\left(2{,}00{,}000 \times \frac{1}{1{,}000}\right)$	200	
Depreciation - Steam boiler	$\left(\frac{50{,}000 - 2{,}000}{10} \times \frac{1}{12}\right)$	400	
Depreciation - Generating plant	$\left(1{,}50{,}000 \times \frac{10}{100} \times \frac{1}{12}\right)$	1,250	
	Total	13,550	13,550

Salaries and wages of boiler house			
20 men × ₹150 per month	= 3,000		
40 women × ₹60 per month	= 2,400	5,400	
Salaries and wages of generating plant			
10 skilled workers × 300 per month	= 3,000		
15 unskilled workers × 100 per month	= 1,500	4,500	9,900
Repairs and maintenance			1,000
Share of administration expenses			1,050
			40,500
Add: Cost of electricity used in generation (*See: Note-1*)			4,500
Total cost of generation			45,000

$$\text{Cost per unit} = \frac{45{,}000}{2{,}00{,}000} = ₹0.225$$

Working Note-1

Let the cost of electricity generated be 'y'.

$$\begin{aligned}\text{Cost of electricity used in generation} &= y \times \frac{1}{10}\\ &= 0.1y\\ y &= 40{,}500 + 0.1y\\ 0.9y &= 40{,}500\\ y &= \frac{40{,}500}{0.9}\\ &= 45{,}000\end{aligned}$$

$$\begin{aligned}\text{Cost of electricity used in generation} &= 45000 \times \frac{1}{10}\\ &= ₹4{,}500\end{aligned}$$

18.8 CINEMA HOUSE

Cinema houses provide entertainment to viewers. The cost unit of a theatre is **man show**. But cinema theatres charge different amount for different group of seats classified as third class, second class, first class, box etc. These seats are to be converted into third class seats giving weightage on the basis of charges levied for each class of seats. The operating expenses include wages and salaries of staff, hire for print, advertisement, insurance, depreciation, carbon, advertisement etc. These expenses are usually classified on variability basis as fixed costs and variable costs.

Illustration-17

The following are the expenses of Orient Theatres of Pune for the year ending 31st March 2009:

(i) Salaries:

- 2 managers ₹6,000 each per month
- 15 gate-keepers and security guards at ₹2,500 per month each
- 3 operators at ₹3,000 per month each
- 2 clerks at ₹3,000 per month each.

(ii) Hire for cinema print ₹50,00,000.

(iii) Advertisement ₹25,000 per annum.

(iv) Lighting and power ₹50,000 per annum.

(v) Depreciation:

(a) at 10% on building costing ₹1.5 crore

(b) at 25% on projector and equipment costing ₹50,00,000.

(vi) Administration and office expenses ₹1,75,000.

(vii) Miscellaneous expenses ₹9,57,200

(viii) Revenue from

(a) parking lots ₹50,000

(b) canteen ₹1,00,000 and

(c) advertisement ₹2,50,000.

The seating capacity of the theatre is 1,000 seats, which is divided into four categories. They are:

Super Class	150 seats
I class	300 seats
II class	350 seats
III class	200 seats

The charges levied for the second class is twice as much as that of third class, the charges for the first class is thrice as that of third class and charges for super class is four times the charges for third class. On average only 90% of the seats are full.

The theatre runs 3 shows daily for 360 days in a year. The management wants to earn a profit of 20% on cost. Entertainment tax is 20% on net charges.

Find the gross ticket rates (including entertainment tax) for each class of seats.

Solution

(i) Computation of man shows

Super Class	= 150 ×3 ×360	= 1,62,000
I Class	= 300 × 3 × 360	= 3,24,000
II Class	= 350 ×3 × 360	= 3,78,000
III Class	= 200 ×3 × 360	= 2,16,000

(ii) Computation of number of equivalent man shows

Super Class	= 1,62,000 × 4 × 90/100	= 5,83,200
I Class	= 3,24,000 × 3 × 90/100	= 8,74,800
II Class	= 3,78,000 × 2 × 90/100	= 6,80,400
III Class	= 2,16,000 × 1 × 90/100	= 1,94,400
Total equivalent man shows		= 23,32,800

Operating Cost Sheet

	₹	₹
Salaries		
Managers = 2 × 6,000 × 12	1,44,000	
Gate-keepers = 15 × 2,500 × 12	4,50,000	
Operators = 3 × 3,000 × 12	1,08,000	
Clerks = 2 × 3,000 × 12	72,000	
Total	7,74,000	7,74,000
Hire for cinema print		50,00,000
Advertisement		25,000
Lighting and power		50,000
Depreciation – building = $\left(1,50,00,000 \times \frac{10}{100}\right)$	15,00,000	
Depreciation – Projector and equipment = $\left(50,00,000 \times \frac{25}{100}\right)$	12,50,000	27,50,000
Administration and office equipment		1,75,000
Miscellaneous expenses		9,57,200
Total Cost		97,31,200
Less : Revenue received:		
Parking lot	50,000	

Canteen	1,00,000	
Advertisement	2,50,000	4,00,000
Net Operating Cost		93,31,200
Add : Profit 20% on cost		18,66,240
Net Collections		1,11,97,440
Add : Entertainment tax - 20% on net collection		22,39,488
Gross Collections		1,34,36,928

Charge per man show per III Class = 1,34,36,928/23,32,800 = ₹5.76

Charge per man show per II Class = 5.76 × 2 = ₹11.52

Charge per man show per I Class =5.76 × 3 = ₹17.28

Charge per man show per Super Class=5.76 × 4 = ₹23.04

18.9 BOILER HOUSE COSTING

Boiler houses are established in many organisations to supply steam to the production departments. For the purpose of apportionment of boiler house costs to various user departments, it is necessary to calculate the cost of operating boiler houses. The expenses are classified on the basis of their nature like fuel, labour, maintenance, supervision, water and fixed overheads. Cost unit is 1,000 lbs of steam.

The following is the specimen of operating cost statement of a boiler house:

		₹
1.	**Fuel and Power:**	
	Coal, gas, power etc.	xxx
2.	**Water:** Cost of production/supply and water treatment cost	xxx
3.	Salaries and wages	xxx
4.	Repairs and maintenance	xxx
5.	**Fixed Overheads:**	
	Depreciation, insurance, interest on capital general overheads apportioned	xxx
	Total Cost	xxx

Illustration-18

The following information is extracted from the books of ABC Ltd relating to its boiler house:

	₹
Cost of coal consumed	20,00,000
Realisation from sale of ash	50,000
Oil	2,00,000
Water	3,00,000
Repairs and maintenance	4,50,000
Salary and wages	6,50,000
Depreciation	5,00,000
Interest on capital	50,000

Number of units of steam produced 20,50,000 lbs. Compute the cost per 1,000 lbs of steam produced.

Solution

Operating Cost Sheet			
		₹	₹
Fixed Costs:			
Salary and wages		6,50,000	
Interest on capital		50,000	
Depreciation		5,00,000	
Total		12,00,000	12,00,000
Variable Costs:			
Cost of coal	= 20,00,000		
Less: Sale of ash	= 50,000	19,50,000	
Oil		2,00,000	
Water		3,00,000	
Repairs and maintenance		4,50,000	
Total		29,00,000	29,00,000
Total operation cost		-	41,00,000

$$\text{Cost per lb of steam} = \frac{41,00,000}{20,50,000} = ₹2.00$$

Cost per 1000 lb of steam = 1,000 × 2 = ₹2,000.

18.10 OPERATION COSTING

A product may pass through different stages within a process or department like cutting, shearing, processing, boring, grinding, welding, etc. The method of costing followed to find the cost of each operation is called operation costing. Operation costing is an extension of process costing. The total cost of each operation is found by adding the cost of materials, labour and production overheads. This cost is transferred to next operation. Total cost of each operation is divided by the number of units produced in each operation. Operation costing helps in accurate computation of product costs. It is an improvement over process costing.

Illustration-19

An article undergoes three successive operations from raw material to finished product stage. The following information is available from the production records of a month:

Operation No.	Number of pieces input	Number of pieces rejected	Number of pieces output
1.	12,000	4,000	8,000
2.	13,200	1,200	12,000
3.	9,600	1,600	8,000

Find out what should be the input in the first operation in number of pieces to obtain a finished product of 100 pieces after last operation.

Calculate the cost of raw materials required to produce one piece of finished product from the following particulars:

- Weight of finished piece—100 gm per piece
- Price of raw materials—₹10 per kg **(ICWA-Inter)**

Solution

Percentage of rejection on output

$$\text{Operation 1} = \frac{4,000}{8,000} \times 100 = 50\%$$

$$\text{Operation 2} = \frac{1,200}{12,000} \times 100 = 10\%$$

$$\text{Operation 3} = \frac{1,600}{8,000} \times 100 = 20\%$$

Taking final output in operation 3 as 100 units, let us calculate the input of each process in the Reverse method starting from operation 3.

Statement of production and input (units)				
Operation no. (a)	Output (b)	% of rejection (c)	Rejected units (d)	Input units (e) = (b) + (d)
3	100	20%	20	120
2	120	10%	12	132
1	132	50%	66	198

It is seen from the above table if the output of operation 3 is 100 units, the input of operation 1 is 198 units. Therefore if the output in operation 3 is 100 grams per unit, the input for each piece in the operation 1 will be 198 grams.

$$\therefore \quad \text{Cost of raw materials per units} = 198 \times \frac{10}{1000}$$

$$= ₹1.98$$

18.11 COMPREHENSIVE ILLUSTRATIONS

Illustration-20

Mr. Sohan Singh has started transport business with a fleet of 10 taxis. The various expenses incurred by him are given below:

(a)	Cost of each taxi	₹75,000
(b)	Salary of office staff	₹1,500 p.m
(c)	Salary of garage staff	₹2,000 p.m
(d)	Rent of garage	₹1,000 p.m
(e)	Driver salary per taxi	₹400 p.m
(f)	Road tax and repairs per taxi	₹2,160 p.a
(g)	Insurance premium	4% of cost p.a

The life of a taxi is 3,00,000 km and at the end of which it is estimated to be sold at ₹15,000. A taxi runs on an average 4,000 km per month of which 20% it runs empty. Petrol consumption is 9 km per litre of petrol costing ₹6.30 per litre. Oil and sundry expenses amount to ₹10 per 100 km.

Calculate the effective cost of running a taxi per kilometre. If the hire charge is ₹1.80 per kilometre, find out the profit Mr. Sohan Singh may expect to make in the first year of operation.

(ICWA-Inter)

Solution

Statement showing operating cost and profit				
Particulars		**Per 10 tax is (pm)** ₹	**Per taxi (pm)** ₹	**Per km** ₹
Fixed Charges:				
Salary of office staff		1,500	150	
Salary of garage staff		2,000	200	
Rent of garage		1,000	100	
Driver salary	(400 × 10)	4,000	400	
Road tax and repairs	$2,160 \times \frac{10}{12}$	1,800	180	
Insurance	$\left(75{,}000 \times 10 \times \frac{4}{100} \times \frac{1}{12}\right)$	2,500	250	
	Total (A)	12,800	1,280	0.400
Variable Charges:				
Depreciation (WN-1)		8,000	800	0.250
Petrol (WN-2)		28,000	2,800	0.875
Oil and other sundry exp (WN-3)		4,000	400	0.125
	Total (B)	40,000	4,000	1.250
Total Cost (A) + (B)		52,800	5,280	1.650

Total hire charges for the year = 3,200 × 10 × 12 × 1.80
= 6,91,200

Less: Operating cost for the year = 52,800 × 12
= 6,33,600

Profit for the year = 57,600

Profit per effective km = 1.80 − 1.65
= ₹0.15

Computation of effective kilometre per taxi per month

Total km run per taxi per month	4,000 km
Less: 20% empty run	800 km
Effective running kilometres	3,200 km

Working Note:

1. Depreciation $= \dfrac{75{,}000 - 15{,}000}{3{,}00{,}000} \times 4{,}000 \times 10 = 8{,}000$

2. Petrol $= \dfrac{6.30 \times 4{,}000}{9} \times 10 = 28{,}000$

3. Oil and other sundry exp $= \dfrac{10}{100} \times 4{,}000 \times 10 = 4{,}000$

Note: For computing total cost of depreciation, petrol and oil expenses, 4,000 km per taxi has been taken but for calculating cost per km effective running 3,200 km per taxi is used.

Illustration-21

The Kangaroo Transport Ltd operates a fleet of lorries. The records of lorry L-14, reveal the following information for September, 1990:

Days maintained	30
Days operated	25
Days idle	5
Total hours operated	300
Total km covered	2,500
Total tonnage carried	200 (4 tonne load per trip, return journey empty)

The following further information is made available:

A. Operating cost for the month:

Petrol ₹400, oil ₹170, grease ₹90, wages to driver ₹550, wages to Khalasi ₹350.

B. Maintenance cost for the month:

Repairs ₹170, overhaul ₹60, tyres ₹150, garage charges ₹100.

C. Fixed cost for the month based on the estimates for the year:

Insurance ₹50, licence, tax etc., ₹80, interest ₹40, other overheads ₹190.

D. Capital costs:

Cost of acquisition ₹54,000. Residual value at the end of 5 years life is ₹36,000.

Prepare a cost sheet and performance statement showing:

(a) Cost per day maintained,

(b) Cost per day operated,

(c) Cost per kilometre,

(d) cost per hour,

(e) Cost per commercial tonne KM. **(ICWA-Inter, Dec. 1990)**

Solution

Operating cost statement of lorry L-14		
	₹	Total ₹
A. Operating costs:		
Petrol	400	
Oil	170	
Grease	90	
Wages to driver	550	
Wage to Khalasi	350	
	1,560	1,560
B. Maintenance Costs:		
Repairs	170	
Overhaul	60	
Tyres	150	
Garage charges	100	
	480	480
C. Fixed Costs:		
Insurance	50	
Licence, tax, etc.	80	
Interest	40	
Other overheads	190	
	360	360

D. Depreciation $\frac{54{,}000 - 36{,}000}{5} \times \frac{1}{12}$		300
Total cost		2,700

Performance Statement		
		₹
(a) Cost per day maintained	₹2,700 ÷ 30 days	90.00
(b) Cost per day operated	₹2,700 ÷ 25 days	108.00
(c) Cost per kilometre	₹2,700 ÷ 2,500	1.08
(d) Cost per hour	₹2,700 ÷ 300	9.00
(e) Cost per commercial tonne km	₹2,700 ÷ 5,000	0.54

Note:

Commercial tonne km

$$\text{Total km covered} = 2,500$$

$$\text{Effective kilometres (load carrying) } 2{,}500 \div 2 = 1,250$$

$$\begin{aligned}\text{Commercial tonne km} &= \text{effective km} \times \text{load carried}\\ &= 1{,}250 \times 4\\ &= 5{,}000\end{aligned}$$

Illustration-22

A company is considering three alternative proposals for conveyance facilities for its sales personnel who have to do considerable travelling, approximately 20,000 kilometres every year.

The proposals are as follows:

1. Purchase and maintain its own fleet of cars. The average cost of a car is ₹1,00,000
2. Allow the executive to use his own car and reimburse expenses at the rate of ₹1.60 per kilometre and also bear insurance costs.
3. Hire cars from an agency at ₹20,000 per year per car. The company will have to bear costs of petrol, taxes and tyres.

The following further details are available:

Petrol	₹0.60 per kilometre
Repairs and maintenance	₹0.20 per kilometre
Tyre	₹0.12 per kilometre
Insurance	₹1,200 per car per annum
Taxes	₹800 per car per annum

- Life of the car: 5 years with annual mileage of 20,000.
- Resale value: ₹20,000 at the end of the fifth year.

You are required to work out the relative costs of the three proposals and rank them.

(B.Com (Hons.), Delhi University, 2001)

Solution

Comparative operating cost statement

Particulars	Company car per year ₹	Executive own car per km ₹	Hired car per km ₹
Fixed cost:			
Taxes	800	-	0.04
Depreciation	16,000	-	-
Insurance	1,200	0.06	-
Total	18,000	0.06	0.04
Fixed cost per km	0.90	0.06	0.04
Reimbursement cost	-	1.60	1.00
Running cost:			
Petrol	0.60	-	0.60
Repairs	0.20	-	-
Tyre	0.12	-	0.12
Total	1.82	1.66	1.76
Ranking	III	I	II

Illustration-23

A transport company has been given a 20 km long route to run a bus. The bus costs ₹50,000 has been insured at 6% p.a. while annual tax amount to ₹2,000. Garage rent is ₹100 p.m. Yearly repairs will be ₹2,000 and the bus is likely to last for 5 years.

The driver's salary will be ₹3,000 p.a. and that of conductor ₹1,800 p.a. in addition to 10% of the takings as commission. (to be shared by the driver and conductor equally). Cost of stationery will be ₹600 p.a. manager's salary is ₹400 p.m. who also looks after the accounts.

Diesel and oil will be ₹25 per 100 kms. The bus will make 3 round trips carrying on the average 40 passengers on each trip. Assuming 25% profit on takings, calculate the bus fare to be charged from each passenger. The bus runs on an overage 25 days in a month.

(B.Com. (Hons) Delhi University, 2008)

Solution

		Total per month ₹
Fixed charges:		
Taxes	$2{,}000 \div 12$	166.67
Insurance	$50{,}000 \times \frac{6}{100} \times \frac{1}{12}$	250.00
Garage rent		100.00
Salary of driver	$3{,}000 \div 12$	250.00
Salary of conductor	$1{,}800 \div 12$	150.00
Stationery	$600 \div 12$	50.00
Manager's salary		400.00
	Total (A)	1,366.67
Variable costs:		
Depreciation	$\frac{50{,}000}{5} \times \frac{1}{12}$	833.33
Repairs	$2{,}000 \div 12$	166.67
Diesel and oil	$\frac{25}{100} \times 3{,}000$	750.00
	Total (B)	1,750.00
Total cost before commission (A) + (B)		3,116.67
Commission 10% of takings (10/65 on cost before commission)		479.49
	Total cost	3,596.16

Add: Profit 25% on takings (25/75 on total cost)	1,198.72
Total takings	4,794.88
Bus fare per passenger km $\frac{4,794.88}{1,20,000}$ = ₹0.03999573	0.04
Fare per passenger = 0.03999573 × 20 =₹0.80 (Approx)	0.80

Workings

(1) Total km = No. of trips × Trip distance × No. of days
= 3 × 40 × 25 = 3,000

(2) Total passenger km = Total km × Passenger capacity
= 3,000 × 40 = 1,20,000

Illustration-24

There are two warehouses for storing finished goods in a factory. Warehouse 'A' is at a distance of 10 km and warehouse of 'B' at a distance of 15 km from the factory. A fleet of 5-tonne lorries is engaged in transporting the finished goods from the factory. The records show that the lorries average a speed of 30 km per hour when running and regularly takes 40 minutes to load at the factory. At warehouse A unloading takes 30 minutes per load while at warehouse 'B' it takes 20 minutes per load.

Driver wages, depreciation, insurance and taxes amount to ₹18 per hour operated. Fuel, oil, tyres and maintenance cost ₹2.40 per kilometre.

You are required to prepare a statement showing the cost per tonne km for carrying the finished goods to the two warehouses. **(ICWA-Inter)**

Solution

Standing charges are to be calculated on the basis of time taken per trip. Hence we compute operating time per trip.

Statement showing operating time per trip

(i) Warehouse 'A':

Running time per trip of 20 km at 30 km speed per hour	40 minutes
Loading time	40 minutes
Unloading time	30 minutes
Total operating time (or 1 hour 50 minutes)	110 minutes

(ii) Warehouse 'B':

Running time per trip of 30 km at 30 km speed per hour	60 minutes
Loading time	40 minutes
Unloading time	20 minutes
Total operating time (or 2 hours)	120 minutes

Operating cost statement

(i) Warehouse 'A':

	₹
(a) Standing charges per trip for 1 hour 50 minutes at ₹18 per hour	33
(b) Running expenses 20 km × ₹2.40	48
Total cost	81
Tonne km = 10 km × 5 tonnes	50
Cost per tonne km = 81 ÷ 50	1.62

(ii) Warehouse 'B':

(a) Standing charges per trip for 2 hours at ₹18 per hour	36
(b) Running expenses 30 km × ₹2.40	72
Total cost per trip	108
Tonne km = 15 km ×.5 tonnes	75
Cost per tonne km = 108 ÷ 75	1.44

Illustration-25

SMS is a public school having 5 buses each plying in different directions for the transport of the school students. In view of large number of students availing of its bus service, the buses work two shifts both in the morning and in the afternoon. The buses are garaged in the school. The work-load of the students has been so arranged that in the morning the first trip picks up senior students and the second trip plying an hour later picks up the junior students. Similarly in the afternoon the first trip drops the junior students and an hour later the second trip takes senior students home.

The distance travelled by each bus one way is 8 km. The school works 25 days in a month and remains closed for vacation in May, June and December. Bus fee, however, is payable by the students for all the 12 months in a year.

The details of expenses for a year are as under:

- Driver's salary ₹450 per month per driver.
- Cleaner's salary ₹350 per month per cleaner.

(Salary payable for all 12 months, one cleaner employed for all the five buses)

- Licence fees, taxes etc. ₹860 per bus per annum
- Insurance ₹1,000 per bus per annum
- Repairs and maintenance ₹3,500 per bus per annum
- Cost price of the bus ₹1,50,000 each
- Life - 12 years
- Scrap value ₹30,000
- Diesel costs ₹2.00 per litre

Each bus gives an average mileage of 4 km per litre of diesel. The seating capacity of each bus is 50 students. Students picked up and dropped within a range of 4 km of distance from the school are charged half fare and fifty percent of the student travelling in each trip are in this category. Ignore interest. Since the charges are to be based on average cost, you are required to:

1. Prepare a statement showing the expenses of operating a single bus and the fleet of 5 buses for a year.
2. Work out the average cost per student per month in respect of:
   (a) Students coming from a distance of up to 4 km from the school and
   (b) Students coming from a distance beyond 4 km from the school.

Solution

Operating cost statement

Particulars		Per bus per annum ₹	For 5 buses per annum ₹
Fixed Costs:			
Driver's salary	(450 × 12)	5,400	27,000
Cleaner's salary	$(350 \times 12 \times \frac{1}{5})$	840	4,200
Licence fees and taxes etc		860	4,300
Insurance		1,000	5,000
	Total (A)	8,100	40,500
Running Expenses:			
Repairs and maintenance		3,500	17,500

Depreciation	(1,50,000 – 30,000) ÷ 12	10,000	50,000
Diesel cost (WN 2)		7,200	36,000
	Total (B)	20,700	1,03,500
Total operating cost (A+B)		28,800	1,44,000
Operating cost per month		2,400	12,000
Total students in terms of half fare paying students (See WN 1)		150	750
Operating cost per half fare student		$\frac{2,400}{150}$ = ₹16.00	$\frac{12,000}{750}$ = ₹16.00
Operating cost per full fare student		₹32.00	₹32.00

Working Note

(1) Total number of students equal to half fare students

Full fare students 50 × 50/100 = 25 students × 2 × 2	100
Half fare students 50 × 50/100 × 2	50
Total half fare students	150

(2) Diesel cost per bus per month

Trip distance (up and down) = 8 × 2	16 km
No. of trips per day (Morning 2 + afternoon 2)	4 trips
Distance travelled per day = 16 × 4	64 km
Distance covered in a month = 64 × 25	1,600 km
Distance covered per annum = 1,600 × 9 months	14,400 km
Diesel cost ₹2 per litre	for 4 km
Diesel cost for 14,400 km = 14,400 × 2/4	₹7,200

Illustration-26

A vehicle costs ₹5,00,000 and its life is estimated at 5 years, after which its residual value is estimated at ₹60,000. Standing charges per annum are estimated at the following figures:

Insurance ₹22,500, licence ₹5,000 and administration overheads ₹17,500.

Fuel costs ₹30 per litre and based on an estimated kilometres 30,000, the cost of lubricant is ₹4,500. The estimated mileage per litre of fuel is 15 km. A set of tyre costs ₹9,000, its expected life is 30,000 km. Driver is paid ₹600 per week of 44 hours and is entitled to a fortnight paid holiday per annum. The company's contribution towards National Insurance Scheme is ₹60 per week. For each night spent away from home, the driver is paid a subsistence allowance of ₹75.

It is estimated that the vehicle will run 250 days per annum and depreciation is regarded as running expenses. Repairs over the life of the vehicle is estimated at ₹75,000.

Required:

(a) Compute the figures which may be used as a basis for quoting when the company wants to make a profit 20% on cost.

(b) Prepare a quotation for a journey of 250 kilometres and return, assuming no return load and a total time of 2 days.

Solution

Operating cost statement	
	Total per annum ₹
Standing charges:	
Insurance	22,500
Licence	5,000
Administration overheads	17,500
National insurance for 52 weeks at ₹60 per week	3,120
Driver's wages for 52 weeks at ₹600 per week (Including paid holiday)	31,200
Total	79,320
Standing charges per day $\frac{79,320}{250}$ = ₹317.28	
Running expenses:	Per km
Depreciation = $\frac{5,00,000 - 60,000}{5} = \frac{88,000}{1,50,000}$	0.5867
Tyre = $\frac{9,000}{30,000}$	0.3000
Fuel = 30 ÷ 15	2.0000
Lubricant 4,500 ÷ 30,000	0.1500
Repairs = 75,000 ÷ 1,50,000	0.5000
	3.5367

Quotation for the journey of 250 km and return

	₹
Standing charges for 2 days = 317.28 × 2	634.56
Running expenses for 500 miles (both up and down (500 × 3.5367)	1,768.35
Subsistence allowance for 1 night	75.00
Total cost	2,477.91
Add: Profit 20% on cost	495.58
Quotation for the journey	2,973.49

Illustration-27

(Air Transport)

In order to develop tourism, ABCL Airlines has been given permit to operate three flights in a week between X and Y cities (both side). The airlines operates a single aircraft of 160 seats capacity. The normal occupancy is estimated at 60% through out the year of 52 weeks. The one-way fare is ₹7,200. The cost of operation of flights are:

- Fuel cost (variable) - ₹96,000 per flight.
- Food served on flight on non-chargeable basis - ₹125 per passenger.
- Commission - 5% of fare applicable for all bookings.

Fixed costs:

- Aircraft lease - ₹3,50,000 per flight
- Landing charges - ₹72,000 per flight

Required:

(i) Calculate the net operating income per flight.

(ii) The airlines expects that its occupancy will increase to 108 passengers per flight if the fare is reduced to ₹6,720. Advise whether this proposal is to be implemented or not.

(CA-PE II, May 2005)

Solution

(i)

Operating income statement per flight		
		₹
Variable cost:		
Fuel cost		96,000
Cost of food served	(96 × 125)	12,000
Commission	(7,200 × 96 × 5/100)	34,560
	Total	1,42,560
Fixed costs:		
Aircraft lease		3,50,000
Landing charges		72,000
	Total (B)	4,22,000
	Total operating cost (A) + (B)	5,64,560
Revenue from passenger fare	(7,200 × 96)	6,91,200
Net operating income		1,26,640

(ii)

Net operating income		
	₹	₹
Revenue from passenger fare (108 × 6,720)		7,25,760
Less: Operating costs:		
(a) Variable cost:		
Fuel cost	96,000	
Food (108 × 125)	13,500	
Commission (7,25,760 × 5/100)	36,288	
Total	1,45,788	
(b) Total fixed cost	4,22,000	5,67,788
Net operating income		1,57,972

[**Advice:** The proposal to reduce the fare to increase the occupancy is acceptable because the profit increases to ₹1,57,972 from ₹1,26,640]

18.12 EXERCISE

I. Objective Type Questions

A. State whether the following statements are true or false

(i) Operating costing is a method used to measure cost of services rendered.

(ii) Operation costing and operating costing are same.

(iii) Operating costing is also called service costing

(iv) Ordinary measurement units are used to measure the quantum of service rendered.

(v) Operating costing is another variant of unit costing.

(vi) Method of costing followed in hotels is process costing.

(vii) There are definite rules for classification of operating costs.

(viii) Operating costing is followed in industries where raw materials pass through a series of operations.

[**Ans: True:** (i), (iii), (v) **False:** (ii), (iv), (vi), (vii), (viii)]

B. Fill in the blanks

(i) The quantity of ______________ product will be more than that of ______________.

(ii) The method of costing followed in service industries is ______________.

(iii) The cost statement prepared in service industries is called ______________.

(iv) Depreciation charged on operation basis is classified as ______________ cost.

(v) ______________ cost units are used to ascertain the cost of services provided.

(vi) The cost unit followed in passenger transport is ______________.

[**Ans:** (i) Main, by-product, (ii) operating or service costing, (iii) operating cost statement, (iv) variable, (v) composite, (vi) passenger KM]

Theory Questions

A. Short answer type questions

1. What is service costing ?
2. What is the cost unit applied in goods transport?
3. What is operating cost statement?
4. What is Daily Log Sheet?
5. What is operation costing?
6. Explain the cost units followed in various service organizations.
7. Explain the features of services costing.
8. Explain the main difficulty in service costing.
9. Select a suitable cost unit in the following:

(i) Hospital, (ii) City bus transport,
(iii) Hotels providing lodging facility **(CA- Inter)**

10. "The more kilometers you travel with your own vehicle, the cheaper it becomes". Comment briefly on this statement.

B. Long answer type questions

1. What is service costing? Explain the features of operating costing.
2. What is the objective of operating costing? List out the industries where operating costing is followed.
3. What is operation costing? Compare it with process costing.

III. Practical Problems

A. Short answer type questions

1. A transport company operates 3 buses between two towns, the distance between the towns are 70 km. The seating capacity of the buses is 55 passengers. They make two round trips per day. The buses operate on all the days in the month of August, 2008. On average 80% of seats are occupied.

   Calculate the total km and passenger km.

   [**Ans:** Total km - 26,040, Total passengers km - 11,45,760]

2. APN Bus Service Ltd run the following buses in Tamilnadu.

	Seating capacity
25 buses	40 passengers
40 buses	45 passengers

   On an average each bus covers a distance of 250 km daily. 90% of the seats are occupied on an average. All buses operate 25 days a month and 10% of the buses are kept away from the road for repairs.

   Find the effective total passenger km.

   [**Ans:** Passenger km - 1,41,75,000]

3. A bus started from Delhi for Mussorie with 50 passengers on board. 20 passengers got off at Dehradun and the bus proceeded with the remaining passengers. In the evening the same bus left Mussoorie with 50 passengers, 10 passengers got off at Dehradun and the bus resumed its journey with remaining passengers for Delhi. The distance between Delhi and Dehradun is 280 km, and between Dehradum to Mussoorie is 20 km.

Compute the passenger km and cost per passenger km, if the total cost of running the bus comes out to be ₹5,000. **(B.Com. (Hons.) Delhi University)**

[**Ans:** Passenger km - 26,800 and Cost per passenger km - 19 paise]

4. A city municipality arranges for the removal of its garbage by means of vehicle transport. The following vehicles are maintained.

No. of vehicles	Specification
30	5 tonne lorries
40	3 tonne lorries
50	2 tonne lorries
20	4 tonne lorries

On an average each lorry makes 5 trips a day and each trip covers an average distance of 6 km. Each lorry carries garbage of 50% of its capacity. On an annual average, 10% of lorries are laid-up for repairs every day. The conservancy work is carried out daily. Calculate tonne-km per month. **(B.Com. (Hons.) Delhi University)**

[**Ans:** Tonne km - 1,82,250]

5. Mr. Anand runs a truck. It runs between two cities which are 300 km apart. The truck starts with a load of 10 tonnes and returns with a load of 7 tonnes on the same day. It operates on an average 25 days in a month.

Calculate tonne km.

[**Ans:** Tonne km - 1,27,500]

Commercial tonne KM and Absolute tonne KM

6. A truck starts with a load of 12 tonnes from city 'X', unloads 3 tonnes enroute in the city 'Y' and proceeds to city 'Z' with balance load. On return journey it starts with a load of 10 tonnes from city 'Z' to city 'X' direct. The distance from city 'X' to 'Y' is 80 km, from city 'Y' to 'Z' is 100 km. and from city 'Z' to 'X' is 150 km.

Compute Absolute tonne km and commercial tonne km.

[**Ans:** Absolute tonne km - 3,360; Commercial tonne km - 3,410]

7. A lorry runs between two towns which are 60 km apart. The lorry makes three trips a day. Average load carried is 8 tonnes and 30% of the time it runs empty. It runs 27 days in a month. Calculate tonne km.

[**Ans:** Tonne km - 54,432]

Room days

8. A lodging house has 150 rooms. During summer 90% of the rooms are occupied and in winter only 50% of the rooms are full. Take 7 months for summer and 5 months for winter. Assume 30 days a month on average.

Compute room days.

[**Ans:** Room days - 39,600]

9. Globe International Ltd., a hotel gives the following details about the number of rooms in the hotel and their occupancy during different seasons:

	Summer	**Winter**
50 Single room suites	100%	90%
70 Double room suites	90%	60%
40 Family room suites	80%	50%

The number of months of summer and winter are 8 months and 4 months respectively. Take 30 days a month. The rental charges for double rooms suites are twice the rate of single room suites. The rental charges for family rooms is thrice the single room suites.

Compute room days equivalent to single room suites.

[**Ans:** Equivalent single room days - 87,960]

10. There are 1,100 seats in a cinema theatre, divided into 4 types as follows:

Balcony	200 seats
First class	350 seats
Second class	300 seats
Third class	250 seats

The ticket rates for second class is twice the rate for third class, the rate for first class is thrice the rate for third class and the rate for balcony is four times the rate for third class. Daily three shows are run for 360 days in a year with 75% seats occupied.

Compute number of man shows equal to third class.

[**Ans:** Man shows - 21,87,000]

Standard Load

11. A truck carries synthetic water storage tanks weighing 2 tonnes occupying the whole of the loading space. The loading capacity of the truck is 8 tonnes. The total distance covered in a month is 3,000 km.

Find the total standard tonne km.

[**Ans:** Standard tonne km - 24,000]

12. From the following information calculate total km and passenger km:

No. of buses	: 5
Days operated in the month	: 25

Trips made by each bus : 4
Distance of route : 20 km long (one side)
Capacity of the bus : 50 passengers
Normal passenger travelling capacity : 90%

(B.Com., Madras University)

[**Ans:** Total km - 20,000, total passenger km - 9,00,000]

B. Comprehensive problems

1. A transport company is running 4 buses between two towns which are 50 km. away from each other. Seating capacity of each bus is 40 passengers. The following particulars are given from their books for April 2008:

	₹
Wages of operators and drivers	2,400
Salaries	1,000
Diesel, oil	4,000
Repairs and expenses	800
Insurance and tax	1,600
Depreciation	2,600
Interest	2,000

Actual passengers carried were 75% of the seating capacity. All the buses ran on all the days of the month. Each bus made one round trip per day.

Find out the cost per passenger km. **(B.Com., Madras University)**

[**Ans:** Passenger km - 3,60,000; Cost per passenger km - ₹0.04]

2. Vignesh Travellers, a transport company is running two buses between two places 150 kilometres apart. The seating capacity of each bus is 40 passengers. The following particulars are taken from their books for the month of April:

	₹
Wages of drivers, conductors and cleaners	3,000
Salary of office and supervisory staff	1,500
Diesel and oil	6,000
Repairs	1,500
Tax and insurance	2,000
Depreciation	3,000
Interest and other bank charges	2,500

The actual passengers carried were 75% of the seating capacity. The bus ran on all the days. Each bus made a to and fro trip.

Find out the cost per passenger km.

[**Ans:** Cost per passenger km - ₹0.036; Passenger km - 5,40,000]

Cost per kilometre

3. From the following data calculate the cost per kilometre of a vehicle:

	₹
Value of vehicle	1,50,000
Road licence fees per year	1,000
Insurance charges per year	2,000
Garage rent per year	6,000
Driver wages per month	2,000
Cost of petrol per litre	₹32
Kilometre per litre	16

Proportionate charges for tyre and maintenance per km - ₹0.50.

Estimated life - 1,50,000 km.

Estimated annual kilometres - 20,000 km.

Ignore interest on capital.

[**Ans:** Cost per km - ₹5.15]

4. Sri Narayanan owns a fleet of taxies and following information is available from the records maintained by him:

No. of taxies	10
Cost of each taxi	₹2,00,000
Salary of manager	₹6,000 p.m.
Salary of accountant	₹4,000 p.m.
Salary of cleaner	₹2,000 p.m.
Salary of mechanic	₹4,000 p.m.
Garage rent	₹2,000 p.m.
Insurance premium	6% p.a.
Annual tax	₹6,000 per taxi
Driver salary	₹2,000 p.m. per taxi
Annual repairs	₹2,000 per taxi

Total life of a taxi is about 2,00,000 km. A taxi runs in all 3,000 km. in a month of which 30% of it runs empty. Petrol consumption is 10 km at ₹30 per litre.

Calculate the cost of running a taxi per km.

[**Ans:** Cost per km - ₹8.32]

5. A transport company operates a bus service on 25 km long route. Purchase price of the chassis was ₹8.5 lakh and it was furnished at cost of ₹1.5 lakh. It will have residual value of ₹2 lakh at the end of 5 years of normal working life. Annual road tax amount to ₹24,000. While the insurance premium is valued at 2.5% of the total cost of the bus. Annual repairs is estimated at ₹30,000. Garage rent is payable at ₹4,000 per month. Tyre and tube will cost 50 paise per km.

   Salaries of one driver and one conductor will be ₹3,500 and ₹2,500 per month respectively. In addition, they will receive 10% of the collection as commission, which will be shared between the driver and conductor in the ratio of 60:40.

   Other administrative salaries and expenses will cost ₹47,000 per annum. Diesel, oil and lubricants will cost at ₹4.50 per km.

   The bus will make 4 round trips per day for 25 days in a month, carrying 42 passengers in each trip.

   Assuming 20% profit on takings, prepare,

   (a) Operating statement for a year, including fixed and variable cost,

   (b) Cost per passenger km, with working notes, and

   (c) Fare per passenger km and fare per one way trip.

   (ICWA-Inter, June 2008, adapted)

   [**Ans:**

   (a) Fixed cost per year - ₹2,16,000, variable cost before commission per year - ₹4,90,000, driver and conductor commission - ₹1,00,857; Profit - ₹2,01,714; takings per year - ₹10,08,571.

   (b) Cost per passenger km - ₹0.32.

   (c) Fare per passenger km - ₹0.40 and fare per passenger per one way trip - ₹10]

6. A person owns a bus, which runs between Delhi to Chandigarh and back for 10 days in a month. The distance from Delhi to Chandigarh is 150 miles. The bus completes the trip from Delhi to Chandigarh and back the same day. The bus goes another 10 days in a month towards Agra. The distance from Delhi to Agra is 120 miles. The trip is also completed on the same day. For the rest 4 days of its operation in a month it runs in the local city. Daily distance covered in the city is 40 miles. Calculate the rate the person should charge from a passenger when he wants to earn the profit of $33\frac{1}{3}\%$ on his takings. The other information is given below:

	₹
Cost of the bus	60,000
Depreciation	20%
Salary of driver	350 p.m.
Salary of conductor	350 p.m.

Salary of part-time accountant	160 p.m.
Insurance	1,680 p.m.
Diesel consumption 4 miles per litre costing	₹10
Token tax	₹600 p.m.
Lubricant oil ₹10 per 100 miles	
Repairs and maintenance	₹500 p.m.
Permit fees	₹284 p.m.
Normal capacity	50 persons

This bus is generally occupied 90% of the capacity when it goes to Chandigarh and 80% when it goes to Agra. It is always full when it runs within the city, passenger tax is 20% of his net takings. **(B.Com., Bangalore University, April 2002)**

[**Ans:** Rate per passenger km - ₹0.14]

7. Pooja Transport runs a mini bus with a capacity of 25 seats. The bus runs between two towns which are 25 km apart. It runs for 30 days in a month and on an average 80% of seating capacity is utilised. The bus makes two round trips each day.

	₹
Cost of the bus	5,00,000
Estimated scrap value at the end of its useful life of 10 years	20,000
Driver's salary per month	3,000
Conductor's salary per month	2,500
Manager's salary per month	2,000
Cleaner's salary per month	1,500
Garage rent per annum	10,800
Life tax	24,000
Rent, lighting etc. per month	500
Repairs per month	1,200
Diesel, oil etc. per month	12,000

The profit expected was $33\frac{1}{3}\%$ of takings. The driver and the conductor are given 10% of profit as bonus to be divided equally between the two.

Prepare a statement to show:

(a) Operating cost per passenger km

(b) The fare per passenger km.

(B.Com., Bangalore University, April 2004)

[**Ans:**

(a) Operating cost per passenger km - ₹0.464;

(b) Bus fare per passenger km - ₹0.70]

8. The Road Transport Company which keeps a fleet of lorries shows the following information:

km run for April 2009	30,000
Wages for April	₹2,000
Petrol, oil etc.	₹4,000

Depreciation to be allowed at 25% on original cost of ₹1,00,000

Repairs for the month	₹6,000
Garage rent etc. for the month	₹1,000
Licence, insurance etc. for the year:	₹6,000

Prepare operating cost statement for April 2009 showing the total cost and variable cost per running km. **(B.Com., Madras University)**

[**Ans:** Total cost - ₹15,583; variable cost (including depreciation) - ₹12,083; cost per running km - ₹0.52]

9. Union Transport Company supplies the following details in respect of a truck of 5 tonne capacity:

- Cost of truck ₹4,50,000
- Estimated life 10 years
- Diesel, oil, grease ₹75 per trip each way
- Repairs and maintenance ₹2,500 per month
- Driver wages ₹2,500 per month
- Cleaner wages ₹1,250 per month
- Insurance ₹24,000 per year
- Tax ₹12,000 per year
- General supervision charges ₹24,000 per year.

The truck carries goods to and from the city covering distance of 50 miles each way. On onward trip freight is available to the extent of full capacity and on return 20% of capacity.

Assuming that the truck runs on an average 25 days a month, work out:

(a) Operating cost per tonne mile

(b) Rate per tonne per trip that the company should charge if a profit of 50% on freightage is to be earned. **(CA-Inter)**

[**Ans:** Operating cost per tonne mile - ₹2.50, rate per tonne mile ₹5, rate per tonne per trip (one way) - ₹250]

10. Mr. Anand owns a vehicle and provides the following data:

Cost of vehicle	₹7,50,000
Estimated life	3,00,000 lakh km
Loading capacity	10 tonnes
Annual mileage run	40,000 km
Driver wages per hour	₹20
km run per hour	30
Cost of diesel	₹30 per litre
km run per litre of diesel	6 km

A set of tyres costs ₹12,000

Number of tyres in the vehicle - 10

Life of tyres 30,000 km each

Insurance ₹15,000 per annum.

Tax, licence, etc. ₹12,000 per annum.

Oil, lubricants, etc. ₹0.50 per km.

Repairs and maintenance ₹6,000 per month.

Calculate the cost per running km and tonne km.

[**Ans:** Cost per running km ₹13.14, cost per tonne km ₹1.31]

11. Iron ore is transported from two mines 'A' and 'B' and unloaded at points in a railway station. A is at a distance of 10 km and B is at a distance of 15 km from the rail head points. A fleet of lorries of 5 tonnes carrying capacity is used for the transport of ore from mines. Records reveal that the lorries average a speed of 30 km per hour when running and regularly take 10 minutes to unload at the rail head. At mine A loading time averages 30 minutes per load while at mine B loading time averages 20 minutes per load.

    Driver's wages, depreciation, insurance and taxes are found to cost ₹9 per hour operated. Fuel, oil, tyres, repairs and maintenance cost ₹1.20 per km. Draw up a statement showing cost per tonne km of carrying iron ore from each mine. If the coal is of equal quality and price at pit head, from which colliery should the purchases be made? **(CA-Inter, Nov. 2001)**

    [**Ans:** Cost per tonne km - Mine A - ₹0.72 and Mine B - ₹0.66. Coal is to be purchased at mine 'B']

12. A company presently brings coal to its factory from a nearby yard and the rate paid for transportation of coal from the yard located 6 km. away to factory is ₹50 per tonne. The total coal to be handled in a month is 24,000 tonnes.

    The company is considering a proposal to buy its own trucks and has the option of buying either a 10-tonne capacity or a 8-tonne capacity truck.

    The following information is available:

	10-tonne truck	**8-tonne truck**
Purchase price (₹)	10,00,000	8,50,000
Life (years)	5	5
Scrap value at the end of 5th year	Nil	Nil
km per litre of diesel	3	4
Repair/maintenance p.a. per truck (₹)	60,000	48,000
Other fixed expenses p.a. (₹)	60,000	36,000
Lubricants and sundries per 100 km (₹)	20	20

Each truck will daily make 5 trips (to and fro) on an average for 24 days in a month.

- Cost of diesel ₹15 per litre.
- Salary of drivers ₹3,000 per month - two drivers will be required for a truck.
- Other staff expenses ₹1,08,000 p.a.

Prepare a comprehensive cost sheet on the basis of the above data showing transport cost per tonne of operating 10-tonne and 8-tonne truck at full capacity utilisation.

(CA-Final, Nov. 1998)

[**Ans:** Cost per tonne: For 10-tonne truck - ₹29.87, for 8-tonne truck - ₹31.59]

13. Vidya Vikas High School arranges holiday trip to its students. The trip covers important holiday spots in Karnataka and Maharashtra. The trip will take 5 days. Total 50 students joined the trip. The school hired a bus at a charge of ₹4,000 per day inclusive of diesel. Permit fees, entrance fees and food expenses of drivers and an assistant is to be met by the school at ₹150 per driver per day and at ₹100 per day for the assistant. The expenses estimated for the trip are as follows:

    Permit fees for the trip ₹3,500. For visiting amusement parks, zoos and planetarium entrance fees are to be paid at ₹5 per student on 4 occasions. Breakfast, lunch and refreshments are to be provided at ₹75 per student per day. Two teachers are to accompany the students and are paid an allowance of ₹300 per day each. Accommodation facilities for the students are to be arranged at a cost of ₹1,750 for the trip.

    Prepare an operating cost statement for the trips and calculate the amount to be collected from each student for the trip.

    [**Ans:** Rate per student - ₹1,000]

    Note: Assumed two drivers for the bus.

14. Mr. Arvind owns a tractor which he uses for tilling the farm lands on hire. The following are the details of the tractor:

Cost of tractor	₹12,50,000
Estimated life	6 years

Sale value at the end of 6 years	₹2,50,000
Annual repairs and maintenance cost	₹18,000
Cost of tyres and tubes per annum	₹35,000
Sale of old tyres, tubes and spare parts	₹5,000
Wages of a driver	₹4,000 per month
Diesel consumption	4 litres per hour
Cost of diesel	₹30 per litre
Engine oil and lubricants	₹2,500 per month
Cleaning charges	₹160 per month

The tractor runs for 6 hours daily and 20 days in a month on average. If Arvind wants to earn a profit of 30% on his investment annually, what amount he should charge per hour?

[**Ans:** Rate per hour ₹585]

Note:

$$\text{Profit per annum} = 12{,}50{,}000 \times \frac{30}{100}$$
$$= 3{,}75{,}000$$

Profit per month = ₹31,250

Decision making

15. ACME company is considering three proposals for conveyance facilities for its sales staff, who normally travel on an average 20,000 km per annum locally. The proposals are as follows:

    I. Purchase and maintain own fleet of cars: Average cost of a car is ₹2.50 lakh. Petrol consumption is at 12 km/litre. Each has a resale value of ₹50,000 at the end of five years.

    II. Allow the executives to use their own car and reimburse expenses at ₹5 per km and insurance premia.

    III. Hire cars from outside agency for ₹30,000 per year per car. The company shall also bear the cost of petrol (₹3.75 per km), tyre and repairs and maintenance.

    Following data are available for consideration:

    (i) Petrol - ₹45 per litre
    (ii) Repairs and maintenance at 50 paise per km.
    (iii) Insurance ₹4,800 per year per car.
    (iv) Taxes ₹2,400 per year per car
    (v) Tyres at 40 paise per km.
    (vi) Driver's wages and bonus ₹30,000 per annum per car.

    Which of the proposals is acceptable? **(ICWA-Inter, June-2005)**

    [**Ans:** Proposal II should be accepted as the cost per kilometre is minimum at ₹5.24]

16. A practising chartered accountant spends ₹0.90 per kilometre on taxi rate for his clients' work. He is considering two alternatives, the purchase of a new small car or an old big car. The estimated cost figures are:

	New small car ₹	Old big car ₹
Purchase price	35,000	20,000
Sale price	19,000	12,000
Estimated life	5 yrs	5 yrs
Repairs and services per annum	1,000	1,200
Tax and insurance per annum	1,700	700
Petrol consumption per litre	10 km	7 km
Petrol price per litre	3.50	3.50

He estimates that he does 10,000 km annually, which of the three alternatives will be cheaper? If his practice expands and he is to do 19,000 km per annum what should be his decision? At how many km per annum will the costs of two cars break-even and why? Ignore interest and income tax. **(CA-Inter)**

[**Ans:** For 10,000 km old big car is cheaper. For 19,000 km new small car is cheaper, break-even point - 16,000 km]

Note:

$$\text{Break-even point (indifference point)} = \frac{\text{Difference in fixed cost}}{\text{Difference in variable cost per km}}$$

Power generation

17. From the following data, find out in an appropriate cost sheet form the generating cost of electricity per unit in an iron and steel works during the month of April, 2008:

(a) Fuel: Coal at the beginning of month: 500 tonnes. Supply during the month 1,100 tonnes. Balance at the end of month 400 tonnes. Annual contract for the supply of coal F.O.R. celliery at ₹10 per tonne.
Add : 10% to cover freight and handling charges.

(b) Oil: 10 tonnes at ₹250 per tonne.

(c) Water: 50,000 litres. Pumping charges at 25 paise per 100 litres.

(d) Depreciation of steam boiler: Capital value ₹24,000 and the rate of depreciation $12\frac{1}{2}\%$ per annum.

(e) Salaries and Wages of boiler house:

- 10 men at ₹100 per month each.
- 40 coolies at ₹20 per month each.

(f) Recovery on account of sale of ashes: 100 tonnes at ₹1 per ton.

(g) Salaries and wages of the generating station:

- 50 men at ₹100 per month each.
- 20 coolies at ₹20 per month each.

(h) Repairs and maintenance of the generating equipment ₹2,600. Capital value ₹1,20,000 and the rate of depreciation $12\frac{1}{2}\%$ per annum.

(i) Share of administration charges ₹1,750

(j) Number of units generated : 1,46,000

(k) Loss in the process 2,000 units generated. **(B.Com., Madras University)**

[**Ans:** Cost per unit - 20 paise (approx.)]

Cinema theatre

18. Paramount Theatre at Bangalore is a mini theatre with a seating capacity of 500 seats. The seats are classified into 3 categories. They are:

I class	200 seats
II class	200 seats
III class	100 seats

The following are the other relevant information for the month of November 2008:

(a) Salaries and wages

- 2 managers at ₹7,500 per month each
- 12 gate-keepers and attenders - ₹3,000 per month each
- 4 security guards - ₹2,500 per month each
- 4 operators - ₹5,000 per month each
- 2 clerks - ₹3,000 per month each.

(b) Other expenses

Lighting and power	₹1,25,000
Carbon	₹1,00,000
Advertisement	₹60,000
Repairs and maintenance	₹1,00,000
Office expenses	₹75,000
Hire for print	₹2,00,000
Miscellaneous expenses	₹65,067

(c) Depreciation:

- Cost of building ₹90,00,000, depreciation at 5% p.a.
- Cost of projector and equipment ₹60,00,000, depreciation at 25% p.a.
- Cost of furniture and fixtures ₹10,00,000, depreciation at 10% p.a.

- Daily 3 shows are run throughout the year. The theatre operates 360 days a year. The seats are occupied 80% on average. The charges levied are in the ratio of 3 : 2 : 1 for the three classes of seats.

Find the charge to be made for the three classes of seats assuming that the management wants to earn a profit 20% on cost.

[**Ans:** Ticket charge: First class - ₹44.67, Second class - ₹29.78 and Third class - ₹14.89. Total man shows - 79,200. Total cost - ₹9,82,900]

Hotel - Lodging

19. Trident Hotel, Chennai, supplies you the following information:

    (a) Capacity: Single bed rooms - 100, Double bed rooms - 75, and Family rooms - 50.

    (b) Occupancy Ratio:

    i. During summer (30 weeks) - Single room 100%, Double room 90% and family room 80%.

    ii. During winter (22 weeks) - Single room 80%, Double room 70% and family room 60%.

    (c) Salary and wages:

    - 2 managers ₹10,000 per month each
    - 2 accounts clerks ₹3,000 per month each
    - 2 receptionists ₹6,000 per month each
    - Thirty attenders - ₹2,500 per month each
    - Five security guards at ₹5,000 per month each.

    (d) Other expenses:

Lighting and power	₹4,00,000
Interior decoration	₹3,00,000
Licence fees	₹1,50,000
Linen and laundry	₹2,00,000
Repairs and maintenance	₹3,00,000
Depreciation - Building	₹1,00,000
Depreciation - Furniture	₹50,000
Insurance	₹75,000
Water and gardening	₹75,000

    (e) Yearly profit desired at 30% on the total investment of ₹2 crore

    (f) Rent is charged in ratio of 1 : 2 : 3 among the three types of rooms.

Calculate the rent to be charged for each type of room.

[**Ans:** Rent for single bed room ₹79.60, Double bed room ₹159.20 and Family room ₹238.80]

Hospital

20. Surya Sugalaya Hospital supplies you the following information for the year ending 31.03.2009:

    (a) In-patient department has 50 beds of which 90% is full during the year. In-patient department functions on all 365 days in the year.

    (b) Out-patient ward works 300 days in a year. The average number of outpatients visiting the hospital daily is 150. The amount charged for each out-patient is one-fifth of the charge levied for an inpatient.

    (c) Salaries: Administration:

1 Manager	₹15,000 per month
2 Assistant managers	₹8,000 per month each
1 Accountant	₹8,000 per month
4 Clerks	₹5,000 per month each
5 Peons	₹2,000 per month each

    (d) Salaries - Medical:

1 Chief Medical Officer	₹40,000 per month
5 Doctors	₹30,000 per month each
25 Nurses	₹5,000 per month each
15 Ward boys	₹3,500 per month each
30 Attenders and peons	₹2,000 per month each

    (e) Cost of medicines, drugs and chemicals

	₹
Opening stock	2,00,000
Purchases	24,50,000
Closing stock	1,50,000

    (f) Depreciation

	₹
Building	4,00,000
Equipment	3,00,000
Furniture	50,000

    (g) Other expenses:

	₹
Lighting and power	3,00,000

Office expenses	50,000
Telephone expenses	75,000
Cleaning and waste disposal	23,625

Ascertain the cost of service provided to an in-patient and an out-patient per day.

[**Ans:** Cost per out-patient - ₹33 per day and in-patient - ₹165 per day]

Note:

(1) Total cost - ₹41,95,125

(2) No. of equivalent outpatients - 1,27,125

Canteen/Hotel - Boarding

21. Union Transport Company is running a canteen for the benefit of its employees. The following is the information for the month of October, 2008:

(a) Total number of employees using the services of canteen are 750. Out of it 50% of employees took meals once a day for 20 days in the month, another 20% took meals once a day in all the days of month. The balance 30% took tiffin once a day for 25 days in a month. The charge for the tiffin is 80% of the cost of meals.

(b) The expenses for the month are:

i. Wages and salaries:

	₹
1 Manager	15,000 per month
1 Assistant manager	9,000 per month
5 Cooks	7,000 per month each
10 Attenders and assistants	2,000 per month each
1 Clerk	4,000 per month
1 Cashier	4,000 per month
1 Accountant	7,500 per month

ii. Consumable stores and provisions for the month:

	₹
Oil 2 tins costing	2,400 each
Ghee 5 litres	150 per litre
Vegetables	4,500
Rice - 500 kg costing	28 per kg
Atta, maida etc.	4,000
Gas and fuel	8,000
Power and lighting	6,000

Egg, meat etc.	3,000
Miscellaneous expenses	3,500
Subsidy borne by the management	26,500

Find the amount collected from employees per meal and per tiffin.

[**Ans:** Cost per meal - ₹7, cost per tiffin - ₹5.60]

Note:

(1) Total cost - ₹1,43,050

(2) Total equivalent man meals - 16,650

School Bus

22. EPS is a public school having 25 buses each plying in different directions for the transport of its school students. In view of large number of students availing of the bus service, the buses work two shifts daily both in the morning and in the afternoon. The buses are garaged in the school. The workload of the students has been so arranged that in the morning, the first trip picks up senior students and the second trip plying an hour later picks up the junior students. Similarly, in the afternoon, the first trip takes the junior students and an hour later the second trip takes the senior students home.

    The distance travelled by each bus one way is 16 km. The school works 24 days in a month and remains closed for vacations in May and June. The bus fee, however, is payable by the students for all the 12 months in a year.

    The details of expenses for the year 2003-2004 are as under:

Driver's salary payable for all the 12 months	₹5,000 per month per driver
Cleaner's salary payable for all the 12 months	₹3,000 per month per cleaner (One cleaner has been employed for every five buses)
Licence fees, taxes etc.	₹2,300 per bus per annum
Insurance premium	₹15,600 per bus per annum
Repairs and maintenance	₹16,400 per bus per annum
Purchase price of the bus	₹16,50,000 each
Life of the bus	16 years
Scrap value	₹1,50,000
Diesel cost	₹18.50 per litre

Each bus gives an average of 10 km per litre of diesel. The seating capacity of each bus is 60 students. The seating capacity is fully occupied during the whole year.

The school follows differential fees based on distance travelled as under:

Students picked up and dropped within the range of distance from the school	**Bus fees**	**% of students availing this facility**
4 km	25% of full	15%
8 km	50% of full	30%
16 km	Full	55%

Ignore interest. Since the bus fees has to be based on average cost, you are required to:

(a) Prepare a statement showing the expenses of operating a single bus and the fleet of 25 buses for a year.

(b) Work out the average cost per student per month in respect of:

  i. Students coming from a distance upto 4 km from the school

  ii. Students coming from a distance upto 8 km from the school

  iii. Students coming from a distance upto 16 km from the school.

(CA-PE II, May 2004)

[**Ans:**

(a) Operating cost per bus per month ₹2,52,082. Operating cost per fleet of 25 buses per month ₹63,02,050.

(b) i. Average cost per student upto 4 km - ₹59.34

  ii. Average cost per student upto 8 km - ₹118.68

  iii. Average cost per student upto 16 km - ₹237.36.]

Note: Number of equivalent 25% fare paying students = 354 per bus per month.

MARGINAL COSTING 19

- Meaning
- Marginal vs. Direct Costing
- Marginal vs. Absorption costing—Meaning/Differences
- Marginal Costing—Features/Assumptions/Advantages/Disadvantages
- Profit Ascertainment Model Statement using Absorption Costing
- Profit Ascertainment Model Statement using Marginal Costing
- CVP—Analysis
- Break-even Analysis—Meaning/Assumptions
- Margin of Safety—Improvement Steps
- Break-even Chart/Graph
- Cost Break-Even Point/Indifference Point
- Marginal Costing Technique-Applications
- Cost/Non-Cost Factors

Marginal costing is not a method of costing like process costing, job costing, batch costing, etc. rather it is a technique of costing. It is a useful tool in the hands of managements in decision making for maximising the profits of the firms. Marginal costing can be used along with other costing techniques like standard costing and budgetary control. Under marginal costing the difference in the behaviour of costs at various levels of activities of a business is recognised and costs are classified as variable cost and fixed cost.

19.1 COST BEHAVIOUR

Variable cost in total vary in direct proportion to changes in the level of activity. But variable cost per unit remains the same at all levels of activity.

Fixed cost in total remains same at all levels of activity within a certain range of production. But fixed cost per unit changes in inverse proportion to changes in activity levels. Fixed cost is not related to production. It is incurred on time basis. Fixed cost is also called period cost and time cost.

19.1.1 Definitions

Marginal Cost

Marginal cost is defined as "the amount of cost by which the total cost of production changes when the volume of production is changed by one unit from a given level of production". A unit of production may be a single product or a batch of units or a process or a department.

Say, let the present level of production 1,000 units, variable cost of production ₹10,000 and fixed cost ₹5,000. The total cost per unit is ₹15. Let us see what is the total cost if the production is increased by 1 unit.

If the output is increased by one unit:

No. of units	- Variable Cost + Fixed Cost	= Total Cost
for 1,000 units	- ₹10,000 + ₹5,000	= ₹15,000
for 1,001 units	- ₹10,010 + ₹5,000	= ₹15,010
Increase in total cost		= ₹10

The cost of producing one additional unit is ₹10. This is called marginal cost. This increase in cost is due to increase in variable cost only. There is no increase in fixed cost for producing the additional unit. So marginal cost is also called variable costing.

Marginal Costing

CIMA defines marginal costing as "the ascertainment of marginal cost and of the effect on profit of changes in volume or type of output by differentiating between fixed costs and variable costs".

In marginal costing only variable costs are included in the cost of products, processes, operations or departments. Fixed costs, being time cost is charged to profit and loss account of the period.

Marginal Costing and Direct Costing

In marginal costing only variable costs are included in cost of products, processes or operations. In direct costing all direct costs are included. Direct cost may include a fixed cost if it is direct to the product, process or operation. So direct costing is different from marginal costing.

Marginal Costing and Absorption Costing

Absorption costing is also called traditional costing/conventional costing or total costing. In absorption costing no difference is made between variable cost and fixed cost. All costs are included in the cost of production of a product, process or operation. Stock of finished goods and work-in-progress are valued on total cost basis. So fixed cost is included in the cost of inventory. There is no need for classifying costs into variable costs and fixed costs. It is more suitable for small and medium sized firms producing a single product. But absorption costing suffers from certain limitations.

Limitations of absorption costing

1. In absorption costing overheads are apportioned to products, processes or operations using some recovery methods arbitrarily. So overheads charged to products are inaccurate.
2. Fixed cost is a period cost. It should be charged to the period in which it is incurred. But in absorption costing a part of fixed cost of previous period included in opening stock is charged to current period. Similarly a part of fixed cost of current period is transferred to the next period through closing stock.
3. Cost of production per unit at different levels of activity will be different. This does not help the management in decision making.
4. This does not help in preparing flexible budget, tender or quotation.

The following are the differences between marginal costing and absorption costing:

	Basis	Marginal Costing	Absorption Costing
1.	Cost recognition	Only variable cost is included in the total cost.	Both variable costs and fixed costs are included in the total cost.
2.	Classification of costs	Costs are classified into variable and fixed costs.	Costs are classified on functional basis as production, administration, selling and distribution costs.
3.	Treatment of fixed overheads	Fixed overheads are charged to profit and loss account.	Fixed overheads are included in the total cost.
4.	Time of charging fixed overheads	Fixed overheads are charged to the period in which they are incurred.	A part of fixed cost included in stocks are transferred to the next year.
5.	Valuation of inventory	Stocks are valued on variable cost basis only.	Stocks are valued on total cost i.e. both variable and fixed costs are included in stock values.
6.	Decision making	Helpful to management in decision making	Not of much help to management in decision making.
7.	Reporting	It is suitable for internal reporting.	It is suitable for external reporting.
8.	Income recognition	Stock valuation is not acceptable to income tax authorities.	Stock valuation is accepted by tax authorities.

19.1.2 Features of Marginal Costing

1. It is a costing technique used in decision making for profit maximisation.
2. All cost is classified into variable and fixed costs.
3. Semi-variable cost is not recognised in marginal costing.
4. Variable cost is charged to production.
5. Fixed cost is charged to profit and loss account.
6. Inventory is valued on variable cost basis.
7. Profitability of products, processes and operations are ascertained with reference to contribution.
8. Contribution is the excess of the sales revenue over variable cost.
9. Importance is given for maximising contribution.
10. Establishing cost-volume-profit relationship is basic to marginal costing.

19.1.3 Assumptions of Marginal Costing

Marginal costing is based on certain assumptions. Marginal costing will be useful only if the assumptions hold good. The following are the assumptions:

1. Total costs can be easily classified into variable and fixed cost on behaviour basis.
2. Variable cost in total changes in direct proportion to changes in volume of output. Variable cost per unit remains constant at all levels of activity.
3. Fixed cost in total remains constant at all levels of activity.
4. Volume of production is the only factor influencing variable costs.
5. Selling price remains constant at all levels of activity. Management can either increase or reduce the price at its will.
6. Inventory level remains at the same level i.e. production and sales are equal.
7. Both cost and revenue functions are linear. i.e. they vary in direct proportion to changes in activity level.
8. Product mix remains same in case of multiproduct firms.
9. Productivity of all factors of production remain same.

19.1.4 Advantages of Marginal Costing

The following are the advantages of marginal costing:

1. It is easy to understand and people at all levels of management will co-operate.
2. Fixed cost of one period is not carried to another period. Fixed cost is charged to profit and loss account.
3. There is no need for recovery of overhead.
4. It is a useful tool for decision making to maximise the profit.
5. Management can concentrate on variable cost for cost control.
6. It is helpful in evaluating profitability of various products, process and operations.
7. Cost-volume-profit relationship is established for profit planning.
8. Marginal costing technique can be used along with other costing techniques like standard costing and budgetary control.
9. Question of under-absorption or over-absorption of overhead does not arise.

19.1.5 Limitations of Marginal Costing

The following are some limitations of marginal costing:

1. Classification of total costs into variable and fixed cost is difficult. Presence of semi-variable cost makes it more complex.
2. It is assumed that variable cost per unit will remain same at all levels of activity. But when production becomes large, the economies of large scale operation like quantity discount for large purchase of raw materials, improved labour productivity due to introduction of automated machines etc., will result in slight reduction in variable cost per unit.
3. It is also assumed that fixed cost will remain same irrespective of changes in the levels of activity. But fixed cost increases when production increases beyond a certain level of production or due to increase in rates of fixed expenses like rent, insurance, management, staff salary increase etc.
4. In pricing decisions it is assumed that management can increase or reduce prices at its will. But in practice market forces like demand and supply and government regulations influence the price.
5. It is not correct to ignore fixed cost in determining cost of the product, process or operation, when production process takes longer time.
6. Valuation of inventory on marginal cost basis is not acceptable to tax authorities and also not recognised by accounting standard board.

7. Due to employment of large capital, increased automation, increased sales promotion activities etc. result in increased fixed cost. Ignoring large fixed cost in product costing is not advisable.
8. In industries where job costing and contract costing is followed, all costs, both variable and fixed cost are charged to the job or contract. So marginal costing technique is not useful.

Ascertainment of Profit under Marginal Costing and Absorption Costing

(i) Computation of Profit under Absorption Costing

Under absorption costing both variable and fixed cost is included in the total cost. Work-in-progress and finished goods inventory values include fixed also. The following is the proforma for computing profit.

Income Statement

	₹	₹
Sales	-	xxx
Less: Cost of sales:		
Direct materials consumed	xxx	
Direct labour cost	xxx	
Direct expenses	xxx	
Prime Cost	xxx	
Factory overheads: Variable		
Fixed	xxx	
Works Cost	xxx	
Office Administration overheads (fixed and variable)	xxx	
Cost of production	xxx	
Add: Opening stock of finished goods	xxx	
	xxx	
Less: Closing stock of finished goods	xxx	
Cost of goods sold	xxx	
Selling and distribution overheads:		
Fixed	xxx	
Variable	xxx	xxx
Profit/(Loss)		xxx

(ii) Computation of Profit under Marginal Costing

Under marginal costing only variable costs are charged to sales revenue. The surplus of sales revenue over variable cost is called contribution. Fixed cost is charged to contribution. If contribution is more than fixed costs, it is profit. If contribution is less than the fixed cost it is loss. Stock of work-in-progress and finished goods are valued at variable cost of production.

The following is the format of income statement under marginal costing (also called marginal cost statement).

Marginal Cost Statement		
	₹	₹
Sales	-	xxx
Less: Variable cost/marginal cost :		
Direct materials	xxx	
Direct labour	xxx	
Direct expenses	xxx	
Variable factory overheads	xxx	
Total variable cost of manufacturing	xxx	
Add: Opening stock of finished goods	xxx	
	xxx	
Less: Closing stock of finished goods	xxx	
	xxx	
Variable selling and distribution overheads	xxx	xxx
Contribution (sales - variable Cost)	-	xxx
Less: Fixed costs:		
Fixed factory overheads	xxx	
Administration overheads (fixed)	xxx	
Fixed selling and distribution overheads	xxx	xxx
Profit/(Loss)	-	xxx

Note: The following is called marginal cost equation:

$$\text{Sales} - \text{Variable cost} = \text{Contribution}$$

$$\text{Contribution} = \text{Fixed cost} + \text{Profit}$$

$$\text{Sales} - \text{Variable cost} = \text{Fixed cost} + \text{Profit}$$

SITUATION - I

There is no opening or closing stock. (i.e. all goods produced are sold). Profit under both methods of costing will be same.

Illustration-1

XY Ltd. produced and sold 25,000 units in a year. Selling price is ₹65 per unit. The cost information are as below:

Direct materials	₹25 per unit
Direct labour	₹13 per unit
Production overheads:	
Variable	₹2,25,000
Fixed	₹1,00,000
Administration overheads (fixed)	₹75,000
Selling and distribution overheads:	
Variable	₹25,000
Fixed	₹25,000

Prepare income statements showing profit under (a) Absorption costing and (b) Marginal costing.

Solution

(a)

Income Statement (Absorption Costing)		
	₹	₹
Sales (25,000 units × ₹65)		16,25,000
Less: Cost of sales		
Direct materials	6,25,000	
Direct labour	3,25,000	
Production overheads: Variable	2,25,000	
Fixed	1,00,000	
Administration overheads (Fixed)	75,000	
Selling and distribution overheads:		
Fixed	25,000	
Variable	25,000	14,00,000
Profit		2,25,000

(b)

Income Statement (Marginal Costing)		
	₹	₹
Sales (25,000 units × ₹65)		16,25,000
Less: Variable Cost/Marginal Cost		
Direct materials	6,25,000	
Direct labour	3,25,000	
Production overheads: Variable	2,25,000	
Selling and distribution overheads: Variable	25,000	12,00,000
Contribution	-	4,25,000
Less: Fixed costs:		
Production overheads	1,00,000	

Administration overheads	75,000	
Selling and administration overheads	25,000	2,00,000
Profit	-	2,25,000

SITUATION - II

Closing stock is more than opening stock (i.e. sales is less than production). Profit under absorption costing will be more than the profit under marginal costing.

Illustration-2

ABC Ltd. produces and sells product 'Z'. The following are the cost and other relevant data relating to a year:

Opening stock	15,000 units
Production	75,000 units
Sales	70,000 unit at ₹80 per unit
Raw materials	₹15,00,000
Direct labour	₹11,25,000
Factory overheads:	
Variable	₹9,00,000
Fixed	₹7,50,000
Administration overheads (fixed)	₹4,50,000
Selling overheads - Variable	₹3,75,000
Selling overheads - Fixed	₹3,00,000

You are required to ascertain the profit under (a) absorption costing, (b) marginal costing and (c) explain the difference in profit.

Solution

(a)

Income Statement (Absorption Costing)		
	₹	₹
Sales (70,000 units × ₹80)		56,00,000
Less: Cost of sales		
Raw materials	15,00,000	
Direct labour	11,25,000	
Prime cost	26,25,000	

Factory overheads: Variable	9,00,000	
Fixed	7,50,000	
Works cost	42,75,000	
Administration overheads (fixed)	4,50,000	
Cost of production (75,000 units)	47,25,000	
(Cost of production per unit = $\frac{4,72,500}{75,000}$ =₹63)		
Add: Opening stock (15,000 units × ₹63)	9,45,000	
	56,70,000	
Less: Closing stock (20,000 units × ₹63)	12,60,000	
Cost of goods sold	44,10,000	
Selling overheads:		
Variable	3,75,000	
Fixed	3,00,000	50,85,000
Profit	-	5,15,000

(b)

Income Statement (Marginal Costing)		
	₹	₹
Sales (70,000 units × ₹80)		56,00,000
Less: Marginal cost/variable cost		
Raw materials	15,00,000	
Direct labour	11,25,000	
Factory overheads - Variable	9,00,000	
Variable manufacturing cost (75,000 units)	35,25,000	
(Cost of production per unit = $\frac{32,25,500}{75,000}$ = ₹47)		
Add: Opening stock (15,000 units × ₹47)	7,05,000	
	42,30,000	
Less: Closing stock (20,000 units × ₹47)	9,40,000	
Variable manufacturing cost of goods sold	32,90,000	
Add: Selling overheads - Variable	3,75,000	36,65,000
Contribution		19,35,000
Less: Fixed costs:		
Factory overheads - Fixed	7,50,000	
Administration overheads - Fixed	4,50,000	
Selling overheads - Fixed	3,00,000	15,00,000
Profit	-	4,35,000

Note:

Closing stock:	
Opening Stock	15,000 units
Add: Production	75,000 units
Goods available for sale	90,000 units
Sales	70,000 units
Closing stock	20,000 units

Difference in profit = 5,15,000 – 4,35,000
= ₹80,000 (more in absorption costing)

The difference in profit arises due to difference in valuation of stock which is explained below:

	Opening Stock ₹	**Closing Stock** ₹
Value in absorption costing	9,45,000	12,60,000
Value in marginal costing	7,05,000	9,40,000
Difference	2,40,000	3,20,000

Net difference = 3,20,000 – 2,40,000
= ₹80,000

SITUATION - III

(Opening stock is more than closing stock i.e., sales is more than production)

Profit under marginal costing will be more than the profit under absorption costing.

Illustration-3

From the following details of P Ltd. prepare income statements under (a) absorption costing, (b) marginal costing and (c) explain the difference in profits between the two methods:

Opening stock	4,000 units
Production	12,000 units
Sales	13,500 units
Selling price per unit	₹30
Materials cost	₹9 per unit

Direct wages		₹7 per unit
Factory overheads:	Variable	₹3 per unit
	Fixed	₹9,000
Office overheads (fixed)		₹18,000
Selling overheads:	Variable	₹12,000
	Fixed	₹12,000

Solution

(a)

Income Statement (Absorption Costing)		
	₹	₹
Sales (13,500 units × ₹30)		4,05,000
Less: Cost of sales		
Materials cost (12,000 units × ₹9)	1,08,000	
Direct wages (12,000 units × ₹7)	84,000	
Prime cost	1,92,000	
Factory Overheads: Variable	36,000	
Fixed	9,000	
Works cost	2,37,000	
Office overheads (fixed)	18,000	
Cost of production (12,000 units)	2,55,000	
Add: Opening stock $\left(\frac{2,45,000}{12,000} \times 4,000\right)$	85,000	
	3,40,000	
Less: Closing stock $\left(\frac{2,45,000}{12,000} \times 2,500\right)$	53,125	
Cost of goods sold	2,86,875	
Selling overheads: Fixed	12,000	
Variable	12,000	3,10,875
Profit	-	94,125

(b)

Income Statement (Marginal Costing)		
	₹	₹
Sales (13,500 units × ₹30)		4,05,000
Less: Marginal cost/variable cost		
Materials cost	1,08,000	
Direct wages	84,000	

Factory overheads - variable	36,000	
Variable manufacturing cost (12,000 units)	2,28,000	
(Cost of production per unit $= \frac{2,28,000}{12,000} =$ ₹19)		
Add: Opening stock (4,000 units × ₹19)	76,000	
	3,04,000	
Less: Closing stock (2,500 units × ₹19)	47,500	
	2,56,500	
Add: Selling overheads - Variable	12,000	2,68,500
Contribution		1,36,500
Less: Fixed overheads		
Factory overhead - Fixed	9,000	
Administration overhead - Fixed	18,000	
Selling overheads - Fixed	12,000	39,000
Profit	-	97,500

19.2 COST - VOLUME - PROFIT ANALYSIS

Major aim of managements is to maximise the profit of firms. There is close relationship between cost, volume and profit. Understanding the relationship between cost, volume and profit helps the management in production and profit planning. So cost-volume-profit analysis is an effective tool in the hands of a management in taking decisions for maximisation of profits. The various tools used in cost volume profit analysis are:

(i) Profit-volume analysis (P/V ratio),

(ii) Break-even analysis (Break-even point), and

(iii) Margin of Safety (MS Ratio).

19.2.1 Profit-Volume Analysis

In profit-volume analysis, the relationship between contribution and sales is established. It is also called Contribution-Sales Ratio (C/S Ratio) and P/V ratio. It helps to determine the relative profitability of different products, processes, operations and departments. Fixed cost does not affect P/V ratio.

Assumption

Profit-volume analysis is based on the assumption that selling price and variable cost per unit remain unaltered in the short run.

Significance/Importance/Uses of P/V ratio

1. P/V ratio helps to identify the most profitable product, process, operation and department.
2. It helps to find the break-even point.
3. It also helps to determine the sales volume required to earn a certain profit.

The following are the equations used to calculate P/V ratio:

$$\text{(i) P/V Ratio} = \frac{\text{Total Contribution}}{\text{Total Sales}} \times 100$$

$$\text{(ii) P/V Ratio} = \frac{\text{Contribution per unit}}{\text{Selling price per unit}} \times 100$$

$$\text{(iii) P/V Ratio} = \frac{\text{Changes in Profit}}{\text{Changes in Sales}} \times 100$$

$$\text{(iv) P/V Ratio} = \frac{\text{Fixed Cost}}{\text{Break-even Sales}} \times 100$$

$$\text{(v) P/V Ratio} = \frac{\text{Profit}}{\text{Margin of Safety Sales}} \times 100$$

Improvement of P/V Ratio

P/V ratio can be improved by the following measures:

1. Increasing selling price per unit
2. Reducing variable cost per unit
3. In case of multiproduct firms, increase the sales volume of the product having highest P/V ratio in the product mix.

Illustration-4

From the following particulars calculate the present and future P/V ratio:

	₹
Sales	10,00,000
Variable cost	6,00,000
Fixed cost	2,00,000

There is a proposal to reduce the selling price by 10%.

Solution

	₹
Present sales	10,00,000
Less: Variable cost	6,00,000
Contribution	4,00,000

$$\text{Present P/V Ratio} = \frac{\text{Contribution}}{\text{Sales}} \times 100$$
$$= \frac{4,00,000}{10,00,000} \times 100 = 40\%$$

	₹
Present sales	10,00,000
Less: 10% reduction in selling price	1,00,000
Future sales	9,00,000
Less: Variable cost	6,00,000
Future contribution	3,00,000

$$\text{Future P/V Ratio} = \frac{\text{Future Contribution}}{\text{Future Sales}} \times 100$$
$$= \frac{3,00,000}{9,00,000} \times 100 = 33.33\%$$

Note: Reduction in selling price reduces the sales value. Volume of production and variable costs remain the same.

Illustration-5

A company sells its product at ₹15 per unit. In a period, if it produces and sells 8,000 units, it incurs a loss of ₹5 per unit. If the volume is raised to 20,000 units, it earns a profit of ₹4 per unit. Calculate P/V Ratio. **(CA-Inter)**

Solution

(i) Variable cost per unit $= \dfrac{\text{Changes in total cost}}{\text{Changes in no. of units produced}}$

$$= \frac{60,000}{12,000}$$

$= ₹5$

Note:

Total cost at 8,000 units = (Selling price per unit + Loss per unit) × No. of units
= (15 + 5) × 8,000
= ₹1,60,000

Total cost at 20,000 units = Sales – Profit
= 15 × 20,000 – 4 × 20,000
= 3,00,000 – 80,000
= ₹2,20,000

Changes in no. of units produced and sold = 20,000 – 8,000
= 12,000 units

Changes in total cost = 2,20,000 – 1,60,000
= ₹60,000

(ii) Contribution:

	₹
Selling Price	15
Less: Variable cost per unit	5
Contribution per unit	10

(iii) $\text{P/V Ratio} = \dfrac{\text{Contribution}}{\text{Sales}} \times 100$

$= \dfrac{10}{15} \times 100$

$= 66.67\%$

Illustration-6

X Ltd. furnishes the following information for two years:

Year	2010	2011
Sales (₹)	8,00,000	10,00,000
Profit (₹)	90,000	1,20,000

Calculate P/V Ratio, assuming that selling price per unit, variable cost per unit and total fixed cost remained the same during the two years.

Solution

$$\text{P/V Ratio} = \frac{\text{Changes in Profit}}{\text{Changes in Sales}} \times 100$$
$$= \frac{30{,}000}{2{,}00{,}000} \times 100$$
$$= 15\%$$

Working Note

Year	Sales (₹)	Profit (₹)
2010	8,00,000	90,000
2011	10,00,000	1,20,000
Difference	2,00,000	30,000

Illustration-7

A company provides the following information for two years :

Year	2010	2011
Sales (₹)	6,00,000	7,50,000
Cost (₹)	5,40,000	6,60,000

Compute P/V Ratio.

Solution

$$\text{P/V Ratio} = \frac{\text{Changes in Profit}}{\text{Changes in Sales}} \times 100$$
$$= \frac{30{,}000}{1{,}50{,}000} \times 100$$
$$= 20\%$$

Working Note

Changes in profit		
	Sales (₹) – Total cost (₹)	**Profit (₹)**
Year 2010	6,00,000 – 5,40,000 =	60,000
Year 2011	7,50,000 – 6,60,000 =	90,000
	Changes in Profit =	30,000
Changes in Sales	6,00,000 – 7,50,000 =	1,50,000

Illustration-8

Examine whether the following equations are correct:

(a) $\text{Sales} = \dfrac{\text{Contribution}}{\text{P/V Ratio}}$

(b) $\text{Contribution} = \dfrac{\text{P/V Ratio}}{\text{Sales}}$

Solution

(i) $\text{P/V Ratio} = \dfrac{\text{Contribution}}{\text{Sales}}$

$$\text{Sales} = \frac{\text{Contribution}}{\text{P/V Ratio}}$$

Given equation (a) is correct.

(ii) $\text{P/V Ratio} = \dfrac{\text{Contribution}}{\text{Sales}}$

$$\text{Contribution} = \text{Sales} \times \text{P/V ratio}$$

Given equation (b) is incorrect.

19.2.2 Break-even Analysis

Break-even analysis shows the relationship between costs and profits in relation to sales. The level of activity (Sales / Production) at which total sales revenue is equal to the total cost is called break-even point. Hence, there is no profit or loss. So the activity at which there is no profit or loss is called break-even point. Break-even point is also called 'No Profit, No Loss point' or 'Zero Profit, Zero Loss point'. Break-even point helps in production planning and profit planning. It helps to forecast the profit at different levels of activity. It also helps to know the activity levels for earning different amount of profits.

Assumptions of Break-even Analysis

All assumptions of marginal costing techniques apply to break-even analysis also.

Factors affecting break-even analysis are:

1. **Change in fixed cost**

   Reduction in fixed cost will lower the break-even point. Increase in fixed cost increases the break-even point. A firm operating with smaller fixed cost will have a lower break-even point. Such firms stand in a better position during recessionary periods.

2. **Changes in variable cost per unit**

   When variable cost decreases, contribution margin increases. This will bring down the break-even point. Contribution margin decreases when variable cost per unit increases, resulting in higher break-even point.

3. **Changes in selling price per unit**

   When selling price is increased, the contribution margin increases. It brings down the break-even point. If the selling price decreases, it reduces the contribution margin. It will increase the break-even point.

4. **Changing product mix/sales mix**

   In case of a multiproduct company, if the product and sale of a product having higher P/V ratio is increased, it will increase the overall contribution. It pushes down the break-even point.

The following formulas are used for calculating break-even point:

(a) Break-even sales volume (Quantity)

$$\text{Break-even point (Units)} = \frac{\text{Fixed cost}}{\text{Contribution per unit}}$$

(b) Break-even sales value:

i. $\text{Break-even point (₹)} = \dfrac{\text{Fixed cost}}{\text{Contribution per unit}} \times \text{Selling price per unit}$

ii. $\text{Break-even point (₹)} = \dfrac{\text{Fixed cost}}{\text{Total contribution}} \times \text{Total sales}$

iii. $\text{Break-even point (₹)} = \dfrac{\text{Fixed cost}}{\text{P/V Ratio}}$

19.2.2.1 Composite break-even point

When a company produces two or more products, a break-even point calculated for all the products combined together is called composite break-even point. There are two alternative ways of calculating composite break-even point. They are:

- Constant product mix approach
- Variable product mix approach

(i) Constant Product Mix Approach

In this approach, combined contribution is divided in the ratio of sales of each product in the combined sales.

(ii) Variable Product Mix Approach

First, more profitable product is produced to its maximum capacity to recover the fixed cost. Then next less profitable product is taken to recover the balance fixed overheads.

Break-even capacity

Break-even point may also be expressed as a percentage of total capacity. The formula is,

$$= \frac{\text{Break-even point (units)/₹}}{\text{Total capacity (units)/₹}} \times 100$$

Forecasting of sales required to earn a desired profit

It is an extension of break-even analysis. The break-even point formulae are used with small changes. The formulae for calculation of sales required for a desired profit are:

1. Required sales volume (Quantity) :

$$\text{Required sales (Units)} = \frac{\text{Fixed cost + Desired profit}}{\text{Contribution per unit}}$$

2. Break-even sales value:

(a) $$\text{Required sales (₹)} = \frac{\text{Fixed cost + Desired profit}}{\text{Contribution per unit}} \times \text{Selling price per unit}$$

(b) $$\text{Required sales (₹)} = \frac{\text{Fixed cost + Desired profit}}{\text{Total contribution}} \times \text{Total sales}$$

(c) $$\text{Required sales (₹)} = \frac{\text{Fixed cost + Desired profit}}{\text{P/V Ratio}}$$

19.2.3 Margin of Safety

Margin of safety is the excess of actual sales over the BEP sales. Sales upto break point helps in recovering the total cost. Only the margin of safety sales helps a firm to earn profit. A higher margin of safety makes a company more stronger in the sense that it can face recessionary business conditions successfully.

$$\text{Margin of safety sales} = \text{Actual Sales} - \text{BEP Sales}$$

$$\text{Margin of safety ratio (MS Ratio)} = \frac{\text{MS sales}}{\text{Actual sales}} \times 100$$

Improvement of margin of safety

The following steps may be taken to improve the margin of safety.

1. Increasing the sales volume through sales promotion activities.
2. Increasing the selling price, provided demand for the product will not decrease.
3. Reducing fixed cost.
4. Reducing variable cost per unit.
5. Introducing/increasing the sales of a highly profitable product in case of multi-product companies.

Illustration-9

Determine break-even point from the following data:

- Fixed cost - ₹5,00,000
- Variable cost - 75% of sales

What would be the Break-even point in the following situations:

(a) Fixed cost increases by 10%
(b) Fixed cost decreases by 5%
(c) Variable cost increases by 10%
(d) Variable cost decreases by 20%
(e) Selling price increases by 20%
(f) Selling price decreases by 10%

Solution

Present:	
Let sales be	100
(−) Variable cost	75
Contribution	25
P/V Ratio	25%

$$\text{Break-even point (₹)} = \frac{\text{Fixed Cost}}{\text{P/V Ratio}}$$

$$= \frac{5{,}00{,}000}{25} \times 100 = ₹20{,}00{,}000$$

Situation (a):

Fixed cost increases by 10%	
Present fixed cost	₹5,00,000
Add: Increase 10%	₹50,000
New fixed cost	₹5,50,000
P/V Ratio (as at present)	25%

$$\text{Break-even point (₹)} = \frac{\text{New Fixed Cost}}{\text{P/V Ratio}}$$
$$= \frac{5,50,000}{25} \times 100$$
$$= ₹22,00,000$$

Situation (b):

Fixed cost decreases by 5%	
Present fixed cost	₹5,00,000
Less: Decrease 5%	₹25,000
New fixed cost	₹4,75,000
P/V Ratio (as at present)	25%

$$\text{Break-even point (₹)} = \frac{\text{New Fixed Cost}}{\text{P/V Ratio}}$$
$$= \frac{4,75,000}{25} \times 100$$
$$= ₹19,00,000$$

Situation (c):

Variable cost increases by 10%		
Let Sales be		₹100
Less: Variable cost:		
Present	75.0	
Add: Increase 10%	7.5	₹82.50
New contribution		₹17.50

$$\text{New P/V ratio} = \frac{17.5}{100} = 17.5\%$$

$$\text{Break-even point (₹)} = \frac{\text{Fixed Cost}}{\text{New P/V Ratio}}$$
$$= \frac{5,00,000}{17.5} \times 100 = ₹28,57,143$$

Situation (d):

Variable cost decreases by 20%		
Let Sales be		₹100
Less: Variable cost:		
Present	75.0	
Less: Decrease 20%	15.0	₹60
New contribution		₹40

New P/V ratio = 40%

$$\text{Break-even point (₹)} = \frac{\text{Fixed Cost}}{\text{New P/V Ratio}} = \frac{5{,}00{,}000}{40} \times 100$$
$$= ₹12{,}50{,}000$$

Situation (e):

Selling price increases by 20%	
Let present selling price be	₹100
Add: Increase 20%	₹20
New selling price	₹120
Less: Variable cost	₹75
New contribution	₹45

$$\text{New P/V ratio} = \frac{\text{New Contribution}}{\text{New Sales}} \times 100$$
$$= \frac{45}{120} \times 100$$
$$= 37.5\%$$

$$\text{Break-even point (₹)} = \frac{\text{Fixed Cost}}{\text{New P/V Ratio}}$$
$$= \frac{5{,}00{,}000}{37.5} \times 100$$
$$= ₹13{,}33{,}333$$

Situation (f):

Selling price decreases by 10%	
Let present selling price be	₹100
Add: Decrease 10%	₹10
New selling price	₹90
Less: Variable cost	₹75
New contribution	₹15

$$\text{New P/V ratio} = \frac{\text{New Contribution}}{\text{New Sales}} \times 100$$
$$= \frac{15}{90} \times 100$$
$$= 16.67\%$$

$$\text{Break-even point (₹)} = \frac{\text{Fixed Cost}}{\text{New P/V Ratio}}$$
$$= \frac{5{,}00{,}000}{16.67} \times 100$$
$$= ₹29{,}99{,}400 \text{ (or) } ₹30{,}00{,}000$$

Illustration-10

The following information relates to the product of a company:

Selling price per unit	₹30
Variable overheads:	
Manufacturing	₹17
Selling	₹3
Fixed overheads:	
Factory	₹1,50,000
Selling	₹30,000

Calculate:

(a) BEP in amount and in units

(b) Sales to earn a profit of ₹60,000 in value and in units and

(c) Profit or loss if sales are 15,000 units. **(B.Com., Karnataka University)**

Solution

Note:

		₹
Selling price		30
Less: Variable cost		
Manufacturing	17	
Selling	3	20
Contribution per unit		10

Fixed cost:	₹
Factory	1,50,000
Selling	30,000
Total	1,80,000

(a) Break-even point (in units)

$$= \frac{\text{Fixed cost}}{\text{Contribution per unit}}$$

$$= \frac{1,80,000}{10}$$

$$= 18,000 \text{ units}$$

Break-even point (in amount)

$$= \frac{\text{Fixed cost}}{\text{Contribution per unit}} \times \text{Selling price per unit}$$

$$= \frac{1,80,000}{10} \times 30$$

$$= ₹5,40,000$$

(b) Sales to earn a profit of ₹60,000

$$\text{Required sales value (₹)} = \frac{\text{Fixed cost} + \text{Desired profit}}{\text{Contribution per unit}} \times \text{Selling price per unit}$$

$$= \frac{1,80,000 + 60,000}{10} \times 30$$

$$= ₹7,20,000$$

$$\text{Required sales (in units)} = \frac{\text{Fixed cost} + \text{Desired profit}}{\text{Contribution per unit}}$$

$$= \frac{1,80,000 + 60,000}{10}$$

$$= 24,000 \text{ units}$$

(c)

Profit or loss if sales are 15,000 units:	
	₹
Sales (15,000 units × ₹30)	4,50,000
Less: Variable Cost (15,000 units × ₹20)	3,00,000
Contribution	1,50,000
Less: Fixed Cost	1,80,000
Loss	(–) 30,000

Illustration-11

From the following data, calculate (a) break-even point expressed in amount of sales in rupees and (b) number of units that must be sold to earn a profit of ₹60,000 per year.

Sales price	₹20 per unit
Variable manufacturing costs	₹11 per unit
Variable selling cost	₹3 per unit
Fixed factory overheads	₹5,40,000 per year
Fixed selling cost	₹2,52,000 per year

(ICWA-Final)

Solution

Note:

		₹
Selling price		20 per unit
Less: Variable cost		
Manufacturing	11	
Selling	3	14 per unit
Contribution per unit		6 per unit

Fixed cost:	₹
Factory	5,40,000
Selling	2,52,000
Total	7,92,000

$$\text{P/V ratio} = \frac{\text{Contribution}}{\text{Sales}} \times 100$$

$$= \frac{6}{20} \times 100 = 30\%$$

(a) Break-even point (in units):

$$= \frac{\text{Fixed cost}}{\text{Contribution per unit}}$$

$$= \frac{7,92,000}{6}$$

$$= 1,32,000 \text{ units}$$

Break-even point (in amount):

$$= \frac{\text{Fixed cost}}{\text{P/V Ratio}}$$

$$= \frac{7,92,000}{30} \times 100$$

$$= ₹26,40,000$$

(b) No. of units to be sold to earn a desired profit of ₹60,000:

$$\text{Required sales (in units)} = \frac{\text{Fixed cost + Desired profit}}{\text{Contribution per unit}}$$

$$= \frac{7,92,000 + 60,000}{6}$$

$$= 1,42,000 \text{ units}$$

Illustration-12

Indian Plastics makes plastic buckets. An analysis of their accounting reveals:

Variable cost per unit	₹20
Fixed cost	₹50,000 for the year
Capacity	2,000 buckets per year
Selling price per bucket	₹70

Required:

(i) Find the break-even point;

(ii) Find the number of buckets to be sold to get a profit of ₹30,000;

(iii) If the company can manufacture 600 buckets more per year with an additional fixed cost of ₹2,000, what would be the selling price to maintain the profit per bucket as at (ii) above.

(B.Com. (Hons.), Delhi University)

Solution

Note:

	₹
Selling price per unit	70
Less: Variable cost per unit	20
Contribution per unit	50

(i) Break-even point (in units)

$$= \frac{\text{Fixed cost}}{\text{Contribution per unit}}$$

$$= \frac{50{,}000}{50}$$

$$= 1{,}000 \text{ units}$$

$$\text{BEP (₹)} = 1{,}000 \text{ units} \times ₹70$$

$$= ₹70{,}000$$

(ii) No. of buckets to be sold for a desired profit of ₹30,000

$$\text{Required sales (in units)} = \frac{\text{Fixed cost} + \text{Desired profit}}{\text{Contribution per unit}}$$

$$= \frac{50{,}000 + 30{,}000}{50}$$

$$= 1{,}600 \text{ units}$$

$$\text{Profit per unit} = \frac{30{,}000}{1{,}600} = ₹18.75$$

(iii) New selling price per bucket, if sales is increased by 600 buckets more:

Sales in (ii) above	1,600 buckets
Add: Increase	600 buckets
Total	2,200 buckets

Let the new selling price be 'x'.

$$\text{Total sales} = \text{Total fixed cost} + \text{Total variable cost} + \text{Total profit}$$

$$2{,}200 \times x = 52{,}000 + (2{,}200 \times 20) + (2{,}200 \times 18.75)$$

$$2{,}200x = 52{,}000 + 44{,}000 + 41{,}250$$

$$2{,}200x = 1{,}37{,}250$$

$$x = \frac{1{,}37{,}250}{2{,}200} = ₹62.39$$

New selling price = ₹62.39

Illustration-13

The following details are extracted from the books of X Ltd. for two years:

	2010	2011
Sales (₹)	12,00,000	15,00,000
Profit (₹)	2,40,000	3,30,000

Find,

(a) Break-even point sales value;

(b) Sales required to earn a profit of ₹4,00,000;

(c) Profit on a sales value of ₹20,00,000;

(d) Margin of safety ratio for the year 2011.

Solution

Note:

Year	Sales (₹)	Profit (₹)
2010	12,00,000	2,40,000
2011	15,00,000	3,30,000
Difference	3,00,000	90,000

$$P/V \text{ ratio} = \frac{\text{Changes in profit}}{\text{Changes in sales}} \times 100$$

$$= \frac{90{,}000}{3{,}00{,}000} \times 100 = 30\%$$

$$\text{Fixed cost} = \text{Sales} \times P/V \text{ Ratio} - \text{Profit}$$

$$= 12{,}00{,}000 \times \frac{30}{100} - 2{,}40{,}000$$

$$= 3{,}60{,}000 - 2{,}40{,}000 = ₹1{,}20{,}000$$

(a) Break-even point (₹):

$$= \frac{\text{Fixed cost}}{\text{P/V Ratio}}$$

$$= \frac{1{,}20{,}000}{30} \times 100 = ₹4{,}00{,}000$$

(b) Sales required to earn a profit of ₹4,00,000:

$$\text{Required sales (₹)} = \frac{\text{Fixed cost + Desired profit}}{\text{Contribution per unit}}$$

$$= \frac{1{,}20{,}000 + 4{,}00{,}000}{30} \times 100$$

$$= ₹17{,}33{,}333$$

(c) Profit on a sales value of ₹20,00,000

$$\text{Contribution} = \text{Sales} \times \text{P/V Ratio}$$

$$= 20{,}00{,}000 \times \frac{30}{100}$$

$$= ₹6{,}00{,}000$$

$$\text{Profit} = \text{Contribution} - \text{Fixed cost}$$

$$= 6{,}00{,}000 - 1{,}20{,}000$$

$$= ₹4{,}80{,}000$$

(d) Margin of safety ratio for the year 2011

$$\text{Margin of safety} = \text{Total sales} - \text{BEP Sales}$$

$$\text{(MS Sales)} = 15{,}00{,}000 - 4{,}00{,}000$$

$$= ₹11{,}00{,}000$$

$$\text{Margin of safety ratio} = \frac{\text{MS Sales}}{\text{Total sales}} \times 100$$

$$= \frac{11{,}00{,}000}{15{,}00{,}000} \times 100$$

$$= 73.33\%$$

Illustration-14

A Ltd. produces and sells 20,000 units at present. Selling price per unit is ₹60. Variable cost is ₹40 per unit. Fixed cost is ₹3,00,000. Find the present break-even point and also the new selling price if the break-even point is reduced by 2,000 units.

Solution

	₹
Selling price per unit	60
Less: Variable cost per unit	40
Contribution per unit	20

$$\text{Break-even point (in units)} = \frac{\text{Fixed cost}}{\text{Contribution per unit}}$$

$$= \frac{3,00,000}{20}$$

$$= 15,000 \text{ units}$$

New selling price:	
Present BEP	15,000 units
Less: Decrease	2,000 units
New BEP	13,000 units

$$\text{Sales at BEP} = \text{Variable cost} + \text{Fixed cost} + \text{Nil profit}$$

$$\text{BEP sales for 13,000 units} = (13,000 \times 40) + 3,00,000 + 0$$

$$= 5,20,000 + 3,00,000$$

$$= ₹8,20,000$$

$$\text{New selling price p/u} = \frac{8,20,000}{13,000}$$

$$= ₹63.08 \text{ (Approx.)}$$

19.3 BREAK-EVEN CHART OR GRAPH

Break-even chart is a graphical representation of cost-volume-profit relationship. Break-even chart shows break-even point, margin of safety and profit at different activity levels at a glance. The following are the uses of break-even chart:

1. Break-even chart shows the relationship between cost, sales and profit.
2. It shows profit of a firm when it operates at different activity levels.
3. We can ascertain the capacity level at which a firm reaches break-even point.
4. It shows margin of safety.
5. It also shows angle of incidence clearly.

Construction of break-even chart

1. On the X-axis (horizontal line) production/sales (units) is shown using a suitable scale.
2. On the Y-axis (vertical line) costs and sales revenue is shown using suitable scale.
3. Fixed cost line is drawn. It starts from Y-axis above 0 point and runs parallel to X-axis.
4. Total cost for different activity level is plotted in the graph. Total cost line starts from Y axis at fixed cost point and runs in straight line between X- and Y-axis.
5. Sales revenue for different activity level is plotted in the graph. Sales line starts from 0 point and runs in straight line between X- and Y-axis.
6. Total cost line intersects sales line at a point, which is known as break-even point.
7. The area lying between total cost line and sales line above the BEP is profit area.
8. The area lying between total cost line and sales line below the break-even point is loss area.
9. The angle formed between total cost line and sales line above BEP is called angle of incidence.

Illustration-15

Draw a break-even chart from the following information:

	₹
Variable cost per unit	10
Selling price per unit	20
Total fixed expenses	1,50,000

Solution

Prepare a table showing costs and sales revenue for different levels of activity. Levels of activities are chosen at random:

Activity level (Output units)	Fixed cost ₹	Variable cost ₹	Total cost ₹	Sales revenue ₹
0	1,50,000	-	-	-
5,000	1,50,000	50,000	2,00,000	1,00,000
10,000	1,50,000	1,00,000	2,50,000	2,00,000
15,000	1,50,000	1,50,000	3,00,000	3,00,000
20,000	1,50,000	2,00,000	3,50,000	4,00,000
25,000	1,50,000	2,50,000	4,00,000	5,00,000
30,000	1,50,000	3,00,000	4,50,000	6,00,000

We get the following chart after plotting the above data in the graph.

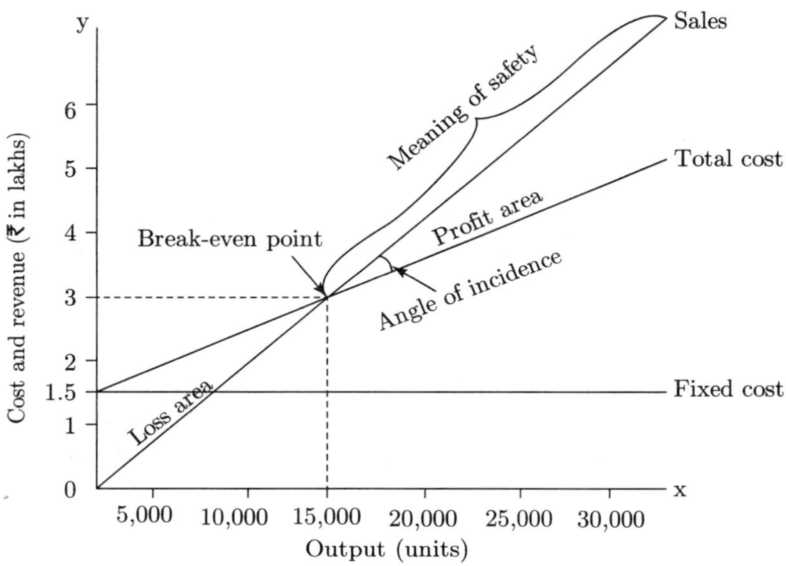

Break-even chart

There is an alternative way of preparing a break-even chart. Variable cost line and sales line are drawn first. Both lines start from 0 point and lie between X- and Y-axis in straight lines. Total cost line is drawn. It starts from Y-axis at fixed cost point. Total cost line lies above variable cost line parallelly. The area between total cost line and variable cost line stands for fixed cost. The break-even chart will appear as below:

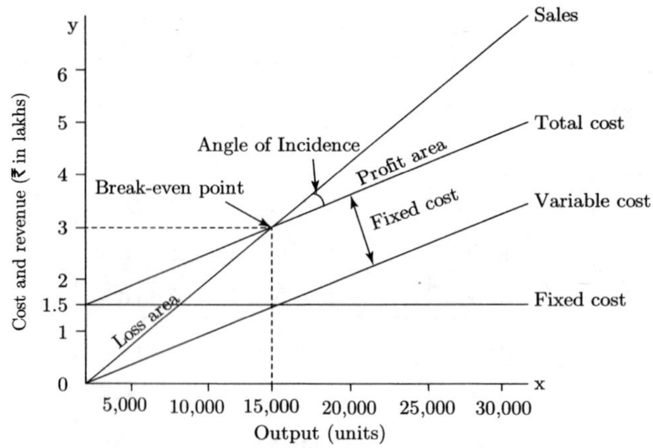

Break-even point chart

19.3.1 Special Break-even Charts

Break-even charts are drawn highlighting certain specific points. They are:

(a) Contribution break-even chart
(b) Cash break-even chart
(c) Control break-even chart
(d) Analytical break-even chart
(e) Profit break-even chart
(f) Product-wise break-even chart

(a) Contribution Break-even Chart

Under ordinary break-even chart only profit/loss at different activity levels is shown. In the contribution break-even chart contribution earned at different activity levels can be known. Taking information given in *Illustration-15*, let us draw the contribution break-even chart:

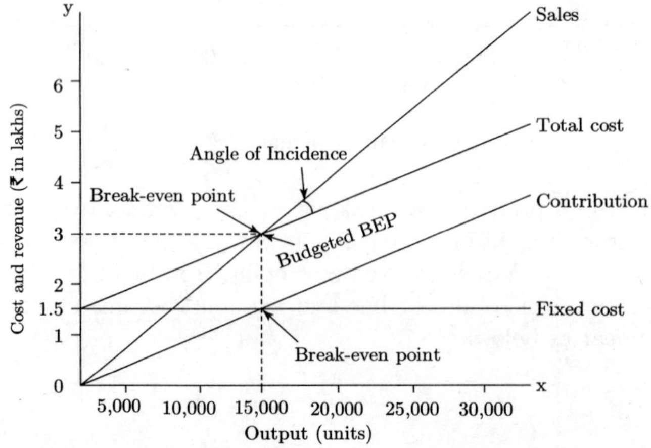

Contribution break-even chart

(b) Cash Break-even Chart

In cash break-even chart only cash fixed expenses are taken. Non-cash fixed expenses like depreciation etc., are deducted from the total fixed cost. The following is the formula for cash break-even point:

$$\text{Cash BEP (in units)} = \frac{\text{Cash fixed cost}}{\text{Contribution per unit}}$$

Taking information in *Illustration-15* and assuming cash fixed cost as ₹1,25,000, let us draw a chart:

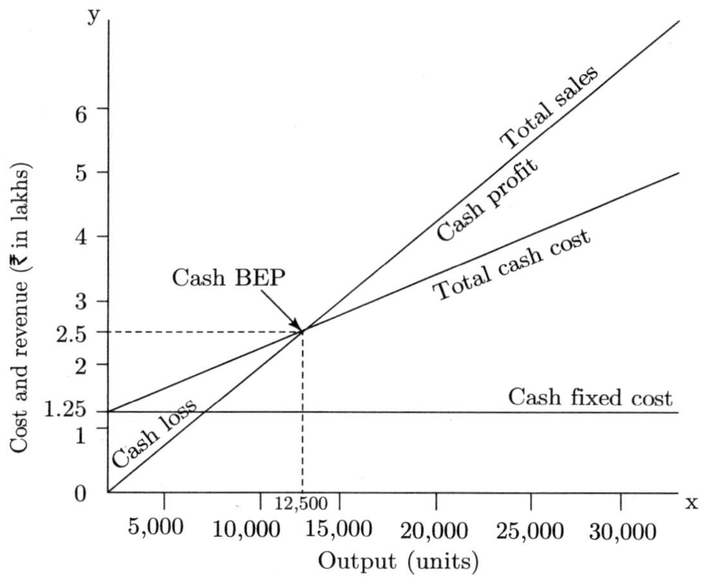

Cash break-even chart

(c) Control Break-even Chart

Controlling costs is one of the major aim of a management. Actual cost data and budgeted cost data are used for drawing control break-even chart. Control break-even chart helps to find the cost and profit variances.

Illustration-16

Draw a control break-even chart from the following information:

Budgeted variable cost	₹10
Budgeted selling price	₹20
Budgeted fixed cost	₹1,50,000
Actual variable cost	₹15
Actual selling price	₹25
Actual fixed cost	₹2,00,000

Solution

Prepare a table showing budgeted and actual costs and sales for various activity levels.

Output unit	Budgeted			Actual			
	Fixed cost ₹	Variable cost ₹	Total cost ₹	Fixed cost ₹	Variable cost ₹	Total cost ₹	Sales ₹
0	1,50,000	-	1,50,000	2,00,000	-	2,00,000	-
5,000	1,50,000	50,000	2,00,000	2,00,000	75,000	2,75,000	1,25,000
10,000	1,50,000	1,00,000	2,50,000	2,00,000	1,50,000	3,50,000	2,50,000
15,000	1,50,000	1,50,000	3,00,000	2,00,000	2,25,000	4,25,000	3,75,000
20,000	1,50,000	2,00,000	3,50,000	2,00,000	3,00,000	5,00,000	5,00,000
25,000	1,50,000	2,50,000	4,00,000	2,00,000	3,75,000	5,75,000	6,25,000
30,000	1,50,000	3,00,000	4,50,000	2,00,000	4,50,000	6,50,000	7,50,000

$$\text{Budgeted BEP (units)} = \frac{\text{Budgeted fixed cost}}{\text{Budgeted contribution p/u}}$$

$$= \frac{1{,}50{,}000}{10} = 15{,}000 \text{ units (or) ₹}3{,}00{,}000$$

$$\text{Actual BEP (units)} = \frac{\text{Actual fixed cost}}{\text{Actual contribution p/u}}$$

$$= \frac{2,00,000}{10} = 20{,}000 \text{ units (or) ₹}5{,}00{,}000$$

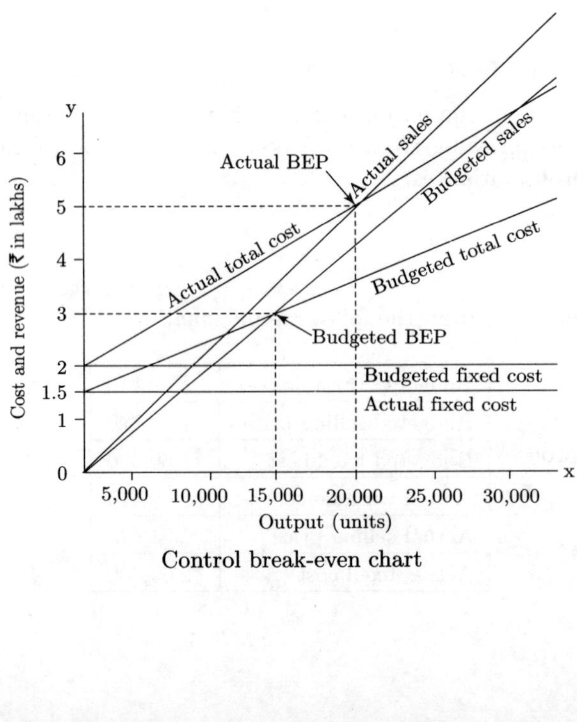

Control break-even chart

(d) Analytical Break-even Chart

Analytical break-even chart shows the details of marginal cost like direct materials, direct labour and variable overheads. The appropriation of profits like proposed dividend, transfer to reserves and balance in profit and loss accounts are shown. A model analytical break-even chart is shown below:

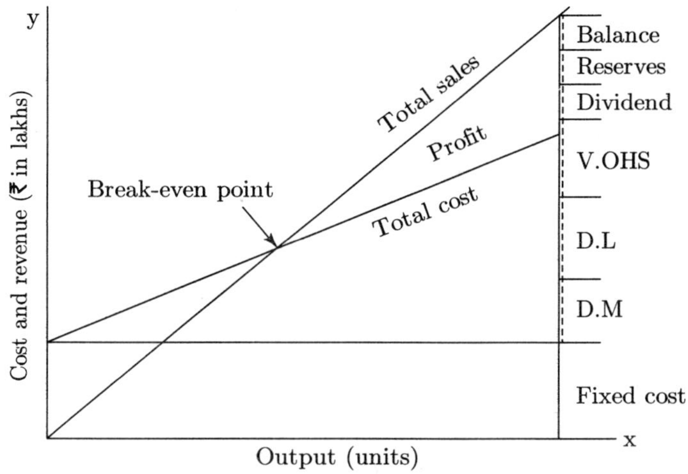

Analytical break-even chart

(e) Profit Break-even Chart/Profit/Volume (P/V) Graph

Profit break-even chart is a special graph. Profits and losses are plotted on the Y-axis. Sales revenue (₹)/Production (units) line is drawn horizontally starting at zero profit point in Y-axis. Then profits/losses at different activities are plotted and a straight line is drawn. The point where the profit line intersects sales/production line is called break-even point. The area between sales/product line and profit line below BEP is loss area. The area between sales line and profit line above BEP is profit area. This graph shows profit/loss at different activity levels. Taking the information in *Illustration-17*, let us draw a P/V graph.

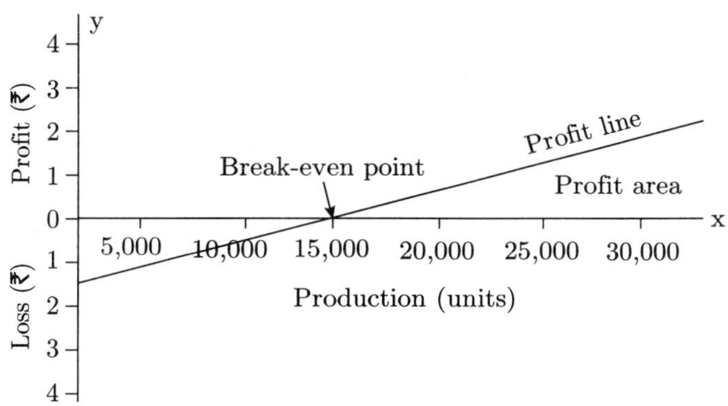

Profit break-even chart

(f) Product-wise Break-even Chart

Separate break-even charts may be prepared for each product in case of multi-product firms. It involves an arbitrary apportionment of fixed cost over different products.

19.3.2 Cost Break-Even Point/Indifference Point

Cost BEP is that level of activity at which total cost/profit of two options are same. Management can choose any of the options at this level. So this level is also called indifference point. If activity level is below indifference point, the option with lower fixed cost will be in a better position. If activity level is above the indifference point, the option with lower variable cost per unit (i.e. higher P/V ratio) will earn more profit. The following formulae are used for calculating indifference point:

(a) $\text{Indifference point (in ₹)} = \dfrac{\text{Difference in fixed cost}}{\text{\% Difference in variable cost}}$

$\text{or} = \dfrac{\text{Difference in Fixed Cost}}{\text{Difference in P/V Ratio}}$

(b) $\text{Indifference point (in units)} = \dfrac{\text{Difference in fixed cost}}{\text{Difference in variable cost per unit}}$

$\text{or} = \dfrac{\text{Difference in fixed cost}}{\text{Difference in contribution per unit}}$

Illustration-17

A Ltd. has two machines 'X' and 'Y' producing similar products. Their cost structure and other details are given below:

	Machine 'X'	Machine 'Y'
Full capacity	1,00,000 units	1,50,000 units
Fixed cost	₹1,50,000	₹4,00,000
Variable cost per unit	₹35	₹30
Selling price per unit	₹60	₹60

Required:

1. Calculate break-even point of each machinery
2. Calculate indifference point of these machineries
3. Evaluate the machineries when they produce and sell
   (a) 40,000 units and
   (b) 60,000 units.

Solution

1. Break-even point (in units)

$$= \frac{\text{Fixed cost}}{\text{Contribution per unit}}$$

$$\text{Machinery 'X'} = \frac{1,50,000}{25}$$

$$= 6,000 \text{ units}$$

$$\text{Machinery 'Y'} = \frac{4,00,000}{30}$$

$$= 13,333 \text{ units}$$

Note:

	Machine 'X' ₹	**Machine 'Y'** ₹
Selling price per unit	60	60
Less: Variable cost	35	30
Contribution per unit	25	30

2. Indifference point (in units)

$$= \frac{\text{Difference in fixed cost}}{\text{Difference in variable cost per unit}}$$

$$= \frac{2,50,000}{5}$$

$$= 50,000 \text{ units}$$

3. (a) Profitability if production is 40,000 units

Marginal Cost Statement

	Machine 'X' ₹	**Machine 'Y'** ₹
Sales (40,000 units × ₹60)	24,00,000	24,00,000
Less: Variable cost	14,00,000 (40,000 × 35)	12,00,000 (40,000 × 30)
Contribution	10,00,000	12,00,000
Less: Fixed cost	1,50,000	4,00,000
Profit	8,50,000	8,00,000

Ans: Machine 'X' is in better position because its fixed cost is lower.

So when production and sales is below the indifference point, the machine having lower fixed cost earns more profit.

(b) Profitability if production is 60,000 units

Marginal Cost Statement

	Machine 'X' ₹	Machine 'Y' ₹
Sales (60,000 units × ₹60)	36,00,000	36,00,000
Less: Variable cost	21,00,000 (60,000 × 35)	18,00,000 (60,000 × 30)
Contribution	15,00,000	18,00,000
Less: Fixed cost	1,50,000	4,00,000
Profit	13,50,000	14,00,000

Ans: Machine 'Y' earns more profit, because its variable cost per unit is lower.

When sales/production is above the indifference point, option with lower variable cost per unit will earn more profit.

The following is the summary of formulae and equations used in marginal costing technique:

1. Marginal Cost Equation

Sales – Variable cost = Contribution

Contribution = Fixed cost + Profit

Sales – Variable cost = Fixed cost + Profit

2. Contribution

(a) Contribution = Sales – Variable cost

(b) Contribution = Fixed cost + Profit/(–) Loss

(c) Contribution = Sales × P/V ratio

(d) $\text{Contribution} = \dfrac{\text{Profit}}{\text{MS Ratio}}$

3. P/V Ratio

(a) $\text{P/V ratio} = \dfrac{\text{Contribution}}{\text{Sales}} \times 100$

(b) $\text{P/V ratio} = \dfrac{\text{Contribution per unit}}{\text{Selling price per unit}} \times 100$

(c) $\text{P/V ratio} = \dfrac{\text{Changes in profit}}{\text{Changes in sales}} \times 100$

(d) $\text{P/V ratio} = \dfrac{\text{Fixed cost}}{\text{Break-even sales}} \times 100$

(e) $\text{P/V ratio} = 1 - \dfrac{\text{Variable cost}}{\text{Sales}} \times 100$

4. Break-even point

(a) $\text{Break-even point (units)} = \dfrac{\text{Fixed cost}}{\text{Contribution per unit}}$

(b) $\text{Break-even point (₹)} = \dfrac{\text{Fixed cost}}{\text{Contribution}} \times \text{Sales}$

(c) $\text{Break-even point (₹)} = \dfrac{\text{Fixed cost}}{\text{P/V Ratio}}$

5. Required sales for a desired profit

(a) $\text{Required sales (units)} = \dfrac{\text{Fixed cost + Desired profit}}{\text{Contribution per unit}}$

(b) $\text{Required sales (₹)} = \dfrac{\text{Fixed cost + Desired profit}}{\text{Contribution}} \times \text{Sales}$

(c) $\text{Required sales (₹)} = \dfrac{\text{Fixed Cost + Desired profit}}{\text{P/V Ratio}}$

6. Margin of safety

(a) MS Sales (₹) = Total sales − BEP sales

(b) $\text{MS Sales (₹)} = \dfrac{\text{Profit}}{\text{P/V Ratio}}$

(c) $\text{Margin of safety (Units)} = \dfrac{\text{Profit}}{\text{Contribution per unit}}$

(d) $\text{Margin of safety ratio (MS Ratio)} = \dfrac{\text{MS Sales}}{\text{Actual sales}} \times 100$

7. Fixed cost

(a) Fixed cost = Contribution − Profit

(b) Fixed cost = BEP Sales × P/V ratio

(c) Fixed cost = Sales × P/V ratio − Profit

8. Variable cost

(a) Variable cost = Sales − Contribution

(b) Variable cost = Sales × Complement of P/V ratio

9. Sales

(a) Sales = Total Cost + Profit/(−) Loss

(b) $\text{Sales} = \dfrac{\text{Contribution}}{\text{P/V ratio}}$

10. Profit

(a) Profit = Contribution − Fixed cost

(b) Profit = MS Sales × P/V ratio

(c) Profit = Sales × P/V ratio − Fixed cost

11. Indifference point/Cost BEP

(a) $\text{Indifference point (in ₹)} = \dfrac{\text{Difference in fixed cost}}{\text{\% Difference in variable cost}}$

$\text{or} = \dfrac{\text{Difference in fixed cost}}{\text{Difference in P/V ratio}}$

(b) $\text{Indifference point (in Units)} = \dfrac{\text{Difference in fixed cost}}{\text{Difference in variable cost per unit}}$

$\text{or} = \dfrac{\text{Difference in fixed cost}}{\text{Difference in contribution per unit}}$

19.4 APPLICATION OF MARGINAL COSTING TECHNIQUE

Management has to take many decisions involving production planning and profit planning. The following are the areas where the marginal costing technique helps the management:

1. Key factor or limiting factor
2. Shut down or continue
3. Profitable sales mix/product mix
4. Accepting orders at a price below total cost
5. Sell or process further
6. Fixing/alteration of selling price
7. Plant merger

8. Make or buy
9. Discontinuance of a product
10. Maintaining a desired level of profit

19.4.1 Key Factor or Limiting Factor

A firm may be producing two or more products. The firm has to limit the production and sales of the products due to certain limiting factors. In case of lack of demand for the firm's product, production is to be limited to the extent of sales potential. In some other cases some factors of production may be scarce like raw materials, skilled labour, power, finance etc. Then production is to be limited to the extent of scarce resources available. The basic question is—how much of each product is to be produced to maximise the profit of the firm.

In such situations, first calculate the contribution per unit of each product. Next, per unit contribution is to be converted into per unit contribution of limiting factor (i.e. limiting factor contribution). Then rank the products based on highest limiting factor contribution.

	Limiting Factors	Limiting Factor Contribution
1.	Sales demand in units (equal for all products)	Contribution per unit of products
2.	Sales demand in units (unequal demand for products)	Contribution per unit × no. of units (i.e. total contribution of each product)
3.	Sales demand (in value):	
	a) Sales value equal for all products	P/V ratio
	b) Sales value unequal for the products	Sales × P/V ratio (i.e. total contribution of each product)
4.	Power	Contribution per unit of power
5.	Raw materials:	
	a) Raw material quantity given	Contribution per unit of material
	b) Raw material value only given	% contribution on value of materials consumed
6.	Labour	Contribution per unit of labour time

Illustration-18

The following particulars are extracted from the records of a company:

	Product 'A' (per unit)	Product 'B' (per unit)
Sales	₹100	₹120
Consumption of materials	2 kg	3 kg

Materials cost	₹10	₹15
Direct wages cost	₹15	₹10
Direct expenses	₹5	₹6
Machine hours used	3 hours	2 hours
Overhead expenses:		
Fixed	₹5	₹10
Variable	₹15	₹20

Direct wages per hour is ₹5. Comment on the profitability of each product (both use the same raw material) when,

(i) Total sales potential in units is limited

(ii) Total sales potential in value is limited

(iii) Raw material is in short supply

(iv) Production capacity (in terms of machine hours) is the limiting factor.

Solution

Marginal Cost Statement

Particulars	₹	₹	**Product 'A' (per unit)** ₹	**Product 'B' (per unit)** ₹
Sales			100	120
Less: Variable cost				
Materials	10	15		
Direct wages	15	10		
Direct expenses	5	6		
Variable overheads	15	20	45	51
Contribution per unit			55	69
Contribution per kg of material			$\frac{55}{2}$=₹27.50	$\frac{69}{3}$= ₹23
Contribution per machine hour			$\frac{55}{3}$ ₹18.33	$\frac{69}{2}$ ₹34.50
P/V Ratio			55%	57.5%

Ranking of Products:		
(i) Sales potential in unit is limited (Basis - Contribution per unit)	Rank - II	Rank - I
(ii) Sales potential in value is limited (Basis - P/V ratio)	Rank - II	Rank - I
(iii) Raw material in short supply (Basis - contribution per kg. of material)	Rank - I	Rank - II
(iv) Production capacity (Machine hour) is limited (Basis - contribution per machine hour)	Rank - II	Rank - I

Illustration-19

From the following data, which product would you recommend to be manufactured in a factory, time being the key factor:

	Product 'A' (per unit) ₹	**Product 'B'** (per unit) ₹
Direct material	24	14
Direct labour at ₹1 per hour	2	3
Variable overheads at ₹2 per hour	4	6
Selling price	100	110
Standard time to produce	2 hours	3 hours

(B.Com., - Madras University)

Solution

Marginal Cost Statement

Particulars	₹	₹	**Product 'A'** (per unit) ₹	**Product 'B'** (per unit) ₹
Sales			100	110
Less: Variable cost				
Direct materials	24	14		
Direct labour	2	3		
Variable overheads	4	6	30	23

Contribution per unit	70	87
Contribution per hour	$\frac{70}{2}$ = ₹35	$\frac{87}{3}$ = ₹29

Ans: Contribution per unit is higher for Product 'B'. But contribution per unit of limiting factor—contribution per hour is higher for product 'A'. So product 'A' is more profitable and recommended for production.

Illustration-20

The following particulars are taken from the records of a company engaged in manufacturing two products—A and B, from a certain material:

	Product 'A' (per unit) ₹	Product 'B' (per unit) ₹
Sales	2,500	5,000
Materials cost (₹50 per kg)	500	1,250
Direct labour (₹30 per hour)	750	1,500
Variable overhead	250	500
Total fixed overheads	₹10,00,000	

Comment on the profitability of each product when,

(i) Total sales value is limited

(ii) Raw material is in short supply

(iii) Production capacity is a limiting factor.

(iv) Total availability of raw material is 20,000 kg and maximum sales potential of each product is 1,000 units, find the product mix to yield the maximum profit.

(ICWA-Inter)

Solution

Particulars	Product 'A' (per unit) ₹	₹	Product 'B' (per unit) ₹	₹
Sales		2,500		5,000
Less: Variable cost:				
Materials cost	500		1,250	
Direct labour	750		1,500	

Variable overheads	250	1,500	500	3,250
Contribution per unit		1,000		1,750
Contribution per kg of material	$\frac{1,000}{10} = ₹100$		$\frac{1,750}{25} = ₹70$	
Contribution per labour hour	$\frac{1,000}{25} = ₹40$		$\frac{1,750}{50} = ₹35$	
P/V Ratio $\left(\frac{C}{S} \times 100\right)$	40%		35%	

Ranking of Products:	Product A	Product B
(i) Total sales value is limiting factor (Basis - P/V ratio)	Rank - I	Rank - II
(ii) Raw material in short supply (Basis - contribution per kg. of raw material)	Rank - I	Rank - II
(iii) Production capacity is limiting factor (Basis - contribution per hour)	Rank - I	Rank - II

(iv) Product Mix

Product 'A' is more profitable when raw material is limiting factor. So first utilise the available material to produce product 'A' to the maximum (i.e. 1,000 units) and with balance materials available produce product 'B'.

	Total material available	20,000 kg
Less:	Material required for producing 1,000 units of product 'A' (1,000 units × 10 kg)	10,000 kg
	Balance material available for producing product 'B'	10,000 kg
	Number of units of product 'B' produced with 10,000 kg material	$\frac{10,000}{25} = 400$ units

Recommended product mix is:

Product 'A'	1,000 units
Product 'B'	400 units

19.4.2 Shutdown or Continue

Sometimes the business operations of a firm may be adversely affected due to economic slowdown or adverse market conditions. The firm may incur loss temporarily. In such a situation the firm has to decide whether to continue the business or shutdown completely or partially. Some fixed cost can be avoided by shutdown. But some additional costs are to be incurred like plant maintenance cost, retrenchment compensation or subsistence allowance to employees and re-opening expenses. If contribution earned is more or equal to avoidable fixed cost, it is better to continue the business. If contribution is less than the avoidable fixed cost, it is better to shutdown the business.

Apart from monetary considerations, the following non-monetary factors should also be considered:

(i) Losing the market to competitors.

(ii) Heavy sales promotion costs to regain the lost market.

(iii) Shut-down may affect the firm's image in the market.

(iv) Difficulty in recruitment of new employees.

(v) Relationship with clients and distributors may also be affected.

The following is the formula for calculating shut-down point.

$$\text{Shut-down point (in ₹)} = \frac{\text{Avoidable fixed cost}}{\text{P/V Ratio}}$$

$$\text{Shut-down point (in units)} = \frac{\text{Avoidable fixed cost}}{\text{Contribution per unit}}$$

Illustration-21

Due to adverse market conditions, a company is expected to operate at 30% of its capacity in the forthcoming year. Its full capacity is 10,000 units. Selling price is ₹25 per unit. Variable cost is ₹18. The present fixed cost of the firm is ₹60,000. If the firm shuts down its operations, there will be a saving of ₹35,000 in fixed cost and at the same time the firm has to incur additional expenses of ₹7,000 for reopening its operations. Calculate the shut-down point and advise the company as to whether it should continue or shut down its operations.

Solution

$$\text{Shut-down point (in units)} = \frac{\text{Avoidable fixed cost}}{\text{Contribution per unit}}$$

$$= \frac{28{,}000}{7} = 4{,}000 \text{ units}$$

Marginal Cost Statement

	Expected level of operation (3,000 units) ₹	**Shut-down point** (4,000 units) ₹
Sales - ₹25 per unit	75,000	1,00,000

Less:		
Variable cost (₹18 per unit)	54,000	72,000
Contribution	21,000	28,000
Present fixed cost	60,000	-
Shut-down fixed cost	-	32,000
Loss	(39,000)	(4,000)

Advice: The firm is operating below the shut-down point. If it shuts down its operations it can avoid a loss of ₹35,000 (i.e. 39,000 – 4,000).

Working Note

1.

Shut-down fixed cost:	₹
Present fixed cost	60,000
Less: Savings in fixed cost	35,000
	25,000
Add: Additional cost	7,000
	32,000

2.

Avoidable fixed cost:	₹
Savings in fixed cost	35,000
Less: Additional fixed cost	7,000
Avoidable fixed cost	28,000

3. Contribution per unit = Selling price per unit – Variable cost per unit
= 25 – 18 = ₹7

19.4.3 Profitable Sales Mix/Product Mix

A company may produce two or more products. Then the company has to decide the amount of sales of each product in the total sales to maximise the company's profit. Compute the P/V Ratio of each product. The sales of the products having highest P/V Ratio should be increased. The product having low P/V Ratio should be discontinued, if possible or reduce the sales of that product to the extent of minimum commitment in the market.

Illustration-22

The following set of information is presented to you by your client AB Ltd., producing two products X and Y.

	X	Y
1. Direct materials per unit (₹)	20	18
2. Direct wages per unit (₹)	6	4
3. Sale price per unit (₹)	40	30

4. Fixed overheads during the period is expected to be ₹1,600. Variable overheads recovered at 100% of direct wages.

5. Proposed sales mix:

(i) 100 units of X and 200 units of Y

(ii) 150 units of X and 150 units of Y

(iii) 200 units of X and 100 units of Y

As a cost accountant you are requested to present to the management of AB Ltd., the following:

(a) The unit marginal cost and unit contribution

(b) The total contribution and the resultant profit from each of the above sales mixes.

(c) The proposed sales mixes to earn a profit of ₹300 and ₹600 with the total sales of X and Y being 300 units. **(ICWA-Inter)**

Solution

(a) Statement showing marginal cost and contribution per unit

	Product 'X' (per unit) ₹	Product 'Y' (per unit) ₹
Selling price	40	30
Marginal cost:		
Direct material	20	18
Direct wages	6	4
Variable overhead	6	4
Total	32	26
Contribution	8	4

(b) Statement showing profitability of each sales mix

Sales Mix (i)

	X (100 units) ₹	Y (200 units) ₹	Total (300 units) ₹
Total contribution	800	800	1,600
Less: Fixed cost	-	-	1,600
Profit			Nil

Sales Mix (ii)

	X (150 units) ₹	Y (150 units) ₹	Total (300 units) ₹
Total contribution	1,200	600	1,800
Less: Fixed cost	-	-	1,600
Profit			200

Sales Mix (iii)

	X (200 units) ₹	Y (100 units) ₹	Total (300 units) ₹
Total contribution	1,600	400	2,000
Less: Fixed cost	-	-	1,600
Profit			400

(c) Case (i) Proposed sales mix to earn a profit of ₹300

$$\text{Let the number of units of product X be} = p$$

$$\text{Then number of Y units sold} = 300 - p$$

$$\text{Total contribution} = \text{Fixed cost} + \text{Profit}$$

$$= 1{,}600 + 300$$

$$= ₹1{,}900$$

(or)

$$\text{Total contribution} = \text{Contribution of X} + \text{Contribution of Y}$$
$$1{,}900 = p \times 8 + (300 - p)4$$
$$1{,}900 = 8p + 1{,}200 - 4p$$
$$4p = 700$$
$$p = \frac{700}{4}$$
$$= 175 \text{ units}$$
$$\text{No. of units of product Y} = 300 - 175$$
$$= 125 \text{ units}$$

Sales Mix:

No. of units – X = 175 units and Y = 125 units

Case (ii)

Let the number of units of product X be = p

$$\text{Then total units of product Y} = 300 - p$$
$$\text{Total contribution} = \text{Fixed cost} + \text{Profit}$$
$$= 1{,}600 + 600$$
$$= ₹2{,}200$$

$$\text{Total contribution} = \text{Contribution of X} + \text{Contribution of Y}$$
$$2{,}200 = p \times 8 + (300 - p)4$$
$$2{,}200 = 8p + 1{,}200 - 4p$$
$$4p = 1{,}000$$
$$p = \frac{1{,}000}{4}$$
$$= 250 \text{ units}$$
$$\text{No. of units of product Y} = 300 - 250$$
$$= 50 \text{ units}$$

Sales Mix:

No. of units – product X = 250 units and product Y = 50 units

Illustration-23

Vijendra Hard Chrome Products manufactures and sells 4 types of products under the brand names of A, B, C and D.

The sales mix in the value comprises $33\frac{1}{3}\%$, $41\frac{2}{3}\%$, $16\frac{2}{3}\%$ and $8\frac{1}{3}\%$ of A, B, C and D respectively. The total budgeted sales are ₹60,000 per month.

Operating costs of the enterprise are as follows :

Product A	60% of sale price
Product B	68% of sale price
Product C	80% of sale price
Product D	40% of sale price
Fixed cost	₹14,700 per month

The firm proposes to change the sales mix for the next month as follows and it is estimated that the total sales would be maintained at the same level as in the current month:

Product A	25%
Product B	40%
Product C	30%
Product D	5%

You are required to calculate:

(i) Break-even point for the products on an overall basis for the current month;

(ii) Break-even point for the products on an overall basis for the next month assuming that the proposal is implemented; and

(iii) Explain the shift in the break-even point to a new position.

(B.Com. (Hons.), Delhi University)

Solution

(i)

Marginal Cost Statement - Current month sales mix

	Products				Total
	A	B	C	D	
% of sales mix	$33\frac{1}{3}\%$	$41\frac{2}{3}\%$	$16\frac{2}{3}\%$	$8\frac{1}{3}\%$	100%
Sales (₹)	20,000	25,000	10,000	5,000	60,000
Operating cost (Variable cost) (₹)	12,000	17,000	8,000	2,000	39,000
Total contribution (₹)					21,000
Less: Fixed cost (₹)					14,700
Profit (₹)					6,300

$$\text{P/V ratio} = \frac{21{,}000}{60{,}000} \times 100$$

$$= 35\%$$

$$\text{Current month BEP (₹)} = \frac{\text{Fixed cost}}{\text{P/V ratio}}$$

$$= \frac{14{,}700}{35\%} = ₹42{,}000$$

(ii)

Marginal Cost Statement - Next month					
	Products				Total
	A	B	C	D	
% of revised sales mix	25%	40%	30%	5%	100%
Sales (₹)	15,000	24,000	18,000	3,000	60,000
Variable cost (₹)	9,000	16,320	14,400	1,200	40,920
Total contribution (₹)					19,080
Less: Fixed cost (₹)					14,700
Profit (₹)					4,380

$$\text{P/V ratio} = \frac{19{,}080}{60{,}000} \times 100$$

$$= 31.8\%$$

$$\text{Current month BEP (₹)} = \frac{\text{Fixed cost}}{\text{P/V ratio}}$$

$$= \frac{14{,}700}{31.8\%} = ₹46{,}226$$

(iii)

Reason for increase in BEP				
	Products			
	A	B	C	D
P/V Ratio (complement to variable cost ratio)	40%	32%	20%	80%
Current month sales mix	$33\frac{1}{3}\%$	$41\frac{2}{3}\%$	$16\frac{2}{3}\%$	$8\frac{1}{3}\%$

Next month sales mix	25%	40%	30%	5%
Change in sales mix	$(-)8\frac{1}{3}\%$	$(-)1\frac{2}{3}\%$	$(+)13\frac{1}{3}\%$	$(-)3\frac{1}{3}\%$

The sales of product C whose P/V ratio is the lowest increases but the sales of products A, B and D whose P/V ratios are higher than that of C, decreases. This is the reason for increase in BEP.

Illustration-24

SI Industries manufactures three products: P, Q and R. The projected figures as per the budget are as under:

Product	Sales value (₹)	P/V Ratio (%)
P	6,00,000	40
Q	10,00,000	30
R	24,00,000	50

The fixed overheads for the corresponding period are estimated at ₹19,14,000.

You are required to prepare a statement showing projected loss, if any, on the basis of the above information, suggest to the management the change in the volume of sales for each product assuming the same sales mix as considered in the budget in order to eliminate the loss.

Solution

Marginal Cost Statement for Budgeted Sales mix

Product	Sales value (₹)	Sales mix (%)	P/V ratio (%)	Contribution (₹)
P	6,00,000	$\frac{6,00,000}{40,00,000} \times 100 = 15$	40	2,40,000
Q	10,00,000	$\frac{10,00,000}{40,00,000} \times 100 = 25$	30	3,00,000
R	24,00,000	$\frac{24,00,000}{40,00,000} \times 100 = 60$	50	12,00,000
	40,00,000	100	-	17,40,000
Less: Fixed expenses				19,14,000
Loss				1,74,000

Additional contribution required from each product for no loss:

$$\text{Product P - } 1{,}74{,}000 \times \frac{15}{100} = ₹26{,}100$$

$$\text{Product Q - } 1{,}74{,}000 \times \frac{25}{100} = ₹43{,}500$$

$$\text{Product R - } 1{,}74{,}000 \times \frac{60}{100} = ₹1{,}04{,}400$$

$$\text{Total} = ₹1{,}74{,}000$$

Additional sales value required for no loss:

$$= \frac{\text{Contribution}}{\text{P/V ratio}}$$

$$\text{Product P - } \frac{26{,}100}{40\%} = ₹65{,}250$$

$$\text{Product Q - } \frac{43{,}500}{30\%} = ₹1{,}45{,}000$$

$$\text{Product R - } \frac{1{,}04{,}400}{50\%} = ₹2{,}08{,}800$$

$$\text{Total} = ₹4{,}19{,}050$$

19.4.4 Accepting Orders at a Price Below the Total Cost

Normally a firm will sell its products at a price which will recover the total cost and earn a desired profit on capital employed. Sometimes a firm may be operating below its capacity. In such situations a bulk order from a new customer, an order from government departments or order from a foreign buyer may be received at a price below the normal selling price or even below the total cost. Under absorption costing, the firm will reject the order saying that it will bring loss to the firm. Under marginal costing the firm may decide to accept the order if the price offered is more than the variable cost or at least equal to the variable cost. The reason for this decision is:

(a) Goods are produced only utilizing spare capacity available,

(b) There will be no fixed costs for this additional production. Only variable costs are incurred.

(c) Accepting the special orders will not affect the price in its regular market.

Illustration-25

Due to economic slow down, a firm is producing and selling 25,000 units which is only 50% of its full capacity.

The present cost details are as follows: Raw materials per unit ₹5, Direct labour ₹4 per unit, Direct expenses ₹3. Variable overheads per unit ₹4 and fixed costs ₹5 per unit. Total cost per unit ₹21. The goods are sold in the local market at ₹26 per unit.

The firm receives an export order for 20,000 units at a price of ₹17.50. Since the price is below the total cost, the firm hesitates to accept the order fearing that this order will result in loss.

As a cost accountant advise the firm about the viability of accepting the export order and also state the minimum price the firm may quote for the export order at no profit or no loss basis.

Solution

Detailed Marginal Cost Statement

Particulars	Local Market (25,000 units) ₹	Export Market (20,000 units) ₹	Total (45,000 units) ₹
Sales (A)	6,50,000 (25,000 × 26)	3,50,000 (20,000 × 17.5)	10,00,000
Variable costs:			
Raw material (₹5 per unit)	1,25,000	1,00,000	2,25,000
Direct labour (₹4 per unit)	1,00,000	80,000	1,80,000
Direct expenses (₹3 per unit)	75,000	60,000	1,35,000
Variable overheads (₹4 per unit)	1,00,000	80,000	1,80,000
Total (B)	4,00,000	3,20,000	7,20,000
Contribution (A – B)	2,50,000	30,000	2,80,000
Less: Fixed cost (25,000 × 5)	1,25,000	-	1,25,000
Profit	1,25,000	30,000	1,55,000

The export order should be accepted because it brings an additional profit of ₹30,000.

The minimum price that the firm may quote for the export order is ₹16, equal to the variable cost.

Illustration-26

A company manufacturing electric motors at a price of ₹6,900 each, is made up as follows:

	₹
Direct materials	3,200
Direct labour	400
Variable overheads	1,000
Fixed overheads	200

Depreciation	200
Variable selling overheads	100
Royalty	200
Profit	1,000
Net price	6,300
Central excise duty	600
Total price	6,900

(i) A foreign buyer has offered to buy 200 such motors at ₹5,000 each. As a cost accountant of the company would you advise the acceptance of the offer?

(ii) What should the company quote for a motor to be purchased by a company under the same management if it should be at cost?

Solution

(i)

Marginal Cost statement for export order		
		₹
Export price (per unit)		5,000
Less: Variable cost:		
Direct materials	3,200	
Direct labour	400	
Variable overheads	1,000	
Royalty	200	4,800
Contribution		200

The foreign order is profitable and it may be accepted. Additional contribution per unit is ₹200. So the total contribution will increase by ₹40,000 (i.e. 200 × 200).

Note:

Assumptions

1. No additional fixed cost is incurred for the export order.
2. Depreciation is charged on time basis, hence fixed cost.
3. Excise duty is not levied on export sales.
4. No selling overhead is incurred for export order.
5. Royalty is payable on production basis.

(ii) Supply at cost price to a company under the same management:

	₹
Direct materials	3,200
Direct labour	400
Variable overheads	1,000
Depreciation	200
Fixed overheads	200
Excise duty	600
Royalty	200
	5,800

Price to be quoted at cost = ₹5,800.

Fixing price at below marginal cost

The following are some special circumstances where a firm may decide to sell its products even below the variable cost for a short period:

1. Severe economic recessionary condition.
2. Utilisation of existing inventory of surplus raw material, if sale of raw material may result in more loss.
3. To meet cut-throat competition.
4. Introduction of a new product in the market.
5. Introduction of the existing product in a new market.
6. Distribution of limited quantity of a new product as a sales promotion activity.

Sales at a price below the variable cost cannot be made for a longer period or on a regular basis.

19.4.5 Sell or Process Further

Certain raw materials pass through different distinct stages of production. The product may be sold after the final stage of production.

The product, which is in a semi-finished condition, may have market at the end of any of the intermediary stages of production. Now the management has to decide whether the product should be sold at any of the intermediary stage or should be further processed and sold at final stage only. If the additional revenue generated is more than the additional cost of further processing, the product should be sold after further processing. (*See* chapter Joint Products and By-products)

19.4.6 Fixation and Alteration of Selling Price

Fixation of selling price is an important function of management. Correct pricing is important for survival of a business. The price should recover the total cost and earn a reasonable profit on the capital employed. The price, once fixed, has to be either increased or reduced due to change in economic conditions like economic recession or boom, to meet the competition from other producers, change in the cost of production etc.

Before changing the price, the management has to consider the price fixed by competitors, the market conditions and the effect on sales volume and profit.

Illustration-27

A factory engaged in manufacturing plastic buckets is working at 40% capacity and produces 10,000 buckets p.a. The present cost break-up for one bucket is materials ₹10, labour ₹3, and overheads ₹5 (60% is fixed).

The selling price per bucket is ₹20. If it is decided to work the factory at 50% capacity, the selling price falls by 3%. At 90% capacity, the selling price falls by 5%, accompanied by a similar fall in the price of materials.

Calculate the profit at 50% and 90% capacities and also the BEP at those capacity productions.

(CA-Inter)

Solution

Marginal Cost Statement				
	50% capacity (12,500 units)		90% capacity (22,500 units)	
	Per unit (₹)	Total (₹)	Per unit (₹)	Total (₹)
Sales	19.40	2,42,500	19.00	4,27,500
Less: Variable costs				
Material	10.00	1,25,000	9.50	2,13,750
Wages	3.00	37,500	3.00	67,500
Variable overheads (40%)	2.00	25,000	2.00	45,000
Contribution	4.40	55,000	4.50	1,01,250
Fixed overheads				
(₹3 × 10,000 units)	-	30,000	-	30,000
Profit	-	25,000	-	71,250

$$\text{Break-even point (in units)} = \frac{\text{Fixed cost}}{\text{Contribution per unit}}$$

$$\text{At 50\% capacity} = \frac{30{,}000}{4.40} = 6{,}818 \text{ units}$$

$$(\text{or}) = ₹1{,}32{,}270 \text{ (i.e. } 6{,}818 \times ₹19.40)$$

$$\text{At } 90\% \text{ capacity} = \frac{30{,}000}{4.50}$$

$$= 6{,}667 \text{ units}$$

$$(\text{or}) = ₹1{,}26{,}673 \text{ (i.e. } 6{,}667 \times ₹19)$$

Illustration-28

The following figures are extracted from the books of a manufacturing concern for the year 2011-2012:

Production and sales	20,000 units
Direct materials	₹12 per unit
Direct wages	₹8 per unit
Variable overheads	₹5 per unit
Selling price	₹30 per unit
Fixed cost	₹40,000

The company makes the following two proposals:

(a) Increase in selling price by 10% followed by 10% decrease in sales volume in units.

(b) Decrease in selling price by 10% followed by 15% increase in sales volume in units.

Find the effect on profit of the above proposals.

Solution

Marginal Cost Statement

Particulars	**Present**	**Proposal (a)**	**Proposal (b)**
No. of units	20,000	18,000	23,000
Selling price per unit (₹)	30.00	33.00	27.00
Total sales (₹) (A)	6,00,000	5,94,000	6,21,000
Less: Variable cost:			
Direct materials (₹12 per unit)	2,40,000	2,16,000	2,76,000
Direct wages (₹8 per unit)	1,60,000	1,44,000	1,84,000
Variable overheads (₹5 per unit)	1,00,000	90,000	1,15,000
Total (B)	5,00,000	4,50,000	5,75,000
Contribution (A – B)	1,00,000	1,44,000	46,000
Less: Fixed cost	40,000	40,000	40,000
Profit	60,000	1,04,000	6,000

Illustration-29

You are given the following data for a company for the year 2011-12:

Direct Materials	₹20 per unit
Direct Labour	₹16 per unit
Variable overheads	₹12 per unit
Selling price	₹65 per unit
Fixed cost	₹90,000
Sales volume	10,000 units

Find the new selling price if the company wants to maintain the present profit in the following two situations:

(a) Sales volume increases to 13,000 units and

(b) Sales volume decreases to 8,500 units

Solution

Marginal Cost Statement - Present		
		₹
Sales (10,000 units × ₹65)		6,50,000
Less: Variable cost:		
Direct materials (20 × 10,000)	2,00,000	
Direct labour (16 × 10,000)	1,60,000	
Variable overheads (12 × 10,000)	1,20,000	4,80,000
Contribution		1,70,000
Less: Fixed cost		90,000
Profit		80,000

Statement showing new selling price		
	Situation (a) (13,000 units) ₹	**Situation (b) (8,500 units)** ₹
Variable cost:		
Direct materials (₹20 per unit)	2,60,000	1,70,000
Direct labour (₹16 per unit)	2,08,000	1,36,000
Variable overheads (₹12 per unit)	1,56,000	1,02,000

Total variable cost	6,24,000	4,08,000
Fixed overheads	90,000	90,000
Total cost	7,14,000	4,98,000
Profit desired	80,000	80,000
Total sales	7,94,000	5,78,000
Selling price per unit	$\frac{7,94,000}{13,000}$ = ₹61.08	$\frac{5,78,000}{8,500}$ = ₹68

19.4.7 Plant Merger

A company may have two or more production facilities at different places. The fixed cost and variable cost of the factories may differ from one another. The factories may also be operating at different capacity levels. The management may want to know the break-even point, P/V ratio and margin of safety of all plants put together. Find the sales of each plant at 100% capacity level and total it. Also deduct the total variable cost of all plants at 100% capacity from the total sales. We get the total contribution at 100% capacity level. Now calculate P/V ratio, break-even point and margin of safety.

Illustration-30

A Ltd. and B Ltd. operating in same business decide to merge and form a new company AB Ltd. The following details are extracted from the two companies:

	A Ltd. ₹	**B Ltd.** ₹
Sales	25,00,000	18,00,000
Variable costs	15,00,000	10,00,000
Fixed costs	6,00,000	2,00,000
Capacity of operation	90%	75%

You are required to calculate:

(i) Break-even sales and break capacity of AB Ltd.

(ii) Profit of AB Ltd. when it operates at 80% capacity.

(iii) Sales and capacity level if the company AB Ltd. wants to earn profit equal to the profits of A Ltd. and B Ltd.

Solution

Marginal Cost Statement			
	A Ltd. ₹	B Ltd. ₹	AB Ltd.
Sales at 100% capacity	27,77,778	24,00,000	51,77,778
Less: Variable cost at 100% capacity	16,66,667	13,33,333	30,00,000
Contribution	11,11,111	10,66,667	21,77,778
Less: Fixed cost	6,00,000	2,00,000	8,00,000
Profit	5,11,111	8,66,667	13,77,778
P/V ratio	$\frac{11,11,111}{27,77,778} \times 100 = 40\%$	$\frac{10,66,667}{24,00,000} \times 100 = 44.44\%$	$\frac{21,77,778}{51,77,778} \times 100 = 42.06\%$

(i) Break-even sales of AB Ltd $= \dfrac{\text{Fixed cost}}{\text{P/V ratio}}$

$$= \frac{8,00,000}{42.06\%}$$

$$= ₹19,02,045$$

$$\text{Break-even capacity} = \frac{19,02,045}{51,77,778} \times 100$$

$$= 36.73\%$$

(ii) Profit when AB Ltd. operates at 80% capacity

$$\text{Profit} = 80\% \text{ capacity sales} \times \text{P/V ratio} - \text{Fixed cost}$$

$$= 51,77,778 \times \frac{80}{100} \times \frac{42.06}{100} - 8,00,000$$

$$= ₹9,42,219$$

(iii) Required sales to earn a profit of ₹10,00,000 (i.e. 4,00,000 + ₹6,00,000) (See WN-3)

$$= \frac{\text{Fixed cost} + \text{Desired profit}}{\text{P/V ratio}}$$

$$= \frac{8,00,000 + 10,00,000}{42.06\%}$$

$$= ₹42,79,600$$

$$\text{Capacity level} = \frac{42,79,600}{51,77,778} \times 100$$

$$= 82.65\%$$

Working Note

1. Sales at 100% capacity

$$\text{A Ltd.} = 25{,}00{,}000 \times \frac{100}{90}$$
$$= ₹27{,}77{,}778$$

$$\text{B Ltd.} = 18{,}00{,}000 \times \frac{100}{75}$$
$$= ₹24{,}00{,}000$$

2. Variable Cost at 100% capacity

$$\text{A Ltd.} = 15{,}00{,}000 \times \frac{100}{90}$$
$$= ₹16{,}66{,}667$$

$$\text{B Ltd.} = 10{,}00{,}000 \times \frac{100}{75}$$
$$= ₹13{,}33{,}333$$

3. Profits of A Ltd. and B Ltd.

	A Ltd. ₹	**B Ltd.** ₹
Sales	25,00,000	18,00,000
Less: Variable cost	15,00,000	10,00,000
Contribution	10,00,000	8,00,000
Less: Fixed Cost	6,00,000	2,00,000
Profit	4,00,000	6,00,000

Illustration-31

A company has two plants at location I and II, operating at 100% and 75% of their capacities respectively. The company is considering the proposal to merge the two plants at one location to optimise available capacity. The following details are available in respect of the two plants, regarding their present performance/operations:

	Location I	**Location II**
Sales (₹ in lakhs)	200	75
Variable cost (₹ in lakhs)	140	54
Fixed cost (₹ in lakhs)	30	14

For decision making purposes you are required to work out the following information:

(a) The capacity at which the merged plant will break-even.

(b) The profit of the merged plant working at 80% capacity.

(c) Sales required if the merged plant is required to earn an overall profit of ₹22 lakhs.

(ICWA-Inter)

Solution

Marginal Cost Statement (₹ in lakhs)			
Particulars	**Plant I at 100% capacity** ₹	**Plant II at 100% capacity** ₹	**Merged Plant at 100% capacity** ₹
Sales	200	100	300
Less: Variable cost	140	72	212
Contribution	60	28	88
Less: Fixed cost	30	14	44
Profit	30	14	44
P/V ratio	$\frac{60}{200} \times 100 = 30\%$	$\frac{28}{100} \times 100 = 28\%$	$\frac{88}{300} \times 100 = 29.33\%$

(a) $$\text{Break-even sales} = \frac{\text{Fixed cost}}{\text{P/V ratio}} = \frac{44}{29.33\%} = ₹150 \text{ lakhs}$$

$$\text{\% of BEP capacity} = \frac{150}{300} \times 100 = 50\%$$

(b) The profit when merged plant operates at 80% capacity

$$\text{Sales at 80\% capacity (₹ in lakhs)} - \left(300 \times \frac{80}{100}\right) = 240.00$$

$$\textbf{Less: } \text{Variable cost at 80\% capacity (₹ in lakhs)} - \left(212 \times \frac{80}{100}\right) = \underline{169.60}$$

Contribution = 70.40

Less: Fixed cost = 44.00

Profit (₹ in lakhs) = 26.40

(c) Sales required from merged plant to earn a profit of ₹22 lakh

$$\text{Required sales} = \frac{\text{Fixed cost} + \text{Desired profit}}{\text{P/V ratio}}$$

$$= \frac{44 + 22}{29.33\%} = ₹225 \text{ lakh}$$

Working Note

1. Sales of plant II at 100% capacity $= 75 \times \frac{100}{75} =$ ₹100 lakh

2. Variable cost of plant II at 100% capacity $= 54 \times \frac{100}{75} =$ ₹72 lakh

19.4.8 Make or Buy

A manufacturer of capital goods, vehicles, computers etc., may need many component parts for fitting in the final product. The manufacturer may not produce all the component parts required. So he has to decide what component parts are to be produced internally and what component parts are to be purchased from outside suppliers. The following factors should be considered while making the decision:

I. Cost Factors

1. If the market price of the component is lower than the variable cost of production, it is better to buy from the market.

2. If the market price of the component is higher than the variable cost of production, it is better to produce internally.

   Other cost factors are:

   (a) Utilisation of spare capacity

   (b) Employment of surplus labour

   (c) Additional capital required and additional production facilities available, in case the company decides to produce the component.

   (d) If special technical know-how is used for producing a component, the component should be produced locally to safeguard the secrecy of technical know-how.

   (e) Certain components are to be purchased from suppliers for want of technical know-how or small scale of operation, e.g., tyres and tubes, batteries etc. fitted in a car.

II. Non-Cost Factors

1. Quality of component purchased from suppliers.

2. The capacity and reliability of suppliers as to regular and timely supply of components.

3. Fluctuation in quantity of components required due to seasonal factors.

4. Agreement with trade unions.

Illustration-32

A manufacturing company finds that while the cost of making a component part is ₹10, the same is available in the market at ₹9 with an assurance of continuous supply. Give your suggestion whether to make or buy the component. Give also your views in case the supplier reduces the price from ₹9 to ₹8. The cost information is as follows:

	₹
Materials	3.50
Direct labour	4.00
Other variable expenses	1.00
Fixed expenses	1.50
	10.00

(B.Com., Madras University)

Solution

Variable cost of manufacturing	
	₹
Materials	3.50
Direct labour	4.00
Other variable expenses	1.00
	8.50

Decision - Market Price ₹9.00
The cost of production is lower than the market price. It is profitable to produce the component. Production will give a contribution of ₹0.50 per unit.

Decision - Market Price ₹8.00
The cost of production is higher than the market price. It is profitable to buy the component.

Note: In case of decision to produce, if the fixed cost increases due to the increased production facility, the increase in fixed cost should also be considered for decision making.

Illustration-33

An automobile manufacturing company finds that while the cost of making in its own workshop, Part No. 0028 is ₹6.00 each, the same is available in market at ₹5.60 with an assurance of continuous supply. Write a report to the Managing Director giving your views whether to make or buy this part. Give also your views in case the supplier reduces the price from ₹5.60 to ₹4.60. The cost data is as follows:

	₹
Materials	2.00
Direct labour	2.50
Other variable expenses	0.50
Depreciation and other fixed costs	1.00
	6.00

(B.Com., Madras University)

Solution

Variable Cost of Part No. 0028	
	₹
Materials	2.00
Direct labour	2.50
Other variable expenses	0.50
	5.00

(i) If market price is ₹5.60:

Market price is higher than the variable cost of manufacture. So it is profitable to produce the product in the company. There will be a savings of ₹0.60 per unit (i.e. ₹5.60 – 5.00).

(ii) If the market price is ₹4.60:

Market price is lower than the variable cost of manufacture. So it is profitable to buy from the market. There will be a savings of ₹0.40 per unit (i.e. ₹5.00 – 4.60).

19.4.9 Discontinuance of a Product

In case of a multi-product company, some products may be highly profitable, some products may be less profitable and there may be negative contribution from a product. Then the management has to take cost control measures to improve the contribution. If this is not possible, the product giving negative contribution should be discontinued. The idle production facility may be utilised to increase the production of other products or may be let out to other producers. Similarly if there is a possibility of introducing a new product with higher contribution, the product with lower contribution may also be discontinued.

Illustration-34

The cost per unit of three products, A, B and C of a company are given below:

Particulars	Products A ₹	B ₹	C ₹
Direct materials	20	16	18
Direct labour	12	14	12
Variable expenses	8	10	6
Fixed expenses	6	6	4
Total cost	46	46	40
Profit	18	14	12
Sales	64	60	52
No. of units produced	10,000	5,000	8,000

Production arrangements are such that if one product is given up, the production of others can be raised by 50%. The directors propose that C should be given up because contribution from that product is the lowest. Present suitable analysis of the data indicating whether the proposal should be accepted. **(B.Com., Madras University)**

Solution

Marginal Cost Statement - Present

Particulars	Products A (10,000 units) ₹	B (5,000 units) ₹	C (8,000 units) ₹	Total ₹
Sales (A)	6,40,000	3,00,000	4,16,000	13,56,000
Less: Variable costs				
Direct materials	2,00,000	80,000	1,44,000	4,24,000
Direct labour	1,20,000	70,000	96,000	2,86,000
Variable expenses	80,000	50,000	48,000	1,78,000
Total (B)	4,00,000	2,00,000	2,88,000	8,88,000
Contribution (A – B)	2,40,000	1,00,000	1,28,000	4,68,000
Less: Fixed cost	-	-	-	1,22,000
Profit	-	-	-	3,46,000

Note:

Fixed Cost

A = 10,000 × 6 = ₹60,000

B = 5,000 × 6 = ₹30,000

C = 8,000 × 4 = ₹32,000

Total = ₹1,22,000

Marginal cost statement - if product A is discontinued			
Particulars	**Products**		**Total**
	B (7,500 units) ₹	**C (12,000 units)** ₹	₹
Sales (A)	4,50,000	6,24,000	10,74,000
Less: Variable cost			
Direct materials	1,20,000	2,16,000	3,36,000
Direct labour	1,05,000	1,44,000	2,49,000
Variable expenses	75,000	72,000	1,47,000
Total 'B'	3,00,000	4,32,000	7,32,000
Contribution (A – B)	1,50,000	1,92,000	3,42,000
Less: Fixed cost			1,22,000
Profit	-	-	2,20,000

Marginal cost statement - if product B is discontinued			
Particulars	**Products**		**Total**
	A (15,000 units) ₹	**C (12,000 units)** ₹	₹
Sales (A)	9,60,000	6,24,000	15,84,000
Less: Variable cost			
Direct materials	3,00,000	2,16,000	5,16,000
Direct labour	1,80,000	1,44,000	3,24,000
Variable expenses	1,20,000	72,000	1,92,000
Total 'B'	6,00,000	4,32,000	10,32,000
Contribution (A – B)	3,60,000	1,92,000	5,52,000
Less: Fixed cost	-	-	1,22,000
Profit	-	-	4,30,000

Marginal cost statement - if product C is discontinued			
Particulars	**Products**		**Total**
	A (15,000 units)	**B (7,500 units)**	
	₹	₹	₹
Sales (A)	9,60,000	4,50,000	14,10,000
Less: Variable cost			
Direct materials	3,00,000	1,20,000	4,20,000
Direct labour	1,80,000	1,05,000	2,85,000
Variable expenses	1,20,000	75,000	1,95,000
Total 'B'	6,00,000	3,00,000	9,00,000
Contribution (A - B)	3,60,000	1,50,000	5,10,000
Less: Fixed cost	-	-	1,22,000
Profit	-	-	3,88,000

Answer:

Profit is higher when product 'B' is discontinued. So product C should not be discontinued, product B may be discontinued.

Illustration-35

A limited company manufactures three different products and the following information has been collected from the books of accounts:

	Products		
	S	**T**	**Y**
Sales mix	35%	35%	30%
Selling price per unit (₹)	30	40	20
Variable cost per unit (₹)	15	20	12

The company has currently under discussion, a proposal to discontinue the manufacture of product Y and replace it with product M, when the following results are anticipated:

	Products		
	S	**T**	**M**
Sales mix	50%	25%	25%
Selling price (₹)	30	40	30
Variable cost (₹)	15	20	15

- Total fixed cost ₹1,80,000
- Total sales ₹6,00,000

Will you advise the company to change-over to production of M? Give reasons for your answer.

(CA-Inter)

Solution

Marginal cost statement - Present				
Particulars	**Products**			**Total**
	S $\left(\frac{2,10,000}{30} = 7,000 \text{ units}\right)$ ₹	**T** $\left(\frac{2,10,000}{40} = 5,250 \text{ units}\right)$ ₹	**Y** $\left(\frac{1,80,000}{20} = 9,000 \text{ units}\right)$ ₹	₹
Sales (35 : 35 : 30)	2,10,000	2,10,000	1,80,000	6,00,000
Less: Variable cost	1,05,000	1,05,000	1,08,000	3,18,000
Contribution	1,05,000	1,05,000	72,000	2,82,000
Less: Fixed cost	-	-	-	1,80,000
Profit	-	-	-	1,02,000

Marginal cost statement - Product Y replaced with Product M				
Particulars	**Products**			**Total**
	S $\left(\frac{3,00,000}{30} = 10,000 \text{ units}\right)$ ₹	**T** $\left(\frac{1,50,000}{40} = 3,750 \text{ units}\right)$ ₹	**M** $\left(\frac{1,50,000}{30} = 5,000 \text{ units}\right)$ ₹	₹
Sales (50 : 25 : 25)	3,00,000	1,50,000	1,50,000	6,00,000
Less: Variable cost	1,50,000	75,000	75,000	3,00,000
Contribution	1,50,000	75,000	75,000	3,00,000
Less: Fixed cost	-	-	-	1,80,000
Profit	-	-	-	1,20,000

Answer: The directors proposal to introduce product M in place of product Y is acceptable. The profit increases from ₹1,02,000 to ₹1,20,000.

Illustration-36

A manufacturer is thinking whether he should drop one item from his product line and replace it with another. Below are given his present cost and output data:

Products	Price per unit ₹	Variable cost per unit ₹	% of sales
Bookshelves	60	40	30%
Tables	100	60	20%
Beds	200	120	50%

- Total fixed cost per year ₹7,50,000
- Total sales last year ₹25,00,000

The change under consideration consists in dropping the line of tables in favour of cabinets. If this drop and change is made, the manufacturer forecasts the following cost and output data:

Products	Price per unit ₹	Variable cost per unit ₹	% of sales
Bookshelves	60	40	50%
Cabinets	160	60	10%
Beds	200	120	40%

- Total fixed cost per year ₹7,50,000
- Total sales this year ₹26,00,000

Solution

Marginal Cost Statement - Last year				
Particulars	Products			Total
	Bookshelf $\left(\frac{7,50,000}{60} = 12,500 \text{ units}\right)$ ₹	Table $\left(\frac{5,00,000}{100} = 5,000 \text{ units}\right)$ ₹	Bed $\left(\frac{12,50,000}{200} = 6,250 \text{ units}\right)$ ₹	₹
Sales (30 : 20 : 50)	7,50,000	5,00,000	12,50,000	25,00,000
Less: Variable cost	5,00,000	3,00,000	7,50,000	15,50,000

Contribution	2,50,000	2,00,000	5,00,000	9,50,000
Less: Fixed cost	-	-	-	7,50,000
Profit	-	-	-	2,00,000

Marginal Cost Statement - This year				
Particulars	**Products**			**Total**
	Bookshelf $\left(\frac{13,00,000}{60} = 21,667 \text{ units}\right)$ ₹	**Cabinet** $\left(\frac{2,60,000}{160} = 1,625 \text{ units}\right)$ ₹	**Bed** $\left(\frac{10,40,000}{200} = 5,200 \text{ units}\right)$ ₹	₹
Sales (50 : 10 : 40)	13,00,000	2,60,000	10,40,000	26,00,000
Less: Variable costs	8,66,680	97,500	6,24,000	15,88,180
Contribution	4,33,320	1,62,500	4,16,000	10,11,820
Less: Fixed cost	-	-	-	7,50,000
Profit	-	-	-	2,61,820

Answer: Profit increases from ₹2,00,000 to ₹2,61,820 when cabinet is introduced in the place of table. So this proposal is acceptable.

19.4.10 Maintaining a Desired Level of Profit

When competition increases a firm has to take counter actions like reducing the selling price, increase sales promotion expenses or offer more discount to distributors. In case of temporary slow down in business a firm may take steps to introduce a new product, discontinue an existing product etc. In the above situations management may be interested in maintaining the profit earned at present. For decision making all relevant costs (i.e. variable and fixed costs) and change in revenues are to be considered.

Illustration-37

Quality Products Ltd., manufacture and market a single product. The following data are available:

	Per unit (₹)
Materials	16
Conversion costs	12

Dealer's margin	4
Selling price	40
Fixed costs - ₹5 lakhs	
Present sales - 90,000 units	
Capacity utilisation - 60 percent	

There is acute competition. Extra efforts are necessary to sell. Suggestions have been made for increasing sales

(a) by reducing the selling price by 5 percent;

(b) by increasing the dealer's margin by 25 percent over the existing rate.

Which of these two suggestions would you recommend, if the company desires to maintain the present profit? Give reasons.

Solution

Marginal Cost Statement - Present		
	₹	₹
Sales (90,000 units × ₹40)		36,00,000
Less: Variable cost		
Materials (90,000 × 16)	14,40,000	
Conversion costs (90,000 × 12)	10,80,000	
Dealers' margin (90,000 × 4)	3,60,000	28,80,000
Contribution		7,20,000
Less: Fixed cost		5,00,000
Present profit		2,20,000

Suggestion (a)

Reducing the sale price by 5%		
	₹	Per unit ₹
Present selling price		40
Less: 5% reduction		2
New selling price		38
Less: Variable cost		
Materials	16	
Conversion cost	12	
Dealers' margin	4	32
Contribution		6

$$\text{Required sales volume (in units) to maintain the present profit} = \frac{\text{Fixed cost + Desired profit}}{\text{Contribution per unit}}$$
$$= \frac{5,00,000 + 2,20,000}{6}$$
$$= \frac{7,20,000}{6}$$
$$= 1,20,000 \text{ units}$$

Suggestion (b)

Increasing dealers' margin by 25%		
	₹	Per unit ₹
Selling price		40
Less: Variable cost		
Materials	16	
Conversion cost	12	
Dealers' margin	5	33
Contribution		7

$$\text{Required sales volume (in units) to maintain the present profit} = \frac{\text{Fixed cost + Desired profit}}{\text{Contribution per unit}}$$
$$= \frac{5,00,000 + 2,20,000}{7}$$
$$= \frac{7,20,000}{7}$$
$$= 1,02,857 \text{ units}$$

Answer: Present profit is ₹2,20,000. As per suggestion (a) 1,20,000 units are to be sold and as per suggestion (b) 1,02,857 units are to be sold to maintain the present profit. The suggestion (b) is acceptable because the present profit can be maintained by selling lesser number of units compared with suggestion (a).

Illustration-38

The comparative profit statement of two quarters of a firm is as below:

	Quarter I	**Quarter II**
No. of units sold	2,500	3,750
	₹	₹
Direct materials	87,500	?
Direct wages	62,500	?

Fixed and variable factory overheads	75,000	95,000
Sales	2,75,000	?
Profit	50,000	66,250

In the second quarter, the direct material price has increased by 20%. There was a savings of ₹5,000 in fixed overheads in the second quarter. The other costs and selling price remained the same. Determine the quantity that should have been sold in the second quarter to maintain the same amount of profit per unit as in the first quarter.

Solution

(a)

Segregation of fixed and variable overheads		
Quarter	**Fixed and variable OHS**	**No. of units**
II	95,000	3,750
Add: Savings in fixed cost	5,000	-
	1,00,000	
I	75,000	2,500
Difference	25,000	1,250

$$\text{Variable overheads per unit} = \frac{\text{Difference in overheads}}{\text{Difference in no. of units}}$$

$$= \frac{25{,}000}{1{,}250}$$

$$= ₹20$$

(b)

Fixed overheads in Quarter II	
Total overheads in Quarter I	₹75,000
Less: Variable overheads (2,500 units × ₹20)	₹50,000
Fixed overheads in Quarter I	₹25,000
Less: Savings in fixed overheads in Quarter II	₹5,000
Fixed overheads in Quarter II	₹20,000

(c)

Contribution per unit in Quarter II			
Selling price per unit $\left(\frac{2,75,000}{2,500}\right)$			₹110
Less: Variable cost per unit:			
Direct materials $\left(\frac{87,500}{2,500}\right)$	35		
Add: 20% increase	7	42	
Direct wages $\left(\frac{62,500}{2,500}\right)$		25	
Variable overheads		20	₹87
Contribution per unit in Quarter II			₹23

(d) Number of units to be sold in Quarter II to earn the per unit profit as in Quarter I

$$\text{Let no. of units to be sold be} = x$$

$$\text{Total contribution per unit} = 23 \times x = 23x$$

$$\text{Profit per unit in quarter I} = \frac{50{,}000}{2{,}500} = ₹20$$

$$\text{Total profit in quarter II} = 20 \times x = 20x$$

$$\text{Contribution} - \text{Profit} = \text{Fixed cost}$$

$$= 23x - 20x = 20{,}000$$

$$3x = 20{,}000$$

$$x = \frac{20{,}000}{3} = 6{,}667 \text{ units}$$

No. of units to be sold to earn profit per unit as in quarter I = 6,667 units

19.5 COMPREHENSIVE ILLUSTRATIONS

19.5.1 Calculation of P/V Ratio, BEP, Profit, Required Sales and Margin of Safety

Illustration-39

The sales turnover and profit during two years were as follows:

Year	Sales	Profits
2010	1,70,000	25,000
2011	1,90,000	30,000

You are required to calculate:

(i) P/V ratio
(ii) Break-even point
(iii) Sales required to earn a profit of ₹40,000
(iv) Profit when sales are ₹2,75,000
(v) Margin of safety at a profit of ₹60,000 and MS Ratio
(vi) Variable cost of the two periods. **(B.Com., Madras University)**

Solution

$$\text{(i) P/V ratio} = \frac{\text{Changes in profit}}{\text{Changes in sales}} \times 100$$
$$= \frac{5{,}000}{20{,}000} \times 100 = 25\%$$

Note:

Year	Sales (₹)	Profits (₹)
2010	1,70,000	25,000
2011	1,90,000	30,000
Changes	20,000	5,000

$$\text{(ii) Break-even point} = \frac{\text{Fixed cost}}{\text{P/V ratio}}$$
$$= \frac{17{,}500}{25\%} = ₹70{,}000$$

Note:

$$\text{Fixed cost} = \text{Sales} \times \text{P/V ratio} - \text{Profit}$$
$$= 1{,}70{,}000 \times \frac{25}{100} - 25{,}000$$
$$= 42{,}500 - 25{,}000$$
$$= ₹17{,}500$$

(iii) Sales required to earn a profit of ₹40,000

$$\text{Required sales} = \frac{\text{Fixed cost} + \text{Desired profit}}{\text{P/V ratio}}$$
$$= \frac{17{,}500 + 40{,}000}{25\%} = ₹2{,}30{,}000$$

(iv) Profit when sales are ₹2,75,000

$$\begin{aligned}\text{Contribution} &= \text{Sales} \times \text{P/V ratio}\\ &= 2{,}75{,}000 \times \frac{25}{100}\\ &= ₹68{,}750\\ \text{Profit} &= \text{Contribution} - \text{Fixed cost}\\ &= 68{,}750 - 17{,}500\\ &= ₹51{,}250\end{aligned}$$

(v) Margin of Safety at a profit of ₹60,000

$$\begin{aligned}\text{Margin of safety} &= \frac{\text{Profit}}{\text{P/V ratio}}\\ &= \frac{60{,}000}{25\%} = ₹2{,}40{,}000\\ \text{MS Ratio} &= \frac{\text{Margin of safety}}{\text{Total sales}} \times 100\\ &= \frac{2{,}40{,}000}{3{,}10{,}000} \times 100 = 77.42\%\end{aligned}$$

Note:

$$\begin{aligned}\text{Sales for a profit of ₹60,000} &= \frac{\text{Fixed cost} + \text{Profit}}{\text{P/V ratio}}\\ &= \frac{17{,}500 + 60{,}000}{25\%}\\ &= \frac{77{,}500}{25\%} = ₹3{,}10{,}000\end{aligned}$$

(vi) Variable cost for two periods:

$$\begin{aligned}\text{\% of variable cost} &= \text{Complement of P/V ratio}\\ &= 100 - 25 = 75\%\\ \text{Variable cost} &= \text{Sales} \times \text{\% of variable cost}\\ \text{For 2010} &= 1{,}70{,}000 \times \frac{75}{100}\\ &= ₹1{,}27{,}500\end{aligned}$$

$$\begin{aligned}\text{For 2011} &= 1{,}90{,}000 \times \frac{75}{100}\\ &= ₹1{,}42{,}500\end{aligned}$$

Illustration-40

The following informations relate to production and sales of an article for January and February 2011:

	January (₹)	February (₹)
Sales	38,000	65,000
Profit	-	3,000
Loss	2,400	-

Calculate:

(a) Break-even point

(b) Sales to earn a profit of ₹5,000 and margin of safety

(c) Profit made when sales are ₹1,00,000. **(B.Com., Madras University)**

Solution

$$\textbf{(a) Break-even point} = \frac{\text{Fixed cost}}{\text{P/V Ratio}}$$

$$= \frac{10{,}000}{20\%} = ₹50{,}000$$

Note:

$$\text{(i) P/V ratio} = \frac{\text{Changes in profit}}{\text{Changes in sales}} \times 100$$

$$= \frac{5{,}400}{27{,}000} \times 100$$

$$= 20\%$$

(ii) Changes in profit and sales:

Month	Sales	Profit/ (Loss)
January	38,000	(2,400)
February	65,000	3,000
Changes	27,000	5,400

(iii) Fixed Cost:

$$\text{Contribution} = \text{Sales} \times \text{P/V ratio}$$
$$= 65{,}000 \times \frac{20}{100}$$
$$= 13{,}000$$

$$\text{Fixed cost} = \text{Contribution} - \text{Profit}$$
$$= 13{,}000 - 3{,}000$$
$$= ₹10{,}000$$

(b) Sales required to earn a profit of ₹5,000

$$= \frac{\text{Fixed cost} + \text{Desired profit}}{\text{P/V ratio}}$$
$$= \frac{10{,}000 + 5{,}000}{20\%}$$
$$= \frac{15{,}000}{20\%} = ₹75{,}000$$

$$\text{Margin of safety} = \text{Total sales} - \text{BEP sales}$$
$$= 75{,}000 - 50{,}000$$
$$= ₹25{,}000$$

(c) Profit made when sales are ₹1,00,000

$$\text{Contribution} = \text{Sales} \times \text{P/V ratio}$$
$$= 1{,}00{,}000 \times \frac{20}{100} = ₹20{,}000$$

$$\text{Profit} = \text{Contribution} - \text{Fixed Cost}$$
$$= 20{,}000 - 10{,}000$$
$$= ₹10{,}000$$

Illustration-41

The following costs and sales of a manufacturing company for the first half and second half of 2010 and 2011 are given :

	First half (₹)	**Second half** (₹)
Sales	24,00,000	30,00,000
Total costs	21,80,000	26,00,000

You are asked to determine:

(i) Contribution/Sales ratio of the firm

(ii) Annual fixed costs

(iii) Break-even point

(iv) Margin of safety as percentage of sales **(ICWA-Inter)**

Solution

(i) Contribution/Sales Ratio $= \dfrac{\text{Changes in profit}}{\text{Changes in sales}} \times 100$

$$= \frac{1{,}80{,}000}{6{,}00{,}000} \times 100$$

$$= 30\%$$

(ii) Annual fixed cost

Half yearly fixed cost = Half yearly sales × P/V ratio – Profit

$$= 24{,}00{,}000 \times \frac{30}{100} - 2{,}20{,}000$$

$$= 7{,}20{,}000 - 2{,}20{,}000$$

$$= ₹5{,}00{,}000$$

Annual fixed cost $= 5{,}00{,}000 \times 2$

$$= ₹10{,}00{,}000$$

(iii) Break-even point $= \dfrac{\text{Fixed cost}}{\text{P/V ratio}}$

$$= \frac{10{,}00{,}000}{30\%}$$

$$= ₹33{,}33{,}333$$

(iv) Margin of safety = Total sales – BEP sales

$$= 54{,}00{,}000 - 33{,}33{,}333$$

$$= ₹20{,}66{,}667$$

% of margin of safety $= \dfrac{\text{Margin of safety sales}}{\text{Total sales}} \times 100$

$$= \frac{20{,}66{,}667}{54{,}00{,}000} \times 100$$

$$= 38.27\%$$

Note:

1. Profit = Sales - Total cost

   First half = 24,00,000 - 21,80,000 = ₹2,20,000

   Second half = 30,00,000 - 26,00,000 = ₹4,00,000
2. Changes in profit = 4,00,000 - 2,20,000 = ₹1,80,000
3. Changes in sales = 30,00,000 - 24,00,000 = ₹6,00,000

Illustration-42

A company has annual fixed cost of ₹1,40,00,000. In the year 2007-2008, sales amounted to ₹6,00,00,000 as compared with ₹4,50,00,000 in the preceding year 2006-07. Profit in 2007-08 is ₹42,00,000 more than that in 2006-07, on the basis of the above information, answer the following:

(i) At what level of sales the company would break-even?

(ii) Determine profit/loss on a forecasted sales volume of ₹8,00,00,000.

(iii) If there is a reduction selling price by 10% in the financial year 2008-09 and the company wants to earn the same amount of profit as in 2007-08, what would be the required sales volume?

(ICSI-Executive level)

Solution

(i) **Break-even point** $= \dfrac{\text{Fixed cost}}{\text{P/V ratio}}$

$$= \frac{1{,}40{,}00{,}000}{28\%}$$

$$= ₹5{,}00{,}00{,}000$$

Note:

(a) Changes in sales = 6,00,00,000 − 4,50,00,000 = ₹1,50,00,000

(b) Changes in profit (given) = ₹42,00,000

(c) P/V ratio $= \dfrac{\text{Changes in profit}}{\text{Changes in sales}} \times 100$

$$= \frac{42,00,000}{1,50,00,000} \times 100 = 28\%$$

(ii) **Profit/Loss on a sales of ₹8,00,00,000**

$$= \text{Sales} \times \text{P/V ratio} - \text{Fixed cost}$$

$$= 8{,}00{,}00{,}000 \times \frac{28}{100} - 1{,}40{,}00{,}000$$

$$= 2{,}24{,}00{,}000 - 1{,}40{,}00{,}000$$

Profit = ₹84,00,000

(iii) Required sales volume

Required sales to earn a profit amount as in the year 2007-08:

$$= \frac{\text{Fixed cost} + \text{Desired profit}}{\text{New P/V ratio}}$$

$$= \frac{1{,}40{,}00{,}000 + 28{,}00{,}000}{20\%}$$

$$= \frac{1{,}68{,}00{,}000}{20\%}$$

$$= ₹8{,}40{,}00{,}000$$

Working Note

1.

Let present selling price be	100
Less: Reduction in price 10%	10
New selling price	90
(−) Variable cost (complement of P/V Ratio) (i.e. 100 – 28)	72
New contribution	18

$$\text{New P/V ratio} = \frac{C}{S} \times 100$$

$$= \frac{18}{90} \times 100 = 20\%$$

2. Profit for the year 2007-08:

$$\text{Contribution} = \text{Sales} \times \text{P/V ratio}$$

$$= 6{,}00{,}00{,}000 \times \frac{28}{100}$$

$$= ₹1{,}68{,}00{,}000$$

$$\text{Profit} = \text{Contribution} - \text{Fixed cost}$$

$$= 1{,}68{,}00{,}000 - 1{,}40{,}00{,}000$$

$$= ₹28{,}00{,}000$$

Illustration-43

A retail dealer in garments is currently selling 24,000 shirts annually. He supplies the following details for the year ended 31st December, 2011:

	₹
Selling price per unit	40
Variable cost per unit	25

Fixed costs:	
Staff salary for the year	1,20,000
General office costs for the year	80,000
Advertising cost for the year	40,000

As a cost accountant of the firm you are required to answer each part of the following independently:

(i) Calculate the break-even point and margin of safety in sales revenue and number of shirts sold.

(ii) Assume that 20,000 shirts were sold in a year. Find out the net profit of the firm.

(iii) If it is decided to introduce a selling commission of ₹3 per shirt, how many shirts would require to be sold in a year to earn a net income of ₹15,000.

(iv) Assuming that for the year 2012 an additional staff salary of ₹33,000 is anticipated and price of a shirt is likely to be increased by 15%, what would be the break-even point in number of shirts and sales revenue? **(B.Com. (Hons.), Delhi University)**

Solution

(i) Break-even point (in units) $= \dfrac{\text{Fixed costs}}{\text{Contribution per unit}}$

$= \dfrac{2,40,000}{15}$

= 16,000 shirts

Break-even point (in ₹) = 16,000 × 40

= ₹6,40,000

Current sales = 24,000 shirts

Or 24,000 × ₹40 = ₹9,60,000

Margin of safety sales (in ₹) = Present sales – BEP sales

= 9,60,000 – 6,40,000

= ₹3,20,000

Margin of safety in units = 24,000 – 16,000

= 8,000 shirts

Note: Contribution per unit = Selling price per unit – Variable cost per unit

= 40 – 25

= ₹15

(ii)

	₹	₹
Sales amount for 20,000 shirts (20,000 × 40)		8,00,000
Less: Variable cost (20,000 × 25)		5,00,000
Contribution		3,00,000
Less: Fixed costs:		
Staff salary	1,20,000	
General office cost	80,000	
Advertisement cost	40,000	2,40,000
Profit		60,000

(iii) No. of shirts to be sold to earn a profit of ₹15,000

$$\text{Required sales (units)} = \frac{\text{Fixed cost + Profit desired}}{\text{New contribution per unit}}$$

$$= \frac{2{,}40{,}000 + 15{,}000}{12}$$

$$= 21{,}250 \text{ shirts}$$

Note: New contribution per shirt:

	₹	₹
Selling price per unit		40
(−) Selling commission	3	
Variable cost	25	28
New contribution		12

(iv) $$\text{Break-even point (in units)} = \frac{\text{New fixed costs}}{\text{New contribution per unit}}$$

$$= \frac{2{,}73{,}000}{21}$$

$$= 13{,}000 \text{ shirts}$$

$$\text{Break-even point (in ₹)} = 13{,}000 \times 46$$

$$= ₹5{,}98{,}000$$

Note

1. New fixed cost:

	₹
Current fixed cost	2,40,000
Add: Additional staff salary	33,000
New fixed cost	2,73,000

2. New contribution per unit:

	₹
Current selling price	40 per unit
Add: 15% increase	6 per unit
New selling price	46 per unit
Less: Variable cost	25 per unit
New contribution	21 per unit

Illustration-44

A company is planning to instal a water bottling plant. The estimated annual sales would be 50,000 bottles. Sale price will be ₹27 per bottle.

The cost estimates are as under:

	Total cost p.a. (₹)	**Fixed portion** (%)
Materials cost	5,00,000	Nil
Wages	3,00,000	50%
Factory overheads	2,00,000	40%
Administration & selling overheads	1,60,000	60%

Over and above, 10% of the sale price is to be paid to the sales agency as commission:

(i) Calculate break-even point and

(ii) What should be the sale price if the desired profit is 10% of sales? **(ICWA-Inter)**

Solution

(i)

Statement showing contribution per unit		₹	₹
Selling price per unit		-	27.00
Less: Variable costs per unit:			
Materials	$\left(\frac{5,00,000}{50,000}\right)$	10.00	
Wages	$\left(\frac{3,00,000}{50,000} = 6 \times \frac{50}{100}\right)$	3.00	

Factory overheads $\left(\frac{2,00,000}{50,000} = 4 \times \frac{40}{100}\right)$	1.60	
Administration and selling overheads		
$\left(\frac{1,60,000}{50,000} = 3.20 \times \frac{60}{100}\right)$	1.92	
Sales agency commission $\left(\frac{10}{100} \times 27\right)$	2.70	19.22
Contribution	-	7.78

Statement showing total fixed cost	
	₹
Wages $\left(3,00,000 \times \frac{50}{100}\right)$	1,50,000
Factory overheads $\left(2,00,000 \times \frac{40}{100}\right)$	80,000
Administration and selling overheads $\left(1,60,000 \times \frac{60}{100}\right)$	96,000
Total	3,26,000

$$\text{Break-even point (in units)} = \frac{\text{Fixed cost}}{\text{Contribution per unit}} = \frac{3,26,000}{7.78} = 41,902 \text{ bottles}$$

$$\text{Break-even point (in ₹)} = 41,902 \times 27 = ₹11,31,354$$

(ii)

Selling price per bottle if profit desired is 10% of sales	
Statement of Cost:	₹
Variable cost (19.22 × 50,000)	9,61,000
Fixed cost	3,26,000
Total cost	12,87,000
Profit 10% on sale price (i.e. $\frac{10}{90}$ on cost price)	1,43,000
Total sales	14,30,000

$$\text{Selling price per bottle} = \frac{14,30,000}{50,000} = ₹28.60$$

Illustration-45

Two companies P Ltd. and Q Ltd. producing and selling similar products forecasted their profit and loss account for the next year, which is as follows :

	P Ltd.		Q Ltd.	
	₹	₹	₹	₹
Sales	-	3,00,000	-	3,00,000
Less: Variable cost	2,00,000		2,25,000	
Fixed expenses	50,000	2,50,000	25,000	2,50,000
Estimated profit	-	50,000	-	50,000

Calculate:

(a) P/V ratio, break-even point and margin of safety for both the companies.

(b) Sales required to earn a profit of ₹30,000 for both companies.

(c) Under the following situations, which company will show better results (i) increase in sales and (ii) decrease in sales.

Solution

(a)

$$\text{P/V ratio} = \frac{\text{Contribution}}{\text{Sales}} \times 100$$

$$\text{P Ltd.} = \frac{1{,}00{,}000}{3{,}00{,}000} \times 100$$

$$= 33.33\%$$

$$\text{Q Ltd.} = \frac{75{,}000}{3{,}00{,}000} \times 100$$

$$= 25\%$$

$$\text{Break-even point} = \frac{\text{Fixed cost}}{\text{P/V ratio}}$$

$$\text{P Ltd.} = \frac{50{,}000}{33.33/100} = ₹1{,}50{,}000$$

$$\text{Q Ltd.} = \frac{25{,}000}{25/100} = ₹1{,}00{,}000$$

$$\text{Margin of safety} = \text{Total sales} - \text{BEP sales}$$

$$\text{P Ltd.} = 3{,}00{,}000 - 1{,}50{,}000$$

$$= ₹1{,}50{,}000$$

$$\text{Q Ltd.} = 3{,}00{,}000 - 1{,}00{,}000$$

$$= ₹2{,}00{,}000$$

(b) Sales required to earn a profit of ₹30,000 $= \dfrac{\text{Fixed cost} + \text{Desired profit}}{\text{P/V ratio}}$

$$\text{P Ltd.} = \frac{50{,}000 + 30{,}000}{33.33/100}$$

$$= ₹2{,}40{,}000$$

$$\text{Q Ltd.} = \frac{25{,}000 + 30{,}000}{25/100}$$

$$= ₹2{,}20{,}000$$

(c) **(i) Increase in Sales:**

Company P Ltd. stands to earn more profit when sales are increasing because it has higher P/V ratio.

(ii) Decrease in Sales:

Company Q Ltd. is in a better position. Because its break-even point is lower. Q Ltd. will not incur loss even if sales decrease to ₹1,00,000. But P Ltd. will incur loss if sales decreases to ₹1,00,000 because its break-even point is ₹1,50,000.

19.5.2 Profit Planning

Illustration-46

The Young Hotel has annual fixed costs applicable to room of ₹15,00,000 for a 300 rooms hotel with average daily room rates of ₹40 and average variable cost of ₹6 for each room rented.

The hotel operates 365 days per year. It is subject to income tax rate of 30 percent. It is required to:

(i) calculate the number of rooms the hotel must rent to earn a net income after tax of ₹10,00,000; and

(ii) compute the break-even point in terms of number of rooms rented.

(B.Com. (Hons.), Delhi University)

Solution

(i) Number of rooms to be rented out to earn an after-tax profit of ₹10,00,000

Let income before tax be	100
Less: Tax	30
Profit after tax	70

$$\text{Desired profit before tax} = \frac{10{,}00{,}000 \times 100}{70}$$
$$= ₹14{,}28{,}571$$

$$\text{Contribution per room per day} = 40 - 6$$
$$= ₹34$$

$$\text{No. of rooms to be rented out} = \frac{\text{Fixed cost} + \text{Profit desired before tax}}{\text{Contribution per room per day}}$$
$$= \frac{15{,}00{,}000 + 14{,}28{,}571}{34}$$
$$= 86{,}134 \text{ rooms annually or } \frac{86{,}134}{365}$$
$$= 236 \text{ rooms daily}$$

$$\text{(ii) Break-even point in rooms} = \frac{\text{Fixed cost}}{\text{Contribution per room per day}}$$
$$= \frac{15{,}00{,}000}{34}$$
$$= 44{,}118 \text{ rooms per year or } \frac{44{,}118}{365}$$
$$= 121 \text{ rooms daily}$$

Illustration-47

Garden Product Ltd. manufactures the 'Rain Pour' garden spray. The accounts of the company for the year 2010 are expected to reveal a profit of ₹14,00,000 from the manufacture of 'Rain-Pour' after charging fixed cost of ₹10,00,000. The Rain Pour is sold for ₹50 per unit and has a variable unit cost of ₹20.

Market sensitivity tests suggest the following responses to price changes:

Alternatives	Selling price reduced by	Quantity sold increased by
A	5%	10%
B	7%	20%
C	10%	25%

Evaluate these alternatives and state which, on profitability consideration, should be adopted for the forthcoming year, assuming that cost structure remains unchanged from 2010.

(B.Com. (Hons.), Delhi University)

Solution

Statement of Profit				
Particulars	Present	Alternatives Proposed		
		A	B	C
	₹	₹	₹	₹
Selling price per unit	50.00	47.50	46.50	45.00
Less: Variable cost	20.00	20.00	20.00	20.00
Contribution per unit	30.00	27.50	26.50	25.00
No. of units sold	80,000 units	88,000 units	96,000 units	1,00,000 units
Total contribution	24,00,000	24,20,000	25,44,000	25,00,000
Less: Fixed cost	10,00,000	10,00,000	10,00,000	10,00,000
Profit	14,00,000	14,20,000	15,44,000	15,00,000

Answer: Profit under alternative B is the highest. So alternative B should be accepted.

Working Note

1. Computation of number of units sold in 2010:

$$\text{Total contribution} = \text{Fixed cost} + \text{Profit}$$
$$= 10,00,000 + 14,00,000$$
$$= ₹24,00,000$$

$$\text{Contribution per unit} = \text{Selling price} - \text{Variable cost}$$
$$= 50 - 20$$
$$= ₹30$$

$$\text{No. of units sold in 2010} = \frac{\text{Total contribution}}{\text{Contribution per unit}}$$
$$= \frac{24,00,000}{30}$$
$$= 80,000 \text{ units}$$

2. Number of units under alternatives:

$$A = 80,000 + 10\% = 88,000 \text{ units}$$
$$B = 80,000 + 20\% = 96,000 \text{ units}$$
$$C = 80,000 + 25\% = 1,00,000 \text{ units}$$

Illustration-48

An analysis of X Ltd cost records gives the following information:

	Variable cost (% of sales)	Fixed cost (₹)
Direct materials	32.8	-
Direct labour	28.4	-
Factory overheads	12.6	1,89,000
Distribution overheads	4.1	58,400
General administration overheads	1.1	66,700
Budgeted sales for the next year		18,50,000

You are required to determine:

(a) Profit at the budgeted sales value

(b) Break-even sales value

(c) Profit if actual sales (i) drop by 10%, (ii) increase by 5% from budgeted sales.

(B.Com., Madras University)

Solution

(a) Statement showing budgeted profit

Budgeted sales	18,50,000
Less: Variable costs (79% on Sales)	14,61,500
Contribution	3,88,500
Less: Fixed costs (1,89,000 + 58,400+66,700)	3,14,100
Budgeted profit	74,400

$$\text{P/V ratio} = \frac{3{,}88{,}500}{18{,}50{,}000} \times 100 = 21\%$$

(b) $$\text{Break-even point} = \frac{\text{Fixed cost}}{\text{P/V ratio}} = \frac{3{,}14{,}100}{21/100} = ₹14{,}95{,}714$$

(c) (i) Profit when sales drop by 10%

	₹
Budgeted sales	18,50,000
Less: 10% drop	1,85,000
New sales	16,65,000

Less: Variable cost 79% on Sales	13,15,350
Contribution	3,49,650
Less: Fixed cost	3,14,100
Profit	35,550

(ii) Profit when sales increase by 5%

	₹
Budgeted sales	18,50,000
Less: 5% increase	92,500
New sales	19,42,500
Less: variable cost 79% on Sales	15,34,575
Contribution	4,07,925
Less: Fixed cost	3,14,100
Profit	93,825

Illustration-49

From the following data, calculate:

(i) Break-even point expressed in amount of sales in rupees.

(ii) Number of units that must be sold to earn a profit of ₹60,000 per year.

(iii) How many units must be sold to earn a net profit of 10% on sales.

Sales price	₹20 per unit
Fixed factory overheads	₹5,40,000 per unit
Fixed selling costs	₹2,52,000 per unit
Variable manufacturing costs	₹11 per unit
Variable selling costs	₹3 per unit

Solution

(i) $\text{Break-even point (in rupees)} = \dfrac{\text{Fixed cost}}{\text{Contribution per unit}} \times \text{Selling price per unit}$

$$= \frac{7{,}92{,}000}{6} \times 20$$

$$= ₹26{,}40{,}000$$

Note:

Contribution per unit = Sales – Variable cost

$= 20 - (11 + 3) = ₹6$

(ii) Number of units to be sold to earn a profit of ₹60,000

$$= \frac{\text{Fixed cost} + \text{Desired profit}}{\text{Contribution per unit}}$$

$$= \frac{7{,}92{,}000 + 60{,}000}{6}$$

$$= 1{,}42{,}000 \text{ units}$$

(iii) Number of units to be sold to earn a profit of 10% on Sales

Let the number of units to be sold be 'x'

$$\text{Total Sales} = \text{Total variable cost} + \text{Total fixed cost} + \text{profit}$$

$$20x = (14 \times x) + 7{,}92{,}000 + (20 \times x)\frac{10}{100}$$

$$20x = 14x + 7{,}92{,}000 + 2x$$

$$20x - 14x - 2x = 7{,}92{,}000$$

$$4x = 7{,}92{,}000$$

$$x = \frac{7{,}92{,}000}{4}$$

$$= 1{,}98{,}000 \text{ units}$$

Number of units to be sold = 1,98,000 units

Illustration-50

Titan Engineering is operating at 70 percent capacity and presents the following information:

Break-even point	₹200 crores
P/V ratio	40%
Margin of safety	₹50 crores

Titan's management has decided to increase production to 95 percent capacity level with the following modifications.

(i) The selling price will be reduced by 8 percent.

(ii) The variable cost will be reduced by 5% on sales.

(iii) The fixed cost will increase by ₹20 crore, including depreciation on additional plant, but excluding interest on additional capital.

(iv) Additional capital of ₹50 crore will be needed for capital expenditure and working capital.

Required:

(a) Indicate the sales figure, with the working, that will be needed to earn ₹10 crore over and above the present profit and also meet 20 percent interest on the additional capital.

(b) What will be the revised.

(i) Break-even point,

(ii) P/V ratio,

(iii) Margin of safety.

Solution

(a) Sales required to earn an additional profit of ₹10 crore (i.e. Total ₹30 crore)

$$= \frac{\text{Fixed cost} + \text{Desired profit}}{\text{P/V ratio}}$$

$$= \frac{110 + 30}{45/100}$$

$$= ₹311.11 \text{ crore}$$

(b) (i) Revised BEP $= \dfrac{\text{Fixed cost}}{\text{Revised P/V ratio}}$

$$= \frac{110}{45/100}$$

$$= ₹244.45 \text{ crore}$$

(ii) Revised P/V ratio = 45% (*see* working Note. 6)

(iii) Margin of safety = Total sales – BEP sales

$$= 311.11 - 244.45$$

$$= ₹66.66 \text{ crore}$$

Working Note

1. Present sales = BEP sales + Margin of safety

$$= 200 + 50$$

$$= ₹250 \text{ crore}$$

2. Variable cost % = 60% (Complement of P/V ratio)

$$\text{Variable cost} = 250 \times \frac{60}{100}$$

$$= ₹150 \text{ crore}$$

3. Fixed cost = BEP sales × P/V ratio

$$= 200 \times \frac{40}{100}$$

$$= ₹80 \text{ crore}$$

4. Profit = Sales – Variable cost – Fixed cost

$$= 250 - 150 - 80$$

$$= 20 \text{ crore}$$

5. Revised fixed cost:

Present fixed cost	80 crore
Increase in fixed cost	20 crore
Interest on additional capital $\left(50 \times \frac{20}{100}\right)$	10 crore
Total	110 crore

6. Revised P/V ratio:

Let the present price be		100
Less: 8% reduction		8
New Selling price		92
Present variable cost 60% on selling price	55.2	
Less: Decrease 5% on Sales $\left(92 \times \frac{5}{100}\right)$	4.6	50.6
New Contribution		41.40

$$\text{Revised P/V ratio} = \frac{\text{New contribution}}{\text{New selling price}} \times 100$$
$$= \frac{41.40}{92} \times 100$$
$$= 45\%$$

19.5.3 Key Factor

Illustration-51

A company manufactures and markets three products x, y and z. All the three products are made from the same set of machines. Production is limited by machine capacity. From the data given below, indicate priorities for products x, y and z with a view to maximising profits:

Particulars	Products		
	x ₹	y ₹	z ₹
Raw materials cost per unit	11.25	16.25	21.25
Direct labour cost per unit	2.50	2.50	2.50
Other variable costs per unit	1.50	2.25	3.55
Selling price per unit	25.00	30.00	35.00
Standard machine required per unit in minutes	39 minutes	20 minutes	28 minutes

(CA-Inter)

Solution

Marginal Cost Statement			
Particulars	**Products**		
	x ₹	y ₹	z ₹
Selling Price (A)	25.00	30.00	35.00
Variable costs:			
Raw materials	11.25	16.25	21.25
Direct labour	2.50	2.50	2.50
Other variable cost	1.50	2.25	3.55
Total (B)	15.25	21.00	27.30
Contribution Per unit (A - B)	9.75	9.00	7.70
Standard machine time per unit	39 minutes	20 minutes	28 minutes
Contribution per machine hour	$\frac{9.75}{39} \times 60 =$ ₹15.00	$\frac{9}{20} \times 60 =$ ₹27.00	$\frac{7.70}{28} \times 60$ ₹= 16.50
Ranking	III	I	II

Answer: Machine hour is limiting factor. Product y earns highest contribution per machine hour. Hence, product y should be given priority in production over the other products.

Illustration-52

From the following particulars, find out the most profitable product mix and prepare a statement of profitability of that product mix:

Particulars	Product A	Product B	Product C
Units budgeted to be produced and sold	1,800	3,000	1,200
Selling price per unit	₹60	₹55	₹50
Direct materials	5 kg	3 kg	4 kg
Direct labour	4 hrs	3 hrs	2 hrs
Variable overheads	₹7	₹13	₹8
Fixed overheads	₹10	₹10	₹10
Cost of direct materials per kg	₹4	₹4	₹4
Direct labour hour rate	₹2	₹2	₹2
Maximum possible units of sale	4,000	5,000	1,500

All the three products are produced from the same direct materials using the same type of machines and labour, which is the key factor, is limited to 18,600 hours. **(CA-Inter)**

Solution

Marginal Cost			
Particulars	**Product A (Per unit) ₹**	**Product B (Per unit) ₹**	**Product C (Per unit) ₹**
Selling Price (A)	60	55	50
Variable costs:			
Direct materials	20	12	16
Direct wages	8	6	4
Variable overheads	7	13	8
Total (B)	35	31	28
Contribution per unit (A − B)	25	24	22
Contribution per direct labour hour	$\frac{25}{4}$ = ₹6.25	$\frac{24}{3}$ = ₹8	$\frac{22}{2}$ = ₹11
Ranking	III	II	I

Marginal cost statement - Budgeted Production and Sales				
Particulars	**Product A (1,800 units) ₹**	**Product B (3,000 units) ₹**	**Product C (1,200 units) ₹**	**Total ₹**
Total contribution	45,000 (25 × 1,800)	72,000 (24 × 3,000)	26,400 (22 × 1,200)	1,43,400
Less: Fixed cost	18,000 (10 × 1,800)	30,000 (10 × 3,000)	12,000 (10 × 1,200)	60,000
Total profit	-	-	-	83,400

Computation of most profitable product mix	
Total machine hours available	18,600 hrs
Less: Machine hours utilised for producing 1,500 units of product C (1,500 × 2) (i.e. - Ranked I)	3,000 hrs
Balance hours	15,600 hrs
Less: Machine hours utilised for producing 5,000 units of product 'B' (5,000 × 3) (i.e. - Ranked II)	15,000 hrs
Balance hours available utilised to produce 150 units of product 'A' (600 ÷ 4 = 150 units)	600 hrs

Profitable product Mix:

Product 'A' - 150 units
Product 'B' - 5,000 units
Product 'C' - 1,500 units

Statement of profit for the profitable product mix			
Product	**No. of Units**	**Contribution per unit (₹)**	**Total Contribution (₹)**
A	150	25	3,750
B	5,000	24	1,20,000
C	1,500	22	33,000
Total contribution			1,56,750
Less: Fixed overheads			60,000
Profit			96,750

Illustration-53

A company engaged in plantation activities has 200 hectares of land which can be used for growing jointly or individually tea, coffee and cardamom. The yield per hectare of the different crops and their selling price per kg are as under:

	Yield (kg)	**Selling price per kg (₹)**
Tea	2,000	20
Coffee	500	40
Cardamom	100	250

The relevant cost data are given below:

(A)

Variable Cost per kg.			
	Tea (₹)	**Coffee (₹)**	**Cardamom (₹)**
Labour charges	8	10	120
Packing materials	2	2	10
Other costs	4	1	20
Total cost	14	13	150

(B)

Fixed costs per annum	
	₹
Cultivation and growing cost	10,00,000
Administration cost	2,00,000
Land revenue	50,000
Repairs and maintenance	2,50,000
Other costs	3,00,000
Total cost	18,00,000

The policy of the company is to produce and sell all the three kinds of products and the maximum and minimum area to be cultivated per product is as follows:

	Hectares	
	Maximum	**Minimum**
Tea	160	120
Coffee	50	30
Cardamom	30	10

Calculate the most profitable product mix and the maximum profit which can be achieved.

(ICWA-Inter)

Solution

Marginal Cost Statement			
Particulars	**Tea** ₹	**Coffee** ₹	**Cardamom** ₹
Selling price per kg.	20	40	250
Less: Variable cost	14	13	150
Contribution per kg.	6	27	100
Yield per hectare	2,000 kg.	500 kg.	100 kg.
Contribution per hectare	₹12,000	₹13,500	₹10,000
Ranking	II	I	III

Calculation of Most profitable product mix	
Total area available	200 hectares
Less: Minimum area allotted to the crops:	
Tea - 120 hectares	

Coffee - 30 hectares Cardamom - 10 hectares	160 hectares
Balance area available - to be allotted to most profitable crops (subject to maximum limit)	40 hectares
Less: 20 hectares allotted to coffee	20 hectares
Balance area 20 hectares allotted to tea	20 hectares

Most Profitable Product Mix	
Tea (120 + 20)	140 hectares
Coffee (30 + 20)	50 hectares
Cardamom	10 hectares
Total	200 hectares

Statement showing maximum profit from suggested product mix			
Crops	**Area** (hectares)	**Contribution per Hectare** (₹)	**Total** (₹)
Tea	140	12,000	16,80,000
Coffee	50	13,500	6,75,000
Cardamom	10	10,000	1,00,000
Total contribution	-	-	24,55,000
Less: Fixed cost	-	-	18,00,000
Maximum profit	-	-	6,55,000

19.5.4 Make or Buy

Illustration-54

A TV manufacturer finds that while it costs him ₹625 each to make a component, the same is available in the market at ₹575 each, with an assurance of continuous supply.

The break-down of cost of manufacture is as follows:

	₹
Material	275
Labour	175

Other variable costs	50
Fixed costs	125
	625

(a) Should he make or buy the component?

(b) What would be your decision if the supplier offers the component at ₹485 each.

(B.Com., Madras University)

Solution

Variable Cost of manufacture

	₹
Material	275
Labour	175
Other variable costs	50
	500

Decision Making

(a) If the market price is ₹575, it is profitable to produce the component because there will be a savings of ₹75 per component.

(b) If the market price is reduced to ₹485, it is profitable to buy from the market because there will be savings of ₹15 per unit.

Illustration-55

Remember Ltd. has an annual production of 50,000 units for a motor component. The company's cost structure is as given below:

	₹
Material	270
Labour (25% fixed)	180
Other variable costs	90
Fixed costs	135
Total cost	675

(i) The purchase manager has an offer from a supplier who is willing to supply the component at ₹540 per unit. Should the component be purchased and production stopped?

(ii) Assume the resources now used for this component manufacture are to be used to produce another new product for which the selling price is ₹485 per unit. For producing this new product material price would be ₹200 per unit. 90,000 units of this product can be produced at the same cost basis for labour and expenses. Discuss whether it would be advisable to divert the resources to manufacture that new product on the footing that the component presently being produced would instead of being produced, be purchased from the market.

(B.Com., Madras University)

Solution

(i) Variable cost of production of motor component

	Per unit (₹)
Materials	270
Labour - variable 75%	135
Expenses - variable	90
Total	495

Price quoted by supplier ₹540.

Decision: If price quoted by the supplier is ₹540 per unit, it is profitable to produce the component. There will be savings of ₹45 per unit.

(ii) Contribution from new product

		₹
Selling price per unit		485
Less: Variable cost per unit:		
Materials	200	
Labour - 75% variable	135	
Expenses - variable	90	425
Contribution		60

(iii) Statement of profit/loss

Total contribution from new product (90,000 × 60)	₹54,00,000
Less: Opportunity cost (i.e. contribution foregone from component (50,000 × 45)	₹22,50,000
Net contribution	₹31,50,000

Decision: The proposal to produce a new product after discontinuing the motor component is acceptable. This proposal gives an additional contribution of ₹31,50,000.

Illustration-56

A company is purchasing annually 10,000 units of a component at ₹9 per unit. There is a proposal to make the component within the factory itself. Studies show that the machine required to make the component will cost ₹1,50,000 with a life of 10 years at the end of which the scrap value is likely to be ₹15,000. Space for the machine can be easily found but will have a notional annual rent of ₹1,500. The amount required for the machine will have to be withdrawn from a fixed deposit account earning interest at 10% p.a. Insurance will be 0.5% of machine cost and power consumption ₹6,000 per annum. Materials will cost ₹1.80 per unit and a contingent of 5 workers at ₹600 p.m. each will be needed in addition to a supervisor costing ₹1,000 p.m.

Comment on the proposal from the costing point of view.

Solution

Statement showing cost of production of 10,000 components	
	₹
Materials (10,000 units × ₹1.80)	18,000
Wages (5 workers × ₹600 × 12)	36,000
Supervisor (₹1,000 × 12)	12,000
Power	6,000
Insurance	750
Depreciation	13,500
Interest	15,000
Total cost	1,01,250

$$\text{Cost of production per unit} = \frac{1{,}01{,}250}{10{,}000}$$
$$= ₹10.13$$

Cost of purchase of the component ₹9.00.

Decision: Cost of production is higher than the purchase cost. It is advisable to continue to purchase the component.

19.5.5 Optimum Sales Mix

Illustration-57

Given the following information you are required to:

(a) Calculate and present the marginal product cost and contribution per unit and

(b) State which of the alternative sales mix you would recommend to the management and why?

Selling price per unit	- Product X - ₹25
	- Product Y - ₹20
Direct materials	- Product X - ₹8
	- Product Y - ₹6
Direct wages	- Product X - 24 hours at ₹0.25 per hour
	- Product Y - 16 hours at ₹0.25 per hour
Fixed overhead	- ₹750
Variable overhead	- 150% of direct wages

Alternative sales mixes:

(i) 250 units of X and 250 units of Y

(ii) Nil units of X and 400 units of Y

(iii) 400 units of X and 100 units of Y

Solution

(a)

Statement showing Marginal Cost and Contribution per unit

	Product 'X' (per unit)	**Product 'Y' (per unit)**
Selling price (A)	25	20
Less: Variable cost/Material cost		
Direct materials	8	6
Direct wages	6	4
Variable overheads	9	6
Total (B)	23	16
Contribution per unit (A-B)	2	4

Profitability of alternative sales mixes:

Sales mix (i)

	Product X (250 unit) ₹	**Product Y (250 unit) ₹**	**Total (500 unit) ₹**
Contribution	500 (250 × 2)	1,000 (250 × 4)	1,500
Less: Fixed cost	-	-	750
Profit			750

Sales Mix (ii)

	Product Y (400 units) ₹
Contribution (400 × 4)	1,600
Less: Fixed cost	750
Profit	850

Sales mix (iii)

	Product X (400 unit) ₹	**Product Y (100 unit) ₹**	**Total (500 unit) ₹**
Contribution	800	400	1,200
Less: Fixed cost	-	-	750
Profit			450

Alternative II sales mix is recommended because it gives highest profit.

19.5.6 Accepting Special Orders at Price Below Cost

Illustration-58

The cost sheet of a product is given as under:

	Per unit (₹)
Direct material	10
Direct wages	6
Factory overheads:	
Fixed	1
Variable	1
Administration expenses	1.50
Selling and distribution overheads:	
Fixed	0.50
Variable	1.00
	21.00

The selling price is ₹24.

The above figures are for the output of 50,000 units. The capacity of the firm is 65,000 units. A foreign customer is desirous of buying 15,000 units at a price of ₹20 per unit. Advise the manufacturer whether the offer should be accepted. What will be your advice if the order was from a local merchant?

Solution

Variable cost of manufacture	
	Per unit (₹)
Direct materials	10
Direct wages	6
Factory overheads - variable	1
Selling and distribution overheads variable	1
	18

Marginal Cost Statement			
Particulars	**Local Market 50,000 units**	**Export order 15,000 units**	**Total 65,000 units**
Selling price p/u	₹24	₹20	-
Sales	12,00,000	3,00,000	15,00,000
Less: Variable cost (₹18 per unit)	9,00,000	2,70,000	11,70,000
Contribution	3,00,000	30,000	3,30,000
Less: Fixed cost	1,50,000	-	1,50,000
Profit	1,50,000	30,000	1,80,000

Export order is acceptable because it gives a profit of ₹30,000 over the present profit of ₹1,50,000.

If the order comes from a local merchant the order should not be accepted because it will affect the local market.

Illustration-59

A factory produces 24,000 units. The cost sheet gives the following information:

	₹
Direct materials	1,20,000
Direct wages	84,000
Variable overheads	48,000
Semi-variable overheads	28,000
Fixed overheads	80,000
Total cost	3,60,000

The product is sold at ₹20 per unit.

The management proposes to increase the production by 3,000 units for sales in the foreign market. It is estimated that the semi-variable overheads will increase by ₹1,000. But the product will be sold at ₹14 per unit in the foreign market. However, no additional capital expenditure will be incurred. The management seeks your advice as a cost accountant. What will be your advice?

Solution

Marginal Cost Statement

Particulars	**Local Market 24,000 units**	**Export order 3,000 units**	**Total 27,000 units**
Selling price p/u	₹20	₹14	-
Sales (A)	4,80,000	42,000	5,22,000
Variable cost:			
Direct materials (₹5 per unit)	1,20,000	15,000	1,35,000
Direct wages (₹3.50 per unit)	84,000	10,500	94,500
Variable overheads (₹2 per unit)	48,000	6,000	54,000
Semi-variable overheads	28,000	1,000	29,000
Fixed overheads	80,000	-	80,000
Total Cost (B)	3,60,000	32,500	3,92,500
Profit (A - B)	1,20,000	9,500	1,29,500

The export order gives a profit of ₹9,500. So it is profitable to accept the export order.

Illustration-60

A manufacturer of a certain product has been selling exclusively in the Indian market upto now. The company has just received its first export enquiry and wants to quote as competitively as the circumstances will allow. The latest Indian Cost Sheet is given below:

	Per unit (₹)
Raw materials	34
Direct labour	13
Services	6
Works overhead	7
Office overheads	2
Total costs	62

Add: Profit earned in India	6
Selling price	68

The management is thinking of quoting a selling price somewhere between ₹62 and ₹68 per unit for this export order. One of the directors suggests quoting even a lower price based on the principles of Marginal Costing. As the firm's cost accountant, you are required to suggest the lowest price the management could quote on these principles. State clearly any assumptions that you may make on the above facts, and also any other costs or facts.

Solution

Variable cost of manufacture per unit

	₹
Raw materials	34
Direct labour	13
Services	6
Total	53

The lowest export price company can quote on no profit no loss basis is ₹53.

Assumptions:

1. Service cost is assumed to be variable.
2. Works overhead and office overheads are assumed to be fully fixed.
3. There is sufficient spare capacity to produce additional units for export order.
4. There are some additional costs like insurance, transport and special packing for export order. These likely expenses to be added to total variable cost while fixing export price.
5. There are incentives for exports made. This should also be taken into account while accepting export order.

Illustration-61

X Ltd. is currently operating at 80% of its capacity and produces and sells 40,000 units annually. The cost details are as below:

	₹
Direct wages	60,000
Direct materials	80,000

Overheads:	
Fixed	84,000
Variable	42,000
	2,66,000

The selling price per unit is ₹8.75. In the present market conditions there is hardly any chance for selling more locally. A special export order for 10,000 units at ₹6 per unit is received.

(a) Would it be prudent for the company to accept the order at this price?

(b) What is the price beyond which it would be profitable to accept this order?

Solution

Statement showing variable cost

	₹
Direct wages	60,000
Direct materials	80,000
Overheads:	
Variable	42,000
	1,82,000

Variable cost per unit $= \frac{1,82,000}{40,000} =$ ₹4.55

Export price ₹6

Contribution from export order $= 6 - 4.55$

= ₹1.45 per unit

(a) It is profitable to accept the export order. Total profit from export order will ₹14,500 (i.e. 10,000 units x ₹1.45)

(b) Any price above ₹4.55 (i.e. variable cost) is acceptable.

19.5.7 Discontinuing a product line

Illustration-62

The Skyrock Ltd. produces and sells three types of products P, Q and R. The management committee has decided to discontinue the production of Q. Since there is not much profit in it. From the following set of information find out the profitability of the products and give your short comments on the decision of the management:

Products	Selling price per unit (₹)	Direct materials per unit (₹)	Direct wages		
			Dept. A (₹)	Dept. B (₹)	Dept. C (₹)
P	300	60	20	15	10
Q	275	30	20	20	10
R	305	70	12	10	20

The absorption rate of overheads on direct wages are:

	Dept. A	Dept. B	Dept. C
Variable overheads	150%	120%	200%
Fixed overheads	200%	240%	150%

(ICWA-Inter)

Solution

Marginal Cost Statement			
Particulars	**Products**		
	Prod. P ₹	**Prod. Q** ₹	**Prod. R** ₹
Selling price (A)	300	275	305
Variable costs:			
Direct material	60	30	70
Direct wages			
Dept. A	20	20	12
Dept. B	15	20	10
Dept. C	10	10	20
Variable overheads:			
Dept. A (150% of direct wages)	30	30	18
Dept. B (120% of direct wages)	18	24	12
Dept. C (200% of direct wages)	20	20	40
Total variable cost (B)	173	154	182
Contribution per unit (A - B)	127	121	123

Less: Fixed cost			
Dept. A (200% of direct wages)	40	40	24
Dept. B (240% of direct wages)	36	48	24
Dept. C (150% of direct wages)	15	15	30
Profit	36	18	45
P/V ratio	42%	44%	40%

Decision:

The contribution per unit is lower in case of product Q. But its P/V ratio is highest. The management's decision to discontinue product Q is not correct. By increasing the production and sale of product Q the company can increase its profit at a faster rate than the other products.

Illustration-63

A company is manufacturing and selling three products X, Y and Z. The details of production and sales for the year ended 31.12.2001 were as follows:

	Products		
	X	**Y**	**Z**
No. of units sold	10,000	12,000	16,000
Selling price per unit (₹)	40	36	32
Direct materials per unit (₹)	16	15	14
Direct labour per unit (₹)	8	6	7
Variable overheads per unit (₹)	8	6	7
Allocated fixed overheads per unit (₹)	5	5	5

Since product Z is causing loss, the management is considering the following options for the next year:

(a) Stop production of Z and continue production of X and Y.

(b) Stop production of Z. Reduce selling price of X by 5%. It is expected that sales of X will increase by 50%.

(c) Stop production of Z and increase production of Y by 20% and sell the entire production by incurring an extra sales promotion expenditure of ₹10,000.

(d) Introduce a new product W in place of Z. Expected sales of W will be about 9,000 units at ₹30 per unit. The cost profile of W is given below:

Direct materials ₹10, direct labour ₹6, and variable overhead ₹6.

Additional facilities are not required for (b), (c) and (d).

You are required to analyse the current working results on marginal costing lines, examine each of the options under consideration and suggest the best option, together with your comments on each.

(ICWA-Inter)

Solution

Marginal Cost Statement - Present position				
Particulars	**Product X (10,000 units)** ₹	**Product Y (12,000 units)** ₹	**Product Z (16,000 units)** ₹	**Total** ₹
Sales (A)	4,00,000	4,32,000	5,12,000	13,44,000
Variable Costs:				
Direct materials	1,60,000	1,80,000	2,24,000	5,64,000
Direct labour	80,000	72,000	1,12,000	2,64,000
Variable overheads	80,000	72,000	1,12,000	2,64,000
Total (B)	3,20,000	3,24,000	4,48,000	10,92,000
Contribution (A – B)	80,000	1,08,000	64,000	2,52,000
Less: Fixed cost	50,000	60,000	80,000	1,90,000
Profit/(Loss)	30,000	48,000	(16,000)	62,000
P/V ratio	20%	25%	12.5%	-
Present contribution per unit	₹8	₹9	₹4	-

Option (a) Stop production of Z

Income Statement	
	₹
Contribution: Product X	80,000
Product Y	1,08,000
Total contribution	1,88,000
Less: Total fixed cost	1,90,000
Loss	(2,000)

Option (b) Stop production of Z and reduce selling price of X by 5%.

Contribution:

Income Statement	
Product X:	₹
Present selling price per unit	40
Less: 5% reduction in price	2
New selling price	38

Less: Variable cost per unit :		
Direct materials	16	
Direct labour	8	
Variable overheads	8	32
Contribution per unit		6
Number of units sold at present		10,000
Add: 50% increase		5,000
		15,000
Total contribution – Product X (15,000 × 6)		90,000
Total contribution – Product Y (as at present)		1,08,000
Total Contribution		1,98,000
Less: Total fixed cost		1,90,000
Profit		8,000

Option (c) Stop production of Z and increase production of Y by 20%

		₹
Contribution – Product X (10,000 ×8)		80,000
Contribution – Product Y (14,400 ×9)		1,29,600
Total contribution		2,09,600
Less: Present fixed cost	= 1,90,000	
Add: Increase in sales		
Promotion expenses	= 10,000	2,00,000
Profit		9,600

Option (d) Introducing product 'W' in the place of Z

	₹
Contribution – Product X (10,000 × 8)	80,000
Contribution – Product Y (12,000 × 9)	1,08,000
Contribution – Product W (9,000 × 8)	72,000
Total contribution	2,60,000
Less: Fixed cost	1,90,000
Profit	70,000

Note:

Contribution per unit of Product 'W'

	₹
Selling price per unit	30
Less: Variable cost	

Direct materials	- 10	
Direct labour	- 6	
Variable overheads	- 6	22
Contribution		8

Decision:

Profits under options (a), (b) and (c) are less than the present profit. Under option (d) profit is higher than the present profit. So the best option is option (d).

19.5.8 Key Factor and Product Mix

Illustration-64

From the following particulars, find the most profitable product mix and prepare statement of profitability of that product mix:

	Product A	Product B	Product C
Units budgeted to be produced and sold	1,800	3,000	1,200
Selling price per unit	₹60	₹55	₹50
Requirements per unit:			
Direct materials	5 kg.	3 kg.	4 kg.
Direct labour	4 hrs.	3 hrs.	2 hrs.
Variable overheads	₹7	₹13	₹8
Fixed overheads	₹10	₹10	₹10
Direct material price per kg	₹4	₹4	₹4
Direct labour hour rate	₹2	₹2	₹2
Maximum possible units of sales	4,000 units	5,000 units	1,500 units

All the three products are produced from the same direct material using the same type of machines and labour. Direct labour hour which is the key factor is limited to 20,000 hours.

Solution

Statement showing contribution and ranking of products			
Particulars	**Product A per unit** ₹	**Product B per unit** ₹	**Product C per unit** ₹
Selling price (A)	60	55	50
Variable costs:			
Direct materials	20	12	16

Direct labour	8	6	4
Variable overheads	7	13	8
Total (B)	35	31	28
Contribution (A – B)	25	24	22
No. of labour hours	4 hrs.	3 hrs.	2 hrs.
Contribution per labour hour	$\frac{25}{4}$ = ₹6.25	$\frac{24}{3}$ = ₹8	$\frac{22}{2}$ = ₹11
Ranking	III	II	I

Calculation of most profitable product mix		
		Required labour hours
1)	First Produce - I ranked product C to the maximum possible (1,500 × 2)	3,000
2)	Next Produce - II ranked product B to the maximum possible (5,000 × 3)	15,000
	Total hours used	18,000
	Total hours available	20,000
	Balance 2,000 hrs. available is used to produce 400 units of Product C $\left(\frac{2,000}{5} = 400 \text{ units}\right)$	2,000

Suggested Product Mix is:

Product A - 400 units
Product B - 5,000 units
Product C - 1,500 units

Statement of Profit for the suggested product mix				
Particulars	**Product A (400 units)** ₹	**Product B (5,000 units)** ₹	**Product C (1,500 units)** ₹	**Total** ₹
Contribution per unit	25	24	22	-
Total contribution	10,000	1,20,000	33,000	1,63,000
Less: Budgeted fixed overheads	-	-	-	60,000
Total profit	-	-	-	1,03,000

Note: Budgeted fixed overheads

	₹
Product 'A' - 1,800 × 10	18,000
Product 'B' - 3,000 × 10	30,000
Product 'C' - 1,200 × 10	12,000
Total	60,000

Illustration-65

A company manufactures three products, the budgeted quantity, selling price and unit costs are as under:

	Products		
	A per unit ₹	**B per unit** ₹	**C per unit** ₹
Raw materials at ₹20 per kg.	80	40	20
Direct wages at ₹5 per hour	5	15	10
Variable overheads	10	30	20
Fixed overheads	9	22	18
Budgeted production in units	6,400	3,200	2,400
Selling price per unit	₹140	₹120	₹90

Required:

(i) Present a statement of budgeted profit

(ii) Set optimal product mix and determine the profit, if the supply of raw materials is restricted to 18,400 kg.

(iii) A supplier comes forward to supply 20,000 kg of raw materials at a premium of ₹15 per kg. This supply is over and above the stocks of 18,400 kg available with the company. State whether the company should accept the entire quantity or any part of it. If not, what lowest price should be negotiated? **(CA-Inter)**

Solution

Statement of contribution per unit of Key factor and Ranking of Products			
Particulars	**Products**		
	A per unit ₹	**B per unit** ₹	**C per unit** ₹
Selling Price (A)	140	120	90
Variable Costs:			

Raw materials	80	40	20
Direct wages	5	15	10
Variable overheads	10	30	20
Total (B)	95	85	50
Contribution per unit (A − B)	45	35	40
Raw materials per unit	4 kg	2 kg	1 kg
Contribution per kg of raw materials	$\frac{45}{4}$ = ₹11.25	$\frac{35}{2}$ = ₹17.50	$\frac{40}{1}$ = ₹40
Ranking	III	II	I

(i)

Statement showing budgeted profit				
	Products			**Total**
Particulars	**A**	**B**	**C**	**₹**
Budgeted production	6,400 units	3,200 units	2,400 units	-
Contribution per unit	₹45	₹35	₹40	-
Total contribution	₹2,88,000	₹1,12,000	₹96,000	4,96,000
Less: Fixed overheads	-	-	-	1,71,200
Budgeted profit	-	-	-	3,24,800

Note: Fixed Overheads

	₹
Product A - (6,400 × 9)	57,600
Product B - (3,200 × 22)	70,400
Product C - (2,400 × 18)	43,200
Total	1,71,200

(ii)

Statement showing optimum product mix		
		Materials Required (kg.)
1)	First produce - I ranked product C to the maximum (2,400 × 1)	2,400
2)	Next produce - II ranked product B to the maximum (3,200 × 2)	6,400
	Materials used	8,800

	Total materials available	18,400
	Balance material 9,600 kg is used to produce 2,400 units of Product A $\left(\frac{9,600}{4} = 2,400 \text{ units}\right)$	9,600

Suggested Product Mix is:

Product A - 2,400 units
Product B - 3,200 units
Product C - 2,400 units

Statement of Profit for the suggested product mix				
Particulars	**Product A (2,400 units)** ₹	**Product B (3,200 units)** ₹	**Product C (2,400 units)** ₹	**Total** ₹
Contribution per unit	45	35	40	-
Total Contribution	1,08,000	1,12,000	96,000	3,16,000
Total fixed cost	-	-	-	1,71,200
Profit	-	-	-	1,44,400

(iii)

Total Raw Materials requirements for budgeted production	
	₹
Product A - (6,400 units × 4 kg)	25,600
Product B - (3,200 units × 2 kg)	6,400
Product C - (2,400 units × 1 kg)	2,400
Total	34,400
Less: Materials in hand	18,400
Shortage of materials	16,000

The company should buy only 16,000 kg of materials from a supplier at premium.

(It will be used to produce Product A)

Statement showing maximum price that can be offered for raw materials

Present price per kg.	₹20
Add: Premium	₹15
Price offered	₹35

Raw material required per unit of product A = 4 kg	
Raw material premium per unit of product A = (4 × 15)	₹60
Current contribution	₹45
Loss per unit	₹15

$$\text{Loss per kg. of material} = \frac{15}{4} = ₹3.75$$

If premium is reduced below ₹11.75 per kg (i.e. 15 – 3.75), the raw materials may be purchased. So the maximum price should be below ₹31.75 (i.e. 20 + 11.75). It may be ₹31 or any lower price negotiated.

19.5.9 Plant Merger

Illustration-66

X, Y and Z are locations of plants owned by a single company. Contemplating the merger of plants they want you to find out (i) the capacity of the merged plant at break-even, (ii) profits at 80% capacity after merger, and (iii) sales for a desired profit of ₹35 lakh after merger of plants. The details pre-merger are as under:

	X	Y	Z
Capacity utilisation	100%	80%	60%
Turnover (₹)	400 lakh	290 lakh	160 lakh
Variable costs (₹)	250 lakh	200 lakh	80 lakh
Fixed costs (₹)	80 lakh	50 lakh	60 lakh

(ICWA-Inter)

Solution

Marginal Cost Statement at 100% capacity of merged plants (₹in lakhs)				
Particulars	**Products**			**Total (₹)**
	X - 100% capacity (₹)	**Y - 100% capacity (₹)**	**Z - 100% capacity (₹)**	
Turnover	400	$\left(\frac{290}{80} \times 100\right) =$ 362.50	$\left(\frac{160}{60} \times 100\right) =$ 266.67	1,029.17
Less: Variable cost	250	$\left(\frac{200}{80} \times 100\right) =$ 250.00	$\left(\frac{80}{60} \times 100\right) =$ 133.33	633.33

Contribution	150	112.50	133.34	395.84
Less: Fixed cost	80	50.00	60.00	190.00
Profit	70	62.50	73.34	205.84

(i)

$$\text{Break-even point} = \frac{\text{Fixed cost}}{\text{Contribution}} \times \text{Sales}$$

$$= \frac{190}{395.84} \times 1{,}029.17$$

$$= ₹494 \text{ lakh}$$

$$\text{Break-even capacity} = \frac{494}{1{,}029.17} \times 100 = 48\%$$

(ii)

Profit at 80% capacity	₹(lakhs)
Sales at 80% capacity $\left(1,029.17 \times \frac{80}{100}\right)$	823.33
Less: Variable cost $\left(633.33 \times \frac{80}{100}\right)$	506.66
Contribution	316.67
Less: Fixed cost	190.00
Profit at 80% capacity	126.67

(iii) **Sales for a desired profit of ₹35 lakh**

$$= \frac{\text{Fixed cost} + \text{Desired Profit}}{\text{Contribution}} \times \text{Sales}$$

$$= \frac{190 + 35}{395.84} \times 1{,}029.17$$

$$= ₹585 \text{ lakh}$$

Illustration-67

There are two similar plants under the same management. The management wants to merge these two plants. The following particulars are available:

	Factory I	**Factory II**
Capacity operated	100%	60%
Sales	₹300 lakh	₹120 lakh

Variable costs	₹220 lakh	₹90 lakh
Fixed costs	₹40 lakh	₹20 lakh

You are required to calculate:

(a) What would be the capacity of the merged plant to be operated for the purpose of the break-even and

(b) What would be the profitability on working at 75% of merged capacity?

(ICWA-Inter)

Solution

Marginal Cost Statement of merged plant at 100% capacity			
			(₹in lakhs)
Particulars	**Factory I** 100% capacity ₹	**Factory II** 100% capacity ₹	**Merged plant** 100% capacity ₹
Sales	300	$\left(\frac{120}{60} \times 100\right) = 200$	500
Less: Variable cost	220	$\left(\frac{90}{60} \times 100\right) = 150$	370
Contribution	80	50	130
Less: Fixed cost	40	20	60
Profit	40	30	70

(i)

$$\text{Break-even point} = \frac{\text{Fixed cost}}{\text{Contribution}} \times \text{Sales}$$

$$= \frac{60}{130} \times 500 = ₹230.77 \text{ lakh}$$

$$\text{Break-even capacity} = \frac{230.77}{500} \times 100 = 46.15\%$$

(ii)

Profit at 75% capacity	₹(lakhs)
Sales at 75% capacity $\left(500 \times \frac{75}{100}\right)$	375.00
Less: Variable cost $\left(370 \times \frac{75}{100}\right)$	277.50
Contribution	97.50
Less: Fixed cost	60.00
Profit at 75% capacity	37.50

19.5.10 Indifference Point

Illustration-68

PQ Ltd. has been offered a choice to buy a machine between A and B. You are required to compute:

(a) Break-even point for each of the machine

(b) Level of sales at which both machines earn equal profits

(c) Range of sales at which one is more profitable than the other.

Relevant data are given below:

	Machine A	Machine B
Annual output (in units)	10,000	10,000
Fixed cost (₹)	30,000	16,000
Profit (₹)	30,000	24,000

Market price of the product is expected to be ₹10 per unit.

(ACS - Inter)

Solution

(a)

Computation of Break-even Point		
	Machine A (₹)	**Machine B (₹)**
Fixed cost	30,000	16,000
Add: Profit	30,000	24,000
Total contribution	60,000	40,000
Contribution per unit	₹6	₹4

$$\text{Break} - \text{even point} = \frac{\text{Fixed cost}}{\text{Contribution per unit}}$$

$$\text{Machine A} = \frac{30{,}000}{6} = 5{,}000 \text{ units or } ₹50{,}000$$

$$\text{Machine B} = \frac{16,000}{4} = 4{,}000 \text{ units or } ₹40{,}000$$

(b) Sales level where both machines earn equal profit

This involves computation of indifference point.

$$\text{Indifference point (in units)} = \frac{\text{Difference in fixed cost}}{\text{Difference in contribution per unit}}$$

$$= \frac{30{,}000 - 16{,}000}{6 - 4} = \frac{14{,}000}{2} = 7{,}000 \text{ units}$$

Verification:

	Machine A (₹)	**Machine B (₹)**
Contribution	42,000 (7,000×6)	28,000 (7,000×4)
Less: Fixed cost	30,000	16,000
Profit	12,000	12,000

(c)

$$\text{P/V Ratio} = \frac{\text{Contribution per unit}}{\text{Selling price per unit}}$$

$$\text{Machine A} = \frac{6}{10} \times 100 = 60\%$$

$$\text{Machine B} = \frac{4}{10} \times 100 = 40\%$$

Machine A will be more profitable for sales range above 7,000 units, because its P/V Ratio is higher.

Machine B will be more profitable in the sales range from 4,000 units to 6,999 units, because its break-even point is lower.

19.5.11 Miscellaneous

Illustration-69

(Flexible Budget)

Prepare a budget for 70% capacity from the following cost data at 40% capacity:

Direct materials cost	₹20 lakh
Administrative overheads	₹8 lakh
Direct HR cost	₹30 lakhs
Factory overheads	₹24 lakh
Selling overheads	₹14 lakh
Sales	₹120 lakh

Materials cost gets reduced by 20% at 70% capacity utilisation. Factory overheads are 50% fixed. Administration overheads 60% are fixed and selling overheads 40% are fixed. 70% capacity production could be sold only if there is a reduction of 10% in sales price.

Also calculate (a) P/V ratio, (b) Break-even point and (c) Margin of safety at 70% capacity utilisation. **(ICWA-Inter adapted)**

Solution

Budget for 70% capacity utilisation (₹in lakhs)

		₹
Sales (WN-1)	(A)	189.0
Variable Costs:		
Direct materials (See WN-2)		28.0
Administrative overheads (See WN-3)		5.6
Direct HR cost (See WN-4)		52.5
Factory overheads (See WN-5)		21.0
Selling overheads (See WN-6)		14.7
	Total (B)	121.8
	Contribution C (A – B)	67.2
Fixed Costs:		
Administration overheads		4.8
Factory overheads		12.0
Selling overheads		5.6
	Total D	22.4
	Profit (C – D)	44.8

(a) $\text{P/V ratio} = \dfrac{\text{Contribution}}{\text{Sales}} \text{x } 100$

$= \dfrac{67.2}{189} \times 100$

$= 35.56\%$

(b) $\text{Break-even point} = \dfrac{\text{Fixed cost}}{\text{P/V ratio}}$

$= \dfrac{22.4}{35.56/100}$

$= ₹62.99$ lakh

(c) Margin of safety = Actual sales – BEP Sales

$$= 189 - 62.99$$

$$= ₹126.01 \text{ lakh}$$

Working Note

1. Sales at 40% capacity = 120 lakhs

   Sales at 70% capacity = $\left(\frac{120}{40} \times 70\right)$ = 210 lakh

   Less: 10% reduction in sale price = 21 lakh

   Adjusted sales at 70% = 189 lakh

2. Direct materials at 40% capacity = 20 lakh

   Direct materials at 70% capacity = $\left(\frac{20}{40} \times 70\right)$ = 35 lakh

   Less: 20% reduction in cost = 7 lakh

   Adjusted materials cost = 28 lakhs

3. Total administration overheads at 40% capacity = 8 lakh

   60% fixed = $8 \times \frac{60}{100}$ = 4.8 lakh

   40% variable = $8 \times \frac{40}{100}$ = 3.2 lakh

   Variable administration overheads at 70% capacity = $\left(\frac{3.2}{40} \times 70\right)$

   = ₹5.6 lakh

4. Direct HR cost at 40% capacity = ₹30 lakh

   Direct HR cost at 70% capacity = $\frac{30 \times 70}{40}$ = ₹52.5 lakh

   Direct HR cost is fully variable.

5. Factory overheads at 40% capacity = ₹24 lakh

   Fixed factory overheads 50% = $\frac{24 \times 50}{100}$ = ₹12 lakh

   Variable factory overheads 50% = $\frac{24 \times 50}{100}$ = ₹12 lakh

   Variable factory overheads 70% capacity = $\frac{12 \times 70}{40}$ = ₹21 lakh

6. Selling overheads at 40% capacity = ₹14 lakh

Fixed selling overheads 40% $= \frac{14 \times 40}{100}$ = ₹5.6 lakh

Variable selling overheads 60% $= \frac{14 \times 60}{100}$ = ₹8.4 lakh

Variable selling overheads 70% capacity $= \frac{8.4 \times 70}{40}$ = ₹14.7 lakh

19.6 EXERCISE

I. Objective Type Questions

A. State whether the following statements are true or false

(i) Marginal costing is also known as direct costing.

(ii) A key factor, which at a particular time or over a period will not limit the activities of the organisation.

(iii) Variable cost per unit remains constant.

(iv) Fixed cost per unit remains constant.

(v) Total variable cost does not increase in proportion to output.

(vi) Administration costs are mostly fixed.

(vii) In make or buy decisions only cost factors are relevant.

(viii) Marginal costing can be used with process costing.

(ix) In marginal costing, valuation of stock is done on variable cost basis.

(x) Profit = Sales - Contribution.

(xi) P/V ratio $= \frac{\text{Profit}}{\text{Sales}} \times 100$

(xii) In absorption costing, valuation of stock is done on total cost basis.

(xiii) In absorption costing, total cost is analysed as variable cost and fixed cost.

(xiv) Semi-variable cost is recognised in marginal costing.

(xv) Profit = Margin of Safety × P/V ratio

(xvi) Sales = Contribution ÷ P/V ratio

(xvii) Marginal costing is a method of costing.

(xviii) Absorption costing is more suitable for decision making than marginal costing.

(xix) Marginal costing is a technique of cost control.

(xx) Profit in marginal costing will be more when sales is more than production.

(xxi) Cost - Volume - Profit relationship is a more comprehensive term than break-even analysis.

(xxii) Contribution and incremental revenue are same.

(xxiii) The valuation of stock is higher in absorption costing than in marginal costing.

(xxiv) Angle of incidence is the angle between sales line and total cost in a break-even chart.

(xxv) Variable cost is also called marginal cost.

(xxvi) An increase in volume of production will result in reduction in unit variable cost.

(xxvii) Changes in fixed cost will affect break-even point.

(xxviii) Marginal cost is the difference between the total cost and fixed cost.

(xxix) The difference between budgeted output and actual output is margin of safety.

(xxx) By lowering fixed cost P/V ratio can be improved.

[**Ans: True:** (iii), (vi), (viii), (ix), (xii), (xv), (xvi), (xix), (xx), (xxi), (xxiii), (xxiv), (xxv), (xxvii), (xxviii), (xxx)

False: (i), (ii), (iv), (v), (vii), (x), (xi), (xiii), (xiv), (xvii), (xxviii), (xxii), (xxvi), (xxix)]

B. Fill in the blanks

(i) Marginal costing is also called ______________ costing.

(ii) Marginal cost does not include ______________ cost.

(iii) Stocks are valued on total cost basis in ______________ costing.

(iv) Fixed cost is not included in valuation of stock in ______________ costing.

(v) In marginal costing fixed costs are charged to ______________

(vi) Sales revenue and total cost is equal at ______________.

(vii) If closing stock of finished goods is more than the opening stock of finished goods profit will be more in ______________ costing.

(viii) Variable cost per unit remains ______________ at all levels of output.

(ix) Actual sales in excess of BEP sales is called ______________.

(x) The chart showing the cost-volume-profit relationship is called ______________

(xi) Profit planning and cost control is possible under ______________ costing.

(xii) ______________ factor influences the entire activities of an organization.

(xiii) The angle formed between sales line and total cost line above the break-even point in a BEP chart is called ______________.

(xiv) Margin of safety × P/V ratio is ______________

(xv) In buy or make decision ______________ and ______________ factors are considered.

(xvi) Contribution minus ______________ cost is profit.

(xvii) At break-even point, the contribution is equal to ______________.

(xviii) In an ordinary break-even chart fixed cost line runs parallel to ______________.

(xix) Sales × P/V ratio is equal to ______________.

(xx) At break-even point contribution is equal to ______________.

[**Ans:** (i) variable, (ii) fixed, (iii) absorption, (iv) marginal, (v) profit and loss account, (vi) BEP, (vii) absorption, (viii) constant, (ix) margin of safety, (x) break-even chart, (xi) marginal, (xii) key/limiting, (xiii) angle of incidence, (xiv) profit, (xv) cost; non-cost, (xvi) fixed, (xvii) fixed cost, (xviii) x-axis, (xix) contribution, (xx) fixed cost]

II. Theory Questions

A. Short answer type questions

1. What is marginal cost?
2. Explain contribution.
3. Define marginal costing.
4. What is absorption costing?
5. What is break-even point?
6. What is break-even chart?
7. What is P/V ratio?
8. Explain Cost-Volume-Profit analysis.
9. What is key factor / limiting factor?
10. What is margin of safety?
11. Explain indifference point.
12. What is angle of incidence?
13. Explain the difference between fixed cost and variable cost.
14. State how the following independent situations will affect the P/V Ratio.
    (a) An increase in physical sales volume.
    (b) An increase in fixed cost.
    (c) A decrease in variable cost per unit.
    (d) A decrease in the contribution margin.

(e) An increase in the selling price per unit.

(f) A decrease in the fixed cost.

(g) A 10% increase in both selling price and variable cost per unit.

(h) A 10% increase in selling price per unit and 10% decrease in physical sales volume.

(i) A 50% increase in variable cost per unit and 50% decrease in fixed cost.

(j) An increase in angle of incidence.

[**Ans:** 14. (a) No change, (b) No change, (c) Increase in P/V Ratio, (d) Decrease in P/V Ratio, (e) Increase in P/V ratio, (f) No change, (g) No change, (h) Increase in P/V ratio, (i) Decrease in P/V ratio, (j) Increase in P/V ratio]

B. Long answer type questions

1. Explain the differences between absorption costing and marginal costing.
2. Define marginal costing. Explain the assumptions of marginal costing.
3. What are the managerial uses of marginal costing? Explain.
4. Cost-Volume-Profit analysis is a very useful technique to management for cost control and profit planning. Explain.
5. Define marginal cost and marginal costing. How variable costs and fixed costs are treated in marginal costing?
6. What are the advantages and limitations of marginal costing?
7. What is contribution and P/V ratio? Describe its uses to management.
8. What is break-even points? What is its importance?
9. What are the advantages of break-even analysis?
10. What are the assumptions underlying break-even point?
11. What are the limitations of break-even analysis?
12. Write short notes on:

    (a) Break-even analysis,

    (b) Break-even point,

    (c) Importance of break-even point.
13. What is margin of safety? Explain its importance to management.
14. Explain the ways by which profit volume ratio can be improved.
15. What is marginal cost? What are the circumstances under which price may be fixed below the marginal cost.

16. Discuss the significance of the following terms in relation to marginal costing:
    (a) Profit/volume ratio,
    (b) Break-even point and
    (c) Margin of safety.
17. "Marginal costing is a valuable aid for managerial decisions". Discuss.
18. List out the advantages and assumptions of break-even chart.
19. What is key factor? Explain its significance.
20. Explain the various cost factors and non-cost factors in "Make or Buy" decisions.
21. Explain various situations under which prices may be fixed below the cost.
22. Define break-even chart. Explain various types of break-even charts.
23. Explain the various factors to be considered in plant "Shut down" decisions.
24. What are the differences between marginal costing and direct costing?

III. Practical Problems

A. Short answer type questions

1.

Selling price per unit	₹40
Variable cost per unit	₹25
Fixed cost	₹3,60,000

Calculate (a) P/V ratio, (b) Break-even point.

[**Ans:** (a) P/V ratio - 37.5%, (b) BEP - 24,000 units or ₹9,60,000]

2. Fixed cost ₹4,20,000; Selling price per unit ₹50; Variable cost ₹35.

   Find out (a) Break-even point in units and (b) New break-even point if selling price is reduced by 10%.

   [**Ans:** (a) Break-even point - 28,000 units; (b) New BEP - 42,000 units]

3. Sales ₹10,000; Variable Cost 75% of sales, Profit ₹1,000.

   Find (a) Break-even sales; (b) What would be the sales volume to realize a profit ₹1,500.

   [**Ans:** (a) BEP sales ₹6,000; (b) Sales volume ₹12,000]

4. Sales ₹5,00,000; Fixed cost ₹1,00,000 and break-even point ₹4,00,000.

   Find (a) P/V ratio, (b) Profit

   [**Ans:** (a) P/V ratio - 25%; (b) Profit - ₹25,000]

5. Fixed cost ₹1,00,000; Profit ₹25,000; Break-even point ₹2,00,000.

   Find the sales.

   [**Ans:** Sales - ₹2,50,000]

6. The ratio of variable cost to Sales is 75%. The break-even point occurs at 60% of capacity sales. Find the capacity sales when fixed costs are ₹1,00,000. Also compute profit at 80% capacity sales.

   [**Ans:** Capacity sales ₹6,66,667; Profit at 80% Capacity ₹33,333]

7. P/V ratio - 40%, Margin of Safety - 30%, Sales volume ₹5,00,000.

   Find the profit.

   [**Ans:** Profit ₹60,000]

8. Margin of safety ₹50,000; MS ratio - 25%, P/V ratio - 40%.

   Find (a) Break-even sales; (b) Fixed cost; (c) Profit.

   [**Ans:** (a) BEP - ₹1,50,000; (b) Fixed cost - ₹60,000; (c) Profit ₹20,000]

9. Fixed cost ₹60,000; Profit ₹40,000. P/V ratio 40%. Find sales.

   [**Ans:** Sales ₹2,50,000]

10.

Selling price	₹75 per unit
Variable cost	₹50 per unit
Fixed expenses	₹3,00,000

   Calculate: (a) P/V ratio, (b) Break-even point in units; (c) New selling price per unit if break-even point is reduced to 8,000 units.

   [**Ans:** (a) P/V ratio 33.33%; (b) BEP 12,000 units, (c) Selling price per unit ₹87.50]

11. A plant produces a product which costs ₹3 per unit when produced in quantities of 10,000 units and ₹2.50 per unit when produced in quantities of 20,000 units. You are asked to estimate fixed cost.

    [**Ans:** Fixed cost ₹10,000]

12. The profit volume ratio of a company is 40% and its margin of safety is 50%. Work out the net profit if sales volume is ₹8,00,000.

    [**Ans:** Profit ₹1,60,000]

13. A company has a P/V ratio of 40%. By what percentage must sales be increased to offset (i) 10% reduction in selling and (ii) 20% reduction selling price.

    [**Ans:** (i) 33 1/3%; (ii) 100%]

14.

Sales	₹12,00,000
P/V Ratio	40%

Find variable cost.

[**Ans:** Variable cost ₹7,20,000]

15. X Ltd. earned a profit of ₹50,000 on a sales of ₹4,00,000 in the first quarter of the year 2009-2010. In the next quarter the profit and sales are ₹70,000 and ₹5,00,000 respectively.

    Find (a) P/V ratio and (b) Fixed cost.

    [**Ans:** (a) P/V ratio - 20%; (b) Fixed cost - ₹30,000]

16. From the following data calculate (a) P/V Ratio, (b) Profit and (c) Sales volume required to earn a profit of ₹5,000.

Sales	₹20,000
Fixed cost	₹4,000
Break-even point	₹10,000

[**Ans:** (a) P/V ratio - 40%, (b) Profit - ₹4,000; (c) Sales - ₹22,500]

17. X Ltd. has two factories A and B producing the same article whose selling price is ₹200. Other details are :

	A	B
Capacity in units	10,000	15,000
Variable cost (₹)	120	150
Fixed expenses	2,50,000	3,00,000

Determine:

(a) BEP of each factory

(b) P/V ratio of each factory and

(c) Composite P/V ratio.

[**Ans:** (a) BEP - A) 3,125 units; B) 6,000 units; (b) P/V ratio - A) 40%; B) 25%; (c) Composite P/V ratio - 31%]

18. In a purely competitive market, 10,000 pocket transistors can be manufactured and sold and certain profit is generated. It is estimated that 2,000 pocket transistors need be manufactured and sold in a monopoly market to earn the same profit.

    Profit under both the conditions is targeted at ₹2,00,000. The variable cost per transistor is ₹100 and the total fixed cost is ₹37,000.

    You are required to find out the selling price both under monopoly and competitive conditions.

    (ICWA-Inter)

    [**Ans:** Selling price - Monopoly condition ₹218.50 per unit; Competitive condition - ₹123.70 per unit]

B. Comprehensive Practical Problems

Absorption Costing

1. The following information is extracted from the books of X Ltd:

	2008-09	2009-10	2010-11
Installed capacity (units)	20,000	20,000	20,000
Opening stock (units)	-	-	2,000
Closing stock (units)	-	2,000	-
Production (units)	15,000	18,000	16,000
Selling price per unit (₹)	40	40	40
Fixed cost for the year (₹)	1,00,000	1,00,000	1,00,000
Variable cost per unit	₹25	₹25	₹25

You are required to prepare statements showing profit or loss for the above three years under (a) Absorption costing; and (b) Marginal costing.

Ans:

	2008-09	2009-10	2010-11
Profit - Absorption costing	1,25,000	1,51,111	1,58,889
Profit - Marginal costing	1,25,000	1,40,000	1,70,000

P/V Ratio, BEP, Margin of Safety, etc.

2. The following information is extracted from the books of Best Ltd. for the year 2010-11 :

Fixed cost	₹75,000
Variable cost	₹1,25,000
Number of units sold	10,000
Selling price per unit	₹30

Calculate (a) P/V ratio; (b) Break-even point; (c) Margin of Safety ratio; (d) Sales required to earn a profit ₹50,000.

[**Ans:** (a) P/V ratio - 58.33%; (b) Break-even point - ₹1,28,580; (c) Margin of Safety ratio - 57.14%; (d) Sales required - ₹2,14,298]

3. The following information is extracted from the books of Prime Ltd.

Year	Sales (₹)	Profit (₹)	Loss (₹)
2009	5,00,000	-	10,000
2010	6,00,000	15,000	-

Calculate (a) P/V ratio; (b) Fixed cost; (c) Break-even point; (d) Sales required to earn a profit of ₹30,000; (e) Margin of Safety and MS ratio for sales in (d) above.

[**Ans:** (a) P/V ratio -25%; (b) Fixed cost -₹1,35,000; (c) Break-even point - ₹5,40,000; (d) Sales required - ₹6,60,000; (e) Margin of Safety Sales - ₹1,20,000 and MS ratio - 18.18%]

4. X Ltd. sells 1,000 units of a product per month. The selling price is ₹25 per unit. The variable cost is ₹16 per unit. Fixed cost is ₹4,000 per month. To meet the increased competition, they want to reduce the price by 10%.

   Calculate (a) Present and future P/V ratio. (b) Also find the number of units that the company should sell to maintain the present profit.

   [**Ans:** (a) P/V ratio - (i) Present 36%; (ii) Future 28.89%; (b) Sales -1,231 units]

5. Best Ltd. provides the following information relating to the manufacture of a product:

	Per unit (₹)
Selling price	58
Direct materials	20
Direct wages	14
Variable overheads	6
Fixed overheads per year	72,000

   (a) Find BEP and P/V ratio. (b) If Sales is 20% and 30% above the break-even point, what would be the profits?

   [**Ans:** (a) BEP - 4,000 units (or) ₹2,32,000. P/V ratio - 31.03%; (b) Profit - (i) ₹14,387.52; (ii) ₹21,586.48]

6. H Ltd. produced and sold 20,000 cycles last year at a price of ₹2,000 each. The cost structure per cycle is as follows:

	₹
Direct materials	600
Direct wages	500
Variable overheads	300
Fixed overheads	200
Total cost	1,600
Profit	400
Sales	2,000

   Due to heavy competition the price has to be reduced to ₹1,900 for the coming year. Assuming no change in cost rates, find out how many extra cycles to be sold to ensure the same amount of total profits as in the last year.

   [**Ans:** Extra cycles to be sold 4,000]

7. M Ltd. manufactures and sells four products namely P, Q, R and S. The sales mix of the products in total sales are: 40%, 25%, 20% and 15% of P, Q, R and S respectively. Total budgeted sales is ₹10,00,000.

   Variable costs as % of sales are:

P	70%
Q	60%
R	65%
S	50%

   Fixed costs are ₹2,00,000

   Calculate BEP of the products on overall basis and also find out the net profit on budgeted sales.

   [**Ans:** BEP ₹5,47,945; Net profit - ₹1,65,000]

8. The following details are extracted from the books of a company for two years:

	Sales (₹)	Total cost (₹)
2009-10	25,00,000	20,40,000
2010-11	31,00,000	25,20,000

   Calculate:

   (a) P/V ratio
   (b) Fixed cost
   (c) Break-even point
   (d) Sales required to earn a profit of ₹6,50,000
   (e) Profit on sales volume of ₹40,00,000 and margin of safety ratio.

   [**Ans:** (a) P/V ratio - 20%; (b) Fixed cost - ₹40,000; (c) break-even point - ₹2,00,000; (d) Sales - ₹34,50,000; (e) Profit - ₹7,60,000 and MS Ratio 95%]

9. A company has an annual fixed cost of ₹2,10,000. In 2010 sales amounted to ₹8,00,000 as compared with ₹6,50,000 in 2009. Profit in 2010 was ₹63,000 higher than that in 2009.

   (a) At what level of sales does the company break-even.
   (b) Determine profit or loss on a forecasted sales volume of ₹10,00,000.
   (c) If there is a reduction in selling price by 10% in 2011 and the company desires to earn the same amount of profit as in 2010, what would be the required sales volume?

   [**Ans:** (a) BEP ₹5,00,000; (b) Profit - ₹2,10,000; (c) Sales- ₹9,44,882]

10. A firm producing and selling product M, sells 12,000 units per annum at a selling price of ₹20 per unit. Variable cost per unit is ₹10 per unit. Annual fixed cost is ₹72,000. Market research shows that there is a great demand for the product if the price can be reduced. It is estimated that 60,000 units can be sold, if price is reduced to ₹12.50.

Advise the management in this regard.

[**Ans:** Proposal to reduce the price is acceptable because profit increases by ₹30,000]

11. The following information is taken from the books of Premier Ltd:

Sales	₹5,00,000
Variable cost	₹3,00,000
Fixed cost	₹1,20,000

(a) Find out the P/V ratio, BEP and Margin of Safety.

(b) Calculate the effect on the above of the following:

i. 15% increase in fixed cost.

ii. 10% decrease in fixed cost.

iii. 10% decrease in variable cost.

iv. 20% increase in variable cost.

v. 10% decrease in fixed cost and 10% increase in variable cost.

vi. 10% increase in sales volume.

vii. 15% decrease in sales volume.

viii. 20% increase in fixed cost and 20% decrease in variable cost.

Ans:

	P/V ratio	**BEP (₹)**	**MOS (₹)**
(a)	40%	3,00,000	2,00,000
(b) (i)	40%	3,45,000	1,55,000
(ii)	40%	2,70,000	2,30,000
(iii)	46%	2,60,870	2,39,130
(iv)	28%	4,28,571	71,429
(v)	34%	3,17,647	1,82,353
(vi)	40%	3,00,000	2,50,000
(vii)	40%	3,00,000	1,25,000
(viii)	52%	2,76,923	2,23,077

Sales Mix

12. The following information is taken from the records of Sri Ram Ltd:

	Products	
	A (₹)	**B (₹)**
(i) Direct materials (₹) per unit	35	42
(ii) Direct wages per unit	18	20
(iii) Selling price per unit	85	100

(iv) Fixed overheads for the year	₹25,000
(v) Variable overheads 100% of Direct wages	
(vi) Proposed sales mix: (i) 500 units of A and 1,000 units of B (ii) 750 units of A and 750 units B (iii) 1,000 units of A and 500 units B	

Calculate:

(a) The unit marginal cost and unit contribution.

(b) The total contribution and profit from each of the above sales mixes.

Ans:

(a) Marginal cost per unit: A -₹71 and B - ₹82; Contribution per unit: A - ₹14 and B - ₹18.

(b)

	Contribution (₹)	Profit (₹)
Sales mix (i)	25,000	5,000
Sales mix (ii)	24,000	4,000
Sales mix (iii)	23,000	3,000

Make or Buy

13. Ride Well Cycles Ltd. purchases 20,000 bells per annum from an outside supplier at ₹5 each. The management feels that these be manufactured and not purchased. A machine costing ₹50,000 will be required to manufacture the item within the factory. The machine has an annual capacity of 30,000 units and life of 5 years. The following additional information is available:

Materials cost per bell	₹2.00
Labour cost per bell	₹1.00
Variable overheads	100% of labour cost

You are required to advise whether:

(a) The company should continue to purchase the bells from outside supplier or should make them in the factory; and

(b) Should the company accept an order to supply 5,000 bells to the market at a selling price of ₹4.50 per unit? **(ACS - Inter)**

Ans:

(a) Cost of production ₹4.50 per bell. It is better to produce the bell.

(b) The order to supply 5,000 bells should be accepted because there will be a profit of ₹0.50 per bell

14. Auto Ltd. manufactures motor cars. At present it manufactures 10,000 units of component X.123. The following are the cost details of manufacturing 10,000 units of the above component.

Direct materials	₹7,00,000
Direct labour	₹7,00,000
Variable factory overheads	₹5,00,000
Fixed factory overheads	₹6,00,000

An outside supplier offers to supply the component at a price of ₹210 per unit. There will be a savings of ₹1,00,000 in fixed cost.

Required:

(a) Should the component be continued to be manufactured in the factory or purchased from outside supplier. The capacity released cannot be put to any other use.

(b) In case the released capacity can be leased to other manufacturers at a rent of ₹2,50,000. What would be your decision?

[**Ans:** (a) Purchase the component, savings ₹10 per component, (b) purchase the component and lease out released capacity, savings ₹15 per unit]

15. Key factory/limiting factor. The following information is taken from the records of Vision Ltd.

Particulars	**Products**	
	A (per unit)	**B (per unit)**
Selling price	₹200	₹300
Raw material consumed	3 kg	5 kg
Materials cost	₹40	₹60
Direct wages	₹40	₹50
Direct expenses	₹10	₹15
Machine hours used	5 hours	8 hours
Overhead expenses:		
Fixed	₹15	₹20
Variable	₹20	₹50

Direct wages is ₹10 per hour. Comment on the profitability of each product when the:

(a) Total sales potential in units is limited.

(b) Total sales potential in value is limited.

(c) Raw material is in short supply.

(d) Production capacity in terms of machine hours is limited.

(e) Production capacity in terms of labour hours is limited.

Ans: Product Rankings

	Limiting factor	A	B	Basis of ranking
(a)	Sales (units)	II	I	Contribution per unit
(b)	Sales (Value)	I	II	P/V Ratio
(c)	Raw material	I	II	Contribution per kg of material
(d)	Machine hours	I	II	Contribution per machine hour
(e)	Labour hours	II	I	Contribution per labour hour

16. A market gardener is planning his production for next season and he asked you, as a cost accountant, to recommend the optimal product mix of vegetable production for the coming year.

He has given you the following data relating to the current year:

	Potatoes	Turnips	Parships	Carrots
Area occupied (in acres)	50	40	60	50
Yield per acre (in tonnes)	20	16	18	24
Selling price per tonne (₹)	1,000	1,250	1,590	1,350
Variable cost per acre:				
Fertilisers (₹)	70	50	90	80
Seeds (₹)	30	40	60	50
Pesticides (₹)	50	40	40	50
Direct wages (₹)	800	900	1,000	1,140

The land which is being used for production for carrots and parships can be used for either crop, but not for potatoes and turnips. The land being used for potatoes and turnips can be used for either crop, but not for carrots and parships. In order to provide adequate market service, the gardener must produce each year at least 80 tonnes each of potatoes and turnips and 72 tonnes each of parships and carrots. Annual fixed cost ₹25,00,000.

(a) You are required to prepare a statement to show:
   i. The profit for the current year
   ii. The profit for the production mix, which would you recommend?

(b) Assuming that the land could be cultivated in such a way that any of the above crops could be produced and there was no market commitment, you are required to:
   i. Advise the market gardener on which crop he could concentrate his production;
   ii. Calculate the profit if he were to do so, and
   iii. Calculate the break-even point sales in terms of rupees.

[**Ans:** (a) (i) Profit ₹24,11,100; (ii) Profit ₹26,18,300; (b) (i) carrot; (ii) Profit ₹37,16,000; (iii) Break-even point ₹26,06,178]

17. The following particulars are extracted from the records of a company:

Particulars	Products	
	A (per unit)	B (per unit)
Sales (₹)	100	120
Consumption of material	2 kg	3 kg
Materials cost (₹)	10	15
Direct wages (₹)	15	10
Direct expenses (₹)	5	6
Machine hours used (Hours)	3	2
Overhead expenses:		
Fixed (₹)	5	10
Variable (₹)	15	20

Direct wages per hour is ₹5.

(a) Comment on the profitability of each product (both use the same raw material) when:
   i. Total sales potential is limited.
   ii. Raw material is in short supply.
   iii. Production capacity (in terms of machine hours) is the limiting factor.

(b) Assuming raw material as the key factor, availability of which is 10,000 kg. and maximum sales potential of each product being 3,500 units, find out the product mix which will yield the maximum profit. **(ICWA-Inter)**

[**Ans:** (a) (i) Product B, (ii) Product A, (iii) Product B, (b) Sales mix 3,500 units of product A and 1,000 units of Product B]

Accepting orders below total cost

18. A Ltd. operating at 50% of its capacity produces and sells 10,000 units at a price of ₹10 per unit. The cost details are as follows:

	₹
Materials	25,000
Wages	25,000
Variable overheads	15,000
Fixed overheads	10,000
	75,000

A foreign buyer offers to buy 10,000 units at a unit price of ₹7.25.

Due to increase in volume of production material price of all materials decreases by 2%. Wage rates remains constant but due to employment of new workers, labour efficiency decreases by

3% on all production.

Prepare a statement showing changes in profit if export order is accepted. Advise the management whether export order should be accepted or not.

[**Ans:** Profit increases from ₹25,000 to ₹32,000 if export order is accepted. So it is profitable to accept the export order.]

19. A company currently operating at 80% capacity gives the following particulars:

	₹
Sales	32,00,000
Direct materials	10,00,000
Direct labour	4,00,000
Variable overheads	2,00,000
Fixed overheads	13,00,000

An export order has been received that would utilise half the capacity of the factory. The order cannot be split i.e., it has to be taken in full and executed at 10% below the normal domestic price or rejected totally.

The alternatives available to the management are:

(a) Reject the order and continue with the domestic sales only (as at present) or

(b) Accept the order, split the capacity between overseas and domestic sales and turn away excess domestic demand or

(c) Increase the capacity so as to accept the export order and maintain the present domestic sales by

i. Buying an equipment that will increase the capacity by 10%. This will result in increase of ₹1,00,000 in fixed costs and

ii. Work overtime to meet balance of required capacity. In that case labour will be paid at one and a half times the normal wage rate.

Prepare a comparative statement of profitability and suggest the best alternative.

(CA-Inter)

[**Ans:** Profit - Alternative (a) ₹3,00,000; Alternative (b) ₹5,00,000; and alternative (c) ₹9,50,000. Alternative (c) is more profitable and should be accepted.]

Discontinuing product line

20. AB Ltd. produces and sells three products X, Y and Z. Their cost details are as follows :

Particulars	**Products**		
	X (₹)	**Y (₹)**	**Z (₹)**
Sales	3,00,000	4,50,000	5,00,000

Costs: Direct materials	1,00,000	1,75,000	1,90,000
Direct Labour	48,000	62,000	1,76,000
Variable overheads	41,000	54,000	95,000
Fixed overheads	65,000	90,000	70,000
Total Cost	2,54,000	3,81,000	5,31,000

As the total cost of product 'Z' is more than the sales revenue, the management wants to discontinue the product. Total fixed cost will be same even after discontinuing the product Z. Advise whether it is advisable to discontinue the product.

[**Ans:** Product 'Z' gives a contribution of ₹39,000. Profit will decrease from ₹84,000 to ₹45,000 if product Z is discontinued. So product Z should be continued.]

Plant merger

21. Two manufacturing companies which have the following operating details decide to merge:

	Company 1	**Company 2**
Capacity utilisation	90%	60%
Sales (₹ in lakhs)	540	300
Variable costs (₹ in lakhs)	396	225
Fixed costs (₹ in lakhs)	80	50

Assuming that the proposal has been implemented, Calculate:

(a) Break-even sales of the merged plant and capacity utilisation at that stage.

(b) Profitability of the merged plant at 80% capacity utilization.

(c) Sales turnover of the merged plant to earn a profit of ₹75 lakh.

(d) When the merged plant is working at a capacity to earn a profit of ₹75 lakh what percentage increase in selling price is required to sustain an increase of 5% in fixed overheads. **(CA-Inter)**

[**Ans:** (a) BEP ₹501.75 lakh, % of capacity at BEP 45.61%, (b) Profit ₹98 lakh, (c) Sales ₹791.23 lakh, (d) 3.17%]

Indifference point

22. X Ltd. wants to buy a machine to replace labour. Two machines i.e., A and B are available. Both machines have the capacity to produce 25,000 units. Their operating costs are as follows:

	Machine A (₹)	**Machine B (₹)**
Fixed costs	60,000	90,000
Variable cost per unit	7.00	5.50

Find the indifference point.

[**Ans:** Indifference point - 20,000 units]

23. Y Company has just been incorporated and plans to produce a product that will sell for ₹10 per unit. Preliminary market surveys show that the demand will be around 10,000 units per year.

The company has the choice of buying one of the two machines, each of which has a capacity of 10,000 units per year. Machine A would have fixed costs of ₹30,000 per year would yield a profit of ₹30,000 per year on the sale of 10,000 units. Machine B would have fixed costs of ₹18,000 per year and would yield a profit of ₹22,000 per year on the sale of 10,000 units.

Variable costs behave linearly for both machines.

Required:

(a) Break-even sales for each machine.

(b) Sales level where both machines are equally profitable.

(c) Range of sales where one machine is more profitable than the other. **(ICWA-Inter)**

[**Ans:** (a) BEP: A - 5,000 units, B - 4,500 units, (b) Sales level 6,000 units, (c) Sales range: B - 4,500 to 6,000 units, A - above 6,000 units]

Exploring new market

24. The following extracts are taken from the sales budget of a company for the current year:

		(₹ in '000)
Sales - 40,000 units at ₹25 per unit		1,000
Selling costs :		
Advertising	100	
Salesmen salary	80	
Travelling expenses	50	
Rent of sales office	10	
Others	10	250

The management is considering a proposal to establish a new market in the eastern region in the next year. It is proposed to increase the advertising expenditure by 25% and appoint an additional sales supervisor at a salary of ₹30,000 per year to establish a market. This will involve additional travelling and travelling expenses shall increase by 10%.

Target annual sales volume at the existing selling price for the new market is 10,000 units. The estimated variable cost of production is ₹12 per unit. Should the company try to establish the new market? **(ICWA-Inter)**

[**Ans:** It is profitable to explore the new market. Profit from new market ₹70,000.]

Shut-down point

25. XY Ltd. operating at its normal capacity produces and sells 50,000 units per year. The unit cost of manufacturing at normal capacity is as follows:

	₹
Direct materials	15.00
Direct labour	5.00
Variable overheads	6.50
Fixed overheads	10.00
Total	36.50

Each unit of the product is sold at ₹44 per unit. Variable selling expenses amount to ₹2.25 per unit.

Due to economic slow-down, the company expects to sell only 10,000 units in the next year. The management wants to shut down the plant temporarily. The unavoidable fixed cost amounts to ₹1,60,000. The additional cost of plant shut-down is ₹15,000 and re-opening cost amounts to ₹20,000.

Whether the plant should be shut down? What is the shut-down point?

[**Ans:** Shut down point - 20,000 units, the plant should be shut down.]

26. AB Ltd. sells its product at ₹25 per unit. In a period, it produces and sells 10,000 units, it incurs a loss of ₹7.50 per unit. If the volume is raised to 25,000 units it earns a profit of ₹6 per unit.

    (a) Calculate break-even point in terms of rupees and in terms of units.

    (b) Find out the margin of safety and profit if the volume of sales is 35,000 units.

    (c) If minimum fixed costs are ₹75,000, irrespective of the level of production, find out the shut-down point.

    [**Ans:** (a) Break-even point - ₹3,75,000 or 15,000 units (b) Margin of safety ₹5,00,000 and profit ₹3,00,000; (c) Shut-down point 10,000 units]

Break-even chart

27. From the following data prepare a break-even chart:

Budgeted output	1,00,000 units
Fixed expenses	₹2,00,000
Variable expenses per unit	₹8
Selling price per unit	₹16

If the selling price is reduced to ₹14.40. What will be the new break-even point.

[**Ans:** BEP - 25,000 units, New BEP 31,250 units]

BUDGETS AND BUDGETARY CONTROL

20

- Meaning
- Features
- Budgetary control - Meaning/Objectives/Advantages/Limitations
- Various terms
- Classifications
  - Period
  - Conditions
  - Coverage
  - Capacity
  - ZBB - Advantages & Disadvantages
  - Performance budget - Advantages & Disadvantages
- Evaluation of performance budget - Control ratios
- Fixed vs Flexible budget - Differences
- Budget reports

20.1 INTRODUCTION

Budget is an effective tool for controlling cost and activities in the hands of the management of an enterprise. Budget is an expression of an enterprise's policy in financial and/or quantitative terms.

Budget is defined as "a financial and/or quantitative statement prepared and approved prior to a defined period of time of the policy to be pursued during that period for the purpose of attaining a given objective. It may include income, expenditure and employment of capital."

20.1.1 Features of a Budget

The above definition reveals the following features of a budget:

1. It is goal oriented. It is aimed at achieving the objectives of an enterprise.
2. It is future oriented. It is prepared and approved prior to a defined period of time.
3. It is an expression of policies and plans in monetary and physical terms.
4. It helps in estimating income and expenditure for the budget period.
5. It also estimates the capital to be employed for achieving the predetermined goals.

Budgeting

Budgeting refers to the process of preparing budgets and employing it for effective control of an enterprise. It includes analysis of a company's strength, weaknesses and opportunities available. It also helps in formulating well defined objectives and policies and plans. It is used as a tool in guiding and controlling the operations of an enterprise.

20.2 BUDGETARY CONTROL

Budgetary control is defined as "the establishment of budgets, relating to the responsibilities of executives to the requirements of a policy and the continuous comparison of actuals with budgeted results either to secure by individual action the objective of that policy or to provide a base for its revision".

From the above definition, we may conclude that budgetary control uses the budgets to control the activities of a firm to achieve the predetermined goals. It includes continuous measurement of actual performance and comparing it with the budgets. It reveals the deviation of actual performance from the budgeted activities. Then corrective actions are taken if deviations are due to internal deficiencies. If deviations are due to external / uncontrollable factors, the budgets are revised.

20.2.1 Objectives of Budgetary Control

1. **Planning**

   Budgeting is a part of planning process. The activities of the firm are determined in advance. Planned activity helps in guiding and motivating the employees. It also analyses the future activities and helps in formulation of business policies and strategies and business goals.

2. Coordination

Budgets are prepared in consultation with the people in various departments. Thus the various functions of different departments are balanced and integrated together. Each department understands the problems of other departments.

3. Optimum employment of capital

The resources required for achieving the firm's objectives are estimated and are made available.

4. Responsibility accounting

Each individual is entrusted with well defined responsibilities and they are made accountable.

5. Control

It provides mechanism for continuous measurement of actual performance and comparing it with the budgeted performance. It thus provides basis for taking corrective action.

20.2.2 Advantages of Budgetary Control

1. Budgetary control helps in framing the policies and goals in precise terms.
2. Well defined goals guide and motivate the employees.
3. Employees co-operate with the management in achieving the goals.
4. It helps to coordinate the activities of various departments.
5. It helps in fixing responsibilities of various people of the firm.
6. It helps in the efficient utilisation of economic resources and thus avoids wastages.
7. It increases the operating efficiency of a firm.
8. It provides suitable basis for introducing standard costing and variance analysis.
9. It also helps to evaluate the performance of individuals and their departments.
10. It helps in introducing responsibility accounting.

20.2.3 Differences between Budget and Forecast

Basis	Budget	Forecast
1. Object	Budget is used as a tool for planning and controlling a firm's operations.	Forecast aims at ascertaining the conditions that will prevail in a future period.
2. Sequence	Budgets are based on forecasts of future events.	Forecasts are made before the budgets are prepared.
3. Coverage	Budgets are prepared for important activities of a firm.	It does not cover any defined events. It is related with determining the future probabilities.

4. Time	Budgets are prepared for a definite period of time.	There is no time limit.
5. Performance	Budgets are meant for actual implementation for achieving a firm's objectives.	It is concerned with assessing future conditions.

20.2.4 Limitations of Budgetary Control

1. Budget is a plan of action for a certain future period. Budgets may become unsuitable due to change in the conditions forecasted.

2. Budget is a plan. It lays down what is to be done and how it is to be done. It curtails freedom of action and innovation of executives.

3. Success of budgetary control depends on the cooperation of all the people in a concern. Sometimes it may be lacking.

4. Budgetary control is a costly process for small and medium concerns.

5. Budgetary control itself will not bring success which depends upon the efficiency of the management.

Budget Committee

It is a group of people responsible for preparing budgets. People from various departments are nominated to this committee. Chief executive officer or a board member will head the committee.

This committee will review the budgets prepared by various departments. Necessary changes are made in the budget to ensure that the budgets prepared by various departments are in harmony with the firm's policies and aims.

Budget Manual

Budget manual is a handbook or booklet. It gives a brief note on the objectives and benefits of a budget. It contains guidelines for preparing budgets. It also fixes the responsibility for preparing budgets. It contains rules and regulations for preparing budgets.

Budget Period

Budgets may be prepared for any period of time. It may be a week, a month or a year. A definite period for which a budget is prepared is called budget period.

Budget Factor

It is also known as the key factor or limiting factor or principal factor. A budget key factor influences the level of all the activities. Budgets for various activities are prepared on the basis of budget key factor. A budget key factor is a resource like materials, labour, power or capital whose availability is in short supply. Such resources which are scarce is called budget factor. For example, a firm may have production facility to produce 1,00,000 units of a product. But raw materials may be available for producing only 60,000 units. Then all the other budgets are to be prepared for 60,000 units only.

20.3 CLASSIFICATION OF BUDGETS

Budgets are classified on various basis. They are:

1. Period
   (a) Long-term budgets
   (b) Short-term budgets
2. Conditions
   (a) Basic budgets
   (b) Current budgets
3. Coverage
   (a) Functional budgets
   (b) Master budgets
4. Capacity
   (a) Fixed budgets
   (b) Flexible budgets
5. Others
   (a) Zero based budgeting
   (b) Performance budgeting

1. Period Basis

(a) Long-term budget
Long-term budgets are prepared for a period exceeding one year. They are only forward looking plans. They act as a guidelines for preparing short term budgets. Long-term budgets are not meant for immediate implementation.

(b) Short-term budget
A budget prepared for a period less than a year is called short-term budget. Short term budgets are prepared for actual implementation and it has a practical value.

2. Conditions Basis

(a) Basic budget

Essentially it is a long-term budget. The conditions and assumptions for preparing budgets should remain unaltered for a long period. Basic budgets are like long-term budget act as a guidelines for preparing short-term budgets.

(b) Current budget

A budget prepared for a short time is called a current budget. It is meant for actual implementation. Conditions prevailing at the present are the basis for preparing these budgets.

3. Coverage Basis

Functional Budgets

Functional budgets are the budgets prepared for various activities of a firm. The following are a list of functional budgets:

i. Materials budget
ii. Production budget
iii. Sales budget
iv. Labour budget
v. Administration overheads budget
vi. Capital expenditure budget
vii. Research and development cost budget
viii. Selling overheads budget
ix. Plant utilisation budget
x. Cash budget

20.3.1 Materials Budget

Materials budget takes two forms. These are: 1. Materials requirement budget and 2. Materials purchase budget.

Materials requirement budget

This budget is prepared on the basis of production budget. The quantity, quality and their availability are taken into consideration. The standard prices of direct materials are also fixed. This budget shows the requirements of various materials for the budgeted production.

Materials purchase/procurement budget

In addition to the particulars of materials required for production, the stock of materials available at the beginning and the desired level of stock to be maintained at the end of the budget period is also considered. Total quantity of materials to be purchased and their cost is ascertained.

Purchase order schedule is prepared considering economic order quantity, reorder levels and safety stocks to be maintained.

Illustration-1

AB Ltd. produces two products 'M' and 'N'. It budgets to sell 5,000 units of 'M' and 7,000 units of 'N' during the first quarter of the forthcoming year. The stock at the beginning of the budget period is expected to be 2,000 units of 'M' and 3,000 units of 'N'. The stock level desired at the closing of the budget period is 2,500 units of 'M' and 3,400 units of 'N'.

Materials 'A' and 'B' are mixed in production of product 'M'. 2 units of material 'A' and 3 units of material 'B' are used to produce one unit of product 'M'.

Materials 'X', 'Y' and 'Z' are mixed to produce product 'N'. 2 units of material 'X', 3 units of materials 'Y' and 5 units of material 'Z' are used in the production of each unit of product 'N'.

The standard prices of materials A, B, X, Y and Z are ₹7, ₹9, ₹8, ₹12 and ₹15 respectively.

Prepare a budget showing the quantity of materials required for budgeted production and their cost.

Solution

Materials Requirement Budget					
	Product 'M'		**Product 'N'**		
	Material 'A'	**Material 'B'**	**Material 'X'**	**Material 'Y'**	**Material 'Z'**
Production (units)	5,500	5,500	7,400	7,400	7,400
Materials requirement per unit of product (units)	2	3	2	3	5
Quantity of materials required	11,000	16,500	14,800	22,200	37,000
Standard price per unit	₹7	₹9	₹8	₹12	₹15
Total cost of materials required (₹)	77,000	1,48,500	1,18,400	2,66,400	5,55,000

Note

Production Budget		
Particulars	**Product 'M'**	**Product 'N'**
Sales budgeted (units)	5,000	7,000
Add: Closing stock (")	2,500	3,400
	7,500	10,400
Less: Opening stock (")	2,000	3,000
Production (")	5,500	7,400

Illustration-2

It is estimated that A Ltd. will have the following raw materials inventory as on 01.04.2011:

Name of material	Quantity	Price	Amount
		₹	₹
P	1,000 units	5	5,000
Q	25 tons	75	1,875
R	3,000 kg	4	12,000
S	2,000 litres	7	14,000
T	5,000 kg	9	45,000
	Total		77,875

The management summarised the requirements of raw materials for various departments as follows:

Materials	Departments			
	I	II	III	IV
P (Units)	20,000	2,000	-	7,000
Q (tons)	-	20	15	35
R (kg)	7,000	9,000	6,000	12,000
S (litres)	3,000	5,000	13,000	-
T (kg)	6,000	-	15,000	4,000

The following inventory is expected on 31.03.2012:

P - 1,500 units; Q - 22 tonnes, R - 3,500 kg; S - 5,000 litres and T - 6,000 kg

Assuming prices of material will remain constant, prepare materials purchase budget.

Solution

Materials Purchase Budget for the year 2011-12					
Particulars	**Materials**				
	P (units)	**Q (tonnes)**	**R (kg)**	**S (litres)**	**T (kg)**
Materials required for production in various departments	29,000	70	34,000	21,000	25,000
Add: Closing stock of materials (on 31.3.2012)	1,500	22	3,500	5,000	6,000
	30,500	92	37,500	26,000	31,000

Less: Opening stock of materials (on 1.4.2011)	1,000	25	3,000	2,000	5,000
Purchase quantity	29,500	67	34,500	24,000	26,000
Std. price per unit (₹)	5	75	4	7	9
Value of materials to be purchased (₹)	1,47,500	5,025	1,38,000	1,68,000	2,34,000

20.3.2 Production Budget

Production budget helps in determining the production of various products during the budget period. Production budget is prepared after taking into consideration the following factors:

1. Budgeted sales as per sales budget.
2. Plant capacity available in the factory.
3. Stock of finished goods in the beginning of the budget period and desired closing stock of finished goods at the end of the budget period.
4. Management's decisions relating to what to produce and what to buy from outside.
5. Seasonal variation in sales and production.
6. Level of stock to be maintained at production point and distribution and sales points.
7. Production scheduling which minimises the cost of production.

Production budget is prepared in terms of physical units.

Production Cost Budget

Production cost budget shows the cost of producing a product during the budget period. The various production costs are direct materials, direct labour and factory overheads. Materials cost is ascertained from materials cost budget, labour cost is ascertained from labour cost budget. Factory overheads is ascertained from factory overheads budget. Factory overheads is also analysed into fixed and variable overheads.

20.3.3 Sales Budget

Sales budget is the most important of all other functional budgets. Sales budget is the basis for preparing materials purchase budget, production budget, labour cost budget and overheads cost budget. Any inaccuracy in sales budget will affect correctness of other functional budgets. Sales budget is to be prepared with due care. The following factors are considered while preparing sales budget:

1. Reports received from salesmen and distributors.
2. Competition from other companies.
3. Sales mix in case of a multi-product company.
4. Geographical area covered. Export sales to different destinations and domestic sales in different regions.
5. Government regulations like restriction on exports, price regulations, etc.
6. Economic conditions like recession or boom.
7. Type of customers to whom products are sold-to retail customers; to manufacturers, to govt. departments etc.
8. Type of marketing like, direct marketing or selling through wholesalers, retailers etc.
9. Seasonal variation in demand for products.
10. Pricing policy of the firm and sensitivity of customers to change in prices.

Sales Forecast

A sales forecast is prepared after considering the above factors. Various techniques are used for making a sales forecast. They are, a simple projection of the past experience and present conditions into future, market survey and statistical methods. Sales budget may be prepared in physical units and/or sales value basis also.

Illustration-3

Sri Ram Ltd., manufactures two products A and B and sells them in two regions, North and South. The actual sales for the current year were:

Product	North	South
A	4,000 units at ₹9	6,000 units at ₹9
B	8,000 units at ₹15	10,000 units at ₹15

A market survey was conducted for preparing sales budget for the next year. It was found that product 'A' is under-priced and an increase in price by ₹1, it will find a steady market. Product 'B' is found to be over-priced and if the price is reduced by ₹2, sales can be increased by 10%. The management decides to give effect to the above price changes.

Sales manager has estimated on the basis of reports received from salesman, sales will increase from current levels as follows over and above the effect of price changes:

Product	North	South
A	+10%	+5%
B	+10%	+15%

Further, with the help of intensive sales promotion activities, additional sales can be made as follows:

Product	North	South
A	500 units	750 units
B	1,200 units	800 units

Prepare a sales budget for the next year.

Solution

Sales Budget for the Next Year							
Product	North			South			Total value
	No. of units	Price ₹	Value ₹	No. of units	Price ₹	Value ₹	₹
A	4,900	10	49,000	7,050	10	70,500	1,19,500
B	10,880	13	1,41,440	13,450	13	1,74,850	3,16,290
Total	-	-	1,90,440	-	-	2,45,350	4,35,790

Working Note

No. of units budgeted

Product 'A':

North	$4{,}000 \times \frac{110}{100}$	4,400 units
Add: Increase		500 units
	Total	4,900 units
South	$6{,}000 \times \frac{105}{100}$	6,300 units
Add: Increase		750 units
	Total	7,050 units

Product 'B':

North	$8{,}000 \times \frac{110}{100} \times \frac{110}{100}$	9,680 units
Add: Increase		1,200 units
	Total	10,880 units
South	$10{,}000 \times \frac{110}{100} \times \frac{115}{100}$	12,650 units
Add: Increase		800 units
	Total	13,450 units

20.3.4 Direct Labour Budget

Labour budget may be classified into three types as (a) labour requirement budget, (b) labour recruitment budget and (c) labour cost budget.

(a) Labour Requirement Budget

Production budget is the basis for preparing labour requirement budget. Total labour required for completing the budgeted production is estimated for each grade of workers. Normal idle time, plant capacity available and overtime policy of the management is considered before deciding the number of workers required in each grade of workers.

(b) Labour Recruitment Budget

This budget is based on labour requirement budget. The following factors are also considered before recruitment. They are number of workers working at present in each grade, expected labour turnover, promotional policy of the management, skilled labour availability and training required for new workers.

Utmost care should be exercised before the requirement. Shortage of labour will adversely affect the production. In Indian environment, it will be very difficult to retrench excess workers or unsuitable workers.

(c) Labour Cost Budget

Different rates of pay are fixed for different grades of workers. The skill required, experience, availability of workers and wages rates prevailing in the surroundings for similar workers are considered before fixing the labour rates. Labour cost is estimated based on number of workers required and their standard wage rates.

Illustration-4

A company budgets to produce 600 dozen articles of a product during the first week of September, 2011. The company follows a 40 hour working week. The following are the other details:

Operation no.	Time per article	Grade of worker	Wage rate per hour ₹
1	15 minutes	A	12.00
2	25 minutes	B	15.00
3	10 minutes	C	10.00
4	30 minutes	D	25.00
5	20 minutes	E	15.00

From the above information prepare a labour requirement budget and a labour cost budget showing labour cost per dozen articles.

Solution

Labour Requirement Budget				
Operation No.	Time per article	Grade of worker	Time required for 600 dozen articles	No. of workers required
1	15 minutes	A	$\frac{15 \times 600 \times 12}{60} = 1{,}800$ hrs	$\frac{1{,}800}{40} = 45$
2	25 minutes	B	$\frac{25 \times 600 \times 12}{60} = 3{,}000$ hrs	$\frac{3{,}000}{40} = 75$
3	10 minutes	C	$\frac{10 \times 600 \times 12}{60} = 1{,}200$ hrs	$\frac{1{,}200}{40} = 30$
4	30 minutes	D	$\frac{30 \times 600 \times 12}{60} = 3{,}600$ hrs	$\frac{3{,}600}{40} = 90$
5	20 minutes	E	$\frac{20 \times 600 \times 12}{60} = 2{,}400$ hrs	$\frac{2{,}400}{40} = 60$
			Total	300

Labour Cost Budget for a Week			
Grade of worker	Total hours per week	Wage rate per hour ₹	Total labour cost ₹
A	1,800	12	21,600
B	3,000	15	45,000
C	1,200	10	12,000
D	3,600	25	90,000
E	2,400	15	36,000
		Total	2,04,600

20.3.5 Administration Overheads Budget

Administration is responsible for planning, guiding and controlling the operations of an organisation. The cost of running different divisions/sections in the office is to be established separately to fix the responsibility for increase in costs. Administration overheads are relatively stable. So it is easy to prepare this budget.

20.3.6 Capital Expenditure Budget

Capital expenditure budget is basically a long-term budget. It is an estimate of expenditure to be incurred for creating production facilities like plant, machinery and factory building. This budget is based on the demand for the products in the future, managements business expansion plan and modernisation of production facilities. Capital expenditure budget requires large capital. Cash generation capacity of the new assets is the main criterion in preparing this budget.

20.3.7 Research and Development Budget

This budget is also a long-term budget. It also requires heavy expenditure. The research is of two types i.e., pure research and applied research. Pure research is undertaken to increase the knowledge. So cost-benefit analysis cannot be applied. Applied research is undertaken for producing definite results like developing a new process, product, etc. The expenditure on applied the research is compared with the progress made in the research. The cost benefit ratio is applied while preparing this budget.

20.3.8 Selling Overheads Budget

Selling overheads budget is based on the sales budget. It is a semi-variable cost where one part is fixed and the other part is variable. Advertisement is discretionary. It depends on the management policy. In case of new products heavy expenditure is to be incurred. In case of declining sales due to new competition advertisement cost is to be increased to meet the increased competition. In normal conditions a minimum advertisement is to be maintained. The distribution cost is volume based and hence variable. Separate budgets may be prepared for fixed cost and variable cost.

20.3.9 Plant Utilisation Budget

This budget shows the details of production facilities available in each department. It reveals the overloading in some departments. Then alternative arrangements are made to meet the production budget. In some departments there may be under-utilisation of production facilities. Steps may be taken to utilise unutilised capacities like sub-leasing etc.

20.3.10 Cash Budget

Cash budget is also called financial budget or Ways and means budget. Cash budget is an estimate of cash flows. It is essentially a short-term budget. It consists of two divisions. In the first division the estimated cash inflows like cash sales, receipts from customers, income from investment and other receipts are shown. In the second division the estimated cash outflows like payment for cash purchase, payment to creditors, employees, overhead expenses, capital expenditure, payment of tax, dividends, interest on loans etc. are shown. Usually it is prepared month-wise or quarter.

Advantages of Cash Budget

1. It helps to find the estimated cash balance or shortage at the end of each budget period.
2. It helps to make advance arrangements to ensure availability of minimum cash balance required.
3. It also helps the management to decide whether short-term or long-term borrowings are to be made in case of deficit.
4. In case surplus cash is available steps may be taken to invest them in income earning securities.
5. Cash budget is a tool in the hands of the management to effectively plan working capital management.

Illustration-5

The following are the estimated transactions of Z Ltd. for the forthcoming period from March 2011 to September 2011:

Month	Sales	Purchases	Wages	Production overheads	Administration overheads	Selling overheads
	₹	₹	₹	₹	₹	₹
March	3,45,000	1,10,000	44,000	35,000	27,000	25,000
April	3,66,000	1,23,000	47,000	40,000	28,000	27,000
May	3,91,000	1,34,000	50,000	44,000	28,000	30,000
June	4,12,000	1,56,000	53,000	47,000	29,000	34,000
July	4,39,000	1,47,000	58,000	51,000	30,000	36,000
August	4,52,000	1,53,000	62,000	54,000	32,000	38,000
September	4,11,000	1,45,000	66,000	59,000	32,000	40,000

(i) Cash Sales is 50% of total sales. Half of credit sales is expected to be received in the month following sales and the other half of credit sales is expected to be collected in the second month following sales. Sales commission 5% payable on cash sales in the month following the sales.

(ii) All purchases are on credit and expected to be paid in the second month following the purchase.

(iii) All wages are paid in the first week of the next month following the month in which wages are incurred.

(iv) Half of all overheads are paid in the same month and the rest is paid in the following month.

(v) A dividend of ₹60,000 is declared in the month of April and is expected to be paid in the month of June.

(vi) A machinery is purchased for ₹1,00,000 in March, 2011. Payment is expected to be made in two equal instalments in the months of May and June.

(vii) Advance tax payable is ₹75,000 per quarter in June and September.

(viii) Cash balance expected on 1st May 2011 is ₹45,000.

Prepare a cash budget for 5 months from May 2011.

Solution

Cash Budget

	May ₹	June ₹	July ₹	August ₹	September ₹
Receipts:					
Opening cash balance	45,000	1,03,600	25,075	1,34,525	2,27,800
Cash sales	1,95,500	2,06,000	2,19,500	2,26,000	2,05,500
Receipt from customers (W.N. 1)	1,77,750	1,89,250	2,00,750	2,12,750	2,22,750
Total	4,18,250	4,98,850	4,45,325	5,73,275	6,56,050
Payments:					
Creditors	1,10,000	1,23,000	1,34,000	1,56,000	1,47,000
Wages	47,000	50,000	53,000	58,000	62,000
Production overheads	42,000	45,500	49,000	52,500	56,500
Administration overheads	28,000	28,500	29,500	31,000	32,000
Selling overheads	28,500	32,000	35,000	37,000	39,000
Sales commission	9,150	9,775	10,300	10,975	11,300
Dividend paid	-	60,000	-	-	-
Plant and machinery	50,000	50,000	-	-	-
Advance tax	-	75,000	-	-	75,000
Total	3,14,650	4,73,775	3,10,800	3,45,475	4,22,800
Closing cash balance	1,03,600	25,075	1,34,525	2,27,800	2,33,250

Working Note-1: Receipt from customers

	March ₹	April ₹	May ₹	June ₹	July ₹	Aug ₹	Sep ₹
Credit sales (50% of sales)	1,72,500	1,83,000	1,95,500	2,06,000	2,19,500	2,26,000	2,05,500
Receipt from customers:							
First half of credit sales	-	86,250	91,500	97,750	1,03,000	1,09,750	1,13,000

Second half of credit sales	-	-	86,250	91,500	97,750	1,03,000	1,09,750
Total receipt from customers	-	-	1,77,750	1,89,250	2,00,750	2,12,750	2,22,750

(b) Master Budget

Master budget is a summary of all functional budgets. It gives an overall view of the firm's plan of action for the budget period. In a master budget a summary of functional budgets are incorporated. Master budget takes two forms - a budgeted profit and loss account and budgeted balance sheet. In the budgeted profit and loss account all cost and revenues of all functional budgets are shown in summary form. It reveals the forecasted profit or loss for the budget period. In budgeted balance sheet all assets and liabilities are shown.

Advantages of Master Budget

i. It gives a consolidated view of profit or loss for the budget period.
ii. It reveals the financial position of the firm at the end of the budget period.
iii. It acts as a check on the accuracy of individual budgets.

4. Capacity basis

(a) Fixed Budgets

Fixed budget is prepared for a specific level of activity forecasted. It is prepared on the assumption that actual activity will not vary from budgeted activity level. If the actual activity is different from the budgeted activity, the fixed budget becomes useless. In the fixed budget no provision is made for its modification to suit the actual level of activity. Fixed budget becomes impracticable when future conditions change. It does not help the management in exercising control over the firms activities.

(b) Flexible Budget

Flexible budget is also called variable budget. In a flexible budget provisions are made to modify the budgeted cost and revenue for any level of activity of the firm's operations. So a flexible budget prepared for one level of activity can be altered for any level of activity. For the purpose of preparing flexible budget the costs are classified as variable, semi-variable and fixed costs. Variable cost will vary in direct proportion to the level of activity. Fixed cost remains same for all activity levels. Semi-variable cost changes but less than proportionately to change in activity level. So detailed estimate is made for determining semi-variable cost for different levels of activities.

Advantages of Flexible Budget

i. It gives a consolidated picture of all functional budgets.
ii. It helps to ascertain the profit or loss for budget period.
iii. It helps to check the arithmetical accuracy of all budgets.
iv. It helps to find the financial position of the business by preparing a budgeted balance sheet.

v. A projected cash flow statement can also be prepared to find the liquidity position of the business.

The differences between fixed and flexible budgets

Basis	Fixed Budget	Flexible Budget
1. Activity level	It is prepared for a specific activity level.	It is prepared for many activity levels.
2. Rigidity	It is rigid. It cannot be modified for activity levels other than the budgeted activity level.	It is flexible. It can be modified for any activity level.
3. Cost analysis	Costs are not classified on the basis of variability.	Cost are classified as variable, fixed and semi-variable on the basis of their variability.
4. Conditions	It is prepared on the assumption that the operating level will not change.	It is prepared that future activity level may change.
5. Practical application	Fixed budget can be used only when the actual activity level matches the budgeted level.	It can be applied for all activity levels.
6. Cost control	It does not help to control the cost and business operation.	It helps to control cost and business operations.
7. Cost estimation	As the costs are not classified on the basis of their variability it is difficult to estimate the cost for a particular level of activity.	Costs are analysed on the basis of their variability, so it helps to estimate the cost for any level of activity. So it is easy to submit tenders and quotations.
8. Decision making	It does not help in decision making because actual activity level changes most of the time.	It helps the management in decision making through accurate estimation of cost.
9. Variance analysis	Variance analysis to find the cause for difference in cost is difficult, as the activity level differs from budget.	It is possible to introduce standard costing and variance analysis. Actual cost can be compared with estimated cost for an actual activity level.

Illustration-6

Draw up a flexible budget for overhead expenses on the basis of the following data and overhead rates at 70%, 80% and 90% plant capacity:

	Capacity levels		
	70% (₹)	80% (₹)	90% (₹)
Variable overheads:			
Indirect labour	-	12,000	-
Stores including spares	-	4,000	-
Semi-variable overheads:			
Power (30% fixed)	-	20,000	-
Repairs and maintenance (60% fixed)	-	2,000	-
Fixed Overheads:			
Depreciation	-	11,000	-
Insurance	-	3,000	-
Salaries	-	10,000	-
Total overheads	-	62,000	-
Estimated direct labour hours	-	1,24,000	-

Solution

Flexible Budget

	Capacity levels		
	70% (₹)	80% (₹)	90% (₹)
Variable overheads:			
Indirect labour	10,500	12,000	13,500
Stores including spares	3,500	4,000	4,500
Semi-variable overheads:			
Power: Fixed 30%	6,000	6,000	6,000
Variable 70%	12,250	14,000	15,750
Repairs and maintenance: Fixed 60%	1,200	1,200	1,200
Variable 40%	700	800	900
Fixed overheads:			
Depreciation	11,000	11,000	11,000
Insurance	3,000	3,000	3,000
Salaries	10,000	10,000	10,000
Total overheads	58,150	62,000	65,850
Estimated direct labour hours	1,08,500	1,24,000	1,39,500
Direct labour hour rate (Total OHS/No. of labour hours)	₹0.536	₹0.500	₹0.472

5. Others

(a) Zero Based Budgeting (ZBB)

ZBB was introduced by Peter A. Phyrr in Texas Instruments Incorporation, USA in the year 1969-70. Jimmy Carter applied ZBB techniques in government budgeting in the State of Georgia during '70s when he was the Governor of this State. He introduced ZBB technique at national level during '80s when he became the president of USA.

ZBB differs from traditional budgeting in selecting the projects or activities for inclusion in the budgets. In traditional budgeting ongoing projects or activities are automatically included in the budget for the next year with adjustment for inflation. Additionally new activities and projects are added in the budgets. But in ZBB continuing projects or activities from the past are not automatically included in the current budget. The new budgets are prepared afresh from the start (scratch or zero base, hence ZBB). Each project or activity is to be justified of its necessity for its inclusion in the budget. No past activity is included the current budgets unless there is justification for its inclusion. It is an effective tool of planning and control of activities and costs during the budget period.

Steps in ZBB

i. The overall objective of the an enterprise is sub-divided into goals for each department, project or activity.

ii. The activities and projects are grouped into decision packages. Decision package includes a project/activity or a number of related activities/projects in respect of which departmental managers has to take decisions for its inclusion in the projects.

iii. The decision packages are ranked on the basis of their merits/benefits.

iv. The scarce resources are allocated to activities/projects based on their merits.

v. Evaluate the actual performance with budgeted activities.

vi. Take executive actions in case of adverse deviation from budgeted activity.

Advantages of ZBB

i. It helps in prioritising the activities or projects for inclusion in the budget.

ii. It eliminates the low priority or unwanted projects/activities. Thus it helps to reduce wasteful expenditure.

iii. It helps to allocate scare resources for gaining maximum benefit.

iv. It helps to establish cost benefit relationship in the activities/projects included in budgets.

v. It helps in fixing responsibilities on the departmental managers for the successful implementation of the budget. Every departmental manager is made accountable.

vi. As every departmental manger is involved in the process of planning. It helps to motivate them to involve themselves in the successful implementation of the budget.

vii. There is better integration of departmental objectives with overall objectives.

Limitations of ZBB budgeting

i. As it involves detailed presentation of various projects with justification for inclusion in the budget, it puts much pressure on the departmental heads.

ii. Departmental managers may not co-operate fearing that their inefficiencies may be exposed.

iii. Ranking of decision packages is subjective and leads to different decisions.

iv. There are some activities like legal, advertising, research and social responsibility activities, they cannot be justified on merit basis even though they cannot be avoided.

(b) Performance Budgeting

Performance budgeting establishes a link between the amount of costs incurred and the output achieved. Under performance budgeting objectives are established for each function or programme. A person in charge of a function or programme is made responsible for achieving the objectives within the budgeted expenditure. Usually objectives to be obtained are fixed in physical terms (say, number of units to be produced or number of units to be sold).

Under traditional budgeting expenditure to be incurred is given prominence rather than objectives to be achieved in physical terms. Importance is given for controlling the cost within budgeted level in the traditional budgeting. Less importance is given for achieving the objectives.

In performance budgeting responsibility accounting is made possible.

Steps involved in performance budgeting

i. Total activity is classified into various programmes and functions.

ii. Objectives are established in physical terms for each programme and function.

iii. Cost-benefit relationship is applied for ranking the projects before scarce resources are allocated.

iv. Responsibility is fixed on departmental or divisional officers.

v. Measurement unit and method of measuring the performance is fixed.

vi. Establish a suitable reporting system so that the top management can evaluate the actual performance.

vii. Suitable control mechanism is established for taking corrective action in case of adverse variance.

Advantages of performance budgeting

i. Precise objectives of various functions are established.

ii. A clear linkage is established between resources expended and objectives to be achieved in physical terms.

iii. Cost-benefit analysis is made for ranking the functions for making best use of scare resources.

iv. Control ratios are used to find the deficiency in performance.

v. Better coordination is established between the top management and the lower management.

vi. Clear-cut responsibility is fixed on the executives.

20.4 CONTROL RATIOS

Main step in budgeting is measuring the performance and evaluating the performance for comparison with budgeted performances. Various ratios are used to evaluate actual performance for locating deviations from budgeted activity level. They are:

1. **Budgeted Capacity Usage Ratio**

   It establishes relationship between budgeted number of working hours and maximum possible number of working hours. The formula is:

$$= \frac{\text{Budgeted hours}}{\text{Maximum possible hours in the budget period}} \times 100$$

$$\text{or} = \frac{\text{Budgeted output}}{\text{Practical (maximum) capacity}} \times 100$$

2. **Actual Capacity Usage Ratio**

   It establishes relationship between actual hours worked and budgeted hours. The formula is:

$$= \frac{\text{Actual Hours}}{\text{Budgeted Hours}} \times 100$$

$$\text{or} = \frac{\text{Actual Output}}{\text{Standard Output}} \times 100$$

   Note: Standard output is the budgeted output for actual hours worked, calculated as follows:

$$\text{Standard output} = \frac{\text{Budgeted output}}{\text{Budgeted hours}} \times \text{Actual hours}$$

3. **Efficiency Ratio**

   It establishes relationship between the standard hours and the actual hours. The formula is:

$$= \frac{\text{Standard hours}}{\text{Actual hours}} \times 100$$

$$\text{or} = \frac{\text{Actual output}}{\text{Standard output}} \times 100$$

   Note: Standard hours are the budgeted hours for actual output calculated as below:

$$\text{Standard hours} = \frac{\text{Budgeted Hours}}{\text{Budgeted Output}} \times \text{Actual output}$$

4. **Activity Ratio**

   It shows the relationship between standard hours and budgeted hours:

$$= \frac{\text{Standard hours}}{\text{Budgeted hours}} \times 100$$

$$\text{or} = \frac{\text{Actual output}}{\text{Budgeted output}} \times 100$$

5. Calendar Ratio

It shows the relationship between the actual days worked and the budgeted days. The formula is:

$$= \frac{\text{Actual days}}{\text{Budgeted days}} \times 100$$

$$\text{or} = \frac{\text{Standard output}}{\text{Budgeted output}} \times 100$$

Note: If the ratio is 100% or more the variance is favourable. If the ratio is less than 100% the variance is adverse.

Illustration-7

Following data is available for X Ltd.

Standard working hours	8 hours per day of 5 days per week
Maximum capacity	50 employees
Actual working	40 employees
Budgeted hours expected to be worked per 4 weeks	6,400 hours
Standard hours expected to be earned per 4 weeks	8,000 hours
Actual hours worked in 4-week period	6,000 hours
Standard hours earned in the 4-week period	7,000 hours

The related period is 4 weeks. In this period there was one special holiday due to national event. Calculate the following ratios:

1. Efficiency ratio
2. Activity ratio
3. Calendar ratio
4. Budgeted capacity usage ratio
5. Actual capacity usage ratio

Solution

1. **Efficiency Ratio** $= \frac{\text{Standard hours}}{\text{Actual hours}} \times 100$

$$= \frac{7{,}000}{6{,}000} \times 100$$

$$= 116.67\%$$

2. Activity Ratio $= \dfrac{\text{Standard hours}}{\text{Budgeted hours}} \times 100$

$$= \frac{7{,}000}{6{,}400} \times 100$$

$$= 109.38\%$$

3. Calendar Ratio $= \dfrac{\text{Actual days}}{\text{Budgeted days}} \times 100$

$$= \frac{19}{20} \times 100$$

$$= 95\%$$

4. Budgeted Capacity Usage Ratio $= \dfrac{\text{Budgeted hours}}{\text{Maximum possible hours in the budget period}} \times 100$

$$= \frac{6{,}400}{8{,}000} \times 100 = 80\%$$

5. Actual Capacity Usage Ratio $= \dfrac{\text{Actual hours}}{\text{Budgeted hours}} \times 100$

$$= \frac{6{,}000}{6{,}400} \times 100 = 93.75\%$$

20.5 BUDGET REPORTS

Success of a budgeting process lies in taking corrective action when there is adverse deviation from budgeted activity level. Budgeting being a short-term planning is waste without proper control over the actual performance. This control function is possible only when the top management receives feedback from the lower levels about the actual performance. So provision is to be made in budgets for sending performance reports at periodical intervals. These reports enable the management in evaluating the actual performance and taking control measures where necessary. So budget reports are fundamental to budgetary control. The following are the essential features of a budget report:

1. **Materiality**

   All important informations which are essential for judging the actual performance should be included in the reports.

2. **Time Factor**

   Informations are useful only when they are provided when it is required. So reports are to be submitted at the appointed time.

3. **Accuracy**

   The informations given in performance reports should be accurate. It gives a correct basis for management to take suitable corrective measures.

4. Appropriateness

The reports are to be submitted to those who will use it. Only relevant informations are to be sent to the related executives. Giving unwanted information leads to waste of time of the top executives.

5. Clarity

The report should be clear and to the point.

The following are the various reports prepared and submitted,

1. Top Management

These are presented in the form of annual reports.

(a) Balance sheet
(b) Profit and loss account
(c) Cash flow statement
(d) Statement showing working capital
(e) Capital expenditure
(f) Sales, production reports.

2. Sales Management

Actual sales reports should include the following informations like product-wise sales, territory-wise sales, selling price, types of customers, quantity discounts offered, bad debts, doubtful debts, selling expenses and market conditions. These reports are presented either monthly or quarterly.

3. Production Management

Production reports are also presented either weekly, monthly or quarterly. These reports should include the details of labour efficiency achieved, plant utilisation, productions overheads incurred, material usage and scrap reports.

20.6 COMPREHENSIVE ILLUSTRATIONS

Illustration-8

(Materials purchase budget)

The Sales Manager of a company estimates to sell 75,000 units of a product in the next year.

- The production manager has presented the following information:
  - Two kinds of raw materials A and B are required for manufacturing the product. Each unit of the product requires 3 units of 'A' and 4 units of 'B'.
- The estimated opening balances at the commencement of the next year are:

- Finished product 15,000 units, Material 'A' 18,000 units and Material 'B' 23,000 units.

- The desirable closing balance at the close of the next year are:
  - Finished product 18,000 units, Material 'A' 20,000 units and Material 'B' 25,000 units.

Draw a quantitative chart showing materials purchase budget for the next year.

Solution

Materials Purchase Budget		
Particulars	**Materials 'A' (units)**	**Materials 'B' (units)**
Materials required for production (See WN-2)	2,34,000	3,12,000
Add: Desired closing balance	20,000	25,000
	2,54,000	3,37,000
Less: Stock at the commencement of the year	18,000	23,000
Raw materials purchase quantity	2,36,000	3,14,000

Working Note

1.

No. of finished units production	
Estimated sales	75,000 units
Add: Desired closing balance	18,000 units
	93,000 units
Less: Opening stock	15,000 units
Finished goods production	78,000 units

2.

Materials required for production		
Particulars	**Materials 'A'**	**Materials 'B'**
Materials requirement per unit of finished goods	3 units	4 units
No. of finished goods production	78,000 units	78,000 units
Materials required for production	2,34,000 units	3,12,000 units

Illustration-9

(Production budget and production cost budget)

The following information has been made available from the records of Emkey Industries Ltd. for six months ending 31st December 2009 and for January 2010:

1. Expected sales (units) in each month:

July, 2009	1,500 units
August, 2009	1,600 units
September, 2009	1,700 units
October, 2009	2,000 units
November, 2009	2,200 units
December, 2009	2,100 units
January, 2010	2,300 units

2. There will be no stock of work-in-progress either at the beginning or at the end of any month.
3. Finished units equal to half the sales of next month will be in stock at the end of each month (including June, 2009).
4. Budgeted production and production cost for the year ending 31st December, 2009 are as below:

Production	25,000 units
Direct materials per unit	₹20
Direct wages per unit	₹8
Annual production overheads:	
Fixed	₹1,20,000
Variable	₹2,37,500

You are required to prepare:

(a) A production budget for each of six months of 2009, and

(b) A summarised production cost budget for the same period.

Solution

(a)

Production Budget for 6 months						
	July	**Aug**	**Sep**	**Oct**	**Nov**	**Dec**
Sales (units)	1,500	1,600	1,700	2,000	2,200	2,100
Add: Closing stock (units)	800	850	1,000	1,100	1,050	1,150
	2,300	2,450	2,700	3,100	3,250	3,250
Less: Opening stock (units)	750	800	850	1,000	1,100	1,050
Production (units)	1,550	1,650	1,850	2,100	2,150	2,200

Total production for six months - 11,500 units

(b)

Summarised Production Cost Budget for 6 months	
	₹
Direct materials (11,500 × 20)	2,30,000
Direct wages (11,500 × 8)	92,000
Prime cost	3,22,000
Production overheads:	
Fixed	60,000
Variable (₹9.50 per unit)	1,09,250
Production cost	4,91,250

Illustration-10

(Materials purchase budget)

Shangrila Food Products Ltd. has prepared the sales budget for the first 5 months of 2011:

	Sales Budget (Units)
January	10,800
February	15,600
March	12,200
April	10,400
May	9,800

The inventory of finished products at the end of every month is to be equal to 25% of the sales estimate of next month. On January 1, 2011, there were 2,700 units of product in hand. There is no stock of work-in-progress at the end of any month.

Every unit of product requires two types of materials in the following quantities:

Material 'A'	4 units
Material 'B'	5 units

Materials equal to one half of the next month production are to be in hand at the end of every month. This requirement was met on 1st January 2011.

Prepare a materials requirement budget for the first quarter of 2011 in a logical form showing the quantities of each type of material to be purchased.

(B.Com. (Hons.), Delhi University)

Solution

Materials Requirement Budget and Materials Purchase Budget						
Particulars	**Materials 'A'**			**Materials 'B'**		
	Jan	**Feb**	**Mar**	**Jan**	**Feb**	**Mar**
Production (units) (See WN-1)	12,000	14,750	11,750	12,000	14,750	11,750
Materials required per unit	4	4	4	5	5	5
Materials required for production (units)	48,000	59,000	47,000	60,000	73,750	58,750
Add: Desired closing stock	24,500	23,500	20,500	36,625	29,375	25,625
	72,500	82,500	67,500	96,625	1,03,125	84,375
Less: Stock at the beginning	24,000	24,500	23,500	30,000	36,625	29,375
Materials to be purchased (units)	48,500	58,000	44,000	66,625	66,500	55,000

Working Note-1

Production Budget (units)				
	Jan	**Feb**	**Mar**	**Apr**
Sales (units)	10,800	15,600	12,200	10,400
Add: Desired closing stock	3,900	3,050	2,600	2,450
	14,700	18,650	14,800	12,850
Less: Opening stock	2,700	3,900	3,050	2,600
Production	12,000	14,750	11,750	10,250

Illustration-11

(Production cost budget)

P Ltd. produced 20,000 units of a product in the first six months of 2011. The following are the expenses incurred during the six months ending 30th June 2011:

Direct materials	₹4,00,000
Direct labour	₹3,20,000
Factory overheads - variable	₹2,60,000
Factory overheads - fixed	₹1,60,000

The company decides to prepare a production cost budget for the second six months of year 2011. The following changes are expected during the second half of the year 2011:

(i) Production expected to increase by 25%

(ii) Direct materials price decrease by 2%

(iii) Labour rate increase by 10%

(iv) Labour efficiency will be lower by 3%

(v) Variable overheads will increase by 5% and

(vi) Fixed overheads will increase by ₹40,000

Solution

Production cost budget for six months ending 31st December, 2011	
	₹
Direct materials $\left(4{,}00{,}000 \times \frac{25{,}000}{20{,}000} \times \frac{98}{100}\right)$	4,90,000
Direct labour $\left(3{,}20{,}000 \times \frac{25{,}000}{20{,}000} \times \frac{110}{100} \times \frac{103}{100}\right)$	4,53,200
Prime cost	9,43,200
Production overheads	
- Variable $\left(2{,}60{,}000 \times \frac{25{,}000}{20{,}000} \times \frac{105}{100}\right)$	3,41,250
- Fixed (1,60,000 + 40,000)	2,00,000
Production cost	14,84,450

Illustration-12

(Selling overhead budget)

Prepare a sales overhead budget for the months of January, February and March from the estimates given below:

	₹
Advertisement	2,500
Salaries of the sales department	5,000

Expenses of the sales department	1,500
Counter salesman's salary and dearness allowances	6,000

Commission to counter salesmen at 1% on their sales.

Travelling salesman's commission at 10% of their sales and expenses at 5% on their sales. The sales during the period were estimated as follows:

Month	Counter Sales ₹	Travelling Salesmen's sales ₹
January	80,000	10,000
February	1,20,000	15,000
March	1,40,000	20,000

(B.Com. (Hons), Delhi University)

Solution

Sales Overhead Budget			
Month	**January** (₹)	**February** (₹)	**March** (₹)
Estimated sales	90,000	1,35,000	1,60,000
Variable overheads:			
Commission to counter salesmen - 1% on their sales (₹)	800	1,200	1,400
Travelling salesman's commission - 10% on their sales (₹)	1,000	1,500	2,000
Travelling salesman's expenses - 5% on their sales (₹)	500	750	1,000
Total variable overheads (A)	2,300	3,450	4,400
Fixed overheads:			
Advertisement	2,500	2,500	2,500
Salaries of sales department	5,000	5,000	5,000
Expenses of sales department	1,500	1,500	1,500
Counter salesman salary and DA	6,000	6,000	6,000
Total fixed overheads (B)	15,000	15,000	15,000

Total sales overhead (A+B)	17,300	18,450	19,400
% of sales overheads on total sales	$\frac{17,300}{90,000} \times 100$ = 19.22%	$\frac{18,450}{1,35,000} \times 100$ = 13.67%	$\frac{19,400}{1,60,000} \times 100$ = 12.13%

Illustration-13

(Production budget)

From the following data, prepare a production budget for the ABC Co. Ltd:

Stocks for the budget period

Product	As on 1st Jan.	As on 30th June
A	8,000 units	10,000 units
B	9,000 units	8,000 units
C	12,000 units	14,000 units

Requirement as per sales budget

Product A	60,000 units
Product B	50,000 units
Product C	80,000 units

Normal loss in production

Product A	4%
Product B	2%
Product C	6%

(B.Com., Calicut University)

Solution

Production Budget for six months ending 30th June				
Particulars	Products			Total (Units)
	A (units)	B (units)	C (units)	
Budgeted sales	60,000	50,000	80,000	1,90,000
Add: Closing stock	10,000	8,000	14,000	32,000

	70,000	58,000	94,000	2,22,000
Less: Opening stock	8,000	9,000	12,000	29,000
Production (net)	62,000	49,000	82,000	1,93,000
Add: Loss in production	$\left(62{,}000 \times \frac{4}{96}\right)$ = 2,583	$\left(49{,}000 \times \frac{2}{98}\right)$ = 1,000	$\left(82{,}000 \times \frac{6}{94}\right)$ = 5,234	8,817
Gross production	64,583	50,000	87,234	2,01,817

Illustration-14

(Flexible budget)

For production of 10,000 automatic irons, the following are the budgeted expenses:

	Per unit (₹)
Direct materials	60
Direct labour	30
Variable overheads (production)	25
Fixed overheads (₹1,50,000)	15
Variable expenses (direct)	5
Selling expenses (10% fixed)	15
Administration expenses (₹50,000 rigid for all levels of production)	5
Distribution expenses (20% fixed)	5
Total cost per unit	160

Prepare a budget for production of 6,000, 7,000 and 8,000 units, showing distinctly marginal cost and total cost. **(CA-Inter)**

Solution

Flexible Budget						
Particulars	**Production levels**					
	6,000 units		**7,000 units**		**8,000 units**	
	Total (₹)	**Per unit (₹)**	**Total (₹)**	**Per unit (₹)**	**Total (₹)**	**Per unit (₹)**
Direct materials	3,60,000	60.00	4,20,000	60.00	4,80,000	60.00

Direct labour	1,80,000	30.00	2,10,000	30.00	2,40,000	30.00
Direct variable expenses	30,000	5.00	35,000	5.00	40,000	5.00
Variable overheads:						
Production	1,50,000	25.00	1,75,000	25.00	2,00,000	25.00
Selling	81,000	13.50	94,500	13.50	1,08,000	13.50
Distribution	24,000	4.00	28,000	4.00	32,000	4.00
Marginal cost (A)	8,25,000	137.50	9,62,500	137.50	11,00,000	137.50
Fixed overheads:						
Production	1,50,000	25.00	1,50,000	21.43	1,50,000	18.75
Administration	50,000	8.33	50,000	7.14	50,000	6.25
Selling	15,000	2.50	15,000	2.14	15,000	1.88
Distribution	10,000	1.67	10,000	1.43	10,000	1.25
Total fixed overheads (B)	2,25,000	37.50	2,25,000	32.14	2,25,000	28.13
Total Cost (A + B)	10,50,000	175.00	11,87,500	169.64	13,25,000	165.53

Illustration-15

(Flexible budget)

The cost sheet of a company based on a budgeted volume of sales of 3,00,000 units per quarter is:

Direct materials	₹5 per unit
Direct labour	₹2 per unit
Factory overheads (50% fixed)	₹6 per unit
Selling and administration overheads (1/3 variable)	₹3.00 per unit

The selling price is ₹18 per unit. When the budget was discussed, it was felt that the company would be able to achieve only a volume of 2,50,000 units of production and sales per quarter. The company therefore decided that an aggressive sales promotion campaign should be launched to achieve the following operations:

Proposal I: Sell 4,00,000 units per quarter by spending ₹2,00,000 on special advertising. In this case, the fixed overheads will increase by ₹4,00,000 per quarter.

Proposal II: Sell 5,00,000 units per quarter by reducting the selling price by ₹2 per unit on sales. In this case, the variable selling and administration overheads will increase by 5%. Direct materials cost will be reduced by 1% due to purchase price discounts and fixed factory cost will increase by ₹2,00,000.

You are required to prepare a flexible budget at 2,50,000, 4,00,000 and 5,00,000 units of output per quarter and calculate the profit at each of the levels of output.

Solution

Flexible Budget

Particulars	Budget	Proposal I	Proposal II
Sales (units)	2,50,000	4,00,000	5,00,000
Selling price p/u	₹18	₹18	₹16
Sales (₹)	45,00,000	72,00,000	80,00,000
Variable cost:			
Materials (See WN-1)	12,50,000	20,00,000	24,75,000
Labour cost (₹2 per unit)	5,00,000	8,00,000	10,00,000
Variable production overheads (₹3 p/u)	7,50,000	12,00,000	15,00,000
Variable selling and administration overheads (₹1 p/u)	2,50,000	4,00,000	5,25,000
Total variable cost	27,50,000	44,00,000	55,00,000
Contribution (Sales - Variable cost)	17,50,000	28,00,000	25,00,000
Fixed costs:			
Factory overheads (See WN-3)	9,00,000	13,00,000	11,00,000
Selling and administration overheads	6,00,000	8,00,000	6,00,000
Total fixed costs	15,00,000	21,00,000	17,00,000
Profit (contrition - fixed cost)	2,50,000	7,00,000	8,00,000

Working Note

	Present	Proposal I	Proposal II
1) Materials	$2,50,000 \times 5 =$ ₹12,50,000	$4,00,000 \times 5 =$ ₹20,00,000	$5,00,000 \times 5 \times \frac{99}{100} =$ ₹24,75,000
2) Variable selling overheads	$2,50,000 \times 1 =$ ₹2,50,000	$4,00,000 \times 1 =$ ₹4,00,000	$5,00,000 \times 1 \times \frac{105}{100} =$ ₹5,25,000
3) Fixed factory overheads	$3,00,000 \times 3 =$ ₹9,00,000	₹9,00,000 + 4,00,000 = ₹13,00,000	₹9,00,000 + 2,00,000 = ₹11,00,000

Illustration-16

(Materials purchase budget)

Draw a material procurement budget (quantitative) from the following information: Estimated opening balance at the commencement of the next year:

Finished product	5,000 units
Materials 'A'	12,000 units
Materials 'B'	20,000 units

Materials on order at the commencement of the next year:

Material 'A'	7,000 units
Material 'B'	11,000 units

The desirable closing balances at the end of the next year:

Finished product	7,000 units
Materials 'A'	15,000 units
Materials 'B'	25,000 units

Materials on order at the end of the next year:

Material 'A'	8,000 units
Material 'B'	10,000 units

One unit of finished product requires 2 units of materials 'A' and 3 units of materials 'B'. Estimated sales is 40,000 units.

Solution

Production Budget	
Estimated sales	40,000 units
Add: Closing stock	7,000 units
	47,000 units
Less Opening stock	5,000 units
Estimated production	42,000 units

Materials Procurement Budget (Quantitative)		
Particulars	**Materials 'A' (Units)**	**Materials 'B' (Units)**
Materials required for production	84,000 (42,000 × 2)	1,26,000 (42,000 × 3)
Add: Closing balances of materials	15,000	25,000
Closing materials on order	8,000	10,000
	1,07,000	1,61,000
Less: Opening balances of materials	(12,000)	(20,000)
Opening balances of materials on order	(7,000)	(11,000)
Materials to be purchased	88,000	1,30,000

Illustration-17

(Cash budget)

A firm expects to have ₹25,000 in bank on 1st May, 2011 and requires you to prepare an estimate of cash position during the three months - May to July 2011. The following information is supplied to you:

Month	Sales ₹	Purchases ₹	Wages ₹	Factory expenses ₹	Office expenses ₹	Selling expenses ₹
March	50,000	30,000	6,000	5,000	4,000	3,000
April	56,000	32,000	6,500	5,500	4,000	3,000
May	60,000	35,000	7,000	6,000	4,000	3,500
June	80,000	40,000	9,000	7,500	4,000	4,500
July	90,000	40,000	9,500	8,000	4,000	4,500

Other informations

1. 20% of sales is for cash and remaining sales is collected in the month following that of sale.
2. Supplier supply goods at two-month credit.
3. All expenses are paid in the month following the one in which they are incurred.
4. The company pays dividends to shareholders and bonus to workers of ₹10,000 and ₹15,000 respectively in the month of May.
5. Plant has been ordered and is expected to be received in June. It costs ₹80,000 and is payable on receipt.
6. Income tax ₹25,000 is payable in July.

Solution

Cash Budget			
Particulars	**May** ₹	**June** ₹	**July** ₹
Opening balance	25,000	7,800	(−) 60,700
Receipts:			
Cash sales (20% of current sales)	12,000	16,000	18,000
Credit sales (80% of previous month)	44,800	48,000	64,000
Total	81,800	71,800	21,300
Payments:			
Purchases	30,000	32,000	35,000
Wages	6,500	7,000	9,000
Factory expenses	5,500	6,000	7,500
Office expenses	4,000	4,000	4,000
Selling expenses	3,000	3,500	4,500
Dividend to shareholders	10,000	-	-
Bonus to workers	15,000	-	-
Plant	-	80,000	-
Income tax	-	-	25,000
Total	74,000	1,32,500	85,000
Closing balance / (−) overdraft	7,800	(−) 60,700	(−) 63,700

Illustration-18

(Cash budget)

XYZ Ltd. has given the following particulars. You are required to prepare a cash budget for the three months ending on 31st December, 2011.

1.

Month	Sales ₹	Purchases ₹	Wages ₹	Overheads ₹
August	40,000	20,400	7,600	3,800
September	42,000	20,000	7,600	4,200
October	46,000	19,600	8,000	4,600
November	50,000	20,000	8,400	4,800
December	60,000	21,600	9,000	5,000

2. Credit terms are:

   (a) 10% of sales are on cash basis. 50% of credit sales are collected next month and the balance in the following month:

   (b) Creditors

      – Materials 2 months
      – Wages 1/5 month
      – Overheads 1/2 month

3. Cash balance on 1st October, 2011 is expected to be ₹8,000.

4. A machinery will be installed in August, 2011 at a cost of ₹1,00,000. The monthly instalment of ₹5,000 is payable from October onwards.

5. Dividend at 10% on preference share capital of ₹3,00,000 will be paid on 1st December, 2011.

6. Advance to be received for sale of vehicle ₹20,000 in December.

7. Income tax (Advance) to be paid in December ₹5,000. **(ACS-Inter)**

Solution

Cash Budget

Particulars	October ₹	November ₹	December ₹
Opening cash balance	8,000	11,780	18,360
Receipts:			
Cash sales	4,600	5,000	6,000
Collection from debtors (WN-1)	36,900	39,600	43,200
Advance for sale of vehicle	-	-	20,000
Total	49,500	56,380	87,560
Payments:			
Creditors for materials	20,400	20,000	19,600
Wages (WN-2)	7,920	8,320	8,880
Overheads (WN-3)	4,400	4,700	4,900
Machinery - instalment	5,000	5,000	5,000
Preference dividend	-	-	30,000
Advance of income tax	-	-	5,000
Total	37,720	38,020	73,380
Closing cash balance	11,780	18,360	14,180

Working Note

1.

Collections from debtors					
	Aug	Sep	Oct	Nov	Dec
Total sales	40,000	42,000	46,000	50,000	60,000
Credit sales (90% of sales)	36,000	37,800	41,400	45,000	54,000
50% of credit sales	18,000	18,900	20,700	22,500	27,000
Collections from Debtors:					
First 50% of credit sales (previous month)	-	18,000	18,900	20,700	22,500
Second 50% of credit sales (two months earlier)	-	-	18,000	18,900	20,700
Collections from debtors	-	-	36,900	39,600	43,200

2.

Payment of wages			
	October ₹	November ₹	December ₹
4/5 of current month	6,400	6,720	7,200
1/5 of previous month	1,520	1,600	1,680
Total	7,920	8,320	8,880

3.

Payment of overheads			
	October ₹	November ₹	December ₹
1/2 of current month	2,300	2,400	2,500
1/2 of previous month	2,100	2,300	2,400
Total	4,400	4,700	4,900

Illustration-19

(Cash budget)

Based on the following information prepare a cash budget for ABC Ltd.:

Month	1st Quarter ₹	2nd Quarter ₹	3rd Quarter ₹	4th Quarter ₹
Opening cash balance	10,000	-	-	-
Collection from customers	1,25,000	1,50,000	1,60,000	2,21,000
Payments:				
Purchase of materials	20,000	35,000	35,000	54,200
Other expenses	25,000	20,000	20,000	17,000

Salary and wages	90,000	95,000	95,000	1,09,200
Income tax	5,000	-	-	-
Purchase of machinery	-	-	-	20,000

The company desires to maintain a cash balance of ₹15,000 at the end of each quarter. Cash can be borrowed or repaid in multiples of ₹500 at an interest of 10% p.a. The management does not want to borrow cash more than what is necessary and wants to repay as early as possible. In any event loans cannot be extended beyond four quarters. Interest is computed and paid when the principal is repaid. Assume that borrowings take place at the beginning and repayments are made at the end of the quarters. **(ICWA-Inter)**

Solution

Cash Budget

Particulars	**1st Quarter** ₹	**2nd Quarter** ₹	**3rd Quarter** ₹	**4th Quarter** ₹
Opening cash balance	10,000	15,000	15,000	15,325
Receipts:				
Collection from customers	1,25,000	1,50,000	1,60,000	2,21,000
Total (A)	1,35,000	1,65,000	1,75,000	2,36,325
Payments:				
Purchase of materials	20,000	35,000	35,000	54,200
Other expenses	25,000	20,000	20,000	17,000
Salary and wages	90,000	95,000	95,000	1,09,200
Income tax	5,000	-	-	-
Purchase of machinery	-	-	-	20,000
Total (B)	1,40,000	1,50,000	1,50,000	2,00,400
Difference (A - B)	(–) 5,000	15,000	25,000	35,925
Desired closing balance	15,000	15,000	15,000	15,000
Deficiency	20,000	-	-	-
Borrowings (Equal to deficiency in multiplies of ₹500)	20,000	-	-	-
Surplus	-	-	10,000	11,000
Repayment (principal)	-	-	9,000	-
Interest on repayment (See WN-1)	-	-	675	1,100
Closing balance	15,000	15,000	15,325	23,825

Working Note-1

Calculation of interest on loans repaid:

$$3\text{rd Quarter} = 9{,}000 \times \frac{10}{100} \times \frac{3}{4} = 675$$

$$4\text{th Quarter} = 11{,}000 \times \frac{10}{100} = 1{,}100$$

Illustration-20

(Master budget)

A glass manufacturing company requires you to calculate and present the budget for the next year from the following information:

Sales	
Toughened glass	₹3,00,000
Bent toughened glass	₹5,00,000
Direct materials cost	60% of sales
Direct wages	20 workers at ₹150 per month each

Factory overheads	
Indirect labour	
- Works manager	₹500 per month
- Foreman	₹400 per month
Stores and spares	$2\frac{1}{2}$% on sales
Depreciation on machinery	₹12,600 p.a
Light and power	₹5,000 p.a
Repairs etc.	₹8,000 p.a
Other sundries	10% on daily wages

Administration, selling and distribution expenses ₹14,000 p.a.

(B.Sc., Bharathidasan University)

Solution

Master Budget		
Particulars		**₹**
Sales		
- toughened glass		3,00,000
- bent toughened glass		5,00,000
Total		8,00,000
Costs for the year:		
Direct materials	(60% of sales)	4,80,000
Direct wages	(20 × 150 × 12)	36,000
Prime cost		5,16,000
Factory overheads:		
Stores & spares		20,000
Light and power		5,000
Repairs		8,000
Works manager's salary		6,000
Foreman salary		4,800
Depreciation on machinery		12,600
Other sundries - 10% of wages		3,600
Works cost		5,76,000
Selling and administration expenses		14,000
Total cost		5,90,000
Profit (b/f)		2,10,000
Sales		8,00,000

20.7 EXERCISE

I. Objective Type Questions

A. State whether the following statements are true or false

(i) Zero based budgeting is superior to traditional budget.

(ii) Master budget is a consolidation of all functional budgets.

(iii) Traditional budget does not consider previous year budget as base.

(iv) Fixed budget is prepared for a single activity level only.

(v) Sales budget is the basic budget for preparing all other budgets.

(vi) There is no difference between estimate and forecast.

(vii) A budget manual is a summary of all functional budgets.

(viii) Only short term budgets has practical value.

(ix) In the performance budget a linkage is established between various costs incurred and the results obtained.

(x) Limiting factor is a major constraint on all the operational activities of an organization.

[**Ans: True:** (i), (ii), (iv), (v), (viii), (ix), (x); **False:** (iii), (vi), (vii)]

B. Fill in the blanks

(i) A budget that can be modified for different levels of activities is called ______________.

(ii) A summary of all functional budgets is called ______________.

(iii) A document which gives direction and guidelines for preparing budgets is called ______________.

(iv) Budgets prepared for a period less than one year is called ______________.

(v) A budget prepared for a single level of activity is called ______________.

(vi) A budget prepared afresh every time without considering the past budget is called ______________.

(vii) ______________ Budget estimates the quantity and/or value of materials to be purchased.

(viii) The factor which influences the activity level of all budgets is called ______________.

(ix) The main objectives of budgetary control are ______________ and ______________.

[**Ans:** (i) Flexible budget, (ii) Master budget, (iii) Budget manual, (iv) Short-term budget, (v) Fixed budget, (vi) Zero based budget, (vii) Materials purchase, (viii) Budget factor/Key factor/Limiting factor, (ix) Planning, control.]

II. Theory Questions

A. Short answer type questions

1. What is budget period?
2. What is budget manual?
3. What is budget factor?
4. Define budgetary control.
5. Explain budget committee.
6. What is a fixed budget?
7. What is flexible budget?
8. What is zero based budgeting?

9. What are the objectives of budgetary control?

10. What is budget report?

11. Explain cash budget.

B. Long answer type questions

1. Define 'budget' and 'budgetary control'. Explain the merits and limitations of budgetary control.

2. What is a functional budget? Explain the various functional budgets.

3. Define and explain the term 'flexible budget'. How is a flexible budget constructed and what difficulties would you expect in the compilation? Explain the usefulness of a flexible budget to a management. **(ICWA-Inter)**

4. Write short notes on: (a) Cash budget, (b) Performance budgeting, (c) Materials procurement budget and (d) Sales budget. **(B.Com., Madras University)**

5. Explain with examples the three control ratios used for performance evaluation.

6. What are the advantages of cash budgeting? **(B.Com., Calicut University)**

7. What are various control ratios? Explain their uses. **(B.Com., Mysore University)**

8. Define budget and budgetary control. Explain their advantages and limitations. **(B.Com., Mysore University)**

9. What is a zero based budget? Explain its features and its merits over conventional budgeting. **(B.Com. (Hons.), Delhi University)**

10. What is performance budgeting? Explain its advantages.

11. What do you understand by budgeting? What types of budgets are prepared in an organization? **(ICWA-Inter)**

12. List the various functional budgets prepared in a business. **(CA-Inter)**

Practical Problems

A. Short answer type questions

1. A company expects to sell 1,500 units of a product in a budget period. The desirable closing balance is 300 units. The company is estimated to have an opening balance of 200 units. The labour hours required for producing one unit of the product is 3 hours. Normal idle time is estimated at 10% time paid for. Calculate the budgeted labour hours required.

   [**Ans:** 5,333 hours]

2. A Ltd. budgets to sell 12,500 units of a product in the next year. The stock at the beginning of the next year is estimated at 3,500 units. The company desires to maintain a stock of 5,000 units at the end of the next year. From the past experience, it is found that 2% of units introduced in the process is lost normally at the end of the manufacturing process. Prepare a production budget (Gross).

   [**Ans:** 14,286 units]

3. X Ltd. produced 60,000 units during the current year. The opening stock is 16,000 units and closing stock is 5,000 units. The goods are sold at ₹20 per unit. In the forthcoming year, it is estimated that sales will go up by 20%. Selling price is also expected to increase by 10%. Prepare a sales budget for the next year.

   [**Ans:** Budget sales 85,200 units; Sales value ₹18,74,400]

4. Prepare a production budget for 3 months ending March 31, 2011 for a factory producing four products, on the basis of the following information:

Types of Product	Estimated stock on 01.01.2011	Estimated sales from Jan-Mar 2011	Desired closing stock on 31, March 2011
A	2,000	10,000	3,000
B	3,000	15,000	5,000
C	4,000	13,000	3,000
D	3,000	12,000	2,000

   [**Ans:** A - 11,000 units, B - 17,000 units, C - 12,000 units and D - 11,000 units]

5. A sales manager of a company estimates to sell 25,000 units of a product in the next year. The estimated stock at the beginning of the next year is 7,000 units and desired closing balance for the next year is 4,000 units.

   Two raw materials are used in the production of the product. They are material 'X' and material 'Y'. 4 units of material 'X' and 5 units of material 'Y' are mixed to produce one unit of the product. Raw material 'X' costs ₹5 per unit and material 'Y' cost ₹9 per unit.

   The stock of materials at the beginning of the next year is - Material X - 5,000 units and Y - 7,000 units.

   The stock of materials desired at the end of the next year is - Material X - 10,000 units and material Y - 12,000 units).

   Prepare a materials purchase budget for next year.

   [**Ans:** Production 22,000 units; Purchase - Material X - 93,000 units and Material Y - 1,15,000 units, Value of material to be purchased - Material X - ₹4,65,000 and Material Y - ₹10,35,000]

6. The repairs and maintenance cost of machinery is ₹45,000 when production is 6,000 units. The repairs and maintenance cost is ₹39,000 when the production is 5,000 units. Find the repairs and maintenance cost for a budgeted production of 9,000 units.

   [**Ans:** ₹63,000]

7. From the following information, prepare materials purchase budget for January, 2011:

	Material 'X' (units)	Material 'Y' (units)
Estimated stock on 01.01.2011	25,000	32,000
Estimated stock on 31.01.2011	36,000	40,000
Estimated consumption during January, 2011	2,37,000	2,93,000
Standard price p/u	₹3	₹5

   [**Ans:** Purchase quantity - Material X - 2,48,000 units and Material Y - 3,01,000 units; Purchase value - Material X - ₹7,44,000; Material Y - ₹15,05,000]

B. Comprehensive Practical Problems

1. **(Flexible Budget)** A company produces a standard product. The estimated cost per unit are as follows:

Raw materials	₹4.00
Wages	₹2.00
Variable overheads	₹5.00

   Semi-variable costs are:

Indirect materials	₹235
Indirect labour	₹156
Repairs	₹570

   The variable costs per unit included in semi-variable cost are:

Indirect materials	₹0.05
Indirect labour	₹0.08
Repairs	₹0.10

   The fixed cost are:

Factory	₹2,000
Administration	₹3,000
Selling and distribution	₹2,500

The above costs are for 70% of normal capacity producing 700 units. The selling price is ₹10 per unit. Prepare a flexible budget for 80% and 100% normal capacities from the above information. **(B.Com., Bangalore University)**

[**Ans:** Loss: at 70% capacity - ₹9,161; at 80% capacity - ₹9,284 and at 100% capacity - ₹9,350]

2. **(Flexible Budget)** The following data are available in a manufacturing company for an yearly period:

	(₹ in lakhs)
Fixed expenses:	
Wages and salaries	9.5
Rent, rates and taxes	6.6
Depreciation	7.4
Sundry administration expenses	6.5
Semi-variable expenses (at 50% capacity)	
Maintenance and repairs	3.5
Indirect labour	7.9
Sales department salaries	3.8
Sundry administration expenses	2.8
Variable expenses: (at 50% capacity)	
Materials	21.7
Labour	20.4
Other expenses	7.9
	98.0

Assume that the fixed expenses remain constant at all levels of production. Semi-variable expenses remain constant between 45% and 65% of capacity, increasing by 10% between 65% and 80% capacity and by 20% between 80% and 100% capacity.

Sales at various levels are: (₹ in lakhs)

50% capacity	100
60% capacity	120
75% capacity	150
90% capacity	180
100% capacity	200

Prepare flexible budget for the year and forecast the profit at 60%, 75%, 90% and 100% of capacity.

[**Ans:** Profit: 50% capacity - ₹2 lakh, 60% capacity - ₹12 lakh, 75% capacity - ₹25.20 lakh, 90% capacity - ₹38.40 lakh and 100% capacity - ₹48.40 lakh]

3. **(Flexible Budget)** ABC Ltd has prepared the budget for the production of one lakh units of the only commodity manufactured by it for a costing period as follows:

	(₹ in lakhs)
Raw materials	2.52
Direct labour	0.75
Direct expenses	0.10
Works overhead (60% fixed)	2.25
Administration overheads (80% fixed)	0.40
Selling overheads (50% fixed)	0.20

Prepare a flexible budget for 60,000, 70,000 and 80,000 units.

[**Ans:** Total cost: 60,000 units - ₹4,44,000, 70,000 units - ₹4,88,500, 80,000 units - ₹5,33,000]

4. **(Flexible Budget)** From the following data, prepare a flexible budget for production of 40,000 units and 75,000 units, distinctly showing variable cost and fixed cost as well as total cost. Also show element-wise cost per unit. Budgeted output is 1,00,000 units and budgeted cost per unit is as follows:

	₹ (per unit)
Direct materials	95
Direct labour	50
Production overheads (variable)	40
Production overheads (fixed)	5
Selling overheads (10% fixed)	10
Administration overheads (fixed)	5
Distribution overheads (20% fixed)	15

(B.Com. (Hons.), Delhi University)

[**Ans:** Total cost - 40,000 units ₹96,40,000, 75,000 units - ₹1,68,50,000]

5. **(Flexible Budget)** X company produces a standard product. The estimated cost per unit are given below:

	₹
Materials	10
Direct wages	8
Direct expenses	2
Variable overheads	3
	23

Semi-variable overheads at 100% activity level (10,000 units) are estimated to be ₹40,000 and these overheads vary in steps of ₹2,000 for each change in output of 1,000 units. Fixed overheads are estimated at ₹50,000. The selling price per unit is also estimated at ₹40. Prepare a flexible budget at 50%, 70% and 90% levels of activity.

(B.Com., Bangalore University)

Ans:

	50%	70%	90%
Total cost	₹1,95,500	₹2,45,000	₹2,95,000
Profit	₹5,000	₹35,000	₹65,000

6. **(Cash Budget)** XYZ Ltd, produces goods mostly for stock during April to June 2011. Prepare a cash budget for the above period indicating bank overdraft the company may require at the end of each month. The following are the budgeted figures of the company.

(a)

Month	**Sales** ₹	**Purchase** ₹	**Wages** ₹	**Overheads** ₹
February	5,40,000	5,75000	55,000	25,000
March	5,88,000	6,10,000	61,000	30,000
April	6,13,000	6,47,000	67,000	33,000
May	6,51,000	7,20,000	74,000	40,000
June	6,94,000	7,30,000	80,000	44,000

(b) Cash sales is 40% of total sales. 50% of credit sales is collected in the month following the sales and the remaining 50% of credit sales collected in the second month following the sales.

(c) Sales commission at 5% on total sales is paid in the month following the sales.

(d) All purchases are on 2 month credit.

(e) $\frac{1}{2}$ wages are paid in the same month and the balance in the next month.

(f) $\frac{1}{4}$ overheads are paid in the same month and the balance in the next month.

(g) Cash at bank on April 1, 2011 is estimated at ₹55,000.

[**Ans:** Overdraft required: April - ₹60,550, May - ₹1,85,750, June - ₹3,26,500)

7. **(Cash Budget)** From the following information relating to X Ltd, prepare a cash budget for the half year ended 30th September, 2011:

(a) Budgeted sales and costs:

Month	**Sales** ₹	**Purchase** ₹	**Wages** ₹	**Overheads** ₹
March	1,50,000	90,000	18,000	31,000
April	1,40,000	1,20,000	28,000	35,400

May	1,54,000	84,000	20,800	36,500
June	1,68,000	1,36,000	22,200	36,500
July	1,82,000	1,28,000	30,000	37,000
August	2,04,000	1,51,000	28,000	37,500
September	2,40,000	1,62,000	25,000	38,000

(b) Other informations

i. Bank balance on 01.04.2011 was ₹72,000

ii. A loan instalment of ₹25,000 is payable from July to December, 2011.

iii. Sales commission at 5% on sales is payable in the following month of sales.

iv. ₹50,000 is expected from distributors as advance deposits in the month of July.

v. 50% of sales are on credit. The credit terms 1 month.

vi. 50% of purchases are on each basis and the balance is payable in the next month.

vii. 25% of overheads are payable in the month following their incidence.

viii. Wages are payable on the first day of the following month.

[**Ans:** Closing cash balance/(Over draft): April - ₹52,200; May - ₹25,975; June - ₹11,975; July - ₹12,500; August - (₹35,475); September - (₹71,050)]

8. **(Cash Budget)** Prepare a cash budget for three months ending 30th June, 2011 from the information given below:

(a)

Month	Sales ₹	Materials ₹	Wages ₹	Overheads ₹
February	14,000	9,600	3,000	1,700
March	15,000	9,000	3,000	1,900
April	16,000	9,200	3,200	2,000
May	17,000	10,000	3,600	2,200
June	18,000	10,400	4,000	2,300

(b) Credit terms are:

Sales/debtors - 10% of sales are on cash, 50% of the credit sales are collected next month and the balance in the following month.

Creditors

- Materials - 2 months
- Wages - $\frac{1}{4}$ month
- Overheads $\frac{1}{2}$ month

(c) Cash and bank balance on 1.4.2011 is expected to be ₹6,000

(d) Other relevant information is :

i. Plant and machinery will be installed in February 2011 at a cost of ₹96,000. The monthly instalments of ₹2,000 is payable from April onwards.

ii. Dividend at 5% on preference share capital of ₹2,00,000 will be paid on 1st June.
iii. Advance to be received for sale of vehicles ₹9,000 in June.
iv. Dividends from investments amounting to ₹1,000 are expected to be received in June.
v. Income tax (advance) to be paid in June, is ₹2,000. **(ICWA-Inter)**

[**Ans:** Closing balance: April - ₹3,950, May - ₹3,000, June - ₹300]

9. **(Cash Budget)** From the following information, prepare cash budget for the months of January to April:

	Expected Sales ₹		Expected Purchases ₹
January	60,000	January	48,000
February	40,000	February	80,000
March	45,000	March	81,000
April	40,000	April	90,000

Wages are to be paid to workers at ₹5,000 per month. Balance at Bank on 1st January ₹8,000. It has been decided by the management that:

(a) In case of deficit fund within a limit of ₹10,000, arrangement can be made with the bankers.

(b) In case deficit fund exceeding ₹10,000 but within the limit of ₹42,000, issue of debenture is preferred.

(c) In case of deficit fund exceeding ₹42,000, issue of shares is preferred (considering the fact that it is within the limit of authorised capital). **(M.Com., Madras University)**

[**Ans:** Closing cash balance: January - ₹15,000; Issue of debentures: February - ₹30,000; March - ₹41,000; Issue of shares: April - ₹55,000]

10. **(Cash Budget)** Prepare cash budget for July to December, 2011 from the following information:

(a) The estimated sales, expenses etc. are as follows: (₹ in lakh)

Months	**June** ₹	**July** ₹	**Aug** ₹	**Sept** ₹	**Oct** ₹	**Nov** ₹	**Dec** ₹
Sales	34	40	40	50	50	60	65
Purchases	24	16	17	20	20	25	28
Wages and salaries	12	14	14	18	18	20	22
Miscellanies expenses	5	6	6	6	7	7	7
Interest received	2	-	-	2	-	-	2
Sale of shina	-	-	20	-	-	-	-

(b) 20% of the sales are on cash with 3% cash discount and the balance on credit.

(c) 1% of credit sales are returned by the customers. 2% of net receivable constituted bad debts. 50% of good accounts receivable are collected in the month following the sales with 1% cash discount, 30% of good accounts receivable are collected in the 2nd month following the sales and the rest in the 3rd month following the sales.

(d) The time lag in the payment of miscellaneous expenses and purchases is one month. Wages and salaries are paid fortnightly with a time lag of 15 days.

(e) The company keeps a minimum cash balance of ₹25.00 lakh. Cash in excess of ₹27.00 lakh is invested in 9% government securities in the multiple of ₹1 lakh. Interest is receivable on monthly basis. Shortfalls in the minimum cash balance are made good by borrowings from banks in multiple of ₹2 lakh and repaid by the same amount. The rate of interest is 12% p.a. (compound interest)

(f) Opening cash balance is ₹26 lakhs.

(g) Sales in the month of April and May was ₹44 and 40 lakh respectively.

Ans:

	July ₹	Aug ₹	Sept ₹	Oct ₹	Nov ₹	Dec ₹
Closing balance (₹)	26.96	27.10	27.87	27.43	27.27	27.49
Borrowings	6	-	-	-	-	-
Repayment with interest	-	6.12	-	-	-	-
Investment in govt. bands	-	15	2	1	3	4

11. **(Production and Production Cost Budget)** Gama Engineering Company Ltd manufactures two products 'X' and 'Y'. An estimate of the number of units to be sold in the first seven months of 2011 is given below:

	Product 'X' (Units)	Product 'Y' (Units)
January	5,500	4,400
February	5,600	4,400
March	5,800	4,200
April	6,000	4,000
May	6,200	3,800
June	6,200	3,800
July	6,000	3,900

It is anticipated that:

(a) There will be no stock of work-in-progress at the end of any month.

(b) Finished units equal to half the anticipated sales for the next month will be in stock at the end of each month (including December 2010).

The budgeted production and production cost for the year ending 31st December, 2011 are as follows:

	Product 'X'	Product 'Y'
Production (units)	90,000	65,000
Direct materials per unit (₹)	21	18
Direct wages per unit (₹)	8	10
Variable factory overheads (₹)	4,50,000	3,25,000
Fixed factory overheads (₹)	3,40,000	4,10,000

You are required to prepare:

(a) A production budget showing number of units produced each month and

(b) A summarised production cost budget for 6 months from January to June 2011.

[**Ans:** Production: X - 35,550 units, Y - 24,350 units, Production Cost: X - ₹13,78,700, Y - ₹10,08,550]

12. **(Production Budget and Materials Purchase Budget)** As a cost accountant of Modern Manufacturing Company, you are asked to prepare a quarterly production budget and direct materials purchase budget for the accounting year 1st April 2011 to 31st March 2012. The following information is relevant:

(a) The company manufactures only two products 'A' and 'B'

(b) The sales volume forecast (in units):

2011-2012	A	B
Quarter - I	5,000	4,500
Quarter - II	4,000	5,000
Quarter - III	4,500	5,500
Quarter - IV	5,500	4,000
2012-13		
Quarter - I	4,000	5,000

(c) Raw materials requirement forecast:

Two raw materials X and Y are used in the manufacture of the two products. Standard quantity and price of these materials are as below:

Standard quantities:

- Raw materials X - 4 units for each unit of Product 'A' at ₹15 per unit.
- Raw materials Y - 5 units for each unit of Product 'B' at ₹10 per unit.

(d) It is planned that the closing stock at the end of each quarter should be maintained at a level equal to half the expected sales for the next quarter for both the products. The raw materials stock at the end of each quarter should be equal to half of the material consumed in the next quarter for both materials.

(e) Stock of product 'A' and 'B' at the end of Quarter-I in financial year 2012-13 is estimated at 3,000 units and 3,250 units respectively.

[**Ans:** Total production: Product 'A' - 18,500 units and Product 'B' - 19,250 units.
Total value of purchase: Material 'X' - ₹11,25,000 Material 'Y' - ₹9,87,500]

13. **(Production Budget and Direct Labour Hour Budget)** A Ltd manufactures a single product 'P' with a single grade of labour. The sales budget and finished goods stock budget for the 1st quarter ending 30.06.2011 are as follows:

Sales	1,400 units
Opening stock	100 units
Closing stock	140 units

It is budgeted that 10% of finished work will be scrapped.

The standard direct labour content of product 'P' is 3 hours. The budgeted productivity ratio for direct labour is only 80%.

The company employs 36 direct operatives, who are expected to average 144 working hours each in the first quarter.

You are required to prepare:

(a) Production budget

(b) Direct labour budget

(c) Comment on the problem that your direct labour budget reveals and suggest how this problem might be overcome.

[**Ans:** (a) Production (gross) - 1,600 units, (b) Shortage of direct labour hour - 816 hours]

14. **(Sales Overhead Budget)** Prepare a sales overhead budget for the month of January, February and March from the estimates given below:

Advertisement	₹12,500
Salaries of the sales department	₹15,000
Expenses of sales department	₹10,500
Counter salesman salaries and DA	₹16,000

Commission to counter salesman at 1% on their sales.

Travelling salesman's commission at 10% of their sales and expenses at 5% on their sales.

The sales during the period estimated as follows:

Month	Counter Sales ₹	Travelling Salesman's Sales ₹
January	2,80,000	1,10,000
February	3,20,000	1,15,000
March	3,40,000	1,20,000

[**Ans:** Total sales costs: January - ₹73,300; February - ₹74,450, March - ₹75,400]

15. **(Control Ratios)** Calculate (a) Efficiency ratio, (b) Activity ratio and (c) Capacity ratio, from the following figures:

Budgeted production	88 units
Standard hours per unit	10
Actual production	75 units
Actual working hours	600

(B.Com. (Hons.), Delhi University)

[**Ans:** Efficiency ratio - 125%; Activity ratio - 85.23% and Capacity ratio - 68.10%]

16. **(Control Ratios)** In a manufacturing shop product 'X' requires 2.5 man-hours and product 'Y' requires 6 man-hours. In a month of 25 working days of 8 hours a day, 2,000 units of 'X' and 1,000 units of 'Y' were produced. The company employs 50 workers in the shop and the budgeted man-hours are 1,08,000 for the year. You are required to workout the capacity ratio, activity ratio and efficiency ratio. **(ICWA-Inter)**

[**Ans:** Capacity ratio - 111.11%; Activity ratio - 122.22% and Efficiency ratio - 111%]

Standard Costing and Variance Analysis

21

- Standard Costing - Meaning
- Types of Standards
- Installation of Standard Costing - Pre-requisites
- Standard Vs. Estimated Cost - Differences
- Standard Costing and Budgetary Control
- Standard Costing - Advantages / Dis-advantages
- Establishment of Standard Cost and Elements of Costs
- Variance Analysis - Meaning
- Classification of Variance
- Revision Variance
- Two / Three and Four Variance Method of analysis - Causes and Responsibilities
- Accounting Methods in Standard Costing
- Standard Cost - Reporting
- Variance Control - Through Ratio Analysis

21.1 INTRODUCTION

The main objective of a business concern is to minimise the cost and maximise the profits. The management of a manufacturing concern has to evaluate the operating efficiency and take corrective actions to control cost. Historical costing fails to help the management in cost control. Standard costing is a technique of cost accounting. It aids the management in controlling costs. It can be used with any method of costing.

Standard Cost: Meaning

Standard cost is a predetermined cost. It is fixed for each element of cost. It is developed scientifically after a careful study of all operating conditions. Standard cost is an ideal cost that should be attained at a high level of efficiency.

ICMA - London defines "Standard cost is a predetermined cost which is calculated from managements standard of efficient operation and the relevant necessary operation".

According to the above definition, standard cost is the reasonable cost that should be achieved under a reasonable level of efficiency which a management desires. It involves measuring the costs at a particular level of operation under specified conditions.

Standard Costing

Standard costing is a technique of cost accounting used for cost control. ICMA - London defines standard costing as "the preparation and use of standard costs, their comparison with actual cost and the analysis of variances to their causes and points of incidence".

Actual costs are measured and compared with standard cost to measure the operating efficiency. It discloses the deviation of actual costs from standard costs. The difference between standard costs and actual cost is called cost variances. It indicates the production efficiency. The variances are classified as favourable and unfavourable on the basis of its impact on profit. When actual costs are more than the standard cost it is called unfavourable variance since it impacts profit unfavourably. If actual costs are less than the standard cost, it is called favourable variance, because it has a favourable impact on profit. The variances are to be analysed as to their causes and remedial steps are to be taken. Thus standard costing involves the following steps:

1. Establishing standard costs for each element of cost.
2. Determining actual costs.
3. Comparison of actual cost with standard cost and finding the variances.
4. Analysing the variances as to their causes and classifying them into controllable and uncontrollable variances.
5. Preparation and submission of variance report to management for taking appropriate action.

21.1.1 Types of Standards

The term standard is used in different contexts. It may be classified as follows:

1. **Ideal standards**

   Ideal standard is established assuming that plants can be operated at 100% efficiency. No discount is allowed for normal loss of materials, normal idle time in case of labour and utilisation of full capacity. Ideal standard is impractical to achieve. So it is of no practical use. It will lead to frustration on the part of employees. As unfavourable variance becomes a normal feature and no importance may be given.

2. **Normal standards**

   Normal standards are standards fixed after giving allowances for normal loss of material and labour time. At the same time it is set for an efficiency level that can be achieved with higher effort. It is practically any achievable standard. So it is useful to the management.

3. **Basic standards**

   Basic standards are set for a long period's of time. A base year is selected for establishing basic standards. It will remain unaltered. It is suitable in industries where operating conditions are stable for long period. It is also suitable where production range is small and production process is longer. But in most of the industries business conditions will change often, so this standard has no practical use. But it may be used as base to measure the trends in business conditions like changes in price of materials, labour rate and production efficiency.

4. **Current standards**

   Current standards are simple estimation of what the actual cost will be under current conditions prevailing. These costs will be revised when operating conditions change. So this is useful only for short period. This standard is achievable if anticipated conditions prevail. These standards are used by business houses for cost control and decision making.

21.1.2 Prerequisites for Installation of Standard Costing

The following are prerequisites for establishing standard costing:

1. **Establishing cost centres**

   The area of operation of a business is to be divided into various cost centres. This helps in fixing standards for various cost centres. The actual costs are collected in relation to each cost centre. Deviations between standard cost and actual cost are ascertained for each cost centre. This helps in establishing responsibility for adverse deviations. Person in charge of a cost centre knows his responsibility.

2. **Degree of standard**

   Standards should be established scientifically. A standard which is practically useful should be established.

3. **Period**

   Period for use of standard should be fixed clearly and a suitable standard should be selected.

4. **Level of efficiency**

   The level of efficiency selected for fixing standards should be attainable with a reasonable standard of efficiency. Fixing a too high level of efficiency cannot be achieved and it will lead to frustration.

5. **Volume of production**

   Fixed overhead standards will vary when volume of production varies. So it is necessary to estimate a volume of production that can be achieved. Expected sales volume and available capacity should be considered for fixing volume of production.

6. **Classification of accounts**

   Expenses are to be grouped under proper classifications and codes are to be assigned. This helps in easy collection of actual cost and compare it with standard cost for determining deviations.

21.1.3 Standard Costs and Estimated Costs

Both standard costs and estimated costs are predetermined costs. But they differ in the following aspects:

	Estimated Cost	Standard Cost
1.	It is an estimation of what the cost will be	It is an estimation of what the cost should be
2.	It does not aim at cost control	It is a management tool to control cost
3.	Past experience and future changes anticipated are the basis for fixing estimated cost.	Standard cost are fixed scientifically.
4.	It is usually established by accounting department.	Standards are established by engineering and production planning department.
5.	Estimated costs are not entered in account books.	Standard costs are entered in account books.
6.	Estimated cost may be fixed for the business as a whole (or) for a division.	Standard costs are established for each element of cost.
7.	Responsibility for deviation is not established.	Responsibility is fixed for adverse deviations.
8.	Actual costs and estimated costs are not compared for the purpose of of cost control.	Actual costs and standard costs are compared to ascertain deviations. Deviations are analysed as to their causes.

21.1.4 Standard Costing and Budgetary Control

Both standard costing and budgetary control are techniques of cost control. Predetermined costs are established and compared with actual costs to ascertain deviations in costs. Deviations in cost are analysed as to their causes and remedial steps are taken to control the costs. They are independent of each other. Existence of both will be more useful to the management in decision making and cost control. But they differ in following respects:

	Budgetary Control	Standard Costing
1.	Budgets are prepared both for costs and revenue	It is established for cost only.
2.	It is prepared for a business as a whole or for part of an undertaking	It covers all elements of costs.
3.	Budgets are based on estimated costs and revenues based on past experience.	It is a scientific estimation of what the costs should be?
4.	It is an expression of business policies and plans in quantitative or monetary terms or both.	It is a predetermination of costs on scientific basis.
5.	Budgets are prepared for a specific period.	Standards once established may be used for a long period, if operating conditions remain same.
6.	Budgets are not part of account books	Standard costs are part of account books.
7.	Budgets fix maximum of expenses to be incurred during the budget period	No maximum limit is fixed for expenses.

Advantages of standard costing

1. **Cost control**

   Standard costing is an effective tool in the hands of the management in cost control. Predetermined standard costs are compared with actual cost and remedial steps are taken in case of substantial adverse variations in costs.

2. **Measurement of efficiency**

   Standards are the benchmark for evaluating individual performance. It helps to identify and measure the efficiency of individuals.

3. **Incentives to personnel**

   Standard costing helps to identify and measure the efficiency of individuals. It helps to introduce incentive schemes to those who achieve higher efficiency.

4. **Management by exception**

   Only abnormal deviations from standards are brought to the notice of management. Thus management's attention is drawn to more important matters only. It helps in quick remedial action.

5. **Fixing responsibility**

   It helps to identify the people responsible for inefficiency. Standard costing helps in identifying people responsible for inefficiency.

6. **Utilisation of production facilities**

   Standard cost helps in standardisation and effective utilisation of production facilities.

7. **Standardisation of production procedures**

   Establishing standards helps in simplifying and standardisation of methods of production. It helps to increase production efficiency.

8. **Useful for planning and budgeting**

   Standard costing helps in introducing budgetary control. It also helps in preparing future plans.

9. **Effective delegation of authority and responsibility**

   Standard costing helps to identify who is responsible for what. This helps in effective delegation of authority and fixing responsibilities.

10. **Motivation to employees**

    Setting standards leads to consulting and seeking co-operation of people from various departments. It creates cost consciousness among people. It motivates the employees in achieving the standards.

11. **Economy in accounting**

    Initial costs in establishing standards are more. But these standards can be used over a long period. Using standard cost reduces cost of accounting.

Limitations or disadvantages of standard costing

1. **Costly**

   For small and medium sized firms the cost of establishing and operation of standard costing is prohibitive.

2. **Difficulty in setting standards**

   Setting standards is difficult in industries where works of different nature are taken up according to customers requirements.

3. **Changing business conditions**

   Business conditions are dynamic and are subject to continuous changes. Standards set once may not be useful when business conditions change considerably.

4. **Suitability**

   It may be suitable for industries where work done are of repetitive nature. But it is more difficult to introduce in industries where work carried out is of non-repetitive nature.

5. **Analysing of variances**

   There is great difficulty in classifying variations into controllable and non-controllable variances.

6. **Rigidity**

   Standards once set are treated as benchmark for comparing actual performance. Over a period of time standards become rigid and are not changed even when operating conditions change.

21.2 SETTING UP OF STANDARDS

Standard costs are established for each element of cost. Standard costs are established in respect of the following elements of cost:

1. Direct materials
2. Direct labour
3. Overheads:
   (a) variable
   (b) fixed

1. **Standard materials cost**

   Materials cost depends upon the quantity of materials consumed and its price. It involves setting up of two standards viz., (i) Materials quantity standard and (ii) Materials price standard.

   (a) Materials quantity standards

   Engineering and production planning department establishes standard quantity of materials required for production of a product. Input-output ratio, quality of materials, standard mix of materials, normal wastage and production efficiency are considered in fixing materials quantity standard.

   (b) Materials price standards

   Estimating standard price of materials is very difficult. Materials prices depend on various factors like demand and supply, quality, government regulations, quantity discounts, normal loss and stores overhead. Management must analyse the materials price in the past and fix the expected price in the future. If there is a fixed price supply contract with suppliers, the price agreed will be used as standard price.

2. **Standard labour cost**

   Labour cost depends on labour time and wage rates. Setting labour cost standard involves setting (i) Labour time standard and (ii) Labour rate standard.

(a) Labour rate standard

Wage rate depends on qualification, experience and skill of employees, the company's wage policy, the contract between the management and employees made at the time of recruitment and the agreement between the labour union and the management. The complications involved in doing a job and responsibility also decide the wage rates.

(b) Labour time standard

Standard time required for doing a work or a job may be fixed on the basis of past experience, time and motion study or experimentation. Using average time taken in the past may not be objective and accurate. Standard time fixed under time and motion study or by experimentation will be more reliable and objective.

21.3 OVERHEAD STANDARDS

Overheads consist of a variety of items. Many people are connected with controlling these expenses. Storekeeper is responsible for controlling storage expenses of materials, personnel department is responsible for controlling indirect labour costs etc. Some overhead item will vary in direct proportion to changes in volume of production, some overhead items will vary but less proportionately than change in volume of production and some overhead items remain constant irrespective of changes in volume of production. It is very difficult to establish standards for each overhead item. Instead, overhead budgets are prepared and is used as standards. Fixed overhead rate per unit changes is inverse proportion to change in volume of production. So it is essential to establish budgeted level of production.

21.4 VARIANCE ANALYSIS

C.I.M.A - London defines variance as "The difference between a standard cost and the comparable actual cost incurred during a period".

Variance is the deviation of actual cost from standard cost. It is the difference between the standard cost and actual cost. Ascertaining the variances, analysing as to their causes and taking corrective actions are the foundation of standard costing. Installation of standard costing is a waste without variance analysis.

Variances are calculated for each element of cost. The variances are classified into different categories on different basis as below:

1. On the basis of impact on profit

(a) Favourable variances

When actual cost is less than the standard cost, it has a favourable impact on profit. Such variances are called favourable variances.

(b) Unfavourable variances

When actual cost is more than the standard cost, it has an adverse impact on profit. Such variances are called unfavourable or adverse variances.

2. On the basis of controllability

(a) Controllable variances

When an individual working in a company is made responsible for a variance, it is called controllable variance. Controllable variances are caused by factors internal to the organisation.

(b) Uncontrollable variances:

Uncontrollable variances arise due to factors external to the organisation. No individual within an organisation is responsible for these variances.

3. On the basis of elements of cost:

(a) Direct material cost variances
(b) Direct labour cost variances
(c) Overhead variances.

4. On the basis of sales revenue:

(a) Sales variances with reference to turnover
(b) Sales variances with reference to profit.

21.5 COMPUTATION OF VARIANCES

21.5.1 Direct Materials Cost Variances

Direct material cost variance is the difference between the standard cost of materials for actual output and actual cost of materials incurred. The materials cost variances arise due to many factors. They are classified as follow:

1. Material cost variance (MCV)
2. Material price variance (MPU)
3. Material usage variance (MUV)
4. Material mix variance (MMV)
5. Material yield or sub-usage variance (MYU or MSUV)

1. Material cost variance (MCV)

The difference between standard materials cost for actual output and materials cost incurred is the material cost variance. It is the total or aggregate variance. It arises due to price and quantity differences. The formula for calculating material cost variance is as follows:

$$\text{MCV} = \text{Standard price} \times \text{Standard quantity for actual output} - \text{Actual quantity} \times \text{Actual price}$$

(or)

$$= \text{Standard cost} - \text{Actual cost}$$

Materials cost variance is subdivided into material price variance and material usage or quantity variance.

2. **Material price variance (MPV)**

Material price variance arises due to difference between standard price and actual price. The formula for calculating material price variance is as follows:

$$\text{MPV} = \text{Actual quantity} \times \text{Standard price} - \text{Actual quantity} \times \text{Actual price}$$

(or)

$$= \text{Actual quantity (Standard price} - \text{Actual price)}$$

3. **Material usage (or quantity) variance (MUV)**

Material usage variance arises due to difference between actual quantity of materials used and standard quantity of materials specified for actual output. The formula for calculating material usage variance is as follows:

$$\text{MUV} = \text{Standard price} \times \text{Standard quantity for actual output} - \text{Standard price} \times \text{Actual quantity}$$

(or)

$$= \text{Standard price (Standard quantity for actual output} - \text{Actual quantity)}$$

Material usage variance arises when actual quantity of material used is different from standard quantity specified for actual output. It also arises when more than one material is used in production and they may be mixed in a proportion different from standard proportion. It also arises when output obtained is different from standard output. Material usage variance is further subdivided into material mix variance and material yield variance.

4. **Material mix variance (MMV)**

More than one material may be mixed in a certain ratio to produce an article. Actual materials mix may be in a different ratio than the standard ratio specified. The following is the formula for calculating material mix variance:

$$\text{MMV} = \text{Standard price} \times \text{Revised actual quantity} - \text{Standard price} \times \text{Actual quantity}$$

(or)

$$= \text{Standard price (Revised actual quantity} - \text{Actual quantity)}$$

Note:

Revised actual quantity = Actual mix × Standard mix ratio

5. **Material yield variance (MYV)**

Material yield variance arises when the actual output obtained is different from the standard yield specified for actual quantity of materials used. The following is the formula for computing material yield variance.

$$\text{MYV} = \text{Standard price} \times \text{Standard quantity} - \text{Standard price} \times \text{Revised actual quantity}$$

Alternatively material yield variance may be calculated by using the following formulae:

MYV = Standard materials cost per unit of output(Actual yield
– Standard yield for actual input)

(or)

= Average standard material price (Standard quantity for actual output
– Actual quantity)

For reducing number of calculations and time taken to calculate variances, calculate the following amounts and ascertain the variance:

Step-1: Actual cost of actual materials used:

= Actual price × Actual quantity of materials used

Step-2: Standard cost of actual materials used:

= Standard price × Actual quantity of materials used

Step-3: Standard cost of actual materials used, had it been used in standard mix ratio:

= Standard price × Total weight of actual mix × Standard mix ratio

Step-4: Standard cost of standard quantity of materials for actual output:

= Standard price × Standard quantity for actual output

After the calculation of above amounts variances are calculated as follows:

1. Material cost variance (MCV)

   = (SP × SQ) – (AP × AQ)

   = (4) – (1)

2. Material price variance (MPV)

   = SP × AQ – AP × AQ

   = (2) – (1)

3. Material usage variance (MUV)

   = (SP × SQ) – (SP × AQ)

   = (4) – (2)

4. Material mix variance (MMV)

   = SP × RAQ – SP × AQ

   = (3) – (2)

5. Material yield variance (MYV)

$$= SP \times SQ - SP \times RAQ$$

$$= (4) - (3)$$

where,

SP = Standard price
SQ = Standard quantity for actual output
AP = Actual price
AQ = Actual quantity
AP = Actual price
RAQ = Revised actual quantity

The material variances may be presented in a chart as follow:

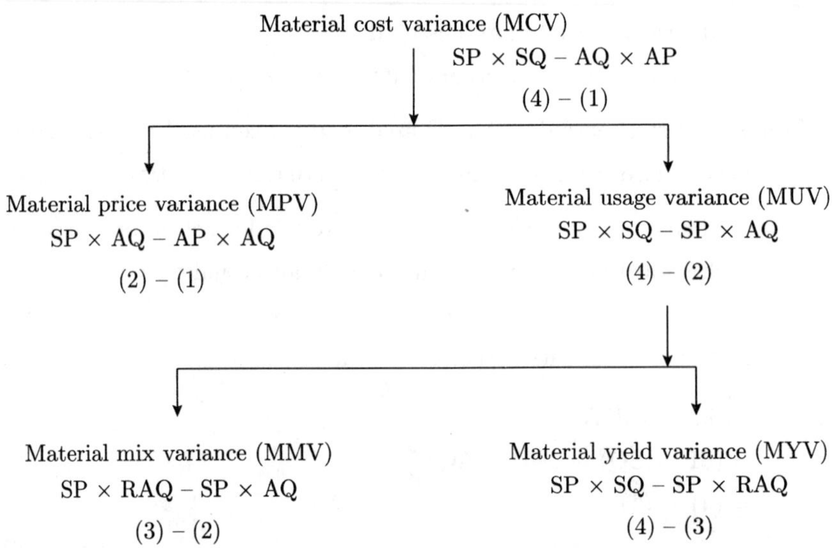

Alternatively:

The above variances may be presented in a line diagram as follows:

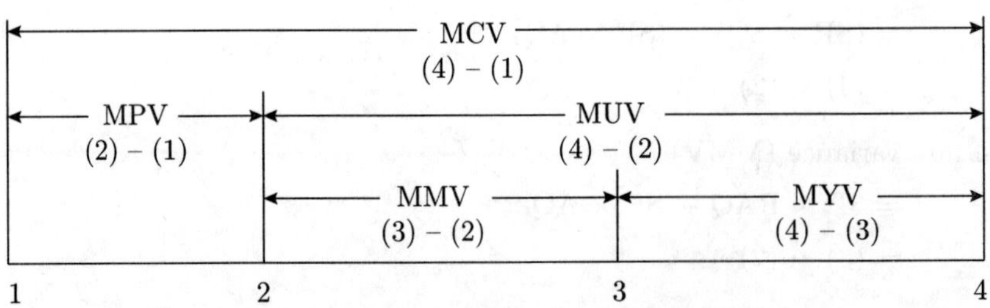

Note:

If the variance is positive, it is called favourable variance. If the variance is negative, it is called unfavourable variance.

Illustration-1

Standard price of a material is ₹15 per unit and actual price is ₹13.50 per unit. Material purchased amounted to 600 units and closing stock of materials is 50 units. Standard quantity is 500 units. Compute material variances.

Solution

Calculations:

1. Actual cost of materials used

   $= \text{Actual price} \times \text{Actual quantity used}$

   $= 13.50 \times 550 = ₹7{,}425$

2. Standard cost of materials used

   $= \text{Standard price} \times \text{Actual quantity used}$

   $= 15 \times 550 = ₹8{,}250$

3. Standard cost of materials used, had it been used in standard mix ratio – Not applicable – No material mix.

4. Standard cost of standard quantity for actual output.

   $= \text{Standard price} \times \text{Standard quantity}$

   $= 15 \times 500 = ₹7{,}500$

Variances:

1. Material cost variances (MCV)

   $= 4 - 1$

   $= 7{,}500 - 7{,}425 = 75 \text{ (F)}$

2. Material price variance (MPV)

   $= 2 - 1$

   $= 8{,}250 - 7{,}425 = 825 \text{ (F)}$

3. Material usage variance (MUV)

   $= 4 - 2$

   $= 7{,}500 - 8{,}250 = 750 \text{ (A)}$

Verification:

$$MCV = MPV + MUV$$

$$75\ (F) = 825\ (F) + 750\ (A)$$

$$75\ (F) = 75\ (F)$$

Note

1. Favourable variances are designated by capital letter 'F' and adverse variance are designated by capital letter 'A'.
2. Material mix variance and material yield variance are calculated when two or more materials are used in production.
3. Material price variance may be calculated for quantity of materials purchased. Material purchase price variance is calculated as follows:

$$\begin{aligned} MPPV &= \text{Quantity purchased (Std price} - \text{Actual price)} \\ &= 600(15 - 13.50) \\ &= 900(F) \end{aligned}$$

4. $$\begin{aligned} \text{Actual quantity used} &= \text{Quantity purchased} - \text{Closing stock} \\ &= 600 - 50 \\ &= 550 \text{ units} \end{aligned}$$

Illustration-2

X Ltd produces a product requiring materials 'M'. Standard quantity of materials is 3 kg per unit of the product. Standard price of the materials is ₹10 per kg. During the period the company produced 1,500 units of product using 4,800 kg materials 'M' at ₹9 per kg. Compute material variances.

Solution

Calculations:

1. Actual cost of materials used

$$= \text{Actual price} \times \text{Actual quantity used}$$

$$= 9 \times 4{,}800 = ₹43{,}200$$

2. Standard cost of materials used

$$= \text{Standard price} \times \text{Actual quantity used}$$

$$= 10 \times 4{,}800 = ₹48{,}000$$

3. Standard cost of materials used, had it been used in standard mix ratio – Not applicable – No material mix.

4. Standard cost of standard quantity for actual output.

   = Standard price × Standard quantity

   = 10 × 4,500 = ₹45,000

   Note

   Standard quantity = 1,500 units × 3 kg = 4,500 kg

Variances:

1. Material cost variance (MCV)

   = 4 − 1

   = 45,000 − 43,200 = 1,800 (F)

2. Material price variance (MPV)

   = 2 − 1

   = 48,000 − 43,200 = 4,800 (F)

3. Material usage variance (MUV)

   = 4 − 2

   = 45,000 − 48,000 = 3,000 (A)

Verification:

MCV = MPV + MUV

1,800 (F) = 4,800 (F) + 3,000 (A)

1,800 (F) = 1,800 (F)

Illustration-3

A furniture manufacturing company uses 20 square feet of mica per table. Standard price of mica is ₹12 per square feet. The company produced 100 tables using 2,200 square feet of mica at a price of ₹13.50 per square feet.

Compute material variances.

Solution

Calculations:

1. Actual cost of materials used

   = AP × AQ

   = 13.50 × 2,200 = ₹29,700

2. Standard cost of materials used

$$= SP \times AQ$$
$$= 12 \times 2{,}200 = ₹26{,}400$$

3. Standard cost of materials used, had it been used in standard mix ratio – Not applicable – No material mix.

4. Standard cost of standard quantity for actual output.

$$= SP \times SQ$$
$$= 12 \times 2{,}000 = ₹24{,}000$$

Note

SQ = 100 tables × 20 sq.ft = 2,000 sq.ft

Variances:

1. Material cost variance (MCV)

$$= 4 - 1$$
$$= 24{,}000 - 29{,}700 = 5{,}700\ (A)$$

2. Material price variance (MPV)

$$= 2 - 1$$
$$= 26{,}400 - 29{,}700 = 3{,}300\ (A)$$

3. Material usage variance (MUV)

$$= 4 - 2$$
$$= 24{,}000 - 26{,}400 = 2{,}400\ (A)$$

Verification:

MCV = MPV + MUV

5,700 (A) = 3,300 (A) + 2,400 (A)

5,700 (A) = 5,700 (A)

Illustration-4

The following is the standard specifications of materials for production of one unit of a product:

Materials A	3 kg at ₹12 per kg
Materials B	2 kg at ₹9 per kg

Production during a month amounted to 1,000 units. The following are the details of materials actually used:

Materials A	3,300 kg at ₹13.20 per kg
Materials B	1,800 kg at ₹8.40 per kg

Compute material variances.

Solution

Calculations:

1. Actual cost of materials used = AP × AQ

Material A	13.20 × 3,300	₹43,560
Material B	8.40 × 1,800	₹15,120
	Total	₹58,680

2. Standard cost of materials used = SP × AQ

Material A	12 × 3,300	₹39,600
Material B	9.00 × 1,800	₹16,200
	Total	₹55,800

3. Standard cost of materials used, had it been used in standard proportion = SP × Actual mix × Standard mix ratio

Material A	12 × 5,100 × 3/5	₹36,720
Material B	9.00 × 5,100 × 2/5	₹18,360
	Total	₹55,080

4. Standard cost of standard quantity for actual output = SP × SQ

Material A	12 × 3,000	₹36,000
Material B	9.00 × 2,000	₹18,000
	Total	₹54,000

Variances:

1. Material cost variances (MCV)

$$= 4 - 1$$

$$= 54{,}000 - 58{,}680 = 4{,}680 \text{ (A)}$$

2. Material price variance (MPV)

$= 2 - 1$

$= 55{,}800 - 58{,}680 = 2{,}880$ (A)

3. Material usage variance (MUV)

$= 4 - 2$

$= 54{,}000 - 55{,}800 = 1{,}800$ (A)

4. Material mix variance (MMV)

$= 3 - 2$

$= 55{,}080 - 55{,}800 = 720$ (A)

5. Material yield variance (MYV)

$= 4 - 3$

$= 54{,}000 - 55{,}080 = 1{,}080$ (A)

Verification:

(a) MCV = MPV + MUV

4,680 (A) = 2,880 (A) + 1,800 (A)

4,680 (A) = 4,680 (A)

(b) MUV = MMV + MYV

1,800 (A) = 720 (A) + 1,080 (A)

1,800 (A) = 1,800 (A)

Illustration-5

A Ltd follows standard costing system. The following are the details of standard mix of materials used in production:

Materials	Standard qty (units)	Standard price per unit ₹	Total ₹
P	25	4.00	100
Q	15	6.00	90
R	10	7.50	75
			265

The above standard is expected to produce 25 units of a finished product. The following are the details of materials actually used:

Material P	8,500 units at ₹3.75 per unit
Material Q	3,000 units at ₹7.00 per unit
Material R	5,500 units at ₹8.00 per unit

Actual output during the period was 8,000 units.

Calculate material variances.

Solution

Calculations:

1. Actual cost of materials used = AP × AQ

Material P	3.75 × 8,500	₹31,875
Material Q	7.00 × 3,000	₹21,000
Material R	8.00 × 5,500	₹44,000
	Total	₹96,875

2. Standard cost of materials used = SP × AQ

Material P	4.00 × 8,500	₹34,000
Material Q	6.00 × 3,000	₹18,000
Material R	7.50 × 5,500	₹41,250
	Total	₹93,250

3. Standard cost of materials used, had it been used in standard proportion = SP × Actual mix × Standard mix ratio

Material P	4.00 × 17,000 × 25/50	₹34,000
Material Q	6.00 × 17,000 × 15/50	₹30,600
Material R	7.50 × 17,000 × 10/50	₹25,500
	Total	₹90,100

4. Standard cost of standard quantity for actual output = SP × SQ

Material P	4.00 × 8,000	₹32,000
Material Q	6.00 × 4,800	₹28,800
Material R	7.50 × 3,200	₹24,000
	Total	₹84,800

Note

Standard quantity for actual output

Material P	25/25 × 8,000	8,000 units
Material Q	15/25 × 8,000	4,800 units
Material R	10/25 × 8,000	3,200 units

Variances:

1. Material cost variances (MCV)

   = 4 − 1

   = 84,800 − 96,875 = 12,075 (A)

2. Material price variance (MPV)

   = 2 − 1

   = 93,250 − 96,875 = 3,625 (A)

3. Material usage variance (MUV)

   = 4 − 2

   = 84,800 − 93,250 = 8,450 (A)

4. Material mix variance (MMV)

   = 3 − 2

   = 90,100 − 93,250 = 3,150 (A)

5. Material yield variance (MYV)

   = 4 − 3

   = 84,800 − 90,100 = 5,300 (A)

Verification:

(a) MCV = MPV + MUV

12,075 (A) = 3,625 (A) + 8,450 (A)

12,075 (A) = 12,075 (A)

(b) MUV = MMV + MYV

8,450 (A) = 3,150 (A) + 5,300 (A)

8,450 (A) = 8,450 (A)

Illustration-6

A manufacturing concern which has adopted standard costing furnishes the following information:

Standard:

Materials per 70 kg of finished products - 100 kg of material
Price of material - ₹10 per kg.

Actual:

Output	- 2,10,000 kg
Material used	- 2,80,000 kg
Cost of material	- ₹25,20,000

Calculate:

(a) Material usage variance

(b) Material price variance

(c) Material cost variance

(B.Com., Madras University)

Solution

Calculation:

1. Actual cost of materials used

$$= AP \times AQ$$
$$= ₹25,20,000 \text{ (given)}$$

2. Standard cost of materials used

$$= SP \times AQ$$
$$= 10 \times 2,80,000 = ₹28,00,000$$

3. Standard cost of materials used, had it been used in standard mix ratio - Not applicable - No material mix.

4. Standard cost of standard quantity for actual output

$$= SP \times SQ$$
$$= 10 \times 3,00,000 = ₹30,00,000$$

Note

Standard quantity for actual output

$$= \frac{100}{70} \times 2,10,000 = 3,00,000 \text{ kgs}$$

Variances:

1. Material Usage Variance (MCV)

$= 4 - 2$

$= 30,00,000 - 28,00,000 = 2,00,000$ (F)

2. Material Price Variance (MPV)

$= 2 - 1$

$= 28,00,000 - 25,20,000 = 2,80,000$ (F)

3. Material Cost Variance (MCV)

$= 4 - 1$

$= 30,00,000 - 25,20,000 = 4,80,000$ (F)

Verification:

MCV = MPV + MUV

4,80,000 (F) = 2,80,000 (F) + 2,00,000 (F)

4,80,000 (F) = 4,80,000 (F)

Illustration-7

The standard cost of certain chemical mixture is:

35% material A at ₹25 per kg.
65% material B at ₹36 per kg.

A standard loss of 5% is expected in production. During a period the following materials are used:

125 kg of material A at ₹27 per kg and
275 kg of material B at ₹34 per kg.

The actual output was 365 kg

Calculate:

(a) Material cost variance

(b) Material price variance

(c) Material mix variance

(d) Material yield variance

(B.Com. (Hons.), Delhi University)

Solution

Calculation:

1. Actual cost of materials used = AP × AQ

Material A	27 × 125	₹3,375
Material B	34 × 275	₹9,350
	Total	₹12,725

2. Standard cost of materials used = SP × AQ

Material A	25 × 125	₹3,125
Material B	36 × 275	₹9,900
	Total	₹13,025

3. Standard cost of materials used, had it been used in standard mix ratio

= Std. Price × Actual mix × Standard mix ratio

Material A	25 × 400 × 35/100	₹3,500
Material B	36 × 400 × 65/100	₹9,360
	Total	₹12,860

4. Standard cost of standard quantity for actual output = SP × SQ

Material A	25 × 134.474	₹3,361.85
Material B	36 × 249.734	₹8,990.42
	Total	₹12352.27 (or) ₹12,352.00

Note:

(i) Total standard mix assumed as equal to actual mix = 400 kg

(ii) Standard output = Total standard mix − 5% normal loss

= 400 kg − 20 kg = 380 kg

(iii) Standard quantity for standard output of 380 kg is:

Material A = Total standard mix × 35/100

= 400 × 35/100 = 140 kg

Material B = Total standard mix × 65/100

= 400 × 65/100 = 260 kg

(iv) Standard quantity for actual output of 365 kg is:

$$\text{Material A} = 140 \times 365/380 = 134.474 \text{ kg.}$$
$$\text{Material B} = 260 \times 365/380 = 249.734 \text{ kg.}$$

Variances:

1. Material cost variance (MCV)

   $= 4 - 1$

   $= 12{,}352 - 12{,}725 = 373$ (A)

2. Material price variance (MPV)

   $= (2) - (1)$

   $= 13{,}025 - 12{,}725 = 300$ (F)

3. Material mix variance (MUV)

   $= 3 - 2$

   $= 12{,}860 - 13{,}025 = 165$ (A)

4. Material yield variance (MYV)

   $= 4 - 3$

   $= 12{,}352 - 12{,}860 = 508$ (A)

Verification:

MCV = MPV + MMV + MYV

373(A) = 300 (F) + 165 (A) +508 (A)

= 373 (A)

(b) Direct Labour Cost Variance:

Direct labour cost variance arises due to the following factors:

1. Actual wage rate paid may be different from standard wage rate.
2. Actual time taken may be different from standard time.
3. When workers of different grades are used, the actual number of workers in each grade may be different from number of workers specified for each grade in the standard.
4. Actual output may be different from the standard output.
5. Labour time might have been lost due to abnormal reasons like power failure, non-availability of materials, machine breakdown etc.

The labour cost variances are classified as follows:

1. Labour cost variance (LCV)
2. Labour rate variance (LRV)
3. Labour efficiency variance (LEV)
4. Labour mix variance (LMV)
5. Labour idle time variance (LITV)
6. Labour yield variance (LYV)

1. Labour cost variance (LCV)

Labour cost variance is the difference between actual labour cost and standard labour cost specified for a volume of output. This is total variance. This variance arises due to change in wage rate, time taken, composition of labour force or idle time. The following is the formula for calculating labour cost variance:

$$= \text{Standard rate} \times \text{Standard time for actual output} - \text{Actual rate} \times \text{Actual time}$$

(or)

$$= \text{Standard labour cost} - \text{Actual labour cost}$$

2. Labour rate variance (LRV)

Labour rate variance arises when the actual wage rate is either more or less than the standard wage rate. It is a sub-division of labour cost variance. Labour rate variance is calculated by using the following formula:

$$= \text{Actual time} \times \text{Standard rate} - \text{Actual time} \times \text{Actual rate}$$

(or)

$$= \text{Actual time (Standard rate} - \text{Actual rate)}$$

3. Labour efficiency variance (LEV)

Labour efficiency variance arises when actual time taken is either more or less than the standard time specified for actual output achieved. The following formula is used for calculating labour efficiency variance:

$$= \text{Standard rate} \times \text{Standard time for actual output} - \text{Standard rate} \times \text{Actual time}$$

(or)

$$= \text{Standard rate (Standard time for actual output} - \text{Actual time)}$$

Labour efficiency variance is subdivided into labour mix variance, Labour Idle time variance and labour yield variance.

4. Labour mix variance (LMV)

Labour mix variance arises when actual number of workers in each grade of labour is either more or less than the number of workers specified for each grade of labour in the standard. This variance is calculated as follows:

= Standard rate × Revised actual time − Standard rate × Actual time

(or)

= Standard rate (Revised actual time − Actual time)

Note: Revised actual time = Total time of actual mix × Standard labour mix ratio

Labour mix variance is also called labour gang variance or labour composition variance.

5. Labour idle time variance (LITV)

This variance arises when labour time is lost due to abnormal reasons like power failure, non-availability of raw material, accident etc. This variance is always adverse. The following formula is used for calculating idle time variance:

= Standard rate × Actual idle time.

6. Labour yield variance (LYV)

This variance arises when the actual output achieved is different from standard output specified. This variance is calculated by using the following formula:

= Standard rate × Standard time for actual output − Standard rate × Revised actual time

(or)

= Standard rate (Standard time for actual output − Revised Actual time)

Note: To reduce number of calculations and time, first calculate the following amounts in the order given and calculate the variances in a step model as follows:

Calculations:

1. Actual wages paid for actual time

   = Actual no. of workers × Actual hours × Actual rate

2. Standard wages for actual time

   = Actual number of workers × Actual hours × Standard rate

3. Standard wages for actual time utilised

   = Actual number of workers × Actual hours utilised × Standard rate

4. Standard wages for actual time, had the workers been engaged in standard mix ratio:

   = Standard number of workers × Actual hours utilised × Standard rate

5. Standard wages for standard time for actual output (or) Standard wage for actual production

   = Standard rate × Standard time for actual production

   (or)

   = Standard labour cost per unit of output × Actual production

Variances:

1. Labour cost variance (LCV)

   = 5 − 1

2. Labour rate variance (LRV)

   = 2 − 1

3. Total labour efficiency variance (LEV)

   = 5 − 2

4. Labour idle time variance (LITV)

   = 3 − 2

5. Labour mix variance (LMV)

   = 4 − 3

6. Labour yield variance (LYV)

   = 5 − 4

The labour variance may be shown in a chart form as below:

Labour cost variance (LCV)
Standard wages for actual production – Actual wages
(5) – (1)

Labour rate variance (LRV)
Standard wages for actual time – Actual wages
(2) – (1)

Total labour efficiency variance (LEV)
Standard wages for actual production – Standardwages for actual time
(5) – (2)

Labour idle time variance (LITU)
Std. wages for actual time utilized – Standard wages for actual time (3) – (2)

Labour mix variance (LMV)
Std. wages for actual time had labour been used in Std.mix (A) – Std. wages for actual time utilized
(4) – (3)

Labour yield variance (LYV)
Std. wages for actual production – Std. wages for actual time utilized (5) – (4)

Alternatively the variances may be shown in a line diagram as follow:

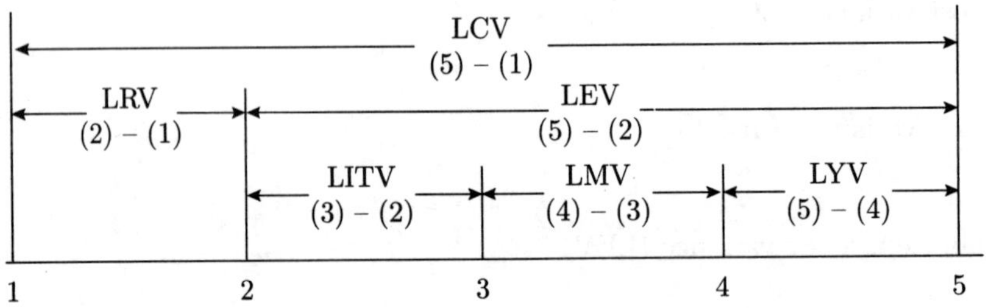

Note:

1. If the answer is in positive figure (i.e. actual cost is less), the variance is called favourable and denoted by capital letter 'F'.
2. If the answer is in negative figure (i.e. actual cost is more), the variance is called adverse and denoted by capital letter 'A'.

Verification:

The correctness of variances can be proved by the following steps

1. LCV = LRV + LEV
2. LEV = LITV + LMV + LYV

Illustration-8

The standard wage rate of a particular grade of labour is ₹7.50. During a period 650 hours were actually worked and 200 units of a product were produced. The standard time allowed is 3 hours per unit. The actual wage rate amounted to ₹8 per hour worked.

Compute Labour Variances.

Solution

Calculations:

1. Actual wages paid for actual time

   = AR × AT

   = 8 × 650 = ₹5,200

2. Standard wages for actual time

   = SR × AT

   = 7.50 × 650 = ₹4,875

3. Standard wages for actual time utilized

   = SR × AT unitlised

   = 7.50 × 650 = ₹4,875

4. Standard wages for actual time, had labour been used in standard mix ratio – Not applicable – No labour mix

5. Standard wages for standard time for actual output.

   = SR × ST

   = 7.50 × 600 = ₹4,500

Note: Standard time for actual output (ST) = 3 × 200 = 600 hours

Variances:

1. Labour cost variance (LCV)

   = 5 – 1

   = 4,500 - 5,200 = 700 (A)

2. Labour rate variance (LRV)

   = 2 – 1

   = 4,875 -5,200 = 325 (A)

3. Labour efficiency variance (LEV)

   = 5 – 2

   = 4,500 – 4,875 = 375 (A)

Verification:

LCV = LRV + LEV

700 (A) = 325(A) + 375 (A)

700 (A) = 700 (A)

Illustration-9

The following information is obtained from standard cost card:

Labour rate	= ₹6.00 per hour
Hours	= 3 hours per unit.

Actual production data are:

Units produced = 500

Labour rate = ₹6.75 per hour

Hours worked = 1,400 hours

Calculate labour cost variances and analyse it.

Solution

Calculations:

1. Actual wages paid for actual time

   = AR × AT

   = 6.75 × 1,400 = ₹9,450

2. Standard wages for actual time

   = SR × AT

   = 6.00 × 1,400 = ₹8,400

3. Standard wages for actual time utilized

   = SR × AT

   = 6.00 × 1,400 = ₹8,400

4. Standard wages for actual time, had labour been used in standard mix ratio – Not applicable – No labour mix

5. Standard wages for standard time for actual output.

   = SR × ST

   = 6.00 × 1,500 = ₹9,000

Note: Standard time for actual output (ST) = 3 × 500 = 1,500 hrs.

Variances:

1. Labour cost variance (LCV)

   = 5 – 1

   = 9,000 – 9,450 = 450 (A)

2. Labour rate variance (LRV)

   = 2 – 1

   = 8,400 – 9,450 = 1,050 (A)

3. Labour efficiency variance (LEV)

$$= 5 - 2$$

$$= 9{,}000 - 8{,}400 = 600 \text{ (F)}$$

Verification:

LCV = LRV + LEV

450 (A) = 1,050(A) + 600 (F)

450 (A) = 450(A)

Illustration-10

The following information is taken from the records of a factory.

Standard:

Number of workers	- 75
Wage rate	- ₹10 per hour
Standard output per hour	- 10 units

Actual:

Number of workers	- 80
Wage rate	- ₹12 per hour
Output	- 340 units

The factory operates 44 hours in a week. Due to power failure 2 hours were lost.

Calculate labour variances.

Solution

Calculations:

1. Actual wages paid for actual time

$$= \text{AR} \times \text{AT}$$

$$= 12.00 \times 3{,}520 = ₹42{,}240$$

2. Standard wages for actual time

$$= \text{SR} \times \text{AT utilised}$$

$$= 10.00 \times 3{,}520 = ₹35{,}200$$

3. Standard wages for actual time utilised

$= SR \times AT$ (utilised)

$= 10.00 \times 3{,}360 =$ ₹33,600

4. Standard wages for actual time, had labour been used in standard mix ratio - Nil

5. Standard wages for standard time for actual output.

$= SR \times ST$

$= 10.00 \times 3{,}400 =$ ₹34,000

Note:

1. Standard time for actual out (ST) $= 10 \times 340 = 3{,}400$ hrs

2. Actual time = Actual number of workers × Working hours in a week

$= 80 \times 44 = 3{,}520$ hours

3. Idle time $= 80 \times 2 = 160$ hours

4. Actual time utilized $= 3{,}520 - 160 = 3{,}360$ hours

Variances:

1. Labour cost variance (LCV)

$= 5 - 1$

$= 34{,}000 - 42{,}240 = 8{,}240$ (A)

2. Labour rate variance (LRV)

$= 2 - 1$

$= 35{,}200 - 42{,}240 = 7{,}040$ (A)

3. Labour efficiency variance (LEV)

$= 5 - 2$

$= 34{,}000 - 35{,}200 = 1{,}200$ (A)

4. Labour idle time variance (LITV)

$= 3 - 2$

$= 33{,}600 - 35{,}200 = 1{,}600$ (A)

5. Labour mix variance (LMV)

$= 4 - 3 =$ Nil

Note: Value of step 4 is nil. Hence value of step 3 is used in the place of step 4.

6. Labour yield variance (LYV)

   = 5 − 4

   = 34,000 − 33,600 = 400 (F)

   Note: Value of step 4 is nil. Hence value of step 3 is used in the place of step 4.

Verification:

1. LCV = LRV + LEV

   8,240(A) = 7,040 (A) + 1,200 (A)

   8,240(A) = 8,240(A)

2. LEV = LMV + LITV + LYV

   1,200 (A) = Nil + 1,600 (A) + 400 (F)

   1,200 (A) =1,200 (A)

Illustration-11

Calculate labour variances from the following information:

Standard hours: 8,000 hrs, Standard wages: ₹30 per hour
Actual hours: 10,000 hrs, Actual wage rate: ₹25 per hour.

Time lost due to non-availability of power is 400 hours

Calculate labour variances.

Solution

Calculations:

1. Actual wages paid for actual time

   = AR × AT

   = 25 × 10,000 = ₹2,50,000

2. Standard wages for actual time

   = SR × AT

   = 30 × 10,000 = ₹3,00,000

3. Standard wages for actual time utilized

   = SR × AT utilised

   = 30 × 9,600 = ₹2,88,000

4. Standard wages for actual time, had labour been used in standard mix ratio – Not applicable – No labour mix

5. Standard wages for standard time for actual output.

$$= \text{SR} \times \text{ST}$$

$$= 30 \times 8{,}000 = ₹2{,}40{,}000$$

Variances:

1. Labour cost variance (LCV)

$$= 5 - 1$$

$$= 2{,}40{,}000 - 2{,}50{,}000 = 10{,}000\ (\text{A})$$

2. Labour rate variance (LRV)

$$= 2 - 1$$

$$= 3{,}00{,}000 - 2{,}50{,}000 = 50{,}000\ (\text{F})$$

3. Labour efficiency variance (LEV)

$$= 5 - 2$$

$$= 2{,}40{,}000 - 3{,}00{,}000 = 60{,}000\ (\text{A})$$

4. Labour idle time variance (LITV) – NIL

$$= 4 - 2$$

$$= 2{,}88{,}000 - 3{,}00{,}000 = 12{,}000\ (\text{A})$$

Note: Value of step 4 is nil. Hence value of step 3 is used in the place of step 4.

5. Labour mix variance (LMV) – Nil

6. Labour yield variance (LYV) / Labour sub-efficiency variance (LSEV)

$$= 5 - 4$$

$$= 3{,}40{,}000 - 2{,}88{,}000 = 48{,}000\ (\text{A})$$

Verification:

1. LCV = LRV + LEV

   10,000 (A) = 50,000 (F) + 60,000 (A)

   10,000 (A) = 10,000 (A)

2. LEV = LMV + LITV + LYV

   60,000 (A) = Nil + 12,000 (A) + 48,000 (A)

   60,000 (A) = 60,000 (A)

Illustration-12

Standard hours for manufacturing two products M and N are 15 hours and 20 hours per unit respectively. Both products require identical kind of labour and the standard wage rate per hour is ₹5. In the year 2009, 10,000 units of M and 15,000 units of N were manufactured. The total labour hours actually worked were 4,50,500 and the actual wage bills came to ₹23,00,000. This included 12,000 hrs paid for at ₹7 per hour and 9,400 hours paid for at ₹7.50 per hour, the balance having been paid at ₹5 per hour.

You are required to calculate the labour variances: **(ICWA-Inter)**

Solution

Calculations:

1. Actual wages paid for actual time

   $= AR \times AT$

   $=$ ₹23,00,000 (given)

2. Standard wages for actual time

   $= SR \times AT$

   $= 5 \times 4{,}50{,}500 =$ ₹22,52,500

3. Standard wages for actual time utilized

   $= SR \times AT$

   $= 5 \times 4{,}50{,}500 =$ ₹22,52,500

4. Standard wages for actual time, had labour been used in standard mix ratio – Not applicable – No labour mix

5. Standard wages for standard time for actual output.

   $= SR \times ST$

   $= 5 \times 4{,}50{,}000 =$ ₹22,50,000

Note: Standard time for actual output

Product M $= 10{,}000 \times 15 = 1{,}50{,}000$ hrs
Product N $= 15{,}000 \times 20 = 3{,}00{,}000$ hrs
Total Std time $= 4{,}50{,}000$ hrs

Variances:

1. Labour cost variance (LCV)

   $= 5 - 1$

   $= 22{,}50{,}000 - 23{,}00{,}000 = 50{,}000$ (A)

2. Labour rate variance (LRV)

$= 2 - 1$

$= 22{,}52{,}500 - 23{,}00{,}000 = 47{,}500$ (A)

3. Labour efficiency variance (LEV)

$= 5 - 2$

$= 22{,}50{,}000 - 22{,}52{,}500 = 2{,}500$ (A)

Verification:

LCV = LRV + LEV

50,000 (A) = 47,500 (A) + 2,500 (A)

50,000 (A) = 50,000 (A)

Illustration-13

A gang of workers normally consists of 30 men, 15 women and 10 children. They are paid at standard hourly rate as under.

Men - ₹0.80

Women - ₹0.60

Children - ₹0.40

In a normal working week of 40 hours, the gang is expected to produce 2,000 units of output.

During the week ending on 31st December, 2008, the gang consisted of 40 men, 10 women and 5 children. The actual wages paid were at ₹0.70, ₹0.65 and ₹0.30 respectively. Four hours were lost due to abnormal idle time and 1,600 units were produced.

Calculate labour variances.

Solution

Calculations:

1. Actual wages paid for actual time = AR × AT

Men	0.70 × 1,600	₹1,120
Women	0.65 × 400	₹260
Children	0.30 × 200	₹60
	Total	₹1,440

2. Standard wages for actual time = SR × AT

Men	0.80 × 1,600	₹1,280
Women	0.60 × 400	₹240
Children	0.40 × 200	₹80
	Total	₹1,600

3. Standard wages for actual time utilized = SR × AT utilized

Men	0.80 × 1,440	₹1,152
Women	0.60 × 360	₹216
Children	0.40 × 180	₹72
	Total	₹1,440

4. Standard wages for actual time, had labour been used in standard mix ratio

Men	0.80 × 1,980 × 1,200/2,200	₹864
Women	0.60 × 1,980 × 600/2,200	₹324
Children	0.40 × 1,980 × 400/2,200	₹144
	Total	₹1,332

5. Standard wages for standard time for actual output = SR × ST

Men	0.80 × 960	₹768
Women	0.60 × 480	₹288
Children	0.40 × 320	₹128
	Total	₹1,184

Note:

1. Actual time = No. of workers × Normal time per week

Men	40 × 40	1,600
Women	10 × 40	400
Children	5 × 40	200
	Total	2,200 hrs

2. Idle time = Actual no. of workers × idle hours

Men	40 × 4	160 hrs
Women	10 × 4	40 hrs
Children	5 × 4	20 hrs

3. Actual time utilised = Actual time − Idle time

Men	1600 − 160	1,440 hrs
Women	400 − 40	360 hrs
Children	200 − 20	180 hrs
	Total	1,980 hrs

4. Standard time for standard output of 2,000 units = Standard no. of workers × Normal hours per week.

Men	30 × 40	1,200 hrs
Women	15 × 40	600 hrs
Children	10 × 40	400 hrs
	Total	2,200 hrs

5. Standard time for actual output of 1,600 units = Standard time × Standard output

Men	1,200 × 1,600/2,000	960 hrs
Women	600 × 1,600/2,000	480 hrs
Children	400 × 1,600/2,000	320 hrs
	Total	1,760 hrs

Variances:

1. Labour cost variance (LCV)

   = 5 − 1

   = 1,184 − 1,440 = 256 (A)

2. Labour rate variance (LRV)

   = 2 − 1

   = 1,600 − 1,440 = 160 (F)

3. Labour efficiency variance (LEV)

   = 5 − 2

   = 1,184 − 1,600 = 416(A)

4. Labour idle time variance (LITV)

   = 3 − 2

   = 1,440 − 1,600 = 160 (A)

5. Labour mix variance (LMV)

   = 4 − 3

   = 1,332 − 1,440 = 108 (A)

6. Labour yield variance (LYV)/Labour sub-efficiency variance (LSEU)

$$= 5 - 4$$
$$= 1{,}184 - 1{,}332 = 148\ (A)$$

Verification:

1. LCV = LRV + LEV

   256 (A) = 160 (F) + 416 (A)

   256 (A) = 256 (A)

2. LEV = LMV + LITV + LYV

   416 (A) = 160 (A) + 108 (A) + 148 (A)

   416 (A) = 416 (A)

21.6 REVISION VARIANCE

Sometimes standards are changed when a particular type of material is not available. Substitute material is used when price of a particular material has increased steeply. Similarly there may be shortage of particular a grade of labour. In such circumstances revision variance is calculated. Thereafter variances are calculated using revised standard as the real standard.

Illustration-14

The standard labour cost for producing 200 units of product 'x' is:

25 men of grade I for 10 hours at ₹8 per hour
15 men of grade II for 15 hours at ₹6 per hour.

Actual production is 2,000 units. Due to shortage of grade I labour the standard mix had to be revised as 200 hours and grade II as 250 hours for producing 200 units.

Actual hours paid for were:

Grade I - 1,900 hrs at ₹10 per hour
Grade II - 2,400 hrs at ₹7 per hour.

50 hours of Grade I and 100 hours of Grade II were lost due to power failure. Calculate labour revised variance and other labour variances.

Solution

Revised labour cost variance = Original standard cost of actual production − Revised standard cost of actual production

$$= 33{,}500 - 31{,}000 = 2{,}500\ (F)$$

Note:

1. **Original standard cost of actual production:**

   Original standard cost for 200 units = No. of works × Hrs × Rate

Grade I	25 × 10 × 8	₹2,000
Grade II	15 × 15 × 6	₹1,350
	Total	3,350 hrs

   Original standard cost for 2,000 units (actual production)

$$= \frac{3{,}350}{200} \times 2{,}000 = ₹33{,}500$$

2. **Revised standard cost for actual production:**

   Revised standard cost for 200 units = Hrs × Rate

Grade I	200 × 8	₹1,600
Grade II	250 × 6	₹1,500
	Total	3,100 hrs

   Revised standard cost for 2,000 unit (actual production)

$$= \frac{3{,}100}{200} \times 2{,}000 = ₹31{,}000$$

II. Calculation of other labour cost variances

Calculations:

1. Actual wage paid for actual time = AR × AT

Grade I	10 × 1,900	₹19,000
Grade II	7 × 2,400	₹16,800
	Total	₹35,800

2. Standard wages for actual time = SR × AT

Grade I	8 × 1,900	₹15,200
Grade II	6 × 2,400	₹14,400
	Total	₹29,600

3. Standard wages for actual time utilised = SR × AT utilised

Grade I	8 × 1,850	₹14,800
Grade II	6 × 2,300	₹13,800
	Total	₹28,600

Note: Actual time utilized = Actual time − Time lost due to power failure.

Grade I	1,900 − 50	1,850 hrs
Grade II	2,400 − 100	2,300 hrs

4. Standard wages for revised actual hours = SR × Revised actual hours

Grade I	8 × 1,911	₹15,288
Grade II	6 × 2,289	₹14,334
	Total	₹29,622

Note: Revised actual hours = Total actual time × Standard proportion

Grade I	4,300 × 2,000/4,500	1,911 hrs
Grade II	4,300 × 2,500/4,500	2,389 hrs

Standard hours

Grade I	200/200 × 2,000	2,000 hrs
Grade II	250/200 × 2,000	2,500 hrs

5. Standard wages for actual production = ₹31,000

   (See note 2. to Revised labour cost variance).

Variances:

1. Labour cost variance (LCV)

   = 5 − 1

   = 31,000 − 35,800 = 4,800 (A)

2. Labour rate variance (LRV)

   = 2 − 1

   = 29,600 − 35,800 = 6,200(F)

3. Labour efficiency variance (LEV)

   = 5 − 2

   = 31,000 − 29,600 = 1,400 (F)

4. Labour idle time variance (LITV)

$$= 3 - 2$$
$$= 28{,}600 - 29{,}600 = 1{,}000 \text{ (A)}$$

5. Labour mix variance (LMV)

$$= 4 - 3$$
$$= 29{,}622 - 28{,}600 = 1{,}022 \text{ (F)}$$

6. Labour yield variance (LYV)

$$= 5 - 4$$
$$= 31{,}000 - 29{,}622 = 1{,}378 \text{ (F)}$$

Verification:

1. LCV = LRV + LEV

   4,800 (A) = 6,200 (A) + 1,400 (F)

   4,800 (A) = 4,800 (A)

2. LEV = LITV + LMV + LYV

   1,400 (F) = 1,000 (A) + 1,022 (F) + 1,378 (F)

   1,400 (F) = 1,400 (F)

21.7 OVERHEAD VARIANCES

Overheads are classified on the basis of behaviour as variable overhead and fixed overhead. Variable overhead is total changes in direct proportion to changes in output. Changes in volume of output has no impact on variable overhead variance. Variable overhead rate per unit remain same at all levels of output. But changes in the rates of variable overheads and efficiency level will cause variances in variable overheads. Fixed overheads remain constant in total irrespective of changes in volume of output. But fixed overhead rate per unit will change in inverse proportion to changes in level of output. Much care should be taken in estimating the expected level of output. If actual output changes widely, the under- or over-absorption of fixed overhead will also be wide. So change in volume of output, rates of fixed overheads and efficiency give rise to fixed overhead variances.

21.7.1 Variable overhead Variances

There are three variable overhead variances. They are,

1. Variable overhead cost variance
2. Variable overhead expenditure variance
3. Variable overhead efficiency variance.

1. Variable overhead cost variance (VOH Cost Variance)

It is an aggregate or total variance. The difference between actual variable overhead and budgeted variable overhead for actual production (recovered overheads) is called variable overhead cost variance. The variable overhead expenditure variance and variable overhead efficiency variance are sub-divisions of variable overhead cost variance. The following is the formula for calculating variable overhead cost variance:

= Std VOH rate per unit × Actual output − Actual VOH rate per unit × Actual output

(or)

= Std VOH rate per hour × standard hours for actual output − Actual VOH rate per hour × Actual hours

(or)

= Standard variable overheads − Actual variable overheads

2. Variable overhead expenditure variance (VOH Exp. Variance)

This variance is also known as spending variance or budget variance. The difference between actual varible overhead and Budgeted variable overhead for actual hours (Standard overheads). The following formula is applied for calculating this variance.

= Std VOH rate per hour × Actual hours − Actual VOH Rate per hour × Actual hours

(or)

= Std VOH rate per unit × actual output in standard hours − Actual VOH rate per unit × Actual output

(or)

= Standard variable overheads − Actual variable overheads

3. Variable overhead efficiency variance (VOV efficiency variance)

This variance arises due to differences between actual efficiency level achieved and the budgeted efficiency level established. The following is the formula for calculation VOH efficiency variance:

= Std VOH rate per unit × Actual output − Std overhead rate per unit × Std output for actual hours

(or)

= Std VOH rate per hour × Standard hours for actual output − Standard VOH rate per hour × Actual hours

(or)

= Recovered VOHS − Standard VOHS

21.7.2 Fixed Overhead variances

The following are the various classification of fixed overhead variances:

1. Fixed overhead cost variance (FOH Cost Variance)

It is an aggregate or total variance. The difference between actual fixed overheads and budgeted fixed overheads for actual production. It is further subdivided into expenditure variance and volume variance. The following is the formula for calculating fixed overhead cost variance:

= Std FOH rate per unit × Actual output − Actual FOH rate per unit × Actual output

(or)

= Std FOH rate per hour × Standard hours for actual output − Actual FOH rate per hour × Actual hours

(or)

= Recovered FOHS − Actual FOHS

2. Fixed overhead expenditure variance (FOH Exp. Variance)

It araises due to variation of actual fixed overheads from budgeted fixed overheads. This variance is also known as spending variance or budget variance.

The following is the formula for calculating fixed overhead expenditure variance:

= Budgeted fixed overheads − Actual fixed overheads.

3. Fixed overhead volume variance (FOH Volume Variance)

This variance arises when actual output deviates from budgeted output. The following formula is used for calculating fixed overhead volume variance:

= Standard FOH rate per unit × Actual output - Budgeted FOHS

(or)

= Standard FOH rate per hour × Standard hours for actual output − Budgeted FOHs

(or)

= Recovered FOHS − Budgeted FOHS

The fixed overhead volume variance is further subdivided into calendar variance, capacity variance and efficiency variance.

4. Fixed overhead calendar variance (FOH Calendar Variance)

This variance arises when actual number of working days during budget period is different from budgeted working days. The following is the formula for calculating fixed overhead calendar variance:

= Possible fixed overheads − Budgeted fixed overheads.

Note:

1. Possible Fixed Overheads = Standard FOH rate per hour × Possible hours

2. Possible hours = Standard working hours per day × Actual number of working days

5. Fixed Overhead Capacity variance (FOH Capacity Variance)

It is a portion of volume variance. It arises due to difference between actual capacity utilized and budgeted capacity. The following formula is used for calculating fixed overhead capacity variance:

= Standard FOH rate per unit × Standard output for actual hours − Budgeted FOH

(or)

= Standard FOH rate per hour × Actual hours − Budgeted FOHS.

(or)

= Standard FOHS − Budgeted FOHS.

6. Fixed Overhead Efficiency variance (FOH Efficiency Variance)

It is a portion of volume variance. It arises due to difference between actual efficiency and budgeted efficiency. The following formula is used for calculating fixed overhead efficiency variance:

= Standard FOH rate per unit × Actual output − Standard FOH rate per unit × Standard output for actual hours

(or)

= Standard FOH rate per hour × Standard hours for actual output − Standard FOH rate per hour × Actual hours

(or)

= Recovered FOHS − Standard FOHS.

Note: The term budgeted overheads and standard overheads are not used in same sense. They stand for different amounts in the calculation of overhead variances. Sometimes standard overhead is given in the sum. It represents only budgeted fixed overheads. Standard fixed overhead is calculated always as given above.

Before attempting variances, one should be familiar with the following basic terms:

1. **Standard overhead rate:** This rate may be expressed for per hour or per unit.

$$\text{Standard overhead rate per hour} = \frac{\text{Budgeted overheads}}{\text{Budgeted hours}}$$

$$\text{Standard overhead rate per unit} = \frac{\text{Budgeted overheads}}{\text{Budgeted output (units)}}$$

2. $\text{Standard hours for actual output} = \dfrac{\text{Budgeted hours}}{\text{Budgeted output}} \times \text{Actual output}$

3. $\text{Standard output for actual hours} = \dfrac{\text{Budgeted output}}{\text{Budgeted hours}} \times \text{Actual hours}$

4. Standard overhead rate per day $= \dfrac{\text{Budgeted overheads}}{\text{Budgeted days}}$

To reduce number of calculations and time, calculate the following amounts in the given order and calculate the variances as given below:

I. Calculation for variable overhead variances:

1. Actual variable overheads (usually given)
2. Standard variable overheads

   = Standard variable overhead per unit × standard output for actual time.

   (or)

   = standard variable overhead rate per hour × Actual hours
3. Recovered variable overheads

   = Standard variable overhead rate per unit × Actual output

   (or)

   = Standard variable overhead rate per hour × Standard hours for actual output.

Variances:

1. Variable overhead cost variance (VOHCV) = 3 − 1
2. Variable overhead expenditure variance (VOH Exp.V) = 2 − 1
3. Variance overhead efficiency variance (VOH Eff.U) = 3 − 2

Verification:

VOHCV = VOH Exp. V + VOH Eff.V

The variable overhead variances may be shown in a chart-form as follows:

Variable overhead cost variance
Recovered VOHS – Actual VOHS
(3) – (1)

Variable overhead expenditure variance
Standard VOHS - Actual VOHS
(2) – (1)

Variable overhead efficiency variance
recovered VOHS – Standard VOHS
(3) – (2)

II. Calculations for fixed overhead variances

1. Actual fixed overheads (usually given)
2. Budgeted fixed overheads (usually given)
3. Budgeted fixed overheads for actual days

   = Budgeted FOH rate per day × Actual days.
4. Standard fixed overheads

   = Standard fixed overhead rate per hour × Actual hours

   (or)

   = Standard FOH rate per unit × Standard output for actual hours
5. Recovered fixed overheads = Standard overhead rate per unit × Actual output

   (or)

   = Standard overhead rate per hour × Standard hours for actual output.

Variances:

1. Fixed overhead cost variance (FOHCV)

   $= 5 - 1$
2. Fixed overhead expenditure variance (FOH Exp.V)

   $= 2 - 1$
3. Fixed overhead volume variance (FOH Vol.V)

   $= 5 - 2$
4. Fixed overhead calendar variance (FOH.Cal.V)

   $= 3 - 2$
5. Fixed overhead capacity variance (FOH.Cap. V)

   $= 4 - 3$
6. Fixed overhead efficiency variance (FOH.Eff.V)

   $= 5 - 4$

The fixed overhead variances may be shown in a chart-form as shown below:

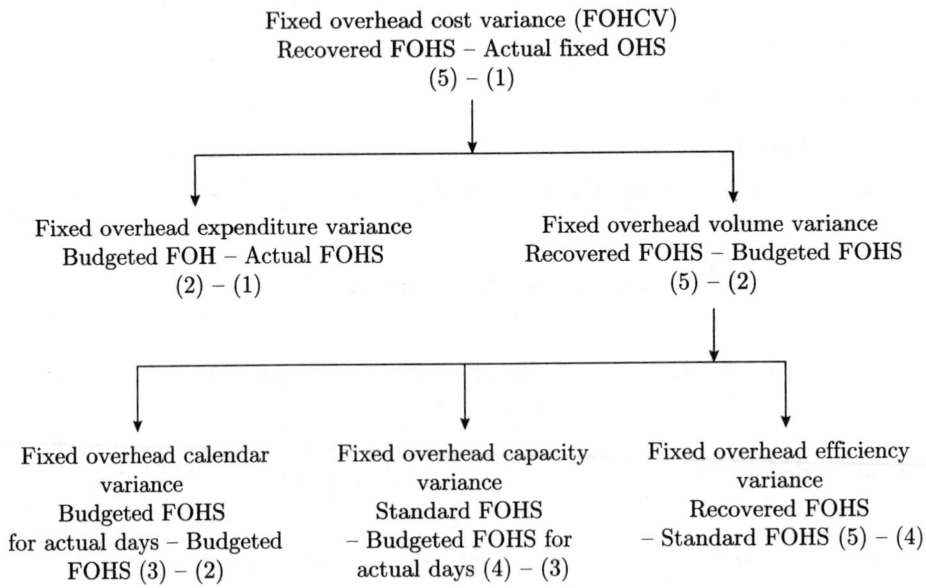

Verification:

1. FOHCV = FOH Exp.V + FOH. Vol.V
2. FOH Vol.V = FOH Cal.V + FOH.Cap.V + FOH.Eff.V

Illustration-15

(Variable OH variances)

From the following data calculate overhead cost variances:

	Standard	Actual
Labour hours	15,000	18,000
Units of output	7,500	6,000
Variable overhead (₹).	3,000	4,500

Solution

Calculations:

1. Actual variable overheads - ₹4,500

2. Standard variable overhead:

$= \text{Standard VOH. rate per hour} \times \text{Actual hours}$

$= 0.20 \times 18{,}000 = ₹3{,}600$

3. Recovered VOHS:

$= \text{Standard VOH. rate per hour} \times \text{Standard hours for actual output}$

$= 0.20 \times 12{,}000 = ₹2{,}400$

Note:

(i) $$\text{Standard VOH rate per hour} = \frac{\text{Budgeted VOHS}}{\text{Budgeted hours}} = \frac{3{,}000}{15{,}000} = ₹0.20$$

(ii) $$\text{Standard hours for actual output} = \frac{\text{Budgeted hours}}{\text{Budgeted output}} \times \text{Actual output} = \frac{15{,}000}{7{,}500} \times 6{,}000 = 12{,}000 \text{ hrs}$$

Variances:

1. VOH cost variance (VOHCV)

$= 3 - 1$

$= 2{,}400 - 4{,}500 = 2{,}100 \text{ (A)}$

2. VOH expenditure variance (VOH.Exp.V)

$= 2 - 1$

$= 3{,}600 - 4{,}500 = 900 \text{ (A)}$

3. VOH efficiency variance (VOH.Eff.V)

$= 3 - 2$

$= 2{,}400 - 3{,}600 = 1{,}200 \text{ (A)}$

Verification:

VOHCV = VOH Exp.V + VOH.Eff.V

2,100 (A) = 900 (A) + 1,200 (A)

2,100 (A) = 2,100 (A)

Illustration-16

Budgeted output (units)	1,00,000
Budgeted hours	25,000
Budgeted variable overheads	₹75,000
Actual output (units)	95,000
Actual hours worked	22,500
Actual variable overheads	₹72,000

Calculate variable overhead variances.

Solution

Calculations:

1. Actual variable overheads - ₹72,000
2. Standard variable overhead:

   = Standard VOH rate per hour × Actual hours

   = 3 × 22,500 = ₹67,500
3. Recovered overheads:

   = Standard VOH rate per hour × Standard hours for actual output

   = 3 × 23,750 = ₹71,250

Note:

(i) $\text{Standard VOH rate per hour} = \dfrac{\text{Budgeted VOHS}}{\text{Budgeted hours}}$

$$= \frac{75,000}{25,000} = ₹3$$

(ii) $\text{Standard hours for actual output} = \dfrac{\text{Budgeted hours}}{\text{Budgeted output}} \times \text{Actual output}$

$$= \frac{25,000}{1,00,000} \times 95,000 = 23,750 \text{ hrs}$$

Variances:

1. VOH cost variance (VOHCV)

   = 3 − 1

   = 71,250 − 72,000 = 750 (A)

2. VOH expenditure variance (VOH.Exp.V)

$$= 2 - 1$$

$$= 67{,}500 - 72{,}000 = 4{,}500 \text{ (A)}$$

3. VOH efficiency variance (VOH.Eff.V)

$$= 3 - 2$$

$$= 71{,}250 - 67{,}500 = 3{,}750 \text{ (F)}$$

Verification:

VOHCV = VOH Exp.V + VOH.Eff.V

750 (A) = 4,500 (A) + 3,750 (F)

750 (A) = 750 (A)

Illustration-17

The following informations are extracted from the books of A Ltd for a period:

	Budget	Actual
Labour hours	20,000	24,000
Units of output	10,000	9,000
Fixed overhead (₹)	12,000	15,000

Solution

Calculations:

1. Actual fixed overheads = ₹15,000
2. Budgeted fixed overheads = ₹12,000
3. Budgeted fixed overheads for actual days - Nil
4. Standard fixed overheads

   = Standard FOH Rate per hour × Actual hours

   = 0.60 × 24,000 = ₹14,400

5. Recovered fixed overheads

   = Standard FOH rate per hour × Standard hours for actual output

   = 0.60 × 18,000 = ₹10,800

Workings:

(i) Standard FOH rate per hour $= \dfrac{\text{Budgeted FOHS}}{\text{Budgeted hours}}$

$$= \frac{12{,}000}{20{,}000} = ₹0.60$$

(ii) Standard hours for actual output $= \dfrac{\text{Budgeted hours}}{\text{Budgeted output}} \times \text{Actual output}$

$$= \frac{20{,}000}{10{,}000} \times 9{,}000 = 18{,}000 \text{ hrs}$$

Variances:

1. FOH cost variance

$= 5 - 1$

$= 10{,}800 - 15{,}000 = 4{,}200$ (A)

2. FOH. expenditure variance

$= 2 - 1$

$= 12{,}000 - 15{,}000 = 3{,}000$ (A)

3. FOH. volume variance

= 5-2

$= 10{,}800 - 12{,}000 = 1{,}200$ (A)

4. FOH calendar variance

$= 4 - 3 =$ NIL

5. FOH capacity variance

$= 4 - 2$

$= 14{,}400 - 12{,}000 = 2{,}400$ (F)

Note: Value of step 3 is nil, hence value of previous step 2 is taken.

6. FOH efficiency variance

$= 5 - 4$

$= 10{,}800 - 14{,}400 = 3{,}600$ (A)

Verification:

1. FOHCV = FOH Exp.V + FOH.Vol.V

4,200 (A) = 3,000 (A) + 1,200 (A)

4,200 (A) = 4,200 (A)

2. FOH.Vol.V = FOH.Cap.V + FOH.Eff.V

   1,200 (A) = 2,400 (F) + 3,600 (A)

   1,200 (A) = 1,200 (A)

Illustration-18

(Fixed overhead variance)

The following information is available from the records of a factory:

	Budget	Actual
Fixed overhead for June (₹)	10,000	12,000
Production in June (units)	2,000	2,100
Standard time per unit (Hrs)	10	-
Actual hours worked in June	-	22,000

Compute:

(i) Fixed overhead cost variance

(ii) Expenditure variance

(iii) Volume variance

(iv) Capacity variance

(v) Efficiency variance **(CA-Inter)**

Solution

Calculations:

1. Actual fixed overheads = ₹12,000
2. Budgeted fixed overheads = ₹10,000
3. Budgeted fixed overheads for actual days - Nil
4. Standard fixed overheads

   = Standard fixed overhead rate per unit × Standard output for actual hours

   = 5 × 2,200 = ₹11,000

5. Recovered fixed overheads

= Standard fixed overhead rate per unit × Actual output

= 5 × 2,100 = ₹10,500

Workings:

(i) Standard fixed overhead rate per unit $= \dfrac{\text{Budgeted fixed overhead}}{\text{Budgeted output}}$

$= \dfrac{10{,}000}{2{,}000} = ₹5$

(ii) Standard output for actual hours $= \dfrac{\text{Actual hours}}{\text{Budgeted hours per unit}}$

$= \dfrac{22{,}000}{10} = 2{,}200$ units

Variances:

1. Fixed overhead cost variance

= 5 – 1

= 10,500 – 12,000 = 1,500 (A)

2. Fixed overhead expenditure variance

= 2 – 1

= 10,000 – 12,000 = 2,000 (A)

3. Fixed overhead volume variance

=5 – 2

= 10,500 – 10,000 = 500 (F)

4. Fixed overhead calendar variance - Nil

5. Fixed overhead capacity variance

= 4 – 2

= 11,000 – 10,000 = 1,000 (F)

6. Fixed overhead efficiency variance

= 5 – 4

= 10,500 – 11,000 = 500 (A)

Verification:

1. FOHCV = FOH Exp. V + FOH Vol. V

   1,500 (A) = 2,000 (A) + 500 (F)

   1,500 (A) = 1,500 (A)

2. FOH.Vol.V = FOH Cap. V + FOH Eff. V

   500(F) = 1,000 (F) + 500 (A)

   500(F) = 500 (F)

Illustration-19

(FOH variances)

In department A of a plant, the following data are submitted for the week ended on 31st March, 2009:

Standard output for 40 hours per week	1,400 units
Budgeted fixed overheads	₹1,400
Actual output	1,200 units
Actual hours worked	32 hours
Actual fixed overhead	₹1,500

You are required to prepare a statement of variances. **(ICWA-Inter)**

Solution

Calculations:

1. Actual fixed overheads = ₹1,500
2. Budgeted fixed overheads = ₹1,400
3. Budgeted fixed overheads for actual days - Nil
4. Standard fixed overheads

   = Standard fixed overhead rate per unit × Standard output for actual hours

   = 1 × 1,120 = ₹1,120

5. Recovered fixed overheads

   = Standard fixed overhead rate per unit × Actual output

   = 1 × 1,200 = ₹1,200

Workings:

(i) Standard fixed overhead rate per unit $= \dfrac{\text{Budgeted fixed overhead}}{\text{Budgeted output}}$

$$= \frac{1{,}400}{1{,}400} = ₹1.00$$

(ii) Standard output for actual hours $= \dfrac{\text{Budgeted output}}{\text{Budgeted hours}} \times \text{Actual output}$

$$= \frac{1{,}400}{40} \times 32 = 1{,}120 \text{ units}$$

Variances:

1. Fixed overhead cost variance

$= 5 - 1$

$= 1{,}200 - 1{,}500 = 300$ (A)

2. Fixed overhead expenditure variance

$= 2 - 1$

$= 1{,}400 - 1{,}500 = 100$ (A)

3. Fixed overhead volume variance

$=5 - 2$

$= 1{,}200 - 1{,}400 = 200$ (A)

4. Fixed overhead calendar variance - Nil

5. Fixed overhead capacity variance

$= 4 - 2$

$= 1{,}120 - 1{,}400 = 280$ (A)

6. Fixed overhead efficiency variance

$= 5 - 4$

$= 1{,}200 - 1{,}120 = 80$ (F)

Verification:

1. FOHCV = FOH Exp.V + FOH.Vol.V

   300 (A) = 100 (A) + 200 (A)

   300 (A) = 300 (A)

2. FOH.Vol.V = FOH.Cap.V + FOH.Eff.V

   200 (A) = 280 (A) + 80 (F)

   200 (A) = 200 (A)

Illustration-20

(FOH and VOH variances - No. of days given and reconciliation statement)

The following information was obtained from the records of a manufacturing unit using standard costing system:

	Budget	**Actual**
Production (units)	4,000	3,800
Working days	20	21
Fixed overheads (₹)	40,000	39,000
Variable overheads (₹)	12,000	12,000

You are required to calculate the following overhead variances:

(a) Variable overhead variances

(b) Fixed overhead variances

i. Expenditure variance

ii. Volume variance

iii. Efficiency variance

iv. Calender variance

Solution

(a) Variable overhead variance:

Calculations:

1. Actual variable overheads = ₹12,000
2. Standard variable overheads = Nil
3. Recovered variable overheads = Standard variable overhead rate per unit × Actual output

$= 3 \times 3{,}800 =$ ₹11,400

Variance: Variable overhead cost variance

$= 3 - 1$

$= 11{,}400 - 12{,}000 = 600$ (A)

(b) Fixed overhead variance:

Calculation:

1. Actual fixed overheads = ₹39,000
2. Budgeted fixed overheads = ₹40,000

3. Standard fixed overheads for actual days

$$= \text{Standard fixed overhead per day} \times \text{Actual days}$$
$$= 2{,}000 \times 21 = ₹42{,}000$$

4. Standard fixed overheads = Nil

5. Recovered fixed overhead

$$= \text{Standard fixed overhead rate per unit} \times \text{Actual output}$$
$$= 10 \times 3{,}800 = ₹38{,}000$$

Workings:

1. Standard variable overhead rate per unit $= \dfrac{\text{Budgted VOHS}}{\text{Budgeted output}}$

$$= \frac{12{,}000}{4{,}000} = ₹3$$

2. Standard fixed overhead rate per unit $= \dfrac{\text{Budgted FOHS}}{\text{Budgeted output}}$

$$= \frac{40{,}000}{4{,}000} = ₹10$$

3. Standard fixed overhead rate per day $= \dfrac{\text{Budgted FOHS}}{\text{Budgeted days}}$

$$= \frac{40{,}000}{20} = ₹2{,}000$$

Variances:

1. FOH expenditure variance

$$= 2 - 1$$
$$= 40{,}000 - 39{,}000 = 1{,}000 \text{ (F)}$$

2. FOH volume variance

$$= 5 - 2$$
$$= 38{,}000 - 40{,}000 = 2{,}000 \text{ (A)}$$

3. FOH efficiency variance

$$= 5 - 3$$
$$= 38{,}000 - 42{,}000 = 4{,}000 \text{ (A)}$$

4. FOH calender variance

$$= 3 - 2$$

$$= 42{,}000 - 40{,}000 = 2{,}000\ (F)$$

(c) Reconciliation statement

		₹
Standard fixed overhead		38,000
Add: Adverse variances		
Fixed overhead efficiency variance		4,000
		42,000
Less: Favourable variance		
Fixed overhead expenditure variance	1,000 (F)	
Fixed overhead calendar variance	2,000 (F)	3,000 (F)
Actual fixed overheads		39,000

21.8 SALES VARIANCES

Management of a manufacturing company has to reduce the operating cost and maximise the revenue. To increase the sales revenue, management prepares the sales budget. The budgeted sales revenues are compared with actual sales. The variances are analysed for their causes. When adverse sales variances arise due to controllable factors, corrective steps are initiated. The sales variances are calculated with references to sales volume and with reference to profit. As sales variances are computed by using budgeted variances, sales variances are also called budgeted variances.

21.8.1 Type of Sales Variances

When actual sales is more than the budgeted sales, it has a favourable impact on profit. So when actual sales is more, it is called favourable variance and when actual sales is less than budgeted sale, it is an unfavourable variance. In sales variances the terms budget and standard is used interchangeably. Sales variances are broadly classified into two groups as: (A) Sales variances with reference to sales volume and (B) Sales variances with reference to profit.

A Sales variances with reference to sales volume

The following are the various variances calculated with reference to sales value

1. Sales value variance

Sales value variance is an aggregate variance. It arises when actual sales is different from then budget sales. It arises due to change in actual units sold and actual price. The following formula is used for calculating sales value variance.

$$= \text{Budgeted units} \times \text{Budgeted price} - \text{Actual units} \times \text{Actual price}$$

(or)

$$= \text{Budgeted sales} - \text{Actual sales}$$

The sales value variance is subdivided into sales price variance and sales volume variance.

2. Sales price variance

This variance arises when the actual selling price is different from budgeted selling price. The following formula is used for calculating sales price variance:

$$= \text{Actual quantity} \times \text{Budgeted price} - \text{Actual quantity} \times \text{Actual price}$$

(or)

$$= \text{Budgeted sales for actual quantity} - \text{Actual sales}$$

3. Sales volume variance

This variance arises due to difference between actual units sold and budgeted sales units. The following formula is used for calculating sales volume variance.

$$= \text{Budgeted units} \times \text{Budgeted price} - \text{Actual units} \times \text{Actual price}$$

$$= \text{Budgeted sales} - \text{Budgeted sales for actual quantity}$$

Sales volume variance in further sub-divided into sales mix variance and sales quantity variance.

4. Sales mix variance

Sales mix variance arises when two or more products are sold and actual sales quantity is in different proportion from budgeted proportion. The following formula is used computing sales mix variance:

$$= \text{Budgeted price} \times \text{Revised budgeted quantity} - \text{Actual price} \times \text{Actual quantity}$$

(or)

$$= \text{Budgeted sales for revised budgeted quantity} - \text{Actual sales}$$

5. Sales quantity variance

$$= \text{Budgeted price} \times \text{Budgeted units} - \text{Budgeted price} \times \text{Revised budgeted quantity}$$

(or)

$$= \text{Budgeted sales} - \text{Budgeted sales for revised budgeted quantity}$$

Verification:

1. Sales value variance = Price variance + Volume variance
2. Volume variance = Mix variance + Quantity variance

Alternatively sales variances may be calculated by following the following steps. First calculate the following amounts and then calculate the variances:

Calculations:

1. Actual sales value = Actual units sold × Actual price
2. Budgeted sales for actual quantity = Actual units sold × Budgeted price.
3. Budgeted sales value, had sales been made in budgeted proportion

   = Revised budgeted quantity × Budgeted price.

   (or)

   = Actual mix × Budgeted mix ratio × Budgeted price
4. Budgeted sales = Budgeted units × Budgeted price

Note:

$$\text{Revised budgeted quantity} = \frac{\text{Total weight actual mix}}{\text{Total weight of standard mix}} \times \text{Budgeted quantity of a product}$$

Variances:

1. Sales value variance

   $= 4 - 1$
2. Sales price variance

   $= 2 - 1$
3. Sales volume variance

   $= 4 - 2$
4. Sales mix variance

   $= 3 - 2$
5. Sales quantity variance

   $= 4 - 3$

The sales variance may be shown in a chart as given below:

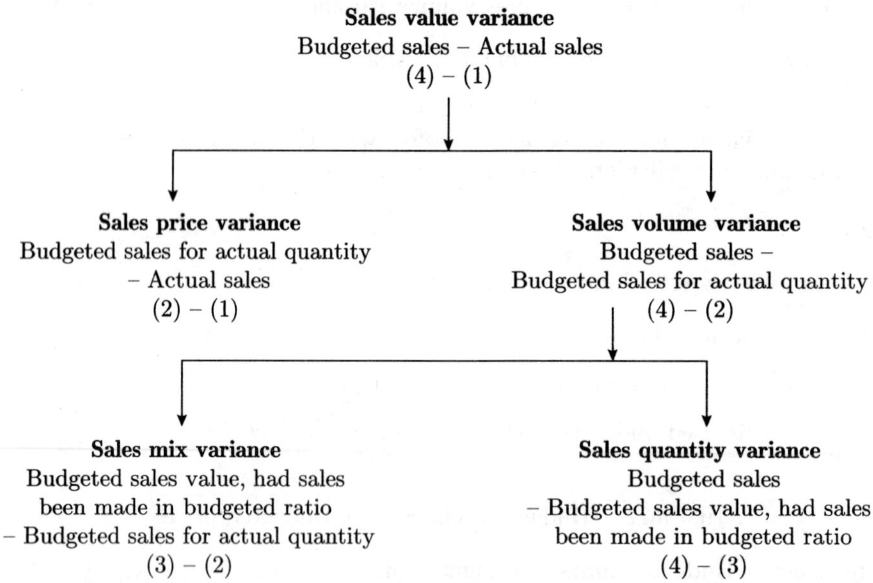

B. **Sales variances with reference to profit**

The following are the classification of sales variances with references to profit:

1. Profit value variance

This variance is an aggregate variance. This variance arises due to change in quantity sold and change in the rate of profit. The following is the formula for calculating profit value variance:

= Budgeted quantity × Budgeted profit per unit − Actual quantity × Actual profit per unit

(or)

= Budgeted profit − Actual profit

Profit value variance is further sub divided into profit price variance and profit volume variance.

2. Profit price variance

Profit price variance araises when the actual rate of profit is different from budgeted rate of profit. The following is the formula for calculating this variance.

= Actual quantity × Budgeted profit per unit − Actual quantity × Actual profit per unit

(or)

= Budgeted profit for actual quantity - Actual profit.

3. Profit volume variance

This variance arises when the actual quantity sold is different from budgeted quantity. The following formula is used for calculating this variance:

= Budgeted quantity × Budgeted profit per unit − Actual quantity × Budgeted profit per unit

(or) = Budgeted profit − Budgeted profit for actual quantity.

4. Profit mix variance

This variance arises when two or more products are sold and actual proportion of products is different from the budgeted proportion. The following is the formula for calculating of profit mix variance.

− Budgeted profit per unit × Revised budgeted quantity − Budgeted profit per unit × Actual quantity.

= Budgeted profit for revised budgeted quantity − Budgeted profit for actual quantity.

5. Profit quantity variance

It is a part of the profit mix variance. The following formula is used for calculating this variance:

= Budgeted quantity × Budgeted profit − Budgeted profit × Revised budgeted quantity.

(or) = Budgeted profit − Budgeted profit for revised budgeted quantity.

Alternatively the sales profit variances may be calculated in the following step. First calculate the following amounts and then calculate the variances.

Calculations:

1. Actual Profit = Actual quantity × Actual profit per unit.

   Note:

   (a) Actual profit per unit = Actual selling price per unit − Budgeted cost per unit.

   (b) Actual cost is not considered for calculating actual profit.

2. Budgeted profit for actual quantity

   = Actual quantity × Budgeted profit per unit

3. Budgeted profit, had actual sales been made in the standard mix ratio.

   = Budgeted profit per unit × Revised budged quantity

4. Budgeted profit

   = Budgeted quantity × Budgeted profit per unit.

Note:

$$\text{Revised budgeted quantity} = \frac{\text{Total weight actual mix}}{\text{Total weight of budgeted mix}} \times \text{Budgeted quantity of a product}$$

Illustration-21

AB Ltd furnishes the following particulars relating to budgeted sales and actual sales for October 2009:

Product	Budget		Actual	
	Quantity (Units)	Selling Price Per unit (₹)	Quantity (Units)	Selling Price Per unit (₹)
A	3,000	12	3,200	11
B	2,500	20	3,000	22
C	1,000	10	800	9

Compute sales variances.

Solution

Calculations:

1. Actual sales = Actual quantity × Actual price

		₹
Product A	3,200 × 11	35,200
Product B	3,000 × 22	66,000
Product C	800 × 9	7,200
	Total	1,08,400

2. Budgeted sales for actual quantity = Actual quantity × Budgeted price

		₹
Product A	3,200 × 12	38,400
Product B	3,000 × 20	60,000
Product C	800 × 10	8,000
	Total	1,06,400

3. Budgeted sales for actual quantity, had actual sales been made in budgeted sales mix ratio:

= Revised budgeted quantity × Budgeted price

		₹
Product A	3,230.77 × 12	38,769
Product B	2,692.31 × 20	53,846
Product C	1,076.92 × 10	10,769
	Total	1,03,384

Note:

$$\text{Revised budgeted quantity} = \frac{\text{Total weight of actual mix}}{\text{Total weight of budgeted mix}} \times \text{Budgeted quantity of a product}$$

$$\text{Product A} = \frac{7{,}000}{6{,}500} \times 3{,}000 = 3{,}230.77\,\text{units}$$

$$\text{Product B} = \frac{7{,}000}{6{,}500} \times 2{,}500 = 2{,}692.31\,units$$

$$\text{Product C} = \frac{7{,}000}{6{,}500} \times 1{,}000 = 1{,}076.92\,\text{units}$$

4. Budgeted sales = Budgeted quantity × Budgeted price

		₹
Product A	3,000 × 12	36,000
Product B	2,500 × 20	50,000
Product C	1,000 × 10	10,000
	Total	96,000

Variances:

1. Sales value variance

= 4 − 1

= 96,000 − 1,08,400 = 12,400 (F)

2. Sales price variance

= 2 − 1

= 1,06,400 − 1,08,400 = 2,000 (F)

3. Sales volume variance

= 4 – 2

= 96,000 – 1,06,400 = 10,400 (F)

4. Sales mix variance

= 3 – 2

= 1,03,384 – 1,06,400 = 3,016 (F)

5. Sales quantity variance

= 4 – 3

= 96,000 – 1,03,384 = 7,384 (F)

Proof:

1. Value variance = Price variance + Volume variance

12,400 (F) = 2,000 (F) + 10,400 (F)

12,400 (F) = 12,400 (F)

2. Volume variance = Mix variance + Quantity variance

10,400 (F) = 3,016 (F) +7,384 (F)

10,400 (F) = 10,400 (F)

Illustration-22

The budgeted sales and actual sales for a period in respect of three products are given below:

Product	Budget			Actual		
	Quantity	Price (₹)	Value (₹)	Quantity	Price (₹)	Value (₹)
A	1,000	5	5,000	1,200	6	7,200
B	750	10	7,500	700	9	6,300
C	500	15	7,500	600	14	8,400

Calculate sales variances. **(CA-Inter)**

Solution

Calculations:

1. Actual sales = Actual quantity × Actual price

		₹
Product A	1,200 × 6	7,200
Product B	700 × 9	6,300
Product C	600 × 14	8,400
	Total	21,900

2. Budgeted sales value for actual quantity = Actual quantity × Budgeted price

		₹
Product A	1,200 × 5	6,000
Product B	700 × 10	7,000
Product C	600 × 15	9,000
	Total	22,000

3. Budgeted sales value for actual quantity, had actual sales been made in standard proportion
= Revised budgeted quantity × budgeted price

		₹
Product A	1,111.11 × 5	5,555.55
Product B	833.33 × 10	8,333.30
Product C	555.56 × 15	8,333.40
	Total	22,222.25 (or) 22,222

$$\text{Revised budgeted quantity} = \frac{\text{Total weight of actual mix}}{\text{Total weight of standard mix}} \times \text{Budgeted quantity of a product}$$

$$\text{Product A} = \frac{2{,}500}{2{,}250} \times 1{,}000 = 1111.11\text{units}$$

$$\text{Product B} = \frac{2{,}500}{2{,}250} \times 750 = 833.33 \text{ units}$$

$$\text{Product C} = \frac{2{,}500}{2{,}250} \times 500 = 555.56 \text{ units}$$

4. Budgeted sales = Budgeted quantity × Budgeted price.

		₹
Product A	1,000 × 5	5,000
Product B	750 × 10	7,500
Product C	500 × 15	7,500
	Total	20,000

Variances:

1. Sales value variance

   = 4 – 1

   = 20,000 – 21,900 = 1,900 (F)

2. Sales price variance

   = 2 – 1

   = 22,000 – 21,900 = 100 (A)

3. Sales volume variance

   = 4 – 2

   = 20,000 – 22,000 = 2,000 (F)

4. Sales mix variance

   = 3 – 2

   = 22,222 – 22,000 = 222 (A)

5. Sales quantity variance

   = 4 – 3

   = 20,000 – 22,222 = 2,222 (F)

Verification:

1. Sales value variance = Sales price variance + Sales volume variance

   1,900 (F) = 100 (A) + 2,000 (F)

   1,900 (F) = 1,900 (F)

2. Sales volume variance = Sales mix variance + Sales quantity variance

   2,000 (F) = 222 (A) + 2,222 (F)

   2,000 (F) = 2,000 (F)

Illustration-23

A company uses standard costing system. The sales and cost data for a period are as under:

Product	Budget			Actual		
	Quantity	Price (₹)	Value (₹)	Quantity	Sales (₹)	Value (₹)
A	1,280	20 p/u	16 p/u	650	12,350	18 p/u
B	3,200	12 p/u	10 p/u	3,900	50,700	12 p/u
C	1,920	16 p/u	13 p/u	1,950	29,250	13 p/u

Calculate:

1. Sales variances with reference to turnover.
2. Sales variances with reference to sales margin. **(CA-Inter-Adapted)**

Solution

A. Sales variances with reference to turnover

Calculations:

1. Actual sales = Actual quantity × Actual price

	₹
Product 'A'	12,350 (given)
Product 'B'	50,700 (given)
Product 'C'	29,250 (given)
Total	92,300

2. Budgeted sales for actual quantity = Actual quantity × Budgeted price

		₹
Product 'A'	650 × 20	13,000
Product 'B'	3,900 × 12	46,800
Product 'C'	1,950 × 16	31,200
	Total	91,000

3. Budgeted sales value for actual quantity, had sales been made in standard sales mix ratio

= Revised budgeted quantity × Budgeted price.

		₹
Product 'A'	1,300 × 20	26,000
Product 'B'	3,250 × 12	39,000
Product 'C'	1,950 × 16	31,200
	Total	96,200

Note:

$$\text{Revised budgeted quantity} = \frac{\text{Total weight of actual mix}}{\text{Total weight of budgeted mix}} \times \text{Budgeted quantity of a product}$$

$$\text{Product 'A'} = \frac{6{,}500}{6{,}400} \times 1{,}280 = 1{,}300 \text{ units}$$

$$\text{Product 'B'} = \frac{6{,}500}{6{,}400} \times 3{,}200 = 3{,}250 \text{ units}$$

$$\text{Product 'C'} = \frac{6{,}500}{6{,}400} \times 1{,}920 = 1{,}950 \text{ units}$$

4. Budgeted sales = Budgeted quantity × Budgeted price

		₹
Product 'A'	1,280 × 20	25,600
Product 'B'	3,200 × 12	38,400
Product 'C'	1,920 × 16	30,720
	Total	94,720

Variances:

1. Sales value variance

   = 4 – 1

   = 94,720 – 92,300 = 2,420 (A)

2. Sales price variance

   = 2 – 1

   = 91,000 – 92,300 = 1,300 (F)

3. Sales volume variance

$= 4 - 2$

$= 94{,}720 - 91{,}000 = 3{,}720\ (A)$

4. Sales mix variance

$= 3 - 2$

$= 96{,}200 - 91{,}000 = 5{,}200\ (A)$

5. Sales quantity variance

$= 4 - 3$

$= 94{,}720 - 96{,}200 = 1{,}480\ (F)$

Verification:

1. Sales value variance = Sales price variance + Sales volume variance

$2{,}420\ (A) = 1{,}300\ (F) + 3,\ 720\ (A)$

$2{,}420\ (A) = 2{,}420\ (A)$

2. Sub-volume variance = Sales mix variance + Sales quantity variance

$3{,}720\ (A) = 5{,}200\ (A) + 1{,}480\ (F)$

$3{,}720\ (A) = 3{,}720\ (A)$

B. Sales variances with reference to sales margin

Calculation:

1. Actual profit = Actual quantity × Actual profit per unit

		₹
Product 'A'	650 × 3	1,950
Product 'B'	3,900 × 3	11,700
Product 'C'	1,950 × 2	3,900
	Total	17,550

2. Budgeted profit for actual quantity = Actual quantity × Budgeted profit per unit

		₹
Product 'A'	650 × 4	2,600
Product 'B'	3,900 × 2	7,800
Product 'C'	1,950 × 3	5,850
	Total	16,250

3. Budgeted profit for actual quantity, had sales been made in standard sales mix ratio:

= Revised budgeted quantity × Budgeted profit per unit

		₹
Product 'A'	1,300 × 4	5,200
Product 'B'	3,250 × 2	6,500
Product 'C'	1,950 × 3	5,850
	Total	17,550

4. Budgeted profit = Budgeted quantity × Budgeted profit per unit

		₹
Product 'A'	1,280 × 4	5,120
Product 'B'	3,200 × 2	6,400
Product 'C'	1,920 × 3	5,760
	Total	17,280

Workings:

1. Budgeted profit = Budgeted price – Budgeted cost

Product A = 20 – 16 = 4
Product B = 12 – 10 = 2
Product C = 16 – 13 = 3

2. Actual profit = Actual selling price − Budgeted cost

$$\text{Product A} = \frac{12{,}350}{650} = 19 - 16 = \text{rupee } 3$$

$$\text{Product B} = \frac{50{,}700}{3{,}900} = 13 - 10 = \text{rupee } 3$$

$$\text{Product C} = \frac{29{,}250}{1{,}950} = 15 - 13 = \text{rupee } 2$$

3.

$$\text{Revised budgeted quantity} = \frac{\text{Total weight actual mix}}{\text{Total weight of budgeted mix}} \times \text{Budgeted quantity of a product}$$

$$\text{Product A} = \frac{6{,}500}{6{,}400} \times 1{,}280 = 1{,}300 \text{ units}$$

$$\text{Product B} = \frac{6{,}500}{6{,}400} \times 3{,}200 = 3{,}250 \text{ units}$$

$$\text{Product C} = \frac{6{,}500}{6{,}400} \times 1{,}920 = 1{,}950 \text{ units}$$

Variances:

1. Margin value variance

   = 4 − 1

   = 17,280 − 17,550 = 270 (F)

2. Margin price variance

   = 2 − 1

   = 16,250 − 17,550 = 1,300 (F)

3. Margin volume variance

   = 4 − 2

   = 17,280 − 16,250 = 1,030 (A)

4. Margin mix variance

   = 3 − 2

   = 17,550 − 16,250 = 1,300 (A)

5. Margin quantity variance

   = 4 − 3

   = 17, 280 − 17,550 = 270 (F)

Verification:

1. Margin value variance = Margin price variance + Margin volume variance

$$270 \text{ (F)} = 1{,}300 \text{ (F)} + 1{,}030 \text{ (A)}$$
$$270 \text{ (F)} = 270 \text{ (F)}$$

2. Margin volume variance = Margin mix variance + Margin quantity variance

$$1{,}030 \text{ (A)} = 1{,}300 \text{ (A)} + 270 \text{ (F)}$$
$$1{,}030 \text{ (A)} = 1{,}030 \text{ (A)}$$

Two-variance, Three-variance and Four-variance methods of analysis

Two-variance , three-variance and four-variance analysis is not a separate method of calculating variances. They refer to depth of analysis of variances.

Two-variance analysis

(i) **Materials cost variance**

Materials cost are analysed into price and quantity variances only.

(ii) **Labour cost variance**

Labour cost are analysed into rate and efficiency variances only.

(iii) **Overhead variances**

Overhead variances are analysed into expenditure and volume variances only.

Three-variance analysis:

Under three variance analysis, the analysis is taken still deeper.

(i) **Materials cost variance**

In material cost variances, variances are analysed into price, usage and mix variances.

(ii) **Labour cost variance**

In case of labour cost variances, the variances are analysed into labour rate, efficiency and mix variances.

(iii) **Overhead variance**

Under three-variance analysis, overhead variances are further analysed into expenditure, efficiency and capacity variances.

Four-Variance analysis

(i) **Material cost variance**

Materials cost variance is analysed into price, usage, mix and yield variances.

(ii) **Labour variance**

Labour variance is further analysed into rate, efficiency, capacity and yield variances.

(iii) **Overhead variance**

Overhead variance is analysed into expenditure variance, fixed overhead efficiency variance, variable overhead variance and fixed overhead capacity variances.

The choice of variance analysis approach depends on the requirements of the management.

Causes of variances and responsibility:

Variance	Possible causes	Persons responsible
	1. Material Cost Variances	
Material price variance	(a) Change in market price (b) Rush order or emergency purchase. (c) Inefficient purchase like not availing discount, placing order for uneconomic quantity etc. (d) Increase in stores overhead. (e) Non-availability of material. (f) Change in quality and specification of materials	Uncontrollable Stores / purchase / production manager Purchase manager Stores manager Uncontrollable Production manager
Material usage variance	(a) Poor quality of material (b) Scrap, spoilage and defectives (c) Wrong mix (d) Defective machines, tools and equipment.	Production manager / purchase manager Foreman / machine operator Production manager Maintenance engineer
	2. Labour Cost Variance	
Labour rate variance	(a) Change in wage rates (b) Use of different grades of workers	Uncontrollable Foreman/production manager

Labour efficiency variance	(a) Insufficient training (b) Bad working conditions (c) Incorrect instruction (d) Faulty planning and scheduling (e) Poor quality material	Foreman/production manager Production manager Foreman Production manager Purchase manager
Idle time variance	(a) Machinery break down (b) Power failure (c) Non-availability of materials	Maintenance engineer Uncontrollable Purchase manger / storekeeper
	3. Overhead Variance	
Overhead expenditure variance	(a) Increase in rates of overheads (b) Poor cost control (c) Change in methods of production (d) Change in production policy	Uncontrollable Departmental manager Production manager Top management
Overhead efficiency variance	(a) Inefficiency of workmen (b) Ineffective supervision (c) Ineffective production scheduling (d) Poor working condition of machines (e) Old and obsolete machinery	Personnel manager Foremen Foremen / Planning Engineer Production manager / Maintenance engineer Top management
Overhead capacity variance	1. Lack of orders 2. Lockouts and strikes 3. Power cut, non-availability of materials, shortage of labour	Uncontrollable / Sales manager Uncontrollable / Top management Uncontrollable

21.9 ACCOUNTING METHODS

There are two methods of accounting for recording the transactions under standard costing. They are:

1. Single plan
2. Partial plan.

Under the single plan variances are recorded immediately when a transaction takes place. Variances are immediately reported to the management. Under partial plan transactions are recorded initially at historical cost. Transfers from various control accounts to work-in-progress account are made at standard cost and variances are calculated only at the end of the period. The following are scheme of entries under both methods:

Transaction	**Partial Plan**	**Single Plan**
1. Purchase of raw material	Materials control a/c Dr To General ledger adjustment a/c	Raw material control a/c Dr Material purchase price variance a/c (Adv) Dr To General ledger adjustment a/c To Material purchase price variance a/c (Fav)
2. Issue of raw material for production	Work-in-progress control a/c Dr To Raw materials control a/c	Work-in-progress control a/c Dr Material usage variance a/c (Adv) Dr To General ledger adjustment a/c To Material usage variance a/c (Fav)
3. Payment of wages	Wages control a/c Dr To General ledger adjustment a/c	Wages control a/c Dr Labour rate variance (Adv) Dr To General ledger adjustment a/c To Labour rate variance a/c (Fav)
4. Direct wages incurred for production	Work-in-progress control a/c Dr To Wages control a/c	Work-in-progress control a/c Dr Labour - efficiency variance (Adv) a/c Dr To Wages control a/c To Labour efficiency variance a/c (Fav)
5. Overheads incurred	Overhead control a/c Dr To General ledger adjustment a/c	Overhead control a/c Dr To General ledger adjustment a/c
6. Overhead absorbed	Work-in-progress control a/c Dr Overhead variance a/c (Adv) Dr To Overhead control a/c To Overhead variance a/c (Fav)	Work-in-progress control a/c Dr Overhead variance a/c (Adv) Dr To Overhead control a/c To Overhead variance a/c (Fav)
7. At the end of the period	**(a) Favourable variance:** Work-in-progress control a/c Dr To Material price / material usage variance **(b) Adverse variance:** Material price / material usage variance Dr To Work-in-progress control a/c	No entry

21.10 STANDARD COST-REPORTING

Variances computed are to be investigated for the specific causes to enable management to take corrective action. Prompt action on the part of the management is the base of standard costing. So variance report is to be prepared keeping the following points in mind:

1. Regular reporting of variances
2. The top management should be informed of the desired performance standards
3. Actual performance level achieved
4. Detailed analysis of variances
5. Variances requiring management attention should be highlighted
6. The magnitude of variance should be pointed out.

21.10.1 Standard Cost Report

Standard cost report is usually prepared in a profit and loss statement format. The following is a format of standard costing profit and loss account:

Standard costing profit and loss report for the month of xxx

Particulars	**Total**	**Dept A**	**Dept B**	**Dept C**
A. Sales	xxx	xxx	xxx	xxx
Less:				
B. Standard cost of sales	xxx	xxx	xxx	xxx
C. Standard profit (A–B)	xxx	xxx	xxx	xxx
D. Add/ Deduct variance:				
Material: Price	xxx	xxx	xxx	xxx
Usage	xxx	xxx	xxx	xxx
Labour: Rate	xxx	xxx	xxx	xxx
Efficiency	xxx	xxx	xxx	xxx
Variable overhead:				
Expenditure	xxx	xxx	xxx	xxx
Efficiency	xxx	xxx	xxx	xxx
Fixed overhead:				
Expenditure	xxx	xxx	xxx	xxx
Volume	xxx	xxx	xxx	xxx
Total (D)	xxx	xxx	xxx	xxx
E. Actual profit (C – D)	xxx	xxx	xxx	xxx

Note: All adverse variances are deducted from standard profit and all favourable variances are added to standard profit.

21.10.2 Disposal of Variances

Variances may be disposed under any one of the following methods:

1. All variances are transferred to costing profit and loss account. This procedure is followed when variances are small.

2. Variances may be distributed proportionately over cost of sales, stock of work-in-progress and stock of finished goods. This method is followed when the amount of variances are substantial.

3. In the third method price variance is distributed over cost of sales, stock of work-in-progress and stock of finished goods. Quantity variance in transferred to costing profit and loss account.

21.10.3 Control of Variances through Ratio Analysis

Cost variances reported to the management in absolute terms may not be of much help to the management. It is necessary that variances are reported in a common measurement term. For easy and quick comprehension, variances are reported in ratios. The following are some of the ratios computed for reporting to management:

1. Efficiency ratio $= \dfrac{\text{Standard hours for actual output}}{\text{Actual hours}} \times 100$

   This ratio is useful in measuring production efficiency.

2. Activity ratio $= \dfrac{\text{Standard hours for actual output}}{\text{Standard hours for budgeted production}} \times 100$

   This ratio helps in measuring actual activity level compared to budgeted activity level.

3. Calendar ratio $= \dfrac{\text{Actual number of working days in budget period}}{\text{Budgeted days in budget period}} \times 100$

   This reveals the difference in actual number of working days compared to budgeted days.

4. Capacity usage ratio $= \dfrac{\text{Actual hours worked}}{\text{Maximum possible hours}} \times 100$

   It reveals the difference in actual hours worked from maximum working hours available

5. Capacity utilisation ratio $= \dfrac{\text{Actual hours worked}}{\text{Budgeted hours}} \times 100$

   This shows the difference in hours worked and hours budgeted.

COMPREHENSIVE ILLUSTRATIONS

Illustration-24

(Material variances - Opening and closing stock) Vivek Ltd produces an article by blending two basic raw materials. It operates a standard costing system and the following standards have been set for raw materials:

Material	Standard mix	Standard price per kg
		(₹)
A	40%	4.00
B	60%	3.00

The standard loss in processing is 15%.

During April, 2008, the company produced 1,700 kg of finished product.

The position of stock and purchase for the month of April 2008 is as under.

Material	Stock on 1.4.2008 kg	Stock on 30.4.2008 kg	Purchase during April kg	Cost ₹
A	35	5	800	3,400
B	40	50	1,200	3,000

Calculate the following variances:

(a) Material price variance

(b) Material usage variance

(c) Material yield variance

(d) Material mix variance

(e) Total material cost variance **(C.A-Inter)**

Solution

Calculations:

1. Actual cost of materials used = Act. Price × Act. quantity

		₹
Material 'A'	4.00 × 35	140.00

Material 'A'	4.25 × 795	3,378.75
Material 'B'	3.00 × 40	120.00
Material 'B'	2.50 × 1,150	2,875.00
	Total	6,513.75

Note:

i. Materials used = Op. stock + Purchase - Cl. stock

Material A = 35 + 800 - 5 = 830 kg

Material B = 40 + 1,200-50 =1,190 kg

ii. Actual price = $\frac{\text{Purchase cost}}{\text{Quantity purchased}}$

Material A	3,400/800	₹4.25
Material B	3,000/1,200	₹2.50

2. Standard cost of material used = Standard price × Actual quantity

		₹
Material A	4 × 830	3,320
Material B	3 × 1,190	3,570
	Total	6,890

3. Standard cost of materials used, had it been used in standard mix ratio

= Total actual quantity × Standard mix ratio × Standard price

		₹
Material A	$2{,}020 \times \frac{40}{100} \times 4$	3,232
Material B	$2{,}020 \times \frac{60}{100} \times 3$	3,636
	Total	6,868

4. Standard cost of standard quantity for actual output = Std. price × Std. qty for actual output

		₹
Material 'A'	4 × 800	3,200
Material 'B'	3 × 1,200	3,600
	Total	6,800

Note:

Standard quantity for actual output (Total) $= \frac{100}{85} \times 1{,}700 = 2{,}000$ kg

Standard quantity material A $= 2{,}000 \times \frac{40}{100} = 800$ kg

Standard quantity material B $= 2{,}000 \times \frac{60}{100} = 1{,}200$ kg

Variances:

1. Material price variance (MPV)

   $= 2 - 1$

   $= 6{,}890 - 6{,}513.75 = 376.25$ (F)

2. Material usages variance (MUV)

   $= 4 - 2$

   $= 6{,}800 - 6{,}890 = 90$ (A)

3. Material mix variance (MMV)

   $= 3 - 2$

   $= 6{,}868 - 6{,}890 = 22$ (A)

4. Material yield variance (MYV)

   $= 4 - 3$

   $= 6{,}800 - 6{,}868 = 68$ (A)

5. Material cost variance (MCV)

   $= 4 - 1$

   $= 6{,}800 - 6{,}513.75 = 286.25$ (F)

Verification:

1. MCV = MPV + MUV

   286.25 (F) = 376.25 (F) + 90 (A)

   286.25 (F) = 286.25 (F)

2. MUV = MMV + MYV

   90 (A) = 22 (A) + 68 (A)

   90 (A) = 90 (A)

Illustration-25

(Material Variances) The standard material inputs required for 1,000 kg of a finished output are given below:

Material	Quantity (kg)	Standard rate per kg
P	450	20
Q	400	40
R	250	60
Total input	1,100	
Less: Standard loss	100	
Standard output	1,000	

Actual production in a period was 20,000 kg of the finished product for which the actual quantities of materials used and the prices paid thereof are as under:

Material	Quantity used (kg)	Purchase price per kg
P	10,000	19
Q	8,500	42
R	4,500	65

Calculate material cost, price, usage, mix and yield variances. Also prepare reconciliation statement.

Solution

Calculations:

1. Actual cost of materials used = Actual price × Actual quantity

		₹
Material P	19 × 10,000	1,90,000
Material Q	42 × 8,500	3,57,000
Material R	65 × 4,500	2,92,500
	Total	8,39,500

2. Standard cost of materials used = Standard price × Actual quantity.

		₹
Material P	20 × 10,000	2,00,000
Material Q	40 × 8,500	3,40,000
Material R	60 × 4,500	2,70,000
	Total	8,10,000

3. Standard cost of materials used, had it been used in standard proportion

= Total actual quantity × Standard mix ratio × Std. price

		₹
Material P	$23{,}000 \times \frac{450}{1100} \times 20$	1,88,182
Material Q	$23{,}000 \times \frac{400}{1100} \times 40$	3,34,545
Material R	$23{,}000 \times \frac{250}{1100} \times 60$	3,13,636
	Total	8,36,363

4. Standard cost of standard quantity for actual output

= Standard price × Standard quantity for actual output

		₹
Material P	20 × 9,000	1,80,000
Material Q	40 × 8,000	3,20,000
Material R	60 × 5,000	3,00,000
	Total	8,00,000

Note:

Total standard quantity for actual output $= \frac{1{,}100}{1{,}000} \times 20{,}000 = 22{,}000$ kg

Standard quantity of material for actual output:

$$P = 22{,}000 \times \frac{450}{1{,}100} = 9{,}000 \text{ kg}$$

$$Q = 22{,}000 \times \frac{400}{1{,}100} = 8{,}000 \text{ kg}$$

$$R = 22{,}000 \times \frac{250}{1{,}100} = 5{,}000 \text{ kg}$$

Variances:

1. Material Cost Variance (MCV)

   $= 4 - 1$

   $= 8{,}00{,}000 - 8{,}39{,}500 = 39{,}500$ (A)

2. Material Price Variance (MPV)

   $= 2 - 1$

   $= 8{,}10{,}000 - 8{,}39{,}500 = 29{,}500$ (A)

3. Material Usage Variance (MUV)

   $= 4 - 2$

   $= 8{,}00{,}000 - 8{,}10{,}000 = 10{,}000$ (A)

4. Material Mix Variance (MMV)

   $= 3 - 2$

   $= 8{,}36{,}363 - 8{,}10{,}000 = 26{,}363$ (F)

5. Material Yield Variance (MYV)

   $= 4 - 3$

   $= 8{,}00{,}000 - 8{,}36{,}363 = 36{,}363$ (A)

Verification:

1. MCV = MPV + MUV

   39,500 (A) = 29,500 (A) + 10,000 (A)

   39,500 (A) = 39, 500 (A)

2. MUV = MMV + MYV

   10,000 (A) = 26,363 (F) + 36,363 (A)

   10,000 (A) = 10,000 (A)

Illustration-26

(Labour Variances) A gang of workers normally consist of 30 men, 15 women and 10 boys. They are paid at standard rate as under:

Men - ₹4.00 per hour
Women - ₹3.00 per hour
Boys - ₹2.00 per hour

In a normal working week of 40 hours, the gang is expected to produce 2,000 units of output. During the week ended 31st March 2009 the gang consisted of 40 men, 10 women and 5 boys. The actual wages paid were at the rate of ₹3.50, ₹3.25 and ₹1.50 per hour respectively. 4 hours were lost due to abnormal idle time and 1,600 units were produced.

Calculate: (i) Labour cost variance, (ii) Labour rate variance, (iii) Labour efficiency variance, (iv) Labour mix variance, (v) Labour idle time variance, (vi) Labour yield variance.

(B.Com. (Hons.), Delhi - adapted)

Solution

Calculations:

1. Actual wages for actual time = Act. no. of workers × Act. hours × Act. rate

		₹
Men	40 × 40 × 3.50	5,600
Women	10 × 40 × 3.25	1,300
Boys	5 × 40 × 1.50	300
	Total	7,200

2. Standard wages for actual time = Act. no. of workers × Act. hours × Std. rate

		₹
Men	40 × 40 × 4	6,400
Women	10 × 40 × 3	1,200
Boys	5 × 40 × 2	400
	Total	8,000

3. Standard wages for actual hours utilised = Actual no. of workers × Act. hours utilised × Std. rate

		₹
Men	40 × 36 × 4	5,760
Women	10 × 36 × 3	1,080
Boys	5 × 36 × 2	360
	Total	7,200

4. Standard wages for actual time utilised had labour been used in Standard mix ratio = Std. no. of workers × Actual hours utilised × Std. rate

		₹
Men	30 × 36 × 4	4,320
Women	15 × 36 × 3	1,620
Boys	10 × 36 × 2	720
	Total	6,660

5. Standard wages for standard time for actual output (or) Standard wages for actual production

= Standard labour cost per unit × Actual production

= 3.40 × 1,600 = ₹5,440

Note:

$$\text{Standard labour cost per unit} = \frac{\text{Standard wages}}{\text{Standard production}}$$

Standard wages = Std. No. of workers × Std. time × Std. rate

		₹
Men	30 × 40 × 4	4,800
Women	15 × 40 × 3	1,800
Boys	10 × 10 × 2	200
	Total	6,800

$$\text{Standard labour cost per unit} = \frac{6{,}800}{2{,}000} = \text{rupee } 3.40$$

Variances:

1. Labour cost variance (LCV)
   $= 5 - 1$
   $= 5{,}440 - 7{,}200 = 1{,}760$ (A)
2. Labour rate variance (LRV)
   $= 2 - 1$
   $= 8{,}000 - 7{,}200 = 800$ (F)
3. Labour efficiency variance (LEV)
   $= 5 - 2$
   $= 5{,}440 - 8{,}000 = 2{,}560$ (A)
4. Labour idle time variance (LITU)
   $= 3 - 2$
   $= 7{,}200 - 8{,}000 = 800$ (A)
5. Labour mix variance (LMV)
   $= 4 - 3$
   $= 6{,}660 - 7{,}200 = 540$ (A)
6. Labour yield variance
   $= 5 - 4$
   $= 5{,}440 - 6{,}660 = 1{,}220$ (A)

Verification:

1. LCV = LRV + LEV
   1,760 (A) = 800 (F) + 2,560 (A)
   1,760 (A) = 1,760 (A)
2. LEV = LITV + LMV + LYV
   2,560 (A) = 800 (A) + 540 (A) + 1,220 (A)
   2,560 (A) = 2,560 (A)

Illustration-27

(Labour variances) From the data given below, calculate labour variances for the two departments:

	Dept. A.	Dept. B
Actual gross wages (₹)	2,000	1,800
Standard hours produced	8,000	6,000
Standard rate per hour (₹)	0.30	0.35
Actual hours worked)	8,200	5,800

(ICWA - Inter)

Solution

Calculations:

1. Actual wages paid for actual hours = Act. time × Act. rate

   Dept. A = ₹2,000 (given)

   Dept. B = ₹1,800 (given)

2. Standard wages for actual hours = Act. hours × Std. rate

   Dept. A = 8,200 × 0.30 = ₹2,460

   Dept. B = 5,800 × 0.35 = ₹2,030

3. Standard wages for actual hours utilised:

   - No idle time, not applicable.

4. Standard wages for actual hours utilised, had labour been utilised in standard mix ratio:

   - No labour mix, not applicable.

5. Standard wages for standard time = Std. time × Std. rate

   Dept. A = 8,000 × 0.30 = ₹2,400

   Dept. B = 6,000 × 0.35 = ₹2,100

Variances:

1. Labour cost variance (LCV)

   = 5 − 1

   Dept. A = 2,400 − 2,000 = 400 (F)

   Dept. B = 2,100 − 1,800 = 300 (F)

2. Labour rate variance (LRV)

   = 2 – 1

   Dept. A = 2,460 – 2,000 = 460 (F)

   Dept. B = 2,030 – 1,800 = 230 (F)

3. Labour efficiency variance (LEV)

   = 5 – 2

   Dept. A = 2,400 – 2,460 = 60 (A)

   Dept. B = 2,100 – 2,030 = 70 (F)

Verification:

LCV = LRV + LEV

Dept. A = 400 (F) = 460 (F) + 60 (A)

400 (F) = 400 (F)

Dept. B = 300 (F) = 230 (F) + 70 (F)

300 (F) = 300 (F)

Illustration-28

(Fixed overhead variance) From the following calculate the fixed overhead cost variance, fixed overhead expenditure variance and fixed overhead volume variance:

Budgeted fixed overhead for March 2009	₹3,00,000
Budgeted production for the month	25,000 units
Actual production for the month	27,000 units
Actual fixed overheads incurred	₹3,60,000

Solution

Calculations:

1. Actual fixed overheads - ₹3,60,000 (given)
2. Budgeted fixed overheads - ₹3,00,000 (given)
3. Not applicable - Working days not given
4. Not applicable - Working hours not given

5. Budgeted fixed overheads for actual production

$$= \text{Bud. fixed overheads per unit} \times \text{Act. production}$$
$$= 12 \times 27{,}000 = ₹3{,}24{,}000$$

Note:

$$\text{Bud. fixed OHS per unit} = \frac{\text{Bud. FOHS}}{\text{Bud. production}}$$
$$= \frac{3{,}00{,}000}{25{,}000} = ₹12$$

Variances:

1. Fixed overhead cost variance

$$= 5 - 1$$
$$= 3{,}24{,}000 - 3{,}60{,}000 = 36{,}000\ (A)$$

2. Fixed overhead expenditure variance

$$= 2 - 1$$
$$= 3{,}00{,}000 - 3{,}60{,}000 = 60{,}000\ (A)$$

3. Fixed overhead volume variance

$$= 5 - 2$$
$$= 3{,}24{,}000 - 3{,}00{,}000 = 24{,}000\ (F)$$

Verification:

Cost variance = Exp. variance + Volume variance

36,000 (A) = 60,000 (A) + 24,000 (F)

36,000 (A) = 36,000 (A)

Illustration-29

(Material and labour variances) A company producing only one product provides the following information:

Standard cost per unit of product:

Materials - 4 kg. at ₹8 per kg.

Labour - 6 hours at ₹10 per hour

Budgeted production for the month of July 2009 was 2,000 units but actual production amounted to 2,200 units.

The company purchased 10,000 units of raw materials at a total cost of ₹83,000. The actual cost data for the month of July 2009 is as follows:

Materials used in production - 9,000 kg.

Labour hours worked - 9,000 hours at total wages of ₹93,600.

Calculate material and labour variances.

Solution

Material Variances

Calculations:

1. Actual cost of materials used:

$$= \text{Act. price} \times \text{Act. Qty.}$$
$$= 8.30 \times 9{,}000 = ₹74{,}700$$

Note:

$$\text{Actual price} = \frac{\text{Total cost of materials purchased}}{\text{Quantity purchased}}$$
$$= \frac{83{,}000}{10{,}000} = ₹8.30$$

2. Standard cost of materials used:

$$= \text{Std. Price} \times \text{Act. Qty.}$$
$$= 8 \times 9{,}000 = ₹72{,}000$$

3. No material mix – Not applicable.

4. Standard cost of standard quantity for actual production:

$$= \text{Std. Price} \times \text{Std. Qty for actual output}$$
$$= 8 \times 8{,}800 = ₹70{,}400$$

Note:

Standard quantity for actual output = 4 × 2,200 = 8,800 kg.

Variances:

1. Material cost variance (MCV)

$$= 5 - 1$$
$$= 70{,}400 - 74{,}700 = 4{,}300 \text{ (A)}$$

2. Material price variance (MPV)

$= 2 - 1$

$= 72{,}000 - 74{,}700 = 2{,}700$ (A)

3. Material usage variance (MUV)

$= 4 - 2$

$= 70{,}400 - 72{,}000 = 1{,}600$ (A)

Verification:

MCV = MPV + MUV

4,300 (A) = 2,700 (A) + 1,600 (A)

4,300 (A) = 4,300 (A)

Labour Variances:

Calculations:

1. Actual wages paid for actual hours:

= Act. rate × Act. hours

= ₹93,600 (given)

2. Standard wages for actual hours:

= Std. rate × Act. hours

$= 10 \times 9{,}000 =$ ₹90,000

3. No idle time – Not applicable.

4. No labour mix – Not applicable.

5. Standard wages for standard time for actual output:

= Std. rate × Std. time for actual output

$= 10 \times 13{,}200 =$ ₹1,32,000

Note: Std. time for actual output $= 6 \times 2{,}200 = 13{,}200$ hrs.

Variances:

1. Labour cost variance (LCV)

$= 5 - 1$

$= 1{,}32{,}000 - 93{,}600 = 38{,}400$ (F)

2. Labour rate variance (LRV)

   = 2 − 1

   = 90,000 − 93,600 = 3,600 (A)

3. Labour efficiency variance (LEV)

   = 5 − 2

   = 1,32,000 − 90,000 = 42,000 (F)

Verification:

LCV = LRV + LEV

38,400 (F) = 3,600 (A) + 42,000 (F)

38,400 (F) = 38,400 (F)

Illustration-30

(Material and labour variances) The following details relating to the product X during the month of March 2009 are available. You are required to compute the material and labour cost variances and also to reconcile the standard and the actual costs with the help of such variances.

Standard cost per unit:

Materials - 50 kg. at ₹40 per kg.

Labour - 400 hours at ₹1 per hour

Actual cost for the month:

Materials - 4,900 kg. at ₹42 per kg.

Labour - 39,600 hours at ₹1.10 per hour

Actual production - 100 units.

(ICWA-Inter)

Solution

Material Variances:

Calculations:

1. Actual cost of materials used:

   = Act. price × Act. Qty.

   = 42 × 4,900 = ₹2,05,800

2. Standard cost of materials used:

   = Std. Price × Act. Qty.

   = 40 × 4,900 = ₹1,96,000

3. No material mix - Not applicable.

4. Standard cost of standard quantity for actual output:

   = Std. price × Std. qty. for actual output

   = 40 × 5,000 = ₹2,00,000

Note: Std. quantity for actual output = 50 × 100 = 5,000 kg.

Variances:

1. Material cost variance (MCV)

   = 4 − 1

   = 2,00,000 − 2,05,800 = 5,800 (A)

2. Material price variance (MPV)

   = 2 − 1

   = 1,96,000 − 2,05,800 = 9,800 (A)

3. Material usage variance (MUV)

   = 4 − 2

   = 2,00,000 − 1,96,000 = 4,000 (F)

Verification:

MCV = MRV + MUV

5,800 (A) = 9,800 (A) + 4,000 (F)

5,800 (A) = 5,800 (A)

Labour Variances:

Calculations:

1. Actual wages paid for actual hours:

   = Act. rate × Act. hours

   = 1.10 × 39,600 = ₹43,560

2. Standard wages for actual hours:

   = Std. rate × Act. hours

   = 1 × 39,600 = ₹39,600

3. No idle time - Not applicable.
4. No labour mix - Not applicable.
5. Standard wages for standard time for actual output:

$$= \text{Std. rate} \times \text{Std. time for actual output}$$
$$= 1 \times 40{,}000 = ₹40{,}000$$

Note:

Std. time for actual output = 400 × 100 = 40,000 hrs.

Variances:

1. Labour cost variance (LCV)

$$= 5 - 1$$
$$= 40{,}000 - 43{,}560 = 3{,}560 \text{ (A)}$$

2. Labour rate variance (LRV)

$$= 2 - 1$$
$$= 39{,}600 - 43{,}560 = 3{,}960 \text{ (A)}$$

3. Labour efficiency variance (LEV)

$$= 5 - 2$$
$$= 40{,}000 - 39{,}600 = 400 \text{ (F)}$$

Verification:

LCV = LRV + LEV

3,560 (A) = 3,960 (A) + 400 (F)

3,560 (A) = 3,560 (A)

Illustration-31

(Overhead variances) The following information is available from the records of a factory:

	Budget	Actual
Fixed overhead for June (₹)	10,000	12,000
Production in June (units)	2,000	2,100
Standard time per unit (hours)	10	-
Actual hours worked in June	-	22,000

Compute:

(i) Fixed overhead cost variance; (ii) Expenditure variance

(iii) Volume variance; (iv) Capacity variance

(v) Efficiency variance

(CA-Inter)

Solution

Calculations:

1. Actual fixed overheads - ₹12,000 (given)
2. Budgeted fixed overheads - ₹10,000 (given)
3. Not applicable - Working days not given
4. Standard fixed overheads:
$$= \text{Std. Fixed OH rate per hour} \times \text{Actual hours}$$
$$= 0.50 \times 22{,}000 = ₹11{,}000$$
5. Recovered fixed overheads:
$$= \text{Std. fixed overheads per hour} \times \text{Std. hours for actual production}$$
$$= 0.50 \times 21{,}000 = 10{,}500 \text{ output}$$

Note:

1. $$\text{Std. fixed OHS rate per hour} = \frac{\text{Bud. FOHS}}{\text{Bud. hours}}$$
$$= \frac{10{,}000}{20{,}000} = ₹0.50$$
2. $$\text{Std. hours for actual production} = \frac{\text{Bud. Hours.}}{\text{Bud. Prod.}} \times \text{Act. Prod.}$$
$$= \frac{20{,}000}{2{,}000} \times 2{,}100 = 21{,}000 \text{ hrs.}$$

Variances:

1. Fixed overhead cost variance
$$= 5 - 1$$
$$= 10{,}500 - 12{,}000 = 1{,}500 \text{ (A)}$$
2. Fixed overhead expenditure variance
$$= 2 - 1$$
$$= 10{,}000 - 12{,}000 = 2{,}000 \text{ (A)}$$

3. Fixed overhead volume variance

$= 5 - 2$

$= 10{,}500 - 10{,}000 = 500$ (F)

4. Fixed overhead capacity variance

$= 4 - 2$

$= 11{,}000 - 10{,}000 = 1{,}000$ (F)

5. Fixed overhead efficiency variance

$= 5 - 4$

$= 10{,}500 - 11{,}000 = 500$ (A)

Verification:

1. Cost variance = Exp. variance + Volume variance

   1,500 (A) = 2,000 (A) + 500 (F)

   1,500 (A) = 1,500 (A)

2. Volume variance = Capacity variance + Efficiency variance

   500 (F) = 1,000 (F) + 500 (A)

   500 (F) = 500 (F)

Illustration-32

(Overhead variances) From the following data calculate overhead variances:

	Budget	Actual
Number of working days	23	25
Man hours per day	10,000	11,000
Output per machine hour in units	1	0.9
Overhead cost (₹)	3,45,000	3,75,000

Solution

Calculations:

1. Actual overheads - ₹3,75,000 (given)
2. Budgeted overheads - ₹3,45,000 (given)

3. Budgeted overhead for actual days:

$$= \text{Bud. overhead per day} \times \text{Actual working days}$$

$$= 15{,}000 \times 25 = ₹3{,}75{,}000$$

4. Standard fixed overheads:

$$= \text{Std. fixed rate per hour} \times \text{Actual hours}$$

$$= 1.50 \times 2{,}75{,}000 = ₹4{,}12{,}500$$

Note:

(a) $$\text{Std. fixed OHS rate per hour} = \frac{\text{Bud. FOHS}}{\text{Bud. Hours}}$$

$$= \frac{3{,}45{,}000}{2{,}30{,}000} = ₹1.50$$

(b) Budgeted hours = 23 × 10,000 = 2,30,000 hrs.

(c) Actual hours = 25 × 11,000 = 2,75,000 hrs.

(d) $$\text{Fixed overheads per day} = \frac{\text{Bud. OHS}}{\text{Bud. days}} = \frac{3{,}45{,}000}{23} = ₹15{,}000$$

5. Recovered fixed overheads:

$$= \text{Std. overheads rate per hour} \times \text{Std. hours for actual output}$$

$$= 1.50 \times 2{,}47{,}500 = ₹3{,}71{,}250$$

Note:

(a) Actual production = Actual hours × 0.9

= 2,75,000 × 0.9 = 2,47,500 units.

(b) Std. hours for actual production = 2,47,500 × 1

= 2,47,500 hrs.

Variances:

1. Fixed overhead cost variance

$$= 5 - 1$$

$$= 3{,}71{,}250 - 3{,}75{,}000 = 3{,}750 \text{ (A)}$$

2. Fixed overhead expenditure variance

$$= 2 - 1$$

$$= 3{,}45{,}000 - 3{,}75{,}000 = 30{,}000 \text{ (A)}$$

3. Fixed overhead volume variance

$$= 5 - 2$$

$$= 3{,}71{,}250 - 3{,}45{,}000 = 26{,}250 \text{ (F)}$$

4. Fixed overhead calendar variance

$$= 3 - 2$$
$$= 3{,}75{,}000 - 3{,}45{,}000 = 30{,}000 \text{ (F)}$$

5. Fixed overhead capacity variance

$$= 4 - 3$$
$$= 4{,}12{,}500 - 3{,}75{,}000 = 37{,}500 \text{ (F)}$$

6. Fixed overhead efficiency variance

$$= 5 - 4$$
$$= 3{,}71{,}250 - 4{,}12{,}500 = 41{,}250 \text{ (A)}$$

Verification:

1. Cost variance = Exp. variance + Volume variance

   3,750 (A) = 30,000 (A) + 26,250 (F)

   3,750 (A) = 3,750 (A)

2. Volume variance = Calendar variance + Capacity variance + Efficiency Variance

   26,250 (F) = 30,000 (F) + 37,500 (F) + 41,250 (A)

   26,250 (F) = 26,250 (F)

Illustration-33

(Sales variances) From the following data relating to budgeted and actual sales of a company for a particular period, calculate relevant sales variances:

Product	Budget			Actual		
	Quantity (Unit)	**Price** (₹)	**Amount** (₹)	**Quantity** (Unit)	**Price** (₹)	**Amount** (₹)
A	5,000	5	25,000	6,000	6	36,000
B	4,000	6	24,000	5,000	5	25,000
C	3,000	7	21,000	4,000	8	32,000

Solution

Calculations:

1. Actual sales value = Act. qty. × Act. price

		₹
Product A	6,000 × 6	36,000
Product B	5,000 × 5	25,000
Product C	4,000 × 8	32,000
	Total	93,000

2. Bud. sales value for actual quantity = Act. qty. × Bud. price

		₹
Product A	6,000 × 5	30,000
Product B	5,000 × 6	30,000
Product C	4,000 × 7	28,000
	Total	88,000

3. Bud. sales value, had sales been made in budgeted mix ratio = Revised bud. qty. × Bud. price

		₹
Product A	6,250 × 5	31,250
Product B	5,000 × 6	30,000
Product C	3,750 × 7	26,250
	Total	87,500

Note:

$$\text{Revised budgeted quantity} = \frac{\text{Total weight of act. mix}}{\text{Total weight of bud. mix}} \times \text{Bud. qty}$$

$$\text{Product A} = \frac{15{,}000}{12{,}000} \times 5{,}000 = 6{,}250$$

$$\text{Product B} = \frac{15{,}000}{12{,}000} \times 4{,}000 = 5{,}000$$

$$\text{Product C} = \frac{15{,}000}{12{,}000} \times 3{,}000 = 3{,}750$$

4. Bud. sales value for bud. qty.= Bud. qty. × Bud. price

		₹
Product A	5,000 × 5	25,000
Product B	4,000 × 6	24,000
Product C	3,000 × 7	21,000
	Total	70,000

Variances:

1. Sales value variance

   = 4 − 1

   = 70,000 − 93,000 = 23,000 (F)

2. Sales price variance

   = 2 − 1

   = 88,000 − 93,000 = 5,000 (F)

3. Sales volume variance

   = 4 − 2

   = 70,000 − 88,000 = 18,000 (F)

4. Sales mix variance

   = 3 − 2

   = 87,500 − 88,000 = 500 (F)

5. Sales quantity variance

   = 4 − 3

   = 70,000 − 87,500 = 17,500 (F)

Verification:

1. Value variance = Price variance + Volume variance

   23,000 (F) = 5,000 (F) + 18,000 (F)

   23,000 (F) = 23,000 (F)

2. Volume variance = Mix variance + Quantity variance

   18,000 (F) = 500 (F) + 17,500 (F)

   18,000 (F) = 18,000 (F)

Illustration-34

X Ltd. had the following budgeted and actual sales for the month of June 2009:

Product	Budget		Actual		Standard Cost per unit (₹)
	Quantity (Unit)	Price (₹)	Quantity (Unit)	Price (₹)	
X	5,000	15	4,500	16	14
Y	6,500	12	7,000	13	10
Z	8,000	9	8,500	8	7

Calculate sales variances according to profit method.

Solution

Calculations:

1. Actual margin realised = Act. qty. × Act. profit per unit

		₹
X	4,500 × 2	9,000
Y	7,000 × 3	21,000
Z	8,500 × 1	8,500
	Total	38,500

2. Bud. margin for actual quantity sold = Act. qty. × Bud. profit per unit

		₹
X	4,500 × 1	4,500
Y	7,000 × 2	14,000
Z	8,500 × 2	17,000
	Total	35,500

3. Bud. margin for act. qty. had sales been made in bud. mix ratio = Revised bud. qty. × Bud. profit per unit

		₹
X	5,128.21 × 1	5,128
Y	6,667.67 × 2	13,335
Z	8,205.13 × 2	16,410
	Total	34,873

Note:

$$\text{Revised budgeted quantity} = \frac{\text{Total weight of act. mix}}{\text{Total weight of bud. mix}} \times \text{Bud. qty}$$

$$\text{Product A} = \frac{20{,}000}{19{,}500} \times 5{,}000 = 5{,}128.21$$

$$\text{Product B} = \frac{20{,}000}{19{,}500} \times 6{,}500 = 6{,}667.67$$

$$\text{Product C} = \frac{20{,}000}{19{,}500} \times 8{,}000 = 8{,}205.13$$

4. Bud. margin for bud. qty. = Bud. qty. × Bud. margin

		₹
X	5,000 × 1	5,000
Y	6,500 × 2	13,000
Z	8,000 × 2	16,000
	Total	34,000

Note:

(a) Budgeted margin = Bud. price – Std. cost

$$X = 15 - 14 = 1$$
$$Y = 12 - 10 = 2$$
$$Z = 9 - 7 = 2$$

(b) Actual margin = Act. price – Std. cost

$$X = 16 - 14 = 2$$
$$Y = 13 - 10 = 3$$
$$Z = 8 - 7 = 1$$

Variances:

1. Profit value variance

$= 4 - 1$

$= 34{,}000 - 38{,}500 = 4{,}500$ (F)

2. Profit price variance

$= 2 - 1$

$= 35{,}500 - 38{,}500 = 3{,}000$ (F)

3. Profit volume variance

$= 4 - 2$

$= 34{,}000 - 35{,}500 = 1{,}500$ (F)

4. Profit mix variance

$= 3 - 2$

$= 34{,}873 - 35{,}500 = 627$ (F)

5. Profit quantity variance

$= 4 - 3$

$= 34{,}000 - 34{,}873 = 873$ (F)

Verification:

1. Value variance = Price variance + Volume variance

4,500 (F) = 3,000 (F) + 1,500 (F)

4,500 (F) = 4,500 (F)

2. Volume variance = Mix variance + Quantity variance

1,500 (F) = 627 (F) + 873 (F)

1,500 (F) = 1,500 (F)

Illustration-35

(All Variances) A company producing a standard product is facing declining sales and dwindling profits. It has therefore decided to introduce a standard cost system to control cost. To motivate the workers to improve the productivity, the management has also decided to introduced an incentive scheme under which employees are paid 20% of the standard cost of the materials saved and also 40% of the labour time saved valued at standard labour rate.

The following are the details of the standard cost of a product:

Standard cost per unit	Amount (₹)
Direct materials: 10 kg at ₹12 each	120
Direct labour: 3 hours at ₹10 each	30
Variable overheads: 3 hours at ₹5 each	15
Fixed overheads (based on a budgeted output of 10,000 units)	25
	190
Selling price per unit	240

During one particular month 9,600 units of the product were manufactured and sold incurring the following actual cost:

	Amount (₹)
Direct materials: 90,000 kg	12,10,000
Direct labour: 25,000 hrs	2,54,000
Variable overheads: 25,000 hrs	1,47,000
Fixed overheads: 25,000 hrs	2,50,000
Total cost	18,61,000
Net profit	4,19,000
Sales	22,80,000

Required: A) Variances that occurred during the month, duly reconciling the standard profits of actual production with actual profits. B) Bonus amount earned by the workers during the month under incentive scheme.

Solution

(1) Material variances

Calculations:

1. Actual cost of materials used = ₹12,10,000

2. Std. cost of material used = Act. qty × Std. price

   = 90,000 × 12 = ₹10,80,000

3. Not applicable – No material mix

4. Std. cost of std. quantity for actual output

   = Std. price × Std. qty for actual output

   = 12 × 96,000 = ₹11,52,000

   Note: Std. qty for actual output = 9,600 × 10 = 96,000 kg

Variances:

1. Material cost variance (MCV)

   = 4 – 1

   = 11,52,000 – 12,10,000 = 58,000 (A)

2. Material price variance (MPV)

   = 2 – 1

   = 10,80,000 – 12,10,000 = 1,30,000 (A)

3. Material usage variance (MUV)

   = 4 – 2

   = 11,52,000 – 10,80,000 = 72,000 (F)

(2) Labour variance:

Calculations:

1. Actual wages paid = ₹2,54,000
2. Standard wages for actual hours

   = Act. hours × Std . rate

   = 25,000 × 10 = ₹2,50,000

3. Not applicable, no idle time
4. Not applicable, no labour mix
5. Std. wages for standard time for actual output

   = Std. time for actual production × Std. rate

   = 28,800 × 10 = ₹2,88,000

   Note: Std. time for actual production = 9,600 × 3 = 28,800 hrs.

Variances:

1. Labour cost variance (LCV)

   = 5 – 1

   = 2,88,000 – 2,54,000 = 34,000 (F)

2. Labour rate variance (LRV)

$= 2 - 1$

$= 2{,}50{,}000 - 2{,}54{,}000 = 4{,}000$ (A)

3. Labour efficiency variance (LEV)

$= 5 - 2$

$= 2{,}88{,}000 - 2{,}50{,}000 = 38{,}000$ (F)

(3) Variable overhead variances

Calculations:

1. Actual variable OHS = ₹1,47,000
2. Std. variable overheads:

   = Variable OH. rate per hour × Act. hours

   $= 5 \times 25{,}000 =$ ₹1,25,000
3. Recovered variable overheads

   = Variable OH. rate per unit × Actual output

   $= 15 \times 9{,}600 =$ ₹1,44,000

Variances:

1. Variable overhead cost variance

   $= 3 - 1$

   $= 1{,}44{,}000 - 1{,}47{,}000 = 3{,}000$ (A)
2. Variable overhead expenditure variance

   $= 2 - 1$

   $= 1{,}25{,}000 - 1{,}47{,}000 = 22{,}000$ (A)
3. Variable overhead efficiency variance

   $= 3 - 2$

   $= 1{,}44{,}000 - 1{,}25{,}000 = 19{,}000$ (F)

(4) Fixed overhead variances

Calculations:

1. Actual fixed overheads = ₹2,50,000
2. Budgeted fixed overheads = ₹2,50,000

3. Not applicable, working days not given

4. Not applicable

5. Recovered fixed overhead

$$= \text{Std. FOH. rate per unit} \times \text{Actual output}$$
$$= 25 \times 9{,}600 = ₹2{,}40{,}000$$

Variances:

1. FOH cost variance

$$= 5 - 1$$
$$= 2{,}40{,}000 - 2{,}50{,}000 = 10{,}000 \text{ (A)}$$

2. FOH expenditure variance

$$= 2 - 1$$
$$= 2{,}50{,}000 - 2{,}50{,}000 = \text{Nil}$$

3. FOH volume variance

$$= 5 - 2$$
$$= 2{,}40{,}000 - 2{,}50{,}000 = 10{,}000 \text{ (A)}$$

(5) Sales variance:

Calculations:

1. Actual sales value

$$= \text{Actual qty} \times \text{Act. price} = ₹22{,}80{,}000 \text{ (given)}$$

2. Bud. sales value of act. qty

$$= \text{Act. qty} \times \text{Std price}$$
$$= 9{,}600 \times 240 = 23{,}04{,}000$$

3. Not applicable No sales mix

4. Not applicable, bud. qty not available.

Variances:

Sales price variance $= 2 - 1$

$$= 23,\ 04{,}000 - 22{,}80{,}000 = 24{,}000 \text{ (A)}$$

Analysis of variances:

Particulars	Adverse variance ₹	Favourable variance ₹
Material price	1,30,000	-
Material usage	-	72,000
Labour rate	4,000	-
Labour efficiency	-	38,000
Variable OH. cost	3,000	-
Fixed OH cost	10,000	-
Sales price	24,000	-
Total	1,71,000	1,10,000
Net variance	61,000 (A)	

Reconciliation of standard profit with actual profit:

	₹
Standard profit for actual production (9,600 × 50)	4,80,000
Less: Net variance (A)	61,000
Actual profit	4,19,000

Illustration-36

(Computation of missing informations-Sales variance)

Compute the missing data indicated by the question marks from the following:

	Product 'R'	Product 'S'
Sales Quantity:		
Standard (units)	?	400
Actual (units)	500	?
Price per unit:		
Standard (₹)	12	15
Actual (₹)	15	20
Sales price variance	?	?
Sales volume variance	1200 (F)	?
Sale value variance	?	?

Sales mix variance for both products together was ₹450 (F)

Solution

Calculation for Product 'R'

1. Actual sales value = Act. qty × Act. price

   Product R = 500 × 15 = ₹7,500

2. Budgeted sales value for actual quantity = Act. qty × Bud. price

   Product R = 500 × 12 = ₹6,000

3. Not applicable, No sales mix

4. Bud. sales for bud. qty = Bud. qty × Bud. Price

   Product R = $x \times 12 = 12x =$ ₹4,800 (See 6 below)

5. Sale price variance = 2 – 1

   = 6,000 – 7,500 = 1,500 (F)

6. Sales volume variance = 4 – 2

   $$(-)1,200(\text{F}) = 12x - 6,000$$

   $$(-)12x = (-)6,000 + 1,200$$

   $$12x = 4,800$$

7. Std. qty of R = $x = 4,800/12 = 400$ units.

   Bud. sales value for bud. qty = 400 × 12 = ₹4,800

8. Sales value variance of 'R' = 4 – 1

   = 4,800 – 7,500 = 2,700 (F)

Workings for product 'S'

Note:

1. Revised bud. qty $= \dfrac{\text{Total weight of act. mix}}{\text{Total weight of std.mix}} \times$ Budgeted quantity

   $$\text{R} = \frac{500+x}{800} \times 400 = \frac{500+x}{2}$$

   $$\text{S} = \frac{500+x}{800} \times 400 = \frac{500+x}{2}$$

2. Total weight of actual mix

Act. qty of R	500
Act qty of S	x
Total	$500 + x$

3. Total weight of bud. mix

Bud. qty R	400 units
Bud. qty S	400 units
Total	800 units

4. Bud. sales for revised bud. qty (Calculation - 3) = Bud. price × Revised bud. qty.

$R = 12 \times \frac{500 + x}{2}$	$3{,}000 + 6x$
$S = 15 \times \frac{500 + x}{2}$	$3{,}750 + 7.5x$
Total	$6{,}750 + 13.5x$

5. Bud. Sales value for act. qty (Calculation 2) = Act. qty × Bud. price

R = 500 × 12	6,000
$S = x \times 15$	$15x$
Total	$6{,}000 + 15x$

6. Sales mix variance = Calculation 5 − Calculation 4

$$450\,(F) = 6{,}000 + 15x - 6{,}750 + 13.5x$$
$$1.5x = 1{,}200$$
$$x = 800$$

Actual quantity of S = 800 units.

Calculation for products 'S'

1. Actual sales value = Act. qty × Act. price

   S = 800 × 20 = ₹16,000

2. Bud. sales value for Act. qty. = Act. qty × Bud. price

   S = 800 × 15 = ₹12,000

3. Bud. sales value for act. qty, had sales been made in bud. sales mix ratio

   = Revised bud. qty × Bud. price

   S = 850 × 15 = ₹12,750

Note:

$$\text{Revised budgeted quantity} = \frac{\text{Total weight of act. mix}}{\text{Total weight of std.mix}} \times \text{Budget quantity}$$

$$R = \frac{1{,}700}{800} \times 400 = 850 \text{ units}$$

4. Bud. sales value for bud. qty = Budget qty × Bud. price

$$S = 400 \times 15 = ₹6{,}000$$

Variances of Product S:

1. Sales price variance

$$= 2 - 1$$
$$= 12{,}000 - 16{,}000 = 4{,}000 \text{ (F)}$$

2. Sales volume variance

$$= 4 - 2$$
$$= 6{,}000 - 12{,}000 = 6{,}000 \text{ (F)}$$

3. Sales value variance

$$= 4 - 1$$
$$= 6{,}000 - 16{,}000 = 10{,}000 \text{ (F)}$$

21.11 EXERCISE

I. Objective Type Questions

A. State whether the following statements are true or false

(i) Introduction of standard costing is not necessary when budgetary control is in use.
(ii) Budgetary control is complementary to standard costing.
(iii) Budgetary control and standard costing are independent cost control systems.
(iv) Aims of budgetary control and standard costing are same.
(v) Standard costing is also known as historical costing.
(vi) Ideal standard is also known as practical standard.
(vii) Standard costing aims at avoiding wastages.
(viii) Variance analysis is the base of standard costing.
(ix) Material cost variance is favourable when actual materials cost is more.
(x) Sales variance is favourable when actual sales is more.
(xi) Budgeted sales and standard sales are synonymous.
(xii) Recovered overheads and absorbed overheads mean the same thing.
(xiii) Idle time variance is always unfavourable.
(xiv) Standard costing helps in applying management by exception principle.
(xv) Responsibility accounting is possible under standard costing.
(xvi) Sales quantity variance is an aggregate of all sales variances.

(xvii) Variances due to external factors are classified as uncontrollable variances.

(xviii) Basic standard remains unchanged for a long period of time.

(xix) Material mix variance is a part of material usage variance.

(xx) Labour rate variance is a part of labour efficiency variance.

[**Ans: True:** (ii), (iii), (iv), (vii), (viii), (x), (xi), (xii), (xiii), (xiv), (xv), (xvii), (xviii), (xix); **False:** (i), (v), (vi), (ix), (xvi), (xx)]

B. Fill in the blanks

(i) Standard cost is ______________ cost.

(ii) The cost that ought to be incurred under prevailing condition is called ______________.

(iii) The limitations of ______________ costing led to introduction of standard costing.

(iv) Variances due to decrease in actual cost is called ______________ variances.

(v) The total of material price variance and material usage variance is ______________.

(vi) Labour variance arising due to abnormal loss of labour time is called ______________.

(vii) The variance due to difference in actual labour hours worked and budgeted labour hours is called ______________.

(viii) Standard costing and ______________ are complementary to one another.

(ix) Calculating what the cost will be which is based on past cost is called ______________.

(x) Variances arising due to internal factors is called ______________ variances.

[**Ans:** (i) Predetermined, (ii) Standard cost, (iii) Historical, (iv) Favourable, (v) Material cost variance, (vi) Labour idle time variance, (vii) Labour efficiency variance, (viii) Budgetary control, (ix) Estimated cost, (x) Controllable]

II. Theory Questions

A. Short answer type questions

1. What is standard cost?
2. What is predetermined cost?
3. What is estimated cost?
4. Explain ideal standard.
5. When fixed overhead calendar variance arises?
6. What is material cost variance?

7. What is labour mix variance?
8. What is material usage variance?
9. Explain the causes for material price variances.
10. What is standard quantity of material for actual output?
11. What are sub-divisions of labour efficiency variance?
12. What are controllable variances?
13. What are uncontrollable variances?

B. Long answer type questions

1. What is standard costing? Explain the prerequisites for introducing standard costing.
2. Explain the differences and similarities between standard costing and budgetary control.
3. Explain the various types of standard costs.
4. What are the basic objectives of standard costing?
5. Explain the advantages and limitations of standard costing.
6. What is variance analysis? Why is it called a tool of management?
7. Explain the term variance and distinguish between controllable and uncontrollable variances.
8. Explain the main methods of standard cost accounting and explain them.
9. Explain and distinguish single plan and partial plan in standard costing.
10. Explain the procedure for disposition of variances.
11. What is variance in standard costing? How does the analysis of variance help the management? **(B.Com., Andra University)**
12. What is material price variance? Explain the causes for material price variance. **(B.Com., Madurai Kamaraj University)**
13. Explain the difference between standard cost and estimated cost.
14. What is two-, three- and four-variance analysis of overheads?
15. What do you understand by the following in the context of operating a standard cost system? (i) Ideal standard; (ii) Average standard; (iii) Attainable standard **(ICWA Inter)**

III. Practical Problems

A. Short answer type questions

1. Given that the cost standards for material consumption are 40 kg at ₹10 per kg. Compute the variances when the actuals are 48 kg at ₹12 per kg.

   [**Ans:** MPV - ₹96(A), MUV - ₹80(A), MCV - ₹176(A)]

2. The budgeted and actual materials are as follows:

Product	Budget		Actual	
	Quantity (Unit)	Price (₹)	Quantity (Unit)	Price (₹)
X	600	3	800	4
Y	800	4	600	3

   Calculate material variances.

   (B.Com., Madras University)

   [**Ans:** MCV - Nil; MPV - 200 (A); MUV - 200 (F); MMV - 200 (F); MYV - Nil]

3. From the data given below, calculate:

   (a) Material cost variance

   (b) Material price variance

   (c) Material usage variance

Particulars	Standard quantity (units)	Standard price (₹)	Actual quantity (units)	Actual price (₹)
Material A	1,050	2.00	1,100	2.25
Material B	1,500	3.25	1,400	3.50
Material C	2,100	3.50	2,000	3.75

   (B.Com., Madras University)

   [**Ans:** MCV - 550 (A); MPV - 1,125 (A); MUV - 575 (F)]

4. Calculate labour variances from the following:

   Standard hours: 100 hrs at ₹5 per hour Actual hours 95 at ₹7 per hour.

   [**Ans:** LCV - 165 (A); LRV - 190 (A); LEV - 25 (F)]

5. Calculate labour variances from the following:

Product	Budget			Actual		
	Hours	Rate (₹)	Amount (₹)	Hours	Rate (₹)	Amount (₹)
Men	800	3	2,400	600	2.50	1,500
Women	200	2	400	500	2.00	1,000
Total	1,000	-	2,800	1,100	-	2,500

[**Ans:** LCV - 300 (F); LRV - 300 (F); LEV - Nil; LMV - 280 (F); LYV - 280 (A)]

6. The standard and actual labour force required for completing a job is given as follows:

Particulars	Std. hours	Std. rate (₹)	Actual hours	Actual rate (₹)
Men	45	50	48	55
Women	50	40	45	40

Calculate:

(a) Labour cost variance

(b) Labour rate variance

(c) Labour efficiency variance

[**Ans:** LCV - 190 (A); LRV - 240 (A); LEV - 50 (F)]

7. From the following data, calculate the labour variances:

Actual gross wages	₹4,000
Standard hours produced	16,000
Standard rate per hour	30 paise
Actual hours worked	16,000

[**Ans:** LCV - 800 (F); LRV - 800 (F); LEV - Nil]

8. From the following information calculate:

(a) Material usage variance

(b) Material cost variance

(c) Material price variance

Standard:

- Materials for 70 kg of finished product 100 kg.
- Price of materials - Re. 1 per kg.

Actual:

- Output - 2,10,000 kg.
- Material used 2,80,000 kg.
- Cost of material ₹2,52,000

[**Ans:** MCV - 48,000 (F); MPV - 28,000 (F); MUV - 20,000 (F)]

9. The following data relates to standard and actual labour force:

- Standard rate of wages per hour ₹10
- Standard hours - 300
- Actual rate of wages per hour ₹12
- Actual hours - 200

Calculate:

(a) Labour cost variance
(b) Labour rate variance
(c) Labour efficiency variance

[**Ans:** LCV - 600 (F); LRV - 400 (A); LEV - 1,000 (F)]

10. From the following information calculate:

(a) Labour cost variance
(b) Labour rate variance
(c) Labour efficiency variance.

Standard	Actual
28 hours	26 hours
₹4 per hour	₹4.50 per hour

[**Ans:** LCV - 5 (A); LRV - 13 (A); LEV - 8 (F)]

11. A company produces one product and the standard cost card contains the following information:

	Budget	**Actual**
Output for the month (units)	4,000	4,400
Fixed overhead (₹)	26,000	26,000
Variable overhead (₹)	24,000	34,000

Calculate overhead variances.

[**Ans:** VOH Cost variance - 7,600 (A); FOH Cost Variance - 2,600 (F); FOH Exp. Variance - Nil; FOH Efficiency variance - 2,600 (F)]

12. From the following data calculate sales variances:

Product	Budget		Actual	
	Quantity (Units)	Price (₹)	Quantity (Units)	Price (₹)
X	1,500	30	2,000	29
Y	1,000	50	700	50

[**Ans:** Sales value variance - 2,000 (A); Sales price variance - 2,000 (A); Sales volume variance - Nil; Sales mix variance - 7,600 (F); Sales quantity variance - 7,600 (A)]

13. The budgeted and actual sales of a concern manufacturing a single product are furnished below:

Budgeted sales: 10,000 units at ₹4.00 per unit

Actual sales: 5,000 units at ₹3.50 per unit

8,000 units at ₹4.00 per unit

Calculate sales variances.

[**Ans:** Value variance - 9,500 (F); Price variance - 2,500 (A); Volume variance - 12,000 (F)]

B. Comprehensive Practical Problems

Material Variances:

1. The standard material cost to produce one tonne of chemical X is:
   - 300 kg of material A at ₹10 per kg
   - 400 kg of material B at ₹5 per kg
   - 500 kg of material C at ₹6 per kg

   During a period, 100 tonnes of mixture X were produced from the usage of:
   - 35 tonnes of material A at a cost of ₹9,000 per tonne
   - 42 tonnes of material B at a cost of ₹6,000 per tonne
   - 53 tonnes of material C at a cost of ₹7,000 per tonne

   Calculate price, usage and mix variance. **(B.Com. (Hons.), Delhi University)**

   [**Ans:** MPV - 60,000 (A); MUV - 78,000 (A); MMV - 11,333 (A)]

2. A company manufactures a particular chemical, the standard material cost being:
   - 40% of material X at ₹20 per kg
   - 60% of material Y at ₹30 per kg
   - A standard loss of 10% is expected in production. During one month 182 kg of chemical were produced from the use of 90 kg of material X at ₹18 per kg and 110 kg at ₹34 per kg

Calculate the following variances for the month:

(a) Material price variance
(b) Material mix variance
(c) Material yield variance
(d) Material cost variance. **(B.Com., Madras University)**

[**Ans:** MPV - 260 (A); MMV - 100(F); MYV - 58 (F); MCV - 102 (A)]

3. From the following information compute:

(a) Material mix variance
(b) Material price variance
(c) Material usage variance.

Product	Budget			Actual		
	Quantity (Unit)	Unit price (₹)	Total (₹)	Quantity (Unit)	Price (₹)	Total (₹)
A	4	1.00	4.00	2	3.50	7.00
B	2	2.00	4.00	1	2.00	2.00
C	2	4.00	8.00	3	3.00	9.00
Total	8	-	16.00	6	-	18.00

[**Ans:** MMV - 4 (A); MPV - 2 (A); MUV - Nil]

4. Mixers Ltd. is engaged in producing a standard mix using 60 kg of Chemical X and 40 kg of Chemical Y. The standard loss of production is 30%. The standard price of X is ₹5 per kg and of Y is ₹10 per kg.

The actual mixture and yield were as follows:

- X - 80 kg at ₹4.50 per kg.
- Y - 70 kg at ₹8.00 per kg.
- Actual yield 115 kg.

Calculate all material variances.

[**Ans:** MCV - 230 (F); MPV - 180(F); MUV-50 (F); MMV - 50(A); MYV-100(F)]

5. A company produces a finished product by using three basic raw materials. The following standards have been set for raw materials:

(a) Material A - 25% at ₹4 per kg.
(b) Material B - 35% at ₹3 per kg
(c) Material C - 40% at ₹2 per kg.

The standard loss in process is 20% of input. During a particular month, the company produced 2,400 kg of finished product. The details of stock and purchases for the month are as under:

Materials	Opening stock (kg)	Closing stock (kg)	Purchases during the month (kg)	Cost of purchases (₹)
A	200	350	800	3,600
B	150	200	1,000	3,500
C	300	200	1,100	1,980

The opening stock was valued at standard cost. You are required to compute:

(a) Material price and cost variances when

i. variance is calculated at the point of issue on FIFO basis

ii. variance is calculated at the point of issue on LIFO basis.

(b) Material usage, mix and yield variances. **(CA-Inter)**

[**Ans:** MCV - FIFO -255(F); LIFO - 120(F); MPV - FIFO - 445(A); LIFO - 580(A); MUV - 700 (F); MMV - 130(F); MYV - 570 (F)]

Note: 1) Actual cost of act. quantity

(a) FIFO Basis:

Material A - From op. stock at std. cost = 200 × 4.00 = ₹800

- From purchases = 450 × 4.50 = ₹2,025

Material B - From op. stock at std. cost = 150 × 3.00 = ₹450

- From purchases = 800 × 3.50 = ₹2,800

Material C - From op. stock at std. cost = 300 × 2.00 = ₹600

- From purchases = 900 × 1.80 = ₹1,620

Total = ₹8,295

(b) LIFO Basis:

Material A - From purchases = 650 × 4.50 = ₹2,925

Material B - From purchases = 950 × 3.50 = ₹3,325

Material C - From op. stock at std. cost = 100 × 2.00 = ₹200

- From purchases = 1100 × 1.80= ₹1,980

Total = ₹8,430

6. A company is manufacturing a chemical product making use of four different types of raw materials as follows:

Raw material	Share of total input (%)	Cost of raw material per kg (₹)
A	40%	50

B	30%	80
C	20%	90
D	10%	100

There is an inevitable normal loss of 10% during the processing.

For April 2007, the management furnishes the following information:

Raw material	Quantity consumed (kg)	Cost of material per kg (₹)
A	42,000	48
B	31,000	80
C	18,000	92
D	9,000	110

Output obtained for the month was 92,000 kg.

Calculate:

(a) Material cost variance
(b) Material price variance
(c) Material mix variance
(d) Material yield variance
(e) Material usage variance **(ICWA-Inter)**

[**Ans:** MCV - 2,18,000(F) MPV - 42,000 (A); MMV - 1,00,000(F); MYV - 1,60,000 (F); MUV - 2,60,000 (F)]

Labour Variances:

7. Find out different labour variances from the following particulars:

Standard	Actual
Output - 2,000 units	Output - 2,500 units
Rate of wages: ₹12 per unit	Wages paid - ₹25,000
Standard time - 150 hours	Time taken - 140 hours

[**Ans:** LCV - 5,000 (F); LRV - 2,600 (A); LEV - 7,600 (F)]

8. A group of workers consisting 30 men above 30 years of age, 15 females above 30 years of age and 10 youths of age between 20-30 are paid standard hourly rate as follows:

- Males - ₹80 per hour
- Females - ₹60 per hour
- Youth - ₹40 per hour

In a normal working week of 40 hours, the group is expected to produce 2,000 units of output. During a week, the group consisting of 40 males, 10 females and 5 youth produced 1,600 units. They were paid wages at ₹70 for males, ₹65 for females and ₹30 for youth per hour.

4 hours were lost due to abnormal idle time.

Calculate:

(a) Wage variance
(b) Wage rate variance
(c) Labour efficiency variance
(d) Labour mix variance
(e) Labour idle time variance. **(ICWA-Inter)**

[**Ans:** Wage variance - 25,600 (A); LRV - 16,000 (F); LEV - 41,600 (A); LMV - 10,800 (A); LITV - 16,000 (A)]

9. The standard time and rate for a unit component A are given below:

- Standard hours - 18
- Standard rate - ₹10 per hour

The actual data and related information are as under:

(a) Actual production - 1,000 units
(b) Actual hours - 18,400 hours
(c) Actual rate - ₹9.75 per hour

Calculate:

(a) Labour cost variance
(b) Labour rate variance
(c) Labour efficiency variance.

[**Ans:** LCV - 600 (F); LRV - 4,600 (F); LEV - 4,000 (A)]

10. The details regarding composition and weekly wage rate of labour force engaged on a job scheduled to be completed in 30 weeks are as under:

Category of workers	**Standard**		**Actual**	
	No. of labourers	**Weekly wage rate (₹)**	**No. of labourers**	**Weekly wage rate (₹)**
Skilled	75	60	70	70
Semi-skilled	45	40	30	50
Unskilled	60	30	80	20

The work is actually completed in 32 weeks. Calculate various labour variances.

[**Ans:** LCV - 13,000 (A); LRV - 6,400 (A); LEV - 6,600 (A); LMV - 9,600(F); LREV - 16,200(A)]

Material and Labour Variances:

11. From the following particulars of a manufacturing company, compute material and labour variances:

    - An input of 100 kg of material yields a standard output of 10,000 units.
    - Standard price per kg of material ₹20.
    - Actual quantity of material issued and used by production department 10,000 kg.
    - Actual price per kg of material ₹21 per kg.
    - Actual output 9,00,000 units.
    - Number of employees 200.
    - Standard wage rate per employee per day ₹40.
    - Standard daily output per employee - 100 units.
    - Total number of days worked 50 days.
    - Idle time paid and included in the above-half day for each employee.
    - Actual wage rate per day ₹45.

    [**Ans:** MCV - 30,000(A); MPV - 10,000 (A); MUV - 20,000 (A); LCV - 90,000(A); LRV - 50,000 (A); LEV - 40,000 (A); LITV - 4,000 (A); LYV - 36,000(A)]

12. The following standards have been set to manufacture a product: Direct Materials:

    - Material X - 3 units at ₹8 per unit = ₹24
    - Material Y - 4 units at ₹10 per unit = ₹40
    - Material Z - 5 units at ₹12 per unit = ₹60
    - Direct labour - 5 hours at ₹9 per hour = ₹45
    - Standard prime cost = ₹169

    The company manufactured and sold 5,000 units of the product during the year. Direct materials cost was as follows:

    - Material X - 15,500 units at ₹7.75 per unit
    - Material Y - 19,000 units at ₹11.00 per unit
    - Material Z - 26,000 units at ₹12.50 per unit

The company worked for 26,000 direct labour hours during year. For 4,000 of these hours was paid at ₹10 per hour while the remaining were paid at standard rate. Calculate material and labour variances.

[**Ans:** MCV - 34,125(A); MPV - 28,125(A); MUV - 6,000(A); MMV - 833(A); MYV - 5,167(A); LCV - 13,000(A); LRV - 4,000(A); LEV - 9,000(A)]

Overhead Variances:

13. From the following data compute fixed overhead variances for the month of March, 2009:

    - Fixed overheads budgeted (₹) - 5,000
    - Budgeted output (Units) - 2,500
    - Actual production (units) - 2,700
    - Actual fixed overheads incurred (₹) - 6,000

    [**Ans:** Cost variance - 600 (A); Exp. variance - 1,000 (A); Volume variance -400(F)]

14. Kolkata Furniture manufactures modular tables, chairs and office desks. The standard labour time required per unit of table, chair and desks are 4 hours, 2 hours and 8 hours respectively. The budgeted production per week is 140 standard hours and budgeted fixed overheads per week is ₹70,000.

    During a particular week the firm achieved the following output:

    - Tables - 8 nos.
    - Chairs - 8 nos.
    - Desks - 9 nos.

    The actual fixed overheads amounted to ₹75,000.

    Calculate:

    (i) Fixed overhead total variance

    (ii) Fixed overhead expenditure variance

    (iii) Fixed overhead volume variance **(ICWA-Inter)**

    [**Ans:** Cost variance - 15,000 (A), Exp. variance - 5,000 (A), Volume variance - 10,000 (A)]

15. ABC Enterprises has normal monthly machine hour capacity of 100 machines working 8 hours per day for 25 working days in a month. The standard time required to manufacture one unit of the product is 4 hours. The budgeted fixed overhead is ₹1,50,000. In a month just concluded, the company worked for average 750 machine hours per day. The production was 4,500 units. The actual fixed overhead was ₹1,60,000. Actual days worked during the month 24 days.

    You are required to compute:

    (a) Efficiency variance

    (b) Capacity variance

    (c) Calendar variance

(d) Expenses variance

(e) Volume variance

(f) Total fixed overhead variance

(ICWA-Inter)

[**Ans:** Efficiency variance - Nil, Capacity Variance - 9,000 (A), Calender variance - 6,000 (A), Exp.Variance - 10,000 (A), Volume variance - 15,000 (A), Total FOH variance - 25,000 (A)]

16. The following data is taken from the books of X Ltd, relating to standard and actual VOHs for a period:

	Budget	**Actual**
Output (units)	400	360
Production hours	8,000	7,000
Variable OHS (₹)	10,000	9,150

[**Ans:** Cost variance - 150 (A), Exp.variance 400 (A), Eff. variance - 250 (F)]

17. A manufacturer operating a standard costing system had the following data in respect of a month:

	Standard	**Actual**
Number of working days	25	27
Man hours per month	5,000	5,400
Output in units	500	525
Fixed overheads (₹)	2,500	2,400

Calculate overhead variances.

[**Ans:** Cost variance - 225(F), Exp. variance - 100 (F), Volume variance - 125 (F), Calendar variance - 200 (F), Capacity variance - Nil, efficiency variance - 75(A)]

Sales Variances:

18. The following data relating to budgeted and actual sales figures for the month of Jan 2009, of X Ltd are as follows:

Product	**Budgeted**		**Actual**	
	Quantity (units)	**Selling Price (₹)**	**Quantity (units)**	**Selling Price (₹)**
M	2,000	15	2,200	17
N	1,000	20	900	18
O	3,000	10	3,500	8

Calculate sales variances.

[**Ans:** Value variance - 1,600 (F), Price variance - 4,400 (A), Volume variance - 6,000 (F), Mix variance - 2,000 (A) Quantity variance - 8,000 (F)]

19. The budgeted sales for one month and the actual results obtained are as under:

Product	Budget			Actual		
	Qty (Nos.)	Rate (₹)	Amount (₹)	Qty (Nos.)	Rate (₹)	Amount (₹)
A	1,000	100	1,00,000	1,200	125	1,50,000
B	700	200	1,40,000	800	150	1,20,000
C	500	300	1,50,000	600	300	1,80,000
D	300	500	1,50,000	400	600	2,40,000
Total	2,500	-	5,40,000	3,000	-	6,90,000

Calculate:

(a) Sales value variance
(b) Sales price variance
(c) Sales volume variance
(d) Sale mix variance

(B.Com.,Madras University)

[**Ans:** Value variance - 1,50,000 (F), Price variance - 30,000 (F), Volume variance - 1,20,000 (F), Mix variance - 12,000 (F), Quantity variance - 1,08, 000 (F)]

20. The budgeted and actual sales of a concern manufacturing and marketing a single product are furnished below:

Budgeted sales - 10,000 units at ₹4 per unit
Actual sales - 5,000 units at 3.50 per unit
- 8,000 units at ₹4.00 per unit.

Calculate sales variances.

[**Ans:** Value variance - 9,500 (F), Price variance - 2,500 (A), Volume variance - 12,000 (F)]

21. From the following details relating to a product calculate:

(a) Total overhead cost variance
(b) Efficiency variance

	Budgeted	Actual
Overhead (₹)	1,800	2,000
Period (Hours)	4,300	4,000
Number of days	22	20
Production (units)	-	425

Standard hours per unit - 10 hours

Standard overhead per hour - ₹0.50

[**Ans:** Total OH. cost variance - 221 (A), Efficiency variance - 221 (A)]

All variances:

22. Z E D has a standard costing system for its single output. Their standard cost for 100 units produced are as follows:

	₹
Materials - 100 kg at ₹10 per kg -	1,000
Labour - 40 hours at ₹20 per hour	800
Variable factory overhead at ₹10 per standard direct labour hour	400
Fixed factory overhead - at ₹5per Standard director labour hour	200
	2,400

The following operating data were taken for May, 2005.

(a) 500 units were manufactured

(b) Normal volume is 220 direct labour hours.

(c) 520 kg of material at ₹11.00 were consumed

(d) 190 labour hours at ₹19.00 were used.

(e) Actual variable overheads ₹2,090

(f) Actual fixed overheads ₹1,150

You are required to calculate the different cost variances.

(ICWA-Inter)

[**Ans:** MCV - 720 (A) , MPV - 520 (A), MUV-220 (A), LCV - 390 (F), LRV = 190 (F), LEV - 200 (F), VOH cost - 90(A), VOH exp - 190 (A), VOH. efficiency - 100 (F), FOH. Cost - 150 (A), FOH Exp. - 50 (A), FOH. Volume-100(A), FOH capacity 150 (A), FOH. Efficiency - 50 (F)]

23. The following information is available from the cost records of a company for February, 2009:

	₹
Material purchased : 20,000 pieces	88,000
Materials consumed : 19,000 pieces	
Actual wages paid for 4,950 hours	24,750

Factory overhead incurred	40,000
Factory overhead budgeted	40,000
Units produced - 1,800	

Standard rates and prices are:

- Direct material rate ₹4 per piece
- Standard input 10 pieces per unit
- Direct labour rate - ₹4 per hour
- Standard requirements 2.5 hour per hour.
- Overhead ₹8 per labour hour.

Required:

(a) Show the standard cost card

(b) Compute all material, labour and overhead variances

(CA-Inter)

[**Ans:** MCV - 11,600 (A) , MPV - 7,600 (A), MUV-4,000 (A), LCV - 6,750(A), LRV - 4,950 (A), LEV - 1,800(A), FOH cost - 4,000 (A), FOH exp - Nil, FOH. Volume - 4,000 (A), FOH. capacity - 400 (A), FOH Efficiency - 3,600 (A)]

MISCELLANEOUS TOPICS 22

- ☞ Uniform costing and inter-firm comparison
- ☞ Activity based costing
- ☞ Transfer pricing
- ☞ Cost control and cost reduction
- ☞ Life cycle cost - LCC

22.1 UNIFORM COSTING AND INTER-FIRM COMPARISON

22.1.1 Uniform Costing

22.1.1.1 Meaning

Uniform costing is not a distinct method of cost accounting like marginal costing or ABC. It is one of the latest techniques of costing and cost control. It refers to acceptance and adherence of identical costing principles and procedures by all or many units in the same industry by mutual agreement.

CIMA (London) defines "Uniform costing is the use by several undertakings of the same costing systems, i.e., the same basic costing methods and superimposed principles and techniques".

As defined by Prof. Glover, "It is a system of uniform application of the principles of a costing method agreed upon and adopted by the whole or majority of the manufacturers or executives in any specific industry".

In simple words it refers to the system which is uniformly followed by many companies of the same industry in order to benefit comparison and competition.

22.1.1.2 Objectives

The following can be taken as the objectives of uniform costing. It may vary from industry to industry and hence cannot be taken as comprehensive but can be illustrative.

- ✧ To compare cost among the members of the same industry
- ✧ To measure own efficiency in comparing with industry standards
- ✧ To measure own efficiency in comparing with competitors
- ✧ To identify and eliminate unnecessary actions to create healthy competition
- ✧ To increase the productivity of men and machine
- ✧ To maintain and provide uniform data to the fovernment as and when required by adopting standards
- ✧ To follow same method of valuation of stocks
- ✧ To follow same method of apportionment of overheads
- ✧ To follow same method of depreciation
- ✧ To have standard "format" for various reports and statements.

22.1.1.3 Advantages

- Helps to maintain high standard of operation since industry design (uniform costing design/system) is carried by highly qualified people
- Helps for improvements and act as a benchmark for achievements
- Helps for comparison with industry standards and with competitors
- Helps for more reliability of data and information due to automation
- Helps to contribute more towards R & D due to high standards
- Helps to reduce wastages
- Helps for high productivity which will lead to high returns
- Helps to have a good and fair wage structure
- Helps to reduce labour turnover
- Helps cost reduction which in turn will reduce the price
- Helps to have standard improved quality products and services
- Helps for proper after sales service

- Helps to provide proper data to the government and other statutory bodies
- Helps to save from developing own system for each units in the industry separately since uniform system is designed.
- Helps trade associations to negotiate with government in assistance or concessions in the matter of taxation, subsidies, duties etc.
- Helps to have a reliable price for the whole industry.

22.1.1.4 Disadvantages

- ✧ System needs co-ordination from all members in the industry to be successful. Lack of co-ordination makes the system not to have the concept "uniform costing".
- ✧ Unrealistic or ambiguous data provided by one or more units will defeat the system
- ✧ Not practical and suitable in the competitive world since every unit wants to prove themselves with their own system
- ✧ Large units will benefit by exploiting small units.

22.1.1.5 Essential requisites for uniform costing

- Mutual trust and confidence among all members in the industry is a must
- Rules and regulations of costing, accounting treatments, principles to be followed etc. should be agreed and accepted by all members
- Classification and codification of accounts to be followed, should be designed as if it suits all organisations, say, big, medium and small.
- Operational difficulties should be considered while designing.
- Exchange of ideas, methods, know-how etc. should be frequent to maintain uniformity.
- Big firms should take the lead to help medium and small firms.

22.1.2 Inter-firm Comparison

22.1.2.1 Meaning

It is defined as "a management technique by the use of which it is made possible for an organization to compare its performance with that of the other units engaged in the same activity in the same industry". In other words it is a technique or method of evaluation and is based upon comparison of productivity, efficiency, cost, profit etc. between different units of the same industry. To put differently it is a technique of evaluating the performance, efficiency, costs and profits of firms in an industry. It consists of voluntary exchange of information, data concerning costs, prices, profits, productivity and overall efficiency among firms engaged in similar type of operations for the purpose of bringing improvement in efficiency and indicating the weaknesses. This comparison is possible when uniform costing is in operation. The comparison can be carried out in the following two methods.

(a) Through published information

(b) By exchange of information between units systematically and scientifically

Out of the mentioned methods the first method which is through published information can be from annual accounts, published reports, bulletins, speeches or statements or interviews given by top executives in journals, newspapers etc. But by this way it is not possible to have a proper inter-firm comparison since there are many drawbacks. Hence the ideal method of comparison is through exchange of information as mentioned in the second point. Under this systematic method, a code number is allotted to every member unit of the industry and all units should provide scientific data honestly and regularly. A team of professionally qualified accountants and consultants are employed to look into the administration and processing of the data collected in order to make user friendly information (e.g. ratio, ranks, grades, percentage etc.) for comparison with the Code number allotted to each member unit instead of the name of the member unit. Inter-firm comparison will be a success, provided if uniform costing is followed properly so that firms can be compared systematically and scientifically.

22.1.2.2 Essentials requisites of inter-firm comparison

- Uniform costing should be properly followed (all points mentioned in uniform costing essentials should be considered)
- Compulsory membership system should be followed
- Central analysis process (central body) with qualified professionals is a must. Centralisation of operation helps to have effective operation since data are collected and analysed in a systematic and scientific manner in order to compare firms. They function as a separate body and will do things for all member units.
- Data should be given by each member unit at frequent intervals and it should be authentic and proper.
- Code number system should be followed as it helps to maintain reports given by individual member units confidentially.

22.1.2.3 Advantages

- Helps meaningful comparison due to fixation of performance standards
- Helps each member unit to know the strength and weaknesses in relation to others
- Helps each member unit to take remedial measures for necessary things

- Helps to accept and apply new techniques in production methods
- Helps to increase productivity
- Helps to increase profit
- Helps to improve quality of product
- Helps to decrease unnecessary costs
- Helps in decision making
- Helps in R & D
- Helps government and other bodies to know the true fact of the industry

22.1.2.4 Disadvantages

- ❖ Possibility of misuse of collected information
- ❖ Member unit may not provide accurate data or may filter data to maintain secrecy
- ❖ Member unit may not provide data on time
- ❖ Not easy to compare due to intangible factors
- ❖ Member unit may not cooperate for comparison

22.2 ACTIVITY BASED COSTING (ABC)

22.2.1 Evolution

ABC is based on George Staubus Activity Costing and Input-Output Accounting. The concept of ABC was developed in the manufacturing sector of the United States during 1970s and 1980s. During this time the Consortium for Advanced Management-International (CAM-I), provided a formative role for studying and formalising the principles that have become more formally known as Activity-Based Costing. ABC lost ground in 1990s to alternative metrics such as balanced scorecard and economic value added. Various opinions were thrown open towards ABC specifying the impact of having ABC Model. In particular to quote the following can be considered.

- ✧ Manually driven ABC was an inefficient use of resources
- ✧ It is expensive and difficult to implement for small gains and a poor value and so alternative methods should be used
- ✧ It focuses on cost allocation in operational management
- ✧ It helps to segregate fixed costs, variable cost and overhead cost which helps to identify "cost drivers"

ABC methodology assigns an organisation's resource costs through activities to the products and services provided to its customers. It is generally used as a tool for understanding product and customer cost and profitability based on the production or performing processes.

22.2.2 Meaning

CIMA defines ABC as, "Cost attribution to cost units on the basis of benefit received from indirect activities"

Example: Ordering, handling, quality assurance etc.

It can also be defined as "the collection of financial and operational performance information tracing the significant activities of the firm to product costs".

ABC is a special costing model that identifies activities in an organization and assigns the cost of each activity with resources to all products and services according to the actual consumption by each activity.

22.2.3 Objectives and Purposes or Why ABC?

- To bring more accuracy in calculation of cost of products and services as compared with traditional costing system, since all products are not produced equally,
  - (a) As some products are produced in large batches and some in small batches
  - (b) As manufacturing overhead costs have increased significantly and they no longer correlate with the productive machine hours or direct labour hours.
- To understand product and customer cost
- To understand profitability based on the production or performing processes
- To have a structured analysis in respect of complex processes
- To provide wealth of information to the management in order to help in decision making
- To eliminate non-value adding activities due to diversity of products
- To increase value adding activities since diversity of customer demands are growing rapidly

22.2.4 Merits

The merits of ABC are separated into "specific" and "general" for easy understanding.

22.2.4.1 Specific

- Helps to identify and eliminate those products and services that are unprofitable and lower the prices of those that are overpriced

- Helps to allocate more resources on profitable products, departments and activities
- Helps in strategic decisions such as pricing, outsourcing etc.,
- Helps to identify cause and effect relationships to objectively assign costs
- Is a modeling process applicable for full and partial views
- Helps to control costs at any pre-product-level (level) and on a departmental level.

22.2.4.2 General

- Helps for better management
- Helps in budgeting and performance measurement
- Helps to ensure product or customer profitability
- Helps to improve product quality
- Helps to manage costs
- Helps to justify investments in latest technology
- Helps by supporting other innovations like TQM and JIT systems.

22.2.5 De-merits

- Expensive in nature
- Slow processes in services and administrations as it involves more staff time
- Not possible to allocate certain overheads to products and customers [e.g., Executive Salary]
- A complex system and so not suitable for small organisations
- Requires to maintain lot of files and records

22.2.6 Various Terms

22.2.6.1 Cost driver

CIMA defines "cost driver is any factor which causes a change in the cost of an activity, e.g., the quality of parts received by an activity is a determining factor in the work required by that activity and therefore affects the resources required. An activity may have multiple cost drivers associated with it."

In other words it refers to a factor that creates or drives the cost of an activity or it refers to the factors which determine the cost of an activity. It is thus a link between activities and the cost.

Examples:

1. For running machinery — Machine hours (operating) are the driver.
2. For library — Issue and receipts of books will be the driver
3. Customer order processing — Number of customers / Number of orders will be the drivers

22.2.6.2 Activity cost pool

CIMA defines "cost pool is the point of focus for the costs relating to a particular activity in an activity based costing system".

Cost pool is similar to the concept of cost centre. Cost pool is the total cost assigned to an activity. In other words it is the total sum of all costs assigned to an activity.

Examples:

1. Library cost — Includes case of library, cost of issue, receipts, ordering, stock taking etc., — Pooled under "library"

22.2.6.3 Activity based budgeting

ABB is different from the traditional budgeting in the sense that it provides a strong link between the objectives of organization and objectives of a particular activity. In other words, it involves identification of activities and dividing them in value adding and non-value adding activities and then eliminating the non-value activities in due course. It requires identification of activities of the organization, establishing the factors which cause costs, the cost drivers and then collecting the costs of the activities in cost pools.

22.2.6.4 Activity based accounting

ABA can be defined as "collection, recording, analysis, control and reporting of activity related costs rather than departmental or cost centers related costs". It involves activities like

1. Activity based budgeting
2. Cost management based on activities
3. Performance measurement of activities
4. Cost reduction through elimination of non-value adding activities and
5. Initiating innovative and advance measures for reduction of costs

22.2.6.5 Activity based management

ABM is a tool of management that involves analysing and costing activities with the goal of improving efficiency and effectiveness. ABM is a set of action that management can take based on information from ABC system to increase and improve profitability. ABM attempts on cost driver analysis, activity analysis and performance analysis for its continuous improvement.

22.2.7 Steps to be followed in ABC System

ABC is an economic model that identifies the cost pools or activity centres in an organization and assigns costs to cost drivers based on the number of each activity used. The implementation of the ABC system can be implemented with the following steps.

ABC Module

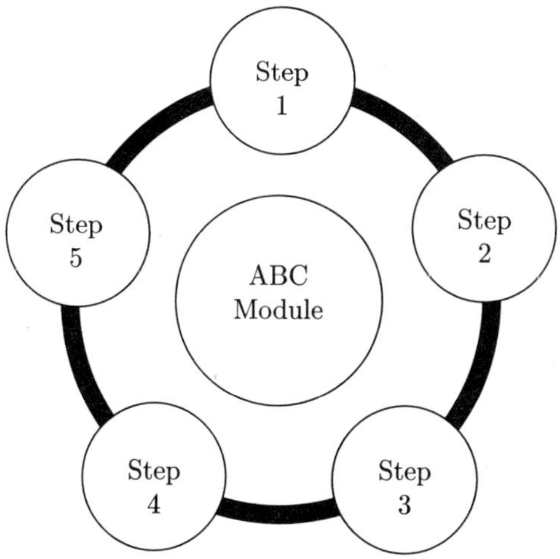

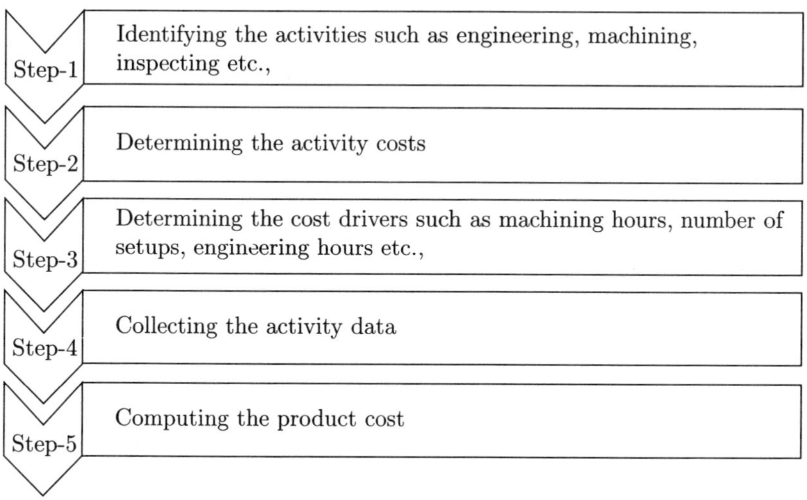

22.2.8 Conventional Costing and ABC - Differences

S.No	Conventional Costing	ABC
1	Actual cost of production and cost of related services cannot be determined accurately	Actual cost of production and cost of related services can be determined accurately

2	Cause and effect relationship to objectively allocate costs are not possible	Cause and effect relationship to objectively allocate costs are possible
3	No concept of "cost driver"	Concept of "cost driver" plays a vital role
4	No linkage between activities and the costs	Linkage between activities and the costs
5	Division of fixed and variable cost may not be realistic	Division of fixed and variable cost are realistic
6	Simple system	Complex system
7	Beneficial for small organizations	Beneficial for big organizations

22.3 TRANSFER PRICING

22.3.1 Meaning

"Transfer pricing" is one of the important tools in the hands of the management for performance evaluation of a division or department. It has become necessary in highly decentralised companies where number of division or department is created as a part of the decentralised organization. In the present context all organisations have more divisions and departments which make transfer pricing a must for the management to measure the performance.

"Transfer price" is that notional value at which goods and services are transferred between divisions in decentralised organisations. Transfer prices are normally set for intermediate products, which are goods and services that are supplied by the selling division to the buying division. In big organisations each division is treated as a profit centre as a part and so their profitability is measured by fixation of "transfer price" for inter divisional transfers.

In simple words a "transfer price" is what one part of a company charges another part of the same company for goods or services. TP is the price that the 'selling' division charges the 'buying' division for the product. Since objects that float usually flow downstream, the selling division is called the "upstream division" and the buying division is called the "downstream division". The transfer generates journal entries on the books of both divisions, but usually no money changes hands. The transfer price becomes an expense for the "downstream division" and revenue for the "upstream division".

22.3.2 Methods of Transfer Pricing

The following are the three main methods of transfer pricing

1. Market based transfer price
2. Cost-based transfer price
    (a) Actual cost

(b) Standard cost

(c) Budgeted cost

(d) Full cost or total cost

(e) Variable cost (marginal cost)

3. Negotiated Transfer Price

22.4 COST CONTROL AND COST REDUCTION

22.4.1 Meaning

"Cost control" is operated through setting standards of targets and comparing actual performance therewith, with a view to identify the deviations from standard norms and taking corrective actions in order to ensure that future performance conforms to standard norms. In other words it can be explained that it is a scientific management technique to control and reduce the costs of doing business. It is more of an activity than a theory. Every industry and company has its own standards to control costs.

"Cost reduction" is a continuous process of critical cost examination, analysis and challenge of standards. In this each aspect of businesses such as products, process, procedures, methods, organization, personnel etc., are critically examined and reviewed with a view of improving efficiency and effectiveness and reducing the costs.

22.4.2 Cost Control and Cost Reduction - Differences

- Cost control aims at achieving the pre-determined costs whereas cost reduction aims at reducing the unit cost of goods
- Cost control concentrates on variance analysis by comparing actual with the standards fixed whereas in cost reduction there is no such comparison
- Cost control does not challenge the standards whereas cost reduction challenges the standards for improvements
- Cost control is a preventive function whereas cost reduction is a corrective function

22.5 LIFE CYCLE COST - LCC

22.5.1 Meaning

LCC is the total cost of ownership of machinery and equipment, including its cost of acquisition, operation, maintenance and conversion. It is a summation of cost estimates from inception to disposal for both equipment and projects as determined by an analytical study and estimate of total costs experienced in annual time increments during the project life with consideration for the time value of money.

LCC is an economic model over the project life span. It is said that the best balance among cost elements is achieved when the total LCC is minimised. LCC provides best results when engineering art and science are merged with good judgement to build a sound business case for action.

Under LCC the businesses should summarise LCC results in NPV (net present value) format considering depreciation, taxes and the time value of money. But for government organisations there is no need to consider depreciation and taxes but time value of money should be considered for LCC decisions.

22.5.2 LCC Process (Fabryck)

LCC includes every cost that is appropriate and appropriateness changes with each specific case which is tailored to fit the situation. LCC follows a process / steps as shown below.

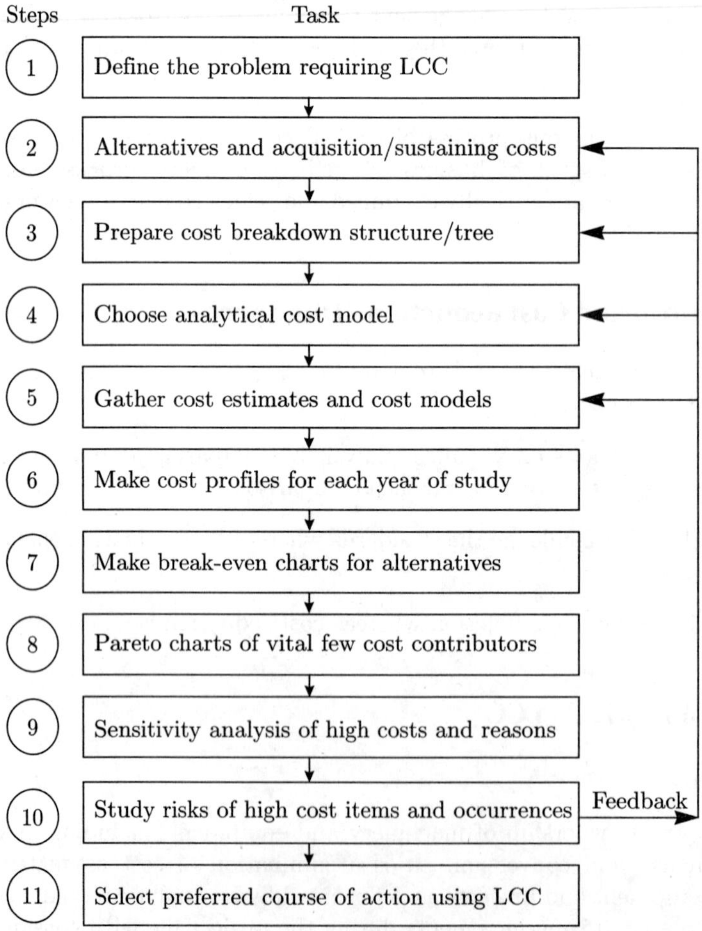

22.5.3 LCC Tree

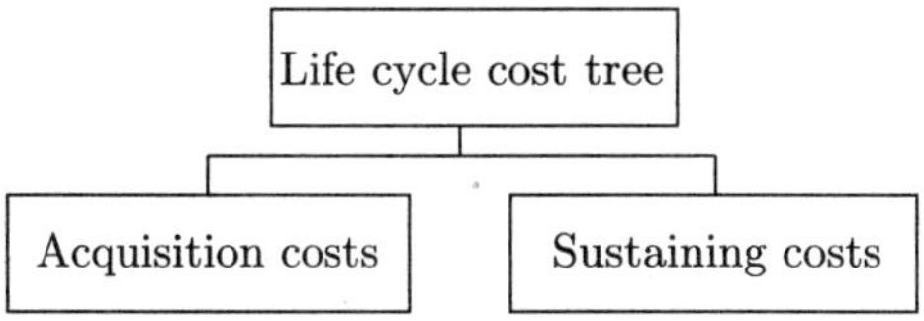

LCC tree combines acquisition and sustaining costs as shown above. Acquisition and sustaining costs are not mutually exclusive. If equipment is acquired acquisition should be sustained and things can't sustain without acquisition of the item. Acquisition and sustaining costs are found by gathering the correct inputs, building the input database, evaluating the LCC and conducting sensitivity analysis to identify cost drivers. Both acquisition costs and sustaining costs have various sub components as follows:

Acquisition Cost Tree

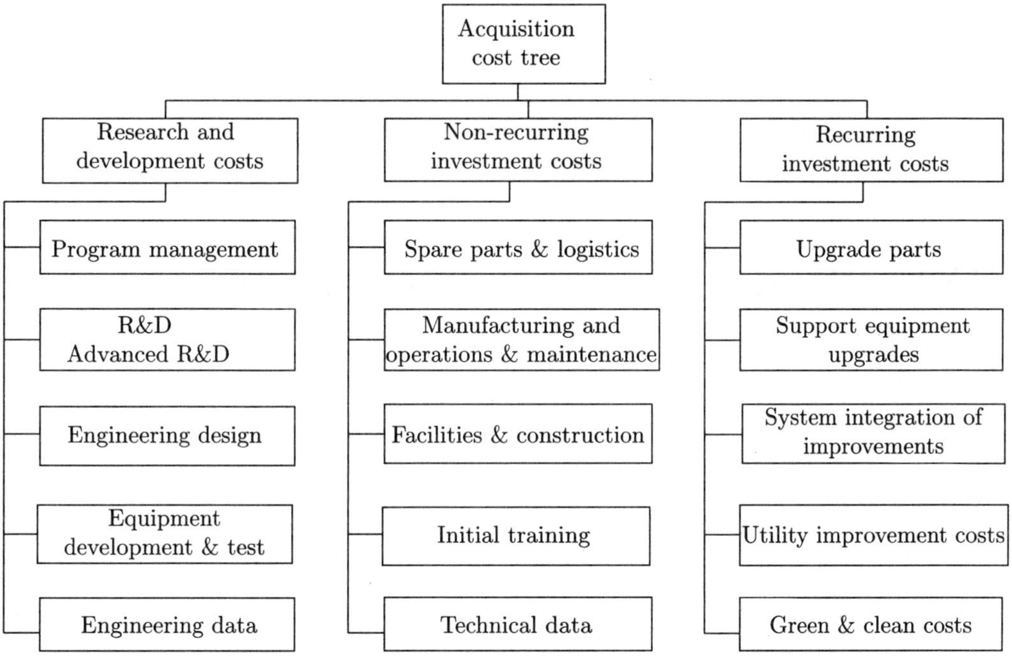

Sustaining Cost Tree

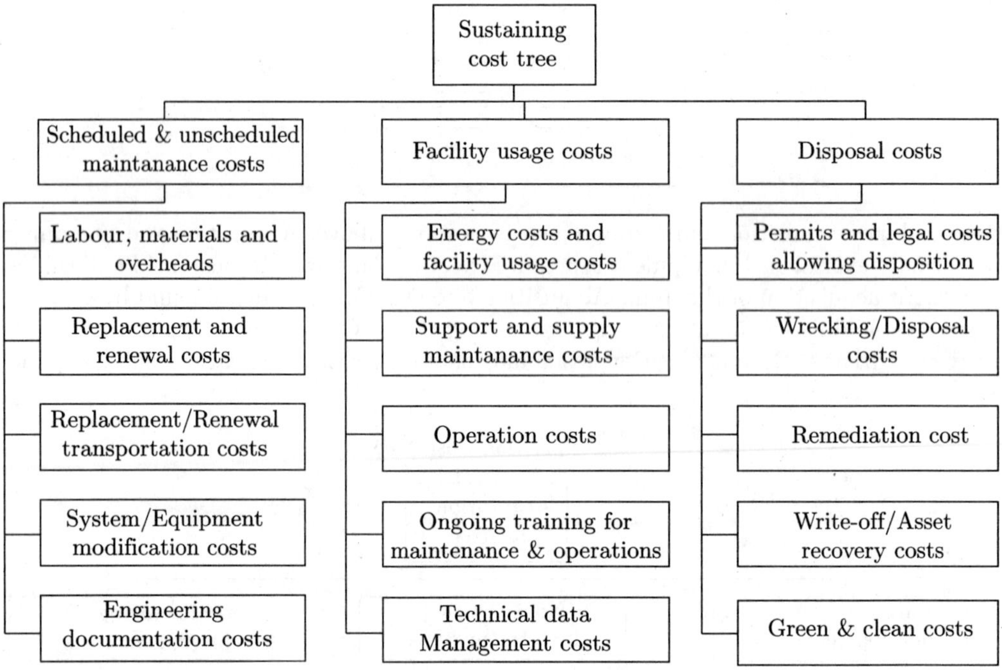

22.6 EXERCISES

Short Questions

1. Write short notes:
   (a) Uniform costing
   (b) Inter-firm comparison
   (c) ABC
   (d) Cost driver
   (e) Activity cost pool
   (f) Activity based budgeting
   (g) Activity based accounting
   (h) Activity based management
   (i) Transfer pricing
   (j) Cost control
   (k) Cost reduction
   (l) LCC

(m) Acquisition costs

(n) Sustaining costs

2. Explain uniform costing with its merits and demerits.
3. Explain inter-firm comparison with its merits and demerits
4. Bring out the objectives of uniform costing.
5. Discuss the requisites for uniform costing
6. Discuss the requisites of inter-firm comparison
7. Explain the advantages and disadvantages of inter-firm comparison
8. Explain the objectives of ABC.
9. Bring out the differences of conventional costing and ABC
10. What is transfer pricing? What are the various methods of transfer pricing.
11. What is LCC tree?
12. Explain the components of acquisition cost tree.
13. Explain the components of sustaining cost tree.

Essay Questions

1. Discuss how uniform costing and inter-firm comparison are related with suitable examples.
2. Discuss the evolution of ABC with its merits and demerits.
3. Why ABC is a must? Discuss.
4. Explain the merits and demerits of ABC.
5. Explain the steps to be followed in ABC system.
6. Differentiate cost control and cost reduction.
7. Discuss the process of LCC.
8. Discuss LCC Tree with its various components.

INDEX

O

P